Comparative Tort Law

Cases, Materials, and Exercises

Thomas KADNER GRAZIANO

Translations by Andrew Tettenborn,
Christopher Booth, Molly Reid et al.

LONDON AND NEW YORK

First published 2018
by Routledge
2 Park Square, Milton Park, Abingdon, Oxon, OX14 4RN

and by Routledge
711 Third Avenue, New York, NY 10017

Routledge is an imprint of the Taylor & Francis Group, an informa business

© 2018 Thomas Kadner Graziano

The right of Thomas Kadner Graziano to be identified as author of this work has been asserted by him in accordance with sections 77 and 78 of the Copyright, Designs and Patents Act 1988.

All rights reserved. No part of this book may be reprinted or reproduced or utilised in any form or by any electronic, mechanical, or other means, now known or hereafter invented, including photocopying and recording, or in any information storage or retrieval system, without permission in writing from the publishers.

Trademark notice: Product or corporate names may be trademarks or registered trademarks, and are used only for identification and explanation without intent to infringe.

British Library Cataloguing-in-Publication Data
A catalogue record for this book is available from the British Library

Library of Congress Cataloging-in-Publication Data
Names: Kadner Graziano, Thomas, 1961– author.
Title: Comparative tort law : cases, materials and exercises / Thomas Kadner Graziano.
Description: Abingdon, Oxon ; New York, NY : Routledge, 2018. | Includes bibliographical references and index.
Identifiers: LCCN 2017035786 | ISBN 9781138567726 (hardback) | ISBN 9781138567733 (pbk.) | ISBN 9781351340625 (epub) | ISBN 9781351340618 (mobipocket)
Subjects: LCSH: Torts—Europe. | LCGFT: Casebooks.
Classification: LCC KJC1640 .K33 2018 | DDC 346.403—dc23
LC record available at https://lccn.loc.gov/2017035786

ISBN: 978-1-138-56772-6 (hbk)
ISBN: 978-1-138-56773-3 (pbk)
ISBN: 978-0-203-70555-1 (ebk)

Typeset in Times New Roman
by Apex CoVantage, LLC

Visit the eResources: http://www.routledge.com/9781138567733

Comparative Tort Law

Comparative Tort Law promotes a 'learning by doing' approach to comparative tort law and comparative methodology. Each chapter starts with a case scenario followed by questions and expertly selected material, such as: legislation, extracts of case law, soft law principles, and (where appropriate) extracts of legal doctrine. Using this material, students are invited to:

- solve the proposed scenario according to the laws of several jurisdictions;
- compare the approaches and solutions they have identified;
- evaluate their respective pros and cons; and
- reflect upon the most appropriate approach and solution.

This book is essential reading for all students and scholars of comparative tort law and comparative law methodology and is the ideal companion for those wishing to both familiarise themselves with real-world materials and understand the many diverse approaches to modern tort law.

Thomas KADNER GRAZIANO is Professor of Law at the University of Geneva and visiting professor at KU Leuven. He holds a doctoral degree from Goethe-University Frankfurt, an LLM degree from Harvard Law School, and a professorial degree from Humboldt-University of Berlin. He was a faculty member of the DUKE-Geneva Institute in Transnational Law (2004, 2010) and has held visiting professorships, teaching comparative law at the Universities of Potsdam (1997), Poitiers (2006), Florida (1996, 2006–10), Exeter (2007–08), Kaunas (2009, 2013, 2014), Vilnius (2014), Lausanne (2015), KU Leuven (since 2015), and Renmin (People's) University of China (Beijing and Suzhou, 2016), and has taught seminars in comparative law at the Universities of Johannesburg (2015) and Luxembourg (since 2016). He is Fellow of the European Centre of Tort and Insurance Law (ECTIL), Vienna, and has acted as an expert on comparative law and comparative private international law, including for the European Parliament and in international proceedings before the UN Security Council's Compensation Commission.

Contents

Preface vii
Acknowledgements x
Translations xv
List of abbreviations xxii

PART A
Introduction 1

Chapter 1   Tort law in the 21st century – the purpose of this book   3

Chapter 2   A case-oriented and multilateral approach to the teaching, studying, and learning of comparative law: the approach used in this book   5

Chapter 3   Is it legitimate and beneficial for judges to compare?   19

Chapter 4   The Principles of European Tort Law – a brief introduction and analysis   46

PART B
Case studies 69

Chapter 5   Conditions and limits of extra-contractual liability – cable cases   71

Chapter 6   Fault-based liability and the required standard of care: the case of damage caused by minors   115

Chapter 7   Fault-based liability in action: challenges of establishing fault (and alternative regimes) – the example of sports accidents   158

Chapter 8	Liability without fault – a ruptured water main: *casum sentit dominus*?	192
Chapter 9	Most common cases: traffic accidents	229
Chapter 10	Liability in cases of uncertain causation – "all or nothing" or partial compensation in relation to the probability of causation?	277
Chapter 11	Damage suffered by secondary victims: the case of psychiatric injury, "nervous shock", or "post-traumatic stress disorder (PTSD)" following the loss or severe injury of a loved one	317
Chapter 12	Damage suffered by secondary victims: damages for pure emotional harm following the loss or severe injury of a loved one	343
Chapter 13	Liability for others – the case of liability of parents for damage caused by their children	389
Chapter 14	Pure economic loss: the case of liability for wrongful information and advice	419
Chapter 15	Protection of privacy and the purposes of tort law	449
Chapter 16	Damage to public goods: the case of damage to the environment, pure ecological damage in particular	499
Chapter 17	Comparative tort litigation – an introduction, with a focus on the costs of lawsuits	537
Chapter 18	Cross-border torts: coordinating legal diversity through Private International Law – an introduction	570
Chapter 19	Epilogue: tort law in context – and potential alternatives to tort liability	592

Table of codal and statutory provisions   610
Index   617

Preface

"On reading each author, I acquired a habit of following all his ideas, without suffering my own or those of any other writer to interfere with them, or entering into any dispute on their utility. I said to myself, 'I will begin by laying up a stock of ideas, true or false, but clearly conceived, till my understanding shall be sufficiently furnished to enable me to compare and make choice.'"[1]

The present book provides an introduction both to comparative tort law and to the use of comparative methodology. The chapters and case studies in Part B address fundamental and highly topical issues of tort law and provide solutions to these issues from various national tort law systems, the Principles of European Tort Law (PETL), and the Draft Common Frame of Reference (DCFR).

The reader is invited to study both tort law and comparative methodology using a *case-oriented* and *problem-based* approach.[2] The sources provided (e.g. extracts from national civil codes or statutes, court decisions, and extracts of academic writing from different countries) set out the law as it applies in a large range of jurisdictions. The book is based on the firm conviction that to discuss and analyse the issues on a truly European level, it is necessary to compare not only UK, French, and German law, but also as many other jurisdictions as feasible, useful, manageable, and beneficial. Limiting our comparison to the European "big three" is even less justifiable once we enter into, or continue with, an exchange of ideas with lawyers and colleagues in other parts of the world, such as China, the USA, and Canada.

The jurisdictions in each case study were chosen because they were considered to be representative of the range of solutions that are currently applied. Similar approaches and solutions may also be found in other countries.

---

1 Jean Jacques Rousseau (1712–1778, *Oevres complètes*, Coll. Bibliothèque de la Pléiade, Paris: Gallimard, 1995–95, Vol. 1, "Les Confessions VI", p. 237. In the *French* original: "En lisant chaque auteur, je me fis une loi d'adopter et suivre toutes ses idées sans y mêler les miennes ni celle d'un autre, et sans jamais disputer avec lui. Je me dis, commençons par me faire un magasin d'idées, vraies ou fausses, mais nettes, en attendant que ma tête en soit assez fournie pour pouvoir les comparer et choisir." Translation: *The Complete Confessions of Jean-Jacques Rousseau* (Book VI) (translated by S. W. Orson), New York: Walter J. Black, 1929.
2 For more information on the approach used, see the introduction below, pp. 3 f., 5 ff.

I am grateful to MAIJA HIRVI for information on Finnish law and SICEN HU on Chinese law (Chapter 5), JERCA KRAMBERGER ŠKERL on Slovenian law (Chapter 7), YI SHEN on Chinese law (Chapter 9), JIŘÍ HRÁDEK on Czech law and DANGUOLE KLIMKEVICIUTE on Lithuanian law (Chapter 12), YUE ZHAO on Chinese law (Chapter 13), JANNO LAHE on Estonian law and FANGYING ZHENG on Chinese law (Chapter 14), JANNO LAHE on Estonian law (Chapter 15), LIESBETH ENNEKING on Dutch, NAOMI SAVIOZ on Belgian, and LIANSHI LIU on Chinese law (Chapter 16), and HANNES MEYLE on German law (Chapter 17).

The statutes and code provisions are provided in their original language accompanied by an English translation. With a view to concentrating on the main issues, most of the academic literature and case law has been reproduced without the original footnotes. Readers who wish to possess further information and references are invited to consult the books and case reports cited. For the purpose of keeping the volume of the book manageable and user-friendly, we eventually decided to place the original language versions of court decisions and extracts of academic writing in languages other than English on a companion website. It is available at: http://www.routledge.com/9781138567733. French and German language versions of this book, published by Helbing Lichtenhahn, Basel, will follow soon.

In order for the publication of this book to succeed, it was essential to have precise translations of the materials. Some of these materials (in particular, extracts of civil codes and statutes) were already available in English. Many other texts (in particular, court decisions, much of the academic literature, and some of the code provisions and statutes) needed to be translated into English. Most of these materials were translated by Professor ANDREW TETTENBORN (University of Swansea), CHRISTOPHER BOOTH (LLB Sheffield, and research assistant at the University of Geneva since 2015), and MOLLY REID (MA in French-English Legal Translation, University of Geneva, and now freelance translator in London). Their work notably included translating decisions of the French *Cour de cassation* and the German *Bundesgerichtshof*. Due to the very cryptic drafting style of the former, and the intricacies often exposed by the latter, these translations required a perfect understanding of not only English law and legal language, but also the respective foreign law. In addition, since many of these legal terms and notions have no linguistic counterpart, it was necessary at times to transpose (often complex) legal ideas to produce an accurate translation of the text. This task is certainly one of the most demanding aspects of legal translation. With a perfect understanding of the foreign materials, ANDREW TETTENBORN, CHRISTOPHER BOOTH, and MOLLY REID succeeded brilliantly in this highly demanding task. Their contribution, as well as the work of TATU V. HOCKSELL, SICEN HU, DANGUOLE KLIMKEVICIUTE, JERCA KRAMBERGER ŠKERL, EMMA LIDÉN, MARLENA WISNIAK, FANGYING ZHENG, and YUE ZHAO, who translated selected materials from their respective jurisdictions, was absolutely fundamental to the success of this book.[3]

I would like to express my particular gratitude to the members of my team (previous and current) at the University of Geneva for their most valuable contributions and critical comments, fundamental for the success of this project: FELIX ADEN, CHRISTOPHER BOOTH, RACHEL HARRISON, NIKOLAS HERTEL, PATRICK KEINERT, HANNES MEYLE, ADELINE MICHOUD, RACHEL NGO NTOMP, DR MICHEL REYMOND, and student assistants DINO VAJZOVIC and ARNE P. WEGNER.

Last but not least, many thanks to my secretary VERA BELARBI for her most reliable multilingual corrections of the text.

---

3 For a list of the translations and the respective translator, see below, pp. xv.

The book uses a multilateral comparative method.[4] It would have been impossible to cover as many, and to provide references to so many, jurisdictions without the impressive comparative research which is being carried out at the European Centre of Tort and Insurance Law in Vienna (ECTIL, founding director: HELMUT KOZIOL) and by its members and fellows. I am very grateful for the opportunity to be part of this international community of likeminded scholars from all over Europe and beyond.

The materials in this book were last updated in spring 2017. The book is part of a new kind of pedagogic material and of a new educational comparative strategy. I would be grateful for any comments regarding the users' experiences and for any suggestions, criticism, or further information.

Thomas KADNER GRAZIANO
Geneva, February 2018

---

4 For further information on the method used, see below, pp. 5 ff.

Acknowledgements

The author and the publisher wish to thank the following persons and institutions for permission to reproduce extracts of copyright material (in the order in which they appear in the materials):

Helmut Koziol for

- Helmut Koziol, in: European Group on Tort Law (ed.), *PETL – Text and Commentary*, 2005, Art. 2:102 n. 9 (epigraph).

Palgrave and Ken Oliphant for

- Alastair Mullis/Ken Oliphant, *Torts*, 4th ed., 2011.

Verlag Franz Vahlen and Dirk Looschelders for

- Dirk Looschelders, *Schuldrecht, Besonderer Teil*, 12th ed., 2017.

Stämpfli and Franz Werro for

- Franz Werro (in collaboration with Josiane Haas), *La responsabilité civile*, 2nd ed., 2011.

Stämpfli for

- Henri Deschenaux/Pierre Tercier, *La responsabilité civile*, 2nd ed., 1982.

Peter Wetterstein for

- Peter Wetterstein, Compensation for Pure Economic Loss in Finnish Tort Law, *Scand. Stud. L.* 2001, 565.

Lextenso and Alain Bénabent for

- Alain Bénabent, *Droit civil. Les obligations*, 16th ed., 2017.

Lextenso for

- Bertrand Fages, *Droit des obligations*, 7th ed., 2017.

De Gruyter and Bénédict Winiger, H. Koziol, B.A. Koch, R. Zimmermann, Ernst Karner, and Ken Oliphant for

- Bénédict Winiger/Helmut Koziol/Bernhard A. Koch/Reinhard Zimmermann (eds.), *Digest of European Tort Law, Vol. II: Essential Cases on Damage*, 2011.

- Bénédict Winiger/Ernst Karner/Ken Oliphant (eds.), *Digest of European Tort Law, Vol. III: Misconduct*, 2017.

Sellier (www.otto-schmidt.de) for

- Christian von Bar/Eric Clive (eds.), *Principles, Definitions and Model Rules of European Private Law – Draft Common Frame of Reference (DCFR), Full Edition, Vol. 4*, 2009.

Miquel Martin Casals for

- Miquel Martin Casals, Comparative Report, in: *Children in Tort Law, Part I: Children as Tortfeasors*, Wien/New York: Springer, 2006, pp. 423 ff., n. 3 (epigraph).

Hans-Leo Weyers for

- Josef Esser/Hans-Leo Weyers, *Schuldrecht, Band II, Besonderer Teil, Teilband 2: Gesetzliche Schuldverhältnisse*, 8th ed., 2000.

Jan Sramek Verlag and Helmut Koziol for

- Helmut Koziol, *Basic Questions of Tort Law from a Germanic Perspective*, 2012.

American Law Institute for

- The American Law Institute, *Restatement of the Law – Torts (3rd): Liability for Physical and Emotional Harm*, Vol. 1, 2013.
- *Restatement of the Law, Torts (2nd)*, 1979.

Pierre Wessner for

- Pierre Wessner, La responsabilité pour faute: une conception non surprenante, des conditions d'application novatrices, *HAVE/REAS* 2005, 252, at 253 (epigraph, in French with English translation).

C.H. Beck for

- Franz J. Säcker/Roland Rixecker/Hartmut Oetker (eds.), *Münchener Kommentar zum Bürgerlichen Gesetzbuch*, Vol. 6, 7th ed., 2017.

Jonathan Gruber for

- Jonathan Gruber, *Public Finance and Public Policy*, 5th ed., New York: Worth Publishers, 2015, p. 395 (epigraph).

LexisNexis (Litec) and Philippe Brun for

- Philippe Brun, *Responsabilité civile extra-contractuelle*, 4th ed., 2016.

LexisNexis (Litec)

- Boris Starck/Henri Roland/Laurent Boyer, *Obligations, 1. Responsabilité délictuelle*, 5th ed., 1996.

Helbing Lichtenhahn Verlag and Bénédict Winiger for

- Bénédict Winiger, *La responsabilié aquilienne en droit commun – Damnum Culpa Datum*, 2002.

Helbing Lichtenhahn Verlag, Franz Werro and Luc Thévenoz for

- Luc Thévenoz/Franz Werro (eds.), *Commentaire Romand, Code des obligations I*, 2nd ed., 2012.

Helbing Lichtenhahn Verlag and Christoph Müller for

- Christoph Müller, *La responsabilité civile extracontractuelle*, 2013.

Sweet & Maxwell for

- Tony Weir, *A Casebook on Tort*, 10th ed., 2004.
- W.V.H. Rogers, *The Law of Tort*, 2nd ed., 1994.
- Paula Giliker/Silas Beckwith, *Tort*, 6th ed., 2017.

Pierre Widmer for

- European Group on Tort Law (eds.), *Principles of European Tort Law – Text and Commentary*, 2005, p. 65 (Pierre Widmer), and Art. 4:103 n. 1 (Pierre Widmer) (epigraphs).

Agathe Lepage for

- Agathe Lepage, Réparation du préjudice résultant d'une atteinte à la vie privée: refus de prendre en compte les profits réalisés par le journal, *D.* 2000, 269 (epigraph, in German version with English translation).

Tilman Hoppe for

- *Persönlichkeitsschutz durch Haftungsrecht*, 2001, p. 206 (epigraph, in German version with English translation).

Mohr Siebeck and Christoph Oertel for

- Christoph Oertel, *Objektive Haftung in Europa – Rechtsvergleichende Untersuchung zur Weiterentwicklung der verschuldensunabhängigen Haftung im europäischen Privatrecht*, 2010.

Oxford University Press for

- Simon Deakin/Angus Johnston/Basil Markesinis, *Markesinis and Deakin's Tort Law*, 7th ed., 2013.
- Lord Denning, *What next in the Law*, 1982.

Bloomsbury Professional Ltd (an imprint of Bloomsbury Publishing Plc) for

- Bryan McMahon/William Binchy, *Law of Torts*, 4th ed., 2013.

Dalloz and Eric Savaux for

- Jacques Flour/Jean-Luc Aubert/Eric Savaux, *Les obligations. 2. Le fait juridique, Quasi-contrats. Responsabilité délictuelle*, 14th ed., 2011.

Dalloz for

- Henri Capitant et al., *Les grands arrêts de la jurisprudence civile, Tome 2*, 13th ed. by François Terré/Yves Lequette, 2015.

Giuffré for

- Pietro Rescigno (a cura di), *Codice Civile, Tomo II*, 9th ed., 2014.

Springer Verlag and B. Winiger, H. Koziol, B.A. Koch and R. Zimmermann for

- Bénédict Winiger/Helmut Koziol/Bernhard Koch/Reinhard Zimmermann (eds.), *Digest of European Tort Law, Vol. I: Essential Cases on Natural Causation*, 2007.

Thomson Reuters (Thomson Aranzadi) and Esthér Gómez Calle for

- Luis Fernando Reglero Campos (Coordinador), *Tratado de Responsabilidad Civil*, 4th ed. 2008.

West Academic Publishing for

- Kenneth S. Abraham, *The Forms and Functions of Tort Law*, 4th ed., 2012.

Erich Schmidt Verlag for

- Michael Kloepfer, Umweltschutz als Aufgabe des Zivilrechts – aus öffentlich-rechtlicher Sicht, *Jb.UTR* 1990, 35 at 43 (epigraph, in German version with English translation).

Igitur and Liesbeth Enneking for

- Berthy van den Broek/Liesbeth Enneking, Public interest litigation in the Netherlands, *Utrecht L. Rev.* 2014, 77.

Wolters Kluwer and Memlouk Malik for

- Memlouk Malik, La loi n° 2016–1087 du 8 août 2016 et la réparation du préjudice écologique, *BDEI* 2016, 30.

Alexandre Guyaz and Muriel Vautier Eigenmann for

- Alexandre Guyaz and Muriel Vautier Eigenmann, Le dommage purement économique, in: Franz Werro and Vincent Brulhart (éds.), *Le dommage dans tous ses états sans le dommage corporel ni le tort moral*, 2013.

Duncker & Humblot for

- Thomas Kadner Graziano, *Der Ersatz ökologischer Schäden – Ansprüche von Umweltverbänden*, 1995.

Jethro K. Lieberman, for

- Jethro K. Lieberman, The Litigious Society, 1981 (epigraph).

Stephen C. Yeazell for

- Stephen C. Yeazell/Joanna C. Schwartz, *Civil Procedure*, 9th ed., 2016, pp. 340–342 (epigraph)

John H. Langbein for

- John H. Langbein, The German Advantage in Civil Procedure, *U. Chi. L. Rev.* 1985, 823.

De Gruyter and Jean-Sébastien Borghetti for

- Jean-Sébastien Borghetti, The culture of Tort Law in France, *JETL* 2012, 158.

Mårten Schultz for

- Mårten Schultz, Disharmonization: A Swedish Critique of Principles of European Tort Law, *EBLR* 2007, 1305.

Steven Shavell for

- Steven Shavell, *Economic Analysis of Accident Law*, 2007.

Contains public sector information licensed under the Open Government Licence v3.0

- Lord Dyson, Master of the Rolls, *Magna Carta and Compensation Culture*, speech at the High Sheriff of Oxfordshire's Annual Law Lecture, Magna Carta Trust, 13th October 2015, Judiciary of England and Wales, HMSO, 2015.

Every effort has been made to trace copyright holders and to obtain their permission for the use of copyright material. The author apologises for any omissions in the above list and would be grateful if notified of any addition that should be incorporated in future reprints or editions of this book.

Translations

ANDREW TETTENBORN

Chapter 5

- DIRK LOOSCHELDERS, *Schuldrecht, Besonderer Teil*, 4. Aufl., Köln: Carl Heymanns Verlag, 2010, n° 1166 *et seq.*
- Bundesgerichtshof (BGH), 4.2.1964, BGHZ 41, 123.
- FRANZ WERRO (in collaboration with JOSIANE HAAS), *La responsabilité civile*, 2e éd., Berne: Stämpfli, 2011, n° 252–253, 297, 307–309.
- Tribunal Fédéral, 2.3.1976, ATF 102 II 85.
- BERTRAND FAGES, *Droit des obligations*, 3e ed., Paris: L.G.D.J., 2011, n° 366 ss.
- Cour de cassation (2e civ.), 8.5.1970 (Société Allamigeon Frères et Lacroix c. Lafarge), Cass. civ. 2, 08.05.1970, n°69–11446, Bull. 1970 n° 160.
- Cour de cassation (2e civ.), 28.4.1965 (Marcailloux c. R.A.T.V.M.), D. 1965 Jur. 777.

Chapter 6

- JOSEF ESSER/HANS-LEO WEYERS, *Schuldrecht, Band II, Besonderer Teil, Teilband 2: Gesetzliche Schuldverhältnisse*, 8. Aufl., Heidelberg: C.F. Müller, 2000, § 55 III
- Bundesgerichtshof (BGH), 28.02.1984, NJW 1984, 1958
- Bundesgerichtshof (BGH), 10.03.1970, NJW 1970, 1038
- Bundesgerichtshof (BGH), 24.04.1979, NJW 1979, 2096
- Bundesgerichtshof (BGH), 11.10.1994, BGHZ 127, 186

Chapter 7

- Bundesgerichtshof, 11.1.1972, BGHZ 58, 40
- GERHARD WAGNER, in: *Münchener Kommentar zum BGB*, 6. Aufl., München: C.H. Beck, 2013, § 823, Rn. 563 ff.
- Tribunal Fédéral, 7.2.1956, ATF 82 II 25
- Cour de cassation (chambres réunies), 13.2.1930 (*arrêt Jand'heur*), in: HENRI CAPITANT et al., *Les grands arrêts de la jurisprudence civile, Tome 2*, 12th ed. by FRANÇOIS TERRÉ et YVES LEQUETTE, Paris: Dalloz, 2007–08, no. 199 avec introduction et observations
- Cour d'Appel de Colmar, 18.9.1992 (*New Hampshire Unat SA c. Hugel*), *La Semaine Juridique (J.C.P.)* 1993, IV, no. 1711
- Résumé de Cour d'appel de Paris, 23.5.1985, Gaz. Pal. 1986, 1, somm. 41
- BORIS STARCK/HENRI ROLAND/LAURENT BOYER, *Obligations, 1. Responsabilité délictuelle*, 5th ed., Paris: Litec, 1996, N. 626–641

- Cour de cassation/Hof van Cassatie, 26.05.1904, *Pasicrisie belge (Pas.)* 1904, I, 246
- Cour de cassation/Hof van Cassatie, 27.11.1969, *Pasicrisie belge (Pas.)* 1970, I, 277

Chapter 8

- Kantonsgericht Sankt Gallen, 23.02.2005, BZ.2002.44

Chapter 10

- Bundesgericht, 12.12.1961 i.S. X. gegen P., BGE 87 II 364
- Brandenburgisches Oberlandesgericht, 08.04.2003, NJW-RR 2003, 1383; VersR 2004, 1050
- OLG Hamm, 26.08.1998, VersR 2000, 325
- Bundesgerichtshof, 9. Zivilsenat, 16.06.2005, BGHZ 163, 223
- Bundesgerichtshof, 9. Zivilsenat, 09.06.1994, BGHZ 126, 217

CHRISTOPHER BOOTH

Chapter 6

- Obligationenrecht, Art. 54
- Bundesgericht, 27.06.1990 (G. c. Staatsanwaltschaft und Obergericht des Kantons Aargau), BGE 116 Ia 162
- CHRISTOPH MÜLLER, *La responsabilité civile extracontractuelle*, Basel: Helbing Lichtenhahn, 2003, Kapitel 2, Nr. 242–244.
- Tribunal fédéral, 21.01.1964 (Zufferey c. O. Kull et Cie), ATF 90 II 9
- Tribunal fédéral, 11.07.1978 (Maillard contre Guye et Gutknecht), ATF 104 II 184
- Tribunal fédéral, 06.12.1977 (A. contre hoirs X.), ATF 103 II 330
- ABGB §§ 21, 176
- PETER APATHY/ANDREAS RIEDER, *Bürgerliches Recht, Band III, Schuldrecht, Besonderer Teil*, 4. Aufl., Wien/ New York: Springer, 2010, § 13/31 ff.
- Oberster Gerichtshof (OGH), 23.03.1976, Az. 5Ob 536/76, SZ 49/47 (Leitsatz)
- Oberster Gerichtshof (OGH), 20.10.1988, Geschäftszahl 7 Ob 36/88
- Oberster Gerichtshof (OGH), 18.12.2009, Geschäftszahl 7 Ob 83/09h
- Cour de cassation, Assemblée plénière, 09.05.1984, n° 82–92.934, Bulletin criminel 1984 n° 162 (arrêt Djouab)
- Cour de cassation, 12.12.1984, n° de pourvoi: 82–12627, Bulletin 1984 II N° 193 (arrêt Molina)
- Cour de cassation, Assemblée plénière, 09.05.1984, n° de pourvoi: 80–14994, Bulletin 1984 Assemblée plénière n° 1 (arrêt Gabillet)
- ALAIN BÉNABENT, *Droit civil. Les obligations*, 12th ed., Paris: Montchrestien, 2010, n° 542, 545
- Codice civile, Arts. 2046, 2047

Chapter 8

- CHRISTOPH OERTEL, *Objektive Haftung in Europa*, Tübingen: Mohr Siebeck, 2010, pp. 322–323

Chapter 13

- PETER RUMMEL (Hrsg.), *Kommentar zum Allgemeinen Bürgerlichen Gesetzbuch, 2. Band*, 3. Aufl., Wien: Manz, 2002, § 1309 n. 9 (REISCHAUER)
- PHILIPPE BRUN, *Responsabilité civile extracontractuelle*, 3e éd., Paris: LexisNexis Litec, 2014, nos. 429 ff.
- L. FERNANDO REGLERO CAMPOS (Coordinador), *Tratado de Responsabilidad Civil*, 3e edición, Madrid: Thomson Aranzadi, 2006, XI n° 3–6, 38 (ESTHER GÓMEZ CALLE)
- Bundesgerichtshof, 6. Zivilsenat, 10.07.1984, NJW 1984, 2574
- Bundesgerichtshof, 6. Zivilsenat, 24.03.2009, NJW 2009, 1952
- Bundesgerichtshof, 6. Zivilsenat, 24.03.2009, NJW 2009, 1954

Chapter 14

- Schweizerisches Bundesgericht, 26.11.1985, BGE 111 II 471
- Bundesgerichtshof, 12.02.1979, NJW 1979, 1595
- *Münchener Kommentar zum BGB*, 6th ed., München: C.H. Beck, 2013, § 826, nos. 66–68 (GERHARD WAGNER)
- ABGB, § 1300
- Oberster Gerichtshof, 28.03.2002, 8b246/01m
- Oberster Gerichtshof, 30.06.2010, 9 Ob 49/09k
- Oberster Gerichtshof, 31.08.2010, 4 Ob 137/10s
- Cour de cassation Com., 09.01.1978, n° 76–13.107, Bull. civ. IV n°12
- FRANCOIS GRUA, Banquier – Responsabilité en matière de service – Services annexes, Fourniture de renseignements, in: *Juris-Classeur Banque – Crédit – Bourse*, Fascicule 335–340, 29, juillet 2011
- ALEXANDRE GUYAZ et MURIEL VAUTIER EIGENMANN, Le dommage purement économique, in: Franz Werro and Vincent Brulhart (éds.), *Le dommage dans tous ses états sans le dommage corporel ni le tort moral*, Bern: Staempfli, 2013, 195 ff., 201, 206

Chapter 15

- Cour d'appel de Paris, 25.01.2006, D. 2006, 2706
- Cour de cassation, 1ère civ., 27.02.2007, n° 06–10.393, Bull. 2007 I, n° 85
- Cour d'appel de Toulouse, 25.05.2004, CCE n° 1/2005, comm. 17
- Bundesgerichtshof, BGH, 25.05.1954, BGHZ 13, 334
- Bundesgerichtshof, BGH, 05.03.1963, NJW 1963, 902
- DIRK LOOSCHELDERS, Schuldrecht, Besonderer Teil, 11th ed., Köln: Carl Heymanns Verlag, 2016, nos. 1234 ff.
- Bundesgerichtshof, BGH, 15.11.1994, BGHZ 128, 1 (Caroline von Monaco I)
- Bundesgerichtshof, BGH, 05.10.2004, NJW 2005, 215
- Bundesverfassungsgericht, BVerfG, 08.03.2000, Az. 1 BVR 1127/96, NJW 2000, 2187
- JOSEF ESSER/HANS-LEO WEYERS, *Schuldrecht, Band II, Besonderer Teil, Teilband 2: Gesetzliche Schuldverhältnisse*, 8th ed., Heidelberg: C.F. Müller, 2000, § 53
- Bundesgericht, 07.12.2006, Schnyder gegen Ringier AG und Kraushaar, BGE 133 III 153
- Bundesgerichtshof, BGH, 04.06.1992, BGHZ 118, 312

Chapter 16

- Loi fédérale sur la chasse et la protection des mammifères et oiseaux sauvages (Loi sur la chasse, LChP), Art. 23
- Loi fédérale sur la protection de l'environnement, Art. 55
- Tribunal fédéral/Bundesgericht, 20.02.2004, Case 4C.317/2002 /ech (La Fondation X. c. La Masse en faillite de feu A.)
- Tribunal fédéral, 15.12.1964 (Etats de Fribourg et de Vaud contre Fibres de verre SA et Höganäsmetoder A.B.), ATF 90 II 417
- Cour de cassation de Belgique, 11.06.2013 (P. P. et P. S. L. V. contre L'inspecteur régional de l'urbanisme et Milieusteunpunt Huldenberg, association sans but lucratif), Arrêt NDEG P. 12.1389.N, Pas., 2013, n° 361
- Cour constitutionnelle belge, 21.01.2016, F-20160121-1, 7/2016
- Rechtbank Rotterdam 15.03.1991, NJ 1992, 91 (Borcea) (together with THOMAS KADNER GRAZIANO)
- Code civil, Arts. 1246–1249, 1251
- Code de l'environnement, Arts. L141-1, L142-2
- Cour de cassation, 16.11.1982, n° 81-15550 (Centre ornithologique Rhône-Alpes c. association communale de chasse agréée de Saint-Martial, Ardèche), Bull. 1982.1.282 n° 331 = R.J.E. 1984, 225
- Tribunal de Grande Instance de Paris, 16.01.2008, aff. 9934895010
- Cour de cassation, chambre criminelle, 25.09.2012, n° du pourvoi 10-82.938, arrêt 3439
- MEMLOUK MALIK, La loi n° 2016-1087 du 8 août 2016 et la réparation du préjudice écologique, *Bulletin de Droit de l'Environnement Industriel (BDEI)*, 01.11.2016, N° 65, pp. 30-38

Chapter 17

- Bundesgerichtshof, BGH, 30.05.2006, NJW 2006, 2490 at 2491
- SIMON MARKUS BECK/TOBIAS SCHEEL, *Zivilprozessrecht im Assessorexamen*, 4. Aufl., München: C.H. Beck, 2007, Rn. 635, 636
- Gesetz über die Vergütung der Rechtsanwältinnen und Rechtsanwälte, Rechtsanwaltsvergütungsgesetz, RVG, §§ 1 (1), 2 (1) and (2), 3a (1), 13 (1) und Anlage 2 zu 13 (1) S. 3
- Bundesverfassungsgericht, 17.10.1990, 1 BvR 283/85, BVerfGE 83, 1 (14)
- Bundesverfassungsgericht, 15.06.2009, 1 BvR 1342/07, NJW-RR 2010, 259 (260)
- CHRISTOPH HOMMERICH/MATTHIAS KILIAN/HEIKE JACKMUTH/THOMAS WOLF, Quersubventionierung im RVG: Fiktion oder Wirklichkeit?, *AnwBl* 2006, 407
- STEFAN HARDEGE/BERND WAAS, *Rechtsanwaltsvergütung in Europa*, Studie für die Bundesrechtsanwaltskammer, Köln, 2008, S. 48 und 51
- Bundesverfassungsgericht, 12.12.2006, 1 BvR 2576/04, BVerfGE 117, 163
- JULIA VON SELTMANN, *Beck'scher Online-Kommentar RVG*, 35. Edition, Stand: 01.06.2016, RVG § 4a
- MATTHIAS KILIAN, Brennpunkte des anwaltlichen Berufsrechts, *NJW* 2014, 1499 (1500)
- HANS-JOCHEM MAYER, Entwicklungen zum Rechtsanwaltsvergütungsgesetz 2007–2011, *NJW* 2011, 1563 at 1565
- MATTHIAS KILIAN, Erfolgshonorare: Gründe für die verhaltene Nutzung durch die Anwaltschaft, *AnwBl* 10/2014, 815 at 817

Chapter 18

- Schweizerisches Bundesgericht, 11.11.2008, BGE 135 III 92

Chapter 19

- Hannes Leitlein, Geburtshilfe: Das Ende der Hebammen, *DIE ZEIT online*, 14.07.2015

Molly Reid

Chapter 6

- Tribunal Fédéral, 21.01.1964 (Zufferey contre O. Kull et Cie), ATF 90 II 9
- Tribunal Fédéral, 11.07.1978, ATF 104 II 184 (Maillard contre Guye et Gutknecht)

Chapter 9

- Cour de cassation, 2e ch. civ., 28.03.1994, Bull. civ. II, n° 110
- Daniel de Callatay et Nicolas Estienne, De la faute inexcusable à la faute intentionnelle, in: Pierre Jadoul et Bernard Dubuisson (sous la dir.), *L'indemnisation des usagers faibles de la route*, Bruxelles: Larcier, 2002, p. 101–137
- J. O. Dalcq, L'indemnisation des dommages corporels des piétons et des cyclistes, *Journal des tribunaux (J.T.)* 1994, p. 665–672

Chapter 10

- Court of Cassation, 18.03.1969 (Y ... vs. Widow Karoubi), First Civil Chamber, Bull. civ. II. no 117
- Cour de cass. (le ch. civ.), 9.4.2002, Bull. civ. 2002 I, No. 116 p. 89
- Hof van Cassatie van België, 05.06.2008, Arrest Nr. C.07.0199
- Tribunal federal, 13.06.2007, BGE 133 III 462

Tatu V. Hocksell

Chapter 5

- Korkein Oikeus, 12.12.2003, KKO 2003:124, R2001/939

Sicen Hu

Chapter 5

- 上诉人黔江区永安建筑有限责任公司与被上诉人黔江区民族医院、黔江区供电有限责任公司财产损害赔偿纠纷案, Chongqing No. 5 Intermediate People's Court, Civil litigation, 26.12.2005, www.law-lib.com/cpws/cpws_view.asp?id=200401143652
- Xiaoming XI and the Tort Law Study Group of the Supreme People's Court of the People's Republic of China, *Tort Law of the People's Republic of China – The*

understanding and application of provisions, Beijing: People's Court Press, 2010, pp. 20–26
- YUNSONG GE, Civil rights protected by Tort Law, *China Legal Science* 3/2010, 37 at 51

THOMAS KADNER GRAZIANO

Chapter 6

- Corte di Cassazione, 28.04.1975, n. 1642, Resp. Civ. Prev., 1976, 136
- Codice civile, Art. 2047

Chapter 7

- Codice civile, Art. 2051
- ARIANE FRY, La responsabilité en droit du sport, in: FRANÇOIS GLANSDORFF/PATRICK HENRY (dir.), *Droit de la responsabilité: Domaines choisis*, Liège: Anthémis, 2010, p. 93 ff.
- GIORGIO CIAN/ALBERTO TRABUCCHI, *Commentario breve al Codice civile*, 9a ed., Padova: CEDAM, 2009, Art. 2050, 2051
- MARCO BONA/ANDREA CASTELNUOVO/PIER GIUSEPPE MONATERI: *La responsabilità civile nello sport*, Milano: IPSOA, 2002, N. 3.4.1.
- MICHAEL WILL and VLADIMIR VODINELIĆ, Generelle Verschuldensvermutung – das unbekannte Wesen. Osteuropäische Angebote zum gemeineuropäischen Deliktsrecht?, in: *European Tort Law – Liber amicorum for Helmut Koziol*, Frankfurt am Main et al.: Peter Lang, 2000, p. 307–344

Chapter 9

- OLG Naumburg, 29.12.2011–4 U 65/11
- BGH, 15.01.1957, BGHZ 23, 90
- Hoge Raad, 28.02.1992 (IZA/Vrerink), Nederlands Jurisprudentie (NJ) 1993, 566
- GIORGIO CIAN (a cura di), *Commentario breve al Codice civile*, 9° ed., Milano: Cedam, 2009, Art. 2054
- PIETRO RESCIGNO (a cura di), *Codice Civile, Tomo II (Artt. 1754–2969)*, Milano: Giuffré, 2008, Art. 2054

Chapter 16

- Rechtbank Rotterdam 15.03.1991, NJ 1992, 91 (Borcea) (with CHRISTOPHER BOOTH)

DANGUOLE KLIMKEVICIUTE

Chapter 8

- Russian Civil Code, Art. 1079

Chapter 12

- Lietuvos Aukščiausiojo Teismo civilinių bylų skyriaus išplėstinės teisėjų kolegijos, 18.04.2005 nutartis c.b. *L. Z., M. Z., V. Z., G. Z. v. VšĮ Marijampolės ligoninė*, No. 3K-7–255/2005
- Lietuvos Aukščiausiojo Teismo Civilinių bylų skyriaus teisėjų kolegijos, 23.02.2010 nutartis c.b. *I. J. and others v. Public Institution Vilnius City University Hospital*, No. 3K-3–59/2010

JERCA KRAMBERGER ŠKERL

Chapter 7

- Supreme Court of Slovenia, 25.05.2013, case n° II Ips 787/2009

EMMA LIDÉN

Chapter 5

- Høyesterett, 29.09.1955, Staten v/Forsvarsdepartementet mot Dagfinn Strøm, Rt-1973–1268

MARLENA WISNIAK

Chapter 9

- OLG Düsseldorf, 15.12.2003–1 U 51/02
- BGH, 15.01.1957, BGHZ 23,90

YUE ZHAO

Chapter 13

- SHENGMING WANG, *Commentaries on Tort Law of the People's Republic of China* (王胜明, 中华人民共和国侵权责任法释义（第二版）), 2nd ed., Beijing: Legislative Affairs Commission of the National Congress of the People's Republic of China, Collection of Commentaries on Laws of the People's Republic of China, 2010, p. 161

FANANGYING ZHENG

Chapter 14

- ZHANG Min'an, GONG Saina, 专业人士所承担的过错侵权责任, 法学评论 2002, Vol. 6, p. 146

Abbreviations

A.B.A. Sec. Ins. Negl. & Comp. L. Proc.	American Bar Association. Section of Insurance, Negligence and Compensation Law. Proceedings
ABGB	Allgemeines Bürgerliches Gesetzbuch (Austrian Civil Code)
AC	Appeal Cases
AcP	Archiv für die civilistische Praxis (German law journal)
aff.	affaire (Case)
AJDA	L'Actualité Juridique de Droit Administratif (French weekly law review)
AJP/PJA	Aktuelle juristische Praxis/Pratique juridique actuelle (Swiss law journal)
al.	Alinéa (Section)
All ER	The All England Law Reports
All ER Annual Review	All England Law Reports Annual Review
Am. J. Comp. L.	The American Journal of Comparative Law
Anglo-Am. L. Rev.	The Anglo-American Law Review
Anm.	Anmerkung (Note)
AnwBl.	Anwaltsblatt (German legal journal)
Ariz. L. Rev.	Arizona Law Review
Art.	Article
Arts.	Articles
ATF	Arrêt du Tribunal Fédéral (Decisions of the Swiss Federal Supreme Court of Justice, official collection)
Aufl.	Auflage (Edition)
BDEI	Bulletin de Droit de l'Environnement Industriel (French bulletin on the law of the industrial environment)
BeckRS	Beck online Rechtsprechung (German Electronic database of court decisions in beck online)
BG	Bundesgericht (Swiss Federal Supreme Court of Justice)
BGB	Bürgerliches Gesetzbuch (German Civil Code)
BGBl.	Bundesgesetzblatt (German Federal Law Gazette)
BGE	Entscheidungen des Schweizerischen Bundesgerichts, amtliche Sammlung (Decisions of the Swiss Federal Supreme Court of Justice, official collection)
BGH	Bundesgerichtshof (Decisions of the German Federal Supreme Court, official collection)

BGHZ	Entscheidungen des Bundesgerichtshofs in Zivilsachen (Decisions of the German Federal Supreme Court, official collection in civil matters)
BRAK-Mitt.	BRAK-Mitteilungen (Legal journal published by the German Federal Lawyers' Association)
Brook. J. Int'l L.	Brooklyn Journal of International Law
Bull.	Bulletin
Bull. Civ.	Bulletin des arrêts de la Cour de cassation, Chambres civiles (Official collection of the case law of the French Court of Cassation)
BVerfG	Bundesverfassungsgericht (German Federal Constitutional Court)
BVerfGE	Entscheidungen des Bundesverfassungsgerichts (Official collection of the decisions of the German Federal Constitutional Court)
BVerwG	Bundesverwaltungsgericht (German Federal Administrative Court)
BW	Burgerlijk Wetboek (Dutch Civil Code)
BYU J. Pub. L.	Brigham Young University Journal of Public Law
Cal.W.L.Rev	California Western Law Review
Camp	Reports of cases determined at nisi prius, in the courts of King's Bench and Common Pleas, and on the Home Circuit, by John Campbell
Cass. Civ.	Cour de cassation, Chambre civile (French Court of Cassation, civil chamber)
CC	Code civil (Civil Code), Codice civile (Italian Civil Code), Código civil (Portuguese Civil Code), Código civil (Spanish Civil Code)
C. cass.	Cour de cassation (French Court of Cassation)
CEDH	Cour européenne des droits de l'homme (European Court of Human Rights)
CESL	Common European Sales Law
China Legal Sci.	China Legal Science
Civ.	Chambre civile (Civil chamber)
CJ-STJ	Colectânea de Jurisprudência – Acórdãos do Supremo Tribunal de Justiça (Collection of Cases of the Portuguese Supreme Court)
CJUE	Court of Justice of the European Union/Cour de justice de l'Union européenne
C.L.J.	Cambridge Law Journal
CLR	Commonwealth Law Reports
CMLR	Common Market Law Review
CO	Code des obligations (Swiss Code of Obligations)
Colum. L. Rev.	Columbia Law Review
Com.	Commercial Chamber
Comm.	Committee
comp.	compare

Cong.	Congress
cons.	considerant (recital)
Const. Comment.	Constitutional Commentary
Corte Cass.	Corte di cassazione (Italian Court of Cassation)
Corte di Cass. SS UU	Corte di cassazione, sezioni unite (Italian Court of Cassation, Joint Divisions)
CPC	Swiss Federal Act on Civil Procedure
Cr. App. R. (S.)	Criminal Appeal Reports (Sentencing)
CUP	Cambridge University Press
D.	Recueil Dalloz (French weekly law journal) and Recueil Dalloz de doctrine, de jurisprudence et de législation, 1945–1964 (French law journal)
DAR	Deutsches Autorecht (German law journal)
DCFR	Draft Common Frame of Reference
Digest I	Digest of European Tort Law, Vol. 1: Essential Cases on Natural Causation
Digest II	Digest of European Tort Law, Vol. 2: Essential Cases on Damage
Digest III	Digest of European Tort Law, Vol. 3: Essential Cases on Misconduct
dir.	Directeurs (Directors)
DÖV	Die öffentliche Verwaltung (German law journal on public and administrative law)
DP	Recueil periodique et critique Dalloz (French law review)
DR	Danno e responsabilità (Italian law review)
D.S.	Recueil Dalloz Sirey de doctrine, de jurisprudence et de législation, since 1965 (French law journal)
Duke Envtl. L. & Pol'y F.	Duke Environmental Law & Policy Forum
Duke J. Comp. & Int'l L.	Duke Journal of Comparative & International Law
Duke L. J.	Duke Law Journal
EBLR	European Business Law Review
ECR	European Court Reports
ed.	Edition/editor
Edin. L. Rev.	The Edinburgh Law Review
eds.	Editors
EJRR	European Journal of Risk Regulation
EllDni	Elliniki Dikaiosini (Greek Justice)
Env. L. Rev.	Environmental Law Review
ER	English Reports
ERPL	European Review of Private Law
et al.	Et alii (and others)
EuR	Europarecht (German law journal on European law)
Eur. J. L. & Econ.	European Journal of Law and Economics
EWCA Civ	England & Wales Court of Appeal, Civil Division
EWHC	England & Wales High Court
EWiR	Entscheidungen zum Wirtschaftsrecht (German legal journal)
Ex Ch	Exchequer Law Report
FED	Forsikringsretlig og Erstatningsretig Domssamling (Danish law journal)

fn.	Footnote
fns.	Footnotes
Foro it.	Foro italiano (Italian law journal)
FSR	Fleet Street Reports
Ga. J. Int'l. & Comp. L.	Georgia Journal of International and Comparative law
Gaz. Pal.	Gazette du Palais (French law journal)
GD	Guida al Diritto (Italian law journal)
Geo. J. Int'l L.	Georgetown Journal of International Law
Giur it	Giurisprudenza italiana (Collection of Italian court decisions)
Giust. Civ.	Giustizia civile (Italian law journal)
GKG	Gerichtskostengesetz (German Act on the Costs of Court Procedures)
GPR	Zeitschrift für Gemeinschaftsprivatrecht (German law journal)
Harv. Int'l. L. J.	Online Harvard International Law Journal Online
Harv. L. Rev.	Harvard Law Review
Harv. Univ. Press	Harvard University Press
HAVE/REAS	Haftung und Versicherung/Résponsabilité et Assurances (Swiss law journal)
H.C.A.	High Court of Australia
HGB	Handelsgesetzbuch (German Commercial Code)
HL	House of Lords
HR	Hoge Raad (Dutch Supreme Court)
Hr	Høyesterett (Norwegian Supreme Court)
ibid.	ibidem (in the same place)
I.B.L.J.	International Business Law Journal
ICLQ	International and Comparative Law Quarterly
IEHC	High Court of Ireland
IESC	Supreme Court of Ireland
ILRM	Irish Law Reports Monthly
InDret	InDret (Spanish/Catalan review on the analysis of law)
Int. Lawyer	The International Lawyer (American law journal)
Int'l J. Baltic L.	International Journal of Baltic Law
Int'l J. Children's Rts.	International Journal of Children's Rights
Int'l Jud. Observer	International Judicial Observer
Int. T.L.R.	International Trade Law and Regulation
IPRspr	Die deutsche Rechtsprechung auf dem Gebiet des internationalen Privatrechts (The German case law in the field of Private International Law – Annual German law journal on the German judicature on Private International Law)
IR	Irish Reports
JAAPL	The Journal of the American Academy of Psychiatry and the Law
JBl.	Juristische Blätter (Austrian Law Journal)
J.B.L.	The Journal of Business Law
Jb.UTR	Jahrbuch des Umwelt- und Technikrechts (Yearbook for environmental law and technology law, Germany)
J.C.P.	Juris-Classeur périodique, La Semaine Juridique (French law journal)

J.D.I.	Journal de Droit International (Clunet)
JdT	Journal des Tribunaux (Swiss journal on the jurisprudence of the Swiss Federal Court)
JETL	Journal of European Tort Law
JHBL	Journal of Health & Biomedical Law
J. L. & Econ.	Journal of Law and Economics
J. Legal Stud.	The Journal of Legal Studies
J. Leg. Ed.	Journal of Legal Education
J.P.I.L.	Journal of Personal Injury Law (before 2000: Journal of Personal Injury Litigation)
J Priv Int L	Journal of Private International Law
JR	Juristische Rundschau (German law journal)
JRP	Journal für Rechtspolitik (Austrian journal on legal politics)
J.S.P.	Journal of Social Policy
J.T.	Journal des tribunaux (Belgian law journal)
JTL	Journal of Tort Law
JURA	Juristische Ausbildung (German law journal)
JuS	Juristische Schulung (German law journal)
JZ	Juristen Zeitung (German law journal)
Kap.	Kapitel (chapter)
K.B.	King's Bench Division
KKO	Korkein oikeus (Finnish Supreme Court)
La. L. Rev.	Louisiana Law Review
LDIP	Loi fédérale sur le droit international privé (Swiss Code on Private International Law)
LG	Landgericht (German court of 1st instance and court of appeal, depending of the value in dispute)
LJ	Lord Justice, Lady Justice
LMCLQ	Lloyd's Maritime and Commercial Law Quarterly
LORPM	Ley orgánica 5/2000, de 12 de enero, reguladora de la responsabilidad penal de los menores (Spanish Criminal Liability of Minors Act)
L.Q.R.	Law Quarterly Review
Misc.2d	Miscellaneous Reports 2d series
MJ	Maastricht Journal of European and Comparative Law
MLR	The Modern Law Review
N.E.	North Eastern Reporter
NIPR	Nederlands Internationaal Privaatrecht (Dutch law journal on Private International Law)
NJ	Nederlandse Jurisprudentie (Collection of Dutch court decisions)
NJA	Nytt Juridiskt Arkiv (Dutch law journal)
NjW	Nieuw Juridisch weekblad (Belgian law journal)
NJW	Neue Juristische Wochenschrift (German law journal)
NJW-RR	Neue Juristische Wochenschrift – Rechtsprechungs-Report (German law journal)
NoV	Nomiko Vima (Greek law journal)
NuR	Natur und Recht (German law journal)

N.Y.	New York Reports
N.Y.S.2d	West's New York Supplement
NZV	Neue Zeitschrift für Verkehrsrecht (German legal journal)
Ø	Østre Landsret (High Court of Eastern Denmark)
OGH	Oberster Gerichtshof (Austrian Supreme Court of Justice)
OHADA	Organisation for the Harmonisation of Business Law in Africa
OJ	Official Journal of the European Union
OJLS	Oxford Journal of Legal Studies
OLG	Oberlandesgericht (German Appellate Court)
OR	Obligationenrecht (Swiss Code of Obligations)
OSNC	Orzecznictwo Sadu Najwyzszego Izba Cywilna
OSNC ZD	Orzecznictwo Sadu Najwyzszego Izba Cywilna – Zbiór Dodatkowy
OSP	Orzecznictwo Sadów Polskich
OUP	Oxford University Press
p.	page
p.a.	per annum (per year)
para./paras.	Paragraph/paragraphs
Pas.	Pasicrisie belge (Collection of Belgian case law)
PECL	Principles of European Contract Law
PETL	Principles of European Tort Law
PIL	Private International Law
PILA	Swiss Private International Law Act
P.I.Q.R	Personal Injuries and Quantum Reports
PN	Professional Negligence
pp.	pages
Q.B.	Queen's Bench Division
Quinnipiac L. Rev.	Quinnipiac Law Review
RabelsZ	Rabels Zeitschrift für ausländisches und internationales Privatrecht (German comparative law journal)
R.C.D.	Revue des contrats (French law journal)
R.C.J.L.	Revue critique de législation et de jurisprudence (French law journal)
RDIC	Revue de droit international et de droit comparé (Belgian comparative law review)
Res.	Resolution
Resp. Civ. Prev.	Responsabilità civile e previdenza (Italian law journal)
Rev. Const. Stud.	Review of Constitutional Studies
Rev. crit. DIP	Revue critique de droit international privé (French publication on Private International Law)
Rev. int. de droit comparé	Revue internationale de droit comparé
RG	Rettens Gang (Norwegian law journal)
RGAR	Revue Générale des Assurances et des Responsabilités (Belgian law journal)
RIS	Austrian Rechtsinformationssystem, www.ris.bka.gv.at
RIW	Recht der internationalen Wirtschaft (German law journal)
RJ	Repertorio de Jurisprudencia Aranzadi (Spanish law report)

R.J.E.	Revue Juridique de l'Environnement (French environmental law review)
r+s	Recht und Schaden (German law journal)
Rt	Norsk Retstidende (Norwegian law journal)
R.T.R.	Road Traffic Reports
RVG	Rechtsanwaltsvergütungsgesetz (German Act on the Remuneration of Lawyers)
RW	Rechtskundig weekblad (Belgian law journal)
S.	Seite/Seiten (page/pages)
San Diego L. Rev.	San Diego Law Review
SC	Supreme Court
Scand. Stud. L.	Scandinavian Studies in Law (Swedish law journal)
SC (HL)	Session Cases (House of Lords)
S.C.R.	Supreme Court Reports
Sect.	Section
sent.	Sentence
Sess.	Session
sez.	Sezione (Section)
SGB	Sozialgesetzbuch (German Social Security Code)
SLT	Scots Law Times
somm.	Sommaire (Summary)
So. 2d	Southern Reporter
SpuRt	Zeitschrift für Sport und Recht (German law journal)
Stbg	Die Steuerberatung (German legal journal)
StGB	Strafgesetzbuch (Criminal Code)
St. Louis U. L. J.	St. Louis University Law Journal
STS	Sentencia del Tribunal Supremo (Official collection of judgments of the Spanish Supreme Court)
StVG	Straßenverkehrsgesetz (German Road Traffic Act)
Subcomm.	Subcommittee
Suffolk U. L. Rev	Suffolk University Law Review
SVG	Straßenverkehrsgesetz/Loi fédérale sur la circulation routière (Swiss Road Traffic Act)
SVR	Straßenverkehrsrecht (German law journal on traffic law)
SZ	Entscheidungen des Österreichischen Obersten Gerichtshofes in Zivil- und Justizverwaltungssachen (Decisions of the Austrian Supreme Court of Justice in civil matters and in matters of administration of justice)
SZW/RSDA	Schweizerische Zeitschrift für Wirtschaftsrecht/Revue Swisse de droit des affaires (Swiss law journal)
TF	Tribunal Fédéral (Swiss Federal Supreme Court of Justice)
TS	Tribunal Supremo (Spanish Supreme Court)
Tul. L. Rev.	Tulane Law Review
U	Ugeskrift for Retsvaesn (Danish law journal)
U. Chi. L. Rev.	The University of Chicago Law Review
UCL Juris. Rev.	UCL Jurisprudence Review
U. Ill. L. Rev.	University of Illinois Law Review
UKHL	United Kingdom House of Lords

U. Miami L. Rev.	University of Miami Law Review
UNIDROIT	International Institute for the Unification of Private Law (www.unidroit.org)
Unif. L. Rev.	Uniform Law Review/Revue de droit uniforme (UNIDROIT)
U. Pa. L. Rev.	University of Pennsylvania Law Review
U. Rich. L. Rev.	University of Richmond Law Review
U.S.	United States Reports
UTLJ	University of Toronto Law Journal
Utrecht L. Rev.	Utrecht Law Review
V	Vestre Landsret (High Court of Western Denmark)
Va. L. Rev.	Virginia Law Review
Verf.	Verfasser (author)
VersR	Versicherungsrecht (German law journal)
VG	Verwaltungsgericht (German administrative court of first instance)
VJIL	Virginia Journal of International Law
Vol.	Volume
VVG	Versicherungsvertragsgesetz (German Insurance Contracts Act)
Wake Forest L. Rev.	The Wake Forest Law Review
Willamette J. Int'l L. & Disp. Resol.	Willamette Journal of International Law and Dispute Resolution
Willamette L. Rev.	Willamette Law Review
WLR	Weekly Law Reports
WM	Zeitschrift für Wirtschafts- und Bankrecht, Wertpapier-Mitteilungen (German law journal)
Wm. Mitchell L. Rev.	William Mitchell Law Review
Wm. & Mary L. Rev.	William & Mary Law Review
Yale L. J.	The Yale Law Journal
YbPIL	Yearbook of Private International Law
Zak	Zivilrecht aktuell (Austrian law journal)
ZaöRV	Zeitschrift für ausländisches öffentliches Recht und Völkerrecht (German law journal on foreign public law and international law)
ZEuP	Zeitschrift für Europäisches Privatrecht (German comparative law journal)
ZfgK	Zeitschrift für das gesamte Kreditwesen (German law journal)
ZfRV	Zeitschrift für Rechtsvergleichung (Austrian comparative law journal)
zfs	Zeitschrift für Schadensrecht (German law journal)
ZGB	Zivilgesetzbuch (Civil Code)
ZGS	Zeitschrift für das gesamte Schuldrecht (German law journal)
ZPO	Zivilprozessordnung (German Code of Civil Procedure)
ZVglRWiss	Zeitschrift für Vergleichende Rechtswissenschaft (German comparative law journal)
ZVR	Zeitschrift für Verkehrsrecht (Austrian law journal)
ZZP	Zeitschrift für Zivilprozess (German law journal on civil procedure)

Part A

Introduction

Chapter 1

Tort law in the 21st century – the purpose of this book

The present book provides an introduction to tort law in all its diversity. It invites the reader to study both comparative tort law and comparative methodology by using a *case-oriented* and *problem-based* approach.

Part A first introduces the approach to comparative law and comparative methodology that is used throughout the book, sets out the choice of jurisdictions included in Part B of the book, and makes some proposals of how to work with the book.[1] The following chapter of Part A addresses the questions of who might use comparative law in practice and, in particular, whether it is legitimate and beneficial for judges (and, as the case may be, for lawyers) to use comparative law in their daily practice.[2] The final chapter of Part A provides a brief introduction to the Principles of European Tort Law (PETL), the needs which they serve, and the purposes for which they are designed.[3] The PETL were presented in 2005 by an international group of tort law specialists and are based on a broad comparative basis which included all European and some extra-European jurisdictions. Today they may, alongside the provisions of Book VI of the Draft Common Frame of Reference (DCFR), serve as a rich source of inspiration for legislators, courts, and legal practitioners.

The 15 chapters of Part B, the central part of the book, each start with a case scenario taken from the case law of a European country and raising a highly topical issue of tort law. Targeted questions follow that guide the readers in their work with each case. The questions are followed by materials that allow the reader to solve the case scenario under different national jurisdictions as well as under the PETL and the DCFR. The materials (extracts from national civil codes, statutes, court decisions, and – where necessary for the understanding of the materials – from academic writing) are provided in the original version with English translations. They present the current state of the law in a large number of jurisdictions.[4]

The *first step* in each chapter is to analyse and solve the case scenario under the different national laws, the PETL, and the DCFR. The *second step* is to compare the approaches to the issue found in the materials and to discover if any common principles exist for the issue in question. Where the national approaches and solutions diverge, the reader is, in a *third tep*, invited to compare them, to analyse their respective pros and cons, and to discuss

---

1 Part A, Chapter 2, pp. 5 ff.
2 Chapter 3, pp. 19 ff.
3 Chapter 4, pp. 46 ff.
4 Part B, Chapter 17, pp. 537 ff., deals with some fundamental issues of tort litigation from a comparative perspective. Lastly, Chapter 18, pp. 570 ff., addresses the question of how the different tort law systems are coordinated in cross-border cases. It provides some basic background information on Private International Law (or Choice of Law) in torts.

which of the approaches and solutions might be the most appropriate to resolve the problem at hand from a comparative and international perspective.

The book invites the reader to work with legal materials from different countries such as continental civil codes, statutes, and court decisions (decisions e.g. of the English Court of Appeal and the House of Lords, now the Supreme Court, the French and Belgian Courts of Cassation, the German and Swiss Federal Supreme Courts of Justice, as well as decisions of lower courts of these countries, in addition to decisions from other European jurisdictions such as Ireland, the Netherlands, Norway, Finland, Austria, Lithuania, and Slovenia, as well as extracts of decisions from the Court of Justice of the European Union, the Supreme Courts of different States in the USA, of Australia, Canada, and China) as well as the relevant provisions of the PETL and the DCFR. The choice of materials is guided by the interest that the respective materials present for the approach to, and the solution of, the issue under examination. The materials further allow the reader to directly encounter any particularities in the form and style of foreign legal materials.

In current comparative literature, one often still finds the presumption that, despite all differences in form and style, when facing the same legal issue, different jurisdictions usually eventually reach similar results.[5] The work with the materials in this book shows that this presumption is wrong – even in comparable societies that share the same basic political, moral, and economic values.

When working with the book, the reader is offered the opportunity to reflect on the differences and similarities inherent in tort law in the 21st century, to compare the different approaches and solutions for the given problem, to analyse the pros and cons of different approaches, and to choose between these options and hereby obtain a comparative perspective.

The comparative approach taught in the book prepares the student to take inspiration from the laws of different countries and jurisdictions when working as a future lawyer or judge, and prepares him or her to work in an international environment that is characterised by legal diversity. The book is based on the firm conviction that comparative law and comparative methodology cannot be taught with a purely theoretical approach. The book therefore promotes the approach of *learning by doing*, which is as close as can be to practical work in the field of comparative law.

Last but not least, working with the book should also help students to better understand their foreign colleagues and their legal backgrounds, and to feel at home in a world populated with very diverse legal thinkers.

---

5 This statement is usually accompanied by a reference to the groundbreaking work of K. ZWEIGERT/H. KÖTZ, *An Introduction to Comparative Law*, 3rd ed. (translated by T. WEIR), Oxford: OUP, 1998.

Chapter 2

A case-oriented and multilateral approach to the teaching, studying, and learning of comparative law

The approach used in this book[1]

I. Introduction

Comparative law is a well-established discipline today.[2] However, uncertainties remain regarding the teaching and learning *method* as well as the *content* of courses on comparative law and on comparative methodology. Matthias Reimann, comparatist at the University of Michigan at Ann Arbor, wrote a few years ago that "[w]hile comparative law has been a considerable success in terms of producing a wealth of knowledge, it has [. . .] failed to mature into an up-to-date, well-defined, and coherent discipline".[3] "[C]omparatists still have no overall theoretical framework explaining, *what* kind of 'law' to compare for what purpose, what to prove or disprove through comparison, and, most embarrassingly, *how* exactly to go about it."[4] In the 1980s, Karl H. Neumayer had already written that "[i]n no other discipline [. . .] does such uncertainty reign as in comparative law regarding the

---

1 The following text was first published in: *ERPL* 2015, 927–944. The text was updated, in particular with respect to the general topic of the present book: tort law.
2 For the situation in Europe, see E. HONDIUS, Comparative Law in the Court-Room: Europe and America Compared, in: A. Büchler/M. Müller-Chen(eds.), *Festschrift für Ingeborg Schwenzer zum 60. Geburtstag*, Vol. 1, Bern: Stämpfli, 2011, p. 759: "The increasing legal co-operation within Europe has led to a growing awareness of foreign law"; p. 765: "From an esoteric elective course, Comparative Law has developed into a mainstream subject"; see also M. REIMANN, The Progress and Failure of Comparative Law in the Second Half of the Twentieth Century, *Am. J. Comp. L.* 2002, 671 at 691 f.; R. MICHAELS, Im Westen nichts Neues? 100 Jahre Pariser Kongress für Rechtsvergleichung – Gedanken anlässlich einer Jubiläumskonferenz in New Orleans, *RabelsZ* 2002, 97 at 112: "Rechtsvergleichung ist *en vogue*. [. . .] Auch in der Praxis ist die Rechtsvergleichung wichtig geworden; sie wird von Gesetzgebern (etwa in den osteuropäischen Transformationsstaaten) und Richtern in zunehmendem Masse genutzt. Schliesslich ist auch die Rechtsangleichung und – vereinheitlichung wesentlich von der Rechtsvergleichung inspiriert worden"; see already R. BUXBAUM, Die Rechtsvergleichung zwischen nationalem Staat und internationaler Wirtschaft, *RabelsZ* 1996, 201: "Europa [erlebt] eine Blüte der Rechtsvergleichung, die in diesem Jahrhundert ihresgleichen sucht".
3 REIMANN (fn. 2), at p. 686. He continues: "Witness, for example, the structure and content of our standard books. They usually begin by talking about the character, history, goals, benefits, and tools of comparative law; almost suddenly, they lay these matters completely aside and launch into descriptions of legal families and traditions; then they add discussions of particular substance topics, and, along the way, they provide a fair amount of information about foreign law. The unifying theme in all this is hard to see. [. . .] When comparatists reiterate their standard lists of their subject's necessity, purposes, tools, and benefits, these mantras are too imprecise and long as to be virtually all-inclusive. The only agreement, it seems, is that anything goes, a few basic prohibitions aside." See also MICHAELS (fn. 2), at p. 106.
4 REIMANN (fn. 2), at p. 689.

teaching method and the content of the courses".⁵ Other authors have noticed a lack of manuals and casebooks intended for a modern and interactive⁶ teaching of comparative law. Edith Friedler has written on the situation in the USA that "recent efforts to give comparative law a facelift are directed more towards scholars than classroom teachers. They bring to mind Roscoe Pound's insistence that this is a discipline for academics and legislators, not for law school class."⁷ Antoine Bullier, comparatist at the University Paris 1, Panthéon Sorbonne, has recently observed that for students and future lawyers and judges, it is often not evident that using the comparative methodology can lead to immediate and tangible results, or that comparative law knowledge can really be useful for the students' future careers.⁸

Added to these uncertainties are new challenges stemming from greater mobility of people and the internationalisation of trade and law. On this point, Michael Waxman noted in the *Journal of Legal Education* that "the inexorable shift to transnational and global legal practice demands a comparable shift in our methods of teaching Comparative Law".⁹

There is thus a need for discussion as to the subject and the method of comparative law teaching. In fact, with a small number of exceptions,¹⁰ in comparative law there is generally no predefined knowledge that each student is supposed to have acquired at the end of his

---

5 K. H. NEUMAYER, Rechtsvergleichung als Unterrichtsfach an deutschen Universitäten, in: H. Bernstein/U. Drobnig/H. Kötz (eds.), *Festschrift für Konrad Zweigert zum 70. Geburtstag*, Tübingen: Mohr Siebeck, 1981, p. 501 at 507. Translated from German: "An den deutschen Universitäten wird kein Lehrgebiet durch eine so große Divergenz in den Methoden des Unterrichts und der Auswahl des Vortragsstoffes verunsichert wie die Rechtsvergleichung".

6 It seems that only specialised courses offer students the opportunity to work with an *active* and *case-oriented* comparative method, while most general comparative law courses are still taught *ex cathedra*. Courses on *comparative methodology* still seem to be rare.

7 E. Z. FRIEDLER, Shakespeare's Contribution to the Teaching of Comparative Law – Some Reflections on *The Merchant of Venice*, La. L. Rev. 2000, 1087. She continues: "[proposals for] new approaches to comparative law [...] contain exciting ideas about new ways to look at comparative law, but a case book or other teaching tool has yet to materialize as a result of these efforts". See, however, the *Ius Commune Casebooks for the Common Law of Europe*, ed. by W. VAN GERVEN et al., aimed at advanced comparative law students, or the books of the author of the present book. Friedler refers to ROSCOE POUND, The Place of Comparative Law in the American Law School Curriculum, Tul. L. Rev. 1933–1934, 161–170. According to Pound, a course on comparative law "has no place in the ordinary curriculum for the first degree in law. That curriculum is too crowded already." Nor did he think that "it has a place in a graduate curriculum". See also p. 168: "I should feel that comparative law is for the research workers; for the relatively few who are specially and immediately engaged in advancing knowledge".

8 A. BULLIER, Le droit comparé dans l'enseignement – Le droit comparé est-il un passe-temps inutile?, *RDIC* 2008, 163 at 164: "cette matière souffre d'un déficit d'image [...] Les juristes sont avant tout des internistes. Ils veulent donner des solutions immédiates et tangibles à leurs étudiants ou clients. La spéculation intellectuelle, si elle est appréciée, ne correspond plus à un monde où l'efficacité et le rendement sont considérés comme essentiels et aller voir ailleurs relève de la curiosité intellectuelle comme pour les digressions élégantes et stimulantes de la philosophie ou de la théorie générale du droit".

9 M. WAXMAN, Teaching Comparative Law in the 21st Century: Beyond the Civil/Common Law Dichotomy, *J. Leg. Ed.* 2001, 305.

10 In particular, the different legal cultures and traditions, their historical origins and particularities, usually form a part of any macro-comparative law course, see K. ZWEIGERT/H. KÖTZ, *An Introduction to Comparative Law*, 3rd ed. (translated by T. WEIR), Oxford: OUP, 1998; R. DAVID/M. GORÉ/C. JAUFFRET-SPINOSI, *Les grands systèmes de droit contemporains*, 12th ed., Paris: Dalloz, 2016; A. GAMBARO/R. SACCO, *Sistemi Giuridici Comparati*, 3rd ed., Turin: Utet Giuridica, 2008; A. GAMBARO/R. SACCO/L. VOGEL, *Le droit de l'occident et d'ailleurs*, Paris: L.G.D.J., 2011; G. CUNIBERTI, *Grands systèmes de droit contemporains*, 3rd ed., Paris: L.G.D.J., 2015; H. P. GLENN, *Legal Traditions of the World: Sustainable Diversity in Law*, 5th ed., Oxford: OUP, 2014.

or her studies. The content of the comparative law course, as well as the methodology, are left to the appreciation of the teacher who, on the one hand, benefits, in that regard, from a large educational freedom. On the other hand, he or she faces the challenge of making, among the vast amount of foreign and comparative materials, a selection that is manageable for the students, and of using a teaching method that meets the needs of students and that adequately prepares them for their future professional practice.

With regard to the question of how to teach and learn comparative law, it appears appropriate to first analyse the *practical requirements* and *challenges* comparatists are facing today. On this basis, it is then considered how students can be prepared for these practical challenges and what consequences might be drawn when it comes to teaching and learning the subject.

II. Practical requirements: from a national and bilateral method to a *multilateral comparative law methodology*

Comparative law has always been employed for the study of different legal cultures, to gain further knowledge and broaden one's own horizons, to better understand one's own law, to relativise the solutions in force in one's own jurisdiction, and to identify notions of justice existing across borders (comparative law in its capacity as *école de vérité*).[11] During large parts of the 20th century, when jurists used comparative methodology, their *starting point* was often *one single jurisdiction* or *one single system of law*, usually the one in which they were trained, which then served as the *point of reference* for the comparison. In practice, the purpose of comparison was often to fill in gaps in national law, to improve it or to reform it. The jurisdiction(s) for comparison was (or were) traditionally chosen among the main representatives of the ancient 'legal families', namely French law, German law, and Common Law (in particular English or US law), occasionally also Swiss law. One could call this traditional method a *national*[12] and *bilateral* approach to comparative law. It is still used in numerous comparative law theses published today.

This approach may still be relevant for some comparative research. In recent years and decades, however, further challenges and tasks have been placed at the centre of debate and the horizon for comparatists has broadened accordingly.

1. Range of jurisdictions to be compared

A first shift concerns the jurisdictions to take into account when comparing – even when the comparison is made with the traditional purpose of improving a single domestic law.

The distinctions between the major codifications that have marked a whole 'legal family', such as the French *Code civil* or the German *BGB*, and the other members of those

---

[11] ZWEIGERT/KÖTZ (fn. 10), at p. 15; DAVID/GORÉ/JAUFFRET-SPINOSI (fn. 10), at nos. 3 ff.
[12] See ZWEIGERT/KÖTZ (fn. 10), at p. 29: "This presents comparative law with a challenge. No longer can it confine itself to making proposals for the reform of national law, valuable though that is, for as long as it does so, it will inevitably be tainted with nationalism, regarding national legal systems as given and fixed, and looking to divergences and convergences only to see what can be of use to them"; H. KÖTZ, Alte und neue Aufgaben der Rechtsvergleichung, *JZ* 2002, 257 at 259; G. P. ROMANO speaks of a "comparaison [. . .] *nationaliste*, puisqu'elle sert la cause du seul législateur national qui la pratique", Les justiciables face à la comparaison des droits: vers la démocratisation d'un droit savant, in: E. Cashin Ritaine/L. Franck/S. Lalani(eds.), *Legal Engineering and Comparative Law*, Vol. 1, Zurich et al.: Schulthess, 2008, p. 95 at 101.

families have significantly increased in many respects over the last decades. Even in the early 1970s, Vlad Constantinesco stated that "it is obvious that some derived legal systems may achieve a level of originality which requires them to also be taken into account when comparing".[13] In Europe, for example, this is true today of Belgian, Italian, Spanish, and Portuguese law, in relation to French law, and most notably of Dutch law since the reform of the Civil Code of the Netherlands. The same is true of Swiss and Austrian law with respect to German law.

Many jurisdictions have recently modernised their codifications, or even put entirely new codifications into force, stemming from important comparative work, with provisions that are often more finely shaded than those of the main representatives of the traditional legal families.[14] These new codifications contain new solutions and cover certain issues for the first time explicitly in black-letter rules. To give just one example: in contract law, the problem of conflicting standard terms and conditions is not regulated explicitly in any of the traditional codifications. The Dutch Civil Code, the Polish Civil Code, the Estonian Law of Obligations, the Lithuanian Civil Code, and the new Romanian Civil Code, on the contrary, contain modern rules on that question; these rules differ significantly from one another, hereby making them even more interesting for comparison.[15] Case law in these countries has also gone its own ways in many aspects.

Limiting the comparison to the principal representatives of the traditional legal families disregards these developments. Today, restricting the comparison to, for example, e.g. French, German, and English law ultimately leaves it to pure chance whether the comparison actually produces the most stimulating or convincing solution with regard to the issue under examination.[16]

In addition, a number of internationally recognised sets of 'principles' (or restatements) have been developed over the last three decades containing high-quality law compiled through comparative research. To avoid having to reinvent the wheel again and again, there should be a widespread consensus that these principles are now also to be included in the comparison, alongside national or international legal provisions and case law.

Restricting comparison to one or a small number of jurisdictions is thus hard to justify in today's world, even if the comparison pursues the traditional purpose of optimising one single domestic law. When it comes to dealing with such a variety of jurisdictions, it is

---

13 L.-J. CONSTANTINESCO, *Rechtsvergleichung, Bd. 2: Die rechtsvergleichende Methode*, Köln: Carl Heymanns Verlag, 1972, p. 50: "Tatsächlich ist es offensichtlich, dass manche abgeleiteten Rechtsordnungen einen Stand der Originalität erreichen können, der den Vergleicher zu ihrer unmittelbaren Untersuchung verpflichtet".

14 To mention just a few examples: the *Dutch* Civil Code (le Burgerlijk Wetboek) of 1992 or the recent codifications in the three Baltic States, see e.g. R. SCHULZE/F. ZOLL (eds.), *The Law of Obligations in Europe: A New Wave of Codifications*, Munich: Sellier, 2013; beyond Europe, see e.g. the *Quebec* Civil Code of 1994, the *Chinese* Contract Act of 1999, which is widely inspired by the UNIDROIT Principles of International Commercial Contracts, or the *Chinese* Property Act of 2007 and the *Chinese* Tort Law Act of 2009.

15 See Art. 6:225 (3) of the *Dutch* Burgerlijk Wetboek, § 40 (1) of the Law of Obligations of *Estonia*, and Art. 6.179 of the *Lithuanian* Civil Code, the latter being strongly inspired by Art. 2.1.22 of the UNIDROIT-Principles on International Commercial Contracts. See also § 385 of the *Polish* Civil Code; Art. 1202 Civil Code of *Romania*.

16 Indeed, the "Principles of European Contract Law" and the 2009 draft "Common Frame of Reference" do often not follow the traditional solutions known of the main representatives of the ancient legal families, but have chosen more differentiated solutions, which are inspired by those found in smaller jurisdictions. For examples, see T. KADNER GRAZIANO, *Comparative Contract Law: Cases, Materials and Excercises*, Basingstoke/New York: Palgrave Macmillan, 2009, pp. 7–30.

necessary to employ a *multilateral* comparative method that allows the comparative lawyer to take into consideration, and draw conclusions from, the most recent and modern developments on an international and comparative scale and allows him or her to benefit from the considerable legal diversity existing today.

2. Transnationalisation, or even globalisation, of trade and legal practice

A second change follows from the transnationalisation, or even the globalisation, of trade, legal practice, and legal issues and challenges. In numerous situations today,[17] jurists are required, together with colleagues from other jurisdictions, to act in a context of legal diversity and to analyse legal issues in a European or even worldwide context, to compare a wide range of different solutions in force in different jurisdictions, to research international tendencies, to identify the most convincing solution on an international level or to suggest solutions acceptable for actors with various legal backgrounds. There is in fact an increasing "necessity of collaboration amongst jurists of all traditions in the resolution of many problems in the world".[18]

With respect to these challenges, traditional bilateral comparison is an inadequate tool. To rise to this challenge, and to cope with a multitude of laws and information, it is necessary to replace the bilateral approach with a *multilateral* comparative method.

3. Search for common principles of law and renewal of the ius commune Europaeum

Last but not least, there are the projects of a variety of research groups aimed to renew the *ius commune Europaeum* or even search for globally accepted (or acceptable) principles of law. In this work, from the outset the national law loses its role as a reference point for the comparison. On the contrary, these research groups operate a multilateral comparison *par excellence*. With respect to this research, Matthias Reimann has stated from a US perspective: "In Western Europe, comparative legal studies have [. . .] gained a momentum and a significance unprecedented in the last hundred years. [. . .] From an American perspective, one may [. . .] look across the Atlantic with envy these days. Comparative law in Europe is a hot topic. It is practically relevant, self-confident, and enjoys a high profile."[19]

In order to research common principles of law and establish a multilateral comparative overview, it is necessary for the comparatist to adopt, from the beginning of the analysis, the view that the solution provided by each jurisdiction for a legal question has, in principle, the same value as the others. To reach this objectivity, one must abandon the national point of view and adopt a bird's eye perspective of the compared objects, or, in other terms, one must adopt a *supranational comparative perspective* while doing multilateral research.

---

17 See the examples on pp. 10–12.
18 GLENN (fn. 10), at p. xxvi, continuing: "[T]here now appears to be no area of law free of the possibility of extra-jurisdictional complication".
19 REIMANN (fn. 2), at pp. 691–692.

4. *Objective: contributing to mutual understanding and allowing an informed choice while being fully aware of all possible solutions and their pros and cons*

The purpose of the use of a multilateral comparative method is, on the one hand, to contribute to a mutual understanding between jurists, judges, and lawyers across borders. On the other hand, the purpose is not necessarily to harmonise or unify law. Applying a multilateral methodology from a supranational perspective allows us to work with numerous laws in order to identify a convincing solution for the issue under examination. The outcome of the comparative research could, where necessary or useful, be introduced in international legislation or case law,[20] but it could also be used as a source of inspiration for national legislation or domestic court decisions,[21] or for parties when looking for a solution that is acceptable at a transnational level.

Whether the multilateral comparative research method is used by a judge, a legislator, or private parties, and whether it is used on a national or international level,[22] the method is, and the benefits to be derived from it are, the same. To resolve a specific legal issue, this method reveals a diversity of possible solutions as well as their respective advantages and disadvantages, and it allows us to discover developments and tendencies on an international and comparative scale. It thus allows us to make an informed choice while being fully aware of (ideally: all) possible solutions and their pros and cons for the legal issue under examination.

III. Three examples from international and comparative legal practice

Multilateral comparison from a supranational perspective is not limited to the activity of a (national or international) legislator. The method can also be helpful, or even necessary in deciding a specific dispute. The range of situations which require a multilateral and supranational comparative method is vast: it extends from armed conflicts of our time to situations raising fundamental private law issues. In the following chapter, three practical examples from the author's practice as a comparative law expert will be presented. They all required a multilateral comparison from an international perspective.[23]

1. The *first example* is related to the most important damages claim that was ever made: in breach of international law, a State invaded another and caused widespread damage. An international force intervened and compelled the first State to withdraw from the occupied territories. Once the war was over, the State that had been invaded, as well as neighbouring States, asked the occupying State for reparation of the damage suffered during the war.

    This case concerned the invasion of Kuwait by Iraq and the subsequent Gulf War in 1990–91. The case was brought before the United Nations Security Council which set up a subsidiary organ, the *United Nations Compensation Commission*, in 1991 at

---

20 See the first and second examples below, pp. 10–11.
21 See the example of the *Australian* case raising the issue of the "loss of a chance", below, pp. 11–12.
22 Parties to litigation can also benefit from this method. On this subject, see ROMANO (fn. 12).
23 The cases are reproduced with the consent of the parties concerned.

the European headquarters of the United Nations in Geneva.[24] According to the regulation established for this procedure, the occupying State was obliged to compensate the neighbouring States and their nationals, in particular regarding health impairments. However, the regulation did not specify in detail the conditions under which the neighbouring States could claim compensation for the injuries and damage done at distance and suffered by their nationals (e.g. damage related to post-traumatic stress disorder, PTSD).

To resolve this issue, it was necessary to undertake a multilateral comparison from a supranational perspective. The aim was to research whether there existed common legal principles for compensation of damage suffered at distance in the different tort law systems in the world. Such common principles could thereafter serve as sources of inspiration to guide the United Nations Compensation Commission when applying the regulation governing its decision.

2. The *second example* is also related to public international law: a State occupies neighbouring land. In breach of international law, colonies are built in the occupied territories and infrastructure is created. After several decades, the occupying State withdraws from these territories. The question then is what the rights and obligations of the occupying State are with respect to the colonies and the infrastructure created there.

The issue presented itself when Israel withdrew from the Gaza strip. It had to be resolved in application of the Hague Convention (IV) respecting the Laws and Customs of War on Land of 1907 and its annex[25] and the 1949 Fourth Geneva Convention relative to the Protection of Civilian Persons in Time of War.[26] According to Art. 55 of the 1907 Hague Convention, the occupying State shall be regarded as *usufructuary* of the occupied territories.[27] There was no international case law specifying the notion of usufructuary and the usufructuary's rights and obligations. However, the national laws that had served as models for Art. 55 of the 1907 Hague Convention have detailed provisions on usufructuary and a rich body of case law interpreting the rights and obligations of the usufructuary.

There again a multilateral comparison of as many jurisdictions as possible which recognise the notion of usufructus offered an interesting perspective into the research of an appropriate solution. In this second example regarding interpretation of international law, the option of only taking one single jurisdiction as a point of reference for comparison was ruled out from the beginning. When interpreting international law, the comparative perspective is necessarily multilateral and supranational.

3. The *third example* raises a fundamental issue of tort law. A 6-year-old girl is admitted to hospital. Through negligence, the doctors delay the necessary exams. When the exams are finally carried out, a brain tumour is diagnosed. The girl is operated on, but suffers severe and permanent brain damage. She claims damages from the

---

24 www.uncc.ch.
25 In particular Arts. 42 to 56 of the Hague Convention.
26 In particular section III of the Geneva Convention.
27 Art. 55 states: The occupying State shall be regarded only as administrator and usufructuary of public buildings, real estate, forests, and agricultural estates belonging to the hostile State, and situated in the occupied country. It must safeguard the capital of these properties, and administer them in accordance with the rules of usufruct.

doctors. The question is whether the doctors' negligence was the cause of her irreversible brain damage.

According to the applicable law, the girl had to establish that it was *more probable than not* that the damage could have been avoided but for the doctors' negligence. The girl couldn't fulfil this requirement and so, according to the traditional rules, the claim could not succeed. The doctors' fault had nevertheless prevented her from having a *chance* to avoid the damage.

This case was brought before the Australian courts. It raised, for the first time in Australian law, the issue of whether it is possible to claim damages for the "loss of a chance".[28] This question had already been discussed, and decided, in a number of foreign jurisdictions. During the procedure before the High Court of Australia, the judges invited the lawyers to present the solutions to the problem found in other jurisdictions, in particular in the USA, the UK, Canada, and jurisdictions on the European continent.

In this third example, comparison was used with a *traditional purpose* which is to find inspiration to deal with and solve an issue raised in a national legal framework. However, to carry out the research required by the court, the lawyers and comparative law experts had to analyse and compare not only one, two, or three, but a large number of jurisdictions worldwide. To manage such a multitude of information and solutions with the greatest possible objectivity, it was necessary to master a multilateral method and adopt, when comparing, a supranational vision of comparative law.[29]

Such extensive multilateral comparison is not restricted to court practice in Australia. In the case law of the UK House of Lords (or, since 2009, the Supreme Court for the UK), approximately one-quarter to one-third of rulings since 1995 have resorted to the comparative method.[30] As in the High Court of Australia ruling, English case law rarely confines its comparison to only one foreign jurisdiction; quite the contrary, courts look for inspiration in as large a number of foreign jurisdictions as possible. Since about 1995, the House of Lords has frequently compared not only with jurisdictions belonging to the Common Law tradition, but also with continental laws.

This research is carried out first and foremost in order to discover and demonstrate the diversity of solutions from which the courts may choose; another purpose is to know if there exist common principles on the international level which could later serve as a source of inspiration for the solution of the issue in the domestic law. If a solution found abroad is adopted or domestic case law overruled, reference to foreign law provides further legal support for the court's judgment. If, on the other hand, a solution applied abroad is eventually rejected, this decision is made in full awareness

---

28 High Court of Australia, *Tabet* v. *Gett*, 21.04.2010, [2010] H.C.A. 12. Extracts below, Part B, Chapter 10, p. 295.
29 For comparative information on this subject, see Part B, Chapter 10, and – with many further references, T. KADNER GRAZIANO, Loss of a Chance in European Private Law – "All or Nothing" or Partial Liability in Cases of Uncertain Causation, *ERPL* 2008, 1009–1042; T. KADNER GRAZIANO, "Alles oder nichts" oder anteilige Haftung bei Verursachungszweifeln – Zur Haftung für "perte d'une chance" und eine Alternative. Urteile des schweizerischen Bundesgerichts vom 13.6.2007, des belgischen Hof van Cassatie vom 5.6.2008, des Supreme Judicial Court of Massachusetts vom 28.7.2008 und des High Court of Australia vom 21.4.2010 mit Anmerkung und einem Lösungsvorschlag, *ZEuP* 2011, 171–200; G. MÄSCH, *Chance und Schaden*, Tübingen: Mohr Siebeck, 2004; C. Müller, *La perte d'une chance*, Bern: Stämpfli, 2002.
30 See M. NOUNCKELE, Aux frontières de la comparaison, *RDIC* 2012, 393–420.

of all options and their respective pros and cons, i.e. on a higher level of knowledge and with greater insight.[31]

4. Numerous other situations require a multilateral comparison from a supranational perspective: in the European Union, during the preparation of every substantive legislation project, the European Commission asks for comparative work taking into account the laws of all 28 EU Member States. For the Court of Justice of the European Union and the European Court of Human Rights, multilateral comparison is daily work.

One could also mention the work of the International Institute for the Unification of Private Law (UNIDROIT), the work of the groups that have prepared the Draft Common Frame of Reference (DCFR), or the work of the European Group of Tort Law (EGTL) which has culminated in the publication of the Principles of European Tort Law (PETL). The works of these and many more groups researching European or even worldwide common principles of law, as well as a number of national legislation projects, were all preceded by vast multilateral comparative research. Finally, on a smaller scale: any choice of law in an international case may require carrying out a multilateral and supranational comparison to identify the most appropriate system for the issue at hand.

IV. Case-oriented comparative law teaching and learning – the approach used in this book

These practical requirements on the national, as well as international, level should have repercussions on the teaching, studying, and learning of comparative law. The question is how to prepare today's students, who are tomorrow's lawyers, judges, and jurists, to face the challenges posed by these situations and by the internationalisation of law and the legal practitioner's work. How can they be prepared to use a multilateral approach to comparative law?

Such an approach to comparative law requires future comparatists to have specific methodological abilities and experiences, to have some basic knowledge of different legal cultures, to know about their historical development and particularities, and – ideally – to have good language skills.

1. Methodological abilities

The multilateral method requires the ability to research, to work with, and to benefit from information and materials from many jurisdictions at the same time. One does not learn such a method with a purely theoretical approach, or, as Denis Tallon has stated: *"il est difficile d'enseigner une méthode dans l'abstrait"*.[32] On the contrary, it is arguably only by way

---

31 For the purposes and the benefits of judicial comparison, see below, Chapter 3, pp. 34 ff.
32 Translation: "It is difficult to teach a method in the abstract." In: DENIS TALLON, Quel droit comparé pour le XXIème siècle?, *Unif. L. Rev.* 1998, 703–709; see also A. FLESSNER, Die Bedeutung der Rechtsvergleichung im Kollisionsrecht: "Die *Rechtsvergleichung* muss zunehmend der internationalen Rechtsberatung und Rechtsgestaltung dienen; sie muss deshalb auch die rechtsberatenden Praktiker erreichen. [. . .] Insgesamt muss der akademische Unterricht vom Erzählen und Staunen über die juristischen Weltwunder mehr auf das Üben, die [. . .] Eigenarbeit mit ausländischen Quellen und Texten umgestaltet werden", in: A. Gamber/B. Verschragen (eds.), *Rechtsvergleichung als juristische Auslegungsmethode*, Vienna: Jan Sramek Verlag,

of *learning by doing* that these abilities can be acquired, i.e. through the students' active work with foreign legal materials on *practical case scenarios*.

The functioning of the multilateral and supranational comparative teaching method, i.e. the method used in this book, shall in the following be illustrated in taking contract and tort law, i.e. the topic of the present book, as examples. To teach the multilateral and supranational comparative method, contract law and tort law are particularly appropriate, given the number of materials that these fields offer for comparison, namely:

- national laws;
- international or interregional law (in contract law and with respect to sales: the United Nations Convention on Contracts for the International Sale of Goods, CISG); and
- international non-State rules and principles (in contract law: in particular, the "Principles of European Contract Law", the "UNIDROIT Principles of International Commercial Contracts", and the "Draft Common Frame of Reference (DCFR)"; in tort law: the "Principles of European Tort Law" and, again, the "Draft Common Frame of Reference (DCFR)").

The materials used in the basic course on comparative law and on (multilateral) comparative methodology may thus be drawn from contract or tort law, but they may also very well be drawn from any other field of law, including administrative or criminal law.

In a case-oriented approach to comparative law, such as the one used in the present book, the *starting point* for the analysis is a *case scenario* raising one of the above-mentioned issues that then guides the students through their work with the legal materials. The students are thus placed in a situation that is as close to practical comparative work as possible.

The following considerations are based on my experience of teaching comparative law at universities in several Eastern and Western European countries, the USA, China, and South Africa. The relevant teaching material developed in Geneva[33] does not give preference to any particular jurisdiction and can thus be used in any country or jurisdiction.

In comparative contract law, for example, our first case is inspired by a Swiss Federal Supreme Court decision: the latest computers are displayed in a shop window at a very attractive price. A customer enters the shop and declares he is buying a computer. Another customer has seen the computers advertised in promotional material (or on the

---

2013, p. 1 at 20; see also CONSTANTINESCO (fn. 13), at p. 29: "Nur wer selbst eine sich auf fremdes Recht erstreckende Untersuchung durchgeführt hat, wer sich selbst darum bemüht hat, die Geheimnisse fremder Rechte und ihrer Rechtsterminologie zu enträtseln, kann etwas Gültiges über die rechtsvergleichende Methode aussagen. Alle, die Rechtsvergleichung ohne Fremdsprachenkenntnisse und ohne die Kenntnis des fremden Rechts, d.h. ohne eigene rechtsvergleichende Studien betreiben und die sich nur auf rechtsvergleichende Monographien stützen, die andere Autoren in ihrer eigenen Sprache geschrieben haben, improvisieren lediglich über eine Sache, die sie nicht kennen. [. . .] Einzig und allein die persönliche Erfahrung in der Anwendung der rechtsvergleichenden Methode kann die wirklichen methodologischen Probleme aufdecken. Vorstellungskraft und Spekulation sind hier keine Hilfe. Die methodologischen Erkenntnisse, die durch persönliche Erfahrung erworben werden, sind eine Sache; die Vergleichung durch eine Zwischenperson ist eine andere." See also MICHAELS (fn. 2), at p. 111: "Über Nutzen und Berechtigung all dieser [theoretischen] Ansätze mag man geteilter Meinung sein. Vor allem fehlt bei allem theoretischen Niveau dieser neuen Ansätze häufig die Rückbindung an praktische Rechtsvergleichung. Kritiker herkömmlicher und Proponenten neuer Methoden verzichten viel zu häufig darauf zu zeigen, wie ihre Methoden praktisch angewandt werden können und zu welchen – vielleicht neuen – Ergebnissen sie führen".

33 See the present book and KADNER GRAZIANO (fn. 16).

Internet) that gives all the relevant information including the price. He contacts the salesperson and states that he would buy one of the computers. The salesperson no longer wants to sell the computer at the advertised price. Has a contract been formed?[34]

In torts, our first case is inspired by the English case *Spartan Steel* v. *Martin Contractors*: a construction company is doing work on a road in the vicinity of a factory producing stainless steel. The construction company carelessly damages a cable that supplies electricity to the steel factory. The cable is owned by a third party. The power is off for 14 hours, disrupting the steel company's 24-hour-a-day operations. The steel factory claims compensation of (a) physical damage to melted material which was in the furnace when the power supply was cut; (b) loss of profit that would have been made had this melt had been properly completed; and (c) loss of further profit caused by the standstill of the factory.[35]

With regard to all issues dealt with in our case scenarios, the laws differ considerably from one jurisdiction to the other.

The *first question* in each exercise invites the students to look for the rules and solutions to the case scenario that are applied in the different national and international legal systems and in the soft law principles, and then *solve the case under the diverse sources*.

In each chapter, the students will discover information on the current state of the law in as many legal systems as was considered useful to fully grasp the variety of solutions available for the issue under examination in a comparative perspective. The material provided is composed of legal provisions as well as extracts from court rulings and academic writings which allow the case to be solved in relation to each system of law.[36] The materials give no priority or preference to any particular jurisdiction.[37] The diversity of legal provisions and case law, as well as the layout of the materials, invites the student to take distance from the law of his or her own country and adopt a supranational view.

The materials provided in the present book (provisions from civil codes and statutes, extracts of court decisions, extracts of academic literature from different countries, and provisions of soft law principles) set out the law as it applies in England and Wales, France, Germany, the USA, Switzerland, and – depending on the topic addressed – a selection of other countries, such as Italy, the Netherlands, Belgium, Austria, Spain, Greece, Poland, Lithuania, Estonia, as well as China, and the Canadian province of Quebec. When resolving the cases, students familiarise themselves with court rulings emanating from a large number of jurisdictions.

The second question in each exercise invites the reader to *regroup* the solutions which fundamentally differ from one another and *to systematise them accordingly*. By doing this,

---

34 Other exercises in the comparative contracts course relate to the issues whether the contract is formed, or can be modified, by simple will of the parties or if other requirements exist (such as a *"cause"* or "consideration"); whether there is an obligation to maintain an offer or if the offerer is free to revoke his offer; whether in scenarios of "battle of forms" general terms and conditions, and if so which ones, are integrated to the contract; whether and under which conditions the parties can demand performance of the contract or if, on the contrary, breach of the contract results in the payment of damages only; whether in the case of delivery of non-conforming goods a right to claim damages should depend on the seller's fault; whether there is a right, or a possibility, for revision of the contract in case of a change of circumstances; and what are the conditions for good faith acquisition of movables, see above (fn. 16).

35 See below, Part B, Chapter 5, pp. 71 ff.

36 It goes without saying that it is the responsibility of the authors of the relevant literature to ensure that all necessary information is provided for the respective jurisdictions to address the issue under examination.

37 One of the consequences of this approach is that the manuals used for teaching can easily be used in many different countries.

the complexity of working with 10, or even 15, systems of law is reduced or focused in each exercise on three or four solutions that fundamentally differ from one another.[38]

The students are thereafter invited to *compare these solutions* and to identify possible common principles for the issue under examination. In cases where the national solutions diverge, the students are invited to *weigh up their respective advantages and disadvantages* and to finally *suggest a solution* which seems most appropriate to them.

2. Acquiring a basic knowledge of the fundamental characteristics of different legal cultures: combining micro- and macro-comparison[39]

When working with the case scenarios, students are introduced to identifying, applying, and then comparing the approaches and solutions provided by different jurisdictions to a single case and legal issue. They are also invited to analyse and compare the rules, principles, and reasoning on which these solutions rely (*micro-comparison*).

Each time that two or three cases have been addressed and worked with, an *ex cathedra* lecture might be offered where the students receive basic information on the different legal cultures. This helps them to better understand the materials provided and grasp the reasons for the diversity of the laws, and to understand the statutes and case law they are working with. In those parts of the course, information and explanations can be provided on the different legal cultures and traditions, on their historical origins and particularities, as well as on different styles in legislation and case law (*macro-comparison*). In those more theoretical parts of the course, students will benefit from the experience they have already gained when actively working with the case scenarios and with foreign law.[40]

3. Challenges due to the diversity of languages

The multilateral method *ideally* requires good knowledge of foreign languages. Solid reading skills of English, French, and German, for example, allows the comparative lawyer to access materials from nine European jurisdictions, as well as legal materials from the USA, many other Common Law jurisdictions, and many members of the ancient French legal family. Adding Spanish gives access to one more European, and numerous Latin American, jurisdictions.

In the present book, information on Common Law jurisdictions is provided solely in its original English language version, whereas materials from other countries (codal or

---

38 Experience shows that for a single question of law, rarely more than three or four fundamentally different solutions are applied.
39 *Macro-comparison* is about general issues of comparative law such as classification of the different jurisdictions, their historical developments and particularities, the organisation of their respective judicial processes, different legislative techniques, and styles of codification, etc., see for instance, ZWEIGERT/KÖTZ (fn. 10), at p. 4. *Micro-comparaison*, on the contrary, deals with rules and principles of law which allow us to solve specific issues and problems, and the comparison of the solution of these problems under different laws, see e.g. ZWEIGERT/KÖTZ (fn. 10), at p. 5.
40 It is in these parts of the course, given *ex cathedra*, that micro- and macro-comparison will merge. See also E. ÖRÜCÜ, Developing Comparative Law, in: E. Örücü/D. Nelken (eds.), *Comparative Law: A Handbook*, Oxford: Hart Publishing, 2007, p. 57: "Ideally macro-comparison and micro-comparison should merge, since the micro-comparative topic must be placed within the entire legal system." For more information, students are advised to read or consult an introduction to comparative law (above fn. 10).

statutory provisions, court rulings, extracts of academic writings) are accompanied by a translation. To better grasp and understand the particularities of the different legal systems, students are invited to read the materials, whenever possible, in the original language version. Doing comparative law thus offers them, at the same time, the opportunity to improve their knowledge of foreign legal languages.[41]

V. Benefits of the presented approach

The proposed method of teaching, studying, and learning comparative law offers several benefits and advantages:[42]

- Students study comparative law with a *learning by doing* approach and actively train themselves using comparative methodology.
- They overcome their discomfort when approaching foreign materials and working with materials from jurisdictions unknown to them until then.
- When solving case scenarios under different laws, students learn to take a step back from the jurisdiction in which they are rooted and they learn to favour a critical view, putting the solution in force in their country into perspective. They experience that the rule provided in their own jurisdiction for a specific legal issue is not the only reasonable rule to follow, but just one of several ways to address and solve the specific legal problem.[43]

    In comparative contract law, for example, students having studied in the UK, the USA, or Germany learn that – contrary to the rules in force in their countries – it is indeed possible to regard the exposure of goods in shops or even advertisements as binding offers, and that some (good) arguments may speak in favour of this solution. Students having studied in France, Belgium, or Common Law countries make the experience that the formation of contracts need not necessarily be made depend on the existence of a "*cause*" or "consideration" – and that more targeted devices to control contractual agreements may work just as well or even better while fully respecting the intention of the parties and achieving a maximum of legal certainty. With respect to the transfer of property of movables, students having studied in Germany, Greece, or South Africa learn that the abstraction principle, deeply rooted in these jurisdictions, is a rare exception from a comparative perspective. Students having studied in Belgium, Switzerland, or Germany learn that, contrary to the laws of Belgium, Switzerland, and Germany, the seller's liability is strict in France, England, the USA, and China, and that (very) good reasons speak in favour of this solution; etc., etc.
- Students thus get familiar with many different jurisdictions and with different styles of legal reasoning. This enables them to better understand foreign colleagues, to

---

41 See also A. BULLIER, Le droit comparé dans l'enseignement – Le droit comparé est-il un passe-temps inutile?, *RDIC* 2008, 163 at 166: "Le droit comparé ne peut, en aucun cas, faire l'impasse sur le problème de la langue qui véhicule concepts, traditions, réflexes et façons de dire et de comprendre les choses. Le cours de droit comparé sait-il initier les étudiants à la traduction juridique?"; see also CONSTANTINESCO (fn. 13), at p. 29.
42 Experience shows that this approach works not only in seminars with a small number of participants, but also in larger classes. In Geneva, between 60 and 160 students take the comparative law course which is taught with this method, at the KU Leuven some 200 students follow the course.
43 Students hereby obtain a "vaccination [...] against the error that the dogmatic figures of their own law are identical with 'natural law'", KÖTZ (fn. 12), at p. 262. (Translated from German: "Die Studierenden erhalten so eine Schutzimpfung [...], die [sie] gegen den Irrtum feit, es seien die dogmatischen Figuren ihrer Rechtsordnung mit dem Naturrecht identisch").

- better exchange with colleagues trained in a number of other jurisdictions,[44] and to have a discussion on legal issues in an international context (e.g. European or even worldwide). In fact, the proposed methodology teaches a comparative legal science which is detached from the contingencies related to one or the other local law and should thus be thought-provoking.
- By the end of the course, students should have acquired the ability and skill to work with materials from many jurisdictions at the same time and to look for, and bring to light, ideally, a range of possible solutions to any issue under examination, or, as the case may be, to possibly discover common principles of law regarding this issue that exist throughout Europe or other parts of the world.
- During the work with the case scenarios and the discussions about pros and cons of the approaches and solutions found in the materials, students will learn to benefit from learning experiences from other jurisdictions. They can hereby make an informed choice, ideally, among several available options, when required to solve a specific legal issue.
- The proposed method thus emphasises the practical benefits that may be associated with the use of the comparative method. It shows that the use of this method can generate immediate and tangible results and that comparative law can be truly efficient.
- Last but not least, the students will be prepared, and will dispose of the necessary methodological tools, to handle scenarios such as the two public international law cases or the civil liability case described above,[45] as well as many other domestic or transnational scenarios.

Mastering a multilateral and supranational comparative method should thus facilitate the students' future work in a multijurisdictional world, populated with very diverse legal thinkers – be it in their work as lawyers, judges, or jurists in a national framework or institution, or in an international organisation and context. James Gordley, comparatist at Tulane University in New Orleans, has written: "A student confronted with only one solution to a legal problem has a tendency to assume it is the right one. When he is confronted with two, he is encouraged to think."[46] One could add: when a student has acquired the capacity to compare the solutions of three, four, or even more jurisdictions and to give these jurisdictions equal weight in his or her analysis, he or she is enabled to *think internationally*.

---

44 ÖRÜCÜ (fn. 40), at p. 43 and p. 45: "Comparative law gives [them] a tool of communication."
45 Above, pp. 10–12.
46 J. GORDLEY, Comparative Law and Legal Education, *Tul. L. Rev.* 2000–2001, 1003 at 1008.

Chapter 3

Is it legitimate and beneficial for judges to compare?

The comparative method taught in this book allows us to compare solutions from different countries and legal systems and to use them as source of inspiration when looking for solutions to legal problems. In the legislative process, a purely domestic perspective has long been considered outdated. In fact, national and international legislatures have always relied on, and benefited from, significant comparative research during the drafting stage of private law legislation. When interpreting domestic law, courts in a certain number of jurisdictions also draw inspiration from foreign solutions and increasingly from "common principles" of law derived from comparison. In other jurisdictions, it is still less common for the judge to take inspiration from the comparative approach when deciding cases according to their domestic law.

The question of whether it is legitimate for the judge to use the comparative method is fundamental to the role that this method can play in practice. If the use of the comparative method is legitimate for the judge, and if judges take inspiration from foreign law and "common principles" derived from comparison, the comparative method becomes not only a precious tool for the judge, but also for lawyers who could also find inspiration in foreign legal systems when it comes to interpreting the law, filling its gaps, or suggesting solutions to new legal problems in the interest of their clients.

Before getting to the heart of the comparative law exercises that constitute Part B of this book, it seems appropriate to give some thought to the question of who could use this method and, notably, whether it is legitimate and useful for the judge to compare. This chapter thus analyses the arguments for and against the legitimacy of judicial comparison when it comes to applying domestic law. It further considers the benefits that may be derived from comparison by the judge.

I. Introduction[1]

In the early 21st century, it might seem surprising to still ask the question whether it is legitimate for judges to use the comparative method in their reasoning. The experience of teaching comparative law shows, however, that students, i.e. the judges and lawyers of tomorrow, despite the insights and the intellectual pleasure they derive from comparing laws, often doubt whether it is legitimate for courts to use comparative methodology. They also have doubts concerning the benefits they might be able to derive from the comparative

---

1 This chapter was first published in *ERPL* 2013, 687–716. It was reprinted (with permission of Kluwer Law International) in an extended version in: D. Fairgrieve/M. Andenas (eds.), *Courts and Comparative Law*, Oxford: OUP, 2015, pp. 25–53.

method in their future practical life as lawyers. In contrast, they quickly recognise the use of comparative law with regard to legislation, whether on a national or international level, given that national and international legislators regularly rely on comparative studies when preparing legislation. Judges and lawyers[2] in some countries also still question the legitimacy of the use of comparative methodology by the courts.

The following reflections address the question of whether it is *legitimate* for the judge to resort to the comparative method in addition to the classic methods of determining and interpreting domestic law. If it is legitimate, is it *beneficial* for the courts to use the comparative method? And if so, do the benefits of the comparative method justify the sometimes considerable effort that the comparative approach demands?

A practical example serves to illustrate that these questions are far from purely theoretical: the economy of a central European State undertakes privatisation. A foreign investor buys one of the largest companies in that country. The company, which is of national importance (and too big to fail), risks bankruptcy but is saved by State investment in the region of several billion dollars. The State accuses the foreign investor of not having taken necessary measures to save the company, measures that the investor had been obliged to take under the privatisation contract. The State therefore claims damages in the region of several billion dollars for the investments made to save the company.

The case is to be decided on the application of provisions of the civil code of the State concerned. There is little doctrine and no case law interpreting the applicable articles (provisions concerning contractual and tortious liability). That being said, in neighbouring countries' codes, there are similar provisions which have been widely commented on and often applied by their courts. These codes served as an inspiration to the state's legislator at the time of codification of its domestic Civil Law.[3]

In such a case, is it legitimate for the court to take inspiration from foreign codes, statutory law, case law, and legal doctrine when dealing with the issue under the applicable domestic law? Would lawyers be able to use, in the interest of their clients, other legal systems as a source of inspiration and support when proposing a certain interpretation of the law to the judges?

These questions are not limited to Europe. A very animated discussion among judges of the Supreme Court of the USA has helped in putting this issue on the agenda of judges, comparatists, and lawyers.[4]

This chapter analyses the arguments for and against the *legitimacy* of the comparative method when it comes to applying domestic law (in section II), and the *benefits* that may be derived from comparison by the judge. Numerous decisions from courts around

---

[2] When teaching comparative law to lawyers, their scepticism regarding the use of comparative law frequently vanishes only when studying cases in which the courts used this method in their reasoning.
[3] For more case scenarios, see Chapter 2, pp. 10–12.
[4] The discussion in the *USA* focuses on the comparative method in constitutional law. In Europe, the legitimacy of judicial comparison has hardly ever been discussed. See e.g. C. McCrudden, A Common Law of Human Rights? Transnational Judicial Conversations on Constitutional Rights, *OJLS* 2000, 499 at 503: a topic "relatively ignored in the theoretical literature"; R. Reed, Foreign Precedents and Judicial Reasoning: the American Debate and British Practice, *L.Q.R.* 2008, 253 at 259: The current discussion in the USA "has no parallel in the United Kingdom or elsewhere in the common law world". In the USA, the topic is also regarded as "under-theorized", R. Hirschl, The Question of Case Selection in Comparative Constitutional Law, *Am. J. Comp. L.* 2005, 125.

Europe illustrate the *reasons* that lead to the use of comparative methodology and the multiple *aims* that the courts pursue by using this method (in section III).

II. Comparative law – a method at the disposal of the courts?

1. Is it legitimate to use comparative law? – arguments against the use of comparative methodology by courts

Some arguments seem to speak against the use of the comparative method by the courts when interpreting national law.[5]

a) A lack of democratic legitimacy

According to a first argument, the judge is bound by the law, but only his or her domestic law as well as international law in force in his or her country. Only the national legislator and, where required, an international legislator, would have the necessary democratic legitimacy to guide the judge in his or her decision. Foreign law failed to respect this democratic legitimacy and would not, in light of this fact, be capable of either binding, convincing, or even serving as an inspiration to the national judge, in the interpretation of his or her own domestic law.[6]

b) The legal system – a national system

According to a second argument, every domestic legal provision or precedent should be interpreted within its own context, that of a national system.[7] In many continental legal systems, Civil Law is codified in a coherent system, the system of the national code, whereas in Common Law countries, case law constitutes a body of jurisprudence with its own coherence. It is claimed that an interpretation that takes inspiration from foreign sources is potentially harmful to national legal systems.

---

[5] For an emphatic statement against the use of comparative law by *US* Federal courts, see A. SCALIA, Keynote Address: Foreign Legal Authority in the Federal Courts, in: American Society of International Law, Proceedings of the 98th Annual Meeting (American Society of International Law), 2004, 305, www.jstor.org/pss/25659941.

[6] A. SCALIA, Commentary, *St. Louis U. L. J.* 1996, 1119 at 1122: "[we] judges of the American democracies are servants of our peoples, sworn to apply [. . .] the laws that those peoples deem appropriate. We are not some international priesthood empowered to impose upon our free and independent citizen supra-national values that contradict their own." In the USA, some critics have argued that an "unchecked comparative practice" was "subversive of the whole concept of sovereignty", see: Appropriate Role of Foreign Judgments in the Interpretation of American Law: Hearing on H.R. Res. 568 before the Subcomm. on the Constitution of the House Comm. on the Judiciary, 108th Cong., 2nd Sess. 77, 2004, at 72 (testimony of Prof. J. RABKIN, Cornell Univ.); see also E. YOUNG, Foreign Law and the Denominator Problem, *Harv. L. Rev.* 2005, 148 at 163: "[I]mporting foreign law into the domestic legal system through constitutional interpretation circumvents the institutional mechanism by which the political branches ordinarily control the interaction between the domestic and the foreign"; D. PFEFFER, Depriving America of Evolving Its Own Standards of Decency? An Analysis of the Use of Foreign Law in Eighth Amendment Jurisprudence and Its Effect on Democracy, *St. Louis U. L. J.* 2007, 855, e.g. at 879; Z. LARSEN, Discounting Foreign Imports: Foreign Authority in Constitutional Interpretation & the Curb of Popular Sovereignty, *Willamette L. Rev.* 2009, 767, e.g. at 784.

[7] In this sense see SCALIA (fn. 6).

c) Specificities of the national situation

According to another argument, each legal provision, as well as each judgment interpreting a provision and applying the law in a specific case, is always the result of a weighing of interests. It is argued that this weighing of interests necessarily takes place within the national context, taking into account the specificities of the situation in the country concerned and the cultural context in which the decision will take effect. In this sense, Antonin Scalia, judge of the Supreme Court of the USA, in a judgment concerning US constitutional law, expressed the opinion that looking at foreign law is, at best, of no importance and, at worst, dangerous. According to him, the Supreme Court of the USA "should not impose foreign moods, fads or fashions on Americans".[8] In the majority opinion of the Court, Justice Kennedy, who frequently uses the comparative method, had referred to English law and the case law of the European Court of Human Rights. According to Justice Scalia, in his dissenting opinion, such considerations of foreign law would be "meaningless dicta".[9]

d) Legal science – a largely national science

Over the last few years, certain courts have once again emphasised the fact that, although *comparativa est omnis investigatio* and "all forms of higher knowledge consist of comparison",[10] the law remains a largely national science. The Federal Supreme

---

8 In *Lawrence et al.* v. *Texas* 539 U.S. 558, [2003], 598 (on the constitutionality of a statute of the State of Texas prohibiting certain sexual acts between persons of the same sex; held that this law violates the "Due Process Clause" of the US Constitution), at p. 598: "The Court's discussion of these foreign views (ignoring, of course, the many countries that have retained criminal prohibitions on sodomy) is therefore meaningless dicta. Dangerous dicta, however, since 'this Court ... should not impose foreign moods, fads, or fashions on Americans'." With reference to *Foster* v. *Florida*, 537 U.S. 990, note (2002) (J. Thomas): "Justice Breyer has only added another foreign court to his list while still failing to ground support for his theory in any decision by an American court." *Ibid.*, at 990: "While Congress, as a *legislature*, may wish to consider the actions of other nations on any issue it likes, this Court's Eighth Amendment jurisprudence should not impose foreign moods, fads, or fashions on Americans."

9 *Ibid.*, at p. 573; see also L. Blum, Mixed Signals: The Limited Role of Comparative Analysis in Constitutional Adjudication, *San Diego L. Rev.* 2002, 157, e.g. at 163; B. Lucas, Structural Exceptionalism and Comparative Constitutional Law, *Va. L. Rev.* 2010, 1965; E. Young (fn. 6), at p. 148. The *US* Supreme Court has, however, a long tradition when it comes to using the comparative method, see e.g. M. Minow, The Controversial Status of International and Comparative Law in the United States, *Harv. Int'l. L. J. Online*, 27.08.2010, at I.: "[N]o one disagrees that United States judges have long consulted and referred materials from other countries as well as international sources; yet for the past nine or so years, citing foreign and international sources provoked intense controversy"; V. Jackson, Constitutional Comparisons: Convergence, Resistance, Engagement, *Harv. L. Rev.* 2005, 110; G. Calabresi/S. Dotson Zimdahl, The Supreme Court and Foreign Sources of Law: Two Hundred Years of Practice and the Juvenile Death Penalty Decision, *Wm. & Mary L. Rev.* 2005, 743. See on the debate in the US also A. Barak, Comparative Law, Originalism and the Role of a Judge in a Democracy: A Reply to Justice Scalia, *The Fulbright Convention*, 29 January 2006 (Speech delivered at the Fulbright Israel/USIEF 50th Anniversary Symposium: International Influences on National Legal Systems, The Hebrew University of Jerusalem, 29 January 2006); M. Rosenfeld, Le constitutionnalisme comparé en mouvement: d'une controverse américaine sur les références jurisprudentielles au droit étranger, in: P. Legrand (ed.), *Comparer les droits, résolument*, Paris: PUF, 2009, p. 561; I. Eisenberger, Wer fürchtet sich vor einem Verfassungsrechtsvergleich? Gedanken zur Rechtsvergleichung in der Judikatur des US Supreme Court, *JRP* 2010, 216 at 217: "Rechtsvergleichung am SC ist beinahe so alt wie die Institution selbst. Ebenso alt wie die Rechtsvergleichungspraxis ist die Kritik daran".

10 M. Freeland, Introduction: Comparative and International Law in the Courts, in: G. Canivet/M. Andenas/D. Fairgrieve (eds.), *Comparative Law before the Courts*, London: BIICL, 2005, p. xvii.

Administrative Court of Germany accordingly declared in a 1992 judgment that "[d]ie Rechtswissenschaft ist eine national geprägte Wissenschaft"[11] (legal science is a nationally characterised science). A German court of appeal expressly supported this view in a judgment in 2004. This case related to the legitimacy of an agreement reached between a lawyer and his client concerning legal fees calculated according to the final result, *Erfolgshonorare* or contingency fees,[12] valid in US law but prohibited and hitherto deemed contrary to moral and legal standards by German law.

e) Lack of knowledge of foreign law and linguistic barriers

According to yet another argument, it is evident that the national legislator would not expect courts to have knowledge of foreign law. This knowledge would, however, be necessary to correctly employ the comparative method. Given that judges did not know or, at best, only knew a little foreign law, use of the comparative method would open the door to error, to danger of an incorrect understanding, and to a false interpretation of foreign law.[13] Added to which, there were often also linguistic barriers that made understanding foreign law particularly difficult and multiplied the risks of error.[14] Because of language barriers, one US author (and comparatist) has made the proposal to leave aside "foreign-language law" when comparing.[15] Last but not least, the judge would simply not have the time and resources necessary to systematically carry out comparative research.[16]

---

11 BVerwG, 30.06.1992 (on the recognition of a Polish Master of Laws degree), NJW 1993, 276.
12 OLG Celle, 26.11.2004, NJW 2005, 2160 f.: "Rechtsvergleichung kann Gemeinsamkeiten und Unterschiede der Rechtsordnungen deutlich machen. Sie kann auch dem Richter eine Auslegungshilfe im Sinne einer 'fünften Auslegungsmethode' . . . sein. Die praktische Bedeutung einer solchen Vorgehensweise ist freilich bislang sehr gering geblieben. Außerhalb des durch Kollisionsnormen bestimmten Bereichs können im Wege der Rechtsvergleichung gewonnene Erkenntnisse nur dort einfließen, wo das eigene Recht 'offen' ist und damit Interpretationsspielräume lässt . . . Auch darf die Bindung des Richters an Recht und Gesetz (Art. 20 III GG) nicht in Frage gestellt werden und muss weiter bedacht werden, dass mit der Übertragung von Rechtsgrundsätzen einer fremden Rechtsordnung, und zwar besonders dann, wenn diese einer anderen Rechtsfamilie angehört, in die eigene Rechtsordnung vorsichtig umzugehen ist".
13 See on this argument E. Hondius, Comparative Law in the Court-Room: Europe and America Compared, in: A. Büchler/M. Müller-Chen (eds.), *Festschrift für Ingeborg Schwenzer zum 60. Geburtstag*, Vol. 1, Bern: Stämpfli, 2011, 759 at 769: "The high quality of the [foreign] expert opinions is apparent from the reports on Dutch law. And yet . . . when reading the expert opinion on Dutch law, I sometimes know almost for certain that a Dutch court would decide differently now"; McCrudden (fn. 4), at p. 526; Reed (fn. 4), at p. 264.
14 Reed (fn. 4), at p. 264: "[M]any British judges (and counsel) are effectively monolingual, so that decisions must either come from an English-speaking jurisdiction or be translated . . . [M]ost of the world's case law is in reality inaccessible to most British lawyers"; Young (fn. 6), at p. 166: both decision costs and error costs "seem likely to be high for American courts dealing with foreign materials, given language and cultural barriers and most American lawyers' lack of training in comparative analysis". See on this issue also J. Bell, Le droit comparé au Royaume-Uni, in: X. Blanc-Jouvan et al., *L'avenir du droit comparé, un défi pour les juristes du nouveau millénaire*, Paris: Société de Législation comparée, 2000, p. 283; B. Markesinis/J. Fedtke, The Judge as Comparatist, *Tul. L. Rev.* 2005–2006, 11 at 114.
15 J. Stapleton, Benefits of Comparative Tort Reasoning: Lost in Translation, *JTL* 2007, 6 at 33, introducing the notion of "comparative foreign-language law": "[T]he general indifference of North American and Australasian courts and practitioners to the tort law of foreign-language jurisdictions seems a wise response from inescapable phenomena. For them there is no more to be reliably derived from foreign-language jurisdictions than from English-speaking ones [. . .]: moreover, there are added perils of misinterpretation"; published also in: M. Andenas/D. Fairgrieve, *Tom Bingham and the Transformation of the Law: A Liber Amicorum*, Oxford: OUP, 2009, p. 773.
16 See the example given by Hondius (fn. 13), p. 759 at 773.

f) The danger of cherry picking

Some have voiced criticism of the courts' over-selective citing of foreign law. It would always be possible to find support in some countries for a solution that is favoured by the courts. In contrast, diverging solutions in other countries would not always be invoked. In certain cases, the courts relied on the comparative argument, whereas they rejected comparison when the solution found in foreign law differs from that which is preferred by the court. Here the argument in question is that of cherry picking. It is used frequently by critics of the comparative approach in recent discussion in the USA and notably by judge Antonin Scalia.[17]

All of these arguments therefore seem to speak against the use of the comparative method by the courts.

2. Widening horizons – arguments in favour of the use of comparative methodology by the courts

The question thus is, on the one hand, whether, and to what extent, these arguments are convincing; and on the other hand, whether there are arguments favouring the use of comparative law by the judge when interpreting and applying domestic law.

a) Cherry picking – an apprehension that has not been confirmed by court practice

The danger of cherry picking is not unique to the comparative argument. The risk exists just as well in relation to differing opinions in doctrine and case law which can also be used and cited very selectively by courts.[18] Therefore, provided that the comparative method is used as seriously and in an equally balanced manner as every other method of interpretation, the danger of cherry picking does not question the legitimacy of comparison. In fact, numerous examples show that courts choose the jurisdictions for comparison very carefully

---

17 SCALIA (fn. 5), at p. 309: "Adding foreign law [. . .] is much like legislative history, which ordinarily contains something for everybody and can be used or not used, used in one part or in another, deemed controlling or pronounced inconclusive, depending upon the result the court wishes to reach [. . .] The Court's reliance has also been selective as to when foreign law is consulted *at all*"; *ibid.*: "To invoke alien law when it agrees with one's own thinking, and ignore it otherwise, is not reasoned decision-making but sophistry", dissenting opinion in *Roper* v. *Simmons*, US SC, 543 U.S. 551 [2005], 627; see also Chief Justice of the US SC J. ROBERTS: "Foreign law, you can find anything you want. If you don't find it in the decisions of France or Italy, it's in the decisions of Somalia or Japan or Indonesia or wherever. As somebody said in another context, looking at foreign law for support is like looking over a crowd for support and picking out your friends [. . .] And that actually expands the discretion of the judge. It allows the judge to incorporate his or her own personal preferences, cloak them with the authority of precedent [. . .] and use that to determine the meaning of the Constitution", in: US Senate Judiciary Committee, Hearing on the Nomination of John Roberts to be Chief Justice of the Supreme Court, Transcript, Day Two, Part III, 13.09.2005, www.washingtonpost.com/wp-dyn/content/article/2005/09/13/AR2005091301210.html; see also R. POSNER, *Legal Affairs*, July/August 2004, www.legalaffairs.org/issues/July-August-2004/feature_posner_julaug04.msp.

18 See R. GLENSY, Which Countries Count? *Lawrence* v. *Texas* and the Selection of Foreign Persuasive Authority, *VJIL* 2005, 357 at 401 ff.; MCCRUDDEN(fn. 4), at p. 517: "[T]here are also increasing numbers of judges in particular jurisdictions who appear to consider it important to distinguish judgments of foreign courts if they go against the conclusions that the judge intends to reach"; S. BREYER, Judge of the US Supreme Court, in: U.S. Association of Constitutional Law Discussion: Constitutional Relevance of Foreign Court Decisions (2005), Transcript by Federal News Service, Washington, DC, www.freerepublic.com/focus/f-news/1352357/posts.

and do not hesitate to cite foreign law in situations where the solution under foreign law differs from that preferred by the court. In these cases, comparative law is used in order to highlight the specificities of one's own domestic law.[19]

b) Increasingly accessible information on foreign law

In order to avoid error and misunderstanding as to the content of foreign law, and so that the court has a solid basis for the use of the comparative method, it is effectively essential that the judge is provided with trustworthy, sound, and reliable information on the substance of foreign law.[20]

For numerous points of law, this information is now available. First of all, and most obviously, the Internet makes access to information on foreign law and foreign case law much easier. Moreover, several institutions, research groups, and numerous comparatists substantially contribute to the circulation of knowledge on foreign law. To name just some of the particularly active institutions and groups, it is possible to mention the International Institute for the Unification of Private Law (UNIDROIT), the Commission on European Contract Law, the Study Group on a European Civil Code, the Research Group on Existing EC Private Law, the Academy of European Private Lawyers, the Trento Group working on a Common Core of European Private Law, the European Group of Tort Law, the European Centre of Tort and Insurance Law (ECTIL), as well as the Leuven and Maastricht group of researchers working under the leadership of Walter van Gerven on the "Ius Commune Casebooks for the Common Law of Europe". Some of these groups count among their members researchers from all European jurisdictions, and others consist of researchers from around the world. They seek to make available entire libraries containing reliable and up-to-date information on foreign laws. A large majority of this information is published in English, thus facilitating access.[21] It is also possible to mention the numerous comparative analyses that are published in European law journals, such as the *European Review of Private Law* (ERPL), the *Maastricht Journal of European and Comparative Law*, the *Columbia Journal of European Law*, the *Zeitschrift für Europäisches Privatrecht* (ZEuP), and the *Rivista di diritto pubblico comparato ed europeo*, published in English, German, and Italian, respectively.

Providing reliable information on foreign and comparative law, in easily accessible languages, is therefore the responsibility of comparatists and researchers using a comparative approach in their publications. English judges have expressly noted that without these publications, comparison would not have been possible for the court.[22] In a case

---

19 For examples and references see below, pp. 38 ff. For criteria for choosing the jurisdiction for comparison, see e.g. McCrudden (fn. 4), at pp. 517 ff.; Reed (fn. 4), at pp. 264, 271; Glensy (fn. 18), at pp. 401 ff.; A. Friedman, Beyond Cherry-Picking: Selection Criteria for the Use of Foreign Law in Domestic Constitutional Jurisprudence, *Suffolk U. L. Rev.* 2011, 873.
20 McCrudden (fn. 4), at p. 527: "(in general) a judge or court in one jurisdiction will not use case law from another jurisdiction unless it is considered to be comparable, and unless the judge or court feels adequately informed about the other jurisdiction"; see also T. Bingham, *Widening Horizons: The Influence of Comparative Law and International Law on Domestic Law*, Cambridge: CUP, 2010, p. 5, who reminds us incidentally that "few human activities are free from the risk of error and judicial decision-making is no exception".
21 A reading proficiency in *English*, *French*, and *German* gives access to the law of *nine* European jurisdictions in the original language, and beyond that to further Common Law jurisdictions as well as to further jurisdictions belonging to the *French* legal tradition.
22 See e.g. Lord Goff of Chieveley, *White* v. *Jones*, [1995] 2 AC 207, All ER 691 at 705 (HL): "[I]n the present case, thanks to material published in our language by distinguished comparatists, German as well as English,

brought before the court, it is also possible for this comparative research to be carried out on an ad hoc basis by comparative law institutions and lawyers[23] (or their trainees) trained in comparative law.[24] Christopher McCrudden recalls that when "lawyers appearing before the courts, or clerks assisting the judge, give the judge confidence, then the decisions of foreign systems are more likely to be cited".[25]

Thanks to this information on foreign law, error and misunderstanding in the substance of foreign law can be avoided. Consequently, this argument does not question the legitimacy and practicability of comparison either.

Ruth Bader Ginsburg, judge at the US Supreme Court, has stated in this respect: "[W]e should approach foreign legal materials with sensitivity to our differences, deficiencies, and imperfect understanding, but imperfection, I believe, should not lead us to abandon the effort to learn what we can from the experience and good thinking foreign sources may convey."[26]

c) Access to foreign law – the Private International Law argument

In cross-border cases which present closer links with a foreign legal system than with the law of the jurisdiction in which a legal action is brought, the forum's Private International Law sometimes obliges the court to resolve the case solely on the application of foreign law. The existence of Private International Law rules clearly shows that the legislators believe it is possible for the national judge to be informed about the substance of foreign law in a reliable and trustworthy way.[27]

d) The comparative methodology – a method of interpretation like any other

It is clear that the national legislator does not expect courts or lawyers to know foreign law as they know domestic law. It is equally clear that judges and lawyers cannot resort to the comparative method in *every* case.

---

we have direct access to publications which should sufficiently dispel our ignorance of German law and so by comparison illuminate our understanding of our own".

23 This was the case e.g. in *Tabet* v. *Gett*, [2010] H.C.A. 12, www.austlii.edu.au/au/cases/cth/HCA/2010/12. html or the *English* case *A and Others* v. *the National Blood Authority* [2001] 3 All ER 289. See also H. Kötz, Alte und neue Aufgaben der Rechtsvergleichung, *JZ* 2002, 257 at 259: lawyers "sind sich offenbar noch nicht genügend des Umstands bewusst, dass ein für ihre Mandanten günstiger Rechtsstandpunkt sich in vielen Fällen auf rechtsvergleichende Argumente stützen lässt"(apparently lawyers are not yet sufficiently aware that they can use comparative law in order to further the interests of their clients); Hondius (fn. 13), p. 759 at 777; for *England* e.g. Lord Steyn, *The Constitutionalisation of Public Law*, London: Constitution Unit, 1999, p. 51 at 58: "Law Lords expect a high standard of research and interpretation from barristers [. . .] For example, if the appeal involves a statutory offence we would expect counsel to be familiar with [. . .] comparative material from, say, Australia and New Zealand".
24 For a method of teaching comparative law that prepares the students for this task, see Chapter 2, pp. 5 ff., and the method taught in this book.
25 McCrudden (fn. 4), at p. 526.
26 R. Bader Ginsburg, A Decent Respect to the Opinions of [Human]kind: The Value of a Comparative Perspective in Constitutional Adjudication, *C.L.J.* 2005, 575 at 580.
27 In some jurisdictions, such as *Switzerland*, the judge establishes the content of foreign law *ex officio*, see Art. 16 sect. 1 LDIP; in other jurisdictions, he or she can require that the parties contribute to the establishment of the content of foreign law or, for certain areas of law, that they establish its content altogether, see Lord Collins of Mapesbury et al. (eds.), *Dicey, Morris & Collins on The Conflict of Laws*, 15th ed., London: Sweet & Maxwell, 2016, Vol. 1, §§ 9R-001 ff.; see also E. Örücü, Comparative Law in Practice: The Courts and the Legislator, in: E. Örücü/D. Nelken (eds.), *Comparative Law: A Handbook*, Oxford: Hart, 2007, p. 411 at 414, 418.

In situations where such knowledge is not available or accessible, the court cannot be expected to use the comparative approach. However, in cases where content of foreign law is brought to the attention of the court, the judges are in a position to build on this knowledge and to use the comparative arguments when interpreting domestic law.[28]

The fact that the comparative method can be used in some cases and not in others is not unique to this method. While the literal rule and perhaps also the purposive approach are methods of interpretation that are always available to the court, this is not the case for other methods of statutory interpretation. This is true notably in relation to the historical interpretation, which draws inspiration from the legislative history of the law, and the systematic interpretation, both of which will assist the judge, much like the comparative method, in his or her search for a solution to specific problems in some cases and not in others.

e) Revival of a European legal science

The argument that legal science is a largely national science is another argument against the use of comparative law that barely convinces. Throughout a large part of the 20th century, in countries such as Germany and France, legal science was effectively a widely national science. However, in other countries, notably the UK as well as some countries in continental Europe, such as the Netherlands, Belgium, Austria, and Switzerland, legal science has never been limited to a single national law. On the contrary, the doctrine in these jurisdictions, and to some extent also the court practice, has a long history of using the comparative approach.[29] In the second half of the 20th century, more and more legal scientists argued in favour of an internationalisation (or more accurately, a *re-internationalisation*[30]) of legal science.[31] These pleas were eventually successful and we observe today a renaissance of a truly international science of law in Europe. In law, ideas and solutions are circulating across borders again.

f) The judge's freedom to choose his or her methods of determining the law – revival of the idea of justice that transcends borders

Another argument against the use of the comparative method asserts that every law and judgment is the result of a weighing of interests which would necessarily have to take place within each country's own cultural context.[32] This argument overlooks the fact that, these days, the national legislators themselves rely on extensive comparative research in practically every

---

28 For the important role that lawyers might play in this respect, see above, pp. 25–26.
29 References below, pp. 34 ff. See also Hondius (fn. 13), at p. 759 at 765: "It has been suggested that, if one wishes to consider legal research a science, [focusing on domestic developments] is the wrong attitude. Science knows no borders, and legal science is no exception."
30 Before the period of the codification of the law started on the continent, legal discourse on the continent was truly European in using the same language, Latin; see e.g. R. ZIMMERMANN, *The Law of Obligations. Roman Foundations of the Civilian Tradition*, Oxford: Clarendon Press, 1996; R. ZIMMERMANN, Das römisch-kanonische ius commune als Grundlage europäischer Rechtseinheit, *JZ* 1992, 8; H. COING, *Die ursprüngliche Einheit der europäischen Rechtswissenschaft*, Wiesbaden: Franz Steiner Verlag, 1968, pp. 10, 17; for the situation in Private International Law, see T. KADNER GRAZIANO, *Gemeineuropäisches Internationales Privatrecht*, Tübingen: Mohr Siebeck, 2002, pp. 46–59.
31 For references see e.g. T. KADNER GRAZIANO, *Comparative Contract Law: Cases, Materials and Excercises*, Basingstoke/New York: Palgrave Macmillan, 2009, pp. 7 ff.
32 See above, pp. 21–22, with references.

important legislative procedure and, at any rate, in matters of private law. To cite just a few recent examples: the recent codifications in the Baltic States have largely taken inspiration from comparative studies. The Estonian legislator has followed the example of the German Civil Code in his new codification of the Law of Obligations (and has introduced e.g. a general part in the new Law of Obligations and has, e.g. in torts, codified the essence of a century of German case law). The legislator has also widely taken inspiration from Swiss law, Dutch law, the laws of Quebec and Louisiana, the United Nations Convention on Contracts for the International Sale of Goods (CISG), the Principles of European Contract Law, and the UNIDROIT Principles of International Commercial Contracts.[33] The new Lithuanian Civil Code of 2000 takes inspiration, among others, from the codifications and statutes of the Netherlands, Quebec, Germany, France, Italy, Switzerland, Sweden, Latvia, Japan, and Russia, as well as from the CISG and the UNIDROIT Principles.[34] Polish law has recently taken inspiration from German and Dutch law, as well as the CISG and the Principles of European Contract Law. In Central and Eastern European countries, the comparative method plays such an important role in modern legislation that it was affirmed that "the main method used for private law in today's legislative drafting is the comparative method".[35]

In 2002, the German Civil Code (the BGB) experienced the most important reform since it came into force in 1900.[36] Initiated by a European Directive, the drafting process of this reform took inspiration from a wide range of European jurisdictions.[37]

In China, important law reforms have taken place over the last 15 years, in particular with the adoption of the Chinese Contract Act of 1999, the Law of Property Act of 2007, and the Tort Law Act of 2010. Among the sources of inspiration for the Contract Act were the codifications of Germany, Japan, and Taiwan, the English Common Law, and US law, as well as the CISG, the UNIDROIT Principles of International Commercial Contracts, and the Principles of European Contract Law.[38] The new Law of Property Act drew inspiration from the laws of Germany, France, Japan, and Taiwan and from some aspects of English and US law.[39] In 2010, a first draft version of a Chinese Civil Code was presented. The structure of the draft code was inspired by the example of the Pandects and by Dutch law.[40]

These varied examples show that preparing legislation in the field of private law does not take place in a context that is purely specific to each state, but within the context of a Europe-wide discussion, or, in the case of Chinese law, the CISG and the UNIDROIT Principles, on a worldwide scale.

The fact that the legislator uses the comparative method in the preparation of domestic law has an important implication for its interpretation: if the legislator takes inspiration from foreign law, because he or she is inspired by an *idea of justice existing beyond State borders*,

---

33 P. VARUL, Legal Policy Decisions and Choices in the Creation of New Private Law in Estonia, *Juridica International* 2000, 104 ff.
34 S. SELELIONYTE-DRUKTEINIENE/V. JURKEVICIUS/T. KADNER GRAZIANO, The Impact of the Comparative Method on Lithuanian Private Law, *ERPL* 2013, 959.
35 VARUL (fn. 33), at p. 107.
36 Gesetz zur Modernisierung des Schuldrechts, BGBl. 2001, I, 3138.
37 See U. Huber, Das geplante Recht der Leistungsstörungen, in: W. Ernst/R. Zimmermann (eds.), *Zivilrechtswissenschaft und Schuldrechtsreform*, Tübingen: Mohr Siebeck, 2001, pp. 104 ff.; P. SCHLECHTRIEM, Das geplante Gewährleistungsrecht, in: *Ibid.*, pp. 205 ff.
38 L. HUIXING, *The Draft Civil Code of the People's Republic of China, English Translation*, Leiden/Boston: Martinus Nijhoff, 2010, p. XIX with examples.
39 *Ibid.*, p. XX.
40 *Ibid.*, p. XXII.

the judge must be able to follow this approach when applying the law. In this sense, Art. 1 (2) of the Swiss Civil Code expressly states that "*à défaut d'une disposition applicable, le juge prononce selon le droit coutumier et, à défaut d'une coutume, selon les règles qu'il établirait s'il avait à faire acte de législateur*" (in the absence of a provision, the court shall decide in accordance with customary law and, in the absence of customary law, in accordance with the rule that it would make as legislator). This provision expresses a general idea according to which the judge is invited to resort to the same sources of inspiration and methods used by the legislator, notably including the comparative method.[41] This is true, as is explicitly stated in Art. 1 (2) of the Swiss Civil Code, in the absence of a legal provision. In many jurisdictions, it is recognised today that this also applies in cases of uncertainty of the law and when interpreting it, since filling gaps in the law and interpreting it are merely two sides of the same coin.[42] The Swiss Federal Court has consequently stated that

> when interpreting the law, all traditional methods of interpretation are to be taken into consideration (systematic, purposive, and historic [. . .] as well as comparative), all of which are used by the Federal Court in a pragmatic way without giving priority or preference to one of these methods over the others.[43]

In the same spirit, the highest court in Germany, the Federal Constitutional Court, has repeatedly confirmed that the judge is not bound when it comes to choosing his or her methods of determining the law. In the 1990s the Constitutional Court held: "Article 20 (3) of the Fundamental Law [Grundgesetz, i.e. the German Constitution] requires that the judge decide 'according to law and justice'. The Constitution does not prescribe a particular method of interpretation (or even a purely literal interpretation)."[44] The court further held that

> [t]he courts are bound only by the law and they are not required to follow an opinion that is prevailing in legal doctrine, nor are they obliged to follow the precedents of higher courts; on the contrary, they can follow their own legal opinion and perception of the law [. . .] The judge is required to decide according to law and justice (Art. 20 (3) Constitution); with respect to the prohibition of arbitrary decisions, the judge has to give reasons for his decision [. . .] In any case, the judge must show that the decision is based on an in depth legal analysis; his view also must not be deprived of objective reasons.[45]

In a 1953 ruling, the Federal Constitutional Court expressly recognised the use of the comparative method by the courts to fill gaps in domestic law and to interpret it.[46]

---

41 Article 1 (2) of the *Swiss* Civil Code was inspired by the works of the *French* legal scientist François Gény and thus is itself the fruit of an influence across borders, see F. Gény, *Méthode d'interprétation et sources en droit privé positif*, Vol. 2, 2nd ed., Paris: L.G.D.J., 1919, pp. 326 ff., no. 204; see also T. Henninger, *Europäisches Privatrecht und Methode*, Tübingen: Mohr Siebeck, 2009, p. 80, with further references.
42 K. Zweigert, Rechtsvergleichung als universale Interpretationsmethode, *RabelsZ* 1949, 5 at 9.
43 *Swiss* Federal Supreme Court, 13.01.1998, ATF 124 III 266: "4. [. . .] bei der Auslegung [sind] alle herkömmlichen Auslegungselemente zu berücksichtigen (systematische, teleologische und historische [. . .]; auch rechtsvergleichende [. . .]), wobei das Bundesgericht einen pragmatischen Methodenpluralismus befolgt und es ablehnt, die einzelnen Auslegungselemente einer Prioritätsordnung zu unterstellen [. . .]"; *French* translation in *JdT* 1999 I 414.
44 BVerfG, 30.03.1993, BVerfGE 88, 145; NJW 1993, 2861 at 2863.
45 BVerfG, 19.07.1995, NJW 1995, 2911.
46 BVerfGE 3, 225 at 244: "Im übrigen haben die Gerichte sich der erprobten Hilfsmittel, nämlich der Interpretation und Lückenfüllung, unter Verwertung auch der rechtsvergleichenden Methode bedient".

In other jurisdictions on the continent, legal provisions defining methods of statutory interpretation by the judge are limited to stating general principles, emphasising the freedom of the judge to interpret and, if necessary, to develop the law.[47]

For Common Law and mixed jurisdictions, Robert Reed, judge at the Supreme Court of the United Kingdom, has noted with respect to the freedom of judges to choose their sources of inspiration:

> Scottish and English judges have for centuries drawn on ideas developed in other jurisdictions (both common law and civilian) [. . .] Judicial reasoning has been seen as a process of rational inquiry, in which there are not in principle any sources of ideas which are off-limit. Judicial reasoning in this country has not been thought of in national terms, with non-national sources of ideas being regarded as suspect: on the contrary, it has long been thought sensible to consider how others, from Ancient Rome onwards, have resolved similar problems. If judges are free to take account of the views of academic lawyers writing in law reviews, whether they are based in Cambridge, England, or Cambridge, Massachusetts, there would seem to be no reason why the opinions of foreign courts should be off-limits.[48]

The courts consequently benefit from a substantial freedom in their choice of the methods they apply to determine the law and they are free with respect to the choice of their sources of inspiration. Numerous examples cited in the third part of this chapter show that in many jurisdictions, judges use the comparative method to fill gaps in domestic law and when interpreting it, without questioning the legitimacy of comparison.[49]

g) Choice of the most convincing solution while respecting the national legal system

The argument that the use of the comparative method risks harming the national legal systems also remains unconvincing. It is true that, in every interpretation of domestic law, the system of the domestic law (be it a national codification or a case law system) must be respected as far as possible. This aim can be achieved through systematic interpretation which is one of the principal methods of interpretation of law. Indeed, like every other method of interpretation, the comparative interpretation must allow an interpretation and development of the law so that, out of the possible solutions, the most convincing is chosen while preserving coherence within the domestic system of law.[50]

---

47 See e.g. §§ 6 f. of the *Austrian* Civil Code (*ABGB*), Art. 1 f. of the *Spanish* Civil Code (*Código civil*), Art. 1 f. of the *Portuguese* Civil Code (*Código civil*), Art. 1 of the introductory provisions of the *Italian* Civil Code (*Codice civile*), Art. 6 of the *Russian* Civil Code, Art. 1.3 ff. of the *Lithuanian* Civil Code, Art. 4 f. of the *Latvian* Civil Code; see also T. HENNINGER (fn. 41), e.g. at pp. 437 ff. with further references.

48 REED (fn. 4), at p. 261 f.; MCCRUDDEN (fn. 4), at p. 527: "the decision whether to use foreign judicial decisions seems largely in the realm of judicial discretion".

49 For references see below, pp. 34 ff.

50 See e.g. G. CANIVET, The Use of Comparative Law before the French Courts, in: Canivet/Andenas/Fairgrieve (fn. 10), p. 181 at 183 ff.; ZWEIGERT (fn. 42), at pp. 16 ff.; H. UNBERATH, Comparative Law in the German Courts, in: Canivet/Andenas/Fairgrieve (fn. 10), p. 307 at 316; see, however, A. FLESSNER, Juristische Methode und Europäisches Vertragsrecht, *JZ* 2002, 14: in a period of a renaissance of a common European legal science and of a European *ius commune*, the systematic interpretation of domestic law should lose its importance when it comes to determining the law.

h) The authority of foreign law – a persuasive authority

It is clear that the judge is bound by domestic law as well as by any provisions of international law in force in his or her country. Neither foreign statutory law nor foreign case law has democratic legitimacy in the judge's country. In relation to the use of the comparative method, two consequences follow from this:

Firstly, when the text of domestic law in force in the judge's country is clear and its interpretation does not leave any room for doubt, the judge is bound by his or her country's law. In principle, he or she cannot deviate from the result prescribed by the law in order to reach another result by using the comparative method; this is even true in cases where the judge finds this other result more adequate, appropriate, and fair, taking into account all the interests at stake.[51] In such a case, it is in principle[52] the role of the legislator (national or international) to solve the problem (if there is a problem). But aren't situations rare where interpretation of domestic law doesn't leave space for doubt or a margin of appreciation for the judge? Numerous uncertainties in domestic law, the demands of interpretation, as well as, in some cases, conflicts between traditional rules of Civil Law and constitutional values, make the scope of application of the comparative methodology very large.

Secondly, foreign legislation and case law can never *bind* the national judge. The authority of foreign law can only be a *persuasive authority*.[53] The more the values in one country and another are similar or shared, the more important is the persuasive authority of the other country's law.[54] The more a certain issue is politically sensitive, and the more particular circumstances in a given country led to the adoption of a specific rule or result, the less

---

51 See e.g. *Bell* v. *Peter Browne & Co.*, [1990] 2 Q.B. 495 (Mustill LJ) with respect to the concurrence of liability in contract and tort: "Other legal systems seem to manage quite well by limiting attention to the contractual obligations which are, after all, the foundation of the relationship between the professional man and his client [citing *French* law] [. . .] Nevertheless the [*English*] law is clear and we must apply it"; see for the discussion in the USA, Jackson (fn. 9), at p. 125: "[T]he legitimacy of looking to foreign experience will vary with the issue, depending on the specificity and history or our constitutional text, the degree to which the issue is genuinely unsettled, and the strength of other interpretative sources".

52 For this rule and its limits, see e.g. the *Swiss* Federal Supreme Court, 28.11.2006, ATF 133 III 257 ("parrots case"), 265 cons. 2.4: "*Ergibt die Auslegung eines Bundesgesetzes auf eine Rechtsfrage eine eindeutige Antwort, so ist diese gemäss Art. 19 Bundesverfassung für das Bundesgericht und die anderen rechtsanwendenden Behörden massgebend. Diese dürfen daher nicht mit der Begründung von Bundesrecht abweichen, es [. . .] entspreche nicht dem (künftig) wünschbaren Recht [. . .] Eine Abweichung von einer Gesetzesnorm ist jedoch zulässig, wenn der Gesetzgeber sich offenkundig über gewisse Tatsachen geirrt hat oder sich die Verhältnisse seit Erlass des Gesetzes in einem solchen Masse gewandelt haben, dass die Anwendung einer Rechtsvorschrift rechtsmissbräuchlich wird*" (Translation: If the interpretation of a federal law leads to a clear result, then, according to Art. 19 of the Federal Constitution, the Federal courts and all other law-applying authorities are bound by it. They cannot deviate from federal law arguing that the result under this legal provision is [. . .] undesirable. It is, however, possible to deviate from a legal provision in cases where the legislator has obviously committed an error or when the circumstances have changed since the enactment of the provision to the point that its application would constitute an abuse of right).

53 See e.g. P. K. Tripathi, Foreign Precedents and Constitutional Law, *Colum. L. Rev.* 1957, 319 at 346: "When a judge looks to foreign legal systems for analogies that shed light on any of the new cases before him, he is looking to legal material which he is absolutely free to reject unless it appeals to his reason"; Jackson (fn. 9), at p. 114: "Transnational sources are seen as interlocutors, offering a way of testing and understanding one's own traditions and possibilities by examining them in the reflection of others"; A. Parrish, Storm in a Teacup: The U.S. Supreme Court's Use of Foreign Law, *U. Ill. L. Rev.* 2007, 637 at 674: "Foreign law is persuasive authority: nothing more, nothing less"; and S. Yeazell, When and How U.S. Courts Should Cite Foreign Law, *Const. Comment.* 2009, 59 at 69: "[I]ts persuasiveness has nothing to do with its origin."

54 For criteria for choosing the jurisdiction for comparison, see the references in fn. 19.

willing will judges be to draw inspiration from foreign law and experience. This is possibly the reason why the use of comparative law in certain constitutional issues before the US Supreme Court has been particularly controversial and disputed over the last years, whereas the use of this same method goes without saying in matters of private law in the USA.[55]

i) Soft harmonisation of the law within the context of regional integration

Finally, the use of the comparative method is justified nowadays in Member States of the European Union, by the membership of these countries in the Union. According to Art. 3 (3) of the Treaty on European Union, the Union sets itself the objective, among others, of establishing an internal market and promoting economic cohesion among Member States. The convergence of provisions applicable to economic relations contributes notably to the achievement of this aim, in areas such as contract law, tort law, and, for certain questions, property law. In such matters, a comparative interpretation can result in 'soft harmonisation' of the law which constitutes, at least for some matters, an interesting alternative to harmonisation through enacting legislation. In relation to this, Walter Odersky, the former President of the German Federal Supreme Court of Justice, has written:

> The national judge has not only the right to rely on interpretations from other legal systems and courts in his judgment, but also the right, when applying domestic law, and naturally when weighing up all interests and points of view to be taken into consideration in the interpretation and development of the law, to attach a certain importance to the fact that the solution in consideration contributes to the harmonisation of European law. Following this reasoning, the judge may, if needs be, follow the solution from another legal system as the result of a weighing of interests. With the progressive process of European integration, the judge should use this reasoning more and more often.[56]

According to Christopher McCrudden, the impulse to use comparative law "will be strongest [. . .] when the integration is set out explicitly as a political programme, with institutional characteristics, such as in Europe. Indeed, the comparative method is there explicitly built into the fabric of judicial decision-making."[57]

3. Intermediate conclusions

In the search for a solution to a legal dispute, the judge benefits from substantial freedom to choose his or her sources of legal knowledge and inspiration. In a large number of countries, judges are nowadays convinced that comparative law is one of the legitimate methods of interpretation of domestic law, and rightly so. The examples cited in the following section will show that national courts draw inspiration from foreign solutions when interpreting

---

55 See fn. 9. The persuasive authority of the comparative argument loses weight if the fundamental values differ from one jurisdiction to the other, see e.g. Scalia (fn. 5), at p. 310: "If there was any thought absolutely foreign to the founders of our country, surely it was the notion that we Americans should be governed the way Europeans are. And nothing has changed".
56 W. ODERSKY, Harmonisierende Auslegung und europäische Rechtskultur, *ZEuP* 1994, 3 (translation from German).
57 McCRUDDEN (fn. 4), at pp. 521 f. (quote on p. 522).

domestic law. Indeed, important innovations notably in English, German, Austrian, Swiss, and US judicial law have taken inspiration from comparison with solutions that are in force abroad.[58]

In current US discussion, Ruth Bader Ginsburg, judge of the US Supreme Court, has written:

> The US judicial system will be poorer, I believe, if we do not both share our experience with, and learn from, legal systems with values and a commitment to democracy similar to our own [. . .] [W]e are not so wise that we have nothing to learn from other democratic legal systems newer to judicial review for constitutionality.[59]

Sonia Sotomayor, appointed in 2009 to the US Supreme Court, stated in the year of her appointment: "[T]o the extent that we have freedom of ideas, international law and foreign law will be very important in the discussion of how to think about the unsettled issues of our legal system."[60] Sandra Day O'Connor expressed the opinion that the judges on the court will "find [them]selves looking more frequently to the decisions of other constitutional courts [. . .] All of these courts have something to teach [. . .] about the civilizing functions of constitutional law."[61]

Following an analysis of the use of the comparative method by courts in Europe, undertaken at the British Institute of International and Comparative Law, Mads Andenas, Duncan Fairgrieve, Guy Canivet (at that time *Premier Président* of the French *Cour de cassation*), and the English judge of the House of Lords, Lord Goff of Chieveley, summarised the analysis in relation to the current role of the comparative method before European courts: "Comparative law is increasingly recognized as an essential reference point for judicial decision-making."[62] According to Canivet, "the use of comparative law is essential to the fulfilment of a supreme court's role in a modern democracy".[63] Andenas and Fairgrieve come to the conclusion that, "[c]ourts make use of comparative law, and make open reference to it, to an unprecedented extent . . . Comparative law has become a source of law."[64] Tom Bingham concludes that: "Judicial horizons have widened and are widening."[65]

---

58 See the references below, in section III of this chapter.
59 BADER GINSBURG (fn. 26), at p. 576, www.supremecourt.gov/publicinfo/speeches/viewspeech/sp_08-02-10.
60 In: S. GROVES, Questions for Justice Sotomayor on the Use of Foreign and International Law, The Heritage Foundation, July 6, 2009, www.heritage.org/research/reports/2009/07/questions-for-judge-sotomayor-on-the-use-of-foreign-and-international-law, note 12 and accompanying text (Transcript of Judge S. SOTOMAYOR's April 2009 Speech to the American Civil Liberties Union of Puerto Rico).
61 S. DAY O'CONNOR, Broadening our Horizons: Why American Judges and Lawyers Must Learn about Foreign Law, *Int'l Jud. Observer* 1997, 2. The following judges of the *US* Supreme Court have favoured the use of the comparative method by the court in recent years: Justices Day O'Connor, Stevens, Souters, Kennedy, Bader Ginsburg, Breyer, and Sotomayor. The following have spoken against the use of this method: Chief Justices Rehnquist and Roberts and Justices Scalia, Thomas, and Alito.
62 In: Canivet/Andenas/Fairgrieve (fn. 10), at pp. v and vii.
63 *Ibid.*, p. 181.
64 *Ibid.*, p. xxvii.
65 BINGHAM (fn. 20), at p. 3.

III. Comparative law in court practice

1. Introduction

If it is legitimate to compare, is it beneficial and appropriate for the courts to resort to the comparative method? Do the benefits of the comparative method justify the sometimes considerable effort that the comparative approach demands?

In some countries, judges are nowadays convinced of the benefits of this method. An analysis of around 1,500 judgments of the Swiss Federal Supreme Court has shown that in around 10% of cases, the court refers to one or more foreign legal systems for the purpose of comparison.[66] In matters concerning tort law, over the last few years, the percentage of the Federal Court's judgments that use the comparative approach has exceeded 20%.[67] In other countries on the continent, the courts occasionally resort to the comparative method.[68]

In English law, judgments in which the judges cite not only decisions from other Common Law jurisdictions but also the laws, judgments, and doctrine from continental Europe have multiplied over the last few years.[69] According to a recent study, for the period of 1996

---

[66] See the excellent analysis by A. GERBER, Der Einfluß des ausländischen Rechts in der Rechtsprechung des Bundesgerichts, in: Institut Suisse de Droit Comparé (ed.), *Perméabilité des ordres juridiques*, Zürich: Schulthess, 1992, pp. 141–163.

[67] T. KADNER GRAZIANO, Entwicklungstendenzen im schweizerischen ausservertraglichen Haftungs- und Schadensrecht, in: P. Jung (ed.), *Aktuelle Entwicklungen im Haftungsrecht*, Zurich: Schulthess, 2007, p. 1, no. 3.

[68] For *France* see R. LEGEAIS, L'utilisation du droit comparé par les tribunaux, *Rev. int. de droit comparé* 1994, 347; CANIVET (fn. 50), at p. 181, in particular pp. 190 ff. Canivet reminds us, however, that the very particular style of reasoning of the *French Cour de cassation* does not allow the judge to reveal his sources of inspiration, p. 187. For *Spain*: J. CANIVELL, Comparative Law before the Spanish Courts, in: Canivet/Andenas/Fairgrieve (fn. 10), at pp. 211 ff. For *Germany*: H. KÖTZ, Der Bundesgerichtshof und die Rechtsvergleichung, in: A. Heldrich/K. J. Hopt (eds.), *50 Jahre Bundesgerichtshof: Festgabe aus der Wissenschaft*, Vol. 2, Munich: C. H. Beck, 2000, p. 825; U. DROBNIG, The Use of Foreign Law by German Courts, in: U. Drobnig/S. van Erp (eds.), *The Use of Comparative Law by the Courts*, The Hague: Kluwer Law International, 1999, p. 127, with references for the period from 1950 to 1980; U. DROBNIG, Rechtsvergleichung in der deutschen Rechtsprechung, *RabelsZ* 1986, 610; UNBERATH (fn. 50). For the influence of *German* law on *English, Swiss,* and *Austrian* law, see: K. SCHIEMANN, Aktuelle Einflüsse des deutschen Rechts auf die richterliche Fortbildung des englischen Rechts, *EuR* 2003, 17; H. HONSELL, Rezeption der Rechtsprechung des Bundesgerichtshofs in der Schweiz, in: *50 Jahre Bundesgerichtshof*, above, Vol. 2, p. 927; H. KOZIOL, Rezeption der Rechtsprechung des Bundesgerichtshofs in Österreich, in: *50 Jahre Bundesgerichtshof*, above, Vol. 2, p. 943; for *Dutch* law: HONDIUS (fn. 13), at p. 764. See also the contributions in: CANIVET/ANDENAS/FAIRGRIEVE (fn. 10); T. KOOPMANS, Comparative Law and the Courts, *ICLQ* 1996, 545; MARKESINIS/FEDTKE (fn. 14), at p. 11.

[69] See M. NOUNCKELE, De la légitimité de la comparaison par les juges – Etude de la jurisprudence de la House of Lords de 1996 à 2005 (study prepared at the University of Louvain-la-Neuve, 2011); E. ÖRÜCÜ, Comparative Law in Practice: The Courts and the Legislator, in: Örücü/Nelken (fn. 27), at p. 411; ibid., Comparative Law in British Courts, in: Drobnig/van Erp (fn. 68), at p. 253; K. SCHIEMANN, Recent German and French Influences on the Development of English law, in: R. Schulze/U. Seif (eds.), *Richterrecht und Rechtsfortbildung in der Europäischen Rechtsgemeinschaft*, Tübingen: Mohr Siebeck, 2003, p. 189. See e.g. the *English* cases: *Woolwich Building Society v. Inland Revenue Commissioners (No. 2)*, [1993] AC 70, [1992] 3 *All ER* 737 (HL): citing *German* law; *Henderson v. Merrett Syndicates Ltd*, [1995] 2 AC 145; *White v. Jones*, [1995] 2 AC 207, 1 All ER 691: comparison with the laws of *Germany, New Zealand,* California, the *USA, France,* and the *Netherlands*; *Antwerp United Diamonds BVBA v. Air Europe*, [1996] Q.B. 317, [1995] 3 All ER 424: comparison with *Dutch* and *Belgian* case law; *Hunter v. Canary Wharf Ltd*, [1997] AC 655; *Kleinwort Benson Ltd v. Lincoln CC*, [1999] 2 AC 349; *McFarlane v. Tayside Health Board*, [2000] 2 AC 59; *Arthur JS Hall & Co v. Simons*, [2002] 1 AC 615, [2000] 3 All ER 673; *Alfred McAlpine Construction Ltd v. Panatown Ltd*, [2001] 1 AC 518: comparison with *German* law; *Greatorex v. Greatorex*, [2000] 4 All ER 769, [2000] 1 WLR

to 2005, between 25% and 33% of House of Lords decisions have included comparative references to other legal systems.[70] Some of the judgments that have benefited from looking beyond borders are among the most prominent cases in English legal history, such as *Hadley v. Baxendale*,[71] which concerned the scope of damages for breach of contract. Tom Bingham, former judge of the House of Lords, wrote in relation to this judgment that

> sometimes seen as a fine flowering of common law jurisprudence, the immediate source of the rule [in *Hadley v. Baxendale*] were the French Code Civil, Pothier's Treatise on the Law of Civil Obligations, Kent's Commentaries, and Sedgwick's Treatise on Damages, none of them works of indigenous origin.[72]

Comparison is no longer limited to private law.[73] An increasing number of public or constitutional law courts have also resorted to the comparative method. In the USA, Justice Scalia, despite being opposed to the comparative approach, has stated:

> In many [. . .] cases, opinions for the Court have used foreign law for the purpose of interpreting the Constitution [. . .] I expect [. . .] that the Court's use of foreign law in the interpretation of the Constitution will continue at an accelerating pace [. . .] [U]se of comparative law in our constitutional decisions is the wave of the future.[74]

1970; *A v. National Blood Authority*, [2001] 3 All ER 289; *Fairchild v. Glenhaven Funeral Services Ltd*, [2003] 1 AC 32, [2002] UKHL 22, [2002] 3 All ER 305 (HL), damage following exposure to asbestos: comparison with the laws of *Germany, Austria, Norway, Canada, Australia, Italy, South Africa*, and *Switzerland*; *Campbell v. Mirror Group Newspapers Ltd*, [2004] AC 457, [2004] 2 All ER 995, liability for the invasion of personality rights and the violation of a person's privacy: comparison with *German* and *French* law; *The Starsin*, [2004] 1 AC 715, [2003] 2 All ER 785; *Douglas and Others v. Hello! Ltd*, [2005] EWCA Civ 595; *National Westminster Bank plc. v. Spectrum Plus Ltd*, [2005] UKHL 41: comparison with the laws of the *USA, India, Ireland*, and *Canada*.

70 NOUNCKELE (fn. 69).
71 [1854] 9 *Ex Ch* 341.
72 BINGHAM (fn. 20), at p. 5. See for the *USA* e.g. MINOW (fn. 9) (text following fns. 135 and 136). She stresses that *Brown v. Board of Education*, 347 U.S. 483 (1954), one of the most famous decisions of the *US* Supreme Court, has benefited, among others, from foreign input; see also GLENSY (fn. 18), at p. 361: "United States Courts have, from the founding of the nation to the present day, referenced foreign legal sources in a variety of different contexts [. . .] [E]xamples can be taken from almost every period of this nation's history", with numerous references.
73 See e.g. C. MCCRUDDEN, Judicial Comparativism and Human Rights, in: Örücü/Nelken (fn. 27), at p. 371: "Courts are playing an impressive role in the creation of what some see as a 'common law of human rights' or, in the context of Europe, 'a ius commune of human rights'"; McCrudden (fn. 4), at pp. 499 ff.; A.-M. SLAUGHTER, A Global Community of Courts, *Harv. Int'l L. J.* 2003, 191; P. HÄBERLE, Grundrechtsgeltung und Grundrechtsinterpretation im Verfassungsstaat – Zugleich zur Rechtsvergleichung als "fünfte Auslegungsmethode", *JZ* 1989, 913; S. BAER, Verfassungsrechtsvergleichung und reflexive Methode: Interkulturelle und intersubjektive Kompetenz, *ZaöRV* 2004, 735; C. FUCHS, Verfassungsvergleichung durch den Verfassungsgerichtshof, *JRP* 2010, 183 (for *Austria*): "Dass Verfassungsvergleichung auch für Verfassungsgerichte ein beachtliches Erkenntnispotential bergen kann, ist [. . .] heute weithin anerkannt. Der VerfGH zieht rechtsvergleichende Argumente in der – unausgesprochenen – Annahme ihrer grundsätzlichen Zulässigkeit und Leistungsfähigkeit zur Problemlösung heran".
74 SCALIA (fn. 5), at pp. 307 ff.; see also BADER GINSBURG (fn. 26), at p. 591: "Recognizing that forecasts are risky, I nonetheless believe we will continue to accord 'a decent Respect to the Opinions of [Human]kind' as a matter of comity in a spirit of humility."

Based on an international survey, Christopher McCrudden, constitutional lawyer at Queen's College, University of Belfast, found: "It is now commonplace in many jurisdictions as well as for courts to refer extensively to the decisions of foreign jurisdictions when interpreting human rights guarantees."[75]

The Constitution of the Republic of South Africa of 1996 expressly invites courts to use the comparative method in matters concerning fundamental rights. The provision states: "When interpreting the Bill of Rights, a court, tribunal or forum [. . .] (b) must consider international law; and (c) may consider foreign law."[76] The Constitutional Court of South Africa is consequently today among the most active actors regarding a transnational judicial discourse.[77]

2. Benefits of using the comparative methodology

The reasons to resort to the comparative method, the aims pursued by the courts by comparing, and the assets of this method are plentiful.[78]

a) Positioning the national law in the international legal landscape

In some cases, courts cite foreign and international law in order to show that the national law is fully in line with modern solutions or international trends. This is frequently the case in Central or Eastern European countries that have recently reformed and re-codified their law.

An example is the case law of the Lithuanian Supreme Court. The court has frequently referred to the UNIDROIT Principles of International Commercial Contracts, the Principles of European Contract Law, the Principles of European Tort Law, and the Draft Common Frame of Reference, usually with the aim of showing that the new Lithuanian Civil Code is fully in line with these modern soft law principles.[79]

b) Complementary to the historical method of interpretation

Courts often cite foreign law or soft law principles that have served as an inspiration to the national legislator for their own legislation. In these cases, the comparative method plays a support role which complements the historical method of interpretation of domestic law.[80]

---

75 McCrudden (fn. 4), at p. 506.
76 Full text: "When interpreting the Bill of Rights, a court, tribunal or forum (a) must promote the values that underlie an open and democratic society based on human dignity, equality and freedom; (b) must consider international law; and (c) may consider foreign law."
77 See McCrudden(fn. 4), at p. 506 with references in fn. 26.
78 See Gerber (fn. 66), at pp. 150 ff. ("*Gründe für das Heranziehen ausländischen Rechts*").
79 The Court has referred to the UNIDROIT Principles on International Commercial Contracts in 20 cases, to the Principles of European Contract Law (PECL) in 11 cases, to the Draft Common Frame of Reference (DCFR) in one case, and to Principles of European Tort Law (PETL) in three cases explicitly, in others implicitly, see Selelionyte-Drukteiniene/Jurkevicius/Kadner Graziano (fn. 34), with references; McCrudden (fn. 4), at p. 518, diagnoses a "pedagogical impulse" in comparative constitutionalism; see also A.-M. Slaughter, A Typology of Transjudicial Communication, *U. Rich. L. Rev.* 1994, 99 at 134: "The court of a fledgling democracy, for instance, might look to the opinions of courts in older and more established democracies as a way of binding its country to this existing community of states."
80 Gerber (fn. 66), at p. 151. See e.g. the *Swiss* cases TF, 03.04.1914, ATF 40 II 249 at 256; TF, 05.04.1938, ATF 64 II 121 at 129, or the *German* cases BGHZ 21, 112 at 119, and BGHZ 24, 214 at 218 f.

In two decisions of 2010 and 2011, the Supreme Court of Lithuania stated that the provisions of the Lithuanian Civil Code which were adopted under the influence of the UNIDROIT Principles shall be interpreted in the light of the Principles.[81]

To cite another example: in a landmark case of 2006, the Federal Court of Switzerland had to rule on the scope of damages for breach of contract. A parrot breeder had bought six parrots for his breeding farm. They were infected with a virus that was subsequently transmitted to the other birds in the breeding farm. As a result, all birds died and the breeder suffered a loss of around 2 million Swiss francs. He brought a claim for damages against the seller of the infected birds. The claim raised the issue of the scope and the limits of the seller's contractual liability.

The Swiss Federal Court awarded damages and, in defining the scope of contractual liability under Art. 208 (2) and (3) of the Swiss Code of Obligations, drew inspiration from the French author Pothier's *Treatise on the Law of Obligations* as well as from Art. 1150 of the French Civil Code, which were already known and had inspired the legislator when the Swiss Code of Obligations was being prepared.[82] The best-known English case concerning the scope of damages for breach of contract, *Hadley* v. *Baxendale*,[83] dating back to 1854, equally takes inspiration from Pothier's *Treatise on the Law of Obligations* and Article 1150 of the French Civil Code. In 1894, the Supreme Court of the USA in turn adopted the principles from *Hadley* for US law.[84]

Pothier's work, Art. 1231–3 (former Art. 1150) of the French Civil Code,[85] the English case of *Hadley* v. *Baxendale*, US case law (and notably that of the Supreme Court of the USA), and, last but not least, the Swiss Federal Court's judgment in 2006 are thus all based on the same idea of justice concerning the scope of contractual liability, an idea of justice existing well beyond national borders.

c) Discovering the diversity of solutions from which the court can choose

Courts use the comparative approach in order to discover and demonstrate the diversity of solutions in force in different jurisdictions and from which the court can choose when interpreting domestic law.[86]

Recent English case law has given, in some cases, an impressive comparative overview. For example, in *Fairchild* v. *Glenhaven*, the House of Lords found inspiration in not only Californian, Canadian, Australian, and South African law, and in the US Restatement of the Law, but also cited German, Greek, Austrian, Dutch, Norwegian, French, Italian, and Swiss law.[87] In *Kleinwort Benson Ltd* v. *Lincoln City Council*, the court referred to US law,

---

81 See SELELIONYTE-DRUKTEINIENE/JURKEVICIUS/KADNER GRAZIANO (fn. 34), with references.
82 TF, 28.11.2006, ATF 133 III 257. For the opposite situation, see the *Swiss* case TF, 22.5.2008, ATF 134, 497 c. 4.2.3, 4.3, 4.4.2: *Swiss* law, notably Art. 418 of the *Swiss* CO, served as a source of inspiration for Art. 89b of the *German* Commercial Code (HGB); the *Swiss* Federal Court then took inspiration from *German* legal doctrine and case law on Art. 89b HGB when interpreting Art. 418 of the *Swiss* CO.
83 See fn. 71.
84 *Primrose* v. *Western Union Tel. Co.*, 154 U.S. 1 [1894].
85 Art. 1231–3 of the *Code civil* provides: "Le débiteur n'est tenu que des dommages et intérêts qui ont été prévus ou qui pouvaient être prévus lors de la conclusion du contrat, sauf lorsque l'inexécution est due à une faute lourde ou dolosive".
86 See also SCALIA (fn. 5), at p. 309: "Adding foreign law to the box of available legal tools is enormously attractive to judges because it vastly increases the scope of their discretion."
87 [2003] 1 AC 32.

and notably, the Restatement of the Law, as well as Canadian, Australian, South African, German, Italian, and French law.[88] In *Arthur Hall* v. *Simons*, the House of Lords compared the case with US and Canadian law and other continental European legal systems, as well as Australian and New Zealand case law.[89] In *White* v. *Jones*, the House of Lords referred to New Zealand, Australian, US, Canadian, German, French, and Dutch law.[90]

The Federal Supreme Court of Switzerland frequently analyses and cites the laws of countries that border Switzerland, namely, French, German, Austrian, and Italian law.[91]

Sometimes, the comparative overview is established by the court itself. More frequently, the courts rely on comparative studies previously published by comparatists. Comparison thus widens the horizon and completes the picture of possible interpretations and solutions that are available to the courts to resolve a specific question. By using the comparative method, judges complete and improve the quality of their reasoning. Anne-Marie Slaughter observed in this respect:

> For [. . .] judges, looking abroad simply helps them to do a better job at home, in the sense that they can approach a particular problem more creatively or with greater insight. Foreign authority [. . .] provides a broader range of ideas and experience that makes for better, more reflective opinions. This is the most frequent cited rationale advanced by judges regarding the virtues of looking abroad.[92]

d) Illustrating the aims and particularities of the domestic solution

In numerous judgments, courts cite foreign solutions in order to confront them with the solution that they have found for their own domestic law. They hereby illustrate the aims and particularities of their domestic law.[93]

By way of example, it's possible to mention a decision of the Federal Supreme Court of Germany (*BGH*) concerning the protection of personality rights and the right to privacy (*Caroline de Monaco*). Here the court compared German and French law, observing that the scope of the right to privacy is more limited in German law than in French law when opposed to the freedom of press.[94] A German court of appeal provides another illustration in which the court cited US practice with respect to contingency fee agreements (i.e. agreements according

---

88 [2002] 2 AC 349.
89 [2002] 1 AC 615.
90 [1995] 2 AC 207, 1 All ER 691.
91 Out of numerous examples, see e.g. the cases TF, 20.04.1972, *Kienast c. Gubler*, ATF 98 II 73 (validity of a testament); TF, 23.04.2009, ATF 135 III 433, c. 3.3 (contractual penal clauses): change of case law inspired by *Italian* and *German* law and legal doctrine.
92 SLAUGHTER (fn. 73), at p. 201.
93 Compare GERBER (fn. 66), at p. 154; JACKSON (fn. 9), at p. 117: "[C]omparison can shed light on the distinctive functioning of one's own system [. . .] considering the questions other systems pose may sharpen understanding of how we are different", p. 128: "engagement with foreign law [. . .] does not necessarily mean adoption, but thoughtful, well-informed consideration"; MINOW (fn. 9), text following fn. 56: "Looking at what others do may sharpen our sense of our differences rather than produce a sense of pressure to conform"; YOUNG (fn. 6), at p. 158: "If American courts were to conclude that only domestic practice is relevant, then their judges might feel pressure to distinguish American *mores* [. . .] from the views they encounter on their European sabbaticals".
94 BGH 19.12.1995, BGHZ 131, 332 at 337 (taking inspiration from *US* law) and at 344 (opposing *French* law); for this use of the comparative method, see also the *Swiss* cases TF, 04.06.1981, ATF 107 II 105 at 111; TF, 18.05.1973, ATF 99 IV 75 at 76.

to which the lawyer's fees depend on the outcome of the case). The court ultimately sets out that such agreements would be irreconcilable with the role of lawyers in German civil procedure.[95]

In *Kuddus* v. *Chief Constable of Leicestershire Constabulary*, the UK House of Lords notes that exemplary or punitive damages do not exist either in continental Civil Law systems, such as German and French law, nor in mixed legal systems which are influenced by both civil and common laws, such as Scots and South African law. The court therefore observes that, for the matter in question, it is "unhelpful to look at the position in other jurisdictions".[96]

In *Awoyomi* v. *Radford*, the Queen's Bench Division of the English High Court refers to case law from the European Court of Justice (ECJ) concerning the immediate or future effects of a change in case law (the question of prospective overruling), before deciding that the case law of the ECJ could be materially distinguished from English law.[97]

The question of pre-contractual liability was addressed in the case of *Chartbrook* v. *Persimmons Homes*. The House of Lords invoked the Principles of European Contract Law, the UNIDROIT Principles of International Commercial Contracts, and the CISG to highlight that the philosophy on which these regulations are founded differs from English contract law.[98]

It is also possible to mention judgments from the Swiss Federal Court concerning the conditions for the transfer of personal property. The court decided that, in contrast to German law (expressly indicating Art. 931 of the BGB), in Swiss law the ownership of movables cannot be passed on by the assignment of an action for recovery of the object.[99] The Federal Court therefore demonstrates that another outcome would be possible and practicable, but that there are reasons why it is not favoured by the court.

In another, nowadays classic case, the Swiss Federal Court explicitly abandoned a solution formerly taken from German law according to which the transfer of ownership is separate from the validity of the contract of sale. The court thus discarded the abstraction principle, a pillar of German property law.[100]

In a case concerning a legal action brought by an environmental protection foundation, the Swiss Federal Supreme Court came to the conclusion that French legislation and case law, which was cited by the court of first instance, "*ne se concilient pas avec l'état actuel de notre legislation*"[101] (cannot be reconciled with the current state of our legislation).

These examples show that the use of comparative law by courts is not at all limited to situations where the foreign solution is the one favoured by the courts. On the contrary, when

---

95 OLG Celle, 26.11.2004, NJW 2005, 2160. See, however, the *German* case: BVerfG, 12.12.2006, 1 BvR 2576/04, BVerfGE 117, 163, NJW 2007, 979 (contingency fees admitted under specific circumstances).
96 [2002] 2 AC 122, [2001] UKHL 29.
97 [2007] EWHC 1671 (Q.B.) no. 15 (per Lloyd Jones J).
98 *Chartbrook Ltd* v. *Persimmons Homes Ltd*, [2009] AC 1101, [2009] UKHL 38, no. 39 (per Lord Hoffmann). See also the case *Agnew* v. *Länsförsäkringsbolagens*, [2001] 1 AC 223 (HL): Lord Justice Millet states that with respect to pre-contractual liability there is a fundamental difference between *English* law on the one hand and *French* and *German* law on the other.
99 TF 02.12.2005, ATF 132 III 155, c. 6.1.1 et 6.1.3: "*Das deutsche Recht [. . .] anerkennt die Abtretung des Herausgabeanspruchs als Ersatz für eine Übergabe. [. . .] [Für das schweizerische Recht ist] festzuhalten, dass durch eine Abtretung des Herausgabeanspruchs das Eigentum an einer Fahrnissache nicht übertragen werden kann, da dies mit dem Traditionsprinzip nicht zu vereinbaren ist*".
100 TF, 29.11.1929, *Grimm c. Masse en faillite Näf-Ackermann*, ATF 55 II 302.
101 TF, 20.02.2004, *La Fondation X. c. La Masse en faillite de feu A*, ou "*Gypaète barbu République V*", 4C.317/2002/ech.

the court's solution differs from another country's solution, the comparative approach can cause the court to expose national particularities and historical and cultural divergences that lead the court to favour one solution over another. In these cases, the comparative method contributes to a greater transparency and a better quality of reasoning. McCrudden concludes with respect to this purpose of judicial comparison:

> a use of foreign [. . .] law does not mean that the approach taken in the other jurisdiction will necessarily be *adopted*, just that it is *considered* [. . .] Even where the *result* of the foreign judicial approach has not been adopted, it has often been influential in sharpening the understanding of the court's view on domestic law.[102]

e) Countering the argument that a certain solution will lead to harmful results

The experiences in other jurisdictions are frequently cited by courts to counter the argument that a certain solution or interpretation of the law would have harmful or disastrous results.

Illustrations of this use of the comparative method are particularly common in English and US case law. For example, according to an old Common Law rule, someone who makes a payment following a mistake of law rather than a mistake of fact cannot seek restitution of the payment. In *Kleinwort Benson Ltd* v. *Lincoln City Council*, the House of Lords abandoned this solution. The comparative approach was used to counter the argument that a right to restitution would result in a flood of litigation.[103]

In the English case *Arthur Hall* v. *Simons*, the court considered the question of immunity of legal professionals for conduct during legal procedures. The court referred to the experiences of other countries in order to show that such immunity is not justified by practical needs, and the court subsequently abandoned the immunity.[104]

This use of the comparative method has furthermore been considered legitimate even by those who are in general opposed to the use of comparative law by the courts. In this respect, Justice Scalia has written:

> I suppose foreign statutory and judicial law can be consulted in assessing the argument that a particular construction of an ambiguous provision in a federal statute would be disastrous. If foreign courts have long been applying precisely the rule argued against, and disaster has not ensued, unless there is some countervailing factor at work, the argument can safely be rejected.[105]

---

102 McCrudden (fn. 4), at p. 512.
103 [2002] 2 AC 349, 375 C (per Lord Goff): "For the present purpose, however, the importance of this comparative material is to reveal that, in civil law systems, a blanket exclusion of recovery of money paid under a mistake of law is not regarded as necessary. In particular, the experience of these systems assists to dispel the fears expressed in the early English cases that a right of recovery on the ground of mistake of law may lead to a flood of litigation."
104 *Arthur JS Hall & Co* v. *Simons*, [2002] 1 AC 615 (see the opinions of Lord Bingham and Lord Hope).
105 Scalia (fn. 5), at p. 306, see also p. 307: "[T]he argument is sometimes made that a particular holding will be disastrous. Here [. . .] I think it entirely proper to point out that other countries have long applied the same rule without disastrous consequences."

f) Legal support for value judgments of the court

Often references to foreign law also play a role in highlighting that the solution favoured by the court is already recognised by other legal systems as being unbiased and fair, even if the legal approach to reaching this solution may differ from one country to another. This use of the comparative argument is particularly common and useful for the court when the decision is based on value judgments. In these situations, references to foreign legislation and case law provide *legal* support for the court's balancing of conflicting values.[106] In the English case *Alfred McAlpine Construction Ltd* v. *Panatown Ltd*, Lord Goff of Chieveley stated in this sense: "I find it comforting (though not surprising) to be told that in German law the same conclusion would be reached as I have myself reached on the facts of the present case."[107]

Here it is possible to refer once again to the famous English case of *Fairchild* v. *Glenhaven Funeral Services Ltd*. In this case, the court discussed liability of employers following the exposure of their employees to asbestos.[108] Inhaling asbestos fibres caused the employees to develop cancer. However, they had worked consecutively for several employers who had all exposed them to asbestos. This resulted in uncertainty as to where they had contracted the illness. According to traditional rules, the claim would have been rejected because the employees could not prove causation with the probability which is traditionally required. While searching for a solution that was favourable to the claim, the House of Lords found support in numerous foreign jurisdictions. In relation to this litigation, Lord Bingham observed:

> Development of the law [. . .] cannot of course depend on a head-count of decisions and codes adopted in other countries of the world, often against a background of different rules and traditions. The law must be developed coherently, in accordance with principles so as to serve, even-handedly, the ends of justice. If, however, a decision [. . .] offends one's basic sense of justice, and if consideration of international sources suggests that a different and more acceptable decision would be given in most other jurisdictions, whatever their legal tradition, this must prompt anxious review of the decision in question. In a shrinking world [. . .] there must be some virtue of uniformity of outcome whatever the diversity of approach in reaching that outcome.[109]

---

106 See e.g. A. BARAK, Constitutional Human Rights and Private Law, *Rev. Const. Stud.* 1996, 218 at 242: Comparative law "grants comfort to the judge and gives him the feeling that he is treading on safe ground, and it also gives legitimacy to the chosen solution"; SLAUGHTER (fn. 73), at p. 201: "Evidence of like-minded foreign decisions could enhance the legitimacy of a particular opinion on the domestic constituency that a particular court seeks to persuade"; Jackson (fn. 9), at p. 119.

107 *Alfred McAlpine Construction Ltd* v. *Panatown Ltd*, [2001] 1 AC 518 (per Lord GOFF OF CHIEVELEY). For other recent examples of this use of the comparative method, see the *UK* cases *Robinson* v. *Jones (Contractors) Ltd*, [2012] Q.B. 44, [2011] EWCA Civ 9, nos. 49 and 78 (LJ JACKSON); *D* v. *East Berkshire Community Health NHS Trust, MAK* v. *Dewsbury Healthcare NHS Trust, RK* v. *Oldham NHS Trust*, [2005] 2 AC 373, [2005] UKHL 23: same outcome in *Australian* law (no. 89, Lord NICHOLLS) and the law of *New Zealand* (no. 113 and 114, Lord RODGER), dissenting opinion by Lord BINGHAM who refers to *French* and *German* law (no.49): "no flood of claims in these countries". See, on this use of the comparative method, and criticising it, SCALIA (fn. 5), at p. 309: "It will seem much more like a real legal opinion if one can cite authority to support the philosophic, moral, or religious conclusions pronounced. Foreign authority can serve that purpose." See for *Switzerland* GERBER (fn. 66), at p. 157.

108 [2003] 1 AC 32. On this and the following cases BINGHAM (fn. 20), at pp. 9 ff.

109 *Fairchild* v. *Glenhaven Funeral Services Ltd*, [2003] 1 AC 32, [2002] UKHL 22, [2002] 3 All ER 305 at 334.

This use of the comparative method can also be found in a recent judgment of the Swiss Federal Court which concerned the capacity of beneficiaries of a will. The court found confirmation for its solution in three out of four of its bordering countries' legal systems (German, Austrian, and Italian law, in contrast with French law).[110]

g) Legal support when changing an established case law or when confronting new problems

In some of the most famous examples of comparison in case law, courts have resorted to the comparative method in order to justify fundamental changes to domestic case law or to confront new problems and to introduce new institutions or remedies.

It is possible to mention many cases where courts have used the comparative method to justify changes to the law: we have already seen the case *Kleinwort Benson Ltd* v. *Lincoln City Council*,[111] in which the House of Lords abandoned the Common Law rule according to which it was only possible to claim restitution of money paid following a mistake in fact as opposed to a mistake of law. Here the court also found support in several foreign jurisdictions for overturning the precedent.

In *White* v. *Jones*, the court considered the question of contractual or tortious liability of a solicitor in relation to pure economic loss suffered by the claimant following the solicitor's professional negligence. The House of Lords observed that despite the conceptual difficulties, in many jurisdictions (the court cited German, French, Dutch, Canadian, US, Australian, and New Zealand law), it is possible to find a favourable solution for the claimant in either the law of contract or the law of tort ("Many jurisdictions have found a remedy in the situation in which the present plaintiffs find themselves"). The court subsequently introduced liability for negligence of legal professionals in English tort law.[112]

In two landmark cases, the Supreme Court of Austria consecutively allowed, in Austrian law, liability for nervous shock and damages for immaterial harm following the loss of a close relation (damages for bereavement).[113] The court cited, as sources of inspiration and to support overruling previous case law, Swiss, French, Italian, Spanish, Scots, Greek, Yugoslavian, Belgian, and Turkish law. The court found information on these laws in the writings of comparatists. It seems that the desire to avoid isolation and to support majority trends in Europe was not the least of motivations for the Austrian Supreme Court.

In some decisions, foreign solutions are cited *obiter dictum* to draw attention to new problems that have not yet been dealt with by the national legislator or by domestic case law. In these situations, the aim is to encourage the legislator and doctrine to examine the problem and to work out a solution.[114]

---

110 TF, 06.02.2006, ATF 132 III 305: "*Auch in ausländischen Rechtsordnungen wird [. . .] die rechtswidrige Beeinträchtigung des freien erblasserischen Willens als Erbunwürdigkeit erfasst (z.B. in § 2339 des deutschen BGB, in § 542 des österreichischen ABGB und in Art. 463 des italienischen Codice civile, nicht hingegen in den Art. 727 ff. des französischen Code civil).*" For other examples of the use of the comparative method for the same purpose, see GERBER (fn. 66), at pp. 155 ff.
111 [2002] 2 AC 349.
112 *White* v. *Jones*, [1995] 2 AC 207, 1 All ER 691, see the opinion of Lord GOFF OF CHIEVELEY.
113 OGH, ZVR 1995, 46 and OGH, 16.05.2001, JBl. 2001, 660.
114 See GERBER (fn. 66), at p. 152 and e.g. the cases TF, 10.05.1932, ATF 58 II 151 at 156 (company law); TF, 20.01.1981, ATF 107 II 57 at 66 (copyright); TF, 21.12.1982, ATF 108 II 475 at 484 f.

More commonly, the court itself will introduce a new solution. A well-known illustration can be found in decisions in Germany that recognised personality rights and the right to privacy as an absolute right, protected by the means of tort liability (§ 823 (1) of the BGB and Art. 2 (1) of the Basic Law for the Federal Republic of Germany). The Federal Supreme Court of Germany[115] as well as the German Constitutional Court[116] found support in foreign laws when introducing a protection of personality rights and of privacy ("*Allgemeines Persönlichkeitsrecht*").[117]

In an English case in 1991 the court still stated that "[i]t is well known that in English law there is no right to privacy".[118] If the judgments of the Court of Appeal and the House of Lords, notably in *Douglas and others* v. *Hello! Ltd*[119] and *Naomi Campbell* v. *Mirror Group Newspapers Ltd*,[120] were to change the law, it would be largely thanks to the case law of the European Court of Human Rights and – last but not least – the influence of comparative law.[121]

Another example is provided by the decisions concerning claims brought by parents, and indeed children, against doctors for damages following an unwanted birth. The issue of medical malpractice for "wrongful life", "wrongful birth", or "wrongful pregnancy" has been considered by the courts in many jurisdictions over the last few years.

In Germany, the landmark case in this matter, published in the official collection under the English title "wrongful life", drew inspiration from the case law of the English Court of Appeal as well as US law.[122] The Swiss Federal Supreme Court took inspiration from German and Dutch case law, distinguishing itself from case law of the UK House of Lords and the Supreme Court of Austria.[123] In another landmark decision, the Supreme Court of Austria in turn took inspiration from French, Italian, Scots, and Danish law, while distinguishing German, Dutch, Belgian, and Spanish law.[124] Dutch case law took German law into consideration, and in turn, exerted an influence on Scots law.[125] In France, on the initiative of the judges of the *Cour de cassation*, the case "*Perruche*" was preceded by comparative studies on liability for wrongful life and wrongful birth, from which it drew inspiration.[126] In truth, judgments relating to this issue that have not referred to foreign case law are very rare.

In Germany, an important procedural innovation, namely the publication of dissenting opinions of judges in the Federal Constitutional Court's judgments, has drawn inspiration from Anglo-Saxon law.[127]

---

115 BGH, 05.03.1963, BGHZ 39, 124 at 132; BGH, 19.12.1995, BGHZ 131, 332 (*Caroline de Monaco*): protection of privacy, reference to *US* law. For further examples, see Kötz (fn. 68), at pp. 832 ff.
116 BVerfG, 14.02.1973, BVerfGE 34, 269 at 289, 291.
117 See H. Ehmann, Das Allgemeine Persönlichkeitsrecht – Zur Transformation unmoralischer in unerlaubte Handlungen, in: Heldrich/Hopt (fn. 68), p. 613 at 628, no. 81 and at p. 640.
118 *Kaye* v. *Robertson*, [1991] FSR 62 (Glidewell, LJ).
119 [2005] EWCA Civ 595.
120 [2002] EWCA Civ 1373.
121 Starting with the case: *Von Hannover* c. *l'Allemagne*, no. 59320/00, CEDH 2004-VI.
122 BGH, 18.01.1983 (wrongful life), BGHZ 86, 240 at 249 ff.
123 20.12.2005, ATF 132 III 359; case note J. Essebier, "Wrongful Birth" in der Schweiz, *ZEuP* 2007, 888.
124 OGH, 14.09.2006, 6 Ob 101/06f; see also OGH 25.05.1999, 1 Ob 91/99k (comparison with *German* law).
125 Hondius (fn. 13), at p. 764.
126 C. cass., 17.11.2000, D. 2001, 332: report of the *avocat général* Pierre Sargos, J.C.P. 2000 II, No. 10438, p. 2302; conclusions de l'avocat général Jerry Sainte Rose, J.C.P. 2000 II, No. 10438, pp. 2308 ff.; Canivet (fn. 50), at pp. 190 ff.; C. cass. 19.11.2002 (*Epoux Brachot* c. *Banque Worms*), J.C.P. 2002 II No. 10201, and avocat général J. Sainte Rose, J.C.P. 2002 II No. 10201.
127 P. Egbert, Für und Wider das Minderheitsvotum, *DÖV* 1968, 513.

h) Legal discourse on an international scale and 'soft harmonisation'

It is possible to identify an eighth and final effect (and perhaps also a final objective) of comparison by the courts. In the aforementioned decisions, as well as in many others, courts draw inspiration from the laws of jurisdictions sharing the same values. In some cases, the courts adopt in their case law a truly European or even a global perspective. By demonstrating such open-mindedness, judges pave the way for discussion of legal problems on a European, or indeed a global, scale, thus creating a genuine European or even global community of lawyers who are able to comfortably discuss with each other.[128] In situations where this discussion leads to shared beliefs and solutions, comparison contributes to "soft harmonisation" of the law on a supranational scale.[129]

IV. Conclusions

From these reflections, a number of conclusions can be drawn:

1. If the applicable domestic law is clear and does not lend itself to interpretation, the judge is bound and can only with great difficulty and exceptionally deviate from the result prescribed by his or her domestic law by using the comparative approach.
2. None of the arguments against the legitimacy of the comparative approach are convincing. For the numerous cases in which domestic law has gaps or lends itself to interpretation, the comparative method is at the disposal of judges who may use it to find inspiration when interpreting domestic law.
3. Nowadays, it is possible that the comparative method constitutes (as it already does in a certain number of countries) a *fifth method of interpretation*, alongside the classical methods of interpretation, namely the literal, historical, systematic, and purposive approaches (or, depending on the country, alongside interpretation in conformity with principles of the national constitution or EU law also).
4. Neither foreign legislation nor foreign case law binds the judge when interpreting his or her country's law. Consequently, foreign law is only a *persuasive authority* and may only guide the judge as such.
5. The aforementioned case law bears witness to the fact that courts, and notably supreme courts, pursue several objectives when using the comparative approach. Courts use the comparative approach:

    - in order to demonstrate that the domestic law is fully in line with modern international trends;
    - to complement the historical method of interpretation of domestic law;
    - to discover and demonstrate the diversity of solutions from which the courts may choose;

---

128 With regard to transnational judicial comparison in the field of human rights SLAUGHTER (fn. 79), at pp. 121 f.: "courts around the world [are] in colloquy with each other"; SLAUGHTER (fn. 73), at p. 193: with respect to certain questions she observes a "constitutional cross-fertilization" and an "emerging global jurisprudence"; *ibid.* at p. 202: "The practice of citing foreign decisions reflects a spirit of genuine transjudicial deliberation within an newly self-conscious transnational community"; see in Europe: C. WITZ, Plaidoyer pour un code européen des obligations, *D.* 2000, Chroniques, 79 at 81.

129 See e.g. *Cheah* v. *Equiticorp Finance Group Ltd*, [1992] 1 AC 472, [1991] 4 All ER 989 (Lord BROWNE-WILKINSON): "It is manifestly desirable that the law on this subject should be the same in all common law jurisdictions"; *Attorney General* v. *Sport Newspapers Ltd*, [1992] 1 All ER 503 (High Court, Q.B.); *Smith* v. *Bank of Scotland*, [1997] SC 111 (120) (HL); ÖRÜCÜ (fn. 27), at pp. 415, 421, 425.

- to benefit from experiences made abroad and to avoid reinventing the wheel again and again;
- to sharpen one's own understanding of certain legal problems and to compare the national solution with differing foreign solutions in order to highlight the particularities of the domestic law;
- to counter arguments that a given solution will lead to harmful or disastrous results;
- to find legal support for a value judgment by the court; and finally,
- to justify changes to domestic case law or to confront new problems, introduce new institutions or remedies.

6. Insofar as judges agree to take inspiration from foreign law or international principles derived from comparison, the comparative method will also become an important tool for lawyers who wish to use it in court in the interest of their clients.
7. So that the court has a solid base for use of the comparative method, it is essential to provide judges with reliable, solid, and trustworthy information as to the content of foreign law. This responsibility falls with the researchers and comparatists who use the comparative approach in their publications. Regarding a case before the court, this comparative research could also be undertaken, and information provided, on an ad hoc basis by comparative law institutions or by lawyers or their staff trained in comparative law.
8. With the progressive programme of European integration, and notably in matters affecting economic relationships, the judge could use the comparative interpretation while pursuing the aim of soft harmonisation which provides an alternative to legislative harmonisation ("bottom-up" instead of "top-down" approach to harmonisation).
9. By using the comparative method, courts contribute to the establishment of a legal discourse that transcends borders. They hereby contribute to the creation of a genuine European or even global community of lawyers who are able to comfortably communicate with each other about topical legal issues.

Thus, the widespread belief in the judiciary of the legitimacy and the multiple benefits of judicial comparison is well founded. With respect to this topic, Thomas Bingham has most aptly made the following point:

> In no other field of intellectual endeavour – be it science, medicine, philosophy, literature, architecture, art, music, engineering or sociology – would ideas or insights be rejected simply because they were of foreign origin . . . [I]t would be strange if [in the field of law] alone practitioners and academics were obliged to ignore developments elsewhere, or at least to regard them as of no practical consequence. Such an approach can only impoverish our law; it cannot enrich it.[130]

Martha Minow, former Dean of Harvard Law School, has stated in the same sense: "Neglecting development in international and comparative law could vitiate the vitality, nimbleness, and effectiveness of [our own] law or simply leave us without the best tools and insights as we design and run institutions, pass legislation, and work to govern ourselves."[131]

---

[130] BINGHAM (fn. 20), at p. 6; in the same sense e.g. A. BARAK, Judge of the Supreme Court of Israel, A Judge on Judging: The Role of a Supreme Court in a Democracy, *Harv. L. Rev.* 2002, 16 at 111: "Indeed, the importance of comparative law lies in extending the judge's horizons."

[131] Fn. 9, III. Reclaiming the Chance to Learn.

Chapter 4

The Principles of European Tort Law – a brief introduction and analysis[1]

The following chapter provides an introduction to the materials that will be used throughout the book. Most scholars and students are aware of the fact that individual nation-states have developed their own tort law systems. Perhaps not all scholars are yet familiar with the non-binding instruments that have been presented since the mid-1990s in the field of tort law, in particular the Principles of European Tort Law (PETL) that were drafted and presented by the European Group on Tort Law (EGTL). For this reason, the present chapter provides a brief introduction to the PETL, their strengths, and some issues to work on or reconsider.

I. Starting point: differences between national legal systems in tort law

In the area of tort liability, there is still very little harmonisation of the law and even less uniform law.[2] The rules on tort law are primarily of national origin and vary considerably from one country to another.[3] In May 2005, confronted with this diversity of national laws,

---

1 A previous French language version of this chapter was published in B. WINIGER (ed.), *La responsabilité civile de demain/Europäisches Haftungsrecht morgen*, Zurich: Schulthess, 2008, pp. 219–247.
2 See for EU law in this area, however, H. KOZIOL/R. SCHULZE (eds.), *Tort Law of the European Community*, Wien/New York: Springer, 2008.
3 During the work of the European Group on Tort Law, the founder of the Group, J. SPIER, noted e.g. the existence of a genuine "fossé qui sépare le système anglais des systems continentaux" ("gulf separating the English system from continental systems"), La faisabilité d'un droit européen de la responsabilité délictuelle, in: F. Milazzo (ed.), *Diritto romano e terzo millennio – Radice e prospettive dell'esperienza giuridica contemporanea (a cura di Francesco Milazzo)*, Napoli: Edizioni Scientifiche Italiane, 2004, p. 239. In tort law, for many issues such a "gulf" can also be noticed between many continental jurisdictions and *French* law. The reason is that *French* law provides very extensive protection e.g. for purely economic loss and non-pecuniary loss, and the scope of strict liability is also very broad when compared to other continental systems, see the information provided in this book and the outcomes of the case studies. See also e.g. R. ZIMMERMANN, *Roman Law, Contemporary Law, European Law*, Oxford: OUP, 2001, pp. 112 ff. For numerous distinctions between European jurisdictions in tort law, see C. VON BAR, *Gemeineuropäisches Deliktsrecht*, Erster Band, München: C. H. Beck, 1996, Zweiter Band, München: C. H. Beck, 1999; C. VON BAR, *The Common European Law of Torts*, Vol. 1 and 2, Oxford: Clarendon Press, 1998 and 2000; C. VAN DAM, *European Tort Law*, 2nd ed., Oxford: OUP, 2013, pp. 218 ff.; for a brief overview of the differences between national laws that pose the most common problems in cross-border situations, see T. KADNER GRAZIANO, *Gemeineuropäisches Internationales Privatrecht*, Tübingen: Mohr Siebeck, 2002, pp. 105 ff.; T. KADNER GRAZIANO, *Europäisches Internationales Deliktsrecht*, Tübingen: Mohr Siebeck, 2002, pp. 10 ff.; T. KADNER GRAZIANO, *La responsabilité délictuelle*

the European Group on Tort Law, a private group of researchers in tort law,[4] set out for the first time in the modern history of private law to present rules or "principles" on all key elements[5] of tort law.[6]

The *precedent* for any research on "principles" of private law is found in projects carried out in *contract* law. This chapter will thus briefly recall the results stemming from the research on principles of *contract* law, hereby illustrating the role that "principles" of law, researched and elaborated from a comparative perspective, can play in the development and practice of law. Next we will ask ourselves whether the principles of tort law will be able to play a similar role in European tort law and, finally, we will analyse provisions of the Principles of European Tort Law (PETL) which may need to be revised and adapted in order to achieve similar success.

II. The precedent set in contract law: Principles of European Contract Law (PECL) and the Principles of International Commercial Contracts (UNIDROIT Principles)

In 1995, the Commission on European Contract Law, a private group of researchers specialising in contract law that was started and chaired by Prof. Ole Lando in the 1980s, presented the first draft of the "Principles of European Contract Law" (PECL or Lando Principles[7]). In the same year, the International Institute for the Unification of Private Law, an independent intergovernmental organisation based in Rome, published their "Principles of International Commercial Contracts" (UNIDROIT Principles[8]). A few years later, more comprehensive versions of both sets of principles were published.[9] These principles have several functions and pursue several objectives:

---

en droit international privé européen, Bâle/Genève/Munich: Helbing Lichtenhahn/Bruxelles: Bruylant/Paris: L.G.D.J., 2004, pp. 10 ff.

4 See the website of the European Group of Tort Law at www.egtl.com.

5 "[They are] at least as comprehensive as most or any of the systems of municipal tort law they are designed to repeat if not replace," G. WAGNER, The Project of Harmonizing European Tort Law, *CMLR* 2005, 1269 at 1287.

6 On the Group's work, see www.egtl.org/ and e.g. J. SPIER, in: European Group on Tort Law (ed.), *Principles of European Tort Law – Text and Commentary*, Wien/New York: Springer, 2005, pp. 12 ff.; J. SPIER, in: Milazzo (fn. 3), at pp. 239 ff.; H. KOZIOL, Die "Principles of European Tort Law" der "European Group on Tort Law", *ZEuP* 2004, 234; B. KOCH, The Work of the European Group on Tort Law: The Case of "Strict Liability", *InDret Working Paper No. 129*, Barcelona 2003, www.indret.com; for academic commentary on the PETL, see www.egtl.org/ (section "Publications").

7 Commission on European Contract Law (President: OLE LANDO), *Principles of European Contract Law*, edited by O. LANDO and H. BEALE, The Hague/London/Boston: Kluwer Law International, 2002, e.g. at www.jus.uio. no/lm/eu.contract.principles.parts.1.to.3.2002/ or www.law.kuleuven.be/personal/mstorme/PECL.html.

8 UNIDROIT, International Institute for the Unification of Private Law, *Principles of International Commercial Contracts*, Rome: International Institute for the Unification of Private Law (UNIDROIT), 2016 edition; www.unilex.info/.

9 In 2002 for the European Principles, as well as in 2004, 2010, and 2016 for the UNIDROIT Principles, see references in fns. 7 and 8. For an instructive account of the 2004 version of the UNIDROIT Principles, see E. CASHIN RITAINE/E. LEIN (eds.), *The UNIDROIT Principles 2004: Their Impact on Contractual Practice, Jurisprudence and Codification*, Zürich: Schulthess, 2007; M. J. BONELL, *The UNIDROIT Principles in Practice: Caselaw and Bibliography on the UNIDROIT Principles of International Commercial Contracts*, 2nd ed., Ardsley, NY: Transnational Publishers, 2006; for the 2010 edition, see the contributions in: *Unif. L. Rev.* 2011, 16(3);

1. Since their publication, the PECL, as well as the UNIDROIT Principles, have served as a *source of inspiration* for many national legislatures during reform of their national laws, particularly in Central and Eastern European countries but also, for example, in China. These principles have therefore considerably contributed to *improvements in domestic legislation*.[10]

   Given that the different countries' legislatures have used the *same source of inspiration*, the Principles have also contributed to *soft harmonisation* of contract law on a European as well as a global level. For example, the Chinese Contract Law Act of 2009 and the contract law in the new civil codes of some Eastern and Central European countries were influenced by the UNIDROIT Principles.[11] In the context of unification of the law on a supranational level, there is a proposal for a uniform contract law for West African countries that are part of the Organisation for the Harmonisation of Business Law in Africa (OHADA)[12] which also largely follows the model set by the UNIDROIT Principles.[13]

   Lawyers familiar with the UNIDROIT Principles or the European Principles will not be surprised by, and quickly feel familiar with, the Chinese Contract Law Act of 2009, for example, as well as with the draft for a future contract law for OHADA. The contract law principles have thus created common standards and European, or even global, rules and solutions for this area.

2. It should also be kept in mind that, following several initiatives of the European Parliament and beginning in 2001, the European Commission has supported and conducted work in the field of contract law, leading to the Draft Common Frame of Reference (DCFR)[14] in 2009, and the draft Common European Sales Law (CESL) in 2011,[15] a proposed optional instrument[16] for the sale of goods. These two instruments

---

S. Vogenauer, *Commentary on the UNIDROIT Principles of International Commercial Contracts (PICC)*, 2nd ed., Oxford: OUP, 2015; for the PECL, see M. W. Hesselink, The Principles of European Contract Law: Some Choices Made by the Lando Commission, *Global Jurist Frontiers* 2001, Article 4.

10 J. A. Estrella Faria, The Influence of the UNIDROIT Principles of International Commercial Contracts on National Laws, *Unif. L. Rev.* 2015, 238–270; Cashin Ritaine/Lein (fn 9). Multiple national reports on the experience under the UNIDROIT Principles, along with statistics, are to be found in a special issue of the *Unif. L. Rev.* (fn 9). For a recent and more general overview of the law of obligations in European countries, see R. Schulze (ed.), *The Law of Obligations in Europe, a New Wave of Codifications*, München: Sellier, 2013. On the uniformity of sales laws in the context of the interpretation of the 1980 Vienna Convention on Contracts for the International Sale of Goods, see F. Ferrari, Tendance insulariste et lex forisme malgré un droit uniforme de la vente, *Rev. crit. DIP* 2013, 323–358.

11 See e.g. Jing Xi, The Impact of the UNIDROIT Principles on Chinese Legislation, in: Cashin Ritaine/Lein (fn. 9), at pp. 107–118.

12 OHADA was created by the Treaty on the Harmonisation of Business Law in Africa, signed on 17 October 1993 in Port Louis, Mauritius. Today OHADA is made up of 17 countries and is open to every state on the African continent, see www.ohada.com.

13 See M. Fontaine, Un projet d'harmonisation du droit des contrats en Afrique, in: Cashin Ritaine/Lein (fn. 9), at pp. 95 ff.

14 The text of the DCFR is available at http://ec.europa.eu/justice/policies/civil/docs/dcfr_outline_edition_en.pdf.

15 COM(2011), 635.

16 On the arguments for and against, and the scope of application of, a future European contract code, see e.g. by the author of this book: Le futur de la Codification du droit civil en Europe: harmonisation des anciens Codes ou création d'un nouveau Code?, in: J.-P. Dunand/B. Winiger (eds.), *Le Code civil français dans le droit européen*, Bruxelles: Bruylant, 2005, p. 257, with numerous references; in *German* language: Die Zukunft der Zivilrechtskodifikation in Europa – Harmonisierung der alten Gesetzbücher oder Schaffung eines neuen? – Überlegungen anlässlich des 200. Jahrestages des französischen Code civil, *ZEuP* 2005, 523; more

are also largely inspired by the PECL and the UNIDROIT Principles. Even if, for the moment, the works have not resulted in the adoption of a comprehensive instrument of EU community law in the field of contract law,[17] the PECL and the UNIDROIT Principles remain of primary importance when it comes to identifying sources of inspiration in the field of contract law.

3. Finally, according to an almost globally applied principle, the contracting parties can choose the law that applies to their contract. To the extent that this national law is non-mandatory, the parties can also opt for the application of soft law and model rules, in particular the PECL or the Principles of International Commercial Contracts.[18]

---

recently M. PICAT/S. SOCCIO, Harmonisation of European Contract Law: Fiction or Reality?, *I.B.L.J.* 2011, 371; Y. LEQUETTE, Le Code européen est de retour, *R.C.D.* 2011, 1028; L. MILLER, The Common Frame of Reference and the Feasibility of a Common Contract Law in Europe, *J.B.L.* 2007, 378; S. PAPOUTSI, The Unification of Private Law in Europe: Questioning the Economic and Legal Cultural Arguments, in: S. Besson/N. Levrat (eds.), *European Legal (Dis)orders*, Genève: Schulthess, 2012, p. 131; J. LE BOURG, Un code européen des obligations?, in: C. Quézel-Ambrunaz (ed.), *Les défis de l'harmonisation européenne du droit des contrats*, Chambéry: Université de Savoie, 2012, p. 141; L. MOCCIA (ed.), *The Making of European Private Law: Why, How, What, Who*, München: Sellier, 2013; P. PICHONNAZ, Un droit européen des contrats unifiés, 20 ans de travaux pour un constat d'échec?, in: A. Epiney/S. Affolter (eds.), *Die Schweiz und die europäische Integration: 20 Jahre Institut für Europarecht*, Zürich: Schulthess, 2015, p. 235; B. ZELLER, Anatomy of EU Contract Harmonization: Where Do We Stand?, *Int. T.L.R.* 2015, 41. More specifically on the CESL: H. EIDENMÜLLER/N. JANSEN/E.-M. KIENINGER/G. WAGNER/R. ZIMMERMANN, The Proposal for a Regulation on a Common European Sales Law: Deficits of the Most Recent Textual Layer of European Contract Law, *Edin. L. Rev.* 2012, 301; M. LEHMANN (ed.), *Common European Sales Law Meets Reality*, München: Sellier, 2015, and also the contributions in *ZEuP* 2012, 681 ff.

17 Regarding perspectives for the future, see e.g. P. SVOBODA, The Common European Sales Law – Will the Phoenix Rise from the Ashes Again?, *ZEuP* 2015, 689; for another excellent update, see PICHONNAZ (fn. 16).

18 See e.g. C. CHAPPUIS, The Significance of the UNIDROIT Principles for International Contract Practice, in: M. Fontaine/D. Philippe (eds.), *Contrats internationaux et arbitrage*, Bruxelles: Larcier, 2014, p. 29, in particular pp. 34–38; for the possibility of opting for the application of the PECL as the rules applicable to a cross-border contract, see Art. 3 of the Hague Principles on Choice of Law in International Commercial Contracts, and the official commentary to Art. 3, in: https://assets.hcch.net/docs/5da3ed47-f54d-4c43-aaef-5eaf-c7c1f2a1.pdf (pp. 40 ff.); M. PERTEGÁS et al. (for the Permanent Bureau of the Hague Conference on Private International Law), Choice of Law in International Commercial Contracts: Hague Principles?, *Unif. L. Rev.* 2010, 883; G. SAUMIER, The Hague Principles and the Choice of Non-State "Rules of Law" to Govern an International Commercial Contract, *Brook. J. Int'l L.* 2014, 1; S. C. SYMEONIDES, Party Autonomy and Private-Law Making in Private International Law: The Lex Mercatoria that Isn't, in: University of Athens (ed.), *Essays in Honour of Konstantinos D. Kerameus*, Athens: Ant. N. Sakkoulas/Bruxelles: Bruylant, 2009, p. 1397; S. C. Symeonides, L'autonomie de la volonté dans les Principes de La Haye sur le choix de la loi applicable en matière de contrats internationaux, *Rev. crit. DIP* 2013, 807 at 832–835; P. DE VAREILLES-SOMMIÈRES, Autonomie et ordre public dans les Principes de La Haye sur le choix de la loi applicable aux contrats commerciaux internationaux, *J.D.I.* 2016, 409 at 432–441; D. MARTINY, Die Haager Principles on Choice of Law in International Commercial Contracts – Eine weitere Verankerung der Parteiautonomie, *RabelsZ* 2015, 624 at 636–639; J. A. MORENO RODRIGUEZ, Contracts and Non-State Law in Latin America, *Unif. L. Rev.* 2011, 877; G. P. ROMANO, Le choix des Principes UNIDROIT par les contractants à l'épreuve des dispositions impératives, in: CASHIN RITAINE/LEIN (fn. 9), at pp. 35 ff.; W.-H. ROTH, Zur Wählbarkeit nichtstaatlichen Rechts, in: H.-P. Mansel/T. Pfeiffer/H. Kronke/C. Kohler/R. Hausmann (eds.), *Festschrift für Erik Jayme, Band I*, München: Sellier, 2004, pp. 757 ff.; F. SCHÄFER, Die Wahl nichtstaatlichen Rechts nach Art. 3 Abs. 2 des Entwurfs einer Rom I VO – Auswirkungen auf das optionale Instrument des europäischen Vertragsrechts, *GPR* 2006, p. 54 ff.; R. MICHAELS, What Is Non-State Law? A Primer, in: M. A. Helfand (ed.), *Negotiating State and Non-State Law: The Challenge of Global and Local Legal Pluralism*, Cambridge: CUP, 2015, p. 41; R. MICHAELS, Non-State Law in the Hague Principles on Choice of Law in International Commercial Contracts, in: K. Purnhagen/P. Rott (eds.), *Varieties of European Economic Law and Regulation: Liber Amicorum for Hans Micklitz*, 2014, p. 43;

The case law that applies these Principles, or that takes inspiration from them, is becoming increasingly rich, particularly but not only in international arbitration.[19] In international relationships, the Principles offer the parties neutral rules and avoid surprise for foreign parties that might arise from the application of national legal systems. Parties to an international contract may consequently have significant reason for choosing the Principles over a national law that is foreign to them.

Given this experience with contract law, the question may be raised as to whether the PETL may be able to play a similar role in tort law as the European Principles and UNIDROIT Principles currently play in contract law.[20] This raises the following questions:

- What are the particular strengths and weaknesses of the PETL?
- May the PETL also serve as a source of inspiration for national legislative reform and soft harmonisation of tort law across Europe?
- Do they offer neutral rules that could serve as inspiration for judges and arbitrators, just like the PECL?
- Could the tort principles be chosen by the parties, particularly in cross-border situations?
- What further improvements may be necessary or helpful so that the PETL can, in the future, play the same role as the PECL and the UNIDROIT Principles currently play in contract law?

III. The strengths of the Principles of European Tort Law

The experience in contract law shows us that the success of PETL depends on their quality and the extent to which they manage to either identify common rules or, alternatively, establish compromises between the differences in the national legal systems or suggest convincing new approaches. We will start our analysis with the strengths of the PETL and then focus on some issues that may possibly have to be reconsidered.

1. Pioneering work

The first strength of the PETL is that they represent a *pioneering work*.[21] Tort law is an area that has considerably diversified since the end of the 19th century and in which the national systems present a wide range of approaches and solutions that are, depending on the specific topic, quite different from one another.[22] For the first time in the modern history of private law, a group of researchers succeeded in producing common principles of European tort law,

---

R. MICHAELS, Privatautonomie und Privatkodifikation – Zu Anwendbarkeit und Geltung allgemeiner Vertragsrechtsprinzipien, *RabelsZ* 1998, 580 ff.

19 The text of the UNIDROIT Principles is available at www.unilex.info.
20 For a comparison of both instruments, see R. ZIMMERMANN, Principles of European Contract Law and Principles of European Tort Law: Comparison and Points of Contact, in: H. Koziol/B. C. Steininger (eds.), *Yearbook European Tort Law 2003*, Vienna/New York: Springer, 2004, pp. 2 ff.
21 See e.g. F. WERRO, Les Principes de droit européen de la responsabilité civile en deux mots: contenu et critique, *HAVE/REAS* 2005, 248 at 250: "Une grande première"; M. SCHULZ, Disharmonization: A Swedish Critique of Principles of European Tort Law, *EBLR* 2007, 1305: "a landmark in the academic discussion on the future of European tort law", and 1306: "the first published proposal on common principles of European tort law formutated by academics".
22 See references, above (fn. 3).

despite all the differences between national laws and the gulf separating, for example, the English Law of Torts from continental systems, as well as the French legal systems from the Germanic systems.

The first and the greatest strength of the PETL thus lies in the fact that they provide, for the first time, a *tertium comparationis* and a *reference* for future discussions and deliberations on tort law in Europe and beyond in the same way that the contract law principles do.

2. A wide comparative basis

A second strength of the PETL is the method that was used to prepare them. The PETL were developed on the basis of a broad comparative study. During their preparation, not only were the laws of many EU Member States represented as sources of inspiration, but also Swiss law and the laws of the USA and two mixed legal systems, South Africa, and Israel.[23] In the works following their publication, the laws of the twenty-eight Member States of the European Union as well as the laws of Norway and Switzerland have been taken into consideration.[24] In the works of the European Group on Tort Law (EGTL), as well as in the research done at the European Centre of Tort an Insurance Law (ECTIL), all European jurisdictions, including Central and Eastern European legal systems that had previously only been taken into consideration to a limited extent in comparative law, have been present.

Today, such a broad comparative view is essential for the success of any project on common principles of European law, for the outcome of the research to be acceptable, and for support to be found throughout Europe.

3. Practical approach

A third strength of the PETL lies in the fact that, during the preparatory phase of the PETL, the Group worked with materials, case scenarios, and leading cases taken from court practice throughout Europe. In tort law, English lawyers reason by using precedents, whereas, on the continent, legal discussion in relation to specific cases takes a provision of the civil code as their starting point. However, continental civil codes and statutes contain fewer and less detailed provisions on torts than on contract law, for example. In tort law, continental lawyers thus also make a wide use of, and reason with respect to, precedents and leading cases from their respective jurisdictions. The European Group on Tort Law consequently based its work on the analysis of numerous precedents and has identified a number of criteria that are commonly used throughout the European legal systems. These criteria have been included in the PETL.

In the Group's publications, as well as those of the members of the research group brought together within the European Centre of Tort and Insurance Law in Vienna, we find many

---

23 See references, above (fn. 6). See however the critical assessment by SCHULZ (fn. 21), at pp. 1305 ff., criticising an underrepresentation of Nordic and possibly also Central and Eastern European jurisdictions and their particular approaches in the preparation of the PETL.
24 Compare e.g. the wide range of jurisdictions covered by the Yearbooks of European Tort Law and the Digest of European Tort Law, see B. WINIGER/H. KOZIOL/B. KOCH/R. ZIMMERMANN (eds.), *Digest of European Tort Law, Volume 1: Essential Cases on Natural Causation*, Wien/New York: Springer, 2007; *Volume 2: Essential Cases on Damage*, Berlin/Boston: Walter de Gruyter, 2011; B. WINIGER/E. KARNER/K. OLIPHANT (eds.), *Volume 3: Essential Cases on Misconduct*, Berlin/Boston: De Gruyter, 2018.

specific cases, as well as their solutions, in a wide range of jurisdictions and under the PETL. Thus, a veritable European library of tort law has been created.[25] These materials make the search for existing solutions considerably easier on a European level and allow for easier comparative reasoning when studying a specific case. These materials are, in turn, very useful when working with, and interpreting, the PETL.

4. The basic requirements for tort liability

When we turn from the methods of their elaboration to the content of the PETL, we discover that they contain (in the order of their respective sections):

I. A Basic Norm;
II. General Conditions of Liability (including provisions on damage, protected interests, and causation);
III. Rules on the Bases of Liability (including chapters on liability based on fault, strict liability, and liability for others);
IV. Defences (including provisions on justifications and the effect of the contributory conduct or activity of the victim);
V. Rules on Multiple Tortfeasors; and
VI. Remedies (containing rules on pecuniary as well as non-pecuniary loss).

Arguably the first question that requires an answer when European tort principles are drafted is which *basic norm* and which *conditions* would be included in the tort law system. The conditions for extra-contractual, delictual, or tortious liability, and therefore the starting point for every analysis of a tort case, vary considerably from one European country to another. This is the case not only between continental law and English law, but also between the individual continental jurisdictions.[26] Section 823 (1) of the German Civil Code (*Bürgerliches Gesetzbuch, BGB*), the basic tort liability provision in the German Civil Code, in principle only protects against breaches of "absolute rights" which are listed exhaustively in this provision. If the victim cannot invoke a breach of an absolute right (i.e. injury to life, health, property, freedom or any other "absolute" right), the analysis of the claim stops and must be rejected.[27] Articles 1240 to 1242 (the former Arts. 1382 to 1384) of the French *Code civil*, on the other hand, provide two general clauses for tort liability that, in principle, do not distinguish between breaches of absolute rights and pure economic loss.[28] The text of Art. 41 of the Swiss Code of Obligations seems to follow the French model of a general tort liability clause. However, Swiss case law and doctrine take inspiration from German law, and an injury is only considered unlawful if it infringes upon one of the victim's absolute rights.[29]

The starting point for an action in tort law thus varies considerably between French law and those jurisdictions that follow the French approach on the one hand, and German law and the jurisdictions which are influenced by the German approach on the other. English Common Law provides yet another approach by identifying several different specific torts

---

25 See the list of publications, available at: www.ectil.org.
26 See the materials provided in Part B and in particular Chapter 5 of this book.
27 Compare Part B, Chapter 5, pp. 81 ff. Exceptions: § 823 (2) BGB and, in the case of breach of "good morals", § 826 BGB.
28 Part B, Chapter 5, pp. 96 ff.
29 Part B, Chapter 5, pp. 87 ff.

when analysing extra-contractual liability. However, numerous comparative law studies, as well as some of the case studies in Part B of the present book, show that even if the basic starting point of each national legal system varies considerably from one system to the next, the scope of protection does not necessarily differ in specific cases.[30]

A simple example that we'll see in Part B of this book[31] illustrates this fact. Following a road traffic accident, several drivers in other cars found themselves caught up in a traffic jam. As a result, one of the drivers arrives late to work, even though he was not directly involved in the accident. Following this delay, he misses an attractive business opportunity and suffers a significant loss of profits. In such a case, under German law, the driver who has been delayed is unable to invoke the breach of an absolute right (i.e. injury to health or property, as pure economic interests are not protected). In Swiss law, the injury wouldn't be considered unlawful (property being an absolute right but, as in German law, there is, in principle, no protection against 'pure' economic loss in itself). In these countries, the claim for damages cannot succeed as it is "purely economic" loss.

In English law, a claim for compensation of lost profits would also fail in such a case. From the perspective of an English lawyer, the person who caused the accident would not have owed a *duty of care* to the drivers who were merely delayed by the traffic jam.[32]

It is only in French law that the claim would stand any chance of succeeding, given that French law does not categorically distinguish between the breach of an absolute right and purely economic loss.[33]

In all jurisdictions, the victim of an accident whose health or body has been injured will be protected by tort law,[34] while in the large majority of European jurisdictions, people who are delayed by a traffic jam cannot be reimbursed for loss of profits.[35] Even if the fixed approaches for refusing these claims vary, the result would probably be the same in many, if not most, jurisdictions.

---

30 See e.g. G. WAGNER, Grundstrukturen des Europäischen Deliktsrechts, in: R. Zimmermann (ed.), *Grundstrukturen des europäischen Deliktsrechts*, Baden-Baden: Nomos, 2003, p. 189 at pp. 224 ff.; W. VAN GERVEN/J. LEVER/P. LAROUCHE, *Cases, Materials and Text on National, Supranational and International Tort Law*, Oxford: Hart Publishing, 2000, pp. 71 ff.; N. JANSEN, Principles of European Tort Law?, Grundwertungen und Systembildung im europäischen Haftungsrecht, *RabelsZ* 2006, 732 at 738; C. VAN DAM (fn. 3).
31 Part B, Chapter 4, second scenario.
32 For the conditions of the duty of care, see *Caparo* v. *Dickman*, [1990] 1 All ER 568 (HL). For an analysis of the duty of care and, in particular, economic loss under *English* law, see S. DEAKIN/A. JOHNSTON/B. MARKESINIS, *Markesinis and Deakin's Tort Law*, 7th ed., Oxford: Clarendon Press, 2013, p. 139; and also J. STAPLETON, Duty of Care and Economic Loss – A Wider Agenda, *L.Q.R.* 1991, 249.
33 See the decision of the *French* Court of Cassation reproduced in Part B, Chapter 5, p. 99: C. cass. (2ᵉ civ.), 28.04.1965, *Marcailloux* c. *R.A.T.V.M.*, D. 1965 Jur. 777. If the action were to be refused, it would be in terms of causation, indirect damage, or uncertain damage, see P. MALAURIE/L. AYNÈS/P. STOFFEL-MUNCK, *Les obligations*, 8th ed., Paris: Défrénois Lextenso ed., 2016, nos. 241 ff.; A. BÉNABENT, *Droit civil – Les obligations*, 12th ed., Paris: Montchrestien, 2010, nos. 675 ff.; TERRÉ/SIMLER/LEQUETTE, *Droit civil – Les obligations*, 11th ed., Paris: Dalloz, 2013, nos. 700 ff.
34 In *German*, *Swiss*, and *French* law, in respect of road traffic accidents, special laws on strict liability apply, either instead of the general rules of tort law (*Swiss* and *French* law) or concurrently with them (*German* law), see § 7 of the *German* Road Traffic Act (*Strassenverkehrsgesetz*); Art. 58 of the *Swiss* Road Traffic Act; Law No. 85–677 of 5 July 1985, aiming at the improvement of the conditions of road traffic accident victims and the acceleration of the compensation procedure (Law Badinter). As for the protected interests and the damages due, the special rules do not differ from the three countries' general tort rules. See the materials *infra*, Part B, Chapter 9, pp. 229 ff.
35 This outcome is certain, particularly, in *German*, *Swiss*, and *English* law; *French* law is very likely to present the exception, see the materials in Chapter 9, pp. 233 ff.

This case, like many others, shows that bodily integrity as well as life, property and certain other so-called absolute rights enjoy greater protection in tort law than purely economic interests such as the interest in making a profit.

Article 2:102 of the PETL confirms this hierarchy of protected interests[36] by stating:

(1) The scope of protection of an interest depends on its nature; the higher its value, the precision of its definition and its obviousness, the more extensive its protection.
(2) Life, bodily or mental integrity, human dignity and liberty enjoy the most extensive protection.
(3) Extensive protection is granted to property rights, including those in intangible property.
(4) Protection of pure economic interests or contractual relationships may be more limited in scope. In such cases, due regard must be had especially to the proximity between the actor and the endangered person, or to the fact that the actor is aware of the fact that he will cause damage even though his interests are necessarily valued lower than those of the victim.

In Article 2:102 of the PETL we thus find a scale of protected values, rights, and interests which is the same as in most European national legal systems without, however, the rigidity of German law or the extreme open-endedness of the French *Code civil*.[37]

5. Wide range of criteria

A fifth strength of the PETL is the wide range of criteria provided to decide specific cases, without turning into a casuistic analysis that would abandon the abstract nature that is essential for all modern European codifications or statutes. Two examples may be used to illustrate this feature.

a) The wide range of criteria can, for example, be illustrated with the help of Articles 4:102 and 4:103 of the PETL concerning liability based on fault. To know whether a fault has been committed, Article 4:102 of the PETL provides a long list of criteria, in particular:

- the nature and value of the protected interest involved (hierarchy of values as established by Art. 2:102);
- the dangerousness of the activity;
- the expertise to be expected of a person carrying it on;
- the foreseeability of the damage;
- the relationship of proximity or special reliance between those involved;

---

36 It may, however, very well be questioned whether there is indeed a hierarchy between the protected interests, comp. Jansen (fn. 30), at pp. 762 f.
37 One might wonder whether the protection of the interests at the top of the list is truly "more extensive" than the protection of those at the bottom of the scale. In European jurisdictions, absolute rights such as ownership benefit from complete protection that hardly differs from the protection of bodily and mental integrity and liberty. However, in respect of non-pecuniary loss, the protection of things placed at the top of the list is indeed more extensive.

- the availability and the costs of precautionary or alternative methods;
- the ages of persons alleged to be liable; and
- extraordinary circumstances which may have made it more onerous to conform to the required standard in the specific case.

In this provision, as in many others, the Principles have chosen a "flexible system" (*"système mobile"*, *"Bewegliches System"*[38]) that makes it possible to undertake a flexible analysis of the criteria for tort liability and weigh up the unique features of specific cases.[39]

b) Another particularly delicate question in tort law is to know under which conditions there is a "duty to protect others from damage" and under which conditions a failure to act would constitute a "fault".

In Article 4:103, the PETL establish criteria that are as precise as possible to facilitate making decisions in specific cases. For example, the following are among the elements that may contribute to creating an obligation to act positively:

- a dangerous situation, created or controlled by the actor;
- a special relationship between the parties; or
- the seriousness of the harm on the one side and the ease of avoiding the damage on the other side.

The fact that the criteria that need to be taken into consideration when solving a case are expressly mentioned in the PETL should contribute to legal certainty across Europe, while leaving judges a margin of appreciation in specific cases.

As such, these criteria already exist and are used in the practice of tort law in Europe. What is new is that these criteria have been identified through a European-wide comparative study and research and introduced into the PETL. The style of the PETL preserves the abstract character of a codified system, while still providing a series of criteria that leaves enough leeway for the judge for further development of the law. The explicit reference to this precise range of criteria which act to guide the judge is even more important since a European court which could oversee the uniform application of common rules in torts will certainly not exist in the next years, or even decades.

6. Relatively straightforward application in many specific cases

A sixth strength of the PETL is that they apply, arguably more easily than most existing codifications, to resolve some of the most difficult cases we currently face in tort law without even needing much case law to clarify them.

---

38 Taking inspiration from the *Austrian* jurist W. WILBURG, *Die Elemente des Schadensrechts*, Marburg an der Lahn: Elwert, 1941; W. WILBURG, *Entwicklung eines beweglichen Systems im bürgerlichen Recht*, Graz: Verlag Jos. A. Kienreich, 1950; see also F. BYDLINSKI, *Juristische Methodenlehre und Rechtsbegriff*, 2nd ed., Wien/New York: Springer, 1991, pp. 529 ff; F. BYDLINSKI/H. KREJCI/B. SCHILCHER/V. STEININGER (eds.), *Das Bewegliche System im geltenden und künftigen Recht*, Wien/New York: Springer, 1986.

39 See B. KOCH, Die "Grundsätze des europäischen Deliktsrechts", in: Winiger (fn. 1), at pp. 205–218.

a) The example of the case Fairchild v. Glenhaven

To illustrate this point, we can refer to the English case of *Fairchild* v. *Glenhaven* that was decided by the UK House of Lords in 2002.[40] Over the course of his professional life, Mr Fairchild had worked consecutively for several employers. Each employer, unlawfully and wrongfully, exposed him to asbestos dust and fibres. Later, Mr Fairchild suffered from a fatal cancer linked to asbestos exposure.

According to expert opinion, the illness might have been caused by the exposure to asbestos by the first employer, by the second, or both. Also, the possibility of it being caused by one single fibre of asbestos wasn't dismissed. Given that asbestos is also present in the atmosphere, there was also a very small possibility that the illness could have been caused by natural exposure.

In all European legal systems, establishing a claim for damages requires the claimant to prove that, in the absence of the defendant's activities, the damage would not have occurred. This is the famous *conditio sine qua non* rule which has been reproduced in Article 3:101 of the PETL, which states that "[a]n activity or conduct [. . .] is a cause of the victim's damage if, in the absence of the activity, the damage would not have occurred". It was, however, impossible for Mr Fairchild to prove which employer had caused the illness (it may have been either of the employers that caused his disease) and to demonstrate that in the absence of exposure from any one of the employers he would not have become ill.

If it had been possible for Mr Fairchild to establish that *cumulative exposure* had been necessary to cause the damage, each exposure would have been a *conditio sine qua non* and the employers would be liable *in solidum* under the rules of several legal systems, as well as under the PETL.[41] However, in *Fairchild*, the victim was unable to prove this because it was equally possible that the exposure by one single employer had caused the illness. According to the traditional rules and requirements on causation, his claim should thus have failed.

Given that, in situations like *Fairchild*, the "but for" or *conditio sine qua non* test cannot be met, establishing liability poses significant problems under all national tort liability systems. However, refusing the claim also appears unjust, considering that each employer had unlawfully and wrongfully exposed Mr Fairchild to a considerable risk of fatal illness and that Mr Fairchild had indeed eventually become a victim of this illness.

In many European jurisdictions, the solution to this case is likewise far from obvious – although in most systems the view is shared that rejecting the claim would be the worst of all options. Based on broad multilateral comparative research, and taking into account the laws of a multitude of jurisdictions, the UK House of Lords finally allowed the claim and held the defendants jointly liable given that they had each contributed to the risk of getting the illness, that they had considerably increased this risk, and that he had eventually contracted the disease.[42]

The PETL devote seven articles to causation (Articles 3:101 to 3:106), as well as two articles to the conduct of multiple tortfeasors (Articles 9:101 and 9:102). These provisions are based as far as possible on the findings in various European legal systems. Where the courts had not yet made a finding, or where the solutions in force were considered unsatisfactory

---

40 [2002] UKHL 22; (2003) 1 AC 32; reproduced in WINIGER/KOZIOL/KOCH/ZIMMERMANN (fn. 24), at 6a.12.5 with commentary by K. OLIPHANT; see also the case of *Barker* v. *Corus UK (Ltd)*, [2006] UKHL 20; [2006] AC 572; and e.g. R. KIDNER, *Casebook on Torts*, 11th ed., Oxford: OUP, 2010, pp. 62–65; see also G. WAGNER, Asbestschäden – Bismarck was right, *ZEuP* 2007, 1122.
41 Art. 9:101 (1) 2 lit. b) PETL.
42 See the reference, above (fn. 40).

by the Group's members, innovative solutions representing minority approaches were adopted by the Group.[43] Thus, in respect of alternative cause, Article 3:103 (1) of the European Principles provides that:

> [i]n case of multiple activities, where each of them alone would have been sufficient to cause the damage, but it remains uncertain which one in fact caused it, each activity is regarded as a cause to the extent corresponding to the likelihood that it may have caused the victim's damage.

In *Fairchild*, in the hypothesis that exposure by one or the other of the employers had been sufficient to cause the illness, each employer would be liable according to Article 3:303 of the PETL *in proportion to the danger* posed to the victim.

With respect to the slight possibility that the illness had been caused by a natural exposure to asbestos, the commentary to the PETL suggests that such issues can be ignored when attributing liability,[44] provided that clearly more significant probabilities can be identified – a solution that corresponds to the practice of the large majority of courts in Europe.

Therefore, the case would be resolved by applying Article 3:103 of the PETL, and each employer would be partially liable in proportion to the unlawful exposure that Mr Fairchild suffered with that employer.[45]

It may still be argued that it cannot be excluded that the damage was caused by an accumulation of exposure. In a case where cumulative exposure caused the illness, every exposure would be a cause (*conditiones sine qua non*) of the illness and, as we have seen, the employers would be liable *in solidum*. If we compare the hypothesis according to which the illness had been caused by cumulative exposure and the hypothesis according to which the illness had been caused by one of the fibres at one of the employers' sites, it is the second that leads to less serious liability. If doubt remains as to the choice between one of the two hypotheses, as in the case of *Fairchild*, it is liability defined according to Article 3:103 of the PETL *in proportion to the danger* to which each employer has exposed the victim that would be less significant for the defendant and that would have to be accepted (given that the requirements for liability *in solidum* cannot be proved by the victim).

The solution to the *Fairchild* case (just as to many other scenarios), which to this day poses serious legal difficulties in numerous European jurisdictions,[46] would become

---

43 J. Spier, in: European Group on Tort Law (fn. 6), at Art. 3:102 nos. 9 ff.; also, see P. Loser, Causation – Kausalität, *HAVE/REAS* 2005, 250 at 251. For an economic analysis of the PETL's provisions on causation, see R. van den Bergh/L. T. Visscher, The Principles of European Tort Law: The Right Path to Harmonization? *ERPL* 2006, 511 at 527 ff.

44 J. Spier, in: European Group on Tort Law (fn. 6), Art. 3:201 nos. 15, 12.

45 This solution has also been upheld by the House of Lords in *Baker* v. *Corus* (above, fn. 40). Just like Mr Fairchild, Mr Baker had worked consecutively for multiple (two) employers. He had also worked as a self-employed plasterer for a while. During all of these periods, he had been exposed to asbestos fibres. Mr Baker died from mesothelioma, a cancer linked to asbestos exposure. During the tort action against his final employer, the first employer went bankrupt. The House of Lords held each employer responsible *in proportion to the danger* to which they had exposed the victim – just as provided by Art. 3:103 of the PETL. The *UK* legislator, however, modified this solution and re-established, for cases of mesothelioma, *in solidum* liability of employers, or in other words, the solution foreseen in *Fairchild*, see Compensation Act 2006, Sect. 3, www.legislation.gov.uk/acts/acts2006/ukpga_20060029_en_1.htm.

46 See H. Koziol, in: Winiger/Koziol/Koch/Zimmermann (fn. 24), Vol. 1, at 6a.29.6 ff.; for *German* and *Dutch* law in this area, see also Wagner (fn. 40), at pp. 1129 ff.

relatively straightforward if the precise and partly innovative PETL provisions on causation were applied. Given the uncertainty and gaps in this area of the current law, the PETL could – if used as a source of inspiration – thus contribute considerably to legal certainty.[47]

b) Findings from the preparation stage of the Digest of European Tort Law, Vol. I – III

Once the PETL had been presented, the European Centre of Tort and Insurance Law (ECTIL) in Vienna started a project leading to the *Digest of European Tort Law*, a collection of court decisions including the case law of almost all European jurisdictions.

The first volume of the *Digest* concerned natural causation.[48] Within the framework of this project, many cases that have proved problematic for national courts have been identified and then analysed according to almost 30 national legal systems, as well as the PETL. The analysis under the PETL has shown that, just like the *Fairchild* case, many other cases can be resolved in a relatively straightforward manner by applying the PETL's text and commentary on causation.[49]

Among these cases are scenarios that are currently being discussed in several jurisdictions under the heading of "loss of a chance" or "*perte d'une chance*".[50] Here again, the PETL and in particular the rules and commentary on causation, in a straightforward manner, allow us to achieve certain, equitable outcomes.[51] This result is remarkable given the considerable difficulties that many national jurisdictions currently encounter in these cases.

The experiences made, and the results found by using the PETL in the course of the work on the second and third volumes of the *Digest of European Tort Law* are similarly positive.[52]

7. Other aspects

Among the numerous other strengths of the PETL, we can point to:

a)   The fact that the PETL address and solve certain issues that have long been problematic, or unsolved, in many national jurisdictions. For example, Article 2:104 of the PETL provides that certain "expenses incurred to prevent threatened damage amount to recoverable damage in so far as reasonably incurred".

   In the Germanic legal family, for example, tort liability is only admissible in the event of injury to a so-called absolute right (life, health, liberty, property, or other

---

47   See LOSER (fn. 43), at p. 252.
48   WINIGER/KOZIOL/KOCH/ZIMMERMANN (fn. 24), Vol. 1.
49   See WINIGER/KOZIOL/KOCH/ZIMMERMANN (fn. 24), Vol. 1, at Chapters 4 ff., nos. 28 respectively (by T. KADNER GRAZIANO).
50   See, from a comparative perspective, T. KADNER GRAZIANO, The "Loss of a Chance" in European Private Law – "All or nothing" or partial compensation in cases of uncertainty of causation, *ERPL* 2008, 1009–1042; in French: T. KADNER GRAZIANO, La "perte d'une chance" en droit privé européen: "tout ou rien" ou réparation partielle du dommage en cas de causalité incertaine, in: C. Chappuis/B. Winiger (eds.), *Les causes du dommage*, Genève/Zurich/Bâle: Schulthess, 2007, pp. 218–248.
51   For an application of the PETL to cases in relation to "loss of a chance", see T. KADNER GRAZIANO, in: WINIGER/KOZIOL/KOCH/ZIMMERMANN (fn. 24), Vol. 1, at 10.28.1 ff.; also, see H. KOZIOL, in: *ibid.*, at 10.29.2,8; J. SPIER, in: European Group on Tort Law (fn. 6), at Art. 3:106, no. 7.
52   WINIGER/KOZIOL/KOCH/ZIMMERMANN (fn. 24), Vol. 2; WINIGER/KARNER/OLIPHANT (fn. 24).

rights that enjoy protection towards any potential injurer). Damages for expenses incurred to avoid damage occurring poses significant problems in these countries given that this amounts to "pure economic" loss.[53]

A rule such as Article 2:104 of the PETL would allow an easy solution to the problem of preventive expenses. Such provisions are still rare.

b) We might also mention some clear positions taken in the PETL, and indeed innovations, in response to certain points which should help to animate discussion, such as:

- the provisions (already mentioned above) allowing for (partial) compensation in alternative causation or "loss of a chance"[54] scenarios which would be a significant innovation for certain European legal systems, such as in German[55] or Swiss[56] law (see the materials in Chapter 10 of Part B of this book);
- Article 4:201 of the PETL which establishes fault-based liability with a reversal of the burden of proof for particularly dangerous activities – this provision confirms that the difference between fault-based liability and strict liability is now a question of degree, and no longer of principle;[57]
- an innovative provision on enterprise liability at Article 4:202, with a reversal of the burden of proof;[58] and
- the fact that, among the aims of tort liability, Article 10:101 includes not only the compensation of victims but also the prevention of damage.[59] On the contrary, and in line with most, if not all, continental European tort law systems, the PETL refuse to recognise punishment as one of the aims of tort liability.[60]

IV. Aspects to reconsider and gaps to fill?

Having reviewed some of the many assets of the PETL, we will now raise the question as to which aspects could be reviewed or reconsidered in light of critical response to the PETL in legal literature.

---

53 For the limits of liability for pure economic loss, see *infra*, Part B, Chapters 5 and 14.
54 See references, above (fns. 50 and 51).
55 See R. ZIMMERMANN/J. KLEINSCHMIDT, this idea [i.e. the loss of a chance] is practically non-existent in the case law of [German] courts, in: WINIGER/KOZIOL/KOCH/ZIMMERMANN (fn. 24), Vol. 1, at 10.2.7.
56 C. MÜLLER, La perte d'une chance, Bern: Stämpfli, 2002, nos. 241 and 249; in 2007, the *Swiss* Federal Supreme Court dealt for the first time expressly with the issue of "loss of a chance", but for procedural reasons left the question open: TF, 13.06.2007, 4A.61/2007, www.bger.ch.
57 H. KOZIOL (fn. 6), at p. 238: "keine scharfen Gegensätze [. . .], vielmehr ein fliessender Übergang"; JANSEN (fn. 30).
58 See, in respect of this liability, O. WAESPI, Die Unternehmens- und Hilfspersonenhaftung gemäss den Principles of European Tort Law, *HAVE/REAS* 2005, 255–259.
59 See on this provision e.g. G. WAGNER (fn. 5), at p. 1302; from the perspective of an economic analysis of the law, VAN DEN BERGH/VISSCHER (fn. 43), at pp. 521 ff.
60 H. KOZIOL (fn. 6), at p. 237: eine "deutliche Absage an so genannte Ersatzleistungen, die ausschliesslich der Prävention oder Sanktion dienen, wie insbesondere die [. . .] *punitive damages*". Contrast with Art. 1 of the Tort Law Act of the *People's Republic of China*: "In order to protect the legitimate rights and interests of parties in civil law relationships, clarify the tort liability, prevent and *punish tortious conduct*, and promote social harmony and stability, this Law is formulated" (emphasis added), text of the provision below, Part B, Chapter 5, p. 100.

1. Different language versions

A first weakness concerns some of the translations of the PETL that were produced from the original English version to other languages. For the PETL to fully convince European lawyers, it seems to be of primary importance that the quality of drafting of their several language versions is the same as the original English language version and that the texts in other language versions are on a level equivalent to the national codifications that the lawyers in the respective countries are used to. It seems that some improvement could still be done in this respect.[61]

2. Commentary and notes

A second criticism concerns not the text but, rather, the commentary to the PETL.[62]

For the PETL to be easy to use, it is important that all the materials useful for interpreting and applying them are easily accessible. If we compare the commentary to the PETL with the commentary and notes published in relation to the PECL the UNIDROIT Principles of International Commercial Contracts, or the Common Frame of Reference,[63] the commentaries on many of the PETL's articles could be further expanded and accompanied with more detailed comparative notes and further examples. Materials published by the Group both during the preparatory phase of the PETL and post-release[64] often have more references and examples than the commentary to the PETL that was published in 2005. Therefore, drafting a more comprehensive commentary to the PETL that would, for example, follow the model of the commentaries to the PECL or the Common Frame of Reference might be considered.

When interpreting and applying legal provisions and "principles of law", it is obviously of great help to know the *rationales and reasons* that underlie the respective provisions. While the commentaries to the instruments in contract law do not offer any justification for the choice of the solutions that were adopted, the commentary to the PETL, published in 2005, is already more transparent with regard to the reasons leading to the choices made by the Group and the rationales of the provisions. A future, more detailed, commentary of the PETL could continue in this direction, by providing the reasons that guided the Group's choices and the rationales of each provision. It could hereby contribute to transparency and further facilitate the interpretation of the PETL's provisions.

A further possibility, and option for consideration, would be to coordinate the commentaries on certain articles so that they truly become the Group's commentary instead of representing the personal stances taken by each commentator.[65]

3. Some incoherencies?

A third point to reconsider is some incoherencies that could be removed.

---

61 This concerns e.g. the *German* version as well as the *French* version; also, see the critique by N. Jansen, Principles of European Tort Law: Text and Commentary, *ZEuP* 2007, 398 at 399 in relation to the *Chinese* translation; P. Giliker, European Tort Law: Five Key Questions for Debate, *ERPL* 2009, 285, referring e.g. to the difficulty of translating, or transposing, even such basic notions as 'tort' from one language into the other.
62 See Jansen (fn. 30), at pp. 755 f.
63 Above (fn. 14).
64 The list of publications can be accessed on the website of the European Centre of Tort and Insurance Law (ECTIL), www.ectil.org/.
65 Compare the critical comments e.g. by Jansen (fn. 30), at p. 755.

Among the protected interests mentioned in Art. 2:102 of the PETL, we find life, bodily or mental integrity, human dignity, liberty, property, and, to a lesser extent, economic interests and contractual relationships.

Article 10:301 of the PETL on compensation of damage provides compensation for non-pecuniary damage, particularly in cases of injury "to human dignity [. . .] or other personality rights". Therefore, we might wonder whether these "other personality rights" are also to be included in the "protected interests" listed at Art. 2:102 of the PETL. Moreover, does the European Convention on Human Rights, and especially Art. 8, not also require the right to a "private life" to be categorised as a protected interest in tort law?

4. Minimalist strict liability

The main weakness of the PETL concerns Chapter 5 of Title III, containing provisions on strict liability.

The situation in Europe in respect of strict liability is especially disparate.[66] Consequently, it is extremely difficult to see clearly and identify common principles in this area (see Part B of this book, Chapter 8). Confronted by the diverging current law, Art. 5:101 (1) PETL provides that:

> A person who carries on an abnormally dangerous activity is strictly liable for damage characteristic to the risk presented by the activity and resulting from it.

According to section (2) (b) of the same provision:

> An activity is abnormally dangerous if [. . .] it is not a matter of common usage.

In contrast to the laws of most European jurisdictions,[67] the European Group on Tort Law decided not to list specific instances of strict liability in the PETL. Instead, it favoured a general provision.[68] The text of this provision is inspired by the US Restatement on Torts

---

[66] See C. OERTEL, *Objektive Haftung in Europa: eine rechtsvergleichende Untersuchung zur Weiterentwicklung der verschuldensunabhängigen Haftung im europäischen Privatrecht*, Tübingen: Mohr Siebeck, 2010; B. C. STEININGER, *Verschärfung der Verschuldenshaftung. Übergangsbereiche zwischen Verschuldens- und Gefährdungshaftung*, Wien: Verlag Österreich, 2007; see also the overview provided by F. WERRO/V. V. PALMER/A.-C. HAHN, Strict Liability in European Tort Law: Is There a Common Core?: Synthesis and Survey of the Cases and Results, in: F. Werro/V. V. Palmer(eds.), *The Boundaries of Strict Liability in European Tort Law*, Durham, NC: Carolina Academic Press/Bern: Stämpfli/Bruxelles: Bruylant, 2004, p. 387; JANSEN (fn. 30), at pp. 741 ff.; T. KADNER GRAZIANO, Haftung(en) ohne Verschulden – die transnationale Perspektive, in: C. Chappuis/B. Winiger (eds.), *Responsabilités objectives*, Zurich: Schulthess, 2003, pp. 85–106; for the reasons for this diversity, see R. ZIMMERMANN, in: KOZIOL/STEININGER (fn. 20), at p. 8.
[67] See below, Part B, Chapter 8.
[68] For the reasons that guided the Group, see B. KOCH/H. KOZIOL, Generalklausel für die Gefährdungshaftung, *HAVE/REAS* 2002, 368 f.: "Die bisher in vielen Rechtsordnungen gebräuchliche Vorgehensweise, für einzelne Gefahrenquellen Sondergesetze zu erlassen, führt zu einer der Gerechtigkeit widersprechenden Verschiedenbehandlung gleichartiger Fälle." Dadurch kommt es "zu nicht sachgerechten Unterschieden, weil die Sondergesetze untereinander ohne ersichtlichen Grund voneinander abweichen. Beruhen die Gefährdungshaftungen auf einem einheitlichen Grundgedanken, so erfordert es die Gerechtigkeit, sie auch einheitlich in derselben Weise zu regeln. Das kann letztlich nur durch eine Generalklausel verwirklicht werden"; B. KOCH/H. KOZIOL, *InDret* 2003, 4.3.: one observes a "German hodgepodge of singular statutes which leave out comparable risks (such as motor boats or dams) and thereby lead to inacceptable discrepancies". For

(especially the final draft of its 3rd Edition[69]). However, in the Common Law, the scope of application of strict liability is traditionally extremely limited. Just as in Art. 5:101 of the PETL, strict liability is limited to "abnormally dangerous activities" that are not "of common usage". Neither road traffic nor railway usage falls within the scope of application of strict liability according to the PETL, despite the fact that there is almost unanimity in Europe on the fact that liability should be strict in these two cases.

The PETL's provisions on strict liability consequently do not at all correspond to the current state of tort law in Europe. Despite the general clause approach, they adopt a solution that is extremely limited from a continental perspective.[70] For the large majority of jurisdictions such a limited scope of application for strict liability would be a step backwards in respect of the law currently in force. To avoid this effect, the PETL refer, in Arts. 5:101 (4) and 5:102, to national laws that can, according to Art. 5:102 (1):

> provide for further categories of strict liability for dangerous activities even if the activity is not abnormally dangerous.

It is submitted that such a provision is contrary to the very idea and aim behind the PETL, which is to propose common solutions instead of referring back to national laws.[71] Here it has apparently not yet been possible for the European Group of Tort Law to build bridges and find a compromise between continental legal systems and the Common Law.

---

arguments for and against a general provision, see W. H. VAN BOOM, Some Remarks on the Decline of *Ryland v. Fletcher* and the Disparity of European Strict Liability Regimes, *ZEuP* 2005, 618 at 630 ff., with numerous references.

69 See Part B, Chapter 8, p. 215, and: The American Law Institute, *Restatement of the Law, Torts (3rd): Liability for Physical Harm* (Proposed Final Draft No. 1), § 20, Abnormally Dangerous Activities: "(a) A defendant who carries on an abnormally dangerous activity is subject to strict liability for physical harm resulting from the activity. (b) An activity is abnormally dangerous if: (1) the activity creates a foreseeable and highly significant risk of physical harm even when reasonable care is exercised by all actors; and (2) the activity is not a matter of common usage". See also the current version of the Restatement: *Restatement of the Law, Torts (2nd)*, 1979, Chapter 21: Abnormally dangerous activities, § 519 General Principle: "(1) One who carries on an abnormally dangerous activity is subject to liability for harm to the person, land or chattels of another resulting from the activity, although he has exercised the utmost care to prevent the harm. (2) This strict liability is limited to the kind of harm, the possibility of which makes the activity abnormally dangerous." § 520. Abnormally Dangerous Activities: "In determining whether an activity is abnormally dangerous, the following factors are to be considered: (a) existence of a high degree of risk of some harm to the person, land or chattels of others; (b) likelihood that the harm that results from it will be great; (c) inability to eliminate the risk by the exercise of reasonable care; (d) extent to which the activity is not a matter of common usage; (e) inappropriateness of the activity to the place where it is carried on; and (f) extent to which its value to the community is outweighed by its dangerous attributes. [. . .]".

70 For a critical appreciation of the strict liability regime in the PETL, see e.g. F. SCHLÜCHTER, Einige Bemerkungen zur Regelung der Gefährdungshaftung in den Artikeln 5:101 und 5:102 PETL, *HAVE/REAS* 2005, 260: "Art. 5: 101 [. . .] setzt für die Annahme einer aussergewöhnlichen Gefahr voraus, dass die Tätigkeit nicht allgemein gebräuchlich ist. Diese Voraussetzung beschränkt die Anwendung der Generalklausel auf 'exotische' Tätigkeiten, was dem Zweck der Generalklausel gerade entgegenläuft"; JANSEN (fn. 30), at pp. 764 ff.; VAN DEN BERGH/VISSCHER (fn. 43), at pp. 531 ff.; for a more positive appreciation of these provisions in the PETL, see WAGNER (fn. 5), at pp. 1282 f.; see JANSEN (fn. 61), at p. 399: "In rechtspolitisch heiklen Fragen halten die PETL sich freilich zu Recht mit Aussagen zurück", who cites the example of strict liability.

71 See also F. PANTALEÓN, Principles of European Tort Law: Basis of Liability and Defences: A Critical View "from Outside", *InDret* 2005, Working Paper n° 299, p. 7.

During the Group's work on strict liability, a more comprehensive proposal was put forward that more closely corresponded to the current European situation.[72] However, for some of the Group's members who were used to a very restricted scope of strict liability in their own jurisdictions, the proposal went too far.[73]

A reform proposal for Austrian tort law[74] took inspiration from a previous proposal for the PETL which had been firmly rejected by some members of the European Group and ultimately not been included in the PETL, while improving and simplifying the proposal.[75] The Austrian reform proposal might, in turn, serve as a basis for the Group's future discussions.

Following the presentation of the PETL in 2005, further comparative research was undertaken in the area of strict liability. One of the results of this research is, in the first place, the observation that a large majority of European jurisdictions have in common that they apply strict liability for sources of particularly serious or high risk. The second observation is that often parties benefit from this liability when exposed to such risks without creating comparable risks themselves. These parties thus find themselves in a situation where the creation of risk of damage is *unreciprocated*. This study has therefore identified a common European principle according to which strict liability applies in situations where there is a *particularly high and unreciprocated risk* of damage.[76]

This principle can indeed be illustrated by numerous examples. For example, it explains why the keeper of a car is strictly liable towards pedestrians and cyclists, whereas, in many countries, elements of fault are applied to liability between drivers and keepers of cars. This principle also explains why liability of aeroplanes or for paragliding in the event of a collision with other similar machines often relies on fault, whereas liability for damage suffered by victims on the ground is often strict.[77] Moreover, this principle helps us to explain why tort liability on ski slopes is fault-based in the large majority of countries[78] despite the numerous, and often serious, injuries that are caused when participating in this sport.[79]

Consequently, the Austrian reform proposal and such comparative studies could very well serve as sources of inspiration to complete the PETL in the area of strict liability.

5. Too much freedom, openness and uncertainty?

According to some critics, the PETL admittedly provide many criteria for deciding specific cases. However, many provisions would leave too much discretion for application in specific cases, which would impair the foreseeability of the outcome in a given case.[80] One

---

72 Text in: B. Koch/H. Koziol, Generalklausel für die Gefährdungshaftung, *HAVE/REAS* 2002, 368 at 369 f.
73 See *ibid.*, at p. 371; H. Koziol (fn. 6), at p. 236.
74 I. Griss/G. Kathrein/H. Koziol (eds.), *Entwurf eines neuen österreichischen Schadensersatzrechts*, Wien/New York: Springer, 2006.
75 See Koch/Koziol (fn. 72), at p. 371.
76 C. Oertel, Principes européens de la responsabilité civile: quel modèle pour décrire le champ d'application de la responsabilité sans faute?, in: C. Chappuis/B. Foëx/T. Kadner Graziano (eds.), *L'harmonisation internationale du droit*, Genève/Zurich/Bâle: Schulthess, 2007, p. 279 at 292, n. 62; Oertel (fn. 66).
77 References in Oertel (fn. 66).
78 References in T. Kadner Graziano, The Distribution of Social Costs of Ski Accidents through Tort Law: Limits of Fault-Based Liability in Practice – and Alternative Regimes, *JETL* 2016, 1.
79 See scenario and materials in Part B, Chapter 7, pp. 158 ff.
80 The "Principles are too willing to sacrifice hard and fast rules for consideration of the equities of the particular case at hand. [...] With all respect for the wisdom of judges, the Principles should supply more guidance";

might wonder in particular whether the very common use of the word "may" in the wording of many provisions of the PETL is truly necessary. In fact, the text of the PETL uses the term "may" 23 times.[81] In identical contexts, an Austrian proposal for reform which was heavily influenced by the PETL often uses stricter terms.

One could point to the example of pure economic interests. According to Article 2:102 (4) of the PETL, the extra-contractual "[p]rotection of pure economic interests or contractual relationships *may* be more limited in scope".[82] In different national systems, these interests are in fact protected in a limited number of specific cases, but not in many other situations.[83] This shows that, from a comparative point of view, the protection of purely economic interests *is* clearly less comprehensive than the protection of absolute rights.[84]

On the one hand, it seems difficult to codify specific instances of pure economic loss that merit (or do not merit) legal protection. This is the reason why the European Group on Tort Law chose not to list the specific cases in which these interests are protected, but rather to list criteria which are to be taken into consideration when defining the scope of application and the extent of protection for purely economic interests. On the other hand, principles guiding liability for pure economic loss have recently been identified and suggested for further academic discussion.[85] They could arguably now be used for shaping a specific rule on economic loss. A more detailed commentary to the PETL, some examples, and more significant comparative notes would also be useful in this respect.

6. Gaps and further action

Just like the first drafts of the PECL and the UNIDROIT Principles, the PETL still leave a number of questions open, such as State liability,[86] the burden of proof (the burden of proof is generally considered a procedural issue by the authors of the PETL[87]), limitation periods, and (social, third party, and first party) insurance and compensation funds.[88]

"To allow for [. . .] loopholes is different from constructing the whole cathedral of the law in form of a Swiss cheese, with holes all over, which allow for equitable considerations to be brought in. It seems that the balance struck by the Principles is tilted too far towards equity, to the detriment of legal certainty", WAGNER (fn. 5), at pp. 1289 f.; in the same respect, JANSEN (fn. 61), at p. 399; JANSEN (fn. 30), at pp. 752 ff: "bewegliche Systeme bieten Argumente statt Entscheidungen".

81 WAGNER (fn. 5), at p. 1287: "The three letter word 'may' [. . .] appears no less than 23 times in the text of the Principles"; R. ZIMMERMANN, in: KOZIOL/STEININGER (fn. 20), p. 2 at 11, also criticises "the surprisingly vague term 'may' in the first sentence of Art. 2:102 (4) PETL"; JANSEN (fn. 30), at pp. 759 ff.
82 Emphasis added.
83 Although the cases in question are more or less similar from one country to another, they are not, however, identical, see W. VAN BOOM/H. KOZIOL/C. WITTING (eds.), *Pure Economic Loss*, Wien/New York: Springer, 2004; M. BUSSANI/V. V. PALMER (eds.), *Pure Economic Loss in Europe*, Cambridge: CUP, 2003; E. BANAKAS (ed.), *Civil Liability for Pure Economic Loss*, London et al.: Kluwer Law International, 1996.
84 See Part B, Chapters 5 and 14.
85 H. KOZIOL, Recovery for Pure Economic Loss in the European Union, *Ariz. L. Rev.* 2006, 871 at pp. 882 ff., suggesting *"Ten Commandments of Liability for Pure Economic Loss"*.
86 See e.g. PANTALEÓN (fn. 71), at p. 3.
87 For an exception, see Art. 2:105, 2nd sent.: "Proof of damage: Damage must be proved according to normal procedural standards. The court may estimate the extent of damage where proof of the exact amount would be too difficult or too costly".
88 S. FUHRER, Wem helfen die Principles?, *HAVE/REAS* 2005, 262, furthermore regrets that the Principles do not take a stance on insurance issues: "Das ist nachvollziehbar [. . .], letztlich aber dennoch bedauerlich. [. . .] Zu denken ist an Themen wie direktes Forderungsrecht, Versicherungsobligationen oder Regressrecht". For a critical commentary, see PANTALEÓN (fn. 71), at p. 2; see however: A. FENYVES/C. KISSLING/S. PERNER/D. RUBIN (eds.), *Compulsory Liability Insurance from a European Perspective*, Vienna: Springer, 2016; G. WAGNER (ed.), *Tort Law and Liability Insurance*, Wien: Springer, 2005; U. MAGNUS (ed.), *The Impact of Social Security*

In respect of limitation periods, for example, the European tort liability systems differ significantly from each other. For the same case, the limitation period can range from one year in some jurisdictions to ten (or more) years in others.[89] In cross-border cases, many disputes over the applicable law to tort liability are brought before the courts in Europe solely because the limitation period for the action would have expired under one of the national laws under consideration but not under the other. Given the enormous practical importance of this issue, a rule on limitation periods would thus be most desirable for the next version of the PETL.[90]

The European Group on Tort Law is well aware of the need to close these gaps. In fact:

> [f]ollowing the original publication of the PETL (with commentary) in 2005, the Group reconvened in 2009 to work on expanding the PETL's scope and updating and refining its content in the light of subsequent scholarly debates and developments in national and EU law.[91]

Over the last years, the Group and related scholars have indeed published articles and studies "on topics not addressed in the initial edition of the PETL or otherwise warranting consideration".[92] The EGTL is about to start works that shall culminate "with the publication of a revised and expanded edition of the PETL".[93]

V. Conclusions

To come back to the question of whether the PETL could play the same role as the PECL and the UNIDROIT Principles of International Commercial Contracts have been playing in contract law as a source of inspiration for legislators and courts, the following conlusions may be reached.

1. Quality

Just like the principles in contract law, the PETL include neutral and well-balanced rules that are the result of intensive, multilateral comparative research that has taken many European and some extra-European jurisdictions into account. The rules are of great quality

---

on Tort Law, Wien: Springer, 2003; see also J. Dute/M. G. Faure/H. Koziol (eds.), *No-Fault Compensation in the Health Care Sector*, Wien: Springer, 2004; S. Klosse/T. Hartlief (eds.), *Shifts in Compensating Work-Related Injuries and Diseases*, Vienna: Springer, 2007; K. Oliphant/G. Wagner (eds.), *Employers' Liability and Workers' Compensation*, Vienna: Springer, 2012.

89 For a comparative overview see C. Salm, *Limitation Periods for Road Traffic Accidents*, European Parliamentary Research Service/European Added Value Unit, PE 581.386, July 2016, www.europarl.europa.eu/RegData/etudes/STUD/2016/581386/EPRS_STU(2016)581386_EN.pdf.

90 See, with numerous references and a proposed solution on the level of Private International Law, T. Kadner Graziano, Die kumulative Anknüpfung der Verjährung "*in favorem actionis*" – Ein Vorschlag zum Opferschutz in grenzüberschreitenden Fällen, *RIW* 2007, 336 ff.

91 The Group's "Current Work Programme" is available at: www.egtl.org/.

92 On the burden of proof, see: V. Ulfbeck/M.-L. Holle, Tort Law and Burden of Proof – Comparative Aspects: A Special Case for Enterprise Liability?, in: H. Koziol/B. C. Steininger (eds.), *European Tort Law 2008*, Vienna/New York: Springer, 2009, pp. 26–48; I. Giesen, The Burden of Proof and other Procedural Devices in Tort Law, in: *ibid.*, at pp. 9–67; E. Karner, The Function of the Burden of Proof in Tort Law, in: *ibid.*, at pp. 68–78; R. W. Wright, Proving Facts: Belief versus Probability, in: *ibid.*, at pp. 79–105.

93 See fn. 91.

and, just like the principles of contract law, many national peculiarities have disappeared (except in the field of strict liability).

Like the first versions of the PECL and the UNIDROIT Principles, the PECL still have some gaps which could be filled in their second version.

2. Source of inspiration for national and international legislatures

Given their quality in general, the PETL, just like the PECL, may serve as a source of inspiration for national legislative reform.[94] One example may be provided by a reform proposal for Austrian tort law which was largely inspired by the PETL.[95]

At the EU level, in the field of contract law, a first attempt to create a uniform European instrument failed in 2014 when the EU Commission took the proposal for a Common European Sales Law (CESL), based on the Draft Common Frame of Reference (DCFR), off its agenda.[96] In the light of this, a European act on tort law, for example applicable to cross-border scenarios,[97] still seems a faraway option.[98] However, the development of new technologies, such as the introduction of autonomous cars, may create new incentives for harmonisation or unification of rules on extra-contractual liability in the EU, at least in some areas such as road traffic accidents.[99] With regard to developments in this area, the minimalist rules in the PETL regarding strict liability are particularly regrettable.

3. Source of inspiration for the courts

Just like the PECL and the UNIDROIT Principles, the PETL have all the assets required to serve as a source of inspiration with persuasive authority for judges and arbitrators. For example, the supreme courts of Spain and the Baltic countries have repeatedly taken inspiration from the PETL.[100]

---

94 In the same respect, see WAGNER (fn. 5), at pp. 1290 ff., with the warning: "However, it is much to be hoped that the flurrying diversity existing within the several European laws of tort and delict will not be buried under the weight of the Principles. The competing solutions offered for one and the same problem still provide a rich treasure for any decision-maker who strives to base his judgement on a broad consideration of the available solutions and a consideration of their respective advantages and disadvantages."
95 GRISS/KATHREIN/KOZIOL (fn. 74).
96 Commission Work Programme 2015 – A New Start, COM(2015) 910 final. For the moment, contract law thus seems to have lost its role as pacemaker, see WAGNER (fn. 5), at pp. 1297 f.: "Contract law as pacemaker". See however SVOBODA (fn. 17).
97 In the area of tort liability, the need for harmonised rules makes itself felt, just as in contract law, especially, if not solely, in cross-border cases, also, see FUHRER (fn. 88): "Mit nationalem Recht lassen sich Fälle ohne Auslandsbezug befriedigend lösen. Schwierigkeiten bereiten dagegen die (immer häufiger vorkommenden) grenzüberschreitenden Fälle"; VAN DEN BERGH/VISSCHER (fn. 43).
98 On the arguments for and against harmonisation or unification in this area, see WAGNER (fn. 5), at pp. 1270 ff.; VAN DEN BERGH/VISSCHER (fn. 43), at pp. 514 ff.; U. MAGNUS, Europa und sein Deliktsrecht, Gründe für und wider die Vereinheitlichung des ausservertraglichen Haftungsrechts, in: H. Koziol/J. Spier (eds.), Liber Amicorum Pierre Widmer, Wien/New York: Springer 2003, pp. 221 ff.
99 For road traffic accidents, see below, Part B, Chapters 9 and 18 (the latter with many references regarding the new technologies) and T. KADNER GRAZIANO/C. OERTEL, Ein europäisches Haftungsrecht für Schäden im Strassenverkehr? – Eckpunkte de lege lata und Überlegungen de lege ferenda, ZVglRWiss 2008, 113–163.
100 See for Spain M. MARTIN CASALS, The Impact of the Principles of European Tort Law (PETL) in Spanish Case Law, JETL 2010, 306, with references; for Lithuania, see S. SELELIONYTÉ-DRUKTEINIENÉ/V. JURKEVICIUS/T. KADER GRAZIANO, The Impact of the Comparative Method on Lithuanian Private Law, ERPL 2013, 959 ff., with references.

However, in order to become a widely used source of inspiration, the PETL need to be known to a wider public. The success of the PETL will therefore very much depend on the willingness of academics in Europe to not only present their national law in their fundamental courses on extra-contractual liability, but also some foreign laws and the European Principles. The success of the PETL will likewise depend on the willingness of European doctrine to refer not only to national provisions but also to use the PETL as a reference point and a source of inspiration. In the case studies in Part B of this book, the PETL will regularly be taken into consideration.

VI. The future?

There are numerous strengths to the PETL, as well as a few points to reconsider and gaps to fill. Among all of its strengths, the most important is that the PETL offer a *reference* and a *tertio comparationis* for any discussion on tort law at a European level, and even beyond Europe. The success of the PECL and of the UNIDROIT Principles for International Commercial Contracts shows that the benefit of having "Principles of Law" is well worth the effort needed to produce, present, and, where necessary, improve and complete them.

Part B

Case studies

Chapter 5

Conditions and limits of extra-contractual liability – cable cases

"[T]he world is full of harm for which the law furnishes no remedy."[1]

"Pure economic loss is a financial loss which does not result from physical injury to the plaintiff's own person or property."[2]

Scenario 1

A construction company is doing work on a road in the vicinity of a factory producing stainless steel. The construction company carelessly damages a cable that supplies electricity to the steel factory. The cable is owned by a third party. The power is off for 14 hours, disrupting the steel company's 24-hour-a-day operations. The steel factory claims damages under three heads:

(a) physical damage to melted material which was in the furnace when the power supply was cut and which the factory's workers tried to save. The *damage to the melted material* amounts to 15,000;
(b) loss of the 10,000 *profit* that would have been made *on the same melted material* if the melt had been properly completed; and
(c) loss of 40,000 *profit* the factory would have been able to make *on four more melts* which could have been put through the furnace, had the power remained on.[3]

Scenario 2

On a public motorway, a driver negligently causes a collision. Following the accident, the traffic is blocked. In one of the cars impeded by this event, a businessman is delayed for two hours. He consequently misses a meeting and the conclusion of a very promising deal.

He claims damages for loss of profit from the person who caused the collision.

---

1 Lord RODGER, in: *D* v. *East Berkshire Community Health NHS Trust*, HL, 21.04.2005, [2005] 2 AC 373 at [100].
2 See e.g. EUROPEAN GROUP ON TORT LAW (ed.), *PETL – Text and Commentary*, Vienna/New York: Springer, 2005, Art. 2:102 n. 9 with further references (HELMUT KOZIOL).
3 An illustration of this scenario is displayed on p. 110. Scenario of the English case: *Spartan Steel & Alloys Ltd* v. *Martin & Co (Contractors) Ltd*, Court of Appeal (Civil Division), 22.06.1972, [1973] 1 Q.B. 27; *Digest III*, 3b/12/1 with comments by K. OLIPHANT/V. WILCOX; *Digest II*, 6/12/1 with comments by K. OLIPHANT. Similar cases happened in many, if not most, jurisdictions, see – further to the materials provided in this chapter – for **Scotland**: *Dynamco Ltd* v. *Holland and Hannen and Cubitts (Scotland) Ltd.*, Court of

Questions

1) The construction company and the steel factory are in no contractual relationship with each other. In *English* law, the tort of *negligence* is nowadays by far the most important basis for claims in extra-contractual, delictual, or tortious liability. What are the conditions for a claim in negligence following the leading case *Donoghue* v. *Stephenson*? Which criteria (or control devices) are employed to limit liability in tort?

2) How is the above cable case solved in English law? Why is the £ 400 loss in *Spartan Steel* regarded as recoverable damage, whereas the further lost profit of £ 1767 is non-recoverable "pure economic loss"? Which policy arguments does the court use to justify this outcome?

3) What are the requirements for a claim in extra-contractual or delictual liability[4] in *German* law? What are the limits of such liability? What are the conditions and limits of such liability under *Swiss* law? How would you decide the cable case scenario in these jurisdictions?

4) Compare Arts. 1043 and 1045 of the *Estonian* Code of Obligations of 2002 with the state of the law in Germany and Switzerland. In what respects do the Estonian provisions follow the Swiss approach, in which respect are they influenced by German law?

5) What solution to the *first scenario* would you suggest under the *Swedish* Tort Liability Act? Explain.

6) Which result did the *Norwegian* Supreme Court reach in the country's leading cable case and which were the decisive criteria for the court?

7) In the leading *Finnish* case, a tortfeasor damaged a power line intentionally. Three companies consequently suffered property damage and loss of income due to the lack of power supply. Which decision did the Finnish Supreme Court reach regarding their claim and how did the court argue?

8) What conditions have to be fulfilled under Arts. 1240 and 1241 (former Arts. 1382 and 1383) of the *French* Civil Code (*Code civil*) for a tort claim to succeed? How would you solve the cable case under French law?

Session (Inner House), 15.07.1971, SC 257, 1972 SLT 38 (Inner House of the Court of Session), *Digest II*, 5/13/1 with comments by M. Hogg; *Digest III*, 3b/13/1 with comments by M. Hogg; **Netherlands**: Hoge Raad (*Supreme Court*), 01.07.1977, NJ 1978/84, *Digest III*, 3b/8/1 with comments by S.D. Lindenbergh: gas pipeline damaged (pure economic loss awarded, even if the number of potential victims is large); Hoge Raad (*Supreme Court*), 18.04.1986, NJ 1986, 567, *Digest II*, 6/8/1 with comments by S. D. Lindenbergh/H. T. Vos: previous case law confirmed; **Denmark**: Vestre Landsret (*Western Court of Appeal*), 08.11.1961, U 1962.190 V: power lines damaged, poultry farm loses 3,000 eggs, contractor held liable for property damage; *Digest III*, 3b/16/4; Østre Landsret (*Eastern Court of Appeal*), 20.01.2003, U 2004.2389 H, *Digest II*, 5/15/4–6 with comments by V. Ulfbeck/K. Siig: pure economic loss awarded (however: parties were in contractual relationship); **Italy**: Corte di Cassazione, Sezioni Unite (*Court of Cassation, Joint Divisions*), 24.06.1972, no 2135 (*Pasta case*), Giur it. 1973, I,1,c 1124, note by G. Visintini; Foro it. 1973, I,1,100, note by V. M. Caferra, *Digest II*, 5/9/1 with comments by N. Coggiola/B. Gardella Tedeschi/M. Graziadei, *Digest III*, 3b/9/1 with comments by N. Coggiola/B. Gardella Tedeschi/M. Graziadei; **Spain**: Tribunal Supremo (*Supreme Court*), 31.01.2012, RJ 2012/2031; *Digest III*, 3b/10/1 with comment by M. Martin Casals/J. Ribot; **Greece**: Efeteio Kritis (*Crete Court of Appeal*), 427/11.09.2007, EllDni 2008, 22; *Digest III*, 3b/5/1 with comments by E. G. Dacoronia (following a breakdown in power supply, 4,360 hens die of suffocation; electricity company liable for 70% of damage, 30% concurrent liability of victim because it had not properly maintained safety generator).

4 On liability without fault, also called strict liability or objective liability, see below, Chapters 8 and 9.

9) What outcome would you suggest in the *second scenario* under *English* and under *German* law (and arguably most other laws)? What would be the outcome under *French* law in light of the materials provided, and in particular with respect to the judgment of the *Cour de cassation* in the case *Marcailloux* c. *R.A.T.V.M.* (this decision still applies to the law in France)?

10) In *China*, important law reforms have taken place over the last 15 years, with the adoption of, in particular, the Chinese Contract Law Act of 1999, the Law of Property Act of 2007, and – in the field of extra-contractual liability – the Tort Law Act of 2009. For 2020, the draft of a Civil Code is on the agenda.

What are the conditions for a claim in extra-contractual liability in Chinese law? In the case reproduced in the materials, the appellate court eventually rejected the claim against the construction company. What role may comparative law have played for the reasoning of the court?

11) In 2005, a group of tort law specialists (the European Group on Tort Law) presented the *Principles of European Tort Law (PETL)*.[5] The PETL were prepared on a wide comparative basis, including most European jurisdictions and some jurisdictions from other parts of the world.[6] What are the conditions for a claim under the PETL to succeed? How would you decide the cable case under the PETL?

12) In 2009, a group of European academics presented the *Draft Common Frame of Reference (DCFR)*. The DCFR proposes a Model Code of European Private Law covering the law of contracts, torts, benevolent intervention in another's affairs, unjust enrichment, property law, and trusts.[7] How would the cable case be solved under the DCFR?

13) Compare the conditions for a claim in extra-contractual liability under English, German, Swiss, Estonian, and French law, as well as under the PETL and the DCFR. In what respects are the approaches of the PETL and the DCFR similar to the national laws and to each other, and in what respects do they differ? What are the strengths and weaknesses of the different approaches in the national tort law systems, the PETL, and the DCFR?

---

5 EUROPEAN GROUP ON TORT LAW (fn. 2). Full text available at: http://egtl.org/.
6 See above, Part A, Chapter 4, pp. 46 ff.
7 Full text available at: http://ec.europa.eu/justice/policies/civil/docs/dcfr_outline_edition_en.pdf.

Table of contents

I. England and Wales
1. ALASTAIR MULLIS/KEN OLIPHANT, *Torts*, 4th ed., Basingstoke/New York: Palgrave Macmillan, 2011, nos. 2.1–2.3, 3.1 ....p. 76
2. Court of Appeal (Civil Division), *Spartan Steel & Alloys Ltd* v. *Martin & Co (Contractors) Ltd*, 22.06.1972, [1972] EWCA Civ 3, [1973] Q.B. 27, [1972] 3 All ER 557 ....p. 78
3. House of Lords, *Murphy* v. *Brentwood District Council*, 26.07.1990, [1991] 1 AC 398 at 487 ....p. 81

II. Ireland
Supreme Court of Ireland, *Glencar Exploration plc* v. *Mayo County Council*, 19.07.2001, [2002] 1 ILRM 481, [2002] 1 IR 84, [2002] 1 IR 112, [2001] IESC 64 ....p. 81

III. Germany
1. Bürgerliches Gesetzbuch, BGB (*Civil Code*), §§ 249, 252, 823 ....p. 81
2. DIRK LOOSCHELDERS, *Schuldrecht, Besonderer Teil (Law of Obligations, Special part)*, 12th ed., Köln: Carl Heymanns Verlag, 2017, nos. 1166 ff. ....p. 83
3. Bundesgerichtshof, BGH (*Federal Supreme Court of Justice*), 04.02.1964, BGHZ 41, 123 ....p. 86

IV. Switzerland
1. Code des obligations/Obligationenrecht (*Code of Obligations*), Art. 41 ....p. 87
2. Code penal/Strafgesetzbuch (*Criminal Code*), Art. 239 (1) and (2) ....p. 87
3. FRANZ WERRO (avec la collaboration de JOSIANE HAAS), *La responsabilité civile (Civil Liability)*, 2nd ed., Berne: Stämpfli, 2011, nos. 252–253, 297, 307–309 ....p. 88
4. Tribunal fédéral/Bundesgericht (*Federal Supreme Court of Justice*), 02.03.1976, ATF 102 II 85 ....p. 89

V. Estonia
Võlaõigusseadus (*Code of Obligations*), §§ 1043, 1045 ....p. 90

VI. Sweden
Skadeståndslagen (*Tort Liability Act*), Ch. 1 § 2, Ch. 2 §§ 1 and 2, Ch. 5 § 7 ....p. 91

VII. Norway
Høyesterett (*Supreme Court*), 10.11.1973, Staten v/Forsvarsdepartementet mot Dagfinn Strøm (*The State, Ministry of Defense* v. *Dagfinn Strøm*), Rt-1973-1268 ....p. 92

VIII. Finland

1. Vahingonkorvauslaki (*Tort Liability Act*), Ch. 2 § 1, Ch. 5 § 1 ....p. 93
2. PETER WETTERSTEIN, Compensation for Pure Economic Loss in Finnish Tort Law, *Scand. Stud. L.* 2001, 565–580 ....p. 94
3. Korkein Oikeus (*Supreme Court*), 12.12.2003, KKO 2003:124, R2001/939 ....p. 95

IX. France

1. Code civil (*Civil Code*), Arts. 1240, 1241 (former Arts. 1382 and 1383) ....p. 96
2. BERTRAND FAGES, *Droit des obligations (Law of Obligations)*, 7th ed., Paris: L.G.D.J., 2017, nos. 369 ff. ....p. 97
3. Cour de cassation, 2ᵉ civ. (*Court of Cassation, 2nd civil chamber*), 08.05.1970 (*Société Allamigeon Frères et Lacroix c. Lafarge*), n°69–11.446, Bull. 1970 n° 160 ....p. 98
4. Cour de cassation, 2ᵉ civ. (*Court of Cassation, 2nd civil chamber*), 28.04.1965 (*Marcailloux c. R.A.T.V.M.*), D. 1965 Jur. 777 ....p. 99

X. People's Republic of China

1. 中华人民共和国侵权责任法 (*Tort Law Act*), Arts. 1, 2, 6 (1) ....p. 99
2. 电力法 (*Electric Power Law*), Art. 60 ....p. 100
3. XIAOMING XI and the Tort Law Study Group of the Supreme People's Court of the People's Republic of China, 中华人民共和国侵权责任法、条文理解与适用 (*Tort Law of the People's Republic of China – The understanding and application of provisions*), Beijing: People's Court Press, 2010, pp. 20–26 ....p. 101
4. Chongqing Fourth Intermediate People's Court (Civil Division), 26.12.2005, 上诉人黔江区永安建筑有限责任公司与被上诉人黔江区民族医院、黔江区供电有限责任公司财产损害赔偿纠纷案 (*Yong'An Construction Company [appellant] v. Quianjiang National Hospital and Quianjiang Power Supply Company*) ....p. 102
5. YUNSONG GE, 侵权责任法，保护的民事利益 (*Civil rights protected by the Tort Law Act*), *China Legal Science* 3/2010, 37 at 51 ....p. 103

XI. Principles of European Tort Law (PETL)

1. PETL, Arts. 1:101, 2:101, 2:102 ....p. 103
2. BÉNÉDICT WINIGER/ERNST KARNER/KEN OLIPHANT (eds.), *Digest of European Tort Law, Vol. III: Misconduct*, Berlin: De Gruyter, 2018, nos. 3b/30/1ff. (by THOMAS KADNER GRAZIANO) ....p. 104

XII. Draft Common Frame of Reference (DCFR)

1. DCFR, Arts. VI. – 1:101, 1:103, 2:101, 2:206, 2:208 (1), 3:102 ....p. 108
2. CHRISTIAN VON BAR/ERIC CLIVE (eds.), *Principles, Definitions and Model Rules of European Private Law – Draft Common Frame of Reference (DCFR), Full Edition*, Vol. 4, Munich: Sellier, 2009, Art. VI. 2:206, Illustration 4, p. 3317 ....p. 109

Materials[8]

I. England and Wales

1. ALASTAIR MULLIS/KEN OLIPHANT, *Torts*, 4th ed., 2011, nos. 2.1–2.3, 3.1

Negligence: introduction

2.1 Origins

It all began in August 1928. The scene was Minchella's cafe in Paisley, near Glasgow. A certain Mrs Donoghue had gone in for a drink. This is her story: a friend bought her a bottle of ginger beer; she began to drink it; then, as her friend topped up her tumbler, she watched in horror as the decomposed remnants of a snail floated out with the ginger beer; she suffered shock and an upset stomach.[9] Now, Mrs Donoghue's injuries may seem of less than earth-shattering importance to us today, but it is to these unlikely beginnings that the modern law of negligence owes its existence. Mrs Donoghue, unable to sue Minchella in the law of contract because she had not bought the bottle herself [. . .], brought an action in tort against the manufacturer, Stevenson. She alleged that he had been negligent in producing the drink. In response, Stevenson denied that those injured by a negligently manufactured product had any right to recover damages outside certain exceptional categories (e.g. inherently or patently dangerous products like firearms). The case reached the House of Lords, which found in favour of Mrs Donoghue. It was not a unanimous decision: two powerful dissents were registered. Neither was the decision of the majority clear and unambiguous in every respect: was it to be a rule confined to defective products or was it to have wider effect? Today, however, its status is unquestioned and its effect plain for all to see, for *Donoghue v Stevenson* [1932] AC 562 is the case that changed the face of the law of negligence.

Up to that time, liability for negligent conduct had been recognised only in certain carefully defined circumstances, for example where innkeepers were careless in looking after property in guests' rooms or where fire damage resulted from negligence. The courts allowed actions for damages in these cases because – they said – the special circumstances gave rise to a 'duty of care'. The significance of *Donoghue v Stevenson*, and of Lord Atkin's speech in particular, was that it sought to unify these disparate duties of care in a single general theory. Lord Atkin noted [. . .]:

"[I]n English law there must be and is some general conception of relations giving rise to a duty of care, of which the particular cases found in the books are but instances. The

---

[8] For the original language versions of the materials reproduced in this chapter, see the companion website at www.routledge.com/9781138567733.

[9] *Note by the author*: similar situations still occur. For example, take the following incident reported in the Swiss daily newspaper *20 minuten*, 12.08.2016, p. 2, *"Tote Maus in Salatbeutel entdeckt"*: in a branch of Migrolino in Gland, Switzerland, a lady bought a ready-to-eat pre-packaged salad. While her friends were eating the salad, she discovered a dead mouse in the packaging (to make up for the incident, Migrolino offered the friends a free meal in a restaurant).

liability for negligence ... is no doubt based upon a general public sentiment of moral wrongdoing for which the offender must pay. But acts or omissions which any moral code would censure cannot in a practical world be treated so as to give a right to every person injured by them to demand relief. In this way rules of law arise which limit the range of complainants and the extent of their remedy. The rule that you are to love your neighbour becomes in law: You must not injure your neighbour, and the lawyer's question: Who is my neighbour? receives a restricted reply. You must take reasonable care to avoid acts or omissions which you can reasonably foresee would be likely to injure your neighbour. Who then, in law, is my neighbour? The answer seems to be persons who are so closely and directly affected by my act that I ought reasonably to have them in contemplation as being so affected when I am directing my mind to the acts or omissions which are called in question."

2.2 The elements of the tort of negligence

Negligence is a common word, referring to a type of fault that is often treated as synonymous with 'carelessness'. But since *Donoghue v Stevenson* [1932] AC 562 it has also become the name of a self-contained tort with its own internal framework of rules. The elements of liability in the tort of negligence can be outlined as follows:

- The defendant must owe the claimant a *duty of care*;
- The defendant must be in *breach* of that duty (ie she must be careless or negligent);
- The breach of duty must *cause* the claimant *loss*;
- The loss caused must not be too *remote* (ie it must be within the foreseeable risk for which the defendant is responsible);
- The defendant must not be able to raise any *defence* to the claimant's action.

[...]

The duty of care concept

3.1 The nature of the duty of care concept

Not every instance of carelessness resulting in harm will lead to liability in the tort of negligence. As Lord Rodger observed in *D v East Berkshire Community Health NHS* Trust [2005] 2 AC 373 at [100]: 'the world is full of harm for which the law furnishes no remedy.' Liability is limited by reference to various 'control devices' [...] of which the most significant is the duty of care. The existence of a duty of care is a precondition of liability in negligence; it is what transforms *factual* responsibility for carelessly causing harm into *legal* responsibility.

In most cases encountered in practice – for example, cases of foreseeable physical injury suffered in accidents at work or on the roads – the existence of a duty of care is clearly established by the authorities. [...]

Deviation from the 'typical' case of physical injury caused by positive act, by one private individual to another, may necessitate a more cautious approach to the imposition of liability and bring the duty of care issue 'into play'. There may be doubts as to whether the loss of which the claimant complains should be recoverable (especially in cases of mental injury[10] or pure economic loss). [. . .]

The duty of care concept marks out these cases – the 'atypical' cases – in which it cannot be taken for granted that the defendant should pay compensation for carelessly caused harm. And it determines whether the special circumstances of these cases are sufficient to outweigh the claimant's moral claim to compensation. Hence the concept's role is essentially negative. As Lord Goff stated in *Smith v Littlewoods Organisation Ltd* [1987] 1 AC 241, 270, 'nowadays . . . the broad general principle of liability for foreseeable damage is so widely applicable that the function of the duty of care is not so much to identify cases where liability is imposed as to identify those where it is not'. The duty of care question is raised in order to deny liability even where the defendant was at fault, and even if that fault caused the claimant harm. To deny the existence of a duty of care is to shield the defendant from liability no matter how culpable her carelessness and no matter how severe the claimant's injury.

2. Court of Appeal (Civil Division), *Spartan Steel & Alloys Ltd* v. *Martin & Co (Contractors) Ltd*, 22.06.1972, [1972] EWCA Civ 3, [1973] Q.B. 27, [1972] 3 All ER 557

Spartan Steel and Alloys Ltd *v.* Martin & Co (Contractors) Ltd

COURT OF APPEAL (The Master of the Rolls, Lord Denning;
Lord Justice Edmund-Davies and Lord Justice Lawton)

THE MASTER OF THE ROLLS (Lord Denning): Spartan Steel have a factory in Birmingham where they manufacture stainless steel. The factory obtains its electricity by a direct cable from a power station of the Midlands Electricity Board.

In June 1969 contractors called Martins were doing work on a road about a quarter-of-a-mile away. They were going to dig up the road with a big power-driven excavating shovel. They made inquiries about the place of the cables, mains, and so forth, under the road. They were given plans showing them. But unfortunately their men did not take reasonable care. The shovel damaged the cable which supplied electricity to the Spartan works. The Electricity Board shut down the power whilst they mended the cable.

The factory was at that time working continuously for twenty-four hours all round the clock. The electric power [. . .] was off for 14½ hours [. . .].

At the time when the power was shut off, there was an arc furnace in which metal was being melted in order to be converted into ingots. Electric power was needed throughout in order to maintain the temperature and melt the metal. When the power failed, there was a danger that the metal might solidify in the furnace and do damage to the lining of the furnace. So the plaintiffs used oxygen to melt the material and poured it from a tap out of the furnace. But this meant that the melted material was of much less value. The physical damage was assessed at £ 368.

---

10 *Note by the author*: see below, Chapters 11 and 12.

In addition, if that particular melt had been properly completed, the plaintiffs would have made a profit on it of £ 400.

Furthermore, during those 14½ hours, when the power was cut off, the plaintiffs would have been able to put four more melts through the furnace: and, by being unable to do so, they lost a profit of £ 1,767.

The plaintiffs claim all those sums as damages against the contractors for negligence. [. . .] [T]he defendants admitted that they had been negligent. The contest was solely on the amount of damages. The defendants [. . .] admit that they are liable for the £ 368 physical damages. They did not greatly dispute that they are also liable for the £ 400 loss of profit on the first melt, because that was truly consequential on the physical damages [. . .]. But they deny that they are liable for the £ 1,767 for the other four melts. They say that was economic loss for which they are not liable. The Judge rejected their contention and held them liable for all the loss. The defendants appeal to this Court. [. . .]

At bottom I think the question of recovering economic loss is one of policy. Whenever the Courts draw a line to mark out the bounds of duty, they do it as matter of policy so as to limit the responsibility of the defendant. Whenever the Courts set bounds to the damages recoverable – saying that they are, or are not, too remote – they do it as matter of policy so as to limit the liability of the defendants.

In many of the cases where economic loss has been held not to be recoverable, it has been put on the ground that the defendant was under no duty to the plaintiff. Thus where a person is injured in a road accident by the negligence of another, the negligent driver owes a duty to the injured man himself, but he owes no duty to the servant of the injured man – see Best v. Fox (1952) A.C. at page 731: nor to the master of the injured man – Inland Revenue Commissioners v. Hambrook (1956) 2 Q.B. 656 at page 660; nor to anyone else who suffers loss because he had a contract with the injured man – see Simpson v. Thomson (1877) 3 A.C. at page 289: nor indeed to anyone who only suffers economic loss on account of the accident – see Kirkham v. Boughey (1958) 2 Q.B. at page 341. [. . .]

In other cases, however, the defendant seems clearly to have been under a duty to the plaintiff, but the economic loss has not been recovered because it is too remote. Take the illustration given by Mr. Justice Blackburn in Catton v. Stockton (1875) L.R. 10 Q.B. at page 457, when water escapes from a reservoir and floods a coalmine where many men are working. Those who had their tools or clothes destroyed could recover but those who only lost their wages could not. [. . .]. In such cases if the plaintiff or his property had been physically injured, he would have recovered, but as he only suffered economic loss, he is held not entitled to recover. This is, I should think, because the loss is regarded by the law as too remote – see King v. Phillips (1953) 1 Q.B. at pages 439–440.

On the other hand, in the cases where economic loss by itself has been held to be recoverable, it is plain that there was a duty to the plaintiff and the loss was not too remote. Such as [. . .] when a banker negligently gives a reference to one who acts on it, the duty is plain and the damage is not too remote – see Hedley Byrne & Co. v. Heller & Partners [1964] AC 465.[11]

---

11 *Note by the author*: see below, Chapter 14, pp. 419 ff.

The more I think about these cases, the more difficult I find it to put each into its proper pigeon-hole. Sometimes I say "There was no duty". In others I say: "The damage was too remote". [. . .] It seems to me better to consider the particular relationship in hand, and see whether or not, as matter of policy, economic loss should be recoverable, or not. [. . .]

So I turn to the relationship in the present case. It is of common occurrence. The parties concerned are: the Electricity Board who are under a statutory duty to maintain supplies of electricity in their district; the inhabitants of the district, including this factory, who are entitled by statute to a continuous supply of electricity for their use; and the contractors who dig up the road. Similar relationships occur with other statutory bodies, such as gas and water undertakings. The cable may be damaged by the negligence of the statutory undertaker, or by the negligence of the contractor, or by accident without any negligence by anyone: and the power may have to be cut off whilst the cable is repaired, or the power may be cut off owing to a short-circuit in the power house, and so forth. If the cutting off of the supply causes economic loss to the consumers, should it as matter of policy be recoverable? And against whom? [. . .]

The second consideration is the nature of the hazard, namely, the cutting of the supply of electricity. This is a hazard which we all run. It may be due to a short circuit, to a flash of lightning, to a tree falling on the wires, to an accidental cutting of the cable, or even to the negligence of someone or other. And when it does happen, it affects a multitude of persons: not as a rule by way of physical damage to them or their property, but by putting them to inconvenience, and sometimes to economic loss. The supply is usually restored in a few hours, so the economic loss is not very large. Such a hazard is regarded by most people as a thing they must put up with – without seeking compensation from anyone. Some there are who install a standby system. Others seek refuge by taking out an insurance policy against breakdown in the supply. But most people are content to take the risk on themselves. When the supply is cut off, they do not go running round to their solicitor. They do not try to find out whether it was anyone's fault. They just put up with it. They try to make up the economic loss by doing more work next day. This is a healthy attitude which the law should encourage.

The third consideration is this: If claims for economic loss were permitted for this particular hazard, there would be no end of claims. Some might be genuine, but many might be inflated, or even false. A machine might not have been in use anyway, but it would be easy to put it down to the cut in supply. It would be well-nigh impossible to check the claims. If there was economic loss on one day, did the applicant do his best to mitigate it by working harder next day? And so forth. Rather than expose claimants to such temptation and defendants to such hard labour – on comparatively small claims – it is better to disallow economic loss altogether, at any rate when it stands alone, independent of any physical damage.

The fourth consideration is that, in such a hazard as this, the risk of economic loss should be suffered by the whole community who suffer the losses – usually many but comparatively small losses – rather than on the one pair of shoulders, that is, on the contractor on whom the total of them, all added together, might be very heavy.

The fifth consideration is that the law provides for deserving cases. If the defendant is guilty of negligence which cuts off the electricity supply and causes actual physical damage to person or property, that physical damage can be recovered – see Baker v. Crow Carrying Co. Ltd. (unreported) Feb. 1st., 1960 C.A., referred to by Lord Justice Buckley in 1971, 1 Q.B. at page 356; and also any economic loss truly consequential on the material damage – see British Celanese v. Hunt (1969) 1 W.L.R. 959; S.C.M. (United Kingdom) Ltd. v. Whittall & Son Ltd. (1971) 1 Q.B. 337. Such cases will be comparatively few. They will be readily capable of proof and will be easily checked. They should be and are admitted.

These considerations lead me to the conclusion that the plaintiff should recover for the physical damage to the one melt (£ 368), and the loss of profit on that melt consequent thereon (£ 400): but not for the loss of profit on the four melts (£ 1,767), because that was economic loss independent of the physical damage. I would, therefore, allow the appeal and reduce the damages to £ 768.

[Lord Justice Lawton (concurring specially with an opinion), Lord Justice Edmund-Davies (dissenting)].

Damages reduced to £ 768 [. . .].

3. House of Lords, *Murphy* v. *Brentwood District Council*, 26.07.1990, [1991] I AC 398 at 487

Lord Oliver: [. . .] The infliction of physical injury to the person or property of another universally requires to be justified. The causing of economic loss does not. If it is to be categorized as wrongful it is necessary to find some factor beyond the mere occurrence of the loss and the fact that its occurrence could be foreseen. [. . .]

II. Ireland

Supreme Court of Ireland, *Glencar Exploration plc* v. *Mayo County Council*, 19.07.2001, [2002] I ILRM 481, [2002] I IR 84, [2002] I IR 112, [2001] IESC 64

[. . .] 84. [. . .] [I]n general, for a defendant to be found guilty of negligence the careless act must have caused personal injury to, or damage the property of, the plaintiff. The law of negligence normally does not afford redress to those who have suffered what has come to be described in the authorities as 'economic loss' simpliciter. [. . .][12]

III. Germany

1. Bürgerliches Gesetzbuch, BGB (*Civil Code*)

Book 2 of the BGB on the Law of Obligations (§§ 241–853) contains, in the first place, a *general part* with provisions applying to all types of obligations (§§ 241–432). When analysing a claim in extra-contractual liability, it must first be determined whether the conditions of a claim under one of the provisions of the special part, for example § 823, are met. Once the duty to compensate is established under, for example, § 823, the general provisions (§§ 241 ff.) determine the precise content of this obligation.

---

12 For an Irish cable case, see: *Irish Paper Sacks Ltd* v. *John Sisk & Son (Dublin) Ltd*, High Court, 18.05.1972, *Digest II*, 5/14/1 with comments by E. QUILL; *Digest III*, 3b/14/7 with comments by E. QUILL: no duty of care to avoid pure economic loss.

Buch 2: Recht der Schuldverhältnisse [§§ 241–853]

Abschnitt 1: Inhalt der Schuldverhältnisse

Titel 1. Verpflichtung zur Leistung

§ 249. Art und Umfang des Schadensersatzes. (1) Wer zum Schadensersatz verpflichtet ist, hat den Zustand herzustellen, der bestehen würde, wenn der zum Ersatz verpflichtende Umstand nicht eingetreten wäre.
(2) Ist wegen Verletzung einer Person oder wegen Beschädigung einer Sache Schadensersatz zu leisten, so kann der Gläubiger statt der Herstellung den dazu erforderlichen Geldbetrag verlangen. [. . .]

§ 252. Entgangener Gewinn. Der zu ersetzende Schaden umfasst auch den entgangenen Gewinn. Als entgangen gilt der Gewinn, welcher nach dem gewöhnlichen Lauf der Dinge oder nach den besonderen Umständen, insbesondere nach den getroffenen Anstalten und Vorkehrungen, mit Wahrscheinlichkeit erwartet werden konnte.

Abschnitt 8: Einzelne Schuldverhältnisse [§§ 433–853]

Titel 27. Unerlaubte Handlungen

§ 823. Schadensersatzpflicht. (1) Wer vorsätzlich oder fahrlässig das Leben, den Körper, die Gesundheit, die Freiheit, das Eigentum oder ein sonstiges Recht eines anderen widerrechtlich verletzt, ist dem anderen zum Ersatz des daraus entstehenden Schadens verpflichtet.
(2) Die gleiche Verpflichtung trifft denjenigen, welcher gegen ein den Schutz eines anderen bezweckendes Gesetz verstößt. Ist nach dem Inhalte des Gesetzes ein Verstoß gegen dieses auch ohne Verschulden möglich, so tritt die Ersatzpflicht nur im Falle des Verschuldens ein.

Translation

Book 2: Law of Obligations [§§ 241–853]

Part 1: Content of the obligation

Title 1. Duty to perform or to compensate

§ 249. Measure and quantification of compensation. (1) Whosoever is liable to compensate loss has to restore the situation that would exist had the circumstance that gave rise to the claim for compensation not occurred.
(2) Where damages have to be paid because of an injury to a person or damage to property, the injured party may claim the amount of money necessary to remedy the damage instead of claiming restoration by the tortfeasor. [. . .]

§ 252. Lost profits. The loss to be compensated also includes lost profits. Profits are deemed 'lost' if they could have been anticipated with sufficient likelihood on the basis

of the usual course of events or the special circumstances of the case, in particular the preparations made and precautions taken.

Part 8: Types of obligations [§§ 433–853]

Title 27. Torts

§ 823. Duty to compensate loss. *(1) Whosoever unlawfully injures, intentionally or negligently, the life, body, health, freedom, property or other right of another person, has an obligation to the other person to compensate the resulting loss.*
(2) The same obligation is incurred by a person who infringes a statutory provision that is intended to protect another person. Where the infringement of the statutory provision does not require fault, the obligation to compensate loss only arises where there is fault.

2. Dirk Looschelders, Schuldrecht, Besonderer Teil (Law of Obligations, Special Part), 12th ed., 2017, nos. 1166 ff

Part 7. Extra-contractual liability in damages

§ 56 Overview

1166   Extra-contractual liability in damages is dealt with in Book 2, Part 27 of the BGB (§§ 823–853) under the rubric of *"Torts"* (*Unerlaubte Handlungen*).

This term is appropriate in so far as the provisions of §§ 823 ff. are overwhelmingly concerned with conduct which is contrary to law (*rechtswidrig*) and intentional or negligent (*schuldhaft*). [. . .] Outside of the BGB there are numerous specific statutes establishing strict liabilities, according to which a person may find himself liable without fault in respect of danger caused to another.[13] [. . .] These instances have now gained such an enormous practical significance that it makes sense to speak in terms of a ***two-track approach*** in German tort law. [. . .]

II. Fundamental distinctions

1168   Extra-contractual liability cannot be considered one-sidedly, with a view of only providing the fullest possible protection for the ***injured party's rights or interests***. Such an attitude would be in conflict with the potential wrongdoer's own constitutionally-guaranteed ***freedom of action and right to pursue his own personal development*** (see the "Fundamental Law" [having the role of the German Constitution], Art. 2 (1)).

1. The principle of fault-based liability

Faced with a conflict between the protection of the victim's interests and the defendant's freedom of action, the legislator has determined that, as a matter of principle, a defendant should only have to answer for the consequences of *fault* on his part. [. . .] The potential defendant's freedom of action and right to personal development is thus safeguarded by providing that he is not responsible for harm that (while assuming

---

[13] See below, Chapters 8 and 9.

him to be an average member of his particular community) he can neither foresee nor avoid. The starting point of the idea of fault is that of a behaviour which is *contrary to law*. On this basis, what is necessary is an infringement of a juridical norm which either forbids the conduct concerned or requires the actor to behave differently. Hence the establishment in BGB, §§ 823 ff., of a system of liability for culpable behaviour contrary to law.

> **Comparative note:** In most other European jurisdictions, the principle that liability is based on fault also forms the basis of extra-contractual liability. Underlying this is the view, characteristic of the Enlightenment, that the individual should be burdened with a liability to compensate others' losses only if the harm he caused was something which, as an autonomous subject, he could have had in mind and prevented. [. . .]

2. No general protection against pure economic loss or of freedom of action

1170 A second important decision by the legislator is that, under BGB § 823 (1), protection against interference with one's interests (whether deliberate or negligent) is in principle limited. It applies only to the *fundamental personal interests* (life, body, health and freedom), together with other absolute rights (notably ownership). There is no general guarantee against pure economic loss as such, and of the freedom to run one's affairs as one pleases. Interference with these interests is in general compensable only in the case of the infringement of a relevant *protective provision* (BGB § 823 (2)) or where there is a *deliberate injury to the claimant's interest by an act contrary to good morals* (BGB § 826). When considered from the point of view of a potential defendant, this means that in the absence of an applicable protective provision, there is no need, as a rule, to have regard to others' abstract patrimonial interests or their freedom to conduct their affairs as they wish.

3. Limitation of the circle of those entitled to claim

1171 By linking tort liability with the infringement of an interest specifically recognised by law, the legislator has taken the position that the category of potential claimants should be clearly restricted. As a matter of principle, this entitlement is given only to a claimant who has suffered the infringement of a legally protected interest *personal to him*. If he suffers pure economic loss following the infringement of someone else's legally protected interests, he will not be compensated under BGB § 823 (1).

> **An example** (see BGH, NJW 2003, 1040): M and F, who were figure-skaters, had over many years developed into a well-matched and internationally successful duo. M was injured in a traffic accident caused by the negligence of S. The result was that F temporarily lost the benefit of skating with her partner. The BGH denied her claim against S's liability insurers for losses she had sustained as a result of having to withdraw from competitions, thus being deprived of prize money and sponsorship income. The reason was that F's specific legally-protected rights [in German law also called "absolute rights"] had not been infringed as a result of the accident. [. . .]

III. The system of tort law in the BGB

1172 Numerous foreign legal systems possess a *general tort clause*, according to which one must compensate for the damage he intentionally or negligently caused to another person. Thus, the French *Code civil* of 1804 expresses the basic rule of tortious liability as follows: "*Tout fait quelconque de l'homme, qui cause à autrui un dommage, oblige celui par la faute duquel il est arrivé, à le réparer*".[14] A general clause of similar significance appears in the Austrian ABGB of 1811 (§ 1295 (1)). By contrast, the German legislator has sought to provide judges with a more precise test to be applied to issues of tort liability. A notable result of this has been the suppression of any generalised liability for pure economic loss and the restriction of the capacity to sue to those suffering direct and unmediated harm. A further consequence is the presence in the BGB of not one but **three basic situations giving rise to tort liability**, i.e. §§ 823 (1), 823 (2) and 826 (known as the "small general clauses" (*kleine Generalklauseln*)) [. . .].

From the point of view of legal policy, both these contrasting approaches give rise to **converse problems**. Wide general clauses mean that judges are forced to take steps to constrain liability for pure economic loss, and limit the categories of those who can claim, so as to prevent the river of liability from turning into a flood. By contrast, German case law faces the necessity of developing specific institutional means to **expand the scope of liability in order to cover specific instances of pure economic loss.**[15] [. . .]

Section 2. Liability under BGB § 823 (1)

§ 57 Liability: fundamental questions

1173 The central rule of tort liability is BGB § 823 (1). Here, the legislator has set out the **vital legally protected interests**, which are protected against infringement by any culpable conduct contrary to law, independently of whether the claimant can point to any specific provision aimed at their protection. The predominant view is that § 823 should be approached through a **three-stage enquiry**, under which – much as in criminal law – three questions have to be kept separate: namely, the establishment of the necessary facts, whether the defendant's act was contrary to law, and whether there was fault. [. . .]

I. Factual issues and acts "contrary to law"

1174 At the factual stage, we are concerned with two questions. One is whether the defendant, by his behaviour, **infringed one of the interests enumerated** in BGB § 823 (1) in a way objectively attributable to what he did, and as such there exists an adequate causal relation between the defendant's act and the infringement (*haftungsbegründende Kausalität*). The second is whether damage flowed from the infringement, again in a way that can be objectively established as attributable to the defendant's act and in circumstances where there exists an adequate causal relation (*haftungsausfüllende Kausalität*). [. . .] If these conditions are satisfied, this is an indication that the conduct was **"contrary to law"** ("*Widerrechtlichkeit*"). However, here one must still apply the test of whether, exceptionally, there is some legal justification for the defendant's conduct which may affect matters. [. . .]

---

14 *Any act of man, which causes damage to another, obliges the person by whose fault it occurred, to compensate it.*

15 See below, Chapter 14.

3. Bundesgerichtshof, BGH (*Federal Supreme Court of Justice*), 04.02.1964, BGHZ 41, 123

A person who negligently severs a power line leading from an electrical substation is liable to a user, who is cut off as a result, for damage occasioned to the latter through spoilage of things which depend on an uninterrupted supply of electricity (in this case, eggs in an electric incubator).

BGB § 823.

Judgment

In March 1960, the first defendant was carrying out road-widening work for the authorities on the provincial highway between K and M. On 14th March [. . .] it employed a team of workmen, under the direction of a foreman, to fell some roadside trees. At about 13.30, one of the trees crashed into a power line belonging to the *Rheinisch-Westfälische Elektrizitätswerke (RWE)* that was situated on the plaintiff's property, where the plaintiff operated a poultry-rearing business. As a result, there was a failure of the electricity supply to an incubator loaded with eggs.

According to the plaintiff's evidence, the outage lasted six hours. As a result of the outage, only a handful of the 3600 eggs hatched, all of which premature and therefore had no financial value. The plaintiff might have expected a yield of 3000 chicks had there been no outage. The loss suffered was estimated at 1800 DM, on the basis of a selling price of 0.60 DM per chick; [. . .]

The lower court allowed the claims, on the basis that the incompetent tree-felling operation had led directly to damage to the plaintiff's property (see BGB § 823 (1)). [. . .]

The grounds of appeal put forward against this judgment are not sufficient to justify setting it aside.

A person is liable under BGB § 823 (1) for damage to persons or property, whether the relevant causal event led to the damage directly, or whether it did so by starting a chain of events leading to it. If a person collides with a motor-car which, as a result, cannons into a vehicle in front, he is responsible for the damage to both vehicles; in such a case, the damage suffered by both owners is direct. The situation is different where damage caused directly to one person has extended consequences as regards his legal relationships with some third party (as is the case where the latter is deprived of the victim's service); [. . .]

If a thing cannot survive without a constant supply of water, electricity, or something similar, then, from a legal standpoint, a person destroys it if he interrupts the supply. If he culpably disrupts arrangements for irrigating a garden or heating a greenhouse, he must answer for any resulting damage to the plants in it, whoever those plants belong to. The same goes for the interruption of the supply of electricity if the things that depend on its constant availability suffer as a result; in particular, products that rely on a supply of electricity in order to keep them at a constant temperature (whether this involves warming or cooling) to prevent them from spoilage, fall into this category. If spoilage results from the negligent severing of the necessary electricity cable and, as a result, the product's sales value is reduced or eliminated, then this loss to the plaintiff's patrimony is a matter of loss consequential to damage to property, which falls under BGB § 823 (1).

It would be different if the electrical outage had not caused damage to an existing thing, but instead had given rise to a temporary impossibility of producing more things of a given description. In so far as this is the situation, it is an instance of pure economic loss. [The German Federal Supreme Court of Justice has admitted that, under certain conditions, an unjustified interference with an established and operative business can be qualified as an infringement of an absolute right, protected under § 823 (1) BGB) (*Eingriff in den eingerichteten und ausgeübten Gewerbebetrieb*). However, the infringement needs to be *directed against* the operation of the business in order to fall under § 823 (1)]. In the present case, compensation cannot be obtained under the header of unjustified interference with an established and operative business either, the reason being that the severing of the cable is *not directed against* the operation of the plaintiff's business (see BGHZ 29, 65).[16] [. . .]

In the present case, the eggs in the process of incubation were effectively destroyed, or at least grievously damaged. It follows that the court below was right to view the case as one of damage to property with a direct effect on the plaintiff. [. . .]

IV. Switzerland

1. Code des obligations/Obligationenrecht (*Code of Obligations*)[17]

A. Principes généraux. I. Conditions de la responsabilité

Art. 41. (1) Celui qui cause, d'une manière illicite, un dommage à autrui, soit intentionnellement, soit par négligence ou imprudence, est tenu de le réparer.
(2) Celui qui cause intentionnellement un dommage à autrui par des faits contraires aux mœurs est également tenu de le réparer.

Translation

A. General Principles. I. Conditions of liability

Art. 41. (1) Whoever unlawfully causes damage to another, whether wilfully or negligently, is obliged to provide compensation.
(2) Whoever wilfully causes damage to another in an immoral manner is likewise obliged to provide compensation.

2. Code pénal/Strafgesetzbuch (*Criminal Code*)[18]

Art. 239. **Entrave aux services d'intérêt général.** (1) Celui qui, intentionnellement, aura empêché, troublé ou mis en danger l'exploitation [. . .] d'un établissement ou d'une installation servant à distribuer au public l'eau, la lumière, l'énergie ou la

---
16 Emphasis added. See also BGH 09.12.1958, BGHZ 29, 65.
17 The Code of Obligations is the fifth book of the Swiss Civil Code. For historical reasons, it was adopted as a separate code.
18 In the criminal laws of most other European jurisdictions, there are no similar provisions.

chaleur, sera puni d'une peine privative de liberté de trois ans au plus ou d'une peine pécuniaire.
(2) La peine sera une peine privative de liberté de trois ans au plus ou une peine pécuniaire si le délinquant a agi par négligence.

Translation

Art. 239. Obstruction to services of public interest. *(1) Whoever intentionally prevents, disturbs or endangers the operation [. . .] of a facility or an installation for distributing water, light, power, or heat to the public, shall be sentenced to up to three years of imprisonment or to a monetary penalty.*
(2) The penalty shall be up to three years of imprisonment or a monetary penalty if the offender has acted negligently.

3. FRANZ WERRO (avec la collaboration de JOSIANE HAAS), *La responsabilité civile (Civil liability)*, 2nd ed., 2011, nos. 252–253, 297, 307–309

[. . .] Liability for one's own conduct

253   Art. 41 CO covers all cases where there is no specific rule of law attaching liability to the person who causes the loss concerned. Hence, this article is considered as instituting a **general clause on liability for fault**. [. . .]

I. Wrongfulness [. . .]

A. The objectivity of the concept [. . .] of wrongfulness

297   Traditionally, a wrongful act is defined as one which violates, without any justification, a norm which protects another person's interests. [. . .] When understood in this sense, wrongfulness can result either from the infringement of an absolute right of the victim (result-based wrongfulness [*illicéité de résultat, Erfolgsunrecht*]), or from the violation of a behavioural norm which is aimed at protecting the victim against the type of pure economic loss suffered by him (conduct-based wrongfulness [*illicéité de comportement, Verhaltensunrecht*]). [. . .]

B. The objective conception: extent and limits

1. Result-based wrongfulness (*L'illicéité de résultat*)

Result-based wrongfulness follows from the **infringement of an absolute right** of the victim. By absolute rights, we mean rights that can be enforced against the whole world (*erga omnes*), and which enjoy the unconditional protection of the law. These are personality rights, real rights, and intellectual property rights. By way of contrast, a person's right to preserve his wealth is not protected in itself. From that, it follows that the mere act of diminishing another's wealth is not recognized as a wrongful act.

The same applies for violations of relative rights, such as the ability to recover a debt due from someone else. [. . .]

307 On this point, Swiss law has been influenced by **German law**. Indeed, under § 823 (1) of the German Civil Code, an obligation to compensate loss that was deliberately or negligently caused arises only where the victim's life, bodily integrity, liberty, property or some analogous right of his is affected. **French law** knows no such restriction. On the contrary, under Art. [1240 (former Art. 1382)] of the French Civil Code, any act that is objectively negligent (and thus contrary to law) is capable of creating liability for the person responsible.

2. Conduct-based wrongfulness (*L'illicéité de comportement*)

308 Conduct-based wrongfulness arises where damage is occasioned through the **violation of a legal norm of behaviour which is aimed at safeguarding the victim** against the specific kind of loss which he has suffered. Wrongfulness of this kind allows a claimant to obtain compensation for loss or damage which would otherwise not amount to an infringement of any of his absolute rights, and protects also against pure economic loss.

309 Protective norms of this sort can be found **throughout the whole legal system**, and particularly in criminal law [see e.g. Criminal Code, Arts. 137 (unlawful appropriation), 146 (fraud), 305bis (money-laundering)], in administrative law, and in private law. [. . .]

4. Tribunal fédéral/Bundesgericht (*Federal Supreme Court of Justice*) 02.03.1976, ATF 102 II 85[19]

Extract from the judgment of the 1ˢᵗ Civil chamber, dated 02.03.1976:
Conrad Zschokke S.A. v. Baumgartner Papiers S.A. and another.

A.- On 26ᵗʰ February 1973, an employee of Conrad Zschokke SA severed a high-tension underground cable using a backhoe while carrying out excavation work in Crissier. The cable, which was owned by the *Service intercommunal de l'électricité de Chavannes, Crissier, Ecublens et Renens* (SIE), supplied substations where high-voltage current was transformed into electricity suitable for the use of its customers, including two companies, Baumgartner Papiers SA and Zinguerie de Renens SA. The rupture of the high-tension cable had the effect of depriving these enterprises of electricity for some hours.

Before embarking on their work, Conrad Zschokke made no enquiries to SIE about the route of electric cables which might be present in the area where they were excavating.

B.- Baumgartner Papiers and Zinguerie de Renens brought proceedings against Conrad Zschokke, claiming CHF 23,100 plus interest and CHF 6,526 respectively [. . .].

Extract from the court's reasoning:

[. . .] 5.- According to the decided cases, liability in tort does not necessarily require infringement of a subjective right [such as ownership]. Art. 41 (1) of the Code of Obligations

---

[19] See also the further cases: TF, 16.05.1975, ATF 101 Ib 252; TF, 11.03.1980, ATF 106 II 75.

(CO) provides that anyone who culpably infringes a legal provision must compensate the damage he thereby occasions to another, even where there is no question of a subjective right of the victim being affected. It is enough if the legal provision infringed by the defendant has as its aim the protection of the rights adversely affected by the act in question [. . .].

6. – [. . .] *c)* The defendant argues that the plaintiffs have suffered only indirect damage, since they have simply been deprived of electricity which the direct victim, SIE, was bound to supply to them; SIE was unable to satisfy its contractual obligation because of the damage it had itself suffered.

However, this argument is only good if one takes the view that Art. 239 of the Criminal Code is not aimed, among other things, at protecting the private interests of the customers of a company whose objective is to provide the public with electricity. The question of whether the plaintiffs have suffered direct or indirect harm thus overlaps with the issue of the wrongful nature of the act concerned. Now, we have seen that – contrary to the appellant's arguments – Art. 239, while undoubtedly aimed at protecting the general interest, also envisages the protection of customers' private interests in being supplied with electricity. As the cutting of the cable affected this interest of the plaintiffs, it follows that they are direct victims of a tort and as such can demand that the defendant compensate the damage they have suffered. [. . .]

In so far as they base their claim on [Art. 41 (1) CO together with] Art. 239 [(1) or (2) of the Criminal Code], the plaintiffs' position differs fundamentally from that of a creditor who, while prevented from invoking the protective effect of a criminal provision, is simply in a position where he is deprived of the benefit of performance of a contractual obligation because his contractual partner is the victim of a tort. In such a case it is only the contractual partner, directly injured by the tort, who can obtain compensation from the person responsible; this is to the exclusion of the creditor, who is merely victim of a loss as a consequence of the non-performance of the contractual obligation due to him [. . .].

V. Estonia

Võlaõigusseadus *(Code of Obligations)*[20]

§ 1043. **Õigusvastaselt tekitatud kahju hüvitamine.** Teisele isikule (kannatanu) õigusvastaselt kahju tekitanud isik (kahju tekitaja) peab kahju hüvitama, kui ta on kahju tekitamises süüdi või vastutab kahju tekitamise eest vastavalt seadusele.

§ 1045. **Kahju tekitamise õigusvastasus.** (1) Kahju tekitamine on õigusvastane eelkõige siis, kui see tekitati:
    1) kannatanu surma põhjustamisega;
    2) kannatanule kehavigastuse või tervisekahjustuse tekitamisega;
    3) kannatanult vabaduse võtmisega;
    4) kannatanu isikliku õiguse rikkumisega;
    5) kannatanu omandi või sellega sarnase õiguse või valduse rikkumisega;
    6) isiku majandus- või kutsetegevusse sekkumisega;
    7) seadusest tulenevat kohustust rikkuva käitumisega;
    8) heade kommete vastase tahtliku käitumisega. [. . .]

---

20 Adopted on 26.09.2001, in force since 01.07.2002.

Translation

§ 1043. Compensation for unlawfully caused damage. A person (tortfeasor) who unlawfully causes damage to another person (victim) shall compensate for the damage if he or she is culpable of causing the damage or is otherwise liable for causing the damage pursuant to law.

§ 1045. Unlawfulness of causing damage. (1) Damage is unlawful in particular when it is caused by:
1) causing the death of the victim;
2) causing bodily injury or damage to the health of the victim;
3) deprivation of the liberty of the victim;
4) violation of a personality right of the victim;
5) violation of the right of ownership or a similar right or right of possession of the victim;
6) interference with the economic or professional activities of a person;
7) behaviour which violates a duty arising from law;
8) intentional behaviour contrary to good morals. [...]

VI. Sweden

Skadeståndslagen (*Tort Liability Act*)

1 kap. Inledande bestämmelser.
[...] 2 § Med ren förmögenhetsskada förstås i denna lag sådan ekonomisk skada som uppkommer utan samband med att någon lider person- eller sakskada.

2 kap. Skadeståndsansvar på grund av eget vållande.
1 § Den som uppsåtligen eller av vårdslöshet vållar personskada eller sakskada skall ersätta skadan.
2 § Den som vållar ren förmögenhetsskada genom brott skall ersätta skadan.

5 kap. Skadeståndets bestämmande.
[...] 7 § Skadestånd med anledning av sakskada omfattar ersättning för
1. sakens värde eller reparationskostnad och värdeminskning,
2. annan kostnad till följd av skadan,
3. inkomstförlust eller intrång i näringsverksamhet.

Translation

Chapter 1: Introductory provisions.
[...] *§ 2.* Pure economic loss in the present Act means such economic damage as arises without anyone having suffered personal or property damage.

Chapter 2: Liability arising from negligence.

§ 1. Anyone who intentionally or by negligence causes personal damage or property damage shall be liable to pay compensation for such loss.

§ 2. Anyone who causes pure economic loss through crime[21] shall be liable to pay compensation for such loss.[22]

Chapter 5: Assessment of damages.

[. . .] § 7. Compensation for property damage shall include:
1. *the value of the property or the repair expenses together with compensation for diminution in value;*
2. *other costs caused by the injury; and*
3. *income loss or infringement of professional activities.[23]*

VII. Norway

Høyesterett (*Supreme Court*), 10.11.1973, Staten v/ Forsvarsdepartementet mot Dagfinn Strøm (*The State, Ministry of Defense v. Dagfinn Strøm*), Rt-1973-1268[24]

[*Note by the author: during a military manoeuvre, an aeroplane negligently caused damage to a power cable and a large number of consumers were left without power. Due to the power cut, A's rainbow trout breeding plant suffered damage as a result of an inoperative electric pump. The State acknowledged responsibility for the damage to the power cord, but denied that it was liable for the damage to A's plant. The Supreme Court ruled four-to-one that the required proximate cause was not fulfilled. The damages were derivative and indirect, and a risk assessment in the present case leads to the conclusion that A should be the one to carry the risk.*]

It is beyond doubt that the central conditions of tort liability, causation and foreseeability, are fulfilled in this particular case. As far as this Court understands, the appellant [the State] does not contest this point, but does nevertheless question whether, among a multitude of potential outcomes, the individual's own particular damage was foreseeable. Regardless of foreseeability of the damage, doubts arise as to the proximity which is also required to establish causation.

Proximate cause represents the core issue in this case, and it was this issue that both parties' final arguments focused on. This Court agrees with the respondent that several different

---

21 Assume that there is no relevant applicable criminal provision in Swedish law.
22 For damages for pure economic loss under Swedish law, see e.g. M. SCHULTZ, *EBLR* 2007, 1305 (quote at 1317): "In the preparatory work of the Act, a source of interpretation often used in Swedish law, the legislator stated that this rule was not to be interpreted *e contrario*. [. . .] However, in the practice of the courts the rule has nevertheless been interpreted in just this way, so that pure economic loss generally will only be compensated where the defendant's action was criminal (for example fraudulent)".
23 For Swedish cable cases, see: Högsta domstolen (*Supreme Court*), 04.04.1966, NJA 1966, 210 (companies owing a cable suffered damage to cable and economic loss consequential to injury to property: damages awarded); HD 07.03.1988, NJA 1988, 62 (victim not the owner of the cable; compensation for property damage awarded but not for pure economic loss), *Digest II*, 5/17/5 and 9 with comments by H. ANDERSSON.
24 Comments by B. ASKELAND, *Digest II*, 5/16/5, and by A. M. FRØSETH/B. ASKELAND, *Digest III*, 3b/17/5.

factors must be taken into account and that the final outcome must result from a consideration of all relevant factors. However, contrary to the respondent's assertions, the Court reaches the conclusion that there is ample reason to determine that a sufficiently proximate cause did not exist in this case. Although one could doubtlessly anticipate considerable damage as a result of a broken cable, this probability is of an abstract and diffuse character in relation to the actual damage in question. This is because the damage caused is not directly related to the object itself, nor to immediate interests related to the object affected by the electricity cut, but rather caused as a consequence of contractual relationships that can vary with time and location. Most often, this lies far beyond what the tortfeasor could reasonably be aware of or have control over. The damage is, as it has been said, "derivative and indirect". The unpredictable nature of the damage, which under unfavourable conditions can lead to ruinous awards in compensation, is another and significant factor that makes it problematic to set the boundaries of liability too wide. The fact that, in this case, the amount in question is modest is obviously not a factor that can be considered when determining the limits of liability. The Court agrees with the appellant that it is the potential for damage that must be the determining factor. [. . .]

The Court's conclusion that the damage suffered does not qualify for compensation can be supported by a risk analysis. If we are to ask ourselves who should be responsible to carry the risk of the damage in question, there is little doubt as to the answer. Those individuals or companies exposed to the risk will also possess a greater or lesser degree of control over their own situation. They need to consider the extent and likelihood of potential damage and take relevant physical or legal precautions. The information that has come to light about the respondent is somewhat revealing. He was aware that his company was extremely vulnerable in the case of a power cut and he could have prevented the damage through simple and inexpensive precautions. The reality is very different for the one causing the damage, who might not be in the same situation as the State, a municipality, or other economically powerful institution. He or she will in most situations be almost powerless to prevent liability, and could face claims for compensation that would not only be ruinous, but could also significantly discourage undertakings for the good of society. The proposed distribution of risk appears to be fair in view of the standard power company practice of setting a disclaimer to exclude liability in the case of power outages caused by human error.

VIII. Finland

1. Vahingonkorvauslaki (*Tort Liability Act*)

> **2 LUKU. Vahingon aiheuttajan korvausvastuu. 1 §.** Joka tahallisesti tai tuottamuksesta aiheuttaa toiselle vahingon, on velvollinen korvaamaan sen, jollei siitä, mitä tässä laissa säädetään, muuta johdu. [. . .]
>
> **5 LUKU. Korvattava vahinko. 1 §.** Vahingonkorvaus käsittää hyvityksen henkilö- ja esinevahingosta sekä 4 a ja 6 §: ssä säädetyin edellytyksin kärsimyksestä. Milloin vahinko on aiheutettu rangaistavaksi säädetyllä teolla tai julkista valtaa käytettäessä taikka milloin muissa tapauksissa on erittäin painavia syitä, käsittää vahingonkorvaus hyvityksen myös sellaisesta taloudellisesta vahingosta, joka ei ole yhteydessä henkilö- tai esinevahinkoon.

Translation

> **Chapter 2. Liability of a Person Causing Injury or Damage. § 1.** *A person who deliberately or negligently causes injury or damage to another shall be liable for damages, unless the provisions of this Act entail otherwise. [. . .]*
>
> **Chapter 5. Damages. § 1.** *Damages shall provide compensation for personal injury and damage to property [. . .]. Where the injury or damage has been caused by an act punishable by law [. . .], or in other cases where there are particularly weighty reasons for so providing, damages shall also include compensation for economic loss that is not connected to personal injury or damage to property.*

2. PETER WETTERSTEIN, Compensation for pure economic loss in Finnish Tort Law, *Scand. Stud. L.* 2001, 565–580[25]

3.1.3 "A particularly weighty reason"

When the Tort Act was being drafted it was considered important that pure economic losses could be compensated – albeit exceptionally – also outside the situations mentioned above, that is, losses caused by criminal conduct or by a public organ in the exercise of its authority. It was felt that some room should be left for the development of this branch of law through court practice. According to the Tort Act Chap. 5, § 1 compensation can be awarded if there exists a "particularly weighty reason". The somewhat unclear legislative history of the provision and the "open" wording "particularly weighty reason" cause problems of interpretation. It is not an easy task to try to find criteria for its interpretation. However, some guidelines have been suggested in the literature. The degree of fault or negligence on part of the person/activity causing the economic loss is relevant. For instance, intentional behaviour (e.g., acts contrary to good practice) or gross negligence may trigger the obligation to compensate pure economic loss. Furthermore, the scope of the loss, its implication for the person suffering damage, and his possibilities to protect himself against such loss may be of relevance. [. . .]

Regarding the practice of the Supreme Court, reference can be made to the following decisions:

1983 II 187: Using advertisements in newspapers, a labour organisation had executed a blockade against an employer who had dismissed an employee. The purpose of the blockade was to put pressure on the employer. By intervening in the dispute between the employer and the employee, who had resort to legal remedies, the organisation caused economic loss to the employer. The Supreme Court considered that the organisation had acted contrary to good practices. However, because also the employer had acted improperly, there was no "particularly weighty reason" for awarding compensation for pure economic loss.

1991:79: An editor had written a newspaper article similar to a product test, in which he and another person expressed their views on baby carriages manufactured by five different producers. The article had given the readers the impression of an impartial test and contained wrongful information about one of the imported baby carriages. The article was

---

25 Full text available at: www.scandinavianlaw.se/pdf/41-23.pdf.

published well noticeable in a context dealing with child care in a widely spread newspaper. The Supreme Court considered that there was a "particularly weighty reason" to oblige the editor and the editor-in-chief of the newspaper, who had acted against good editing practice, to pay compensation for pure economic loss to the importer of the baby carriage.

[...] 1992:44: An attorney was considered having negligently caused economic loss to heirs, when he had assisted in selling assets belonging to the estate without checking that a will had become valid at law. The Supreme Court considered that there was a "particularly weighty reason" to award compensation for the loss, because an attorney has a special obligation to act carefully and properly, and to take into consideration also the interests of other heirs to an estate, not only those of his own client.

It can be concluded that there is a great deal of uncertainty awaiting guiding precedents. The interpretation of "particularly weighty reason" is left to the courts and their consideration of the circumstances in casu. The wording of the provision indicates, however, that compensation for pure economic loss should not be awarded too lightly. The criteria suggested in the literature (cited supra), which also to some extent seem to have been approved in court practice, offer help for the interpretation. [...]

3. Korkein Oikeus (*Supreme Court*), 12.12.2003, KKO 2003:124, R2001/939[26]

Compensation for damage – damage caused to others
A intentionally shot at and destroyed the insulators of a power line. He was later convicted of gross vandalism by a criminal tribunal. The damage to the power line led to a sudden drop in voltage, followed by a shutdown in the electricity supply of the surrounding area, the result of which was that several industrial companies had to rely on their emergency backup systems. They were left with damage to their machinery and experienced a loss of production. The Supreme Court decided in a majority opinion that A could not be found liable for the losses suffered by the industrial companies who were reliant upon the electricity supply. [...]

[At first instance, the Imata District Court found A liable for the damage caused to the industrial companies X Ltd., Y Ltd. and Z Ltd. which were reliant upon the electricity supply. Upon appeal, the Kouvola Court of Appeal reversed the decision and dismissed the claim brought by the three companies against A.]

SUPREME COURT RULING

Grounds
[...] The question before us is whether A is liable to pay compensation for the damage to property and financial losses resulting from his actions. [...]

A should have been aware that damaging a power line could cause serious disturbances in the electricity distribution network. The damage which A was able to foresee is to be deemed equivalent in nature and scale to that of a typical power line failure.

---

[26] See also: *Digest II*, 5/18/1–9 with comments by S. HAKALETHO-WAINIO; *Digest III*, 3b/19/1 with comments by P. KORPISAARI.

Chapter 5 of the Tort Liability Act, which contains the relevant provisions on compensation for damage, does not identify who is entitled to receive compensation. Under this chapter, it is well-established that anyone who suffers direct damage to property as a result of the damaging event is to be entitled to compensation. Subsequent damage to property of a third party is to be covered only in a limited number of well-defined situations. [. . .]

In judgment KKO 1994:94, on the application of § 6 of the Aviation Act (139/1923), the Supreme Court considered whether a loss of production and start-up expenses caused by a broken power line which resulted in a power outage for the surrounding companies relying on its supply, could be considered as property damage within the scope of the aforementioned act. The Court found no basis to suggest that ownership of the power line was an absolute requirement in claiming compensation. Nevertheless, the right to compensation is for the most part to be limited to situations where the damaged lines are so closely situated in proximity and purpose to the industrial company subject to the power cut that the industrial consumer has, for all intents and purposes, a de facto right of use over the latter. Since electricity supply outages can entail exceptionally widespread and unforeseeable losses, the burden of which are often too overwhelming and unreasonable to be put on the shoulders of the person responsible, such exceptions should be kept as restrained and strict as possible from the outset, even where there is pressure to expand the scope of tort liability.

The Supreme Court is nevertheless of the opinion, for the reasons set out above, that the scope of compensation should not be broadened. Energy distribution may be disrupted for many reasons and the energy distributer may, for instance, restrict its liability in regards to power outages by including exclusion clauses in its supply contracts [an option which may not be available to those who are otherwise deemed liable for the interruption of an electricity supply]. [. . .]

[. . .] The damage suffered by the companies was caused by a failure of their energy supply, and not directly by the actions of A. The companies did not have a right of use over the power lines or any similar right and they were, in fact, in the same position as any other consumer.

For these reasons, the Supreme Court concludes that the damage which A caused by his actions was third party damage, and therefore no compensation is available.

Decision

The decision of the Court of Appeal is upheld.

IX. France

1. Code civil (*Civil Code*)

> **Art. 1240 [ancien art. 1382].** Tout fait quelconque de l'homme, qui cause à autrui un dommage, oblige celui par la faute duquel il est arrivé, à le réparer.
>
> **Art. 1241 [ancien art. 1383].** Chacun est responsable du dommage qu'il a causé non seulement par son fait, mais encore par sa négligence ou par son imprudence.

Translation

Art. 1240 [former Art. 1382]. Any act of a person, which causes damage to another, obliges the person by whose fault it occurred, to compensate it.

Art. 1241 [former Art. 1383]. Everyone is liable for the damage he or she causes not only by his or her intentional act, but also by his or her negligent conduct or by his or her imprudence.

2. BERTRAND FAGES, *Droit des obligations (Law of obligations)*, 7th ed., 2017, nos. 369 ff

Part I
The requirements for tortious liability

369. the list of requirements. – Tortious liability presupposes damage [. . .], behaviour giving rise to liability [. . .], and a causal link between the behaviour and the damage [. . .].

Chapter I
Loss and damage

370. No liability without damage. – Damage or loss (the words are used interchangeably to refer to the effects, financial or otherwise, of interference with persons or patrimony) is the first, most important, and indeed necessary condition of civil liability. Such liability cannot exist at all unless there is some damage to be compensated. In contract [. . .] as in tort, there is therefore no such thing as liability without damage. The burden of proving damage is on the victim. [. . .]

Section 1
Types of compensable damage

371. Eagerness to provide compensation. – The instinct of French tort law is that all varieties of loss ought to be fully compensated. The law makes no attempt at any precise definition of relevant loss; faced with all the varied interests that may be affected by a wrongful act, it refuses to create any distinction between those which are, and those which are not, compensable under the law of tort. The resulting position is thus claimant-friendly, but it also means that the French law of compensation possesses a "breadth of scope unknown in almost any other foreign legal system". [. . .]

Section 2
What amounts to compensable damage?

376. Certainty. – To be compensable, damage must be certain. From this, it follows that the existence of a genuine harm suffered by the victim is of crucial importance. The plaintiff must, in principle, be in a position to demonstrate a loss or deterioration in comparison with some previous position. Put another way, there must be, in some sense, a "before" and an "after": you cannot lose what you never could have had.

As with the law of contract [. . .], the requirement that damage be certain means in particular that there is liability only if it is clear that damage has already been occasioned (actual damage) or that it will be suffered at some point (prospective loss). Certain damage is thus to be distinguished from the mere possibility of future damage, which is too speculative to be subject to compensation. [. . .]

378. Other required characteristics? – Apart from being certain and arising from a legitimate interest, it is sometimes said that damage must be direct. This is not entirely untrue, but it merely takes us back to the requirement of a causal connection, which is another necessary condition of liability [. . .].

Chapter 2
The causal connection

379. The proof of causation. – As a general rule, there can only be liability if the defendant's alleged behaviour is linked to the plaintiff's damage by a relation of cause and effect, known as a causal link; this is a necessary condition of liability. The burden of establishing this causal link is on the plaintiff, who is required to provide the judge with sufficient evidence to demonstrate its existence. If this evidence is not persuasive and the connection between the damage and the defendant's alleged behaviour remains in doubt, the plaintiff will lose.

Nevertheless, the plaintiff is not required to provide scientific evidence: it is enough for him to produce a collection of positive and negative indications that make it probable that there was a causal connection. [. . .]

3. Cour de cassation, 2ᵉ civ. (*Court of Cassation, 2ⁿᵈ civil chamber*), 08.05.1970 (*Société Allamigeon Frères et Lacroix c. Lafarge*), n°69-11.446, Bull. 1970 n° 160

Allamigeon Frères et Lacroix Co. v. Lafarge

THE COURT: – On the single ground of appeal: – Whereas, according to the judgment below, in the course of work being carried out by a contractor, Lafarge, a gas pipeline belonging to the *Compagnie française du méthane*, and supplying a factory owned by the *Société Allamigeon Frères et Lacroix*, was ruptured by a bulldozer; that this caused a loss of profits, since the factory was put out of action; and that the factory owner sued Lafarge for compensation; Whereas Lafarge appealed, arguing that the court of appeal held him liable and thereby failed to draw the correct legal conclusion from its findings of fact, according to which the damage was indirect and as such not actionable;

Whereas however, having held that the facts were beyond dispute and that the claim was based on Arts. [1240, 1241 (former Arts. 1382 and 1383)] of the Civil Code, the judgment stated that the damage suffered by the *Société Allamigeon Frères et Lacroix* had all the appearances of a direct consequence of the rupturing of the pipe, since it was the damage to the pipe that led to the shutting down of the factory; and hence, there was a clear and direct connection between the loss complained of and the act causing it; Whereas it follows that in deciding as it did, the court reached its decision on good legal grounds and the appellant's criticisms of the judgment are unfounded;

For these reasons: the Court dismisses the appeal against the judgment of the Appellate Court of Bordeaux dated 15.01.1969.

4. Cour de cassation, 2ᵉ civ. (*Court of Cassation, 2ⁿᵈ civil chamber*), 28.04.1965 (*Marcailloux c. R.A.T.V.M.*), D. 1965 Jur. 777

COURT OF CASSATION
(2ⁿᵈ civil chamber)

28 April 1965

CIVIL LIABILITY, LOSS AND DAMAGE, CERTAINTY OF LOSS, LOSS OF INCOME, PUBLIC TRANSPORT UNDERTAKING, VEHICLES, COLLISION, TRAFFIC HOLD-UP.

The person responsible for a collision which gave rise to traffic congestion was rightly held liable to compensate the loss suffered by a public transport company whose vehicles were delayed by the congestion and which as a result suffered a loss of fare income.

(*Marcailloux and Another* v. *R.A.T.V.M.*)

JUDGMENT

THE COURT; – On the first ground of appeal: – Whereas, according to the final findings of the first instance judge, certain buses owned by the *Régie autonome des transports de la ville de Marseille* (R.A.T.V.M.) were delayed as a result of the congestion of their route within the city; that alleging that Mr Marcailloux was responsible for this congestion, which had caused it a loss of fare income, R.A.T.V.M. sued him and his insurers, *Compagnie Le Patrimoine*, for compensation; – Whereas the judgment is attacked for having granted R.A.T.V.M.'s claim [. . .] without addressing neither the duration of the congestion nor the quantification of the damage which the defendants consider speculative and indirect; – However, whereas the judgment accepted that the road was blocked for a period of time owing to a collision for which Mr Marcailloux was responsible, and that the plaintiff's buses were delayed as a consequence; that the judgment made clear that the delay was the cause of a diminution of fare income amounting to a loss to R.A.T.V.M. that was certain; – Whereas in deciding in favour of R.A.T.V.M. on the basis of these statements and allegations, under which R.A.T.V.M. had established that the halting of its buses, for which Mr Marcailloux was responsible, had caused a reduction in its fare income which amounted to a loss that was neither speculative nor indirect, the judge thus applied the law correctly;. . . [. . .]

X. People's Republic of China

1. 中华人民共和国侵权责任法 (*Tort Law Act*)[27]

第一章 一般规定

第一条 为保护民事主体的合法权益，明确侵权责任，预防并制裁侵权行为，促进社会和谐稳定，制定本法。

---

27 Adopted on 26 December 2009, in force since 1 July 2010.

第二条 侵害民事权益，应当依照本法承担侵权责任。

本法所称民事权益，包括生命权、健康权、姓名权、名誉权、荣誉权、肖像权、隐私权、婚姻自主权、监护权、所有权、用益物权、担保物权、著作权、专利权、商标专用权、发现权、股权、继承权等人身、财产权益。

第二章 责任构成和责任方式

第六条 行为人因过错侵害他人民事权益，应当承担侵权责任。
[...]

Translation

Chapter I. General provisions

Art. 1. In order to protect the legitimate rights and interests of parties in civil law relationships, clarify the tort liability, prevent and punish tortious conduct, and promote social harmony and stability, this Law is formulated.

Art. 2. Those who infringe upon civil rights and interests shall be subject to liability in tort according to this Law.

"Civil rights and interests" used in this Law shall include the right to life, the right to health, the right to name, the right to reputation, the right to honour, right to self-image, right of privacy, marital autonomy, guardianship, ownership, usufruct, security interest, copyright, patent right, exclusive right to use a trademark, right to discovery, equities, right of succession, and other personal and property rights and interests.

Chapter II. Establishing liability [...]

Art. 6. (1) One who is at fault for infringement upon a civil right or interest of another person shall be subject to tort liability. [...]

2. 电力法 (*Electric Power Law*)[28]

第九章 法律责任

第六十条 因电力运行事故给用户或者第三人造成损害的，电力企业应当依法承担赔偿责任。

电力运行事故由下列原因之一造成的，电力企业不承担赔偿责任：

（一）不可抗力；

（二）用户自身的过错。

---

28 Adopted on 28 December 1995, amended on 27 August 2009 and on 24 April 2015. Original version in Chinese available at www.npc.gov.cn/wxzl/gongbao/2015-07/03/content_1942878.htm. English translation available at www.npc.gov.cn/englishnpc/Law/2007-12/12/content_1383731.htm.

因用户或者第三人的过错给电力企业或者其他用户造成损害的，该用户或者第三人承担赔偿责任。

Translation

Chapter IX. Legal responsibility

  Art. 60. (1) *Power supply companies that cause their users or third parties to suffer damage as a result of electrical fault shall be liable to pay compensation for their losses under the law.*
  (2) Such companies shall hold no liability for compensation if an electrical fault is caused by one of the following factors:
    a) Force majeure;
    b) The user's own fault.
  (3) If damage is caused to a power supply company or other users due to the fault of a user or third party, the latter shall instead be liable to pay compensation under the law.

3. XIAOMING XI and the Tort Law Study Group of the Supreme People's Court of the People's Republic of China, 中华人民共和国侵权责任法 条文理解与适用 (*Tort Law of the People's Republic of China – The understanding and application of provisions*), Beijing: People's Court Press, 2010, pp. 20–26[29]

Art. 2 [of the Tort Law Act]. Understanding of the provision [. . .]

2) Civil rights and interests

[. . .] Rights include [. . .], for instance, property rights, the right to life, right of name, etc. Civil interests are those interests which are protected by the law, even if they are not prescribed as "rights" in the law, including personal legal interests and property interests (for instance, commercial secrets, pure economic interests). [. . .] According to this approach, tort law should not impose legislative restrictions on the scope of protected rights and interests [. . .]. [. . .] [T]he Tort Law Act maintains [this approach]. [. . .]

4) Civil interests protected in the Tort Law Act

[. . .] Overprotection of pure economic interests may limit the individual's freedom and liberty; in many situations, it is impossible to determine the number of potential plaintiffs

---

29 *Note by the author*: this book is authored by Judge X. XIAOMING of the Supreme People's Court of China (who participated in the drafting of the Tort Law Act) and a study group composed of judges. Combining the original intention of the legislator with court practice, the book gives explanations to each article in the Tort Law Act and discusses how to apply it in practice (*the author thanks* SICEN HU, *Geneva/Wuhan, for this information*).

as well as the degree of damage. If we were to impose liability for any negligent act and any damage to the world at large, the responsible party would be unable to shoulder the burden and the court might face a flood of litigation. [. . .]. In regard to Chinese law, even though the Tort Law Act does indeed protect civil rights and interests, such interests by their very nature cannot be protected without restriction. In order to determine which civil interests are thus protected by the Tort Law Act, the court may consider the following factors:

a. whether the civil interest is protected by any *lex specialis*.
b. the subjective state of the responsible party at the time of the infringement. If the conduct was intentional, then the infringed civil interest is generally deemed to be protected.
c. whether the victim had a close relationship with the responsible party at the time of the infringement (foreseeability).
d. individual freedom. If by overemphasizing the protection of the victim's interests, we might limit individual freedom, breaking the balance between the protection of the victim's legal interests and individual freedom.

4. Chongqing Fourth Intermediate People's Court (Civil Division), 26.12.2005, 上诉人黔江区永安建筑有限责任公司与被上诉人黔江区民族医院、黔江区供电有限责任公司财产损害赔偿纠纷案 (*Yong'An Construction Company [appellant] v. Quianjiang National Hospital and Quianjiang Power Supply Company*)[30]

Facts: On 15th July 2005, at 21:00, the Yong'An Construction Company was executing work it had been contracted to perform at a riverbank. It negligently damaged a cable that had been installed underground by the Qianjiang Power Supply Company, causing Qianjiang National Hospital to suffer a 26-hour power outage. Qianjiang National Hospital (plaintiff) claims a loss of profit estimated at 25,000 Yuan. The Court of First Instance admitted the plaintiff's claim, holding that the construction company in question was liable to cover the 25,000 Yuan of economic loss suffered by Qianjiang National Hospital.

Claims of the parties: The appellant challenges the decision of the Court of First Instance and claims that it was not liable for the economic loss suffered by Quianjiang National Hospital (the appellee). The appellee hospital argues that the conduct of the construction company (the appellant) constituted a tortious act and therefore the Court should apply the compensational provisions found in the "General Principles of Civil Law of the People's Republic of China" [the predecessor of the Tort Law Act].[31]

Reasoning of the judges: [. . .] Tort law should not provide all rights and interests with the same degree of protection. There must be some distinction – the protection of "human life" is to be afforded the highest priority; the protection of "property" is less preferential; the protection of "economic interests" is the least preferential. [. . .] Damages awarded for the loss of an economic interest are limited to situations of harm to a personal or property right.

---

30 Decision in Chinese available at www.law-lib.com/cpws/cpws_view.asp?id=200401143652.
31 The General Principles of Civil Law were adopted in 1986, and have been in force since 1 January 1987. The provisions of the Tort Law Act, which came into force in July 2010, now prevail over those of the General Principles of Civil Law. See the notice published by the Supreme People's Court on 30 June 2010, available at: www.law-lib.com/law/law_view.asp?id=316994.

In other words, economic loss is generally not recoverable unless it is consequential to damage to some personal right or property right. [...] In deciding whether economic loss is recoverable in the circumstances, the following factors should be taken into account: a) that power supply companies are under a statutory duty to supply electricity and they are generally not liable for economic loss suffered by consumers; b) that power outages happen fairly often and are a rather commonplace event. Following an outage, the supply of electricity is usually restored within a few hours and economic damage is therefore comparatively small. This is regarded by most people as a simple fact of life they must put up with. c) If claims for economic loss were permitted for this particular hazard, there would be no end to potential claims and the responsible party would be imposed with an extremely heavy burden. This outcome appears unfair and presents no socioeconomic benefit.

To sum up, economic loss, except for that loss which arises from damage to personal or property rights, is not recoverable. The expression "damage" as found in Art. 60 (3) of the Electric Power Law should be read as "loss or damage arising from injury to personal or property rights".

The loss of profit claimed by Qianjiang National Hospital belongs to a category of pure economic loss for which the construction company in question is not liable.

Decision: The ruling of the Court of First Instance is annulled.

5. YUNSONG GE, 《侵权责任法》保护的民事利益 (Civil rights protected by the Tort Law Act), China Legal Science 3/2010, 37 at 51

[...] Art. 6 (1) of the Tort Law Act provides a general clause for tort liability. A literal and historical interpretation leads to the conclusion that the Act protects all kinds of rights and interests in private law, and protects them equally. This interpretation would however bring about serious negative effects. Therefore, a teleological reduction must be applied, and it is submitted that namely the restrictive interpretation of German law shall be applied. [...]

XI. Principles of European Tort Law (PETL)[32]

I. PETL

TITLE I. Basic Norm

Art. 1:101. Basic norm. (1) A person to whom damage to another is legally attributed is liable to compensate that damage.
(2) Damage may be attributed in particular to the person
 a) whose conduct constituting fault has caused it; or
 b) whose abnormally dangerous activity has caused it; or
 c) whose auxiliary has caused it within the scope of his functions.

---

32 For background information on the PETL, see above, Part A, Chapter 4.

TITLE II. General Conditions of Liability

Art. 2:101. Recoverable damage. Damage requires material or immaterial harm to a legally protected interest.

Art. 2:102. Protected interests. (1) The scope of protection of an interest depends on its nature; the higher its value, the precision of its definition and its obviousness, the more extensive is its protection.
(2) Life, bodily or mental integrity, human dignity and liberty enjoy the most extensive protection.
(3) Extensive protection is granted to property rights, including those in intangible property.
(4) Protection of pure economic interests or contractual relationships may be more limited in scope. In such cases, due regard must be had especially to the proximity between the actor and the endangered person, or to the fact that the actor is aware of the fact that he will cause damage even though his interests are necessarily valued lower than those of the victim.
(5) The scope of protection may also be affected by the nature of liability, so that an interest may receive more extensive protection against intentional harm than in other cases.
(6) In determining the scope of protection, the interests of the actor, especially in liberty of action and in exercising his rights, as well as public interests also have to be taken into consideration.

2. Bénédict Winiger/Ernst Karner/Ken Oliphant (eds.), *Digest of European Tort Law, Vol. III: Misconduct*, 2018, nos. 3b/30/1 ff. (by Thomas Kadner Graziano)

3b. The Nature and Value of the Protected Interest Involved

Facts

1   A, a construction company, is doing work on a road in the vicinity of V, a company producing stainless steel. A carelessly damages a cable that supplies electricity to V's factory. The cable is owned by a third party. The power is off for 14 hours, disrupting V's 24-hour-a-day operations. V claims damages under three heads:

2   (a) physical damage to melted material which was in the furnace when the power supply was cut and which V's workers tried to save. The damage to this material amounts to € 15,000;

3   (b) loss of the € 10,000 profit that would have been made on the same melted material if the melt had been properly completed;

4   (c) loss of € 40,000 profit V would have been able to make on four more melts which could have been put through the furnace, had the power remained on.[33]

---

[33] Scenario of the ***English*** case: *Spartan Steel & Alloys Ltd v. Martin & Co (Contractors) Ltd*, Court of Appeal (Civil Division) 22.06.1972, [1973] 1 Q.B. 27; *Digest III*, 3b/12/1–6 with comments by K. Oliphant/V. Wilcox; see also: *Digest II*, 6/12/1–3 with comments by K. Oliphant.

Solution

5 **a) Solution According to the PETL.** In the above scenario, the damaged cable was owned by a primary victim (rather than by V). A negligently injured the primary victim in the property of its cable, and for this it can claim damages under the PETL and arguably all European national jurisdictions.

6 V, a secondary victim who did not own the cable, was deprived of its energy supply and consequently suffered physical damage to the material which was in the furnace in the amount of € 15,000. V is thus claiming € 15,000 for damage to *property*.

7 Had V been able to properly complete the melt, it would have been able to sell the material for a profit of € 10,000. This € 10,000 is thus *loss* which is *consequential to damage to property*.

8 Last but not least, V is claiming € 40,000 for loss of profit it would have been able to make on four more melts, had the power supply not been cut. The loss of € 40,000 in profit, suffered by V, does *not* follow from the damage to V's property. It is, on the contrary, *pure economic loss* not resulting from physical injury to V's property but from the fact that the V's activities were interrupted as a consequence of the damage to the power cable owned by a third party.

9 This case raises the issue of the extent to which a party (in the above scenario: the construction company A) is required to avoid different categories of loss, and in particular whether it is required to avoid causing 'pure economic loss' to third parties (in the scenario: V).

10 In a first group of European jurisdictions, indirect loss suffered by a secondary victim (steel company V) would not be recoverable even if damage was caused to the secondary victim's property. The arguments provided for this (comparably restrictive) attitude is that the circle of potential secondary victims may be very wide, and so the burden on the person claimed to be liable may be very heavy to the point of being ruined by a flood of claims, and that the victim could have taken precautions in view of a shortage of electricity supply.[34]

11 In a second group of jurisdictions, no distinction would be made in principle in the above scenario between the primary and secondary victims and between damage to property and pure economic loss. The whole loss claimed by the steel company would be recoverable. These jurisdictions focus primarily on the victim's interest in compensation and, in particular, the victim's interest in an uninterrupted supply of essential commodities such as electricity, gas etc.[35]

---

34 See the reasoning in the ***Norwegian*** case: Hr (*Norwegian Supreme Court*), 29.09.1955, Rt 1955, 872, and 10.11.1973, Rt 1973, 1268; *Digest III*, 3b/17/5 with comments by A. M. Frøseth/B. Askeland [. . .].

35 See for ***Dutch*** law: HR (*Dutch Supreme Court*), 01.07.1977, ECLI:NL:HR:1977:AB7010, NJ 1978/84 (Van Hees/Esbeek); *Digest III*, 3b/8/1ff. with comments by S. D. Lindenbergh; for ***French*** law: Cass. Civ. 2 (*Court of Cassation, 2nd civil chamber*), 08.05.1970 (Société Allamigeon Frères et Lacroix c. Lafarge), n°69–11446, Bull. 1970 n° 160; for ***Italian*** Law: Corte di Cass. SS UU (*Court of Cassation, Joint Divisions*), 24.06.1972, no 2135 (*Pasta case*), Giur it. 1973, I,1,c 1124; Foro it. 1973, I1,100; *Digest III*, 3b/9/1 with comments by N. Coggiola/B. Gardella Tedeschi/M. Graziadei; see also *Digest II*, 5/9/1 with comments by N. Coggiola/B. Gardella Tedeschi/M. Graziadei.

12 Most European courts would reach a third outcome, hereby making a fundamental distinction in the above scenario between positions (a) and (b) on the one hand, and position (c) on the other. Damage to property and financial loss consequential to damage to property which was foreseeable and avoidable for a reasonable person in the circumstances (positions (a) and (b)) is recoverable in these jurisdictions, even if the chain of causation is long. However, there is, in principle, no duty to avoid pure economic loss (position (c)). The damage of € 15,000 resulting from the impairment of material which was in the furnace, as well as the € 10,000 loss, which is consequential to the damage to the factory's property in the material, would be recoverable in these jurisdictions. On the contrary, the defendant would not be liable for the further loss of profit in the amount of € 40,000 (the so-called *pure economic loss*).[36]

13 According to these systems, the further loss of € 40,000 would only be recoverable if the person alleged to be liable violated a provision which specifically protected the victim against this type of (pure economic) loss.[37]

14 Under the PETL, the reasoning would start with the fact that V suffered physical damage to the metal that was in the furnace when the cable was cut. Just like the owner of the cable, V has suffered damage to its property. Given that property rights enjoy extensive protection under Art. 2:102(3) PETL, that the PETL make no fundamental distinction regarding the length of the chain of causation and that they make no fundamental distinction between primary and secondary victims when it comes to damage to property,[38] under the PETL, A was required to take reasonable care with respect to the protection of property of secondary victims such as V. Experience shows that carelessly digging in the vicinity of roads and factories entails a risk of cutting the supply of essential commodities, so in this respect the damage to V would have been foreseeable. A was carrying out its professional activities, it should have had the expertise necessary to avoid this damage, and could have avoided it at reasonable cost and effort by surveying the location of underground power lines (see the criteria provided in Art. 4:102(1) PETL). Following this line of reasoning, V could successfully claim compensation for the damage to the steel that was in the furnace when the cable was cut (position (a)).

15 Under the PETL, once liability for damage to property is established, the liable person has to restore the victim "so far as money can, to the position he would have been in if the wrong complained of had not been committed", Art. 10:101(1) 1st sent PETL. Under this line of reasoning, the damage to V's property would thus include V's loss of profit which is consequential to the property damage, that is, the loss of the 10,000 profit that would have been made if the melt had been properly completed

---

36 See for **England and Wales**: *Spartan Steel & Alloys Ltd v. Martin & Co (Contractors) Ltd*, Court of Appeal (Civil Division), 14.12.1971, [1973] 1 Q.B. 27; *Digest III*, 3b/12/1 with comments by K. OLIPHANT/V. WILCOX; *Digest II*, 6/12/1–3 with comments by K. OLIPHANT; for **Ireland**: *Irish Paper Sacks Ltd v. John Sisk & Son (Dublin) Ltd*, High Court, 18.05.1972; *Digest III*, 3b/14/7 with comments by E. Quill: no duty of care to avoid pure economic loss; see also *Digest II*, 5/14/1 with comments by E. QUILL; for **Scotland**: *Dynamco Ltd v. Holland and Hannen and Cubitts (Scotland) Ltd.*, 15.07.1971, SC 257, 1972 SLT 38 (Inner House of the Court of Session); *Digest III*, 3b/13/1 with comments by M. HOGG; *Digest II*, 5/13/1 with comments by M. HOGG; for **Germany**: BGH (*Federal Supreme Court of Justice*), 04.02.1964, BGHZ 41, 123 (chicken case).

37 Which is the situation for cable cases e.g. in **Switzerland**, see: Tribunal Fédéral Suisse (*Federal Supreme Court of Switzerland*), 02.03.1976, ATF 102 II 85; *Digest III*, 3b/4/7 ff. with comments by B. WINIGER/A. CAMPI/C. DURET/J. RETAMOZO.

38 See *Digest II*, 5/29/9 with comments by T. KADNER GRAZIANO.

(position (b)). This solution under the PETL would be in line with the second and third solutions found in the national jurisdictions.

16 The last question is whether A was also required not to cause pure economic loss to third parties (in the scenario: V) and, consequently, whether it is required to compensate V's further loss in the amount of 40,000. As we have seen above, the PETL list the factors relevant in assessing whether the required standard of conduct has been attained in Art. 4:102(1). According to this provision, "[t]he required standard of conduct" depends, among other criteria, "on the nature and value of the protected interest involved". Art. 2:102 PETL defines the protected interests and provides in para. (4) that "[p]rotection of *pure economic interests* or contractual relationships may be more limited in scope. In such cases, due regard must be had especially to the proximity between the actor and the endangered person, or to the fact that the actor is aware of the fact that he will cause damage even though his interests are necessarily valued lower than those of the victim".[39]

17 Under the PETL, the duty to protect others from pure economic loss "may" thus be less intensive than the duty to avoid injury to life, bodily or mental integrity, human dignity, liberty and property rights (compare Art. 2:102 (1)-(3) PETL). In the above scenario, A and V were not in a relationship with each other and A was not "aware" of the fact that it was causing damage to V (see the criteria in Art. 2:102(4) PETL). Thus, it may very well be argued that under the PETL A did not have a duty to protect V against further loss suffered due to the standstill of V's operations. This outcome would be in line with the majority view in European jurisdictions.

18 A further argument for treating victims who suffer property damage differently from victims suffering pure economic loss under the PETL is the number of potential victims. The number of victims who may suffer pure economic loss due to a shortage in energy supply is much larger than that of victims who may suffer damage to property. In national jurisdictions, liability for (pure economic) loss in 'cable case' situations has been rejected in particular in situations where the number of potential secondary victims was large and the defendant risked being ruined by a flood of claims should he have been held liable.[40] The large number of potential claimants is arguably another reason why national courts are reluctant to hold electricity companies liable in tort vis-à-vis their clients in cases where they negligently interrupted the power electricity supply for the customers.[41]

19 Last but not least, under Art. 8:101(1) PETL (contributory conduct or activity), it may be argued (just as courts do in some jurisdictions) that V could or should have taken precautions against the cutting of energy supply, hereby avoiding the occurrence of damage to its property (with the effect that such liability is reduced), and against the

---

39 Emphasis added.
40 See in particular the reasoning of the *Norwegian* Supreme Court, *Digest III*, 3b/17/6 with comments by A. M. FRØSETH/B. ASKELAND.
41 See e.g. the **Spanish** case: Sentencia del Tribunal Supremo (*Judgment of the Supreme Court*), 31.01.2012, RJ 2012\2031; *Digest III*, 3b/10/1 with comments by M. MARTIN CASALS/J. RIBOT; contrast with the **Greek** case: Efeteio Kritis (*Crete Court of Appeal*), 427/11.09.2007, *EllDni* 2008, 22; *Digest III*, 3b/5/1 with comments by E. G. Dacoronia: following a breakdown in power supply, 4,360 hens die of suffocation; the electricity company is held liable for 70% of damage, with 30% concurrent liability of the victim because they had not properly maintained their safety generator.

occurrence of pure economic loss (which may be another argument to exclude liability for such loss altogether).[42]

20 Thus, it may very well be argued that under the PETL A was required to take all reasonable care to avoid V from suffering *property damage* as well as the *loss of earning consequential to this property damage*, whereas A was not required to prevent V from suffering *pure economic loss* following a shortage in power supply. The case may then illustrate the less extensive protection of pure economic interests under the PETL, when compared to the protection of body, health, or property rights, for instance.

XII. Draft Common Frame of Reference (DCFR)

1. DCFR

Book VI: Non-contractual liability arising out of damage caused to another

Chapter 1: Fundamental provisions

VI. – 1:101: Basic rule. (1) A person who suffers legally relevant damage has a right to reparation from a person who caused the damage intentionally or negligently or is otherwise accountable for the causation of the damage.
(2) Where a person has not caused legally relevant damage intentionally or negligently that person is accountable for the causation of legally relevant damage only if Chapter 3 so provides. [. . .]

Chapter 2: Legally relevant damage

Section 1: General

VI. – 2:101: Meaning of legally relevant damage. (1) Loss, whether economic or non-economic, or injury is legally relevant damage if:
   (a) one of the following rules of this Chapter so provides;
   (b) the loss or injury results from a violation of a right otherwise conferred by the law; or
   (c) the loss or injury results from a violation of an interest worthy of legal protection.
(2) In any case covered only by sub-paragraphs (b) or (c) of paragraph (1) loss or injury constitutes legally relevant damage only if it would be fair and reasonable for there to be a right to reparation [. . .], as the case may be, under VI. – 1:101 (Basic rule) [. . .].
(3) In considering whether it would be fair and reasonable for there to be a right to reparation [. . .] regard is to be had to the ground of accountability, to the nature and proximity of the damage or impending damage, to the reasonable expectations of the person who suffers or would suffer the damage, and to considerations of public policy.

---

42 See the reasoning of the *Norwegian* Supreme Court, above, VII.

(4) In this Book:
  (a) economic loss includes loss of income or profit, burdens incurred and a reduction in the value of property; [...]

Section 2: Particular instances of legally relevant damage

VI. – 2:201: Personal injury and consequential loss. [...]

VI. – 2:203: Infringement of dignity, liberty and privacy. [...]

VI. – 2:204: Loss upon communication of incorrect information about another. [...]

VI. – 2:205: Loss upon breach of confidence. [...]

VI. – 2:206: Loss upon infringement of property or lawful possession. (1) Loss caused to a person as a result of an infringement of that person's property right or lawful possession of a movable or immovable thing is legally relevant damage.
(2) In this Article:
  (a) loss includes being deprived of the use of property;
  (b) infringement of a property right includes destruction of or physical damage to the subject-matter of the right (property damage), disposition of the right, interference with its use and other disturbance of the exercise of the right.

VI. – 2:207: Loss upon reliance on incorrect advice or information. [...]

VI. – 2:208: Loss upon unlawful impairment of business. (1) Loss caused to a person as a result of an unlawful impairment of that person's exercise of a profession or conduct of a trade is legally relevant damage. [...]

VI. – 3:102: Negligence. A person causes legally relevant damage negligently when that person causes the damage by conduct which either:
  (a) does not meet the particular standard of care provided by a statutory provision whose purpose is the protection of the person suffering the damage from that damage; or
  (b) does not otherwise amount to such care as could be expected from a reasonably careful person in the circumstances of the case.

2. CHRISTIAN VON BAR/ERIC CLIVE (eds.), *Principles, Definitions and Model Rules of European Private Law – Draft Common Frame of Reference (DCFR), Full Edition,* Vol. 4, 2009, Art. VI. 2:206, Illustration 4, p. 3317

Illustration 4

A construction company carrying out road works negligently cuts through a subsurface electricity cable. Legally relevant damage is suffered as a result by the electricity company, which is the owner of the cable, but not by a business at whose head office work is consequently temporarily interrupted. The negligent impact on its contractual relationship with the electricity company does not establish legally relevant damage. The situation is different where, as a result of the power cut, property is damaged or destroyed, e.g. heated metal cools down or (in a private household) the contents of a freezer are spoiled.

I. Illustration of scenario I

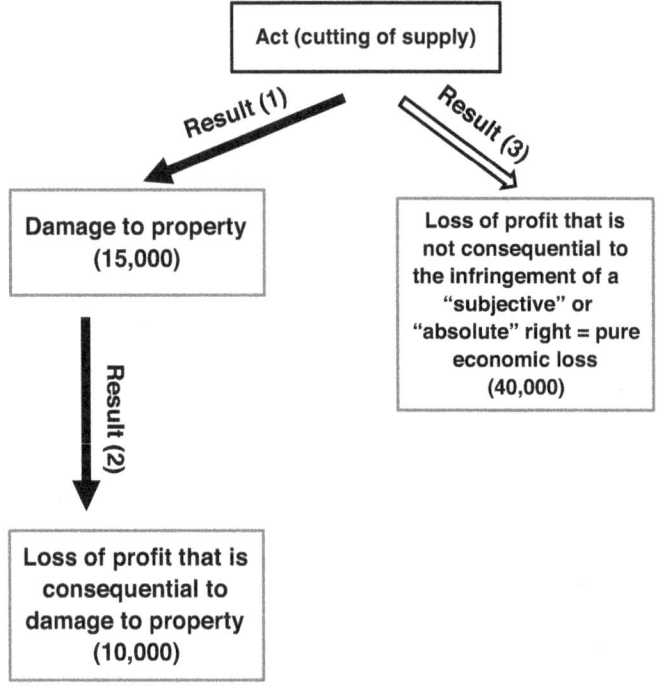

Figure 5.1

Table 5.1

	Conditions of extra-contractual liability
English law: tort of "negligence"	• **Duty of care*** • Breach • Damage • Causation • Foreseeability ** In principle, no duty of care to avoid "pure economic loss".*
German law: § 823 (1) BGB	• Act of the defendant • **Infringement of life, body, health, freedom, property or any other absolute right*** • Causation between the defendant's act and the infringement • Damage • Causation between infringement and damage • Unlawfulness (indicated if an absolute right was infringed) • Fault (intent or negligence) ** In principle, no protection against "pure economic loss".*

Swiss law: Art. 41 (1) CO	• Act of the defendant • Damage • Causation • **Unlawfulness (indicated in case that an absolute right was infringed)*** • Fault (intent or negligence) * *In principle, it is not unlawful to cause "pure economic loss" except if a special provision aiming at the protection of the particular victim (such as Art. 239 of the Criminal Code) is infringed by the defendant's conduct.*
French law: Arts. 1240, 1241 Civil Code	• Act of the defendant • Damage (certain and actual)* • Causation • Fault * *In principle, no distinction is made between injury to absolute or subjective rights and any other legally protected interest.*

II. Outcome of case scenarios

Scenario a)

Table 5.2

	Damage to property	Loss of profit through damage to property	Pure economic loss
England and Wales	✓	✓	X
Ireland	✓	✓	X
Germany	✓	✓	X
Switzerland	✓	✓	✓ (exceptionally because of Art. 239 (2) Criminal Code *cum* Art. 41 (1) CO)
Estonia	✓	✓	X
Sweden	✓	✓	X (except existence of a criminal disposition)
Norway	X	X	X
Finland	X	X	X
France	✓	✓	✓
China	✓	✓	X
PETL	✓	✓	X
DCFR	✓	✓	X

Table 5.3

Property loss + Loss of profit consequential to damage to property + Pure economic loss	Property loss + Loss of profit consequential to damage to property ≠ Pure economic loss	No compensation at all
• **French law** (Art. 1240 Code Civil; 1970 *Lafarge* case). • **Swiss law:** if there is an unlawful conduct (Art. 239 (2) Criminal Code, Art. 41 (1) Code of Obligations).	• **English law:** *Spartan Steel* case. • **Irish law:** *Glencar Exploration* case. • **German law:** (§§ 823, 249 (2), 252 BGB). • **Estonian law** (§§ 1043, 1045 Code of Obligations). • **Swedish law:** (kap. 2 § 1–2 SKL), except in the event that a criminal provision in the sense of kap. 2 § 2 exists. • **Chinese law:** *Yong'An Construction Case.* • **PETL** (Art. 2:102 (4)). • **DCFR** (Art. VI. – 2:206)	• **Norwegian law:** the *Dagfinn Strøm* case. • **Finnish law:** (LUKU 2 § 1, LUKU 5 § 1; and judgment KKO 2003:124).

Scenario b)

Liability exists only in French law; in all other jurisdictions examined above, there is no liability.

Bibliography

On cable cases

GÜNTER HAGER, Haftung bei Störung der Energiezufuhr, *JZ* 1979, 53–58; FILIPPO RANIERI, *Europäisches Obligationenrecht*, 3. Aufl., Wien/New York: Springer, 2009, pp. 1409–1538; KARSTEN SCHMIDT, Integritätsschutz von Unternehmen nach § 823 BGB – Zum "Recht am eingerichteten und ausgeübten Gewerbebetrieb", *JuS* 1993, 985–992; JAAP SPIER (ed.), *The Limits of Expanding Liability: Eight Fundamental Cases in a Comparative Perspective*, The Hague/London/Boston: Kluwer Law International, 1998, Case 2.

On pure economic loss[43]

EFSTATHIOS K. BANAKAS (ed.), *Civil Liability for Pure Economic Loss*, London: Kluwer, 1994; WILLIAM BISHOP, Economic Loss in Tort, *OJLS* 1982, 1; WILLEM H. VAN BOOM/HELMUT KOZIOL/CHRISTIAN A. WITTING (eds.), *Pure Economic Loss*, Wien: Springer, 2004; MAURO BUSSANI/VERNON VALENTINE PALMER (eds.), *Pure Economic Loss in Europe*, Cambridge: CUP, 2011; MAURO BUSSANI/VERNON VALENTINE PALMER (eds.), *Pure Economic Loss: New Horizons in Comparative Law*, London: Routledge-Cavendish, 2009; BRUCE FELDTHUSEN, *Economic Negligence: The Recovery of Pure Economic Loss*, 4th ed., Scarborough, ON: Carswell, 2000; WALTER VAN GERVEN/JEREMY LEVER/PIERRE LAROUCHE, *Cases, Materials and Text on National, Supranational and International Tort Law*, Oxford et al.: Hart, 2000, pp. 208–247; DAVID GRUNING, Pure Economic Loss in American Tort Law: An Unstable Consensus, *Am. J. Comp. L. (Supplement Issue Fall)* 2006, 187–208; HELMUT KOZIOL (ed.), *Unification of Tort Law: Wrongfulness*, The Hague/London/Boston: Kluwer Law International, 1998; D. MARSHALL, Liability for Pure Economic Loss Negligently Caused: French and English Law Compared, *ICLQ* 1975, 748; CEES VAN DAM, *European Tort Law*, 2nd ed., Oxford: OUP, 2002, pp. 208–218; JAN VAN DUNNÉ, Liability for Pure Economic Loss: Rule Or Exception? A Comparatist's View of the Civil Law: Common Law Split on Compensation of Non-physical Damage in Tort Law, *ERPL* 1999, 397; GERHARD WAGNER, in: *Münchener Kommentar Band 6: Schuldrecht Besonderer Teil*, 7th ed., München: C. H. Beck, 2017, § 823 paras 370–379; PETER WETTERSTEIN, Compensation for Pure Economic Loss in Finnish Tort Law, *Scand. St. L.* 2001, pp. 565–580; CHRISTIAN WITTING, Distinguishing between Property Damage and Pure Economic Loss in Negligence: A Personality Thesis, *Legal Studies* 2001, 481–514; GE YUNSONG, Pure Economic Loss in China, *Peking University Law Journal* 2013, 69–104.

On different Tort Law cultures and their specificities

HAKAN ANDERSSON, The Tort Law Culture(s) of Scandinavia, *JETL* 2012, 210; JEAN-SÉBASTIAN BORGHETTI, The Culture of Tort Law in France, *JETL* 2012, 158; GERT BRÜGGEMEIER, European Civil Liability Law outside Europe: The Example of the Big Three: China, Brazil, Russia, *JETL* 2011, 1; GERT BRÜGGEMEIER, *Common Principles of Tort Law: A Pre-Statement of Law*, London: BIICL, 2004, pp. 1–42; JÖRG FEDTKE, The Culture of German Tort Law, *JETL* 2012, 183; PAULA GILIKER, Codifying Tort Law: Lessons from the Proposals for Reform of the French Civil Code, *ICLQ* 2008, 561; H. PATRICK GLENN, Comparative Legal Families and Comparative Legal Traditions, in: Mathias Reimann/Reinhard Zimmermann, *The Oxford Handbook of Comparative Law*, Oxford: OUP, 2006, Chapter 12; IRMGARD GRISS, How Judges Think: Judicial Reasoning in Tort Cases from a Comparative Perspective, *JETL* 2013, 247; DAVID IBBETSON, Harmonisation of the Law of Tort and Delict: A Comparative

---

43 See also below, Chapter 14, with further references.

and Historical Perspective, in: Reinhard Zimmermann (ed.), *Grundstrukturen des Europäischen Deliktsrechts*, Baden-Baden: Nomos, 2003, pp. 83–104; NILS JANSEN, Duties and Rights in Negligence: A Comparative and Historical Perspective on the European Law of Extracontractual Liability, *OJLS* 2004, 443; RICHARD LEWIS/ANNETTE MORRIS, Tort Law Culture in the United Kingdom: Image and Reality in Personal Injury Compensation, *JETL* 2012, 230; ULRICH MAGNUS, Why Is US Tort Law so Different?, *JETL* 2010, 328; BASIL MARKESINIS, *A Comparative Introduction into the German Law of Torts*, 3rd ed., Oxford: Clarendon Press, 1994; KEN OLIPHANT, Cultures of Tort Law in Europe, *JETL* 2012, 147; MÅRTEN SCHULTZ, Disharmonization: A Swedish Critique of Principles of European Tort Law, *EBLR* 2007, 1305 (Nordic countries); CEES VAN DAM, *European Tort Law*, 2nd ed., Oxford: OUP, 2002, Part I Systems of Liability, pp. 3–166; WALTER VAN GERVEN/JEREMY LEVER/PIERRE LAROUCHE, *Cases, Materials and Text on National, Supranational and International Tort Law*, Oxford et al.: Hart, 2000, Introduction and Chapter One; WALTER VAN GERVEN, Bridging the Unbridgeable: Community and National Tort Laws after Francovich and Brasserie, *ICLQ* 1996, 507; CHRISTIAN VON BAR (ed.), *Deliktsrecht in Europa, Systematische Einführungen, Gesetzestexte, Übersetzungen*, Köln et al.: Carl Heymanns, 1994; CHRISTIAN VON BAR, *Gemeineuropäisches Deliktsrecht Erster Band*, München: C. H. Beck, 1996; CHRISTIAN VON BAR,*The Common European Law of Torts Volume One*, Oxford: OUP, 1998; GERHARD WAGNER, Grundstrukturen des Deliktsrechts, in: Reinhard Zimmermann (ed.), *Grundstrukturen des Europäischen Deliktsrechts*, Baden-Baden: Nomos, 2003, pp. 189–340; GERHARD WAGNER, Comparative Tort Law, in: Mathias Reimann/Reinhard Zimmermann, *The Oxford Handbook of Comparative Law*, Oxford: OUP, 2006, Chapter 31.

Chapter 6

Fault-based liability and the required standard of care

The case of damage caused by minors[1]

"[T]he child, by reason of his physical and mental immaturity, needs special safeguards and care, including appropriate legal protection [. . .]."[2]

"[T]he protection offered to children by national legislators in the area of tort law varies widely from country to country [and] is one of the least harmonised as well as intricate areas of tort law."[3]

Scenario

During the school holidays, two children – Stephen and his friend Daniel – are playing in the garden with bows and arrows. They make the bows out of string and pliable inch-thick ash branches and then use twigs for arrows. Initially they set up an archery target on a tree and do target practice at different ranges. Later on, they started play-fighting. It is at this moment that an arrow shot by Stephen strikes Daniel in his right eye. Daniel's right eye has to be surgically removed and replaced by a prosthetic one.

Daniel, represented by his parents, is looking to claim damages from Stephen. Is Stephen liable for the damage that he caused to his friend, assuming that the two boys are:
  (a) 6 years old;
  (b) 9 years old;
  (c) 14 years old?
Both children are of normal development for their age.[4]

---

1 On liability of parents for damage caused by their children, see Chapter 13.
2 Declaration of the Rights of the Child, proclaimed by General Assembly Resolution of the United Nations 1386(XIV) of 20 November 1959, Preamble.
3 M. MARTIN CASALS, Comparative Report, in: *Children in Tort Law, Part I: Children as Tortfeasors*, Wien/New York: Springer, 2006, pp. 423 ff., n. 3.
4 Inspired by the case: Schweizerisches Bundesgericht (*Swiss Federal Supreme Court of Justice*), 10.03.1977, BGE 103 II 24. Similar cases are to be found in many other jurisdictions. Further to the materials reproduced below, see e.g. for *Austria*: OGH, 18.12.2009, 2 Ob 83/09h (eye injury caused with a wooden stick); *Croatia*: Supreme Court of the Republic of Croatia, No Rev-x 570/09–2, 17.02.2009; *Digest III*, 8/26/1 with comments by M. BARETIC (eye injury caused by shot with gas gun); *Slovenia*: Vrhovno sodišče Republike Slovenije (*Slovenian Supreme Court*), 08.03.2012, II Ips 882/2008; *Digest III*, 8/27/1 with comments by B. NOVAK/G. DUGAR (eye of a 4-year-old girl injured with sharp branch of a shrub); the *Czech Republic*: Nejvyšší soud České republiky (*Supreme Court of the*

Questions

1) In most European jurisdictions, fault-based liability is the principal pillar of extra-contractual liability, at least in theory.[5] Fault-based liability is based on the idea that the individual who is held responsible for the harm could, and should, have behaved differently and that he or she thus acted carelessly or, in other words, with negligence[6] when causing the harm.

   a) Some jurisdictions determine whether an individual has acted carelessly or with negligence by adopting an *objective standard* of care, while others resort to a *subjective standard*. What is the difference between the two?

   b) What is the position of the *English*, *Swiss*, and *German* legal systems in relation to this issue? What is the position of *Austrian* law?

   c) What arguments can you think of in support of a subjective standard of care, and which arguments speak in favour of an objective standard? Can you imagine any situations in which these two standards might lead to different results? Bear in mind that in many jurisdictions an individual may in fact be deemed to act carelessly or with negligence when engaging in an activity despite having the

---

Czech Republic), 20.02.2003, 25 Cdo 1333/2001; *Digest III*, 8/24/1 with comments by L. TICHÝ/J. HRÁDEK (eye injury caused by shot with airgun); **Estonia**: Tartu Circuit Court, 13.05.2012, Judgment No 2–09–55061; *Digest III*, 14/20/1 with comments by J. LAHE/T. TAMPUU (loss of an eye caused by throwing a mobile phone); **Poland**: Sąd Najwyższy (*Supreme Court*), 11.01.2001, IV CKN 1469/00, OSNC 2001/9/129, OSP 6/2002 item 81; *Digest III*, 8/23/1 with comments by E. BAGIŃSKA/I. ADRYCH-BRZEZIŃSKA (a boy aged 13 injures a girl with a firecracker and she partially loses vision); **Sweden**: Högsta domstolen (*Supreme Court*) 03.02.1977, NJA 1977, 186; *Digest III*, 8/18/1 with comments by H. ANDERSSON (a 3-year-old boy throws a metal piece with sharp edges at another boy causing him to lose an eye); Högsta domstolen (*Supreme Court*), 08.11.1974, NJA 1974, 585; *Digest III*, 14/18/1 with comments by H. ANDERSSON (eye injury suffered at a ball game when club smashed into player's eye); **Denmark**: Østre Landsret (*Eastern Court of Appeal*), 21.12.2001, FED 2001.2682 Ø; *Digest III*, 8/16/4 with comments by V. ULFBECK/A. EHLERS/K. SIIG (10-year-old hits someone in the eye during a game of crazy golf, causing eye injuries); **Finland**: Korkein oikeus (*Supreme Court*), 04.03.1983, KKO 1983 II 26, R81/382, 884/82; *Digest III*, 8/19/1 with comments by P. KORPISAARI (15-year-old intentionally shoots at someone with an air rifle, causing him to lose an eye).

Equally frequent are scenarios involving children starting fires and causing serious damage to property, see e.g. the cases for **Switzerland**: Bundesgericht (*Federal Supreme Court of Justice*), 06.12.1974, ATF 100 II 332; **Germany**: Bundesgerichtshof (*Federal Supreme Court of Justice*), 28.02.1984, NJW 1984, 1958 (see below, III. 2. b.); OLG (*Court of Appeal*) Brandenburg, 25.02.2010, 12 U 123/09; **Austria**: Oberster Gerichtshof (*Supreme Court*), 20.10.1988, 7 Ob 36/88 (see below, IV. 2. b.); Oberster Gerichtshof, 17.10.1993, 1 Ob 546/94; **France**: Cour de cassation, assemblé plénière (*Court of Cassation, full assembly*), 09.05.1984, n° 82–92.934 (see below, p. 143); **Finland**: Korkein oikeus (*Supreme Court*), 23.05.1984, 1984 II 93, S83/217, 4230/83 (7-year-old children start a fire when playing); **Norway**: Høyesterett (*Supreme Court*), 14.12.2004, Rt 2004, 1942 (on the liability of parents).

5 In the most frequent cases of extra-contractual liability, road traffic accidents, most systems impose liability without fault or, in other terms, strict or objective liability, see below, Chapter 9.
6 In English law, the term "negligence" firstly refers to a type of fault that is often treated as synonymous with "carelessness". Secondly, it also refers to separate tort with various conditions and rules, see e.g. A. MULLIS/K. OLIPHANT, *Torts*, 4th ed., Basingstoke/New York: Palgrave Macmillan, 2011, n. 2.2, and Chapter 5, pp. 76 ff.

knowledge that he or she lacks the requisite skills to carry it out safely (so-called *Übernahmeverschulden*).[7]

2) Even in jurisdictions which apply an objective standard of care, such a standard is to be assessed according to the individual's specific situation (i.e. with regard to his or her knowledge, skills, profession, and age), particularly in cases involving minors. Taking this into account, in your view how would the above scenario be solved under *English law*?

3) The vast majority of civil codes in continental Europe contain specific provisions on the liability of minors.[8] However, such regimes may vary considerably from one country to another.

    a) What criteria are used under *Swiss* law and *German* law in order to restrict the liability of minors? Using the information provided in the materials, what outcome do you think these two jurisdictions would come to in response to our case?

    b) What would be the outcome of our case if you were to apply *Austrian* law? What role does the age limit found in § 21 (2) and § 176 of the ABGB play in solving our case? How about the first hypothesis of § 1310 ABGB?

4) Over the years, the *French Cour de cassation* gradually held minors to a more and more stringent standard, eventually arriving at a very severe standard of care in the mid-1980s.

    a) Would Stephen be held liable for the harm that he caused to his friend under French law?

    b) Contrast the objective standard of care as applied by the French courts with the objective notion of care for the liability of minors applied in other jurisdictions. What is the rationale behind the severe French approach?[9]

5) Contrast with the *Italian* attitude in respect of liability of minors.

6) *Some European jurisdictions* apply the criteria of the child's capacity of judgement (or discernment), while others use fixed age limits and/or presumptions of liability. Which range of criteria and, in particular, different age limits, do you identify in section VII of the materials?

7) What is the approach of the *USA* under the Restatement of the Law, Torts (3rd)?

---

7 See also the materials below, p. 138, and e.g. P. WIDMER, in: European Group on Tort Law (ed.), *PETL – Text and Commentary*, Vienna/New York: Springer, 2005, Art. 4:101 n. 19 and Art. 4:102 nos. 5 and 9: "someone who purports to carry out a 'dangerous' activity knowing that he does not have the necessary ability, commits a fault on embarking on the activity disregarding his insufficient 'expertise' and leading others to believe (falsely) that he is able to accomplish his task." See also § 2912 (2) of the new *Civil Code of the Czech Republic*: "If a tortfeasor demonstrates special knowledge, skill or diligence, or undertakes to perform an activity for which special knowledge, skill or diligence is required, and fails to apply these special qualities, he is presumed to be acting negligently."
8 Exceptions include, e.g. the French and Belgian Civil Codes.
9 See also below, Chapter 19, pp. 596 ff.

8) If the minor is not held liable by virtue of his or her age or lack of capacity, in several jurisdictions he or she may still be held liable *in equity*. Would the outcome in equity under *German, Austrian, French, Swedish,* or *Estonian* law be affected if the individual held responsible for the harm were covered by third-party *liability insurance*, or indeed if the victim had *first-party insurance*? Do the responses raised within the materials conform to the general principle that insurance coverage follows liability?

9) Produce a systematic summary of the different approaches concerning:
   – the standard of care in general;
   – the liability of minors, comparing and contrasting each approach.

   Of all the systems studied, which approach would you recommend in regards to
   – subjective or objective standards of care in general?
   – the liability of minors?

   Give reasons for your answer.

Table of contents

I. England and Wales

1. ALASTAIR MULLIS/KEN OLIPHANT, *Torts*, 4th ed., Basingstoke/
   New York: Palgrave Macmillan, 2011, n° 8.2 .... p. 122
2. Court of Appeal (Civil Division), *Mullin* v. *Richards*, 06.11.1997,
   [1998] 1 All ER 920 .... p. 122
3. Court decisions from other Common Law jurisdictions, cited as
   persuasive authority: High Court of Ontario/Canada, *Tillander* v.
   Gosselin, [1967] 1 OR 203 .... p. 125

II. Switzerland

1. The required standard of care (in general)
   a) Bundesgericht/Tribunal fédéral (*Federal Supreme Court
      of Justice*), 27.06.1990, BGE 116 Ia 162 at 169–170 .... p. 125
   b) CHRISTOPH MÜLLER, *La responsabilité civile extracontractuelle
      (Extra-contractual liability)*, Basel: Helbing Lichtenhahn, 2013,
      nos. 242–244 .... p. 126
2. Liability of minors (in particular)
   a) Code civil/Zivilgesetzbuch (*Civil Code*), Arts. 16, 18, 19 (3) .... p. 126
   b) Code des obligations/Obligationenrecht (*Code of Obligations*),
      Art. 54 .... p. 127
   c) Tribunal fédéral/Bundesgericht (*Federal Supreme Court of Justice*),
      21.01.1964 (*Zufferey* c. *Kull*), ATF 90 II 9 .... p. 127
   d) Tribunal fédéral/Bundesgericht (*Federal Supreme Court of Justice*),
      11.07.1978 (*Maillard* c. *Guye et Gutknecht*), ATF 104 II 184 .... p. 129
3. Liability in equity
   Tribunal fédéral/Bundesgericht (*Federal Supreme Court of Justice*),
   06.12.1977 (*A.* c. *hoirs X.*), ATF 103 II 330 .... p. 130

III. Germany

1. The required standard of care (in general)
   a) Bürgerliches Gesetzbuch, BGB (*Civil Code*), § 276 .... p. 130
   b) JOSEF ESSER/HANS-LEO WEYERS, *Schuldrecht, Band II, Besonderer
      Teil, Teilband 2: Gesetzliche Schuldverhältnisse (Law of Obligations,
      Vol. II, Special Part, 2. Legal Obligations)*, 8th ed., Heidelberg:
      C. F. Müller, 2000, § 55 III .... p. 130
2. Liability of minors (in particular)
   a) Bürgerliches Gesetzbuch, BGB (*Civil Code*), §§ 828, 829 .... p. 131
   b) Bundesgerichtshof, BGH (*Federal Supreme Court of Justice*),
      28.02.1984, NJW 1984, 1958 .... p. 132
   c) Bundesgerichtshof, BGH (*Federal Supreme Court of Justice*),
      10.03.1970, NJW 1970, 1038 .... p. 134

3 Liability in equity
Bundesgerichtshof, BGH (*Federal Supreme Court of Justice*),
24.04.1979, NJW 1979, 2096 .... p. 134

IV. Austria

1. The required standard of care (in general)
   a) Allgemeines bürgerliches Gesetzbuch, ABGB (*General Civil Code*),
      §§ 1294, 1295 (1), 1297, 1306 .... p. 136
   b) HELMUT KOZIOL, *Basic Questions of Tort Law from a Germanic Perspective*, Wien: Jan Sramek Verlag, 2012, nos. 6/81–6/83 .... p. 137
   c) PETER APATHY/ANDREAS RIEDER, *Bürgerliches Recht, Band III, Schuldrecht, Besonderer Teil (Civil Law, Vol. III, Law of Obligations, Special Part)*, 4th ed., Wien/New York: Springer, 2010, §§ 13/31 ff. .... p. 138
   d) Oberster Gerichtshof, OGH (*Supreme Court of Justice*), 23.03.1976, 5 Ob 536/76, SZ 49/47 (Leitsatz/*basic principle*) .... p. 138

2. Liability of children (in particular)
   a) Allgemeines bürgerliches Gesetzbuch, ABGB (*General Civil Code*),
      §§ 21, 176, 1310 .... p. 139
   b) Oberster Gerichtshof, OGH (*Supreme Court of Justice*), 20.10.1988, 7 Ob 36/88 .... p. 139

3. Liability in equity
   Oberster Gerichtshof, OGH (*Supreme Court of Justice*), 18.12.2009, 7 Ob 83/09h .... p. 141

V. France

1. Cour de cassation, Assemblée plénière (*Court of Cassation, full assembly*), 09.05.1984, n° 82–92.934, Bulletin criminel 1984 n° 162 (*arrêt Djouab/Djouab case*) .... p. 143
2. Cour de cassation (*Court of Cassation*), 12.12.1984, n° 82–12.627, Bull. 1984 II n° 193 (*arrêt Molina/Molina case*) .... p. 143
3. Cour de cassation, Assemblée plénière (*Court of Cassation, full assembly*), 09.05.1984, n° 80–14.994, Bull. 1984 n° 1 (*arrêt Gabillet/Gabillet case*) .... p. 144
4. ALAIN BÉNABENT, *Droit civil. Les obligations (Civil Law. Obligations)*, 15th ed., Paris: Montchrestien, 2016, nos. 529, 532 .... p. 144

VI. Italy

1. Codice civile (*Civil Code*), Arts. 2046, 2047 .... p. 145
2. Corte di Cassazione (*Court of Cassation*),
   28.04.1975, n. 1642, Resp. Civ. Prev., 1976, 136 .... p. 146

VII. Liability of children: codal or statutory provisions of various continental jurisdictions (English translations)

1. Burgerlijk Wetboek (*Dutch Civil Code*), Arts. 6:164, 6:165 (1) .... p. 146
2. Võlaõigusseadus (*Estonian Code of Obligations*), § 1052 .... p. 146

3. Гражданский кодекс Российской Федерации (*Russian Civil Code*), Arts. 1073, 1074 .... p. 147
4. Kodeks cywilny (*Polish Civil Code*), Arts. 426, 428 .... p. 147
5. Αστικός Κώδικας (*Greek Civil Code*), Arts. 916–918 .... p. 147
6. Obligacijski zakonik (*Slovenian Code of Obligations*), Art. 137 .... p. 148
7. Civillikums (*Latvian Civil Code*), Arts. 1637, 1780 .... p. 148
8. Código civil (*Portuguese Civil Code*), Arts. 488, 1366 .... p. 148
9. Codul civil (*Romanian Civil Code*), Art. 1366 .... p. 148
10. Erstatningsansvarsloven (*Danish Liability for Damages Act*), § 24a .... p. 149
11. Vahingonkorvauslaki (*Finnish Tort Liability Act*), § 2 .... p. 149
12. Skadeserstatningsloven (*Norwegian Compensatory Damages Act*), § 1–1 .... p. 149
13. Skadeståndslagen (*Swedish Tort Liability Act*), § 4 .... p. 149
14. ЗАКОН ЗА ЗАДЪЛЖЕНИЯТА И ДОГОВОРИТЕ (*Bulgarian Law on Obligations and Contracts*), Art. 47 (1) .... p. 150
15. Zákon občanský zákoník (*Czech Civil Code*), § 2920 .... p. 150
16. Zákon občanský zákoník (*Slovak Civil Code*), § 422 .... p. 150

VIII. USA

The American Law Institute, *Restatement of the Law – Torts (3rd): Liability for Physical and Emotional Harm*, Vol. 1, §§ 1 to 36, St. Paul, Minnesota: American Law Institute Publishers, 2013, § 10. Children

IX. Principles of European Tort Law

1. PETL, Arts. 4:101, 4:102 .... p. 152
2. BÉNÉDICT WINIGER/ERNST KARNER/KEN OLIPHANT (eds.), *Digest of European Tort Law, Vol. III: Misconduct*, Berlin: De Gruyter, 2018, nos. 1/30/1 ff., 8/30/1 ff. (by THOMAS KADNER GRAZIANO) .... p. 152

X. Draft Common Frame of Reference

DCFR, Art. VI. – 3:103 .... p. 154

Materials[10]

1. England and Wales

1. ALASTAIR MULLIS/KEN OLIPHANT, *Torts*, 4th ed., 2011, n° 8.2

Breach of the duty of care

8.2 The objective standard of care

In general, the law requires defendants in negligent actions to attain an objective standard of care demanded by the activity in question and declines to accept excuses that are founded on the defendant's inability to measure up to that standard. The question to be asked is, 'What level of care and skills was required by the activity which the defendant was pursuing?' rather than 'What could the particular defendant have done?' [...] The reason for this approach was clearly expressed by the great American judge and jurist Oliver Wendell Holmes (1881):

> The standards of the law are standards of general application. The law takes no account of the infinite varieties of temperament, intellect and education which make the internal character of a given act so different in different men. It does not attempt to see men as God sees them ... [W]hen men live in society, a certain average of conduct, a sacrifice of individual peculiarities going beyond a certain point, is necessary to the general welfare. If, for instance, a man is borne hasty and awkward, is always having accidents and hurting himself, or his neighbours, no doubt his congenital defects will be allowed for in the courts of Heaven, but his slips are no less troublesome to his neighbours than if they sprang from guilty neglect. His neighbours accordingly require him, at his proper peril, to come up to their standard, and the courts which they establish decline to take his personal equation into account.

[...] However, it appears that age and certain other physical characteristics will be taken into account. [...]

2. Court of Appeal (Civil Division), *Mullin v. Richards*, 06.11.1997, [1998] 1 All ER 920

TERESA JANE MULLIN v. HEIDI RICHARDS

IN THE SUPREME COURT OF JUDICATURE CCRTF 96/1359/C
IN THE COURT OF APPEAL (CIVIL DIVISION)
ON APPEAL FROM THE BIRMINGHAM COUNTY COURT
(HIS HONOUR JUDGE POTTER)

Royal Courts of Justice, Strand, London WC2

---

10 For the original language versions of the materials reproduced in this chapter, see the companion website at www.routledge.com/9781138567733.

Thursday, 6 November 1997

LORD JUSTICE HUTCHISON: On 29 February 1988 at Perry Beeches Secondary School in Birmingham two fifteen year old schoolgirls Teresa Jane Mullin and Heidi Richards who were friends and were sitting side by side at their desk were engaged in playing around, hitting each other's white plastic 30 cm rulers as though in a play sword fight, when one or other of the rulers snapped and a fragment of plastic entered Teresa's right eye with the very unhappy result that she lost all useful sight in that eye, something that must be a source, I am sure, of great distress to her and her family.

Teresa brought proceedings against Heidi [. . .]. [T]he Judge [. . .] concluded that each had been guilty of negligence, that Teresa's injury was the foreseeable result and that, accordingly, her claim against Heidi succeeded subject to a reduction of 50% for contributory negligence.

Against that decision Heidi now appeals to this court. [. . .]

The Judge therefore had to determine whether negligence had been proved [. . .]; [. . .]

I would summarise the principles that govern liability in negligence in a case such as the present as follows.[11] In order to succeed the plaintiff must show that the defendant did an act which it was reasonably foreseeable would cause injury to the plaintiff, that the relationship between the plaintiff and the defendant was such as to give rise to a duty of care, and that the act was one which caused injury to the plaintiff. In the present case, as it seems to me, no difficulty arose as to the second and third requirements because Teresa and Heidi were plainly in a sufficiently proximate relationship to give rise to a duty of care and the causation of the injury is not in issue. The argument centres on foreseeability. The test of foreseeability is an objective one; but the fact that the first defendant was at the time a 15 year old schoolgirl is not irrelevant. The question for the Judge is not whether the actions of the defendant were such as an ordinarily prudent and reasonable adult in the defendant's situation would have realised gave rise to a risk of injury, it is whether an ordinarily prudent and reasonable 15 year old schoolgirl in the defendant's situation would have realised as much. In that connection both counsel referred us to, and relied upon, the Australian decision in *McHale* v *Watson* [1966] 115 C.L.R. 199 and, in particular, the passage in the judgment of Kitto J on pages 213 and 214 [. . .]:

> "The standard of care being objective, it is no answer for him, [that is a child] any more than it is for an adult, to say that the harm he caused was due to his being abnormally slow-witted, quick-tempered, absent-minded or inexperienced. But it does not follow that he cannot rely in his defence upon a limitation upon the capacity for foresight or prudence, not as being personal to himself, but as being characteristic of humanity at his stage of development and in that sense normal. By doing so he appeals to a standard of ordinariness, to an objective and not a subjective standard."

[. . .] It is perhaps also material to have in mind the words of Salmon LJ in the case of *Gough* v *Thorne* [. . .] where the learned Lord Justice at page 1391 said this:

> "The question as to whether the Plaintiff can be said to have been guilty of contributory negligence depends on whether any ordinary child of 13 can be expected to have done

---

11 *Note by the author:* on the elements of the tort of "negligence" see above, Chapter 5, pp. 76 ff.

any more than this child did. I say "any ordinary child". I do not mean a paragon of prudence; nor do I mean a scatter-brained child; but the ordinary girl of 13."

I need say no more about that principle as to the way in which age affects the assessment of negligence because counsel are agreed upon it and, despite the fact that we have been told that there has been a good deal of controversy in other jurisdictions and that there is no direct authority in this jurisdiction, the approach in *McHale* seems to me to have the advantage of obvious, indeed irrefutable, logic. [. . .]

Applying those principles to the facts of the present case the central question to which this appeal gives rise is whether on the facts found by the Judge and in the light of the evidence before him he was entitled to conclude that an ordinary, reasonable 15 year old schoolgirl in the first defendant's position would have appreciated that by participating to the extent that she did in a play fight, involving the use of plastic rulers as though they were swords, gave rise to a risk of injury to the plaintiff of the same general kind as she sustained. [. . .]

[. . .] [T]he question of actual foreseeability (that is to say the application of that correct approach in law to the facts) raises, in my judgement, great difficulties. [T]here certainly was no evidence as to the propensity or otherwise of such rulers to break or any history of their having done so. There was evidence [. . .] that ruler fencing was commonplace. [. . .]

[. . .] I would hold no justification for attributing to the participants the foresight of any significant risk of the likelihood of injury. They had seen it done elsewhere with some frequency. They had not heard it prohibited or received any warning about it. They had not been told of any injuries occasioned by it. They were not in any sense behaving culpably. [. . .] Taking the view therefore that the learned Judge [. . .] was wrong in his view and there was no evidence on which he could come to it, I would allow the appeal and direct that judgment be entered for the first defendant. I have to say that I appreciate that this result will be disappointing to the plaintiff for whom one can have nothing but sympathy, because she has suffered a grave injury through no fault of her own. But unfortunately she has failed to establish in my view that anyone was legally responsible for that injury and, accordingly, her claim should have failed.

LADY JUSTICE BUTLER-SLOSS: I agree [. . .] and since there has been little earlier authority on the proper approach to the standard of care to be applied to a child, I would like to underline the observations of my Lord, Hutchison LJ, and rely upon two further passages in the persuasive judgment of Kitto J in the Australian case in the High Court of Australia in *McHale* v *Watson* [. . .]:

> "[. . .] [N]ormality is, for children, something different from what normality is for adults; the very concept of normality is a concept of rising levels until "years of discretion" are attained. [. . .]"

> "[. . .] in the absence of relevant statutory provision, children, like everyone else, must accept as they go about in society the risks from which ordinary care on the part of others will not suffice to save them. One such risk is that boys of twelve may behave as boys of twelve;"

and I would say that girls of 15 playing together may play as somewhat irresponsible girls of 15.

[. . .] The appeal is allowed [. . .].[12]

3. Court decisions from other Common Law jurisdictions, cited as persuasive authority: High Court of Ontario/Canada, *Tillander* v. *Gosselin*, [1967] 1 OR 203

English published case law on tortious liability of younger children is rare and the English Court of Appeal made heavy use of foreign case law in *Mullin* v. *Richards*. English legal doctrine[13] also refers to court decisions from other Common Law jurisdictions (such as the Canadian case *Tillander* v. *Gosselin*) as persuasive authority. In this case, a three-year-old child grabbed a baby, who at the time had been lying in a pram, and dragged it over a distance of 30 metres. When the parents found the baby, they discovered that it had suffered a fractured skull. A damage claim was brought against the three-year-old child. The Court held:

> "Grant, J.: In this action, the defendant's tender age at the time of the alleged assault satisfies me that he cannot be cloaked with the mental ability of the ordinary reasonable man and hence negligence cannot be imputed to him. That same condition satisfies me that he cannot be said to have acted deliberately and with intention when the injuries were inflicted upon the infant plaintiff. I do not believe that one can describe the act of a normal three-year-old child in doing injury to the baby plaintiff in this case as a voluntary act on his part. [. . .] The defendant child [. . .] would not have the mental ability at the age of three to appreciate or know the real nature of the act he was performing. A child of that age emulates or imitates the actions of those about him rather than making his own decisions. In the present case there could be no genuine intent formulated in his mind to do harm to the child plaintiff or to perform whatever act he did that caused the injury."[14]

II. Switzerland

1. The required standard of care (in general)

a) Bundesgericht/Tribunal fédéral (*Federal Supreme Court of Justice*), 27.06.1990, BGE 116 Ia 162 at 169–170

2. [. . .] c) According to Art. 41 (1) CO,[15] "any person who unlawfully causes damage to another, whether wilfully or negligently, is obliged to provide compensation". [. . .] In order to establish

---

12 Similar conclusions were reached by the Court of Appeal in *Orchard* v. *Lee*, [2009] EWCA Civ 295 at [19]; see *Digest III*, 8/12/3 with comments by K. Oliphant/V. Wilcox: "it is the idiosyncrasies of the *class* to which the defendant belongs that are relevant and not the latter's personal idiosyncrasies".
13 See e.g. C. T. Walton (general ed.), *Charlesworth & Percy on Negligence*, 13th ed., London: Sweet & Maxwell, 2014, nos. 3–63, 3–65 and fns. 165, 167.
14 See for Ireland the case: *McNamara* v. *Electricity Supply Board*, [1975] IR 1; *Digest III*, 8/14/1 with comments by E. Quill: The applicable standard is that of a reasonable child of the same level of development and understanding (in the context of contributory negligence of an 11-year-old boy who was seriously injured while playing in an electricity sub-station near his home, to which he had gained access by climbing over an inadequate fence).
15 For the text of this provision, see above, Chapter 5, p. 87.

carelessness or negligence in tort law, the individual's conduct must cause damage and be considered blameworthy enough to attach liability to the individual. The conduct in question is to be evaluated according to an objective standard, i.e. it is to be compared with what is to be expected from an ordinary law-abiding citizen acting in similar circumstances. Conduct is considered blameworthy, and therefore negligent, if it deviates from what may be considered ordinary and appropriate conduct [. . .]. The question of whether such conduct deviates from that which is considered ordinary is [. . .] the "objective aspect" of fault. The subjective aspect consists, on the other hand, of evaluating whether the person in question possessed the required capacity of judgement (*Urteilsfähigkeit/capacité de discernement*) or mind (*Zurechnungsfähigkeit/responsabilité*). An individual who does not have such capacity cannot be held liable for his or her actions. However, on the grounds of equity, the Court may still order an individual to pay full or partial compensation for the damage he or she has caused even if he or she does not possess the required capacity of judgement (*Urteilsfähigkeit*) within the meaning of Art. 54 (1) CO.

b) Christoph Müller, *La responsabilité civile extracontractuelle (Extra-contractual liability)*, 2013, nos. 242–244

242 An objective assessment. An individual's conduct is to be assessed according to an objective standard, that of the reasonable and prudent person. Purely subjective notions such as tiredness, stress, absent-mindedness, family and work problems, etc. are not to be taken into account. The individual's intellectual capacity and professional skills (e.g. any prior training) shall also be disregarded.

243 Criticism. Legal scholars often criticise this objective assessment of fault. Such an approach does indeed make it difficult to differentiate between wrongfulness (*illicéité, Rechtswidrigkeit*) and fault, since both notions are assessed objectively based on how the reasonable and prudent person would have acted. An objective standard thus leads, it is argued, to the same breach of an obligation being examined twice (once in order to establish wrongfulness and again to establish fault). In addition, it has been criticised that an individual who is held liable under fault-based liability may not even have been at fault were a subjective standard applied instead; he would thus in fact be held strictly liable; this is most prevalent where an action is brought against an individual whose intellectual capacity is lower than that of the average person. [. . .] The majority view, however, is that the objective standard should be retained, primarily because it protects the interests of the victim and facilitates claims in (extra-contractual) civil liability.

244. An assessment based on the facts. The conduct of the individual in question is then to be evaluated in response to the facts of the case; for this we must compare the conduct with a reasonable and prudent person with the same characteristics (e.g. age, sex, profession, dangerousness of the activity, etc.) as the defendant. Thus, the court must identify how the reasonable and prudent person would have acted, considering the circumstances of time and place under which the individual acted (or failed to act).

2. Liability of minors (in particular)

a) Code civil/Zivilgesetzbuch (*Civil Code*)

> **Art. 16. Discernement.** Toute personne qui n'est pas privée de la faculté d'agir raisonnablement en raison de son jeune âge, de déficience mentale, de troubles psychiques,

d'ivresse ou d'autres causes semblables est capable de discernement au sens de la présente loi.

Art. 18. Absence de discernement. Les actes de celui qui est incapable de discernement n'ont pas d'effet juridique; demeurent réservées les exceptions prévues par la loi.

Art. 19. Personnes capables de discernement [...]. Principe. [...] 3. Ils sont responsables du dommage causé par leurs actes illicites.

Translation

Art. 16. Capacity of judgement. A person is capable of judgement within the meaning of the law if he or she does not lack the capacity to act rationally by virtue of being under age or because of a mental disability, mental disorder, intoxication, or similar circumstances.

Art. 18. Lack of capacity of judgement. A person who does not possess capacity of judgement cannot create legal effects by his or her actions, unless the law provides otherwise.

Art. 19. Persons capable of judgement [...]. Principle. [...] 3. They are liable in damages for wrongful acts.

b) Code des obligations/Obligationenrecht (Code of Obligations)

Art. 54. Responsabilité des personnes incapables de discernement. 1. Si l'équité l'exige, le juge peut condamner une personne même incapable de discernement à la réparation totale ou partielle du dommage qu'elle a causé. [...]

Translation

Art. 54. Liability of persons incapable of judgement. 1. On the grounds of equity, the court may order a person to provide full or partial compensation for damage even if he or she does not possess the required capacity of judgement. [...]

c) Tribunal fédéral/Bundesgericht (Federal Supreme Court of Justice), 21.01.1964 (Zufferey c. Kull), ATF 90 II 9

Extract from the judgment of the 1st Civil chamber, dated 21.01.1964: Zufferey v. O. Kull and Partners

A. – a) In May 1954, the public limited company *L'Energie de l'Ouest-Suisse* (Western Swiss Energy) hired a specialist Zurich-based partnership, O. Kull and Partners, to construct a section of high-voltage line through Chandolin, Riddes and Morgins. For this purpose, pylon no. 41 was erected [...] in close proximity to a public footpath. 44 metres high, weighing 12 tonnes, and standing on four concrete foundations [. . .], the pylon was fixed in place by huge nuts, screws and washers. The completion of this task remained on hold for more than five months, during which time anyone could loosen the screws by hand, even after the final adjustment (sealing) of the pylon. [. . .]

b) Pierre Zufferey, born on 20th November 1942, started at St. Maurice School in 1954. He turned out to be a mediocre student [. . .], but his development was average. In January 1955, a [member of the school's teaching staff] organised a walk with some of the pupils, one of whom was Pierre Zufferey [then aged 12]. [The boy was lingering] around pylon no. 41 and, within the space of ten minutes and without the use of any tools or rocks, managed to unscrew three of the four foundations. [. . .]

The following night, a sudden gust of wind violently toppled the pylon. It was completely destroyed.

B. – [. . .] Kull and Partners filed an action against Zufferey for the damage caused [. . .].

[. . .] The Civil Court for the Canton of Vaud ordered Pierre Zufferey to pay damages equivalent to 50% of the losses incurred [considering the contributory negligence of the plaintiff, who should have fixed the screws in such a manner that a child could not have loosened them by hand].

C. – Zufferey requests that the Federal Court overturn this ruling and dismiss the claim [. . .].

Legal considerations:

3. [. . .] The child shall be liable for harm caused by his or her unlawful acts when he or she is capable of judgement (*capable de discernement*) (Art. 19 (3) CC). Unlike other jurisdictions, Swiss law does not envisage a minimum age for liability. A person is deemed to have the capacity to act rationally (Art. 16 CC) when he or she is able to realise the significance of his or her actions and is perfectly capable of ignoring those who wish to influence his or her behaviour. This capacity is to be assessed on a case-by-case basis. The judge must categorically determine for any given action [. . .] whether he or she had this capacity at the moment that he carried out the act which gave rise to the claim. [. . .] The capacity of judgement (*capacité de discernement*) is generally presumed; any person who claims to lack capacity must prove it. Nevertheless, in practice the younger the child is, the weaker this presumption will be up to a point where there is eventually almost no presumption whatsoever. [. . .]

4. On 27th January 1955, the appellant was aged twelve and two months. He is responsible for his unlawful act if he understood that day the dangerous nature of his behaviour. It is not necessary that he foresaw all the possible consequences. It merely suffices that he was aware that his actions could compromise the strength and support of the pylon and hence create a danger. The Cantonal Court applied this line of reasoning correctly [. . .] and set out the problem very well. [. . .] [T]he appellant was indeed found to be of a normal maturity for his age [. . .]. In the Court's opinion, a boy of his age knew, without experience in mechanical studies, what a nut and screw were, and that the latter joins two sections in a way that stops them from separating; he should know this in particular from playing with his toys and bicycle. The size of the nuts, furthermore, ought to have brought to his attention the importance of their function. [. . .] [T]he judges of previous instance (correctly) interpreted the Civil Code in holding that the appellant possessed the required capacity of discernment (*capacité de discernement*). [. . .]

6. By virtue of Art. 44 (1) CO,[16] the judge can reduce or even preclude the award in damages when the actions of the injured party have contributed to bringing about the harm or exacerbating it. In this case, the fault committed by the injured party is severe, especially compared with that of the appellant. [. . .]

7. [. . .] [With regard to the seriousness of Pierre Zufferey's fault] the Federal Court [. . .] shall not apportion compensation beyond a sixth of the loss [. . .].

For these reasons, the Federal Supreme Court

Partially accepts the appeal, amending the disputed ruling accordingly, and orders the defendant and appellant to pay the plaintiff [. . .] the sum of 5,000 Swiss francs[17] [. . .]

d) Tribunal fédéral/Bundesgericht (*Federal Supreme Court of Justice*), 11.07.1978 (*Maillard c. Guye et Gutknecht*), ATF 104 II 184

On 4th March 1972, three nine-year old children – Stéphane Guye, André Maillard and Jean-Fred Gutknecht – were playing with a bow, cobbled together with a stick and some string, and an arrow made out of a small flagstaff. Their game involved taking turns at shooting one of the participants with the arrow who, once hit, would then take control of the bow and shoot. This is how Maillard, who had been hit by Gutknecht, came into possession of the bow. Maillard subsequently aimed at Guye, who ran off. When he had retreated by roughly 3 metres, Guye stopped and turned around. At this moment, Maillard's sped arrow flashed into his right eye. He permanently lost sight in this eye. [. . .]

Stéphane Guye has brought proceedings against André Maillard claiming 105,573 Swiss francs with interest, plus an additional 20,000 for his non-material harm [. . .].

Legal considerations:

2. [. . .] All three being nine years old, the Guye, Maillard and Gutknecht children ought to have been aware of the associated risks (see ATF 100 II 332 ss., admitting that 9 year old children playing with sparklers could incur liability in tort for the damage which they had caused; ATF 70 II 136 ss., concerning the liability of a 10 year old child who was cutting wood with an axe and injured a young girl). Their game was all the more dangerous given that they were not aiming at a target, but instead looking to hit one of their friends. Even if the game's rules had stated that the player must not shoot too high or too close, they had enough awareness to realise that this rule had a chance of being lost in the excitement of the game and that it would not be enough to prevent an accident from happening.

By participating in an activity where they could, and should, have recognised the dangers involved, the three children committed a joint act of negligence, the significance of which

---

16 Art. 44 (1) CO provides: "*Where the injured party consented to the action which caused the loss or damage, or circumstances attributable to him helped give rise to or aggravated the loss or damage, or otherwise worsened the position of the liable party, the court may reduce the amount of compensation or even dispense with it entirely*".

17 Today worth around CHF 18,000.

is admittedly somewhat mitigated by virtue of their young age, but one which nevertheless establishes their liability [. . .].

3. Liability in equity

Tribunal fédéral/Bundesgericht (*Federal Supreme Court of Justice*), **06.12.1977 (A. c. hoirs X.), ATF 103 II 330**

4. [. . .] aa) On grounds of equity, under Art. 54 (1) CO the Court may order an individual to pay complete or partial compensation for any damage caused, even if he or she does not possess the required capacity of judgement (*capacité de discernement*). This provision establishes strict liability in response to the risks that such individuals pose to third parties; the judge will decide on the grounds of equity if, and to what extent, this individual should be ordered to pay compensation for the damage caused by his or her actions, whether the claim is contractual or tortious (ATF 102 II 230). It is especially important to take into account the financial situation of the two parties at the time of the judgment (ATF 102 II 231 considered 3b and citations), and whether the damage suffered by the injured party is insured, wholly or partially, by a third party (ATF 71 II 231s. 6).

III. Germany

1. The required standard of care (in general)

a) Bürgerliches Gesetzbuch, BGB (*Civil Code*)

> § 276. **Verantwortlichkeit des Schuldners.** (1) Der Schuldner hat Vorsatz und Fahrlässigkeit zu vertreten [. . .].
> (2) Fahrlässig handelt, wer die im Verkehr erforderliche Sorgfalt außer Acht lässt. [. . .]

Translation

> *§ 276. **Responsibility of the obligor.** (1) The debtor is responsible for intention and negligence [. . .].*
> *(2) A person acts negligently if he or she fails to exercise reasonable care. [. . .]*

b) JOSEF ESSER/HANS-LEO WEYERS, Schuldrecht, Band II, Besonderer Teil, Teilband 2: Gesetzliche Schuldverhältnisse (*Law of Obligations, Vol. II, Special Part, 2. Legal Obligations*), 8th ed., 2000, § 55 III

III. Fault [. . .]

Fault. § 823 (1) BGB requires intentional or negligent conduct in order to establish liability. Intent and negligence were considered [. . .] the central preconditions for establishing fault, leading naturally to an individual's liability. This is why this system was called "liability for fault" – however not entirely consistently. The reason for the inconsistency is that if we look at the second sentence of § 276 (1), whereby an individual is obliged to exercise "objective" reasonable care, then it cannot be said as a result that liability always actually relies on the individual's personal fault.

[...] [The] question then arises: is the individual's personal fault *ever* required to establish liability? Except for a [very limited number of] specific instances, the answer is *no*: at no point in the BGB (i.e. the Civil Code), is the individual's actual blameworthiness mentioned as a necessary requirement of liability. The resulting discrepancy between civil and criminal law should nevertheless not be overstated. In cases where at first glance it seems doubtful whether an individual's behaviour is indeed blameworthy, in most instances this will be a situation in which *no-one* in that person's place could have acted any differently (cases of overwhelming fatigue not otherwise due to fault, "shock-related conduct", etc.); the actual circumstances shall then already be taken into account when determining the objective standard of care that is required within the wording of § 276 [...] of the BGB.

2. Liability of minors (in particular)

a) Bürgerliches Gesetzbuch, BGB (*Civil Code*)

> § 828. Minderjährige. (1) Wer nicht das siebente Lebensjahr vollendet hat, ist für einen Schaden, den er einem anderen zufügt, nicht verantwortlich.
> (2) Wer das siebente, aber nicht das zehnte Lebensjahr vollendet hat, ist für den Schaden, den er bei einem Unfall mit einem Kraftfahrzeug, einer Schienenbahn oder einer Schwebebahn einem anderen zufügt, nicht verantwortlich. Dies gilt nicht, wenn er die Verletzung vorsätzlich herbeigeführt hat.
> (3) Wer das 18. Lebensjahr noch nicht vollendet hat, ist, sofern seine Verantwortlichkeit nicht nach Absatz 1 oder 2 ausgeschlossen ist, für den Schaden, den er einem anderen zufügt, nicht verantwortlich, wenn er bei der Begehung der schädigenden Handlung nicht die zur Erkenntnis der Verantwortlichkeit erforderliche Einsicht hat.
>
> § 829. Ersatzpflicht aus Billigkeitsgründen. Wer [...] für einen von ihm verursachten Schaden auf Grund [des §] 828 nicht verantwortlich ist, hat gleichwohl, sofern der Ersatz des Schadens nicht von einem aufsichtspflichtigen Dritten erlangt werden kann,[18] den Schaden insoweit zu ersetzen, als die Billigkeit nach den Umständen, insbesondere nach den Verhältnissen der Beteiligten, eine Schadloshaltung erfordert und ihm nicht die Mittel entzogen werden, deren er zum angemessenen Unterhalt [...] bedarf.

Translation

> *§ 828. Minors. (1) Persons below the age of 7 are not responsible for loss they inflict on others.*
> *(2) Persons who have reached the age of 7, but have not yet reached the age of 10, are not liable for loss they inflict on others in an accident involving a motor vehicle, a railway or a cableway. This does not apply where the loss was inflicted intentionally.*

---

18 Zur Haftung von Eltern für Schäden, die von ihren Kindern verursacht wurden, siehe unten, Kapitel 13.

(3) A person who has not yet reached the age of 18 is, to the extent that his or her responsibility is not excluded under subsection (1) or (2), not responsible for damage he or she inflicts on others if, when committing the damaging act, he or she does not have the insight required to recognise his or her responsibility.

§ 829. Duty to compensate loss for equitable reasons. *Whosoever bears no responsibility for loss caused [. . .] because of the rule in § [. . .] 828, nonetheless has to compensate the loss – unless compensation can be obtained from a third person who was under a duty to supervise*[19]*– to the extent that equity requires such compensation under the circumstances, having regard in particular to the entirety of the circumstances of the parties, provided he or she is not deprived of the means which he or she requires for reasonable subsistence [. . .].*

b) Bundesgerichtshof, BGH (*Federal Supreme Court of Justice*), 28.02.1984, NJW 1984, 1958

Facts

[. . .] On 18th December 1977, a barn belonging to [A, a farmer] burnt down. The fire was caused by a candle which had been lit there jointly by the defendants and had ignited a pile of hay. The defendants, both aged 10 at the time, were classmates. They had been playing in the hayloft of the barn. Since it was dark inside they then looked to add some light. With this in mind, they went away and bought [. . .] some candles; another boy offered them a box of matches. They hid these items in the loft and the first defendant's parents' garage respectively. On 18th December, they came back to the barn, this time attempting to fix a lit candle to one of the beams, using candle wax to stick it down. This did not work since the candle kept falling down, eventually setting fire to some loose hay lying on the barn floor. The defendants' efforts to beat out and smother the flames were unsuccessful, and the whole barn was consumed in the fire. There was also agricultural machinery, together with a harvester and other farming equipment in the barn. [. . .] Both defendants have liability insurance. [. . .]

Grounds for the decision

[. . .] II. [. . .] The court of appeal [i.e. the lower court] correctly found that both defendants were legally responsible in tort liability (§ 828 [3] BGB).

a) According to well-established case law, it is sufficient for the individual claimed to be liable to have a general understanding that his conduct may lead to some kind of danger. Conversely, a judge does not need to examine whether the minor in question was able to appreciate the full legal and economic consequences of his behaviour [. . .]. Concerning legal liability, this Court maintains the view [. . .], in line with the wording of § 828 [3] BGB, that liability depends solely upon whether the young person possesses the required capacity of judgement (*capacité de discernement*), i.e. whether the individual is old enough to appreciate the dangers inherent to his actions and to acknowledge that

---

[19] For the liability of parents for damage done by their children, see below, Chapter 13.

he may be responsible for any consequences stemming from them; it is not a question of whether the young person in question is able to act in accordance with that capacity. The obligation to pay damages under civil liability law is subject to criteria that are distinctly different from those applied in criminal law [. . .]. If a minor, given his particular state of development, possesses the required capacity of judgement (*capacité de discernement*) – a capacity which the law presumes young people to have from the age of seven – then he shall be fully liable in so far as he is also at fault within the meaning of § 276 BGB. On the other hand, if he can demonstrate that at the time of the act he lacked the required capacity of judgement (*capacité de discernement*), he does not need [. . .] to answer for the consequences of his act. Unlike criminal law, diminished responsibility is not a concept which the civil law recognises. In civil law a minor is thus much more likely to be found liable for the damage he has caused than in criminal law. In effect, this is because in civil liability it is much more appropriate to hold all persons equally accountable for their actions [. . .]. The obligation to compensate a loss should not depend upon whether the person causing the harm is capable of complying with the required standard. In this respect the purpose of liability law is that the risk of harm shall not be borne by the party who suffered the harm.

b) The court of appeal came to the conclusion, after consultation with relevant experts, that [. . .] given the defendants' stage of development, they were still able to appreciate that they were at fault and that they had to take responsibility for their actions. They must have been aware that handling lit candles in a barn could be dangerous. Therefore, the legal presumption for capacity of judgement (*capacité de discernement*) as prescribed under § 828 [3] BGB has not been rebutted. It is hereby held that the present Court does not detect an error in the application of the law.

2. Conversely, the reasoning by which the court of appeal denied negligence on the part of the defendants (in invoking § 276 BGB) cannot be said to be free from error.

a) When examining whether an act committed by a minor is a negligent one, the court of appeal was indeed correct to start from the premise that when assessing the intellectual maturity of a child it is important to compare the child in question with a child of the same age-group (*Gruppenfahrlässigkeit*, or "category-based liability"). [. . .]

b) The court of appeal's findings of fact do not leave any doubt as to the capacity of judgement (*capacité de discernement*) of the defendants – the single deciding factor here – and hence it can be said with certainty that their conduct amounted to negligence. Even though the court of appeal found that the mental development of both minors was equivalent to that of the average eight year old children, it still follows that the Court made no legal error in concluding that they possessed the required capacity of judgement (*capacité de discernement*), as outlined above. From a perspective of civil liability law the only relevant factor is whether it is possible for the average child of this age-group to demonstrate the requisite degree of care or whether their immaturity precludes their taking the necessary precautions to prevent the danger arising. The tendency of a child of this age to get caught up in the excitement of a game, or indeed the child's compulsion to explore and experiment [. . .] might prohibit him from achieving such a standard. The court of appeal clearly gave weight to this fact when it [. . .] remarked that during the course of their playing the defendants were so caught up in their idea to install and light candles in order to illuminate the hayloft that they had forgotten, or suppressed, all consideration of the inherent danger in what they were doing.

[. . .] The only legally relevant question [. . .] is whether, after they had gone ahead with planning and preparing to light up their hayloft – something they knew to be dangerous and forbidden – they might, taking into account the level of maturity to be expected of typical children of their age, have avoided the danger by abandoning the game to light up the barn at an early stage. This Court [i.e. the BGH] is justified in drawing from its own expertise in order to conclude that this is an act that can be expected of eight-year-olds. Their urge to play is not so overwhelming from the outset that once – like these defendants – they have got hold of the idea of lighting candles in a hayloft, all caution is then thrown to the wind. [. . .]

For these reasons the plaintiff's claim fully succeeds. [. . .]

c) Bundesgerichtshof, BGH (*Federal Supreme Court of Justice*), 10.03.1970, NJW 1970, 1038

When deciding whether a young person has been negligent, [. . .] the issue is not one of personal blameworthiness, but rather what degree of care would be (objectively) expected of a young person in his age-group. With this limitation in mind, the court must assess what represents typical conduct for a young person.

3. Liability in equity

Bundesgerichtshof, BGH (*Federal Supreme Court of Justice*), 24.04.1979, NJW 1979, 2096

On 22nd July 1974, the plaintiff – then aged four – was playing at a campsite in Denmark. He suffered an injury when the defendant, aged six-and-three-quarters, threw a stick about 50 cm long and 2–3 cm thick in his direction. The stick flew into his eye and he lost his sight in it. [. . .]

The plaintiff [. . .] is relying on § 829 BGB to sue the defendant for an appropriate award of damages for his injury. The defendant is insured against liability by his father under a family liability policy. [. . .]

Grounds for the decision

I. 1. [. . .] For a claim to be afforded on the basis of § 829 BGB, an appreciation of all the surrounding circumstances [must] be such that the interests of justice require that the victim be compensated [. . .]. The invocation of this provision is always subject to the [requirement] of an "economic imbalance": i.e. the person alleged to be liable for the damage must be considerably wealthier than the victim. [. . .]

In the present case [. . .] there is [. . .] no such indication of an "economic imbalance". The defendant's father is an auditor by profession; the plaintiff's father a businessman. The defendant, who has one sister, does not possess any assets at present. His parents own a family house which is subject to a mortgage.

2. When carrying out an examination of the financial situation of each party, the court of appeal expressed the view that the judge may take into account the fact that the injurer has liability insurance as a factor – among others – in order to establish this former's liability in equity.

a) [. . .] This Court has consistently noted that the presence of cover by [non-compulsory] liability insurance is not to be taken into account when it comes to deciding *whether* the defendant is liable, but may only have an influence on the amount that is due once liability is established [. . .].[20]

b) [. . .] In the present case, equity does not "require" the defendant to pay compensation. It may indeed be true that the consequences of the [plaintiff's] injury are serious but this, undoubtedly, is not enough in and of itself to afford a claim under § 829 BGB on the mere basis of the existence of insurance cover. Such a factor might at most be taken into account if the attack and its effects are proved to be so drastic that they justified invocation of that provision on an exceptional basis [. . .]. However, this was not the case here. According to the findings of the court of appeal, the injury occurred while the children were playing at a campsite when the defendant threw a stick at the plaintiff. Should a risk relating to a game of this sort indeed materialise, it is possible to protect against the resulting harm by contracting coverage through general accident (i.e. first party) insurance. [. . .] Liability for an economically weaker victim and the payment of damages under § 829 BGB is only required when the person causing the damage possesses substantial assets in his own right.

As a result the plaintiff's claim must be rejected [. . .].

II. The plaintiff has further requested before the lower court that the Court declares that the defendant be obliged to pay him a suitable amount in compensation for the child's pain and suffering in the future, if and in so far as the interests of justice then demand it.

[. . .] 2. [. . .] This declaratory claim has been permitted as far as it falls within the requirements of § 829 BGB, since it cannot be ruled out that someday the defendant may come into the possession of substantial assets (e.g. from inheritance, marriage, donation, capital gains, etc., or indeed as a result of professional earnings) which would make it fair that he should then pay the plaintiff damages, if and in so far as equity at that time requires it. [. . .]

---

20 *Note by the author*: in other related judgments, it has also been held that "it is necessary to bear in mind the purpose of liability insurance, which is aimed primarily at *protecting the interests of the insured faced with a claim*, and not at *creating liability in its own right*". See BGH (*Federal Supreme Court of Justice*) 11.10.1994, BGHZ 127, 186 (191), referring to BGH 18.12.1979, BGHZ 76, 279 (283) (emphasis added). – These principles do *not* apply with respect to mandatory liability insurance, see BGH 11.10.1994, BHGZ 127, 186: "[. . .] III. [. . .] 2. [. . .] bb) These restrictions [derived from the 1979 decision on the relevance of non-compulsory insurance] cannot be [. . .] applied to [. . .] mandatory motor insurance. The purpose of the latter is primarily to protect the interests of the injured party [. . .] and to make sure that victims of road accidents receive compensation. Injured parties should be offered the most comprehensive protection possible in any given circumstance, including cases where the person responsible for their injury does not have the means to pay compensation. [. . .] The unique status of motor insurance, by which all road users are required by law to be covered, also means that when interpreting § 829 BGB the court is justified in taking the existence of insurance into account. The fact that this involves a breach of the principle of separation (*Trennungsprinzip*), under which the insurer's liability arises from the liability of the insured and not vice versa, is not of great importance here. In this situation, for a claim to be made under § 829 BGB, the purpose of compulsory motor insurance – i.e. to give protection to victims of road accidents – must override such a principle. [. . .]".

IV. Austria

1. The required standard of care (in general)

a) Allgemeines bürgerliches Gesetzbuch, ABGB (*General Civil Code*)

> **Quellen der Beschädigung.**
> § 1294. Der Schade entspringt entweder aus einer widerrechtlichen Handlung, oder Unterlassung eines anderen; oder aus einem Zufall. Die widerrechtliche Beschädigung wird entweder willkürlich, oder unwillkürlich zugefügt. Die willkürliche Beschädigung aber gründet sich teils in einer bösen Absicht, wenn der Schade mit Wissen und Willen; teils in einem Versehen, wenn er aus schuldbarer Unwissenheit, oder aus Mangel der gehörigen Aufmerksamkeit, oder des gehörigen Fleißes verursacht worden ist. Beides wird ein Verschulden genannt.
>
> **Von der Verbindlichkeit zum Schadensersatz: 1) Vom Schaden aus Verschulden.**
> § 1295. (1) Jedermann ist berechtigt, vom Beschädiger den Ersatz des Schadens, welchen dieser ihm aus Verschulden zugefügt hat, zu fordern; der Schade mag durch Übertretung einer Vertragspflicht oder ohne Beziehung auf einen Vertrag verursacht worden sein. [...]
>
> § 1297. Es wird aber auch vermutet, dass jeder welcher den Verstandesgebrauch besitzt, eines solchen Grades des Fleißes und der Aufmerksamkeit fähig sei, welcher bei gewöhnlichen Fähigkeiten angewendet werden kann. Wer bei Handlungen, woraus eine Verkürzung der Rechte eines Anderen entsteht, diesen Grad des Fleißes oder der Aufmerksamkeit unterlässt, macht sich eines Versehens schuldig.
>
> **3) aus einer schuldlosen oder unwillkürlichen Handlung.**
> § 1306. Den Schaden, welchen jemand ohne Verschulden oder durch eine unwillkürliche Handlung verursacht hat, ist er in der Regel zu ersetzen nicht schuldig.

Translation

> *Sources of damage.*
> *§ 1294. Damage arises either from another person's unlawful act or omission or from pure coincidence. Unlawfully inflicted damage is caused either voluntarily or involuntarily. The voluntary infliction of damage is based either on malicious intent, if the damage is caused knowingly and willingly; or on negligence, if the damage was caused by culpable ignorance, or by a lack of proper care or diligence. Both are to be termed fault.*
>
> *On the liability to compensate: 1) On Damage caused by fault.*
> *§ 1295. (1) Every person is entitled to claim compensation from the wrongdoer for the damage the latter has culpably inflicted upon him or her; the damage may have been caused by the breach of a contractual duty or independently of any contract. [...]*

§ 1297. It is also presumed that every person of sound mind is capable of exerting the degree of diligence and care that can be applied by a normally competent person. Whosoever fails to attain this degree of diligence and care in the course of acts causing prejudice to another person's rights is guilty of negligence.

3) resulting from an act without fault or through an involuntary act.
§ 1306. A person is generally not liable for the damage he or she has caused without fault or through an involuntary act.

b) HELMUT KOZIOL, *Basic Questions of Tort Law from a Germanic Perspective*, 2012, nos. 6/81–6/83

B. Subjective or objective assessment of fault?

1. The principle of subjective assessment

6/81 According to § 1294 ABGB there is negligence if the perpetrator acted without exercising due care and diligence.

The finding that the perpetrator has acted negligently encompasses in its original meaning the accusation that there has been *blameworthy will*. Such an accusation can only be levelled against the specific perpetrator in the event that he had exercised his will duly and properly, he would have recognised that he was acting dangerously and wrongfully and also provided it would have been possible for him to act differently. Therefore, fault is contingent upon a *subjective* assessment of blameworthy will. Hence, in principle a subjective standard of assessment must also be applied: it is necessary to examine whether the specific perpetrator on the basis of his personal abilities would have been able to recognise the occurrence of the damage and the wrongfulness and been able to act accordingly. Only if his individual abilities would have been adequate to avoid the damage, can a *personal accusation of blameworthy will* be levelled; and only then can fault in the strict sense be affirmed.

6/82 With respect to the *degree of care and diligence*, however, the law requires that the assessment standard be objective: § 1294 ABGB stipulates that due diligence and care must be exercised. Likewise § 1297 ABGB provides that anyone who does not exercise the degree of diligence and care that can be exercised by someone with ordinary abilities is guilty. [. . .]

6/83 A widely held opinion, prevailing nowadays in Germany and predominantly advocated in Switzerland, takes the view that in relation to the subjective abilities of a person, the normative carelessness standard must always be *objective*. According to this view, it is not the individual abilities of the person which are decisive but rather the average abilities and knowledge typical for such a group of persons. However, this departs from the basis for personal culpability in respect of blameworthy will and attaches liability to an objectively established lack of understanding or lack of abilities:

Someone equipped by nature with below average abilities is thus subject to a type of strict liability – albeit contingent upon objectively deficient conduct, such liability being based on the increased dangerousness emanating from a person not adequately equipped with ability.

Ultimately this leads – at least insofar as the participation in general interactions necessary for an existence compatible with human dignity is concerned – to liability for existing, which will affect such a person particularly seriously given that he is already disadvantaged. [. . .]

c) Peter Apathy/Andreas Rieder, *Bürgerliches Recht, Band III, Schuldrecht, Besonderer Teil (Civil Law, Volume III, Law of Obligations, Special Part)*, 4th ed., 2010

13/31   Fault requires (subjectively) **blameful individual conduct** that not only the reasonable man, but also the *individual who caused the harm*, could and should have prevented. [. . .]

13/34   Negligence arises where an individual can be blamed for not having adhered to the standards that are [. . .] objectively required of him (§ 1297). [. . .] An objective standard is applied so that the individual at fault may not rely upon the argument that the conduct was fully in line with his or her everyday behaviour regarding his own affairs. However, fault must be assessed in line with the personal skillset of the individual. If the individual in question is not capable of achieving or maintaining such a standard, then he or she shall not be held liable for any consequences stemming from the conduct. Since, according to § 1297 1st sent., it is assumed that "every person of sound mind is capable of exerting the degree of diligence and care that can be applied by a normally competent person", the burden of proof is to be shifted onto the individual to prove that he or she did not subjectively have the capacity required to comply with the objective standard of care expected, e.g. because of a temporary disturbance of consciousness.

Experts have to act according to the skills required of the average practitioner in the relevant field, without being able to exonerate themselves for lack of technical knowledge. They are however free to prove that it was impossible for them to conform to the reasonable standard of care of their profession, e.g. because of a subjective disturbance of consciousness (SZ 37/157).

d) Oberster Gerichtshof, OGH (*Supreme Court of Justice*), 23.03.1976, 5 Ob 536/76, SZ 49/47 (Leitsatz/*basic principle*)

Whoever [. . .] shall, knowingly or by negligence, try his or her hand at an activity which is generally carried out by an expert, and which clearly poses dangers for a non-professional without the appropriate skillset (in this particular case, connecting a washing machine to a water pipe), shall be liable to compensate for any damage he or she causes.[21]

---

21 *Note by the author*: so-called *Übernahmeverschulden* (negligence for engaging in an activity without adequate skills).

2. Liability of children (in particular)

a) Allgemeines bürgerliches Gesetzbuch, ABGB (*General Civil Code*)

§ 21. (1) Minderjährige und Personen, die aus einem anderen Grund als dem ihrer Minderjährigkeit alle oder einzelne ihrer Angelegenheiten selbst gehörig zu besorgen nicht vermögen, stehen unter dem besonderen Schutz der Gesetze.
(2) Minderjährige sind Personen, die das achtzehnte Lebensjahr noch nicht vollendet haben; haben sie das vierzehnte Lebensjahr noch nicht vollendet, so sind sie unmündig.

§ 176. Soweit einem minderjährigen Kind nicht bereits früher ein Verschulden zugerechnet werden kann (§ 1310), wird es mit der Erreichung der Mündigkeit nach den schadensersatzrechtlichen Bestimmungen verschuldensfähig.

§ 1310. Kann der Beschädigte auf solche Art den Ersatz nicht erhalten; so soll der Richter mit Erwägung des Umstandes, ob dem Beschädiger, ungeachtet er gewöhnlich seines Verstandes nicht mächtig ist, in dem bestimmten Falle nicht dennoch ein Verschulden zur Last liege; [. . .]; oder endlich, mit Rücksicht auf das Vermögen des Beschädigers und des Beschädigten; auf den ganzen Ersatz, oder doch einen billigen Theil desselben erkennen.

Translation

§ 21. (1) Minors and persons who, for reasons other than their age, are unable to take proper care of their affairs, are to benefit from special protection under the law.
(2) Minors are persons who have not yet reached 18 years of age; where such minors are under 14 years old, they are held to have not yet attained the age of discretion.

§ 176. If a minor is not able to be attributed with fault on the basis of other provisions (§1310), it shall be attributed with fault once it reaches the age of discretion.

§ 1310. If the person harmed cannot obtain compensation in such a manner, the judge shall award complete compensation, or an equitable part thereof, taking [firstly] into account whether some fault can be imputed to the injurer under the particular circumstances, notwithstanding the fact of him normally not having capacity; [. . .]; or, [thirdly and] lastly, the financial means of the injurer and of the person harmed.

b) Oberster Gerichtshof, OGH (*Supreme Court of Justice*), 20.10.1988, 7 Ob 36/88

Grounds for the decision

[The defendant, then aged 6 ½, set fire to an inn while playing with a friend of the same age. The fire destroyed the top floor and the roof of the ground floor.] The defendant, an ordinary child with standard cognitive ability for his age, had found matches on his elder sister's bedside table which he subsequently tested on a sheet of paper. The flames then set fire to the bedroom curtains. The [defendant] had never shown any particular interest in fire or matches in the past. He had never indicated that he wanted to play with fire nor did he tend to approach lit fires.

Legal considerations

According to § [176] of the General Civil Code (ABGB), for a child to commit an act of negligence the court must have regard to his or her capacity and age, which must in principle be at least 14 according to § 21 (2) ABGB. Children are, however, not completely unaccountable for their faults. Rather, according to § 1310 ABGB, it is still necessary for the court in the given case to assess whether the child was somehow at fault in his or her actions. If so, the boy will be held liable for the damage he caused. However, this concept of fault-based liability under § 1310 ABGB, much like its counterpart, liability without fault, only comes into play if it is not possible to request compensation from the child's parents or legal guardian (§ 1309 ABGB); their liability is therefore only subsidiary (Koziol, Österreichisches Haftpflichtrecht, 2 II 309).[22]

[. . .] In the present case, it was not possible to obtain compensation from the child's parents for a breach of their duty of supervision [. . .]. On the other hand, given that we usually consider children under 14 years of age to be immune from liability for their acts, their liability in negligence is an exception (EvBl. 1988–1995). The liability of a minor – in particular one under 7 years of age – within the framework of § 1310 ABGB is to be examined by taking into account his or her intellectual capacity and how he or she acted in the circumstances (ZVR 1983/215, EFSlg. 31.515, and more). The younger the child is, the less likely the court is to rule that he or she had the sufficient intellectual capacity in the circumstances; it is very rarely the case that a child under 7 is to be held liable for his or her acts (Reischauer in Rummel, ABGB, para. 4 of § 1310).

In a Supreme Court decision (7 Ob 763/81; EFSlg. 38.579), the Court ruled that it could not be expected from a child below school age (here the child was not yet six at the time of the act) to have any real awareness of the dangers posed by fires. The tendency of children to copy the actions of others must not be disregarded; it is a perfectly normal behaviour for a child to do things which might not be permitted.

In a Supreme Court decision (7 Ob 502/82; RZ 1982 to 1967), the Court argued that it can be assumed that an ordinary child of six-and-a-half is able to understand the basic dangers of playing with matches, but that to expect a child to recognise that throwing a lit match out of a parked car could cause a fire in its engine compartment was beyond the understanding of a child of that age.

In a decision of the Court (6 Ob 579/78; EFSlg 31.516), a child of eight who set fire to a bucket of flammable liquid was not held liable since it could not be expected from him to understand that such conduct represented a threat to people and property.

It may indeed be the case that a child, such as the defendant, who is scarcely six-and-a-half years old and does not yet attend school, still has the basic understanding that playing with matches is "dangerous". Nevertheless, children will be children, and it is perfectly natural

---

22 For the liability of parents for damage done by their children, see below, Chapter 13.

for a child of this age to have an irresistible urge to play, being unaware of the potential consequences of what he or she is doing despite any warning from adults (EvBl. 1988/95); moreover, it may not be excluded that the child might be acting against his or her better judgement (EFSlg. 36.170 und EvBl. 1988/95) and, for that reason, the child may not comprehend that his or her conduct in the circumstances may damage property or put it at risk (Reischauer, ibid para. 3).

In the case of the defendant, his age meant that he was not in the position to understand the dangers which could result from setting fire to a sheet of paper. Therefore the lower court correctly decided that he was not liable for any damage caused. An equitable solution based on the third and final line of § 1310 ABGB must also be ruled out. A right of a minor (as a third-party beneficiary under a liability insurance policy) to receive compensation from his parents' liability insurer would indeed constitute part of the minor's patrimony in the sense of § 1310 3rd hypothesis (SZ 47/43), but such a right does not exist here. [. . .]

The burden of proving that the person who caused the damage does indeed have the means to pay compensation, or that the damage is covered by liability insurance, is on the injured party (Reischauer in Rummel, ABGB, Rz 11 § 1310). As a result, if it cannot be said with complete certainty that the injurer is to receive payment [from a liability insurer] for the compensation which he is liable to pay, i.e. if there is the slightest doubt concerning exclusion of risks, it would not appear equitable to order the injurer to pay damages. Any doubts over the validity of certain conditions of the insurance policy are therefore to be borne by the injured party.

3. Liability in equity

Oberster Gerichtshof, OGH (*Supreme Court of Justice*), 18.12.2009, 7 Ob 83/09h

Grounds for the decision:

On 21st August 2006, the defendant, at that time barely five years old, was playing "knights" with a friend in a field next to the housing estate where his family lived. [. . .] The game consisted of striking a tree with a stick which was around 30 cm long and 2–3 cm thick. The boy was following his mother's instructions not to hit his friends with the stick, and only to aim at the tree.

The plaintiff, who was of the same age as the other boys, arrived midway through the game when he came back from shopping with his mother. His mother was in the apartment putting away the shopping and planned to join the children as soon as this was done. Meanwhile the plaintiff went to play with the other children. The defendant, who at that moment was hitting the stick against the tree, saw the plaintiff arrive. When the latter came within about 3 m of the action, the stick broke and a piece of wood flew into his eye.

The plaintiff suffered a painful injury to this eye [. . .].

The two children are normally developed for their age. The defendant has a private civil liability insurance policy. The plaintiff has first party insurance against accidents, but his insurer refuses to pay out.

The plaintiff therefore requests [. . .] that the defendant pay compensation for his damage, amounting to 7,244.86 EUR [. . .].

Legal considerations

The Court hereby considers that:

1. Now, at third instance, the parties have agreed on the point that, in the present circumstances, the mothers of the young children did not breach their duty of surveillance; likewise the defendant, according to the level of understanding that can be expected of a child of five, is not liable for the injury caused to the plaintiff. The only provision which may therefore potentially establish the liability of the defendant is § 1310, 3rd hypothesis ABGB. Subsequently, damages may only be awarded upon consideration of the financial means of the injurer and of the reparations which ought to be paid to the injured party.

2. In order to establish liability on the basis of § 1310 ABGB, it must be held that an individual with full capacity would be held liable in similar circumstances (EvBl 1974/234; ZVR 1985/127; 5 Ob 529/95; 4 Ob 65/99h; RIS-Justiz RS0027662). [Here this is indeed the case.] [. . .]

3. The discretionary power afforded under the third hypothesis of § 1310 ABGB does not confine the judge to a simple analysis of the financial means of the respective parties. The judge will indeed look to ascertain which party would most easily support the costs in damages in view of their respective financial situations (5 Ob 529/95; 4 Ob 2, 107/96Y = SZ 69/156; RIS-Justiz RS0027582). A reasonable discretion is left to the judge to affix the level of compensation afforded to the plaintiff, which, if needs be, may even correspond to the full amount of damages (9 Ob 181 / 00h = ZVR 2001/82; 2 Ob 167/03b; RIS justice RS0027590). In addition, however, the judge is to take as many additional factors into account as possible when deciding what is fair in the circumstances, for instance the existence of liability insurance on the part of the injurer or the conduct or potential contributory negligence of the victim (2 Ob 167/03b; *Reischauer* supra § 1310 Rz 10).

The defendant [. . .] does not dispute the plaintiff's assertion that the latter was unable to obtain an award of damages from his insurer under his accident insurance policy. We must therefore move on to consider the fact that the defendant was covered by a civil liability policy at the time of the act. The Supreme Court has consistently held that the ability to claim under a liability insurance policy falls within the meaning of "financial means" within § 1310 ABGB. (1 Ob 161 / 05s; RIS-Justiz RS0027608). As long as the personal liability policy covers the costs of the harm, the injurer does not have to pay out of his or her own pocket (5 Ob 529/95; *Reischauer* supra § 1310 Rz 10a).

This principle also applies for the defendant. The plaintiff asserts that the defendant's policy covers all costs relating to the alleged harm and the defendant does not contest this assertion, one which was in fact never disputed during the proceedings. Given the existence of such a policy and insurance coverage, the duty to pay compensation for the plaintiff's harm does not place an economic burden upon the defendant.

The defendant no longer argues that the plaintiff had been contributorily negligent, and rightly so [. . .]. Nevertheless, when examining whether a payment of damages to the plaintiff is required by equity, it must be borne in mind that, whereas from an objective standpoint the defendant has breached his duty of care, the plaintiff has approached a source of (obvious) danger (although he cannot be blamed for this negligent act due to his age) [. . .]. This Court affirms the decision of the court of first instance, holding that it would be appropriate, in the interests of equity, to reduce the award of damages by half. [. . .]

V. France

1. Cour de cassation, Assemblée plénière (*Court of Cassation, full assembly*), 09.05.1984, n° 82–92.934, Bulletin criminel 1984 n° 162 (*arrêt Djouab/Djouab case*)

THE COURT; [. . .] – On the single ground of appeal: Whereas the child D . . . , born on 14th December 1970, and his parents [. . .] contest the judgment [. . .] which declared D . . . liable for starting a fire by which he deliberately destroyed and damaged property including a *Saviem* lorry and buildings belonging to the private company Bertin-Mandal constructors (*Etablissements Bertin-Mandal*) in Nouzonville on the nights of 24th and 25th April 1980 [. . .]; whereas, according to the appellant's assertions, [. . .] it must, in accordance with general principles of law, be established that the child blamed for having committed the act understood and wilfully carried out that act; that any breach of the law requires in fact that the person acted with insight and deliberately; that the Court of Appeal took an overly-restricted view in its categorical assertion that the fire was voluntarily lit by the 9-year-old D . . . without first asking whether the accused was at all aware of the tort for which he was held responsible;

Whereas, however, [. . .] the Court of Appeal held in its distinguished capacity that the child had "deliberately started the fire", and, by that fact alone, legally justified its decision;

For these reasons: dismisses the appeal.

2. Cour de cassation (*Court of Cassation*), 12.12.1984, n° 82–12.627, Bull. 1984 II n° 193 (*arrêt Molina/Molina case*)

THE COURT; [. . .] – On the single ground of appeal, divided into two parts: whereas, according to the judgment which forms the subject of this appeal, Jean-Claude B . . . , aged seven, who was playing in a school playground with Nicolas Y . . . of the same age, pushed the aforementioned who fell, struck a bench and sustained an injury [. . .]; whereas the ruling declaring Jean-Claude B . . . C . . . negligent for the harm caused to Nicolas Y . . . X . . . is first contested on the assertion that the capacity of judgement (*capacité de discernement*) of the seven-year-old child had not been considered, misinterpreting the findings of M.B . . . stating that the case in question involved seven-year-old children who were, by this very fact, bereft of this capacity, and secondly, on the assertion that the push essential to the game did not represent a violent one, that the presence of a bench in the playground did not transform the game of tag into a dangerous one, that any potential violence in the push could not be inferred from an examination of the victim, that by failing to work out if Jean-Claude B . . . was capable of judgement (*capable de discernement*) and by inferring liability for any consequences that would flow from said act, the judgment violated Article 1382 [now Article 1240] of the Civil Code;[23]

Whereas, however, the decision identifies that the child Jean-Claude B . . . pushed Nicolas Y . . . into a bench in the school playground with such force that he sustained a ruptured spleen and internal haemorrhaging; that in regard to these particular facts, the Court of Appeal was not required to establish whether the child Jean-Claude B . . . was capable of judgement (*capable de discernement*), and thereby established and qualified the fault which he had committed; from which follows that the appeal is not well-founded;

---

23 For the text of this provision, see above, Chapter 5, pp. 96–97.

For these reasons, dismisses the appeal against the decision made by the Court of Appeal of Toulouse on 5th March 1982;

3. Cour de cassation, Assemblée plénière (*Court of Cassation, full assembly*), 09.05.1984, n° 80–14.994, Bull. 1984 n° 1 (*arrêt Gabillet/Gabillet case*)

THE COURT; – On the single ground of appeal: Whereas, according to the contested decision [. . .] on 30th June 1975 the child Eric X . . ., then aged three, while falling from a homemade swing which had been constructed with a plank which at this moment broke, blinded his friend Philippe Y . . . in one eye with a stick that he had been holding in his hand; [. . .] Whereas the spouses X . . . appeal the decision declaring Eric X . . . liable on the basis of Art. 1384 (1) [now Art. 1242 (1)] of the Civil Code[24] since, according to the appellants' assertions, the accusation of alleged liability implies a capacity of judgement (*faculté de discernement*); [. . .]

Whereas, however, in deciding that the child Eric had the use, direction and control of the stick, the Court of Appeal was not, despite the very young age of this child, required to subsequently examine whether he was capable of judgement (*capable de discernement*) and therefore applied the law correctly;

For these reasons, dismisses the appeal against the decision made by the Court of Appeal of Agen on 12th May 1980;

4. Alain Bénabent, *Droit civil. Les obligations* (*Civil Law. Obligations*), 16th ed., 2017

§ 1. A GRADUAL DISINTEGRATION OF THE REQUIREMENT OF FAULT

532 Development of the doctrine: reduction from three components down to two. Traditionally based on moral considerations, fault required three elements: firstly, an act had to be established; secondly, this act would need to be legally defined as one which was not in conformity with what is required of a good citizen; and finally some personal attribution of fault was required, the defendant not being held liable if he were not aware of his or her act. Some authors refer to the material, legal, and moral elements of fault. The latter element, after a long and protracted transformation, can now be considered obsolete: fault has now become a **purely objective notion**, requiring conduct which the court deems to be wrongful, but then ignoring examination of any psychological dispositions of its author. [. . .]

535 Moral element abandoned. Admittedly, civil wrongs have never required intent, i.e. a willingness to harm, as is often the case in criminal liability: besides, Art. [1241, former 1383] expressly addresses negligence or carelessness.[25] But is it not necessary to at least require awareness of one's acts? The traditional doctrine considered that liability could only be established for a person whose behaviour was such that "fault could be attributed to him", i.e. if he was capable of being aware of the consequences

---

24 For the text of this provision which, according to French case law, establishes a liability without fault, see below, Chapter 7, p. 171.
25 For the text of this provision, see above, Chapter 5, pp. 96–97.

of his acts. How then can the court declare the act of someone who is mentally ill, or of a very young child, to be wrongful if he or she does not know right from wrong? This is a moral perspective of fault inspired by criminal liability. However, from a purely civil perspective which aims at remedying a harm rather than punishing a wrong, this concept had a few major pitfalls: it left the victim without any reparation for an act which would ordinarily be considered wrongful, simply because he was misfortunate enough that the act was performed by a person who was not aware of what he or she was doing. Moreover, with the growth of the insurance industry, the conviction gained ground that it was for these "irresponsible individuals", or their relatives, to take out their own insurance covering their harmful acts; acts which are all the more likely given their condition – the idea being that the "risks" associated with their condition must be supported by them, and not by their victims.[26] [. . .] Our substantive law, for these reasons, is now purely objectively-orientated, detached from the condition of the author of the harm. [. . .]

[. . .] Case law extended this practice to *very young children* in a series of cases decided by the Full Assembly of the Court of Cassation on 9th May 1984.

We can now therefore clearly distinguish fault in civil law from fault in criminal law through its criterion of moral culpability: even if we cannot *hold* someone *criminally liable* because he was not conscious of his acts, we can, by contrast, *seek damages under civil law* for harm resulting from those acts.

VI. Italy

1. Codice civile (*Civil Code*)

Art. 2046. Imputabilità del fatto dannoso. Non risponde delle conseguenze dal fatto dannoso chi non aveva la capacità d'intendere o di volere al momento in cui lo ha commesso, a meno che lo stato d'incapacità derivi da sua colpa.

Art. 2047. Danno cagionato dall'incapace. In caso di danno cagionato da persona incapace d'intendere o di volere, il risarcimento è dovuto da chi e tenuto alla sorveglianza dell'incapace, salvo che provi di non aver potuto impedire il fatto.
Nel caso in cui il danneggiato non abbia potuto ottenere il risarcimento da chi è tenuto alla sorveglianza, il giudice, in considerazione delle condizioni economiche delle parti, può condannare l'autore del danno a un'equa indennità.

Translation

Art. 2046. Attribution of liability for an act causing damage. *Any person who lacks the capacity to understand and intend his or her actions is not liable for any damage stemming therefrom except where he or she negligently brought about his or her own incapacity.*

---

26 *Note by the author:* in France, liability insurance is extremely widespread to the extent that almost every French citizen is covered, see below, Chapter 19, pp. 596 ff.

> *Art. 2047. Damage caused by a person lacking capacity. In the event that damage is caused by a person who lacks the capacity to understand and intend his or her actions, compensation is due from his or her guardian unless the latter can prove that such actions could not have been prevented.*
>
> *If the injured party is unable to secure compensation from the guardian, the judge may, upon consideration of the financial circumstances of each party, order the person who caused the damage to pay equitable compensation.*

2. Corte di Cassazione (*Court of Cassation*), 28.04.1975, n. 1642, Resp. Civ. Prev., 1976, 136[27]

With respect to the capacity of judgement of minors, the Italian Corte di Cassazione has decided:

[T]he judge must not only keep in mind the age of the minor and the precise facts of the case, but must also consider his intellectual development, his physical development [. . .], the strength of character, the ability of the minor to realise the illegality of its action, [and] the ability of will with regard to the attitude to self-determination.

VII. Liability of children: codal or statutory provisions of various continental jurisdictions (English translations)

1. Burgerlijk Wetboek (*Dutch Civil Code*)

> *Art. 6:164. The conduct of a child under fourteen years of age cannot be attributed to him as a tortious act.*[28]
>
> *Art 6:165. (1) The fact that the conduct of a person of fourteen years of age or older can be considered as an act that was done under the influence of a mental or physical disability does not exclude the possibility of attributing that act to him as a tortious act. [. . .]*

2. Võlaõigusseadus (*Estonian Code of Obligations*)

> *§ 1052. Restrictions on liability. (1) A person under 14 years of age shall not be liable for damage caused by himself or herself. [. . .]*
>
> *(3) A person who, pursuant to subsections (1) [. . .] of this section, is not liable for damage shall nevertheless be liable for damage caused by himself or herself if it would be unjustified with regard to the victim to release the person from liability considering*

---

[27] Confirmed e.g. by Corte Cass., 26.07.2001, n. 8740, Foro it. 2001, 3098; GD 2001, 41, 47; DR 2002, 3, 283; Corte Cass., 26.10.2001, n. 8740, Giust. Civ. 2002, I, 710.

[28] For the strict liability of parents for damage done by their children under 14 years of age, see below, Chapter 13.

the tortfeasor's age, state of development and mental state, the type of act, the financial situation of the persons concerned, including existing insurance or insurance which such persons could normally be presumed to have, and also other circumstances.

3. Гражданский кодекс Российской Федерации (*Russian Civil Code*)

Art. 1073. Liability for the Injury Inflicted by Minors under the Age of 14 Years.
(1) Parents (adopters) or guardians shall be liable for the injury inflicted by minors who have not attained 14 years of age, unless they prove that the injury has been inflicted not through their fault. [. . .]

Art. 1074. Liability for the Injury Inflicted by Minors between 14 and 18 Years.
(1) Minors at the age from 14 to 18 years shall bear liability for the inflicted injury on general grounds. [. . .]

4. Kodeks cywilny (*Polish Civil Code*)

Art. 426. *A minor who has not attained the age of thirteen years is not liable for any damage he causes.*[29]

Art. 428. *Where a perpetrator is not liable for damage due to his age or mental or physical condition, and there are no persons responsible for his supervision, or when redress for the damage cannot be obtained from them, the injured person may demand complete or partial redress for the damage from the perpetrator himself if it follows from the circumstances, in particular from a comparison of the financial circumstances of the injured person and those of the other person, that the principles of community life so require.*

5. Αστικός Κώδικας (*Greek Civil Code*)

Art. 916. *A person who has not attained ten years of age shall not be liable for the damage he has caused.*

Art. 917. *A person who has attained ten years but not fourteen years of age shall be liable for the damage he has caused except if he acted without discretion. [. . .]*

Art. 918. *A person who has caused damage but is not liable according to the provisions of articles 915 to 917 may be obliged by the court, after consideration of the position of the parties, to pay reasonable damages if the damage caused cannot be compensated in any other way.*

---

29 For case law and further information, see *Digest III*, 8/23/1–24 with comments by E. BAGINSKA/I. ANDRYCH-BRZEZINSKA.

6. Obligacijski zakonik (*Slovenian Code of Obligations*)

*Art. 137. **Liability of minors.*** *(1) Minors under the age of seven shall not be liable for any damage they inflict.*
(2) Minors aged seven and over but under fourteen shall not be liable for damage, unless it is shown that they were capable of accounting for their actions when the damage was inflicted.
(3) Minors aged fourteen and over shall be liable according to the general rules on liability for damage.[30]

7. Civillikums (*Latvian Civil Code*)

Art. 1637. Children under seven years of age [. . .] shall not be held liable for delicts. [. . .]

Art. 1780. Losses that have been caused by children who are not more than seven years of age [. . .] shall be compensated for from the property of these persons to the extent that they are not deprived of the means needed for their maintenance. If losses have occurred through the negligence of a person whose duty it is to supervise the aforementioned persons, such person shall be primarily liable regarding the losses, to the extent of his or her own property.

8. Código civil (*Portuguese Civil Code*)

*Art. 488. **Imputability.*** *(1) A person who for any reason was incapable of understanding or of forming intent when the injurious event occurred, shall not be liable for its consequences, unless he wilfully caused himself to be in that condition, and the condition was temporary.*
(2) Persons who are aged less than seven years [. . .] shall be deemed not to bear any liability.[31]

9. Codul Civil (*Romanian Civil Code*)

*Art. 1366. **Liability of minors and of incapacitated persons.*** *(1) Neither a minor who is under the age of 14 nor an incapacitated person is liable for damage, unless his or her discernment at the time of the wrongfulness is proven.*
(2) A minor who has reached the age of 14 years is liable for the damage, unless it is proven that he or she lacked discernment at the time the wrongfulness was committed.

---

30 On this provision, see *Digest III*, 8/27/3ff., with comments by B. Novak/G. Dugar.
31 For more information and Portuguese case law, see *Digest III*, 8/11/1ff with comments by A. Pereira/S. Rodrigues/P. Morgado.

10. Erstatningsansvarsloven (*Danish Liability for Damages Act*)

§ 24a. Children under 15 years of age shall be liable to pay compensation for wrongful acts in accordance with the same rules as for persons over that age. The compensation can be reduced or even excluded completely, however, in so far as it is found reasonable to do so due to lack of development on the part of the child, the nature of the act and the circumstances in general, including the relationship between the ability of the party who caused the loss and the injured party to bear the loss and the prospects of obtaining compensation from another source.[32]

11. Vahingonkorvauslaki (*Finnish Tort Liability Act*)

§ 2. If the injury or damage has been caused by a person under 18 years of age, he or she shall be liable for damages to an amount that is deemed reasonable in view of his or her age and maturity, the nature of the act, the financial means of both the person causing the injury and the victim, and any other circumstances.[33]

12. Skadeserstatningsloven (*Norwegian Compensatory Damages Act*)

§ 1–1. Children's liability. Children and youths under 18 years of age are liable to compensate damage or injury which they cause intentionally or negligently, provided such obligation is considered reasonable in view of their age, development, conduct, financial means and other circumstances.[34]

13. Skadeståndslagen (*Swedish Tort Liability Act*)

§ 4. Anyone who [. . .] causes damage before he is 18 years of age shall pay compensation to the extent that this is reasonable in view of his age and development, the nature of the act, his liability insurance coverage at the time, his other economic circumstances, and any other relevant factors. [. . .][35]

---

32 For more information and Danish case law, see *Digest III*, 8/16/1ff with comments by V. Ulfbeck/A.Ehlers/K. Siig.

33 See e.g. the case: Korkein oikeus (*Supreme Court*), 04.03.1983, 1983 II 26, R81/382, 884/82; *Digest III*, 8/19/1 with comments by P. Korpisaari (15-year-old intentionally shoots at another person with an air rifle, causing him to lose an eye: in view of the intent, the nature of the act, and the fact that the minor was fully able to understand the risk of injury, no adjustment was made and the minor was held to be fully liable); contrast with: KKO, 23.5.1984, 1984 II 93, S83/217, 4230/83 (7-year-old children playing with fire; held: they were to pay a combined sum of 20,000 Finnish markka for damage amounting to 250,268.36 Finnish markka).

34 See e.g. the case: Høyesterett (*Supreme Court*), 08.03.2000, Rt 2000, 433; *Digest III*, 8/17/1 with comments by H. Andersson (an 11-year-old boy follows a friend on his bicycle and collides with a pedestrian; held: not liable because not acting acted negligently due to his young age and low level of maturity).

35 On this provision with further references, see *Digest III*, 8/18/3f with comments by H. Andersson.

14. ЗАКОН ЗА ЗАДЪЛЖЕНИЯТА И ДОГОВОРИТЕ
(Bulgarian Law on Obligations and Contracts)

> *Art. 47 (1) A person who lacks the capacity to understand or control his actions shall not be liable for any damage he causes while in such a state unless his lack of capacity was caused through his own fault. [. . .]*

15. Zákon občanský zákoník *(Czech Civil Code)*

> *§ 2920. Liability of a minor. (1) A minor who has not yet acquired full legal capacity [. . .] shall provide compensation for the damage caused if he was capable of controlling his behaviour and assessing its consequences [. . .].*
> *(2) If a minor who has not yet acquired full legal capacity [. . .] was incapable of controlling his behaviour and assessing its consequences, the victim is entitled to compensation if it is fair with regard to the property situation of the tortfeasor and victim.*

16. Zákon občanský zákoník *(Slovak Civil Code)*

> *§ 422. (1) A minor [. . .] is liable for the damage he causes if he is capable of controlling his conduct and judging its consequences, while anyone who has a duty to exercise supervision over such a person shall be jointly and severally liable with him. If a person who, due to his age [. . .], is incapable of controlling his own conduct or judging its consequences, causes damage, liability for such damage shall be borne by the person whose duty it was to exercise supervision over him.*
> *(2) A person obliged to exercise supervision shall exempt himself from liability if he proves that he did not act below the proper standard of supervision. [. . .]*

VIII. USA

The American Law Institute, *Restatement of the Law – Torts (3rd): Liability for Physical and Emotional Harm*, Vol. 1, §§ 1 to 36, St. Paul, Minnesota: American Law Institute Publishers, 2013, § 10. Children[36]

§ 10. Children

(a) A child's conduct is negligent if it does not conform to that of a reasonably careful person of the same age, intelligence, and experience, except as provided in Subsection (b) and (c).

---

36 The Restatements of the Law promulgated by the American Law Institute are "[v]ery valuable and often very influential for the development of the case law" in the USA. "There are restatements for most areas of the law, often already in a second or third revised version. They synthesize the case law and, in form and presentation,

(b) A child less than five years of age is incapable of negligence.
(c) The special rule in subsection (a) does not apply when a child is engaging in a dangerous activity that is characteristically undertaken by adults.

Comment:

a. Coverage. A "child" is a person below the age of majority as specified by the particular jurisdiction. In most states, the age of majority has been reduced from 21 to 18. [. . .]

b. Rationale. Children are less able than adults to maintain an attitude of attentiveness towards the risks their conduct may occasion and the risks to which they may be exposed. [. . .] Acknowledging this, tort law refines the characterization of negligence [. . .] to take account of these realities. [. . .]

All American jurisdictions accept the idea that a person's childhood is a relevant circumstance in negligence determinations. Jurisdictions divide, however, on the best way to take childhood into account. The very substantial majority of all jurisdictions accept the flexible rule set forth in Subsection (a). A considerable minority of [approximately 10] jurisdictions pursue a different approach. Under that approach, for children above 14 there is a rebuttable presumption in favour of the child's capacity to commit negligence; for children between seven and 14, there is a rebuttable presumption against capacity; children under the age of seven are deemed incapable of committing negligence [rule of sevens].

The difference between the approaches taken in Subsection (a) and the minority approach is narrowed by the presence of Subsection (b) providing that children under five years of age are incapable of negligence and by essentially all jurisdictions' acceptance of Subsection (c), providing that children are treated as adults when they engage in dangerous adult acts [such as driving a car, a tractor, and a motorcycle, and operating other motorised vehicles].

c. Evidence of age, intelligence, and experience. [. . .] Evidence about experience typically focuses on the child's experience with the particular activity that has given rise to the accident – what the child knows about the activity, how frequently the child has engaged in it, and what instructions the child has received from parents or other adults as to which precautions are needed. [. . .]

While American jurisdictions are unanimous in regarding the child's age, intelligence, and experience as all relevant [and hence apply a largely subjective standard], courts in Australia and England evidently follow a different approach: they take into account the specific fact of the actor's age, but then apply an objective test relating to children of the same age that does not inquire into the specifics of the actor's intelligence and experience. While this approach loses something by way of individualization, it otherwise has much to commend it. The approach simplifies litigation by eliminating the need for evidence as to the child's precise intelligence and experience, and it avoids the odd result of having

---

resemble a civil law code. In this way, they facilitate a quick overview of the current law in any particular area of law." They are not binding for the courts but have a great persuasive authority. Many of them are "so reliable in their analysis of case law that attorneys and judges often cite to them instead of the case law on which they are based", P. HAY, *The Law of the United States: An Introduction*, London: Routledge, 2017, p. 12 no. 32.

testimony from the child's parents and teachers, as to the child's commendable intelligence and experience [. . .]. Moreover, [. . .] the Australian approach avoids the awkward result of penalizing the family in which the parents have a more responsible job in providing the child with appropriate instruction. In the future, American jurisdictions might wish to consider experimenting with this approach. [. . .]

IX. Principles of European Tort Law

1. PETL

> **Art. 4:101. Fault.** A person is liable on the basis of fault for intentional or negligent violation of the required standard of conduct.
>
> **Art. 4:102. Required Standard of Conduct.** (1) The required standard of conduct is that of the reasonable person in the circumstances, and depends, in particular, on the nature and value of the protected interest involved, the dangerousness of the activity, the expertise to be expected of a person carrying it on, the foreseeability of the damage, the relationship of proximity or special reliance between those involved, as well as the availability and the costs of precautio.nary or alternative methods.
> (2) The above standard may be adjusted when due to age, mental or physical disability or due to extraordinary circumstances the person cannot be expected to conform to it.
> (3) Rules which prescribe or forbid certain conduct have to be considered when establishing the required standard of conduct.

2. BÉNÉDICT WINIGER/ERNST KARNER/KEN OLIPHANT (eds.), *Digest of European Tort Law, Vol. III: Misconduct*, 2018, nos. 1/30/1 ff. and 8/30/1 ff. (by THOMAS KADNER GRAZIANO)

1. General overview

1   Misconduct – understood as the failure to meet a given standard of required conduct as a basis of tortious liability – is in some jurisdictions addressed under the heading "wrongfulness" or "unlawfulness" (*Rechtswidrigkeit, illicéité*) on the one hand, and "fault" (*Verschulden, faute*) on the other, whereas other jurisdictions focus instead on one single key requirement, called "breach of a duty of care" in some jurisdictions and "fault" (*faute*) in others.

2   **a) Solution according to the PETL.** The text of the PETL does not employ the terminology "wrongful", "wrongfulness", "unlawful" or "unlawfulness" in establishing civil liability. Instead, the PETL "merge wrongfulness with fault" and subsequently focus on the "most traditional, most widespread and – apparently – most important criterion" required for misconduct to trigger liability: the concept of fault. [. . .]

4   In Art. 4:101 PETL, fault is defined as an "intentional or negligent violation of the required standard of conduct". Pursuant to Art. 4:102(1) PETL, "[t]he required standard of conduct is that of the reasonable person in the circumstances". The individual person is required to behave as a "reasonable person in the circumstances",

independently of his or her individual capacities. The PETL thus use an objective (as opposed to a subjective) notion and standard of fault.

5   The attribution of damage based on fault relies on the idea that the tortfeasor is somehow blameworthy for the damage done. It has been said, and rightly so, that if fault-based liability uses an objective standard of care, liability is detached from individual blameworthiness. For those who are incapable of meeting the required standards, fault-based liability may then come close to strict liability for damage done. However, an objective standard of care is in accordance with the prevailing trend of modern-day European tort law systems. It gives priority to the interests of the victim and facilitates claims in extra-contractual liability. Victims who are not adequately equipped with the means to meet the required standards can, and should, contract liability insurance. Therefore, unlike criminal law, fault in tort law does not necessarily look to blame the individual for causing the damage.

6   This being said, the PETL reserve the possibility in Art. 4:102 (2) that the objective notion of fault may be tempered in order to avoid an excessive hardship in the evaluation of a person's effective possibilities to behave as the standard would have required, notably by taking into account the age of the tortfeasor. Here again however, the standard of care that is applied remains objective with respect to the relevant group of tortfeasors. The PETL thus require, for example, that a minor respects the standard of care that can be expected from minors of his age, as opposed to looking into his particular subjective state of development.

7   Tort law systems that require the criteria of both "wrongfulness" and "fault", and which apply an objective standard of care, may face difficulties when it comes to distinguishing wrongfulness from (objectively determined) fault. The test applied to determine wrongfulness and fault may be similar, or even identical, to one another. By focusing exclusively on fault, as opposed to requiring wrongfulness as a separate and additional condition for liability, the PETL avoid such problems and preclude any overlap between the two criteria. [...]

10 When it comes to determining whether particular conduct corresponds to the required standard or whether, conversely, it constitutes fault (in other words, whether it represents a breach of the duty to conduct oneself as required), Art. 4:102 (1) PETL provides a list of criteria such as "the nature and value of the protected interest involved, the dangerousness of the activity, the expertise to be expected of a person carrying it out, the foreseeability of the damage, the relationship of proximity or special reliance between those involved, as well as the availability and the costs of precautionary or alternative methods". [...]

8. Age

Various scenarios

Facts

1   V, a minor, is injured when A, another minor of 6/9/14 years of age, shoots him in the eye with a gas pistol, an air gun or an arrow and causes him to go blind in one eye. In other cases, minors of the same ages set fire to a building when playing, causing considerable damage to property belonging to a third party. [...]

8   a) **Solution according to the PETL** [...]

11 Contrary to many of the national tort law systems mentioned above, the PETL do not fix a specific age limit below which a minor is exempt from liability. Instead, they use a "flexible system" according to which "the question whether or not a person had sufficient insight and control of his or her behaviour has to be answered from case to case, according to the concrete mental development of that person".

12 In the first of the above scenarios, a minor of 6/9/14 years of age shot one of his friends in the eye with a gas pistol, an air gun or an arrow, and caused him to go blind in one eye. In the following scenario, minors of the same ages set fire to buildings when playing and caused considerable damage to property belonging to a third party. The official commentary to the PETL sets out that "[g]enerally speaking, and in the absence of special disabilities, one can normally assume that a child of fourteen, and even one of nine years, is capable to realise the danger of playing with matches, while a six year old child is not". The commentary further states that "[t]here are situations – like e.g. playing with matches or fireworks or other dangerous toys (such as "airsoft guns" or even handmade bows and arrows) or the manner in which one has to behave on streets and places open to the traffic – where even relatively young children are normally aware of the risk and able to act in consequence of such insight".

13 According to the commentary, in the above scenario, the minors of 14 and 9 years of age would very likely be taken to have violated the standard of conduct required from them under the PETL, whereas the 6-year-old child would arguably not be held to have violated the standard required from an average child of his age. [...]

15 [...] [I]n situations in which a minor who caused damage is not liable due to a lack of capacity to foresee the consequences of his acts, in many jurisdictions he may still have to pay (some) compensation, if this is deemed to be reasonable, when taking into consideration both parties' economic situations. The PETL do not contain a similar rule.

X. Draft Common Frame of Reference

> **Art. VI. – 3:103: Persons under eighteen.** (1) A person under eighteen years of age is accountable for causing legally relevant damage [...] only in so far as that person does not exercise such care as could be expected from a reasonably careful person of the same age in the circumstances of the case.
> (2) A person under seven years of age is not accountable for causing damage intentionally or negligently.
> (3) However, paragraphs (1) and (2) do not apply to the extent that:
> (a) the person suffering the damage cannot obtain reparation under this Book from another; and
> (b) liability to make reparation would be equitable having regard to the financial means of the parties and all other circumstances of the case.

Table of solutions

A. Major systems of extra-contractual, tortious, or delictual liability

- Fault-based liability (for basic information, see Chapters 5–7)
- Liability without fault/strict liability/objective liability (see below, Chapters 8 and 9)

B. Standards of care

- *Objective*: England, Germany, Switzerland, France
- *Subjective*: Austria (in general), see however OGH 23.03.1976 ("*Übernahmeverschulden*")
- *Subjective*: Italy, US Restatement (both with respect to liability of minors)

C. Liability of minors

Table 6.1

1. General test of reasonableness	2. Capacity of judgement or other general criteria (no age limits fixed)	3. Systems using age limits	4. Equitable compensation taking into account the parties' economic situation	5. Minors treated like adults
• **Denmark** for minors under 15 years of age, § 24a Liability for Damages Act • **Finland** for minors under 18 years of age, § 2 Tort Liability Act • **Sweden** for minors under 18 years of age, § 4 Tort Liability Act	*Capacity of judgement* • **Switzerland** Arts. 16, 18, 19 Civil Code • **Italy** Art. 2047 Civil Code • **Bulgaria** Art. 47 (1) Law on Obligations and Contracts • **Czech Republic** § 2920 (1) Civil Code • **Slovakia** Art. 422 Civil Code	*Immunity from liability* • **USA** under 5 years, Restatement, § 10 (b); under 7 years some jurisdictions ("rule of sevens") • **Germany** under 7 years, § 828 (1) Civil Code • **Slovenia** under 7 years, Art. 137 (1) Code of Obligations • **Latvia** under 7 years, Art. 1637 (1) Civil Code	*Capacity of judgement (for certain age groups)* • **USA** over 5 years, Restatement, § 10 (a) and (b) • **USA**, some jurisdictions, 7–14 years: lack of capacity presumed; from 14 years onwards: capacity presumed • **Slovenia** 7–14 years: lack of capacity presumed, Art. 137 (2) Code of Obligations	• **Switzerland** Art. 54 (1) Code of Obligations • **Germany** § 829 Civil Code • **Austria** § 1310 3rd alt. Civil Code • **Czech Republic** § 2920 (2) Civil Code • **Italy** Art. 2047 (2) Civil Code • **Estonia** § 1052 (3) Code of Obligations	• **France**

(Continued)

Table 6.1 (Continued)

1.	2.		3.	4.	5.
General test of reasonableness	**Capacity of judgement or other general criteria (no age limits fixed)**		**Systems using age limits**	**Equitable compensation taking into account the parties' economic situation**	**Minors treated like adults**
	Other general criteria • **England** negligence: foreseeability, depending on age • **PETL** Art. 4:102 (2) (adjustment of standard of care according to age)	• **Portugal** under 7 years, Art. 488 (2) Civil Code • **DCFR** under 7 years, Art. VI. 3:103 (2) • **Germany** under 10 years for damage suffered in motor traffic accident, § 828 (2) Civil Code • **Greece** under 10 years, Art. 916 Civil Code • **Poland** under 13 years, Art. 426 Civil Code • **The Netherlands** under 14 years, Art 6:164 Civil Code • **Estonia** under 14 years, § 1052 (1) Code of Obligations • **Russia** under 14 years, Art. 1073–1074 Civil Code	• **Greece** 7–14 years: capacity presumed, Art. 917 Civil Code • **Romania** under 14 years: lack of capacity presumed; from 14 years onwards: capacity presumed, Art. 1366 (1) and (2) Civil Code • **Austria** under 14 years, §§ 176 and 21 (2) Civil Code • **Germany** 7–18 years: capacity presumed, § 828 (3) Civil Code • **DCFR** 7–18 years, Art. VI. – 3:103 (1)	• **Poland** Art. 428 Civil Code • **Greece** Art. 918 Civil Code	

Bibliography

CHRISTIANE BIRR, *Die Haftung Minderjähriger im Zivilrecht, Deliktshaftung – Gefährdungshaftung – Aufsichtspflichten*, Berlin: Erich Schmidt, 2005; RAINER BORGELT, *Das Kind im Deliktsrecht: Zur Bedeutung der individuellen Reife für persönliche Haftung und Mitverschulden*, Regensburg: Roderer, 1995; MANFRED DÄHLER, Das Verschulden bei der Haftungsbegründung, Schadenersatzbemessung und als Entlastungsgrund, in: Stephan Weber (ed.), *Personen-Schaden-Forum 2014: Kind als Täter und Opfer*, Zürich: Schulthess, 2014, pp. 15–36; DAN B. DOBBS, *The Law of Torts*, St. Paul/Minnesota: West, 2000, §§ 124–127; NUNO FERREIRA, The Harmonisation of Private Law in Europe and Children's Tort Liability: A Case of Fundamental and Children's Rights Mainstreaming, *Int'l J. Children's Rts.* 2011, 571–594; ANNE-MARIE GALLIOU-SCANVION, *L'enfant dans le droit de la responsabilité délictuelle*, Villeneuve d'Ascq: Presses universitaires du Septentrion, 2001; KLAUS GOELCKE, *Die unbegrenzte Haftung Minderjähriger im Deliktsrecht*, Berlin: Duncker & Humblot, 1997; MATTHIAS KILIAN, Die deliktische Verantwortlichkeit Minderjähriger nach § 828 BGB nF, *ZGS* 2003, 168–173; HELMUT KOZIOL (ed.), *Unification of Tort Law: Wrongfulness*, The Hague/London/Boston: Kluwer, 1998; HELMUT KOZIOL, *Basic Questions of Tort Law from a Germanic Perspective*, Vienna: Jan Sramek Verlag, 2012, pp. 200–209; HELMUT KOZIOL, Kinder als Täter und Opfer: Kernfragen rechtsvergleichend betrachtet, in: Stephan Weber (ed.), *Personen-Schaden-Forum 2014: Kind als Täter und Opfer*, Zürich: Schulthess, 2014, pp. 89–113; HERBERT LANG, Die Haftung Minderjähriger – alle Fragen geklärt?, *r+s* (special edition) 2011, 63–69; MARIE-CHRISTINE LEBRETON, *L'enfant et la responsabilité civile*, Rouen: Publications des Universités de Rouen et du Havre, 1999; DIRK LOOSCHELDERS, Verfassungsrechtliche Grenzen der deliktischen Haftung Minderjähriger, *VersR* 1999, 141–151; MIQUEL MARTIN CASALS (ed.), *Children in Tort Law, Part I: Children as Tortfeasors*, Wien/New York: Springer, 2006; MIQUEL MARTIN CASALS (ed.), *Children in Tort Law, Part II: Children as Victims*, Wien/New York: Springer, 2007; FRÉDÉRIQUE NIBOYET, *Die Haftung Minderjähriger und ihrer Eltern nach deutschem und französischem Deliktsrecht zwischen Dogmatik und Rechtspolitik*, Berlin: Duncker & Humblot, 2001; PETER H. M. RAMBACH, *Die deliktische Haftung Minderjähriger und ihrer Eltern im französischen, belgischen und deutschen Deliktsrecht*, Apeldoorn: Maklu/Zürich: Schulthess, 1994; ROLF STÜRNER, Zivilrechtliche Haftung junger Menschen – fortbestehender Reformbedarf im deutschen Recht?, in: Haimo Schack (ed.), *Gedächtnisschrift für Alexander Lüderitz*, München: C. H. Beck, 2000, pp. 789–810; CEES VAN DAM, *European Tort Law*, 2nd ed., Oxford: OUP, 2002, pp. 269–277; CHRISTIAN VON BAR, *Gemeineuropäisches Deliktsrecht, Zweiter Band*, München: C. H. Beck, 1999, pp. 76–101; CHRISTIAN VON BAR, *The Common European Law of Torts, Volume Two*, Oxford: OUP, 2000, pp. 84–111; GERHARD WAGNER, in: *Münchener Kommentar Band 6: Schuldrecht Besonderer Teil*, 7th ed., München: C. H. Beck, 2017, § 823 paras. 28–56; FRANZ WERRO, *La capacité de discernement et la faute dans le droit suisse de la responsabilité. Etude critique et comparative*, 2e éd., Fribourg: Ed. Universitaires, 1986; PIERRE WIDMER (ed.), *Unification of Tort Law: Fault*, The Hague/London/Boston: Kluwer Law International, 2005; PIERRE WIDMER/WILLEM VAN BOOM, *Unification of Tort Law: Fault*, The Hague: Kluwer Law International, 2005; BÉNÉDICT WINIGER/ERNST KARNER/KEN OLIPHANT (eds.), *Digest of European Tort Law, Vol. III: Misconduct*, Category 8/1–31, 2017 (forthcoming); REINHARD ZIMMERMANN (Hrsg.), *Grundstrukturen des Europäischen Deliktsrechts*, Baden-Baden: Nomos, 2003, S. 256–269 (by GERHARD WAGNER).

Chapter 7

Fault-based liability in action
Challenges of establishing fault (and alternative regimes) – the example of sports accidents

"By a wrong we here mean every fault, whether of commission or of omission, which is in conflict with what men ought to do, either from their common interest or by reason of a special quality. From such a fault, if damage has been caused, by the law of nature an obligation arises, namely that the damage should be made good."[1]

"[L]a responsabilité pour faute [...] continue d'offrir la protection minimale aux victimes qui n'ont pas à disposition un moyen plus efficace."[2]

Scenario 1

Two skiers are at the top of a steep descent. They first start off on separate, parallel tracks, before finally colliding. One of the skiers is seriously injured. No witnesses are available. In these circumstances it cannot be established which of the skiers was further down on the run when the collision occurred.

The injured skier claims damages from the other for the injuries suffered.[3]

---

1 HUGO GROTIUS (1583–1645), *De Iure Belli ac Pacis*, 2, 17, 1. Translation by F. W. KELSEY, Oxford: Clarendon Press, 1925. In Latin: "Maleficium hic appellamus culpam omnem, sive in faciendo, sive in non faciendo, pugnantem cum eo quod aut homines communiter, aut pro ratione certae qualitatis facere debent. Ex tali culpa obloigatio naturaliter oritur, si damnum datum est, nempe ut id resarciatur".
2 PIERRE WESSNER, La responsabilité pour faute: une conception non surprenante, des conditions d'application novatrices, *HAVE/REAS* 2005, 252, at 253 (translation: *Liability based on fault continues to offer minimal protection to victims who do not have a more effective remedy available*). With reference to G. VINEY, Pour ou contre un principe général de responsabilité pour faute?, *Osaka U.L. Rev.* 2002, 33, at 36: "le principe général de responsabilité pour faute [...] continue à définir la protection minimale mise à la disposition de toutes les victimes qui ne disposent pas d'un instrument plus efficace".
3 Inspired by the French case: Cour d'Appel de Colmar, 18.09.1992 (*New Hampshire Unat SA c. Hugel*), J.C.P. 1993, IV, n° 1711 (see below, pp. 173–174). In terms of absolute numbers, the subject of ski accidents is far from insignificant: approximately 38,000 to 39,000 skiers domiciled in **Germany** are involved in ski or snowboard accidents resulting in personal injury every year. About 6,700 of them, representing 17%, are injured in collisions, with an upward trend in recent years. In **Switzerland**, the number of victims injured in winter sports is as high as the number of victims of road traffic accidents: in 2012 e.g., 82,360 victims were injured in Switzerland in road traffic accidents compared with 82,920 on ski slopes. Of them, 50,600 were alpine skiing; 14,070 snowboarding; 6,860 sledding; 930 ski touring; 4,520 cross-country skiing; and 5,950 others, with an average cost of CHF 7,600 per ski accident. Almost 4,000 of these victims, corresponding to 6%, were injured in collisions with other skiers. Whereas, in Switzerland, about 6,300 pedestrians are injured in road traffic accidents every year (an average of 1,575 every three months), about 4,000 persons are injured in ski collisions in a little more

Scenario 2

Jockeys are competing in a horse race. After the second to last jump, the first and the second jockey approach a left-hand bend. They take a line that leaves no room for the third horse on the bend. The latter shies, turns right, and obstructs the fourth horse, following closely behind, which is brought down and whose jockey is seriously injured.

The stewards find the jockeys of the first two horses guilty of careless riding "because they had not left enough room for the third horse to come round the inside rail". They are both suspended for three racing days.

The injured jockey brings a claim for damages against the jockeys who were riding the first two horses.[4]

---

than three winter months. The total costs of skiing accidents amount to more than CHF 369 million per year. In other countries, the number of ski accidents is also considerable, with 35,000 injuries per year in *Italy*, 12% (or about 4,200) of which are due to collisions with other skiers, and about 150,000 injuries per year in *France* (numerous references in T. KADNER GRAZIANO, The Distribution of Social Costs of Ski Accidents through Tort Law: Limits of Fault-based Liability in Practice – and Alternative Regimes, *JETL* 2016, 1, at 3–4).

4 Scenario of the English case: *Caldwell* v. *Maguire and Fitzgerald*, Court of Appeal, 27.06.2001, [2002] P.I.Q.R. P6 (see below, pp. 188–189).

Questions[5]

1) Sports accidents are, second to traffic accidents,[6] one of the most common causes of personal injury brought before the courts.[7] The fact that some sports frequently lead to injury, and that the participants in these sports deliberately engage in this activity while being well aware of the risks involved, has led to the proposal that legal liability should be limited or excluded on the basis of acceptance of risk of injury. If we take, for example, German law, does the fact that the defendant has *deliberately engaged in an activity bearing a considerable risk of injury* limit or, indeed, exclude liability?

   What role do the rules of sports associations play when it comes to determining the standard of care owed in tort law?

2) In most jurisdictions, liability for sports accidents is *fault-based* and the action will only succeed if the victim can establish and, where necessary, provide proof that the defendant committed a "fault". For the victim it may, however, often be difficult to establish the fault of the other party. How did the *German* courts deal with this difficulty and how did they solve the skiing accident reported in the materials? What were the consequences of the claimant's contributory negligence? What would have been the outcome if it could not have been established at all which of the skiers, if either, was at fault?

3) How did the *Swiss* Federal Supreme Court of Justice solve the case of the skiing accident included in the materials? Why did the injured skier receive compensation for only 50% of the damage suffered?

4) In what is possibly the most famous *French* tort law case, the *Jand'heur* case, the *Cour de cassation* established a strict liability regime for persons who keep a thing under control. It has been said that "the French regime of liability for things pursuant to Art. 1384 (1) [now Art. 1242 (1)] C. civ. constitutes one of the great distinguishing features of French tort law [. . .]."[8] What are the conditions and limits for liability of the keeper of a thing or, in other words, of the person who has a thing under control (*gardien de la chose*), according to French law?

   How would you decide the case of the skiing accident under French law? When is liability for sports accidents strict, as opposed to being fault-based in French law?

   On which principle(s) might the strict liability of the *gardien* be based?

5) Articles 1382, 1383, and 1384 (1) of the Belgian Civil Code and Arts. 1240, 1241, and 1242 (1) of the French Civil Code have the same wording. What are the conditions for liability of the *gardien de la chose* according to the case law of the Belgian *Cour de cassation*? Would Art. 1384 (1) of the Belgian Civil Code apply in scenario 1, or would the liability of the skiers be fault-based?

6) *Italy* was one of the first jurisdictions to introduce, in Art. 2050 of the Civil Code of 1942, a general provision on liability for dangerous activities. In light of the

---

[5] It should be noted that in *professional* sports, litigation is often resolved through sports arbitration, which uses its own set of rules, tailored for each discipline in question.
[6] For traffic accidents, see below, Chapter 9, pp. 229 ff.
[7] For ski accidents, see the numbers in fn. 3.
[8] W. van Gerven/J. Lever/P. Larouche, *Cases, Materials and Text on National, Supranational and International Tort Law*, Oxford/Portland: Hart, 2000, p. 539.

information provided in the materials, would you consider this liability to be fault-based (using a presumption of fault), a regime based on liability without fault, or a system in between the two?

Regarding the general rules on tort liability, would you have recommended in Italian law to deal with the case of the skiing accident under the provision on fault-based liability (Art. 2043), the rule on dangerous activities (Art. 2050), the provision on damage done by things (Art. 2051), or the rule on traffic accidents (Art. 2054)? Keep in mind the numbers of victims injured in ski accidents every year (see footnote 3).

In 2003, the *Italian* legislator introduced a special rule for ski collisions that matches the rule for motor traffic accidents in Art. 2054 (2) of the Italian Civil Code. How would you solve the ski accident under Art. 19 of the new Italian Law no 363/2003 of 24 December 2003? Which problem does this provision address and solve?

7) French law, Belgian law, and Italian law all belong to the same "legal family". Do they reach identical solutions in our scenario? What are the benefits of using the classification of "legal families" and what are its limits?[9]

8) Which solution to the skiing accident would you suggest under Arts. 149 and 150 of the *Slovenian* Code of Obligations?

9) In the former socialist legal family, as well as in the new codifications of many former members of this legal family, liability in tort was, and still is, generally fault-based, with fault being presumed.[10] The burden is thus, in principle, on the defendant to prove that he or she was not at fault. What might be the advantages and disadvantages of this approach? Would this approach help reaching a fair outcome in the above scenarios?

Compare with the approach that was already discussed in continental European *ius commune*.

10) In the *UK*, injuries occur more frequently in horse riding than on ski slopes. In the *Caldwell* case, on which the second scenario is based, the competent sports authorities found the defendant riders guilty of careless riding. However, the Court of Appeal rejected the claimant's action for liability in tort. Why?

11) Sports accidents often happen in a split second and witnesses are often not available or their statements may be biased. Compare the solutions of the skiing case under a fault-based system, with or without a presumption of fault, with the application of a system of liability for dangerous activities, and with a strict liability system (such as under French law). What are the respective advantages and disadvantages, and what might be the (social and economic) costs of applying the different approaches? Which approach would you prefer for solving sports accidents? Give reasons.

---

9 On legal families, see K. ZWEIGERT/H. KÖTZ, *An Introduction to Comparative Law*, 3rd ed., Oxford: Clarendon Press, 1998, pp. 63 ff.

10 A presumption of fault has not been adopted in *Poland* and *Romania*, see Art. 415 of the Polish Civil Code (in English translation: *Any person who by his fault has caused damage to another person is obliged to redress it.*) and Art. 1357 of the Romanian Civil Code (in English translation: *(1) Those who cause damage to another person through an illegal act, be it intentional or negligent, have to repair it.*).

Table of contents

I. Germany
1. Bürgerliches Gesetzbuch, BGB (*Civil Code*), §§ 823, 254 (1) .... p. 164
2. GERHARD WAGNER, in: *Münchener Kommentar zum BGB, Band 6 (Munich Commentary on the German Civil Code, Vol. 6)*, 7th ed., München: C.H. Beck, 2017, § 823, nos. 563 ff. .... p. 164
3. Bundesgerichtshof, BGH (*Federal Supreme Court of Justice*), 11.01.1972, BGHZ 58, 40 .... p. 166

II. Switzerland
1. Obligationenrecht/Code des obligations (*Code of Obligations*), Arts. 41 (1), 44 (1) .... p. 168
2. Bundesgericht/Tribunal fédéral (*Federal Supreme Court of Justice*), 07.02.1956, (*Bally* c. *Rosti*), BGE 82 II 25 .... p. 169

III. Czech Republic
Občanský zákoník (*Czech Civil Code*) as of 2014, § 2899 .... p. 170

IV. France
1. Code civil (*Civil Code*), Arts. 1240, 1241, 1242 (1) .... p. 171
2. Cour de cassation, chambres réunies (*Court of Cassation, assembled chambers*), 13.02.1930 (*arrêt Jand'heur/Jand'heur case*), in: HENRI CAPITANT et al., *Les grands arrêts de la jurisprudence civile, Tome 2 (Leading Cases of the Civil Courts, Vol. 2)*, 13th ed. by FRANÇOIS TERRÉ/YVES LEQUETTE, Paris: Dalloz, 2015, n° 202 (with observations) .... p. 171
3. Cour d'appel de Colmar (*Appellate Court of Colmar*), 18.09.1992, (*New Hampshire Unat SA* c. *Hugel*), J.C.P. 1993, IV, n° 1711, and Cour d'appel de Paris (*Appellate Court of Paris*), 23.05.1985, summarised in: Gaz. Pal. 1986, 1, somm. 41 .... p. 173
4. BORIS STARCK/HENRI ROLAND/LAURENT BOYER, *Obligations, 1. Responsabilité délictuelle (Law of Obligations, 1. Torts)*, 5th ed., Paris: Litec, 1996, nos. 626–641 .... p. 174

V. Belgium
1. Code civil/Burgerlijk Wetboek (*Civil Code*), Arts. 1382, 1383, 1384 (1), 1386 .... p. 176
2. Cour de cassation/Hof van Cassatie (*Court of Cassation*), 26.05.1904, Pas. 1904, I, 246 .... p. 177
3. Cour de cassation/Hof van Cassatie (*Court of Cassation*), 27.11.1969, Pas. 1970, I, 277 .... p. 177
4. ARIANE FRY, La responsabilité en droit du sport (*Liability in Sports Law*), in: FRANÇOIS GLANSDORFF/PATRICK HENRY (dir.), *Droit de la responsabilité: Domaines choisis (Liability Law: Selected Topics)*, Liège: Anthémis, 2010, pp. 93 ff. .... p. 178

VI. Italy

1. Codice civile (*Civil Code*), Arts. 2043, 2050, 2051, 2054 .... p. 179
2. Giorgio Cian/Alberto Trabucchi, *Commentario breve al Codice civile (Short Commentary on the Civil Code)*, 11th ed., Padova: CEDAM, 2014, Arts. 2050, 2051 .... p. 180
3. Marco Bona/Andrea Castelnuovo/Pier Giuseppe Monateri, *La responsabilità civile nello sport (Civil Liability in Sports)*, Milano: IPSOA, 2002, n° 3.4.1 .... p. 181
4. Legge 24 dicembre 2003, n. 363: Norme in materia di sicurezza nella pratica degli sport invernali da discesa e da fondo (*Law n° 363/2003 of 24 December 2003*), Art. 19 (1) .... p. 182

VII. Slovenia

1. Obligacijski zakonik (*Code of Obligations*), Arts. 149, 150 .... p. 183
2. Vrhovno sodišče Republike Slovenije (*Supreme Court of Slovenia*), 25.05.2013, case n° II Ips 787/2009 .... p. 183

VIII. Diverse jurisdictions formerly belonging to the socialist legal family

1. Гражданский кодекс Российской Федерации (*Russian Civil Code*), Art. 1064 (1) and (2) .... p. 184
2. Võlaõigusseadus (*Estonian Code of Obligations*), Art. 1050 (1) .... p. 184
3. Obligacijski zakonik (*Slovenian Code of Obligations*), Art. 131 (1) .... p. 184
4. Zakon o obligacionim odnosima (*Serbian Law on Contracts and Torts*), Art. 154 (1) .... p. 185
5. Michael Will/Vladimir Vodinelić, Generelle Verschuldensvermutung – das unbekannte Wesen. Osteuropäische Angebote zum gemeineuropäischen Deliktsrecht? (*A general presumption of fault – the unknown creature. Eastern European contributions to the common European law of torts*), in: *European Tort Law – Liber amicorum for Helmut Koziol*, Frankfurt am Main et al.: Peter Lang, 2000, pp. 307 ff. at 341–342 .... p. 185
6. Obren Stancović, La responsabilité civile selon la nouvelle loi yougoslave sur les obligations (*Civil Liability according to the New Yugoslav Law of Obligations*), Rev. int. de droit comparé 1979, 765 at 765–766 .... p. 186

IX. Historical foundations: Roman law and *ius commune*

Bénédict Winiger, *La responsabilié aquilienne en droit commun – Damnum Culpa Datum (Tortious Liability in Continental European Ius Commune)*, Genève/Bâle/Munich: Helbing Lichtenhahn, 2002, pp. 76 ff. .... p. 186

X. Principles of European Tort Law

PETL, Art. 4:201 .... p. 187

XI. England and Wales

Court of Appeal, *Caldwell* v. *Maguire and Fitzgerald*, 27.06.2001, [2002] P.I.Q.R. P6 .... p. 188

Materials[11]

I. Germany

1. Bürgerliches Gesetzbuch, BGB (*Civil Code*)

§ 823. Schadensersatzpflicht. (1) Wer vorsätzlich oder fahrlässig das Leben, den Körper, die Gesundheit, die Freiheit, das Eigentum oder ein sonstiges Recht eines anderen widerrechtlich verletzt, ist dem anderen zum Ersatz des daraus entstehenden Schadens verpflichtet. [. . .]

§ 254. Mitverschulden. (1) Hat bei der Entstehung des Schadens ein Verschulden des Beschädigten mitgewirkt, so hängt die Verpflichtung zum Ersatz sowie der Umfang des zu leistenden Ersatzes von den Umständen, insbesondere davon ab, inwieweit der Schaden vorwiegend von dem einen oder dem anderen Teil verursacht worden ist. [. . .][12]

Translation

§ 823. Duty to compensate loss. (1) Whosoever unlawfully injures, intentionally or negligently, the life, body, health, freedom, property, or other right of another person, has an obligation to the other person to compensate the resulting loss. [. . .]

§ 254. Contributory negligence. (1) Where fault on the part of the injured person contributes to the occurrence of the damage, liability for damages as well as the extent of compensation to be paid depend on the circumstances, in particular on the extent the damage is mainly caused by one or the other party. [. . .][13]

2. GERHARD WAGNER, in: *Münchener Kommentar zum BGB* (*Munich Commentary on the German Civil Code*), Vol. 6, 7th ed., 2017, § 823, nos. 563 ff.

1. Sports and games

a) Fundamentals

[. . .]

564 Sport has its origins in the combat exercises and war-games once found in warrior societies. Even if sporting activities today no longer serve the purpose of developing fighting skills, but instead satisfy people's craving for a controlled release from a largely hazard-free everyday life, sport remains what it always has been: an activity that is **not without its dangers**. Consequently, the practice of sports entails, all too regularly, accidents and associated lawsuits. All this gives rise to the

---

11 For the original language versions of the materials reproduced in this chapter, see the companion website at www.routledge.com/9781138567733.
12 Für die Definition des Verschuldens in § 276 BGB, siehe oben, Kapitel 6, S. 130–131.
13 For the definition of fault in § 276 BGB, see above, Chapter 6, pp. 130–131.

central question whether voluntary participation in sporting activities should **limit or exclude any legal liability on the basis of acceptance of the risk of injury** associated with it. To answer this question, we have to draw an immediate distinction between contact sports, involving interaction with others, and individual contests, where a number of athletes compete alongside one another. [. . .]

b) Contact sports

565 Tennis and squash certainly demonstrate some of the elements of contact sports, as do typical cases such as **football**, handball and boxing. A discussion of the standard of liability for injuries arising from sports in this category was necessary only because people, relying on the idea of result-based wrongfulness, got into the habit of inferring a breach of the duty of care (*Sorgfaltspflichtverstoß*), and consequently unlawfulness, from the mere injury to a legally-protected interest. In general, they failed to pay sufficient regard to the point that the mere fact that an injury has been inflicted is not necessarily an indication that the person who caused it has been guilty of failure to take proper care. It was for this basic reason that in one judgment [. . .] the BGH considered, in an *obiter dictum*, that taking part in a dangerous sport could be regarded as **"acting on one's own risk or peril"** and thereby **accepting** potential injury.

566 The BGH later drew back from this view, and rightly so. A person engaging in contact sports **in no way consents to infringement of his legal rights**. On the contrary, he has every expectation that his opponents will abide by the rules of the game, and in addition do their very best to prevent injury. Nevertheless, if this criterion is satisfied (e.g. if a footballer suffers serious harm as a result of an entirely lawful tackle by an opponent) there is no question of the latter being liable, for the simple reason that he has not acted without proper care. As a result of this, where sports injuries are concerned, the litigation tends to turn on the question of whether there has been a **breach of the rules of the game**. Thus, with football, the issue is generally whether there has been a **failure to observe the rules** laid down by the DFB [*Deutscher Fußballbund*, or German Football Association] or the FIFA, as the case may be [. . .]. The **burden of proof** of a breach of the rules, or of negligence of the person who caused the injury, is on the injured party, as it is under the general law; the court may thereby take into account the **decisions of the referee** [. . .]. These basic principles have no need of any further reinforcement from the idea of an activity undertaken at one's own risk [. . .]. Instead, they follow from the basic idea of fault liability, under which it is no easy feat to make someone liable for an injury he caused; it is necessary for his behaviour to be wrongful in regard of all the circumstances of the case, which involves demonstrating that there has been a failure to observe the level of care people are entitled to expect in the particular situation. [. . .]

567 [. . .] **Sport federation rules are not binding legal precepts**, and breaches of the duty of care are not confined to infringements of some abstract standard of behaviour as objectified in the rules of the game. Apart from the outwardly obvious features of the activity in hand, it is a matter of the legitimate expectations of those taking part in it: for instance, what reasonable football players are entitled to expect from others by way of precautions against unnecessary injuries. These expectations do not go as far as requiring a behaviour that is guaranteed to prevent any injury – that would generally be illusory – but include the avoidance of serious breaches of the rules of the game and the infliction of deliberate injury (e.g. by a dangerous sliding tackle, or hitting or kicking an opponent other than while trying to get the ball). [. . .]

569   The basic principles outlined here apply not only to professional competitions, but also to adults engaging in sport competitions in their leisure time, in particular to children's sporting activities, starting with football [. . .].

c) Individual sports

570   When it comes to the practice of **individual or sports alongside others**, physical contact between participants is neither required nor desired. It follows that here there can be no question of limitations to legal liability based on assumption of risk or on acting at one's own peril [. . .]. But it is different in the case of **competitive sports** where people have to take into account the possibility of injury even if the rules are observed or broken only in minor respects: take, for example, **car, bicycle or horse racing**. In these instances, it is appropriate to apply the rules described above that were developed for contact sports.

572   When it comes to **skiing accidents,** with which the courts are dealing frequently, they often firstly take into consideration the rules of the International Ski Federation, the **FIS rules** [. . .].

573   However, it does not follow from these rules, and in particular the general rule that you should not injure others, that every skiing accident gives rise to a case of civil liability. Here, as in general, there is **no absolute duty to avoid damage**; on the contrary, the individual is only required to take reasonable care. [. . .] He who observes the duty of controlled skiing but nevertheless commits a mistake, such as a tilting the ski and thus coming off course, is not in breach of a duty of care in tort; he is however in breach if, instead of letting himself fall down to avoid a collision, he attempts to continue skiing in an unreasonable manner. [. . .] Since the violation of a duty of care cannot be inferred from the mere occurrence of a collision, the injured person cannot rely on a presumption of fault and bears the entire burden of proof in this regard.

3. Bundesgerichtshof, BGH (*Federal Supreme Court of Justice*), 11.01.1972, BGHZ 58, 40

a) Liability of skiers (collision of two skiers on a run).
b) A skier must conduct himself in the course of a run in such a way as not to endanger or injure other skiers.

German Civil Code (BGB), § 823.

VI. Civil Senate, 11.1.1972: Th. [defendant] v. Sch. [plaintiff]. VI ZR 187/70

I. *Landgericht* (first instance court), Freiburg
II. *Oberlandesgericht* (appeal court), Karlsruhe

On the afternoon of 10th April 1967, the parties were involved in a skiing accident on the Zeller slope in the vicinity of Feldberg. As a result of the accident, the plaintiff suffered a complex spiral fracture of the femur. [. . .] Immediately before the accident the defendant was skiing downhill in a straight line on the lower third of the Zeller slope, while the plaintiff was simultaneously traversing at an angle of about 45°. Neither party saw the other. Roughly in the middle of the bottom third of the slope, they collided with each other. The precise nature of the collision is a matter of controversy. The defendant fell to his left, down a small drop, and remained unhurt. The plaintiff was thrown to the right and incurred a spiral fracture of the femur.

The plaintiff claimed three-quarters of his losses due to the accident, together with a proportionate award of damages for pain and suffering, from the defendant; he also sought a declaration that the defendant was liable to compensate [. . .] three-quarters of any of his future losses arising from the accident.[14] He argued that the defendant had been skiing straight down at an excessive speed, considerably faster than he had been, and had hit him from behind causing him to twist round and fall. The defendant, he said, was overwhelmingly to blame for the accident. He argued that he himself was guilty of contributory fault to a degree of no more than 25%.

The defendant alleged that he had been skiing in short turns and not in a straight line. He denied that he had failed to keep a proper lookout, or that he had been going too fast. The plaintiff, he said, had been going considerably faster than he had, and had run into him without warning from behind. [. . .]

Grounds of the decision:

The court below held the defendant liable under § 823 (1) BGB. However, it found contributory fault on the plaintiff's part (§ 254 BGB), which it quantified at 50%. [. . .]

2. The question of liability – and the question of whether the plaintiff has to accept that he was contributorily negligent under § 254 BGB – are to be decided, as the court below duly accepted, according to general legal principles. Nevertheless, this does not mean that circumstances particular to the practice of skiing cannot be taken into consideration. [. . .]

As for the duties, whose breach by the defendant is in issue here, they are particular instances of the general duty of care. With respect to a skier on an open run, the content of these rules includes a requirement that he conduct himself so as not to endanger or hurt anyone else, [. . .]. [I]n particular, [they require] that, in so far as there is a possibility of harm to third parties, he should only ski under proper control (i.e. he must temper his speed according to his own capabilities, the difficulty of the terrain, the conditions of the snow, and the extent to which other people are around [. . .]). [. . .] It follows that any skier must keep an eye on the area ahead of him, and on other skiers in, and dashing into, his path; he must take into his calculations the potential obstacles those skiers may present; and he must regulate his speed accordingly, with a view to reacting correctly and quickly to their proximity to his path and being able either to take evasive action or, in some cases, to stop.

3. According to the view taken by the court below [. . .] not only the plaintiff but also the *defendant* has negligently infringed these duties.

a) It is accepted that the defendant did not see the plaintiff (and that the latter did not see him). But the court below was satisfied that the defendant could have seen the plaintiff (as the plaintiff could have seen him), and could have reacted in time so to prevent the accident (i.e. avoid the collision). On the basis of his investigation of the ski slope where the accident had occurred, and assisted by expert advice, the judge at first instance has determined that a straight-line skier such as the defendant would have had a view of the entire expanse of

---

14 *Note by the author*: Such a declaration acts to avert the possibility of the claimant's right to compensation later becoming time-barred.

the lower part of the Zeller slope, except for one part, of no relevance here, lying below what seems to have been the site of the accident. [. . .]

From the fact that the defendant did not see the plaintiff, the first instance judge concluded that he was skiing without keeping a proper lookout. Under the circumstances as established, there is no argument that can properly be taken against this conclusion. [. . .]

c) [. . .] Even the argument of this appeal acknowledges that the rule requiring one skier coming up behind another to set a course which will not put that other in danger [. . .] cannot be invoked by the defendant here. As the court below duly concluded, the plaintiff did not come up "behind" the defendant – any more than the defendant came up behind the plaintiff. Both parties were travelling towards each other at a mutual angle of 45%. In this case, according to the finding at first instance, both parties were travelling at the same speed; during the time before the collision, the defendant was even skiing slightly higher on the slope than the plaintiff. [. . .]

4. The court below found contributory negligence in the plaintiff (§ 254 BGB), which it quantified at 50%. [. . .]

b) In *assessing* the fault on both sides which contributed to the accident, the court below reasoned that the causal contribution was roughly the same on both sides. Indeed, had the parties spotted each other, each would have been bound to take whatever steps he could to avoid the collision [. . .]. [. . .]

On this basis, it reached the conclusion that the contribution of the plaintiff was 50% [and the compensation was reduced accordingly].

c) The appeal against this judgment is ill-founded [and the judgment confirmed].

II. Switzerland

1. Obligationenrecht/Code des obligations (*Code of Obligations*)

Art. 41. (1) Wer einem andern widerrechtlich Schaden zufügt, sei es mit Absicht, sei es aus Fahrlässigkeit, wird ihm zum Ersatze verpflichtet. [. . .]

Art. 44. (1) Hat der Geschädigte in die schädigende Handlung eingewilligt, oder haben Umstände, für die er einstehen muss, auf die Entstehung oder Verschlimmerung des Schadens eingewirkt oder die Stellung des Ersatzpflichtigen sonst erschwert, so kann der Richter die Ersatzpflicht ermässigen oder gänzlich von ihr entbinden. [. . .]

Translation

Art. 41. (1) Any person who unlawfully causes damage to another, whether wilfully or negligently, is obliged to provide compensation. [. . .]

Art. 44. (1) Where the injured party consented to the action which caused the loss or damage, or circumstances attributable to him or her helped give rise to or aggravated the loss or damage, or otherwise worsened the position of the liable party, the court may reduce the amount of compensation or even dispense with it entirely. [. . .]

2. Bundesgericht/Tribunal fédéral (*Federal Supreme Court of Justice*), 07.02.1956 (*Bally c. Rosti*), BGE 82 II 25

Judgment of the 1st Civil Division, dated 7.2.1956: Bally v. Rosti

A.- At about 11 a.m. on Sunday 13th January 1952, Carl Bally, then aged 15, was skiing down a slope between Corviglia and St. Moritz, towards the path connecting Giop with the Salastrains restaurant and guesthouse; he was with a class from the Lyceum Alpinum in Zuoz, under the leadership and direction of an instructor, Mr Schild. The slope led steeply from a hill some 50–80 m above the path, swung left onto a ledge directly above the path, and merged into the path about 30 m beyond the curve and some 20–50 m from the guesthouse.

On the ledge, the snow had been slightly displaced by passing skiers onto the path where it formed a sloping bank. Luigi Rosti, a bank official from Milan, was standing here, on the side of the path facing the hill. He had planted his skis in the snow, had his back to the slope, and was enjoying the view, watching the operation of the ski school on the flatter practice area lying below the path.

Although Bally knew the hard slope perfectly and had spotted Rosti from the hill, he was traversing down the slope so fast that he lost control when taking the bend, careened on to the path, collided with Rosti and his skis, rolled over twice, and flew over Rosti to land about 2 m below the path. The collision was so violent that Rosti was knocked off the path and broke the head of his left femur.

The broken bone had to be nailed. Rosti remained in hospital in Samedan until 1st February 1952. On the 3rd February, he had to be transferred to Milan in order to continue medical treatment because of a wound infection and a general septic condition. The infection led to phlebitis in the femur. Rosti returned to work part-time on 15th April 1952 and full-time on 16th June. But movement in his left leg remains restricted to this day.

B.- On 2nd April 1953, Rosti brought proceedings against Bally [. . .] claiming CHF 70,000 for loss incurred, together with pain and suffering [. . .].[15]

The *Bundesgericht* thus reasons

1. Under Art. 41 (1) of the Code of Obligations (CO), a person is only bound to compensate damage caused to another if he acted wrongfully. The *Obergericht* [appeal court] inferred the wrongfulness of the defendant's conduct from the fact that he had caused serious bodily injury to the claimant without any justification. [. . .]. The defendant is wrong to argue that his conduct should not be regarded as wrongful [. . .]. According to general legal principles, a person who causes a situation which could lead to harm to someone else is bound to take the measures necessary to prevent that harm [. . .].

The defendant has infringed this requirement. [. . .] [He] was bound [. . .] to ski in such a way that no harm could come to the plaintiff. The fact that he formed part of a class under the leadership of a ski instructor did not relieve him of that obligation. He was obliged to set himself a suitable speed, in the light of his own abilities, the steepness of the slope and the snow conditions as he knew them to be (a slope that was firm, well-worn and partly frozen), so that he could avoid going across the slope at the left-hand bend and careering

---

15 Today worth around CHF 302,000.

into the plaintiff. Even someone skiing in a group can, and must, adapt the way he skis in accordance with his own abilities; where experienced skiers take a stretch with small turns, he should turn and lift more, in order to approach a point where there is a known or obvious danger, in such a way that no-one will be endangered. [. . .] Instead of doing this, the defendant was going significantly too fast [. . .]. Had he slowed his pace appropriately, he would not have lost control and crashed. [. . .]

2. Under Art. 41 (1) CO a person is only bound to compensate for a loss if he inflicts it intentionally or negligently. The defendant is alleged [. . .] to be guilty of negligence. The *Obergericht* concluded that he negotiated "a dangerously steep exit onto a path, with clearly inadequate technical skills, and too fast". One cannot agree wholly with this, in so far as no complaint can be mounted against the defendant solely on the basis that he took part in the descent. He was part of a class which he had often been with before; the leader of the class, who was familiar with his ability and level of skill, had not advised him that there were any particular reasons for him to withdraw. The defendant was entitled to assume that he had the capacity to engage in this run, even if his technical skills were not yet fully developed. Nevertheless, as has been pointed out, this did not relieve him from his duty to adapt his speed to the circumstances and to take into account the presence of the plaintiff. [. . .] The objection that even the most skilful can suffer mishaps is not convincing. It is true that even the most astute skier accepts the danger of an accident. If he does not endanger anyone as a result, then he cannot be criticised. But if he has to say to himself that his skiing could injure someone, he must take all reasonable care to prevent this. [. . .] The defendant could and should have been aware that a serious collision with the plaintiff was capable of injuring him badly. The actual outcome did not fall outside people's ordinary experience; nor was it beyond what even a 15 year old high school student ought to have foreseen. Therefore, as a matter of principle, it follows that the defendant is liable to pay compensation. [. . .]

4. Art. 44 (1) CO empowers the judge to reduce damages to a lower sum or to nil, if there are circumstances for which the person suffering the loss must take responsibility, and that have contributed to his damage, aggravated it, or have otherwise worsened the position of the defendant.

The defendant is right to argue that this is such a case, since the plaintiff remained standing in a place where he ought to have realised that there was a danger of collision. [. . .] So he is partly responsible for the collision. Nevertheless, his fault is less serious than that of the defendant.

5. In view of the degree of the defendant's fault and the plaintiff's own contributory fault, it is right to limit the defendant's liability to 50% of the plaintiff's damage. [. . .]

III. Czech Republic

Občanský zákoník (*Czech Civil Code*) as of 2014

§ 2899. Kdo pro sebe přijal nebezpečí oběti, byť tak učinil za takových okolností, že to lze považovat za neprozřetelné, nevzdal se tím práva na náhradu proti tomu, kdo újmu způsobil.

Translation

§ 2899. A person who assumed the risk of becoming a victim, whether or not he or she did so under such circumstances that it could be considered imprudent, did not thereby waive his or her right to compensation against the person who caused the harm.

IV. France

1. Code civil (*Civil Code*)

Art. 1240 [ancien art. 1382]. Tout fait quelconque de l'homme, qui cause à autrui un dommage, oblige celui par la faute duquel il est arrivé, à le réparer.

Art. 1241 [ancien art. 1383]. Chacun est responsable du dommage qu'il a causé non seulement par son fait, mais encore par sa négligence ou par son imprudence.

Art. 1242 al. 1ᵉʳ[ancien art. 1384 al. 1ᵉʳ]. On est responsable non seulement du dommage que l'on cause par son propre fait, mais encore de celui qui est causé par le fait des personnes dont on doit répondre, ou des choses que l'on a sous sa garde. [. . .]

Translation

Art. 1240 [former Art. 1382]. Any act of a person, which causes damage to another, obliges the person by whose fault it occurred, to compensate it.

Art. 1241 [former Art. 1383]. Everyone is liable for the damage he or she causes not only by his or her intentional act, but also by his or her negligent conduct or by his or her imprudence.

Art. 1242 [former Art. 1384]. (1) A person is liable not only for the damage he or she causes by his or her own act, but also for that which is caused by the acts of persons for whom he or she is responsible, or by things he or she has under control. [. . .]

2. Cour de cassation, ch. réun. (*Court of Cassation, assembled chambers*), 13.02.1930 (*arrêt Jand'heur/Jand'heur case*), in: HENRI CAPITANT et al., *Les grands arrêts de la jurisprudence civile, Tome 2 (Leading Cases of the Civil Courts, Vol. 2)*, 13ᵗʰ ed., 2015, n° 202 (with observations)

CIVIL LIABILITY. INANIMATE OBJECTS. PRESUMPTION
OF FAULT. REBUTTABILITY. – Ass. Chamb., 13.02.1930
(D. P. 1930. 1. 57, rapport LE MARC'HADOUR, concl. MATTER,
note RIPERT, S. 1930. 1. 121, note ESMEIN).

(*Jand'heur (a widow)* v. *Les Galeries belfortaises*)

JUDGMENT

The Court: – ... Whereas the presumption of liability in Art. [1242] (1) of the French *Code civil*, affecting a person who has under control a thing which has caused damage to another, can only be rebutted by proof of an overwhelming fortuitous event (*cas fortuit*), *force majeure*, or an unconnected causal event outside of the defendant's responsibility; it is not sufficient herein for the defendant to show that he was in no way at fault, or that the cause of the events leading to the damage remains unknown; – Whereas, on 22nd April 1926, a lorry belonging to the *Société Aux Galeries belfortaises* ran over and injured Lise Jand'heur, a minor; that the judgment under appeal declined to apply the provision referred to, on the basis that an accident occasioned by a motor vehicle in motion, with a person driving and controlling it, was not the act of a thing under someone's control within the terms of Art. [1242] (1) CC, in the absence of proof that there was something actually wrong with the vehicle; and that it was argued that it followed that in order to obtain compensation for the damage suffered, the plaintiff had to prove negligence of the driver;[16] – Whereas however, the law, in applying the presumption stipulated, draws no distinction according to whether the thing occasioning the damage was or was not under human control; nor is it necessary that there be an inherent defect in the thing that caused the damage, given that Art. [1242] ties liability to the control of the thing, and not to the thing itself; – From which it follows that, by deciding in the way which it did, the judgment under appeal [. . .] failed to properly apply the abovementioned text of the law; – For these reasons, the judgment is annulled . . . .

OBSERVATIONS. – This decision is of utmost importance. It embodies a definitive decision that Art. [1242] (1) CC creates a presumption of liability against anyone who has, under his control, a thing that has inflicted damage.

Ever since the end of the nineteenth century, the development of a society based on machines, multiplying the number of accidents whose causes were hard to establish, had been highlighting the inadequacy of fault-based liability under Art. [1240] of the *Code civil*. Thus, from this time onwards, and with the aim of obtaining compensation for victims of injury, the *Cour de cassation* had been inferring from Art. [1242] (1) CC a general principle of liability for things (Civ. 16 juin 1896, *Teffaine*, D. 97. 1. 433, note Saleilles, S. 97. 1. 17, note Esmein). [. . .] From the 1920s onwards, burgeoning motor traffic has given rise to a resurgence of the problem: if a motorist injures a third party, can he be made liable through the application of Art. [1242] (1), or is it necessary to prove that he was at fault under Art. [1240] CC?[17]

[. . .] The judgment of the *chambres réunies* presented above lays this controversy to rest: it rejects a number of restrictive interpretations concerning both the liability for damages caused by things and the nature of the thing itself [. . .].

I. Rejection of restrictive interpretations – [. . .]

A. Liability for things

There can be – it was once argued – no damage done by a thing, unless the thing suffered from some inherent *defect* which is at the origin of the damage. The assembled chambers (*chambres réunies*) reject this analysis. Indeed, they formally proclaim that, in order for

---

16 *Note by the author:* for fault-based liability in French law (Arts. 1240 and 1241 of the Civil Code), see above, Chapter 5, pp. 96 ff.
17 For the current system of liability for traffic accidents in French law, see below, Chapter 9, pp. 251 ff.

Art. [1242] (1) CC to be engaged, it is not necessary for the thing to have any inherent defect likely to cause damage [. . .]. Art. [1242] (1) makes liability dependent on one having the thing under control, and not on the nature of the thing itself. [. . .]

According to another opinion, damage inflicted by a thing is to be contrasted with damage caused *by human actions*. If a thing is operated by human hands, it is merely an instrument at the disposition of its operator; it is simply performing his will. In this situation, the only way to establish liability is under Art. [1240] CC [i.e. the rule on damage for *fault*]. By contrast, where the thing is left to itself, the damage it causes must necessarily be due to its intervention; its *gardien* (keeper or custodian) can then be made liable under Art. [1242] (1). This view amounted to a considerable limitation to the ambit of Art. [1242] (1); all accidents caused by a vehicle being driven by someone would fall outside of it. [. . .].

B. The quality of the thing

Here too, the *chambres réunies* have rejected this restrictive interpretation, deciding that Art. [1242] (1) applies to anyone who has a thing under control; whether the thing is, or is not, under human control makes no difference. Hence, the presumption of liability now applies to any damage caused by a person through the intervention of a thing: be it a car, a bicycle, a firearm, etc . . . . [. . .]

Furthermore, by clear implication, the *chambres réunies* reject the theory that Art. [1242] only covers things that, because of their *dangerous* nature, require effective attention by whoever is in charge of them, such as cars or guns. Under this theory, inoffensive things such as domestic furniture would not be included, since they do not strictly need such attention at all [. . .]. By not requiring dangerousness as a condition of the applicability of Art. [1242], there can be no doubt whatsoever that the *chambres réunies* rejected this restrictive theory. [. . .]

It is worth adding that subsequent case law has decided that damage caused by the *human body* itself can be the subject of a claim for compensation under Art. [1242] (1), when it forms a composite unit with a thing (such as a bicycle, or a pair of skis) that causes it to move in a particular way. In this case, we effectively consider that the instrument causing the damage is not so much the body which comes into direct contact, than the thing which has imparted to it a degree of kinetic energy (Crim. 21 juin 1990, *Bull. crim.*, n° 257, *Rev. trim. dr. civ.* 1991. 124, obs. Jourdain). [. . .]

Mention must be made of the fact that, by the Law of 5.7.1985 on traffic accident victims, the legislator took a number of situations which exemplified liability for things, and indeed constituted its most important area of application, and removed them entirely from the ambit of Art. [1242] (1) CC. [O]ne should therefore beware of the fact that all situations concerning damages for accidents caused by motor vehicles are now not covered by Art. [1242] (1), but by the provisions of the Law of 5.7.1985. [. . .][18]

3. Cour d'appel de Colmar (*Appellate Court of Colmar*), 18.09.1992 (*New Hampshire Unat SA c. Hugel*), J.C.P. 1993, IV, n° 1711

1711 Civil liability. – Liability for things. Two skiers at the top of a steep descent started off one after the other on separate, parallel paths. They both skied in a straight line, before finally colliding. It is impossible, in these circumstances, to determine with certainty which one was further down on the run, and no fault can be established against either.

---

18 See below, Chapter 9, pp. 251 ff.

The skier injured in the accident sued the other for compensation. Noting that the defendant had been mounted on skis, that these skis had provided him with the means of rapid and dynamic movement, and that they were solely under his control, a first instance court held him solely and completely liable under the provisions of Art. [1242] (1) of the Civil Code for the damage resulting from the accident.

By taking account of the dynamic part they played as a means of locomotion, the judge at first instance sufficiently characterised the skis as a cause of the accident, even assuming that there had not been any direct contact between them and the victim.

Finally, the lack of clarity of the circumstances surrounding the accident made it impossible to exonerate the defendant, even partially. (Colmar, *2e ch. civ., 18 sept. 1992; New Hampshire Unat SA c. Hugel et a.: Juris Data, n. 049783*).

To distinguish liability under Art. 1242 (1) from fault-based liability under Arts. 1240 and 1241 CC, see: Appellate Court of Paris, 23.05.1985, summarised in: Gaz. Pal. 1986, 1, somm. 41 with note:

A skier had maintained complete control over his skis, and had not deviated from his trajectory. He hit another skier and injured him. Held: no liability for things under Art. [1242] (1) CC, but liability for negligence under Art. [1240] CC; the conditions for liability under Art. [1240] CC were met [so that there was no need to have recourse to Art. 1242 (1)].

4. BORIS STARCK/HENRI ROLAND/LAURENT BOYER, *Obligations, 1. Responsabilité délictuelle (Law of Obligations, 1. Torts)*, 5th ed., 1996, nos. 626–641

SUBSECTION V

THE BASIS OF LIABILITY FOR DAMAGE DONE BY THINGS

626. – The decided cases here show a distinct concern for practicalities; they deal with particular problems as and when they appear. By contrast, academic writings, characterised by a search for a system, have sought to find a principled justification for this [. . .] head of liability [based on Art. 1242 (1)], which is developing towards becoming a generalised principle of law. We will here present in broad strokes the three explanations which are the most popular among authors. Namely, that this liability is based (§ 1) on risk, (§ 2) on fault, or (§ 3) on a warranty by the *gardien de la chose* (keeper of the thing).

§ 1. – The theory that liability is based on risk

627. – Some writers view liability for things as embodying the triumph of the theory of liability based on risk. [. . .]

On the other hand, the *Cour de cassation* has never invoked this theory and lower courts have only referred to it infrequently. [. . .]

628. – [. . .] The theory of risk-based liability has no acceptable basis, given that liability under this head applies to all types of things without making any differentiation between them. [. . .]

§ 2. – The theory that the liability depends on fault

[. . .] **630. – *Theory of presumed fault.*** – It is said that Art. [1242] (1) of the *Code Civil* provides for a presumption that the person in charge of the thing must have been at fault. This view has been accepted by some writers, and also in a few decided cases. But it does not take long to see what is wrong with it. *A presumption that cannot be rebutted is no presumption at all*. As has been made evident, the person in charge of the thing cannot escape liability, even if he does prove a complete absence of fault on his part. He is not only liable if the cause of the damage is unknown, but also if it is known and he establishes his own blamelessness beyond any doubt: as in the case of some undetectable defect in the thing itself, sudden cardiac arrest, dementia, or justified action in a case of necessity, etc.

631. – *Theory of negligence in supervision.* – To sidestep these objections, a different explanation of liability for things has been advanced. According to this theory, the liability of a person in charge of a thing depends, not on a presumption of fault, but *on the fact that he is actually at fault*: he is guilty of "negligence in supervision". The reasoning goes like this: a person armed with the use, control and management of a thing *is obliged to exercise complete command over it*, so as to prevent it from causing harm to anybody else. If the thing causes an accident or is the instrument through which an accident occurs, this in itself provides proof that the obligation in question to look after it has not been respected; and failure to perform an obligation amounts to fault. Hence, there is no need to show any error committed by the *gardien*: the accident in itself suffices. This explains why the *gardien* cannot escape liability even if he proves that he has exercised an impeccable degree of care: the gist of the action against him is not any lack of due diligence, but the fact that he allowed the thing to escape his control and cause damage as a result. [. . .]

633. – [W]e cannot accept the theory of negligence in supervision, according to which fault is regarded as being proved by the mere fact of an accident. [. . .] The notion of fault would then be free from any subjective element. How can we properly talk of fault, whether moral, civil or social, while saying that it does not carry any implication whatsoever of misconduct on the part of the *gardien*? [. . .]

634. – [. . .] We could offer multiple objections [. . .]. Indeed, once we admit the existence of an obligation to exercise control, why limit it to things we are using? *Why should we not take as our starting point an obligation to exercise control over oneself,* and consequently reason that any act that causes damage to someone else must itself be classified as fault [. . .].

Theoretical analysis gives no support to this idea. Nor do the decided cases. [. . .]

§ 3. – The theory that liability depends on a warranty by the *gardien*

636. – Being aware of all these difficulties, the *Cour de cassation* has made its own attempt to unearth a justification for the enigmatic provision in Art. [1242] (1). It has suggested two formulations worth mentioning here because the second leads us to the warranty theory.

637. – *The formulations of the Cour de cassation.* – To excise any idea that the *gardien de la chose* might escape liability by proving that he was not guilty of negligence, the *Cour de cassation* has, ever since the *Jand'heur* decision, stated that what is at stake is a *presumption of liability*.

Almost every writer agrees that this expression has no discernible meaning. Presumptions involve *facts*, which other *facts* render likely to be true. *An obligation cannot be presumed.* [. . .]

639. – [. . .] [O]ver the last thirty years or so, our highest court has moved towards a different formulation, declaring that Art. [1242] (1) establishes a *liability by operation of the law* against the person in charge of a thing. In using the expression "liability by virtue of law" (*une responsabilité de plein droit*), the *deuxième Chambre civile* gives no further justification; it declines to reveal what it sees as the nature or basis of the *gardien*'s duty. Nevertheless, the fact remains that in moving away from the term "presumption", which it had previously used, the court demonstrates its desire to distance itself from earlier mistakes, which – openly or otherwise – had tended to maintain a connection with the old idea that fault was the only proper basis for civil liability.

Proclaiming that the *gardien*'s liability is a liability by operation of the law (*une responsabilité de plein droit*) amounts to recognition that it is a no-fault liability, while leaving the basis of this liability unexplained. [. . .]

V. Belgium

1. Code civil/Burgerlijk Wetboek (*Civil Code*)

Art. 1382. Tout fait quelconque de l'homme, qui cause à autrui un dommage, oblige celui par la faute duquel il est arrivé, à le réparer.

Art. 1383. Chacun est responsable du dommage qu'il a causé non seulement par son fait, mais encore par sa négligence ou par son imprudence.

Art. 1384. (1) On est responsable non seulement du dommage que l'on cause par son propre fait, mais encore de celui qui est causé par le fait des personnes dont on doit répondre, ou des choses que l'on a sous sa garde. [. . .]

Art. 1386. Le propriétaire d'un bâtiment est responsable du dommage causé par sa ruine, lorsqu'elle est arrivée par une suite du défaut d'entretien ou par le vice de sa construction.

Translation

Art. 1382. Any act of a person, that causes damage to another, obliges the person by whose fault it occurred, to compensate it.

Art. 1383. Everyone is liable for the damage he or she causes not only by his or her intentional act, but also by his or her negligent conduct or by his or her imprudence.

Art. 1384. (1) A person is liable not only for the damage he or she causes by his or her own act, but also for that caused by the act of persons for whom he or she is responsible, or things that are under his or her control. [. . .]

Art. 1386. The owner of a building is liable for the damage caused by its collapse, when it has happened as a result of a lack of maintenance or a defect in its construction.

2. Cour de cassation/Hof van Cassatie (*Court of Cassation*), 26.05.1904, Pas. 1904, I, 246

Whereas, in Art. 1384 [of the Belgian Civil Code (CCB)], the legislator has assimilated injury inflicted by things to injury inflicted by persons; [. . .] that it follows that proof of a defect in the thing in the defendant's charge is, by the same reasoning, applied to the fault of a person for whom he is responsible, a condition of liability under Art. 1384 CCB; that there is no legal presumption that does away with the need for proof in this regard;

Whereas Art. 1386 CCB provides that the owner, and only the owner, is liable for damage caused by the dereliction of a building; that, on a proper reading of the text of this article, liability arises from a defect in the thing attributed to fault;

That, reasoning by reference to any personal fault falling directly under the application of Arts. 1382 and 1383 CCB, it makes no sense to make the *gardien* of a movable liable for damage done by it when it is free from any defect whatsoever; particularly since proof of a defect in a ruined building is a necessary condition, expressly provided for by the law, for the existence of any claim for damage caused by the ruin.

3. Cour de cassation/Hof van Cassatie (*Court of Cassation*), 27.11.1969, Pas. 1970, I, 277

COURT OF CASSATION

1st CH. – **27th November 1969.**

EXTRA-CONTRACTUAL LIABILITY – ART. 1384 (1) CCB – DEFECT IN THE THING – CONCEPT.

The mere fact that a tree-trunk, something that is not in itself defective, has been positioned owing to the fault of a third party so as to be a danger to traffic, does not permit the judge to infer the existence of a defect in it and hold the person who has control of it liable for injury done by it to a third party (Art. 1384 (1) CCB).

(SPRL SCIERIE BENOÎT, ERNEST ET COMPAGNIE V. MAGNAN.)

Summary of the Report of Mr Ganshof van der Meersch, Attorney General (Procureur Général):

The facts of this case are simple: during the night, a motor-car driven by the defendant hit a tree-trunk belonging to the plaintiff, a sawmill operator. The car was damaged and the driver injured. The judge found that the tree-trunk, which was on the roadside verge, protruded 20 cm into the zone reserved for traffic. In addition the judge found that, placed where it was, the trunk was an obstruction to traffic, and that it had not been put there by an employee of the plaintiff, but by one or more persons still unknown; [. . .].

* * *

The judgment under appeal held the plaintiff liable, on the basis of Art. 1384 CCB, for he was the entity in charge of the tree-trunk. Under the terms of this provision, "one is liable" ["*on est responsable*"] for damage caused by things under his control. [. . .]

JUDGMENTS.

THE COURT; – [. . .] On the second ground of appeal, based on a failure to properly apply Arts. 1382, 1383 and 1384 CCB, in particular Art. 1384 (1) [. . .].

Whereas it is apparent from the findings of the judgment under appeal that the motorcar driven by the defendant collided, during the night, with a tree-trunk belonging to the plaintiff company, "trunk which, left on the verge of the road . . . , protruded 20 cm . . . onto the part of the road reserved for vehicles";

That it emerges from the judgment that this interference with the road was not the act of any employee of the plaintiff, but of an unknown third party [. . .];

Whereas, in order to hold the plaintiff liable on the basis of Art. 1384 (1), a provision establishing liability for damage done by things under one's control, the judgment below finds (there being no appeal against this finding) that the plaintiff was, at the time of the accident, the person "solely in charge of its tree-trunk";

Whereas the judgment bases the defendant's liability on the fact that this tree-trunk, which he had under control, for the simple reason that it protruded on the road owing to the fault of a person unknown, suffered from an "external" defect which justified imposing liability on the plaintiff based on this provision;

Whereas the mere fact that a tree-trunk, that is in and of itself harmless, that was under control of the plaintiff at the time of the accident, was positioned so as to be a danger to traffic owing to the fault of a third party did not justify the drawing of an inference that there existed a defect in it;

This appeal is well founded;

For these reasons, the court sets aside the judgment under appeal [. . .] and remits the case to the *Tribunal de première instance* in Arlon [. . .].

4. ARIANE FRY, La responsabilité en droit du sport (*Liability in Sports Law*), in: FRANÇOIS GLANSDORFF/PATRICK HENRY (dir.), Droit de la responsabilité: Domaines choisis (*Liability Law: Selected Topics*), 2010, pp. 93 ff.

C. Liability for damage done by things

[. . .]

a) Liability for damage done by things under one's control

1. According to Art. 1384 (1) *in fine* of the CCB, one is liable for damage done by things under one's control.
2. Only the keeper or custodian (*gardien*) of the thing can be held liable for the damage caused. The custodian is the person who uses the thing for his own account, benefits from it, or has it under his control with the possibility to monitor, direct and control it.
3. The thing must have a defect. This refers to any abnormal characteristics of the thing that, in particular circumstances, is likely to cause injury to a third party. A

feature is abnormal if it makes a thing inappropriate for the purpose for which it was intended. [. . .]

A football field, whose lines drawn in lime had caused severe burns to a player who was making a tackle, was considered defective. [. . .]

4. When the conditions of application of this article are met, the custodian is subject to an irrebuttable presumption of liability from which he can only free himself if he proves that the damage is due to a cause unrelated to the defect of the thing (an overwhelming fortuitous event [*cas fortuit*], an unavoidable occurrence [*force majeure*], or the intervention of a third party or of the victim him- or herself). [. . .]

VI. Italy

1. Codice civile (*Civil Code*)

Art. 2043. Risarcimento per fatto illecito. – Qualunque fatto doloso o colposo che cagiona ad altri un danno ingiusto, obbliga colui che ha commesso il fatto a risarcire il danno.

Art. 2050. Responsabilità per l'esercizio di attività pericolose. – Chiunque cagiona danno ad altri nello svolgimento di un'attività pericolosa, per sua natura o per la natura dei mezzi adoperati, è tenuto al risarcimento, se non prova di avere adottato tutte le misure idonee a evitare il danno.

Art. 2051. Danno cagionato da cosa in custodia. – Ciascuno è responsabile del danno cagionato dalle cose che ha in custodia, salvo che provi il caso fortuito.

Art. 2054. Circolazione di veicoli. (1) Il conducente di un veicolo senza guida di rotaie è obbligato a risarcire il danno prodotto a persone o a cose dalla circolazione del veicolo, se non prova di aver fatto tutto il possibile per evitare il danno.
(2) Nel caso di scontro tra veicoli si presume, fino a prova contraria, che ciascuno dei conducenti abbia concorso ugualmente a produrre il danno subito dai singoli veicoli. [. . .]

Translation

Art. 2043. Damages for tortious liability. – *Any intentional or negligent event that causes unlawful damage to others obliges the person who caused the event to compensate the damage.*

Art. 2050. Liability for dangerous activities. – *Whoever causes damage to another person by carrying out a dangerous activity, being such because of its nature or the type of means used, must compensate the damage, unless he or she proves that he or she has taken all appropriate measures to avoid the damage.*

Art. 2051. Damage caused by things under one's control. – *Every person is liable for damage caused by things which are under his or her control, except if he or she proves unforeseeable circumstances (force majeure).*

> **Art. 2054. Road traffic.** *(1) The driver of a road vehicle must pay for the damage caused to persons or property by its use in traffic, unless he is proven to have made every possible effort to avoid the damage.*
> *(2) In the case of a vehicle collision, unless there is evidence to the contrary, it is presumed that each driver has to the same extent contributed to the damage suffered by each vehicle. [. . .]*

2. Giorgio Cian/Alberto Trabucchi, *Commentario breve al Codice civile (Short Commentary on the Civil Code)*, 11th ed., 2014, Arts. 2050, 2051

Art. 2050

I. General remarks. ■ Liability for dangerous activities is a modern type of liability [. . .] that does not exist in the civil codes of France and Germany [. . .]. ■ The nature of the field of liability under examination has long been controversial. [. . .] The doctrine prevalent nowadays [. . .] regards it as a form of **strict liability**; this also follows from the fact that subjectively [. . .] the person alleged to be liable may not be at fault with regard to the required standards of behaviour [. . .] or more precisely, there is **liability for the creation of risk that was objectively avoidable** [. . .] ■ According to settled case-law, in order to exonerate oneself it is not sufficient to show that there was no breach of the law or of required standards, but it has to be proved that under the circumstances of the case all technically available measures and all possible means were taken to avoid the damage. The rigor with which the courts apply the test for release of liability which actually makes it coincide with **fortuitous event** (*cas fortuit*), strengthens the idea that we are in fact dealing with strict liability. [. . .]

II. Concept of dangerous activity. ■ The legislator has not provided any examples or types of dangerous activities. [. . .] Activities that are considered dangerous are those that involve the **significant possibility of the occurrence of damage**, due to their very nature or due to the means used [. . .]. ■ [. . .] [An] activity that is usually safe does not become dangerous because it is carried out dangerously; this situation is governed by fault-based liability under Art. 2043. ■ **Hunting**, undoubtedly, constitutes a dangerous activity [. . .]. The **organisation of sports competitions**, such as a **motorcycle race** on a circuit open to the public, is certainly a dangerous activity. The decision of the Court of Turin on 11th November 2004 was very controversial [. . .] for it described a match of [the Italian Football League] *Serie A* as a dangerous organisational activity, and excluded at the same time that the behaviour of a fan who injured another fan with the launch of a smoke bomb could be considered an action of a third party for the purposes of the exemption from responsibility of the organisers of the game. ■ With regard to the activity of [horse] **riding**, it was held that the manager of a stable, as operator of a dangerous activity, is liable for damages suffered by participants of riding lessons, if they are beginners or inexperienced riders. [. . .] ■ Non-competitive **skiing** is a sport and recreation activity that does not reach the degree of dangerousness – by itself or due to the equipment used – required to justify the application of article 2050 (App. Bologna 26–2–1976, G. It. 73, I, 2, 964; Ziviz . . . ; Chiné . . . ; *contra* Di Martino . . .). Skiing dangerously may thus lead to liability under the general rule of Art. **2043 CCiv**. [. . .]

Art. 2051

[...] ■ Doctrine has addressed the relationship between liability under Arts. 2050 and 2051, reaching the conclusion that the latter is applicable in the event of damage resulting from dangerous things not operated by humans, whereas Art. 2050 applies when the thing is the tool necessary for carrying out the dangerous activity (MONATERI, *ivi*, 1042; BIANCA, *La resp.*, 716; VISINTINI, *ivi*, 793s.).

3. Marco Bona/Andrea Castelnuovo/Pier Giuseppe Monateri, *La responsabilità civile nello sport (Civil Liability in Sports)*, 2002, n° 3.4.1

3.4.1. *Collision of Skiers: liability and proof*

The liability regime applicable to accidents between skiers is found in Art. 2043 of the Civil Code.

Fault is firstly examined with respect to the rules and standards established by the International Ski Federation, applied in light of the circumstances of the case (conditions of the premises, with particular reference to the snow; the warning signs present; the visibility; the obstacles on the track; the presence of other skiers; the technical skills of the skiers involved in the accident).

The main problem in this type of accident is the **proof** to be provided by the skier claiming damages. In most cases, the dynamics of the accident render its reconstruction very difficult, even if it happened in the presence of witnesses. Often, they were themselves busily skiing and therefore did not pay attention to all the details of the accident, or – in order to help their friends being sued – even unknowingly make witness statements not entirely faithful to what actually occurred. In many respects, in terms of substantive justice and given that it is the classic situation where **both parties are obliged** to adopt appropriate measures **to prevent harm**, the right approach would definitely be to apply, by analogy, the rules of evidence established by Art. 2054 (2) of the Civil Code, a presumption applying in cases in which it is impossible to ascertain the exclusive fault of one of the two skiers or the contributing fault of the other. Some courts have in fact gone this way. A judgment of the Court of Bolzano is particularly notable for it held that "*grammatically and logically, the presumption of fault provided by Art. 2054 of the Civil Code appears ... certainly applicable*", while correctly excluding the reference to the specific rules on road traffic. The Court of Bolzano had to decide on a collision between skiers in a case where it was not possible to determine the course of events. No witnesses were available, nor was it possible to identify in other ways what exactly had happened: "*it was impossible to determine how the accident had happened and who was at fault; therefore, if there is no recourse to a presumption of fault, the action must fail; if, on the other hand, a presumption is applied, it cannot be overcome.*" Having excluded the possibility of using Art. 2050 CCI, the Court of Bolzano argued that there was every reason to examine the case under Art. 2054 of the Civil Code: "*Skiing ... certainly constitutes a means of locomotion structurally designed for movement, even if it is a particular kind of movement*"; "*it is a means of locomotion, which is intended to make it more convenient and fast for people to move, and for people using them, a pair of skis is undoubtedly, so to speak, a vehicle*"; "*that it is not a road vehicle is of little importance, because we do not consider applying the rules on road traffic, but a rule that applies to circulation on land in general*"; [...] "*the fact that skis do not move on their own does not negate their property of being a vehicle; they build* *an entity with the skier who carries or is carried by them, which is also the case for two-wheeled vehicles which cannot keep control by themselves either, and their guidance depends significantly on the movement of the body of the person; it also does not matter that the skis are driven by the sheer force of gravity, applied to the body of the skier, which is common to all vehicles without engine, when going downhill;"* Based on these findings and noting that skiing and driving on the road both have in common "**the risk of traffic**, *which is the reason for presuming fault with respect to both activities*", the Court resolved the case considering that there was contributory negligence by the claimant to the extent of 50%.

The applicability of Art. 2054 CCI [. . .], however, was not accepted by the Italian Supreme Court which, given the close and also historic connection between Art. 2054 of the Civil Code and the Road Traffic Act, held that the rule in question cannot be deemed to extend to the use of skis, *"precisely because the Road Traffic Act does not include them among the vehicles, despite having taken care to list the various types of vehicles and describing their characteristics"*. The Supreme Court has also drawn a clear line of demarcation between vehicles and skis: *"According to common sense a vehicle is a means of transportation for people or things, usually mechanical and driven by man, or without engine and driven by man or animals"; "Skis are, on the other hand, a device that has been used for a long time already, which is spatula-shaped, pliant and curved upwards, and secured to the foot by means of a metallic pincer fixed to the shoe; thus, it constitutes a whole with the legs of the skier and can, in this way, slide on snow-covered slopes . . . This shows that the use of skis gives rise to a movement of people provided with that particular equipment, rather than to a movement of vehicles".*

[. . .] With a few rare exceptions, the argument in support of the application of Art. 2050 CCI has not managed to convince either, which seems acceptable with regard to the relationship between colliding skiers. In this case there is indeed a mutual obligation to avoid damage. It would thus not be sensible to attribute a greater burden of proof to the defendant than that attributed to the person who suffered the damage. [. . .]

Against this background of case law, the question of proof should therefore be discussed **with respect to Art. 2043 CCI** at present. [. . .] The suggested approach to the rules of evidence is essentially based on a **reasonableness test**, with the evidence centred not on the exact dynamics of the accident, but rather on the judge's assessment of how *both* sides should have conducted themselves in the precise case with regard to a *common risk*. If the plaintiff fails to provide evidence on how the collision exactly happened (and it remains for example unclear which party was skiing in a downhill position when the collision occurred), this does not necessarily imply that any liability of the defendant is excluded if a whole series of objective circumstances [. . .] indicate that the latter could also reasonably have foreseen and prevented the accident [. . .].

4. Legge 24 dicembre 2003, n. 363: Norme in materia di sicurezza nella pratica degli sport invernali da discesa e da fondo (*Law no. 363/2003 of 24 December 2003*)

Art. 19. (Concorso di colpa). 1. Nel caso di scontro tra sciatori, si presume, fino a prova contraria, che ciascuno di essi abbia concorso ugualmente a produrre gli eventuali danni. [. . .]

Translation

Art. 19. (Contributory negligence). 1. In the case of a collision between skiers, it is presumed, until evidence to the contrary is provided, that both skiers are equally responsible for any injury caused. [. . .]

VII. Slovenia

1. Obligacijski zakonik (*Code of Obligations*)

5. odsek: ODGOVORNOST ZA ŠKODO OD NEVARNE STVARI ALI NEVARNE DEJAVNOSTI

I. SPLOŠNE DOLOČBE

Domneva vzročnosti. 149. Člen. Za škodo, nastalo v zvezi z nevarno stvarjo oziroma nevarno dejavnostjo, se šteje, da izvira iz te stvari oziroma te dejavnosti, razen če se dokaže, da ta ni bila vzrok.

Kdo odgovarja za škodo. 150. Člen. Za škodo od nevarne stvari odgovarja njen imetnik, za škodo od nevarne dejavnosti pa tisti, ki se z njo ukvarja.

Translation

Subsection 5: Liability for damage from dangerous objects or dangerous activities

I. General provisions

Art. 149. Presumption of causality. Damage occurring in connection with a dangerous object or dangerous activities shall be deemed to originate from the dangerous object or dangerous activities unless it is shown that such was not the cause.

Art. 150. Who is liable for damage. The holder of a dangerous object shall be liable for the damage it causes; the person involved in dangerous activities shall be liable for resulting damage.

2. Vrhovno sodišče Republike Slovenije (*Supreme Court of the Republic of Slovenia*), 25.05.2013, case n° II Ips 787/2009

[. . .] A ski slope is not, in itself, a dangerous thing within the meaning of Art. [149] and skiing is a normal sporting activity that produces, like many other activities, certain dangers and risks. However, these are not of such a nature that they cannot be kept under control if the activity is exercised with due care, in accordance with the applicable safety regulations; this would however have to be the case in order for this activity to be regarded as inherently dangerous under the Code of Obligations. If, on the contrary, an activity is not inherently dangerous, but only becomes dangerous in a certain case because due care had not been exercised and the safety regulations established by the ski operator had been violated, then the case is to be governed exclusively by fault-based liability. [. . .]

VIII. Diverse jurisdictions formerly belonging to the socialist legal family

1. Гражданский кодекс Российской Федерации (*Russian Civil Code*)

> ГК РФ Статья 1064. Общие основания ответственности за причинение вреда. (1) Вред, причиненный личности или имуществу гражданина, а также вред, причиненный имуществу юридического лица, подлежит возмещению в полном объеме лицом, причинившим вред. [. . .]
> (2) Лицо, причинившее вред, освобождается от возмещения вреда, если докажет, что вред причинен не по его вине. [. . .]

Translation

> *Art. 1064. General Grounds for Liability for Damage.* (1) *The injury inflicted on the personality or property of an individual, and also the damage done to the property of a legal entity shall be subject to full compensation by the person who inflicted the damage.* [. . .]
> (2) *A person who has caused harm shall be released from the redress of injury if he or she proves that such injury was not caused through his or her fault.* [. . .]

2. Võlaõigusseadus (*Estonian Code of Obligations*)

> § 1050. Süü vastutuse alusena. (1) Kahju tekitaja ei vastuta kahju tekitamise eest, kui ta tõendab, et ei ole kahju tekitamises süüdi, kui seadusega ei ole sätestatud teisiti. [. . .]

Translation

> *§ 1050. Culpability as basis for liability.* (1) *Unless otherwise provided by law, a tortfeasor is not liable for the causing of damage if the tortfeasor proves that he or she is not culpable of causing the damage.* [. . .]

3. Obligacijski zakonik (*Slovenian Code of Obligations*)

> 131. člen. (1) Kdor povzroči drugemu škodo, jo je dolžan povrniti, če ne dokaže, da je škoda nastala brez njegove krivde. [. . .]

Translation

Art. 131. Basis for liability. *(1) Any person that inflicts damage on another shall be obliged to reimburse it, unless it is proved that the damage was incurred without the culpability of the former. [. . .]*

4. Zakon o obligacionim odnosima (*Serbian Law on Contracts and Torts*)

Član 154. (1) Ko drugome prouzrokuje štetu dužan je naknaditi je, ukoliko ne dokaže da je šteta nastala bez njegove krivice. [. . .]

Translation

Art. 154. Foundations of Liability. *(1) Whoever causes injury or loss to another shall be liable to redress it, unless he or she proves that the damage was caused without his or her fault. [. . .]*

5. Michael Will/Vladimir Vodinelić, Generelle Verschuldensvermutung – das unbekannte Wesen. Osteuropäische Angebote zum gemeineuropäischen Deliktsrecht? (*A general presumption of fault – the unknown creature. Eastern European contributions to the common European law of torts*), in: *European Tort Law – Liber amicorum for Helmut Koziol*, 2000, p. 307 at 341–342

[In jurisdictions belonging to the former socialist legal family, such as, for example, former Yugoslavia] four arguments were put forward in favour of a general presumption of fault in tort liability [*references omitted*]:

First of all, it is easier for the alleged wrongdoer to prove that he or she was not guilty of negligence than for the victim, conversely, to prove the fault of the alleged wrongdoer; "if a person causes a harm, then he or she shall know better than anyone else under what circumstances the injury was caused . . . . " In many cases it will be "difficult" and sometimes even "impossible" or "close to impossible" for the victim to prove the fault of the wrongdoer and to evidence what the wrongdoer knew or what the latter was thinking at the time of the act.

Secondly, without a reversal of the burden of proof, an otherwise deserving victim might lose his or her right to compensation if he or she fails to effectively demonstrate that a fault has been committed. At the same time, a person who has by all means acted negligently will then escape liability or only be partly liable.

Thirdly, why should the injured party have to prove the fault of the party who caused the damage? The injured person is already a victim and was injured by the act of the alleged wrongdoer.

Fourthly, occasionally it is mentioned that a reversal of the burden of proof has beneficial preventive effects. [. . .]

6. OBREN STANCOVIĆ, La responsabilité civile selon la nouvelle loi yougoslave sur les obligations (*Civil Liability according to the new Yugoslav Law of Obligations*), Rev. int. de droit comparé 1979, 765 at 765–766

[. . .] 3. The legislator has inserted a presumption of fault into the regime of subjective liability for tort; the presumption may of course be rebutted [. . .], Art. 154 (1). The legislator assumed that in most cases the person who caused the damage acted with fault and that, accordingly, it makes sense to presume that the former was at fault, while at the same time affording him or her the opportunity to bring proof to the contrary, i.e. to rebut such presumption. The legislator held the view that such a presumption, although placing the injured party into a better position than they may have been before, may not be quite as ground-breaking as one might think in comparison with the traditional regime, which required proof of fault. As was the case under the traditional regime, a victim has to prove that there is causation between the defendant's act and his or her damage (this can never be presumed!), and it is only after such causation has been established that the presumption may arise, deeming the person who caused the damage to be at fault. Furthermore, the courts in large part assess causation and the existence of fault in relying on the same set of facts, meaning that evidence of causation would also, to a certain extent, prove the fault of the person who caused the damage or, at the very least, be an important element when it comes to proving fault [. . .]. [. . .]

IX. Historical foundation: Roman law and *ius commune*

BÉNÉDICT WINIGER, *La responsabilié aquilienne en droit commun – Damnum Culpa Datum (Tortious Liability in Continental European Ius Commune)*, 2002, pp. 76 ff.

D. *Damnum Culpa Datum* and natural law

The original text of the *lex Aquilia* [i.e. the legal source for extra-contractual liability in Roman law] expressly stipulated [. . .] that for the law to intervene, it was necessary to establish *iniuria* [i.e. unlawfulness]. Thus, to succeed in a claim, the plaintiff had not only to show that he had suffered damage, but also had to demonstrate that an unlawful act had been committed. To convince the judge of this fact, he had to demonstrate that the law had been violated. Before very long, Roman case law would allow plaintiffs to submit a variety of different arguments as evidence of a violation of law, most notably demonstrating that the defendant had committed a fault, or that his conduct had been negligent, undisciplined, or indeed reckless. Of these concepts, it would be fault that would emerge victorious.

In the works of Gaius,[19] in particular, fault had become the key concept of the *lex Aquilia*. [. . .] According to Gaius, the plaintiff first had to prove that the damaging act was unlawful: *iniuria occidere*, but for the judge to then infer *iniuria* [i.e. unlawfulness], it became necessary for the plaintiff to demonstrate the defendant's fault or fraudulent conduct.

[. . .] The central role afforded to fault would lead courts to carry out an ever closer examination of the persons involved, the judge being concerned first and foremost with the parties' conduct, but also with their motives, intentions, and even their emotional responses.

---

19 Gaius (AD 120–180, flourished under the reign of Emperor Hadrian), jurist, legal scholar, and author of *The Institutes of Gaius*.

This trend, which would render tortious liability yet more subjective, continued through to the next millennium. [. . .] During the period of *ius commune*, jurists would mainly focus on the teachings of Gaius, and thus more and more emphasis was placed on fault as the key element of liability in tort [. . .]. The shift towards fault would have important consequences. The term *iniuria* [unlawfulness] makes formal reference to the word *ius* [law], and thus to the legal order as a whole. Once *iniuria* was replaced by *culpa* [i.e. fault], the reference was no longer to a legal standard, but to any standard of conduct whatsoever. Jurists of the *ius commune*, and in particular proponents of natural law, would draw from this that the notion of fault and, as follows, tortious liability as a whole, was to be extended to all acts by man. An action could now be brought not only for the infringement of a particular legal standard, but for any kind of damaging act. [. . .]

[. . .] Donellus[20] considered that not only was it impossible to define fault – *quod est infiniti laboris* – but, moreover, that any attempt to do so would be in vain since borderline cases could appear at any time. As a result, he suggested that the courts instead take the opposite approach of identifying criteria excluding a person's fault [. . .], since these could be listed exhaustively.

It was at this point that Donellus brought about a fundamental shift in thinking, by spelling out that any damage inflicted should entail a presumption of fault: "*the starting point is that all damage is inflicted by fault, and as such comes under the full force of the lex Aquilia, if he who inflicted such damage has no defence for what he has done*". By introducing a general presumption of fault, Donellus reversed [. . .] the parties' burdens. If, under the *lex Aquilia*, a plaintiff had previously been obliged to demonstrate the defendant's *iniuria*, the duty now fell upon the defendant to prove his absence of fault. [. . .]

To bypass a requirement of negative proof, which would inevitably be impossible to meet, Donellus was compelled to offer up a number of criteria which would determine when there was to be no *culpa* on the part of the defendant. [. . .]

By exploring the case law [. . .], Donellus developed four main criteria for the defendant to prove the absence of fault: firstly, [. . .] cases where he could not have avoided the damage; secondly, if the law has permitted him to commit the damaging act; thirdly, if the damage was unforeseeable; and finally, if the victim himself was at fault. [. . .]

Donellus [. . .] introduced a new model of tortious liability [. . .]. He first replaced *iniuria* with *culpa*. Then, he put in place a general presumption of fault once damage had occurred. Last but not least, he reversed the roles of the parties who, hereafter, no longer relied upon proving the existence of an *iniuria* but rather on proving the absence of *culpa*. [. . .]

X. Principles of European Tort Law

Section 2. Reversal of the burden of proving fault

Art. 4:201. Reversal of the burden of proving fault in general

(1) The burden of proving fault may be reversed in light of the gravity of the danger presented by the activity.

(2) The gravity of the danger is determined according to the seriousness of possible damage in such cases as well as the likelihood that such damage might actually occur.[21]

---

20 Hugo Donellus, 1527–1591, Calvinist and one of the leading representatives of the legal community, was a scholar in Heidelberg, Leyden, and then Altorf (France).

21 For a commentary to this provision, see: European Group on Tort Law (ed.), *PETL – Text and Commentary*, Vienna/New York: Springer, 2005, Art. 4:201 (by P. Widmer).

XI. England and Wales

Court of Appeal, *Caldwell* v. *Maguire and Fitzgerald*, 27.06.2001, [2002] P.I.Q.R. P6

(Lord Woolf C.J., Judge and Tuckey L.JJ.)

June 27, 2001

Appeal by Peter Harvey Caldwell against the judgment of Holland J., dismissing his claim against Adrian Maguire and Mick Fitzgerald. [. . .]

TUCKEY L.J.: 2 On September 30, 1994, the appellant, Peter Caldwell, who was then a professional jockey, was seriously injured whilst riding in a two mile novice hurdle race at Hexham. Holland J. dismissed his claim for personal injuries against the two respondents who are also professional jockeys and were riding in the same race. [. . .]

4 The accident involved four horses: Fion Corn, ridden by [Peter Caldwell]; Master Hyde, ridden by [. . .], Adrian Maguire; Mr Bean, ridden by [. . .] Mick Fitzgerald; and Royal Citizen, ridden by Derek Byrne. Royal Citizen on the inside, Mr Bean on his right, and Master Hyde on the outside, jumped the second last hurdle of the race together. However, after the jump and as the three horses approached a left-hand bend about 100 yards up the course, Mr Bean and Master Hyde pulled three-quarters of a length ahead of Royal Citizen on their inside and took a line which left no room for Royal Citizen on the bend. [. . .] [Royal Citizen shied and turned right; his jockey was unseated und suffered bruisings. He thereby obstructed and brought down the closely following horse Fion Corc so that his jockey, Peter Caldwell, was seriously injured].

5 Following the race there was a stewards inquiry at which the respondents were found guilty of careless riding "in that they had not left enough room for Byrne to come round the inside rail". They were each suspended for three days. [. . .]

9 Based on statistical evidence, the judge concluded that careless riding was a relatively common offence (the statistics showed that in 1999 there were 129 cases) [. . .]

11 As to the law, the judge said that the "primary guidance" for him must come from the Court of Appeal. He noted that this court had never had to consider an entirely similar situation, but had considered analogous situations in five cases, which he reviewed. From these cases he extracted five propositions:

> [1] Each contestant in a lawful sporting contest (and in particular a race) owes a duty of care to each and all other contestants.
>
> [2] That duty is to exercise in the course of the contest all care that is objectively reasonable in the prevailing circumstances for the avoidance of infliction of injury to such fellow contestants.
>
> [3] [. . .] [I]n the particular case of a horse race the prevailing circumstances will include the contestant's obligation to ride a horse over a given course competing with the remaining contestants for the best possible placing, if not for a win. Such must further include the Rules of Racing and the standards, skills and judgment of a professional jockey, all as expected by fellow contestants.
>
> [4] Given the [. . .] prevailing circumstances the threshold for liability is in practice inevitably high; the proof of a breach of duty will not flow from proof of [. . .]

an error of judgment or from mere proof of a momentary lapse in skill (and thus care) respectively when subject to the stresses of a race. Such are [. . .] incidents inherent in the nature of the sport.

[5] In practice it may therefore be difficult to prove any such breach of duty absent proof of conduct that in point of fact amounts to reckless disregard for the fellow contestant's safety. [. . .]

13 Lord Brennan Q.C. for the appellant accepts the first three of the judge's propositions of law, but says that the last two are unduly restrictive and not supported by the Court of Appeal authorities, which the judge considered. [. . .]

27 Having seen the videos, and carefully considered Lord Brennan's submissions, I do not think that the judge's conclusion can be faulted. The situation he was considering was graphically described in one of the [. . .] Australian cases [. . .] which the judge quoted at the end of his judgment. The Australian judge said:

Thoroughbred horse racing is a competitive business, which is played for high stakes. Its participants are large animals ridden by small men at high speed in close proximity. The opportunity for injury is abundant and the choices available to jockeys to avoid or reduce risk are limited.

28 In such circumstances it is not possible to characterise momentary carelessness as negligence. [. . .] This incident occurred in the last part of a close race. The respondents should, as they admitted and the judge found, have checked to see that the line they were taking was safe. Like the judge, however, I do not think that their failure to do so can be characterised as anything more than an error of judgment, an oversight or a lapse which any participant might be guilty of in the context of a race of this kind. It was the sort of incident which happens quite often. What was unusual about this incident [. . .] "was the exceptional seriousness of the injury sustained by the appellant". The Jockey Club's rules and its findings are of course relevant matters to be taken into account, but, as the authorities make clear, the [Jockey Club's] finding that the respondents were guilty of careless riding is not determinative of negligence. As the judge said, there is a difference between response by the regulatory authority and response by the courts in the shape of a finding of legal liability.

29 For these reasons I [. . .] would dismiss this appeal. In doing so, I express my sympathy for the appellant who sustained very serious injury but, unfortunately, that is an injury for which, as I see it, he cannot be compensated through the courts.

Overview of the range of liability regimes potentially applying[22]

Table 7.1

1.	2.	3.	4.
Classic fault-based liability	*Fault-based liability with presumption of fault*	*Strict liability for a thing under one's control*	*Strict liability for dangerous activities*
• **German law** (§ 823 BGB) • **Swiss law** (Art. 41 CO) • **French law** (Art. 1240 CC) • **Belgian law** (Art. 1382 CC) • **Italian law** (Art. 2050 CC) • **English law** (Tort of negligence)	*Numerous jurisdictions in Central and Eastern Europe, e.g.:* • **Russian law** (Art. 1064 CC) • **Estonian law** (Art. 1050 (1) CO) • **Slovenian law** (Art. 131 (1) CO) • **Serbian law** (Art. 154 (1) Law on Contracts and Torts) *Specific rules, such as:* • Art. 19 (1) of the **Italian** Legge 24.12.2003 n° 363.	• **French law** (Art. 1242 (1) CC) • **Belgian law** (Art. 1384 (1) CC but only if the thing was defective)	• **Italian law** (Art. 2054 CC) • **Slovenian law** (Arts. 149, 150 CO)

---

22 For arguments for and against the application of the individual solutions with regard to ski accidents, see T. KADNER GRAZIANO, The Distribution of Social Costs of Ski Accidents through Tort Law: Limits of Fault-Based Liability in Practice – and Alternative Regimes, *JETL* 2016, 1–26.

Bibliography

On sports accidents

PAUL CAPRARA, Surf's Up: The Implications of Tort Liability in the Unregulated Sport of Surfing, *Cal.W.L.Rev.* 2008, 557–587; GERHARD DAMBECK, 40 Jahre FIS-Regeln, *DAR* 2007, 677–681; ERWIN DEUTSCH, Die Mitspielerverletzung im Sport, *VersR* 1974, 1045–1051; HOLGER FLEISCHER, Reichweite und Grenzen der Risikoübernahme im in- und ausländischen Sporthaftungsrecht, *VersR* 1999, 785; CHRISTIAN FÖRSTER, in: Heinz Georg Bamberger/Herbert Roth (eds.), *Beck'scher Online Kommentar BGB*, 42nd ed., München: C. H. Beck, 2017, § 823 paras 587–588; JOCHEN FRITZWEILER, Sport: Schäden und Beeinträchtigungen, in: JOCHEN FRITZWEILER/BERNHARD PFISTER/THOMAS SUMMERER, *Praxishandbuch Sportrecht*, 3. Aufl., München: C. H. Beck, 2014, Teil 5; BRUCE GARDINER, Liability for Sporting Injuries, *J.I.P.L.* 2008, 16–25; UMBERTO IZZO (ed.), *Safety and Liability Rules in European Ski Areas*, Trento: Università degli Studi di Trento (forthcoming); JEAN-FRANCOIS JOYE/GRÉGOIRE CALLEY/JEAN-FRANCOIS DREUILLE (eds.), *L'accident en montagne*, Chambéry Cedex: Université de Savoie, 2015, pp. 287–312; THOMAS KADNER GRAZIANO, The Distribution of Social Costs of Ski Accidents through Tort Law: Limits of Fault-Based Liability in Practice – and Alternative Regimes, *JETL* 2016, 1–26; DIRK LOOSCHELDERS, Die haftungsrechtliche Relevanz außergesetzlicher Verhaltensregeln im Sport, *JR* 2000, 265; PATRICK MEIER, Haftung der Athleten für Verletzungen im Sport, *VersR* 2014, 800–805; GERHARD KNERR, in: Reinhart Geigel/Kurt Haag (eds.), *Der Haftpflichtprozess*, 27th ed., München: C. H. Beck, 2015, Chapter 37 Beweisführung und Beweiswürdigung; ALEXANDER PFEIFFER, Schneesportunfälle in den Alpen, *SpuRt* 2011, 7–10; VIOLA SÄLZER, *Skiunfälle im organisierten Skiraum*, Lausanne: Université de Lausanne, 2013; ERIKA SCHEFFEN, Zivilrechtliche Haftung im Sport, *NJW* 1990, 2658–2665; HANS-KASPAR STIFFLER, *Schweizerisches Schneesportrecht*, 3. Aufl., Bern: Stämpfli, 2002; FRANZ ZEILNER, *Haftung und Schadensersatzansprüche bei Sportunfällen*, Frankfurt am Main: Peter Lang, 2001.

Chapter 8

Liability without fault – a ruptured water main

Casum sentit dominus?[1]

"*Accidents happen. Injuries occur. People suffer. Frequently nobody is at fault. The problem is one of mechanics, not morals.*"[2]

"*[There is] substantial deadweight loss involved in using the courts as a means to settle injury claims. Since all that [is] at stake [is] a transfer of money from [persons alleged to be liable to victims], all the costs associated with these cases (such as lawyers' fees and other court costs) [are] a waste to society. [A no fault liability scheme], in contrast, does not assign blame for injuries: regardless of whose fault it is, [victims] are entitled to insurance benefits if they are injured [. . .]. As a result of this approach, the transaction costs of the transfer are greatly reduced by the existence of no-fault [liability].*"[3]

Scenario

Jeanne Bierman owns a small house in the city. One morning, at about 6:30 a.m., water leaks into the basement. It damages the boiler, floor, and walls. The source of the flood is a ruptured water main owned by the city and located in front of Mrs Bierman's house. It is impossible to establish the cause of the rupture. The city council manages to establish that all necessary precautions had been taken to avoid ruptures in the water mains, so it cannot be proved that the city council acted negligently.

Mrs Bierman brings a claim for compensation against the city.[4]

---

1 The owner bears the risk of fortuitous damage to his or her property, or: the loss lies where it falls.
2 Judge IRVING YOUNGER, in: *Bierman* v. *City of New York*, Civil Court of the City of New York, 60 Misc.2d 497, 302 N.Y.S.2d 696 (below, pp. 216–217).
3 JONATHAN GRUBER (Massachusetts Institute of Technology, Department of Economics), *Public Finance and Public Policy*, 5th ed., New York: Worth Publishers, 2015, p. 395. In full text: "Moreover, there was substantial deadweight loss involved in using the courts as a means to settle injury claims. Since all that was at stake was a transfer of money from employers to employees, all the costs associated with these cases (such as lawyers' fees and other court costs) were a waste to society. WC [WC = Workers' compensation, a no-fault compensation scheme applied in the USA], in contrast, does not assign blame for injuries: regardless of whose fault it is, workers are entitled to insurance benefits if they are injured on the job. As a result of this approach, the transaction costs of the transfer are greatly reduced by the existence of no-fault WC." Workers' compensation is just one example of a strict liability system, among many others, to which this reasoning can be applied.
4 Scenario based on the New York case: *Bierman* v. *City of New York,* see fn. 2. These cases still happen, see: *London Evening Standard*, 09.07.2013, p. 23: "Burst pipe has ruined our new home – Couple had just finished £ 15,000 work on house [in London] when flood struck"; or *China Daily*, 26.05.2016, p. 12: "Road collapses

Questions

1) Liability without fault, also known as objective or strict liability, is the second pillar of modern tort liability. In which situations do liability without fault regimes apply instead of, or in addition to, fault liability systems, for example, under *German*, *Swiss*, and *English* law? Is the liability under §§ 833 and 836 of the German BGB (and similar provisions in many other jurisdictions) strict? Which criteria are employed for determining whether damage should be covered by strict liability?

   Would Mrs Bierman's claim be examined under a liability without fault regime in German, Swiss, and English law?

2) What are the conditions for liability without fault in the *USA* according to the extracts provided in the materials? What is the scope of strict liability under the *Restatement of Torts (3rd)*? How should the scenario be solved in applying these materials?

3) How was the scenario solved by the *Civil Court of the City of New York*? Which legal principles and policy arguments did the New York judge invoke in his reasoning? In line with this reasoning, where would the limits of strict liability lie? Contrast with the arguments submitted by W.V.H. ROGERS in the extracts provided.

4) Some jurisdictions have introduced a series of strict liability regimes addressing particular types of situations or risks, whereas others use general clauses of strict liability.

   a) What are the approaches used in the *Dutch* Civil Code, Art. 2050 of the *Italian* Civil Code, Art. 1079 of the *Russian* Civil Code, and Arts. 6.266 and 6.270 of the *Lithuanian* Civil Code?

   b) Would these provisions arguably allow Mrs Bierman to successfully claim damages? Argue on the basis of the text of these provisions.

   c) What is the difference between Art. 6.266 of the Lithuanian Civil Code and § 836 (1) of the German BGB?

5) Which criteria should be taken into consideration when deciding whether liability should be strict? What is the advantage of having a series of strict liability provisions establishing rules for particular activities, situations, or risks, and what is the advantage of instead having a general clause on strict liability?

6) How would cases such as that of Mrs Bierman be solved according to your answer to the previous question?

7) What are the positions of the PETL and the DCFR in regard to liability without fault? Which sources of inspiration might the drafters of these provisions have principally used? In what respect do these instruments restate, reflect, or deviate from, the prevailing solutions in the different European jurisdictions?

8) In relation to road traffic accidents, some jurisdictions distinguish between damage caused to pedestrians and cyclists on the one hand (these victims often benefit from strict liability), and damage caused to drivers and keepers of cars on the other (where

---

burying cars. About 200 metres of road running up to the famous Ponte Vecchio [in central Florence] caved in when a major waterpipe it was sitting on broke [. . .]. Around 20 cars fell into the newly created ditch, awash with water, but no one was injured".

elements of fault continue to be used).[5] Also, in aircraft accidents, liability for damage caused by aircrafts to victims on the ground is often strict, whereas damage caused by an aircraft in an aircraft collision is often governed by fault-based liability.[6] Why might this be? Should the absence, or the presence, of *reciprocity of risk* be a factor to be taken into consideration when it comes to deciding where to apply a strict liability system?

9) How would you argue the Bierman case under the proposal *de lege ferenda* reproduced in the annex?

---

5 See, e.g. Art. 436 of the *Polish* Civil Code: according to Art. 436 § 1 in conjunction with Art. 435, the owner/possessor of a motor vehicle is *strictly liable* for damage caused by the operation of the vehicle, unless the damage was caused by *force majeure* or exclusively by the fault of the injured party or of a third person for whom he or she is not liable. However, according to Art. 436 § 2 in conjunction with Art. 415, in case of a collision of vehicles, the liability of the owners/possessors vis-à-vis each other is *fault-based*. For more information on the rules for traffic accidents, see below, Chapter 9, pp. 229 ff., with numerous references. See also Art. 6.270 (5) of the *Lithuanian* Civil Code (below, pp. 220–221).

6 See e.g. Art. 64 (1) of the *Swiss* Federal Aviation Act (below, pp. 203, 205), the situation in *English* law (below, T. WEIR, p. 212), and the law in the *USA* (below, R. A. EPSTEIN, pp. 213–215).

Table of contents

I. Germany

1. JOSEF ESSER/HANS-LEO WEYERS, *Schuldrecht, Band II, Besonderer Teil, Teilband 2: Gesetzliche Schuldverhältnisse (Law of Obligations, Vol. II, Special Part, 2. Legal Obligations)*, 8th ed., Heidelberg: C. F. Müller, 2000, §§ 53, 63 ....p. 197
2. Bürgerliches Gesetzbuch, BGB (*Civil Code*), §§ 833, 836 (1)....................p. 198
3. Specific statutes establishing strict liability (examples)....................p. 199
   a) Haftpflichtgesetz (*Civil Liability Act*), § 1 (1)....................p. 199
   b) Produkthaftungsgesetz (*Product Liability Act*), § 1 (1) 1st sent.....................p. 199
   c) Umwelthaftungsgesetz (*Environmental Liability Act*), § 1 ....p. 199
4. Bundesgerichtshof, BGH (*Federal Supreme Court of Justice*), 15.10.1970, BGHZ 54, 332 (Versagen einer Verkehrssignalanlage [*Malfunctioning Traffic Lights*]) ....p. 200
5. Haftpflichtgesetz (*Civil Liability Act*), § 2 (1) 1st sent....................p. 201
6. WERNER FILTHAUT, Haftpflichtgesetz – Kommentar (*Civil Liability Act – Commentary*), 9th ed., München: C. H. Beck, 2015, § 2 notes 2 and 8 ....p. 202

II. Switzerland

1. HENRI DESCHENAUX/PIERRE TERCIER, *La responsabilité civile (Civil Liability)*, 2nd ed., Berne: Stämpfli, 1982, pp. 42 ff., nos. 30, 33, 35–39 ....p. 202
2. Specific statutes establishing strict liability (examples)....................p. 203
   a) Loi fédérale sur les chemins de fer (*Federal Railway Act*), Art. 40b (1) ....p. 203
   b) Loi fédérale sur l'aviation (*Federal Aviation Act*), Art. 64 (1)....................p. 203
   c) Loi fédérale sur les installations de transport par conduites de combustibles ou carburants liquides ou gazeux (*Federal Act on Pipelines for the Transport of Liquid or Gaseous Fuels*), Arts. 1 (1), 33 (1)....................p. 203
   d) Loi fédérale sur les substances explosibles (Loi sur les explosifs) (*Explosive Substances Act*), Art. 27....................p. 204
   e) Loi fédérale sur la responsabilité du fait des produits (*Product Liability Act*), Art. 1 ....p. 204
   f) Loi fédérale en matière nucléaire (*Federal Act on Nuclear Energy*), Art. 3 (1)....................p. 204
   g) Loi fédérale sur la protection de l'environnement (*Federal Act on the Protection of the Environment*), Art. 59a....................p. 204
   h) Loi fédérale sur l'application du génie génétique au domaine non humain, Loi sur le génie génétique (*Law on the Application of Genetic Engineering in Non-Human Biotechnology, Genetic Engineering Act*), Arts. 30 (1) and (4), 31 ....p. 205
3. Obligationenrecht/Code des obligations (*Code of Obligations*), Art. 58 (1)....................p. 207

4. Franz Werro, in: Luc Thévenoz/Franz Werro (eds.), *Commentaire Romand, Code des obligations I (Commentary to the Code of Obligations I)*, 2nd ed., Genève/Bâle/Munich: Helbing Lichtenhahn, 2012, Art. 58, nos. 1, 2, 8, 23 .... p. 208
5. Kantonsgericht Sankt Gallen (*St. Gallen Cantonal Court*), 23.02.2005, BZ.2002.44 .... p. 208

III. England and Wales

1. W.V.H. Rogers, *The Law of Tort*, 2nd ed., London: Sweet & Maxwell, 1994, pp. 112–115, 124–129 .... p. 209
2. House of Lords, *Read v. J. Lyons & Co. Ltd*, 18.10.1946, [1947] AC 156 ...... p. 212
3. Tony Weir, *An Introduction to Tort Law*, Oxford: OUP, 2006, pp. 91 ff. ...... p. 212
4. Water Industry Act 1991, Sect. 209 (1) and (2) .... p. 213

IV. USA

1. Richard A. Epstein, *Torts*, New York: Aspen, 1999, pp. 333, 344–351 ...... p. 213
2. The American Law Institute, *Restatement of the Law, Torts (3rd), Liability for Physical and Emotional Harm, Vol. 1, §§ 1 to 36*, St. Paul, Minnesota: American Law Institute Publishers, 2013, § 20 ...... p. 215
3. Civil Court of the City of New York, *Bierman v. City of New York*, 60 Misc. 2d 497, 302 N.Y.S.2d 696 .... p. 216

V. The Netherlands, Italy, Russian Federation, Lithuania, Estonia

1. Burgerlijk Wetboek (*Dutch Civil Code*), Arts. 6:173 (1), 6:174, 6:175 (1) and (3) .... p. 217
2. Codice civile italiano (*Italian Civil Code*), Art. 2050 .... p. 219
3. Гражданский кодекс Российской Федерации (*Russian Civil Code*), Art. 1079 (1) and (3) .... p. 219
4. Lietuvos Respublikos Civilinis kodeksas (*Lithuanian Civil Code*), Arts. 6.266, 6.270 (1) and (5) .... p. 220
5. Võlaõigusseadus (*Estonian Code of Obligations*), §§ 1056, 1058 .... p. 221

VI. Principles of European Tort Law

1. PETL, Art. 5:101 (1) – (3) .... p. 222
2. European Group on Tort Law (eds.), *Principles of European Tort Law. Text and Commentary*, Wien/New York: Springer, 2005, Art. 5:101, nos. 9–10 (by B. Koch) .... p. 223

VII. Draft Common Frame of Reference

DCFR, Arts. VI. – 3:202, 3:206 .... p. 223

VIII. Annex: a proposal *de lege ferenda*

Christoph Oertel, *Objektive Haftung in Europa – Rechtsvergleichende Untersuchung zur Weiterentwicklung der verschuldensunabhängigen Haftung im europäischen Privatrecht (Objective Liability in Europe – A Comparative Study on Liability Without Fault in European Private Law and Potential Perspectives)*, Tübingen: Mohr Siebeck, 2010, pp. 322–323 .... p. 225

Materials[7]

I. Germany

1. Josef Esser/Hans-Leo Weyers, *Schuldrecht, Band II, Besonderer Teil, Teilband 2: Gesetzliche Schuldverhältnisse (Law of Obligations, Vol. II, Special Part, 2. Legal Obligations)*, 8th ed., 2000, §§ 53, 63

§ 53 On the Purpose of the Law of Delict

1. In general

[. . .] b) [. . .] The traditional rationale surrounding strict liability (*Gefährdungshaftung*) was that anyone operating, and benefitting from the operation of, something that may be classed as a "source of danger" (such as a motor vehicle, or a nuclear power station) should provide compensation for all typical damage suffered by third parties arising as a result of the operation. Nowadays, the general approach may be summed up as follows: certain defined activities – the "operation" of objective sources of danger such as motor vehicles, but also a good many other things [. . .] – are regarded by the legislator as so dangerous that the associated risks may be placed on those in charge of them, and as a result obliges them to compensate all typical damage which arises from their operation. [. . .]

II. Liability based on the creation of risk (*Gefährdungshaftung*)

The scope of liability for the creation of a risk (*Gefährdungshaftung*) ranges from liability for damage caused by animals held for non-economic purposes (*Luxustiere*) under BGB, § 833 (1), to those outside the BGB, in particular under the laws relating to energy and transport undertakings. Faced with the choice between a general clause of strict liability based on the creation of risk and separate clauses each governing specific risks, the German legislator has preferred the method of listing each relevant situation of risk *on a case by case basis*. The reason for this choice may be that the idea of *Gefährdungshaftung* (liability for the creation of risk) as a self-sufficient principle has only recently achieved theoretical recognition. Other jurisdictions have, in practice, extended the scope of application of provisions that were initially made for other purposes (compare the French *Code Civil*, Art. 1384 [now Art. 1242]), or made use of explicit general clauses (e.g. Art. 1079 of the Russian Civil Code) on "liability for sources of serious danger", thereby leaving it up to the courts to decide which particular situations should fall under the rubric of liability for the creation of a risk (*Gefährdungshaftung*).

The law of delict: strict liability or liability for the creation of a risk (*Gefährdungshaftung*)

§ 63 Basic principles

I. Function and development

[. . .] The aim of fault-based liability is to compensate *unlawful* damage, based on the fact that the interference with the plaintiff's rights, resulting from the defendant's acts, could and should have been avoided by the exercise of reasonable care.

---

[7] For the original language versions of the materials reproduced in this chapter, see the companion website at www.routledge.com/9781138567733.

By contrast, liability for the creation of a risk (*Gefährdungshaftung*) is not concerned with the question of whether the particular behaviour of the defendant is lawful or unlawful: descriptions of what he did as "contrary to law" or "negligent" are therefore irrelevant. Rather, it is intended to cover "accidental losses"; in effect, it is dependent upon the fundamental concept that anyone who benefits from the operation of a source of danger should, at least from an economic point of view, bear the risks connected with it. [...]

2. Bürgerliches Gesetzbuch, BGB (*Civil Code*)[8]

> § 833. **Haftung des Tierhalters.** Wird durch ein Tier ein Mensch getötet oder der Körper oder die Gesundheit eines Menschen verletzt oder eine Sache beschädigt, so ist derjenige, welcher das Tier hält, verpflichtet, dem Verletzten den daraus entstehenden Schaden zu ersetzen. Die Ersatzpflicht tritt nicht ein, wenn der Schaden durch ein Haustier verursacht wird, das dem Beruf, der Erwerbstätigkeit oder dem Unterhalt des Tierhalters zu dienen bestimmt ist, und entweder der Tierhalter bei der Beaufsichtigung des Tieres die im Verkehr erforderliche Sorgfalt beobachtet oder der Schaden auch bei Anwendung dieser Sorgfalt entstanden sein würde.
>
> § 836. **Haftung des Grundstückbesitzers.** (1) Wird durch den Einsturz eines Gebäudes oder eines anderen mit einem Grundstück verbundenen Werkes oder durch die Ablösung von Teilen des Gebäudes oder des Werkes ein Mensch getötet, der Körper oder die Gesundheit eines Menschen verletzt oder eine Sache beschädigt, so ist der Besitzer des Grundstücks, sofern der Einsturz oder die Ablösung die Folge fehlerhafter Einrichtung oder mangelhafter Unterhaltung ist, verpflichtet, dem Verletzten den daraus entstehenden Schaden zu ersetzen. Die Ersatzpflicht tritt nicht ein, wenn der Besitzer zum Zwecke der Abwendung der Gefahr die im Verkehr erforderliche Sorgfalt beobachtet hat. [...]

Translation

> *§ 833. **Liability of an animal keeper.** If a human being is killed by an animal or if the body or the health of a human being is injured by an animal or a thing is damaged by an animal, then the person who keeps the animal is liable to compensate the injured person for the damage arising therefrom. There is no liability if the damage is caused by a domestic animal intended to serve the occupation, economic activity, or subsistence of its keeper, and either the keeper of the animal has exercised reasonable care in supervising the animal, or the damage would still have occurred had this care been exercised.*
>
> *§ 836. **Liability of the owner of a plot of land.** (1) If a human being is killed or if the body or the health of a human being is injured or a thing is damaged by the collapse of a building or any other structure attached to a plot of land or by parts of the building or structure breaking off, then the possessor of the plot of land is liable to compensate*

---

8 Provisions similar to §§ 833 and 836 BGB exist in many other jurisdictions, and are not reproduced in the materials.

the injured person for damage resulting from this, to the extent that the collapse or detachment is a consequence of defective construction or inadequate maintenance. There is no liability if the possessor has observed reasonable care for the purpose of avoiding danger. [. . .]

3. Specific statutes establishing strict liability (examples)[9]

a) Haftpflichtgesetz

§ 1. [Haftung des Bahnbetriebsunternehmers.] (1) Wird bei dem Betrieb einer Schienenbahn oder einer Schwebebahn ein Mensch getötet, der Körper oder die Gesundheit eines Menschen verletzt oder eine Sache beschädigt, so ist der Betriebsunternehmer dem Geschädigten zum Ersatz des daraus entstehenden Schadens verpflichtet.
(2) Die Ersatzpflicht ist ausgeschlossen, wenn der Unfall durch höhere Gewalt verursacht ist. [. . .]

b) Produkthaftungsgesetz

§ 1. Haftung. (1) Wird durch den Fehler eines Produktes jemand getötet, sein Körper oder seine Gesundheit verletzt oder eine Sache beschädigt, so ist der Hersteller des Produkts verpflichtet, dem Geschädigten den daraus entstehenden Schaden zu ersetzen. Im Falle der Sachbeschädigung gilt dies nur, wenn eine andere Sache als das fehlerhafte Produkt beschädigt wird und diese andere Sache ihrer Art nach gewöhnlich für den privaten Ge- oder Verbrauch bestimmt und hierzu von dem Geschädigten hauptsächlich verwendet ist. [. . .]

c) Umwelthaftungsgesetz

§ 1. Anlagenhaftung bei Umwelteinwirkungen. Wird durch eine Umwelteinwirkung, die von einer im Anhang 1 genannten Anlage[10] ausgeht, jemand getötet, sein Körper oder seine Gesundheit verletzt oder eine Sache beschädigt, so ist der Inhaber der Anlage verpflichtet, dem Geschädigten den daraus entstehenden Schaden zu ersetzen. [. . .]

Translations

a) Civil Liability Act

§ 1. [Liability of the railway company.] (1) If, in the operation of a railway or suspension railway, a human being is killed or suffers injury to body or health, or a thing

---

9 See also § 7 of the Road Traffic Act, below, Chapter 9, pp. 244–245.
10 Genannt sind knapp 100 Anlagen auf den Gebieten: Wärmeerzeugung, Bergbau, Energie, zur Herstellung oder Verarbeitung von Steinen und Erden, Glas, Keramik, Baustoffen, Stahl, Eisen und sonstigen Metallen, chemischen Erzeugnissen, Arzneimitteln, Raffination und Weiterverarbeitung von Mineralöl, etc.

is damaged, the company is bound to compensate the injured party for the damage arising therefrom.

(2) The duty to compensate is excluded if the accident was caused by force majeure. [. . .]

b) Product Liability Act

§ 1. Liability. *(1) If, as a result of the defect of a product, a human being is killed, injured, or his or her health is affected, or his or her property is damaged, the manufacturer is obliged to compensate the person who suffered the damage for the resulting harm. In the case of damage to property, this rule only applies if an object other than the defective product is damaged and if this object is normally intended for private use or consumption and has been used by the injured party primarily for this purpose. [. . .]*

c) Environmental Liability Act

§ 1. Facility liability for environmental impacts. *If a person suffers death or injury to his or her body or health, or if property is damaged, due to an environmental impact that issues from one of the facilities named in Appendix 1,*[11] *then the operator of the facility shall be liable for the damage caused to the injured person. [. . .]*

4. Bundesgerichtshof, BGH (*Federal Supreme Court of Justice*), 15.10.1970, BGHZ 54, 332 (Versagen einer Verkehrssignalanlage [*Malfunctioning Traffic Lights*])

[Collision between two cars at a crossroads in Nuremberg caused by a traffic light failure. At the time of the accident, one set of traffic lights was green, and the other was not working. It was impossible to prove that anyone was at fault. Both car owners sued the City of Nuremberg.]

[. . .] III. [. . .] Our legal system makes the duty to compensate dependent on negligent behaviour by the person who caused the damage. The legislator has explicitly provided for strict liability for the creation of risk (*Gefährdungshaftung*) in a few exceptional, closely circumscribed cases, because it regarded an exception to the fault principle as necessary there, compare, for instance, § 1 [. . .] HaftpflG (Civil Liability Act), § 7 StVG (Road Traffic Act),[12] and § 19 LuftVG (Air Traffic Act). By contrast, in other cases where the application of risk-based liability might be expected, and indeed has been called for, [. . .] including in particular situations not too far removed from traffic light failure, the legislator has not taken this as a justification to resort to strict liability for the creation of risk (*Gefährdungshaftung*); and this is despite the fact that such thought must have crossed the legislator's

---

11 In the appendix, approximately 100 facilities are listed in the following fields, namely those for heat generation, mining, energy, for the production or processing of mineral products, glass, ceramics, building materials, steel, iron and other metals, chemical products, pharmaceuticals, refining and processing of mineral oil, etc.
12 See below, Chapter 9, pp. 244–245.

mind. In view of this deliberate decision by the legislator not to act, the judge cannot intervene here. [. . .]

As for the argument based on equity (§ 242 BGB), which appears at the forefront of this appeal, with its reference to the rationale on which the provisions of § 836 BGB is based – that anyone ought to accept liability for damage caused by a thing belonging to him in so far as he ought reasonably to guard against damage on the basis of a fair regard for others' interests – such argument is not sufficient to displace the legal principle of fault-based liability in cases such as the present. Here, it is important to note that the provisions of § 836 BGB do not provide an exception to the fundamental principle of liability based on fault, but rather create a liability based on a presumption of fault, and a rebuttable presumption at that. [. . .][13]

Note by the author: in a judgment dated 25.01.1971 (BGHZ 55, 229), the Federal Supreme Court of Justice affirmed this decision in a case where the plaintiff suffered damage as a result of a bursting water main. The cause of the damage was a latent defect in the material from which the pipe was made. Following this decision, the German legislator took action and extended responsibility under the Civil Liability Act (see below, 5.).

5. Haftpflichtgesetz (*Civil Liability Act*) as of January 1978

§ 2. [**Haftung des Inhabers einer Energieanlage**]. (1) Wird durch die Wirkungen von Elektrizität, Gasen, Dämpfen oder Flüssigkeiten, die von einer Stromleitungs- oder Rohrleitungsanlage oder einer Anlage zur Abgabe der bezeichneten Energien oder Stoffe ausgehen, ein Mensch getötet, der Körper oder die Gesundheit eines Menschen verletzt oder eine Sache beschädigt, so ist der Inhaber der Anlage verpflichtet, den daraus entstehenden Schaden zu ersetzen, [. . .]
(3) Die Ersatzpflicht nach Absatz 1 ist ausgeschlossen. [. . .] 3. wenn der Schaden durch höhere Gewalt verursacht worden ist, es sei denn, dass er auf das Herabfallen von Leitungsdrähten verursacht wurde.

Translation

§ 2. [*Liability of the proprietor of an energy establishment*]. *(1) If a human being is killed or suffers injury to body or health or an object is damaged through the operation of electricity, gas, steam, or liquids escaping from a cable or pipeline or a plant for the provision of such energy or material, the owner of the installation or plant is bound to compensate the damage arising therefrom. [. . .]*
(3) The duty to compensate under subsection 1 is excluded [. . .] 3. if the damage was caused by force majeure, unless it is caused by the fall of cable wires.

---

13 See above, pp. 198–199.

6. WERNER FILTHAUT, *Haftpflichtgesetz – Kommentar (Civil Liability Act – Commentary)*, 9th ed., 2015, § 2

2   The **limitation** of *Gefährdungshaftung*, or risk-based liability, to electrical and gas installations has proved to be [...] too restrictive. Pipes serving not to transport or deliver "gas" as a fuel, but carrying **other gases, steam** (e.g. for communal heating installations) or **liquids** (e.g. water pipes, and pipelines built to carry oil or oil products) have since emerged. These have given rise to a particular risk of damage, not simply because of the nature or quantity of what they transport, but also because of the sheer scale of the networks involved. Victims were not adequately protected since, in order to establish liability, they were obliged to demonstrate fault. [...] As a result, the *Gesetz zur Änderung schadensersatzrechtlicher Vorschriften* [Law amending the Rules on the Right to Compensation for Damage], which entered into force on 1st January 1978, would finally extend *Gefährdungshaftung* (strict liability) to cover these types of installation [...]. [...]

8   [...] Liquids covered by this legislative provision include, for example, oil, oil products, and water (including sewage) [...]. The latter includes water that has undergone a change through domestic or industrial use, and also rainwater. [...]

II. Switzerland

1. HENRI DESCHENAUX/PIERRE TERCIER, *La responsabilité civile (Civil Liability)*, 2nd ed., 1982, pp. 42 ff., nos. 30, 33, 35–39

3.2. Objective or strict liability

30 Parallel to fault-based liability, there are situations where the law obliges a person to compensate damage caused by him even if he is not necessarily at fault [...]. In general, it is on the grounds of equity, together with the development of economic, social and technological conditions, that the legislator has been persuaded to extend the field of civil liability. We refer to "objective liability" or "liability based on causation" (*Kausalhaftungen*). [...]

33 There are a very substantial number of cases on objective liability [...]. According to OFTINGER, they can be divided into two main categories: cases of simple objective liability, and cases of aggravated objective liability.

35 a) **Simple objective liability.** Under the heading of simple objective liability, or liability based *simply on causation* (*milde Kausalhaftungen; gewöhnliche Kausalhaftungen*), are a number of fields of liability instated by the Civil Code and the Code of Obligations: those applying to employers, heads of families,[14] keepers of animals, owners of structures, and building owners. In all these cases, it has been thought appropriate to assume that the relevant person was at fault (something otherwise hard to prove), so as to better assure that the damage suffered by the victim is compensated.

---

14 See below, Chapter 13, pp. 389 ff.

36　The common feature of these heads of liability is that they entail an implicit *breach of a duty to take care*: employers, heads of families, keepers of animals and owners of facilities must exercise a certain amount of control (over persons or things) in order to prevent damage. It follows that it is quite normal to impose strict liability upon them once they are in breach of that duty [the breach being presumed].

37　**b) Aggravated objective liability.** Under the heading of aggravated objective liability or *risk-based liability* (*scharfe Kausalhaftungen*; *Gefährdungshaftungen*) we classify a number of heads of liability created by particular legal regimes: for example, those applying to keepers of motor vehicles;[15] to rail, sea or air transport; or to operators of electrical or nuclear installations.

38　The distinguishing feature of these heads of liability is that they do not necessarily imply any breach of a duty to take care. It is sufficient for the person in question to have caused the particular factual situation to arise: the law then obliges him to pay compensation. These heads of liability were introduced by virtue of the *particular peril* involved in the exercise of certain activities or the pursuit of certain enterprises. This enhanced risk arises from the frequency and/or the gravity of the damage which these activities cause to third parties. Nevertheless, for all their dangers, these activities are regarded as useful and desirable: therefore we allow them, but impose an aggravated regime of liability on those who carry them out.

2. Specific statutes establishing strict liability (examples)[16]

a) Loi fédérale sur les chemins de fer, LCdF

Art. 40b. Principes. (1) Le détenteur d'une entreprise ferroviaire répond du dommage si les risques caractéristiques liés à l'exploitation du chemin de fer ont pour effet qu'un être humain est tué ou blessé ou qu'un dommage est causé à une chose. [...]

b) Loi fédérale sur l'aviation, LA

Art. 64. (1) Le dommage causé par un aéronef en vol aux personnes et aux biens qui se trouvent à la surface donne droit à réparation contre l'exploitant de l'aéronef s'il est établi que le dommage existe et qu'il provient de l'aéronef. [...]

c) Loi fédérale sur les installations de transport par conduites de combustibles ou carburants liquides ou gazeux (Loi fédérale sur les installations par conduites, LIPC)

Art. 1. Champ d'application. (1) La présente loi s'applique aux conduites servant à transporter de l'huile minérale, du gaz naturel ou tout autre combustible ou carburant liquide ou gazeux désigné par le Conseil fédéral, ainsi qu'aux installations telles

---

15　See below, Chapter 9, pp. 229 ff.
16　See also Art. 58 (1) of the Road Traffic Act, below, Chapter 9, pp. 248–249.

que pompes et réservoirs servant à l'exploitation de ces conduites (leur ensemble est appelé ci-après " installations "). [...]

Art. 33. Responsabilité civile. Principe. (1) Lorsque la mort d'une personne, une atteinte à la santé ou un dommage matériel est causé par l'exploitation d'une installation de transport par conduites, par le défaut ou la manipulation défectueuse d'une telle installation qui n'est pas en exploitation, l'entreprise est responsable du dommage. Si l'installation n'appartient pas à l'entreprise, le propriétaire répond solidairement. [...]

d) Loi fédérale sur les substances explosibles (Loi sur les explosifs, LExpl)

Art. 27. Responsabilité. (1) L'exploitant d'une entreprise ou d'une installation où sont fabriqués, entreposés ou utilisés des matières explosives ou des engins pyrotechniques répond des dommages occasionnés par leur explosion. Les dispositions générales du code des obligations traitant des actes illicites sont au surplus applicables.
(2) Celui qui prouve que le dommage est dû à la force majeure ou à la faute grave du lésé ou d'un tiers, est libéré de sa responsabilité. [...]

e) Loi fédérale sur la responsabilité du fait des produits, LRFP

Art. 1. Principe. (1) Le producteur répond du dommage lorsqu'un produit défectueux cause:
a. la mort d'une personne ou provoque chez elle des lésions corporelles;
b. un dommage à une chose ou la destruction d'une chose d'un type qui la destine habituellement à l'usage ou à la consommation privés et qui a été principalement utilisée à des fins privées par la victime.

(2) Il ne répond pas du dommage causé au produit défectueux.

f) Loi sur la responsabilité civile en matière nucléaire, LRCN

Art. 3. Principe. (1) L'exploitant d'une installation nucléaire répond de manière illimitée des dommages d'origine nucléaire causés par des substances nucléaires se trouvant dans son installation. [...]

g) Loi fédérale sur la protection de l'environnement, LPE

Art. 59a. Dispositions générales. (1) Le détenteur d'une entreprise ou d'une installation qui présente un danger particulier pour l'environnement répond des dommages résultant des atteintes que la réalisation de ce danger entraîne. [...]
(2) Présentent en règle générale un danger particulier pour l'environnement, notamment les entreprises et installations suivantes:
a. celles que le Conseil fédéral soumet aux prescriptions d'exécution selon l'art. 10 en raison des substances, des organismes ou des déchets qu'elles utilisent;
b. celles qui servent à éliminer les déchets;
c. celles dans lesquelles sont utilisés des liquides pouvant altérer les eaux;
d. celles qui détiennent des substances dont l'utilisation est soumise à autorisation par le Conseil fédéral, ou pour lesquelles le Conseil fédéral édicte d'autres prescriptions particulières pour protéger l'environnement.

(3) Est libéré de cette responsabilité, celui qui prouve que le dommage est dû à la force majeure ou à une faute grave du lésé ou d'un tiers. [. . .]

h) Loi fédérale sur l'application du génie génétique au domaine non humain (Loi sur le génie génétique, LGG)

Art. 30. Principes. (1) Toute personne soumise au régime de la notification ou de l'autorisation qui utilise des organismes génétiquement modifiés en milieu confiné, qui dissémine de tels organismes dans l'environnement à titre expérimental ou qui les met sans autorisation en circulation, répond des dommages causés par cette utilisation et dus à la modification du matériel génétique de ces organismes. [. . .]
(4) Si le dommage est causé par la mise en circulation autorisée de tout autre organisme génétiquement modifié et qu'il est dû à la modification du matériel génétique de cet organisme, le titulaire de l'autorisation en répond, pour autant que l'organisme soit défectueux. Il répond également des défauts que l'état des connaissances scientifiques et de la technique n'a pas permis de détecter au moment de la mise en circulation de l'organisme concerné.

Art. 31. Dommages causés à l'environnement. (1) Celui qui répond de l'utilisation d'organismes génétiquement modifiés doit également rembourser les frais des mesures nécessaires et adéquates prises pour remettre en état les composantes de l'environnement détruites ou détériorées, ou pour les remplacer par un équivalent.
(2) Lorsque les composantes de l'environnement détruites ou détériorées ne font pas l'objet d'un droit réel ou que l'ayant droit ne prend pas les mesures commandées par les circonstances, le droit à réparation revient à la collectivité publique compétente.

Translations

a) Federal Railway Act

Art. 40b. Principles. (1) If the typical risks related to the operation of the railroad causes the death or the injury of a person or damage to property, the operator of the railway enterprise is liable for the damage. [. . .]

b) Federal Aviation Act

Art. 64. (1) The operator of an aircraft is liable to compensate the damage caused by the aircraft in flight to persons and things on the ground, provided the existence of damage caused by the aircraft has been proved. [. . .]

c) Federal Act on Pipelines for the Transport of Liquid or Gaseous Fuels (Pipeline Act)

Art. 1. Scope of application. (1) The present Act applies to pipelines for the transport of mineral oil, natural gas or any other liquid fuel or gaseous fuel designated by the Federal Council, as well as to installations such as pumps and tanks used to operate these pipelines (further referred to as "installations"). [. . .]

Art. 33. Civil Liability. Principle. (1) *If by the operation of a pipeline system of transport or by a defect or a defective manipulation of a similar system not in operation, a person is killed or is affected in his or her health, or suffers a material damage, the operator is liable. If the system does not belong to the operator, the owner is jointly and severally liable to provide compensation. [. . .]*

d) Federal Explosive Substances Act

Art. 27. Liability. (1) *The operator of a company in which explosive or pyrotechnic equipment is manufactured, deposited or used is liable for the damage caused by its explosion. For the rest, the general provisions of the Code of Obligations regarding obligations in tort apply.*
(2) *Anyone who proves that the damage was caused by force majeure or by gross negligence on the part of the injured party or of a third party is relieved of liability. [. . .]*

e) Product Liability Act

Art. 1. General provisions. (1) *The manufacturer is liable for the damage when a defective product causes:*

a. *death or bodily harm to a person;*
b. *damage or destruction of a thing that, by its nature, is normally destined for private use or consumption and when it has been used by the damaged person mainly for private purposes.*

(2) *He is not liable for the damage caused to the defective product itself.*

f) Federal Act on Nuclear Energy

Art. 3. General Principle. (1) *The operator of a nuclear facility is subject to unlimited liability for the damage of nuclear origin caused by nuclear substances used in the facility. [. . .]*

g) Federal Act on the Protection of the Environment (Environmental Protection Act, EPA)

Art 59a. General provisions. (1) *The operator of an establishment or an installation that represents a special threat to the environment is liable for the loss or damage arising from effects that occur when this threat becomes reality. [. . .]*
(2) *As a rule, the following establishments and installations are regarded as representing a special threat to the environment:*

a. *those that the Federal Council makes subject to the implementing provisions in terms of article 10 on the basis of the substances or organisms used or the waste produced;*
b. *those that are used for waste disposal;*
c. *those in which liquids which may pollute water are handled;*
d. *those in which substances are present for which the Federal Council has introduced a licensing requirement or other special regulations to protect the environment.*

(3) Any person who proves that the loss or damage was caused by force majeure or by gross negligence on the part of the injured party or of a third party is relieved of liability. [. . .]

h) Federal Act on Non-Human Genetic Technology (Genetic Technology Act, GTA)

Art. 30. Principles. (1) Any person who has obtained authorisation or prior notification to handle genetically modified organisms under contained conditions, who then introduces such organisms into the environment for experimental purposes or introduces them into the ecosystem without prior authorisation, is liable for any loss or damage that occurs as a result of such handling due to the modification of the genetic material of these organisms. [. . .]
(4) If any loss or damage caused by the authorised introduction of a genetically modified organism into the ecosystem was caused by such genetic modification, liability is to rest with the licence holder. Such liability also extends to defects that could not have been recognised on the basis of scientific and technical knowledge of the time at which the respective organism was introduced.

Art. 31. Environmental damage. (1) The person who is deemed to be liable for the damage caused by the handling of genetically modified organisms must also bear the costs of any necessary or appropriate measures taken to restore or replace environmental components destroyed or damaged by the organism in question.
(2) If the destroyed or damaged environmental components are not subject to any property right, or if the licence holder does not take all measures required in the circumstances, the relevant public authority has the right to claim compensation.

3. Obligationenrecht/Code des obligations (*Code of Obligations*)

Art. 58. (1) Le propriétaire d'un bâtiment ou de tout autre ouvrage répond du dommage causé par des vices de construction ou par le défaut d'entretien.[17] [. . .]

Translation

Art. 58.(1) The owner of a building or any other structure is liable for any damage caused by defects in its construction or design or by inadequate maintenance.[18] *[. . .]*

---

[17] *Note de l'auteur*: Selon la jurisprudence du Tribunal fédéral, l'art. 58 s'applique en principe aussi aux conduites d'eau, voir par ex. les arrêts suivants: TF, 12.03.1935, BGE 61 II 78; TF, 13.10.2009, 4A_235/2009 (tous deux portent sur des dommages causés par l'eau en raison d'un manque d'entretien de conduites d'eau).

[18] *Note by the author*: Art. 58 also applies to water pipes, see e.g. the cases: TF, 12.03.1935, ATF/BGE 61 II 78; TF, 13.10.2009, 4A_235/2009 (both cases deal with liability for lack of sufficient maintenance and damage caused by water pouring out of a water main).

4. Franz Werro, in: Luc Thévenoz/Franz Werro (eds.), *Commentaire Romand, Code des obligations I (Commentary to the Code of Obligations I)*, 2nd ed., 2012, Art. 58

I. In general

1 Under Art. 58 of the Code of Obligations, "the owner of a building or any other structure is liable for any damage caused by defects in its construction or design or by inadequate maintenance." This article creates a system of "simple objective liability" [...] based upon the breach of an objective duty of care [...]. A breach may be demonstrated by proving that a **structural defect** existed at the time of the damage. [...]

2 [...] [T]he owner **may not exonerate himself** from liability. Thus, the owner cannot escape liability by proving that he or his employees have applied all required care. For this reason, academic authors generally accept that this head of liability is stricter than the relevant systems of simple objective liability. This view would be convincing if the courts limited their examination of the existence of a breach of duty by reference solely to the dangerous nature of the thing. However, in practice, the decision often depends on the level of care that might reasonably have been expected of the owner [...]; the plaintiff does not succeed unless he persuades the judge that the owner failed to show the required level of care. Hence, in a recent decision, the *Tribunal fédéral* exculpated the owner of a defective structure on the basis that the damage to the plaintiff would have occurred even if the owner had behaved with all due care (lack of natural causation) [and consequently did not hold him liable] [...] [NBP: ATF 122 III 229, c.5]. [...]

8 To be classified as a structure, an object must [...] be attached to the land, directly or indirectly, permanently or temporarily. The *Tribunal fédéral* has classified objects as varied as a road, a steam boiler, a water pipe, a telegraph pole, an elevator or scaffolding as structures [...]. [...]

23 The injured party **bears the burden of proving that there was a defect**. This is generally not an issue where the structure has not been destroyed or distorted in the accident or as a result of some later event. Otherwise, the judge may infer the existence of a defect from the damage that occurred. [This is precisely in order to take into account such difficulties of proof]

5. Kantonsgericht Sankt Gallen (*St. Gallen Cantonal Court*), 23.02.2005, BZ.2002.44

FACTS: In May 1999, following unusually heavy rainfall, a landslide occurred. As a result, two houses were damaged. The owner of the houses took the view that the landslide had been triggered by a defective water pipe owned by his neighbour further up the hill. The issue was whether this made his neighbour liable as owner of a structure under Art. 58 of the Code of Obligations (OR).

THE COURT CONSIDERS: The frequency with which checks should be made, or more specifically the circumstances under which such checks are necessary and can be expected to be carried out by the owner of premises, depend on the objective likelihood that a defect may develop which could cause damage to someone else. In the normal course of events, a properly-laid water pipe, properly used, poses no danger to the surrounding environment. It follows that the owner is not generally to be criticised if he limits himself to making occasional checks for leaks.

What caused the breach in the water pipe was the landslide caused by torrential rainfall, which gave rise to a drop of several centimeters along the line followed by the pipe. This was more than the strength of the water pipe could bear; the result was the breach in the pipe. The failure of an Eternit water pipe under the influence of forces such as these is due to the nature of the thing, and cannot be regarded as resulting from any defect in it. It follows that any connection between the damage and a structural defect disappears, and with it the defendant's liability. [. . .]

III. England and Wales

1. W.V.H. ROGERS, *The Law of Tort*, 2nd ed., 1994, pp. 112–115, 124–129

CHAPTER SIX

Strict Liability

[. . .] Given that we are likely to retain for the foreseeable future a major role for tort [as opposed to a system relying on insurance only], what should be its guiding principle? The choice is essentially between reliance on a criterion of fault ("negligence") or its abandonment in favour of a non-fault or "strict" liability. [. . .] Since liability based upon fault may be thought to have at least some connection with generally shared moral values and therefore to be the "natural" position for the law to adopt, what are the arguments for a stricter liability?

A system of strict liability may reduce the issues to be determined in litigation (and hence the cost of the process) and increase the numbers of persons who receive the "full" compensation which the tort system approaches more nearly than social security. The first point must, however, be heavily qualified because in many cases under the present law there is either no difficulty in establishing the facts relating to the defendant's conduct or liability is readily admitted but the matter is bitterly fought on questions of causation and quantum of damages, both of which would continue to be relevant to any strict liability tort system that could be devised. In any event, there is likely to be strong opposition to a system of strict liability unless it makes provision for reduction of damages on account of the plaintiff's contributory negligence and this may produce almost as many disputed issues of fact as the present fault-based system. Further, even if it is true that a system of strict liability is cheaper to administer on a case by case basis [because there is no need to establish and, where necessary, prove fault], American experience with strict products liability indicates a risk that it may lead to an increase in the overall level of litigation. As to the full compensation point, it cannot be assumed (though it often is by critics of the tort system) that increasing the range and quantum of compensation is necessarily an unqualified good for it may impose an excessive burden (either by way of damages awarded and their effect on insurance rates or by way of the costs necessary to prevent injuries) upon the persons carrying out the activity in question. Injury by accident is a misfortune like disease and unemployment and it is unlikely that there will be any society willing to compensate all misfortune so generously as to restore all victims to their prior financial position. Whether the victims of accidents or of particular types of accidents are deserving of special treatment above the "floor" level of social security is a matter of values and politics upon which there are widely differing views.

Another argument advanced in favour of strict liability is that an activity should bear its own costs, including the cost of harms caused by it (in economists' jargon the costs should be "internalised"), no doubt on the basis that he who gets the benefit should also bear the burden. Under this theory the costs of unavoidable accidents are not, as under the law of negligence, left to lie where they fall but are shifted back on to the person conducting the activity. He in turn will no doubt pass them on in his prices to his customers so far as the market will allow him to do so, thereby achieving the desired goal of "loss distribution". Alternatively, if his competitors' prices will not allow him to pass on the cost he will improve his safety procedures or be driven out of business and the other desirable goal of accident prevention thereby served. There are two objections to this approach. First, it is not necessarily the most efficient way of ordering affairs. It may well in some cases be cheaper for, say, an owner of property to cover a risk by loss insurance than to pass it across to the person causing the harm. In this sense a rule of no-liability is the most efficient. [. . .] Unfortunately, efficiency arguments tend to be conducted in a rather rarefied atmosphere in which it is *assumed* that this or that is the cheapest way of proceeding, but in real life we rarely have the data to proceed in this way.

The second objection is that any general rule of strict liability raises serious problems of causation. Suppose a cyclist is blown off course by the slipstream of a passing juggernaut[19] and falls into a drainage ditch, where he drowns. Now under the present law we would simply ask whether the driver of the juggernaut was negligent and if he was, attribute sole responsibility to him (and his employer). It is just about possible that an issue might be raised about whether having an unfenced, deep ditch in that proximity to the highway amounted to negligence but that seems unlikely. If, however, we say that an activity should carry its own costs the picture starts to look different. No doubt we would still say that the death was one of the costs of long-distance road haulage, but is it also attributable to land drainage, to the highway system and to the activity of cycling? And if the last, why not to manufacturing cycles or the goods being carried in the lorry? Such an endless regression is obviously wholly impractical and any strict liability system is likely to adopt, expressly or by implication, some test of "dominant" or "effective" cause or to limit its reach by reference to an additional requirement of abnormality. Thus product manufacturers are not strictly liable under the Consumer Protection Act 1987 for injuries caused by their products but for injuries caused by *defects* in their products. If one cannot design a lawnmower that will cut grass but not cut off toes one is entitled to market it without risk of liability if it is well made in accordance with generally recognised standards of design. No doubt, in 99 per cent of the cases where the plaintiff's action against a lawnmower manufacturer would fail we would be able to say that the accident was not "attributable" to lawnmower manufacture because it was entirely his own fault but in law the manufacturer escapes liability for the more fundamental reason that his product is not defective.

Though strict liability has attracted much attention from theorists it seems unlikely that any common law system will adopt it as a general replacement for liability based upon negligence. It may, however, make advances in particular areas as a result of legislation, as has recently happened here with product liability. The present law seems like an almost

---

19 *Note by the author*: a giant truck.

random collection of isolated instances of liability without fault, some based on the common law and of respectable antiquity (though in some cases modified by statute) others being modern statutory creations. The law has certainly not been designed as a coherent whole according to a plan, though some have discerned in it the shadow of a theme of responsibility for an increased or unusual risk.

Dangerous things: the rule in *Rylands* v. *Fletcher*

The rule in *Rylands* v. *Fletcher* has been regarded as English law's broadest attempt at a principle of strict liability for accidental harms. The case [FN: (1866) L.R. 1 Wx 265; (1868) L.R. 3 H.L. 330] involved flooding of the plaintiff's mine as a result of inadequate measures to stop up shafts on the defendant's land in the vicinity of a reservoir being built for him. Giving judgment for the plaintiff, Blackburn J. enunciated what has come to be known as "the rule" as follows:

> "[A] person who, for his own purposes, brings on his land and collects and keeps there anything likely to do mischief if it escapes must keep it in at his peril, and if he does not do so he is *prima facie* answerable for all the damage which is the natural consequence of its escape. He can excuse himself by showing that the escape was owing to the plaintiff's default; or perhaps that the escape was the consequence of *vis major*, or the act of God."

The effect of the decision of the House of Lords on appeal has been treated as adding a further requirement to the rule, namely that the use of the land in question must be "non-natural". In fact, Lord Cairns L.C. [Lord Chancellor] seems not to have intended this to be an additional requirement [. . .] of strict liability.

[. . .] In England, however, the tendency in modern times has been to cut down the scope of the rule and to insist on a general requirement of negligence. The principal vehicles of this have been the requirement of non-natural user and the defence of act of a third party.

Given some of Blackburn J.'s illustrations in *Rylands* v. *Fletcher* "non-natural" may have been intended quite literally as covering the accumulation of anything brought on to the land, but at least since the decision in *Rickards* v. *Lothian* [FN: [1913] A.C. 263] it has been given the different meaning of a "special use bringing with it increased danger to others . . . not merely the ordinary use of the land or such use as is proper for the general benefit of the community." [T]here are dicta which doubt the applicability of the rule to public authorities carrying out statutory functions [. . .]. No doubt one may feel that to impose strict liability upon such public benefactors is unfair, but that conclusion is wholly inconsistent with a loss-spreading philosophy, public authorities being in a better position than anyone, by reason of their monopoly or quasi-monopoly positions, to spread loss over the community at large. [. . .] Each of us must put up with a certain amount of risk generated by his neighbour's activities because that is the price of his own freedom of action, but there comes a point when this "reciprocity" of risk is exceeded. [. . .]

[. . .] The legislature has saved us from the difficulties and uncertainties which would arise in the application of *Rylands* v. *Fletcher* to some risks by enacting specific legislation. For example there is a strict liability for damage caused by marine oil pollution and ionising radiations [. . .]. It was the growing legislative activity which led the House of Lords in the

Cambridge Water case to decline to begin a process of expanding the scope or strictness of *Rylands* v. *Fletcher*. As Lord Goff put it:

> "As a general rule, it is more appropriate for strict liability in respect of operations of high risk to be imposed by Parliament, than by the courts. If such liability is imposed by statute, the relevant activities can be identified, and those concerned can know where they stand. Furthermore, statute can where appropriate lay down precise criteria establishing the incidence and scope of such liability."

2. House of Lords, *Read v. J. Lyons & Co. Ltd,* 18.10.1946, [1947] AC 156

[*Facts*: The plaintiff, an employee of the Ministry of Defence, inspected a weapons factory when a shell exploded there. She suffered injuries. No negligence was alleged.]

LORD MACMILLAN: [. . .] The action is one of damages for personal injuries. Whatever may have been the law of England in early times I am of the opinion that as the law now stands an allegation of negligence is in general essential to the relevancy of an action of reparation for personal injuries. [. . .] [T]he appellant sought to convince your Lordships that there is a category of things and operations dangerous in themselves and that those who harbour such things or carry on such operations in their premises are liable apart from negligence for any personal injuries occasioned by these dangerous things or operations. [. . .] In my opinion it would be impracticable to frame a legal classification of things as things dangerous and things not dangerous. [. . .] It was suggested that some operations are so intrinsically dangerous that no degree of care however scrupulous can prevent the occurrence of accidents and that those who choose for their own ends to carry on such operations ought to be held to do so at their own peril. [. . .] Should it be thought that this is a reasonable liability to impose in the public interest it is for Parliament so to enact. [. . .]

3. Tony Weir, *An Introduction to Tort Law,* 2006, pp. 91 ff.

COMMON LAW

Whereas strict liability is said to be axiomatic in contract law [. . .] instances in the common law of tort are distinctly rare. [. . .] *Read v Lyons* is a very important case: it can be seen as the corollary of *Donoghue v Stephenson*, for if the latter says that negligence is normally sufficient for liability, the former says that it is normally necessary. [. . .]

STATUTORY LIABILITY

If strict liability is rare at common law, it is relatively common by statute. [. . .] When the harm is due to something under the defendant's control strict liability is quite often imposed explicitly, as it is, for example, on the owner of an aircraft when it or anything from it falls on a grounding, on the operator of a radiation complex for the physical harm done by the escape of radioactive material, on the water authority for the escape of water from a mains, on the ship-owner for oil pollution, and on the producer of products which prove to be defective. These are all statutory claims for compensatory damages, usually in respect of physical harm only, where the quantum of damages is worked out in the normal way. [. . .]

4. Water Industry Act 1991

Sect. 209. Civil liability of undertakers for escapes of water etc.[20](1) Where an escape of water, however caused, from a pipe vested in a water undertaker causes loss or damage, the undertaker shall be liable, except as otherwise provided in this section, for the loss or damage.
(2) A water undertaker shall not incur any liability under subsection (1) above if the escape was due wholly to the fault of the person who sustained the loss or damage or of any servant, agent or contractor of his. [...]

IV. USA

1. RICHARD A. EPSTEIN, *Torts*, 1999, pp. 333, 344–351

Chapter 13
Traditional Strict Liability

[...] The basic negligence principle says that the level of precaution should be in proportion to the level of anticipated risk, taking into account the anticipated severity of harm. Setting fires, keeping animals, blasting, drilling, and mining are all dangerous on both counts: something is likely to go wrong, and when it does, the consequences are likely to be severe. Negligence law thus imposes a very high degree of care, and courts of the use *res ipsa loquitur*[21] to shift the burden of proof from P [the plaintiff] to D [the defendant]. It takes only a short step to dispense with the proof of negligence altogether, by simply holding D strictly liable for the harm, even though his act is lawful and its consequences against his will. [...]

§ 13.3 Ultrahazardous or abnormally dangerous activities

The law of fires and animals establish two specific outposts of strict liability that pave the way for the broader category of cases where a landowner is held responsible for ultrahazardous activities (the preferred term under the original Restatement) or

---

20 *Note by the author*: an "undertaker" under the Water Industry Act 1991 is a company appointed to provide water services to a defined geographic area. The company shall also own the supply system and other infrastructure. The Act was intended to regulate water companies in the private sector responsible for maintaining the public water networks in the UK.
21 *Res ipsa loquitur* ("the thing speaks for itself") is a Common Law maxim derived from Roman law whereby the plaintiff is able to establish a prima facie case by relying solely upon the fact of the accident having occurred. The mere happening of the injury "speaks for itself" since it appears more consistent with negligence on the part of the defendant than any other cause. A common example is that of a person experiencing prolonged pain after undergoing a routine surgical operation, only to find out later on that a scalpel has been left inside his or her abdomen. In such a case, there is no reason for the scalpel to have been left inside the body after the operation without negligence having occurred. See e.g. J. CHARLESWORTH/R. A. PERCY (eds.), *Charlesworth & Percy on Negligence*, 8th ed., London: Sweet & Maxwell, 1990, pp. 421 ff.; A. M. JONES/M. A. DUGDALE (eds.), *Clerk & Lindsell on Torts*, London: Sweet & Maxwell, 2006, pp. 496 ff.

abnormally dangerous activities (the preferred term under the Second Restatement). The origin of this generalization is the epochal English case of *Rylands v. Fletcher* [1868] [. . .]

Although *Rylands* itself met with much judicial resistance, a principle of strict liability for ultrahazardous activities did gain wider acceptance, culminating in the publication of the First Restatement of Torts in 1934, which carved out "ultrahazardous activities" for a strict liability treatment. [. . .]

The comments to this provision [. . .] announce categorical judgments as to what activities are ultrahazardous: the storage and transportation of explosives, blasting, drilling for oil, and (as of 1934) aviation were treated in that category, but the driving of an automobile was not. [. . .]

[. . .] [I]n the Second Restatement published in 1977 [. . .] the first change was largely cosmetic: the phrase "ultrahazardous activities" was replaced with "abnormally dangerous activities" so as to place somewhat less weight on the intrinsic risk associated with a given activity, and more on the social and economic setting in which that activity was conducted. Thus the revised § 519(1) reads: "(1) One who carries on an abnormally dangerous activity is subject to liability for harm to the person, land or chattels of another resulting from the activity, although he has exercised the utmost care to prevent the harm."

On the key question of how these abnormally dangerous actions should be defined, the Second Restatement expands the laundry list of relevant factors under § 520:

> "In determining whether an activity is abnormally dangerous, the following factors are to be considered:
>
> (a) existence of a high degree of risk of some harm to the person, land or chattels of others;
> (b) likelihood that the harm that results from it will be great;
> (c) inability to eliminate the risk by the exercise of reasonable care;
> (d) extent to which the activity is not a matter of common usage;
> (e) inappropriateness of the activity to the place where it is carried on; and
> (f) extent to which its value to the community is outweighed by its dangerous attributes."

[. . .] The question of what activities are abnormally dangerous is still decided category-by-category [. . .], and blasting, drilling, fumigating and radiation are still on the list, while automobile driving is not. [. . .]

The weakness of the Second Restatement's treatment is also revealed by its ad hoc treatment of aircraft injuries. The First Restatement subjected these to strict liability on the ground that aviation was both hazardous in the individual case and, at the time, not an activity of common usage. By 1977 both assumptions were false, given that aviation was safer than driving, even though the latter has been decreed to be a normally dangerous activity subject to the normal negligence rule. One possible response in the Second Restatement [would have been to] place aviation within the province of negligence. Yet exactly the opposite was done: new § 520A declared [. . .] that the strict liability rule applied to "physical harm to land or persons or chattel on the ground . . . caused by the ascent, descent or falling of aircraft, or by the dropping or falling of an object from the aircraft," on grounds that no situation better exemplifies the *active* defendant and the *passive* defendant.[22] Cases of midair collisions have been excluded, for these do resemble traffic accidents in which [the plaintiff's] conduct could play a decisive role. [. . .]

2. The American Law Institute, *Restatement of the Law, Torts (3rd), Liability for Physical and Emotional Harm,* Vol. I, §§ 1 to 36, 2010, § 20[23]

Chapter 4. Strict liability

§ 20. Abnormally Dangerous Activities. (a) An actor who carries on an abnormally dangerous activity is subject to strict liability for physical harm resulting from the activity.
(b) An activity is abnormally dangerous if:
(1) the activity creates a foreseeable and highly significant risk of physical harm even when reasonable care is exercised by all actors; and
(2) the activity is not one of common usage.

[*Note by the author*: the official Comment to the Restatement 3rd mentions blasting (e.) and controlled burn fires (h. [. . .]) as examples of abnormally dangerous activities. It states that "in certain jurisdictions, blasting is essentially the only activity that has been given strict-liability treatment, at least so far" (Reporters's note on 'Comment e. Strict liability for blasting' with references). The Comment further states (g.):

> The absence of a highly significant risk is one of several reasons that courts have been unwilling to impose strict liability for harms caused by leaks from or ruptures in water mains; the likelihood of harm-causing incidents is not especially high, and the level of harm when there is such an incident is generally not severe.

With respect to the requirement that "the activity is not one of common usage" the Comment explains:

> [A]ctivities can be in common use even if they are engaged in by only a limited number of actors. Consider the company that transmits electricity through wires, or distributes gas through mains, to most buildings in the community. The activity itself is engaged in by only one party. Even so, electric wires and gas mains are pervasive within the community. Moreover, most people, though not themselves engaging in the activity, are connected to the activity; electric wires and gas mains reach their homes. Accordingly, the activity is obviously in common usage, and partly for that reason strict liability is not applicable.]

---

22 Emphasis added.
23 With respect to damage to property, the Restatement Torts 2nd is still relevant.

3. Civil Court of the City of New York, *Bierman v. City of New York*, 60 Misc. 2d 497, 302 N.Y.S.2d 696

BIERMAN v. CITY OF NEW YORK
Civil Court of the City of New York, 1969.
60 Misc.2d 497, 302 N.Y.S.2d 696.

IRVING YOUNGER, Judge. Jean Bierman, a lady no longer young, owns a small house at 149 Rivington Street, New York City, where, assisted by Social Security payments, she makes her home.

On February 11, 1968, at about 6:30 a.m., water poured into Mrs Bierman's basement. It damaged the boiler, floor, and walls. The source of the flood was a ruptured water main in front of her house.

She filed a claim for property damage against the City, which responded with a letter stating, in substance, that Consolidated Edison had been working on the main, and hence that Mrs Bierman's grievance, if any, was against Consolidated Edison. Mrs Bierman then commenced an action in [. . .] this Court, against both the City and Consolidated Edison, seeking damages in the amount of $300.[24] [. . .]

Neither the City nor Consolidated Edison offered any evidence. Rather, at the close of Mrs Bierman's case, each moved to dismiss the complaint on the ground that there was no proof of negligence. There was none. Although it has been held that without such proof a plaintiff may not recover for harm caused by a broken water main, George Foltis, Inc. v. City of New York, 287 N.Y. 108, 38 N.E.2d 455 (1941), I find that simple citation of authority will not suffice as a basis for decision here.

This is a Small Claims case, and in Small Claims cases we are adjured "to do substantial justice between the parties according to the rules of substantive law." N.Y.City Civ.Ct.Act, Sec. 1804. The rule of substantive law says that Mrs Bierman may not recover because she cannot prove negligence on the part of the City or of Consolidated Edison. Is this substantial justice? Only a very backward lawyer could think so. Why should a little lady unable to bear the loss nevertheless bear it? Because the metropolis and the great utility were not at fault, we are told. Yet the concept of fault is beside the point. When called upon to decide the rights of a farmer into whose cabbages the flock wandered while the shepherd dallied, a court can preach a sermon on culpability and still appear to reason its way to a just result. But when the task is the allocation of burdens between a plaintiff who is little more than a bystander in his own society and government itself, talk of negligence leaves the highroad to justice in darkness. Accidents happen. Injuries occur. People suffer. Frequently nobody is at fault. The problem is one of mechanics, not morals. The law should therefore turn from fault as a rule of decision. Rather, judges must find a rule to decide whose the cost and whose the compensation so as to satisfy the legislature's command in a case like this "to do substantial justice." Modern legal scholarship provides at least three signposts pointing to such a rule.

(1) Cost-spreading. See Calabresi, "Some Thoughts on Risk Distribution and the Law of Tort", 70 Yale L.J. 499 (1961). The rule should operate to alleviate the expense

---

24 Today worth around US$ 2,000

of accidents. Can Mrs Bierman recover only by proving negligence? Can Mrs Bierman recover only by proving negligence here where no one was negligent? Then she will bear the whole expense and defendants none. Can Mrs Bierman recover without proving negligence? Then defendants will in the first instance bear the whole expense and Mrs Bierman none. That whole expense defendants will thereupon spread among all who benefit from the water main: the City in taxes, Consolidated Edison in Rates. Mrs Bierman obviously can do no such thing. So the defendants should pay. If they must, they argue, they have become insurers. Precisely. Let them charge each person something so that no person pays everything.

(2) Injury-prevention. See Seavey, "Speculations as to 'Respondeat Superior'," in Harvard Legal Essays 433 (1934); Calabresi, "The Decision for Accidents: An Approach to Nonfault Allocation of Costs", 78 Harv.L.Rev.713 (1965). The rule should assign liability to the party who will thereby be moved to take all possible precautions against recurrence of the accident. That party is not Mrs Bierman. It is the defendants.

(3) Fairness. See Ira S. Bushey & Sons, Inc. v. United States, 398 F.2d 167 (2d Cir. 1968). The rule should impress an onlooker as fair. Here, defendants maintained a water main in the street. It was their business to do it. They created a hazard. The hazard gave issue to the accident. I believe that fairness calls for a defendant to pay for accidents which occur because of his business activities. Thus the City and Consolidated Edison should pay Mrs Bierman for her damages here.

I recognize that Mrs Bierman was a beneficiary of defendants' water main. So were many others. There is nothing in Mrs Bierman's use of her share of the water to require that she sustain the entire loss brought about by the accident. At most, she should sustain her share; and that is the result forecast under "cost-spreading", above.

I conclude that "substantial justice" in this case demands a rule of strict liability rather than rule of fault. Accordingly, plaintiff shall have judgment against defendants, jointly and severally, in the sum of $300, together with interest from February 11, 1968.

V. The Netherlands, Italy, Russian Federation, Lithuania, Estonia

1. Burgerlijk Wetboek (*Dutch Civil Code*)

Art. 6:173. (1) De bezitter van een roerende zaak waarvan bekend is dat zij, zo zij niet voldoet aan de eisen die men in de gegeven omstandigheden aan de zaak mag stellen, een bijzonder gevaar voor personen of zaken oplevert, is, wanneer dit gevaar zich verwezenlijkt, aansprakelijk [. . .]. [. . .]

Art. 6:174. (1) De bezitter van een opstal die niet voldoet aan de eisen die men daaraan in de gegeven omstandigheden mag stellen, en daardoor gevaar voor personen of zaken oplevert, is, wanneer dit gevaar zich verwezenlijkt, aansprakelijk [. . .].
(2) [. . .]. Bij openbare wegen rust zij op het overheidslichaam dat moet zorgen dat de weg in goede staat verkeert, bij kabels en leidingen op de kabel- en leidingbeheerder, behalve voor zover de kabel of leiding zich bevindt in een gebouw of werk en strekt tot toevoer of afvoer ten behoeve van dat gebouw of werk.

(3) Bij ondergrondse werken rust de aansprakelijkheid op degene die op het moment van het bekend worden van de schade het werk in de uitoefening van zijn bedrijf gebruikt. [. . .].
(4) Onder opstal in dit artikel worden verstaan gebouwen en werken, die duurzaam met de grond zijn verenigd, hetzij rechtstreeks, hetzij door vereniging met andere gebouwen of werken.
(5) Degene die in de openbare registers als eigenaar van de opstal of van de grond staat ingeschreven, wordt vermoed de bezitter van de opstal te zijn. [. . .]

Art. 6:175. (1) Degene die in de uitoefening van zijn beroep of bedrijf een stof gebruikt of onder zich heeft, terwijl van deze stof bekend is dat zij zodanige eigenschappen heeft, dat zij een bijzonder gevaar van ernstige aard voor personen of zaken oplevert, is aansprakelijk, wanneer dit gevaar zich verwezenlijkt. [. . .] Als bijzonder gevaar van ernstige aard geldt in elk geval dat de stof ontplofbaar, oxyderend, ontvlambaar, licht ontvlambaar of zeer licht ontvlambaar, dan wel vergiftig of zeer vergiftig is [. . .]. [. . .].
(3) Bevindt de stof zich in een leiding, dan rust de aansprakelijkheid uit het eerste lid op de leidingbeheerder, behalve voor zover de leiding zich bevindt in een gebouw of werk en strekt tot toevoer of afvoer ten behoeve van dit gebouw of werk. [. . .]

Translation

Art. 6:173. Liability for dangerous equipment. *(1) The possessor of a movable thing which is known to cause great danger for people and property when it does not meet the standards which in the circumstances may be set for such equipment, is liable if this potential danger is realised [. . .]. [. . .]*

Art. 6:174. Liability for dangerously constructed immovable things. *(1) The possessor of a constructed immovable thing which causes danger for people or other property because it does not meet the standards which in the given circumstances may be set for such things, is liable if this potential danger is realised [. . .].*
(2) [. . .]. With regard to dangerous public roads, liability rests on the public authority that has to ensure that the road is in good condition. With regard to dangerous pipelines, it rests on the management in charge of maintenance, except in so far as the pipelines are situated in a building or construction and serve for the supply or discharge of fluids or other materials for that building or construction.
(3) With regard to underground constructions, liability rests on the person who, at the moment when the damage becomes known, uses this construction in the course of his or her business. [. . .].
(4) For the purpose of this Article, a constructed immovable thing is understood as a building, work or construction, permanently attached to the land, either directly, or by means of a connection with another building, work or construction.
(5) The person who is registered on the public land register as the owner of the constructed immovable thing or of the land to which this thing is attached, is considered to be the possessor of the constructed immovable thing. [. . .]

Art. 6:175. Liability for dangerous substances. (1) The person who, in the course of his or her profession or business, uses a substance or keeps it under his or her control, while it is known that this substance has such characteristics that it poses a particular hazard of a serious nature for persons or property, is liable when this potential danger is realised. [. . .] When a substance is explosive, oxidising, flammable, highly flammable, extremely flammable, toxic, or very toxic [. . .], then it will always be regarded as a substance which poses a particular hazard of a serious nature. [. . .].
(3) Where the substance is to be found in a pipeline, the liability under the first paragraph rests on the management in charge of maintenance, except in so far as the pipeline is situated in a building or construction and serves for the supply or discharge of fluids or other materials on for that building or construction. [. . .][25]

2. Codice civile italiano (*Italian Civil Code*)[26]

Art. 2050. Responsabilità per l'esercizio di attività pericolose. Chiunque cagiona danno ad altri nello svolgimento di una attività pericolosa, per sua natura o per la natura dei mezzi adoperati, è tenuto al risarcimento, se non prova di avere adottato tutte le misure idonee a evitare il danno.

Translation

Art. 2050. Liability for dangerous activity. Whoever causes damage to another person by carrying out a dangerous activity, being such because of its nature or the nature of the means adopted, must pay damages, unless he or she proves that he or she has taken all appropriate measures to avoid the damage.

3. Гражданский кодекс Российской Федерации (*Russian Civil Code*)

Статья 1079. Ответственность за вред, причиненный деятельностью, создающей повышенную опасность для окружающих. (1) Юридические лица и граждане, деятельность которых связана с повышенной опасностью для окружающих (использование транспортных средств, механизмов, электрической энергии высокого

---

25 Further provisions establish strict liability for landfill sites (Art. 6:176 BW) and mining operations (Art. 6:177 BW).
26 On this provision, see also above, Chapter 7, pp. 179 ff.: G. Cian/A. Trabucchi, *Commentario breve al Codice civile (Short Commentary on the Civil Code)*, 11th ed., Padova: CEDAM, 2014, Art. 2050 no. 1 (in English translation): "[. . .] According to settled case-law, in order to exonerate oneself it is not sufficient to show that there was no breach of the law or of required standards, but it has to be proved that under the circumstances of the case all technically available measures and all possible means were taken to avoid the damage. The rigor with which the courts apply the test for release of liability which actually makes it coincide with fortuitous event (force majeure), strengthens the idea that we deal in fact with a strict liability".

напряжения, атомной энергии, взрывчатых веществ, сильнодействующих ядов и т.п.; осуществление строительной и иной, связанной с нею деятельности и др.), обязаны возместить вред, причиненный источником повышенной опасности, если не докажут, что вред возник вследствие непреодолимой силы или умысла потерпевшего. [...]
(3) Владельцы источников повышенной опасности солидарно несут ответственность за вред, причиненный в результате взаимодействия этих источников (столкновения транспортных средств и т.п.) третьим лицам по основаниям, предусмотренным настоящей статьи. Вред, причиненный в результате взаимодействия источников повышенной опасности их владельцам, возмещается на общих основаниях

Translation

Art. 1079. Liability for damage caused by activities creating an increased danger to others. (1) Legal entities and citizens whose activity is associated with an increased risk for others (operation of motor vehicles, machinery, high electric voltage power or nuclear energy, explosives or poisonous materials, etc.; activities in the sphere of construction or other related activity, etc.) must compensate the damage caused by the source of increased danger, unless they prove that the damage was caused by force majeure or was intended by the victim. [...]
(3) The operators of sources of special danger are jointly and severally liable for injury caused by the interaction of these sources (the collision of vehicles, etc.) to third persons on the grounds provided for by Section 1 of this Article. Damage suffered by the operators of sources of increased danger as a result of the interaction of such sources shall be compensated according to the general provisions [Article 1064].

4. Lietuvos Respublikos Civilinis kodeksas (*Lithuanian Civil Code*)

6.266 straipsnis. Statinių savininko (valdytojo) atsakomybė. (1) Žalą, padarytą dėl pastatų, statinių, įrenginių ar kitokių konstrukcijų, įskaitant kelius, sugriuvimo ar dėl kitokių jų trūkumų, privalo atlyginti šių objektų savininkas (valdytojas), jeigu neįrodo, kad buvo šio kodekso 6.270 straipsnio 1 dalyje numatytos aplinkybės.
(2) Preziumuojama, kad pastatų, statinių, įrenginių ar kitokių konstrukcijų savininkas (valdytojas) yra asmuo, viešame registre nurodytas kaip jų savininkas (valdytojas).

6.270 straipsnis. Atsakomybė už didesnio pavojaus šaltinių padarytą žalą.
(1) Asmuo, kurio veikla susijusi su didesniu pavojumi aplinkiniams (transporto priemonių, mechanizmų, elektros ir atominės energijos, sprogstamųjų ir nuodingų medžiagų naudojimas, statybos ir t. t.), privalo atlyginti didesnio pavojaus šaltinio padarytą žalą, jeigu neįrodo, kad žala atsirado dėl nenugalimos jėgos arba nukentėjusio asmens tyčios ar didelio neatsargumo. [...]
(5) Didesnio pavojaus šaltinių valdytojams dėl šių šaltinių sąveikos padaryta žala atlyginama bendrais pagrindais.

Translation

Art. 6.266. Liability of the owner (possessor) of construction works. *(1) If damage was caused by reason of the collapse of buildings, construction works, installations or other structures, including roads, or if the damage was caused by reason of any defect thereof, the owner (possessor) of these objects shall be liable to compensate the damage unless he or she proves the occurrence of the circumstances indicated in Paragraph 1 of Article 6.270 of this Code.*
(2) It shall be presumed that the owner (possessor) of buildings, constructions, installations or other structures is the person indicated as their owner (possessor) in the Public Register.

Art. 6.270. Liability arising from the source of increased danger. *(1) A person whose activities are associated with an increased danger for surrounding persons (operation of motor vehicles, machinery, electric and nuclear energy, use of explosive or poisonous materials, activities in the sphere of construction, etc.) shall be liable to compensate damage caused by the source of increased danger, unless he or she proves that the damage was caused by force majeure, or by the victim's intent or gross negligence. [. . .]*
(5) Damage suffered by the operators of sources of increased danger as a result of the interaction of such sources shall be compensated according to the general provisions.

5. Võlaõigusseadus (*Estonian Code of Obligations*)

§ 1056. Vastutus suurema ohu allikaga tekitatud kahju eest. (1) Kahju põhjustamise korral eriti ohtlikule asjale või tegevusele iseloomuliku ohu tagajärjel vastutab kahju tekitamise eest, sõltumata oma süüst, ohu allikat valitsenud isik. Suurema ohu allikat valitsenud isik vastutab kannatanu surma põhjustamise, talle kehavigastuse või tervisekahjustuse tekitamise või tema asja kahjustamise eest, kui seadusest ei tulene teisiti.
(2) Asja või tegevust loetakse suurema ohu allikaks, kui selle olemuse või selle juures kasutatud ainete või vahendite tõttu võib isegi asjatundjalt oodatava hoolsuse rakendamise korral tekkida suur kahju või võib kahju tekkida sageli. Kui asjale või tegevusele sarnase ohu allika puhul on seadusega juba ette nähtud vastutus, sõltumata allikat valitsenud isiku süüst, eeldatakse, et asi või tegevus on suurema ohu allikas. [. . .]

§ 1058. Ohtliku ehitise või asja omaniku vastutus. (1) Ehitise omanik vastutab selles toodetava, ladustatava või edastatava energia või tule-, kiirgus- või plahvatusohtlike, mürgiste või sööbivate või keskkonnaohtlike ainete tõttu või muul põhjusel ehitisest lähtuva erilise ohu tagajärjel tekkinud kahju eest. Asja omanik vastutab asjast lähtuva tule-, kiirgus- või plahvatusohtlike, mürgiste, söövitavate või keskkonnaohtlike omaduste tõttu või muul põhjusel asjast lähtuva erilise ohu tagajärjel tekkinud kahju eest.
(2) Kui ohtlik ehitis või asi võis kahju põhjustada, eeldatakse, et kahju põhjustati ehitisest või asjast lähtuva erilise ohu tagajärjel. See ei kehti, kui ehitist või asja on nõuetekohaselt käitatud ja käitamine ei olnud häiritud.

(3) Omanik ei vastuta käesoleva paragrahvi lõikes 1 sätestatu alusel, kui: [. . .] 2) kahju on tekkinud vääramatu jõu tõttu; [. . .]

Translation

§ 1056. Liability for damage caused by a source of major danger. *(1) If damage is caused resulting from danger characteristic to a thing that constitutes a major source of danger or from a particularly dangerous activity, the person who manages the source of danger shall be liable for causing of damage regardless of the person's culpability. A person who manages a major source of danger shall be liable for causing death, bodily injury, or damage to the health of a victim, and for damaging a thing of the victim, unless otherwise provided by law.*
(2) A thing or an activity is deemed to be a major source of danger if, due to its nature or to the substances or means used in connection with the thing or activity, major or frequent damage may arise therefrom even if it is handled or performed with due diligence by a specialist. [. . .]

§ 1058. Liability of the owner of a dangerous structure or thing. *(1) The owner of a structure shall be liable for damage caused as a result of a particular danger arising from the structure due to the production, storage or transmission in the structure of energy, substances which are flammable, involve a radiation hazard or can cause combustion, or toxic, corrosive or environmentally hazardous substances, and for damage caused as a result of a particular danger arising from the structure for any other reason. The owner of a thing shall be liable for damage caused as a result of a particular danger arising from the thing due to its flammable, radioactive, combustible, toxic, corrosive or environmentally hazardous characteristics, and for damage caused as a result of particular danger arising from the thing for any other reason.*
(2) If a dangerous structure or thing is a potential cause of damage, it shall be presumed that the damage is caused as a result of particular danger arising from the structure or thing. This does not apply if the structure or thing is operated according to requirements and if the operation thereof is not disturbed.
(3) The owner shall not be liable under the provisions of paragraph 1 of this section, if: [. . .] 2) the damage is caused by force majeure; [. . .]

VI. Principles of European Tort Law

1. PETL

Chapter 5. Strict liability

Art. 5:101. Abnormally dangerous activities. (1) A person who carries on an abnormally dangerous activity is strictly liable for damage characteristic to the risk presented by the activity and resulting from it.

(2) An activity is abnormally dangerous if
(a) it creates a foreseeable and highly significant risk of damage even when all due care is exercised in its management and
(b) it is not a matter of common usage.
(3) A risk of damage may be significant having regard to the seriousness or the likelihood of the damage. [...]

2. European Group on Tort Law (eds.), *Principles of European Tort Law. Text and Commentary*, 2005, Art. 5:101, nos. 9–10 (by B. KOCH)

9   [...] [D]riving a motor car is certainly a matter of common usage and for that reason falls outside the scope of this Article [...], whereas transporting highly explosive chemicals in a huge tanker may not be excluded by this provision. Setting off a few pieces of fireworks on New Year's Eve is a custom practiced by a large number or people, whereas large-scale, long-lasting firework displays with hundreds of rockets and involving substantial organization and coordination is not: Only the prior activity will be a matter of common usage, whereas harm in the course of the latter kind of activity may lead to strict liability. This is obviously even more so for companies producing and storing fireworks. Even though dams are certainly no longer exceptional constructions per se, most of them will nevertheless be "abnormally dangerous" inasmuch as their mere existence constitutes a certain danger which is not commonly achieved by household water butts.

10 [...] Even if only few people pursue an activity which brings about a highly significant risk of harm, it may still be of common usage. This is true, for example, for certain public utilities: Electricity supply is typically provided by only few companies but will still be considered an everyday activity [...]. [...]

21 Since the scope of this article was meant to be limited to extreme types of dangers, only few activities will fall under this rule in practice. [...] A typical example of an ultra-hazardous activity which is not of common usage is blasting [...].

VII. Draft Common Frame of Reference

Book VI. Section 2: Accountability without intention or negligence. [...]

VI. – 3:202. Accountability for damage caused by the unsafe state of an immovable. (1) A person who independently exercises control over an immovable is accountable for the causation of personal injury and consequential loss, loss within VI. – 2:202 (Loss suffered by third persons as a result of another's personal injury or death), and loss resulting from property damage (other than to the immovable itself) by a state of the immovable which does not ensure such safety as a person in or near the immovable is entitled to expect having regard to the circumstances including:
   (a) the nature of the immovable;
   (b) the access to the immovable; and
   (c) the cost of avoiding the immovable being in that state.

(2) A person exercises independent control over an immovable if that person exercises such control that it is reasonable to impose a duty on that person to prevent legally relevant damage within the scope of this Article.

(3) The owner of the immovable is to be regarded as independently exercising control, unless the owner shows that another independently exercises control.

VI. – 3:204. Accountability for damage caused by defective products. [. . .]

VI. – 3:205. Accountability for damage caused by motor vehicles. [. . .]

VI. – 3:206. Accountability for damage caused by dangerous substances or emissions. (1) A keeper of a substance or an operator of an installation is accountable for the causation by that substance or by emissions from that installation of personal injury and consequential loss, [. . .], loss resulting from property damage, and burdens within VI. – 2:209 (Burdens incurred by the State upon environmental impairment), if:

   (a) having regard to their quantity and attributes, at the time of the emission, or, failing an emission, at the time of contact with the substance it is very likely that the substance or emission will cause such damage unless adequately controlled; and

   (b) the damage results from the realization of that danger.

(2) "Substance" includes chemicals (whether solid, liquid or gaseous). Microorganisms are to be treated like substances.

(3) "Emission" includes:

   (a) the release or escape of substances;

   (b) the conduction of electricity;

   (c) heat, light and other radiation;

   (d) noise and other vibrations; and

   (e) other incorporeal impact on the environment.

(4) "Installation" includes a mobile installation and an installation under construction or not in use.

(5) However, a person is not accountable for the causation of damage under this Article if that person:

   (a) does not keep the substance or operate the installation for purposes related to that person's trade, business or profession; or

   (b) shows that there was no failure to comply with statutory standards of control of the substance or management of the installation.

VIII. Annex: a proposal *de lege ferenda*

CHRISTOPH OERTEL, *Objektive Haftung in Europa – Rechtsvergleichende Untersuchung zur Weiterentwicklung der verschuldensunabhängigen Haftung im europäischen Privatrecht (Objective Liability in Europe – A Comparative Study on Liability Without Fault in European Private Law and Potential Perspectives)*, 2010, pp. 322–323

Proposal for a general clause on objective (or strict) liability

§ 1 Basis of liability

(1) A person to whom damage to another is legally attributable is liable to compensate that damage.
(2) Liability is to be based upon:
 a) Fault
 b) Creation of danger [. . .]

§ 2 Liability based on the creation of danger (strict liability)

§ 2.1 Basic principle

(1) Strict liability arises from the creation of, or the control over, a source of danger. The danger may derive from the particular nature or use of an object or from an activity, especially where damage is foreseeable even when exercising a reasonable degree of care.
(2) The damage resulting from a danger being created must be attributable. When assessing whether the damage resulting from a danger being created is attributable, the following aspects shall be taken into account:
 a) The likelihood of damage occurring and the extent of the damage;
 b) The danger created by the injuring party and the injured party respectively;
 c) The possibility of attributing the negative consequences of the activity in question to those benefitting from it;
 d) The possibility of spreading the negative consequences of the activity across all those carrying it out;
 e) The interest in allowing activities which benefit the public good;
 f) Insurability against risk of damage;
 g) Any difficulties which typically arise for particular classes or categories of victims in establishing or proving fault.

§ 2.2 Examples

Damage which occurs as the result of a danger being created shall be attributed to the person having created the danger in particular (but not limited to) where:
 a) the damage in question was caused by a source of exceptional risk. An exceptional risk is present when the source of danger in question is particularly likely to cause damage or has the potential to cause particularly severe damage. Such definition extends in particular to:
  • the operation of land- or water-based vehicles, or aircraft;
  • the operation of facilities for the storage or handling of substances having explosive, corrosive, toxic, radioactive or similar properties or being of large enough quantity to potentially cause serious damage;

- contact with explosive material, weaponry or other similar apparatus;
- mining activities; and
- sports activities which have the potential to cause serious damage due to the equipment used or speeds achieved.

b) the injuring party unilaterally exposed the injured party to a risk of damage without the latter producing an equal and reciprocal risk. Such definition extends in particular to damage inflicted by:
- a motor vehicle or train towards a pedestrian or cyclist;
- an aircraft towards persons on the ground;
- a motor vessel or a motor boat towards a swimmer;
- persons operating facilities within the scope of the second indent of § 2.2 (a) and persons owning or holding property in the vicinity; and
- persons hunting or doing sport in relation to spectators, other persons taking part in the event, or innocent bystanders.

c) the risk was created in the course of a professional economic activity [. . .].

Bibliography

On strict liability

J.-P. WARREN ALLAN, Liability Rules in Accident Law, Liberalism and the Economic Analysis of Law, *UCL Juris. Rev.* 2000, 122–141; RODERICK BAGSHAW, Rylands Confined, *L.Q.R.* 2004, 388; BIRGIT BAUDISCH, *Die gesetzgeberischen Haftungsgründe der Gefährdungshaftung*, Aachen: Shaker, 1998; ANDREAS BLASCHCZOK, *Gefährdungshaftung und Risikozuweisung*, Köln et al.: C. Heymanns, 1993; GERT BRÜGGEMEIER, *Common Principles of Tort Law: A Pre-Statement of Law*, London: BIICL, 2004, pp. 82–92; ERDEM BÜYÜKSAGIS/WILLEM H. VAN BOOM, Strict Liability in Contemporary European Codification: Torn Between Objects, Activities, and Their Risks, *Geo. J. Int'l L.* 2012–2013, 609; ALAN CALNAN, The Fault(s) in Negligence Law, *Quinnipiac L. Rev.* 2007, 695–750; CHRISTINE CHAPPUIS/BÉNÉDICT WINIGER (eds.), *Responsabilités objectives*, Genève/Zurich/Bâle: Schulthess, 2003; VITTORIO DI MARTINO, *La responsabilità civile nelle attività pericolose e nucleari*, Milano: Giuffrè, 1979; BILL W. DUFWA, Tort Law and No-Fault Schemes, in: Helmut Koziol/Jaap Spier (eds.), *Liber Amicorum Pierre Widmer*, Vienna: Springer, 2003, pp. 63–78; RICHARD A. EPSTEIN, *Torts*, New York: Aspen Publishers, 1999, Chapters 3 and 4; JACQUES FLOUR/JEAN-LUC AUBERT/ERIC SAVAUX, *Les obligations – 2. Le fait juridique*, 14e éd., Paris: Sirey, 2011, pp. 311 ff.; JOSHUA GETZLER/RICHARD EPSTEIN, Strict Liability, and the History of Torts, *JTL* 2010, Article 3; ISRAEL GILEAD, On the Justifications of Strict Liability, in: Helmut Koziol/Barbara C. Steininger (eds.), *European Tort Law 2004*, Vienna: Springer, 2005, pp. 28–49; ROBERT FRANCIS VERE HEUSTON/R. A. BUCKLEY, The Return of Rylands v Fletcher, *L.Q.R.* 1994, 506; TONY HONORÉ, *Responsibility and Fault*, Portland: Hart Publishing, 1999; ULRICH HÜBNER, Zur Reform von Deliktsrecht und Gefährdungshaftung, *NJW* 1982, 2041; NILS JANSEN, Principles of European Tort Law? Grundwertungen und Systembildung im europäischen Haftungsrecht, *RabelsZ* 2006, 732; BERNHARD A. KOCH/HELMUT KOZIOL (eds.), *Unification of Tort Law: Strict Liability*, The Hague/London/Boston: Kluwer Law International, 2002; ADOLF LAUFS, Deliktische Haftung ohne Verschulden?: eine Skizze, in: Hans-Bernd Schäfer/Claus Ott, *Lehrbuch der ökonomischen Analyse des Zivilrechts*, Berlin/Heidelberg: Springer, 2013, pp. 181–247; DONAL NOLAN, The Distinctiveness of Rylands v Fletcher, *L.Q.R.* 2005, 421; CHRISTOPH OERTEL, *Objektive Haftung in Europa – Rechtsvergleichende Untersuchung zur Weiterentwicklung der verschuldensunabhängigen Haftung im europäischen Privatrecht*, Tübingen: Mohr Siebeck, 2010, in particular pp. 231 f., 321 ff., 329 ff.; CHRISTOPH OERTEL, Principes européens de la responsabilité civile: quel modèle pour décrire le champ d'application de la responsabilité sans faute?, in: Christine Chappuis/Thomas Kadner Graziano/Bénédict Foex (eds.), *L'harmonisation internationale du droit*, Zürich: Schulthess, 2007, pp. 279–297; KEN OLIPHANT, *Rylands v Fletcher* and the Emergence of Enterprise Liability in the Common Law, in: Helmut Koziol/Barbara C. Steininger (eds.), *European Tort Law 2004*, Vienna: Springer, 2005, pp. 81–120; ELSPETH REID, Liability for Dangerous Activities: A Comparative Analysis, *ICLQ* 1999, 731–756; BAPTISTE RUSCONI, *Quelques considérations sur l'influence de la faute et du fait du lésé dans la responsabilité causale*, Basel: Helbing Lichtenhahn, 1963, pp. 338–363; FABIO SCHLÜCHTER, *Haftung für gefährliche Tätigkeit und Haftung ohne Verschulden – Das italienische Recht als Vorbild für das schweizerische?*, Bern/Stuttgart: Haupt, 1990; BEAT SCHÖNENBERGER, Generalklausel für die Gefährdungshaftung: ein sinnvolles Reformvorhaben?, in: Thomas Sutter-Somm/Felix Hafner/Gerhard Schmid/Kurt Seelmann (eds.), *Risiko und Recht: Festgabe zum Schweizerischen Juristentag 2004*, Basel: Helbing Lichtenhahn/Bern: Stämpfli, 2004, pp. 171–194; BARBARA C. STEININGER, *Verschärfung der Verschuldenshaftung. Übergangsbereiche zwischen Verschuldens – und Gefährdungshaftung*, Wien: Verlag Österreich, 2007; CEES VAN DAM, *European Tort Law*, 2nd ed., Oxford: OUP, 2013, pp. 297–306; CHRISTIAN VON BAR, *Gemeineuropäisches Deliktsrecht, Zweiter Band*, München: C. H. Beck, 1999, pp. 329–392; CHRISTIAN VON BAR, *The Common European Law of Torts, Volume Two*, Oxford: OUP, 2000, pp. 333–432; FRANZ WERRO, Liability for Harm Caused By Things, in: Arthur S. Hartkamp/Martijn W. Hesselink/Ewoud Hondius/Chantal Mak/Edgar Du Perron (eds.), *Towards a European Civil Code*, 4th ed., Alphen aan den Rijn: Kluwer Law International, 2011, pp. 921–943; FRANZ WERRO/VERNON V. PALMER (eds.), *The Boundaries of Strict Liability in European Tort Law*, Durham: Carolina Academic Press/Bern: Stämpfli/Brussels: Bruylant, 2004; MICHAEL WILL, Generelle Verschuldensvermutung – das unbekannte Wesen. Osteuropäische Angebote zum gemeineuropäischen Deliktsrecht?, in:

Ulrich Magnus/Jaap Spier (eds.), *European Tort Law – Liber amicorum for Helmut Koziol*, Frankfurt a.M. et al.: Peter Lang, 2000, pp. 307–344; Bénédict Winiger, Strict Liability: What about Fault?, in: Helmut Koziol/Barbara C. Steininger (eds.), *European Tort Law 2001*, Vienna: Springer, 2002, pp. 2–17; Volker Witte, *Die Verschuldensvermutung im deutschen und europäischen Recht*, Göttingen: Cuvillier, 1998; Claude Zwahlen, Les responsabilités objectives du code des obligations et du code civil, in: Jérôme Bénédict/Frédéric Berthoud/Baptiste Rusconi (eds.), *Responsabilité civile et assurance: études en l'honneur de Baptiste Rusconi*, Lausanne: Bis et Ter, 2000, pp. 481–510.

Chapter 9

Most common cases

Traffic accidents

> "[T]he great majority of cases where damage occurs and (extra-contractual) liability is at stake, are dealt with on a basis where fault plays a marginal role, if any."[1]

Scenario 1

A man is driving his friend's BMW 545i in the direction of a town centre, when he suddenly loses consciousness. His foot is pinned on the accelerator and the car speeds up from 50 km/h to 200 km/h. It goes through a red traffic light and crashes into seven other cars. Several pedestrians, passengers, and other drivers are injured and need treatment in hospital. The driver of the BMW suffers severe injuries but survives the accident.

Between 1999 and 2007, the driver of the BMW had suffered recurrent brain tumours. Following a final operation in 2010, doctors gave him the all-clear. Two days before the accident, he had undergone a medical check-up, including a brain scan, that did not reveal any medical problems. His doctors considered him to be completely healthy. Medical experts confirm that people in his condition usually are, in the absence of any symptoms, entirely capable of driving a car.

The injured pedestrians, passengers, and other drivers are claiming compensation for the damage to their health and property.[2]

---

[1] EUROPEAN GROUP ON TORT LAW (eds.), *Principles of European Tort Law – Text and Commentary.* Wien/New York: Springer, 2005, p. 65 (PIERRE WIDMER).

[2] Inspired by the case of the former Swiss Olympic champion (gold medallist in cycling and track pursuit at the 1980 Olympic Games in Moscow) Robert Dill-Bundi. The accident happened on 22 August 2013 in Aigle, near Montreux, reported e.g. in the Swiss weekly newspaper *L'illustré*, 28.08.2013 cover and pp. 3, 10–19. Similar cases happen in many, if not most, jurisdictions, see e.g. for **Austria**: Oberster Gerichtshof (*Supreme Court*), 21.11.1968, 2 Ob 336/68, SZ 41/16, *Digest III*, 12/3/4 with comments by E. KARNER; for **Belgium**: Cour d'appel de Bruxelles (*Appellate Court of Brussels*), 27.10.1981, RGAR 1983, 10608, *Digest III*, 9/7/1 with comments by B. DUBUISSON/I. DURANT/T. MALENGREAU; for **Ireland**: High Court of Ireland, *Counihan v. Bus Átha Cliath* (Dublin Bus), [2005] IEHC 51, [2005] 2 IR 436, *Digest III*, 9/14/1 with comments by E. QUILL; for **Scotland**: House of Lords, *Waugh v. James K Allan Ltd*, 1964 SC (HL) 102, *Digest III*, 9/13/1 with comments by M. HOGG; for **Poland**: Sąd Najwyższy (*Supreme Court*), 05.02.2002, V CKN 644/00, OSNC 12/2002, p. 15, *Digest III*, 9/23/1 with comments by E. BAGIŃSKA/I. ADRYCH-BRZEZIŃSKA; for **Lithuania**: Lietuvos Aukščiausiasis Teismas (*Lithuanian Supreme Court*), AS v. EM, 08.01.2003, Civil Case No 3K-3–18/2003, *Digest III*, 10/22/6 with comments by J. KIRŠIENE/S. PALEVIČIENE/S. SELELIONYTĖ-DRUKTEINIENE.

Scenario 2

A couple is driving its car through a small town. As they approach a junction, they slow down and then come to a halt to wait for a safe gap in the traffic. They thereby respect all the relevant road traffic rules and regulations. Suddenly, a cyclist approaches from another street. Misjudging his own speed and the situation at the crossing, he crashes into the couple's stationary car. The cyclist suffers injuries; the bicycle and the car are damaged.

The cyclist claims compensation for the injuries suffered and the damage to his bicycle.[3]

The problem is not limited to road traffic accidents, see the further *Austrian* case: Oberster Gerichtshof (*Supreme Court*), 22.04.2010, 2 Ob 33/10g, JBl. 2010, 653, *Digest III*, 12/3/1 with comments by E. KARNER (a helmsman of a cargo ship, who did not have any symptoms of disease when he started working in the preceding days, then feels a sudden discomfort [shivering, pain in the limbs, and nausea] and loses consciousness. When passing out, he touches the helm and knocks the convoy off-course, causing a collision with a railway bridge. The railway company seeks compensation). For a cross-border case raising a similar issue (accident under the influence of an epileptic seizure), see the **German** case: LG Lübeck (*Lübeck Court*), 19.05.2010, IPRspr 2010, Nr. 53, 120 (accident in England, case brought before the German courts, applicable law: English law).

3 See e.g. the *German* case: BGH (*Federal Supreme Court of Justice*), 17.04.2007, BGHZ 172, 83 (a claim *against* the cyclist for the damage done to the couple's car would be governed by the general rules of tort liability [see § 823 BGB and above, Chapter 5]). On liability according to German law: T. KADNER GRAZIANO/J. LANDBRECHT, Ein Straßenverkehrsunfall mit bemerkenswerten Folgen, *JURA* 2014, 624.

Questions

1) Road traffic accidents are the most common cases of extra-contractual liability. Which liability regime applies to traffic accidents in *English* law? Would the claims in the above scenarios have a chance of success, taking into account the information provided in the materials?

2) What outcome would you suggest for the two scenarios under *Irish* law?

3) In many jurisdictions, the high number of injuries to property, health, or even life resulting from road traffic accidents together with the difficulties in proving fault have led to the introduction of objective, or strict, systems of liability. In *German* law, which regime applies to establish the liability of the keeper[4] and/or the driver of a motor vehicle? In the *first scenario*, would the claim of the injured pedestrians against the keeper and/or the driver of the BMW succeed? Would the keepers and the injured drivers of the other cars benefit from strict liability?

    Would the damage claim by the injured cyclist in the *second scenario* succeed? What consequences will the cyclist's own fault have on his claim?

4) Which solutions would you suggest for the two scenarios under *Swiss* law, considering the information provided in the materials?

5) Since the 1930 decision of the *Cour de cassation* in the famous *Jand'heur* case,[5] liability of the keeper of a motor vehicle has been strict in *French* law. In 1985, in order to further improve the situation of traffic accident victims, namely pedestrians and cyclists, and with the purpose of accelerating the compensation process, the French legislator further tightened the standards of liability for road traffic accidents (*Loi Badinter*). How would you decide the claims in the two scenarios under French law?

    Would the cyclist's behaviour in the second scenario have any consequences on his claim for compensation

    a) for injury to his health?
    b) damage to his property?

6) In *Belgian* law, civil liability for road accidents is based on the general rules of Arts. 1382 and 1383 of the Civil Code; with respect to liability under Art. 1384 (1) of the Civil Code, the courts in Belgium require that the damage be caused by a *defective thing*.[6] In addition to these rules and in order to strengthen the position of traffic accident victims, the legislator created (in a *lex specialis*) a right to claim compensation from the insurer of a motor vehicle. Such right exists regardless of whether the driver or keeper of the car is liable under the relevant rules of the Civil Code. Would an action brought by the injured persons against the insurer of the BMW in the *first scenario* succeed under Belgian law?

    Would the claim of the injured cyclist in the *second scenario* succeed? Would the cyclist's behaviour have any consequence for his claim?

---

[4] The keeper is the person who has control over the car and operates it at his or her expenses. The driver is not necessarily the keeper of the car.
[5] See above, Chapter 7, pp. 171 ff.
[6] See above, Chapter 7, pp. 177 ff.

7) Art. 185 of the *Dutch* Road Traffic Act provides a specific liability regime governing the rights of non-motorised road users. The Dutch Supreme Court (*Hoge Raad*) has further strengthened the position of road traffic victims. Under a so-called 100% rule, damage suffered by a child under age 14, in an accident involving a motorised road user, will always be fully compensated (no appeal to force majeure or contributory negligence is permitted).[7] Which type of liability would apply to the victims' claims in the two scenarios above, and what would be the consequence, in the *second scenario*, of the *Hoge Raad's* so-called 50% rule?

8) In most jurisdictions, strict liability has traditionally been governed by special laws.[8] In *Italian* law, on the contrary, the provision on liability for traffic accidents is to be found in the Civil Code. Which kind of liability does Art. 2054 of the Italian Civil Code establish, and what outcomes for our scenarios would you suggest under this rule?

9) How many fundamentally different approaches can you identify in the materials, with respect to

- liability for damage caused by the operation of motor vehicles?
- the effect of the victim's contributory negligence?
- other possibilities for exoneration from liability?

What are the strengths and weaknesses of the different approaches, and which approach would you give preference to? Explain.

10) Some codal or statutory provisions, such as Art. 24b of the *Danish* Liability for Damages Act and Art. 33 of the *Chinese* Tort Law Act of 2009, expressly address the particular situation in which damage is caused following a loss of consciousness. Compare this provision with other relevant materials in the Chapter. Would you recommend legislators in other countries to follow this example?

---

7 Hoge Raad (*Supreme Court*), 24.12.1993 (*Anja Kellenaers*), NJ 1995, 236.
8 See in this chapter the rules on liability of the *German* and *Swiss* Road Traffic Acts, of the *French* Badinter Act, and of the *Dutch* Wegenverkeerswet, as well as numerous provisions reproduced in Chapter 8.

Table of contents

I. **England and Wales**
   1. Lord DENNING, *What Next in the Law*, London: Butterworths, 1982, pp. 126–129 .... p. 236
   2. Court of Appeal, *Carter v. Sheath*, 28.07.1989, [1990] R.T.R. 12 .... p. 237
   3. Court of Appeal, *Mansfield v. Weetabix*, 26.03.1997, [1997] EWCA Civ 1352 .... p. 239
   4. TONY WEIR, *A Casebook on Tort*, 10th ed., London: Sweet & Maxwell, 2004, pp. 170–172 .... p. 239

II. **Ireland**
   BRYAN MCMAHON/WILLIAM BINCHY, *Law of Torts*, 4th ed., Haywards Heath: Bloomsbury Professional, 2013, nos. 1.25, 15.01, 15.03–04, 15.18, 15.20–23, 15.32, 15.39–40, 15.45, 7.17–20 .... p. 241

III. **Germany**
   1. Straßenverkehrsgesetz, StVG (*Road Traffic Act*), §§ 7 (1) and (2), 8, 9, 17 (1) and (2), 18 (1) .... p. 244
   2. Bürgerliches Gesetzbuch, BGB (*Civil Code*), § 254 .... p. 245
   3. MICHAEL KAUFMANN, in: Reinhart Geigel, *Der Haftpflichtprozess (Civil Liability Litigation)*, 27th ed. by Kurt Haag, München: C.H. Beck, 2015, Chapter 25, n. 95 .... p. 246
   4. Bundesgerichtshof, BGH (*Federal Supreme Court of Justice*), 15.01.1957, BGHZ 23, 90 .... p. 246
   5a. OLG Düsseldorf (*Düsseldorf Appellate Court*), 15.12.2003, 1 U 51/02, BeckRS 2005, 13591 .... p. 247
   5b. OLG Naumburg (*Naumburg Appellate Court*), 29.12.2011, 4 U 65/11, VersR 2013, 776 .... p. 248

IV. **Switzerland**
   1. Strassenverkehrsgesetz/Loi fédérale sur la circulation routière, SVG (*Road Traffic Act*), Arts. 58 (1), 59 (1) and (2), 60 (1) and (2), 62 (1) .... p. 248
   2. Bundesgericht/Tribunal fédéral (*Federal Supreme Court of Justice*), 29.05.1979, BGE 105 II 209 .... p. 249

V. **France**
   1. Loi n° 85–677 du 5 juillet 1985 tendant à l'amélioration de la situation des victimes d'accidents de la circulation et à l'accélération des procédures d'indemnisation, Loi Badinter (*Law No. 85–677 of 5th July 1985, Aiming at the Improvement of the Conditions of Road Traffic Accident Victims and the Acceleration of the Compensation Procedure, Badinter Act*), Arts. 1 to 5 .... p. 251
   2. JACQUES FLOUR/JEAN-LUC AUBERT/ERIC SAVAUX, *Les obligations. 2. Le fait juridique, Quasi-contrats. Responsabilité délictuelle*

(Obligations. 2. Legal liability, Quasi-contracts. Tortious Liability),
14th ed., Paris: Sirey, 2011..p. 253
3. Cour de cassation, 2ᵉ civ. *(Court of Cassation, 2nd civil chamber)*,
28.03.1994, n° 92–15.863, Bull. 1994 II, n° 110, p. 63..........................p. 256

VI. Belgium

1. ROGER O. DALCQ, L'indemnisation des dommages corporels des piétons et des cyclistes *(Compensation for Injury to Pedestrians and Cyclists)*, J.T. 1994, 665–672..p. 256
2. Loi du 21 novembre 1989 relative à l'assurance obligatoire de la responsabilité civile en matière de véhicules automoteurs *(Act of 21st November 1989 on Compulsory Motor Vehicle Liability Insurance)*, Art. 29ᵇⁱˢ §§ 1, 2, 5...p. 257
3. BERTRAND DE CONINCK/BERNARD DUBUISSON, L'indemnisation automatique des usagers faibles, victimes d'accidents de la circulation – Rapport belge *(Automatic Compensation for Vulnerable Road Users, Victims of Road Traffic Accidents – Report on Belgium)*, in: L'indemnisation des victimes d'accidents de la circulation en Europe, Recueil des travaux du Groupe de Recherche Européen sur la Responsabilité civile et l'Assurance (GRERCA), Luxembourg: Bruylant, 2012, pp. 25–45..p. 258
4. DANIEL DE CALLATAY/NICOLAS ESTIENNE, De la faute inexcusable à la faute intentionnelle *(From Gross Negligence to Willful Misconduct)*, in: Pierre Jadoul/Bernard Dubuisson (sous la dir.), L'indemnisation des usagers faibles de la route *(Compensation for Vulnerable Road Users)*, Bruxelles: Larcier, 2002, pp. 101–137...........p. 260

VII. The Netherlands

1. Wegenverkeerswet *(Road Traffic Act)*, Art. 185.............................p. 260
2. Hoge Raad *(Supreme Court)*, 28.02.1992 *(IZA/Vrerink)*, NJ 1993, 566..p. 261

VIII. Italy

1. Codice civile *(Civil Code)*, Art. 2054..p. 262
2. GIORGIO CIAN/ALBERTO TRABUCCHI, *Commentario breve al Codice civile (Short Commentary on the Civil Code)*, 11th ed., Padova: CEDAM, 2014, Art. 2054...p. 262
3. PIETRO RESCIGNO (a cura di), *Codice Civile, Tomo II (Civil Code, Vol. II [Commentary])*, 9th ed., Milano: Giuffré, 2014, Art. 2054.......p. 263

IX. Denmark

1. Bekendtgørelse af færdselsloven *(Road Traffic Act)*, § 101............p. 264
2. Erstatningsansvarsloven *(Liability for Damages Act)*, § 24b.........p. 264

X. Estonia

Võlaõigusseadus *(Code of Obligations)*, § 1057...............................p. 265

XI. People's Republic of China

1. 中华人民共和国侵权责任法 (*Tort Law Act*), Arts. 33, 48 ....p. 266
2. 中华人民共和国道路交通安全法 (*Road Traffic Safety Act*), Art. 76 ....p. 266
3. 机动车交通事故责任强制保险条款 (*Compulsory Motor Vehicle Accident Liability Insurance Terms*), Art. 8 ....p. 267

XII. Principles of European Tort Law and Draft Common Frame of Reference

1. PETL, Arts. 4:101, 4:102 (1) and (2), 5:101 (1) and (2) ....p. 268
2. DFCR, Arts. VI – 3:102, 3:205 ....p. 269
3. Bénédict Winiger/Ernst Karner/Ken Oliphant (eds.), *Digest of European Tort Law, Vol. III: Misconduct*, Berlin: De Gruyter, 2018, nos. 9/30/1ff. (by Thomas Kadner Graziano) ....p. 269

Materials[9]

I. England and Wales

1. LORD DENNING, *What Next in the Law*, 1982, pp. 126–129

1 Motors are dangerous things

When I was a boy, all movement on the roads was by horse or on foot. There were the farm wagons going slowly along – with loads of hay – or bags of corn – drawn by two horses. There were the tradesmen's vans going more smartly – with one pony – but stopping every few yards to deliver their wares. There was the occasional gentleman's carriage driven by his coachman. There was the man on his horse coming to do business. So far as I remember there were rarely any road accidents. I never heard of anyone in our parts being injured or killed. The reason was that everything was slower. You could see what was coming. You could hear what was coming. You had time to take avoiding action. No need for split-second decisions. That was the sort of traffic for which the judges of the nineteenth century laid down the rules about liability for road accidents.

So it was for the first twenty years of this century. In 1910 motor-cars were a rarity. My wife's father had the first one registered in London – 'No. 1, London'. You got in the back like a trap. She drove it at the age of eleven. Snorting and smelling, these pre-war vehicles went only about 20 miles an hour. They often broke down. When they were coming, you could easily get out of the way. Even during the First World War my Field Company of Engineers had horses and wagon transport. No motor transport at all.

Now all is different. Motor vehicles are things that are dangerous in themselves. They traverse the roads at great speeds. They go round bends swiftly and silently. You do not hear them coming. They do not hoot. You do not have time to get out of the way. When any emergency arises, the driver has to make a split-second decision – to swerve or to go ahead or to brake. His decision is an exercise of judgement. Even if it turns out to be an error, it cannot always be said to be negligent. It is at most an error of judgement – without negligence. The error may – and sometimes does – kill or maim innocent people. They may be left without witnesses. Even if there are witnesses, they only catch – in that split-second – a brief glimpse of some little part of what happened. One witness sees one part. Another witness sees another part. By the time of the trial each witness has reconstructed in his own mind what he thinks he saw – not what he did see. A judge has to decide between their contradictory accounts. Often it is so close that he might as well toss-up.

2 Compulsory insurance

In 1930 Parliament made a change of great importance. By the Road Traffic Act 1930 it made it compulsory for drivers to insure against liability to third parties: but they were only liable when they were proved to be negligent. This meant that the injured party could be sure of getting any damages that were awarded to him because, even though the driver himself had not the means to pay, the insurance company would do so. It also had much practical effect on the decisions of the courts. All juries came soon to know that the defendants were insured. So did the judges. The result was that they found for the plaintiff in cases where the defendant was only slightly to blame. They would make him liable even for

---

[9] For the original language versions of the materials reproduced in this chapter, see the companion website at www.routledge.com/9781138567733.

an error of judgement. They also had no hesitation in awarding high damages as, after all, it was the insurance company who would pay. Nevertheless, there still remained one great drawback. The plaintiff still had to prove that the driver was negligent. If the plaintiff had no witnesses he could not recover because he could not prove it. [. . .]

4 No need to prove negligence

In the present state of motor traffic, I am persuaded that any civilised system of law should require, as matter of principle, that the person who uses this dangerous instrument on the roads – dealing death and destruction all around – should be liable to make compensation to anyone who is killed or injured in consequence of the use of it. There should be no need for him to prove that he was negligent. There should be liability without proof of fault. To require an injured person to prove fault results in the gravest injustice to many innocent persons who have not the wherewithal to prove it. It is fault enough that the driver should use this dangerous instrument on the roads – thereby putting others at risk.

So I find myself in agreement with one of the best common law judges of my time – Mr Justice Swift – of whom Mr Justice Goddard said in 1938:

> The late Swift J who, at the time of his lamented death, had an unrivalled experience of these cases, said, on more than one occasion, using the vigorous language which characterised him, that if Parliament allowed such potentially dangerous things as motor-cars to use the public streets, it ought also to provide that people who were injured by them through no fault of their own should receive compensation.

2. Court of Appeal, *Carter v. Sheath*, 28.07.1989, [1990] R.T.R. 12

The appeal was argued on 29 June 1989.

Curia adversari vult[10]

JUDGMENT

MANN LJ: There is before the court an appeal against a decision of Ian Kennedy J given at Winchester on 6 September 1988. The judge had before him an issue as to liability in regard to a road traffic accident. [. . .] The judge determined that the defendant driver was guilty of negligence which was causative of the injuries sustained by the pedestrian plaintiff [. . .].

The accident occurred at about 21.15 hours on 7 November 1980. [. . .] The defendant was driving his Renault 4TL along Bitterne Road [Southampton] in an easterly direction [. . .]. He was accompanied by his wife, who sat in the front passenger seat. The judge accepted that the defendant, whom he found to be 'entirely decent and honest,' was driving at about 30 mph in his near side lane, 2 feet to 2 feet 6 inches from the near side kerb. Somewhere near to the Pelican crossing,[11] which was showing a green light in the defendant's favour,

---

10 The court takes time for consideration.
11 *Note by the author:* a Pelican crossing is a type of pedestrian crossing that also features traffic lights for oncoming traffic. Pedestrians use these crossings by pressing a button at one side of the crossing and waiting for the pictogram of the green person to appear; this indicates that the traffic lights are red for the traffic, and that it is safe to cross the road.

the near side of his car, about six to nine inches in, struck the plaintiff, who was thrown a distance upon the carriageway to somewhat short of the northern part of Rampart Road.

At the time of the accident the plaintiff was 13 years old. He was a Boy Scout, and his troop meetings were held at premises in the southern part of Rampart Road. [. . .] On the evening of the accident he was on his way home from a troop meeting with three fellow Scouts. He crossed Bitterne Road at the Pelican crossing whilst the pedestrian light was at red. This he had been cautioned not to do that very evening by both his mother and his Scoutmaster. At all events he did it, and achieved the northern side without incident. [. . .] Whatever [the plaintiff then did], it most sadly had grievous consequences for him. His injuries were to the left side of his body, and he suffered severe brain damage. Whether the injuries were caused by the impact of the car, or the projection on to the road surface, cannot be determined. The plaintiff is unable to act on his own behalf, and sues by his mother.

The judge [of the court of lower instance] remarked:

'The question of liability presents unusual difficulties . . . because of the curious paucity of direct evidence as to what exactly happened.'

It is known that the plaintiff safely crossed Bitterne Road. He left on the southern side his three companions. They were Richard Monk, Colin Norman and Mark Phillips. [. . .] Mark Phillips gave evidence at the trial. He said that the plaintiff, having crossed the road, stood 'on' the west end of the eastern guard rail of the pelican crossing and faced the three who were waiting for the light to change in their favour. Thereafter Mr Phillips looked to the east for on-coming traffic, and heard, but did not see, the impact. [. . .]

The plaintiff can remember nothing of what occurred. The defendant, although observing what must have been the three boys on the south side of Bitterne Road, did not see the plaintiff at all. As he was passing the crossing 'there was a bang on the front of the car as if somebody had thrown a coat into this part of the door fitting where the windscreen and door pillar come down.'

The defendant's wife, who is an experienced driver, saw nothing [. . .].

The critical question, in my judgement, is: ought the defendant to have seen the plaintiff? The judge of the lower court said: 'Why did the defendant not see the plaintiff? He had seen from a distance of three or four cars lengths the boys on the opposite side of the road. He did not see the [plaintiff] on the nearside of the road. But the plaintiff was there to be seen. If one assumes that he may have been bending down, possibly to tie up a shoe lace with his back towards the defendant, thus in the most disadvantageous position for a person to be able to see him, I still cannot understand why the defendant did not see him. I reach the conclusion that, although the defendant is a good and careful driver, on this occasion he made a careless mistake and he did not see a boy who was there to be seen and whom he should have seen had he been looking as carefully as ordinarily he did.'

That the plaintiff was about is undoubted, for he was struck, but was he 'there to be seen?' Where was 'there?' What was he doing there? I do not know the answer to any of these questions. The case is unusual and, in my judgement, upon the evidence, the accident is inexplicable without an answer to the questions I have posed.

Mr Temple, for the defendant, relied on Rhesa Shipping Co SA v Edmunds [1985] 1 WLR 948, 955–956, where Lord Brandon of Oakbrook said: ' . . . the judge is not bound always to make a finding one way or the other with regard to the facts averred [declared] by the parties. He has opened to him the third alternative of saying that the party on whom the burden of proof lies in relation to any averment [declaration] made by him has failed to discharge that burden. No judge likes to decide cases on burden of proof if he can legitimately avoid having to do so. There are cases, however, in which, owing to the unsatisfactory state of the evidence or otherwise, deciding on the burden of proof is the only just course for him to take.'

In my judgement this is a case of the third alternative. The plaintiff has not discharged the burden upon him and on that ground I would, with respect to the judge, allow this appeal. [. . .]

[CROOM-JOHNSON LJ and FOX LJ concurring]

3. Court of Appeal, *Mansfield* v. *Weetabix*, 26.03.1997, [1997] EWCA Civ 1352

LEGGATT LJ: [. . .] [A] 38-ton lorry belonging to the first defendants, Weetabix Ltd., failed to take a sharp bend in the village of Upper Tean near Stoke-on-Trent in Staffordshire and crashed into the shop belonging to the plaintiffs, Mr. and Mrs. Mansfield, causing extensive damage. At the wheel of the lorry was Mr. Terence Tarleton, who has since died [. . .]. Although he had no reason to suspect it, Mr. Tarleton had malignant insulinoma. That resulted in a hypoglycaemic state in which the brain was starved of glucose and so was unable to function properly. That was what caused the accident. [. . .]

In my judgment, the standard of care that Mr. Tarleton was obliged to show in these circumstances was that which is to be expected of a reasonably competent driver unaware that he is or may be suffering from a condition that impairs his ability to drive. To apply an objective standard in a way that did not take account of Mr. Tarleton's condition would be to impose strict liability. But that is not the law. [. . .].

In the present case the plaintiffs may well have been insured. Others in their position may be less fortunate. A change in the law is, however, a matter for Parliament. Meanwhile, since in my judgment Mr. Tarleton was in no way to blame, he was not negligent. I would therefore allow the appeal.[12]

4. Tony Weir, *A Casebook on Tort*, 10th ed., 2004, pp. 170–172

Section 5. – Proof of breach

In his statement of claim a plaintiff must disclose a cause of action, that is, he must aver [declare] facts which, if proved, would entitle him to succeed. If he does not, he may fail right at the outset *(Price v Gregory* [1959] 1 W.L.R. 177; *Fowler v Lanning*, below, p. 322). [. . .]

At the trial itself, the plaintiff must lead some evidence. [. . .]

But all the facts may not emerge – indeed, they rarely do. [. . .] The question then is whether the plaintiff has proved enough. If you do not know what the defendant did (a matter of proof), you cannot decide (a matter of judgement) whether what he did was careless or not. It may, however, be possible to say that it is more probable than not that the defendant was careless; this is an elliptical and confusing way of saying that from the facts proved it is possible to *infer* other facts which, if proved, would entitle one to conclude that the defendant had fallen short of the required standard. [. . .]

---

12 Contrast with the case: High Court, Q.B., *Roberts* v. *Ramsbottom*, 07.02.1979, [1980] 1 WLR 82 (a 65-year-old man was hit by a stroke which deprived him of the capacity to control and drive a car. The defendant was held liable since he had continued to drive although he should have been aware that he was unfit). Case also reported in *Digest III*, 9/12/1 ff. with comments by K. Oliphant/V. Wilcox.

When one can infer from the facts proved that the defendant was careless in some respect not specifically shown, then it is said that *res ipsa loquitur*. [. . .]

If *res ipsa loquitur*[13] [. . .], the defendant will lead evidence. His aim is to show that he behaved properly. [. . .]

Take an example: [. . .] The plaintiff stopped his car quite properly at traffic lights, only to be rear-ended by a Sherpa minibus, driven by the first defendant and owned by the second defendant. The judge found that the Sherpa's brakes had suddenly failed without any warning, and that the driver was not to blame. He held the owner liable, however, despite evidence that the minibus had passed its M.O.T. test[14] a month earlier and had had a "full service" a fortnight before that. The Court of Appeal accepted that the crash was evidence of negligence which required rebuttal, but held that while the M.O.T. test did not rebut the inference, the proof of the "full service" did so. The plaintiff accordingly lost his claim. *Worsley v Hollins* [1991] R.T.R. 252.

In *Widdowson v Newgate Meat Corp.* [1997] Times L.R. 622 neither party gave evidence, the plaintiff because he suffered from a serious mental disorder (he had been found lying in the middle of the nearside lane of a dual carriageway) and the defendant because he thought he had no case to answer, having told the police that he had been travelling at about 60 m.p.h. with headlights on high beam and suddenly collided with something, he knew not what, since he had seen nothing. The trial judge refused to apply *res ipsa loquitur* and dismissed the plaintiff's claim. The Court of Appeal said he was wrong, and that though the maxim rarely applied in traffic cases, it was also not usual for there to be no evidence from either party. Here the plaintiff could tellingly have asserted that it was more likely than not that the effective cause of the accident was the failure of the driver, after a long day, to observe and avoid him, and no plausible explanation had been offered to rebut this inference. The Court assessed contributory negligence at 50 per cent [. . .].

If Widdowson in the case above had been on the sidewalk at the time, there would clearly have been a prima facie case and *a fortiori* if he had been on a pedestrian crossing. But if the defendant proves that the driver was dead at the wheel by reason of a cardiac attack, then the inference of facts indicating negligence (the driver can't have been keeping a proper look-out etc.) vanishes, and the defendant does not then have to go further and show that it was not negligent of the driver to set out when he was about to collapse *(Waugh v James K Allen Ltd*, 1964 S.L.T. 269; [1964] 2 Lloyd's Rep. 1, HL).

The courts are reluctant to hold that traffic accidents take place with no negligence on either side, and incline to find both parties negligent unless there is evidence to the contrary. [. . .]

Sometimes [the incident] remains a mystery. Such a case was *Carter v Sheath* [1990] R.T.R. 12, CA. A boy of 13 on his way back from a Scout meeting left his two companions on one side of the road and crossed safely to the other, though against the lights. Then he was struck and killed by the defendant's car, neither the defendant nor his wife travelling beside him having seen the boy. It was a mystery how the boy came to be back in the road. The accident being entirely unexplained, the defendant was held not liable.

Difficulties of proof have led other countries to adopt strict liability for traffic accidents [. . .] [and] Britain is quite exceptional in denying the claims of traffic accident victims who cannot prove that anyone is to blame for their injuries [. . .].

---

13 *Note by the author*: for more information on the doctrine of *res ipsa loquitur* (the thing speaks for itself), see Chapter 8, p. 213 and fn. 21.
14 The Ministry of Transport test (abbreviated to M.O.T. test) is an annual test of automobile safety and roadworthiness aspects required in Great Britain for most vehicles over three years old.

II. Ireland

1. BRYAN MCMAHON/WILLIAM BINCHY, *Law of Torts*, 4th ed., 2013

CHAPTER 1: OVERVIEW OF THE LAW OF TORTS

V. STRICT LIABILITY, INSURANCE AND OTHER SYSTEMS OF COMPENSATION

[1.25] In the areas of tort law that seem to need most urgent reform nowadays there have been many advocates for a solution based on strict liability. Strict liability already exists in respect of occupational injuries and there have been many suggestions for a similar system in respect of road traffic accidents. [. . .]

CHAPTER 15: NEGLIGENCE ON THE ROADS

I. INTRODUCTION

[15.01] Road accidents have given rise to a huge volume of litigation in this country. The cases are sometimes difficult to reconcile. [. . .] [A]s Lavery J stated in *O'Connell v Shield Insurance Co Ltd*:

> The circumstances to be considered where two moving parties come into collision are infinitely various. The time, the weather, the place, the possibility of view, the light – daylight or artificial – the vehicle or vehicles involved and many other matters will all affect the question of whether there has been a breach of duty.

[. . .]

II. THE DUTY OF THE DRIVER

[15.03] The Courts have frequently stressed the somewhat obvious fact that the duty of the driver varies according to the particular circumstances of the case. [. . .]

The presence of children

[15.04] Children present particular difficulties, not only for drivers and for those who have the duty to keep them under their care, but also for courts. Vigilance is particularly necessary "at a time of day when school children may be 'creeping like snails unwillingly to school' . . . ". The courts have made it plain that a driver is not obliged to avoid hitting a child, in every circumstance, and no liability will attach when the child's movement is wholly unexpected and reasonably unpredictable. To impose such an obligation would:

> . . . make the movement of traffic impossible once it was shown that there were children on a footpath in front of the driver of a vehicle.

III. GENERAL RULES OF BEHAVIOUR ON THE HIGHWAY

[. . .]

Failure to Keep a Proper "Look Out"

[15.18] The failure of either a driver or a pedestrian to keep a proper look out may be negligence (or contributory negligence as the case may be). This issue is usually one for the fact-finder to resolve. As Walsh J stated in the Supreme Court decision of *Nolan v Jennings*:

> It cannot be held as a matter of law that a person must be found guilty of negligence if he fails to observe the whole of an area which it is possible to observe. The test is whether the area he did in fact observe was in the circumstances reasonably sufficient and consistent with his obligation to himself to anticipate the emergence of traffic from [another] street.

[. . .]

[15.20] In *McEleney v McCarron*, the plaintiff, when returning home from a disco by bus in a comatose state of drunkenness, was helped off the bus and propped against a wall. Two young women who knew him tried to get him home but he kept falling, eventually lying with his feet on the path and his torso and head on the road. The women pulled him further in from the road but had not completed this operation when the defendant's car approached. One of the young women signalled to the defendant, who interpreted this as an attempt to thumb a lift, which he was not willing to provide. He then caught a half glimpse of what looked like a shadow adjacent to the young women. This was the plaintiff; the defendant's car came in contact with his head almost immediately and injured him severely.

[15.21] Carney J. imposed liability in negligence. He stated:

> The case comes down to whether the . . . defendant kept a proper look-out. On the defendant's own evidence he did not, for presumably by reason of concentration on the girls he never saw the plaintiff's torso and head on the road until after he had run over it. Accordingly I find the . . . defendant guilty of negligence . . .

[15.22] The Supreme Court reversed this finding. Finlay CJ (Hederman and O'Flaherty JJ concurring) stated:

> It seems to me that the manner in which the conclusion of the learned trial judge is stated would appear to assume that the mere fact that the defendant failed to see, in the very short space which was available and in the short space of time which was available, the torso of the plaintiff lying on the road, of itself, must establish a negligent failure to keep a proper look-out.
>
> I do not think that this is so, and I am satisfied that it would be placing upon the defendant an absolute duty and not what is required by law, namely a duty to take reasonable care.

[15.23] The Chief Justice considered that the defendant's "major obligation" was to keep an eye on the two women whom he understood to be trying to thumb a lift. [. . .] The defendant owed a duty by keeping them under his observation, to ensure that neither of the young women stepped forward to further their apparent intention of trying to get a lift. The defendant's concentration on them "was the proper reasonable care which he should have exercised on that occasion". Once the trial judge concluded that this was the explanation for the defendant's failure to see the part of the plaintiff's body on the road, "it would be a wholly artificial standard of care to hold him guilty of negligence . . .". [. . .]

[15.32] In *Moore v Fullerton*, the Supreme Court, by a majority, upheld Costello J finding that the defendant, who was driving his large, laden lorry through a village at about 12 to 14 miles per hour had not been guilty in striking the plaintiff, a nine year-old boy, who had run out into his path from behind a lorry, which was straightening itself having crossed the road. Finlay CJ was satisfied that to hold the driver liable in these circumstances would be to impose on him an artificially high and unreasonable standard of care.

Road Junctions

[15.39] Accidents at road junctions have given rise to much litigation, if only because of the conflict of evidence that frequently arises in such cases.

[15.40] An intersection of roads of equal status "impose[s] a very high degree of caution on the users of both roads". [. . .]

[15.45] Cyclists coming from a minor road onto a major road will be guilty of contributory negligence if they fail to ensure that they do not cycle into the path of an oncoming vehicle.

CHAPTER 7: THE STANDARD OF CARE

III. PHYSICAL CAPACITIES

[. . .]

[7.17] In *O'Brien v Parker*, the defendant had been involved in a traffic accident in which his car had crashed into the plaintiff's vehicle. There was no dispute that, if no particular individuating circumstances were taken into account, the defendant's driving would be considered negligent. The defence lodged by the defendant, however, asserted that he had "suffered an attack of epilepsy without prior indication or warning" and that "[i]n the circumstances the defendant was not negligent." It appeared from the evidence that the defendant had never previously been treated for epilepsy; that on the fateful day, he had had "certain experiences at home" before driving; that when he was driving, he had a minimal sense of smell and had intense images of light and that he did not recollect the final hundred yards of his journey before collision.

[7.18] What the defendant had suffered was a condition of temporal lobe epilepsy which had manifested itself "out of the blue". The consultant neurologist was of the opinion that the defendant had experienced a complex partial seizure. They would "allow for some consciousness on an objective basis [and] would allow a person suffering from this condition to make a decision. There was a degree of awareness . . .".

[7.19] Counsel for the defendant argued that, where a defendant proved that his or her actions were the result of a sudden illness, the defence of inevitable accident was made out. He conceded that the illness in the case had to result in autonomism or a state of unconsciousness in which the defendant had been left without control of his actions.

[7.20] Lavan J., after a review of some British authorities on the defence of automatism in criminal prosecutions, noted that these decisions had prescribed strict limits to its scope. It was necessary for the defendant to establish "a total destruction of voluntary control on [his or her] part". Impaired, reduced or partial control would not suffice. In the instant case, the defendant had not succeeded in establishing such a total destruction of voluntary control. He had made the decision to drive even though he had experienced "some difficulties" at home. He had when driving been conscious of experiencing some symptoms before the accident had occurred.[15]

III. Germany

1. Straßenverkehrsgesetz, StVG (*Road Traffic Act*)

§ 7. Haftung des Fahrzeughalters.[16](1) Wird bei dem Betrieb eines Kraftfahrzeuges[17] [...] ein Mensch getötet, der Körper oder die Gesundheit eines Menschen verletzt oder eine Sache beschädigt, so ist der Halter verpflichtet, dem Verletzten den daraus entstehenden Schaden zu ersetzen.
(2) Die Ersatzpflicht ist ausgeschlossen, wenn der Unfall durch höhere Gewalt verursacht wird. [...]

§ 8. Ausnahmen. Die Vorschriften des § 7 gelten nicht, [...] 2. wenn der Verletzte bei dem Betrieb des Kraftfahrzeugs [...] tätig war [...].

§ 9. Mitverschulden. Hat bei der Entstehung des Schadens ein Verschulden des Verletzten mitgewirkt, so finden die Vorschriften des § 254 des Bürgerlichen Gesetzbuchs [...] Anwendung [...].

§ 17. Schadensverursachung durch mehrere Kraftfahrzeuge. (1) Wird ein Schaden durch mehrere Kraftfahrzeuge verursacht und sind die beteiligten Fahrzeughalter einem Dritten kraft Gesetzes zum Ersatz des Schadens verpflichtet, so hängt im Verhältnis der Fahrzeughalter zueinander die Verpflichtung zum Ersatz sowie der Umfang des zu leistenden Ersatzes von den Umständen, insbesondere davon ab, inwieweit der Schaden vorwiegend von dem einen oder dem anderen Teil verursacht worden ist.
(2) Wenn der Schaden einem der beteiligten Fahrzeughalter entstanden ist, gilt Absatz 1 auch für die Haftung der Fahrzeughalter untereinander. [...]

§ 18. Ersatzpflicht des Fahrzeugführers. (1) In den Fällen des § 7 Abs. 1 ist auch der Führer des Kraftfahrzeugs [...] zum Ersatz des Schadens nach den Vorschriften der §§ 8 bis 15 verpflichtet. Die Ersatzpflicht ist ausgeschlossen, wenn der Schaden nicht durch ein Verschulden des Führers verursacht ist. [...]

---

15 For further *Irish* cases, see *Digest III*, 9/14/1 ff. with comments by E. QUILL.
16 Nach ständiger höchstrichterlicher Rechtsprechung ist "Halter eines Kraftfahrzeugs, wer es für eigene Rechnung in Gebrauch hat und die Verfügungsgewalt darüber besitzt", BGH, 03.12.1991, VI ZR 378/90, NJW 1992, 900, at 902.
17 § 1 Abs. 2 StVG: Als Kraftfahrzeuge im Sinne dieses Gesetzes gelten Landfahrzeuge, die durch Maschinenkraft bewegt werden, ohne an Bahngleise gebunden zu sein.

Translation

§ 7. Liability of the registered keeper.[18] *(1) Where, in the course of the operation*[19] *of a motor vehicle*[20] *[. . .], a person is killed or suffers injury to his or her body or health, or his or her property is damaged, the keeper of the vehicle is obliged to compensate the injured party for the resulting loss.*
(2) The obligation to compensate does not arise where the accident is caused by force majeure.[21] *[. . .]*

§ 8. Exceptions. The provisions of § 7 do not apply, [. . .] 2. if the injured person was operating the motor vehicle [. . .].

§ 9. Contributory negligence of the injured party. If the injured party contributed to the damage by his or her negligence, § 254 BGB applies [. . .].

§ 17. Contribution among several persons liable to pay compensation. (1) If damage is caused by several motor vehicles and if the keepers of the vehicles involved are bound by law to pay compensation to a third party, the liability to pay compensation of the keepers of the vehicles and the extent of the compensation to be paid between them depends upon the circumstances, especially according to whether the damage has been caused predominantly by one or the other of the parties.
(2) Where damage was inflicted on one of the keepers of the vehicles involved, paragraph (1) is also applicable to the liability of the keepers between themselves. [. . .]

§ 18. Liability of the driver of the motor vehicle. (1) Where § 7 (1) is applicable, the driver of the vehicle [. . .] is also liable to pay compensation according to the provisions of §§ 8 to 15. The obligation to compensate does not arise where the loss was not caused by the driver's fault. [. . .]

2. Bürgerliches Gesetzbuch, BGB (*Civil Code*)

§ 254. **Mitverschulden.** (1) Hat bei der Entstehung des Schadens ein Verschulden des Beschädigten mitgewirkt, so hängt die Verpflichtung zum Ersatz sowie der Umfang des zu leistenden Ersatzes von den Umständen, insbesondere davon ab, inwieweit der Schaden vorwiegend von dem einen oder dem anderen Teil verursacht worden ist. [. . .]

---

18 The keeper is the person who has control of the car and operates it at his expense.
19 The term "in the course of the operation", pursuant to § 7 (1) StVG, is interpreted broadly. A vehicle is generally deemed to be in operation when it is being used for transportation. However, according to the German Supreme Court, the keeper of a vehicle may even be liable e.g. when a defective battery causes a fire in a parked car. Furhter, § 7 (1) StVG covers any damage which is in close temporal and geographical proximity to the operation or operational devices of the car, see BGH, 21.01.2014, VI ZR 253/13.
20 According to § 1 (2) StVG, a motor vehicle is any machine-propelled terrestrial vehicle that does not operate on rails.
21 For an event to be qualified as "force majeure", it must be extraordinary, unavoidable, and extraneous, see e.g. M. BURMANN/R. HESS/K. HÜHNERMANN/J. JAHNKE/H. JANKER, *Straßenverkehrsrecht*, 24th ed., Munich: C. H. Beck, 2016, § 7 Rn. 19. Thus, force majeure only covers exceptional situations like natural disasters, acts of sabotage, and the intentional interference of third parties, such as throwing stones at cars off a motorway bridge, see e.g. C. GRÜNEBERG, in: U. Berz/M. Burmann (eds.), *Handbuch des Straßenverkehrsrechts*, supplement 36, 12/2016, Munich: C. H. Beck, § 7 Rn. 43.

Translation

> **§ 254. Contributory negligence.** *(1) Where fault on the part of the injured person contributes to the occurrence of the damage, liability in damages and the extent of compensation to be paid depend on the circumstances, in particular to what extent the damage is caused mainly by one or the other party. [. . .]*

3. MICHAEL KAUFMANN, in: Reinhart Geigel, *Der Haftpflichtprozess (Civil Liability Litigation)*, 27th ed. by Kurt Haag, 2015, Chapter 25, n° 95

[On § 7 (2) of the Road Traffic Act:] [. . .] Force majeure is an inevitable event, not linked to the operation of the vehicle itself, but affecting the vehicle from the outside. The event is so extraordinary that it could not be prevented by economically reasonable means, even by taking the utmost care. The courts affirm that an event is unavoidable in the case of a child appearing between two parked cars and running into the driver's passing car, if the child is not visible and foreseeable for the driver [. . .]. However, since it is not unusual for children to run between parked vehicles onto the road, this is not a case of force majeure [. . .].

4. Bundesgerichtshof, BGH (*Federal Supreme Court of Justice*), 15.01.1957, BGHZ 23, 90

The defendant's husband was driving his car on G – Rd. in Sp – . Having reached St. Joseph's Church, he steered the car onto the pavement on the right-hand side of the road for no apparent reason. The car then veered across the street and went over the left-hand pavement, where it hit the plaintiffs who were walking there. Finally, the car returned to the road, where it collided with a truck, and came to a standstill. The defendant's husband was severely injured in the collision with the truck and died that same day in the hospital. The autopsy revealed that the cause of his death was a cerebral haemorrhage due to a ruptured aneurysm, unrelated to the accident, and which had initially led to a state of unconsciousness and then resulted in paralysis of the respiratory system. The plaintiffs were severely injured in the accident. They are therefore bringing a claim against the defendant, who is the sole heir of her husband [i.e. of the former keeper of the car]. They are seeking quantified damages and declaratory relief stating that the defendant is liable for any subsequent damage that may result from the accident. [. . .]

Decision:

I . . . In the judgment which forms the subject of this appeal, the Appellate Court rightly notes that the question of whether liability [. . .] is excluded when the driver of a car is physically and psychologically unable to control his acts, or if the strict liability regime of § 7 (1) StVG applies nonetheless, is highly controversial. [. . .]

This court follows the second opinion for cases involving sudden unconsciousness of the car driver. The following considerations are material for the court:

a) According to the legislator, strict liability of the keeper of the car, which goes well beyond ordinary liability (§§ 823 ff. BGB), is justified by the increased danger that the movement of cars, driven by mechanical power, represents to society. [. . .]. As the Court of Appeal rightly stated, such an increase of danger [. . .] results from the interaction between machines and men. The safety of operating a car depends as much on human activity, by making the car move and stop, as it does on the technical structure of the car. Thus, failures in human activity belong to the risk inherent in operating a motor vehicle [. . .]. With regard to the purpose of § 7 [StVG], it is therefore only logical that a physical or mental failure of the driver, which he could not foresee and avoid even with the utmost care, does not free him from liability, just as a technical failure of the car would not exonerate him [. . .]. [. . .]

e) [. . .] The plaintiffs can therefore successfully bring a claim based on § 7 StVG for the damage caused by the accident on 27.7.1953, even though the defendant's husband's sudden unconsciousness was caused by a cerebral haemorrhage that was impossible to foresee even by using the outmost care. [. . .]

5a. OLG Düsseldorf (*Düsseldorf Appellate Court*), 15.12.2003, I U 51/02, BeckRS 2005, 13591

Facts

The cause of the lawsuit is a traffic accident that happened on 28th October 1999 at around 7:15 p.m. [. . .] and resulted in the death of Dr. H. W. K., the husband of Plaintiff 1 and father of Plaintiffs 2 and 3.

Dr. K. rode his racing bike on road K towards Hochneukirch. At the same time, Defendant 1 was approaching from the opposite direction, driving an Audi car with the registration plate HOL-DH 79, which was registered under the name of Defendant 2 [who was the keeper of the car]. A head-on collision occurred in the course of a long bend in the road [. . .] between the bike and the car. Dr. K. was thrown onto the front of the car and subsequently thrown into the air in the direction of Wanlo; he was killed instantly [. . .].

By way of declaratory judgment, the plaintiffs claim damages for the material damage suffered. [. . .]

Decision

[. . .] The legal grounds of the plaintiffs' claim against Defendant 1 [who was driving the car] can be found in §§ 7, [. . .], 18 StVG [. . .].

The legal grounds for the claim against Defendant 2 [the keeper of the car] can be found in § 7 StVG. [. . .]

Defendant 1 could have avoided the accident by not going beyond the line marking and by driving the car exclusively on his own side of the road. He could also have avoided the accident had he respected the speed limit. [. . .]

Nonetheless, the deceased Dr. K. has partially contributed to the occurrence of the head-on collision. [. . .] He failed to stay on the right side of the lane, thus violating traffic regulations, as he moved towards the part of his lane near the line marking [in the middle of the road], shortly before the head-on collision. If he had been cycling on the far right side of his lane, the fatal collision would have been avoided. Therefore, as a consequence of the contributory negligence of Dr. K [§ 254 BGB], the amount of damages that is due to the plaintiffs is reduced by 25%.

5b. OLG Naumburg (*Naumburg Appellate Court*), 29.12.2011–4 U 65/11, VersR 2013, 776

In the case of a car accident that happened at night on an unlit country road, the cyclist's contributory negligence can lead to a reduction of the car driver's liability. In the present case, the cyclist was dressed in dark clothes and was riding a black bicycle without lights, when he was hit from behind by a car. Because of the cyclist's negligence, the car driver was held to be liable for only ¼ of the damage [§ 254 (1) BGB]. [This is so even if the latter drove at a speed that left him unable to bring his car to a standstill at any time within the visible route, thereby violating a duty imposed on all drivers].

IV. Switzerland

1. Strassenverkehrsgesetz/Loi fédérale sur la circulation routière (*Road Traffic Act*)

> **Art. 58. Haftpflicht des Motorfahrzeughalters.** (1) Wird durch den Betrieb eines Motorfahrzeuges ein Mensch getötet oder verletzt oder Sachschaden verursacht, so haftet der Halter für den Schaden.[22] [. . .]
>
> **Art. 59. Ermässigung oder Ausschluss der Halterhaftung.** (1) Der Halter wird von der Haftpflicht befreit, wenn er beweist, dass der Unfall durch höhere Gewalt oder grobes Verschulden des Geschädigten oder eines Dritten verursacht wurde ohne dass ihn selbst oder Personen, für die er verantwortlich ist, ein Verschulden trifft und ohne dass die fehlerhafte Beschaffenheit des Fahrzeuges zum Unfall beigetragen hat.
> (2) Beweist der Halter, der nicht nach Absatz 1 befreit wird, dass ein Verschulden des Geschädigten beim Unfall mitgewirkt hat, so bestimmt der Richter die Ersatzpflicht unter Würdigung aller Umstände. [. . .]
>
> **Art. 60. Mehrere Schädiger.** (1) Sind bei einem Unfall, an dem ein Motorfahrzeug beteiligt ist, mehrere für den Schaden eines Dritten ersatzpflichtig, so haften sie solidarisch.
> (2) Auf die beteiligten Haftpflichtigen wird der Schaden unter Würdigung aller Umstände verteilt. Mehrere Motorfahrzeughalter tragen den Schaden nach Massgabe des von ihnen zu vertretenden Verschuldens, wenn nicht besondere Umstände, namentlich die Betriebsgefahren, eine andere Verteilung rechtfertigen.
>
> **Art. 62. Schadenersatz, Genugtuung.** (1) Art und Umfang des Schadenersatzes sowie die Zusprechung einer Genugtuung richten sich nach den Grundsätzen des Obligationenrechtes über unerlaubte Handlungen. [. . .][23]

---

22 *Anm. des Verf.*: Halter ist, wer die Kontrolle über das Fahrzeug ausübt und es für seine Rechnung betreibt. Nach schweizerischem Recht haftet allein der Halter verschuldensunabhängig. Für den Fahrer gilt dagegen die Verschuldenshaftung des Art. 41 OR, siehe z.B. den Entscheid BG, 15.06.2000, 6S.754/2000, c.3a.
23 Art. 41 OR, siehe oben, Kapitel 5, S. 87.

Translation

Art. 58. Liability of the keeper of the motor vehicle. *(1) If death, bodily injury of a person, or damage to property are caused by a motor vehicle in operation, the keeper is liable for the damage.*[24][. . .]

Art. 59. Reduction or exoneration of the keeper's liability. *(1) The keeper is exonerated of liability if he or she proves that the accident was caused by force majeure or by gross negligence on the part of the injured party or of a third party, on the condition that neither his or her own fault nor the fault of persons for whom he or she is responsible, nor a defect of the motor vehicle have contributed to the accident.*
(2) If the keeper, who cannot exonerate himself of liability according to section 1, proves that a fault of the injured party has contributed to cause the accident, the judge will determine the compensation with due regard to all the circumstances. [. . .]

Art. 60. Multiple liable persons. *(1) Where two or more persons are liable for the damage suffered by a third party in an accident in which a motor vehicle has been involved, they are jointly and severally liable.*
(2) The contribution of each to the compensation is assessed in light of all the circumstances. Where two or more keepers of motor vehicles are liable, their contribution to the compensation will be in proportion to their fault, unless special circumstances, especially the risk of driving vehicles, justify another way of division.

Art 62. Compensation and satisfaction. *(1) The form and extent of the compensation, as well as the attribution of satisfaction, are governed by the principles of the Code of Obligations relating to unlawful acts. [. . .]*[25]

2. Bundesgericht/Tribunal fédéral (*Federal Supreme Court of Justice*), 29.05.1979, BGE 105 II 209

A. – On the morning of 15th June 1976, Raymond Bischof, assistant at the Swiss Federal Institute of Technology Zurich, drove a car that was owned by the Swiss Federation (VW 1600 Variant A). He drove on highway 13, from Sargans towards Chur. Due to maintenance work on the section between Bad Ragaz and Landquart, only one of the two lanes leading to Chur was passable. The vehicles travelling towards Sargans had been diverted into the fast lane of the opposite carriageway. Hence, the cars travelling in the direction of Chur directly passed the cars travelling in the direction of Sargans. This traffic management was marked with road signs in accordance with the relevant regulations.

Approximately 250 meters before the exit at Maienfeld, the vehicle driven by Bischof went into the left-hand lane, where it collided head-on with the Mercedes Benz tipper truck driven in full respect of the rules of the road by Ernst Kalberer, travelling in the opposite direction [. . .]; Bischof was killed on the spot. [. . .] The driver of the truck was not injured. [. . .]

The *Bundesgericht* thus reasoned: [. . .]

---

24 *Note by the author*: the keeper is the person who has control over the car and operates it at his or her expense. In *Swiss* law, a driver who is *not* the keeper is liable under Art. 41 CO (liability for fault), see e.g. BG, 15.06.2000, 6S.754/2000, c.3a. Only the keeper is strictly liable.
25 Art. 41 CO, see above, Chapter 5, p. 87.

3. – When a person is killed by the operation of a motor vehicle, the keeper of the car is liable for the damage by virtue of Art. 58 (1) of the Road Traffic Act (SVG). However, the keeper is exempt from liability if he proves that the accident was caused by force majeure or gross negligence of the injured party or of a third party, on the condition that neither his own fault, nor the fault of persons for whom he is responsible, nor a defect of the motor vehicle have contributed to the accident (Art. 59 (1) of the SVG).

Kressig's truck was involved in the accident. It is undisputed that the driver of the truck was not at fault, that the accident was not due to force majeure, and that the truck was roadworthy. Thus, under Art. 59 (1) of the SVG, it only needs to be examined whether Bischof has caused the accident through gross negligence [in which case the defendant would be released from liability according to Art. 59 (1) Road Traffic Act]. The defendant claims that Bischof had violated elementary precautions and omitted to do what any reasonable person in this situation and under the same circumstances would have done in order to avoid the accident. Art. 59 (1) of the SVG expressly states that the burden to prove gross negligence lies with the defendant.

The contested judgment states that the vehicle driven by Bischof went into the left-hand lane of the carriageway. According to the expert opinion obtained by the court, the accident was not due to a technical defect of the federal vehicle. It can also be excluded that Bischof was blinded at the critical moment. An error on Bischof's part was not apparent either. Neither had he tried to overtake carelessly, nor was he overly tired or intoxicated, nor is there evidence of suicide. However, according to the report of the medical expert, it is possible that Bischof had been afflicted with a malaise or loss of consciousness due to the after-effects of a previous myocardial inflammation, and that this had caused the accident. There is no certainty, but unconsciousness on Bischof's part is with "some probability" the cause of the accident in question.

From these circumstances, identified by the Cantonal Court, it follows that it is not established that Bischof was able to control his acts at the time of the accident. In the interest of the injured party, Art. 59 (1) of the SVG establishes a special burden of proof according to which the defendant has to prove gross negligence on the part of the claimant if he wants to avoid liability; he therefore also has to prove Bischof's capacity to control his acts at the time of the accident. [. . .] It is obvious that Bishop objectively violated a traffic rule when he drove with his vehicle in the opposite lane (Art. 34 (1) SVG), thereby acting illegally. Subjectively, fault does not require that Bischof was aware of this illegality. However, in order for him to be able to violate a duty of care, it is necessary that he was able to control his acts. The latter has not been proven here. If the defendant cannot prove that Bischof was at fault, he is consequently not exempt from liability for the consequences of the accident (Art. 59 (1) SVG).

4. – a) Since several vehicles were involved in the accident in question, their holders are jointly liable for the damage caused (Art. 60 (1) SVG). In the present case, both the claimant, as keeper of the motor car, and Kressig, the keeper of the truck, or his insurer, are jointly liable.

b) According to Art. 60 (2) SVG, the damage is to be distributed between all liable parties, taking into consideration all the circumstances of the case; thereby, regard has to be had in the first place to the fault committed by the keepers of the motor vehicles involved. Only under special circumstances, namely with regard to the risk of operating a vehicle, can a different distribution be justified.[26]

---

26 *Note by the author*: the same principles apply in German law under § 17 (1) StVG.

According to what has been said, none of the keepers of the vehicles involved in the accident was at fault. Under Art. 60 (2) of the SVG, regard has to be had "especially" to the risk of operating a vehicle. [. . .] As such, the existence of a link between the accident and the operating of the vehicle is sufficient to materialise the risk of operating a vehicle. This applies, however, also to the truck involved in the accident. The fact that the truck was in the opposite lane at the time of the accident presented an obstacle for the federal vehicle, that caused the damage to eventually occur. From the judgment under appeal, it follows that both vehicles involved in the accident were driven at a speed of 80 km/h before the accident. The lower court further holds that the truck was fully loaded and thus had a weight of 15 tons, whereas the car only weighed about a ton. [. . .] Due to the much higher weight of the truck, the destructive force released by the truck during the accident was much higher than that emanating from the passenger car; accordingly, the risk of operating the truck is to be estimated as higher.

Given the absence of fault of both drivers and the significantly higher operating risk of the truck, the equal division of the damage between the keepers of both vehicles, such as decided by the lower court, appears to be adequate. [. . .]

V. France

1. Loi n° 85–677 du 5 juillet 1985 tendant à l'amélioration de la situation des victimes d'accidents de la circulation et à l'accélération des procédures d'indemnisation, Loi Badinter (Law No. 85–677 of 5th July 1985, Aiming at the Improvement of the Conditions of Road Traffic Accident Victims and the Acceleration of the Compensation Procedure, Badinter Act)

Chapitre Ier: indemnisation des victimes d'accidents de la circulation

Art. 1. Les dispositions du présent chapitre s'appliquent [. . .] aux victimes d'un accident de la circulation dans lequel est impliqué un véhicule terrestre à moteur [. . .], à l'exception des chemins de fer et des tramways circulant sur des voies qui leur sont propres.

Section I: dispositions relatives au droit à indemnisation

Art. 2. Les victimes, y compris les conducteurs, ne peuvent se voir opposer la force majeure ou le fait d'un tiers par le conducteur ou le gardien d'un véhicule mentionné à l'article 1er.

Art. 3. (1) Les victimes, hormis les conducteurs de véhicules terrestres à moteur, sont indemnisées des dommages résultant des atteintes à leur personne qu'elles ont subis, sans que puisse leur être opposée leur propre faute à l'exception de leur faute inexcusable si elle a été la cause exclusive de l'accident.
(2) Les victimes désignées à l'alinéa précédent, lorsqu'elles sont âgées de moins de seize ans ou de plus de soixante-dix ans, ou lorsque, quel que soit leur âge, elles sont titulaires, au moment de l'accident, d'un titre leur reconnaissant un taux d'incapacité permanente ou d'invalidité au moins égal à 80%, sont, dans tous les

> cas, indemnisées des dommages résultant des atteintes à leur personne qu'elles ont subis.
> (3) Toutefois, dans les cas visés aux deux alinéas précédents, la victime n'est pas indemnisée par l'auteur de l'accident des dommages résultant des atteintes à sa personne lorsqu'elle a volontairement recherché le dommage qu'elle a subi.
>
> **Art. 4.** La faute commise par le conducteur du véhicule terrestre à moteur a pour effet de limiter ou d'exclure l'indemnisation des dommages qu'il a subis.
>
> **Art. 5.** La faute, commise par la victime a pour effet de limiter ou d'exclure l'indemnisation des dommages aux biens qu'elle a subis. [...]

Translation

> *Chapter I: Compensation of Victims of Road Traffic Accidents*
>
> *Art. 1. The provisions of the present chapter apply to victims of a road traffic accident [...] where a terrestrial motor vehicle is involved [...], with the exception of trains and tramways circulating on their own tracks.*
>
> *Section I: Provisions Governing the Right to Compensation*
>
> *Art. 2. The driver or the keeper of a vehicle mentioned in Article 1 may not plead force majeure or the act of a third party against the victims, including drivers.*
>
> *Art. 3. (1) Victims, apart from drivers of terrestrial motor vehicles, shall be compensated for the damage resulting from personal injuries suffered by them, and their own fault may not be pleaded against them, except where their inexcusable fault was the sole cause of the accident.*
> *(2) Where the victims referred to in the preceding subparagraph are under the age of 16 or over the age of 70 or where, irrespective of their age, they are holders of a certificate attesting a degree of permanent incapacity or invalidity of at least 80%, they shall in all cases be compensated for the damage resulting from the personal injuries they have suffered.*
> *(3) Nevertheless, in the cases mentioned in the two preceding subparagraphs, the victim shall not be compensated by the person who caused the accident for the damage resulting from his or her personal injuries, where he or she intentionally brought about the damage suffered.*
>
> *Art. 4. A fault committed by the driver of the terrestrial motor vehicle shall have the effect of limiting or excluding compensation of the damage suffered by him or her.*
>
> *Art. 5. A fault committed by the victim shall have the effect of limiting or excluding compensation for property damage suffered by him or her. [...]*

2. Jacques Flour/Jean-Luc Aubert/Eric Savaux, Les obligations. 2. Le fait juridique, Quasi-contrats. Responsabilité délictuelle (Obligations. 2. Legal liability, Quasi-contracts. Tortious Liability), 14th ed., 2011

The compensation scheme for victims of traffic accidents

320. Genesis of the law of 5th July 1985. – Despite the considerable efforts of the courts to give the principle found in Art. [1242] (1) [i.e. the liability of the keeper of a thing] the broadest possible scope,[27] the actual results were not always satisfactory. This has been the case especially with regard to traffic accidents, in particular since the constant development of traffic led to a multiplication of the number of victims.

The fact that some victims were fully or partially deprived of compensation, because the accident occurred as a result of force majeure or because the victim was (often only slightly) at fault, was increasingly regarded as shocking and unacceptable.

From then on, support for the adoption of a law regulating compensation for damage caused by traffic accidents, following in the example of many other industrialised countries, became increasingly widespread. This very wide movement led to the passing of Law No. 85–677 of 5 July 1985, *aiming at the improvement of the condition of road traffic accident victims and the acceleration of the compensation process.* [. . .]

321. Liability and right to compensation. – Very quickly, the question was raised as to whether the solutions of the new law were merely distortions – by way of exceptions – of Arts. [1240 ff.] that remained applicable or, from a very different perspective, whether they established an autonomous regime replacing these rules.

Autonomy was rationally necessary and actually established: the law defines, for the benefit of the victims of traffic accidents, a *right to compensation* that is independent of the Arts. [1240 ff.] of the Civil Code. [. . .]

§ 1. Conditions for application and scope of the act

[. . .] **324. Traffic accident.** – The law applies exclusively to *traffic accidents*. The understanding of this notion is, however, very broad. [. . .] It is immaterial whether the accident involved only one vehicle and whether it was moving or stationary [. . .].

a) The right to compensation for victims other than drivers

343. Principle of quasi-automatic compensation. – Elimination of force majeure, the intervention of a third party, and fault on the part of the victim. – In line with its purpose, the regime of the 1985 Act ensures that victims other than drivers receive an almost automatic compensation for personal injury.

This principle of compensation is provided by Art. 2 of the Act, according to which "the driver or keeper of a vehicle may not plead force majeure or the act of a third party against the victims, including drivers." It would therefore be pointless to establish that the damage

---

27 See above, Chapter 7, pp. 171 ff.

resulted from an unforeseeable and unavoidable natural event – force majeure – or that it was the act of a third party, similarly unpredictable and irresistible. [. . .]

[Art. 3 (1)] excludes any restriction of the right to compensation based on the victim's contributory fault, even if it may present the character of force majeure. The right to compensation is only excluded in case of *gross negligence* which was *the sole cause of the accident*, and when the victim *voluntarily sought the damage*. It is however necessary to make some qualifications to this observation.

344. Distinction between two categories of victims: victims simply protected and victims entitled to privileged protection. – [. . .] [A]rt. 3 distinguishes two sub-categories among victims other than drivers:

- first, victims entitled to *simple protection* [. . .], representing the majority;
- then, various persons [. . .] entitled to reinforced protection, which allows us to speak of *victims entitled to privileged protection*.

Victims benefit from such privileged status only as long as they are not drivers and are [. . .] under the age of 16 or over the age of 70. [. . .]

As for the victims that are only entitled to simple protection, [the right to compensation] ceases to exist in two cases: when the victim has committed an *inexcusable fault that is the sole cause of the accident* (Art. 3 (1)), or when the victim *voluntarily sought the damage* (Art. 3 (3)). On the other hand, the right to compensation of victims entitled to privileged protection is only compromised when they voluntarily sought the injury. [. . .]

345. The inexcusable fault as sole cause of the accident. – The Court of Cassation very quickly provided a definition of what constitutes *inexcusable fault* in the sense of Art. 3: it is a "deliberate fault of exceptional gravity that puts its author at an unreasonably dangerous risk of which he should have been aware". This formula was adopted in a ruling of the Plenary Assembly of the Court.

The *inexcusable fault as sole cause of the accident* is characterised as an act of the victim creating an unpredictable situation and rendering the accident inevitable for the motorist who committed no fault or negligence.

The cumulative requirements, consisting of an *inexcusable fault* and of this fault being the *sole cause of the accident* [. . .], mean that this exception to compensation is hardly ever applicable.

Indeed it presupposes that the victim acts deliberately, thereby taking a very serious and completely unjustifiable risk. Only particularly risky behaviour that has no plausible explanation satisfies this requirement, as opposed to mere, even serious, imprudence.

Regarding accidents of pedestrians crossing a road, it seems that fault is only considered inexcusable if the victim shows contempt for an obstacle that is deliberately placed to stop the crossing of the lane – such as guardrails. [. . .]

It further implies that the victim is *acting consciously*. This excludes that such fault can be attributed to [. . .] a *child*. [. . .]

It finally implies that the inexcusable fault was the sole cause of the accident. [. . .]

347. Conclusion. – The analyses of these two narrow exceptions to compensation provided by the law show the considerable scope of the right to compensation for victims who are not drivers. This right ensures such category of victims an *almost automatic compensation*. And it is a right to *full compensation*: the right to compensation introduced by the 1985 Act can only be maintained for the whole damage, or it may be completely barred. It is a system of *all or nothing*.

The victim is thus entitled to full compensation and this right cannot be reduced [...] on the pretext that she was at fault. When the principle yields exceptionally, either because the victim voluntarily sought the injury, or because he committed an inexcusable fault that was the sole cause of the accident, there is no compensation *at all*: the right to compensation disappears *completely*. The law says so explicitly in the case where the victim deliberately sought the damage (Art. 3 (3)); the solution is implicit, but certain, in the case of an inexcusable fault.

However, such a loss of the right to compensation may only occur very rarely. [...]

[...] The law thereby clearly dissociates itself from the multiple failures of the right to compensation under Art. [1242] (1). And rightly so: the situations following traffic accidents are sufficiently dramatic that the law does not add further complications. But, under such circumstances, it is hard to conceive that the regime does not apply to *all* victims of traffic accidents, and that the law, on the contrary, offers a much less favourable treatment to *drivers*.

b) The right to compensation of injured drivers

348. Limitation of the right to compensation with regard to the fault committed by the driver. – Like other victims, drivers of motorised vehicles have a right to compensation for their personal injury. They can invoke this right under the 1985 Act against both the drivers and keepers of the vehicles involved. But this right is subject to a very different system of a much more limited scope when compared to the one applying to other victims.

Undoubtedly, under Art. 2, the driver or keeper of a vehicle, who is held liable for the traffic accident, cannot plead *force majeure* or an *act of a third party* against other drivers injured in a traffic accident.

However, according to Art. 4 "fault on the part of the driver of the terrestrial motor vehicle shall have the effect of limiting or excluding compensation of the damage suffered by him". In contrast to the treatment accorded to other victims, any fault committed by the driver, however slight, may limit or even exclude his right to compensation. [...]

350. Critical analysis of the liability regime. – Under the 1985 Act, there are two categories of victims: those having an almost absolute right to full compensation for damages resulting from injury to their person (the *non-drivers*), and those who, in case of the slightest fault, may be deprived of a part, if not all, of their compensation (the *drivers*).

The juxtaposition is shocking, even if we take into consideration that motorists can get personal injury insurance, which may balance out the shortcomings of the compensation scheme imposed on them. [...]

2 Damage to property

351. Right to compensation. Limitation or exclusion, in consideration of the fault of the victim. – [...] With regard to [damage to property], the law makes no distinction between the victims: drivers and non-drivers are subject to the same regime, which is defined in the same terms as the one that applies to drivers with respect to injury suffered to their person. According to Art. 5 (1), the "fault committed by the victim shall have the effect of limiting or excluding compensation for property damage he has suffered." [...]

C. The person owing compensation

352. [...] – The compensation is to be paid by the person designated in Art. 3 (3) as "the person who caused the accident."

[...] Art. 2 shows, in fact, that the author of the accident is either the *driver* of the motor vehicle involved or the *keeper* thereof. In fact, the real debtor is the insurer of the vehicle involved. [...]

3. Cour de cassation, 2ᵉ civ. (*Court of Cassation, 2nd civil chamber*), 28.03.1994, n° 92–15863, Bull. 1994 II, n° 110, p. 63

THE COURT: – On the first argument of the single ground of appeal: In view of Art. 3 of the Law of 5th July 1985; Whereas a fault may only be considered inexcusable, according to this text, insofar as it is deliberate and of exceptional gravity, exposing the person committing it to a danger of which he should have been aware without valid reason; Whereas, according to the confirmatory judgment which forms the subject of this appeal, the bicycle of Mr André X . . . and the motor vehicle of Mrs Cado collided at a crossroads; that Mr X . . . having been killed as a result, Mr X . . .'s next of kin filed a suit against Mrs Cado and her insurance company, *la Concorde*; [...] Whereas, in dismissing this suit, the judgment states that the accident took place at night, as the cyclist rode in a prohibited direction in the dark without lights, cutting across the path of the driver of the motor vehicle, and that the accumulation of entirely unnecessary risks taken by Mr X . . . rendered his fault inexcusable; That, given that these findings do not constitute an inexcusable fault on the part of the victim according to the aforementioned text, the *Cour d'appel* was in breach of the text;

For these reasons, [. . .] dismisses and renders null [. . .] the judgment of 30th March 1992 [. . .] by the Bourges *Cour d'appel*; [. . .].

VI. Belgium

1. Roger O. Dalcq, L'indemnisation des dommages corporels des piétons et des cyclistes (*Compensation for Injury to Pedestrians and Cyclists*), J.T. 1994, 665–672

[...]

II. STUDIES, RESEARCH AND FORMER PROPOSALS

[...]

Traffic accident legislation: the need for amendment

Belgium is one of the few countries in the European Union where road traffic accidents are still subject to the general rules on tort, namely Arts. 1382 and 1383 of the Code Civil. This means that the burden of proof lies solely with the victim [. . .].

[. . .] [T]here was hope that courts might offset lawmakers' inertia, which would have been possible, had our Highest Court agreed to revise its interpretation of Art. 1384 (1) of the Code Civil, and to acknowledge the error in the interpretation of this provision that it made in 1904.[28] [. . .]

---

[28] *Note by the author*: in *Belgian* law, according to a 1904 decision of the *Belgian Cour de cassation*, the liability based on Art. 1384 (1) requires a *defect* of the thing. See above, Chapter 7, pp. 177 ff.

2. Loi du 21 novembre 1989 relative à l'assurance obligatoire de la responsabilité civile en matière de véhicules automoteurs (*Act of 21st November 1989 on Compulsory Motor Vehicle Liability Insurance*)

CHAPITRE V*bis*. – De l'indemnisation de certaines victimes d'accidents de la circulation

Art. 29*bis*. § 1er. En cas d'accident de la circulation impliquant un ou plusieurs véhicules automoteurs [. . .] et à l'exception des dégâts matériels et des dommages subis par le conducteur de chaque véhicule automoteur impliqué, tous les dommages subis par les victimes et leurs ayants droit et résultant de lésions corporelles ou du décès, y compris les dégâts aux vêtements, sont réparés solidairement par les assureurs qui, conformément à la présente loi, couvrent la responsabilité du propriétaire, du conducteur ou du détenteur des véhicules automoteurs. La présente disposition s'applique également si les dommages ont été causés volontairement par le conducteur. [. . .]
Les victimes âgées de plus de 14 ans qui ont voulu l'accident et ses conséquences ne peuvent se prévaloir des dispositions visées à l'alinéa 1. [. . .]

§ 2. Le conducteur d'un véhicule automoteur et ses ayants droit ne peuvent se prévaloir du présent article [. . .].

§ 5. Les règles de la responsabilité civile[29] restent d'application pour tout ce qui n'est pas régi expressément par le présent article.

Translation

CHAPTER Vbis. – On compensation for certain victims of road traffic accidents

*Art. 29bis § 1. In the case of a traffic accident involving one or several motor vehicles [. . .] and with the exception of damage to property and damage sustained by the driver of each motor vehicle involved, all damage sustained by the victims and their beneficiaries and resulting from bodily injuries or death, including damage to clothes, are to be jointly and severally compensated by the insurers who, according to the present Act, insure against the liability of the owner, driver, or holder of the motor vehicles. The present provision also applies if the damage has been caused voluntarily by the driver. [. . .]
Victims older than 14 years who intended the accident and its consequences may not invoke the provisions set out in the first paragraph. [. . .]*

§ 2. The driver of a motor vehicle and his or her beneficiaries may not invoke the present provision [. . .].

§ 5. Civil liability rules[30] remain applicable for everything not expressly covered by the present provision.

---

29 Code civil, arts. 1382–1384 (voir *supra*, Chapitres 5–7).
30 Civil Code, Arts. 1382–1384 (see above, Chapters 5–7).

3. BERTRAND DE CONINCK/ BERNARD DUBUISSON, L'indemnisation automatique des usagers faibles, victimes d'accidents de la circulation – Rapport belge (*Automatic Compensation for Vulnerable Road Users, Victims of Road Traffic Accidents – Report on Belgium*), in: *L'indemnisation des victimes d'accidents de la circulation en Europe, Recueil des travaux du Groupe de Recherche Européen sur la Responsabilité civile et l'Assurance (GRERCA)*, 2012, pp. 25–45

CHAPTER I. GENERAL OVERVIEW

1. The purpose of the law [. . .] that incorporates Art. 29*bis* into the Compulsory Motor Vehicle Insurance Act of 21ˢᵗ November 1989 is to remedy losses resulting from the bodily injury or death of a "vulnerable road user" caused by a road traffic accident in which a motor vehicle is involved. Largely taking inspiration from the French law of the 5ᵗʰ July 1985 (*Loi Badinter*), this law has several aims.

- *The reduction of social security costs*: Strangely, it was economic considerations that allowed for the adoption of this law. The primary objective was indeed to reduce the significant social security costs that road traffic accidents engendered where no liability was incurred or demonstrated. By transferring the burden of compensation to private insurance companies, the money saved proved to be considerable.

- *The protection of victims*: The adoption of this new regime is justified by a concern for making compensation easier and speeding up payouts. It was also about overcoming the numerous obstacles that were slowing down, or sometimes even preventing, compensation payments (difficulty of proving the driver's fault, the impact of the victim's fault).

- *The backlog of cases at court*: It was hoped that the number of disputes brought before the courts would be reduced.

2. [. . .] The current system [dissociates] the compensation of vulnerable road users from the civil liability of motor vehicle drivers. In other words, Art. 29*bis* only allows an action against the insurance company [. . .] and not the driver [or the keeper of the car]. The compensation awarded pursuant to Art. 29*bis* doesn't incur the liability of the latter. Whether right or wrong, it was thought that it would be politically difficult to convince public opinion that it is fair to hold a person liable for a loss that was not caused by his fault. [. . .]

CHAPTER II. CONDITIONS FOR APPLICATION: THE INVOLVEMENT OF A MOTOR VEHICLE IN A ROAD TRAFFIC ACCIDENT WHERE THE VICTIM IS A VULNERABLE ROAD USER

[. . .] 5. The case must [. . .] concern a "road traffic" accident. This concept must receive a broad interpretation. [. . .] Since traffic consists of – voluntary or involuntary – alternating movements and stopping, it is irrelevant whether the vehicle is moving or has stopped. Therefore, the law also applies to parked vehicles. [. . .]

Section 3. The involvement of a motor vehicle

10. [. . .] In relation to the requirement of involvement, the Court of Cassation has held on several occasions that a motor vehicle is involved, as per Art. 29*bis*, when any link exists

between the vehicle and the accident. Direct contact between the vehicle and the victim is sufficient to establish involvement, even when the vehicle is parked. [. . .]

Section 4. The recipients of compensation

12. [. . .] [O]nly the driver of a motor vehicle and his beneficiaries are excluded from the right to receive compensation; all others can benefit from the system and are therefore considered "vulnerable road users".

13. The exclusion of the driver is essentially justified by the fact that "the law is intended to improve the situation of victims, and not of those who are considered as creating the risk" [see the report of reasons for the law (*l'exposé des motifs de la loi*)]. If Art. 29*bis* truly establishes a strict liability system, it would be illogical to allow the person who creates the risk to obtain compensation. Liability is always in respect of another. There is no liability towards oneself. [. . .]

16. Moreover, every "non-driver" who is a direct or indirect victim of a road traffic accident in which a vehicle is involved may therefore benefit from the compensation system established by Art. 29*bis*. [. . .]

Section 5. Who pays compensation?

19. An action pursuant to Art. 29*bis* can only be brought against the insurance company [. . .] The provision doesn't allow the victim to bring an action against the driver, owner [. . .] or the keeper of the vehicle. [. . .] When several vehicles are involved in a road traffic accident, the insurance companies that cover the vehicles are jointly and severally liable (Art. 29*bis*, § 1).

CHAPTER III. RESTRICTIONS TO THE RIGHT TO COMPENSATION

Section 1. Fault that may be invoked against the vulnerable road user [. . .]

20. Given that we are dealing with an automatic compensation system, the only permissible grounds for release from liability are provided by the law. This provides only a single ground which is intentional fault, or, in other words, a fault committed by a victim older than 14 who intended the accident and its consequences (Art. 29*bis*, § 1 (5)). [. . .]

24. Therefore, victims escape the consequences of their own fault that contributed to their loss, except if they intended the accident. By application of the principle of the burden of proof, it is for the person who is liable to pay compensation to prove the victim's intentional fault as grounds for exoneration of liability.

Section 2. Covered losses

25. The law allows for full compensation of all losses resulting from bodily injury or death (medical and hospital expenses, economic and non-pecuniary losses following incapacitation or death). [. . .] However, it excludes all material damage in a larger sense, or, in other words, damage to the vehicle [and] other transported goods [. . .].

Chapter IV. Autonomy of the right to compensation and its relationship with other legal rules

27. According to Art. 29*bis*, § 5, "civil liability rules remain applicable for everything not expressly covered by the present provision".

4. Daniel de Callatay/Nicolas Estienne, De la faute inexcusable à la faute intentionnelle (*From Gross Negligence to Willful Misconduct*), in: Pierre Jadoul/Bernard Dubuisson (dir.), *L'indemnisation des usagers faibles de la route (Compensation for vulnerable road users)*, 2002, pp. 101–137

Section 1. The initial scheme: inexcusable fault

§ 1. Definition of an inexcusable fault

A. The legal text

Prior to its revision of 19th January 2001, Art. 29*bis* § 1 of the Act on Compulsory Motor Vehicle Liability Insurance defined an inexcusable fault as "a deliberate fault of particular gravity, exposing the person having committed it, without valid cause, to a danger of which he should have been aware" [. . .].

This legal definition followed, word for word, the definition given by the second Chamber of the French Court of Cassation for an inexcusable fault.

Section 2. The present scheme: intentional fault

§ 1. Act of 19th January 2001

[. . .] One of the main characteristics of this new legal text is the removal of all references to the concept of "inexcusable fault". Indeed, it replaces the former sect. (5) of Art. 29*bis* § 1 [on inexcusable fault] by the following: "Victims older than 14 years who intended the accident and its consequences may not invoke the provisions set out in the first paragraph". [. . .]

§ 2. Commentary

By replacing the concept of inexcusable fault by that of "deliberate causing the incident and its consequences", the Act of 19th January 2001 clearly means to restrict the loss of the benefits of automatic compensation to the sole cases in which the victim committed an *intentional fault*.

An intentional fault is the gravest of faults. It exceeds an inexcusable fault in that it is characterised by a wish to see the damage done. Thus, it is comparable to self-harm or suicide.

VII. The Netherlands

1. Wegenverkeerswet (*Road Traffic Act*)

Art. 185. (1) Indien een motorrijtuig waarmee op de weg wordt gereden, betrokken is bij een verkeersongeval waardoor schade wordt toegebracht aan, niet door dat motorrijtuig vervoerde, personen of zaken, is de eigenaar van het motorrijtuig of – indien er

een houder van het motorrijtuig is – de houder verplicht om die schade te vergoeden, tenzij aannemelijk is dat het ongeval is te wijten aan overmacht, daaronder begrepen het geval dat het is veroorzaakt door iemand, voor wie onderscheidenlijk de eigenaar of de houder niet aansprakelijk is.
(2) De eigenaar of houder die het motorrijtuig niet zelf bestuurt, is aansprakelijk voor de gedragingen van degene door wie hij dat motorrijtuig doet of laat rijden.
(3) Het eerste en het tweede lid vinden geen toepassing ten aanzien van schade, door een motorrijtuig toegebracht [. . .] aan een ander motorrijtuig in beweging of aan personen en zaken die daarmee worden vervoerd.
(4) Dit artikel laat onverkort de uit andere wettelijke bepalingen voortvloeiende aansprakelijkheid.

Translation

Art. 185. (1) When a motor vehicle that is driven on the road is involved in a traffic accident, and as a result of which damage is inflicted on persons or things not carried in that motor vehicle, the owner of the motor vehicle or – when there is a keeper of the motor vehicle – the keeper must compensate that damage, unless it is plausible that the accident is attributable to circumstances beyond their control [i.e. there is a case of force majeure], including a situation that is caused by someone for whom the owner or the keeper is not liable.
(2) An owner or keeper who is not driving the motor vehicle him or herself is liable for the acts of the person who is driving the motor vehicle.
(3) The first and the second paragraph are not applicable in the case of damage inflicted by a motor vehicle [. . .] on another motor vehicle in motion or on persons or things carried thereby.[31]
(4) This article does not exclude any liability that derives from other statutory provisions.[32]

2. Hoge Raad (*Supreme Court*), 28.02.1992 (*IZA/Vrerink*), NJ 1993, 566

[*Note by the author*: on the dark and rainy night of 24th December 1984, a 67-year-old lady tried to cross a carriageway and was hit and severely injured by a car. The car drove at approximately 40 km/h, which was a little less than the maximum speed permitted by law. When the pedestrian set foot on the carriageway, the car was already so close that its driver could not reasonably be expected to avoid the collision. The Supreme Court of the Netherlands held:]

---

31 The rights of drivers and passengers of other motor vehicles are governed by the Burgerlijk Wetboek (*the Dutch Civil Code*), Arts. 6:162 ff. (i.e. the regime applicable to tortious liability for fault).
32 See the previous note.

3.7 [...] When the owner of the motor vehicle is in principle liable because there is no case of force majeure, but there is an error of a cyclist or a pedestrian [who is the victim of the accident], but no intent or behaviour bordering recklessness on behalf of the cyclist or pedestrian, fairness with respect to the distribution of this damage requires that the owner of the motor vehicle bear at least 50% of the damage, because of the realisation of the risk associated with operating a motor vehicle. He is consequently liable for at least 50% of the damage. For the remaining 50%, it should be considered to what extent the behaviour of the victim contributed to the injury. [...]

VIII. Italy

1. Codice civile (*Civil Code*)

> **Art. 2054. Circolazione di veicoli.** (1) Il conducente di un veicolo senza guida di rotaie è obbligato a risarcire il danno prodotto a persone o a cose dalla circolazione del veicolo, se non prova di aver fatto tutto il possibile per evitare il danno.
> (2) Nel caso di scontro tra veicoli si presume, fino a prova contraria, che ciascuno dei conducenti abbia concorso ugualmente a produrre il danno subìto dai singoli veicoli.
> (3) Il proprietario del veicolo o, in sua vece, l'usufruttuario o l'acquirente con patto di riservato dominio, è responsabile in solido col conducente, se non prova che la circolazione del veicolo è avvenuta contro la sua volontà. [...]

Translation

> *Art. 2054. Road traffic. (1) The driver of a road vehicle must pay for the damage caused to persons or property by its use in traffic, unless he or she is proven to have made every possible effort to avoid the damage.*
> *(2) In the case of a vehicle collision, unless there is evidence to the contrary, it is presumed that each driver has to the same extent contributed to the damage suffered by each vehicle.*
> *(3) The owner of the vehicle (or, in his place, the usufructuary or the hire purchaser) and the driver are jointly and severally liable, unless the former proves that the vehicle was driven against his or her will. [...]*

2. Giorgio Cian/Alberto Trabucchi, *Commentario breve al Codice civile (Short Commentary on the Civil Code)*, 11th ed., 2014, Art. 2054

V. Liability of the driver: criterion for the attribution of liability; grounds for exemption; ∎
The criterion for attribution of liability of the driver is still the subject of both doctrinal and jurisprudential heated debates. In fact, there are those who believe that the provision in question has the mere function of extending the standard of care imposed on the driver to the **slightest fault**; human behaviour and fault would, accordingly, still be prevailing over the simple

custody of the *thing*, and therefore it would be correct to assume that the code establishes a **presumption of fault** and not a strict liability regime [. . .]. According to others, the provision is of procedural character and aims at redistributing the burden of proof [. . .]. ■ According to the most recent doctrinal tendencies, the damage is attributed to the driver on the basis of an **objective criterion** based on the link between the activity of the tortfeasor and the movement of the vehicle; in order to be **exempted from liability**, the causal link between the traffic and the damage needs to be broken, the driver having done "everything possible to avoid the damage" [. . .] meaning that the damage has materialised regardless of the driver's behaviour, for example in cases where the driver is able to demonstrate the exclusive fault of the other driver or force majeure [. . .]. ■ This theory is confirmed by an examination of the case law, according to which the driver is exempted from liability if the **accident was inevitable** [. . .]: see the case C 84/1214, which states that the driver is liable under Art. 2054 for damage related to changes in the environment, including the presence of mud, ice or oil stains; see also C 87/4370 where, in the event of a pedestrian suddenly crossing the road, the liability of the driver was not ruled out even though he was in full respect of the traffic rules, as an effective impossibility of avoiding the harmful event was considered necessary. [. . .] ■ [. . .]. According to the case law, liability may also result from **not foreseeing the recklessness of others** ■ Case law has further established [. . .] that the evidence [. . .] may also be provided **indirectly**, i.e., by showing that the behaviour of the victim was the **sole cause** of the damaging event [. . .], unavoidable for the driver even by the adoption of appropriate emergency manoeuvres [. . .]. ■ Other decisions are more focused on the assessment of the fault of the driver, so that the test would be whether the driver took the **utmost diligence** in order to avoid the accident [. . .]; [. . .]

3. Pietro Rescigno (a cura di), *Codice Civile, Tomo II (Civil Code, Vol. II [Commentary])*, 9th ed., 2014, Art. 2054

2. Driver's liability. Exemption. [. . .]. To free himself from liability, the driver must demonstrate that he has complied with all the rules of the road [. . .]. [. . .] The proof of compliance with traffic rules, however, is not in itself sufficient to free the driver, who must still demonstrate that he was in a situation of objective impossibility of avoiding the accident [. . .], and that he has observed, in his conduct, the most absolute and strict standards of care [. . .], and thus the causation of the damage should be ascribed to force majeure. [. . .] He has also a duty to foresee the fault of others [. . .]. For example, the sudden crossing of a street by a pedestrian not on a crossing is not in itself sufficient to exclude liability, except if the pedestrian has crossed the road so suddenly so as to constitute an unavoidable obstacle not allowing the driver at all to avoid the collision. [. . .] Drowsiness or a sudden illness do not exclude the imputation of liability either, unless they were of an absolutely unpredictable nature [. . .]. However, the responsibility of the driver is based on a presumption of fault and is not strict [. . .]. [. . .] Art. 2054 does not preclude a possible contributory negligence of the injured.

4. Collision of vehicles. The presumption of a similar degree of negligence [of the drivers], established for collisions between vehicles in Art. 2054 (2), operates only where it is not possible to ascertain to what extent the actual conduct of the two drivers has contributed to the event. [. . .] The fault of one of the drivers does not exonerate the other from liability under (1), and is therefore compatible with a partial concurrent liability of the other [. . .]. The Highway Code imposes on the driver the obligation to maintain a safe distance from the vehicle in front, so as to cope with any unexpected eventuality [. . .]; consequently, in the event of a collision between two vehicles proceeding in a line of traffic, the presumption of equal fault does not apply [. . .]; [. . .]

IX. Denmark

1. Bekendtgørelse af færdselsloven (*Road Traffic Act*)

§ 101. *Stk. 1.* Den, der er ansvarlig for et motordrevet køretøj, skal erstatte skader, som køretøjet volder ved færdselsuheld eller ved eksplosion eller brand, der hidrører fra brændstofanlæg i køretøjet.
Stk. 2. Erstatningen for personskade eller tab af forsørger kan nedsættes eller bortfalde, hvis skadelidte eller afdøde forsætligt har medvirket til skaden. Erstatningen kan endvidere nedsættes og i særlige tilfælde bortfalde, hvis skadelidte eller afdøde ved grov uagtsomhed har medvirket til skaden.
Stk. 3. Erstatningen for tingsskade kan nedsættes eller bortfalde, hvis skadelidte forsætligt eller uagtsomt har medvirket til skaden.

Translation

§ 101. (1) A person who is responsible for a motor vehicle must compensate damage caused by the vehicle as a result of a road accident, an explosion, or a fire due to the fuel system.
(2) If an injured person or a deceased intentionally contributes to damage or injury to him or herself, compensation for the injury or loss of dependency may be reduced or excluded. The same applies to situations where the injured person or the deceased has contributed through gross negligence to the damage or injury.
(3) Compensation for property damage may be reduced or excluded if the injured person intentionally or negligently contributed to the damage.

2. Erstatningsansvarsloven (*Liability for Damages Act*)

§ 24b. *Stk. 1.* En person, som på grund af sindssygdom, hæmmet psykisk udvikling, forbigående sindsforvirring eller lignende tilstand har manglet evnen til at handle fornuftmæssigt, er erstatningspligtig for skadegørende handlinger efter samme regler som sjælssunde personer. Dog kan erstatningen nedsættes eller endog helt bortfalde, for så vidt det findes billigt under hensyn til personens sindstilstand, handlingens beskaffenhed eller omstændighederne i øvrigt, derunder navnlig forholdet mellem den skadegørendes og den skadelidendes evne til at bære tabet og udsigten til, at skaden kan fås godtgjort hos andre.
Stk. 2. Har den skadegørende ved misbrug af berusesesmidler eller på lignende måde forbigående hensat sig i en sindstilstand som ovenfor nævnt, er en lempelse i erstatningsansvaret udelukket.

Translation

§ 24b. (1) A person who was unable to act rationally owing to mental illness, impaired mental development, temporary insanity, or a similar condition shall be liable to pay compensation for wrongful acts in accordance with the same rules as for persons of sound mind. The compensation can be reduced or even waived completely, however, in so far as it is found reasonable to do so owing to the person's state of mind, the nature of the act or circumstances in general, including the relationship between the ability of the party causing the loss and the injured party to bear the loss and the prospects of obtaining compensation from another source.
(2) If the person causing the loss has temporarily put him or herself into a state of mind as specified above through the use of intoxicants or by similar means, mitigation of his or her liability in damages shall be ruled out.

X. Estonia

Võlaõigusseadus (Code of Obligations)

§ 1057. **Mootorsõiduki valdaja vastutus.** Mootorsõiduki otsene valdaja vastutab mootorsõiduki käitamisel tekkinud kahju eest, välja arvatud juhul, kui:

(1) kahjustatakse mootorsõidukiga veetavat asja, mida mootorsõidukis viibiv isik ei kanna seljas ega kaasas;
(2) kahjustatakse mootorsõiduki valdajale hoiule antud asja;
(3) kahju põhjustas vääramatu jõud või kannatanu tahtlik tegu, välja arvatud juhul, kui kahju tekkis õhusõiduki käitamisel;
(4) kannatanu osales mootorsõiduki käitamisel;
(5) kannatanut veeti tasuta ja väljaspool vedaja majandustegevust.

Translation

§ 1057. Liability of the owner of a motor vehicle. A direct owner of a motor vehicle shall be liable for any damage caused by the operation of the motor vehicle, unless:

(1) the damage is caused to a thing being transported by the motor vehicle and which is not being worn or carried by a person in the vehicle;
(2) the damage is caused to a thing deposited with the owner of the motor vehicle;
(3) the damage is caused by force majeure or by an intentional act on the part of the victim [. . .];
(4) the victim participates in the operation of the motor vehicle;
(5) the victim is carried without charge and outside the economic activities of the carrier.

XI. People's Republic of China

1. 中华人民共和国侵权责任法 (*Tort Law Act*)

第三十三条　完全民事行为能力人对自己的行为暂时没有意识或者失去控制造成他人损害有过错的，应当承担侵权责任；没有过错的，根据行为人的经济状况对受害人适当补偿。
　　完全民事行为能力人因醉酒、滥用麻醉药品或者精神药品对自己的行为暂时没有意识或者失去控制造成他人损害的，应当承担侵权责任。

第六章　机动车交通事故责任

第四十八条　机动车发生交通事故造成损害的，依照道路交通安全法的有关规定承担赔偿责任

Translation

Art. 33. (1) Where a person with full capacity of judgement causes harm to another person as the result of his or her temporary loss of consciousness or control, he or she shall, if at fault, assume liability in tort; if he or she is not at fault, the victim shall be compensated appropriately according to the economic circumstances of the person who caused the harm.
(2) Where a person with full capacity of judgement causes harm to another person as the result of his or her temporary loss of consciousness or control due to alcohol intoxication or abuse of narcotic or psychoactive drugs, he or she shall assume liability in tort.

Chapter VI. Liability for motor vehicle traffic accident

Art. 48. Where a motor vehicle is involved in a traffic accident and causes harm, liability shall be assumed and compensation awarded according to the relevant provisions of the Road Traffic Safety Law.

2. 中华人民共和国道路交通安全法 (*Road Traffic Safety Act*)[33]

第七十六条　机动车发生交通事故造成人身伤亡的，由保险公司在机动车第三者责任强制保险责任限额范围内予以赔偿；不足的部分，按照下列规定承担赔偿责任：

（一）机动车之间发生交通事故的，由有过错的一方承担赔偿责任；双方都有过错的，按照各自过错的比例分担责任。

33　2011 Amendment.

(二) 机动车与非机动车驾驶人、行人之间发生交通事故，非机动车驾驶人、行人没有过错的，由机动车一方承担赔偿责任；有证据证明非机动车驾驶人、行人有过错的，根据过错程度适当减轻机动车一方的赔偿责任；机动车一方没有过错的，承担不超过百分之十的赔偿责任
。 交通事故的损失是由非机动车驾驶人、行人故意碰撞机动车造成的，机动车一方不承担赔偿责任。

Translation

Art. 76. *Where a motor vehicle is involved in a road traffic accident and causes personal injury or death or damage to property, the insurance company shall pay compensation in line with the amount covered by the compulsory third party liability insurance for the motor vehicle.*[34] *Any remaining sum shall be compensated according to the following provisions:*

1. *Where a traffic accident occurs between motor vehicles, the party at fault shall bear liability; if both parties are at fault, they shall each bear their proper share of liability; and*
2. *Where a traffic accident occurs between a motor vehicle and a non-motorised vehicle or a pedestrian, if the driver of the non-motorised vehicle or pedestrian is not at fault, the motor vehicle driver shall bear liability; however, if there is any evidence that the driver of the non-motorised vehicle or the pedestrian is at fault, the liability of the driver of the motor vehicle driver may be mitigated appropriately in line with the degree of fault; if the driver of the motor vehicle is not at all at fault, he or she shall be liable for no more than 10% of the damage.*

Where the damage is caused by a driver of a non-motor vehicle or pedestrian who deliberately enters into collision with the motor vehicle in question, the driver of the motor vehicle shall bear no liability.

3. 机动车交通事故责任强制保险条款 (*Compulsory Motor Vehicle Accident Liability Insurance Terms*)

Note by the author: According to Art. 23 of the "Regulation on Compulsory Auto Liability Insurance", the amounts covered by mandatory liability insurance are fixed by the "China Insurance Regulatory Commission" in the "Compulsory Motor Vehicle Accident Liability Insurance Terms" (CIRC (2008) No. 3).

第八条 在中华人民共和国境内（不含港、澳、台地区），被保险人在使用被保险机动车过程中发生交通事故，致使受害人遭受人身伤亡或者财产损失，依法

---

34 See the relevant rules below, under heading 3.

> 应当由被保险人承担的损害赔偿责任，保险人按照交强险合同的约定对每次事故在下列赔偿限额内负责赔偿：
>
> （一）死亡伤残赔偿限额为110000元；
> （二）医疗费用赔偿限额为10000元；
> （三）财产损失赔偿限额为2000元；
> （四）被保险人无责任时，无责任死亡伤残赔偿限额为11000元；无责任医疗费用赔偿限额为1000元；无责任财产损失赔偿限额为100元。[...]

Translation

> *Art. 8.* In the territory of the People's Republic of China (excluding Hong Kong, Macao, and Taiwan), where a driver of an insured vehicle is involved in a traffic accident which results in personal injury or property damage for which the insured is liable under the law, the insurer shall award compensation to the victims in line with the following limits in each accident under the Compulsory Motor Vehicle Accident Insurance contract:
>
> (1) The limit of death and disability compensation is 110,000 yuan [app. € 14,700];
> (2) The limit of medical expenses is 10,000 yuan [app. € 1,400];
> (3) The limit of compensation for property damage is 2,000 yuan [app. € 270];
> (4) Where the insured person is not liable for the accident, the limit of compensation for death and disability is 11,000 yuan [app. € 1,470]; the limit of compensation for medical expenses is 1,000 yuan [app. € 134]; the limit of compensation for property damages is 100 yuan [app. € 14]. [...]

XII. Principles of European Tort Law and Draft Common Frame of Reference

1. Principles of European Tort Law (PETL)

> **Art. 4:101. Fault.** A person is liable on the basis of fault for intentional or negligent violation of the required standard of conduct.
>
> **Art. 4:102. Required Standard of Conduct.** (1) The required standard of conduct is that of the reasonable person in the circumstances [...].
> (2) The above standard may be adjusted when due to age, mental or physical disability or due to extraordinary circumstances the person cannot be expected to conform to it. [...]
>
> **Art. 5:101. Abnormally dangerous activities.** (1) A person who carries on an abnormally dangerous activity is strictly liable for damage characteristic to the risk presented by the activity and resulting from it.

(2) An activity is abnormally dangerous if

(a) it creates a foreseeable and highly significant risk of damage even when all due care is exercised in its management and
(b) it is not a matter of common usage. [...]

2. Draft Common Frame of Reference (DCFR)

VI. – 3:102. Negligence. A person causes legally relevant damage negligently when that person causes the damage by conduct which either:

(a) does not meet the particular standard of care provided by a statutory provision whose purpose is the protection of the person suffering the damage from that damage; or
(b) does not otherwise amount to such care as could be expected from a reasonably careful person in the circumstances of the case.

VI. – 3:205. Accountability for damage caused by motor vehicles. (1) A keeper of a motor vehicle is accountable for the causation of personal injury and consequential loss, loss within VI. – 2:202 (Loss suffered by third persons as a result of another's personal injury or death), and loss resulting from property damage (other than to the vehicle and its freight) in a traffic accident which results from the use of the vehicle.
(2) "Motor vehicle" means any vehicle intended for travel on land and propelled by mechanical power, but not running on rails, and any trailer, whether or not coupled.

3. BÉNÉDICT WINIGER/ERNST KARNER/KEN OLIPHANT (eds.), *Digest of European Tort Law, Vol. III: Misconduct*, 2018, nos. 9/30/I ff. (by THOMAS KADNER GRAZIANO)

9. Physical disability

Facts

A is driving his vehicle when, suddenly, he suffers a heart attack which causes him to lose consciousness, resulting in a traffic accident which causes both personal damage and property damage to V. Before the accident, A led a very busy professional life and undertook a cardiac assessment every three months which did not reveal any reason not to drive.[35]

Solution

a) PETL. Art. 4:101 PETL defines fault as an "intentional or negligent violation of the required standard of conduct". According to Art. 4:102(1) PETL, "[t]he required standard

---

35 See the *Belgian* case: Cour d'appel de Bruxelles (*Appellate Court of Brussels*), 27.10.1981, *RGAR* 1983, 10608, *Digest III*, 9/7/1 with comments by B. DUBUISSON/I. DURANT/T. MALENGREAU. Quotes in the text from: European Group on Tort Law (fn. 1), at Art. 4:102 (P. WIDMER), and from C. VON BAR/E. CLIVE, *DCFR*, Art. VI – 3:102, Comments, A. (p. 3402), Art. VI – 5:301, Comments, B. (footnotes omitted).

of conduct is that of a reasonable person in the circumstances". This standard applies independently of the individual's actual capacities. The PETL thus use, in principle, an objective standard of fault.

However, "the Principles reserve the possibility, in para. 2 of Art. 4:102, though only for a particular type of wrongdoers and for 'extraordinary circumstances', that the objective notion of fault – based on the objective standard of conduct – may be tempered in order to avoid an excessive 'hardship' in the evaluation of a person's effective possibilities to behave as the standard would have required". Art. 4:102(2) PETL thus provides that the required standard "may be adjusted when due to age, mental or *physical disability* or due to *extraordinary circumstances* the person cannot be expected to conform to it".

In the above scenario, A suffered a heart attack which caused him to lose consciousness, leading to a traffic accident. If a person suffering from a physical disability has reason to doubt his capacity to engage in an activity which may risk causing damage to others, he is required to act with particular care or if, due to his incapacity the risk is unavoidable, to refrain from such activity. Had there been any previous symptoms that would have caused a reasonable driver in A's position to doubt his capacity to safely drive a car, he would thus have been required to refrain from driving.

In the above scenario, A had regular check-ups on his heart which had not revealed any reason for him to assume that he was impaired from driving a car safely. The sudden attack was totally unforeseeable to him, as it would have been for anyone else in the same circumstances. Under these conditions, it could not have been expected for him, nor any reasonable and competent driver in his position, to abstain from using a car. Under the PETL, driving thus did not violate the required standard of conduct. To hold him liable under these conditions would require a regime of strict liability. Under the PETL, it is thus material whether the disability was a pre-existing or foreseeable condition, or was sudden and unexpected.

In most continental jurisdictions, at least for personal injury caused to third parties, A would be liable according to the rules on strict liability for traffic accidents. Art. 5:101 PETL, on the contrary, limits strict liability to "abnormally dangerous activities" which are not "a matter of common usage".[36] Strict liability as provided by the PETL does not therefore cover damage suffered in traffic accidents.

b) DCFR. The DCFR defines negligence in Art. VI – 3:102 as "conduct which [. . .] (b) does not [. . .] amount to such care as could be expected from a reasonably careful person in the circumstances of the case". Like the PETL, the DCFR thus uses an objective standard of care. The standard "does not turn on the individual abilities of the person acting, rather it is based on what can be reasonably expected of that person".

According to the official commentary to the DCFR, "[p]hysically disabled persons are subject to the same requirements of due care as physically able persons, to the extent that they are aware of their physical disability, and their conduct must be adjusted accordingly. [. . .] A person who must anticipate sudden but short-lived losses of vision due to a chronic circulatory disorder is not permitted to sit at the wheel of a car", for example.

However, negligence as defined by Art. VI – 3:102 DCFR requires human "conduct", that is, an action controlled by human will. An unconscious act is not "conduct" within the meaning of Arts. VI – 3:101 and VI – 3:102.

---

36 See above, pp. 268–269.

If the driver of a car suffers a *sudden and unforeseeable* brain haemorrhage that renders him unconsciousness, then the conduct is not one controlled by human will. The driver cannot therefore be regarded as being in violation of the required standard of care under the DCFR and would not be accountable for having negligently caused damage.

As mentioned above, the result differs where he "should have anticipated having such episodes or reflex actions as a consequence of a physical problem and therefore should have refrained from the activity in question in advance", whereby he would be accountable for his conduct.

Should the driver also be the keeper of the car, he would be liable without negligence under the rule on strict liability for loss suffered "in a traffic accident which results from the use of a vehicle", pursuant to Art. VI – 3:205 DCFR.[37]

Overviews

Table 9.1

Liability regimes for road traffic accidents		
Fault-based liability	**Strict liability**	**Insurance coverage, disconnected from civil liability**
• **English law**: tort "negligence" • **Irish law**: tort "negligence" • **Belgian law**: liability based on Arts. 1382, 1383 Code civil. • For injury to life or to physical integrity supplemented by insurance coverage going beyond tort liability, see "insurance coverage for traffic accidents, disconnected from civil liability"	• **German law**: strict liability of the **keeper** of the car covering injury to life, bodily integrity, and damage to property (§ 7 (1) StVG) [the liability of the driver is fault-based with fault being presumed (§§ 7 ff., 18 (1) StVG)] Limit: force majeure (§ 7 (2) StVG) Contributory fault of the victim is taken into consideration (§§ 9 StVG, 254 BGB) • **Swiss law**: strict liability of the **keeper** of the car covering injury to life, bodily integrity, and damage to property (§ 58 (1) SVG) [the liability of the driver is fault-based] Limit: force majeure etc. (§ 59 (1) SVG) Contributory fault of the victim is taken into consideration (§ 59 (2) SVG) • **French law**: strict liability of the **driver** or **keeper** (= the insured) of the car covering injury to life, bodily integrity, and economic loss (*Loi Badinter*, Arts. 1 ff.) Limit: intentional self-harm of the victim (§ 3 (3) *Loi Badinter*) Contributory fault: 1. Driver: taken into consideration 2. Other victims: only inexcusable fault being the exclusive cause of the accident is taken into consideration (§ 3 (1) *Loi Badinter*) ("all or nothing" approach) 3. Victims below the age of 16 or over 70: not taken into consideration (§ 3 (2) *Loi Badinter*) 4. All victims: taken into consideration for damage to property (§ 5 *Loi Badinter*)	• **Belgian law**: right of accident victims against **insurer** of the driver, owner, or keeper of the car (= the insured) covering injury to life or bodily integrity (*Loi du 21 novembre 1989*, § 29bis) Limit: intentional self-harm of victims older than 14 years Contributory fault: 1. Driver: taken into consideration (Art. 29bis § 1 (1), § 5) 2. Other victims: not taken into consideration (regarding injury to life or physical integrity) 3. All victims: taken into consideration for damage to property (comp. Art. 29bis § 1 (1), § 5)

(*Continued*)

---

37 For the text of this provision, see above, p. 269.

Table 9.1 (Continued)

Liability regimes for road traffic accidents		
Fault-based liability	Strict liability	Insurance coverage, disconnected from civil liability
	• **Dutch law**: strict liability of **keeper or owner** for damage to life, physical integrity or property vis-à-vis victims outside the car that caused the accident, except if victims are carried in another car in motion (*Wegenverkeerswet*, Art. 185 (1)) *Limit*: force majeure and acts of third parties (*Wegenverkeerswet*, Art. 185 (1)) *Contributory fault*: 1. Drivers and passengers of motor vehicles: taken into consideration 2. Victims outside cars (pedestrians, cyclists etc.): 50% of compensation guaranteed, contributory fault only taken into consideration beyond this threshold (*Hohe Raad*, 50% rule) 3. Victims under 14 years: not taken into consideration at all (*Hohe Raad*, 100% rule)	

Table 9.2

Contributory negligence of the victim		
Taken into consideration when determining the amount of compensation	Disregarded when determining the amount of compensation	Intermediate solutions

• **English law**: tort "*negligence*"
• **Irish law**: tort "*negligence*"
• **German law** (§ 9 StVG, § 254 BGB)
• **Swiss law** (§ 59 (2) SVG)
• **French law**: only for drivers
 	
All victims: taken into consideration for damage to property (§ 5 *Loi Badinter*)
• **Belgian law** (Art. 29bis §§ 1 (1), 5): only for drivers
 	
All victims: taken into consideration for damage to property
• **Dutch law**: for drivers and passengers of motor vehicles
	• **French law** (§ 3 (1) *Loi Badinter*): victims having suffered bodily injury, except drivers:
	  • only inexcusable fault being the exclusive cause of the accident is taken into consideration, "all or nothing" approach;
	  • victims below the age of 16 or over 70: not taken into consideration at all, § 3 (2) *Loi Badinter*)
	• **Belgian law**: victims having suffered bodily injury, except drivers
	• **Dutch law**: victims under 14 years, *Hohe Raad*: 100% rule
		• **Dutch law**: victims under 14 years, *Hohe Raad*: 50% rule

Table 9.3

Solutions to the scenarios			
Country	Scenario 1	Scenario 2	The role of contributory negligence in scenario 2
England	Tort 'negligence' requires fault *Mansfield* v. *Weetabix* ➔ No liability		Not considered (because no liability in both scenarios)
Ireland	Tort 'negligence' requires fault *O'Brien* v. *Parker* ➔ No liability		Not considered
Germany	**Keeper is strictly liable** § 7(1) StVG Except in cases of *force majeure*; however, defect of the machine or man <u>not</u> an excuse, BGHZ 23, 90 ➔ Keeper is liable **Liability of driver is fault-based with a presumption of fault** § 18 StVG (includes damage to property) ➔ Driver is not liable		**Liability reduced in proportion to victim's fault** (e.g. 50:50, 60:40, 40:60) § 9 StVG and § 254(1) BGB
Switzerland	**Keeper is strictly liable** Art. 58 (1) SVG Except in cases of *force majeure* or gross negligence, Art. 59 (1) ➔ Keeper is liable **Liability of driver is fault-based** Art. 41 CO ➔ Driver is not liable		**Liability reduced in proportion to victim's fault** (e.g. 50:50, 60:40, 40:60) Art. 60 (2) SVG
France	**Driver/keeper is strictly liable** Art. 1 Loi Badinter No defence; not even force majeure ➔ Driver/keeper is liable		**Personal injury: only inexcusable fault is considered (principle of "all or nothing" applied)** Art. 3(1) Loi Badinter **Property damage: liability reduced in proportion to victim's fault** Art. 5 Loi Badinter
Belgium	**Liability of driver is fault-based** Arts. 1382, 1383 CC ➔ No liability **Insurer pays compensation for bodily injury/death** Art. 29bis. §1 (1) Act of 21 November 1989 ➔ Insurer pays compensation for bodily injury, but not for property damage	**Insurer pays compensation for bodily injury/death** Art. 29bis. §1 (1) Act of 21 November 1989 ➔ Insurer pays compensation for bodily injury of cyclist, but not for property damage (to the bike)	**Personal injury: only inexcusable fault is considered (principle of "all or nothing" applied)** Act of 19 January 2001

(Continued)

Table 9.3 (Continued)

Solutions to the scenarios			
Country	Scenario 1	Scenario 2	The role of contributory negligence in scenario 2
Netherlands	Owner or keeper is strictly liable for damage suffered by pedestrians and cyclists Art. 185 (1), (3) WVW Except in cases of force majeure, Art. 185(1) WVW → Owner or keeper is liable vis-à-vis pedestrians and cyclists		If the victim is a cyclist or pedestrian: for first 50% of damage, victim's fault is disregarded; for second 50% of damage, liability reduced in proportion to victim's fault Hoge Raad decision
Italy	Liability of driver is fault-based with a presumption of fault Art. 2054(1) CC Except if he or she is proven to have made every possible effort to avoid the damage, Art. 2054(1) CC Sudden illness an excuse if absolutely unpredictable → Driver arguably not liable	Liability of driver is fault-based with a presumption of fault Art. 2054(1) CC Except if he or she is proven to have made every possible effort to avoid the damage, Art. 2054(1) CC → Borderline case; driver not liable if there was an objective impossibility of avoiding the accident	Not precluded Art. 2054 CC
Denmark	Keeper is strictly liable § 101(1) RTA → Keeper is liable		Personal injury: only intention or gross negligence is relevant § 101(2) RTA Property damage: intention or negligence are relevant § 101(3) RTA
Estonia	Owner is strictly liable § 1057 Except in cases outlined under § 1057 → Owner is liable		Only intentional act of the victim is relevant § 1057(3)
PETL	No strict liability for road traffic accidents		

Bibliography

PETER BARTRIP, No-Fault Compensation on the Roads in Twentieth Century Britain, *C.L.J.* 2010, 263–286; ROLAND BREHM, *La responsabilité civile automobile*, 2nd ed., Bern: Stämpfli, 2010; PHILIPPE BRUN, *Responsabilité civile extracontractuelle*, 3rd ed., Paris: LexisNexis, 2014, pp. 451–496; JAMES DEMPSEY, Fault at the Crossroads, *A.B.A. Sec. Ins. Negl. & Comp. L. Proc.* 1971, pp. 94–128; Wolfgang Ernst (ed.), *The Development of Traffic Liability*, Cambridge: CUP, 2010; EUROPEAN COMMISSION, Rome II Study on Compensation of Cross-Border Victims in the EU. Compensation of Victims of Cross-Border Road Traffic Accidents in the EU: Comparison of National Practices, Analysis of Problems and Evaluation of Options for Improving the Position of Cross-Border Victims. Final Report Prepared for the European Commission DG Internal Market and Services. Final Version of the Final Report – Part II – Analysis (2008), available at: http://ec.europa.eu/civiljustice/news/docs/study_compensation_road_victims_en.pdf (author: Demolin, Brulard, Barthelemy – Hoche, team leader: JEAN ALBERT); JÖRG FEDTKE, Strict Liability for Car Drivers in Accidents Involving "Bicycle Guerrillas"? Some Comments on the Proposed Fifth Motor Directive of the European Commission, *Am. J. Comp. L.* 2003, 941; GRERCA, *Recueil des travaux du Groupe de Recherche Européen sur la Responsabilité civile et l'Assurance (GRERCA), L'indemnisation des victimes d'accidents de la circulation en Europe*, Brussels: Bruylant, 2015; DESMOND S. GREER, No-Fault Compensation for Personal Injuries Arising from Road Accidents: Developments in the United States, *Anglo-Am. L. Rev.* 1992, 221; THOMAS KADNER GRAZIANO/CHRISTOPH OERTEL, Ein europäisches Haftungsrecht für Schäden im Strassenverkehr? – Eckpunkte de lege lata und Überlegungen de lege ferenda, *ZVglRWiss* 2008, 113–163; VANESSA KRAUSE/MICHAEL NUGEL, Bildung der Haftungsquote bei einem Verkehrsunfall nach deutschem Recht unter Berücksichtigung des Anscheinsbeweises, in: René Schaffhauser (ed.), *Jahrbuch zum Strassenverkehrsrecht 2015*, Bern: Stämpfli, 2015, pp. 65–78; JANNO LAHE/IRENE KULL, Motor Vehicle Operational Risk and Awarding Damages in the Event of a Traffic Accident, *JETL* 2014, 105; HARDY LANDOLT/JAN GYSI, Schockschadenhaftung im Strassenverkehr aus psychiatrischer und juristischer Sicht, in: René Schaffhauser (ed.), *Jahrbuch zum Strassenverkehrsrecht 2014*, Bern: Stämpfli, 2014, pp. 1–28; RICHARD LEWIS, No-Fault Compensation for Victims of Road Accidents: Can It Be Justified?, *J.S.P.* 1981, 161; MELINDA FLORINA LOHMANN, Liability Issues Concerning Self-Driving Vehicles, *EJRR, Special Issue on the Man and the Machine* 2016, 335–340; THOMAS M. MANNSDORFER, Haftung bei Verkehrsunfällen in Grossbritannien, in: René Schaffhauser (ed.), *Jahrbuch zum Strassenverkehrsrecht 2012*, Bern: Stämpfli, 2012, pp. 229–284; THOMAS M. MANNSDORFER, Haftung bei Verkehrsunfällen in Spanien, in: René Schaffhauser (ed.), *Jahrbuch zum Strassenverkehrsrecht 2010*, St. Gallen: Prisma Druck, 2010, pp. 231–284; THOMAS M. MANNSDORFER, Haftung bei Verkehrsunfällen in Frankreich, in: René Schaffhauser (ed.), *Jahrbuch zum Strassenverkehrsrecht 2009*, St. Gallen: Prisma Druck, 2009, pp. 331–408; MIQUEL MARTÍN-CASALS, An Outline of the Spanish Legal Tariffication Scheme for Personal Injury Resulting from Traffic Accidents, in: Helmut Koziol/Jaap Spier (eds.), *Liber Amicorum Pierre Widmer*, Vienna: Springer, 2003, pp. 235–251; RUTH REDMOND-COOPER, No Fault Liability on the French Roads, *J.P.I.L.* 1995, 291; FRANZ WERRO/VINCENT PERRITAZ, Les véhicules connectés: Un changement de paradigme pour la responsabilité civile?, in: Franz Werro/Thomas Probst (eds.), *Journées du droit de la circulation routière*, Bern: Stämpfli, 2016, pp. 1–20; CEES VAN DAM, *European Tort Law*, 2nd ed., Oxford: OUP, 2002, pp. 408–419; CHRISTIAN von Bar, *Gemeineuropäisches Deliktsrecht, Zweiter Band*, München: C. H. Beck, 1999, pp. 397–416; Christian von Bar, *The Common European Law of Torts, Volume Two*, Oxford: OUP, 2000, pp. 398–417; Walter van Gerven/Jeremy Lever/Pierre Larouche, *Cases, Materials and Text on National, Supranational and International Tort Law*, Oxford et al.: Hart, 2000, pp. 583–597.

Chapter 10

Liability in cases of uncertain causation – "all or nothing" or partial compensation in relation to the probability of causation?

> "*An activity or conduct is a cause of the victim's damage if, in the absence of the activity, the damage would not have occurred*".[1]
>
> "*If negligent diagnosis or treatment diminishes a patient's prospects of recovery, a law which does not recognise this as a wrong calling for redress would be seriously deficient today.*"[2]

Scenario 1

A 25-year-old woman experiences a dull ache in her knee, resulting in a burning sensation and a peculiar pain. After three months of frequent visits to her general practitioner, she asks him to refer her to a medical specialist. Instead, she is offered treatment for ligament damage. It takes another three months and some concern from a physiotherapist until she is administered an x-ray. She is then diagnosed with osteosarcoma, a bone cancer that is most common in young and tall people (the woman is 1.78 m tall), and which is thought to be linked to rapid growth. Intensive chemotherapy fails to reduce the size of the cancer and her only chance of survival is to have her right leg amputated.

Following the operation, the woman takes legal action against her general practitioner alleging medical malpractice leading to the loss of a limb. According to a medical expert, the general practitioner negligently delayed the diagnosis by six months, thus increasing the likelihood of the cancer leading to amputation by 25%.[3]

---

1 PETL, Art. 3:101.
2 Lord NICHOLLS OF BIRKENHEAD (dissenting opinion), in: House of Lords, *Gregg* v. *Scott*, 27.01.2005, [2005] 2 AC 176 (see below, pp. 289 ff.).
3 Inspired by a case reported in *The Guardian*, 24.06.2008, Supplement, pp. 18–19, article by B. CHAUNDY: "Something Was Obviously Wrong". For references to further scenarios of unclear causation in medical malpractice cases under the laws of *England, France, Belgium, Germany, Austria, Italy, Spain, the Netherlands, Scotland, Ireland, Lithuania, Hungary*, and *Switzerland*, see T. KADNER GRAZIANO, Loss of a Chance in European Private Law 'All or Nothing' or Partial Liability in Cases of Uncertain Causation, *ERPL* 2008, 1009–1042.

Scenario 2

A woman works as a secretary to the sales manager of a retail chain. She is notified that she is going to be transferred to another section, which will affect her working hours and working conditions. She claims that the transferral is a breach of her contract of employment and contacts a lawyer with the purpose of bringing a claim against her employer. Her lawyer negligently fails to file her claim with the employment tribunal within the required time period. As a result, the action brought on her behalf is dismissed.

She sues the lawyer seeking compensation for her financial loss, which consists of the damages she would likely have been awarded for violation of her employment contract, and the subsequent unemployment benefits she would have been entitled to, had the action been successful. Her lawyer argues that, even if the action had been brought in time, it is more probable than not that she would have lost her claim anyway.[4]

---

[4] See the *Spanish* case: Tribunal Supremo, 09.07.2004, RJ 2004, 5121; *Digest I*, 10/10/5 with comments by J. RIBOT/A. RUDA. For references to further scenarios of uncertain causation in lawyers' liability cases under the laws of *England, Scotland, the Netherlands, Denmark, Portugal, Germany, Spain*, and *Switzerland*, see T. KADNER GRAZIANO (fn. 3).

Questions

To establish civil liability, there must be a link of natural causation between the conduct of the person claimed to be liable and the damages suffered. In other words, the activity must be a *conditio sine qua non* of the victim's injury (sometimes referred to as "causation-in-fact" or "but for" test).

In some jurisdictions, such causal link must be established with *certainty*. In others, it is sufficient to establish a *predominant probability* of the purported cause with regard to the effect – in other words, that it is "more likely than not" that the damage was caused by the act (or omission) of the defendant.

In each of the above scenarios, the person alleged to be liable acted negligently. However, with regard to causation, the claimants cannot establish that the negligence of the medical doctor or lawyer was the *conditio sine qua non* of the damage they suffered with the probability that is generally required. Under traditional approaches to causation, the claims would consequently have to be dismissed.

1) One way of strengthening the position of the victim is to *reverse the burden of proof* with respect to the causal link between the purported cause and the damage suffered by the victim. With respect to the *German* case law provided in the materials, what are the benefits, and what are the shortcomings of such an approach?

    Is there a correlation between the degree of fault (such as gross negligence) and the probability of a causal link between the professional negligence and the damage suffered by the victim?

2) According to the German Federal Supreme Court of Justice, "[t]he principles relating to medical malpractice [...] cannot be applied to contracts with lawyers". Are you convinced by this reasoning? Which approach do the German courts apply to solve cases of lawyer's liability?

3) Another way of strengthening the position of the victim is to *redefine the relevant damage*. In two separate decisions, the *English* courts decided on the application of the "loss of a chance" doctrine for lawyers' and medical liability, respectively.

    a) Explain the "loss of a chance" doctrine and how it solves the problem of uncertainty of causation.
    b) In the *Kitchen* ruling, the English courts applied the "loss of a chance" doctrine to cases of lawyers' liability. Why is this so? How does the court calculate the relevant damages?
    c) In *Gregg* v. *Scott*, the House of Lords was divided on the question of whether the loss of a chance doctrine should be extended to cases of medical malpractice in English law. How did the court ultimately decide? What were the arguments on either side?

4) How would the *first scenario* be solved:

    a) under *Australian* law?
    b) under the law of the US State of *Massachusetts*?

5) What would be the outcome to our two scenarios under *French* and *Belgian* law?

6) Did the *Swiss Tribunal fédéral* ultimately permit use of the doctrine of loss of a chance in cases of medical negligence? Which approach did this Court apply in response to lawyers' liability?

7) How did the *Austrian Oberster Gerichtshof*, and, respectively, the PETL, reason with respect to uncertainty of causation in situations corresponding to our *first scenario*? Which approach is used when facing more than one potential cause of damage?

8) What is the position of the DCFR?

9) Which of the approaches found in the materials would you recommend using in cases of medical malpractice, and which would you recommend for lawyers' liability cases? In what respects are the situations similar, in what respects do they differ?

Table of contents

I. Germany
1. Bürgerliches Gesetzbuch, BGB (*Civil Code*), § 630h (5) ....p. 283
2. OLG Brandenburg (*Brandenburg Appellate Court*), 08.04.2003,
   NJW-RR 2003, 1383; VersR 2004, 1050 ....p. 283
3. OLG Hamm (*Hamm Appellate Court*), 26.08.1998, VersR 2000, 325........p. 284
4. Bundesgerichtshof, BGH, 9. Zivilsenat (*Federal Supreme Court of Justice, 9th Civil Senate*), 16.06.2005, BGHZ 163, 223.............................p. 285
5. Bundesgerichtshof, BGH, 9. Zivilsenat (*Federal Supreme Court of Justice, 9th Civil Senate*), 09.06.1994, BGHZ 126, 217 ....p. 285

II. England and Wales
1. Court of Appeal, *Kitchen* v. *Royal Air Force Association*,
   01.04.1958, [1958] WLR 563 ....p. 287
2. House of Lords, *Gregg* v. *Scott*, 27.01.2005, [2005] UKHL 2,
   [2005] 2 AC 176, [2005] All ER 812...p. 289

III. Australia
High Court of Australia, *Tabet* v. *Gett*, 21.04.2010, [2010] H.C.A. 12............p. 295

IV. Massachusetts, USA
Supreme Judicial Court of Massachusetts, *Matsuyama* v. *Birnbaum*, 23.07.2008,
890 NE 2d 819 ....p. 296

V. France
1. Cour de cassation, 1ère civ. (*Court of Cassation, 1st civil chamber*),
   18.03.1969 (Y . . . c. *Veuve [widow] Karoubi*), n°68–10.252, Bull.
   1969 II, n° 117 ....p. 299
2. Cour de cassation, 1ère civ. (*Court of Cassation, 1st civil chamber*),
   09.04.2002, n°00–13.314, Bull. 2002 I, n° 116 p. 89...........................p. 299

VI. Belgium
Hof van Cassatie/Cour de cassation (*Court of Cassation*),
05.06.2008, Arrest C.07.0199, *RW* 2008–09, afl. 19, pp. 795–799
note by Steven Lierman; also in: NjW 2009, afl. 194, pp. 31–33 ....p. 300

VII. Switzerland
1. Tribunal fédéral/Bundesgericht (*Federal Supreme Court of Justice*),
   13.06.2007, ATF 133 III 462 ....p. 301
2. Bundesgericht/Tribunal fédéral (*Federal Supreme Court of Justice*),
   12.12.1961, BGE 87 II 364 ....p. 303

VIII. Austria
1. Allgemeines bürgerliches Gesetzbuch, ABGB (*General Civil Code*),
   §§ 1302, 1304 ....p. 305

2. Oberster Gerichtshof, OGH, 4. Zivilsenat (*Supreme Court of Justice, 4th Civil Senate*), 07.11.1995, 4 Ob 554/95 (RIS), JBl. 1996, 181 ....p. 305

IX. Principles of European Tort Law
   1. PETL, Arts. 2:101, 2:102 (1) and (2), 3:101, 3:103 (1), 3:106 ....p. 307
   2. Bénédict Winiger/Helmut Koziol/Bernhard Koch/Reinhard Zimmermann (eds.), *Digest of European Tort Law, Vol. I: Essential Cases on Natural Causation*, Wien/New York: Springer, 2007, nos. 10/28/1 ff. (by Thomas Kadner Graziano) ....p. 307

X. Draft Common Frame of Reference
   1. DCFR, Art. VI-2:101(1) to (3) .... p. 310
   2. Christian von Bar/Eric Clive (eds.), *Principles, Definitions and Model Rules of European Private Law – Draft Common Frame of Reference (DCFR), Full Edition*, Vol. 4, Munich: Sellier, 2009, Art. VI – 2:201 Note XII, p. 3192; VI – 2:201 Comment D, p. 3144; VI – 2:201 Comment A, Loss of a chance, p. 3195; VI – 4:101 Comment A, Special rules, p. 3570..p. 311

Materials[5]

I. Germany

1. Bürgerliches Gesetzbuch, BGB (*Civil Code*)

§ 630h. Beweislast bei Haftung für Behandlungs- und Aufklärungsfehler. [. . .]
(5) Liegt ein grober Behandlungsfehler vor und ist dieser grundsätzlich geeignet, eine Verletzung des Lebens, des Körpers oder der Gesundheit der tatsächlich eingetretenen Art herbeizuführen, wird vermutet, dass der Behandlungsfehler für diese Verletzung ursächlich war. [. . .]

Translation

§ 630h. Burden of proof for establishing liability following an error in treatment or incorrect medical advice. [. . .] (5) In the case of gross medical malpractice, it is assumed that the malpractice was the cause of the injury if it is in principle capable of causing an injury to life, body or health of the kind that actually occurred. [. . .]

§ 630h was introduced into the BGB by way of the "Gesetz zur Verbesserung der Rechte von Patienten und Patientinnen vom 20.02.2013" (*Act Intended to Improve the Rights of Patients*) (BGBl. I S. 277). It came into force in February 2013. § 630h confirms long-standing case law of the German courts, see for example:[6]

2. OLG Brandenburg (*Brandenburg Appellate Court*), 08.04.2003, NJW-RR 2003, 1383; VersR 2004, 1050

Grounds for the decision

1 The plaintiff [born on 22nd June 1995] is claiming compensation from the defendant, as operator of the B municipal hospital, for material loss, pain and suffering arising out of her treatment at birth. She contends that the doctor failed to notice a congenital dislocation of the hip (luxation dysplasia), and in particular, failed to immediately start a medical investigation. [. . .].

33 b) In the course of her final examination of the plaintiff, Dr St [the responsible doctor] did not order an immediate ultrasound scan of her hip; nor did she advise the plaintiff's mother of the compelling need for the child to have a consultation as soon as possible with an orthopaedic surgeon for an ultrasound check-up. In these circumstances, this amounts to serious ("gross") medical malpractice. [. . .]

---

[5] For the original language versions of the materials reproduced in this chapter, see the companion website at www.routledge.com/9781138567733.
[6] See the further decisions: BGH, 26.06.1962, VersR 1962, 960; BGH, 11.06.1968, NJW 1968, 2291; BGH, 27.04.2004, BGHZ 159, 48. Recently applied also in a case similar to the *Belgian* scenario of the veterinarian charged with the treatment of a horse (see below, p. 300): BGH, 10.05.2016, VI ZR 247/15.

38 Serious ("gross") malpractice is a significant and fundamental failure to observe approved rules of medical treatment or follow established medical science which, in the objective circumstances of the case, goes beyond what is understandable, and which is absolutely unacceptable on the part of a doctor. [. . .] This is the case here. [. . .]

41 If the evidence reveals some serious ("gross") malpractice that is generally accepted to be at least a potential contributory cause of the injury in issue, it is up to the defendant (doctor or hospital operator) to establish that there is no causal relation between the breach of duty and the injury or illness. In this sense, there is, on the level of causality, a reversal of the burden of proof. [. . .] The presumption that the serious error was the cause of the plaintiff's injury is only rebutted if a causal relation with the injury or ill-health is "entirely implausible". However, this is not the case here. [. . .]

43 [. . .] [T]he expert witness, Prof Dr M, explained in more detail that, in his view, the probability of successful conservative therapy on a Type IV hip dislocation was "extremely low", but overall could be measured at about 10%. However, a 10% overall chance of success cannot justify the conclusion that the existence of a causal relation is for legal purposes "entirely implausible". It follows that here, since a case of serious ("gross") malpractice has been made, the burden of proof associated with a failure in treatment is indeed reversed. [. . .]

45 Hence, on the basis, which must be accepted, that the possibility of successful preventive treatment was not entirely implausible, it must be presumed in favour of the plaintiff that in the absence of the established serious ("gross") malpractice, the "brutal repositioning" of 4th January 1996 would not have been necessary; nor would there have been the subsequent treatment (in hospital), discomfort and permanent disability connected with it. The expert witness, Prof Dr M, – who was found to be convincing by the court – demonstrated that the probability of this was anything up to 10%, and thus it was not entirely implausible. [. . .]

47 e) On the basis of the above reasoning, the defendant, being liable for the injury and illness suffered by the plaintiff, is bound to pay damages for pain and suffering in the amount of € 25,000. [. . .]

3. OLG Hamm (*Hamm Appellate Court*), 26.08.1998, VersR 2000, 325

1   The plaintiff, born on 14th June 1928, was admitted as an in-patient with the St K Foundation in T for hip replacement surgery and was operated on by the first defendant. [. . .]

2   After the completion of the operation on 4th May 1992, where the hip joint was replaced with an internal prosthesis, the affected area became infected with the staphylococcus aureus microbe. As a result, the prosthesis was removed on 22nd June 1992. Residues of the bone cement used in the course of the original operation, as well as a broken-off fragment of a pair of surgical pliers used during the course of the operation remained inside the body. [. . .].

3   Faced with continuing discomfort, the plaintiff was admitted to the E City Clinic for treatment. There, on 4th July 1993, further surgery was undertaken in the affected area and the broken segment of surgical pliers removed. The injury healed in due course, and the implantation of a new left hip joint followed in March 1994.

4   The plaintiff claimed damages [. . .] for pain and suffering in the sum of DM 50,000 [€ 25,000]. [. . .].

Grounds for the decision

[. . .] 31 As the *Landgericht* [lower court] correctly concluded, there was defective medical treatment on the part of the doctors employed by the first defendant, in that after the further surgery on 22nd June 1992, that had not cured the infection, no supplementary operation was carried out on the plaintiff; nor was the plaintiff advised that one should be. [. . .]

37 What is not clear to this court is whether with proper treatment the injury would have successfully healed earlier than it in fact did, in spring 1993. [. . .]

38 Even the fact that the chance of a successful recovery was good, or even very good, has not dispelled this court's doubts as to the prospects of a successful outcome since, according to the expert's view, the chance of a full cure was not clearly greater than 90%. Viewing the matter as a whole, the causal connection alleged by the plaintiff was not established with the degree of certainty that was required for the action to succeed.

39 Since the proven malpractice cannot be regarded as gross negligence, the burden of proof lies with the plaintiff. [Hence, since the plaintiff could not establish a causal connection between the negligent treatment and the delay in her recovery with certainty, her claim was rejected, and her appeal against the decision at first instance was dismissed].

4. Bundesgerichtshof, BGH, 9. Zivilsenat (*Federal Supreme Court of Justice, 9th Civil Senate*), 16.06.2005, BGHZ 163, 223

[. . .] 8 In a liability claim for damages [against a lawyer], if the question as to whether the client has suffered loss as a result of his lawyer's negligent breach of duty depends on the issue of what the outcome of earlier proceedings (hereafter "the previous proceedings") would have been, the court hearing the liability claim [. . .] must take the necessary steps to decide for itself how those previous proceedings ought properly have been decided [. . .].

9 The hypothetical inquiry as to whether the present plaintiff would have been successful in the previous proceedings covers questions not only of law, but of fact as well. [. . .]

5. Bundesgerichtshof, BGH, 9. Zivilsenat (*Federal Supreme Court of Justice, 9th Civil Senate*), 09.06.1994, BGHZ 126, 217

Summary: [. . .] 5. Where lawyers' liability is concerned, even in the case of gross negligence, the client must still prove that the lawyer's breach of duty was the cause of the damage for which he wishes to claim compensation. [. . .]

Grounds for the decision

[. . .] 29 The established case law makes it clear that a lawyer must carry out his instructions in such a way as to safeguard his client's interests in every respect and, as far as possible, avoid any negative consequences to him. [. . .]

30 The lower court decided that there was a causal connection between the breach of duty on the part of the defendant [the lawyer], and the losses the plaintiff [the client] claims compensation for [. . .]. It held that the gross negligence which had been established against

[the lawyer] justified a reversal of the burden of proof of causation; and that the necessary counter-proof had not been successfully provided by him. [. . .]

31 The appeal against this holding must be allowed. [. . .]

42 3. This court agrees with the court below that the defendant [lawyer] was grossly negligent in failing to bring a claim as soon as possible after having received another lawyer's letter declining to pay the sales price [to the plaintiff].[7] Looking at the evidence produced by both parties, there was no sensible reason for the defendant [lawyer] to simply do nothing and await further developments. Nevertheless, this does not mean that the burden of proof as regards causation was transferred to the [defendant] lawyer. [. . .]

44 [. . .] According to a view expressed by some in legal doctrine, [. . .] the burden of proof is to be reversed if it is found that the lawyer has committed gross professional negligence. This point of view takes its support in particular from case law that has developed from medical malpractice [. . .]. The principles relating to medical malpractice, however, cannot be applied to contracts with lawyers.

45 In essence, the aforementioned case law is largely based on the idea that gross medical negligence usually puts patients' health seriously at risk, and as a result goes hand-in-hand with a lack of success in the treatment concerned (see BGHZ 85, 212, 216; 104, 323, 332). In addition, in legal proceedings for medical malpractice, the medical practitioner starts with a very substantial advantage, since the patient has no knowledge of what actually happened in the circumstances of the case, and has no means of appreciating the significance of developments in his physical condition following a failure to receive the expert treatment he was entitled to. This is particularly true where, in order to preserve or restore health, operations on the patient take place when he is unconscious. If the medical practitioner has demonstrated serious negligence, and thereby brought about a situation where there can be no direct knowledge of how matters would have proceeded under proper treatment, it is only appropriate that the parties' interests ought to be rebalanced, so as to transfer the burden of proof to the person whose failure to perform according to his contract gave rise to the plaintiff's evidential difficulties in the first place [. . .].

46 In the case of actions for lawyer's liability, the client is not in a comparable situation. It is simply not apparent that the risk that the client will suffer loss is substantially increased in the case of gross negligence by a lawyer when compared to other forms of negligence. The contract between lawyer and client is often so dependent on individual features of the parties' situation, that the same breach of it can, according to the circumstances, be regarded as slight, middling or gross negligence. In general, however, the degree of negligence does not allow conclusions to be drawn with regard to the question of how likely it is to have caused loss or damage to the client. [. . .] On the contrary, the client's situation depends much more on the specific features of the concrete legal business involved. [. . .]

47 The client, moreover, is not as existentially dependent on his lawyer as is often the case with the patient who undergoes treatment by a doctor. As a result, clarifying the facts of the case is typically not fraught with the same difficulties as the ones generally facing a patient

---

[7] The case arose out of a contract to buy a house, which the buyer had wrongly refused to perform, alleging fraud; the claim against the lawyer was for failure to institute proceedings for damages against the buyer in good time. The buyer had later become insolvent.

entrusting himself to a doctor for treatment. [. . .] Even where the lawyer is guilty of gross negligence, it is not justifiable to reverse the burden of proof in an area which often depends on events and decisions not best known to, and uninfluenced by, the lawyer since they lie entirely within the sphere of his client. Thus, even where the lawyer has acted with gross negligence, the burden of proof is not reversed when considering what the client's position would have been had he received the promised performance [. . .]. [. . .]

II. England and Wales

1. Court of Appeal, *Kitchen v. Royal Air Force Association*, 01.04.1958, [1958] WLR 563

Kitchen v Royal Air Force Association and others

1955 K. No. 1085
Court of Appeal
M.R. Lord Evershed, Parker, and Sellers
1958 Mar. 18, 19, 20, 21, 24, 25, 26, 27, 31; April 1

[. . .] The plaintiff, Hilda Kitchen, was the widow and administratrix of John William Kitchen, who died intestate on May 22, 1945. In this action she claimed damages against [. . .] Donald, Darlington & Nice, a firm of solicitors, for negligence in and about the formulation and prosecution of a claim arising out of the death of her husband against the West Kent Electricity Co. [. . .]

The following statement of facts is summarized from the judgment of Lord Evershed M.R.

The plaintiff's husband, a Leading Aircraftsman in the Royal Air Force, was home on leave with his wife, the plaintiff, in their flat in Renton Drive, St. Mary Cray. At about 8 o'clock in the morning of May 22, 1945, the husband went to the kitchen to prepare his wife a cup of tea, for which purpose he turned on the main switch at the control box. He was electrocuted and died almost at once. The plaintiff was firmly persuaded that the West Kent Electricity Co., now absorbed in the South Eastern Electricity Board, was in some way responsible for her husband's death. After the accident [. . .] [h]er case was sent forward [. . .] to the firm of Donald, Darlington & Nice, the present appellants. [. . .] [T]he appellants had formed the view that the thing to do was to allow time to expire, so barring the plaintiff's claim [. . .].

THE MASTER OF THE ROLLS (Lord Evershed): [. . .] In my judgment, the appellants [Donald, Darlington & Nice] deliberately allowed the time to run out without getting any instructions at all, and knowing that no expert evidence had been obtained. I cannot, for my part, understand how, in the circumstances, a responsible firm of solicitors failed to make any attempt at least to keep the case alive [. . .]. I, therefore, agree with the judge that the case of negligence by the appellants is made out. [. . .]

[. . .] [A]ssuming that she has established negligence, has the plaintiff proved anything other than nominal damages?[8] It is necessary to say something of the nature of the problem which

---

8 *Note by the author*: nominal damages are a small amount of money awarded to recognise that the claimant's rights have been violated, although he or she has not suffered any significant monetary loss that has to be compensated.

(as I understand the law) the court has to solve in determining the measure of damages in such a case as this. Mr. O'Connor's [i.e. the defendant's lawyer's] point is that we have now to consider the question of liability as between the plaintiff and the electricity company (or their successors) as though it were a distinct proceeding within the present action; and Mr. O'Connor says that, if we find on balance against the plaintiff, that is to say, that she fails in her claim against the electricity board (considered as if it were a separate and existing proceeding), then it follows that her damage is no more than nominal. If that is the right approach, it must follow that in any case such as the present the result expressed in terms of money is always all for the plaintiff or nothing. I cannot, for my part, accept that as the right formulation of the problem.

If, in this kind of action, it is plain that an action could have been brought, and if it had been brought that it must have succeeded, of course the answer is easy. The damaged plaintiff then would recover the full amount of the damages lost by the failure to bring the action originally. On the other hand, if it be made clear that the plaintiff never had a cause of action, that there was no case which the plaintiff could reasonably ever have formulated, then it is equally plain that the answer is that she can get nothing save nominal damages for the solicitors' negligence. [. . .]

But the present case falls into neither one nor the other of the categories which I have mentioned. There may be cases where it would be quite impossible to try "the action within the action" as Mr. O'Connor asks. It may be that for one reason or another the action for negligence is not brought till, say, twenty years after the event and in the process of time the material witnesses or many of them may have died or become quite out of reach for the purpose of being called to give evidence.

In my judgment, what the court has to do (assuming that the plaintiff has established negligence) in such a case as the present, is to determine what the plaintiff has by that negligence lost. The question is, has the plaintiff lost some right of value, some chose in action of reality and substance? In such a case, it may be that its value is not easy to determine, but it is the duty of the court to determine that value as best it can. In the present case [. . .] [t]he judge [. . .] concluded that she should be entitled to recover £ 2,000, which was a figure he arrived at as being equivalent to two-thirds arithmetically of the full amount which (admittedly) was the maximum recoverable under the Fatal Accidents Acts. The relevant passage in the judgment is:

"I am not prepared myself to say that there was no hope for this action. [. . .] The more I think about it the more I think that, [. . .] considering that even successful actions may involve a party in some part of the costs, the fair figure at which to estimate the damage which was suffered by the failure to bring this matter to trial or to issue proceedings is the sum of £ 2,000."

[. . .] I think that the plaintiff established that there was a cause of action and that she had lost something of value. So I think on this matter, too, that we should not disturb the judge's finding. In the end, therefore, I would say that this appeal should be dismissed.[9]

Appeal dismissed.

---

9 Parker LJ and Sellers LJ concurring.

2. House of Lords, *Gregg v. Scott*, 27.01.2005, [2005] UKHL 2, [2005] 2 AC 176, [2005] All ER 812[10]

IN THE HOUSE OF LORDS

on appeal from: [2002] EWCA Civ 1471

Thursday 27th January, 2005

Before: Lord Nicholls of Birkenhead, Lord Hoffmann, Lord Hope or Craighead, Lord Philipps of Worth Matravers, Baroness Hale of Richmond

GREGG (FC) (Appellant) v. SCOTT (Respondent)

JUDGMENT

LORD NICHOLLS OF BIRKENHEAD [dissenting opinion]: My Lords, 1. This appeal raises a question which has divided courts and commentators throughout the common law world. [. . .]

2. [. . .] A patient is suffering from cancer. His prospects are uncertain. He has a 45% chance of recovery. Unfortunately his doctor negligently misdiagnoses his condition as benign. So the necessary treatment is delayed for months. As a result the patient's prospects of recovery become nil or almost nil. Has the patient a claim for damages against the doctor? No, the House was told. The patient could recover damages if his initial prospects of recovery had been more than 50%. But because they were less than 50% he can recover nothing.

3. This surely cannot be the state of the law today. It would be irrational and indefensible. The loss of a 45% prospect of recovery is just as much a real loss for a patient as the loss of a 55% prospect of recovery. In both cases the doctor was in breach of his duty to his patient. In both cases the patient was worse off. He lost something of importance and value. But, it is said, in one case the patient has a remedy, in the other he does not.

4. This would make no sort of sense. It would mean that in the 45% case the doctor's duty would be hollow. The duty would be empty of content. For the reasons which follow I reject this suggested distinction. The common law does not compel courts to proceed in such an unreal fashion. I would hold that a patient has a right to a remedy as much where his prospects of recovery were less than 50–50 as where they exceeded 50–50. [. . .]

5. First I must mention the salient facts of this appeal. These are not quite so straightforward or extreme as in the example just given. At the risk of over-simplification they can be summarised as follows. The defendant Dr Scott negligently diagnosed as innocuous a lump under the left arm of the claimant Mr Malcolm Gregg when in fact it was cancerous (non-Hodgkin's lymphoma). This led to nine months' delay in Mr Gregg receiving treatment. During this period his condition deteriorated by the disease spreading elsewhere. The

---

10 Case notes: J. Morgan, A Chance Missed to Recognize Loss-of-a-Chance in Negligence, *LMCLQ* 2005, 281; E. Peel, Loss of a Chance in Medical Negligence, *L.Q.R.* 2005, 364; G. Reid, Gregg v Scott and Lost Chances, *PN* 2005, 78; J. R. Spencer, Case Comment, Damages for Lost Chances: Lost for Good?, *C.L.J.* 2005, 282; J. Stapleton, Loss of the Chance of Cure from Cancer, *MLR* 2005, 996; A. Mullis/D. Nolan, Case Note. *Gregg v. Scott*, *All ER Annual Review* 2005, 479; G. Mäsch, Case Comment, Gregg v. Scott – Much Ado about Nothing?, ZEuP 2006, 656.

deterioration in Mr Gregg's condition reduced his prospects of disease-free survival for ten years from 42%, when he first consulted Dr Scott, to 25% at the date of the trial. [. . .]

15. [. . .] Sometimes, whether a claimant has suffered actionable damage cannot fairly be decided on an all-or-nothing basis by reference to what, on balance of probability, would have happened but for the defendant's negligence. [. . .] What would have happened in the absence of the defendant's negligence is altogether too uncertain for the all-or-nothing approach to be satisfactory. In some cases what the claimant lost by the negligence was the opportunity or chance to achieve a desired result whose achievement was outside his control and inherently uncertain. The defendant's wrong consisted of depriving the claimant of a chance he would otherwise have had to achieve a desired outcome.

[. . .] 17. In order to achieve a just result in such cases the law defines the claimant's actionable damage more narrowly by reference to the opportunity the claimant lost, rather than by reference to the loss of the desired outcome which was never within his control. In adopting this approach the law does not depart from the principle that the claimant must prove actionable damage on the balance of probability. The law adheres to this principle but defines actionable damage in different, more appropriate terms. The law treats the claimant's loss of his opportunity or chance as itself actionable damage. The claimant must prove this loss on balance of probability. The court will then measure this loss as best it may. The chance is to be ignored if it was merely speculative, but evaluated if it was substantial [. . .].

18. Some familiar examples will suffice. A woman who was wrongly deprived of the chance of being one of the winners in a beauty competition was awarded damages for loss of a chance. The court did not attempt to decide on balance of probability the hypothetical past event of what would have happened if the claimant had been duly notified of her interview: Chaplin v Hicks [1911] 2 KB 786. When a solicitor's failure to issue a writ in time deprived a claimant of the opportunity to pursue court proceedings damages were not assessed on an all-or-nothing basis by reference to what probably would have been the outcome if the proceedings had been commenced in time. The court assessed what would have been the claimant's prospects of success in the proceedings which the solicitor's negligence prevented him from pursuing: Kitchen v Royal Air Force Association [1958] 1 WLR 563.[11] When an employer negligently supplied an inaccurate character reference, the employee did not need to prove that, but for the negligence, he would probably have been given the new job. The employee only had to prove he lost a reasonable chance of employment, which the court would evaluate: Spring v Guardian Assurance Plc [1995] 2 AC 296, 327.

19. In Allied Maples Group Ltd v Simmons & Simmons [1995] 1 WLR 1602 a solicitor's negligence deprived the claimant of an opportunity to negotiate a better bargain. The Court of Appeal applied the 'loss of chance' approach. [. . .]

20. Against this background I turn to the primary question raised by this appeal: how should the loss suffered by a patient in Mr Gregg's position be identified? [. . .]

24. Given this uncertainty of outcome, the appropriate characterisation of a patient's loss in this type of case must surely be that it comprises the loss of the chance of a favourable outcome, rather than the loss of the outcome itself. Justice so requires, because this matches medical reality. [. . .] The doctor's negligence diminished the patient's prospects

---

11 See above, pp. 287–288.

of recovery. And this analysis of a patient's loss accords with the purpose of the legal duty of which the doctor was in breach. In short, the purpose of the duty is to promote the patient's prospects of recovery by exercising due skill and care in diagnosing and treating the patient's condition.

25. This approach also achieves a basic objective of the law of tort. The common law imposes duties and seeks to provide appropriate remedies in the event of a breach of duty. If negligent diagnosis or treatment diminishes a patient's prospects of recovery, a law which does not recognise this as a wrong calling for redress would be seriously deficient today. In respect of the doctors' breach of duty the law would not have provided an appropriate remedy. Of course, losing a chance of saving a leg is not the same as losing a leg: see Tony Weir, 'Tort Law' (2002), p 76. But that is not a reason for declining to value the chance for whose loss the doctor was directly responsible. The law would rightly be open to reproach were it to provide a remedy if what is lost by a professional adviser's negligence is a financial opportunity or chance but refuse a remedy where what is lost by a doctor's negligence is the chance of health or even life itself. Justice requires that in the latter case as much as the former the loss of a chance should constitute actionable damage.

[. . .] 42. [. . .] [A] doctor's duty to act in the best interests of his patient involves maximising the patient's recovery prospects, and doing so whether the patient's prospects are good or not so good. In the event of a breach of this duty the law must fashion a matching and meaningful remedy. A patient should have an appropriate remedy when he loses the very thing it was the doctor's duty to protect. To this end the law should recognise the existence and loss of poor and indifferent prospects as well as those more favourable.

43. Application of the all-or-nothing balance of probability approach in the 'Gregg' type of cases would not achieve this object. [. . .] It cannot be right to adopt a procedure having the effect that, in law, a patient's prospects of recovery are treated as non-existent whenever they exist but fall short of 50%. [. . .] The law should not, by adopting the all-or-nothing balance of probability approach, assume certainty where none in truth exists: see Deane J in Commonwealth of Australia v Amann Aviation Pty Ltd (1991) 66 ALJR 123, 147. The difference between good and poor prospects is a matter going to the amount of compensation fairly payable, not to liability to make payment at all. As Dore J said in [in the US case] Herskovits v Group Health Cooperative of Puget Sound (1983) 664 P 2d 474, 477:

"To decide otherwise would be a blanket release from liability for doctors and hospitals any time there was less than a 50 per cent chance of survival, regardless of how flagrant the negligence."

45. This approach would represent a development of the law. So be it. If the common law is to retain its legitimacy it must remain capable of development. It must recognise the great advances made in medical knowledge and skills. It must recognise also the medical uncertainties which still exist. The law must strive to achieve a result which is fair to both parties in present-day conditions. The common law's ability to develop in this way is its proudest boast. [. . .]

46. [. . .] The present state of the law is crude to an extent bordering on arbitrariness. It means that a patient with a 60% chance of recovery reduced to a 40% prospect by medical negligence can obtain compensation. But he can obtain nothing if his prospects were reduced from 40% to nil. This is rough justice indeed. By way of contrast, the approach set

out above meets the perceived need for an appropriate remedy in both these situations and does no more than reflect fairly and rationally the loss suffered by a patient in these situations. [. . .]

59. I would therefore allow this appeal. [. . .]

LORD HOFFMANN: My Lords, [. . .] I would dismiss the appeal.

LORD HOPE OF CRAIGHEAD [dissenting opinion]: My Lords, 92. This is an anxious and difficult case. It is only after many months of deliberation that it has become clear that the majority view is that the appeal must be dismissed. I have reached a different opinion. In agreement with my noble and learned friend Lord Nicholls of Birkenhead, I would allow the appeal [. . .].

LORD PHILLIPS OF WORTH MATRAVERS: My Lords, 169. [. . .] The closer that Mr Gregg comes to being a survivor the smaller is the likelihood that the delay in commencing his treatment has had any effect on his expectation of life. [. . .] On balance of probability I suspect that one is now in a position to conclude that the delay in commencing Mr Gregg's treatment has not affected his prospect of being a survivor [. . .]. [. . .]

190. The complications of this case have persuaded me that it is not a suitable vehicle for introducing into the law of clinical negligence the right to recover damages for the loss of a chance of a cure. Awarding damages for the reduction of the prospect of a cure, when the long term result of treatment is still uncertain, is not a satisfactory exercise. Where medical treatment has resulted in an adverse outcome and negligence has increased the chance of that outcome, there may be a case for permitting a recovery of damages that is proportionate to the increase in the chance of the adverse outcome. That is not a case that has been made out on the present appeal. [. . .]

191. [. . .] I agree with Lord Hoffmann and Baroness Hale that this appeal must be dismissed.

BARONESS HALE OF RICHMOND: My Lords, [. . .] 193. [. . .] It must [. . .] be shown on the balance of probabilities that what the defendant negligently did or failed to do caused the claimant's damage. As Tony Weir (Tort Law, Oxford University Press, 2002, pp 74–75) puts it: "[. . .] Certainty is not required. The essential thing is to persuade the judge that the harm would probably have been avoided if the defendant had acted properly: it does not matter whether he is easily persuaded, because it is obvious, or is persuaded only with difficulty, because the matter is far from clear. The tendency to state the matter in terms of percentages is to be avoided. 'More likely than not' is a matter of persuasion, not of proof."

194. Once persuaded, however, the judge awards the claimant the full value of the damage that has been caused. As Tony Weir goes on to say: "The idea that recovery should be proportional to the cogency of the proof of causation is utterly unacceptable . . ."

195. If it is more likely than not that the defendant's carelessness caused me to lose a leg, I do not want my damages reduced to the extent that it is less than 100% certain that it did so. On the other hand, if it is more likely than not that the defendant's carelessness did not cause me to lose the leg, then the defendant does not want to have to pay damages for the 20% or 30% chance that it did. A 'more likely than not' approach to causation suits both sides.

196. So it matters how the claimant, and the law, define the damage which is the gist of his action. [. . .]

212. This is [. . .] a new case, not covered precisely by previous authority. The appellant himself describes his argument as the 'policy approach'. He recognises that it is a question of legal policy whether the law should be developed as he argues it should be. The wide version of the argument would allow recovery for any reduction in the chance of a better physical outcome, or any increase in the chance of an adverse physical outcome, even if this cannot be linked to any physiological changes caused by the defendant. A defendant who has negligently increased the risk that the claimant will suffer harm in future (for example from exposure to asbestos or cigarette smoke) would be liable even though no harm had yet been suffered. This would be difficult to reconcile with our once and for all approach to establishing liability and assessing damage. Unless damages were limited to a modest sum for anxiety and distress about the future, sensible quantification would have to 'wait and see'. [. . .]

213. The attractions of adopting this reformulation of the gist of the action are many [. . .]. First, the conventional approach to causation is, in theory at least, retained. The claimant still has to prove that it is more likely than not that the negligence led to the damage. But the damage is no longer defined in terms of the outcome – saving the leg or achieving disease free survival. It is defined in terms of the loss or diminution of the chance of saving the leg or achieving disease free survival. [. . .]

215. [. . .] But in the end [. . .] common sense will often suggest that the chances of a better outcome would have been better if the doctor had done what he should have done: for why else should he have done it but to improve the patient's chances? Reformulating the damage in this way could lead to some liability in almost every case.

216. Second, however, many would argue that this is a good thing. One of the objects of the law of negligence is to maintain proper standards, in the workplace, on the roads, in professional conduct, or whatever. If an employer, or a driver, or a professional person can be shown to have taken less care than he should have taken, then he should have to pay damages of some sort. [. . .]

217. But of course doctors and other health care professionals are not solely, or even mainly, motivated by the fear of adverse legal consequences. They are motivated by their natural desire and their professional duty to do their best for their patients. Tort law is not criminal law. The criminal law is there to punish and deter those who do not behave as they should. Tort law is there to compensate those who have been wronged. [. . .] [I]t can never be enough to show that the defendant has been negligent. The question is still whether his negligence has caused actionable damage. [. . .]

218. Third, it can be argued that some kinds of negligence do result in liability for loss of a chance. It has long been established that a solicitor whose negligence deprives the client of a viable claim is liable for damages even though the chances of succeeding in the claim were never better than even: see Kitchen v Royal Air Force Association [1958] 1 WLR 563.[12] The court simply asks what his claim was worth, assesses his chances of success, and discounts the full value by reference to the degree to which those chances were less than 100%. So why should my solicitor be liable for negligently depriving me of the chance of winning my action, even if I never had a better than even chance of success, when my doctor is not liable

---

12 Above, pp. 287–288.

for negligently depriving me of the chance of getting better, even if I never had a better than even chance of getting better? Is this another example of the law being kinder to the medical profession than to other professionals?

[. . .] 220. It is unfashionable these days to distinguish between financial loss and personal injury. Losing the money one has may not be so different from losing the leg one has. But many claims for financial loss do not relate to the money one has but to the money one expected to have – a prospective financial gain. There is not much difference between the money one expected to have and the money one expected to have a chance of having: it is all money. There is a difference between the leg one ought to have and the chance of keeping a leg which one ought to have. There is perhaps an even greater difference between the disease free state one ought to have and the chance of having a disease free state which one ought to have. [. . .]

221. Fourth, it can be argued that an all or nothing approach to outcome based losses is unjust. If it is shown on the balance of probabilities that my doctor caused or failed to prevent my injury or disease, he has to pay 100% of what that injury or uncured disease is worth. But, as Joseph H King argues at (1981) 90 Yale LJ 1353, 1387, "by compensating the 95% chance as though it were 100%, courts overcompensate the plaintiff. Both types of chance should be valued in a way that reflects their probability of occurrence. Such an approach would also promote a more accurate loss allocation."

222. The logic of this argument, however, is that personal injury law should transform itself. It should never be about outcomes but only about chances. It seems to me that this is the real problem we face in this case. How can the two live together?

223. Until now, the gist of the action for personal injuries has been damage to the person. My negligence probably caused the loss of your leg: I pay you the full value of the loss of the leg (say £100,000). My negligence probably did not cause the loss of your leg. I do not pay you anything. Compare the loss of a chance approach: my negligence probably caused a reduction in the chance of your keeping that leg: I pay you the value of the loss of your leg, discounted by the chance that it would have happened anyway. If the chance of saving the leg was very good, say 90%, the claimant still gets only 90% of his damages, say £90,000. But if the chance of saving the leg was comparatively poor, say 20%, the claimant still gets £20,000. So the claimant ends up with less than full compensation even though his chances of a more favourable outcome were good. And the defendant ends up paying substantial sums even though the outcome is one for which by definition he cannot be shown to be responsible.

224. Almost any claim for loss of an outcome could be reformulated as a claim for loss of a chance of that outcome. [. . .]

225. [. . .] [T]he claimants who currently obtain full recovery on an adverse outcome basis might in future only achieve a proportionate recovery. This would surely be a case of two steps forward, three steps back for the great majority of straightforward personal injury cases. In either event, the expert evidence would have to be far more complex than it is at present. Negotiations and trials would be a great deal more difficult. Recovery would be much less predictable both for claimants and for defendants' liability insurers. [. . .] [This change] would cause far more problems in the general run of personal injury claims than the policy benefits are worth.

226. Much of the discussion in the cases and literature has centred round cases where the adverse outcome has already happened. The patient has lost his leg. Did the doctor's

negligence cause him to lose the leg? If not, did it reduce the chances of saving the leg? But in this case the most serious of the adverse outcomes has not yet happened, and (it is to be hoped) may never happen. The approach to causation should be the same for both past and future events. What, if anything, has the doctor's negligence caused in this case? We certainly do not know whether it has caused this outcome, because happily Mr Gregg has survived each of the significant milestones along the way. Can we even say that it reduced the chances of a successful outcome, given that Mr Gregg has turned out to be one of the successful minority at each milestone? [. . .] The complexities of attempting to introduce liability for the loss of a chance of a more favourable outcome in personal injury claims have driven me, not without regret, to conclude that it should not be done.

227. [. . .] I agree that this appeal should be dismissed.

[Appeal dismissed]

III. Australia

High Court of Australia, *Tabet v. Gett*, 21.04.2010, [2010] H.C.A. 12

[*Note by the author*: 6-year-old Rema Tabet is admitted to hospital with a brain tumour. After a delay of one day, the child's brain is scanned. The child is operated on and suffers from severe permanent brain damage. The Court concludes that the tumour and cerebrospinal fluid have led to an increase of pressure in the brain. A quarter of the damage was due with a probability of 40% to the one day delay in the diagnosis. Other causes of permanent damage are the tumour itself, the (skilfully executed) surgery and subsequent treatments. The Court of Appeal concludes that the probability of a causal relationship between the one day delay and a quarter of the damage is about 15%.]

1. **GUMMOW ACJ.** [. . .] 2. The action was brought in negligence alone and there was no claim in contract. [. . .]

47. [. . .] [I]n a negligence action, unlike an action in contract, the existence and causation of compensable loss cannot be established by reference to breach of an antecedent promise to afford an opportunity.

48. In a contract case the plaintiff should be entitled at least to nominal damages for loss of the promised opportunity.

104. **KIEFEL J.** [. . .] 152. The appellant is unable to prove that it was probable that, had treatment [. . .] been undertaken earlier, the brain damage which occurred on 14 January 1991 would have been avoided. The evidence was insufficient to be persuasive. The requirement of causation is not overcome by redefining the mere possibility, that such damage as did occur might not eventuate, as a chance and then saying that it is lost when the damage actually occurs. Such a claim could only succeed if the standard of proof were lowered, which would require a fundamental change to the law of negligence. The appellant suffered dreadful injury, but the circumstances of this case do not provide a strong ground for considering such change. It would involve holding the respondent liable for damage which he almost certainly did not cause.

[Claim for damages dismissed.]

IV. Massachusetts (USA)

Supreme Judicial Court of Massachusetts,
Matsuyama v. Birnbaum, 23.07.2008, 890 NE 2d 819

[Facts: An internist near Boston wrongly diagnoses the symptoms of a 42-year-old patient over several years. He thereby acts negligently. Finally, gastric cancer is detected. The patient dies shortly thereafter, leaving his wife and a small child behind. With an early diagnosis, the patient would have had a 37.5% chance of survival, which he lost completely until the disease was finally discovered.]

MARSHALL, C.J. We are asked to determine whether Massachusetts law permits recovery for a "loss of chance" in a medical malpractice wrongful death action, where a jury found that the defendant physician's negligence deprived the plaintiff's decedent of a less than even chance of surviving cancer. We answer in the affirmative. [. . .] [T]he loss of chance doctrine views a person's prospects for surviving a serious medical condition as something of value, even if the possibility of recovery was less than even prior to the physician's tortious conduct. Where a physician's negligence reduces or eliminates the patient's prospects for achieving a more favorable medical outcome, the physician has harmed the patient and is liable for damages. Permitting recovery for loss of chance is particularly appropriate in the area of medical negligence. [. . .] We conclude that recognizing loss of chance in the limited domain of medical negligence advances the fundamental goals and principles of our tort law. [. . .]

2. Loss of chance. Although we address the issue for the first time today, a substantial and growing majority of the States [in the USA] that have considered the question have indorsed the loss of chance doctrine, in one form or another, in medical malpractice actions [FN: The highest courts of at least twenty States and the District of Columbia have adopted the loss of chance doctrine [references omitted]. Ten States' high courts have, in contrast, refused to adopt the loss of chance doctrine [references omitted]. Other States' high courts have not addressed the issue or have explicitly left the question open [references omitted]. We join that majority to ensure that the fundamental aims and principles of our tort law remain fully applicable to the modern world of sophisticated medical diagnosis and treatment.

[. . .] The doctrine originated in dissatisfaction with the prevailing "all or nothing" rule of tort recovery. [. . .] Under the all or nothing rule, a plaintiff may recover damages only by showing that the defendant's negligence more likely than not caused the ultimate outcome, in this case the patient's death; if the plaintiff meets this burden, the plaintiff then recovers 100% of her damages. Thus, if a patient had a 51% chance of survival, and the negligent misdiagnosis or treatment caused that chance to drop to zero, the estate is awarded full wrongful death damages. On the other hand, if a patient had a 49% chance of survival, and the negligent misdiagnosis or treatment caused that chance to drop to zero, the plaintiff receives nothing. [. . .] Thus, the all or nothing rule provides a "blanket release from liability for doctors and hospitals any time there was less than a 50 percent chance of survival, regardless of how flagrant the negligence."

As many courts and commentators have noted, the all or nothing rule is inadequate to advance the fundamental aims of tort law. [. . .] Fundamentally, the all or nothing approach does not serve the basic aim of "fairly allocating the costs and risks of human injuries," O'Brien v. Christensen, 422 Mass. 281, 288 (1996) [. . .]. The all or nothing rule "fails to deter" medical negligence because it immunizes "whole areas of medical practice from liability". McMackin v. Johnson County Healthcare Ctr., 73 P. 3d 1094, 1099 (Wyo. 2003) [. . .]. It fails to provide the proper incentives to ensure that the care patients receive does not slip below the "standard of care and skill of the average member of the profession practising the specialty". Brune v. Belinkoff, 354 Mass. 102, 109 (1968). And the all or nothing rule fails to ensure that victims, who incur the real harm of losing their opportunity for a better outcome, are fairly compensated for their loss. [. . .]

Courts adopting the loss of chance doctrine also have noted that, because a defendant's negligence effectively made it impossible to know whether the person would have achieved a more favorable outcome had he received the appropriate standard of care, it is particularly unjust to deny the person recovery for being unable "to demonstrate to an absolute certainty what would have happened in circumstances that the wrongdoer did not allow to come to pass". Hicks v. United States, 368 F.2d 626, 632 (4th Cir. 1966).

[. . .] The unsettled boundaries of the [loss of chance] doctrine have left it open to criticisms similar to those that the defendants have leveled here: that the loss of chance doctrine upends the long-standing preponderance of the evidence standard; alters the burden of proof in favor of the plaintiff; undermines the uniformity and predictability central to tort litigation; results in an expansion of liability; and is too complex to administer. [. . .] While these objections deserve serious consideration, the doctrine of loss of chance, when properly formulated, survives these criticisms.

[. . .] The defendants argue that the loss of chance doctrine "lowers the threshold of proof of causation" by diluting the preponderance of the evidence standard [. . .]. [. . .] [I]n a case involving loss of chance, as in any other negligence context, a plaintiff must establish by a preponderance of the evidence that the defendant caused his injury.

However, "injury" need not mean a patient's death. Although there are few certainties in medicine or in life, progress in medical science now makes it possible, at least with regard to certain medical conditions, to estimate a patient's probability of survival to a reasonable degree of medical certainty. [. . .] That probability of survival is part of the patient's condition. When a physician's negligence diminishes or destroys a patient's chance of survival, the patient has suffered real injury. The patient has lost something of great value: a chance to survive, to be cured, or otherwise to achieve a more favorable medical outcome. [. . .]. Thus we recognize loss of chance not as a theory of causation, but as a theory of injury.

[. . .] In order to prove loss of chance, a plaintiff must prove by a preponderance of the evidence that the physician's negligence caused the plaintiff's likelihood of achieving a more favorable outcome to be diminished. That is, the plaintiff must prove by a preponderance of the evidence that the physician's negligence caused the plaintiff's injury, where the injury consists of the diminished likelihood of achieving a more favorable medical outcome. [. . .] The loss of chance doctrine, so delineated, makes no amendment or exception to the burdens of proof applicable in all negligence claims.

We reject the defendants' contention that a statistical likelihood of survival is a "mere possibility" and therefore "speculative". [. . .] [S]urvival rates are not random guesses. They are estimates based on data obtained and analyzed scientifically and accepted by the relevant medical community as part of the repertoire of diagnosis and treatment, as applied to the specific facts of the plaintiff's case . . . . Where credible evidence establishes that the plaintiff's or decedent's probability of survival is 49%, that conclusion is no more speculative than a conclusion, based on similarly credible evidence, that the probability of survival is 51%. [. . .]

The defendants also point out that "[t]he cause, treatment, cure and survivability related to cancer is tremendously uncertain and complex" [. . .]. Such difficulties are not confined to loss of chance claims. A wide range of medical malpractice cases, as well as numerous other tort actions, are complex and involve actuarial or other probabilistic estimates. Wrongful death claims, for example, often require, as part of the damages calculation, an estimate of how long the decedent might have lived absent the defendant's conduct. The calculation of damages in a claim for lost business opportunities may be similarly complex. [. . .] [A]s we noted above, at least for certain conditions, medical science has progressed to the point that physicians can gauge a patient's chances of survival to a reasonable degree of medical certainty, and indeed routinely use such statistics as a tool of medicine. [. . .]

We are unmoved by the defendants' argument that "the ramifications of adoption of loss of chance are immense" across "all areas of tort". We emphasize that our decision today is limited to loss of chance in medical malpractice actions. Such cases are particularly well suited to application of the loss of chance doctrine. [. . .] First, as we noted above, reliable expert evidence establishing loss of chance is more likely to be available in a medical malpractice case than in some other domains of tort law. Second, medical negligence that harms the patient's chances of a more favorable outcome contravenes the expectation at the heart of the doctor-patient relationship that "the physician will take every reasonable measure to obtain an optimal outcome for the patient". [. . .]. Third, it is not uncommon for patients to have a less than even chance of survival or of achieving a better outcome when they present themselves for diagnosis, so the shortcomings of the all or nothing rule are particularly widespread. Finally, failure to recognize loss of chance in medical malpractice actions forces the party who is the least capable of preventing the harm to bear the consequences of the more capable party's negligence. In sum, whatever difficulties may attend recognizing loss of chance as an item of damages in a medical malpractice action, these difficulties are far outweighed by the strong reasons to adopt the doctrine [. . .].

4. Damages. [. . .] A [. . .] challenging issue is how to calculate the monetary value for the lost chance. [. . .] The most widely adopted [method] of valuation is the "proportional damages" approach. [. . .] Under the proportional damages approach, loss of chance damages are measured as "the percentage probability by which the defendant's tortious conduct diminished the likelihood of achieving some more favorable outcome". [. . .] The formula aims to ensure that a defendant is liable in damages only for the monetary value of the portion of the decedent's prospects that the defendant's negligence destroyed. In applying the proportional damages method, the court must first measure the monetary value of the patient's full life expectancy and, if relevant, work life expectancy as it would in any wrongful death case. But the defendant must then be held liable only for the portion of that value that the defendant's negligence destroyed. [. . .]

To illustrate, suppose in a wrongful death case that a jury found, based on expert testimony and the facts of the case, that full wrongful death damages would be $ 600,000 (step 1), that the patient had a 45% chance of survival prior to the medical malpractice (step 2), and that the physician's tortious acts reduced the chances of survival to 15% (step 3). The patient's chances of survival were reduced 30% (i.e., 45% minus 15%) due to the physician's malpractice (step 4), and the patient's loss of chance damages would be $ 600,000 multiplied by 30%, for a total of $ 180,000 (step 5). [. . .]

V. France

1. Cour de cassation, 1ère civ. (*Court of Cassation, 1st civil chamber*), 18.03.1969 (*Y . . . c. Veuve [widow] Karoubi*), n°68–10.252, Bull. 1969 II, n° 117

THE COURT: – On the single ground of appeal: Whereas the judgment which forms the subject of this appeal states that Karoubi, having been treated by doctor Y . . . for simple appendicitis, died a few days later due to uraemia; that his widow attributed his death to negligence on the part of the medical practitioner and brought an action against him; that doctor Y . . . was ordered by the *Cour d'appel*, pursuant to her claim, to pay the widow the sum of 60,000 francs[13] in damages, on the grounds that "by operating immediately and bypassing the testing usually done in similar situations, doctor Y . . . did not give Karoubi the care that he was entitled to receive from a specialist" and that this negligence deprived Karoubi of a chance of survival; Whereas the applicant claims that the *Cour d'appel* undermined its own reasoning by admitting a loss of a chance while at the same time recognising "that the fault upheld as grounds by the Court was not established as the cause of death"; that these grounds were arbitrary and dis not provide a basis for the Court's judgment; However, whereas by upholding the surgeon's fault in the judgment under appeal, the *Cour d'appel* was able to decide, without undermining its own reasoning or deciding arbitrarily, that even if it could not be proved that Y . . .'s negligence was the cause of death, such negligence had nonetheless deprived Karoubi of a chance of survival; As a consequence, the argument cannot be accepted as grounds of appeal;

For these reasons, the Court dismisses the appeal against the judgment of the Aix-en-Provence Court of Appeal rendered on 12th October 1967.

2. Cour de cassation, 1ère civ. (*Court of Cassation, 1st civil chamber*), 09.04.2002, n°00–13.314, Bull. 2002 I, n° 116 p. 89

THE COURT: – On the first argument of the single ground of appeal: In view of [the previous] Art. 1147 of the Civil Code;[14] Whereas in sentencing Mr X . . ., a lawyer, [. . .] to pay the sum of 444,744.36 francs[15] to the Regional Health Fund for the Ile-de-France (*Caisse régionale d'assurance maladie Ile-de-France, CRAMIF*) [. . .], the judgment which forms the subject of this appeal [. . .] states that the case file shows that the loss of a chance suffered by *CRAMIF* through the definitively acknowledged fault of its counsel [i.e. Mr X . . .] is in fact equivalent to the full amount of the sums that *CRAMIF* was required to pay the victim due to the incident that occurred on 29th March 1967; Whereas when the *Cour d'appel* gave this judgment, it was in breach of the aforementioned article, since the compensation for

---

13 Today worth around € 67,500.
14 *Note by the author*: the previous Art. 1147 of the *French* Civil code provided: "A debtor shall be ordered to pay damages, if appropriate, for either the non-performance of the obligation, or for delay in performance, whenever he cannot prove that the non-performance is due to an external cause which cannot be attributed to him, even when there is no bad faith on his part." Now, a similar rule can be found in Art. 1231–1 of the current version of the Code.
15 Today worth around € 82,000.

loss of a chance must be measured according to the lost chance and cannot be equal to the advantage that the realisation of this chance would have brought about;

For these reasons, the Court dismisses and renders null all provisions of the judgment of the *Cour d'appel de Douai* of 17th January 2000 with respect to the parties, restores the case and parties to their state prior to the judgment, and refers them to the *Cour d'appel d'Amiens* for retrial.

VI. Belgium

Hof van Cassatie/Cour de cassation (*Court of Cassation*), 05.06.2008, Arrest Nr. C.07.0199, RW 2008–09, afl. 19, 795–799; NjW 2009, afl. 194, 31–33

[Facts: a veterinarian is charged with the treatment of the famous and very successful race horse Prizrak. He negligently fails to administer a feeding tube. A little while later, the anterior wall of the horse's stomach bursts and, as a result, it dies. According to an expert opinion, the horse would have had an 80% chance of survival had it been treated correctly; the chances of it dying anyway stood at 20%. The plaintiff seeks (pro rata) compensation in line with the value of the horse, the sum of which amounts to € 198,000.] [. . .]

[. . .] JUDGMENT OF THE COURT

1. It is for the person seeking compensation to prove a link of causation between the fault and the damage that occurred, and to establish that, had the fault not been committed, the damage would not have occurred in that manner.

2. The loss of an actual chance of recovery or survival is taken into consideration for damages if the fault is the *conditio sine qua non* of the loss of this chance. The judge may award damages for the loss of a chance to obtain a benefit or avoid a loss, should the defendant's conduct constitute a fault. The judge may therefore compensate the loss of a chance of recovery or survival of an animal if he finds that the owner of an animal in ill health which, had it been given timely care, would have had a chance of recovery or survival, has lost the chance of this outcome through the fault of a veterinarian. [. . .]

4. The judgment [of the appellate judge] states that:

- Given the circumstances, the veterinarian committed a fault by not inserting a gastric tube;
- The horse died as a result of a rupture of the stomach wall;
- The insertion of a gastric tube could probably have prevented the stomach wall from rupturing and, therefore, could have prevented the horse's death;
- The expert evaluated the horse's chance of survival at 80%, had it received the correct treatment.

5. The decision of the appellate judges was that, had the horse been treated correctly, it would have had an actual chance for survival, and that the link of causation between fault and damage, namely the loss of a chance for survival, had been proved; they hereby also dismissed the possibility that the damage would have occurred with certainty in that manner if the veterinarian had not committed the fault.

6. For these reasons, the decision of the appellate judges to allow the respondent's claim for damages for loss of a chance of survival is legally justified. [. . .]

VII. Switzerland

1. Tribunal fédéral/Bundesgericht (*Federal Supreme Court of Justice*), 13.06.2007, ATF 133 III 462

[Facts: at 3:30 a.m., a man arrives in the emergency department of the Cantonal Hospital of Fribourg in Switzerland. He suffers from severe headaches, nausea, vomiting and abdominal pain. A junior doctor diagnoses flu. At 6:30, the patient is discharged at his own request. At 9:55, he is taken back in a lethargic state. Meningitis is now immediately diagnosed and he receives adequate treatment. However, he suffers serious complications. When the patient is discharged weeks later, he is deaf in both ears. Expert opinion reaches the conclusion that the junior doctor had committed a diagnostic error. However, meningitis, even if recognised at an early stage, often results in serious damage. It is therefore impossible to determine whether the harm to the patient could have been prevented if he had not been treated only after a four to five hour delay. A second opinion concludes that the delay in the diagnosis deprived the patient of a chance of recovery, and led to an increased risk of deafness. The patient claims damages against the *Kantonsspital* in the amount of 3 million CHF, inter alia, for the loss of a chance of recovery.]

2.1 The dispute centres around the liability of a public hospital towards a patient for the actions of a doctor employed by the hospital. [. . .]

4.2 [. . .] The Cantonal Court (*cour cantonale*) [. . .] denied the defendant's liability in the absence of a link of natural causation between the conduct of the assistant doctor in question and the damage, namely the after-effects on the applicant. The Administrative Court based its decision on the forensic report [. . .], which stated [. . .] that it was impossible to say, in this particular case, whether prescription of antibiotics four or five hours earlier would have prevented the applicant's loss of hearing.

The loss of a chance doctrine was developed for precisely this type of situation [. . .]; in other words, the benefits at stake – for example, the patient being entirely cured – cannot be ascertained, and thus it is impossible to prove a link of natural causation between an act incurring liability and the damage [. . .]. According to the aforementioned doctrine, the compensable damage consists of the loss of a measurable chance for a person to obtain a benefit or avoid a loss. The amount of damages therefore correspond to the probability for the injured party to obtain such benefit or avoid such loss. The value of the lost opportunity in principle corresponds to the value of what the injured party might have gained (for example, the future income of the patient, were he entirely cured) multiplied by the probability of this coming to pass, calculated statistically (e.g. based on medical studies on the success of a therapeutic method according to the progression of the illness). A causal relationship must exist between the act in question and permanent loss of a chance, rather than between the act and the ultimate full damage to the legally protected right.

In practice, this method limits compensation to an amount corresponding to the degree of probability that the person who is held responsible did indeed cause the damage. [. . .]

4.3 It would appear that there is no precedent to date where the loss of a chance doctrine has been invoked before the Federal Court. [. . .]

Authors who have examined the loss of a chance doctrine are rather favorable to the idea that it be introduced into Swiss law by the courts, for instance by way of Art. 42 (2) CO [. . .].[16]

---

16 Art. 42 CO (*Determining the Loss or Damage*) provides: "(1) A person claiming damages must prove that loss or damage occurred. (2) Where the exact value of the loss or damage cannot be quantified, the court shall

4.4 It now remains to examine whether the cantonal court made its previous ruling arbitrarily when it refused to consider the applicant's claim from the standpoint of the loss of a chance doctrine.[17]

4.4.1 As regards the interpretation and implementation of cantonal legislation [. . .], arbitrariness and infringement of the law are not to be confused. [. . .] It is not within the Federal Court's competence to examine which interpretation of the applicable law the cantonal authority should have given; it must only rule on the defensibility of the manner in which cantonal law was applied or interpreted. A solution is not arbitrary solely because another is conceivable or even preferable [. . .].

4.4.2 [. . .] An act is the natural cause of a result when it is a *conditio sine qua non* thereof. In other words, a link of natural causation exists between two events when the second would not have occurred without the first; [. . .] The existence of a link of natural causation between the act incurring liability and the damage is a question of fact on which the judge must decide according to the rule of balance of probabilities and the "more probable than not test" [as opposed to requiring certainty of causation]. In such a case, the lowering of the burden of proof is justified by the fact that, due to the very nature of the matter, it is not possible to uphold a strict standard of proof, and it would not be reasonable to require that the person bearing the burden of proof establishes causation with certainty.

[In Swiss law], [d]amage is defined as an involuntary decrease in net wealth; it corresponds to the difference between the patrimony actually held by the injured party and his patrimony had the harmful event not taken place [the so-called "difference theory"]. [. . .]

4.4.3 As previously stated, the application of the loss of a chance doctrine recognises that compensation is to be calculated on the basis of the probability – whatever it may be – that the act incurring liability actually caused the injury. It follows that, in the case of delayed or inadequate care, the next of kin of a deceased patient who would have had a one in four chance of survival, had he been given the correct care, could claim compensation for 25% of the damage related to death. This would not be in accordance with the concept of natural causation as defined above by precedent (consid. 4.4.2). In this situation, considering the doctor's act as the natural cause of losing the chance of a favourable outcome, according to the rule of balance of probabilities, would hardly be acceptable when it is established that the illness would have led to the patient's death in three-quarters of the time anyway.

Certainly, a way to avoid this difficulty is simply to define the loss of a chance itself as a recoverable damage. Defining chance as an element of one's patrimony is, however, not an easy thing to do; it is not enough to state that a chance has economic value. The chance is not part of a person's actual patrimony, since it has been lost. It cannot be part of a person's hypothetical patrimony either, since it will either have been transformed into an increase in wealth, or will have disappeared for reasons unknown. Chance is by its very nature temporary, and aspires to become either something or nothing. Due to its dynamic and progressive nature, chance cannot remain a constitutive element of the patrimony.

---

estimate the value at its discretion in the light of the normal course of events and the steps taken by the injured party. [. . .]".

17 *Note by the author*: due to procedural reasons, the review by the *Tribunal fédéral* was limited to the question of whether the non-application of the loss of a chance doctrine by the lower courts was *arbitrary*.

Since the difference principle, applicable to compensation calculations in Swiss law, is based on the state of patrimony at two precise moments, it cannot economically measure a lost chance [. . .]

As a result, the introduction into Swiss law of the loss of a chance doctrine, as developed notably in French case law, is at the very least problematic. In this case, it cannot be concluded that the Administrative Court clearly violated the legal concepts of causation and damage and, in doing so, applied cantonal law in an arbitrary manner. Therefore, the appeal is refused.

2. Bundesgericht/Tribunal fédéral *(Federal Supreme Court of Justice)*, 12.12.1961, BGE 87 II 364

A. – On 15th November 1956, Miss P., born on 13th November 1937, gave birth to a baby boy. She identified G., an unmarried man born in 1930, as the father of the child. [. . .] G. admitted having entertained P. on two occasions at his house, but denied her allegations that they had had sexual intercourse. [. . .]

B. – On 28th/29th November 1957, Dr X [a lawyer] filed a paternity suit against G. in the *Amtsgericht* [local court] in the name of the mother and child, seeking an order that G. indemnify the mother and provide support for the child. [. . .] On 25th March 1958, the *Amtsgericht* granted G.'s application to have the suit dismissed as time-barred, on the basis that Dr X had lodged the proceedings after the expiry of the limitation period provided for [by law].

C. – On 4th April 1960, the mother and child brought proceedings against Dr X [the lawyer], seeking an order for payment of CHF 1189.95[18] to the first plaintiff [the mother] [. . .] and CHF 23,100[19] to the second plaintiff [the child] [. . .]. They alleged that the defendant had been at fault in delaying the institution of paternity proceedings. Although it could not be established with certainty what the outcome of any such proceedings would have been, it should (they argued) be inferred that the court would have upheld the claim. [. . .]

The defendant [. . .] argued [among other things] that it was only possible to infer that the plaintiffs had suffered loss if it were proved as a matter of certainty that they would have succeeded in the paternity suit, which was something not even alleged on their part. [. . .]

The court of appeal of Bern (second civil chamber), deciding the case at first instance, inferred that the defendant, having taken instructions from the plaintiffs, owed them a duty under Art. 398 of the Code of Obligations to execute the business entrusted to him faithfully and carefully. Given that he did not institute the claim before the expiry of the limitation period [. . .], he broke the duty of care that he owed. [. . .] Had he brought the claim in time, the plaintiffs would have had a solid prospect of success in the paternity proceedings. [. . .]

---

18 Today worth around CHF 4,900.
19 Today worth around CHF 95,500.

Considerations

The *Bundesgericht* thus reasoned:

1. The defendant [. . .] was [. . .] under a duty to take care to observe the time limit [. . .] expiring on 15th November 1957. [It was] his obvious duty to manage matters in such a way that there could be no argument over whether proceedings had been brought in time; in other words, [to start proceedings] within the limitation period, which ran until 15 November 1957 (see STAUDINGER, 11th ed., n° 201 der Vorbemerkungen vor § 611 BGB [Preliminary remarks to § 611 BGB of the German Civil Code], p. 1152, stating, on the basis of the German case-law, that in the event of doubt a lawyer must "choose the safer and more certain course of action"). [. . .] All things considered, the defendant cannot escape the allegation that his delay in lodging his claim has caused the dismissal of the paternity proceedings [. . .].

2. The plaintiffs claim as damages the capitalised value of the sums which G. would have been adjudged to pay them had they won their paternity claim against him. The defendant is liable for this sum only on the assumption that the plaintiffs would have succeeded in their paternity suit if proceedings had been brought in time.

Where proceedings fail because of a missed time-bar, it is impossible to establish with absolute certainty what the result would have been if the limitation period had been observed. On the contrary, in such a case one can only speculate. This holds both for the facts, which would have been established in the proceedings in question, and also for the legal outcome to which those facts would have given rise. Nevertheless, this does not prevent evidence being given to the effect that the then plaintiff would have succeeded if the proceedings had been brought in time; and that therefore the loss occasioned by failure to observe the time bar corresponds to the sum which he would have been entitled to had he succeeded in the original proceedings. If, in the process of the action for damages, it emerges that the conditions necessary for a favourable judgment in the original proceedings were fulfilled, the inference that the claim would have succeeded may be so irresistible that it may be regarded as having been proved. Investigating the prospects of success in earlier proceedings in this way is in accordance with both French and German authority (see MAZEAUD & TUNC, *Traité théorique et pratique de la responsabilité civile délictuelle et contractuelle* [French textbook on the theory and practice of liability in contract and delict] Vol. 1, 5th ed. 1957, n° 219, p. 280: " . . . courts examine what the lawsuit was fundamentally worth . . . "; and also STAUDINGER, above, p. 1153 n° 202 [. . .]). [. . .]

In essence, the court of appeal of Bern considered, on the basis of an entirely permissible appreciation of the evidence, what the probable result of the plaintiffs' paternity suit against G. would have been if the defendant had instituted proceedings in time. [. . .] The fact that the plaintiffs in the damages proceedings admitted (entirely correctly) that the result in the paternity suit could not be established with complete certainty does not count against them when weighed against the defendant's case; to prove their loss in their damages claim, it must (as has been said) be enough if it can be inferred that they would in all probability have succeeded in the paternity suit. [. . .]

On this basis, the *Bundesgericht* decides: The appeal is dismissed and the judgment of the court of appeal of Bern [. . .] of 14th June 1961 is affirmed.

VIII. Austria

1. Allgemeines bürgerliches Gesetzbuch, ABGB (*General Civil Code*)

b) **Mehrere Teilnehmer.** [. . .] § 1302. [. . .] [W]enn die Beschädigung in einem Versehen gegründet ist, und die Anteile sich bestimmen lassen, [verantwortet] jeder nur den durch sein Versehen verursachten Schaden. [W]enn aber [. . .] die Anteile der Einzelnen an der Beschädigung sich nicht bestimmen lassen; so haften alle für einen und einer für alle; doch bleibt demjenigen, welcher den Schaden ersetzt hat, der Rückersatz gegen die übrigen vorbehalten.

§ 1304. Wenn bei einer Beschädigung zugleich ein Verschulden von Seite des Beschädigten eintritt; so trägt er mit dem Beschädiger den Schaden verhältnismäßig; und, wenn sich das Verhältnis nicht bestimmen läßt, zu gleichen Teilen.

Translation

b) Multiple participants. [. . .] § 1302. [. . .] [I]f the damage was caused negligently and the contributions to it can be determined, each participant is liable only for the part of the damage caused through his or her negligence. However, if [. . .] the contributions of each to the damage cannot be ascertained, all are liable for one, and one for all; the persons having compensated the damage will nevertheless have a right of recourse against the others.

§ 1304. If, in a case of damage, there is also fault on the part of the person harmed, he or she has to bear the loss proportionally with the injurer, and, if the proportion cannot be determined, in equal shares.

2. Oberster Gerichtshof, OGH, 4. Zivilsenat (*Supreme Court, 4th Civil Senate*), 07.11.1995, 4 Ob 554/95 (RIS), JBl. 1996, 181

Reasoning

The plaintiff was born on 26th February 1988 in the [. . .] regional hospital. At the time of his birth he showed signs of perinatal asphyxia, resulting in seriously arrested psychomental motor development. He will be blind for life.

There were two possible causes of the plaintiff's asphyxia: either serious maternal placental inadequacy, or a double constriction of the umbilical cord which manifested itself at birth. Asphyxia in the plaintiff as a consequence of placental inadequacy could have been prevented if the mother, at the time when she went into labour, had been treated as an in-patient at the [. . .] provincial hospital. As it was, she was admitted as an in-patient on 14th February 1988, but was discharged on 24th February 1988; and this was despite the fact that the placental insufficiency was detectable via the results of [. . .] tests carried out on her as an in-patient; [. . .]

The plaintiff is claiming [damages] from the defendant federal state, in its capacity as operator of the hospital [. . .].

The trial court [. . .] found [. . .] (*inter alia*) as follows:

[. . .] The constriction of the funiculus umbilicalis could not have been detected before birth [. . .]. If it had been discovered any earlier, this would have been a matter of pure chance. It was never established in the course of the proceedings whether the effective cause of the infant's serious asphyxia had been the mother's grave placental inadequacy, or the double constriction in the umbilical cord [. . .].

Legal considerations

[. . .] The instant case has [. . .] a particular distinguishing feature. As regards the cause of the plaintiff's birth defect, there were two possible causes: the insufficiency of the maternal placenta, which could with proper treatment have been prevented from occasioning the plaintiff's perinatal injury and thus could not be regarded as anything other than a matter of clinical negligence, but also the umbilical constriction. It was impossible to establish which of these two factors had actually caused the perinatal injury. As F. Bydlinski has observed, circumstances such as these frequently arise in connection with "medical malpractice", and are associated not only with the peculiar difficulty of establishing reliable causal relationships with previous events affecting the individual living being, but also with the problems of appraising medical practice in the professional context (JBl 1992, 352). In cases like this, involving competing possible causes (see Koziol-Welser, 10 I 369) and raising as they do a contest between, on the one hand, the defendant's negligent behaviour and, on the other, the very real misfortune the injured party [. . .] has to live with, he has repeatedly and convincingly argued that it is appropriate to apply by way of analogy the basic principle deriving from § 1302 ABGB, under which a mere possibility of causation may be accepted as relevant for attribution purposes, combined with the principle of division of liability laid down in § 1304 ABGB (see Franz Bydlinski in JBl 1959, 1 [esp. 8 ff, 13]; Bydlinski, *Probleme der Schadensverursachung* [1964] 87; also Beitzke-FS [1979], 6 [30 ff.] and Frotz-FS [1993], 3 ff. and, following his lead, Koziol, *Haftpflichtrecht* 2 I 66 ff; also, with further references, and contrasting the objections that have been raised to the argument, Welsers, ZfRV 1968, 42 ff).

Furthermore, the Oberster Gerichtshof has very recently followed this theory of F. Bydlinski's, and has provided extensive arguments for doing so. It has stated that, where fault on the defendant's part coexists with factors within the victim's sphere (i.e. mere bad luck and similar events falling within his own sphere), then the damage is to be shared under § 1304 ABGB. In the absence of any clear indication, the shares should be even, that is 50:50 (EvBl 1994/13). [. . .]

The Senate charged with deciding this case accepts [. . .] the theory put forward by F. Bydlinski and Koziol, since it is the only solution to the problem which meets the needs of justice. Were their proposal not accepted, then, in any situation where there is a conflict between proved negligence and a mere accident, all that would be available is a choice between two extreme solutions, neither of which is either sensible or reasonable. One would have to decide either that the plaintiff's claim failed entirely where there was no clear indication which of the two events had in fact caused the damage, or alternatively that the defendant had to pay full compensation to the claimant without his behaviour having been shown to be the cause at all. Both of these solutions would be entirely inconsistent with the ruling principles of Austrian damages law [. . .].

IX. Principles of European Tort Law

1. PETL

Art. 2:101. Recoverable damage. Damage requires material or immaterial harm to a legally protected interest.

Art. 2:102. Protected interests. (1) The scope of protection of an interest depends on its nature; the higher its value, the precision of its definition and its obviousness, the more extensive is its protection.
(2) Life, bodily or mental integrity, human dignity and liberty enjoy the most extensive protection. [. . .]

Art. 3:101. Conditio sine qua non. An activity or conduct (hereafter: activity) is a cause of the victim's damage if, in the absence of the activity, the damage would not have occurred.

Art. 3:103. Alternative causes. (1) In case of multiple activities, where each of them alone would have been sufficient to cause the damage, but it remains uncertain which one in fact caused it, each activity is regarded as a cause to the extent corresponding to the likelihood that it may have caused the victim's damage. [. . .]

Art. 3:106. Uncertain causes within the victim's sphere. The victim has to bear his loss to the extent corresponding to the likelihood that it may have been caused by an activity, occurrence or other circumstances within his own sphere.

2. BÉNÉDICT WINIGER/HELMUT KOZIOL/BERNHARD KOCH/REINHARD ZIMMERMANN (eds.), *Digest of European Tort Law, Vol. I: Essential Cases on Natural Causation*, 2007, nos. 10/28/1 ff. (by THOMAS KADNER GRAZIANO)

Case 1 ("medical malpractice")

Facts

1. A teenage boy falls from a tree in his school playground and sustains an acute traumatic fracture of his left femoral epiphysis. He is taken to hospital but his injuries are not correctly diagnosed and not adequately treated for several days. Afterwards, the boy is found to be suffering from a permanent disability (a vascular necrosis) in his hip joint, resulting from the insufficiency of the blood supply to the epiphysis. The defendant health authority admits negligence but claims that, at the time the plaintiff was taken to hospital, the blood supply had been so interrupted that a vascular necrosis was inevitable.

2. Evidence shows that there has been a 25% chance that a vascular necrosis would not have developed if the plaintiff had been treated without delay.

Solution

a. First step: application of Art. 3:101 PETL

3. The key issue is the question if the activity, conduct or omission of the defendant (*i.e.* the wrong diagnosis and the delay in the treatment) has caused the victim's

damage (*i.e.* the boy's permanent disability). Natural causation in the sense of Art. 3:101 PETL is established if, in case of a correct diagnosis and treatment, the damage would not have occurred.

4 In the present case, as in many other medical malpractice cases, it remains uncertain if the victim's damage would have occurred if the doctor had not committed the fault but if he had correctly diagnosed the injury. The causal link between the negligent activity and the damage to the protected interest (here: the plaintiff's bodily integrity) is not established and the *condition sine qua non–* or "but for"–test of Art. 3:101 PETL is not met.

5 The victim has, however, lost a 25% chance that the injury would not have occurred. Had the defendant acted as required, this chance would not have been lost. As far as the causal link between the activity and the *loss of a chance* is concerned, the *conditio sine qua non*-test of Art. 3:101 PETL is met.

6 It may be argued that in cases of loss of a chance the damage is established once the chance is lost.

7 The Principles have, however, adopted another approach to deal with the issue of lost chances. Under the Principles "[d]amage requires material or immaterial harm to a legally protected interest", Art. 2:101 PETL. The protected interests include life, bodily or mental integrity, human dignity, liberty, property rights and – to a more limited extent – pure economic interests (Art. 2:102 PETL). As far as causation is concerned, the starting point under the Principles is Art. 3:101 PETL stating that the causal link needs to exist, in principle, *not* between an activity (or omission) and the *chance* of a loss or damage but between an activity and a *damage* to an interest that enjoys legal protection under the Principles. Once the causal link between the tortfeasor's activity and the damage to a legally protected interest is established (and once all the other criteria for liability are met), the damage will be, in principle, compensated for entirely.

8 In applying Art. 3:101 PETL the next crucial question is which degree of probability is required to meet the Principles' *conditio sine qua non*-test.

9 The Principles do not specify which degree of probability is required in order to meet the *conditio sine qua non*-test, this issue being, in principle, one of civil procedure. Given that the lowest percentage of probability required in the European tort law systems is 51%, it is suggested that a probability below this degree is not sufficient under the Principles either. In the present case, the probability of causation was far below this line.

10 The next question then is if, in order to take the hurdle of natural causation, in some specific situations the requirement of proving causation may be lowered or the burden of proof may be entirely reversed. In medical malpractice cases some national laws reverse the burden of proof once it is established that the doctor has acted with (gross) negligence and once it is shown that his negligence may have caused the victim's injury.

11 The Principles provide, under certain conditions, for a reversal of the burden of proof as far as the proof of the defendant's fault is concerned (Arts. 4:201 and 4:202 PETL) and they allow, under certain circumstances, that the extent of damage is estimated (Art. 2:105, 2nd sentence PETL), but they do *not* expressly reverse the burden of proof for natural causation.

b. Second step: application of Arts. 3:103(1) and 3:106 PETL

12 The situation of alternative causes with (at least) one of the potential causes lying within the victim's sphere is addressed by Arts. 3:103 (1) and 3:106 PETL.

13 Under Art. 3:103 (1) PETL, in a situation where each of several multiple activities alone would have been sufficient to cause the damage (alternative causes), but where "it remains uncertain which one in fact caused it, each activity is regarded as a cause to the extent corresponding to the likelihood that it may have caused the victim's damage".

14 According to Art. 3:106 PETL, "[t]he victim has to bear his loss to the extent corresponding to the likelihood that it may have been caused by an activity, occurrence or other circumstances within his own sphere." Circumstances in his own sphere may be, for example, a natural event or a disease unrelated to activities of third parties.

15 The boy's permanent disability in his hip joint may have been caused by his falling from the tree exclusively, or it may be the result of the boy's accident and the subsequent medical malpractice. In the first case the boy's accident alone would be the *condition sine qua non* of his injury; in the second case both the boy's accident as well as the following medical fault would be *conditiones sine quibus non*. Each incident, *i.e.* the first accident alone, or the combination of the boy's first accident and the subsequent medical malpractice have been sufficient to cause the injury, and it remains uncertain which one in fact caused it.

16 In such circumstances, according to Arts. 3:103 (1) and 3:106 PETL, the activity of the third party (the negligent treatment) is regarded as a cause of the damage to the extent corresponding to the likelihood that it may have caused the victim's damage. Evidence shows that there was a 25% chance that a vascular necrosis would not have developed if the claimant had been treated without delay. The likelihood that the boy's injury was caused by circumstances within his own sphere *exclusively* (his accidental falling from the tree or physical predispositions of his own) is 75%.

17 Arts. 3:103 and 3:106 PETL lead to a distribution of the loss between the victim and the defendant according to the probabilities of causation: the boy has to bear 75% of the damage whereas 25% will have to be paid by the defendant health authority, provided that the other conditions for liability are met. The case shows that the two articles, applied together, may reduce the threshold for causation in loss of a chance cases to probabilities far below the line of 51%.

Comments

18 [...] [Another] way to deal with the present case would be to shift the burden of proof of causation in medical malpractice cases. If this approach is compared to the one used in Arts. 3:103 and 3:106 PETL, two differences may be noted:

19 First, in the national laws the burden of proof is usually shifted only in cases of particularly serious professional faults, whereas Arts. 3:103 and 3:106 PETL distribute the loss according to the criteria of potential causation independent of the seriousness of the fault committed. Second, whereas the burden of proof approach leads to a shift of the entire loss and hereby follows the "all-or-nothing" approach, Arts. 3:103 and 3:106 PETL distribute losses according to probabilities and hereby avoids the often harsh solution to either compensate for the entire loss or not to compensate at all.

Case 2 ("lawyer's negligence")

Facts

20 A woman works as a secretary to the sales manager of a retail chain. She is notified that she is going to be transferred to another section, affecting her working hours and working conditions. She claims that the transferral is a breach of her contract of employment and contacts a lawyer with the purpose of bringing a claim against her employer. Her lawyer negligently fails to file her claim with the employment tribunal within the required time period. As a result, the action brought on her behalf is dismissed.

21 She sues the lawyer seeking compensation for her financial loss, which consists of the likely award of damages for violating the contract of employment and the subsequent unemployment benefits she would have been entitled to, had the action been successful. Her lawyer argues that it is more probable than not that she would have lost her claim anyway, even if the action had been brought in time.

Solution

22 First of all the woman may want to bring a claim for compensation against her attorney on a contractual basis. As far as non-contractual liability is concerned, given the fact that the woman working as a secretary to the sales manager claims compensation for a pure financial or economic loss, liability under the Principles would be based on Arts. 1:101 (1), (2) a) [basis norm], Art. 2:101, 2:102 (1), (4) [protection against pure economic loss], Arts. 4:101 ff. PETL [fault-based liability].

23 The claimant will not be able to prove the existence of a causal link between the faulty conduct (her attorney's failing to lodge her claim with the labour court within due time) and the damage, as required by Art. 3:101 PETL.

24 According to Arts. 3:103 (1) and 3:106 PETL, the attorney's fault is regarded as a cause to the extent corresponding to the likelihood that it may have caused the woman's damage, and "the victim has to bear his loss to the extent corresponding to the likelihood that it may have been caused . . . by circumstances within [her] own sphere".

25 In the present case the amount of compensation paid by the secretary's employer had her claim been successful as well as the likelihood of success of the claim need to be established. According to Arts. 3:103 (1) and 3:106 PETL, she would then have to bear her loss to the extent corresponding to the likelihood of failure of her claim. The other part of the damage would be considered having been caused by the lawyer who failed to lodge her claim with the labour court within due time.

X. Draft Common Frame of Reference

I. DCFR

> **Art. VI-2:101.** (1) Loss, whether economic or non-economic, or injury is legally relevant damage if: [. . .] (c) the loss or injury results from a violation of an interest worthy of legal protection.

(2) In any case covered only by sub-paragraph [. . .] (c) of paragraph (1) loss or injury constitutes legally relevant damage only if it would be fair and reasonable for there to be a right to reparation [. . .].
(3) In considering whether it would be fair and reasonable for there to be a right to reparation [. . .] regard is to be had to the ground of accountability, to the nature and proximity of the damage or impending damage, to the reasonable expectations of the person who suffers or would suffer the damage, and to considerations of public policy. [. . .]

2. CHRISTIAN VON BAR/ERIC CLIVE (eds.), *Principles, Definitions and Model Rules of European Private Law – Draft Common Frame of Reference (DCFR), Full Edition*, Vol. 4, 2009

Art. VI – 2:201 Note XII, p. 3192: The issue of 'loss of a chance' shall be dealt with in the context of art VI – 2:101 (Meaning of legally relevant damage).

Art. VI – 2:201 Comment D, p. 3144: Art. VI – 2:101(1)(c) "consciously makes space for the further development of the law on non-contractual liability by judges. It also avoids setting down in legislated form certain developments and concepts which are presently still in a state of flux. An example of the latter is liability for the loss of a chance".

Art. VI – 2:201 Comment A, Loss of a chance, p. 3195: "This area is [. . .] left to the judiciary for future developments. [. . .] However, the general rule on legally relevant damage does leave room for characterizing the loss of a chance as an *independent form of damages* for the purposes of the law of non-contractual liability".

Art. VI – 4:101 Comment A, Special rules, p. 3570: "The question of liability for loss of a chance would be *a question concerning legally relevant damage*, not causation; of course the differences of opinion on this issue confirm that these two elements of liability (legally relevant damage and causation) partially intersect".

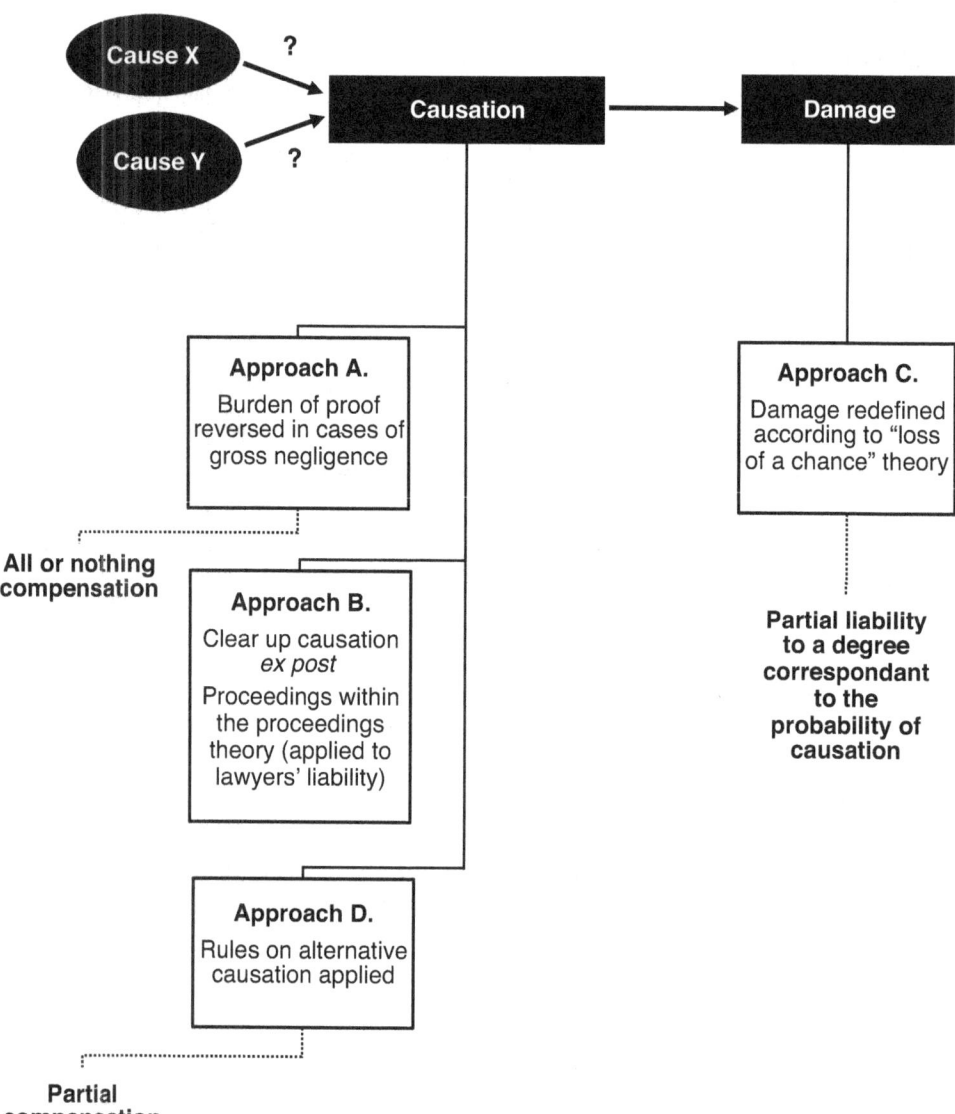

Figure 10.1 Overview: 4 ways of solving the issue of uncertainty of causation

Liability in cases of uncertain causation | 313

Table 10.1

Overview: 5 ways of dealing with uncertainty of causation

A.	B.	C.	D.	E.
Reversal of the burden of proof of causation in case of gross negligence	Clearing up causation ex post (in lawyers' liability scenarios)	Redefining damage and applying the principles on "loss of a chance"	Applying the rules on alternative causation (by way of analogy)	Applying the traditional tests on causation
In case of gross negligence, the burden of proof is reversed → the principle of "*all or nothing*" is applied (full compensation or no compensation). **Applied** e.g. in • *German law* in cases of medical malpractice; rejected for cases of lawyer's liability.	For lawyers' liability scenarios it may be possible to establish causation *ex post* in the liability claim ("proceedings within the proceedings" approach). **Applied** in • *German law*, • *Swiss law*, • *French law*, • many other jurisdictions in cases in which there is no substantial doubt about the outcome of the previous proceedings. **Rejected** in the English case *Kitchen v. Royal Air Force Association*.	All conditions of liability must be established except that of causation between the defendant's act and the ultimate damage to the protected good. → The *loss of a measurable chance* to obtain a benefit or avoid the damage may then itself be *considered legally relevant damage*. • In this case, causation needs to be established between the act attributable to the defendant and the loss of a chance. • The value of the lost chance corresponds to the value of the benefit that the injured party might have gained, or the loss he or she might have avoided, multiplied with the probability of this outcome, calculated statistically. • As a consequence → *pro rata* compensation is due for an amount corresponding to the degree of the chance lost. **Applied** in: • French law, • Belgian law, • English law (e.g. in cases of lawyers' liability; **rejected** in medical malpractice cases); • *21 States in the USA* in medical malpractice cases. **Rejected** in • *German law*, • *English law* (for medical malpractice), • *10 states in the USA* for medical malpractice, and • by the High Court of Australia. Issue not yet ultimately decided in *Swiss law*.	The rules on alternative causation are applied by way of analogy. As a consequence → *partial compensation* is due corresponding to the probability of causation. **Applied** in • *Austrian law* (applied by the 4th Senate of the Supreme Court of Justice; solution not applied by other Senates); • Principles of European Tort Law, Arts. 3:101, 3:106.	The traditional tests on causation are applied (i.e. certainty is required or a "more probable than not" test is applied) → the principle of "*all or nothing*" applies, and the claim rejected.

Table 10.2

	Potential outcome under approach A. (the German approach found in § 630h (5) BGB)		
	Degree of fault	**Probability of causation**	**Outcome**
OLG Brandenburg case	gross negligence	10%	Liability 100%
OLG Hamm case	(medium) negligence	90%	No liability

Bibliography

LAURENT BIERI/PIERRE MARTY, The Discontinuous Nature of the Loss of Chance System, *JETL* 2011, 23; FRANZ BYDLINSKI, Aktuelle Streitfragen um die alternative Kausalität, in: Otto Sandrock (ed.), *Festschrift für Günther Beitzke zum 70. Geburtstag am 26. April 1979*, Berlin/New York: De Gruyter, 1979, pp. 3 ff.; RUI CARDONA FERREIRA, The Loss of Chance in Civil Law Countries: A Comparative and Critical Analysis, *MJ* 2013, 56–74; BRIAN CASACELI, Losing a Chance to Survive: An Examination of the Loss of Chance Doctrine within the Context of a Wrongful Death Action, *JHBL* 2014, 521–552; QUINTEN DE RAEDT, Loss of a Chance in Medical Malpractice: A Double Application, *JETL* 2013, 314; ISABELLE DURANT, Une brève histoire de la théorie de la perte d'une chance en droit belge, *HAVE/REAS* 2008, 72; RICHARD A. EPSTEIN, *Torts*, New York: Aspen Publishers, 1999, Chapter 10; MICHAEL FAURE/VÉRONIQUE BRUGGEMAN, Causal Uncertainty and Proportional Liability, in: Lubos Tichy(ed.), *Causation in Law*, Prague: Univerzita Karlova v Praze, 2007, pp. 105 ff.; HOLGER FLEISCHER, Schadensersatz für verlorene Chancen im Vertrags- und Deliktsrecht, *JZ* 1999, 766; SARAH FULHAM-MCQUILLAN, Judicial Belief in Statistics as Fact: Loss of Chance in Ireland and England, *PN* 2014, 9–31; ISRAEL GILEAD/MICHAEL D. GREEN/BERNARD A. KOCH (eds.), *Proportional Liability: Analytical and Comparative Perspectives*, Vienna: Springer, 2013; ALAIN HIRSCH, Perte de chance et causalité, in: Christine Chappuis/Bénédict Winiger (eds.), *Les causes du dommage*, Genève/Zurich/Bâle: Schulthess, 2007, pp. 279 ff.; NILS JANSEN, The Idea of a Lost Chance, *OJLS* 1999, 271; MICHAEL A. JONES, Proving Causation – beyond the "but for" Test, *PN* 2006, 251–269; THOMAS KADNER GRAZIANO, Loss of a Chance in European Private Law: "All or Nothing" or Partial Liability in Cases of Uncertain Causation, *ERPL* 2008, 1009; THOMAS KADNER GRAZIANO, La 'perte d'une chance' en droit privé européen: 'tout ou rien' ou réparation partielle du dommage en cas de causalité incertaine, in: Christine Chappuis/Bénédict Winiger (eds.), *Les causes du dommage*, Genève/Zurich/Bâle: Schulthess 2007, pp. 217 ff.; THOMAS KADNER GRAZIANO, Alles oder nichts' oder anteilige Haftung bei Verursachungszweifeln – Zur Haftung für perte d'une chance und eine Alternative, *ZEuP* 2011, 171; THOMAS KADNER GRAZIANO, Ersatz für 'entgangene Chancen' im europäischen und im schweizerischen Recht, *HAVE/REAS* 2008, 61; LARA KHOURY, Causation and Risk in the Highest Courts of Canada, England and France, *L.Q.R.* 2008, 103; LARA KHOURY, *Uncertain Causation in Medical Liability*, Oxford: Hart, 2006; HELMUT KOZIOL, Schadensersatz für den Verlust einer Chance?, in: Gerhard Hohloch/Rainer Frank/Peter Schlechtriem (eds.), *Festschrift für Hans Stoll zum 75. Geburtstag*, Tübingen: Mohr Siebeck 2001, pp. 233 ff.; HARDY LANDOLT, Perte d'une chance – verlorene oder vertane Chance?, *HAVE/REAS* 2008, 68; GERALD MÄSCH, *Chance und Schaden*, Tübingen: Mohr Siebeck, 2004; GERALD MÄSCH, Case Comment, Gregg v. Scott – Much ado about nothing?, *ZEuP* 2006, 656; GERALD MÄSCH, Anmerkung zu BGH 16.6.2005, *JZ* 2006, 198; JONATHAN MORGAN, A Chance Missed to Recognize Loss-of-a-Chance in Negligence, *LMCLQ* 2005, 281; CHRISTOPH MÜLLER, La perte d'une chance n'a pas perdu sa chance en droit Suisse, *HAVE/REAS* 2008, 55; CHRISTOPH MÜLLER, *La perte d'une chance*, Berne: Stämpfli, 2002; CHRISTOPH MÜLLER, La perte d'une chance, in: Bénédict Foex/Franz Werro (eds.), *La réforme du droit de la responsabilité civile*, Zürich: Schulthess, 2004, pp. 143 ff.; ALASTAIR MULLIS/DONAL NOLAN, Case Note. Gregg v. Scott, *All ER Annual Review* 2005, 479; EDWIN PEEL, Case Comment, Loss of a Chance in Medical Negligence, *L.Q.R.* 2005, 364–370; CHRISTOPHE QUÉZEL-AMBRUNAZ, *Essai sur la causalité en droit de la responsabilité civile*, Paris: Dalloz, 2010; HELEN REECE, Losses of Chances in the Law, *MLR* 1996, 188; GRAHAM REID, Case Comment, Gregg v. Scott and Lost Chances, *PN* 2005, 78; CHRISTIAN SCHÖBI, Art. 42 Abs. 2 OR: Substanziieren vs. Schätzen – eine Annäherung an die Rechtsfigur der "perte d'une chance"?, in: Anna Böhme/Fabian Gähwiler/Fabiana Theus Simoni/Ivo Zuberbühler (eds.), *Ohne jegliche Haftung – Festschrift für Willi Fischer zum 65. Geburtstag*, Zürich: Schulthess, 2016, pp. 447–458; JAAP SPIER (ed.), *Unification of Tort Law: Causation*, The Hague/London/Boston: Kluwer Law International, 2000; JANE STAPLETON, The Gist of Negligence, Part II, *L.Q.R.* 1988, 389; JANE STAPLETON, Cause in Fact and the Scope of Liability for Consequences, *L.Q.R.* 2003, 388; JANE STAPLETON, Loss of the Chance of Cure from Cancer, *MLR* 2005, 996; HANS STOLL, Schadensersatz für verlorene Heilungschancen vor englischen Gerichten in rechtsvergleichender Sicht, in: Erwin

Deutsch/Ernst Klingmüller/Hans Josef Kullman (eds.), *Festschrift für Erich Steffen zum 65. Geburtstag am 28. Mai 1995 – Der Schadensersatz und seine Deckung*, Berlin/New York: De Gruyter 1995, pp. 465 ff.; Hans Stoll, Haftungsverlagerung durch beweisrechtliche Mittel, *AcP* 1976, 146; Luc Thévenoz, La perte d'une chance et sa réparation, in: Christine Chappuis/Guy Chappuis/Pierre Tercier/Luc Thévenoz/Franz Werro (eds.), *Quelques questions fondamentales du droit de la responsabilité civile: actualités et perspectives*, Berne: Stämpfli, 2002, pp. 237 ff.; Cees van Dam, *European Tort Law*, 2nd ed., Oxford: OUP, 2002, pp. 337–341; Christian von Bar, *Gemeineuropäisches Deliktsrecht, Zweiter Band*, München: C. H. Beck, 1999, pp. 433–503; Christian von Bar, *The Common European Law of Torts, Volume Two*, Oxford: OUP, 2000, pp. 433–498; Tony Weir, Loss of a Chance–Compensable in Tort? The Common Law, in: Olivier Guillod (ed.), *Neuere Entwicklungen im Haftpflichtrecht*, Zürich: Schulthess, 1991, pp. 111 ff.; Pierre Widmer, Chance verpasst?, *HAVE/REAS* 2008, 55; Bénédict Winiger/Helmut Koziol/Bernhard Koch/Reinhard Zimmermann (eds.), *Digest of European Tort Law, Volume 1: Essential Cases on Natural Causation*, Wien/New York: Springer, 2007, no. 10/1–29; Bénédict Winiger/Helmut Koziol/Bernhard Koch/Reinhard Zimmermann (eds.), *Digest of European Tort Law, Volume 2: Essential Cases on Damage*, Berlin/Boston: De Gruyter, 2010, no. 26/1–30.

Chapter 11

Damage suffered by secondary victims

The case of psychiatric injury, "nervous shock", or "post-traumatic stress disorder (PTSD)" following the loss or severe injury of a loved one

> "[T]he nature of ricochet damage is certainly one of the most delicate and polemical questions of the law of liability, as it is envisaged by some as the projection onto an indirect victim of damage suffered by an initial victim, while for others it is, on the contrary, entirely separate damage."[1]

Scenario

Two sisters, aged 19 and 17, and their 21-year-old brother live with their parents, Mr and Mrs Miller, in a small town. The siblings often spend their Saturday evenings in a nightclub in a nearby city. One Saturday night, coming back from the club in their parents' car, they approach a crossroads where they have priority.

From another direction, a young man who has recently received his driver's licence is approaching the crossroads in his Volkswagen Golf GTI. He is slightly drunk. From his car, the young man cannot see if anyone else is approaching from another direction. He deliberately takes a risk and tries to pass the crossroads at 100 km/h, even though he does not have priority. In the middle of the crossroads, his car crashes into the car belonging to the Miller family. The young Mr Miller is killed immediately. His two sisters die three hours later in hospital. The driver of the VW Golf survives the accident. The siblings' parents are informed at 4:00 a.m. by the police that their son has lost his life. At 7:00 a.m., they receive a call from the hospital informing them that the two sisters have also died.

As a result of the accident, Mr and Mrs Miller's lives turn into a nightmare (a national magazine publishes an article about their case entitled: "Our whole life was destroyed"[2]). Since the day of the accident, Mr Miller has needed ongoing medical treatment. He is unable to concentrate, loses his job, and spends several months of the year in hospital. Mrs Miller copes with her problems on her own, trying everything to keep the memory of their children alive.

The young driver who caused the accident is sentenced to two years and three months imprisonment.[3]

---

[1] Advocate General NILS WAHL, Case C-350/14 (*Florin Lazar* c. *Allianz SpA*), opinion of 10.09.2015, n° 35; see also Advocate General MARCO DARMON, Case C-220/88 (*Dumez France* c. *Tracoba*), opinion of 23.10.1989, nos. 23 et 24.
[2] See the German weekly magazine *STERN* 34/1995 ("Unser ganzes Leben wurde zerstört"), by W. METZNER.
[3] Based on the *German* case: OLG Nürnberg (*Nürnberg Appellate Court*), 01.08.1995, *r+s* 1995, 384.

Questions

1) The driver of the Golf GTI who caused the accident would be liable for the damage done to the *primary victims* either under a strict liability regime or under a fault-based system, depending on the jurisdiction and the applicable law.[4] In the present scenario, the primary victims involved in the accident (i.e. the two sisters and their brother) have lost their lives. In the case of a severe accident, damage might also be suffered by certain *secondary victims*. What kinds of damage might Mr and Mrs Miller want compensation for? Consider this issue without consulting the materials.

2) The Millers may wish to claim compensation for, inter alia, psychiatric injury or, in other terms, for "nervous shock" or post-traumatic stress disorder (PTSD), suffered following the tragic accident. What are the conditions for such a claim under
   a) *English* law?
   b) the jurisdictions of *California* and *Florida*?
   c) the *Australian* Civil Liability Act?

   Describe the development that took place in the *USA* with respect to the criteria that are used to limit this liability.

   Would Mr and Mrs Miller's claim succeed in these jurisdictions?

3) What are the conditions of a claim for compensation of damage resulting from nervous shock or PTSD in the jurisdictions of
   a) *France*?
   b) *Germany*?
   c) *Switzerland*?

4) Until 1995, it was well-established case law in *Austria* that secondary victims could not claim damages for post-traumatic stress disorder following the loss or severe injury of a loved one. On which arguments was this position based? What did the Austrian Supreme Court's decision of 16th June 1994 change in this regard, and what reasons did the court give for this change?

5) What common conditions are employed by the jurisdictions represented in the materials to determine, and limit, liability in nervous shock cases?

   It is often assumed that damages are usually awarded more generously in the USA than in Europe. What particular features of the US jurisdictions in the materials may suggest that this is not the case?

6) What are the arguments for and against the different solutions regarding damages for nervous shock? How would you evaluate these arguments, and which criteria would you recommend when it comes to dealing with this issue?

7) In many decisions reproduced in the materials, the courts use the comparative methodology alongside the traditional methods of interpretation. For what purposes is the comparative method used in these decisions, and which benefits do the courts derive when using comparative law in their reasoning? Does the use of comparative law by the courts further the harmonisation of the law across borders?[5]

---

4 See above, Chapter 9.
5 See also above, Part A, Chapter 3, pp. 19 ff., or alternatively: T. KADNER GRAZIANO, Is It Legitimate and Beneficial for Judges to Compare? in: D. Fairgrieve/M. Andenas (eds.), *Courts and Comparative Law*, Oxford: OUP, 2015, pp. 25–53 (reprinted and extended version of an article previously published in *ERPL* 2013, 687–716).

Table of contents

I. **England and Wales**
   House of Lords, *McLoughlin* v. *O'Brian*, 06.05.1982, [1982] UKHL 3, [1982] 2 All ER 298, [1983] 1 AC 410 .... p. 320

II. **USA**
   1. Supreme Court of California, *Dillon* v. *Legg*, 21.06.1968, 441 P. 2nd 912 .... p. 323
   2. Supreme Court of Florida, *Champion* v. *Gray*, 07.03.1985, 478 So. 2nd 17 .... p. 327
   3. Restatement of the Law – Torts (3rd): Liability for Physical and Emotional Harm, 2013, § 48 and Reporters' Note, Comment
      a. Scope and history .... p. 329

III. **Australia**
   Civil Liability Act, Sect. 33 .... p. 330

IV. **France**
   Cour de cassation, 2^{e} civ. (*Court of Cassation, 2nd civil chamber*), 17.05.1973 (*De Allende et Compagnie l'Union et le Phenix Espagnol c. dame Doussinault*), Gaz. Pal. 1974, 71 .... p. 330

V. **Germany**
   1. Bürgerliches Gesetzbuch, BGB (*Civil Code*), §§ 253, 823 (1) .... p. 331
   2. Bundesgerichtshof, BGH (*Federal Supreme Court of Justice*), 11.05.1971, BGHZ 56, 163 .... p. 332

VI. **Switzerland**
   1. Code des obligations/Obligationenrecht (*Code of Obligations*), Arts. 41 (1), 47 .... p. 333
   2. Tribunal fédéral/Bundesgericht (*Federal Supreme Court of Justice*), 11.03.1986 (*G. c. Confédération Suisse*), ATF 112 II 118 .... p. 334

VII. **Austria**
   1. Allgemeines bürgerliches Gesetzbuch, ABGB (*General Civil Code*), §§ 1295 (1), 1325 .... p. 336
   2. Oberster Gerichtshof, OGH (*Supreme Court of Justice*), 16.06.1994, 2 Ob 45/93, ZVR 1995, 116 .... p. 337

VIII. **Sweden**
   Skadeståndslagen (*Tort Liability Act*), Ch. 5, § 2 nos. 1–3 .... p. 338

Materials[6]

I. England and Wales

House of Lords, McLoughlin v. O'Brian, 06.05.1982, UKHL [1982] UKHL 3, [1982] 2 All ER 298, [1983] 1 AC 410

LORD WILBERFORCE: My Lords, this appeal arises from a very serious and tragic road accident which occurred on 19th October 1973 near Withersfield, Suffolk. The appellant's husband, Thomas McLoughlin, and three of her children, George, aged 17, Kathleen, aged 7 and Gillian, nearly 3, were in a Ford motor car: George was driving. A fourth child, Michael, then aged 11, was a passenger in a following motor car driven by Mr. Pilgrim: this car did not become involved in the accident. The Ford car was in collision with a lorry driven by the first respondent and owned by the second respondent. [. . .]. It is admitted that the accident to the Ford car was caused by the respondents' negligence. It is necessary to state what followed in full detail.

As a result of the accident, the appellant's husband suffered bruising and shock; George suffered injuries to his head and face, cerebral concussion, fractures of both scapulae and bruising and abrasions; Kathleen suffered concussion, fracture of the right clavicle, bruising, abrasions and shock; Gillian was so seriously injured that she died almost immediately.

At the time, the appellant was at her home about two miles away; an hour or so afterwards the accident was reported to her by Mr. Pilgrim, who told her that he thought George was dying, and that he did not know the whereabouts of her husband or the condition of her daughter. He then drove her to Addenbrooke's hospital, Cambridge. There she saw Michael, who told her that Gillian was dead. She was taken down a corridor and through a window she saw Kathleen, crying, with her face cut and begrimed with dirt and oil. She could hear George shouting and screaming. She was taken to her husband who was sitting with his head in his hands. His shirt was hanging off him and he was covered in mud and oil. He saw the appellant and started sobbing. The appellant was then taken to see George. The whole of his left face and left side was covered. He appeared to recognise the appellant and then lapsed into unconsciousness. Finally, the appellant was taken to Kathleen who by now had been cleaned up. The child was too upset to speak and simply clung to her mother. There can be no doubt that these circumstances, witnessed by the appellant, were distressing in the extreme and were capable of producing an effect going well beyond that of grief and sorrow.

The appellant subsequently brought proceedings against the respondents. At the trial, the judge assumed [. . .] that the appellant subsequently suffered [. . .] severe shock, organic depression and a change of personality. [. . .]

[. . .] The critical question to be decided is whether a person in the position of the appellant, i.e. one who was not present at the scene of grievous injuries to her family but who comes upon those injuries at an interval of time and space, can recover damages for nervous shock.

[. . .] Although in the only case which has reached this House (*Bourhill* v. *Young* [1943 A.C. 92]) a claim for damages in respect of "nervous shock" was rejected on its facts, the House gave

---

[6] For the original language versions of the materials reproduced in this chapter, see the companion website at www.routledge.com/9781138567733.

clear recognition to the legitimacy, in principle, of claims of that character. As the result of that and other cases, [. . .] the following position has been reached:

1. While damages cannot, at common law, be awarded for grief and sorrow,[7] a claim for damages for "nervous shock" caused by negligence can be made without the necessity of showing direct impact or fear of immediate personal injuries for oneself. [. . .] The arguments on this issue were fully and admirably stated by the Supreme Court of California in *Dillon* v. *Legg* (1968) 29 A.L.R. 3rd, 130.[8]

2. A plaintiff may recover damages for "nervous shock" brought on by injury caused not to him or herself but to a near relative, or by the fear of such injury. So far [. . .], the cases do not extend beyond the spouse or children of the plaintiff [. . .].

3. Subject to the next paragraph, there is no English case in which a plaintiff has been able to recover nervous shock damages where the injury to the near relative occurred out of sight and earshot of the plaintiff. [. . .]

4. An exception from, or I would prefer to call it an extension of the latter case, has been made where the plaintiff does not see or hear the incident but comes upon its immediate aftermath. In *Boardman* v. *Sanderson* [English Court of Appeal] the father was within earshot of the accident to his child and likely to come upon the scene: he did so and suffered damage from what he then saw. In *Marshall* v. *Lionel Enterprises* [1972] 2 Ontario 3 Reports 117 [Ontario High Court], the wife came immediately upon the badly injured body of her husband. And in *Benson* v. *Lee* [1972] V.R. 789 [Supreme Court of Victoria, Australia], a situation existed with some similarity to the present case. The mother was in her home one hundred yards away, and, on communication by a third party, ran out to the scene of the accident and there suffered shock. Your Lordships have to decide whether or not to validate these extensions. [. . .]

Throughout these developments, as can be seen, the courts have proceeded in the traditional manner of the common law from case to case, upon a basis of logical necessity. [. . .] If one continues to follow the process of logical progression, it is hard to see why the present plaintiff also should not succeed. She was not present at the accident, but she came very soon after upon its aftermath. [. . .]

To argue from one factual situation to another and to decide by analogy is a natural tendency of the human and the legal mind. But the lawyer still has to enquire whether, in so doing, he has crossed some critical line behind which he ought to stop. [. . .]

[A]t the margin, the boundaries of a man's responsibility for acts of negligence have to be fixed as a matter of policy. [. . .] Foreseeability, which involves a hypothetical person, looking with hindsight at an event which has occurred, is a formula adopted by English law, not merely for defining, but also for limiting the persons to whom duty may be owed, and the consequences for which an actor may be held responsible. [. . .] [F]oreseeability does not of itself, and automatically, lead to a duty of care [. . .].

[. . .] The policy arguments against a wider extension can be stated under four heads.

---

[7] On this issue, see below, Chapter 12, pp. 343 ff.
[8] See below, pp. 323 ff.

First, it may be said that such extension may lead to a proliferation of claims, and possibly fraudulent claims, to the establishment of an industry of lawyers and psychiatrists who will formulate a claim for nervous shock damages [. . .], for all, or many, road accidents and industrial accidents.

Secondly, it may be claimed that an extension of liability would be unfair to defendants, as imposing damages out of proportion to the negligent conduct complained of. In so far as such defendants are insured, a large additional burden will be placed on insurers, and ultimately upon the class of persons insured – road users or employers.

Thirdly, to extend liability beyond the most direct and plain cases would greatly increase evidentiary difficulties and tend to lengthen litigation.

Fourthly, it may be said – and the Court of Appeal agreed with this – that an extension of the scope of liability ought only to be made by the legislature, after careful research. This is the course which has been taken in New South Wales and the Australian Capital Territory. [. . .]

Fraudulent claims can be contained by the courts, who, also, can cope with evidentiary difficulties. The scarcity of cases which have occurred in the past, and the modest sums recovered, give some indication that fears of a flood of litigation may be exaggerated – experience in other fields suggests that such fears usually are. If some increase does occur, that may only reveal the existence of a genuine social need: that legislation has been found necessary in Australia[9] may indicate the same thing.

But [. . .] there remains, in my opinion, just because "shock" in its nature is capable of affecting so wide a range of people, a real need for the law to place some limitation upon the extent of admissible claims. It is necessary to consider three elements inherent in any claim: the class of persons whose claims should be recognised; the proximity of such persons to the accident; and the means by which the shock is caused. As regards the class of persons, the possible range is between the closest of family ties – of parent and child, or husband and wife, and the ordinary bystander. Existing law recognises the claims of the first: it denies that of the second, either on the basis that such persons must be assumed to be possessed of fortitude sufficient to enable them to endure the calamities of modern life, or that defendants cannot be expected to compensate the world at large. In my opinion, these positions are justifiable, and since the present case falls within the first class, it is strictly unnecessary to say more. I think, however, that it should follow that other cases involving less close relationships must be very carefully scrutinised. I cannot say that they should never be admitted. The closer the tie (not merely in relationship, but in care) the greater the claim for consideration.[10] The claim, in any case, has to be judged in the light of the other factors, such as proximity to the scene in time and place, and the nature of the accident.

As regards proximity to the accident, it is obvious that this must be close in both time and space. It is, after all, the fact and consequence of the defendant's negligence that must be

---

9 See below, p. 330.
10 *Note by the author*: in *English* law, the rule established in the *Alcock* case (see below, Chapter 12, pp. 350 ff.) applies. According to the said rule, there is a presumption of close ties of love and affection between parents and children, and between spouses (and probably fiancés). Other relatives, such as siblings or grandparents, have to prove close ties of love and affection.

proved to have caused the "nervous shock". Experience has shown that to insist on direct and immediate sight or hearing would be impractical and unjust and that under what may be called the "aftermath" doctrine, one who, from close proximity comes very soon upon the scene, should not be excluded. In my opinion, the result in [the Australian case] *Benson v. Lee* was correct and indeed inescapable. It was based, soundly, upon "direct perception of some of the events which go to make up the accident as an entire event, and this includes . . . the immediate aftermath". [. . .]

Finally, and by way of reinforcement of "aftermath" cases, I would accept, by analogy with "rescue" situations, that a person of whom it could be said that one could expect nothing else than that he or she would come immediately to the scene – normally a parent or a spouse, could be regarded as being within the scope of foresight and duty. [. . .]

Lastly, as regards communication, there is no case in which the law has compensated shock brought about by communication by a third party. In *Hambrook* v. *Stokes* [1925] 1 K. B. 141, indeed, it was said that liability would not arise in such a case and this is surely right. It was so decided in *Abramzik* v. *Brenner* (1967) 65 D.L.R. (2nd) 651 [Saskatchewan Court of Appeal, Canada]. The shock must come through sight or hearing of the event or of its immediate aftermath. Whether some equivalent of sight or hearing, e.g. through simultaneous television, would suffice may have to be considered.[11] [. . .]

I would allow her appeal.

[Lord Edmund-Davies, Lord Russell of Killowen, Lord Scarman, Lord Bridge of Harwich concurring with separate opinions]

II. USA

1. Supreme Court of California, *Dillon* v. *Legg*, 21.06.1968, 441 P. 2nd 912

Dillon v. Legg, 441 P. 2d 912 (Supreme Ct. of California)

68 Cal. 2d 728; 441 P. 2d 912, 69 Cal. Rptr. 72; 1968 Cal. LEXIS 201

MARGERY M. DILLON et al., Plaintiffs and
Appellants, v. DAVID LUTHER LEGG, Defendant and Respondent

Sac. No. 7816

Supreme Court of California

June 21, 1968

OPINION BY: TOBRINER. That the courts should allow recovery to a mother who suffers emotional trauma and physical injury from witnessing the infliction of death or injury to her child for which the tortfeasor is liable in negligence would appear to be a compelling proposition. As Prosser points out, "All ordinary human feelings are in favor of her [the

---

11 See the *Alcock* case below, Chapter 12, pp. 350 ff.

mother's] action against the negligent defendant. If a duty to her requires that she herself be in some recognizable danger, then it has properly been said that when a child is endangered, it is not beyond contemplation that its mother will be somewhere in the vicinity, and will suffer serious shock." (Prosser, Law of Torts (3d ed. 1964) p. 353.)

Nevertheless, past American decisions have barred the mother's recovery. Refusing the mother the right to take her case to the jury, these courts ground their position on an alleged absence of a required "duty" of due care of the tortfeasor to the mother. Duty, in turn, they state, must express public policy; the imposition of duty here would work disaster because it would invite fraudulent claims and it would involve the courts in the hopeless task of defining the extent of the tortfeasor's liability. In substance, they say, definition of liability being impossible, denial of liability is the only realistic alternative.

We have concluded that neither of the feared dangers excuses the frustration of the natural justice upon which the mother's claim rests. [. . .]

In the instant case plaintiff's [. . .] cause of action alleged that on or about September 27, 1964, defendant drove his automobile in a southerly direction on Bluegrass Road near its intersection with Clover Lane in the County of Sacramento, and at that time plaintiff's infant daughter, Erin Lee Dillon, lawfully crossed Bluegrass Road. The complaint further alleged that defendant's negligent operation of his vehicle caused it to "collide with the deceased Erin Lee Dillon resulting in injuries to decedent which proximately resulted in her death." [. . .]

Plaintiff's [. . .] cause of action alleged that she, Margery M. Dillon, "was in close proximity to the . . . collision and personally witnessed said collision." She further alleged that "because of the negligence of defendants . . . and as a proximate cause [sic] thereof plaintiff . . . sustained great emotional disturbance and shock and injury to her nervous system" which caused her great physical and mental pain and suffering. [. . .]

[W]e have before us a case that dramatically illustrates the difference in result flowing from the alleged requirement that a plaintiff cannot recover for emotional trauma in witnessing the death of a child or sister unless she also feared for her own safety because she was actually within the zone of physical impact.

[. . .] [T]he complaint here presents the claim of the emotionally traumatized mother, who admittedly was not within the zone of danger, as contrasted with that of the sister, who may have been within it. The case thus illustrates the fallacy of the rule that would deny recovery in the one situation and grant it in the other. In the first place, we can hardly justify relief to the sister for trauma which she suffered upon apprehension of the child's death and yet deny it to the mother merely because of a happenstance that the sister was some few yards closer to the accident. The instant case exposes the hopeless artificiality of the zone-of-danger rule. [. . .]

We turn then to an analysis of the concept of duty, which, as we have stated, has furnished the ground for the rejection of such claims as the instant one. Normally the simple facts of plaintiff's complaint would establish a cause of action: the complaint alleges that defendant drove his car (1) negligently, as a (2) proximate result of which plaintiff suffered (3) physical injury. Proof of these facts to a jury leads to recovery in damages; indeed, such a showing represents a classic example of the type of accident with which the law of negligence has been designed to deal.

The assertion that liability must nevertheless be denied because defendant bears no "duty" to plaintiff begs the essential question whether the plaintiff's interests are entitled to legal protection against the defendant's conduct. [. . .]

The history of the concept of duty in itself discloses that it is not an old and deep-rooted doctrine but a legal device of the latter half of the nineteenth century designed to curtail the feared propensities of juries toward liberal awards. [. . .]

Indeed, the idea of court-imposed restrictions on recovery by means of the concept of "duty" contrasted dramatically with the preceding legal system of feudal society. In the enclosed feudal society, the actor bore responsibility for any damage he inflicted without regard to whether he was at fault or owed a "duty" to the injured person. Thus, at that time, the defendant owed a duty to all the world to conduct himself without causing injury to his fellows. It may well be that the physical contraction of the feudal society imposed an imperative for maximum procurable safety and a corresponding absolute responsibility upon its members.

The Industrial Revolution, which cracked the solidity of the feudal society and opened up wide and new areas of expansion, changed the legal concepts. Just as the new competitiveness in the economic sphere figuratively broke out of the walls of the feudal community, so it broke through the rule of strict liability. In the place of strict liability it introduced the theory that an action for negligence would lie only if the defendant breached a duty which he owed to plaintiff. As Lord Esher said in Le Lievre v. Gould (1893) 1 Q.B. 491, 497: "A man is entitled to be as negligent as he pleases towards the whole world if he owes no duty to them."

We have pointed out that this late 19th century concept of duty, as applied to the instant situation, has led the courts to deny liability. We have noted that this negation of duty emanates from the twin fears that courts will be flooded with an onslaught of (1) fraudulent and (2) indefinable claims. We shall point out why we think neither fear justified.

1. This court in the past has rejected the argument that we must deny recovery upon a legitimate claim because other fraudulent ones may be urged. [. . .]

In the first instance, the argument proceeds from a doubtful factual assumption. Whatever the possibilities of fraudulent claims of physical injury by disinterested spectators of an accident, a question not in issue in this case, we certainly cannot doubt that a mother who sees her child killed will suffer physical injury from shock. "It seems sufficiently obvious that the shock of a mother at danger or harm to her child may be both a real and a serious injury." (Prosser, Law of Torts, supra, at p. 353.)

[. . .] In the second instance, and more fundamentally, the possibility that fraudulent assertions may prompt recovery in isolated cases does not justify a wholesale rejection of the entire class of claims in which that potentiality arises. [. . .]

[. . .] Undoubtedly, ever since the ancient case of the tavernkeeper's wife who successfully avoided the hatchet cast by an irate customer (I de S et ux v. W de S, Y.B. 22 Edw. iii, f. 99, pl. 60 (1348)), defendants have argued that plaintiffs' claims of injury from emotional trauma might well be fraudulent. Yet we cannot let the difficulties of adjudication frustrate the principle that there be a remedy for every substantial wrong.

2. [. . .] In order to limit the otherwise potentially infinite liability which would follow every negligent act, the law of torts holds defendant amenable only for injuries to others which to defendant at the time were reasonably foreseeable.

[. . .] We note, first, that we deal here with a case in which plaintiff suffered a shock which resulted in physical injury and we confine our ruling to that case. In determining, in such a case, whether defendant should reasonably foresee the injury to plaintiff, or, in other terminology, whether defendant owes plaintiff a duty of due care, the courts will take into account such factors as the following: (1) Whether plaintiff was located near the scene of the accident as contrasted with one who was a distance away from it. (2) Whether the shock resulted from a direct emotional impact upon plaintiff from the sensory and contemporaneous observance of the accident as contrasted with learning of the accident from others after its occurrence. (3) Whether plaintiff and the victim were closely related, as contrasted with an absence of any relationship or the presence of only a distant relationship.

The evaluation of these factors will indicate the degree of the defendant's foreseeability: obviously defendant is more likely to foresee that a mother who observes an accident affecting her child will suffer harm than to foretell that a stranger witness will do so. Similarly, the degree of foreseeability of the third person's injury is far greater in the case of his contemporaneous observance of the accident than that in which he subsequently learns of it. The defendant is more likely to foresee that shock to the nearby, witnessing mother will cause physical harm than to anticipate that someone distant from the accident will suffer more than a temporary emotional reaction. All these elements, of course, shade into each other; the fixing of obligation, intimately tied into the facts, depends upon each case.

[. . .] In the instant case, [. . .] [s]urely the negligent driver who causes the death of a young child may reasonably expect that the mother will not be far distant and will upon witnessing the accident suffer emotional trauma. As Dean Prosser has stated: "when a child is endangered, it is not beyond contemplation that its mother will be somewhere in the vicinity, and will suffer serious shock." (Prosser, The Law of Torts, supra, at p. 353. [. . .])

We are not now called upon to decide whether, in the absence or reduced weight of some of the above factors, we would conclude that the accident and injury were not reasonably foreseeable and that therefore defendant owed no duty of due care to plaintiff. In future cases the courts will draw lines of demarcation upon facts more subtle than the compelling ones alleged in the complaint before us.

[. . .] The fear of an inability to fix boundaries has not impelled the courts of England to deny recovery for emotional trauma caused by witnessing the death or injury of another due to defendant's negligence. We set forth the holdings of some English cases merely to demonstrate that courts can formulate and apply such limitations of liability. [The court then discusses the English cases *Hambrock* v. *Stokes Bros.*, *Boardman* v. *Sanderson*, and *Bourhill* v. *Young*] [. . .]

In short, the history of the cases does not show the development of a logical rule but rather a series of changes and abandonments. [. . .] At first they insisted that there be no recovery for emotional trauma at all. [. . .] Retreating from this position, they gave relief for such trauma only if physical impact occurred. [. . .] They then abandoned the requirement for physical impact but insisted that the victim fear for her own safety (Amaya v. Home Ice, Fuel & Supply Co., supra, 59 Cal.2d 295), holding that a mother could recover for fear for her children's safety if she simultaneously entertained a personal fear for herself. [. . .] They stated that the mother need only be in the "zone of danger" [. . .]. The final anomaly would be the instant case in which the sister, who observed the accident, would be granted recovery because she was in the "zone of danger," but the mother, not far distant, would be barred from recovery.

The successive abandonment of these positions exposes the weakness of artificial abstractions which bar recovery contrary to the general rules. As the commentators have suggested, the problem should be solved by the application of the principles of tort, not by the creation of exceptions to them. Legal history shows that artificial islands of exceptions, created from the fear that the legal process will not work, usually do not withstand the waves of reality and, in time, descend into oblivion.

[. . .] To the extent that it is inconsistent with our ruling here, we therefore overrule Amaya v. Home Ice Fuel & Supply Co., supra, 59 Cal.2d 295.

To deny recovery would be to chain this state to an outmoded rule of the 19th century which can claim no current credence. No good reason compels our captivity to an indefensible orthodoxy.

The judgment is reversed.

DISSENT: TRAYNOR, C. J. I dissent for the reasons set forth in Amaya v. Home Ice, Fuel & Supply Co. (1963) 59 Cal.2d 295, 297–315 [. . .]. In my opinion that case was correctly decided and should not be overruled.

DISSENT: BURKE, J. As recently as 1963 this court, in Amaya v. Home Ice, Fuel & Supply Co. [. . .], thoroughly studied and expressly rejected the proposition [. . .] that tort liability may be predicated on fright or nervous shock (with consequent bodily illness) induced solely by the plaintiff's apprehension of negligently caused danger or injury to a third person. [. . .]

So far as has been discovered, in not a single such jurisdiction has an appellate court ruled to the contrary since Amaya. [. . .] Instead, we are offered two English cases [. . .] whose ruling we expressly rejected in Amaya [. . .] and which, as already stated has not been followed or approved by any jurisdiction in this country.

[. . .] The majority, obviously recognizing that they are now embarking upon a first excursion into the "fantastic realm of infinite liability" (Amaya, at p. 315 of 59 Cal.2d), undertake to provide so-called "guidelines" for the future. [. . .]

It appears to me that in the light of today's majority opinion the matter at issue should be commended to the attention of the Legislature of this state. [. . .] [I]f all alleged California tortfeasors, including motorists, home and other property owners, and governmental entities, are now to be faced with the concept of potentially infinite liability beyond any rational relationship to their culpability, then surely the point has been reached at which the Legislature should reconsider the entire subject and allow all interests affected to be heard. [. . .]

2. Supreme Court of Florida, *Champion v. Gray*, 07.03.1985, 478 So. 2nd 17

WALTON D. CHAMPION, Petitioner, v. ROY LEE GRAY, JR., et al., Respondents

No. 62,830

Supreme Court of Florida

478 So. 2d 17; 1985 Fla. LEXIS 3372; 10 Fla. L. Weekly S 164;
10 Fla. L. Weekly S 579; 10 Fla. L. Weekly S 592

March 7, 1985

[. . .] Larry Klein, West Palm Beach, Florida, Amicus Curiae for The Academy of Florida Trial Lawyers; and Joseph W. Little, Gainesville, Florida, Amicus Curiae.

JUDGES: Boyd, C.J., McDonald, Overton, Ehrlich, Shaw, Adkins, Alderman, JJ.

OPINION BY: McDONALD

This is a petition to review Champion v. Gray, 420 So. 2d 348 (Fla. 5th DCA 1982), which certified the following question to this Court as a matter of great public importance:

I. Should Florida abrogate the "Impact Rule" and allow recovery for the physical consequences resulting from mental or emotional stress caused by the defendant's negligence in the absence of physical impact upon the plaintiff?

[. . .] To a limited extent we modify our previous holdings on the impact doctrine and recognize a cause of action within the factual context of this claim.

The complaint in this case alleged that a drunken driver ran his car off the road, striking and killing Karen Champion. Karen's mother, Joyce Champion, heard the impact, came immediately to the accident scene, saw her daughter's body, and was so overcome with shock and grief that she collapsed and died on the spot. Walton Champion, as personal representative of his wife's estate, then brought this action for damages caused by the driver's negligence which led to Mrs. Champion's death. [. . .] [T]he trial court dismissed the complaint. The district court affirmed the dismissal, following the long-standing Florida rule that a plaintiff must suffer a physical impact before recovering for emotional distress caused by the negligence of another. [. . .]

[. . .] The impact doctrine gives practical recognition to the thought that not every injury which one person may by his negligence inflict upon another should be compensated in money damages. There must be some level of harm which one should absorb without recompense as the price he pays for living in an organized society.

We now conclude, however, that the price of death or significant discernible physical injury, when caused by psychological trauma resulting from a negligent injury imposed upon a close family member within the sensory perception of the physically injured person, is too great a harm to require direct physical contact before a cause of action exists. We emphasize the requirement that a causally connected clearly discernible physical impairment must accompany or occur within a short time of the psychic injury. [. . .]

Foreseeability is the guidepost of any tort claim. Because we are dealing with an unusual and non-traditional cause of action in allowing damages caused by psychic injury following an injury to another, however, public policy comes into play and some outward limitations need to be placed on the pure foreseeability rule. We have already referred to the requirement of a significant discernible physical injury. In addition the psychically injured party should be directly involved in the event causing the original injury. If such a person sees it, hears it, or arrives upon the scene while the injured party is still there, that person is likely involved. The English case of McLoughlin v. O'Brian, 2 All ER 298 (1982),[12] adopting a pure foreseeability rule, allowed recovery when a parent suffered psychic injury upon seeing her child in the hospital shortly following an accident. We do not say whether or not we would or would not recognize a claim under such circumstances, but, if so, we would think that this scenario reaches the outer limits of the required involvement in the event. Another factor in the foreseeability requirement is that the secondarily injured party must have an especially close emotional attachment to the directly injured person. A child, a parent, or a spouse would qualify; others may or may not, depending upon their relationship and the circumstances thereof.

The complaint in the case sub judice alleges that Mrs Champion heard the accident, came immediately to the accident scene, and suffered severe emotional distress and shock which led to her death shortly after seeing her injured child. The requirements set out in this opinion have been met. No physical impact to her need be alleged because she suffered discernible physical injuries (death).

Accordingly [. . .] [w]e hold that a claim exists for damages flowing from a significant discernible physical injury when such injury is caused by psychic trauma resulting from negligent injury imposed on another who, because of his relationship to the injured party and his involvement in the event causing that injury, is foreseeably injured.

The district court's decision is quashed, and the district court is directed to remand the case for proceedings consistent with this opinion.

3. Restatement of the Law – Torts (3rd): Liability for Physical and Emotional Harm, 2013

> **§ 48. Negligent Infliction of Emotional Harm Resulting from Bodily Harm to a Third Person.** An actor who negligently causes sudden serious bodily injury to a third person is subject to liability for serious emotional harm caused thereby to a person who: (a) perceives the event contemporaneously, and (b) is a close family member of the person suffering the bodily injury.

[. . .]

Reporters' note

Comment a. Scope and history. The rule stated in this Section for bystander liability was first adopted by the California Supreme Court in Dillon v. Legg, 441 P. 2d 912 (Cal. 1968). Since *Dillon*, a number of courts [. . .] have decided that the open-ended foreseeability approach to bystander liability was unworkable and have instead employed a rule-based approach to bystander claims. [. . .] 29 American jurisdictions now follow *Dillon* or a modified version of the *Dillon* approach [references to the case law of the 29 US States omitted].

Eleven jurisdictions permit bystander recovery only when the plaintiff is in the "zone of danger". [including e.g. New York, references omitted]

---

[12] See above, pp. 320 ff.

Four jurisdictions reject *Dillon* and the "zone of danger" test and follow only the "impact" rule. [...]

The remaining jurisdictions have either not considered the issue, have rejected any rule of liability, have uncertain law, or have pursued a different approach altogether. [...]

III. Australia

Civil Liability Act

> **Sect. 33 – Mental harm – duty of care.** (1) A person (the "defendant") does not owe a duty to another person (the "plaintiff") to take care not to cause the plaintiff mental harm unless a reasonable person in the defendant's position would have foreseen that a person of normal fortitude in the plaintiff's position might, in the circumstances of the case, suffer a psychiatric illness.
> (2) For the purposes of this section
> (a) in a case of pure mental harm, the circumstances of the case to which the court is to have regard include the following:
> (i) whether or not the mental harm was suffered as the result of a sudden shock;
> (ii) whether the plaintiff witnessed, at the scene, a person being killed, injured or put in peril;
> (iii) the nature of the relationship between the plaintiff and any person killed, injured or put in peril;
> (iv) whether or not there was a pre-existing relationship between the plaintiff and the defendant; [...]

IV. France[13]

Cour de cassation, 2ᵉ civ. (*Court of Cassation, 2nd civil chamber*), 17.05.1973, (*De Allende et Compagnie l'Union et le Phenix Espagnol c. dame Doussinault*), Gaz. Pal. 1974, 71

CIVIL LIABILITY [...]. – COMPENSABLE DAMAGE. – NON-PECUNIARY LOSS. – ACCIDENT. – PREGNANT WOMAN. – SUBSEQUENT MISCARRIAGE. – CAUSAL CONNECTION WITH ACCIDENT. – FIRST INSTANCE COURT'S APPRECIATION OF THE FACTS. – AWARD OF DAMAGES. – IMPOSITION OF LIABILITY HELD JUSTIFIED

The trial judges had the final word in determining the issue of a causal connection between the effect on a pregnant woman of an accident suffered by her husband and a miscarriage taking place a few weeks later. They were therefore justified in awarding

---

13 For the strict liability system as basis of liability for road traffic accidents in *French* law, see above, Chapter 9, pp. 251 ff.

damages to the couple in respect of the non-pecuniary harm suffered by them as a result of the miscarriage.

Rejected.

De Allende & Another v. Doussinault

Appeal from a judgment of the Paris *Cour d'appel* dated 18.1.1971

Judgment of the court. – On the single ground of appeal

Whereas, the judgment under appeal concludes that in a collision between a car driven by Mr De Allende and one under the control of Mr Doussinault, the latter was injured; that Mr and Mrs Doussinault, alleging that the emotional shock occasioned to Mrs Doussinault, who was pregnant at the time, at the sight of her husband returning home with torn and blood-spattered clothes, was the cause of her miscarriage some weeks later, have sued Mr De Allende and his insurers (*Compagnie l'Union et le Phénix Espagnol*) for damages reflecting their non-pecuniary harm suffered as a result of the miscarriage; that the trial judges, before whom it was agreed that Mr De Allende had been entirely to blame for the accident in which Mr Doussinault was injured, allowed the claim; that, on appeal by Mrs Doussinault and cross-appeal by Mr De Allende and his insurers, the appeal court confirmed the result, while increasing the amount of damages awarded;

Whereas this judgment is now appealed [. . .];

Whereas, however, having analysed (and in no way misconstrued) the expert's report, the appeal judges outline that, until the accident, Mrs Doussinault's pregnancy was a normal one; that bloody discharges appeared immediately after the accident, and swiftly led to the miscarriage; and that although Mrs Doussinault's health record was somewhat variable owing to her age, it had never previously given cause for concern; that they add that there is serious, precise and corroborating evidence that the shock occasioned to Mrs Doussinault by the accident contributed to, or even determined, the subsequent development in her pregnancy; and that there is therefore a clear relation of cause and effect between the accident and the miscarriage; that, in view of these findings and the terms of the judgment alone, and disregarding the redundant ground of appeal, it follows that the *Cour d'appel*, not contradicting itself and not being bound to accept the conclusions of the expert, provided a suitable legal basis for its decision;

For these reasons: – dismisses the appeal . . .

V. Germany

1. Bürgerliches Gesetzbuch, BGB (*Civil Code*)[14]

§ 253. Immaterieller Schaden. (1) Wegen eines Schadens, der nicht Vermögensschaden ist, kann Entschädigung in Geld nur in den durch das Gesetz bestimmten Fällen gefordert werden.

---

14 See the explanatory comment above, Chapter 5, p. 81. For the strict liability system applicable for road traffic accidents in *German* law, see above, Chapter 9, pp. 244 ff.

(2) Ist wegen einer Verletzung des Körpers, der Gesundheit, der Freiheit oder der sexuellen Selbstbestimmung Schadensersatz zu leisten, kann auch wegen des Schadens, der nicht Vermögensschaden ist, eine billige Entschädigung in Geld gefordert werden.

§ 823. Schadensersatzpflicht. (1) Wer vorsätzlich oder fahrlässig das Leben, den Körper, die Gesundheit, die Freiheit, das Eigentum oder ein sonstiges Recht eines anderen widerrechtlich verletzt, ist dem anderen zum Ersatze des daraus entstehenden Schadens verpflichtet. [...]

Translation

§ 253. Non-pecuniary loss. (1) Compensation for non-pecuniary loss can only be claimed in the cases stipulated by law.
(2) Where compensation is due for injury to body, health, freedom, or sexual self-determination, the injured party can claim an equitable amount of monetary compensation also for non-pecuniary loss.

§ 823. Duty to compensate loss. (1) Whosoever unlawfully injures, intentionally or negligently, the life, body, health, freedom, property, or other right of another person, has an obligation to the other person to compensate the resulting loss. [...]

2. Bundesgerichtshof, BGH (*Federal Supreme Court of Justice*), 11.05.1971, BGHZ 56, 163

27. "Nervous shock damage" caused by the accidental death of a relative

The nervous shock resulting from receiving news of a fatal accident to a relative does not result in a claim for damages against the person responsible for the accident in a case where, although it has ascertainable medical consequences, such effects are no worse than the impairments to health that close relatives are generally likely to suffer in any case as a result of hearing about a death. The protection envisaged by BGB § 823 (1) is limited to injuries to health of a type and severity that go beyond such impairments.[15]
[...]

The claimant's husband, aged 64, was fatally injured on 6th March 1965 by a car driven by the defendant. The claimant, then 50, sought damages in respect to injury to her health which she said she suffered as a result of her husband's death. [...]

Reasoning of the court:

[...] The law regards as impermissible [...] a claim for damage suffered as a result of emotional distress, unless that distress is the outcome of an injury to the claimant's (own) bodily

---

15 The same applies if the claim is not based on § 823 of the Civil Code, but on § 7 of the Road Traffic Act.

integrity or health. It is consistent with this decision of the legislator that an independent claim should be available to someone who, due to the unusually "traumatic" effect of seeing or being informed of an accident, suffers an injury to his physical, mental or emotional health. [. . .]

On the other hand, as we know from general knowledge and experience, it is noteworthy that a highly traumatic event that gives rise to feelings such as grief, sadness and fright, regularly has harmful and often very appreciable effects on a person's physiological processes and emotional functions. It is clear that to regard ill-effects of this sort as amounting to harm to one's health for the purposes of BGB, § 823 (1) would be inconsistent with the intention of the legislator, which is binding on the courts. [. . .] On the contrary, at least in cases where psychiatric injuries were not intended by the person responsible, [. . .] it is necessary to limit liability to those afflictions that are not only regarded in medical circles as amounting to injuries to bodily integrity or health, but are also so viewed according to people's general understanding. [. . .] It follows that we must, as a matter of principle, refuse to compensate illnesses that, even though medically recognisable, do not have the character of a "shock-like" effect on health; thus, the negative (and frequently far from trivial) consequences for a person's general health, ordinarily associated with a deeply-felt bereavement, do not normally provide a sufficient basis for an independent claim for damages.

c) Applying the reasoning criteria contained in these general principles, the judgment under appeal cannot stand. [. . .]

IV. [. . .] Under this reasoning, the lower court may only allow the claim [. . .] in so far as the court is satisfied – if necessary on the basis of a fuller enquiry into the facts – that the news of the accident led directly to the claimant suffering a "traumatic" injury to her physical or psychiatric health that goes beyond feelings of grief, bereavement and depression, which would be a normal reaction to it. [. . .][16]

VI. Switzerland[17]

1. Code des obligations/Obligationenrecht (*Code of Obligations*)

Art. 41. (1) Celui qui cause, d'une manière illicite, un dommage à autrui, soit intentionnellement, soit par négligence ou imprudence, est tenu de le réparer. [. . .]

Art. 47. Le juge peut, en tenant compte de circonstances particulières, allouer à la victime de lésions corporelles ou, en cas de mort d'homme, à la famille une indemnité équitable à titre de réparation morale.

---

16 *Note by the author*: in the case on which the above scenario is based (OLG Nürnberg, 01.08.1995, *r+s* 1995, 384), the Nürnberg Appellate Court awarded Mr Müller DM 60,000 (approximately € 30,000) and Mrs Müller DM 30,000 (approximately € 15,000) for their nervous shock suffered due to the tragic events. These amounts are at the upper end of the amounts for nervous shock in *German* law.
17 For the strict liability system applicable for road traffic accidents in *Swiss* law, see above, Chapter 9, pp. 248 ff.

Translation

> *Art. 41.* (1) *Any person who unlawfully causes damage to another, whether wilfully or negligently, is obliged to provide compensation. [. . .]*
>
> *Art. 47.* *In cases of death or personal injury, the court may award the victim of personal injury or the dependants of the deceased an appropriate sum by way of satisfaction taking into account the specific circumstances of the case.*

2. Tribunal fédéral/Bundesgericht (*Federal Supreme Court of Justice*), 11.03.1986 (*G. c. Confédération Suisse*), ATF 112 II 118

A. – On 23rd August 1982, a Hawker Hunter military aircraft crashed, killing Claude G (born on 4th January 1965) and his brother Frédéric (born on 15th January 1972). Their mother, Alberte, and their brother Alban were injured. At the time, they were picking pears.

Following the deaths, Angiolino G (born in 1931), the father of the persons killed, suffered a bad bout of nervous shock that seriously affected his physical health. He received, and to this day continues to receive, medical treatment. In the spring of 1985, he was accepted to claim disability allowances. [. . .]

B. – The Confederation made a payment by way of satisfaction for loss of a loved one (damages for bereavement) in the sum of CHF 40,000 for each parent, i.e. Alberte and Angiolino in respect of the death of the two children,[18] and CHF 12,000 for Alban in respect of the death of his brother,[19] plus interest.[20] [. . .] However, it did not accept the [. . .] father's claim for damages reflecting his inability to work and permanent illness.

[. . .] At a preliminary hearing on 3rd October 1985, the Confederation accepted that Angiolino suffered from a 50% disability due to the nervous shock he had suffered as a result of the crash. [. . .]

Legal considerations: [. . .]

4. – The plaintiff Angiolino G seeks compensation in respect of his 50% disability stemming from the nervous shock suffered by him as a result of the death of his two sons. He also claims damages for the pain and suffering engendered by this disability. [. . .]

5. – *a)* The defendant Confederation refuses Angiolino's claim for damages for the pain and suffering stemming from his disability. It argues that this is a matter of indirect harm, which does not give rise to a right to compensation. According to its argument, the plaintiff's loss would have been a direct loss if he had actually witnessed the accident and suffered psychological trauma as a result; as it was, however, he was working somewhere else at the time, and was only told what had happened some time later. Hence, the argument

---

18 Today worth around CHF 60,000.
19 Today worth around CHF 18,000.
20 *Note by the author*: for the obligation to pay damages for the loss of a loved one under Art. 47 CO, see below, Chapter 12, pp. 361 ff.

goes, the harm to his health is not the result of the defendant's wrongful act as such, but rather of the death of his two children resulting from the incident.

b) On numerous occasions, the *Tribunal fédéral* has decided that, regarding fault-based liability under Art. 41 CO or strict liability, the law only allows an award of damages in favour of a person directly harmed by the wrongful act. Third parties suffering indirect or reflective damage are barred from such a claim [. . .]. In the case of wrongful death, it has been made clear that the provisions of Arts. 45 and 47 CO in particular are exhaustive,[21] and that those left behind cannot recover damages for any loss they may have suffered indirectly as a result of an accident affecting the property of the deceased [. . .]. The Court has emphasised that Art. 45 (3) CO, allowing survivors to claim compensation for loss of support even though their damage is merely reflective, is of an exceptional nature; the Court has argued that this provision is out of line with the general system inherent in the CO, and should be interpreted narrowly [. . .].

As regards the particular problem of loss caused by nervous shock stemming from the death of a near relative, an 1897 case decided that it was fair to award a sum of money to the father of a child who was accidentally killed, considering that one had to take into account the fact that the father and mother had lost their only child and that, as a result of the death, the mother had suffered a post-traumatic neurosis causing her both material damage and pain and suffering [. . .]. In a 1928 decision, by contrast, the *Tribunal fédéral* was of the view that the heads of damage recoverable in respect of a death had been exhaustively laid down in Arts. 45 and 47 CO; the expenses incurred for the treatment of the nervous shock that was suffered by parents as a result of the accident and the tragic death of their child were therefore [according to this decision] not recoverable [. . .]. [. . .]

d) Decisions by German courts, which are in accordance with the view held by the majority of doctrinal opinions, do in principle allow compensation for damage of the sort in question. Such damage is called "*Schockschaden*" and is regarded as a direct damage. Since 1971, however, the German Federal Supreme Court has limited the ambit of these awards, only allowing for compensation where there is serious harm of a medically recognised kind, and even then limiting those who can sue to a limited class of relatives of the deceased (BGHZ 56 (1971), p. 163 ss; for detailed discussion of the question, see STAUDINGER, BGB, 12th ed., para. 823, nos. 506 ss, 516 ss, 525).

In France, damage of this sort is also compensated. The underlying legal basis, however, is less similar to that in Swiss law than German law (see MAZEAUD, *Traité de la responsabilité civile*, 6th ed., II, nos. 1872–1874; FREI, op.cit., pp. 72 ss).

Austrian case law does not allow for the compensation of "*Schockschaden*", owing to the principle that the legislative provisions dealing with compensation for wrongful death are regarded as regulating the matter exhaustively. But this way of looking at things is criticised by scholars (see RUMMEL, *Kommentar zum ABGB*, Vienna 1984, para. 1325, n. 5).

---

21 *Note by the author*: Art. 45 CO provides (in English translation): "(1) In the event of death, compensation includes all expenses arising and in particular the funeral costs. (2) Where death did not occur immediately, the compensation must also include the costs of medical treatment and losses arising from inability to work. (3) Where others are deprived of their means of support as a result of the death, they must also be compensated for that loss".

e) From the above account of the case law and doctrinal opinions, it follows that one cannot refuse compensation for the damage suffered by Angiolino for the reason advanced by the defendant, namely that this is a matter of "indirect" damage – or, more precisely, reflective loss (known as "*dommage par ricochet*" or "*Reflexschaden*"), signifying damage suffered by a third party as a result of his relationship with the primary victim [. . .].

The existence of the damage here is not in question. Nor is the factual causal link between it and the military aircraft crash. Since what we are dealing with here is the consequences of nervous shock suffered by a father following the accidental killing of his two young sons, the adequacy of the causal connection is undeniable.

The condition that there must have been a wrong, which applies equally in the case of strict liability [. . .], is also met. In effect, wrongfulness is always present when the act complained of infringes any interest protected by an absolute right, such as the right to life, bodily integrity or property. The legal order protects these rights directly, without any need to investigate whether the defendant has been guilty of infringing any particular legal prohibition. [. . .] The person who is himself the victim of an infringement of an absolute right, as with the plaintiff here, is thus directly harmed and can demand that his harm be compensated by the person who caused it. For these purposes, it is irrelevant whether the chain of causation is long or short, or whether the damage is caused to someone directly or rebounds from the immediate victim so as to hurt someone in relation with him. Furthermore, the exclusivity of the regime under Art. 45 CO [. . .] applies only to purely patrimonial damage for which someone other than the deceased seeks compensation; it does not apply to damage affecting the plaintiff's own bodily integrity. [. . .]

f) It follows that the plaintiff Angiolino, whose bodily integrity has been seriously impaired by the military plane crash, has the right to full compensation from the defendant [. . .].

6. – Since his own bodily integrity has been infringed, the plaintiff has a right to claim damages for pain and suffering linked to his own incapacity, this being quite separate from any suffering resulting from the death of his sons. Taking all the circumstances into account [. . .], the judgment in his favour amounts to CHF 20 000,[22] plus interest from the date of the accident. [. . .]

VII. Austria

I. Allgemeines bürgerliches Gesetzbuch, ABGB (*General Civil Code*)

> § 1295. (1) Jedermann ist berechtigt, von dem Beschädiger den Ersatz des Schadens, welchen dieser ihm aus Verschulden zugefügt hat, zu fordern; der Schade mag durch Übertretung einer Vertragspflicht oder ohne Beziehung auf einen Vertrag verursacht worden sein. [. . .]
>
> § 1325. Wer jemanden an seinem Körper verletzt, bestreitet die Heilungskosten des Verletzten, ersetzt ihm den entgangenen, oder, wenn der Beschädigte zum Erwerb unfähig wird, auch den künftig entgehenden Verdienst; und bezahlt ihm auf Verlangen überdies ein den erhobenen Umständen angemessenes Schmerzensgeld.

---

22 Today worth around CHF 30,000.

Translation

§ 1295.(1) Every person is entitled to claim compensation from the wrongdoer for the damage the latter has culpably inflicted upon him or her; the damage may have been caused by the breach of a contractual duty or independently of any contract. [. . .]

§ 1325. Whosoever injures a person's body must bear the costs of healing and compensate him or her for lost earnings, and, if the person harmed loses his or her earning capacity, also for the loss of future earnings, and moreover has to pay, on demand, damages for pain and suffering that are adequate in the circumstances.

2. Oberster Gerichtshof, OGH (*Supreme Court of Justice*), 16.06.1994, 2Ob 45/93, ZVR 1995/46

Grounds for the decision

On 26th May 1990, the first defendant, driving a car insured by the second defendant, negligently caused an accident. The plaintiff, an infant then 20 months old, was sitting in a child seat in the back of a car being driven by her mother Anna B. Anna B was very seriously injured. She was able for the first time to receive a visit from her daughter two weeks after the accident while in intensive care. She stayed in hospital continuously as an in-patient for two months.

[. . .] [T]he abrupt loss of contact with her mother during the latter's hospitalisation had serious psychological effects on the infant. Before the crash, there had been a close relationship between mother and child, manifesting itself in an early achievement of typical developmental abilities. The plaintiff slept alone in her own room. After the traumatic experience of separation from her parent, this was no longer possible. She suffered from anxiety and refused to be left alone. The psychological traumas brought on by this fear of being alone now manifest themselves in great physical discomfort, and they seriously affect the child's physical well-being. The experience of separation is expected to lead to further detrimental effects on the child's psychological development; in the future, these effects are capable of causing the development of anxiety neurosis. What is involved is thus a matter of psychological illness, but one that does not manifest itself in any physical ailment. The child still suffers from anxieties that can only be cured with expert help. [. . .]

Both defendants admitted that the first defendant is solely to blame for the accident [. . .].

The plaintiff seeks [. . .] damages for pain and suffering in the sum of 24 000 [Austrian Schilling][23] [. . .]. The defendants argues that the claim should fail. [. . .]

Legal considerations

[. . .] § 1325 ABGB provides for payment of damages for pain and suffering in the case of bodily injury. This compensates for non-material damage suffered in conjunction with bodily injury (Koziol, *Österreichisches Haftpflichtrecht* 2 II 138), and hence is available if such injury has in fact been caused. The concept of bodily injury is to be understood as

---

23 Today worth around € 1,850.

including any impairment of physical or mental health, or of personal integrity. An externally visible lesion is not required: even internal injuries or nervous harms fall within the concept of bodily injury. So it is already established that harm to the functioning of the brain or the nervous system count as bodily injury (ZVR 1977/54; JBl 1989,41), as does (for example) insomnia (ZBl 1937/114; SZ 20/186), as well as stress and agitation of any kind. But a simple emotional affectation, consisting of no more than discomfort or feelings of unhappiness, is not in itself enough to qualify as bodily injury, nor can it be regarded as equivalent (EvBl 1983/82; Koziol, above, 115). [. . .] A massive psychological impairment of the kind in question here is, however, included, if from a medical perspective the mental harm involved requires treatment. In particular, this is the case where it cannot be expected that the effects will wear off of their own accord, or where it is to be feared that in the absence of medical treatment there will remain a long-term impairment of the subject's health (see Mertens, in *Münchner Kommentar zum Bürgerlichen Gesetzbuch*, Rz 56 zu § 823 BGB).

According to the findings, the plaintiff is suffering from massive symptoms of nervous anxiety resulting from her grievous experience of separation. She cannot deal with these except with professional help, and they entail a risk of further deterioration in her psychological development. The plaintiff's need for medical care makes it abundantly clear that, as far as she is concerned, it is not a case of simple emotional effects impairing mental wellbeing, but rather that we have here an injury to her health with clear clinical significance. This gives rise to a claim for damages. [. . .]

Against the appellant's objection that this case concerns indirect damage for which no compensation can be claimed, the following points are to be made:

It is true that there can be no claim for damages in respect of pure emotional harm not resulting from an injury to one's own body [. . .].[24] In the instant case, however, what we are concerned with is not pure emotional harm resulting from the mother's injury and hospitalisation, but an illness in the plaintiff herself caused as a consequence of her mother's injury; it is therefore a case of compensable damage. Admittedly, in the decisions in ZVR 1958/144, ZVR 1963/147 and SZ 44/39 (= ZVR 1977/27), it was held that no damages were available for shock occasioned by the death of a near relative, on the basis that this was a claim for damage to a third party. Those decisions were however criticised by legal scholars, and rightly so, because where nervous harm is suffered, the third party's absolute right to bodily integrity is impaired, and he can hence be regarded as a direct victim. [. . .]

VIII. Sweden

Skadeståndslagen (*Tort Liability Act*)

> **5 kap. Skadeståndets bestämmande. § 2.** Har personskada lett till döden, skall ersättning betalas för
> 1. begravningskostnad och, i skälig omfattning, annan kostnad till följd av dödsfallet,
> 2. förlust av underhåll,
> 3. personskada som till följd av dödsfallet åsamkats någon som stod den avlidne särskilt nära.

---

24 For the current position in Austrian law, see below, Chapter 12, pp. 365 ff.

Translation

Chapter 5. Determination of damages. *§ 2. Where personal injury has led to death, compensation shall be paid for*
1. funeral expenses and, to a reasonable extent, other costs resulting from the death,
2. loss of support,
3. personal injury which, as a result of the death, is caused to a person who was particularly close to the deceased.

Systematic overviews

I. Damage suffered by secondary victims – liability for "nervous shock"

Table 11.1

Two alternative approaches to the issue of nervous shock				
Accident leading to:	**First approach**	*direct damage,* suffered by primary victim	→	followed by *indirect damage,* suffered by secondary victim
	Second approach	→ primary victim suffering harm to absolute right → secondary victim suffering harm to own absolute right		

Table 11.2

Requirements made in all jurisdictions
1. Loss of life or severe injury suffered by the *primary victim*
2. Psychiatric injury/nervous shock/PTSD suffered by the *secondary victim,* in particular when requiring medical treatment
3. Close tie of love and affection between the *primary* and the *secondary victim,* e.g. spouses or life partners, parents and children (explicitly codified e.g. in Ch. 5 § 2 n. 3 of the Swedish Tort Liability Act: "person who was particularly close to the deceased"; see also Restatement 3rd Torts, § 48(b): "close family member")

Additional proximity test in certain jurisdictions[1]		
The secondary victim must have been present at the scene of the accident, been within "sight or hearing" of the accident, or, in certain jurisdictions, have arrived in the "immediate aftermath" at the accident or in hospital. • **English law** (*McLoughlin v. O'Brian*) • **Case law of California** (*Dillon v. Legg*) • **Case law of Florida** (*Champion v. Gray*) • **Case law of 27 further States in the USA** • **Restatement 3rd Torts, § 48(a)** • **Civil Liability Act of Australia,** Sect. 33	The secondary victim must have been in the 'zone of danger' of the accident. • 11 jurisdictions in the USA (including e.g. New York)	The secondary victim must have suffered a 'physical impact' in the accident. • 4 jurisdictions in the USA

[1] In most (if not all) jurisdictions on the European continent, no such further requirements are made (see e.g. the jurisdictions of *France, Germany, Switzerland, Austria,* or *Sweden,* references above).

II. The use of comparative law by the courts and before the courts (question 7)

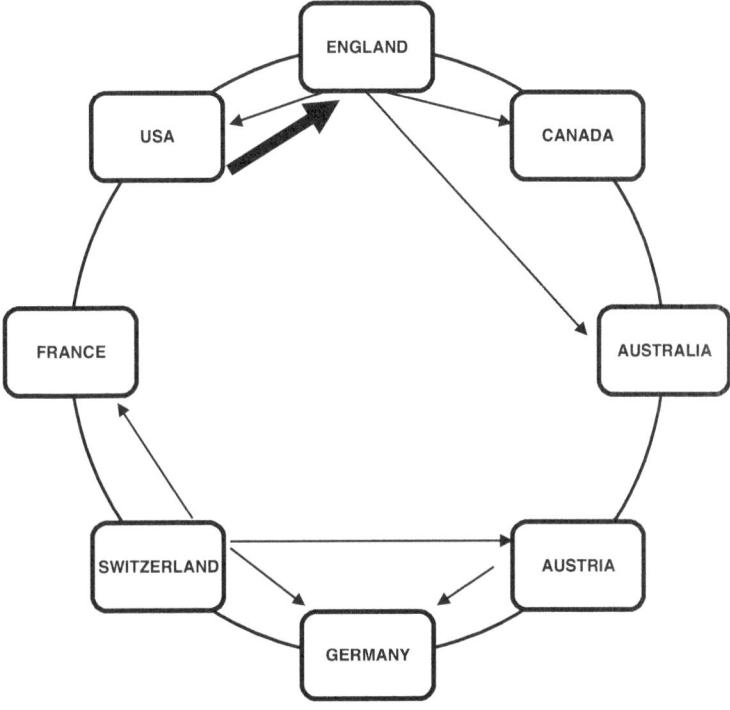

Figure 11.1

References to foreign law are to be found in the following decisions:

- In *McLoughlin v. O'Brian*, the **UK** House of Lords quotes the Supreme Court of California, *Dillon v. Legg*; the Ontario High Court (Canada), *Marshall v. Lionel Enterprises*; the Supreme Court of Victoria (Australia), *Benson v. Lee*; and the Saskatchewan Court of Appeal (Canada), *Abramzik v. Brenner*.
- In *Dillon v. Legg*, the Supreme Court of **California** quotes English case law (*Hambrock v. Stokes Bros.*, *Boardman v. Sanderson*, and *Bourhill v. Young*).
- In *Champion v. Gray*, the Supreme Court of **Florida** quotes the UK House of Lords, *McLoughlin v. O'Brian*.
- In ATF 112 II 118, the **Swiss** Federal Supreme Court of Justice quotes the leading German case BGHZ 56, 163, as well as French and Austrian legal doctrine.
- In 2Ob45/93, the **Austrian** OGH quotes German legal doctrine (*Münchener Kommentar*).

For the range of potential purposes of judicial comparison, and its potential benefits, see above, Part A, pp. 19, at 34 ff.

Bibliography

MARRIOS AMADOU/ANTONY S. HALE, PTSD and the Law of Psychiatric Injury in England and Wales: Finally Coming Closer? *JAAPL* 2003, 327; GERT BRÜGGEMEIER, *Common Principles of Tort Law: A Pre-Statement of Law*, London: BIICL, 2004, pp. 93–108, 112–115, 203–211; GERT BRÜGGEMEIER, *Haftungsrecht: Struktur, Prinzipien, Schutzbereich: ein Beitrag zur Europäisierung des Privatrechts*, Heidelberg: Springer, 2006, pp. 259–262; PHILIPPE BRUN/CHRISTOPHE QUEZEL-AMBRUNAZ, French Tort Law Facing Reform, *JETL* 2013, 78; BELA BONITA CHATTERJEE, Rethinking Alcock in the New Media Age, *JETL* 2016, 272–299; JACQUES DE MOL, *Le dommage psychique – Du traumatisme à l'expertise*, Bruxelles: Larcier, 2012; MELANIE JANSSENS, Nervous Shock Liability: A Comparative Study of the Law Governing the Principle of Nervous Shock in England, the Netherlands, Germany and France, *ERPL* 1998, 77; ERNST A. KRAMER, Schockschäden mit Krankheitswert: noch offene Fragen?, in: Peter Apathy et al. (eds.), *Festschrift für Helmut Koziol zum 70. Geburtstag*, Wien: Jan Sramek, 2010, pp. 743–758; HARDY LANDOLT, Immaterielle Unbill nach Verkehrsunfall unter besonderer Berücksichtigung von Schockschäden, in: René Schaffhauser (ed.), *Jahrbuch zum Strassenverkehrsrecht 2011*, Bern: Stämpfli, 2011, pp. 67–110; HARDY LANDOLT, Ersatzpflicht für "Schockschäden", in: Franco Lorandi/Daniel Staehelin, *Innovatives Recht: Festschrift für Ivo Schwander*, Zürich: Dike, 2011, pp. 361–382; LAW COMMISSION REPORT, *Liability for Psychiatric Illness*, 1998 (Law Com No 249), available at: www.lawcom.gov.uk/wp-content/uploads/2015/04/LC249.pdf (30.05.2017); RAY LEE, *Victims in Nervous Shock: A Primary or Secondary Victim?*, Hong Kong: Legal & Law Community, 2012; ULRICH MAGNUS (ed.), *Unification of Tort Law: Damages*, The Hague: Kluwer Law International, 2001, Question 10; NICHOLAS J. MULLANY, Personal Perception of Trauma and Sudden Shock: South Africa Simplifies Matters, *L.Q.R.* 2000, 29; NICHOLAS J. MULLANY/PETER R. HANDFORD, *Tort Liability for Psychiatric Damage: The Law of "Nervous Shock"*, London: The Law Book Co./Sweet & Maxwell, 1993; NEGLIGENCE REVIEW PANEL (ed.), *Review of the Law of Negligence: Final Report*, Canberra, Commonwealth of Australia, 2002, available at: www.treasury.gov.au/Consultationsand Reviews/Reviews/2002/~/media/Treasury/Consultations%20and%20Reviews/Reviews%20and%20 Inquiries/2002/Review%20of%20the%20Law%20of%20Negligence/Key%20Documents/PDF/Law_Neg_Final.ashx (30.05.2017); JOSEPH A. PAGE, Reflections on Pain-and-Suffering Damages in the United States, in: Aurelia Colombi Ciacchi/Christine Godt/Peter Rott/Lesley J. Smith (eds.), *Haftungsrecht im dritten Millenium/Liability in the Third Millenium, Liber Amicorum Gert Brüggemeier*, Baden-Baden: Nomos, 2009, pp. 193–213; FILIPPO RANIERI, *Europäisches Obligationenrecht: ein Handbuch mit Texten und Materialien*, 3. Aufl., Wien: Springer, 2009, pp. 1539–1622; ROLAND SCHAER, Schockschäden und psychische Überlagerungen, in: Giordano Beati/Efrem Beretta/Roland Schaer (eds.), *Relazioni tra diritto civile e assicurazioni sociali: atti della giornata di studio del 1° giugno 1992*, Lugano: Commissione ticinese per la formazione permanente dei giuristi, 1993, pp. 19–47; F.A. TRINIDADE, Reformulation of the Nervous Shock Rules, *L.Q.R.* 2003, 204; STEPHAN WEBER, Gedanken und Bedenken zu zwei neuen Schockschaden-Urteilen, *HAVE/REAS* 2012, 288–291; FRANZ WERRO/JESSICA MABILLARD, Le prejudice resultant du choc nerveux en cas d'accident de la circulation routiere, in: Franz Werro/Thomas Probst (eds.), *Journées du droit de la circulation routière*, Bern: Stämpfli, 2012, pp. 1–26.

Chapter 12

Damage suffered by secondary victims

Damages for pure emotional harm following the loss or severe injury of a loved one

"The position that, in wrongful death cases, mere injury to feelings should not be compensated is regarded more and more as unacceptable."[1]

Scenario

The semi-final of a national cup competition is scheduled between two professional football clubs. On match day, a large number of spectators approach the stadium. Special stands are reserved for the supporters of the visiting team. As kick-off nears, the front side of the entrances to these stands is clearly overcrowded and seems to be leading to a crush. A few minutes before the start of the game, the security guards who are responsible for crowd control open the gates in order to alleviate this congestion. They then allow an excessively large number of spectators to enter the pens: around 2,000 people are admitted to a pen in which a maximum of 1,600 supporters should be allowed. The incoming supporters push the fans that are already inside the pen, squashing them against the metal fences situated at the pitch-side. In the resulting crush, 96 people are killed and over 400 physically injured.

The following morning, some people are informed by telephone that their loved ones died and are later summoned to identify their bodies.

The company in charge of security admits fault and liability in respect of the spectators injured or killed in the stadium.[2]

---

1 Oberster Gerichtshof, OGH (*Austrian Supreme Court of Justice*), 16.05.2001, JBl. 2001, 660.
2 Scenario inspired by the English case: House of Lords, *Alcock* v. *Chief Constable of South Yorkshire Police*, 28.11.1991, [1991] UKHL 5, [1992] 1 AC 310, [1991] 4 All ER 907. The claim was brought against the police in charge of security in the stadium. The case was in the British press again 23 years later, see: *The Guardian*, 13.09.2012, pp. 1, 2, 5: "Hillsborough: The Reckoning"; *Independent*, 12.09.2012, pp. 1, 6: "Hillsborough: Police Did Doctor Evidence in Bid to Avoid Blame" and 13.09.2012, pp. 1–7: "Hillsborough: At Long Last, the Truth"; *The Times*, 14.09.2012, pp. 1, 9: "Hillsborough Cover-Up: Police to Face Reckoning"; *Daily Mail*, 13.09.2012, pp. 1, 4–7: "Finally the Hillsborough Families Know the Truth: The Police Lied and Lied. Now Will They Get Justice?" After 27 years, a jury eventually determined that the victims were unlawfully killed, that numerous failings by police and the ambulance services contributed to their deaths, and that Liverpool fans did not contribute to the disaster, see www.theguardian.com/uk-news/2016/apr/26/hillsborough-inquests-jury-says-96-victims-were-unlawfully-killed.

In the disaster, among others:

- a woman lost her husband;
- a couple lost their minor son, another couple an adult son;
- a child lost his father; and
- a man lost his brother.

Some of the secondary victims suffer psychiatric illness, nervous shock, or post-traumatic stress disorder (see the subject of Chapter 11), whereas others do not and are thus not deemed to have been impaired in their own health. They all claim damages for their grief and sorrow following the loss of a loved one.

Questions

1) Chapter 11 provided information on the conditions under which different jurisdictions permit claims for *secondary victims* who have suffered psychiatric injury caused by an injury inflicted on a loved one (the *primary victim*). The scenario above is based on the English case *Alcock* v. *Chief Constable of South Yorkshire Police*, in which the claims of those suffering psychiatric harm, nervous shock, or post-traumatic stress disorder were rejected. Why?

2) In the previous chapter, Mrs Miller had (contrary to her husband) not suffered psychiatric illness and would thus not have a claim for nervous shock. Do those who lost a loved one in the disaster have a right to damages for their grief and sorrow, independent of any harm to their *own* health amounting to actual illness? In other words, can secondary victims successfully claim damages for their pure emotional harm or *bereavement*?

   a) What is the answer under *English* Common Law?[3] What about statutory law?

   b) What about *Irish* law and the jurisdictions of *New York* or *Florida*?

   c) Would Mr and Mrs Miller in Chapter 11, be entitled to receive damages for their grief and sorrow due to the loss of their children in these jurisdictions?

3) Look at the jurisdictions of *France, Germany, Switzerland, Austria, Greece, Portugal, Finland, Norway, Poland, Estonia*, the *Czech Republic, Slovenia, Romania*, the Canadian province of *Quebec*, and *Japan*.

   a) Do each of these jurisdictions award damages for grief and sorrow due to the loss of a loved one?

   b) If so, who are the potential beneficiaries of a claim for damages for grief and sorrow due to the loss of a loved one?

   c) In very few jurisdictions, the amount of damages for emotional harm due to the loss of a loved one is fixed by law or statute. The *Czech Republic* has recently stopped using tables. Can you imagine why? What are the advantages and the disadvantages of using tables?

   d) Would the secondary victims also benefit from a claim in these jurisdictions if the primary victim were not killed but severely injured?

4) Several codal or statutory provisions limit damages for grief and sorrow or emotional harm to cases of death of the primary victim. Despite these legislative limitations, it is not uncommon for the courts to extend the scope of damages for emotional harm to cases of (severe) injury of the primary victim. In what respect has the *Lithuanian* Supreme Court extended the scope of application of the Lithuanian Civil Code of 2001 beyond the situations expressly addressed by Art. 6.284 (1)? Compare with the development in Swiss law.

   In its judgments reported in the materials, the Lithuanian Supreme Court does not draw a clear line between nervous shock, on the one hand, and mental grief on the

---

3 See the opinion of Lord ACKNER in *Alcock*, in particular: "The nature of the cause of action", (1) and (3).

other. Likewise, in recent *Swiss* case law, courts only rarely talk of nervous shock and, instead, award damages for the emotional harm suffered by a secondary victim following the loss, or (severe) injury, of a loved one. What may be the advantage of focusing on such damages?

5) In several cases before the European Court of Human Rights, parents claimed damages for bereavement following the loss of an adult son. The young man had died while in a public institution (prison or hospital). The applicable national law only provided bereavement damages for loss of a *minor* child. Before the European Court of Human Rights, the parents argued that their Convention rights had been breached, invoking Art. 2 (in that the public authorities had failed to protect their son's life) and Art. 13 (in that there had been no effective remedy in national law for breach of Convention rights by public institutions) and claimed inter alia bereavement damages for the loss of their *adult* son. What did the Court decide?

6) How is the issue of damages for pure emotional harm following loss or severe injury of a loved one dealt with in the PETL, and what is the position of the DCFR?

7) In March 2015, an Airbus operated by the German airline Germanwings crashed in the French Alps, leading to the death of 150 passengers and crew members. The crash hereafter sparked a public debate regarding the need to introduce bereavement damages into *German* law. At this point in time, the German government had, in fact, already declared its intention to introduce damages for emotional harm following the loss of a loved one into German law.[4] If you were asked to provide advice based on a comparative analysis, how would you answer the following questions:

- Should damages for emotional harm be awarded to secondary victims?
- If so, should they be awarded exclusively for death, or also for the severe injury of a loved one?
- Should they be awarded in case of fault-based liability only (and if so, should liability be limited to gross negligence) or also in cases of strict liability?
- Who should be the beneficiaries?
- Would you recommend fixing the amount by law or statute, or would you leave it to the courts to fix the precise amounts of such damage awards?

Now have a look at the materials under the "Latest news" heading below. In which respect does the new § 844 of the German Civil Code (BGB) correspond to, or differ from, your proposal?

8) In a landmark decision of 2001, the *Austrian* Supreme Court introduced damages for emotional harm following the loss or the severe injury of a loved one into Austrian law. What role does the comparative argument play in this decision? What role does comparative law play in the case law of the Supreme Court of *Canada* regarding compensation for *solatium doloris*?

---

4 See the agreement of the governing coalition: "Deutschlands Zukunft gestalten – Koalitionsvertrag zwischen CDU, CSU und SPD" (*Shaping Germany's Future – Agreement Forming the Governing Coalition*), 18. Legislaturperiode, 16.12.2013, p. 102.

Table of contents

I. England and Wales

1. House of Lords, *Alcock* v. *Chief Constable of South Yorkshire Police*, 28.11.1991, [1991] UKHL 5, [1991] 4 All ER 907, [1992] 1 AC 310 .... p. 350
2. High Court (King's Bench), *Baker* v. *Bolton*, [1808] EWHC K.B. J92, (1808) 1 Camp 493; 170 ER 1033 .... p. 352
3. SIMON DEAKIN/ANGUS JOHNSTON/BASIL MARKESINIS, *Markesinis and Deakin's Tort Law*, 7th ed., Oxford: OUP, 2013, pp. 851–852 .... p. 353
4. Fatal Accidents Act 1976, Sect. 1A .... p. 354

II. Ireland

Civil Liability Act 1961 (revised), Sects. 47 (1), 48 (1), 49 (1) (a) and (b) .... p. 354

III. USA

1. Restatement of the Law – Torts (2nd), 1979, § 925. Actions for Causing Death .... p. 355
2. Wrongful death acts .... p. 356
   a) New York Estates, Powers & Trusts Law – Part 4. Rights of Members of Family Resulting From Wrongful Act, Neglect or Default Causing Death of Decedent, §§ 5–4.1, 5–4.3 .... p. 356
   b) Florida Wrongful Death Act, Sects. 768.16, 768.17, 768.19, 768.21 (2)-(4) .... p. 356

IV. France

1. Code civil (*Civil Code*), Arts. 1240, 1241 (former Arts. 1382, 1383) .... p. 357
2. Cour de cassation (*Court of Cassation*), 22.10.1946 (*Société nationale de Chemins de fers français* c. *Geneix et époux Chamard*), D. 1947, 59 .... p. 357
3. Cour de cassation (*Court of Cassation*), 29.11.1989 (*Balian* c. *Deturmeny*), J.C.P. 1990, pp. 31 ff. .... p. 358

V. Germany

1. Bürgerliches Gesetzbuch, BGB (*Civil Code*), §§ 253, 823 (1) .... p. 359
2. Oberlandesgericht Freiburg (*Freiburg Appellate Court*), 30.06.1953, JZ 1953, 704 .... p. 359

VI. Switzerland

1. Obligationenrecht/Code des obligations (*Code of Obligations*), Arts. 47, 49 .... p. 361
2. Zivilgesetzbuch/Code civil (*Civil Code*), Art. 28 .... p. 362
3. Bundesgericht/Tribunal fédéral (*Federal Supreme Court of Justice*), 22.04.1986, BGE 112 II 220 .... p. 362

VII. Austria

1. Allgemeines bürgerliches Gesetzbuch, ABGB (*General Civil Code*),
   §§ 1295 (1), 1325 .... p. 365
2. Oberster Gerichtshof, OGH (*Supreme Court of Justice*), 16.05.2001,
   JBl. 2001, 660; ZVR 2001, 73/284; ZEuP 2002, 825 .... p. 365

VIII. Greece, Portugal, Finland, Norway, Poland, Estonia, Czech Republic, Slovenia, Romania, Serbia, Japan

1. Αστικός Κώδικας (*Greek Civil Code*), Art. 932 .... p. 369
2. Código civil (*Portuguese Civil Code*), Art. 496 (2)-(4) .... p. 369
3. Vahingonkorvauslaki (*Finnish Tort Liability Act*), § 4a .... p. 370
4. Skadeserstatningsloven (*Norwegian Compensatory Damages Act*),
   § 3–5 (2) .... p. 370
5. Kodeks cywilny (*Polish Civil Code*), Art. 446 §§ 1, 4 .... p. 371
6. Võlaõigusseadus (*Estonian Code of Obligations*), § 134 (3) .... p. 371
7. Občanský zákoník (*Czech Civil Code*), § 444 (3), replaced by
   § 2959 in 2014 .... p. 372
8. Obligacijski zakonik (*Slovenian Code of Obligations*),
   Art. 180 .... p. 373
9. Codul civil (*Romanian Civil Code*), Art. 1391 (1) and (2) .... p. 374
10. Zakon o obligacionim odnosima (*Serbian Law of Contracts
    and Torts Act*), Art. 201 .... p. 374
11. 民法 (*Japanese Civil Code*), Art. 711 .... p. 375

IX. Lithuania

1. Civilinis kodeksas (*Civil Code*), Arts. 6.250, 6.284 (1) .... p. 375
2. Lietuvos Aukščiausiojo Teismo civilinių bylų skyriaus išplėstinės
   teisėjų kolegijos (*Supreme Court, Expanded Panel of Judges of
   the Civil Division*), 18.04.2005, Case No. 3K-7-255/2005 .... p. 376
3. Lietuvos Aukščiausiojo Teismo civilinių bylų skyriaus teisėjų
   kolegijos (*Supreme Court, Panel of Judges of the Civil Division*),
   23.02.2010, Case No. 3K-3-59/2010 .... p. 378

X. Quebec (Canada)

1. Code civil/Civil Code, Art. 1457 .... p. 379
2. Supreme Court of Canada, *Augustus* v. *Gosset*, 03.10.1996, [1996]
   3 S.C.R. 268 .... p. 379

XI. European Convention on Human Rights

1. European Convention on Human Rights, Arts. 2 (1), 3, 13 .... p. 381
2. European Court of Human Rights, *Keenan* v. *the United Kingdom*,
   03.04.2001, Nr. 27229/95, ECHR 2001-III .... p. 382
3. European Court of Human Rights, *Edwards* v. *United Kingdom*,
   14.03.2002, Nr. 46477/99, ECHR 2002-II .... p. 382
4. European Court of Human Rights, *Reynolds* v. *the United Kingdom*,
   13.03.2012, Nr. 2694/08, ECHR 2008 .... p. 383

XII. Principles of European Tort Law
PETL, Art. 10:301 (1) .... p. 384

XIII. Draft Common Frame of Reference
DCFR, Arts. VI. – 2:101 (4), 2:202 (1) .... p. 384

Latest news .... p. 384

Materials[5]

I. England and Wales

1. House of Lords, *Alcock v. Chief Constable of South Yorkshire Police*, 28.11.1991, [1991] UKHL 5, [1991] 4 All ER 907, [1992] 1 AC 310

LORD KEITH OF KINKEL: My Lords, the litigation with which these appeals are concerned arose out of the disaster at Hillsborough Stadium, Sheffield, which occurred on 15 April 1989. On that day a football match was arranged to be played at the stadium between the Liverpool and the Nottingham Forest football clubs. It was a semi-final of the F. A. Cup. The South Yorkshire police force, which was responsible for crowd control at the match, allowed an excessively large number of intending spectators to enter the ground at the Leppings Lane end, an area reserved for Liverpool supporters. They crammed into pens 3 and 4 below the West Stand, and in the resulting crush 95 people were killed and over 400 physically injured. Scenes from the ground were broadcast live on television from time to time during the course of the disaster, and recordings were broadcast later. The Chief Constable of South Yorkshire has admitted liability in negligence in respect of the deaths and physical injuries. Sixteen separate actions were brought against him by persons none of whom was present in the area where the disaster occurred [. . .]. All of them were connected in various ways with persons who were in that area, being related to such persons or, in one case, being a fiancée. In most cases the person with whom the plaintiff was concerned was killed, in other cases that person was injured [. . .]. All the plaintiffs claim damages for nervous shock resulting in psychiatric illness which they allege was caused by the experiences inflicted on them by the disaster. [. . .][6]

LORD ACKNER: My Lords, if sympathy alone were to be the determining factor in these claims, then they would never have been contested. [. . .] It is, however, trite law that the respondent, the Chief Constable of South Yorkshire, is not an insurer against psychiatric illness occasioned by the shock sustained by the relatives or friends of those who died or were injured, or were believed to have died or to have been injured. [. . .]

Since the decision of your Lordships' House in McLoughlin v. O'Brian [1983] 1 A.C. 410,[7] if not earlier, it is established law that: 1. A claim for damages for psychiatric illness resulting from shock caused by negligence can be made without the necessity of the plaintiff establishing that he was himself injured [except for suffering nervous shock] or was in fear of personal injury. 2. A claim for damages for such illness can be made when the shock results: a) From death or injury to the plaintiff's spouse or child or the fear of such death or injury and b) The shock has come about through the sight or hearing of the event, or its immediate aftermath.

---

5 For the original language versions of the materials reproduced in this chapter, see the companion website at www.routledge.com/9781138567733.

6 *Note by the author: Alcock* is a leading English authority on liability for psychiatric illness due to the injury of another (i.e. the topic of Chapter 11, pp. 317 ff.). However, the court also confirms the Common Law position (as opposed to the statutory law) on compensation for grief due to the loss of a loved one.

7 See above, Chapter 11, pp. 320 ff., I.

To succeed in the present appeals the plaintiffs seek to extend the boundaries of this cause of action by: 1. Removing any restrictions on the categories of persons who may sue; 2. Extending the means by which the shock is caused, so that it includes viewing the simultaneous broadcast on television of the incident which caused the shock; 3. Modifying the present requirement that the aftermath must be "immediate". [. . .]

The nature of the cause of action
[. . .] (1) Even though the risk of psychiatric illness is reasonably foreseeable, the law gives no damages if the psychiatric injury was not induced by shock. Psychiatric illnesses caused in other ways, such as from the experience of having to cope with the deprivation consequent upon the death of a loved one, attracts no damages. Brennan J. in the Jaensch case [. . .] gave as examples, the spouse who has been worn down by caring for a tortiously injured husband or wife and who suffers psychiatric illness as a result, but who, nevertheless, goes without compensation; a parent made distraught by the wayward conduct of a brain-damaged child and who suffers psychiatric illness as a result also has no claim against the tortfeasor liable to the child.

(2) Even where the nervous shock and the subsequent psychiatric illness caused by it could both have been reasonably foreseen, it has been generally accepted that damages for merely being informed of, or reading, or hearing about the accident are not recoverable. [. . .]

(3) Mere mental suffering, although reasonably foreseeable, if unaccompanied by physical injury, is not a basis for a claim for damages. To fill this gap in the law a very limited category of relatives are given a statutory right by the Administration of Justice Act 1982 section 3 inserting a new section 1A into the Fatal Accidents Act 1976 to bring an action claiming damages for bereavement.[8] [. . .]

(5) "Shock", in the context of this cause of action, involves the sudden appreciation by sight or sound of a horrifying event, which violently agitates the mind. [. . .]

As regards claims by those in the close family relationships referred to by Lord Wilberforce [in McLoughlin v. O'Brian], the justification for admitting such claims is the presumption, which I would accept as being rebuttable, that the love and affection normally associated with persons in those relationships is such that a defendant ought reasonably to contemplate that they may be so closely and directly affected by his conduct as to suffer shock resulting in psychiatric illness. While as a generalisation more remote relatives and, a fortiori, friends, can reasonably be expected not to suffer illness from the shock, there can well be relatives and friends whose relationship is so close and intimate that their love and affection for the victim is comparable to that of the normal parent, spouse or child of the victim and should for the purpose of this cause of action be so treated. [. . .]

The proximity of the plaintiff to the accident
It is accepted that the proximity to the accident must be close both in time and space. Direct and immediate sight or hearing of the accident is not required. It is reasonably foreseeable that injury by shock can be caused to a plaintiff, not only through the sight or hearing of the event, but of its immediate aftermath.

Only one of the plaintiffs before us was at the ground. However, it is clear from McLoughlin's case that there may be liability where subsequent identification can be regarded as part

---

[8] See below, p. 354.

of the "immediate aftermath" of the accident. Mr. Alcock identified his brother-in-law in a bad condition in the mortuary at about midnight, that is some eight hours after the accident. This was the earliest of the identification cases. Even if this identification could be described as part of the "aftermath", it could not in my judgment be described as part of the immediate aftermath. [. . .] Mrs. McLoughlin had arrived at the hospital within an hour or so after the accident. Accordingly in the post accident identification cases before your Lordships there was not sufficient proximity in time and space to the accident.

The means by which the shock is caused
Lord Wilberforce concluded [in the McLoughlin case] that the shock must come through sight or hearing of the event or its immediate aftermath but specifically left for later consideration whether some equivalent of sight or hearing, e.g. through simultaneous television, would suffice [. . .]. Of course it is common ground that it was clearly foreseeable by the Chief Constable that the scenes at Hillsborough would be broadcast live and that amongst those who would be watching would be parents and spouses and other relatives and friends of those in the pens behind the goal at the Leppings Lane end. However he would also know of the code of ethics which the television authorities televising this event could be expected to follow, namely that they would not show pictures of suffering by recognisable individuals. [. . .] Although the television pictures certainly gave rise to feelings of the deepest anxiety and distress, in the circumstances of this case the simultaneous television broadcasts of what occurred cannot be equated with the "sight or hearing of the event or its immediate aftermath". Accordingly shocks sustained by reason of these broadcasts cannot found a claim. [. . .][9]

Conclusion
[. . .] Brian Henderson was at the ground. His relatives who died were his two brothers. The quality of brotherly love is well known to differ widely – from Cain and Abel to David and Jonathan. I assume that Mr. Henderson's relationship with his brothers was not an abnormal one. His claim was not presented upon the basis that there was such a close and intimate relationship between them, as gave rise to that very special bond of affection which would make his shock-induced psychiatric illness reasonably foreseeable by the Chief Constable. [. . .] The other plaintiff who was present at the ground, Robert Alcock, lost a brother-in-law. He was not, in my judgment, reasonably foreseeable as a potential sufferer from shock-induced psychiatric illness, in default of very special facts and none was established. Accordingly their claims must fail, as must those of the other plaintiffs who only learned of the disaster by watching simultaneous television. I [. . .] would therefore dismiss these appeals.

2. High Court (King's Bench), *Baker v. Bolton*, [1808] EWHC K.B. J92, (1808) 1 Camp 493; 170 ER 1033

This was an action against the defendants as proprietors of a stage-coach, on the top of which the plaintiff and his late wife were travelling from Portsmouth to London, when

---

9 *Note by the author*: for new challenges due to modern technologies, and for potential answers, see B. B. CHATTERJEE, Rethinking Alcock in the New Media Age, *JETL* 2016, 272–299.

it was overturned; whereby the plaintiff himself was much bruised, and his wife was so severely hurt, that she died about a month after in an hospital. The declaration besides other special damage, stated, that "by means of the premises, the plaintiff had wholly lost, and been deprived of the comfort, fellowship, and assistance of his said wife, and had from thence hitherto suffered and undergone great grief, vexation, and anguish of mind".

It appeared that the plaintiff was much attached to his deceased wife [. . .].

But Lord Ellenborough said, the jury could only take into consideration the bruises which the plaintiff had himself sustained, and the loss of his wife's society, and the distress of mind he had suffered on her account, from the time of the accident till the moment of her dissolution [i.e. her death]. In a civil Court, the death of a human being could not be complained of as an injury; and in this case the damages, as to the plaintiff's wife, must stop with the period of her existence. [. . .]

3. SIMON DEAKIN/ANGUS JOHNSTON/BASIL MARKESINIS, *Markesinis and Deakin's Tort Law*, 7th ed., 2013, pp. 851–852

(D) DAMAGES FOR BEREAVEMENT

When the claimant's life expectancy is reduced by an injury and this causes him mental suffering this will be taken into account when assessing his damages for pain and suffering and loss of amenity. [. . .] In 1935 [. . .] the Court of Appeal in *Flint* v. *Lovell* held that there existed an independent heading of damages for loss of expectation of life and the House of Lords, two years later in *Rose* v. *Ford*, held that this right also survived for the benefit of the deceased estate. [. . .] In the case of death the only real function of these damages performed was to give the parents of young children killed in an accident a small sum which they would otherwise not have obtained [. . .].

FN 300: [. . .] In the case of death of a young child [. . .] its parents could recover nothing. Since it could not earn anything its 'value' to its parents was 'nil'. Like Oscar Wilde's cynic, English law knew the 'price' of everything but the value of nothing. Through the medium of damages for the expectation of life 'the meanness of refusing parents damages for their grief was neutralized by the absurdity of giving the dead child a claim for being killed' (J.A. Weir, Compensation for personal injury and death: recent proposals for reform, The Cambridge-Tilburg Law Lectures, First Series (Kluwer, 1978)).

Loss of expectation of life was abolished [. . .] and was replaced by a new claim, 'bereavement' [amending Sect. 1A of the Fatal Accidents Act, below], which gives a fixed sum by way of damages to a spouse for the loss of the other spouse and to parents for the loss of a child. [. . .]

As the parliamentary debates show, the acceptance of this new right raises many problems, philosophical as well as legal. In the first place, the very principle of paying a sum for bereavement is doubtful. As the Lord Chancellor put it: 'there is no sum of money at all that one can nominate which is not an insult to the bereaved person, whether it is £ 10 million or £ 10'. Having said this, he also accepted that others, perhaps the majority, might think otherwise [. . .]. But the sum should, he felt, be fixed. It would be unattractive, if not invidious, for courts to have to calculate a person's grief in money terms. This may explain why the sum is a conventional one, but it does not explain why a similar right was not given to children for the loss of one or both parents. [. . .]

4. Fatal Accidents Act 1976

Sect. 1A Bereavement. (1) An action under this Act may consist of or include a claim for damages for bereavement.
(2) A claim for damages for bereavement shall only be for the benefit –
(a) of the wife or husband or the civil partner of the deceased; and
(b) where the deceased was a minor who was never married or a civil partner –
(i) of his parents, if he was legitimate; and
(ii) of his mother, if he was illegitimate.
(3) [. . .] [T]he sum to be awarded as damages under this section shall be £ 12,980.
(4) Where there is a claim for damages under this section for the benefit of both the parents of the deceased, the sum awarded shall be divided equally between them [. . .].

II. Ireland

Civil Liability Act 1961 (revised)

Part IV

Fatal injuries

47. – (1) In this Part – "dependant" means, in respect of a deceased person whose death is caused by a wrongful act – (*a*) a spouse, civil partner [. . .], parent, grandparent, step-parent, child, grandchild, step-child, brother, sister, half-brother or half-sister of the deceased,
(*b*) [. . .]
(*c*) a person who was not married to or a civil partner of the deceased but who, until the date of the deceased's death, had been living with the deceased as the deceased's cohabitant within the meaning of section 172 of the Civil Partnership and Certain Rights and Obligations of Cohabitants Act 2010 for a continuous period of not less than three years,
who has suffered injury or mental distress as a result of the death;
"wrongful act" includes a crime. [. . .]

48. – (1) Where the death of a person is caused by the wrongful act of another such as would have entitled the party injured, but for his death, to maintain an action and recover damages in respect thereof, the person who would have been so liable shall be liable to an action for damages for the benefit of the dependants of the deceased. [. . .]

49. – (1) (*a*) The damages under section 48 shall be – [. . .] (ii) subject to paragraph (*b*) of this subsection, the total of such amounts (if any) as the judge shall consider reasonable compensation for mental distress resulting from the death to each of such dependants.
(*b*) The total of any amounts awarded by virtue of subparagraph (ii) of paragraph (*a*) of this subsection shall not exceed € 35,000. [. . .]

III. USA

1. Restatement of the Law – Torts (2nd), 1979

§ 925. **Actions for Causing Death.** The measure of damages for causing the death of another depends upon the wording of the statute creating the right of action and its interpretation.

Comment[10]

a. Following the holding in Baker v. Bolton, (1808) [. . .],[11] it was generally agreed that at common law, a person who had suffered pecuniary or other harm from the death of another had no cause of action against the person who caused the death. Thus a spouse, parent or master who had a cause of action against a tortfeasor who *physically harmed* a spouse, child or servant, for expenditures and for loss of services or society resulting from the harm, was denied a right of action for similar loss caused by the *death* of the wife, child or servant. [. . .]

This legal situation was remedied in England in 1846 by a statute commonly known as "Lord Campbell's Act," which provided that for the benefit of certain near relatives who had suffered *pecuniary loss* from the death of a person, the personal representatives should have a cause of action against the one who tortiously caused the death, provided that the deceased would have had a cause of action if he had been merely injured and not killed. Under the provisions of this statute, the amount recoverable depends upon proof of the probable contributions to the beneficiaries by the deceased during the life expectancy. This total amount is divided among the beneficiaries in proportion to the amount of loss suffered by each.

In the United States also, the omission of the common law has been corrected in every state by statutes colloquially known as "wrongful death acts." Most of these are modelled more or less closely on the English Act.[12] [. . .]

e. Harm to feelings. Damages for harm to the feelings of the survivors and compensation for mere loss of association or membership in the family are not granted,[13] although [. . .] damages for loss of advice, care, attention, guidance, or even companionship that has *pecuniary value* may be given. [. . .]

---

10 Emphasis added.
11 See above, pp. 352–353.
12 See the Fatal Accidents Act for *England* and *Wales*, above, p. 354.
13 *Note by the author*: see, however, the Florida Wrongful Death Act below, p. 356.

2. Wrongful death acts

a) New York Estates, Powers & Trusts Law

> **Part 4. Rights of members of family resulting from wrongful act, neglect or default causing death of decedent**
>
> **§ 5–4.1 Action by personal representative for wrongful act, neglect or default causing death of decedent.** 1. The personal representative, duly appointed in this state or any other jurisdiction, of a decedent who is survived by distributees may maintain an action to recover damages for a wrongful act, neglect or default which caused the decedent's death against a person who would have been liable to the decedent by reason of such wrongful conduct if death had not ensued. [. . .]
>
> **§ 5–4.3 Amount of recovery.** (a) The damages awarded to the plaintiff may be such sum as the jury or, where issues of fact are tried without a jury, the court or referee deems to be fair and just compensation for the *pecuniary*[14] injuries resulting from the decedent's death to the persons for whose benefit the action is brought. [. . .]
> (b) [. . .] [I]n addition to damages and expenses recoverable under paragraph (a) above, punitive damages may be awarded if such damages would have been recoverable had the decedent survived. [. . .][15]

See on the other hand:

b) Florida Wrongful Death Act

> **Florida statutes – Title XLV – TORTS – Chapter 768 – NEGLIGENCE – Part I – General Provisions**
>
> **768.16 Wrongful Death Act.** – Sections 768.16–768.26 may be cited as the "Florida Wrongful Death Act."
>
> **768.17 Legislative intent.** – It is the public policy of the state to shift the losses resulting when wrongful death occurs from the survivors of the decedent to the wrongdoer. [. . .]
>
> **768.19 Right of action.** – When the death of a person is caused by the wrongful act, negligence, default, or breach of contract or warranty of any person [. . .], and the event would have entitled the person injured to maintain an action and recover damages if death had not ensued, the person [. . .] that would have been liable in damages if death had not ensued shall be liable for damages as specified in this act notwithstanding the death of the person injured [. . .]. [. . .]

---

14 Emphasis added.
15 *Note by the author*: the rights of family members following the death of a loved one are regulated exclusively by this Act. Further damages are not recoverable.

768.21 Damages. – [. . .] Damages may be awarded as follows: [. . .] (2) The surviving spouse may [. . .] also recover for loss of the decedent's companionship and protection and for mental pain and suffering from the date of injury.
(3) Minor children of the decedent, and all children of the decedent if there is no surviving spouse, may also recover for lost parental companionship, instruction, and guidance and for mental pain and suffering from the date of injury. [. . .]
(4) Each parent of a deceased minor child may also recover for mental pain and suffering from the date of injury. Each parent of an adult child may also recover for mental pain and suffering if there are no other survivors. [. . .]

IV. France

1. Code civil (*Civil Code*)

Art. 1240 (ancien art. 1382). Tout fait quelconque de l'homme, qui cause à autrui un dommage, oblige celui par la faute duquel il est arrivé, à le réparer.

Art. 1241 (ancien art. 1383). Chacun est responsable du dommage qu'il a causé non seulement par son fait, mais encore par sa négligence ou par son imprudence.

Translation

Art. 1240 (former Art. 1382). Any act of a person, which causes damage to another, obliges the person by whose fault it occurred, to compensate it.

Art. 1241 (former Art. 1383). Everyone is liable for the damage he or she causes not only by his or her intentional act, but also by his or her negligent conduct or by his or her imprudence.

2. Cour de cassation (*Court of Cassation*), 22.10.1946 (*Société nationale de Chemins de fers français c. Geneix et époux Chamard*), D. 1947, 59

CIV. 22ND OCTOBER 1946. – CIVIL LIABILITY, NON-PECUNIARY DAMAGE, FATHER, CHILD VICTIM OF NON-FATAL ACCIDENT, DISABILITY

Having found that a father suffered non-pecuniary harm of an exceptional character as a result of feelings of grief that constantly recur whenever he sets eyes on his only daughter, who was injured in a railway accident and is now afflicted with a permanent disability which had the effect of seriously reducing her quality of life, the court below is justified in concluding that, under the provisions of the law which are subject to no relevant restriction, the father is entitled to compensation for harm of this sort; that is, harm which flowed directly from the accident in which his daughter had been injured, and which must be regarded as distinct from any harm suffered by the daughter herself.

[. . .] On the second ground of appeal: – Whereas the appellant contends that non-pecuniary harm is only compensable if it results from the deep and irremediable grief provoked by the loss of a loved one, a parent or a relative who is the victim of a fatal accident; and that for that reason, Mr Geneix has no claim to damages on the basis of a non-fatal injury caused to his daughter;[16] – Whereas, however, the judgment under appeal makes it clear that Mr Geneix had suffered "non-pecuniary harm of an exceptional character" as a result of the grief he has experienced, which constantly recurs whenever he sets eyes on his only daughter who is [. . .] now afflicted with a permanent disability which has the effect of seriously reducing her quality of life; whereas, in so characterising the nature and intensity of the feelings which affected Mr Geneix, the *Cour d'appel* was justified in deciding that, in these circumstances, he was entitled to compensation pursuant to the provisions of the law which contained no relevant restriction, damage of this sort being damage which stems directly from the accident in which his daughter had been injured, and being quite distinct from any damage caused to the daughter herself; that the judgment under appeal provided a proper justification for its decision, and did not act in breach of the provisions cited in the grounds of appeal;

For these reasons, the appeal is dismissed.

3. Cour de cassation (*Court of Cassation*), 29.11.1989 (*Balian c. Deturmeny*), J.C.P. 1990, pp. 31 ff.

Civil liability. – Damage. Compensation. Non-pecuniary damage. Damage occasioned to husband as a result of wife's permanent disablement stemming from surgeon's judicially-established professional negligence. Compensation (yes) [. . .].

The *Cour d'appel* acted contrary to Art. [1240] of the *Code civil* when it dismissed a husband's claim for damages against a surgeon in respect of non-pecuniary damage suffered by himself and his five-year-old daughter. This non-pecuniary damage stemmed from the state of health of the claimant's wife, who was permanently disabled after having undergone considerable pain and suffering as a result of the judicially-established professional error of the surgeon. Even if the distress suffered by the husband and child had been exacerbated by factors extraneous to the fault of the surgeon, the only reason why it occurred in the first place was the situation provoked by the surgeon's negligence. (Appeal from a judgment of the *Cour d'appel* of Aix-en-Provence dated 1.10.1987)

---

16 *Note by the author*: in case of *death*, it has long been recognised in French law that the person responsible for causing the death is liable to pay damages for bereavement to those who had close ties of love and affection with the deceased, see e.g. the case *Cour de cassation*, 13.02.1923, DP 1923, 1.52, note H. Lalou: a father is killed by a horse; the owner is held to pay damages to his three sons and one daughter for their emotional harm due to the loss of their father. For the preceding academic discussion, see M. Chausse, De L'intérêt d' Affection, *R.C.J.L.* 1895, 436; see also Y. Lambert-Faivre, *De la responsabilité encourue envers les personnes autres que la victime initiale: le problème dit du dommage par ricochet*, Lyon: Collection thèses françaises, Université de Lyon, 1959; J. Dupichot, *Des préjudices réfléchis nés de l'atteinte à la vie ou l'intégrité personnelle*, Paris: LGDJ, 1969.

V. Germany

1. Bürgerliches Gesetzbuch, BGB (*Civil Code*)[17]

§ 253. **Immaterieller Schaden.** (1) Wegen eines Schadens, der nicht Vermögensschaden ist, kann Entschädigung in Geld nur in den durch das Gesetz bestimmten Fällen gefordert werden.
(2) Ist wegen einer Verletzung des Körpers, der Gesundheit, der Freiheit oder der sexuellen Selbstbestimmung Schadensersatz zu leisten, kann auch wegen des Schadens, der nicht Vermögensschaden ist, eine billige Entschädigung in Geld gefordert werden.

§ 823. **Schadensersatzpflicht.** (1) Wer vorsätzlich oder fahrlässig das Leben, den Körper, die Gesundheit, die Freiheit, das Eigentum oder ein sonstiges Recht eines anderen widerrechtlich verletzt, ist dem anderen zum Ersatze des daraus entstehenden Schadens verpflichtet. [. . .]

Translation[18]

§ 253. Non-pecuniary loss. (1) Compensation for loss that is non-pecuniary can only be claimed in the cases stipulated by law.
(2) Where compensation is due for injury to body, health, freedom, or sexual self-determination, the injured party can claim an equitable amount of monetary compensation also for non-pecuniary loss.

§ 823. Duty to compensate loss. (1) Whosoever unlawfully injures, intentionally or negligently, the life, body, health, freedom, property, or other right of another person, has an obligation to the other person to compensate the resulting loss. [. . .]

2. Oberlandesgericht Freiburg (*Freiburg Appellate Court*), 30.06.1953, JZ 1953, 704

BGB §§ 823, [253 II].

Where a mother suffers induced depression as a result of negligence causing the death of her child, she has a valid claim for damages.
These damages are not awarded in respect of grief caused by the death of the child, but rather on the basis of physical and emotional injury to her as a consequence of damage to her own health.

Oberlandesgericht FREIBURG, Judgment dated 30.6.1953–2 U 115/52.

On 1st March 1951, Doctor M., a general practitioner, ordered in the defendant's pharmacy 200 ml of medical saline solution plus codeine cough syrup for the claimant's [his wife's] 8½-year-old daughter who was suffering from measles. The defendant pharmacist confused

---

17 Siehe die Erläuterung oben, Kapitel 5, S. 81.
18 See the explanatory comment in Chapter 5, p. 81.

the containers; when making up the saline solution, instead of the necessary 1.8g of sodium chloride, he added the equivalent quantity of codeine. That day, after Dr M. made an enema for the child from half of the supposed saline solution together with seven drops of Sympatol, the child suffered from severe cramps; after fighting for her life for sixteen hours, she died. The autopsy revealed that the death was due to codeine poisoning. The defendant pharmacist was prosecuted and fined 1,000 DM[19] for negligently causing the death of the child. [. . .]

The *Landgericht* decided in favour of the [claimant, i.e. the child's mother], awarding damages in the amount of 2,000 DM, and the defendant appealed. [. . .] On appeal, the *Oberlandesgericht* modified the judgment by reducing the defendant's liability from 2,000 DM to 1,000 DM, but otherwise upheld the decision of the lower court.

Reasoning of the court:

This claim for damages is brought [by the mother of the dead child] pursuant to §§ 823 (1) and [253 (2)] BGB.[20] According to the provisions of the BGB concerning extra-contractual liability, a person has no claim for damages, for either material or non-material harm, if he himself has not suffered injury of some legally-protected right or interest. In such cases, we talk of "indirect" damage, and characterise the regime in §§ 844 and 845 BGB as a strictly limited exception to the basic principle that only those directly damaged can claim compensation.[21] [. . .] However, this consideration must not be allowed to blind us from the fact that even an indirect injury of a legally-protected right or interest is enough to found a claim, provided that an adequate causal relation is shown between it and the tortious act. [. . .] The interests of clarity are best served if we do not ask whether injury or damage is direct or indirect, but rather concentrate on the issue of whether the victim has suffered an injury to a legally-protected right or interest, and if so, whether there is a sufficient causal connection between that injury and the tortious act. [. . .]

The only question, therefore, is whether the claimant herself has suffered injury to her health or bodily integrity as a sufficiently-established result of the death of her child. If so, she has a right to compensation not only for physical injury, but also for non-material harm arising from this damage. [. . .]

It is generally acknowledged that there can be harm to physical or mental health as a result of even a purely emotional affectation. [. . .] On the other hand, mere grief over the

---

19 Today worth around € 3,800.
20 *Note by the author*: BGB § 847, the provision in force at the relevant time and hence the one referred to by the court, was removed in 2002 when the BGB was reformed. The current provisions concerning liability for non-pecuniary loss in respect of injuries to health now appear in BGB § 253 (2), and the citation from the judgment has been altered accordingly.
21 BGB § 844 (Third-party compensation claims in the case of death) provides (in English translation): "(1) In cases where death is caused, the person liable in damages must reimburse the costs of a funeral to the person under a duty to bear these costs.

(2) If the person killed, at the time of the injury, stood in a relationship to a third party on the basis of which he was obliged or might become obliged by operation of law to provide maintenance for that person and if the third party has as a result of the death been deprived of his right to maintenance, then the person liable in damages must give the third party damages by payment of an annuity to the extent that the person killed would have been obliged to provide maintenance for the presumed duration of his life; the provisions of § 843 (2) to (4) apply with the necessary modifications. Liability in damages also arises where the third party at the time of injury had been conceived but not yet born".

BGB § 845 (Compensation claims for lost services) provides (in English translation): "In the case of death or injury to body or health, or in the case of deprivation of liberty, the person liable in damages must give a third party compensation for loss of services by payment of an annuity if the injured person by operation of law was under a duty to the third party to render services in the household or business of the latter. [. . .]".

loss of a near relative, however overwhelming or sustained, is admittedly a matter affecting the emotions, but not of itself an injury to health. However, as soon as a person's emotional devastation transcends mere grief and attains the status of physical or psychological harm, there is a case of injury to health. [. . .] The victim can recover damages for any material or non-material harm consequent on this injury. In this context, the *Landgericht* rightly points out that it is not always easy to establish whether the line has been crossed between simple emotional grief and actual psychological harm. Nevertheless, this argument cannot convince us to consider any other means of assessment. [. . .] Cases of psychiatric injury will normally be limited to particularly tragic situations leading to the death of near relatives;[22] consequently, an award of damages for the immaterial consequences of injuries of this type does not open the door to claims for compensation for grief felt simply because of the death [. . .].

The *Landgericht* rightly responded in the affirmative to the question of whether the claimant herself suffered harm to her health as a result of the defendant's wrong. The expert witness, Dr K, has explained in detail how the child's death and the horrific circumstances surrounding it [. . .] gave rise to an induced depression in a clearly sensitive claimant, leaving her entirely unable to work for four months and only able to work part-time at 40% for a further two; he explained that this was to be regarded as an illness in the psychiatric sense, which was cured only by a trip abroad and by falling pregnant again. [. . .] As to whether there existed a sufficient causal connection between the incorrect preparation of the medicine and the claimant's illness, there can be no doubt whatsoever. Ordinary experience makes it clear that the negligent killing of a child is capable of causing serious harm to the health of a sensitive mother. Furthermore, this was foreseeable to the defendant.

Regarding the amount of the claimant's compensation, the only legally relevant suffering was that which affected the claimant herself as a result of her illness. The defendant correctly argues that the claimant's grief over the death of her child must be left out of consideration in so far as it resulted not from her illness but was attributable simply to the loss of her child and its consequences. [. . .] The *Landgericht*, in fixing the amount of damages at 2,000 DM, unjustifiably based its figure on the overall grief of the claimant over the death of her child, and failed to realise that the harm suffered by the mother justified an award of compensation only on the basis of actual harm to her own health [as opposed to pure emotional harm due to the loss of her child]. As a result, a reduction in the award of damages made by the lower court is appropriate. Having regard to all the circumstances of the case, the Senate considered a payment of 1,000 DM an appropriate reflection of the physical and psychological illness suffered by the claimant following the death of her child.

VI. Switzerland

1. Obligationenrecht/Code des obligations (*Code of Obligations*)

> Art. 47. **Leistung von Genugtuung.** Bei Tötung eines Menschen oder Körperverletzung kann der Richter unter Würdigung der besonderen Umstände dem Verletzten oder den Angehörigen des Getöteten eine angemessene Geldsumme als Genugtuung zusprechen.
>
> Art. 49. **Bei Verletzung der Persönlichkeit.** (1) Wer in seiner Persönlichkeit widerrechtlich verletzt wird, hat Anspruch auf Leistung einer Geldsumme als Genugtuung,

---

22 See also the judgment of the German Federal Supreme Court above, Chapter 11, pp. 332–333.

sofern die Schwere der Verletzung es rechtfertigt und diese nicht anders wiedergutgemacht worden ist.
(2) Anstatt oder neben dieser Leistung kann der Richter auch auf eine andere Art der Genugtuung erkennen.

Translation

Art. 47. Satisfaction. In cases of death or personal injury, the court may award the victim of personal injury or the dependants of the deceased an appropriate sum by way of satisfaction taking into account the specific circumstances of the case.

Art. 49. Injury to Personality Rights. (1) Any person whose personality rights are unlawfully infringed is entitled to a sum of money by way of satisfaction provided this is justified by the seriousness of the infringement and no other measures have been taken to remedy the damage.
(2) The court may order that satisfaction be provided in another manner instead of, or in addition to, monetary compensation.

2. Zivilgesetzbuch/Code civil (*Civil Code*)

Art. 28. (1) Wer in seiner Persönlichkeit widerrechtlich verletzt wird, kann zu seinem Schutz gegen jeden, der an der Verletzung mitwirkt, das Gericht anrufen.
(2) Eine Verletzung ist widerrechtlich, wenn sie nicht durch Einwilligung des Verletzten, durch ein überwiegendes privates oder öffentliches Interesse oder durch Gesetz gerechtfertigt ist.

Translation

Art. 28. (1) Any person whose personality is unlawfully infringed may petition the court for protection against all those causing the infringement.
(2) An infringement is unlawful unless it is justified by the consent of the person whose rights are infringed or by an overriding private or public interest or by law.

3. Bundesgericht/Tribunal fédéral (*Federal Supreme Court of Justice*), 22.04.1986, BGE 112 II 220[23]

Claim by a husband for pain and suffering in respect of harm to his personality resulting from his wife's serious disability following an accident (Art. 28 CC; Art. 47, Art. 49 CO).

---

[23] For the right to damages for emotional harm following the loss of a close family member in *Swiss* law, see already above, Chapter 11, p. 334, under B. (first para.).

A. – On 16th April 1977, C.X.'s wife, E.X., was knocked down and grievously injured by a motorcyclist on a pedestrian crossing in Zurich. As a result of the accident, the victim lost her sight and fell into a state of deep unconsciousness. [. . .] After a while she was able to breathe normally again, but only through an opening in her neck. Although she began to have isolated lucid intervals, the doctors at the time held out little hope of improvement.

In the autumn of 1980, Mrs X was admitted to the Y nursing-home [. . .]. Contrary to her prognosis up until then, she began to be able to express herself in rudimentary speech. In addition, she gained the ability to swallow and recovered the capacity to feed herself; however, she remained dependent on constant care and was still confined to a wheelchair. Although her understanding is impaired, she realises that she is blind. Recovery is out of the question: her life expectancy has been reduced as a result of the accident.

[. . .] Mrs X received, inter alia, pain and suffering damages of CHF 60,000, plus interest, from the insurers of the motorcyclist who had negligently caused the accident. [. . .]

B. – On 10th January 1985, C.X. [her husband] brought a claim against the insurers V, based on Arts. 47 and 49 CO, seeking the payment of CHF 40,000 to compensate for the severe interference with his personal circumstances stemming from the consequences of his wife's accident. On 9th July 1985, the Zurich cantonal commercial court dismissed the claim.

C. – The plaintiff appealed against the judgment of the commercial court, asking for the decision to be reversed and his claim to be upheld. [. . .] The *Bundesgericht* allowed the appeal.

Extract from the court's reasoning:

2. The judgment under appeal was essentially based on the idea that Art. 47 CO limits the defendant's liability [to the case of death of the primary victim], thereby ruling out a claim by relatives in their own right for the reflective loss they suffered in cases of mere injury of the primary victim. A claim based on the general provision of Art. 49 CO (according to the argument) was ruled out, Art. 47 being a *lex specialis*.

a) In its judgment of 11th March 1986, in the case of *G v. Swiss Confederation* (ATF 112 II 121 ff, BGE 112 II 121 ff.), the First Civil Section of the *Bundesgericht* approved the award of damages for pain and suffering to a father who had suffered shock and resulting incapacity as a consequence of the accidental death of two of his sons. The court explicitly rejected the defendant's argument that mere reflective losses could not be the subject of compensation. The court held that a person who suffered injury to an interest protected as an absolute right suffers direct damage, even if another person related to him formed an intermediate link in the chain of causation between the harmful event and the harm he suffered [. . .].[24]

In the present case, there has been an interference with the plaintiff's personal circumstances, which are protected as an absolute right (Art. 28 CC). For that reason, it is impermissible to dismiss the claim for compensation on the grounds that the plaintiff merely suffered indirect harm. Nor can the assumption made by the lower court, that Art. 47 CO is a specific provision excluding the application of Art. 49 CO, be upheld, given that the

---

24 See above, Chapter 11, section VI. 2. In the present case, the husband did not claim to have suffered psychological injury, nervous shock, or PTSD.

plaintiff's argument is that his own personal circumstances [and thus his personality right] have been detrimentally affected. [. . .]

b) Under Art. 49 (1) CO, a person suffering damage to his personal circumstances is entitled to payment of a sum of money as compensation if this sum is justified by the particular gravity of the harm. Under the wording of the provision, a person has a right of action for harm to his circumstances if particular conditions are fulfilled. It should not be inferred from this provision that certain persons are excluded, nor can one infer a restriction on compensation for harm caused in a particular way, or harm of a particular type.

c) In the decision BGE 108 II 433 f., the *Bundesgericht*, in the course of awarding pain and suffering damages to a little girl afflicted with long-term loss of consciousness, also took account of the effect that her injury had on her parents who looked after her. Thus, the court indirectly awarded compensation, not only to the injured person, but also to her near relatives even though they themselves had not made any claim. In doing this, the court did not depart from the previous practice denying relatives of injured parties a claim to damages in their own right; but it had regard to the fact that the grief and anguish of relatives in cases of that sort is possibly greater than in the case of wrongful death, where Art. 47 CO expressly provides for a claim for bereavement damages.

The indirect route taken by the *Bundesgericht* in dealing with injured parties was not without its critics. It led TERCIER to ask, in a discussion of the case, whether it would not be more consistent to afford near relatives their own claim, whether by the analogous use of Art. 47 CO or directly under Art. 49 [. . .].

d) In two judgments, cantonal courts approved, in principle, claims by relatives for compensation of their emotional harm [. . .].

e) French practice has for many years allowed near relatives to bring a claim for non-pecuniary loss in the case of serious personal injury [that had been inflicted on a primary victim] (ZWEIGERT/KÖTZ, Einführung in die Rechtsvergleichung auf dem Gebiete des Privatrechts, Vol. II, 2 ed. 1984, S. 358; MAZEAUD, Traité de la responsabilité civile, 6th ed., II, n. 1874, p. 950). With regard to practice in Italy, there is one known judgment whereby damages for non-pecuniary loss were available to the mother of a minor who was seriously injured in an accident (Tribunale civile, Busto Arsizio, 26.9.1984, Archivio giuridico della circolazione e dei sinistri stradali 1985, pp. 818 ff., noted G. Gussoni, pp. 823–824), on the ground that the pain and anguish suffered by the relatives of a seriously injured person could be as great as, or for that matter even greater than, that in the case of death (p. 280). [. . .][25]

3. From this reasoning, it is plain to see that the plaintiff's right to claim must be upheld. All that remains to be asked is whether the conditions laid down in Art. 49 CO are satisfied in this case. On this point, Basic Principle No 13 recommended by the Committee of Ministers

---

25 *Note by the author*: in recent years, courts in *Italy* have been awarding the highest sums in Europe for bereavement damages. They hereby refer to the Italian Constitution, according to which family ties enjoy the highest legal protection. For the loss of a spouse, the amount awarded can vary between roughly € 43,000 and € 230,000, and in some cases may even be as high as € 300,000. For the loss of a child, parents may receive between € 25,000 and € 196,000. For the loss of a parent, a minor child might receive between € 25,000 and € 158,000. Finally, for the loss of a sibling, the amount awarded by the courts starts at around € 6,000, and may in some cases rise as high as € 90,000; see, with numerous references, M. WENTER, Regulierung von Personenschäden im italienischen Recht, *zfs* 2012, 4; G.CHRISTIANDL/D. HINGHOFER-SZALKAY, Ersatzansprüche für immaterielle Schäden aus Tötung naher Angehöriger – eine rechtsvergleichende Untersuchung, *ZfRV* 2007, 44 at 58 ff.

in the Council of Europe in its Resolution 75–7 dated 14.3.1975 can be taken into account, only envisaging awards to relatives for non-pecuniary loss where their suffering has been exceptional ("*souffrances d'un caractère exceptionnel*") (see J.-F. Egli in Mélanges André Grisel, pp. 325 and 338). The findings of fact in the lower court are sufficient to permit this court to deal with the question: there can be no doubt that the conditions are satisfied.

a) According to the judgment under appeal, at the time of the accident, Mr and Mrs X had been married for 24 years. The accident has entirely destroyed the previous lifelong relationship enjoyed by the plaintiff. The companionship of marriage has been largely eliminated, a matter exacerbated by the fact that the marriage has remained childless. The plaintiff, who devotes his time intensively to caring for his wife, has hardly any time to himself apart from his work in the nursing-home. The fact that Mrs X is at least partly aware of her condition further adds to the burden he has to bear. [...]

b) The claim for CHF 40,000 plus interest at 5% must therefore be upheld.

VII. Austria

1. Allgemeines bürgerliches Gesetzbuch, ABGB (*General Civil Code*)

§ 1295. (1) Jedermann ist berechtigt, von dem Beschädiger den Ersatz des Schadens, welchen dieser ihm aus Verschulden zugefügt hat, zu fordern; der Schade mag durch Übertretung einer Vertragspflicht oder ohne Beziehung auf einen Vertrag verursacht worden sein. [...]

§ 1325. Wer jemanden an seinem Körper verletzt, bestreitet die Heilungskosten des Verletzten, ersetzt ihm den entgangenen, oder, wenn der Beschädigte zum Erwerb unfähig wird, auch den künftig entgehenden Verdienst; und bezahlt ihm auf Verlangen überdies ein den erhobenen Umständen angemessenes Schmerzensgeld.

Translation

§ 1295. (1) Every person is entitled to claim compensation from the wrongdoer for the damage the latter has negligently inflicted upon him or her; the damage may have been caused by the breach of a contractual duty or independent of any contract. [...]

§ 1325. Whosoever injures a person's body must bear the costs of healing and compensate him or her for lost earnings, and, if the person harmed loses his or her earning capacity, also for the loss of future earnings, and moreover has to pay, on demand, damages for pain and suffering that are adequate in the circumstances.

2. Oberster Gerichtshof, OGH (*Supreme Court of Justice*), 16.05.2001, 2 Ob 84/01v, JBl. 2001, 660; ZVR 2001, 73/284; ZEuP 2002, 825

The Supreme Court decides [...] that the appeal fails. [...]

Reasons for the decision

The plaintiffs' eight-year-old daughter, a pedestrian, was knocked down and killed by a truck driven by the first defendant, owned by the second defendant, and insured in respect of liability by the third defendant. The first plaintiff (the father) claimed (*inter alia*) 100,000 Austrian Schilling and the second plaintiff (the mother) claimed 200,000 Austrian Schilling[26] as damages for non-pecuniary loss [. . .].

[. . .] The first plaintiff was told about the accident by a neighbour, and found his daughter still lying in the street where it had happened. The emergency doctor told him that his daughter would not have stood a chance. From a neuropsychiatric and neuropsychological point of view, the parents suffered a psychologically normal grief reaction, but there was no nervous shock or post-traumatic stress disorder. [. . .] The first plaintiff reacted to his daughter's accident with an attack of grief, a reaction which is psychologically normal, understandable and deserving of sympathy. His continuing depression and dissatisfaction at the time he was examined is the product of his continuing grief. [. . .] The second plaintiff, the mother, suffered from overwhelming grief [. . .]. In neuropsychological terms, this was a normal reaction. There was no indication of post-traumatic stress disorder. [. . .]

In its decision, the first instance court found no fault with the first defendant; however, it also held that no adequate exculpatory evidence under § 9 EKHG (Eisenbahn- und Kraftfahrzeughaftpflichtgesetz = *Act on Liability for Damage Caused by Rail and Road Traffic*) had been given (and so the defendant was strictly liable, i.e. liable without fault, according to that provision). [. . .]

An appeal is permissible here, since the question of whether mere harm to the feelings of the near relatives of a deceased person is compensable needs to be discussed. The appeal is, however, ultimately unsuccessful. In essence, the claimants allege that their claim as bereaved parents for damages corresponding to their suffering comes under the scope of compensable damage to third parties, even though they do not suffer any more than ordinary grief and even though they do not claim to suffer any pathological condition. [. . .]

Since its decision in 2 Ob 45/93 (= ZVR 1995/46), the relevant Senate of the Court has accepted that shock suffered by the close relatives of accident victims is compensable. This is because, through being subjected to nervous harm, a relative has suffered interference with his absolutely protected right to bodily integrity, and thus has to be viewed as suffering direct damage.[27] [. . .] Lastly, shock occasioned to a relative has been accepted as compensable even where caused, not by the accident itself, but by being informed about it.

Admittedly, all these cases involved harm to health amounting to actual illness. The existence of an independent claim for suffering caused by the death of a near relative where there was no such injury to the plaintiff's health was denied in the (older) case-law [. . .].

Danzl [. . .], for one, has sided with the established case-law. [. . .] Harrer also denies the possibility of a claim for damages in respect of grief suffered by the bereaved. Similarly, Reischauer [. . .] expresses the view that a claim for damages is to be ruled out on the basis of

---

26 Today worth around € 14,600.
27 See above, Chapter 11, pp. 337–338.

§ 1327 ABGB.[28] The issue, he says, is simply whether the immaterial harm following the loss of a loved one can be regarded as bodily injury within the meaning of § 1325 ABGB[29] [. . .].

On the other hand, Koziol thinks it may be possible, on the basis of value judgments already to be found in the law, to say that there can be an award of compensation to close relatives for (pure) harm to feelings. He [. . .] is in favour of drawing an analogy with § 1327 ABGB. Reaching the same conclusion as Koziol, Karner has advocated the use of Art. 47 of the Swiss CO as a source of inspiration. Lastly, and most recently, Christian Huber has suggested that compensation to relatives for the immaterial harm that they suffer following the loss of a loved one should be separated from damages for shock, and made available whenever there is very substantial mental disruption to them.

A glance at the law in other European countries (see Stoll, Haftungsfolgen im bürgerlichen Recht [1993] 359 f.; Kadner Graziano, Schmerzensgeld für Angehörige – angemessener Ausgleich immaterieller Beeinträchtigungen oder exzessiver Ersatz mittelbarer Schäden? ZEuP 1996, 135, 140 ff; Vorndran, Schmerzensgeld für Hinterbliebene bei der Tötung naher Angehöriger, ZR 1988, 293) shows that, in most jurisdictions, damages for immaterial harm following the loss of a loved one are made available to the relatives of those killed – though admittedly they take different forms. This is true in Switzerland, France, Italy, Spain, England, Scotland, Greece, Yugoslavia, Belgium and Turkey. By contrast, compensation for non-pecuniary loss of this sort is denied in Germany (and, according to Kadner Graziano, in Sweden as well). German case-law permits the compensation of relatives for such harm only where there is a specific and tangible effect on the plaintiff's health [. . .].[30] Indeed, according to Vorndran, in France, the German position is sometimes rejected as being contrary to *ordre public*. [. . .][31]

Taking into account the above matters, the Senate responsible for deciding this case has concluded as follows: the position that, in wrongful death cases, mere injury to feelings should not be compensated is regarded more and more as unacceptable. Distinguishing grief from grief accompanied by illness is frequently problematic. Bereaved parents grieving over the death of children will find it hard to understand the argument that they should have no claim for damages for the immaterial harm which they suffer following their loss because, in the absence of actual illness, what has materialised is simply one of life's general risks which they are expected to shoulder themselves. While minor bodily injuries

---

28 § 1327 provides (in English translation): "If bodily injury results in death, not only must all expenses be compensated, but also what is lost thereby by the surviving dependants for whose maintenance the deceased was obliged to provide by law".
29 *Note by the author*: see in this case above, Chapter 11, pp. 337–338.
30 *Note by the author*: see above, pp. 359 ff.
31 *Note by the author*: in a recent case, according to the relevant provisions of Private International Law, the *Italian* courts had to apply a foreign (*Austrian*) law which did not, at this point in time, provide damages for victims experiencing emotional harm following the loss of a loved one. The Corte di Cassazione held that the refusal to compensate emotional harm following the loss of a daughter/sister who was killed in a road traffic accident violated not only (1) the Italian Constitution, but also (2) Art. 8 of the European Convention on Human Rights (providing a "Right to respect for private and family life"), (3) Art. 7 of the Charter of Fundamental Rights of the European Union (protecting "private and family life"), and (4) as a consequence, Italian *ordre public*, see Corte di Cassazione Civile, sez. III. 22.08.2013, n. 19405, *Foro it.*, 2014, col. 2809 note M. CASORIA (on the application of Austrian law as it existed prior to the 2001 decision of the Austrian Supreme Court of Justice). The Appellate Court of Venice therefore took the decision to apply Italian law, according to which it awarded damages in the amount of € 65,000 for each parent and € 20,000 for each sibling.

such as bruises or sprains automatically give rise to damages for pain and suffering, those damages would not be available in the case of (mere) distress over the loss of a near relative, even though such distress would generally be regarded as much more serious.

It seems particularly outlandish that, if the law specifically allows for compensation for injured feelings under certain conditions where property is damaged (§ 1331 ABGB[32]), it should not do the same in the case of the death of a loved one. Such an absolute limitation on liability cannot be reconciled with the scheme intended by the legislator.

Provided that the danger of an over-expansion of liability can be contained by way of a strict limit on the category of those entitled to claim, it is the opinion of the Senate that there should be no concern about regarding this as a gap in the law that is filled by way of analogy. This solution has to fit in with the values already expressed in the law: radical and comprehensive reform is something only the legislator can undertake. But if we look at §§ 1331 [. . .], 1328 [. . .],[33] and 1329 ABGB [. . .],[34] we can infer from them an underlying current of thought, to the effect that, in order for injured feelings to be compensable in the absence of some bodily injury (§ 1325 ABGB), there should be a requirement of qualified fault [. . .].

The Senate therefore reaches the conclusion that it is only in the case of gross negligence or intentional harm that there can be liability to give compensation for injured feelings resulting from the loss of a close relative, where that loss has not caused any actual harm to the plaintiff's health within § 1325 ABGB. By contrast, in the case of lesser carelessness, and also in the case of strict liability, the necessary serious legal justification for awarding damages for emotional harm following the loss or the severe injury of a loved one is lacking.

In the case before the court, there is no need to fear an explosion of claims for injured feelings, since parents grieving over the accidental death of an eight-year-old child living with them must in any case belong to the small class of persons clearly deserving protection. Here, according to the findings of fact in the court below, the plaintiffs have not suffered any injury to their health; and also, as regards the second and third defendants, they are liable only according to the rules on non-fault (or strict) liability arising under the EKHG. Thus, following the above reasoning, in the absence of gross negligence attributable to the man at the wheel, the defendants cannot be held liable [. . .] to pay damages for the plaintiffs' injured feelings. As a result, this appeal must fail.[35]

---

32 ABGB § 1331 provides (in English translation): "If a person's patrimony is damaged *through intent or conspicuous negligence* of another, the victim is also entitled to claim lost profits and, if the damage was caused through an act forbidden by criminal law, or through wantonness and spitefulness, *such value as is attributable to his particular preferences*"(emphasis added).

33 ABGB § 1328 provides (in English translation): "A person who abuses another either through sexual intercourse or any other sexual act procured by criminal conduct, or otherwise by *deceit, threat or exploitation of a relation of dependency or authority*, must compensate the actual damage suffered and the lost profit, and provide *appropriate compensation for the encroachment suffered*" (emphasis added).

34 ABGB § 1329 provides (in English translation): "Whosoever deprives a person of his liberty through violent abduction, private seizure, or *intentionally* through unlawful arrest, is obligated to restore the person harmed to his previous liberty and to *provide full satisfaction.* [. . .]" (emphasis added).

35 *Note by the author*: in later cases, the requirement of gross negligence was met and the Supreme Court of Justice granted damages for emotional harm, both in cases of loss and of severe and lasting injury of the primary victim, for references see E. KARNER, Trauerschmerz und Schockschäden in der aktuellen Judikatur, *ZVR* 2008, 44.

VIII. Greece, Portugal, Finland, Norway, Poland, Estonia, Czech Republic, Slovenia, Romania, Serbia, Japan

1. Αστικός Κώδικας (*Greek Civil Code*)

Άρθρο 932. Ικανοποίηση της ηθικής βλάβης. Σε περίπτωση αδικοπραξίας, ανεξάρτητα από την αποζημίωση για την περιουσιακή ζημία, το δικαστήριο μπορεί να επιδικάσει εύλογη κατά την κρίση του χρηματική ικανοποίηση λόγω ηθικής βλάβης. Αυτό ισχύει ιδίως για εκείνον που έπαθε προσβολή της υγείας, της τιμής ή της αγνείας του ή στερήθηκε την ελευθερία του. Σε περίπτωση θανάτωσης προσώπου η χρηματική αυτή ικανοποίηση μπορεί να επιδικαστεί στην οικογένεια του θύματος λόγω ψυχικής οδύνης.

Translation

Art. 932. Compensation for moral harm. In the case of a tort, the court may, independent of damages for pecuniary harm, award a reasonable sum as compensation for moral harm. This applies especially to a person who has suffered injury to health, honour, or chastity or was deprived of his or her liberty. In the case of death, this monetary compensation may be awarded to the family of the victim for pain and suffering.[36]

2. Código civil (*Portuguese Civil Code*)

Art. 496. Danos não patrimonias. [. . .] (2) Por morte da vítima, o direito à indemnização por danos não patrimoniais cabe, em conjunto, ao cônjuge não separado de pessoas e bens e aos filhos ou outros descendentes; na falta destes, aos pais ou outros ascendentes; e, por último, aos irmãos ou sobrinhos que os representem.
(3) Se a vítima vivia em união de facto, o direito de indemnização previsto no número anterior cabe, em primeiro lugar, em conjunto, à pessoa que vivia com ela e aos filhos ou outros descendentes.
(4) O montante da indemnização é fixado equitativamente pelo tribunal, tendo em atenção, em qualquer caso, as circunstâncias referidas no artigo 494.º; no caso de morte, podem ser atendidos não só os danos não patrimoniais sofridos pela vítima, como os sofridos pelas pessoas com direito a indemnização nos termos dos números anteriores.

Translation

Art. 496. Non-pecuniary damage. [. . .] (2) Where a victim dies, the right to compensation for non-pecuniary damage shall be available, jointly, to a spouse who is not legally separated from the person and property and to the children or other

---

36 See e.g. the case: Efeteio Larissas (*Larissa Court of Appeal*) 25/2012, *Digest III*, 12/5/1 ff. with comments by E. G. DACORONIA (a 64-year-old lady was killed in a car accident. The brothers were awarded € 10,000 each for the pain and suffering due to the loss of their beloved sister).

descendants; failing the latter, to the parents or other ascendants; and, finally, to the brothers and sisters or nephews and nieces representing them.
(3) If the victim was living in a de facto union, the right to compensation provided in the previous paragraph shall be available in the first place to the person that lived with the victim together with the children and other descendants.
(4) The amount of compensation shall be fixed equitably by the court, having regard in any event to the circumstances mentioned in article 494;[37] in the event of death, regard may be taken not only of non-pecuniary damage suffered by the victim but also of such damage suffered by the persons entitled to compensation by virtue of the previous paragraphs.

3. Vahingonkorvauslaki (*Finnish Tort Liability Act*)

5 LUKU. Korvattava vahinko. [. . .] 4a §. Surmansa saaneen vanhemmilla, lapsilla ja aviopuolisolla sekä muulla näihin rinnastettavalla surmansa saaneelle erityisen läheisellä henkilöllä on oikeus saada korvausta kuolemantapauksen aiheuttamasta kärsimyksestä, jos kuolema on aiheutettu tahallisesti tai törkeästä huolimattomuudesta ja korvauksen tuomitseminen harkitaan kohtuulliseksi ottamalla huomioon surmansa saaneen ja korvausta vaativan välisen suhteen läheisyys, teon laatu sekä muut olosuhteet.

Translation

Chapter 5. Damages. [. . .] *§ 4a. The parents, children, and spouse of a person who has died, as well as any other comparable person who was especially close to the deceased, shall be entitled to damages for the grief arising from the death if the death was caused deliberately or by a grossly negligent act and if the award of such damages is deemed reasonable taking into account the close relationship between the deceased and the person seeking the damages, the nature of the act, and other circumstances.*

4. Skadeserstatningsloven (*Norwegian Compensatory Damages Act*)

§ 3–5. (erstatning (oppreisning) for skade av ikke økonomisk art.) [. . .] (2) Den som forsettlig eller grovt aktløst har voldt en annens død, kan pålegges å betale avdødes ektefelle, samboer, barn eller foreldre slik oppreisning som nevnt i første ledd.

---

37 Art. 494 provides (in English translation): "Where liability is based on fault, compensation may be fixed equitably at an amount lower than that corresponding to the damage caused, provided that the degree of fault of the wrongdoer, the financial situation of the wrongdoer and of the injured party as well as the other circumstances of the case justify doing so".

Translation

§ 3–5. Compensation for non-pecuniary loss. [. . .] (2) A person who intentionally or by gross negligence causes another person's death may be ordered to pay the deceased's spouse, children, or parents such redress for pain and suffering as is mentioned in the preceding paragraph.[38]

5. Kodeks cywilny (*Polish Civil Code*)

446. § 1. Jeżeli wskutek uszkodzenia ciała lub wywołania rozstroju zdrowia nastąpiła śmierć poszkodowanego, zobowiązany do naprawienia szkody powinien zwrócić koszty leczenia i pogrzebu temu, kto je poniósł.
§ 4. Sąd może także przyznać najbliższym członkom rodziny zmarłego odpowiednią sumę tytułem zadośćuczynienia pieniężnego za doznaną krzywdę.

Translation

Art. 446. § 1. If, as a consequence of bodily injury or damage to health the injured person dies, whoever is liable for the damage is liable towards the person that endured the medical and funeral expenses. [. . .]
§ 4. The court may also award an appropriate sum of money as compensation to the immediate members of the deceased's family for non-pecuniary harm that they suffer.

6. Võlaõigusseadus (*Estonian Law of Obligations Act*)

§ 134. Mittevaralise kahju hüvitamise erisused. [. . .] (3) Isiku surma põhjustamise või talle raske kehavigastuse või tervisekahjustuse tekitamisega tekitatud kahju hüvitamise kohustuse korral võivad ka surmasaanu või kahjustatud isiku lähedased isikud nõuda mittevaralise kahju hüvitist, kui hüvitise maksmist õigustavad erandlikud asjaolud. [. . .]

Translation

§ 134. Specifications for compensation for non-pecuniary damage. [. . .] (3) In the case of an obligation to compensate for damage arising from the death of a person or a serious bodily injury or health damage caused to the person, the persons

---

38 *Note by the author*: the preceding paragraph provides for a lump sum payment in an amount that the court finds reasonable as compensation for non-pecuniary loss.

close to the deceased or the aggrieved person may also claim compensation for non-pecuniary damage if payment of such compensation is justified by exceptional circumstances. [. . .]

7. Občanský zákoník (*Czech Civil Code*)

§ 444. [. . .] (3) Za škodu usmrcením náleží pozùstalým jednorázové odškodnìní, a to
a) manželovi nebo manželce 240 000 Kè,
b) každému dítìti 240 000 Kè,
c) každému rodièi 240 000 Kè,
d) každému rodièi pøi ztrátì dosud nenarozeného poèatého dítìte 85 000 Kè,
e) každému sourozenci zesnulého 175 000 Kè,
f) každé další blízké osobì žijící ve spoleèné domácnosti s usmrceným v dobì vzniku události, která byla pøíèinou škody na zdraví s následkem jeho smrti, 240 000 Kè.

Translation

§ 444. [. . .] (3) A lump-sum payment is to be made to the surviving dependants for damage suffered from death, in particular to:
a) the husband or wife, CZK 240,000,[39]
b) each child, CZK 240,000,
c) each parent, CZK 240,000,
d) each parent in the case of the loss of an unborn conceived child, CZK 85,000,
e) each sibling of the deceased, CZK 175,000,
f) each close person living in the same household with the deceased at the time of the occurrence of the incident which led to the injury to health resulting in death, CZK 240,000.

In 2014, § 444 was replaced by the following provision:

§ 2959. Při usmrcení nebo zvlášť závažném ublížení na zdraví odčiní škůdce duševní útrapy manželu, rodiči, dítěti nebo jiné osobě blízké peněžitou náhradou vyvažující plně jejich utrpení. Nelze-li výši náhrady takto určit, stanoví se podle zásad slušnosti.

---

39 Today worth around € 9,000.

Translation

§ 2959. Where death or particularly serious harm to health is caused, the wrongdoer shall redress any mental suffering of the spouse, parent, or child of the injured party or other person close to him or her by means of a monetary sum fully compensating their suffering. If the amount of compensation cannot be determined in this way, it shall be determined in accordance with the principles of equity.[40]

8. Obligacijski zakonik (*Slovenian Code of Obligations*)

180. člen. Osebe, ki imajo v primeru smrti ali težke invalidnosti pravico do denarne odškodnine. (1) Če nekdo umre, lahko sodišče prisodi njegovim ožjim družinskim članom (zakonec, otroci in starši) pravično denarno odškodnino za njihove duševne bolečine.
(2) V primeru posebno težke invalidnosti kakšne osebe lahko sodišče prisodi njenemu zakoncu, otrokom in staršem pravično denarno odškodnino za njihove duševne bolečine.
(3) Takšno odškodnino je mogoče prisoditi tudi bratom in sestram, če je med njimi in umrlim oziroma poškodovanim obstajala trajnejša življenjska skupnost.
(4) Odškodnino iz prvega oziroma drugega odstavka tega člena lahko prisodi sodišče tudi zunajzakonskemu partnerju, če je obstajala med njim in umrlim oziroma poškodovancem trajnejša življenjska skupnost.

Translation

*Art. 180. Persons entitled to monetary compensation in case of death or serious disability. (1) If a person dies the court may award just monetary compensation to his or her immediate family members (spouse, children and parents) for their mental distress.
(2) In the event of a person becoming seriously disabled the court may award his or her spouse, children, or parents just monetary compensation for their mental distress.
(3) Such compensation may also be awarded to siblings if there was a long-term union for life between them and the deceased or injured party.*

---

[40] In recent *Czech* legislation, there has been a conceptual change away from the assessment of damages by law or regulation towards an assessment by the courts. The Czech Constitutional Court even held in 2016 that, in the light of the principle of full compensation, damage awards that are fixed by law, statute, or point-scales and that prevent the judge from determining the compensation according to the circumstances of the particular case is *constitutionally questionable* (Case IV US 3122/2015). The amounts that previously used to be fixed in § 444 of the previous version of the Civil Code continue to be used by Czech courts as guidelines when determining damages under the new § 2959. The author is grateful to Jiří Hrádek, from Charles University Prague, for this information. For an introduction to the new Czech provisions, see J. Hrádek/A. J. Bell, The New Czech Civil Code and Compensation for Damage: Introductory Remarks, *JETL* 2016, 300–307; translation of selected provisions of the new Czech Civil Code, by J. Hrádek/A. J. Bell, in *JETL* 2016, 308. For previous case law see J. Hrádek, Czech Republic, in: H. Koziol/B. C. Steininger (eds.), *Yearbook European Tort Law 2010*, Berlin/Boston: De Gruyter, 2011, pp. 104 ff.

(4) The compensation specified in the first and second paragraphs of this article may be awarded by the court to an extra-marital partner if there was a long-term union for life between the partner and the deceased or injured party.

9. Codul civil (*Romanian Civil Code*)

Art. 1391. Repararea prejudiciului nepatrimonial. (1) În caz de vătămare a integrității corporale sau a sănătății, poate fi acordată și o despăgubire pentru restrângerea posibilităților de viață familială și socială.
(2) Instanța judecătorească va putea, de asemenea, să acorde despăgubiri ascendenților, descendenților, fraților, surorilor și soțului, pentru durerea încercată prin moartea victimei, precum și oricărei alte persoane care, la rândul ei, ar putea dovedi existența unui asemenea prejudiciu. [. . .]

Translation

*Art. 1391. **Non-pecuniary loss.** (1) In cases of the violation of physical integrity or health, compensation may also be granted for diminished opportunities for a family life or social life.*
(2) The court may also grant compensation to ascendants, descendants, brothers, sisters, or a spouse for pain and suffering caused by the death of the victim, and to any person who can prove the existence of such pain or suffering. [. . .]

10. Zakon o obligacionim odnosima (*Serbian Contracts and Torts Act*)

Član 201. Lica koja imaju pravo na novčanu naknadu u slučaju smrti ili teškog invaliditeta. (1) U slučaju smrti nekog lica, sud može dosuditi članovima njegove uže porodice (bračni drug, deca i roditelji) pravičnu novčanu naknadu za njihove duševne bolove. (2) Takva naknada može se dosuditi i braći i sestrama ako je između njih i umrlog postojala trajnija zajednica života. (3) U slučaju naročito teškog invaliditeta nekog lica, sud može dosuditi njegovom bračnom drugu, deci i roditeljima pravičnu novčanu naknadu za njihove duševne bolove. (4) Naknada iz st. 1 i 3 ovog člana može se dosuditi i vanbračnom drugu, ako je između njega i umrlog, odnosno povređenog postojala trajnija zajednica života.

Translation

*Art. 201. **Persons Entitled to Damages in Case of Death or Serious Disability.** (1) In case of death of a person, the court may award to members of his or her immediate family (spouse, children, and parents) equitable damages for their mental suffering.*

(2) Such damages may be also awarded to brothers and sisters should a permanent household unit exist between them and the deceased.
(3) In case of a particularly serious disability of a person, the court may award to his or her spouse, children, and parents an equitable money indemnity for their mental suffering.
(4) The indemnity specified in paragraphs 1 and 3 of the present article may also be awarded to a co-habitee, if a permanent household unit had existed between the co-habitee and the deceased, or injured person.

II. 民法 (Japanese Civil Code)

近親者に対する損害の賠償
第七百十一条
他人の生命を侵害した者は、被害者の父母、配偶者及び子に対しては、その財産権が侵害されなかった場合においても、損害の賠償をしなければならない。

Translation[41]

Compensation for Damage to the Next of Kin.
Art. 711. A person who has taken the life of another must pay damages to the father, mother, spouse, and children of the victim, even when they have not suffered pecuniary damage.

IX. Lithuania

1. Civilinis kodeksas (Civil Code)

6.250. straipsnis. Neturtinė žala. (1) Neturtinė žala yra asmens fizinis skausmas, dvasiniai išgyvenimai, nepatogumai, dvasinis sukrėtimas, emocinė depresija, pažeminimas, reputacijos pablogėjimas, bendravimo galimybių sumažėjimas ir kita, teismo įvertinti pinigais.
(2) Neturtinė žala atlyginama tik įstatymų nustatytais atvejais. Neturtinė žala atlyginama visais atvejais, kai ji padaryta dėl nusikaltimo, asmens sveikatai ar dėl asmens gyvybės atėmimo bei kitais įstatymų nustatytais atvejais. Teismas, nustatydamas neturtinės žalos dydį, atsižvelgia į jos pasekmes, šią žalą padariusio asmens kaltę, jo turtinę padėtį, padarytos turtinės žalos dydį bei kitas turinčias reikšmės bylai aplinkybes, taip pat į sąžiningumo, teisingumo ir protingumo kriterijus.

---

41 The Supreme Court of *Japan* has decided that a person in a similar position to "the father, mother, spouse and children" may also be entitled to the damage award (judgment n° 12.17 of 1974). Grandparents are among these beneficiaries. There are about 40 published cases of mostly lower and some higher courts (i.e. of courts at the intermediate level) on this issue. The author thanks Prof. YOSHIHARU MATSUURA, from Nagoya University, Faculty of Law, for this information.

6.284. straipsnis. Atsakomybė už dėl gyvybės atėmimo atsiradusią žalą. (1) Fizinio asmens mirties atveju teisę į žalos atlyginimą turi asmenys, kurie buvo mirusiojo išlaikomi arba jo mirties dieną turėjo teisę gauti iš jo išlaikymą (nepilnamečiai vaikai, sutuoktinis, nedarbingi tėvai ar kiti faktiniai nedarbingi išlaikytiniai), taip pat mirusiojo vaikas, gimęs po jo mirties. Šie asmenys taip pat turi teisę į neturtinės žalos atlyginimą.

Translation

Art. 6.250. Non-pecuniary damage. (1) Non-pecuniary damage shall be deemed to be a person's suffering, emotional experiences, inconveniences, mental shock, emotional depression, humiliation, deterioration of reputation, diminution of possibilities to associate with others, etc., evaluated by a court in terms of money.

(2) Non-pecuniary damage shall be compensated only in cases provided for by law. Non-pecuniary damage shall be compensated in all cases where it is incurred due to crime, health impairment, or deprivation of life, as well as in other cases provided for by law. The court in assessing the amount of non-pecuniary damage shall take into consideration the consequences of such damage sustained, the gravity of the fault of the person by whom the damage is caused, his or her financial status, the amount of pecuniary damage sustained by the aggrieved person, also any other circumstances of importance for the case, likewise to the criteria of good faith, justice, and reasonableness.

Art. 6.284. Liability to compensation for damage caused by fatal injury. (1) In the event of death of a natural person, the right to compensation for damage caused by the latter's death shall be acquired by the persons who were under his or her support or were entitled to be supported by him or her at the time of his death (minor children, spouses, parents incapable of work or other factual dependents incapable of work), as well as children of the deceased born after his or her death. These persons shall also have the right to compensation for non-pecuniary damage.

2. Lietuvos Aukščiausiojo Teismo civilinių bylų skyriaus išplėstinės teisėjų kolegijos (*Supreme Court, Expanded Panel of Judges of the Civil Division*), 18.04.2005, No. 3K-7–255/2005

[. . .] I. The essence of the dispute

On 30th December 2001, in the Hospital of Marijampolė, V.Z. gave birth to twins, L. and M.Z. Immediately after birth, the newborns were laid on a hot water bottle; the water was so hot that it caused severe physical injuries to the newborns. 20% of L's and 14% of M's body surface were burnt. They had to undergo multiple skin transplantations, L. having three and M. two operations [. . .].

[. . .] Due to the injuries, the newborns suffered considerable physical pain, each of them having to undergo several operations. These injuries have an impact on their current and future development. Following the injuries suffered by the children, their parents (claimants V.Z. and G.Z.) have suffered serious psychiatric shock and needed treatment. G.Z., acting as skin donor, has also experienced a severe physical pain. The mental shock to the claimants was caused by the injury to their children, the following operations and by the increased attention of the public and the media.

V.Z. and G.Z. have brought a claim against the Public Institution Hospital of Marijampolė, among others, for 1,000,000 Litas of non-pecuniary damage, including 400,000 Litas for non-pecuniary damage suffered by each of the children (L. and M.) and 100,000 Litas for non-pecuniary damage suffered by each of their parents (V.Z. and G.Z.).

II. The essence of the first instance and appellate court decisions

On 27th August 2004, the Kaunas Regional Court awarded the full amount that was claimed. [. . .].

The Panel of Judges of the Civil Division of the Lithuanian Court of Appeal [. . .], on 30th November 2004 [. . .], reduced the amount of non-pecuniary damage awarded to L.Z. and M.Z. to 200,000 Litas[42] per child, and the amount awarded to V.Z. and G.Z. to 50,000 Litas[43] each [. . .]. [. . .]

IV. Arguments and interpretations of the Supreme Court

[. . .] Persons related to the injured persons (parents, children, spouse) may suffer significant non-pecuniary harm, characterised by serious detrimental effects. Primarily, this may be the case for those who are emotionally very close to the injured person: individuals (parents, children, spouses) whose relationships with the victims are very close. The quality of the relations between these individuals has to be assessed in every particular case. [. . .] The non-pecuniary damage can be caused by physical suffering, as well as by a difficult emotional experience. In the case of physical injury of newborns, causing them severe, life-threatening physical injuries, damage is done to both the newborns and their parents. This is due to the close relationships between them and the concern about the injury to the helpless newborns. [. . .] In view of the severe injuries suffered by the newborns, non-pecuniary damage was caused to them, their father as the donor, as well as to both parents due to the special emotional and physical connection existing between children and parents. The person who has not suffered physical injuries himself, but who has subsequently grieved following the injuries occasioned to his helpless newborns, is also, in the eyes of the law, entitled to non-pecuniary damage taking into consideration the circumstances of the particular case. [. . .]

The Expanded Panel of Judges of the Civil Division of the Supreme Court of Lithuania [. . .] decides: to leave unchanged the decision adopted on 30th November 2004 by the Panel of Judges of the Civil Division of the Lithuanian Court of Appeals. [. . .]

[A sum of 500,000 Litas (approx. € 145,000) for non-pecuniary damage is awarded: 200,000 Litas (approx. € 58,000) to each of the injured newborn twins, and 50,000 Litas (approx. € 14,500) to each of their parents].

---

42 Today worth around € 58,000.
43 Today worth around € 14,500.

3. Lietuvos Aukščiausiojo Teismo Civilinių bylų skyriaus teisėjų kolegijos (*Supreme Court, Panel of Judges of the Civil Division*) 23.02.2010, Nr. 3K-3-59/2010, Case No. 3K-3-59/2010

[. . .] I. The essence of the dispute

In the present case, a dispute arose regarding a duty of a health care institution to compensate damage inflicted by the death of a patient [a young woman] due to inappropriate treatment.

The claimants are bringing a claim for damages which includes: [. . .]; 3) 175,000 Litas[44] for the non-pecuniary damage of each of the claimants, M.Č. and J.Č., due to the death of their daughter [. . .].

According to the claimants the relationship between the deceased, D.J., and them, her parents, was very strong.

II. The essence of the first instance and appellate court decisions

[. . .] The Panel of Judges of the Civil Division of the Lithuanian Court of Appeals [. . .] awarded a sum of 10,000 Litas [. . .] for each claimant, M.Č. and J.Č. [. . .]

IV. The arguments and interpretations of the Supreme Court

[. . .] Having regard to the practice of the Supreme Court of Lithuania in its interpretation and application of Art. 6.284 (1) of the Civil Code, the right to non-pecuniary damage is also granted to adult children, regardless of their ability to work, if the relationship with the deceased person was close and strong enough [. . .]. To meet these criteria, the relationship needs to be of permanent character, emotionally strong, sincere and close [. . .]. Although the prior decisions of the Supreme Court concerned the award of non-pecuniary damages to adult children (and not for parents as in the case at issue), according to the assessment of the panel of judges, the interpretations as such are also relevant in the present case.

Taking into consideration both Art. 30 (2) of the Constitution of the Republic of Lithuania,[45] and [. . .] the practice interpreting and applying Art. 6.284 (1) of the Civil Code regarding the persons who have the right to non-pecuniary damage, the panel of judges [. . .] holds that the parents of the deceased person also have a right to compensation for non-pecuniary damage, regardless of their ability to work or the right to receive maintenance payments from the deceased person, if their relationship with the deceased person was close and strong. Such relationships are not in themselves identical to [those expressly mentioned in Art. 6.284 (1)]. For this reason, the parents of the deceased person who bring a claim for non-pecuniary damage, have to prove the existence of a close and strong relationship, including its objective and subjective aspects [. . .]. [. . .]

The appellate court indicates in its decision that the relationship between the patient and her parents was close. According to the evaluation of the court, circumstances proving the closeness of these relationships have been provided. After the death of her daughter, the appellant M.Č. became the guardian of her granddaughter. Until her death, [the deceased daughter] D.J. had lived in the apartment of her parents [. . .].

In the case at issue, the appellants M. and J.Č. provided arguments and evidence regarding their pain caused by the unexpected death of their daughter [. . .].

---

44 Today worth around € 50,700.
45 Art. 30 (2) of the *Republic of Lithuania*'s Constitution provides (in English translation): "Compensation for material and moral damage inflicted upon a person shall be established by law".

[For each of the parents of the deceased person a sum of 10,000 Litas[46] for non-pecuniary damage is awarded.]

X. Quebec (Canada)

1. Code civil/Civil Code

Art. 1457. Every person has a duty to abide by the rules of conduct which lie upon him, according to the circumstances, usage or law, so as not to cause injury to another. Where he is endowed with reason and fails in this duty, he is responsible for any injury he causes to another person by such fault and is liable to reparation for the injury, whether it be bodily, moral or material in nature. [. . .]

2. Supreme Court of Canada, *Augustus v. Gosset*, 03.10.1996, [1996] 3 S.C.R. 268

1 L'HEUREUX-DUBÉ J. – This case has its origins in the death of a 19-year-old black youth who was shot by a police officer. The issue is whether the victim's mother can obtain compensatory damages for *solatium doloris* [. . .].

A. Solatium doloris

24 I note that the trial judge refused to award the appellant moral damages for *solatium doloris* but that he nevertheless awarded her $9,000 for loss of moral and financial support. The Court of Appeal, unanimous on this point, held that *solatium doloris* is a type of moral prejudice that is compensable in Quebec civil law, also finding that, in the circumstances, the appellant should receive a larger award of $15,000, according to the majority [. . .].

27 Unlike the common law, the civil law tradition has never denied that an indirect victim can obtain compensation for the moral prejudice resulting from a person's death [. . .].

29 The issue of the recognition of *solatium doloris* in Quebec civil law was raised before this Court for the first time in *Canadian Pacific Railway Co. v. Robinson* (1887), 14 S.C.R. 105. In that unanimous decision, the Court, inspired by a concern to apply the rule of non-recovery for *solatium doloris* uniformly in Canada and by the common law's traditional reluctance to compensate for non-economic losses, refused to award the wife and children of a deceased person any compensation whatsoever for their bereavement. [. . .]

32 [. . .] [T]he Quebec courts subsequently considered *Canadian Pacific Railway Co. v. Robinson, supra,* a "historical error" [. . .]. In light of the specificity of the legal tradition of Quebec, I agree with the Court of Appeal that it was French law, not English law, that

---

46 Today worth around € 2,900.

should have been applied in deciding whether to recognize *solatium doloris* in Quebec civil law [. . .] [I]t is clear that French law has always recognized, at the outset, that compensation is available for the moral prejudice resulting from the death of a close relative or friend [. . .].

34 France and Quebec are not alone in providing compensation for the moral prejudice suffered by third parties due to the death of loved ones. Belgium and Scotland, to give two examples, have also done so: R. André, *La réparation du préjudice corporel* (1986), at pp. 370-71; D. M. Walker, *Principles of Scottish Private Law* (4th ed. 1988), vol. 2, at p. 618. Even a number of common law jurisdictions, including certain states in Australia and the United States, have abandoned the rule that only pecuniary losses may be recovered in the event of death: H. Luntz, *Assessment of Damages* (3rd ed. 1990), at p. 437; R. D. VanHorne, "Wrongful Death Recovery: Quagmire of the Common Law" (1985-86), 34 *Drake L. Rev.* 987, at p. 997.

35 The appellant argued at length, stressing trends in Canadian case law and the state of the law in foreign jurisdictions, that compensation for moral prejudice in the form of *solatium doloris* has always been recognized in French civil law, and should thus also be in Quebec civil law. This argument is without question valid; the Court of Appeal was clearly right to hold that the trial judge had applied an erroneous principle of law in refusing to find that this type of prejudice is compensable in Quebec civil law. It was, therefore, right, according to the test for reviewing the assessment of the prejudice, to intervene to correct the trial judge's judgment in this respect [. . .].

37 [. . .] [T]he *solatium doloris* concept includes all extrapatrimonial damage, both *immediate* grief and the loss of *future* moral support, resulting from the death of a loved one. [. . .]

44 Although it is difficult to quantify a prejudice related to a person's emotional or physical integrity, it is not uncommon for the courts to face this task. For example, this Court recently awarded $300,000 in moral damages for defamation: *Hill v. Church of Scientology of Toronto*, 1995 CanLII 59 (SCC), [1995] 2 S.C.R. 1130; see also *Botiuk v. Toronto Free Press Publications Ltd.*, 1995 CanLII 60 (SCC), [1995] 3 S.C.R. 3. Moreover, the cap on awards of non-pecuniary damages for bodily injury, which was originally set at $100,000 in 1978, is now approximately $243,000: *Andrews v. Grand & Toy Alberta Ltd.*, supra; *Lindal v. Lindal*, 1981 CanLII 35 (SCC), [1981] 2 S.C.R. 629, at pp. 640-41. [. . .]

46 It should be mentioned that in every Canadian province except Quebec, the right to claim damages owing to the death of a third person is governed by special statutes [. . .]. In Alberta, for example, since 1994, the amount fixed "for grief and loss of . . . guidance, care and companionship" is $40,000 for the spouse and parents of the victim and $25,000 for the victim's children: *Fatal Accidents Act*, R.S.A. 1980, c. F-5, s. 8(2). [. . .]

47 It is not hard to understand that the death of one's own child is in all respects an extremely distressing, indeed even traumatizing, event. The suffering that accompanies this unnatural event has no equivalent in intensity aside from the immeasurable joy that can result from the birth of a child. Such suffering is so acute that it seems impossible even to assess it in monetary terms. [. . .]

51 In the case at bar, there is extensive evidence of the grief caused to the appellant by the death of her only surviving child, exacerbated by the facts that, in 1983, she experienced the death of a little girl who had been born very sick and, that, at her age, she cannot hope to have other children. [. . .] In addition, owing to the unforeseeable circumstances of Anthony's death, the appellant was unprepared for her ensuing grief. I would also add that the extensive publicity given to the unfortunate facts at the root of this case certainly did not make it easier for the appellant to resume a normal life. Although I recognize that it is impossible out of context to appraise the feelings resulting from the irreparable circumstance of the death of one's own child, it is my view that an award in the order of $ 25,000[47] might be fair and reasonable in the circumstances of this case; that being said, it remains to the Court of Appeal to fix the quantum, after hearing the parties on this point.

XI. European Convention on Human Rights

Note by the author: In three cases submitted to the European Court of Human Rights, parents had lost an adult son. In *Keenan* v. *United Kingdom*, the claimant's son, who at the time was a prisoner, killed himself while in prison. It was known to the authorities that there was a risk of suicide. In *Edwards* v. *United Kingdom*, the claimants' son was killed by another detainee while held in prison on remand. In the third case, *Reynolds* v. *United Kingdom*, the claimants' son, who suffered from schizophrenia and was a suicide risk, jumped out of a window on the sixth floor of a public hospital and fell to his death. The mothers (in *Keenan* and *Reynolds*) and parents (in *Edwards*), respectively, alleged that the State officials had been negligent and claimed inter alia damages for bereavement. Since the young men in all three cases were adults, Sect. 1A of the Fatal Accidents Act did not grant the parents damages for bereavement under English law.[48]

I. European Convention on Human Rights

Art. 2. Right to life. (1) Everyone's right to life shall be protected by law. [. . .]

Art. 3. Prohibition of torture. No one shall be subjected to torture or to inhuman or degrading treatment or punishment.

Art. 13. Right to an effective remedy. Everyone whose rights and freedoms as set forth in this Convention are violated shall have an effective remedy before a national authority notwithstanding that the violation has been committed by persons acting in an official capacity.

---

47 Today worth around € 16,800.
48 See above, p. 354. See on these cases e.g. J. WRIGHT, The Operational Obligation under Article 2 of the European Convention on Human Rights and Challenges for Coherence – Views from the English Supreme Court and Strasbourg, *JETL* 2016, 58; A. TETTENBORN, Wrongful Death, Human Rights and the Fatal Accidents Act, *L.Q.R.* 2012, 327; M. LUNNEY/K. OLIPHANT, *Tort Law: Text and Materials*, Oxford: OUP, 2008, p. 924.

2. European Court of Human Rights, *Keenan v. the United Kingdom*, 03.04.2001, No. 27229/95, ECHR 2001-III

[. . .] 130. [. . .] The Court considers that, in the case of a breach of Articles 2 and 3 of the Convention, which rank as the most fundamental provisions of the Convention, compensation for the non-pecuniary damage flowing from the breach should in principle be available as part of the range of possible remedies.

131. In this case, the Court concludes that the applicant should have been able to apply for compensation for her non-pecuniary damage [. . .].

132. Moreover [. . .] no effective remedy was available to the applicant in the circumstances of the present case which would have established where responsibility lay for the death of Mark Keenan [her son]. In the Court's view, this is an essential element of a remedy under Article 13 for a bereaved parent.

133. Accordingly, there has been a breach of Article 13 of the Convention. [. . .]

135. [The applicant] claimed an appropriate award for her own grief, emotional loss, distress and bereavement, referring to the shattering effect of losing her only son.

138. [. . .] The applicant, [Mark Keenan's] mother, must [. . .] be regarded as having suffered anguish and distress from the circumstances of his detention and her inability to pursue an effective avenue of redress. Making an assessment on an equitable basis [. . .], the Court awards for non-pecuniary damage the sum of GBP [. . .] 3,000 to the applicant in her personal capacity. [. . .]

3. European Court of Human Rights, *Edwards v. United Kingdom*, 14.03.2002, No.46477/99, ECHR 2002-II

[. . .] 91. Article 13 of the Convention provides: "Everyone whose rights and freedoms as set forth in [the] Convention are violated shall have an effective remedy before a national authority notwithstanding that the violation has been committed by persons acting in an official capacity." [. . .]

97. Where alleged failure by the authorities to protect persons from the acts of others is concerned, Article 13 may not always require that the authorities undertake the responsibility for investigating the allegations. There should, however, be available to the victim or the victim's family a mechanism for establishing any liability of State officials or bodies for acts or omissions involving the breach of their rights under the Convention. Furthermore, in the case of a breach of Articles 2 and 3 of the Convention, which rank as the most fundamental provisions of the Convention, compensation for the non-pecuniary damage flowing from the breach should, in principle, be available as part of the range of redress (see Z and Others v. the United Kingdom [GC], no. 29392/95, § 109, ECHR 2001-V, and Keenan v. the United Kingdom, no. 27229/95, § 129, ECHR 2001-III). [. . .]

101. [T]he Court finds that in this case the applicants did not have available to them [. . .] the possibility of obtaining an enforceable award of compensation for the damage suffered

[. . .]. In the Court's view, this is an essential element of a remedy under Article 13 for a bereaved parent.

102. Accordingly, there has been a breach of Article 13 of the Convention. [. . .]

104. The applicants claim compensation [*inter alia* for their] anguish, severe distress and grief suffered at the loss of their son and the ongoing stress and associated ill-health suffered by the second applicant as a result of the traumatic loss and ongoing frustration at the inability to pursue an effective avenue of redress. [. . .]

106. The Court observes that [. . .] the applicants [that is the parents] must be regarded as having suffered anguish and distress from the circumstances of his death and their inability to obtain an effective investigation or remedy. Making an assessment on an equitable basis and bearing in mind the amounts awarded in other cases, the Court awards the sum of 20,000 pounds sterling (GBP) for non-pecuniary damage. [. . .]

4. European Court of Human Rights, *Reynolds v. the United Kingdom*, 13.03.2012, No. 2694/08, ECHR 2008

[. . .] 60. The Court has examined the applicant's complaint under Article 13 in conjunction with Article 2 of the Convention. In particular, it has considered whether there is an arguable claim of a breach of Article 2 of the Convention and whether civil proceedings for establishing any liability and, if so, awarding non-pecuniary damages were available to the applicant in that respect [. . .].

65. [A]s the mother of an adult child and a non-dependant, the applicant would have been unable to claim damages under the 1976 Act [i.e. the Fatal Accidents Act 1976, in particular Sec. 1A (Damages for Bereavement)[49]] on her own behalf. [. . .] While it is likely that he suffered significant anguish and fear, there is no evidence that this would be regarded as psychiatric "injury" in the sense recognised by domestic law.[50] [. . .] It must be concluded therefore that the applicant had no prospect of obtaining adequate compensation for the non-pecuniary damage suffered by her as a result of the death of her child [. . .].

67. The Court has therefore concluded that the present applicant did not have available to her, prior to the introduction of her application to this Court, civil proceedings to establish any liability and compensation due as regards the non-pecuniary damage suffered by her on her son's death.

68. The Court therefore concludes that there has been a violation of Article 13 in conjunction with Article 2 of the Convention and, consequently, it dismisses the Government's objection as to the applicant's failure to exhaust domestic remedies. [. . .]

73. The Court has found a violation of Article 13 in conjunction with Article 2 (paragraph 67 above) in that domestic law did not afford a civil remedy to the present

---

49 Above, p. 354.
50 Compare above, Chapter 11, pp. 320 ff.

applicant enabling any liability to be established and any appropriate redress to be obtained as regards the non-pecuniary loss sustained by the applicant on the death of her son. The Court [. . .] accepts that the lack of civil remedy likely caused [the applicant] some frustration and distress so that the Court awards the applicant the sum of EUR 7,000 [. . .]. [. . .]

XII. Principles of European Tort Law (PETL)

> **Art. 10:301. Non-pecuniary damage.** (1) Considering the scope of its protection (Article 2:102), the violation of an interest may justify compensation of non-pecuniary damage. This is the case in particular where the victim has suffered personal injury; or injury to human dignity, liberty, or other personality rights. Non-pecuniary damage can also be the subject of compensation for persons having a close relationship with a victim suffering a fatal or very serious non-fatal injury. [. . .]

XIII. Draft Common Frame of Reference (DCFR)

> **VI. – 2:101: Meaning of legally relevant damage.** [. . .] (4) In this Book: [. . .] (b) non-economic loss includes pain and suffering and impairment of the quality of life.
>
> **VI. – 2:202: Loss suffered by third persons as a result of another's personal injury or death.** (1) Non-economic loss caused to a natural person as a result of another's personal injury or death is legally relevant damage if at the time of injury that person is in a particularly close personal relationship to the injured person.

Latest news

On 18th May 2017, the *Deutscher Bundestag* (German Parliament) decided to introduce damages for bereavement into German law. The following new section was added to § 844 of the German Civil Code (BGB). Similar provisions were added to the specific laws dealing with strict liability.

> **§ 844. Ersatzansprüche Dritter bei Tötung.** [. . .] (3) Der Ersatzpflichtige hat dem Hinterbliebenen, der zur Zeit der Verletzung zu dem Getöteten in einem besonderen persönlichen Näheverhältnis stand, für das dem Hinterbliebenen zugefügte seelische Leid eine angemessene Entschädigung in Geld zu leisten. Ein besonderes persönliches Näheverhältnis wird vermutet, wenn der Hinterbliebene der Ehegatte, der Lebenspartner, ein Elternteil oder ein Kind des Getöteten war.

Translation

§ 844. Claims of Third Parties upon Death. [. . .] (3) The person who is liable also has to provide adequate monetary compensation for the emotional harm suffered by any surviving person who had a particularly close relationship with the deceased at the time of the injuring act. A particularly close relationship shall be presumed when the relative in question was the spouse, partner, parent, or child of the deceased.

Systematic overviews

I. Systems which award damages for emotional harm following the loss or (severe) injury of a loved one

A. Relevant injury suffered by the primary victim

Table 12.1

Damages awarded in case of death of the primary victim[1]	Damages awarded in case of death or (very) severe injury of the primary victim[2]
• **English law** (FAA 1976, s.1A(2)) • **Irish law** (CLA 1961 s.48(1)) • **Finnish law** (Tort Liability Act C5 § 4a) • **Norwegian law** (CDA § 3–5) • **Polish law** (CC Art. 446 § 4) • **Romanian law** (CC Art. 1391(2)) • **Greek law** (CC Art. 932) • **Portuguese law** (CC Art. 496(2)) • **Law of Florida** (Wrongful Death Act, Sect. 768.21) • **Japanese law** (CC Art. 711)	• **French law** (CC Art. 1240; CdC 22.10.1946) • **Swiss law** • (CO Art. 47;TF 22.04.1986) • **Austrian law** (OGH 16.05.2001) • **Czech law** (CC § 2959) • **Estonian law** (Law of Obligations § 134) • **Lithuanian law** (Supreme Court 18.04.2005) • **Serbian law** (Contracts and Tort Act Art. 201(1), 201(3)) • **Slovenian law** (Code of Obligations Art. 180(1), 180(2))

1 See further e.g. for *Belgium*: e.g. Cour de cassation/Hof van Kassatie, 07.12.1970, Pas., 1971 I 319; for *Latvia*: Civil Code, Art. 1635; for *Luxemburg*: e.g. 08.05.1896, Pas. lux. 4, 177; 01.02.1984, Pas. lux. 26, 147; for *Bulgaria*: Supreme Court of Cassation, III. Civil Division, 3. 7. 2005, Decision No. 377, Civil Case 3667/2002, in: B. Winiger/H. Koziol/B. A. Koch/R. Zimmermann (eds.), *Digest of European Tort Law, Vol. 2: Essentiel Cases on Damage*, Berlin/Boston: De Gruyter, 2011, 12/27/6; for *Scotland*: Damages (Scotland) Act 2011, Sect. 4 (3) (b); for *Spain* see e.g.: Tribunal Supremo, 19.12.1986, RJ 1986, no. 7682;TS, 15.6.1989, RJ 1989, no. 5123; for *South Korea*, Civil Code, Art. 752.

2 See further, *Italy*: Corte Costituzionale, 11.07.2003, *Foro it.* 2003, 2201; further references in G. Christiandl/D. Hinghofer-Szalkay, Ersatzansprüche für immaterielle Schäden aus Tötung naher Angehöriger – eine rechtsvergleichende Untersuchung, *ZfRV* 2007, 44 at 51 f. and 58 f.;

B. Beneficiaries

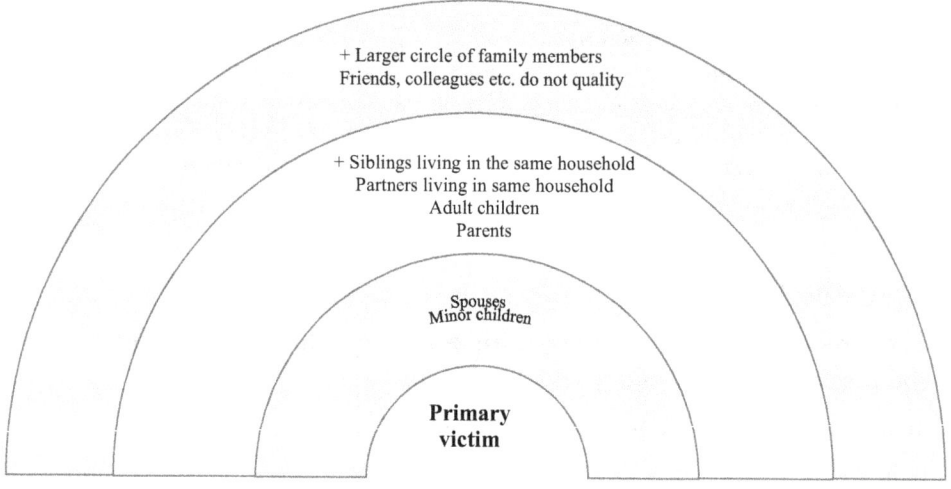

Figure 12.1

C. Relevant system of liability

Table 12.2

Awarded both under fault-based and strict liability	Awarded only under fault-based liability	Awarded only for gross negligence
Most jurisdictions e.g. France, Switzerland	England and Wales	Some jurisdictions e.g. Austria, Finland, Norway, Sweden

D. Amounts

Fixed by the courts

Most jurisdictions

Fixed by law or statute

England and Wales (£ 12,980)
Approach recently abandoned in the Czech Republic

Statute fixes a maximum amount

Ireland (€ 35,000)

II. Systems refusing to award damages for bereavement

Germany (until 2017), New York (for example)[51]

III. Comparative overview for selected countries[52]

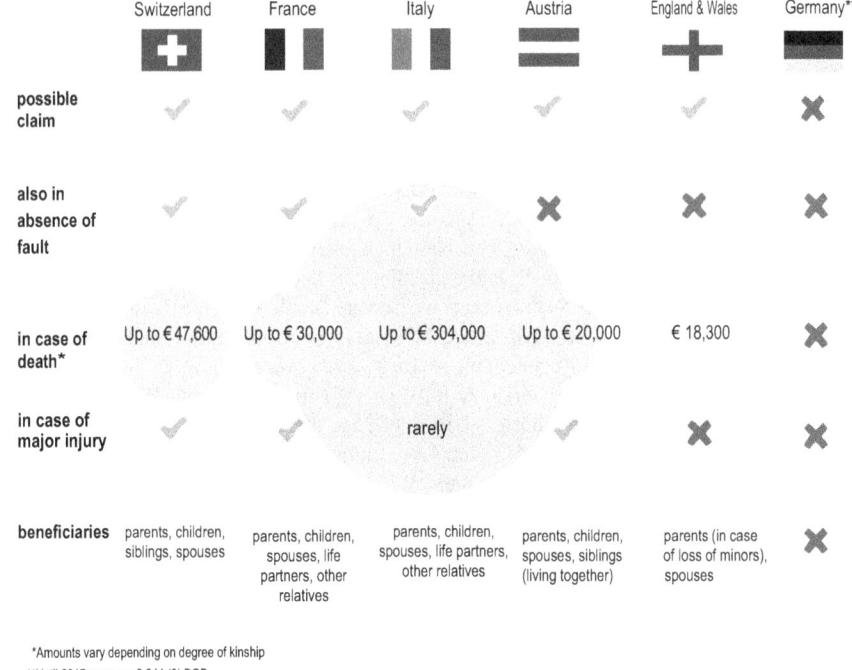

*Amounts vary depending on degree of kinship
**Until 2017; see now § 844 (3) BGB.

Figure 12.2

---

51 Refences above. See further for the *Netherlands*: Hoge Raad, 22.02.2002, NJ 2002, 240, with case notes in *ERPL* 2003, 412.
52 Based on a table previously published in: *DER SPIEGEL*, no. 28/2015 of 04.07.2015, pp. 38 ff.

Bibliography

GERT BRÜGGEMEIER, *Common Principles of Tort Law: A Pre-Statement of Law*, London: BIICL, 2004, pp. 209–211; PETER CANE/PATRICK ATIYAH, *Atiyah's Accidents, Compensation and the Law*, 7th ed., Cambridge: CUP, 2006; KARL-HEINZ DANZL, Der Ersatz ideeller Schäden in Europa und im AGBG am Beispiel des Angehörigenschmerzensgeldes, in: Constanze Fischer-Czermak/Gerhard Hopf/Georg Kathrein/Martin Schauer (eds.), *Festschrift 200 Jahre ABGB*, Wien: Manz, 2011, pp. 1633–1666; DAGMAR HINGHOFER-SZALKAY, Schwerste Verletzung eines Angehörigen: Fortentwicklung des Trauerschmerzengeldes? Mit einem Exkurs zum niederländischen Gesetzesentwurf (unter D) von Margareth Prisching, *ZVR* 2008, 444–450; W.V. HORTON ROGERS, *Damages for Non-Pecuniary Loss in a Comparative Perspective (Tort and Insurance Law)*, New York: Springer, 2001; W.V. HORTON ROGERS, Death and Non-Pecuniary Loss, in: Helmut Koziol/Barbara C. Steininger (eds.), *European Tort Law 2006*, Vienna: Springer, 2008, pp. 52–60; CHRISTIAN HUBER, Kein Angehörigenschmerzensgeld de lege lata – Deutschland auch künftig der letzte Mohikaner in Europa oder ein Befreiungsschlag aus der Isolation, *NZV* 2012, 5–11; THOMAS KADNER GRAZIANO, Angehörigen- oder Trauerschmerzensgeld – Die Würfel fallen, *RIW* 2015, 549–563; THOMAS KADNER GRAZIANO, Angehörigenschmerzensgeld im europäischen Privatrecht – die Schere schliesst sich, *ZEuP* 2002, 834–859; THOMAS KADNER GRAZIANO, Schmerzensgeld für Angehörige – Angemessener Ausgleich immaterieller Beeinträchtigungen oder exzessiver Ersatz mittelbarer Schäden?, *ZEuP* 1996, 135–153; ERNST KARNER, Trauerschmerz und Schockschäden in der aktuellen Judikatur, *ZVR* 2008, 44–49; GIEDRĖ KASMAUKAITĖ, Can Damages Be Recovered for the Loss of Services of a Minor Child?, *Int'l J. Baltic L.* 2005, 15; HELMUT KOZIOL, Die Tötung im Schadenersatzrecht, in: Helmut Koziol/Jaap Spier (eds.), *Liber Amicorum Pierre Widmer*, Vienna: Springer, 2003, pp. 203–219; HELMUT KOZIOL, Wrongful Death: Basic Questions, in: Helmut Koziol/Barbara C. Steininger (eds.), *European Tort Law 2006*, Vienna: Springer, 2008, pp. 28–34; ULRICH MAGNUS (ed.), *Unification of Tort Law: Damages*, The Hague: Kluwer Law International, 2001, Case 9; DONAL NOLAN, Reforming Liability for Psychiatric Injury in Scotland: A Recipe for Uncertainty? *MLR* 2005, 983; ANDREW J. OSWALD/NATTAVUDH POWDTHAVEE, Death, Happiness, and the Calculation of Compensatory Damages, *J. Legal Stud.* 2008, 217; ROBIN L. RABIN, Emotional Distress in Tort Law: Themes of Constraint Third Restatement of Torts, *Wake Forest L. Rev.* 2009, 1197; FILIPPO RANIERI, *Europäisches Obligationenrecht*, 3. Aufl., Wien: Springer, 2009, pp. 1539–1622; HENDRIK SCHULTZKY, Schmerzensgeld für Angehörige – Bericht über das Fachgespräch am 29. November 2011 in München, *VersR* 2011, 857–861; HARVEY TEFF, Liability for Psychiatric Illness: Advancing Cautiously, *MLR* 1998, 849; ANDREW TETTENBORN, Wrongful Death, Human Rights and the Fatal Accidents Act, *L.Q.R.* 2012, 327; GERHARD WAGNER, Angehörigenschmerzensgeld, in: Alexander Bruns et al. (eds.), *Festschrift für Rolf Stürner zum 70. Geburtstag*, Tübingen: Mohr Siebeck, 2013, pp. 231–253; GERHARD WAGNER, Supreme Court, 02.04.2014: Schadensersatz bei Tötungen und Angehörigenschmerzensgeld – Die Rückständigkeit des deutschen Rechts, *ZEuP* 2015, 874–887; CHRISTIANE C. WENDEHORST, Wrongful Death and Compensation for Pecuniary Loss, in: Helmut Koziol/Barbara C. Steininger (eds.), *European Tort Law 2006*, Vienna: Springer, 2008, pp. 35–51; MARKUS WENTER, Die Ansprüche naher Angehöriger von Unfallopfern im italienischen Schadensrecht (mit Anmerkung von GERDA MÜLLER), *zfs* 2012, 1–7; JANE WRIGHT, The Operational Obligation under Article 2 of the European Convention on Human Rights and Challenges for Coherence – Views from the English Supreme Court and Strasbourg, *JETL* 2016, 58; HORST ZINNEN et al., Hoge Raad, Judgment of 22 February 2002 – On Compensation for Psychiatric Injury and Emotional Distress Suffered by Close Relatives, with Case Notes, *ERPL* 2003, 412.

Chapter 13

Liability for others – the case of liability of parents for damage caused by their children

> "*The general rule is that one man is under no duty of controlling another to prevent his doing damage to a third. There are, however, special relations, which are the source of a duty of such nature.*"[1]
>
> "*[N]ous avons tous été enfants avant que d'être hommes.*"[2]

Scenario[3]

On their walk home from school, Vincent and Jonathan, aged 9 and 10, respectively, notice a gap in a temporary fence at a construction site. They enter the site and find a packet of cigarettes with a few cigarettes left inside, along with a box of matches. They decide to start a fire. The flames ignite some nearby flammable materials and the fire quickly spreads; it causes significant damage to the building under construction.

The two boys live with their respective parents, who have always forbidden their children to play with matches, and have taught them about the dangers of lighting fires. Vincent and Jonathan have always behaved normally for their age.

The company that owns the building claims compensation from the parents of the boys.

---

1 Justice Dixon in: High Court of Australia, *Smith v. Leurs*, 22.10.1945, [1945] H.C.A. 27; 70 CLR 256.
2 René Descartes, Discours de la Méthode, in: René Descartes, *Œuvres et lettres* (Textes présentés par André Bridoux), Bibliothèque de la Pléiade, Paris: Gallimard, 1953 (reprint 1978), p. 133. In English translation: "We have all been children before being men".
3 For further cases and scenarios on damage caused by children, see above, Chapter 6, pp. 115 ff.

Questions

Depending on their age and capacity of judgement, minors might not be liable for the damage they have caused.[4] Under certain circumstances, it might instead be possible to request compensation from the minor's parents.

When dealing with the question of whether parents should be held liable for damage caused by their children, the European tort liability regimes provide every conceivable approach, ranging from fault-based liability (with or without a presumption of parents' fault) to strict liability, with intermediate solutions and combinations of different approaches dependant on the age of the child in question.

1) Which liability regime is in general applied in *English* law to the liability of parents for damage caused by their children? Under which conditions may strict liability be employed? Which solution to the above scenario would you suggest in English law?

2) What is the solution of the scenario under *Austrian* law?

3) Which approach is applied in *German* and *Swiss* law? In two German decisions that were decided on the same day, and which were based on the same facts, the parents of the 5 ½-year-old boy were held potentially liable, whereas the parents of the 7 ½-year-old boy were not. Why was this so? How would you solve the above scenario in these jurisdictions?

4) The codal provisions of Germany, Switzerland, France, and Spain all provide for the same system regarding parents' liability. How are the *French* and *Spanish* provisions applied by the courts? Would the parents of Vincent and Jonathan be held liable for the damage caused by their children under French and Spanish law?

5) According to the provisions provided in the materials, which approaches to parents' liability are to be found in *other European countries*, in the *People's Republic of China*, in the *PETL*, and in the *DCFR*? Present these approaches in a systematic manner.

6) What are the advantages and disadvantages of each approach? In your opinion, which liability regime is the most suitable with regard to this issue? Explain.

7) How do the rules on children's liability (see above, Chapter 6) and parents' liability complement each other in the different jurisdictions? Would your answer to question 6 change depending on whether the children are liable for their own acts?

---

4 See above, Chapter 6, pp. 115 ff.

Table of contents

I. England and Wales
1. CHRISTOPHER T. WALTON/SIMON E. WOOD/ROGER COOPER/STEPHEN TODD (eds.), *Charlesworth & Percy on Negligence*, 13th ed., London: Sweet & Maxwell, 2016, pp. 3–214 .... p. 393
2. Lincoln Assizes, *Gorely v. Codd*, 10.06.1966, [1967] 1 WLR 19 .... p. 393
3. Power of Criminal Courts (Sentencing) Act 2000, Sects. 130 (1) (a), 131 (A1) and (1), 137 (1) .... p. 395

II. Austria
1. Allgemeines bürgerliches Gesetzbuch, ABGB (*General Civil Code*), §§ 1308, 1309 .... p. 396
2. PETER RUMMEL/MEINHARD LUKAS (eds.), *Kommentar zum Allgemeinen bürgerlichen Gesetzbuch, Band II (Commentary on the General Civil Code, Vol. II)*, 3rd ed., Wien: Manz, 2002, § 1309 n. 9 (by RUDOLF REISCHAUER) .... p. 396

III. Germany
1. Bürgerliches Gesetzbuch, BGB (*Civil Code*), § 832 (1) .... p. 396
2. Bundesgerichtshof, BGH, 6. Zivilsenat (*Federal Supreme Court of Justice, 6th Civil Senate*), 10.07.1984, NJW 1984, 2574 .... p. 397
3. Bundesgerichtshof, BGH, 6. Zivilsenat (*Federal Supreme Court of Justice, 6th Civil Senate*), 24.03.2009, NJW 2009, 1952 .... p. 399
4. Bundesgerichtshof, BGH, 6. Zivilsenat (*Federal Supreme Court of Justice, 6th Civil Senate*), 24.03.2009, NJW 2009, 1954 .... p. 400

IV. Switzerland
1. Code civil/Zivilgesetzbuch (*Civil Code*), Art. 333 (1) .... p. 401
2. Bundesgericht/Tribunal fédéral (*Federal Supreme Court of Justice*), 07.11.1974 (*Maurer c. Feltscher*), BGE 100 II 298 .... p. 401

V. France
1. Code civil (*Civil Code*), Art. 1242 (former Art. 1384) (4) and (7) .... p. 402
2. Cour de cassation, 2e civ. (*Court of Cassation, 2nd civil chamber*), 19.02.1997 (*Jean-Claude Bertrand c. Philippe Domingues*), n° 94–21.111, J.C.P. 1997 II 22848 .... p. 403
3. PHILIPPE BRUN, *Responsabilité civile extracontractuelle (Tort Law)*, 4th ed., Paris: LexisNexis Litec, 2016, nos. 419, 435–437, 440 .... p. 403

VI. Spain
1. Código civil (*Civil Code*), Arts. 1902, 1903 (1), (2) and (6) .... p. 404
2. Ley orgánica 5/2000, de 12 de enero, reguladora de la responsabilidad penal de los menores (*Criminal Liability of Minors Act*), Art. 61 (3) (LORPM) .... p. 405

3. Luis Fernando Reglero Campos (Coordinador), *Tratado de Responsabilidad Civil (Treatise on Civil Liability)*, 4th ed., Madrid: Thomson Aranzadi, 2008, Chapter XXI, nos. 3–6, 38 (by Esther Gómez Calle) ....p. 405

VII. Codal or statutory provisions of various continental jurisdictions (translations)

1. ЗАКОН ЗА ЗАДЪЛЖЕНИЯТА И ДОГОВОРИТЕ (*Bulgarian Law on Obligations and Contracts*), Art. 48 (1) and (3) ....p. 407
2. Lov om hæftelse for børns erstatningsansvar (*Danish Act on Vicarious Liability for Children*), § 1 ....p. 407
3. Võlaõigusseadus (*Estonian Code of Obligations*), § 1053 ....p. 408
4. Αστικός Κώδικας (*Greek Civil Code*), Art. 923 (1).................p. 408
5. Codice civile (*Italian Civil Code*), Art. 2048 (1) and (3) ....p. 408
6. Burgerlijk Wetboek (*Dutch Civil Code*), Art. 6:169.................p. 408
7. Skadeserstatningsloven (*Norwegian Compensatory Damages Act*), § 1–2 ....p. 409
8. Kodeks cywilny (*Polish Civil Code*), Arts. 426, 427.................p. 409
9. Código civil (*Portuguese Civil Code*), Art. 491 ....p. 409
10. Codul civil (*Romanian Civil Code*), Art. 1372.................p. 410
11. Obligacijski zakonik (*Slovenian Code of Obligations*), Arts. 142 (1), (2) and (4), 145, 146 ....p. 410
12. Гражданский кодекс Российской Федерации (*Russian Civil Code*), Arts. 1073 (1), 1074, 1075.................p. 411

VIII. People's Republic of China

1. 中华人民共和国侵权责任法 (*Tort Law Act*), Art. 32.................p. 411
2. Shengming Wang, 中华人民共和国侵权责任法释义 (*Commentaries on the Tort Law of the People's Republic of China*), 2nd ed., Beijing: Legislative Affairs Commission of the National Congress of the People's Republic of China, Collection of Commentaries on Laws of the People's Republic of China, 2010, p. 161 ....p. 412

IX. Principles of European Tort Law

PETL, Art. 6:101 ....p. 412

X. Draft Common Frame of Reference

DCFR, Art. VI.-3:104 (1) and (3).................p. 413

Materials[5]

I. England and Wales

1. Christopher T. Walton/Simon E. Wood/Roger Cooper/Stephen Todd (eds.), *Charlesworth & Percy on Negligence*, 13th ed., 2016, pp. 3–214

3–214 A parent, as such, is not liable for the negligence of a child [. . .]. Parents, of course, are liable for their own negligence and they are under a duty to exercise such control over their children, as prudent parents would exercise. The age of a child is a material factor to be taken into account. Thus, a father was liable where he gave his son, aged 15, an airgun, with which the boy [. . .] shot the plaintiff in the eye [*Bebee v Sales* (1916)]. A father of a 15-year-old boy, was liable for failing to take reasonable care that his son did not use an airgun in such a way as to injure other persons [*Court v Wyatt* (1960)]. Similarly, where a father allowed his son, aged 12, to possess a .410 shotgun but did not instruct him how to handle it safely when he was in the presence of others, the father was liable when a child was shot. It was no defence that he had forbidden his son to use the gun when he was accompanied by other children [*Newton v Edgerly* (1959)]. On the other hand, a father, who allowed his son, aged 13, to have an air rifle, on the condition that he did not use it outside the house, was not liable when, in disobedience to his orders, his son fired the rifle in an alleyway, injuring a child. The precautions were suitable and would have been adequate, had it not been for the son's disobedience [*Donaldson v McNiven* (1952); *Gorely v Codd* (1967)]. Where a parent knew that there were candles present in the house, he was under a duty to instruct his son, aged 14, as to the caution with which lighted candles should be treated and to supervise him with a view to preventing danger arising from their use [*Jauffur v Akhbar* (1984)]. However, in the case of normal 14-year-old boys, it has been said the duty of care owed by a parent must not be applied so over-cautiously as to stifle initiative and independence, qualities in youngsters that ought to be encouraged [*Porter v Barking and Dagenham LBC* (1990)]. [. . .]

2. Lincoln Assizes,[6] *Gorely v. Codd*, 10.06.1966, [1967] 1 WLR 19

The [. . .] plaintiff, a boy aged 14 ½ years, and the [son of the defendant], a mentally retarded boy of 16 ½ [having a mental age of 9 ½ judging from his academic performance] were out shooting in a field. The infant plaintiff wished to shoot at a bird which was sitting on a fence, but he was prevented from doing so by the [son of the defendant], who pointed his .22

---

5 For the original language versions of the materials reproduced in this chapter, see the companion website at www.routledge.com/9781138567733.
6 The *assizes*, or assize courts, were presided over by English High Court judges "on circuit", a system that may be traced back to the 12th century. They had jurisdiction over all indictable criminal offences, as well as some civil ones. The Courts Act 1971 abolished these courts, replacing them with a single Crown Court. See: S. H. Bailey/J. P. L. Smith/N. W. Taylor, *Smith, Bailey and Gunn on the Modern English Legal System*, 5th ed., London: Sweet & Maxwell, 2007, pp. 77–78; G. Slapper/D. Kelly, *The English Legal System*, 18th ed., Abingdon-on-Thames: Routledge, 2017, p. 308.

air rifle at the infant plaintiff and accidentally discharged it, causing the plaintiff a brain injury. The infant plaintiff [. . .] claimed damages [. . .] from the father of the [. . .] defendant, contending that he was negligent in allowing his son, a boy of subnormal intelligence, to possess an air rifle, and that he had failed to give any or sufficient instruction to his son in the use of the air rifle, and had allowed him to use it without supervision.

NIELD, J. [. . .] There is no doubt in my judgement that the law imposes a high duty upon those who handle firearms, and also upon those who entrust firearms to others or permit others to handle firearms.

[. . .] It is necessary to see whether the [boy's] father [i.e. the defendant] instructed his son in the use of the Diana air rifle which the boy possessed before he acquired the B.S.A. [a much more powerful rifle].

The father struck me as a very responsible [person]. He himself said that he remembered the Diana being bought and that when it was:

> "I went up the garden and instructed John how to use it. We had a shoot at targets, and I, myself, having been in the infantry from 1940 to 1946, knew about firearms. I showed my son how to use it, told him not to point it at anyone, and to be sure that it was not loaded. I permitted my son to use it in the place, but I told him he must not use it on the public highway. I said he could use it in the garden."

and thus I reach the conclusion that [. . .] Mr. Codd gave his son adequate instruction in the use of the Diana.

When the [son of the defendant] acquired this B.S.A., what instruction was he given by his father? Again, Mr Codd, senior, tells me that he realised, as was obvious, that the B.S.A. was a more powerful weapon, and that [. . .] he took his son again in the garden, and said that he would have to be even more careful because this was a more powerful weapon and that a pellet would go farther, and he said: "I gave my son the same instruction as before." We fired it; it worked properly, and there was perhaps three quarters to one hour's practice with the weapon." [He] went on to say [. . .] that his son John was in the school cadet corps, where the use of firearms was permitted and in which some instruction certainly would be given. That was the position on the day before the accident.

Let me consider then the position of the adult defendant to see whether it is the case that he must be held responsible having failed in his duty of care. I observe that the first allegation made against the father is that he failed to give his son proper or sufficient instruction in the use of the air rifle: I am satisfied affirmatively that he gave perfectly proper and sufficient instruction. It is next said that he allowed the son to use the air rifle without any such instruction and without any supervision, but I have dealt with the instruction and I am of the opinion that it was not necessary, having regard to all the circumstances, that the son should be supervised. [. . .]

Finally it is said, and this is perhaps a very important aspect of the allegation, that the father allowed the son, who was to his knowledge of subnormal intelligence, to possess and to use a dangerous weapon, that is to say, the air rifle. It is quite clear as a matter of principle that a person who entrusts a firearm to another must be careful to see that he entrusts it to somebody who is competent, and not to someone who is not responsible by reason of mental illness or otherwise may be said to be incompetent. However, in this case, also there is this retardation in book-learning in the infant [boy], I am quite satisfied [. . .] that that in no way affects his responsibility in other directions and that for purposes of this case he was a perfectly normal boy. [. . .] [I]n activities other than book-learning he is in effect as good as anyone else. [. . .]

There will be judgment for the adult defendant.

3. Power of Criminal Courts (Sentencing) Act 2000

Note by the author: According to English tort law, parents are thus under a duty to exercise such control over their children as prudent parents would exercise. If they violate this duty, they are liable for their own negligence. English criminal law provides additional, separate grounds for compensation claims against parents. Under Sect. 137(1) in conjunction with Sect. 130(1) of the Power of Criminal Courts (Sentencing) Act 2000, if a minor commits an act which is *punishable under criminal law*, his parents may be strictly liable, i.e. liable without fault, for any damage caused:

Sect. 130. (1) A court by or before which a person is convicted of an offence [. . .] may, on application or otherwise, make an order (in this Act referred to as a "compensation order") requiring him –
a) to pay compensation for any personal injury, loss or damage resulting from that offence [. . .]. [. . .]

Sect. 131(A1). This section applies if (but only if) a magistrates' court has convicted a person aged under 18 ("the offender") of an offence or offences.[7]

Sect. 131. (1) The compensation to be paid under a compensation order made by the court in respect of the offence, or any one of the offences, shall not exceed £5,000.

Sect. 137. (1) Where –
a) a child or young person (that is to say, any person aged under 18) is convicted of any offence for the commission of which [. . .] a compensation order may be made, and
b) the court is of the opinion that the case would best be met by [. . .] the making of such an order, whether with or without any other punishment, the court shall order that the [. . .] compensation [. . .] be paid by the parent [. . .] of the child or young person instead of by the child or young person himself, unless the court is satisfied –
(i) that the parent or guardian cannot be found; or
(ii) that it would be unreasonable to make an order for payment, having regard to the circumstances of the case. [. . .][8]

---

[7] The minimum age for criminal liability in England is 10 years, as confirmed in the "Children and Young Persons Act 1933", Sect. 50.

[8] *Note by the author*: the compensation order does not depend on a fault of the parents or on a causal link between the parents' behaviour and the offence committed by the minor, see: High Court of Justice, Q.B., Divisional Court, *The Queen on the Application of "M"* v. *Inner London Crown Court*, 10.02.2003, [2003] EWHC 301, n.78: "Where a child of 13 years of age is convicted of a criminal offence, it can be assumed, in the absence of evidence to the contrary, and there was no such evidence in the present case, that the finances of the child are dependent on the parent or guardian. There is specifically no requirement in the statute that the parent should be at fault; nor is there any requirement for any causal connection between the parent's conduct and the child's criminal offence. The policy underlying the section 137 regime [. . .] is to achieve the recovery of fines, costs and compensation orders imposed on children and young persons in order to protect the public purse and/or, as in this case, the person in favour of whom the compensation order has been made. It is in the public interest that the financial penalty should be recovered from the parent

II. Austria

1. Allgemeines bürgerliches Gesetzbuch, ABGB (*General Civil Code*)

§ 1308. Wenn [. . .] Unmündige jemanden beschädigen, der durch irgendein Verschulden hierzu selbst Veranlassung gegeben hat, so kann er keinen Ersatz ansprechen.

§ 1309. Außer diesem Falle gebührt ihm der Ersatz von denjenigen Personen, denen der Schade wegen Vernachlässigung der ihnen über solche Personen anvertrauten Obsorge beigemessen werden kann.

Translation

§ 1308. If a person, who him or herself induced the injury through any fault on his or her part, is harmed by [. . .] a minor under the age of 14, he or she is not entitled to compensation.

§ 1309. Excepting such a case, he or she is entitled to compensation from those to whom the damage can be attributed on account of the neglect of their supervisory duties over such persons.

2. Peter Rummel (eds.), *Kommentar zum Allgemeinen bürgerlichen Gesetzbuch, Band II* (*Commentary on the General Civil Code, Vol. II*), 3rd ed., 2002, § 1309 n. 9 (by Rudolf Reischauer)

9 [. . .] [T]he victim [must] prove that the parents **violated** [. . .] **their duty of supervision** and that there exists a **causal link** between this violation and the damage suffered. [. . .] Once a violation has been established, the responsibility then lies with the parents to demonstrate their **absence of fault**. [. . .] Case law has established that the plaintiff must prove the combination of circumstances which led to the parents' violation of the duty of supervision (for example [the following quotes are taken from case law]: "it has not emerged that the parents were aware that their child was particularly fond of playing with objects which posed a health and safety risk"; "the child was particularly disobedient"; "there is no reason to believe that the harmful behaviour in question was foreseeable"). [. . .]

III. Germany

1. Bürgerliches Gesetzbuch, BGB (*Civil Code*)

§ 832. **Haftung des Aufsichtspflichtigen.** (1) Wer kraft Gesetzes zur Führung der Aufsicht über eine Person verpflichtet ist, die wegen Minderjährigkeit [. . .] der Beaufsichtigung bedarf, ist zum Ersatz des Schadens verpflichtet, den diese Person einem

---

unless there are special circumstances which make that result inappropriate." A compensation order was, however, regarded as unreasonable where a minor lived in a public institution and the parents did not have any control over him, see Divisional Court, *T.A.* v. *DPP*, 01.04.1996, [1997] 1 Cr. App. R. (S.) 1, 4.

Dritten widerrechtlich zufügt. Die Ersatzpflicht tritt nicht ein, wenn er seiner Aufsichtspflicht genügt oder wenn der Schaden auch bei gehöriger Aufsichtsführung entstanden sein würde. [...]

Translation

§ 832. Liability of persons under a duty to supervise. (1) Whosoever is under a duty to supervise another person who requires supervision by reason of age [...] is under an obligation to compensate the loss unlawfully inflicted by such person on third parties. The obligation to compensate does not arise where he or she has fulfilled his or her duty to supervise or where the loss would have occurred even if the duty to supervise had been fulfilled. [...]

2. Bundesgerichtshof, BGH, 6. Zivilsenat (*Federal Supreme Court of Justice, 6th Civil Senate*), 10.07.1984, NJW 1984, 2574

Facts

1 The plaintiff is claiming damages from the defendant spouses [...] – hereinafter *the defendants* – in accordance with § 832 BGB for the breach of their duty to supervise their son M, who was 8½ years of age at the time when the relevant facts arose.

2 On 23rd October 1979, at around 6:45 pm, a shoe warehouse, which had been set up by the plaintiff inside the premises of a tavern rented out by the defendants, [...] was destroyed in a fire. The fire started in what was once an oil storage room, located under the stage in the functions room of the tavern. Three children had been playing there, namely the co-defendants M, Th, and Mi, [...] who were all aged between 8½ and 9 years old. They had snuck through a window into a "projection booth" next to the stage area which, up until a week before the event, had served as a hangout for a local alcoholic. It was in this room that the children found some matches [...]. They crawled into the oil storage room where they lit a fire with some hay and straw. [...] M dropped a paving slab on the fire to put it out. This was not enough to smother the fire and so, over the next hour and a half to two hours, the fire spread to the stage and consequently set the whole room on fire.

3 The plaintiff sued [...] for an estimated 263,800 DM[9] of damages.

4 The defendants [...] deny [...] having breached their duty of supervision. It is alleged that the defendant father had been working the whole day in his job as a bus driver. The defendant mother meanwhile claims that she had been looking after M while tending to her duties in the tavern. The boy left to go for a bike ride, and then play in the garden. The mother made sure to regularly check up on what he was doing. It has been alleged that M is of normal development for his age and is in no way an unruly child. It is stressed that before this event he had not once played with matches. [...]

---

9 Today worth around € 132,000.

Grounds for the decision

7 The court of appeal was of the opinion that the defendants did not produce sufficient evidence to discharge their obligation under § 832 (1) 2nd sentence of the BGB. [. . .]

9 [The] arguments raised by the court of appeal are not well-founded.

10 1. The court of appeal was correct to base its assertions on the 2nd sentence of § 832 (1) of the BGB, by which the responsibility lies with the defendants to demonstrate either that they had fulfilled their duty of supervision, or that the damage would have occurred even under proper supervision.

11 2. Nevertheless, the court of appeal overemphasised the duty of supervision owed by the parents in stating that, in the given circumstances, the parents ought to have forbidden their 8½ year old son from sneaking into the projection booth altogether, and that they ought to have monitored his actions on a regular basis, such that the children [. . .] could not have got away with sneaking into the room and starting a fire.

12 a) The degree of supervision appropriate for a child depends on his or her age, nature, and disposition. Correspondingly, the minimum standard for what is reasonable and necessary of a parent is to be decided according to what the ordinarily prudent parent would require of their child in the given circumstances to prevent harm such as that in the given case [. . .]. In particular, it is the nature and self-discipline of the child which determine the extent to which he or she is able to adhere to simple dos and don'ts or whether further monitoring is required to ensure good behaviour [. . .]. In this regard, it should be taken into account that there is a close relationship between the child's self-discipline and the degree of supervision which is required: the less self-disciplined the child is, the more rigorous the required supervision and monitoring will be [. . .].

According to [. . .] the defendants' assertions, which are to be considered in their favour, until the incident, M was a child of normal development for his age and was not known for his bad behaviour, especially around matches. For this reason, the court is to impose a standard of supervision equal to that required of a normally developed 8½ year old child living in the countryside. That being said, when a child reaches this age, it is not only unnecessary [. . .] for the parents to follow the child "at every turn", but there is also no need to check what the child is doing at regular half-an-hour intervals, as would be the case for a toddler, for example [. . .]. As a matter of principle, a child of between 8 and 9 years of age, who is of normal development, should be allowed to play outdoors without being supervised, even if the location is such that the parents are not able to immediately step in and intervene.

Children at play have a natural inclination to discover and "conquer" new parts of the world. They need not be forbidden from this unless any particular risk is posed to themselves or those around them. For children of this age, who at this stage are even old enough to make their own way to school, parents are only required to have some basic idea of what they are up to, unless there is any particular reason to believe that further precautions must be taken. Otherwise, a child's capacity to properly develop, most importantly to face up to all life's dangers, is hampered. In the present case, the defendants submitted – without being challenged on this point – that M left the tavern clearly telling his mother that he was going for a bike ride and then going to play in the garden. The parents hereby fulfilled their duty to enquire about the child's activities; they were not then required to make sure that what the child was saying was the truth: the mother therefore cannot be held liable for failing to notice M's spontaneous trip to the old oil storage room. [. . .]

14 c) Nor can the defendant mother [. . .] be said to have violated her duty of supervision by not finding out exactly what M had been doing during the afternoon in question after the latter returned home from playing. It would only be necessary to immediately question the child if there were particular reasons to believe that M had been up to no good. [. . .]

15 d) For the same reasons, it cannot be held that the defendant father breached his duty to supervise M. [. . .]

16 3. Lastly, the court of appeal also erred in the contested decision by stating that the defendants did not fulfil their duty of supervision without any further analysis.

17 a) Parents do indeed have a strict duty to inform their children of the dangers of fire, and particularly playing with matches [. . .]. It is not unheard of for children who are playing around to cause fires. Damage resulting from fires caused by playing children shall, in principle, not be borne by society as a whole. On the contrary, in accordance with the rationale of § 832 BGB, the risks which children pose to those around them [. . .] should first and foremost be attributed to their parents, who are more responsible for the acts of their child than any ordinary member of the public, and whose duty to care for the child's upbringing affords them the opportunity to impart the necessary knowledge about the dangers of playing with fire, particularly inside buildings. The manner in which parents go about doing this in the best way possible is for the most part left to their own judgement. Once the risk does indeed materialise, the responsibility then lies with the parents to present and demonstrate evidence that they had fulfilled their duty to instruct the child in accordance with § 832 BGB. Nevertheless, the court must take into account the inherent difficulty of bringing such proof, since the nature of these life lessons is that they are taught in the private sphere of the family home [. . .]. Thus, the Court is not required to carry out a too rigorous examination of the parents [. . .].

23 The appeal [against the judgment holding the parents liable] is therefore well founded. [. . .]

3. Bundesgerichtshof, BGH, 6. Zivilsenat (*Federal Supreme Court of Justice, 6th Civil Senate*), 24.03.2009, NJW 2009, 1952

Facts

1 The plaintiff is claiming damages from the defendants for the breach of their duty to supervise their son P.

2 On 9th July 2003, P. and his friend M. – aged 5 years 4 months and 7 years 7 months respectively – scratched a total of 17 vehicles parked in the car park of the residential complex in which the defendants lived with their son. The plaintiff's vehicle was among those damaged in the incident. The residential complex contained a playground where P had been playing before the incident. [. . .]

Grounds for the decision

[. . .] 9 2. The court of appeal [. . .] was correct to apply the standard of a normally developed child approaching 5½ years old in determining whether the defendants had complied with their duty of supervision. [. . .]

10 a) In order to ascertain the extent of the defendants' duty of supervision, the court of appeal took into account, and rightly so, the allegations made by the headmistress of the

nursery school which P. attended between 2001 and 2004, that P. was a quiet and unassuming child and had never shown any sign of aggressive behaviour. [. . .]

14 a) Normally developed children of around 5½ years of age may indeed be left unsupervised for a certain amount of time without his or her parents being able to immediately intervene. For the proper development of children, it is important to allow them to play outdoors without being watched "at every turn". [. . .]

15 b) On the other hand, we do not accept the court of appeal's assertion that P. could be left unattended for between 40 and 60 minutes, even after his mother had instructed him not to leave the playground in question. In line with the rationale of § 832 BGB, the risk which children pose to those around them is to be attributed to their parents, who are more responsible for the acts of their child than any ordinary member of the public. [. . .] It is therefore unsuitable to allow a 5-year-old child to play outdoors unsupervised for such a long period of time.

16 Although the second defendant need not have anticipated that the child would damage other people's vehicles with pieces of broken glass, the possibility cannot be ruled out that a 5-year-old child left unsupervised for such a long period of time might, with or without peer pressure from other children, think to leave the playground and get into mischief resulting in damage to third parties. With this in mind, the person responsible for the supervision of the child is therefore required to ensure that the 5½-year-old is checked at regular intervals of no more than 30 minutes. A longer interval than this would not be sufficient to comply with his or her duty of supervision, taking into account a 5-year-old's natural playful exuberance and dynamism, and not losing sight of the fact that children of this age do not wholly understand that they have to be careful with other people's property.

17 4. Finally, the court of appeal did not go far enough in establishing whether, and to what extent, the parents complied with their duty to instruct the child. The court of appeal was, in any case, correct to take the view that the requirements relating to the duty of supervision, in particular to the duty to instruct and look after a child, are based on the foreseeability of the harmful act. [. . .] In view of this fact, the second defendant may not have foreseen that her son would damage people's cars with pieces of broken glass. Nevertheless, this does not exempt her from her duty to regularly instruct her 5½-year-old to respect other people's property and not to damage it. [. . .]

18 The decision of the court of appeal is therefore quashed and the case referred back to the former for retrial and decision. In revising its decision, the court of appeal shall be afforded the opportunity to ascertain [. . .] the duration for which the second defendant did not comply with her duty of supervision [. . .].

Note by the author: Regarding the liability of the 7½-year-old boy for the same events, the Federal Supreme Court of Justice rendered the following decision on the same day:

4. Bundesgerichtshof, BGH, 6. Zivilsenat *(Federal Supreme Court of Justice, 6th Civil Senate)*, 24.03.2009, NJW 2009, 1954

Grounds for the decision

4 The court of appeal ruled that the plaintiff could not claim damages from the defendants under § 832 (1) BGB. While the conditions of the first sentence of § 832 (1) BGB were fulfilled, given that the defendants' son had scratched the plaintiff's car, the defendants had,

according to the court of appeal, nevertheless fulfilled their duty of supervision in accordance with the second sentence of § 832 (1) BGB. [. . .]

10 a) To determine whether the defendants fulfilled their duty of supervision, the court of appeal adopted the standard of a normally developed child of 7 years 7 months of age. The plaintiffs have not claimed at any point during this appeal (*Revision*) that M, for any reason, required a greater degree of supervision. [. . .]

11 b) The Federal Supreme Court of Justice approves the assertion of the court of appeal that there is no fundamental reason to prevent a normally developed child of this age from playing outdoors unsupervised for up to 2 hours, provided that he received instruction not to leave the playground in question. [. . .]

14 c) [. . .] Since it is first and foremost the child's nature and the level of personal responsibility which determine the extent to which he or she is able to adhere to simple dos and don'ts or whether further monitoring is required, [. . .] this Court concludes that M's parents fulfilled their duty of supervision since they had repeatedly urged M to respect other people's property. [. . .] [A] child who has been instructed not to damage other people's property, should be able to appreciate that he has no right to damage someone's car with a piece of glass. Since the defendants were aware of the general whereabouts of their child, and had expressly ordered M not to stray into the parking lot in question, they had done all that could be reasonably expected from them to stop their child from damaging other people's property. [. . .]

IV. Switzerland

1. Code civil (*Civil Code*)

Art. 333. (1) Le chef de la famille est responsable du dommage causé par les mineurs [. . .], à moins qu'il ne justifie les avoir surveillés de la manière usitée et avec l'attention commandée par les circonstances. [. . .]

Translation

Art. 333. (1) If damage is caused by a member of the household who is a minor [. . .], the head of the family is liable unless he or she can show that his or her supervision of the household was as diligent as would normally be expected in the prevailing circumstances. [. . .]

2. Bundesgericht/Tribunal fédéral (*Federal Supreme Court of Justice*), 07.11.1974 (*Maurer c. Feltscher*), BGE 100 II 298

On 7th April 1970, Stéphane Maurer, born in 1955 [then aged 14 or 15], and Anton Mittner were shooting at rats with their air rifles in a local rubbish dump situated just south of the municipality of Felsberg, in a small valley on the Rhine. At around 6 pm, Markus Feltscher, born in 1957, arrived at the dump with another child to bring some rubbish. As they arrived, they could only see Anton Mittner, who was out in the open looking for rats, but didn't notice Stéphane Maurer, who was in a nearby thicket. Maurer saw these two boys arrive but did not otherwise pay too much attention to them. At that moment, Maurer spotted a rat and shot at it. The bullet missed and hit a solid object causing it to ricochet towards Markus Feltscher, who was standing some five to ten metres away, and hit him in his right eye. The injury caused the loss of this eye. [. . .]

[Markus Feltscher has initiated legal proceedings against Stéphane Maurer's father for negligence, and claims CHF 136,528 in damages.]

The Federal Supreme Court of Justice has been keen to underline the importance of affording children the freedom to go out and play, and acknowledges that once a child reaches a certain age, continuous supervision is no longer necessary. The Court also acknowledges that the defendant's son is of sound mind, has behaved well in the past, comes from an honourable family, and is reasonably mature for his age. In addition, an incident two years prior, in which the boy had misfired his rifle and caused a scrape to his younger brother's face, had upset him. However, this in itself was not enough to establish that the child knew all about the dangers associated with handling air rifles. As head of the family, it was the defendant's responsibility to fully explain to his son the dangers of using such a weapon. The fact that a similar incident had already occurred reveals that a warning of this nature and strict discipline were all the more pertinent. The defendant, in not adequately instructing the child of the relevant dangers or taking any appropriate security precautions, and by failing to subsequently seriously warn the child of potential damage, breached his duty of supervision. [. . .] The defendant ought not only to have prohibited his son from shooting directly at people, but should also have actively instructed him never to shoot when people are close enough to potentially get hurt by shrapnel or by shots which ricochet. There is a causal link between the defendant's failure to warn the child of such dangers and the incident itself. The defendant shall therefore be held liable for any damage caused pursuant to Art. 333 CC.

V. France

1. Code civil (*Civil Code*)

> **Art. 1242 (ancien art. 1384).** [. . .] (4) Le père et la mère, en tant qu'ils exercent le droit de garde, sont solidairement responsables du dommage causé par leurs enfants mineurs habitants avec eux. [. . .]
> (7) La responsabilité ci-dessus a lieu, à moins que les pères et mères [. . .] ne prouvent qu'ils n'ont pu empêcher le fait qui donne lieu à cette responsabilité. [. . .]

Translation

> *Art. 1242 (former Art. 1384).* [. . .] *(4) The father and mother, in so far as they exercise parental authority, are jointly and severally liable for the damage caused by their minor children who live with them.* [. . .]
> *(7) The above liability applies, unless the father and mother [. . .] prove that they could not prevent the act which gives rise to that liability.* [. . .]

2. Cour de cassation, 2ᵉ civ. (*Court of Cassation, 2ⁿᵈ civil chamber*), 19.02.1997 (*Jean-Claude Bertrand c. Philippe Dominguez*), n° 94–21.111, J.C.P. 1997 II 22848

Whereas the judgment which held Mr Jean-Claude Bertrand liable in negligence is being appealed on the grounds that the presumption of liability established by Art. [1242] (4) of the Civil Code, whereby parents are held responsible for the acts of their children, may be discarded not only where there is force majeure or where the victim is at fault, but also where the parents in question can prove that they have not committed a fault in the supervision or upbringing of their child; whereas in neglecting to examine whether Mr Jean-Claude Bertrand genuinely breached a duty of supervision, on the basis that force majeure and fault of the victim were the only ways in which the former could be exonerated from liability, the Court of Appeal violated Art. [1242] (4) of the Civil Code; Whereas, however, since the judgment explicitly outlined that only force majeure or fault of the victim could exonerate Mr Jean-Claude Bertrand from the legal liability ("*responsabilité de plein droit*") incurred as a result of the damage caused by his minor son residing with him at that time, the Court of Appeal did not need to examine the existence of a breach of the duty of supervision by the father; the appeal is therefore not well-founded; [. . .]

For these reasons, the appeal is rejected.

3. Philippe Brun, *Responsabilité civile extracontractuelle (Tort Law)*, 4ᵗʰ ed., 2016, nos. 417, 433 ff.

§ 1. – The responsibility of mothers and fathers for the acts of their children

419. – Development. Art. [1242] (4) of the Civil Code, in its current wording [. . .], is still faithful to the legislator's vision of parental liability. Subject to the age of the child, and whether or not he lived with his parents, such liability was entirely warranted by the authority that parents possess over their children, and by the duties of upbringing and supervising arising from that authority. It naturally follows from the above that, just as stated in Sect. (7) of the same article, the obligation to compensate harm would cease to exist if the parents of the child could prove "that they could not have prevented the act that gave rise to liability". The courts applied this approach for many years, but all of this changed at the end of the 20ᵗʰ century under the pressures of social development. The present practice no longer reflects the content, nor the intentions of the aforementioned provisions. [. . .]

B – Limitations to parental liability

435. – The exemption provided for parents under Art. [1242] (7) of the Civil Code discarded. From this provision, which affords the mother or father the opportunity to "prove that they could not prevent the act which gives rise to that liability", we initially inferred that parental liability entailed a presumption of fault in the upbringing and supervision of the child, presumptions which the parents could then rebut by proving that they had acted with all due diligence with regard to both duties. In keeping with the legislator's intentions, this interpretation of Art. [1242] (7) prevailed for many years, as much in legal literature and scholarly debate as in case law. It should nevertheless be noted that [. . .] this rule had always been difficult to apply and that, particularly from the second half of the 20ᵗʰ century onwards, its implementation had become somewhat inconsistent. As a result of the twin presumption of fault, the judge was afforded a wide margin of appreciation: whereas there may have been a very precise idea of the standard required for a parent's duty to supervise his or her child, the same could not be said of the parent's duty of upbringing. [. . .] A chaotic situation resulted in that decisions that were somewhat favourable to parents, and others that were excessively rigid, appeared side by side. It may not be too bold to suggest that [. . .] such a patchwork of decision-making might eventually have led to a revolt against the written law. In the end, by the famous *Bertrand* case dated 19.02.1997, the Second Civil Chamber of the *Cour de cassation* set out the principle [. . .] that "only force majeure or fault of the victim could exonerate the father of the legal liability incurred as a result of the damage caused by the minor son living in his household". By ignoring Sect. (7) of Art. [1242] of the Civil Code [. . .], the Supreme Court sounded the death knell for the presumption of parental fault, given that the rule had now become one of strict liability ("*responsabilité de plein droit*"), and that such liability is, by definition, independent of fault. [. . .]

436.– This reversal of precedent is often cited as one of the most spectacular in the Court's history in the field of civil liability. [. . .] But given that the *Cour de cassation* has thus decided to rewrite Sect. (7) of Art. [1242] of the Civil Code, this raises the question of whether the legislator ought now to intervene. [. . .]

437. – Force majeure or fault of the victim: conditions set out by the court to free parents from liability. The mother or father of a child may no longer escape liability simply by demonstrating a lack of fault on their part. In the eyes of the Court, only force majeure and fault of the victim are valid exemptions. [. . .] [I]t follows that, as demonstrated by an examination of the relevant case law, the conditions absolving parents of liability exist more in theory than they do in practice. [. . .]

440. – Parental liability at a crossroads: the need for reform. Whether this evolution is to be regarded as progress or aberration, case law has abolished the present legal provision. [. . .] The judges of the *Cour de cassation* are renowned for their inclination to take matters into their own hands in tort law; however, this usually arises when the judge wishes to bridge gaps in the law, hereby complementing the law, not contradicting it. [. . .] If this new concept of "all-encompassing" liability is to be embraced, [. . .] we must make sure that financial costs are taken care of appropriately: whether it be by a special compensation fund or by creating a legal obligation to contract insurance.

VI. Spain

1. Códigó civil (*Civil Code*)

> **Art. 1902.** El que por acción u omisión causa daño a otro, interviniendo culpa o negligencia, está obligado a reparar el daño causado.
>
> **Art. 1903.** (1) La obligación que impone el artículo anterior es exigible, no sólo por los actos u omisiones propios, sino por los de aquellas personas de quienes se debe responder. (2) Los padres son responsables de los daños causados por los hijos que se encuentren bajo su guarda. [. . .]
> (6) La responsabilidad de que trata este artículo cesará cuando las personas en él mencionadas prueben que emplearon toda la diligencia de un buen padre de familia para prevenir el daño.

Translation

Art. 1902. *The person who, as a result of an action or omission, causes damage to another by his or her fault or negligence shall be obliged to repair the damage caused.*

Art. 1903. *(1) The obligation imposed pursuant to the preceding article shall be enforceable not only as a result of one's own actions or omissions but also of those of such persons for whom one is liable.*
(2) Parents are liable for damage caused by children under their care. [. . .]
(6) The liability provided in the present article shall cease if the persons mentioned therein should evidence that they acted with all the diligence of an orderly pater familias to prevent the damage.

2. Ley orgánica 5/2000 de 12 de enero reguladora de la responsabilidad penal de los menores (*Criminal Liability of Minors Act*) (LORPM)

Art. 61. [. . .] (3) Cuando el responsable de los hechos cometidos sea un menor de dieciocho años, responderán solidariamente con él de los daños y perjuicios causados sus padres [. . .]. Cuando éstos no hubieren favorecido la conducta del menor con dolo o negligencia grave, su responsabilidad podrá ser moderada por el Juez según los casos.

Translation

Art. 61. [. . .] (3) When the person responsible for the acts is a child under 18 years of age,[10] *his or her parents [. . .] shall be held jointly and severally liable with him or her for the damage caused. If these persons have not encouraged the conduct of the minor with intent or gross negligence, the judge may adjust their liability according to the circumstances of the case.*

3. Luis Fernando Reglero Campos (Coordinador), *Tratado de Responsabilidad Civil (Treatise on Civil Liability)*, 4th ed., 2008, Chapter XXI, nos. 3–6, 38 (by Esther Gómez Calle)

I. THE LIABILITY OF PARENTS

1. The liability of parents for harm caused by the non-criminal acts of their children

[. . .]

1.1. The characteristics of "parental" liability according to Art. 1903 of the Civil Code

3   A) Traditionally, parental liability under Art. 1903 of the Civil Code has been considered a *subjective notion* founded upon the principles of *culpa in vigilando* (a "fault

---

10   *Note by the author*: but not under 14 years. In *Spanish* law, minors below that age are not liable for their criminal acts.

in supervision") and/or *culpa in educando* (a "fault in upbringing"); accordingly, it was underlined that parents were to be held liable for any harm caused by the acts of a child under their care when (and because) the harm, even when directly and incontrovertibly caused by their child, was also in some part due to poor parenting, either in the upbringing or in the supervision of this child; i.e. that the parents contributed, albeit indirectly and generally by omission, to the occurrence of the harm. Therefore, liability is said to arise due to the parent's own act, or rather, the parent's own fault. From the final paragraph of Art. 1903 of the Civil Code, we may infer that parents shall remain free of liability should they evidence that they acted with all due diligence to prevent the harm, i.e. that there was no causal link between the harm and any fault on their part.

4 B) [...] In reality, there has not been a single case in which respondent parents have successfully brought evidence to be absolved of liability under the final paragraph of Art. 1903 of the Civil Code, the result of which is that parents are systematically held liable for any harm caused by their children. This is not dependent upon the age of the child (which, on occasion, is not even mentioned in the judgment), upon the type of activity which brought about the harm, upon the personal circumstances of the parents at the time of that harm (work, number of children, etc.), or upon the attitudes of the parent towards the child (e.g. if they had prohibited the child from performing the act in question). It follows that the assertions made by the Supreme Court, namely that fault is required in order to establish liability *ex* Art. 1903 (2) of the Civil Code, purely stand as the Court's formal acknowledgement that the norm is to be interpreted literally without much wider practical implication, given that *such liability is, in practice, applied objectively.* [...]

5 C) A large share of legal doctrine has praised the Court's objective approach to this issue. These authors criticise the fault requirement in parental liability and deem the principles of *culpa in vigilando* and *culpa in educando* to be inadequate and artificial. Among these critics, there are several who, while acknowledging that the Civil Code – and indeed the wording of Art. 1903 – attributes liability for the parent's fault, nevertheless deem the provision to contain a *slight objective nuance*, or believe that its legal basis has changed over time, now becoming a duty of care which is "objective in practice", or believe that it is based on an " *'ex lege' obligation* linked to the exercise of *patria potestad* ('parental authority')". [...]

6 D) I personally agree with the traditional interpretation that the liability of parents pursuant to Art. 1903 of the Civil Code be based upon fault. The fact that the courts have never found the evidence provided by parents sufficient to exonerate them of liability under the final paragraph does not justify, as I see it, to read into Art. 1903 a meaning which it was not intended to have; [...] Nor do I believe that there are any grounds to establish a rule of objective liability for parents *de lege ferenda*. [...] If, both socially and legally, we are to give children the freedom to engage in certain activities (including objectively dangerous acts such as handling firearms and driving mopeds), why, in the event that such actions cause harm, should we attribute subsequent liability for damages to the child's parents even when it is impossible to hold these parents personally liable? Ultimately, a parent who is aware of such prospect may be inclined to over-supervise and over-control his or her child, instead of slowly allowing the child to develop by encouraging individual responsibility.

2.2. Organic Law 5/2000 of the 12th January, concerning the Criminal Liability of Minors [. . .]

38 [. . .] A minor who is more than 14 years old, and may thus be held criminally liable (by virtue of the present law [. . .]), might also be held liable in civil proceedings, jointly and severally with his or her parents if applicable.

As far as parents are concerned, the essential difference between this regime and that of Art. 1903 of the Civil Code, is that their liability pursuant to Art. 61 (3) of the present law seems to be *objective in nature*, because in no way does it seem conditional upon the existence of any fault on behalf of the parents; [. . .]. Art. 61 (3) of the present law [. . .] introduces a stricter regime of liability for the parents of a minor who has committed an offence (at least in theory: remember the tendency of our courts to establish parental liability de facto objectively under Art. 1903 of the Civil Code).[11]

VII. Codal or statutory provisions of various continental jurisdictions (translations)

1. ЗАКОН ЗА ЗАДЪЛЖЕНИЯТА И ДОГОВОРИТЕ (*Bulgarian Law on Obligations and Contracts*)

Art. 48. *(1) Biological and adoptive parents who exercise parental rights shall be liable for damage caused by their minor children and who still live with them. [. . .]*
(3) The said persons shall not be liable if they were not in a position to prevent the occurrence of the damage.

2. Lov om hæftelse for børns erstatningsansvar (*Danish Act on Vicarious Liability for Children*)

§ 1. (1) A person who has custody of a resident child is liable according to the general rules on tortious liability to compensate an injured person for damage the child has caused, up to a sum of 7,500 DKK[12] for each tortious act or omission committed by the child.
(2) In the case of joint custody, the parents are jointly and severally liable for the amount mentioned in subsection 1.

---

11 *Note by the author*: see also above or e.g. Sentencia del Tribunal Supremo (*Judgment of the Supreme Court*), 10.11.2006, RJ 2006/7170, in: *Digest III*, 8/10/1 ff. with comments by M. MARTIN CASALS/J. RIBOT, in particular at 8/10/5: "courts render it impossible to escape liability by proving that the parents who are held liable for the acts of their children met the required standard of care. [. . .] In spite of the wording of the Code, in practice parents are held liable even without fault. An ever-increasing number of decisions even refer to 'risk' as the grounds for liability of the parents in art 1903 CC".

12 Today worth around € 1,000.

3. Võlaõigusseadus (*Estonian Code of Obligations*)

> *§ 1053. Liability for damage caused by children [. . .]. (1) The parents [. . .] of a person under 14 years of age shall be liable for damage unlawfully caused to another person by the person under 14 years regardless of any fault of the parents [. . .].*
> *(2) The parents [. . .] of a person of 14 to 18 years of age shall also be liable for damage unlawfully caused by the latter to another person, regardless of any fault of the parents [. . .], unless they prove that they have done everything which could be reasonably expected in order to prevent the damage.*

4. Αστικός Κώδικας (*Greek Civil Code*)

> *Art. 923. Liability of a person who supervises another person. (1) Whosoever supervises a person under age [. . .] is liable for the damage that such a person unlawfully causes to a third party unless he proves that he has properly exercised his duty of supervision, or that the damage could not have been avoided. [. . .]*[13]

5. Codice civile (*Italian Civil Code*)

> *Art. 2048. (1) The father and mother, or guardian, are responsible for the unlawful acts caused by their minor children [. . .], who live with them. [. . .]*
> *(3) The persons referred to in the preceding paragraphs are released from liability only if they prove that they have not been able to prevent the acts.*[14]

6. Burgerlijk Wetboek (*Dutch Civil Code*)

> *Art. 6:169. (1) A person who exercises parental authority or legal guardianship over a child under fourteen years of age is liable for damage caused to a third person by the conduct of that child, provided that this conduct would have been regarded as a tortious act of the child but for its age.*[15]

---

13 For case law, see e.g. Athens Court of Appel 777/2005, EllDni 46, 1493; H. Koziol/B. C. Steininger (eds.), *Yearbook European Tort Law 2005*, Vienna/New York: Springer, 2006, Greece, nos. 8/31 ff. with comments by E. Dacoronia (under *Greek* law, the assumption of fault is indeed rebuttable).

14 According to *Italian* case law, the presumption of parents' fault is very hard to rebut, bordering on impossibility, see e.g. G. Alpa, *La responsabilità civile: principi*, Torino: Utet Giuridica, 2010, pp. 409–410: parents are "*sostanzialmente sempre responsabile*" and courts have transformed "*la prova liberatori in una prova impossibile*", limiting the exoneration for children living in the same household essentially to the case of force majeure ("*i genitori si liberano da responsabilità solamente se riescono a provare que il fatto era inevitabile, dal momento che è dispeso da caso fortuito o perché non vi era la coabitazione*").

15 For case law, see e.g. Hoge Raad (*Supreme Court of Justice*), 12.11.2004, NJ 2005, 138; H. Koziol/B. C. Steininger (eds.), *Yearbook European Tort Law 2005*, Vienna/New York: Springer, 2006, The Netherlands, pp. 17 ff., 19, with comments by M. Faure/T. Hartlief: liability under Art. 6:169(1) of the *Dutch* Civil Code requires abstraction of the act in question from the young age of the child.

(2) A person who exercises parental authority or legal guardianship over a child that is fourteen years of age, but not yet sixteen years of age, is liable for damage caused to a third person by the child's fault, unless he cannot be blamed for failing to prevent the child's tortious act.

7. Skadeserstatningsloven (*Norwegian Compensatory Damages Act*)

§ 1–2. Parental liability. (1) Parents are liable to compensate damage or injury caused by their children if they have failed to exercise adequate supervision for the purpose of preventing damage, or otherwise have not acted in a manner that could reasonably be expected of them under the circumstances.
(2) Regardless of any fault of their own, parents are liable for damage or injury caused intentionally or negligently by their children under 18 years of age who are members of their household and under their care, up to 5000 NKR[16] for each damage or injury.

8. Kodeks cywilny (*Polish Civil Code*)

Art. 426. A minor who has not attained the age of thirteen years is not liable for any damage he causes.

Art. 427. A person who, by virtue of a statute or contract, is obliged to supervise a person who, due to his age [. . .], cannot be deemed to be at fault is obliged to redress damage caused by that person, unless he has complied with his duty of supervision, or the damage would have been caused notwithstanding diligent supervision. [. . .]

9. Código civil (*Portuguese Civil Code*)

Art. 491. Liability of persons obliged to supervise another. Persons who, by virtue of law or contract, are obliged to supervise others, due to their natural incapacity, are liable for damage caused by the latter, except where they can prove that they fulfilled their duty of vigilance, or that the damage would have arisen even if they had fulfilled such duty.[17]

An amendment was recently proposed to extend the current strict liability rule of parents and guardians with regard to children under the age of 14 to also cover damage caused by minors over the age of 14. This proposal was rejected on 19 May 2015 in the Upper Chamber, see E. KARNER/B. C. STEININGER (eds.), *Yearbook European Tort Law 2015*, Berlin/Boston: De Gruyter, 2016, The Netherlands, nos. 4–5, with comments by J. EMAUS/A. KEIRSE.

16 Today worth around € 560.
17 For the applicable standards and case law, see e.g. Supremo Tribunal de Justiça (*Supreme Court of Justice*), 03.09.2011, *Digest III*, 8/11/9 ff. with comments by A. G. DIAS PEREIRA/S. RODRIGUES/P. MORGADO: when playing football, the ball arrived on a far-away road and caused a motorcycle accident, leading to severe injuries to the rider. The court rejected the claim against the parents holding that "the interpretation of Art. 491 must take into consideration the 'new family' whereby parents don't have an effective control, and a real physical presence near the children; there is a 'softening of parental authority and a faster acquisition of maturity of children, that imposes an *actualist* interpretation of the norm contained in art 491.' [. . .] [A]rt. 491 shall not be confounded

10. Codul civil (*Romanian Civil Code*)

Art. 1372. Liability for the acts of a minor or of an incapacitated person. *(1) A person who, in accordance with law, a contract or a court order, has an obligation to supervise a minor [. . .] is liable for damage caused by those persons.*
(2) The liability subsists even if the minor [. . .] is not responsible for his or her own acts.
(3) A person under a duty of supervision is exempt from liability only if he or she proves that his or her acts could not have prevented the damaging act. Concerning parents [. . .] the proof of exemption is considered to have been made only if they can prove that the child's act is the result of a cause other than the way they fulfilled their duties arising from the exercise of parental authority.

11. Obligacijski zakonik (*Slovenian Code of Obligations*)

Art. 142. Parental liability. *(1) Parents shall be liable for damage inflicted on another by their child until the child reaches the age of seven, irrespective of culpability.*
(2) They shall be released from liability if grounds for such an exemption, according to the rules on strict liability, are given. [. . .]
(4) Parents shall be liable for damage inflicted on another by a child of theirs who is aged over seven but is not yet of age, unless it is shown that the damage occurred through no culpability of their own.[18]

Art. 145. Special parental liability. *(1) If supervision of a minor is not the responsibility of the parents but of another person, the injured party shall have the right to demand compensation from the parents if the damage occurred for reason of the poor upbringing of the minor, or the poor example or bad habits set by the parents, or if the damage can otherwise be attributed to their culpability.*
(2) If the person responsible for supervision in this case must pay compensation to the injured party, such person shall have the right to demand that the parents reimburse the sum paid out.

Art. 146. Equitable compensation. *(1) If damage was inflicted by a person not liable and therefore compensation cannot be obtained from the person that should have supervised the former, the court may order the injurer to reimburse all the damage or a part thereof if justice demands such particularly in respect of the financial situation of the injurer and the injured party.*
(2) If the damage was inflicted by a minor capable of accounting for his or her actions who cannot reimburse it, the court may, in the interests of equity, and particularly in

---

with a case of strict liability." See on the other hand Supremo Tribunal de Justiça, 23.01.2007, CJ-STJ 2007, pp. 30–34; H. KOZIOL/B. C. STEININGER (eds.), *Yearbook European Tort Law 2007*, Vienna/New York: Springer, 2008, Portugal, nos. 2/22–27, with comments by A. G. DIAS PEREIRA: there is a rebuttable presumption of fault under Art. 491 CC; an inadequate upbringing is considered as non-performance of the duty of supervision giving rise to tort liability (a minor of 16 had suffered head injuries by a stone thrown by another minor; the latter's parents were held liable to pay damages in the amount of € 125,000).

18 On this provision, see e.g. B. NOVAK/G. DUGAR, *Digest III*, 8/27/4.

respect of the financial situation of the parents and the injured party, order the parents to reimburse all the damage or a part thereof even if they are not liable.

12. Гражданский кодекс Российской Федерации (*Russian Civil Code*)

Art. 1073. Liability for the Injury Inflicted by Minors under 14 Years of Age. (1) Parents (or adoptive parents) or guardians shall be liable for the injury inflicted by minors who have not attained 14 years of age, unless they prove that the injury has not been inflicted through their fault. [. . .]

Art. 1074. Liability for the Injury Inflicted by Minors between 14 and 18 Years of Age. (1) Minors between 14 and 18 years of age shall bear liability for the inflicted injury on general grounds.
(2) In the event that such a minor has no income or other property sufficient to redress the injury, the latter shall be redressed in full or in the lacking part by his parents (or adoptive parents) [. . .], unless they prove that the injury has been inflicted not through their fault. [. . .]
(3) The obligation of parents (or adoptive parents) [. . .] to redress the injury inflicted by a minor between 14 and 18 years of age shall cease upon the attainment of majority by the inflictor of injury in cases where before the attainment of majority he acquired income or other property, which are sufficient to redress the injury, or where he acquired legal capacity before the attainment of majority.

Art. 1075. Liability of Parents Deprived in Parental Rights for the Injury Inflicted by Minors. Liability may be imposed by a court of law for the injury inflicted by a minor on his parent during three years after the parent was deprived of his parental rights, if the child's behaviour that entailed the infliction of injury had been the result of the improper exercise of parental duties.

VIII. People's Republic of China

1. 中华人民共和国侵权责任法 (*Tort Law Act*)

第三十二条　无民事行为能力人、限制民事行为能力人造成他人损害的，由监护人承担侵权责任。监护人尽到监护责任的，可以减轻其侵权责任。
有财产的无民事行为能力人、限制民事行为能力人造成他人损害的，从本人财产中支付赔偿费用。不足部分，由监护人赔偿。

Translation

Art. 32. (1) If a person without capacity of judgement, or with limited capacity, causes harm to another person, the parent or guardian shall assume liability in tort. If the parent or guardian has fulfilled his parental duties, his liability in tort may be reduced appropriately.

> *(2) Where a person without capacity of judgement, or with limited capacity, causes harm to another person, the relevant compensation shall first be paid out of his own property. The parent or guardian shall make up for any deficit in the compensation award.*

2. Shengming Wang, 中华人民共和国侵权责任法释义 (Commentaries on the Tort Law of the People's Republic of China), 2nd ed., 2010, p. 161

In accordance with Art. 133 (1) of our *General Principles of the Civil Law*, "[i]f a person without capacity of judgement, or with limited capacity, causes harm to another person, the parent or guardian shall assume liability in tort. If the parent or guardian has fulfilled his parental duties, his liability in tort may be reduced appropriately."[19] [. . .]

Where a person without capacity of judgement, or with limited capacity, causes harm to another person, the parent or guardian shall assume liability in tort. This liability is based on the duty of parental responsibility. Given that there is often a close tie (e.g. a genetic link) between the parent or guardian and the person under his or her authority, the parent or guardian is under a duty to reduce, or even avoid, tortious acts performed by the person under his or her authority through proper upbringing and control. In accordance with this provision, the liability of parents and guardians cannot simply be understood as a strict liability or fault-based liability regime with a presumption of fault. On the one hand, if the parent or guardian is able to prove that he has fulfilled his duty of parental responsibility, his civil liability may merely be reduced, and not exempted entirely, which is to be distinguished from fault-based liability with a presumption of fault. On the other hand, a parent or guardian assumes liability only if the conduct of the person without capacity of judgement, or limited capacity, constitutes a tort, which means that the parent or guardian is not to be held liable for each and every act of the person under his authority. If a person with full capacity of judgement would not be held liable for similar acts, then the parent or guardian shall not be liable if these same actions are performed by the person under his authority. Moreover, a parent or guardian is not liable for all damage caused by the person under his authority. His liability in tort may be reduced if he has fulfilled his duty. In this respect, such duty can also be distinguished from strict liability.

IX. Principles of European Tort Law (PETL)

> **Art. 6:101. Liability for minors or mentally disabled persons.** A person in charge of another who is a minor [. . .] is liable for damage caused by the other unless the person in charge shows that he has conformed to the required standard of conduct in supervision.

---

19 Art. 32 of the Tort Law Act and Art. 133 (1) of the General Principles of the Civil Law have the same wording. Since its entry into force, the former applies as *lex specialis* and thus prevails over the latter. That is why only the Tort Law Act is reproduced here.

X. Draft Common Frame of Reference (DCFR)

Art. VI.-3:104. (1) Parents or other persons obliged by law to provide parental care for a person under fourteen years of age are accountable for the causation of legally relevant damage where that person under age caused the damage by conduct that would constitute intentional or negligent conduct if it were the conduct of an adult. [. . .]

(3) However, a person is not accountable under this Article for the causation of damage if that person shows that there was no defective supervision of the person causing the damage.

Overviews

I. General overview

Fault-based liability of parents: applied in England and Wales, Austria, Norway, Poland (for minors of 13–18 years), the Netherlands (for minors of 16–18 years), and the DCFR (for minors of 14–18 years).

Fault-based liability with a presumption of fault: applied in Bulgaria, Greece, Germany, Italy, Portugal, Romania, Slovenia (for minors of 7–18 years), Switzerland, Poland (for minors up to 13 years), Russia (for minors up to 14 years and for minors of 14–18 years with no own means), and the Netherlands (for minors of 14–16 years), the PETL, and the DCFR (for minors up to 14 years).

Strict liability of parents: applied in France (case law), Spain (case law), Estonia (for minors up to 14 years), the Netherlands (for minors up to 14 years), Slovenia (for minors up to 7 years), Denmark (cap: approximately € 1,000), Norway (cap: approximately € 560), and England (in case of criminal conviction of minors of 10–18 years, maximum £ 5,000).

II. Detailed overview by countries

Table 13.1

	All minors	From ages 10 to 18
England and Wales	Fault-based liability ("tort liability")	Strict liability: In case of criminal liability (Power of Criminal Courts [Sentencing] Act 2000, Sects. 137(1) and 130(1)) • maximum £ 5,000
	All minors	
Austria	Fault-based liability (§ 1309 ABGB)	
	All minors	
Germany	Fault-based liability with presumption of fault (§ 832 (1) BGB)	
	All minors	
Switzerland	Fault-based liability with presumption of fault (Art. 333 (1) CC)	
	All minors	
France	Strict liability (Case law)	
	All minors	**From ages 14 to 18**
Spain	De facto strict liability In theory: fault-based liability with a presumption of fault; In practice: the presumption of parents' fault is de facto irrebuttable (§ 1903 (2), (6) CC and Case law)	Strict liability: In case of criminal liability (§ 61 (3) LORPM)

(Continued)

Table 13.1 (Continued)

Bulgaria	All minors		
	Fault-based liability with presumption of fault (§ 48 (1) and (3) LOC)		
Denmark	All minors		
	Strict liability: Damages up to approximately € 1,000 (§ 1 AVLC)		
Estonia	Up to age 13	From ages 14 to 18	
	Strict liability (§ 1053 (1) CO)	Fault-based liability with presumption of fault (§1053 (2) CO)	
Greece	All minors		
	Fault-based liability with presumption of fault (§ 923 (1) CC)		
Italy	All minors		
	De facto strict liability *In theory*: fault-based liability with a presumption of fault; *In practice*: the presumption of parents' fault is extremely hard to rebut (Art. 2048 CC)		
The Netherlands	Up to age 13	From ages 14 to 15	From ages 16 to 18
	Strict liability (§ 6:169 (1) BW)	Fault-based liability with presumption of fault (§ 6:169 (2) BW)	Fault-based liability (general rules on tort liability: § 6:169 BW)
Norway	All minors		
	Strict liability Damages up to € 560 (§ 1–2 (2) CDA)	→	Fault-based liability Damages above € 560 (§ 1–2 (1) CDA)
Poland	Up to age 13	From ages 14 to 18	
	Fault-based liability (general rules on tort liability; Art. 415 CC)	Fault-based liability with presumption of fault (Arts. 426 and 427 CC)	
Portugal	All minors		
	Fault-based liability with presumption of fault (Art. 491 CC)		
Romania	All minors		
	Fault-based liability with presumption of fault (Art. 1372 CC)		
Slovenia	Up to age 7	From ages 8 to 18	
	Strict liability (§ 142 (1) CO)	Fault-based liability with presumption of fault (§ 142 (4) CO)	
Russia	Up to age 13	From ages 14 to 18	
	Fault-based liability with presumption of fault (§ 1073 (1) CC)	Fault-based liability with presumption of fault **Condition**: the minor is without means (§ 1074 (1) and (2) CC)	

(Continued)

Table 13.1 (Continued)

	All minors	
China	Fault-based liability with presumption of fault **However**, the parent can only reduce his or her liability. Thus, part of the liability will remain *strict* (Art. 32 TLA)	
	All minors	
PETL	Fault-based liability with presumption of fault (Art. 6:101)	
DCFR	**Up to age 13**	**From ages 14 to 18**
	Fault-based liability with presumption of fault (Art.VI.-3:104 (1))	Fault-based liability (general rules on tort liability)

III. Systematic overview

Table 13.2

Fault-based liability	Fault-based liability with a presumption of fault	Strict liability	Strict liability with caps
Application of the general rules on tort liability: **England**: tort "negligence" **Austria**: § 1309 ABGB **The Netherlands**: Art. 6:162 BW (for minors of 16–18 years) **Poland**: Art. 415 (for minors of 14–18 years) **Norway**: § 1-2 (1) CDA **DCFR**: for minors of 14–18 years	**Bulgaria**: § 48 (1), (3) LOC **Estonia**: § 1053 (2) (for minors of 14–18 years) **Germany**: § 832 (1) BGB **Greece**: § 923 (1) CC **Portugal**: Art. 491 CC **Romania**: Art. 1372 CC **Switzerland**: Art. 333 (1) CC **China**: Art. 32 TLA. However, the parent can only reduce his/her liability; thus, part of the liability is *strict*. **PETL**: Art. 6:101 *For certain age groups:* **Slovenia**: § 142 (4) CO (for minors of 8–18 years) **Poland**: §§ 427, 426 CC (for minors up to 13 years) **Russia**: § 1073 (1) CC (for minors up to 13 years), § 1074 (2), (3) CC (for minors of 14–18 years if without means) **The Netherlands**: § 6:169 (2) BW (for minors of 14–15 years) **DCFR**: Art.VI.-3:104 (1) (for minors up to 13 years)	**France**: Case law (ULCA) **Estonia**: § 1053 (1) CO **The Netherlands**: § 6:169 (1) BW (for minors up to 13 years) **Slovenia**: § 142 (1) CO (for minors up to 7 years) **Italy**: Art. 2048 (in theory: fault-based liability with a presumption of fault; in practice the presumption of parents' fault is extremely hard to rebut, making responsibility de facto strict) **Spain**: § 1903 (2), (6) CC and case law (presumption of parents' fault de facto irrebuttable); § 61 (3) LORPM (for minors of 14–18 years, in case of criminal liability of the minor)	**England**: Sects. 137(1) and 130(1) of the Power of Criminal Courts (Sentencing) Act 2000 (in case of criminal liability of the minor of 10–18 years), *cap*: maximum £ 5,000 **Denmark**: § 1, *cap*: approximately € 1,000 **Norway**: § 1-2 (2) CDA, *cap*: approximately € 560

(Continued)

Table 13.2 (Continued)

Fault-based liability	Fault-based liability with a presumption of fault	Strict liability	Strict liability with caps
… combined with a presumption of fault **The Netherlands**: § 6:169 (2) BW (for minors of 14–15 years) **Poland**: Art. 427 with Art. 426 CC (for minors up to 13 years) **DCFR**: Art. VI.-3:104 (1) (for minors up to 13 years)	**… combined with a fault-based liability without presumption of fault** **Poland** (Art. 415 CC): general rules on tort liability apply (for minors of 14–18 years), **The Netherlands** (Art. 6:162 BW): general rules on tort liability apply (for minors of 16–18 years), **DCFR**: general rules on tort liability apply (for minors of 14–18 years)	**… combined with a fault-based liability with a presumption of fault** **Estonia**: § 1053 (2) CO (for minors of 14–18 years) **The Netherlands**: § 6:169 (2) BW (for minors 14–15 years) **Slovenia**: § 142 (4) CO (for minors of 8–18 years)	
… combined with strict liability **The Netherlands**: § 6:169 (1) BW (for minors up to 13 years) **… combined with strict liability and caps** **England**: (in case of criminal liability of the minor 10–18 years), Power of Criminal Courts (Sentencing) Act 2000, Sect. 137(1) and 130(1), maximum £ 5,000 **Norway**: § 1–2 (2) (for minors up to 18 years), maximum app. €560	**… combined with strict liability** **Slovenia**: § 142 (1) CO (for minors up to 7 years) **Estonia**: § 1053 (1) CO (for minors up to 13 years) **The Netherlands**: § 6:169 (1) BW (for minors up to 13 years)	**… combined with a fault-based liability without presumption of fault** **The Netherlands**: general rules on torts apply (for minors of 16–18 years).	

Bibliography

HANS-JOACHIM ALBILT, *Haften Eltern für ihre Kinder? Zur Haftung von Aufsichtspersonen Minderjähriger*, Pfaffenweiler: Centaurus-Verlagsgesellschaft, 1987; ANNETTE ALBRECHT, *Die deliktische Haftung für fremdes Verhalten im französischen und deutschen Recht*, Tübingen: Mohr Siebeck, 2013; FALK BERNAU, *Die Aufsichtshaftung der Eltern nach § 832 BGB – im Wandel! Die Elternhaftung im Lichte des Wandels in der Verfassung, im bürgerlichen Recht und der Gesellschaft*, Berlin: Duncker & Humblot, 2005; CHRISTIANE BIRR, *Die Haftung Minderjähriger im Zivilrecht, Deliktshaftung – Gefährdungshaftung – Aufsichtspflichten*, Berlin: Erich Schmidt, 2005; PHILIPPE BRUN, *Responsabilité civile extracontractuelle*, 3rd ed., Paris: LexisNexis, 2014, pp. 275–330; MARTINA FUCHS, *Die Haftung des Familienhaupts nach Art. 333 Abs. 1 ZGB im veränderten sozialen Kontext*, Zürich/Basel/Genf: Schulthess, 2007; ANNE-MARIE GALLIOU-SCANVION, *L'enfant dans le droit de la responsabilité délictuelle*, Villeneuve d'Ascq: Presses universitaires du Septentrion, 2001; JEAN-PIERRE HELLER/PASCAL OBERSON, Die Haftung des Familienoberhauptes nach Art. 333 Abs. 1 ZGB sowie die Billigkeitshaftung nach Art. 54 Abs. 1 OR, in: Stephan Weber (ed.), *Personen-Schaden-Forum 2014: Kind als Täter und Opfer*, Zürich: Schulthess, 2014, pp. 37–88; SABINE HOHENSINN, *Eltern haften für ihre Kinder! Eine rechtsvergleichende Untersuchung im Hinblick auf die Reform des Schadenersatzrechts*, Wien: Manz, 2009; EWOUD HONDIUS, De la responsabilité délictuelle des enfants et de leurs parents, in: MURIEL FABRE-MAGNAN/ JACQUES GHESTIN/PATRICE JOURDAIN SÉBASTIEN BORGHETTI, *Etudes offertes à Geneviève Viney*, Paris: LGDJ, 2008, pp. 511 ff.; URS KARLEN, *Die Haftung des Familienhauptes nach ZGB 333 und des Tierhalters nach OR 56. Eine vergleichende Betrachtung mit besonderer Berücksichtigung des Sorgfaltsbeweises*, Bern/Frankfurt am Main: Peter Lang, 1980; HELMUT KOZIOL, Kinder als Täter und Opfer: Kernfragen rechtsvergleichend betrachtet, in: Stephan Weber (ed.), *Personen-Schaden-Forum 2014: Kind als Täter und Opfer*, Zürich: Schulthess, 2014, pp. 89–113; MARIE-CHRISTINE LEBRETON, *L'enfant et la responsabilité civile*, Rouen: Publications de l'Université de Rouen, 1999; MIQUEL MARTIN CASALS (ed.), *Children in Tort Law, Part I: Children as Tortfeasors*, Vienna: Springer, 2006; FRÉDÉRIQUE NIBOYET, *Die Haftung Minderjähriger und ihrer Eltern nach deutschem und französischem Deliktsrecht zwischen Dogmatik und Rechtspolitik*, Berlin: Duncker & Humblot, 2001; PETER H. M. RAMBACH, *Die deliktische Haftung Minderjähriger und ihrer Eltern im französischen, belgischen und deutschen Deliktsrecht*, Anvers/Apeldoorn: Maklu, 1994; JAAP SPIER (ed.), *Unification of Tort Law: Liability for Damage Caused by Others*, The Hague/London/New York: Kluwer Law International, 2003; JAAP SPIER (ed.), *The Limits of Expanding Liability – Eight Fundamental Cases in a Comparative Perspective*, The Hague/London/Boston: Kluwer Law International, 1998, Case 8; CEES VAN DAM, *European Tort Law*, 2nd ed., Oxford: OUP, 2002, pp. 493–496.

Chapter 14

Pure economic loss
The case of liability for wrongful information and advice

> "[T]here seems to exist a certain convergence in the European legal systems towards an improved compensation of 'pure economic loss', which is very often a consequence of a breach of confidence, in particular in the field of liability for incorrect or omitted information."[1]
>
> "If liability for negligence exists, a thoughtless slip or blunder, the failure to detect a theft or forgery beneath the cover of deceptive entries, may expose accountants to a liability in an indeterminate amount for an indeterminate time to an indeterminate class."[2]

Scenario

A company instructs an advertising agency to place substantial orders on its behalf for commercial time on television and advertising space in newspapers. Before accepting the order and carrying it out, the advertising agency asks its bank to contact the company's bank and enquire into the company's creditworthiness. The company's bank gratuitously responds to the request, and states that it is a "[r]espectably constituted company" that is "considered good for its normal business engagements".

The advertising agency relies on this assessment and places the order with the television and newspaper companies. It is personally liable for the costs of these orders. Before paying the advertising agency for their services, the company goes into liquidation. As a result, the advertising agency loses a considerable amount of money.

The advertising agency sues the company's bank for damages on the basis that their response had been negligent and painted a false and misleading picture of their client's credit situation.[3]

---

1 EUROPEAN GROUP ON TORT LAW (eds.), *Principles of European Tort Law – Text and Commentary*, Wien/New York: Springer, 2005, Art. 4:103 n. 1 (PIERRE WIDMER).
2 Chief Justice BENJAMIN N. CARDOZO, in: New York Court of Appeals, *Ultramares Corp. v. Touche*, 255 N.Y. 174 (1931), 174 N.E. 441 at 444 (1932).
3 Scenario of the English case: *Hedley Byrne & Co Ltd v. Heller & Partners Ltd*, House of Lords, 28.05.1963, [1964] AC 465.

Questions

1) In most jurisdictions, liability for "pure" economic loss is admitted only under exceptional circumstances.[4] Despite this, in response to the above scenario, a number of jurisdictions might hold the provider of wrongful information or advice liable towards the ultimate user of the information (a third party) for the "pure" economic loss suffered.

   What is the response of *English* and *Irish* law to the question of liability for wrongful information or advice? Why was the claim in the case of *Hedley Byrne* v. *Heller* eventually rejected?

2) Which approaches to this issue are to be found in the materials on *US* law? Can liability be imposed on the supplier of information? How did the US courts define the bank's "pecuniary interest" in providing advice? Compare and contrast the reasoning in the two US decisions provided in the materials.

3) Under *Swiss* law, in order to be held liable, the defendant must, in principle, have infringed one of the victim's absolute rights, or violated a behavioural norm aimed at protecting the victim against the type of loss he or she has suffered.[5]

   a) How does the Swiss Federal Supreme Court of Justice establish "wrongfulness" in cases of incorrect information?

   b) What solution would you suggest to the scenario under Swiss law?

4) Why do *German* courts use contract law to address the issue rather than tort law, despite the lack of direct contract between the parties to the claim?

5) § 1048 of the *Estonian* Code of Obligations, § 2950 of the new Civil Code of the *Czech Republic*,[6] and § 1300 of the *Austrian* ABGB explicitly address cases in which wrongful advice is provided by experts.

   a) Under what conditions is the provider of the information liable vis-à-vis third parties in these jurisdictions?

   b) When is the condition that the advice be given "*against remuneration*" ("*gegen Belohnung*") fulfilled according to the interpretation of the Austrian Supreme Court?

6) Under what conditions is the provider of information liable for its accuracy in *French* law? In the French case reported in the materials, the recipient of the wrongful information brought a claim both against the bank that had issued the wrongful information, and against his own bank who had requested the information for him and had passed it on to him. How were these claims decided?

7) While the PETL do not contain a special provision on liability for wrongful advice, the DCFR does. How might the case be solved under the PETL and under the DCFR?

8) How many fundamentally different approaches and solutions do you identify in the materials regarding liability for wrongful information or advice?

---

4 Compare above, Chapter 5, pp. 76 ff.
5 *Ibid.*
6 In force since 2014.

9) The *Chinese* legislator is planning to introduce a comprehensive Civil Code of the People's Republic of China. At present, the question of liability for wrongful advice or information remains relatively open, as revealed by the Chinese materials. If you were to advise this legislator (or the legislator in any other country), would you recommend to make the liability of the person providing the information or advice depend on whether he acted gratuitously or against remuneration? Explain.

Table of contents

I. England and Wales
1. Court of Appeal, *Candler* v. *Crane*, 15.12.1950, [1951] 2 K.B. 164, [1951] 1 All ER 426, dissenting opinion by Lord DENNING...........p. 424
2. House of Lords, *Hedley Byrne & Co Ltd* v. *Heller & Partners Ltd*, 28.05.1963, [1964] AC 465...........p. 425

II. Ireland
Supreme Court of Ireland, *Glencar Exploration plc* v. *Mayo County Council*, 19.07.2001, [2002] 1 ILRM 481, [2002] 1 IR 84, [2002] 1 IR 112, [2001] IESC 64...........p. 427

III. USA
1. The American Law Institute, Restatement of the Law – Torts (2nd), St. Paul, Minnesota: American Law Institute Publishers, 1979, § 552...........p. 428
2. District Court of Appeal of Florida, 4th District, *Reimsnyder* v. *Southtrust Bank*, N.A., 11.04.2003, 846 So. 2d 1264...........p. 429
3. Supreme Court of Mississippi, *Berkline Corp.* v. *Bank of Mississippi*, 25.07.1984, 453 So. 2d 699...........p. 430

IV. Switzerland
1. Bundesgericht/Tribunal fédéral (*Federal Supreme Court of Justice*), 26.11.1985, BGE 111 II 471...........p. 431
2. ALEXANDRE GUYAZ/MURIEL V. EIGENMANN, Le dommage purement économique (*Pure economic loss*), in: Franz Werro/Pascal Pichonnaz (eds.), *Le dommage dans tous ses états sans le dommage corporel ni le tort moral* (*Compensation of all types of damage – except personal and immaterial damage*), Bern: Stämpfli, 2013, pp. 195 ff. at 201, 206...........p. 433

V. Germany
1. Bürgerliches Gesetzbuch, BGB (*Civil Code*), §§ 675 (2), 823, 826...........p. 434
2. Bundesgerichtshof, BGH (*Federal Supreme Court of Justice*), 12.02.1979, NJW 1979, 1595...........p. 435
3. FRANZ J. SÄCKER/ROLAND RIXECKER/HARTMUT OETKER (eds.), *Münchener Kommentar zum BGB (Munich Commentary on the German Civil Code)*, Vol. 6, 7th ed., München: C. H. Beck, 2017, § 826, nos. 79–81 (by GERHARD WAGNER)...........p. 437

VI. Estonia
Võlaõigusseadus (*Code of Obligations*), §§ 1043, 1045 (1), 1048...........p. 438

VII. Czech Republic
Občanský zákoník (*Civil Code*), § 2950...........p. 439

VIII. Austria

1. Allgemeines bürgerliches Gesetzbuch, ABGB (*General Civil Code*), § 1300 ....p. 440
2. Oberster Gerichtshof, OGH (*Supreme Court of Justice*),
   (a) 30.06.2010, 9 Ob 49/09k, (b) 31.08.2010, 4 Ob 137/10s,
   (c) 20.11.1996, 7 Ob 513/96..p. 440

IX. France

1. Cour de cassation, Com. (*Court of Cassation, Commercial Chamber*), 09.01.1978, n° 76–13.107, Bull. civ. IV, n°12 ....p. 441
2. FRANCOIS GRUA, Banquier – Responsabilité en matière de service – Services annexes, Fourniture de renseignements (*Banker – Liability in relation to a service – Ancillary services, supply of information*), in: *Juris-Classeur Banque – Crédit – Bourse*, Fascicule 335–340, 29, Juillet 2011..p. 443

X. Principles of European Tort Law

1. PETL, Arts. 2:102, 4:102 (1)...p. 443
2. BÉNÉDICT WINIGER/ERNST KARNER/KEN OLIPHANT (eds.), *Digest of European Tort Law, Vol. III: Misconduct*, Berlin: De Gruyter, 2018, nos. 3e/30/1 ff. (by THOMAS KADNER GRAZIANO)..................p. 444

XI. Draft Common Frame of Reference

1. DCFR, Art. VI. – 2:207 ....p. 446
2. CHRISTIAN VON BAR/ERIC CLIVE (eds.), *Principles, Definitions and Model Rules of European Private Law – Draft Common Frame of Reference (DCFR), Full Edition*, Vol. 4, Munich: Sellier, 2009, Art. VI. – 2:207, Comment A., pp. 3345–3347 ....p. 446

XII. People's Republic of China

MIN'AN ZHANG/SAINA GONG, 专业人士所承担的过错侵权责任 (*On Professional Liability in Tort*), Chinese Legal Review 2002, 145 at 146............. p. 447

Materials[7]

I. England and Wales

Note by the author: In the case of *Candler* v. *Crane*, whose facts are similar to those of the above scenario, the Court of Appeal had to decide whether or not a false statement carelessly made by one person to another, and acted on by that other to his detriment, was actionable in the absence of any contractual or fiduciary relationship between the parties. By a majority of 2 to 1, the Court ruled in the negative and rejected the claim for damages. Lord DENNING delivered a dissenting opinion (which was later relied upon by the House of Lords, in the case of *Hedley Byrne* v. *Heller*, to overrule the Court of Appeal's decision in *Candler*):

1. Court of Appeal, *Candler v. Crane*, 15.12.1950, [1951] 2 K.B. 164, [1951] 1 All ER 426

LORD DENNING [dissenting opinion]: Now I come to the great question in the case: did the accountants owe a duty of care to the plaintiff? If the matter were free from authority, I should have said that they clearly did owe a duty of care to him. They were professional accountants who prepared and put before him these accounts, knowing that he was going to be guided by them in making an investment in the company. On the faith of those accounts he did make the investment, whereas if the accounts had been carefully prepared, he would not have made the investment at all. The result is that he has lost his money. In the circumstances, had he not every right to rely on the accounts being prepared with proper care; and is he not entitled to redress from the accountants on whom he relied? I say that he is, and I would apply to this case the words of Knight Bruce, L.J., in an analogous case ninety years ago: "A country whose administration of justice did not afford redress in a case of the present description would not be in a state of civilization". [. . .]

[T]o whom do these professional people owe this duty? I will take accountants, but the same reasoning applies to the others. They owe the duty, of course, to their employer or client; and also I think to any third person to whom they themselves show the accounts, or to whom they know their employer is going to show the accounts, so as to induce him to invest money or take some other action on them. But I do not think the duty can be extended still further so as to include strangers of whom they have heard nothing and to whom their employer without their knowledge may choose to show their accounts. [. . .]

One final word: I think that the law would fail to serve the best interests of the community if it should hold that accountants and auditors owe a duty to no one but their client. [. . .] There is a great difference between the lawyer and the accountant. The lawyer is never called on to express his personal belief in the truth of his client's case; whereas the accountant, who certifies the accounts of his client, is always called on to express his personal opinion as to whether the accounts exhibit a true and correct view of his client's affairs; and he is required to do this, not so much for the satisfaction of his own client, but more for the guidance of shareholders, investors, revenue authorities, and others who may have to rely on the accounts in serious matters of business. [. . .]

---

7 For the original language versions of the materials reproduced in this chapter, see the companion website at www.routledge.com/9781138567733.

2. House of Lords, *Hedley Byrne & Co Ltd* v. *Heller & Partners Ltd*, 28.05.1963, [1964] AC 465

LORD REID: My Lords, this case raises the important question whether and in what circumstances a person can recover damages for loss suffered by reason of his having relied on an innocent but negligent misrepresentation. [. . .]

[*Note by the author*: Lord Reid introduces the facts as set out in the above scenario. However, in the English case, Hedley Byrne's bank began the inquiry by saying that they wanted the information "in confidence and without responsibility" on the part of the bank Heller.]

Before coming to the main question of law, it may be well to dispose of an argument that there was no sufficiently close relationship between these parties to give rise to any duty. It is said that the respondents [Heller] did not know the precise purpose of the inquiries and did not even know whether the National Provincial Bank wanted the information for its own use or for the use of a customer: they knew nothing of the appellants [Hedley Byrne]. I would reject that argument. They knew that the inquiry was in connection with an advertising contract, and it was at least probable that the information was wanted by the advertising contractors. It seems to me quite immaterial that they did not know who these contractors were: there is no suggestion of any speciality which could have influenced them in deciding whether to give information or in what form to give it. I shall therefore treat this as if it were a case where a negligent misrepresentation is made directly to the person seeking information, opinion or advice [. . .].

[. . .] The law ought so far as possible to reflect the standards of the reasonable man, and that is what *Donoghue v. Stevenson*[8] sets out to do. [. . .] [I]t seems to me that there is good sense behind our present law that in general an innocent but negligent misrepresentation gives no cause of action. There must be something more than the mere misstatement. [. . .]

[*Note by the author*: Lord Reid quotes the view of Lord Haldane in *Nocton* v. *Lord Ashburton* [1914] A.C. 932 at 947 and proceeds:] Lord Haldane did not think that a duty to take care must be limited to cases of fiduciary relationship in the narrow sense [. . .]. He speaks of other special relationships, and I can see no logical stopping place short of all those relationships where it is plain that the party seeking information or advice was trusting the other to exercise such a degree of care as the circumstances required, where it was reasonable for him to do that, and where the other gave the information or advice when he knew or ought to have known that the inquirer was relying on him. [. . .]

A reasonable man, knowing that he was being trusted or that his skill and judgment were being relied on, would, I think, have three courses open to him. He could keep silent or decline to give the information or advice sought: or he could give an answer with a clear qualification that he accepted no responsibility for it or that it was given without that reflection or inquiry which a careful answer would require: or he could simply answer without any such qualification. If he chooses to adopt the last course he must, I think, be held to have accepted some responsibility for his answer being given carefully, or to have accepted a relationship with the inquirer which requires him to exercise such care as the circumstances require.

---

8 For information on this case, see above, Chapter 5, pp. 76 ff.

If that is right, then it must follow that *Candler v. Crane, Christmas & Co.* was wrongly decided. There the plaintiff wanted to see the accounts of a company before deciding to invest in it. The defendants were the company's accountants, and they were told by the company to complete the company's accounts as soon as possible because they were to be shown to the plaintiff who was a potential investor in the company. At the company's request the defendants showed the completed accounts to the plaintiff, discussed them with him, and allowed him to take a copy. The accounts had been carelessly prepared and gave a wholly misleading picture. It was obvious to the defendants that the plaintiff was relying on their skill and judgment and on their having exercised that care which by contract they owed to the company, and I think that any reasonable man in the plaintiff's shoes would have relied on that. This seems to me to be a typical case of agreeing to assume a responsibility: they knew why the plaintiff wanted to see the accounts and why their employers, the company, wanted them to be shown to him, and agreed to show them to him without even a suggestion that he should not rely on them. [. . .]

Now I must try to apply these principles to the present case. [. . .] But here the appellants' bank, who were their agents in making the inquiry, began by saying that "they wanted to know in confidence and without responsibility [on the part of the respondents Heller]" [. . .]. So I cannot see how the appellants can now be entitled to disregard that and maintain that the respondents did incur a responsibility to them. [. . .][9]

I am therefore of opinion that it is clear that the respondents never undertook any duty to exercise care in giving their replies. The appellants cannot succeed unless there was such a duty and therefore in my judgment this appeal must be dismissed.

LORD MORRIS OF BORTH-Y-GEST: My Lords, [. . .] [i]n order to recover the damages which they claim Hedleys must establish that the bank owed them a duty, that the bank failed to discharge such duty, and that as a consequence Hedleys suffered loss. [. . .]

My Lords, I consider [. . .] that it should now be regarded as settled that if someone possessed of a special skill undertakes, quite irrespective of contract, to apply that skill for the assistance of another person who relies upon such skill, a duty of care will arise. The fact that the service is to be given by means of or by the instrumentality of words can make no difference. Furthermore, if in a sphere in which a person is so placed that others could reasonably rely upon his judgment or his skill or upon his ability to make careful inquiry, a person takes it upon himself to give information or advice to, or allows his information or advice to be passed on to, another person who, as he knows or should know, will place reliance upon it, then a duty of care will arise. [. . .]

[I]n my judgment, the bank in the present case, by the words which they employed, effectively disclaimed any assumption of a duty of care. They stated that they only responded to the inquiry on the basis that their reply was without responsibility. If the inquirers chose to receive and act upon the reply they cannot disregard the definite terms upon which it was given. They cannot accept a reply given with a stipulation and then reject the stipulation. Furthermore, within accepted principles [. . .] the words employed were apt to exclude any liability for negligence.

I would therefore dismiss the appeal.

---

9 Today, the validity of the disclaimer would need to be analysed under the Unfair Contract Terms Act 1977.

LORD DEVLIN: [. . .] I think [. . .] that there is ample authority to justify your Lordships in saying now that the categories of special relationships which may give rise to a duty to take care in word as well as in deed are not limited to contractual relationships or to relationships of fiduciary duty, but include also relationships which in the words of Lord Shaw in *Nocton v. Lord Ashburton* are "equivalent to contract," that is, where there is an assumption of responsibility in circumstances in which, but for the absence of consideration, there would be a contract. [. . .] [T]he absence of consideration is not irrelevant. Payment for information or advice is very good evidence that it is being relied upon and that the informer or adviser knows that it is. Where there is no consideration, it will be necessary to exercise greater care in distinguishing between social and professional relationships and between those which are of a contractual character and those which are not. It may often be material to consider whether the adviser is acting purely out of good nature or whether he is getting his reward in some indirect form. The service that a bank performs in giving a reference is not done simply out of a desire to assist commerce. It would discourage the customers of the bank if their deals fell through because the bank had refused to testify to their credit when it was good.

[. . .] In the present case the appellants were not [. . .] the customers or potential customers of the bank. Responsibility can attach only to the single act, that is, the giving of the reference, and only if the doing of that act implied a voluntary undertaking to assume responsibility. [. . .]

I shall content myself with the proposition that wherever there is a relationship equivalent to contract, there is a duty of care. [. . .] Where there is a general relationship of this sort, it is unnecessary to do more than prove its existence and the duty follows. Where, as in the present case, what is relied on is a particular relationship created ad hoc, it will be necessary to examine the particular facts to see whether there is an express or implied undertaking of responsibility. [. . .] I regard this proposition as an application of the general conception of proximity. [. . .]

[. . .] A man cannot be said voluntarily to be undertaking a responsibility if at the very moment when he is said to be accepting it he declares that in fact he is not. [. . .] For this reason alone, I would dismiss the appeal.[10]

II. Ireland

Supreme Court of Ireland, *Glencar Exploration plc* v. *Mayo County Council*, 19.07.2001, [2002] 1 ILRM 481, [2002] 1 IR 84, [2002] 1 IR 112, [2001] IESC 64

[Judgments delivered by Keane C.J. and Fennelly J.; Denham, Murray, and McGuinness J.J. concurring.]

JUDGMENT delivered the 19th day of July, 2001, by Keane C.J.

[. . .] 93. The law in Ireland must now be considered. The decisions in both Donoghue v. Stephenson and Hedley Byrne v. Heller & Partners Ltd. have been considered and

---

10 Today, the validity of the disclaimer would need to be analysed under the Unfair Contract Terms Act 1977. For a concise analysis of English case law since *Hedley Byrne*, see e.g. R. KIDNER, *Casebook on Torts*, 11th ed., Oxford: OUP, 2010, Chapter 8.

adopted by our courts in a number of cases and unquestionably represent the law in this jurisdiction. [...]

111. There remains the question of economic loss. The reason why damages for such loss as distinct from compensation for injury to persons or damage to property are normally not recoverable in tort is best illustrated by an example. If A sells B an article which turns out to be defective, B can normally sue A for damages for breach of contract. However, if the article comes into the possession of C, with whom A has no contract, C cannot in general sue A for the defects in the chattel, unless he has suffered personal injury or damage to property within the *Donoghue v. Stephenson* principle. That would be so even where the defect was latent and did not come to light until the article came into C's possession. To hold otherwise would be to expose the original seller to actions from an infinite range of persons with whom he never had any relationship in contract or its equivalent.

112. That does not mean that economic loss is always irrecoverable in actions in tort. As already noted, economic loss is recoverable in actions for negligence misstatement. [...]

III. USA

1. The American Law Institute, Restatement of the Law – Torts (2nd), 1979[11]

§ 552. **Information Negligently Supplied for the Guidance of Others.** (1) One who, in the course of his business, profession or employment, or in any other transaction in which he has a pecuniary interest, supplies false information for the guidance of others in their business transactions, is subject to liability for pecuniary loss caused to them by their justifiable reliance upon the information, if he fails to exercise reasonable care or competence in obtaining or communicating the information. [...]
(2) [...] [T]he liability stated in Subsection (1) is limited to loss suffered (a) by the person or one of a limited group of persons for whose benefit and guidance he intends to supply the information or knows that the recipient intends to supply it; and (b) through reliance upon it in a transaction that he intends the information to influence or knows that the recipient so intends or in a substantially similar transaction. [...]

Comment on Subsection (1): c. Pecuniary interest in the transaction. The rule stated in Subsection (1) applies only when the defendant has a pecuniary interest in the transaction in which the information is given. If he has no pecuniary interest and the information is given purely gratuitously, he is under no duty to exercise reasonable care and competence in giving it. [...]

---

11 The Restatement of the Law (3rd), Liability for economic harm, 2012, has not been adopted yet by the members of The American Law Institute. Further, § 5 of the Draft Restatement (3rd) is in major part identical to § 552 of the Restatement (2nd), with only a few changes which would leave the solution of our case scenario unaffected.

Illustrations:
1. A, seeking information as to the will of B, asks C Trust Company for a copy of the will. C Trust Company is not in the business of supplying copies of wills, and has no interest in giving this one to A, but gratuitously agrees to supply the copy as a favor to A. By a negligent mistake but in good faith it gives A a copy of the will of another person of the same name as B. In reliance on the copy A incurs pecuniary loss. C Trust Co. is not liable to A. [. . .]

2. District Court of Appeal of Florida, 4th District, *Reimsnyder v. Southtrust Bank,* N.A., 11.04.2003, 846 So. 2d 1264

846 So. 2d 1264 (2003)

Eric REIMSNYDER, Appellant,

v.

SOUTHTRUST BANK, N.A. and Carroll Richardson, Appellees.

No. 4D01–4922.

District Court of Appeal of Florida, Fourth District.

June 11, 2003.

WARNER, J.: The issue in this case involves the liability of a bank to a third party for providing a reference as to one of its account customers. The bank officer told the third party that its customer was a reputable company, which the third party contends was a misrepresentation. The third party invested in the company, and six months later the company was ultimately investigated for fraud by the Securities and Exchange Commission. The trial court granted summary judgment in favor of the bank. We affirm, holding that the bank had no duty of care to the third party in accordance with the Restatement (2nd) of Torts, section 552. [. . .]

Section 552 has been interpreted as limiting liability for the supply of false information to those entities that are in the business of supplying a particular type of information or those who have a pecuniary interest in the transaction to which the information pertains. [. . .] However, when the information supplied is "gratuitous," no liability attaches because "the user of the information is not justified in expecting the supplier to have used due care in giving the information." *Cont'l Leavitt*, 857 F.Supp. at 1270 (citing Restatement (2nd) of Torts § 552, comment d. (1977)). The supplier is only charged with the obligation to "speak in good faith and without consciousness of a lack of any basis for belief in the truth or accuracy of what he says." § 552, cmt. a. In other words, the standard is one of honesty. § 552 comment d. [. . .]

Southtrust [was] not in the business of supplying information regarding the financial health of companies. A bank may have information regarding the size of deposits and the creditworthiness of its customers based upon their dealings with the bank, but there is neither evidence, nor did Reimsnyder allege, that Southtrust's business included the dissemination of information regarding the intricacies of its customers' particular businesses. [. . .]

Further, [. . .] Southtrust [did not have] any pecuniary interest in the transaction between Reimsnyder and [the bank's client].

In this case, the bank was not called upon to make a specific representation regarding [its client's] creditworthiness on a particular transaction, and Richardson made no such statements. The bank had no pecuniary interest in the transaction between Reimsnyder and [the bank's client]. Thus, the information was gratuitously supplied, and the bank and Richardson cannot be held liable. As Reimsnyder himself testified, Richardson acted in good faith. Therefore, we conclude that summary judgment was properly rendered. [. . .]

Affirmed.

SHAHOOD and TAYLOR, JJ., concur.

3. Supreme Court of Mississippi, *Berkline Corp.* v. *Bank of Mississippi*, 25.07.1984, 453 So. 2d 699 (1984)

Before ROY NOBLE LEE, P.J., and ROBERTSON and SULLIVAN, JJ.
ROBERTSON, Justice, for the Court.

I.

Berkline Corporation has brought this action charging that Bank of Mississippi made material misrepresentations regarding the credit worthiness of Furniture City, Inc. Berkline says that it reasonably relied upon these representations and made credit sales of furniture to Furniture City and that it has suffered financial loss in consequence thereof.

The Circuit Court [. . .] dismissed the action [. . .]. [. . .] [W]e reverse and remand for further proceedings. [. . .]

III.

We live in a credit era. Consumers, commercial enterprises and government all operate on credit. Though attended by evils, credit makes possible a level of material well-being and economic prosperity otherwise unapproachable.

A common incident of the extension of credit is the credit reference. Consumers as well as commercial enterprises, when seeking to open a new line of credit, are regularly asked for references. [. . .]

Banking institutions play a vital role in our credit economy. Consumers and commercial enterprises alike regularly give banks as credit references. Common sense suggests that the prospective debtor's bank will often be better equipped than anyone else to give creditable credit information.

Banks' motives in serving as credit references can hardly be described as altruistic [. . .]. The bank gives credit information as an accommodation to its customer. The customer obviously needs credit references in order to conduct his own business on credit. By serving as a reference, the bank incurs its customer's favor. The bank thus facilitates its customer's business success and, presumably, receives its own benefits from the customer's economic longevity.

Again generally speaking, banks know that the credit information they give out will be relied upon. They are in a unique position to know of the customer's credit worthiness, and they know or reasonably should know that others so perceive them.

We emphasize that the Bank of Mississippi was under no duty to serve as a credit reference for Furniture City. Upon receipt of the original inquiry from Berkline, the Bank was perfectly free to decline to divulge any information. A bank incurs no liability to anyone when it declines to act as a credit reference.

Where a bank [. . .] undertakes to supply credit information, arguably gratuitously, the bank and its officers are bound to use the skill and expertise which they hold themselves out to the public as possessing. There is ordinarily no reason why factual information given by the bank should not be accurate. When a bank officer makes representations or omissions of material facts false at the time, and where that officer has not exercised reasonable care and diligence to see that the information dispensed is accurate, the bank may incur a liability. [. . .]

The law applicable to cases such as this requires that, in order to recover, a plaintiff such as Berkline must allege and prove by a preponderance of the evidence

(a) A misrepresentation or omission of a fact;
(b) That the representation or omission is material or significant;
(c) That in responding to the credit inquiry the bank officer failed to exercise that degree of diligence and expertise the public is entitled to expect of reasonably competent bank officers;
(d) That it reasonably relied upon the bank's misrepresentation or omission; and
(e) That it suffered damages as a direct and proximate result of such reasonable reliance.
[. . .] Reversed and remanded

IV. Switzerland

1. Bundesgericht/Tribunal fédéral (*Federal Supreme Court of Justice*), 26.11.1985, BGE III II 471

A. – Munich-based A. GmbH was looking to enter into a commercial contract on the sale of textiles with B. AG. It appointed Bank C. in Munich to obtain a credit report on B. AG from the Zurich branch of Bank D. Bank C. subsequently telegrammed Bank D. on 3rd April 1981 for information on the current financial status of the company and, more specifically, to ascertain whether or not the latter could honour commercial debts resulting from the delivery of goods of between DM 300,000 and 500,000. One hour later, Bank D. telegrammed a response. The latter provided the bank with details from the commercial register, and added:

"We have been in a business relationship with this company for a number of years. The account has always had a positive balance and we have therefore seen no reason to take a closer look at the company's financial circumstances. To our knowledge, the company holds almost debt-free assets in German real property. We are not aware that the company has had any difficulties paying off its debts. We therefore recommend entering into a business relationship with them."

[. . .] On the basis of this information, A. GmbH agreed to enter into a contract with B. AG for the delivery of textile [. . .]. [. . .] On 7th July 1981, B. AG went bankrupt. [. . .]

B. – [. . .] [On account of the losses incurred in trading with B AG, A GmbH is now looking to claim compensation] from [Bank D. in Zurich] in the amount of DM 318,752.

The Bundesgericht thus reasons:

[. . .] 2. – According to the case law of the Supreme Court, when information is provided outside the course of a profession and imparted gratuitously, the provider shall not be regarded as having undertaken performance of a contractual obligation; consequently, the parties are only in an extra-contractual relationship (BGE 57-II-85 consid. 2 with commentaries). This is the case in particular with regard to information provided by a bank which issues information outside the scope of a bank-customer relationship [. . .]. [. . .]

3. – Any person in a specialised role who receives a request relating to his area of expertise is obliged – should he agree to respond – to provide truthful information insofar as he recognises that the information in question is, or is likely to be, of great importance to the recipient. He is not permitted to wilfully spread false information, nor may he neglectfully provide information where it should have been plain for him to see that it was inaccurate or imprecise (BGE 57-II-86, 41-II-82 consid. 5). The recipient of the information cannot rely on the bank to carry out a particularly thorough investigation, but can nevertheless rely on the bank to act in good faith, provide information with due care, and faithfully communicate any objective information it possesses (cited Federal Supreme Court decision in SJZ 31/1934–35, p. 187 consid. 4). The information provider may be held liable not only when he provides incorrect statements either neglectfully or against his better judgment, but also when he conceals any facts of which he may be aware which might have altered the final outcome of the recipient's decision to invest (BGE 80-III-54 consid. 4).

4. – a) As the plaintiff quite rightly points out, a bank is perceived by the public as being qualified to provide information on its customers, particularly when taking into consideration that there exists a well-developed information system between banks with regard to data of economic value (Schönle, ibid., p. 387). [. . .] Although the defendant bank claims that it did not have the capacity to examine the financial circumstances of B. AG, this does not change the fact that it was in a position of confidence.

b) Likewise, the fact that the two telegrams were not addressed to A. GmbH, but to the German banks which the latter had appointed, has no fundamental impact on the defendants' liability, even if the telegrams had explicitly stated that the information was only intended for its addressees and was to be treated with confidentiality. The defendants' argument that the information had been disclosed without prior authorisation cannot be accepted by the court since, in accordance with the contested judgment, it is in this court's view that information such as this is generally intended for bank customers and, in line with the principle of good faith, the confidentiality clause has no effect. [. . .]

c) The importance of the information was already clear from the question of whether B AG could honour commercial debts resulting from the delivery of goods of over DM 300,000. [. . .] [The] defendant [should have] realised that the German banks had made the enquiries on behalf of a customer who was going to rely upon the information, especially since the requested information was provided by the Swiss bank of his future business partners. If the defendant wished to avoid liability then it should have clearly expressed in its response that its information was not to be afforded such a great degree of importance. [. . .]

5. – [. . .] The court admits that, by being required to provide information on its own customers, the bank was placed into a delicate situation whereby refusal would not have been well received, but this is of no consequence to the outcome of this decision. [. . .]

9. – [. . .] [The Commercial Court rejected the claim and reasoned inter alia that] while the damage may have stemmed naturally from the bank's actions, causation was nevertheless lacking. A businessman would not usually be expected to risk extending a loan on the basis of this kind of information alone and, for this reason, the plaintiff's own negligence played a role in the chain of causation. [. . .] However, [contrary to the conclusions of the Commercial Court], the fact that A. GmbH relied upon the information in question to sell goods on credit was not in itself so negligent as to break the adequate causal link existing between the damage and the conduct of the defendants. [. . .]

11. – The defendant's final argument was that it had excluded its liability by expressly including the words "without liability on our part" at the footer of the telegram. [. . .] Even if this disclaimer had initially been addressed at the German bank that made the request, it would be inequitable to disregard the clause following the transfer of the information to the customer, even if the transfer was not authorised. [. . .] The Federal Supreme Court denied to take into account a clause that excluded tort liability in SJZ 31/1934–35 (consid. 3 p. 187). Academic commentary suggests the opposite solution [. . .]. It is nevertheless unnecessary to decide this dispute in the present case since, [. . .] for liability to be excluded, the consent of both parties is required. [. . .] [I]t [is] not clear from the contested judgment [whether] A. GmbH's German bank passed on the information with all disclaimers intact to its customer, and indeed this point has not been argued before the Court [. . .]. This in itself rules out the question of whether or not the defendant consented to A. GmbH's liability exclusion clause.

2. ALEXANDRE GUYAZ/MURIEL VAUTIER EIGENMANN, Le dommage purement économique (*Pure Economic Loss*), in: FRANZ WERRO/ PASCAL PICHONNAZ (eds.), *Le dommage dans tous ses états sans le dommage corporel ni le tort moral (Compensation of all types of damage – except personal and immaterial damage)*, 2013, pp. 195 ff. at 201, 206

[. . .] In line with our objective notion of *wrongfulness*, the general consensus is that a rule may be violated in one of two ways, either by injuring an absolute right of the victim (notably life, health, or property) – an injury which is deemed *ipso facto* prohibited by the legal order – or by infringing a standard of conduct which has the purpose of protecting the injured party. The former is referred to as *illicéité de résultat* (result-based wrongfulness), and the latter *illicéité de comportement* (conduct-based wrongfulness). [. . .]

The *Tribunal fédéral* has stated, or at least implied, that *illicéité de comportement* (conduct-based wrongfulness) extends to situations where the injurer provides incorrect advice or imprecise information. In these types of scenario, information may even be provided without the existence of any contractual relationship between the parties. Our Supreme Court is of the opinion that any person in a specialised role who receives a request relating to his area of expertise is obliged – should he agree to respond – to provide truthful information insofar as he recognises that the information in question is, or is likely to be, of great importance to the recipient. He is not permitted to wilfully spread false information, nor may he neglectfully provide information where it should have been plain for him to see that it was inaccurate or imprecise.[12]

V. Germany

1. Bürgerliches Gesetzbuch, BGB (*Civil Code*)

§ 675. **Entgeltliche Geschäftsbesorgung.** [...] (2) Wer einem anderen einen Rat oder eine Empfehlung erteilt, ist, unbeschadet der sich aus einem Vertragsverhältnis, einer unerlaubten Handlung oder einer sonstigen gesetzlichen Bestimmung ergebenden Verantwortlichkeit, zum Ersatz des aus der Befolgung des Rates oder der Empfehlung entstehenden Schadens nicht verpflichtet. [...]

§ 823. **Schadensersatzpflicht.** (1) Wer vorsätzlich oder fahrlässig das Leben, den Körper, die Gesundheit, die Freiheit, das Eigentum oder ein sonstiges Recht eines anderen widerrechtlich verletzt, ist dem anderen zum Ersatz des daraus entstehenden Schadens verpflichtet.
(2) Die gleiche Verpflichtung trifft denjenigen, welcher gegen ein des Schutz eines anderen bezweckendes Gesetz verstößt. [...]

§ 826. **Sittenwidrige vorsätzliche Schädigung.** Wer in einer gegen die guten Sitten verstoßenden Weise einem anderen vorsätzlich[13] Schaden zufügt, ist dem anderen zum Ersatz des Schadens verpflichtet.

---

12 *Note by the author*: in a couple of decisions, notably the cases: Federal Supreme Court of Justice, 15.11.1994, ATF 120 II 331 (Swissair), and Federal Supreme Court of Justice, 10.10.1995, ATF 121 III 350 (Ringer), the *Swiss* Federal Supreme Court has held that there is not only contractual and tort liability, but a *third form of liability*, so-called responsibility based on confidence (*Vertrauenshaftung, responsabilité fondée sur la confiance*). According to the Swiss Supreme Court, this liability is based on the idea that, in cases where a person who is obviously relying on a false perception or a misrepresentation of issues or facts and who risks suffering damage therefrom, the principle of good faith requires that someone who has special knowledge may be under a duty to warn or inform the said person. See e.g. P. LOSER, Die Vertrauenshaftung in der Praxis, in: P. Jung (ed.), *Aktuelle Entwicklungen im Haftungsrecht*, Zürich: Schulthess, 2007, pp. 23 ff.

It is submitted that the case law on "*Vertrauenshaftung*"/ "*responsabilité fondée sur la confiance*" blurs the conditions for, and the limits of, contractual and extracontractual liability, that there is no need for this third type of liability, and that the (few) cases dealt with in *Switzerland* under the principles on "*Vertrauenshaftung*"/"*responsabilité fondée sur la confiance*" can very well be dealt with under either the rules on contractual or on extra-contractual liability. In situations of wrongful information or advice, this "third form of liability" would lead to the same results as the liability based on Art. 41 CO as set out in the above materials (see the considerations of the Federal Supreme Court of Justice in the case: TF, 26.09.2001, 4C.193/2000). The Swiss judge made principles on a third form of liability should thus arguably not be considered for exportation to other jurisdictions.

13 *Anmerkung des Verf.*: Deliktische Haftung aufgrund falscher Auskunftserteilung setzt nicht zwingend Vorsatz voraus; vielmehr erachten deutsche Gerichte zunehmend auch grob fahrlässiges Handeln als ausreichend, vgl. z. B. H. G. BAMBERGER/H. ROTH (Hrsg.), *Beck'scher Online-Kommentar BGB*, 42. Aufl., München: C.H. Beck, 2017, § 826 Rn. 75–79 (C. FÖRSTER).

Translation

§ 675. Nongratuitous management of the affairs of another. [...] *(2) A person who gives another person advice or a recommendation, notwithstanding the responsibility that arises from a contractual relationship, a tort, or another statutory provision, is not obliged to pay compensation for the damage arising from following the advice or the recommendation.* [...]

§ 823. Duty to compensate loss. (1) Whosoever unlawfully injures, intentionally or negligently, the life, body, health, freedom, property, or other right of another person, has an obligation to the other person to compensate the resulting loss.
(2) The same obligation is incurred by a person who infringes a statutory provision that is intended to protect another person. [...]

§ 826. Intentional immoral infliction of loss. Whosoever intentionally[14] inflicts loss on another person in a manner that is contrary to good morals has an obligation to compensate the loss.

2. Bundesgerichtshof, BGH (*Federal Supreme Court of Justice*), 12.02.1979, NJW 1979, 1595

On the liability of a bank for having negligently provided unidentified potential lenders with incorrect information about the creditworthiness of one of its clients.

Facts:

The plaintiff is claiming compensation from the defendant, an international bank, for the losses suffered as a result of incorrect information about the creditworthiness [of one of its clients] issued by its German subsidiary. Around the turn of the year 1971, the plaintiff was looking to invest a sum of DM 130,000. The financial broker *L* advised the latter to invest in *P*, a hotel in the town of M – which had been built and opened by businessman *A* [...] in mid-June of the same year. *A* had taken out a series of loans to construct the hotel, including one from the plaintiff in the amount of DM 2.5 million. [...] To cover a budgeting shortfall of around DM 3.5 million, *A* placed newspaper advertisements and contacted a number of financial intermediaries [...] to attract more investors. [...]

On 3rd February 1971, the broker *L* presented the plaintiff with the following information, which he wrote on the bank's company-headed paper without any address or date: "Hotel *P* is a newly constructed luxury hotel in M – ... The official opening in mid-June 1970 was attended by local dignitaries from the church and the council of M – -. The hotel has around 440 beds and complies with all relevant international standards. ... *A* is the sole proprietor and has proved to be an active and competent hotelier throughout our business relations

---

14 *Note by the author*: in cases of wrongful advice, there is a tendency in *German* court decisions to consider it sufficient under § 826 that the provider of the information acted with gross negligence, rather than having caused the loss intentionally. See e.g. H. G. BAMBERGER/H. ROTH (eds.), *Beck'scher Online-Kommentar BGB*, 42nd ed., München: C.H. Beck, 2017, § 826 nos. 75–79 (C. FÖRSTER).

with him. Moreover, *A* is proprietor of a modern 600-bed hotel in Tenerife, along with 2 health-resorts . . . each of which are of first class. The health-resort . . . is under the medical direction of a well-known professor of prophylaxis at . . . the University of B –. Due to the sharp rise in construction costs and the building of new extensions, *A* requires a cash injection of DM 3.5 million from private investors to cover his additional expenses. [. . .] Our bank has provided *A* with a large-scale secured loan. Due to the increased expenses incurred on a number of his construction projects, *A*'s liquidity is considered precarious for the time being."

On 17th February 1971, the plaintiff handed *L* a cheque for DM 130,000, which was cashed by the defendant bank that very day. [. . .] *A* sank further and further into financial difficulties. [. . .] [O]n 20th April 1972, *A* filed for bankruptcy. The plaintiff received only a scarce sum from the foreclosure of the hotel and nothing from the resulting bankruptcy estate. [. . .]

Grounds of the decision

The lower court found the defendant bank to be contractually liable for the loss. The appeal was rejected.

I. 1. According to the findings of the lower court, the defendant bank consciously and intentionally drafted and published the information with an eye to attracting private investors who could act as lenders for *A*.

a) The lower court reasoned that the information was addressed in both substance and form to a select audience. It had a largely laudatory and promotional effect which would encourage a positive response from private individuals. [. . .] [The information] was deliberately intended to portray the property as a reliable private investment. [. . .]

3. The lower court considered the information to be false, since the defendant bank omitted a number of facts which ought to have been disclosed. The reference to two health-resorts gave the impression that *A* had full ownership of both. In actual fact, they were burdened with the maximum permissible mortgages. In addition, the defendant bank stated that *A* held a large-scale secured loan with them, which was false since this loan had been terminated before the information was presented to the plaintiff. [. . .] The defendant bank does not challenge [. . .] further facts indicating that the information may have been false. [. . .] For a lender, it is important to know the extent of charges existing over the debtor's property before making the decision to grant a loan. Since [. . .] the disclosed information gave the impression that the health-resorts were assets available to lenders in case of financial difficulties of the borrower, in this sense such information was false since each of the properties was burdened with the maximum permissible mortgages. Unlike the appellant, this Court recognises that in reality it is common practice for banks to inform potential lenders about any considerable charges existing over real property. [. . .] When the information on *A*'s creditworthiness was given, the latter had not even paid for any of the hotel furnishings or health-resort facilities; upon deciding to provide information about the creditworthiness of its client, the defendant bank was required, under these circumstances, to [. . .] disclose these facts, since they played an important role in the decision of the lenders. Under these circumstances it was not sufficient for the bank to merely state that *A*'s liquidity was considered precarious for the time being [. . .]. These findings are sufficient to qualify the information provided by the bank as false.

II. Under these circumstances, the defendant is contractually liable to pay damages for the wrongful provision of false information. It is settled case-law that a tacit contractual or quasi-contractual relationship arises between a bank and an enquirer when it is clear that the latter attaches considerable importance to the expert opinion of the former, and intends to rely upon such expert opinion when investing a significant proportion of his assets [. . .]. This also applies to the situation at hand. In this case, there is no doubt that the bank addressed a select audience, namely private investors who might be interested in providing a loan to help finance the Hotel P project. The defendant bank directed the information at this group in particular, since the bank knew that it may lead to a significant economic investment, in which the bank had an interest. This was exactly the reason why they provided the information. The law is to make no distinction in respect of whether the bank addresses the recipient, or vice versa. Given that the bank sought to profit from the information supplied, the provision of the information is to be viewed as a binding contractual statement giving rise to a legal relationship; the person transferring the information merely plays the role of intermediary. Customary practice and the principle of good faith dictate that a contractual relationship has emerged in the present case if, in light of the above, a potential addressee has relied on the information provided and subsequently acted upon it. The appellant contends that the information [. . .] was only intended to land in the hands of a bank, but this is irrelevant since nothing stopped that bank from then passing the information on. It is true that the information was intended for third parties which were, as of that time, unknown to the bank. [. . .] However, in these circumstances there was only a small and foreseeable number of individuals who would obviously have had an interest in such information.

III. 1. Since a contract for information had been formed between the parties, the defendant was obliged to provide objectively correct information. The defendant bank negligently violated this obligation (§§ 276, 278 BGB) since, in its position, it knew or at least ought to have known that the information omitted was, in the circumstances, important for the lender's decision on whether or not to grant a loan. [. . .]

3. Franz J. Säcker/Roland Rixecker/Hartmut Oetker (eds.), *Münchener Kommentar zum BGB (Munich Commentary on the German Civil Code)*, Vol. 6, 7th ed., 2017, § 826, nos. 79–81 (by Gerhard Wagner)

a) Fundamentals

79   In many cases, pure economic loss occurs when an individual acts in reliance of information he has requested and received from a professional who **occupies a qualified position of trust**. Should the information provided by the "expert" prove to be false, then the latter is to be held liable with respect to the **economic losses** suffered by any third parties who were informed of the expert's statements and subsequently made investment decisions to their detriment. [. . .]

b) Liability for wrongful information

80   If an individual provides a third party with information which he knows to be incorrect then he shall be held liable under § 826 [BGB] for committing an act which is contrary to good morals. The same holds true for information which is provided out of the blue,

with lack of due care or in gross negligence where it is obvious that the content therein is important and the provider is able to foresee that the recipient might suffer damage. These rules have particular repercussions for the banking industry, especially in regard to the disclosure of client solvency and creditworthiness records. Should information be provided which is objectively wrong, in the sense that it is incorrect in substance or passed on without due consideration or conscience then, according to § 826, the bank shall be held liable towards the recipient of the information who, in reliance of the information, granted a loan to a party who subsequently went insolvent. [. . .]

81 § 826 now has little practical significance in this field [. . .] since, despite the existence of § 675 (2) [of the Civil Code, BGB], the courts have increasingly extended the scope of contractual liability for wrongful information, by employing the notion of an **implied contract on the provision of information** [. . .]; the formation of this type of contract only has two requirements: one, that the information must clearly be of considerable economic importance to the recipient, who intends to act upon it in making a significant investment, and the other, that the individual providing the information possesses particular expertise or acts in his own economic interests. According to settled case law, when a lending bank produces an incorrect report into its client's financial circumstances and an authorised third party subsequently acts in reliance of such materials, the bank can be held liable to cover his losses since there is an implied contract on the provision of information between the two. It is only in cases where one of the above conditions is not fulfilled that the courts need to examine § 826, which allows a claim when the individual has consciously or recklessly provided false information.

VI. Estonia

Võlaõigusseadus (*Code of Obligations*)

§ 1043. **Õigusvastaselt tekitatud kahju hüvitamine.** Teisele isikule (kannatanu) õigusvastaselt kahju tekitanud isik (kahju tekitaja) peab kahju hüvitama, kui ta on kahju tekitamises süüdi või vastutab kahju tekitamise eest vastavalt seadusele.

§ 1045. **Kahju tekitamise õigusvastasus.** (1) Kahju tekitamine on õigusvastane eelkõige siis, kui see tekitati:
1) kannatanu surma põhjustamisega;
2) kannatanule kehavigastuse või tervisekahjustuse tekitamisega;
3) kannatanult vabaduse võtmisega;
4) kannatanu isikliku õiguse rikkumisega;
5) kannatanu omandi või sellega sarnase õiguse või valduse rikkumisega;
6) isiku majandus- või kutsetegevusse sekkumisega;
7) seadusest tulenevat kohustust rikkuva käitumisega;
8) heade kommete vastase tahtliku käitumisega. [. . .]

§ 1048. **Asjatundja ebaõige arvamuse õigusvastasus.** Teisele isikule varalises küsimuses ebaõiget teavet või ebaõige arvamuse andnud või teabe või arvamuse, vaatamata uutele teadmistele, parandamata jätnud asjatundja käitumine loetakse õigusvastaseks, kui kahju tekitajale kuulub tema kutsealase tegevuse tõttu eriline usaldusseisund ja teabe või arvamuse saaja võis sellele usaldusele tugineda.

Translation

§ 1043. Compensation for unlawfully caused damage. *A person (tortfeasor) who unlawfully causes damage to another person (victim) shall compensate for the damage if he or she is culpable of causing the damage or is otherwise liable for causing the damage pursuant to law.*

§ 1045. Unlawfulness of causing damage. *(1) Damage is unlawful in particular when it is caused by:*
1) causing the death of the victim;
2) causing bodily injury or damage to the health of the victim;
3) deprivation of the liberty of the victim;
4) violation of a personality right of the victim;
5) violation of the right of ownership or a similar right or right of possession of the victim;
6) interference with the economic or professional activities of a person;
7) behaviour which violates a duty arising from law;
8) intentional behaviour contrary to good morals. [. . .]

§ 1048. Unlawfulness of incorrect opinion of expert. *The behaviour of an expert is deemed to be unlawful if the expert provides incorrect information or an incorrect opinion to another person in a financial matter or, regardless of receiving new knowledge concerning the matter, fails to correct the information or opinion already provided, and if the expert enjoys particular trust due to his or her professional activities and the person who was given the information or opinion could expect to rely on such trust.*[15]

VII. Czech Republic

Občanský zákoník (*Civil Code*)

§ 2950. Škoda způsobená informací nebo radou. Kdo se hlásí jako příslušník určitého stavu nebo povolání k odbornému výkonu nebo jinak vystupuje jako odborník, nahradí škodu, způsobí-li ji neúplnou nebo nesprávnou informací nebo škodlivou radou danou za odměnu v záležitosti svého vědění nebo dovednosti. Jinak se hradí jen škoda, kterou někdo informací nebo radou způsobil vědomě.

---

15 In *Estonian* law, there is no case published yet which corresponds to the above scenario. However, § 1048 may apply, and the bank could be held liable in tort vis-à-vis the ultimate recipient of the information, provided that there is no contract between those parties. In cases where the bank knows the precise identity of the ultimate user of the information, the focus may instead lie on § 80 and, more importantly, § 81 (1) of the Code of Obligations. § 80 of the Code of Obligations provides (in English translation): "A contract may prescribe, or the nature of an obligation may indicate, that the obligation is to be performed for the benefit of a third party in lieu of the obligee (contract for the benefit of a third party)." § 81 (1) 1st sent. reads (in English translation): "A contract may prescribe the obligation to take into account the interests or rights of a third party to the same extent as the interests or rights of the obligee." Under both provisions, a third party may seek compensation for breach of contract – under the condition that the identity of the ultimate recipient was known when the information was provided (the author is grateful to Prof. JANNO LAHE, Tartu, for this information on Estonian law).

Translation

> § 2950. *Damage caused by information or advice. A person who offers professional performance as a member of a vocation or profession, or otherwise acts as an expert, shall provide compensation for damage caused by his or her provision of incomplete or incorrect information or harmful advice provided for consideration in a matter related to his or her expertise or skill. Otherwise, only damage intentionally caused by providing information or advice is subject to compensation.*

VIII. Austria

1. Allgemeines bürgerliches Gesetzbuch, ABGB (*General Civil Code*)

> § 1300. Ein Sachverständiger ist [. . .] dann verantwortlich, wenn er gegen Belohnung in Angelegenheiten seiner Kunst oder Wissenschaft aus Versehen einen nachtheiligen Rath ertheilet. Außer diesem Falle haftet ein Rathgeber nur für den Schaden, welchen er wissentlich durch Ertheilung des Rathes dem Anderen verursachet hat.

Translation

> § 1300. *An expert is [. . .] liable if he or she gives advice in a matter pertaining to his or her particular skill or insight against remuneration and hereby negligently causes damage. Any person shall otherwise only bear liability if he or she knowingly causes damage to another.*

2. Oberster Gerichtshof, OGH (*Supreme Court of Justice*)

(a) 30.06.2010, 9 Ob 49/09k

[. . .] According to the first sentence of § 1300 ABGB, an expert is liable if "against remuneration" he mistakenly gives advice which harms another. The word "advice" is to encompass both advice and information [. . .]. Modern-day academic commentary and case law hold that "against remuneration" in the first sentence of § 1300 ABGB is to be understood as meaning that the advice was not given gratuitously; such liability may thus be established even where there is no contractual relationship between the parties to the dispute. The only factor which is important in establishing liability, even in cases of one-off advice, is whether the advice was given gratuitously [. . .]. The basic idea of this approach is to subject those who expect to benefit from providing information to a stricter standard than those who advise purely as a matter of courtesy (VÖLKL, ÖJZ 2006, 97 [101], etc.).

(b) 31.08.2010, 4 Ob 137/10s

[. . .] 2. The defendant is to be held liable [. . .] on the basis of § 1300 1st sent. ABGB.

2.1. According to settled case law, remuneration is not required to establish liability under the 1st sentence of § 1300 ABGB; all that needs to be shown is that the advice or information was not given for purely altruistic (gratuitous) reasons [. . .]. This is especially relevant where the conduct in question is performed in respect of a benefit expected from a third party (notably when expecting commission on a transaction) [. . .].

2.2. The defendant's guarantee that the proposed transaction was [. . .] safe was provided in expectation of commission on the successful conclusion of a business transaction. Thus, the latter cannot be said to have acted for purely altruistic reasons since he had his own economic interests in mind. On this basis, the defendant is to be held liable on the basis of § 1300 1st sent. ABGB, even if his negligent conduct caused the plaintiff to suffer purely economic loss. [. . .]

Note by the author: Regarding liability vis-à-vis third parties, the Austrian Supreme Court has held:

(c) 20.11.1996, 7 Ob 513/96

[. . .] Examining the [. . .] most recent decisions of our courts [. . .], this Senate has come to the conclusion that an expert is under an objective legal duty of care towards a third party wherever he is to expect his expert opinion to be relied upon by the latter. Should the client indicate to the expert that his survey is to be presented to potential lenders or buyers then the expert is to be held liable towards that third party for breach of such duty of care. Accordingly, an expert is to be held liable for any survey which is sufficiently credible to persuade third parties to put faith in it.

In the present case, the client requested the defendant experts to ascertain the market value of the property in question "ready to be submitted to the bank". Consequently, it must have been obvious to the defendants while preparing their proposal that a lending bank would place reliance on the accuracy of their survey in deciding whether or not to extend a loan. [. . .] Since the defendant was aware that his survey was intended to be submitted to a lending bank for acquisition of a mortgage and that the latter would rely upon the accuracy and reliability of such survey, the plaintiff thus enjoys objective legal protection as a third party [. . .]. So long as there is [. . .] a demonstrable causal link between the false survey and the harm suffered by the plaintiff, the defendant is to be held liable towards the plaintiff by virtue of the objective legal duty of care he accepted when preparing a false survey for the latter and hereby causing losses [. . .].

Nevertheless, in the view of this Senate, the plaintiff's own contributory negligence is to be set at 50%. [. . .]

IX. France

1. Cour de cassation, Com. (*Court of Cassation, Commercial Chamber*), 09.01.1978, n° 76–13.107, Bull. civ. IV, n°12

(1) Bank – liability – information of a commercial nature – misinformation – information obtained from another bank. (2) Bank – liability – information of a commercial nature – misinformation – whether mistake can be justified by a duty of confidentiality (denied).

On the second ground of appeal: Whereas, according to the contested judgment's findings, a bill of exchange was drawn by Martinet ("the payee") on a company in Cergy ("the drawee") whose CEO, Mr Keats ("the guarantor"), endorsed it to be paid at its date of maturity on 5th July 1972; in April 1972, the Eric Soutou company looked to discount Martinet's bill but, being aware of its former employee Martinet's financial difficulties, first asked its bank, *Crédit Lyonnais*, to contact the drawee's bank, *Banques Vernes*, to investigate the drawee's creditworthiness; that in the presence of Soutou's CEO, a *Crédit Lyonnais* representative phoned *Banque Vernes*, which replied that "the instrument would be honoured at its due date without any issue"; that Soutou acquired the bill which was subsequently dishonoured; that the drawee entered into insolvency proceedings on 24th October 1972, ultimately leading to the liquidation of its assets along with that of its CEO, Mr Keats, and a suspension of payments backdated to 24th April 1971; that the company Soutou sought compensation from both *Crédit Lyonnais* and *Banque Vernes* for the losses which it subsequently incurred; whereas the judgment is under appeal for having dismissed the claim against *Crédit Lyonnais*, the appellant contending that the role of a bank as provider of information implies that the bank is liable towards its client even if it does nothing more than pass inaccurate information on from a fellow professional;

Whereas, however, the decision under appeal notes that *Crédit Lyonnais* had only been instructed to obtain information from *Banque Vernes* and had not itself been requested to obtain a credit report, nor conduct a credit check since the company in Cergy was not its client, and that the bank carried out this task correctly; in light of this, the court of appeal correctly concluded that the bank committed no fault; this ground of appeal is thus without merit;

Turning now to the first ground of appeal, which is based on two separate arguments founded upon Art. 1382 [now Art. 1240] of the Civil Code [. . .]: whereas, however, the court of previous instance rejected Soutou's claim against *Banque Vernes* holding that the latter had a duty of confidentiality towards its client and had only agreed to provide the information, in conformity with customary banking practice, in derogation from the principles of professional secrecy; that the court found that the disclosed information was not outdated, nor did the bank have any awareness of the drawee's financial difficulties or unduly extend credit to a company on the brink of bankruptcy for its own benefit; that, finally, Soutou had carried out an insecure high-risk transaction and had no right to hold a third party liable for its losses since it could have found out about the business situation of the drawee itself by simply examining whether any registered protests had been made against the latter; Whereas, arguing in this way despite, first, the fact that any negligent act which Soutou may have committed does not, in and of itself, exonerate *Banque Vernes* of its liability; that, moreover, should a bank take the view that it is bound by the limits imposed by banking secrecy and thereby refuse to disclose information on a client, such duty of confidentiality does not entitle the bank to give inaccurate information; finally, in light of the fact that seven protests had been registered against the drawee and the latter been suspended from payments for a year, the court of appeal could not, without undermining its own reasoning, hold that the bank was correct in suggesting that that the instrument would be recoverable without any issue; that by not determining whether *Banque Vernes* had been negligent or acted in an incorrectly light-handed manner in responding to *Crédit Lyonnais*' request as it did and whether this potentially negligent act had, in whole or in part, caused the loss suffered by the Soutou company, the court of appeal thus gave no legal basis for its decision;

For these reasons: the Court quashes the judgment of the Court of Appeal of Paris of 23rd April 1976, but only in relation to the rejected claim of the Soutou company against *Banques*

Vernes; consequently both parties are to be placed in the position they were in before the judgment was rendered and, to ensure a decision in line with the law, the case is thus referred to the Court of Appeal of Orléans [. . .].

2. FRANCOIS GRUA, Banquier – Responsabilité en matière de service – Services annexes, Fourniture de renseignements (*Banker – Liability in relation to a service – Ancillary services, supply of information*), in: *Juris-Classeur Banque – Crédit – Bourse*, Fascicule 335–340, 29, 07/2011

1 Liability of a banker towards a person who requests information or advice

[. . .] 3. – We cannot usually expect a banker to be perfectly accurate when providing information because the materials at his disposal are not always reliable. What's more, he may have been prevented from revealing everything he knew on the grounds of professional secrecy. This is why it is unanimously acknowledged that a banker only takes on an obligation to exercise reasonable means (*obligation de moyens*)[16] [. . .]. It follows that the act of providing inaccurate information is not necessarily a negligent one. Properly seen, negligence is a result of either a lack of due diligence in verifying the information in question, or causing the recipient of the information to draw incorrect conclusions from such information.

The courts have thus decided that when a banker is asked by his client to provide information on whether a prospective contractual partner is solvable, that banker has an obligation to exercise reasonable means (*obligation de moyens*), but does not automatically assume liability for the client's losses (*obligation de résultat*). If the banker is to be held liable then it cannot be the result of the information's inaccuracy alone. However, should a banker accept such an assignment, he is required to exercise all available means to check that the information is accurate before supplying it [. . .]. [. . .]

10. – Liability exclusion clauses – liability exclusion clauses are an option. Nevertheless, in accordance with the general rules of law, such clauses do not exonerate the banker of liability for gross negligence. [. . .]

X. Principles of European Tort Law

1. PETL

> **Art. 2:102. Protected interests.** (1) The scope of protection of an interest depends on its nature; the higher its value, the precision of its definition and its obviousness, the more extensive is its protection.
> (2) Life, bodily or mental integrity, human dignity and liberty enjoy the most extensive protection.

---

16 As opposed to guaranteeing the correctness of the information (which would correspond to an *obligation de résultat*).

(3) Extensive protection is granted to property rights, including those in intangible property.
(4) Protection of *pure economic interests* or contractual relationships may be more limited in scope. In such cases, due regard must be had especially to the proximity between the actor and the endangered person, or to the fact that the actor is aware of the fact that he will cause damage even though his interests are necessarily valued lower than those of the victim.[17][. . .]

Art. 4:102. Required standard of conduct. (1) The required standard of conduct is that of the reasonable person in the circumstances, and depends, in particular, on the nature and value of the protected interest involved, the dangerousness of the activity, the expertise to be expected of a person carrying it on, the foreseeability of the damage, the relationship of proximity or special reliance between those involved, as well as the availability and the costs of precautionary or alternative methods. [. . .]

2. Bénédict Winiger/Ernst Karner/Ken Oliphant (eds.), *Digest of European Tort Law, Vol. III: Misconduct*, 2018, nos. 3e/30/1 ff. (by THOMAS KADNER GRAZIANO)

3e. A relationship of proximity or special reliance between those involved

1   *Facts* [the facts are similar to those of the present chapter.]

Solution

3   **a) Solution According to the PETL.** This scenario raises the question of the extent to which a party (in the above scenario: bank A which is providing information about a client) is required not to cause 'pure economic loss' to the persons ultimately relying on their information (in the scenario: V, which was considering whether to give credit to a client). The case fits into what can be called "liability for false information or [negligent] misrepresentation",[18] which is itself a particularly prominent example of "special reliance" cases.

4   In order to determine the required standard of conduct in cases of "liability for false information or negligent misrepresentation", several provisions of the PETL need to be considered.

5   The first of such provisions is Art. 2:102, which determines the *interests protected* under the PETL. [. . .]

6   Secondly, Art. 4:102(1) PETL, which lists the factors relevant in determining the *required standard of conduct* [. . .].

---

17   Emphasis added.
18   EUROPEAN GROUP ON TORT LAW (fn. 1), at Art. 4:102, n. 29 (P. WIDMER).

7   Last but not least, Art. 4:103 on the *"[d]uty to protect others from damage"*, which provides that "[a] duty to act positively to protect others from damage may exist [. . .] when there is a special relationship between parties or when the seriousness of the harm on the one side and the ease of avoiding the damage on the other side point towards such a duty".

8   In the above scenario, the negligent statement caused V to suffer pure economic loss. On the one hand, "[p]rotection of 'pure economic interests' [. . .] may be more limited in scope" under Art. 2:101 PETL. Moreover, the party issuing the statement and the one relying on it were not in direct contact, and in no particular proximity, with each other. On the contrary, bank A did not even know the identity of the firm for which the statement was issued.

9   On the other hand, there is no interest worth protecting in negligently issuing wrongful statements. When issuing a statement about the financial situation and the creditworthiness of a client, a bank must be aware that a false statement is likely to be relied upon and to cause damage to third parties. It was obvious that the very purpose for requesting the statement was to use it as a basis for an investment decision. If it proved to be wrong, the statement was very likely therefore to cause considerable damage to the person relying upon it. The damage was thus easily foreseeable. A bank is expected to have the required expertise to issue reliable statements about the financial situation of its client. Last but not least, there is a situation of special reliance between a bank issuing a credit statement and a person receiving and relying on it. A reasonable person in the circumstances would either have issued a correct and reliable statement or refrained from issuing a statement at all. Given that banks control the number of statements they issue, there is no danger of an uncontrollable, limitless liability.

10 The commentary to the PETL provides the example of an employer D who issues a favourable letter of reference for an employee who has defrauded a considerable sum of money and was consequently dismissed. In the letter of reference, the employer praises the employee's skills in financial management. Another company P employs him, relying on the letter of reference, and suffers damage when he fails to redeem himself.[19]

11 In the case of the unreliable letter of reference, according to the commentary to the PETL, "it seems likely that, under the Principles, and more specifically by application of Art. 4:101, 4:102 and perhaps 4:103, the first employer D could [. . .] be held liable for the (purely economic) loss of the second employer P. This would mean to admit a duty of D vis-à-vis P (or any other person who could be induced in error by the letter of reference) to provide correct information. Such a duty [. . .] may also be deduced from the general principle of good faith".[20]

12 The same is true in the above scenario where, just as in the example provided in the commentary, the victim was a third party who relied on a false statement. In both cases, the issuer of the information must have been aware that the statement may be relied upon and may cause considerable financial damage if wrong. In both cases, the issuer of the statement was expected to have the required expertise to issue a

---

19 *Ibid.*
20 *Ibid.*

reliable statement. In the above scenario, just as in the example provided in the commentary, a reasonable person in the circumstances would either have issued a correct and reliable statement or refrained from issuing one at all. The person providing the false statement could easily have avoided the (considerable) damage, therefore, by simply refraining from issuing the statement (compare also Art. 4:103 4th hypothesis PETL).

13 The official commentary to the PETL mentions, however, that this position is not unanimous and that some authors deny that there is liability *per se* and that the same authors require instead a "(pre-existing) 'special relationship' between the parties" for there to be liability for false statements.[21]

XI. Draft Common Frame of Reference

1. DCFR

> **VI. – 2:207: Loss upon reliance on incorrect advice or information.** Loss caused to a person as a result of making a decision in reasonable reliance on incorrect advice or information is legally relevant damage if:
> (a) the advice or information is provided by a person in pursuit of a profession or in the course of trade; and
> (b) the provider knew or could reasonably be expected to have known that the recipient would rely on the advice or information in making a decision of the kind made.

2. CHRISTIAN VON BAR/ERIC CLIVE (eds.), *Principles, Definitions and Model Rules of European Private Law – Draft Common Frame of Reference (DCFR), Full Edition*, Vol. 4, 2009, Comment A., pp. 3345–3347

A. General. Policy considerations. As a general principle, there is no liability for advice, recommendation and information. [. . .] The case is otherwise only when the recipient of the information has special cause to rely on the correctness of the information and the provider of the information knows or should know about this special situation in which the recipient of the information is placed. Typical cases concern information about credit-worthiness provided by banks and faulty valuations or certifications. [. . .]

B. The circle of protected recipients of the information. Professional advice or information. Not every provision of information and advice which is defective and relied on by the recipient to the recipient's detriment can lead to liability under this Article. The damage must be caused by provision of information "in pursuit of a profession or in the course of trade". 'Kerbstone' advice falls outside those terms because provision by a professional is not enough; what is required is provision of the defective information or advice in the course of carrying out the profession. In the usual case this will mean in the context of a business activity, albeit irrespective of whether that is remunerated and whether there is a pre-existing contractual relationship with the recipient. [. . .]

---

21 *Ibid.*

[. . .] The person who gives the information or advice certainly does not need to know the actual recipient. [. . .] Nor is it necessary that the recipient received the defective information or advice from the provider directly. [. . .]

C. Reliance. Reasonable reliance. The existence of relevant damage for the purposes of the law on non-contractual liability arises crucially out of the disappointment of a legitimate reliance. It does not suffice that the recipient of the information actually relied on its correctness. This must be accompanied by the element that in the circumstances and in relation to the decision to be made, the recipient might reasonably rely on the information. A reasonable reliance on the accuracy of the information or advice is missing if one has trusted the utterances of a fortune teller, astrologist or similar charlatan. The recipient of information may also not rely on it if the recipient knows or should know that the provider of the information does not wish to vouch for the correctness of the communication. [. . .]

XII. People's Republic of China[22]

MIN'AN ZHANG/SAINA GONG, 专业人士所承担的过错侵权责任 (*On Professional Liability in Tort*), *Chinese Legal Review* 2002, 145 at 146

Chapter 3. The nature of professional liability

[. . .] 2. **Liability of professionals vis-à-vis third parties:** If a professional is negligent and provides false information during his or her service, it may not only be the professional's client who may suffer a loss, but also a third party who has no contractual relationship with the professional. In this respect, does this victim, if it does not have a contractual relationship with the professional, have the right in tort to claim damages for his or her loss? [Chinese] law does not provide a clear answer, but current case-law appears to answer in the negative. Nevertheless, in response to the numerous cases in which third parties suffer loss as a result of professional negligence, some courts have changed their position and ruled that professionals could indeed be held liable in tort vis-à-vis third parties. For example, professionals have been held liable in tort for providing false information. Liability of professionals in tort vis-à-vis third parties has improved the protection of the rights of third parties and has assured that the scope of the professional's duty of care is extended. Thus, this notion is critical in promoting the accountability of professionals and the development of the market economy.

---

22 For the starting point of the analysis, that is Arts. 1, 2, and 6 of the Tort Law Act of the *People's Republic of China*, see Chapter 5, section X, pp. 99–100.

Bibliography

EFSTATHIOS K. BANAKAS (ed.), *Civil Liability for Pure Economic Loss*, London: Kluwer, 1994; WILLIAM BISHOP, Economic Loss in Tort, *OJLS* 1982, 1; WILLEM H. VAN BOOM/HELMUT KOZIOL/CHRISTIAN A. WITTING (eds.), *Pure Economic Loss*, Wien: Springer, 2004; MAURO BUSSANI/VERNON VALENTINE PALMER (eds.), *Pure Economic Loss in Europe*, Cambridge: CUP, 2011; MAURO BUSSANI/VERNON VALENTINE PALMER (eds.), *Pure Economic Loss: New Horizons in Comparative Law*, London: Routledge-Cavendish, 2009; JOCHEN DIRICHS, Die Haftung für die Erteilung einer falschen Kreditauskunft bei Mitwirkung zweier Banken, *WM* 1976, 1078–1081; WERNER F. EBKE/BENEDIKT FECHTRUP, Zur Haftung des Wirtschaftsprüfers bei unrichtigen Auskünften über einen Kreditnehmer gegenüber einer Bank, *JZ* 1986, 1112–1116; VOLKER EMMERICH, Rechtsprechungsübersicht: Keine Haftung einer Bank aus einer falschen, in mittelbarer Stellvertretung für einen Dritten eingeholten Auskunft, *JuS* 1996, 1129–1130; RICHARD A. EPSTEIN, *Torts*, New York: Aspen Publishers, 1999, Chapter 21; BRUCE FELDTHUSEN, *Economic Negligence: The Recovery of Pure Economic Loss*, 4th ed., Scarborough/Ontario: Carswell, 2000; SABINE FEUERBORN, Zur Haftung für Bankauskunft, *EWiR* 1985, 153–154; ERICH HARTMANN/FRANK HEIMANN, Das Problem der sog. Dritthaftung – Möglichkeiten der Haftungsbeschränkung?!, *Stbg* 2002, 527–531; NILS JANSEN, Principles of European Tort Law? Grundwertungen und Systembildung im europäischen Haftungsrecht, *RabelsZ* 2006, 732; JEAN-PHILIPPE KLEIN, Responsabilité de la banque pour renseignements inexactes au sujets d'un gérant externe, *SZW/RSDA* 2013, 220–231; HELMUT KOZIOL, Recovery for Pure Economic Loss in the European Union, *Ariz. L. Rev.* 2006, 871; HELMUT KOZIOL (ed.), *Unification of Tort Law: Wrongfulness*, The Hague/London/Boston: Kluwer, 1998; SIEGBERT LAMMEL, Zur Auskunftshaftung, *AcP* 1979, 337–366; ANTON LEININGER, Haftung für Auskünfte gegenüber Dritten, *Stbg* 1990, 435; PETER LOSER, Die Vertrauenshaftung in der Praxis, in: Peter Jung (ed.), *Aktuelle Entwicklungen im Haftungsrecht*, Zürich: Schulthess, 2007, pp. 23–44; MARK LUNNEY/KEN OLIPHANT, *Tort Law*, 3rd ed., Oxford: OUP, 2008, Chapter 8; D. MARSHALL, Liability for Pure Economic Loss Negligently Caused: French and English Law Compared, *ICLQ* 1975, 748; HANS-JOACHIM MUSIELAK, Die Haftung der Banken für falsche Kreditauskünfte – Zugleich ein Beitrag zur Lehre von den vertraglichen Schutzwirkungen für Dritte, *VersR* 1977, 973–979; PETER MÜSSIG, Falsche Auskunftserteilung und Haftung, *NJW* 1989, 1697–1704; FILIPPO RANIERI, *Europäisches Obligationenrecht*, 3. Aufl., Wien: Springer, 2009, pp. 1409–1538; CATHERINE M. SHARKEY, Tort Liability for Pure Economic Loss: A Perspective from the United States and Some Comparative European Insights, *JETL* 2016, 237–271; HARALD SCHWARTZ, *Internationales Privatrecht der Haftung für Vermögensschäden infolge fahrlässig falsch erteilter Auskunft*, 2. Aufl., München: Herbert Utz Verlag, 2000, pp. 15–150; JAAP SPIER (ed.), *The Limits of Expanding Liability: Eight Fundamental Cases in a Comparative Perspective*, The Hague/London/Boston: Kluwer Law International, 1998; CLAUS STEINER, Bankauskünfte – Zweierlei Maß?, *ZfgK* 1991, 1029–1030; KNUT SUHR, *Schadensersatzhaftung für Rat und Auskunft – Die privatrechtliche Haftung für Vermögensschäden von Banken, Auskunfteien, Rechtsanwälten und anderen für erteilte falsche Auskünfte und Ratschläge in Deutschland, der Schweiz, Frankreich, den Vereinigten Staaten von Amerika und England; Eine rechtsvergleichende Untersuchung*, Dissertation Universität Hamburg, 1970; THIERRY URWYLER, "Reden ist Silber, Schweigen ist Gold" – eine Abhandlung zur Haftung für Rat und Auskunft, in: *Ohne jegliche Haftung – Festschrift für Willi Fischer zum 65. Geburtstag*, Zürich: Schulthess, 2016, pp. 529–540; CEES VAN DAM, *European Tort Law*, 2nd ed., Oxford: OUP, 2013; JAN VAN DUNNÉ, Liability for Pure Economic Loss: Rule or Exception? A Comparatist's View of the Civil Law – Common Law Split on Compensation of Non-Physical Damage in Tort Law, *ERPL* 1999, 397; JÜRGEN VORTMANN, Bankauskunft "im Kundeninteresse" und zugleich "im Eigeninteresse" der anfragenden Bank – zur Haftung bei unrichtiger Auskunftserteilung, *EWiR* 1991, 971–972; HANS P. WALTER, Responsabilité fondée sur la confiance et devoir d'information: 10 ans après, in: Christine Chappuis/Bénédict Winiger (éds.), *La responsabilité pour l'information fournie à titre professionnel*, Zurich: Schulthess, 2009, pp. 153–173; RUDOLF WELSER, *Die Haftung für Rat, Auskunft und Gutachten: zugleich ein Beitrag zur Bankauskunft*, Wien: Manz, 1983.

Chapter 15

Protection of privacy and the purposes of tort law

"*It is well-known that in English law there is no right to privacy.*"[1]

"*[L]a question se pose régulièrement de savoir quelle peut être la sanction la plus dissuasive des atteintes à la vie privée réalisées par une presse dont la vocation est l'indiscrétion.*"[2]

"*Haben die Betroffenen nur Anspruch auf Schmerzensgeld, so hat die Presse keinen Anreiz, von einer Gewinnerzielung durch Persönlichkeitsrechtsverletzung abzusehen. Der Anspruch auf Abschöpfung des Verletzervorteils – [. . .] im Verband mit dem Schmerzensgeldanspruch – verschafft [. . .] den Betroffenen die [. . .] Freiheit, sich selbst entscheiden zu können, ob sie ihre Persönlichkeit einer Vermarktung öffnen wollen.*"[3]

Scenario[4]

A widely distributed magazine publishes an article entitled "Naomi: I am a drug addict." The article recounts that a world-famous model is attending anonymous meetings at a group for drug addicts in order to fight her addiction to alcohol and drugs. Details of the treatment are revealed and photos of her, taken without her consent during the group's sessions by a photographer employed by the newspaper, are published. In the past, she has always claimed that, unlike many others in her profession, she had not taken any drugs and was "clean".

---

1 Lord Justice GLIDEWELL, in: Court of Appeal, *Kaye* v. *Robertson*, 16.03.1990, [1991] F.S.R. 62. The quote continues: "and accordingly there is no right of action for breach of a person's privacy. The facts of the present case are a graphic illustration of the desirability of Parliament considering whether and in what circumstances statutory provision can be made to protect the privacy of individuals." See also P. GILIKER/S. BECKWITH, *Tort*, 6th ed., London: Sweet & Maxwell, Thomson Reuters, 2017, n° 15–002: "Prior to the Human Right Act 1998, it seemed clear that there was no right to privacy in English law".
2 AGATHE LEPAGE, Réparation du préjudice résultant d'une atteinte à la vie privée: refus de prendre en compte les profits réalisés par le journal, D. 2000, 269. Translation: "The question regularly arises as to what may be the most dissuasive sanction for the violation of privacy by a press whose vocation is indiscretion".
3 TILMAN HOPPE, *Persönlichkeitsschutz durch Haftungsrecht*, Berlin: Duncker Humblot, 2001, p. 206. Translation: "If the victim were only entitled to claim damages for non-pecuniary harm, then the press would have no incentive to refrain from making a profit by violating the personality rights of others. Shifting illegally-obtained benefits – in conjunction with compensation for non-pecuniary harm – provides the individual with the freedom to decide by him- or herself whether he or she should commercialise his or her personality rights".
4 Inspired by the English case: House of Lords, *Campbell* v. *MGN Ltd*, 06.05.2004, [2004] UKHL 22, [2004] 2 AC 457, [2004] 2 All ER 995 (extracts below, pp. 457 ff.).

The young woman was unaware of the article prior to its publication and had not consented to the taking of the photos and the publication of the article. The article helped the magazine to increase its sales figures for this issue by an estimated 30%.

She claims damages for infringement of her rights resulting from the publication of the article and photos.

Questions

A. Protection of privacy v. freedom of expression, of information, and of the press – the influence of the European Convention on Human Rights

1) In 1990, in the case *Kaye* v. *Robertson*, the *English* Court of Appeal held that "in English law there is no right to privacy".[5] This finding was subsequently confirmed by the House of Lords in the 2003 decision *Wainwright* v. *Home Office*.[6]

    Article 8 of the European Convention on Human Rights (ECHR) guarantees a "right to respect for private and family life". Human rights are primarily a legal guarantee which protects individuals against the illegal interference of the state. However, the ECHR imposes a positive obligation on all State authorities, including the courts, to act in a way which is compatible with the Convention and to see that the Convention rights are respected. It is thus by way of the courts applying private law remedies that Convention rights may extend to the relationships between private parties (the so-called indirect horizontal effect of Convention rights on third parties).[7]

    In the UK, a Contracting State to the ECHR, the Convention was given effect by the Human Rights Act 1998. How was the case in the scenario resolved in *Campbell* v. *MGN Ltd*, and how is privacy protected in English private law today? Does English law now recognise a "protection of privacy" tort? Describe the impact of the ECHR on English law.

2) Article 9 of the *French* Civil Code explicitly provides for the protection of privacy in private law. How are the freedom of the press and the protection of privacy balanced in French law? What effect might the ECHR, as interpreted by the European Court of Human Rights, have on French law?

3) The *German* BGB does not explicitly refer to personality rights and privacy among the rights and interests which are protected under its tort law provisions. How did the courts in Germany allow such rights to be protected under the law of torts? Which difficulties did they have to overcome?

---

5 See above, fn. 1.
6 See Lord HOFFMANN, in: House of Lords, *Wainwright* v. *Home Office*, 16.10.2003, [2004] 2 AC 406 at para. 33; [2003] 4 All ER 969; [2003] UKHL 53 (strip-search of a mother and son who went to visit another son in a prison, in violation of the prison rules).
7 See e.g. M. HUNT, The "Horizontal Effect" of the Human Rights Act, *P.L.* 1998, 423; R. BUXTON, The Human Rights Act and Private Law, *L.Q.R.* 2000, 1116 at para. 48; H.W.R. WADE, Horizons of Horizontality, *L.Q.R.* 2000, 217; N. BAMFORTH, The True "Horizontal Effect" of the Human Rights Act 1998, *L.Q.R.* 2001, 34; G. PHILLIPSON, The Human Rights Act, "Horizontal Effect" and the Common Law: A Bang or a Whimper?, *MLR* 1999, 824; P. VAN DIJK/F. VAN HOOF/A. VAN RIJN/L. ZWAAK (eds.), *Theory and Practice of the European Convention on Human Rights*, 4th ed., Oxford: Intersentia, 2006, pp. 28 ff.; R. ST. J. MACDONALD/F. MATSCHER/H. PETZOLD (eds.), *The European System for the Protection of Human Rights*, Dodrecht/Boston/London: Martinus Nijhof, 1993, Chap. 9 (by A. CLAPHAM); A. L. YOUNG, Mapping Horizontal Effect, in: D. Hoffman (ed.), *The Impact of the UK Human Rights Act on Private Law*, Cambridge: CUP, 2011, p. 18. See also the English Human Rights Act 1998, Sect. 6 (Acts of public authorities): "(1) It is unlawful for a public authority to act in a way which is incompatible with a Convention right. [. . .] (3) In this section 'public authority' includes (a) a court or tribunal [. . .]".

4) The *Estonian* legislator, when drafting the Code of Obligations of 2002, took inspiration from German law but took care to fill the gaps left by the BGB. Compare the Estonian provisions with those of the BGB.

5) In a case that was eventually brought before the *European Court of Human Rights*, Princess Caroline of Hannover (previously *of Monaco*) brought a petition against the publication of photos in the German tabloid press. The German courts had considered her to be a so-called *absolute Person der Zeitgeschichte* (figure of contemporary society *par excellence*) who enjoyed only limited protection of her privacy (notably when she is at home or in a secluded place away from the public eye) and had rejected most of her claims. How did the European Court of Human Rights (ECtHR) decide the case? Which changes did the decision bring to German law?

6) When balanced against the freedom of the press, the protection of privacy and of personality rights differs considerably from one country to the next. Would you expect the ECHR to lead to a gradual harmonisation of this field among the jurisdictions in Europe? Explain.

B. Fixing the amount of damages and setting the right incentives in tort law

7) How do the German *Bundesgerichtshof* and *Bundesverfassungsgericht* argue with respect to fixing the amounts of damages for violation of privacy and personality rights through the press? In particular, why are the damages awarded by German courts so much higher when compared to those awarded in other countries in similar cases, for example in the UK, France, or Switzerland?

8) The profit made by tortfeasors through the violation of privacy rights may by far exceed the damages that have to be paid out to the victims of such violations. For example, in the English case *Douglas* v. *Hello! Ltd*, at the wedding of two celebrities, a paparazzo illegally took photos and sold six of them for £ 125,000 to *Hello!* magazine which then published the photos, making a benefit that considerably exceeded the amount paid to the pararazzo.[8] The English courts held the defendant publisher liable and awarded compensation to the claimants in the amount of £ 3,750 each as general damages for mental distress.[9] When determining the damage award, the court explicitly rejected claims to take into account either the profit made by the magazine or an amount corresponding to a notional licence fee.[10] In

---

8 The two celebrities had previously sold the exclusive rights to publish photos of their marriage to *OK!* magazine for £ 500,000.
9 High Court (Chancery division), *Douglas* v. *Hello! (No. 3)*, 27.01.2003, [2003] 3 All ER 996; Court of Appeal, 18.05.2005, [2005] 4 All ER 128, [2005] EWCA Civ 595. See also the further case: Court of Appeal, *McKennitt* v. *Ash*, 14.12.2006, [2007] 2 WLR 194, [2006] EWCA civ 1714 (a Canadian folk singer complained of a book, written by a former friend and revealing details about e.g. her personal and sexual relationships, personal feelings, health and diet, vulnerability, and property disputes between the two; damages of £ 5,000 awarded).
10 See Lord PHILLIPS M.R., in: *Douglas* v. *Hello! (No. 3)* (above, fn. 9), at 243–250, e.g. at 244: "It is well established that damages in a case involving unauthorised use of, or unauthorised benefiting from, intellectual property and similar rights can be assessed in a number of different ways. In *General Tire & Rubber Co v Firestone Tyre and Rubber Co Ltd* [. . .], Lord Wilberforce identified the normal categories at least in patent cases. They are the profit, or the royalty, which was or would have been achieved [. . .], and the licence fee which would reasonably have been charged (e.g. where it is not possible to assess the level of profit). [In t]he present case [. . .] in our view none of these normal methods of assessment would be appropriate. [. . .]".

Campbell v. *MGN*, with facts similar to those of the above scenario, the claimant was awarded £ 3,500 for "breach of confidence". The profit made by the defendant largely exceeded this amount. For potential tortfeasors, there might therefore be a lack of incentive to respect the law and it may even be cost-effective from their point of view to continue infringing the privacy rights of others.

In view of this problem, German courts have raised the maximum amount which can be awarded for violation of privacy up to € 400,000.[11] The German approach hereby addresses the problem of setting adequate incentives for tortfeasors (and in particular mass media) to respect the privacy of others. On the other hand, it risks undermining the consistency of damage awards for immaterial harm in general: before this, compensation of this magnitude had usually been reserved for immaterial harm relating to extremely severe injuries to body and health, such as causing the victim to become tetraplegic.[12] Amounts for pain and suffering for victims of severe sexual abuse, for example, range between € 20,000 and € 50,000.[13] Awarding six-figure amounts for immaterial harm to celebrities injured in their privacy rights may thus be perceived as unsuitable and unfair by victims of severe bodily injury who usually receive considerably lower amounts for immaterial harm they suffered (see the arguments made by the Millers before the German Constitutional Court[14]).

This raises the question of the objectives pursued by tort law. What are, or ought to be, the goals and purposes of the law of tort? Think also about the cases, statutory provisions, and court decisions covered in the previous chapters. Is *prevention* a goal of tort law? What are the purposes of tort law according to HANS-LEO WEYERS and KENNETH S. ABRAHAM, respectively? Would you agree with either of these interpretations?

9) How is the problem of illicit gain by tortfeasors addressed, and solved, in *Swiss* law?

To apply the Swiss approach effectively, it is important to possess figures relating to the illegal profit obtained. How does the Swiss Federal Supreme Court solve the plaintiff's issue of providing evidence of the profit obtained by the defendant?

---

11 So far, € 400,000 is the highest amount of damages that has been awarded in Germany following the infringement of privacy rights. A magazine had published 86 fictitious stories about Princess Madeleine of Sweden, see OLG Hamburg, 30.07.2009, Az. 7 U 4/08. In other cases, up to e.g. € 395,000 were awarded, see OLG Köln, 12.07.2016, Az. 15 U 175/15 and 15 U 176/15: stigmatisation of TV host Jörg Kachelmann as "violent serial offender who despises women"; € 200,000, OLG Hamburg, 3 U 60/93: publishing of photos of Caroline of Hannover without authorisation; € 90,000, LG München, 14.11.2001, 9 O 11617/01: computer game violating privacy rights.
12 See e.g. the cases (all accidents resulting in tetraplegia) LG Aachen, 13.06.2000, Az. 9 O 40/00 (€ 409,000); OLG Schleswig, 17.02.2005, Az. 7 U 168/03 (€ 332,340); LG Oldenburg, 11.10.1989, Az. 4 O 1431/89, MDR 1990, 630 = VersR 1990, 1019 (€ 255,000). The arguably highest award amounted to € 614,000 (awarded to a three-year-old child that became tetraplegic after a car accident), see LG Kiel, 11.07.2003, Az. 6 O 13/03, VersR 2006, 279.
13 OLG Hamm, 03.02.1992, Az. 6 U 9/91; LG Hannover, 14.09.2005, Az 8 O 310/05; LG Stuttgart, 16.04.2003, Az. 27 O 113/03; LG Frankfurt, NJW 1998, 2294 (all cases of rape). In a particularly severe case, € 100,000 were awarded, see LG Wuppertal, VersR 2013, 591 (a 16-year-old pregnant girl was kidnapped for 72 hours, repeatedly raped, and threatened with her life).
14 Below, p. 473.

C. Using exemplary or punitive damages as an alternative device to set the right incentives?

10) Awarding "exemplary" or "punitive" damages, in addition to compensatory damages, could be another option to dissuade potential tortfeasors from breaching the law and make sure that tort does not pay.

   Some states in the *USA* allow punitive damages (although they are hardly, if ever, awarded against the press), others prohibit them or allow them only when explicitly authorised by statute, whereas a third group of states allows punitive damage awards but uses a variety of control devices to curtail them.[15]

   > Among these control measures are: (1) maximum caps on awards ranging, according to the state, from $ 50,000 to $ 350,000 or, in some states, $ 5 million; (2) a fixed maximum ratio between punitive and compensatory damage (ranging from 1:1 to 5:1); (3) payment of sums to State agencies, charities etc.[16] rather than to plaintiffs, totally or in part; or (4) mandatory bifurcated trials with separate proceedings for punitive damages determinations.

   What are the purposes and strengths of "punitive damages" as set out by the Court of Appeals of California in the case *Grimshaw* v. *Ford Motor Co.*?

11) A large majority of European jurisdictions refuse to apply punitive damages. Many also refuse to recognise foreign judgments awarding punitive damages insofar as they serve the purpose of punishing the tortfeasor. In cross-border cases, the Private International Law of the EU, namely the Rome II Regulation "on the law applicable to non-contractual obligations", allows a law that is otherwise applicable under the Regulation to be disregarded, insofar as the application of this law would lead to an award of non-compensatory exemplary or punitive damages.[17] Why is this so? What could be gained and what would be at risk if punitive damages were adopted in Europe?

---

15 See below and the appendix to the opinion of Justice RUTH BADER GINSBURG, in: US Supreme Court, *BMW of North America, Inc.* v. *Gore*, 517 U.S. 559 (1996).
16 For example a victims' assistance fund, medical assistance or health care funds, the State university system, a school for the deaf and blind, etc.
17 For the application of the Rome II Regulation in cross-border scenarios in Europe, see below, Chapter 18.

Table of contents

I. Council of Europe: European Convention on Human Rights
European Convention on Human Rights, Arts. 8 (Right to respect for private and family life) and Art. 10 (Freedom of expression) ....p. 457

II. England and Wales
1. House of Lords, *Campbell* v. *MGN Ltd*, 06.05.2004, [2004] UKHL 22, [2004] 2 AC 457, [2004] 2 All ER 995..p. 457
2. PAULA GILLIKER/SILAS BECKWITH, *Tort*, 6th ed., London: Sweet & Maxwell, Thomson Reuters, 2017, nos. 15–002 ff......................................p. 461

III. France
1. Code civil (*Civil Code*), Art. 9 (1) ....p. 462
2. Déclaration des droits de l'homme et du citoyen de 1789 (*Declaration of the Human Rights and the Rights of the Citizen of 1789*), Art. 11........p. 463
3. Cour d'appel de Paris (*Appellate Court of Paris*), 25.01.2006, D. 2006, 2706 ....p. 463
4. Cour de cassation, 1ère civ. (*Court of Cassation, 1st civil chamber*), 27.02.2007, n° 06–10.393, Bull. 2007 I, n° 85, and European Court of Human Rights, 12.06.2014 (*Couderc et Hachette Filipacchi Associés* v. *France*), n° 40454/07 ....p. 464
5. Cour d'appel de Toulouse (*Appellate Court of Toulouse*), 25.05.2004, CCE n° 1/2005, comm. 17..p. 465

IV. Germany
1. Grundgesetz (*Basic Law*), Arts. 1 (1), 2 (1), 5 ....p. 466
2. Bürgerliches Gesetzbuch, BGB (*Civil Code*), §§ 253, 823 (1).....................p. 467
3. Gesetz betreffend das Urheberrecht an Werken der bildenden Künste und der Photographie, Kunsturhebergesetz (*Act Concerning the Copyright of Works of Visual Art and Photography, Art Copyright Act*), §§ 22, 23 (1) ....p. 467
4. Bundesgerichtshof, BGH (*Federal Supreme Court of Justice*), 05.03.1963, NJW 1963, 902 ....p. 468
5. DIRK LOOSCHELDERS, *Schuldrecht, Besonderer Teil (Law of Obligations, Special part)*, 12th ed., Köln: Carl Heymanns Verlag, 2017, nos. 1234 ff..........p. 469
6. Bundesgerichtshof, BGH (*Federal Supreme Court of Justice*), 15.11.1994, BGHZ 128, 1 (Caroline of Monaco I, Fictitious exclusive interview)...p. 471
7. Bundesgerichtshof, BGH (*Federal Supreme Court of Justice*), 05.10.2004, NJW 2005, 215 ....p. 472
8. Bundesverfassungsgericht, BVerfG (*Constitutional Court*), 08.03.2000, Az. 1 BVR 1127/96, NJW 2000, 2187 ....p. 473

V. Estonia
Võlaõigusseadus (*Code of Obligations*), §§ 134 (2), 1043, 1045, 1046............p. 474

VI. European Court of Human Rights

European Court of Human Rights, *Caroline von Hannover* v. *Germany*, 24.06.2004, Nr. 59320/00, [2005] 40 ECHR 1..................p. 475

VII. Goals and purposes of the law of torts

1. Josef Esser/Hans-Leo Weyers, *Schuldrecht, Band II, Besonderer Teil, Teilband 2: Gesetzliche Schuldverhältnisse* (*Law of Obligations, Vol. II, Special Part, 2. Legal Obligations*), 8th ed., Heidelberg: C.F. Müller, 2000, § 53 ....p. 478
2. Kenneth S. Abraham, *The Forms and Functions of Tort Law*, 4th ed., New York: Thomson Reuters, Foundation Press, 2012, pp. 16 ff..........p. 480
3. People's Republic of China, 中华人民共和国侵权责任法 (*Tort Law Act*), Art. 1..................p. 482
4. Principles of European Tort Law, Art. 10:101..................p. 483

VIII. Switzerland

1. Zivilgesetzbuch/Code civil (*Civil Code*), Arts. 28, 28a..................p. 483
2. Obligationenrecht/Code des obligations (*Code of Obligations*), Arts. 49, 419, 423 (1)..................p. 484
3. Bundesgericht/Tribunal fédéral (*Federal Supreme Court of Justice*), 07.12.2006 (*Schnyder* g *Ringier AG and Kraushaar*), BGE 133 III 153..................p. 485

IX. The Netherlands

Burgerlijk Wetboek (*Civil Code*), Art. 6:104..................p. 488

X. Punitive or exemplary damages – alternative devices to set the right incentives?

1. Kenneth S. Abraham, *The Forms and Functions of Tort Law*, 4th ed., New York: Thomson Reuters, Foundation Press, 2012, pp. 258–259..........p. 489
2. Court of Appeals of California, Fourth District, *Grimshaw* v. *Ford Motor Co.*, 29.05.1981, 119 Cal. App.3d 757, 174 Cal. Rptr. 348..................p. 490
3. US Supreme Court, *Exxon Shipping Co.* v. *Baker*, 25.06.2008, 554 U.S. 471 ....p. 492
4. Bundesgerichtshof, BGH (*Federal Supreme Court of Justice*), 04.06.1992, BGHZ 118, 312..................p. 493
5. Regulation (EC) No 864/2007 of the European Parliament and of the Council of 11 July 2007 on the law applicable to non-contractual obligations, [2007] OJ, L 119/40 (Rome II Regulation), Recital 32..........p. 495

Materials[18]

I. Council of Europe: European Convention on Human Rights

Art. 8. Right to respect for private and family life. (1) Everyone has the right to respect for his private and family life, his home and his correspondence.
(2) There shall be no interference by a public authority with the exercise of this right except such as is in accordance with the law and is necessary in a democratic society in the interests of national security, public safety or the economic well-being of the country, for the prevention of disorder or crime, for the protection of health or morals, or for the protection of the rights and freedoms of others.

Art. 10. Freedom of expression. (1) Everyone has the right to freedom of expression. This right shall include freedom to hold opinions and to receive and impart information and ideas without interference by public authority and regardless of frontiers. [. . .]
(2) The exercise of these freedoms, since it carries with it duties and responsibilities, may be subject to such formalities, conditions, restrictions or penalties as are prescribed by law and are necessary in a democratic society, [. . .] for preventing the disclosure of information received in confidence [. . .].

II. England and Wales

1. House of Lords, *Campbell v. MGN Ltd*, 06.05.2004, [2004] UKHL 22, [2004] 2 AC 457, [2004] 2 All ER 995

Campbell v MGN Ltd

HOUSE OF LORDS

[2004] UKHL 22, [2004] 2 AC 457, [2004] 2 All ER 995

HEARING-DATES: 18, 19 February, 6 May 2004

6 May 2004

LORD NICHOLLS OF BIRKENHEAD: [1] My Lords, Naomi Campbell is a celebrated fashion model. Hers is a household name, nationally and internationally. Her face is instantly recognisable. Whatever she does and wherever she goes is news.

[2] On 1 February 2001 the Daily Mirror (the Mirror) newspaper carried as its first story on its front page a prominent article headed: 'Naomi: I am a drug addict.' The article was supported on one side by a picture of Miss Campbell as a glamorous model, on the other side by a slightly indistinct picture of a smiling, relaxed Miss Campbell, dressed in baseball cap and jeans, over the caption: 'THERAPY: Naomi outside meeting.' The article read: SUPERMODEL Naomi Campbell is attending Narcotics Anonymous meetings in a

---

18 For the original language versions of the materials reproduced in this chapter, see the companion website at www.routledge.com/9781138567733.

courageous bid to beat her addiction to drink and drugs. The 30-year-old has been a regular at counselling sessions for three months, often attending twice a day. Dressed in jeans and baseball cap, she arrived at one of NA's lunchtime meetings this week. Hours later at a different venue she made a low-key entrance to a women-only gathering of recovered addicts. Despite her £14 million fortune Naomi is treated as just another addict trying to put her life back together. [. . .]

[3] The story continued inside, with a longer article spread across two pages. [. . .]

[6] The general tone of the articles was sympathetic and supportive with, perhaps, the barest undertone of smugness that Miss Campbell had been caught out by the Mirror. The source of the newspaper's information was either an associate of Miss Campbell or a fellow addict attending meetings of NA. The photographs of her attending a meeting were taken by a freelance photographer specifically employed by the newspaper to do the job. He took the photographs covertly, while concealed some distance away inside a parked car. [. . .]

THE PROCEEDINGS AND THE FURTHER ARTICLES

[8] On the same day as the articles were published Miss Campbell commenced proceedings against MGN Ltd, the publisher of the Mirror. The newspaper's response was to publish further articles, this time highly critical of Miss Campbell. [. . .]

[10] In the proceedings Miss Campbell claimed damages for breach of confidence [. . .].

BREACH OF CONFIDENCE: MISUSE OF PRIVATE INFORMATION

[11] In this country, unlike the United States of America, there is no overarching, all-embracing cause of action for 'invasion of privacy'[19] [. . .] But protection of various aspects of privacy is a fast developing area of the law, here and in some other common law jurisdictions. [. . .] In this country development of the law has been spurred by enactment of the Human Rights Act 1998.

[12] The present case concerns one aspect of invasion of privacy: wrongful disclosure of private information. The case involves the familiar competition between freedom of expression and respect for an individual's privacy. Both are vitally important rights. Neither has precedence over the other. The importance of freedom of expression has been stressed often and eloquently, the importance of privacy less so. But it, too, lies at the heart of liberty in a modern state. A proper degree of privacy is essential for the well-being and development of an individual. And restraints imposed on government to pry into the lives of the citizen go to the essence of a democratic state [. . .].

[13] The common law or, more precisely, courts of equity have long afforded protection to the wrongful use of private information by means of the cause of action which became known as breach of confidence. [. . .] Today this nomenclature is misleading. The breach of confidence label harks back to the time when the cause of action was based on improper use of information disclosed by one person to another in confidence. To attract protection the information had to be of a confidential nature. But the gist of the cause of action was that information of this character had been disclosed by one person to another in circumstances

---

19 *Note by the author*: for the law in the USA, see the groundbreaking article by SAMUEL D. WARREN/LOUIS D. BRANDEIS, The Right to Privacy, *Harv. L. Rev.* 1890, 194.

'importing an obligation of confidence' even though no contract of non-disclosure existed [. . .]. The confidence referred to in the phrase 'breach of confidence' was the confidence arising out of a confidential relationship.

[14] This cause of action has now firmly shaken off the limiting constraint of the need for an initial confidential relationship. In doing so it has changed its nature. [. . .] Now the law imposes a 'duty of confidence' whenever a person receives information he knows or ought to know is fairly and reasonably to be regarded as confidential. Even this formulation is awkward. The continuing use of the phrase 'duty of confidence' and the description of the information as 'confidential' is not altogether comfortable. Information about an individual's private life would not, in ordinary usage, be called 'confidential'. The more natural description today is that such information is private. The essence of the tort is better encapsulated now as misuse of private information.

[15] In the case of individuals this tort, however labelled, affords respect for one aspect of an individual's privacy. That is the value underlying this cause of action. An individual's privacy can be invaded in ways not involving publication of information. Strip searches are an example. The extent to which the common law as developed thus far in this country protects other forms of invasion of privacy is not a matter arising in the present case. It does not arise because, although pleaded more widely, Miss Campbell's common law claim was throughout presented in court exclusively on the basis of breach of confidence, that is, the wrongful publication by the Mirror of private information. [. . .]

[17] The time has come to recognise that the values enshrined in Arts. 8 and 10 are now part of the cause of action for breach of confidence. As Lord Woolf CJ has said, the courts have been able to achieve this result by absorbing the rights protected by Arts. 8 and 10 into this cause of action [. . .] Further, it should now be recognised that for this purpose these values are of general application. The values embodied in Arts. 8 and 10 are as much applicable in disputes between individuals or between an individual and a non-governmental body such as a newspaper as they are in disputes between individuals and a public authority.

[18] In reaching this conclusion it is not necessary to pursue the controversial question whether the convention itself has this wider effect. [. . .] It is sufficient to recognise that the values underlying Arts. 8 and 10 are not confined to disputes between individuals and public authorities.

[19] In applying this approach, and giving effect to the values protected by Art. 8, courts will often be aided by adopting the structure of Art. 8 in the same way as they now habitually apply the Strasbourg court's approach to Art. 10 when resolving questions concerning freedom of expression. [. . .]

THE PRESENT CASE

[23] I turn to the present case and consider first whether the information whose disclosure is in dispute was private. Mr Caldecott QC placed the information published by the newspaper into five categories: (1) the fact of Miss Campbell's drug addiction; (2) the fact that she was receiving treatment; (3) the fact that she was receiving treatment at NA; (4) the details of the treatment – how long she had been attending meetings, how often she went, how she was treated within the sessions themselves, the extent of her commitment, and the nature of her entrance on the specific occasion; and (5) the visual portrayal of her leaving a specific meeting with other addicts.

[24] It was common ground between the parties that in the ordinary course the information in all five categories would attract the protection of Art. 8. But Mr Caldecott recognised that, as he put it, Miss Campbell's 'public lies' precluded her from claiming protection for categories (1) and (2). When talking to the media Miss Campbell went out of her way to say that, unlike many fashion models, she did not take drugs. By repeatedly making these assertions in public Miss Campbell could no longer have a reasonable expectation that this aspect of her life should be private. Public disclosure that, contrary to her assertions, she did in fact take drugs and had a serious drug problem for which she was being treated was not disclosure of private information. As the Court of Appeal noted ([2003] 1 All ER 224 at [43]), where a public figure chooses to present a false image and make untrue pronouncements about his or her life, the press will normally be entitled to put the record straight. [. . .]

LORD HOFFMANN: [. . .] [46] In recent years [. . .] there have been two developments of the law of confidence, typical of the capacity of the common law to adapt itself to the needs of contemporary life. One has been an acknowledgement of the artificiality of distinguishing between confidential information obtained through the violation of a confidential relationship and similar information obtained in some other way. The second has been the acceptance, under the influence of human rights instruments such as Art. 8 of the European Convention for the Protection of Human Rights and Fundamental Freedoms 1950 [. . .], of the privacy of personal information as something worthy of protection in its own right. [. . .]

[50] What human rights law has done is to identify private information as something worth protecting as an aspect of human autonomy and dignity. And this recognition has raised inescapably the question of why it should be worth protecting against the state but not against a private person. There may of course be justifications for the publication of private information by private persons which would not be available to the state – I have particularly in mind the position of the media, to which I shall return in a moment – but I can see no logical ground for saying that a person should have less protection against a private individual than he would have against the state for the publication of personal information for which there is no justification. Nor, it appears, have any of the other judges who have considered the matter.

[51] The result of these developments has been a shift in the centre of gravity of the action for breach of confidence when it is used as a remedy for the unjustified publication of personal information. It recognises that the incremental changes to which I have referred do not merely extend the duties arising traditionally from a relationship of trust and confidence to a wider range of people. [. . .]

[52] These changes have implications for the future development of the law. They must influence the approach of the courts to the kind of information which is regarded as entitled to protection, the extent and form of publication which attracts a remedy and the circumstances in which publication can be justified.

[53] In this case, however, it is unnecessary to consider these implications because the cause of action fits squarely within both the old and the new law. [. . .]

BARONESS HALE: [132] [. . .] The 1998 Act does not create any new cause of action between private persons. But if there is a relevant cause of action applicable, the court as a public authority must act compatibly with both parties' Convention rights. In a case such as this, the relevant vehicle will usually be the action for breach of confidence [. . .].

[133] [. . .] [O]ur law cannot, even if it wanted to, develop a general tort of invasion of privacy. But where existing remedies are available, the court not only can but must balance the competing Convention rights of the parties.

[134] [. . .] How does the scope of the action for breach of confidence accommodate the Article 8 rights of individuals? [. . .] The position we have reached is that the exercise of balancing article 8 and article 10 may begin when the person publishing the information knows or ought to know that there is a reasonable expectation that the information in question will be kept confidential. [. . .]

[137] It should be emphasised that the 'reasonable expectation of privacy' is a threshold test which brings the balancing exercise into play. It is not the end of the story. Once the information is identified as 'private' in this way, the court must balance the claimant's interest in keeping the information private against the countervailing interest of the recipient in publishing it. Very often, it can be expected that the countervailing rights of the recipient will prevail. [. . .]

Note by the author: in Campbell v. MGN it was generally agreed that the fact that the claimant had taken drugs and was in treatment could be published by the newspaper, given that Mrs Campbell had publicly made false statements in this respect. On the other hand, a majority held that publishing the name of the institution where the treatment was delivered, details of the treatment and photos taken without consent violated the claimant in her rights. The claimant was awarded damages in the amount of £ 3,500.[20]

2. PAULA GILLIKER/SILAS BECKWITH, *Tort*, 6th ed., 2017

Chapter 15

PRIVACY (OR MISUSE OF PRIVATE INFORMATION)

15–001 [The tort] defamation protects the reputation of the claimant against untrue statements of facts. The common law has found more difficulty in deciding whether the claimant should be able to obtain a remedy in tort for the publication of *true* facts which the claimant does not wish others to know. [. . .] With the advent of the Human Rights Act 1998, the question has arisen whether English law should now accept a new tort based on invasion of privacy.

Such a tort would be contentious. Whilst it would protect the claimant from invasion of his or her private life, it would be at the expense of the public's right to know and the defendant's freedom of expression, protected by art. 10 of the European Convention on Human Rights (ECHR). At worst, it would give claimants a means of suppressing true, but damaging, information which it is in the public interest to disclose. Yet, it cannot be denied that publication of details of an individual's private life, even when they are accurate, can be distressing. In particular, advances in modern technology have led to an increasing number of intrusions into the private lives of individuals be they public or private figures. Many other countries have accepted the need for laws protecting privacy.

---

20 Following the decision, the claimant's solicitors served bills of costs to the defendants in the amount of £ 1,086,295. Miss Campbell had formed a conditional fee agreement (no win, no fee) with her lawyers in the amount of £ 279,981. For the costs of lawsuits, and the question of who bears them, see below, Chapter 17, pp. 537 ff.

The 1998 Act, which incorporates art. 8, ECHR (right to respect for private and family life), brings to the fore the question of whether, and to what extent, English law should recognise a right to privacy.

Protection of privacy through existing torts

15–002 Prior to the Human Rights Act 1998, it seemed clear that there was no right to privacy in English law. [. . .]

The impact of the Human Rights Act 1998

15–003 In October 2000, the Human Rights Act 1998 came into force in England and Wales. This Act gives domestic legal effect to the vast majority of the rights contained in the European Convention on Human Rights. Under s. 6, the courts (as a public authority) must act in a way which is compatible with the Convention. [. . .]

The question arises whether [Article 8 of the Convention is] sufficient to give claimants a "right" to privacy, or require or empower the courts to develop a tort protecting claimants from invasion of their privacy. The [UK] Government's response was in the negative. [. . .]

This does not prevent, however, the courts choosing to develop the common law in a way which provides greater protection of privacy rights. The subsequent development of the law illustrates two propositions:

- there is still no general tort of invasion of privacy,
- claimants may nevertheless seek a remedy against the publication of private information relating to their personal lives under the action for breach of confidence. [. . .]

(2) The "extended" breach of confidence action

15–006 [. . .] When will information be private? Clearly if a public figure discusses her private life in the press, she will run the risk, as with Ms Campbell, that this will be viewed as a matter of public debate. [A]rt. 8 rights are not [. . .] absolute. The courts will in each case balance the claimant's rights to private and family life against the defendant's freedom of expression. It is clear in *Campbell* that [. . .] neither right has pre-eminence. The test is whether publication pursues a legitimate aim and whether the benefit of publication is proportionate to the harm done by interference with privacy. [. . .]

III. France

I. Code civil (*Civil Code*)

Art. 9. (1) Chacun a droit au respect de sa vie privée [. . .].

Translation

Art. 9. (1) Everyone has the right to respect for his or her private life [. . .].[21]

2. Déclaration des droits de l'homme et du citoyen de 1789 (Declaration of the Human Rights and the Rights of the Citizen of 1789)[22]

Art. 11. La libre communication des pensés et des opinions est un des droits les plus précieux de l'Homme: tout Citoyen peut donc parler, écrire, imprimer librement, sauf à répondre de l'abus de cette liberté dans les cas déterminés par la Loi.

Translation

Art. 11. The free communication of thoughts and opinions is one of the most precious rights of human beings: every citizen can therefore speak, write, and print freely, except to answer for the abuse of this freedom in the cases determined by the Law.

3. Cour d'appel de Paris (Appellate Court of Paris), 25.01.2006, D. 2006, 2706

[*Note by the author*: Regarding the balance between the freedom of the press and the protection of privacy in French law, the French courts have concluded as a general rule:]

[. . .] [W]hen an article which is devoted to a public figure discusses information which is not yet in the public domain, or where its content cannot be deemed entirely trivial, the right

---

21 Note by the author: before Art. 9 was introduced in 1970, the *French* courts had protected privacy under Arts. 1382, 1383 (now Arts. 1240, 1241). In a case decided by the 1st civil chamber of the *Cour de cassation* on 05.11.1996 (Cass., 1st civil chamber., 05.11.1996, n° 94–14.798, D. 1997, jur., p. 403), the Court confirmed that Art. 9 applies independently of Art. 1382 [1240] of the *Code civil*: "[. . .] *according to Article 9 of the Code civil, an invasion of privacy is all that is required to trigger the right to compensation*". A victim whose right to a private life has been violated therefore does not need to prove fault or loss, the mere invasion of privacy is all that is required to trigger the right to compensation; see also Cass., 2nd civil chamber, 05.03.1997, n° 95–14.503.

22 In the decision n° 71–44, handed down on 16 July 1971, the *Conseil constitutionnel français* (*French Constitutional Court*) conferred constitutional status on the preamble to the 1958 Constitution which in turn refers to both the preamble of the 1946 Constitution and the 1789 Declaration of Human Rights and the Rights of the Citizen. The Declaration therefore forms part of the so-called *bloc de constitutionnalité* (constitutional framework), which is recognised as having constitutional status in France, see in particular T. DE BERRANGER/M. DE VILLIERS, *Droit public général*, 7th ed., Paris: LexisNexis/Litec, 2015, p. 387.

to a private life must override the principle of freedom of expression where such article does not contribute to any debate of public interest. [. . .][23]

4. Cour de cassation, 1ère civ. (*Court of Cassation, 1st civil chamber*), 27.02.2007, n° 06–10.393, Bull. 2007 I, n° 85, and European Court of Human Rights, 12.06.2014 (*Couderc et Hachette Filipacchi Associés v. France*), n° 40454/07

[*Note by the author*: For the balance between freedom of the press and protection of privacy in a given case, see the differing approaches taken by the French *Cour de cassation* and the European Court of Human Rights in the case *Couderc et Hachette Filipacchi Associés v. France*:]

Cour de cassation

Whereas, in issue n° 2920 of the weekly magazine *Paris Match*, dated 5th May 2005 [. . .], an interview was published in which Mrs X . . . revealed the birth of a child named Alexandre who was alleged to have been conceived as the result of her relationship with Albert Y . . ., Prince of Monaco; whereas the text was complemented by a number of photographs representing the child and the Prince together; whereas these revelations were declared in large print on the front page of the magazine under the heading "Albert of Monaco: Alexander, the secret child. His mother Nicole tells the whole story"; whereas alleging that his right to a private life and his right to control of his own image had been infringed, Prince Albert brought proceedings against the publishers, the Hachette Filipacchi company ("the company") [. . .]; whereas in the affirmatory ruling under appeal, the Court accepted the claim and ordered the company to pay compensation and publish the decision;

Turning to [. . .] the second ground of appeal, which is based on three separate arguments: Whereas [. . .] the appellants claim that the Court failed to properly apply Art. 9 of the *Code civil* and Art. 10 of the European Convention on Human Rights [. . .]; Whereas, however, every person, whatever his rank, birth, fortune or present or future functions, is entitled to respect for his private life; whereas the judgment notes firstly that, on the date on which the article was published, the child's existence and his descent were unknown to the public, and secondly that the Principality's Constitution rules out the possibility of his accession to the throne, since he was an illegitimate child [. . .] and, lastly, the article contained multiple digressions on the circumstances in which Mrs X . . . and Prince Albert met and about their relationship, the Prince's reaction to the news of the pregnancy and his subsequent attitude towards the child; whereas in the light of these findings and considerations, the Court of Appeal correctly noted the lack of any topical news item or any debate on a matter of public interest which would have justified its being reported at the time of the impugned publication on the grounds of legitimately imparting information to the public; moreover, the publication of photographs of a person to illustrate subsequent content which

---

23 Following the decision by the European Court of Human Rights in the case *Caroline von Hannover v. Germany* (below, pp. 475 ff.), the topic of violation of privacy by mass media seems to have almost disappeared from most leading treatises on the French law of obligations and French tort law, with the notable exception of the treatise of Philippe Le Tourneau, *Droit de la responsabilité et des contrats (Torts and Contract Law)*, 8th ed., Paris: Dalloz, 2010, nos. 1616 ff. Instead, and despite numerous decisions on this topic by the French courts, French legal doctrine now refers almost exclusively to the decisions of the ECHR.

amounts to an invasion of his privacy necessarily infringes his right to control of his own image.

For these reasons: the appeal is rejected; [. . .]

European Court of Human Rights

111. In the present case, the impugned information was not without political import, and could arouse the interest of the public with regard to the rules of succession in force in the Principality (which prevented children born outside marriage from succeeding to the throne). Likewise, the attitude of the Prince, who wished to keep his paternity a secret and refused to acknowledge it publicly [. . .], could, in a hereditary monarchy whose future is intrinsically linked to the existence of descendants, also be of concern to the public. This was equally true with regard to his behaviour in respect of the child's mother [. . .] and the child himself: this information could provide insights into the Prince's personality, particularly with regard to the way in which he approached and assumed his responsibilities.

112. In this context, it is important to reiterate the symbolic role of a hereditary monarchy. In such a monarchy, the Prince embodies the unity of the nation. It follows that certain events affecting the members of the ruling family, while they are part of the latter's private lives, are also part of contemporary history. [. . .]

114. [. . .] [T]he Court considers it useful to emphasise that [. . .] the press is a vector for disseminating debates on matters of public interest, but it also has the role of revealing and bringing to the public's attention information capable of eliciting such interest and of giving rise to such a debate within society. [. . .]

113. Consequently, the Court considers that, although the impugned article admittedly contained numerous details which concerned solely private or even intimate details of the Prince's life, it was also intended to contribute to a debate on a matter of public interest [. . .].

FOR THESE REASONS, THE COURT
1. *Holds*, unanimously, that there has been a violation of Article 10 of the Convention; [. . .]

5. Cour d'appel de Toulouse (*Appellate Court of Toulouse*), 25.05.2004, CCE n° 1/2005, comm. 17

[*Note by the author*: With respect to the elements to be taken into consideration under French law when determining the award in damages, the Toulouse Court of Appeal held that:]

[. . .] [A]ny profits made by the newspaper must be excluded from the assessment of compensation; compensation is not intended to sanction conduct, nor is it to act as a deterrent for press misconduct, but must be assessed in line with the victim's loss in accordance with the general principles of tort law.[24]

---

24 See further on this issue LEPAGE (fn. 2).

Note by the author: the amounts awarded by French courts to celebrities for non-pecuniary harm (*prejudice moral*) resulting from infringement of the right to privacy range between € 3,500 in some cases to as much as € 40,000 in others.[25]

IV. Germany

1. Grundgesetz (*Basic Law*)

Art. 1. (1) Die Würde des Menschen ist unantastbar. Sie zu achten und zu schützen ist Verpflichtung aller staatlichen Gewalt. [. . .]

Art. 2. (1) Jeder hat das Recht auf die freie Entfaltung seiner Persönlichkeit, soweit er nicht die Rechte anderer verletzt und nicht gegen die verfassungsmäßige Ordnung oder das Sittengesetz verstößt. [. . .]

Art. 5. (1) Jeder hat das Recht, seine Meinung in Wort, Schrift und Bild frei zu äußern und zu verbreiten und sich aus allgemein zugänglichen Quellen ungehindert zu unterrichten. Die Pressefreiheit und die Freiheit der Berichterstattung durch Rundfunk und Film werden gewährleistet. Eine Zensur findet nicht statt.
(2) Diese Rechte finden ihre Schranken in den Vorschriften der allgemeinen Gesetze [. . .] und in dem Recht der persönlichen Ehre.

Translation

Art. 1. (1) The dignity of human beings is inviolable. All public authorities have a duty to respect and protect it. [. . .]

Art. 2. (1) Everyone shall have the right to the free development of their personality provided that they do not interfere with the rights of others or violate the constitutional order or moral law. [. . .]

Art. 5. (1) Everyone shall have the right to freely express and disseminate his or her opinions in speech, writing, and pictures and freely to obtain information from generally accessible sources. Freedom of the press and freedom of reporting on the radio and in films shall be guaranteed. There shall be no censorship.
(2) These rights shall be subject to the limitations laid down by the provisions of the general laws and by statutory provisions aimed at [. . .] the obligation to respect personal honour.

---

25 See e.g. Cour d'appel de Toulouse (*Court of Appeal of Toulouse*), 25.05.2004, CCE n° 1/2005, comm. 17 = Juris-Data n° 2004–247730 (High-level sportsman harassed by paparazzi while spending holidays in Saint Tropez with a starlet accustomed to the tabloid press; € 6,000 awarded); Cour d'appel de Versailles (*Court of Appeal of Versailles*), 19.06.2003, Juris-data 2003–250949 (Claudia Schiffer, € 4,000 awarded); Cour d'appel de Versailles (*Court of Appeal of Versailles*), 23.09.1999, CCE n° 2/2000, comm. 25 (French Francs 120,000, corresponding to approximately € 20,000); Tribunal de grande instance de Paris (*High Court of Paris*), 05.05.1999, D. 2000, 269 (€ 20,000 French Francs corresponding to approximately € 3,700 awarded to both a famous singer and his wife); Cour d'appel de Paris (*Court of Appeal of Paris*), 04.01.1988, D.S. 1989, Somm. comm. p. 92 (French Francs 250,000 corresponding to approximately € 40,000 awarded to the French actress Brigitte Bardot).

2. Bürgerliches Gesetzbuch, BGB (*Civil Code*)

§ 253. **Immaterieller Schaden.** (1) Wegen eines Schadens, der nicht Vermögensschaden ist, kann Entschädigung in Geld nur in den durch das Gesetz bestimmten Fällen gefordert werden.
(2) Ist wegen einer Verletzung des Körpers, der Gesundheit, der Freiheit oder der sexuellen Selbstbestimmung Schadensersatz zu leisten, kann auch wegen des Schadens, der nicht Vermögensschaden ist, eine billige Entschädigung in Geld gefordert werden.

§ 823. **Schadensersatzpflicht.** (1) Wer vorsätzlich oder fahrlässig das Leben, den Körper, die Gesundheit, die Freiheit, das Eigentum oder ein sonstiges Recht eines anderen widerrechtlich verletzt, ist dem anderen zum Ersatze des daraus entstehenden Schadens verpflichtet. [...]

Translation

§ 253. Immaterial harm. (1) Monetary compensation for non-pecuniary damage can only be claimed in the cases stipulated by law.
(2) Where compensation is due for injury to body, health, freedom, or sexual self-determination, the injured party may also claim reasonable monetary compensation for non-pecuniary damage.

§ 823. Duty to compensate damage. (1) Whosoever unlawfully injures, intentionally or negligently, the life, body, health, freedom, property, or other right of another person, has an obligation to the other person to compensate the resulting damage. [...]

3. Gesetz betreffend das Urheberrecht an Werken der bildenden Künste und der Photographie, Kunsturhebergesetz (*Act Concerning the Copyright of Works of Visual Art and Photography, Art Copyright Act*)

§ 22. Bildnisse dürfen nur mit Einwilligung des Abgebildeten verbreitet [...] werden. [...]

§ 23. (1) Ohne die nach § 22 erforderliche Einwilligung dürfen verbreitet [...] werden:
1. Bildnisse aus dem Bereiche der Zeitgeschichte; [...]
(2) Die Befugnis erstreckt sich jedoch nicht auf eine Verbreitung [...], durch die ein berechtigtes Interesse des Abgebildeten [...] verletzt wird.

Translation

§ 22. Images shall only be disseminated [...] with the express approval of the person concerned. [...]

> *§ 23. (1) Without the approval of the person concerned, only the following [. . .] can be disseminated: 1. images portraying an aspect of contemporary society; [. . .]*
> *(2) This authorisation does not extend to disseminations [. . .] which would interfere with a legitimate interest of the person [. . .] concerned.*

4. Bundesgerichtshof, BGH (*Federal Supreme Court of Justice*), 05.03.1963, NJW 1963, 902

[*Note by the author*: in a decision handed down in May 1954, the German Federal Supreme Court of Justice recognised for the first time, and with a very short reasoning given the fundamental character of the decision, that every person enjoys a general right of personality not only in constitutional law and against the state, but also in private law, particularly under tort law, and with effect to other private persons.[26] In the following years, in a series of ground-breaking decisions, the BGH awarded monetary compensation for the violation of personality rights – despite the fact that, technically speaking, the wording of § 253 of the BGB limits monetary compensation to the violation of rights that are explicitly enumerated in this provision. In a 1963 decision, the BGH provided their clearest statement regarding this issue:]

[. . .] II. This Court has recognised [. . .] that a claim for [monetary] compensation of immaterial harm can be brought against any person who seriously violates the personality rights of another. [. . .] The Court hereby recognised that the BGB grants a right to monetary compensation for immaterial harm only insofar as the latter is stipulated by law and assumes on this basis that the BGB does not allow monetary compensation of immaterial harm in any other instance. Even in the parliamentary debates that preceded the enactment of the BGB [in 1896], this attitude of the legislator came under steep criticism, as did the inadequate protection afforded to personality and honour under the BGB. [. . .] The [. . .] increase in the protection of the individual's personality rights through court decisions and legal doctrine owes much of its success to the fact that nowadays private law not only focuses on economic damage but increasingly recognises the actionability of infringements of personality rights, and thus, the enjoyment of personality rights has begun to impose more and more limitations on the individual's freedom of action. Aside from this development of legal thinking, this progression in the law has been further emphasised by the fact that we have undergone profound technical and social developments since 1900. Not only have we witnessed entirely new ways of violating personality rights which the legislator could never have predicted, but on top of this we now live in an environment in which the effects of such violations can be long-lasting – not least with the influence and spread of "the mass media". The BGB provision thus no longer appears to be adequate [. . .] to meet the demands for an increase in the [. . .] legal protection of personality rights. With the recognition [by this Court] of a "general personality right" protected by the rules of tort law, the values enshrined in the *Grundgesetz* (Arts. 1 and 2) have finally influenced a fundamental departure from the prevailing view of the legislator in 1900 that monetary compensation should not be granted even in cases of severe violation of personality rights. If the protection of

---

26 Bundesgerichtshof, BGH (*Federal Supreme Court of Justice*), 25.05.1954, BGHZ 13, 334.

human dignity [. . .] is to be taken seriously [. . .], then we can no longer bind judges to the decision which was made by the legislator in 1900 which has the effect of restricting compensation for immaterial harm to such an extent that even serious violations of personality rights are not covered. [. . .] [If we did bind judges to this provision], not only would victims be given the impression that their rights are not protected against unlawful impairments, but also the observance of the limits determined by the law to protect the personality rights of individuals would be seriously jeopardised. In this Court's view, it is for this reason that in almost all jurisdictions in which the dignity of human beings is paramount, monetary compensation is recognised as an adequate private law sanction for the violation of the personality rights of another. Since the freedom of the press is fundamentally important in these jurisdictions, just as in Germany, and is respected despite the existence of a claim for monetary compensation of immaterial harm, the Court rejects the assertion that to admit such compensation for violation of personality rights constitutes an unacceptable interference with the fundamental freedom of the press or an impermissible threat to such freedom. [. . .] [J]ustice [requires] that [the press] pay compensation in satisfaction to any person suffering extensive and irreparable harm through the wrongful impairment of their personality rights in cases where the impairment cannot be remedied otherwise. [. . .]

5. DIRK LOOSCHELDERS, *Schuldrecht, Besonderer Teil (Law of Obligations, Special part)*, 12ᵗʰ ed., 2017, nos. 1234 ff.

§ 59 The general right of personality

1. Historical development

1234   When the **BGB was being drafted**, German legal opinion held a very restrictive notion of the protection of the individual's right to personality. It was for this reason that the legislator deliberately refrained from including a general right of personality or honour among the rights and interests benefitting from protection under § 823 (1) of the BGB. [. . .] The reasoning behind this was: "it would oppose prevailing national opinion . . . to award money for immaterial harm".

1235   After the *Grundgesetz* [i.e. the Constitution] **entered into force**, the courts and academic opinion generally came to the conclusion that the decision of the drafters of the BGB not to protect personality rights was inadequate given that the individual now benefitted from a right to respect for his dignity (Art. 1 (1) of the *Grundgesetz*) and to the free development of his personality (Art. 2 (1) of the *Grundgesetz*). It is for this reason that the *Bundesgerichtshof* recognised the general right of personality as "**other [absolute] right**" under § 823 (1) for the first time in the case *Leserbrief-Entscheidung* dating 25.5.1954. [. . .]

1236   In later decisions, victims were awarded compensation for **immaterial harm** in deliberate breach of § 253 [1]. This claim [. . .] is [. . .] based on a direct application of the Constitution (Arts. 1 (1), 2 (1) of the *Grundgesetz*). [. . .]

1237   Given that this principle emerged out of the Constitution, the legislator, when **reforming the law of damages in 2002** (*Schadensrechtsreform*), abstained from extending damages for immaterial harm to violations of personality rights in § 253 (2). The basis for bringing a claim is therefore § 823 (1) in conjunction with Arts. 1 (1), 2 (1) of the *Grundgesetz*. [. . .]

II. The general right of personality as a framework protection

1238 [. . .] The question of whether an individual's personality right has been infringed must [. . .] be assessed on a case-by-case basis according to a careful **balancing of interests**. Not only can the victim claim protection of his or her fundamental rights, but the tortfeasor may do so too. Alongside the freedom of action (Art. 2 (1) of the *Grundgesetz*), it is particularly important to consider [. . .] the freedom of thought and the freedom of the press (Art. 5 (1) of the *Grundgesetz*). [. . .]

2. The protection of celebrities from the press

1240 The protection of celebrities against infringement of their personality rights by the press is a subject of intense debate. At the centre of this debate is the question: under what conditions is it admissible to publish pictures taken without the knowledge or consent of the subject ("**Paparazzi shots**")?

> **Example** (BGHZ 131, 332; BVerfGE 101, 361; EGMR NJW 2004, 2647): Princess Caroline of Monaco (C) challenges the publication of "paparazzi shots" taken without her knowledge. The photos show C shopping at a market, riding on horseback, and (together with an actor) in a restaurant garden. C argues that the taking of the photos and their dissemination have interfered with her right to respect for her private life.

According to our traditional understanding, those who have a prominent position in public life (e.g. monarchs, politicians, artists, sportspeople), i.e. "figures of contemporary society *par excellence*" (*absolute Personen der Zeitgeschichte*), enjoy only limited protection against images taken without their knowledge or consent. Based on the traditional interpretation of the first sentence of § 23 (1) of the Art Copyright Act (*Kunsturhebergesetz*), these individuals must simply tolerate the fact that pictures taken without their approval may be published. This also applies even if the pictures do not show the person carrying out any public function, but relate to the individual's private life. An exception may only be made where the person in question is at home or has retired to a secluded place. The reason behind this is that the public has more interest in photographical representations of these persons. Stricter standards have been applied for **relatively public figures** of contemporary society who are only in the public eye due to a one-off event. In such situations, the requirement of approval may only be dispensed with where the depictions in question have a factual and temporal connection with the relevant event. [. . .]

1241 The criteria developed by the German courts to protect the personality rights of celebrities have since been criticised by the **European Court of Human Rights** (ECtHR) [see below, VI.].

> **Example:** In the Caroline of Monaco case, the Federal Supreme Court of Justice, with the backing of the Federal Constitutional Court, declared the publication of photos taken of C shopping at a market and riding on horseback as permissible. Nevertheless, the restaurant garden where some of the photos were taken was an area which was closed off to the public where C had retired for a private conversation. The Supreme Court of Justice (*BGH*) affirmed that in the latter respect there had been an unacceptable interference in C's protected private life. However, the

ECtHR later decided that the publication of the riding photos and of the photos at the market was equally inadmissible [see below, VI.].

[. . .]

IV. Legal consequences

[. . .]

2. The compensation of immaterial harm

1245   Regarding immaterial harm, the victim [. . .] may bring a claim for **monetary compensation** on the basis of § 823 (1) in conjunction with Arts. 1 (1), 2 (1) of the *Grundgesetz*. A prerequisite for this claim, however, is that the victim must have suffered a *severe infringement of his personality rights* which cannot be *compensated by any other means* (e.g. retraction). Recent case law has abandoned the requirement of gross negligence. However, the degree of fault can be taken into account when deciding on the relevant severity of the infringement of personality rights.

With respect to **calculating the amount of monetary compensation**, different criteria are applied than those used to assess damages for pain and suffering under § 253 (2), in that the notions of *deterrence* and *profits made* by the tortfeasor come into play. The freedom enjoyed by the press should not be excessively limited, but claims for monetary compensation often far exceed claims for pain and suffering resulting from injuries to body and health. This is notably the case when a celebrity brings a claim for monetary compensation following the commercialisation of her public image [. . .].

6. Bundesgerichtshof, BGH (*Federal Supreme Court of Justice*), 15.11.1994, BGHZ 128, 1

[*Note by the author*: in a case dating from 1994, two German magazines had published fictitious exclusive interviews with Caroline of Monaco. She claimed, inter alia, monetary compensation for immaterial harm caused by the infringement of her personality rights. Regarding the determination of the amount, the BGH held:]

84 [. . .] Awarding monetary compensation following the infringement of a person's general right of personality is not the same as awarding damages for pain and suffering on the basis of § [253] BGB, but instead constitutes a legal remedy derived from the constitutional protection established in Arts. 1 and 2 (1) of the *Grundgesetz* [. . .]. The idea behind offering monetary compensation is that if victims did not have such a claim then many injuries to human dignity and honour would go without sanction and the legal protection of personality rights would suffer as a consequence. Unlike a claim in damages for pain and suffering, monetary compensation following the infringement of the general right to personality places the emphasis on providing satisfaction for the victim [. . .]; [. . .]. The remedy also serves as a means of deterrence [. . .].

85 [. . .] The [Court of Appeal] [. . .] is of the view that, when deciding on the award of monetary compensation for immaterial harm, the judge must not pay attention to whether

the defendant infringed the victim's personality rights in order to make a profit and that the judge should ignore any considerations of deterrence. However, this approach appears to be [. . .] too restrictive. What sets apart this case is that the respondent, through wilful violation of the law, used the personality of the claimant as a means of increasing circulation of its print media and thereby pursued its own commercial interests. If the respondent were not obliged to provide monetary compensation, then the claimant would be largely defenceless against abusive commercial exploitation of his personality in the future; retraction and apologies are to some extent effective measures because they can only be imposed to the extent that they respect the guaranteed freedom of the press as enjoyed by respondents, but they nevertheless provide inadequate protection to the claimant. However, awarding monetary compensation to the claimant will only achieve the goal of preventing future infringements of personality rights if the award also takes into account any profits which were generated through the infringement of the personality rights in question. This does not mean that as a response to the abusive commercialisation of a person's personality we are to transfer any profits made to the victim, but profits which have been gained through infringement of the plaintiff's rights should be taken into account by the court as a factor when deciding on the sum to be awarded. For this reason, the amount awarded must also be large enough to have a genuine preventive effect which deters a person from marketing another person's image. A further factor which can be taken into consideration when evaluating the award is the severity of the infringement to the individual's personality rights. [. . .]

7. Bundesgerichtshof, BGH (*Federal Supreme Court of Justice*), 05.10.2004, NJW 2005, 215

[. . .] II. [. . .] 1. [. . .] The idea behind awarding monetary compensation following the severe infringement of an individual's personality rights is that without such a claim many injuries to human dignity and honour would go without sanction and the legal protection of personality rights would suffer as a consequence. What regularly sets apart such an award from damages for pain and suffering is that the award of monetary compensation focuses on providing satisfaction for the victim. It also serves as a means of deterring potential tortfeasors [. . .]. Some more sceptical scholars have claimed *inter alia* that, given the aim of preventing and deterring future infringements, the award can be likened to a fine and therefore the question is raised as to whether it has *de facto* punitive effect [. . .]; however, the Court has emphasised that monetary compensation has its basis in constitutional and private law and is not a criminal sanction [. . .]. The Constitutional Court has also decided in this respect that when a private law court orders monetary compensation following the infringement of an individual's personality rights, the order is not [. . .] a criminal sanction, however much it might look to be "akin to a fine" [. . .].

In contrast to a State-imposed criminal penalty, the aim of awarding monetary compensation in private law in cases such as these is to ensure the protection of the victim's interests as guaranteed by Arts. 1 and 2 (1) of the *Grundgesetz*. [. . .]

2. [. . .] d) [. . .] In cases where the injuring party has misused the personality of the claimant as a means of increasing circulation of its print media and has thereby pursued its own commercial interests, any profits gained through violation of the law should be taken into account by the court when deciding on the amount to be awarded. The award in such cases must be large enough to have a genuine preventive effect; a further factor which can be

taken into consideration when evaluating the amount is the severity of the infringement to personality rights [. . .]. [. . .]

8. Bundesverfassungsgericht, BVerfG (*Constitutional Court*), 08.03.2000, Az. I BVR 1127/96, NJW 2000, 2187

[*Note by the author*: in the scenario of Chapter 11, the German courts finally awarded the Millers, who had lost their three children in a road traffic accident, compensation for their pain and suffering following their nervous shock in the amount of DM 70,000 (Mr Miller) and DM 40,000 (Mrs Miller).[27] Claims for damages for bereavement were rejected under the German law of the time.[28] The Millers argued that the amounts of these awards violated their constitutional rights under, inter alia, Art. 3 (1) of the Basic Law (*"All persons shall be equal before the law"*). They argued that, in the light of the awards for the violation of personality rights, the amounts awarded for pain and suffering following the severe infringement of their health were unreasonably low, hereby violating (inter alia) Art. 3 (1). The German Constitutional Court rejected this contention and argued as follows:]

9 A clear distinction [. . .] exists between [impairments to physical health and infringements of an individual's right of personality, especially in the case of proceedings brought against the media], and it is constitutionally permitted for the courts to treat the two cases differently. [. . .] The basic idea behind offering monetary compensation is that if victims did not have such a claim then many injuries to human dignity and honour would go without sanction [. . .]. The criteria employed to quantify this award are partially different to those used when awarding damages for pain and suffering. The *Bundesgerichtshof* has held that this amount should be large enough to have a genuine preventive effect on the marketing of another person's image through wilful violation of the law so that the press is deterred from using the personality of the claimant as a means to increase the number of copies it sells and thereby pursue its own commercial interests. The sum awarded should also be linked to the profits generated through the infringement of the personality rights in question. This is not to say that all profits shall be transferred to the victim; rather, the court is to take into account (and only take into account) the profits sought by the injuring party when deciding on the award [. . .]. Thus, in cases where the court is required to calculate monetary compensation following the infringement of an individual's personality rights, deterrence is the decisive factor leading to a significant increase in the award.

10 However, this factor is not to be taken into account in tort law cases where the victim suffers a bodily or shock-related injury as the result of a traffic accident. There are several reasons why the two cases are treated differently. The violation arising from a typical traffic accident is neither intentional, nor is it motivated by the pursuit of commercial interests. [. . .] Equally, we cannot generally expect a potential tortfeasor to stick to road safety guidelines simply because of a rise in compensation costs. Another reason why increased compensation costs barely have any impact is that the obligation to pay compensation does

---

27 See, OLG Nürnberg, 01.08.1995, 3 U 468/95, DAR 1995, 447 = NZV 1996, 367 = r + s 1995, 384. A claim for "revision" of the judgment by the BGH was rejected, BGH, 16.04.1996, VI ZR 308/95.

28 For the state of *German* law at the time, see above, Chapter 12, pp. 384–385, and the "Latest news" there regarding the new § 844 (3) of the BGB.

not fall on the tortfeasor alone, but on his or her liability insurer – as we have seen in the present case. [. . .]

15 In light of all of the above, the Court rejects the plaintiff's contention that the difference in treatment was constitutionally inadmissible. [. . .]

V. Estonia

Võlaõigusseadus (*Code of Obligations*)

§ 134. **Mittevaralise kahju hüvitamise erisused.** [. . .] (2) Isikult vabaduse võtmisest, isikule kehavigastuse tekitamisest, tema tervise kahjustamisest või muu isikuõiguse rikkumisest, sealhulgas isiku au teotamisest, tekkinud kahju hüvitamise kohustuse olemasolu korral tuleb kahjustatud isikule mittevaralise kahju hüvitiseks maksta mõistlik rahasumma. [. . .]

§ 1043. **Õigusvastaselt tekitatud kahju hüvitamine.** Teisele isikule (kannatanu) õigusvastaselt kahju tekitanud isik (kahju tekitaja) peab kahju hüvitama, kui ta on kahju tekitamises süüdi või vastutab kahju tekitamise eest vastavalt seadusele.

§ 1045. **Kahju tekitamise õigusvastasus.** (1) Kahju tekitamine on õigusvastane eelkõige siis, kui see tekitati:
[. . .] 4) kannatanu isikliku õiguse rikkumisega; [. . .]

§ 1046. **Isiklike õiguste kahjustamise õigusvastasus.** (1) Isiku au teotamine, muu hulgas ebakohase väärtushinnanguga, isiku nime või kujutise õigustamatu kasutamine, eraelu puutumatuse või muu isikliku õiguse rikkumine on õigusvastane, kui seadusega ei ole sätestatud teisiti. Õigusvastasuse tuvastamisel tuleb arvestada rikkumise liiki, põhjust ja ajendit, samuti suhet rikkumisega taotletud eesmärgi ja rikkumise raskuse vahel.
(2) Isikliku õiguse rikkumine ei ole õigusvastane, kui rikkumine on õigustatud, arvestades muid seadusega kaitstud hüvesid ja kolmandate isikute või avalikkuse huve. Õigusvastasuse tuvastamisel tuleb sellisel juhul lähtuda erinevate kaitstud hüvede ja huvide võrdlevast hindamisest.

Translation

*§ 134. **Specifications for compensation for non-pecuniary damage.** [. . .] (2) In the case of an obligation to compensate for damage arising from depriving a person of liberty, causing bodily injuries to or damage to the health of a person, or violation of other personality rights, including defamation of a person, the aggrieved person shall be paid a reasonable amount of money as compensation for non-pecuniary damage. [. . .]*

*§ 1043. **Compensation for unlawfully caused damage.** A person (tortfeasor) who unlawfully causes damage to another person (victim) shall compensate for the damage if he or she is culpable of causing the damage or is otherwise liable for causing the damage pursuant to law.*

§ 1045. Unlawfulness of causing damage. (1) Damage is unlawful in particular when it is caused by: [. . .] 4) violation of a personality right of the victim; [. . .]

§ 1046. Unlawfulness of damaging personality rights. (1) The defamation of a person, inter alia by passing undue judgement, by the unjustified use of the name or image of the person, or by breaching the inviolability of the private life or another personality right of the person is unlawful unless otherwise provided by law. When establishing unlawfulness, the type of violation, the reason and motive for the violation, and the gravity of the violation relative to the aim pursued shall be taken into consideration.
(2) The violation of a personality right is not unlawful if the violation is justified considering other legal rights protected by law and the rights of third parties or public interests. In such case, unlawfulness shall be established based on the comparative assessment of different legal rights and interests protected by law.

Note by the author: the Estonian courts apply the Code of Obligations, §§ 1043, 1045 (1) no. 4, and § 134 (2) also to violations of privacy (inter alia the right to informational self-determination and the right to one's word and image). The unlawfulness of an infringement to privacy is governed by § 1046 and the criteria mentioned there; in general, a person has the right to determine if and what information he or she discloses about his or her private life. Compensation awards range from € 100 to € 10,000, with average amounts of approximately € 1,000.[29]

VI. European Court of Human Rights

European Court of Human Rights, *Caroline von Hannover v. Germany*, 24.06.2004, Nr. 59320/00, [2005] 40 ECHR I

[*Note by the author*: Princess Caroline of Hannover (previously *of Monaco*) brought a petition against the publication of photos in the German tabloid press (*Bunte* and *Neue Post*, owned by *Burda* publishing company). The photos showed her in various settings and revealed activities which she carried out in her private life. The German courts, including the German Federal Supreme Court and the Constitutional Court, regarded Caroline of Hannover as a celebrity of particular interest to the general public (a figure of contemporary society *par excellence, absolute Person der Zeitgeschichte*) who was required to tolerate this kind of publication. The German courts rejected most of her claims on the grounds of the public interest in being informed about her behaviour and of freedom of press (including the entertainment press). The European Court of Human Rights held:]

[. . .] b. The general principles governing the protection of private life and the freedom of expression

56. In the present case the applicant did not complain of an action by the State, but rather of the lack of adequate State protection of her private life and her image.

---

29 The author thanks Prof. JANNO LAHE, Tartu, for this information.

57. The Court reiterates that although the object of Article 8 is essentially that of protecting the individual against arbitrary interference by the public authorities, it does not merely compel the State to abstain from such interference: in addition to this primarily negative undertaking, there may be positive obligations inherent in an effective respect for private or family life. These obligations may involve the adoption of measures designed to secure respect for private life even in the sphere of the relations of individuals between themselves [. . .].

The boundary between the State's positive and negative obligations under this provision does not lend itself to precise definition. The applicable principles are, nonetheless, similar. In both contexts regard must be had to the fair balance that has to be struck between the competing interests of the individual and of the community as a whole; and in both contexts the State enjoys a certain margin of appreciation [. . .].

58. That protection of private life has to be balanced against the freedom of expression guaranteed by Article 10 of the Convention. In that context the Court reiterates that the freedom of expression constitutes one of the essential foundations of a democratic society. [. . .]

[. . .] [T]he press plays an essential role in a democratic society. Although it must not overstep certain bounds, in particular in respect of the reputation and rights of others, its duty is nevertheless to impart [. . .] information and ideas on all matters of public interest [. . .].

59. Although freedom of expression also extends to the publication of photos, this is an area in which the protection of the rights and reputation of others takes on particular importance. The present case does not concern the dissemination of "ideas", but of images containing very personal or even intimate "information" about an individual. Furthermore, photos appearing in the tabloid press are often taken in a climate of continual harassment which induces in the person concerned a very strong sense of intrusion into their private life or even of persecution.

60. In the cases in which the Court has had to balance the protection of private life against the freedom of expression it has always stressed the contribution made by photos or articles in the press to a debate of general interest [. . .].

c. Application of these general principles by the court

61. The Court points out at the outset that in the present case the photos of the applicant in the various German magazines show her in scenes from her daily life, thus engaged in activities of a purely private nature such as practising sport, out walking, leaving a restaurant or on holiday. The photos, in which the applicant appears sometimes alone and sometimes in company, illustrate a series of articles with such anodyne titles as "Pure happiness", "Caroline . . . a woman returning to life", "Out and about with Princess Caroline in Paris" and "The kiss. Or: they are not hiding anymore . . . " [. . .].

62. The Court also notes that the applicant, as a member of the Prince of Monaco's family, represents the ruling family at certain cultural or charitable events. However, she does not exercise any function within or on behalf of the State of Monaco or one of its institutions [. . .].

63. The Court considers that a fundamental distinction needs to be made between reporting facts – even controversial ones – capable of contributing to a debate in a democratic society relating to politicians in the exercise of their functions, for example, and reporting details of the private life of an individual who, moreover, as in this case, does not exercise official functions. While in the former case the press exercises its vital role of "watchdog" in a democracy by contributing to "impart[ing] information and ideas on matters of public interest [. . .] it does not do so in the latter case."

64. Similarly, although the public has a right to be informed, which is an essential right in a democratic society that, in certain special circumstances, can even extend to aspects

of the private life of public figures, particularly where politicians are concerned [. . .], this is not the case here. The situation here does not come within the sphere of any political or public debate because the published photos and accompanying commentaries relate exclusively to details of the applicant's private life.

65. As in other similar cases it has examined, the Court considers that the publication of the photos and articles in question, of which the sole purpose was to satisfy the curiosity of a particular readership regarding the details of the applicant's private life, cannot be deemed to contribute to any debate of general interest to society despite the applicant being known to the public [. . .].

66. In these conditions freedom of expression calls for a narrower interpretation [. . .]. [. . .]

68. The Court finds another point to be of importance: even though, strictly speaking, the present application concerns only the publication of the photos and articles by various German magazines, the context in which these photos were taken – without the applicant's knowledge or consent – and the harassment endured by many public figures in their daily lives cannot be fully disregarded [. . .].

69. The Court reiterates the fundamental importance of protecting private life from the point of view of the development of every human being's personality. That protection – as stated above – extends beyond the private family circle and also includes a social dimension. The Court considers that anyone, even if they are known to the general public, must be able to enjoy a "legitimate expectation" of protection of and respect for their private life [. . .].

70. Furthermore, increased vigilance in protecting private life is necessary to contend with new communication technologies which make it possible to store and reproduce personal data [. . .]. [. . .]

72. The Court has difficulty in agreeing with the domestic courts' interpretation of section 23(1) of the Copyright (Arts Domain) Act, which consists in describing a person as such as a figure of contemporary society "par excellence". Since that definition affords the person very limited protection of their private life or the right to control the use of their image, it could conceivably be appropriate for politicians exercising official functions. However, it cannot be justified for a "private" individual, such as the applicant, in whom the interest of the general public and the press is based solely on her membership of a reigning family whereas she herself does not exercise any official functions. [. . .]

74. The Court therefore considers that the criteria on which the domestic courts based their decisions were not sufficient to protect the applicant's private life effectively. As a figure of contemporary society "par excellence" she cannot – in the name of freedom of the press and the public interest – rely on protection of her private life unless she is in a secluded place out of the public eye and, moreover, succeeds in proving it (which can be difficult). Where that is not the case, she has to accept that she might be photographed at almost any time, systematically, and that the photos are then very widely disseminated even if, as was the case here, the photos and accompanying articles relate exclusively to details of her private life.

75. [. . .] In the present case merely classifying the applicant as a figure of contemporary society "par excellence" does not suffice to justify such an intrusion into her private life.

d. Conclusion

[. . .] 79. Having regard to all the foregoing factors, and despite the margin of appreciation afforded to the State in this area, the Court considers that the German courts did not strike a fair balance between the competing interests. [. . .]

FOR THESE REASONS, THE COURT UNANIMOUSLY
Holds that there has been a violation of Article 8 of the Convention; [. . .]

VII. Goals and purposes of the law of torts

Note by the author: when fixing damage awards for the violation of personality rights, the German Federal Supreme Court of Justice and the German Constitutional Court emphasise that these damages shall provide *satisfaction* (*Genugtuung*) for the victim and that they shall have a *preventive effect*. This raises the question of the objectives pursued by tort law. What are, or ought to be, the goals and purposes of the law of tort?

1. Josef Esser/Hans-Leo Weyers, *Schuldrecht, Band II, Besonderer Teil, Teilband 2: Gesetzliche Schuldverhältnisse (Law of Obligations, Vol. II, Special Part, 2. Legal Obligations)*, 8th ed., 2000

§ 53 On the Purpose of the Law of Delict [or Tort]

1. In general. a) Tort law determines whether, and to what extent, a person is required to provide compensation for damage inflicted on another person irrespective of whether there is any contractual relationship between the two. First [. . .], out of all the regular occurrences of day-to-day life, it is important to distinguish those which give rise to claims in compensation. This step is required because not all damage, even where it can be causally linked to a person's conduct, obliges this person to provide compensation even if the latter could have prevented the damage from occurring. [. . .] Under the rules of civil law, compensation may only be granted to persons suffering damage if there is a specific ground for a claim. This principle has come to be known by the maxim "*casum sentit dominus*" (the loss lies where it falls). The courts are required to determine whether there is a ground to impose liability by examining the conditions applicable to the delict [or tort] in question [. . .].

b) The rationale behind *fault-based liability* is that any person who wrongfully interferes with the rights of another should be liable to compensate the latter for any loss or damage resulting from this interference. In *Kantian* philosophy, compensation constitutes a response to the abusive exercise of free will (wrongful conduct or a failure to act). [. . .]

This rational explanation of the rules of tort law has, of course, emerged out of more recent historical *developments*. The historical roots which underpin tort law to this day appear to be deeply ingrained into our very subconscious. At its origin was the idea of retribution [. . .]. Retributive justice gradually became more ordered over the centuries and further developments reveal that step-by-step, through the continual strengthening and outsourcing of executive power, punishment and atonement became conceptually and organisationally separate from compensation and compensatory damages. A tort was initially casuistically framed as a moral wrong which represented a palpable and massive violation of fundamental legal rights of another. Compensatory damages have only become a general remedy for negligence in more recent times with the growth in population density and increased interaction. The earliest, and today somewhat naïve, approaches to theoretical understanding and reliance on general principles are a product of the Enlightenment, leading to the emergence the Great legal codes containing the first abstract rules on liability for tort (general tort liability clauses, *Generaltatbestände*). With them begins the success of the principle of fault-based liability in the history of ideas [. . .].

In the nineteenth century, fault-based liability corresponded to the trend of contemporary discussion. It seemed to fit into an image of the economically competent, responsible and proficient citizen. Indeed, in response to this new liberal economy which promoted unrestricted individual activity as a means to enhance economic productivity, tort law based on fault would only slightly curtail this freedom by imposing the consequence of liability. [. . .]

a) If the "relevance" of a field of law is to be determined by the number of cases governed under it and the basic function it performs for the community, then one can conclude somewhat simplistically that in practice [. . .] the tort law of today has two main focuses. One focus lies in the attribution of damage caused by accidents [. . .]. Tort law thus regulates the award of compensation for damage caused by various injuries to health and property occurring in all aspects of daily life, from accidents on the road to those on the ski slope, from the occasionally serious consequences of children at play to water pollution and harm which is the cruel result of pharmaceutical drugs. [. . .]

b) The second important role which tort law performs is that of defining and setting the boundaries between *individual freedom* and *liability* based on the current state of societal development. [. . .] With regard to this second role, when defining the scope of tort law a battle is fought between the legal recognition and protection of certain goods and interests on the one hand, and the freedom of action on the other; in this respect, tort law plays a central and crucial role for the development of society. [. . .]

The most important *conflict* of this demarcation has for quite some time been that between individual privacy, its protection from commercial exploitation or disclosure to the public, and the potential to generate profits and revenue for firms, enterprises, or practices utilising such commodities, and the protection of such potential against competitors or other impairments to business. [. . .]

It is important at this point to call into question the often baseless assertions and allegations made by those claiming that fault-based liability has a *preventive effect*. This is not to say that fault-based liability does not play a role in controlling human conduct in certain sectors. For decades, large firms, organisations, associations etc. have been forced to produce a growing tide of circulars and directives following court decisions implementing new "duties to implement safety precautions". Where accidents can be avoided through proper planning and organisation, the economic consequences of potential liability may indeed have a preventive effect. Nevertheless, in many hazardous situations which are difficult, if not impossible to foresee (e.g. road traffic accidents), the psychological prerequisites for an independent role and effect of liability – which would go beyond the fear of punishment or individual self-interest – are usually lacking. Moreover, [. . .] the rules governing liability are often of no economic consequence to those concerned, and as such they offer no incentive. The firm and undifferentiated belief that the law of liability has a general, independent preventive effect is a subjective judgment and can hardly be upheld in light of the relevant counter-arguments. [. . .] It may be that this belief is related to the rational assumption that – even if a preventive effect of civil liability cannot be empirically proven for many sectors – civil liability applied by the courts in any case encourages and decrees a certain standard of conduct desirable for our community of legal subjects. However, this conclusion is no more verifiable than the other.

A sounder theoretical approach than that of a general preventive effect is the widely-discussed *economic* proposition according to which the fact that the burden of the accident is shifted onto the tortfeasor's shoulders ensures that activities that are more dangerous are performed less frequently for the simple reason that less dangerous activities will be "cheaper" to perform. It cannot be denied that such a correlation may indeed exist. The typical case is that of a product which is manufactured in such a way that it carries an extremely high risk of liability (resulting in high liability insurance premiums) competing on the market with another product manufactured for the same cost but in a harmless way and therefore having almost negligible liability insurance premiums. It is however still important to test whether the assumptions used in this model hold true before any sensible proposals can be made for the practice of liability law. There remains much work to be done. [. . .]

The fact that the burden of loss is shifted to the tortfeasor may imply a further purpose of tort law, namely that tort law serves to *punish* the tortfeasor. Given everything that has been stated above, it need not be explained in more detail that this aim is not only largely unattainable under contemporary tort law but also undesirable in the absence of the constitutional safeguards provided by our criminal law system which would act to protect the tortfeasor. [. . .]

2. KENNETH S. ABRAHAM, *The Forms and Functions of Tort Law*, 4th ed., 2012, pp. 16 ff.

III. The nature of tort law

Fields of law normally do not come labelled with a self-designated character or set of goals. [. . .] Some scholars argue that tort law is, and should be, rights-based. On this view, tort law is about redressing, or providing recourse for, wrong. It is about a relationship between a wrongdoer and a victim. Others see tort law's functions as more instrumental: to prevent wrongs, or to compensate those who suffer loss. For many instrumentalists, tort law is, or should be, concerned among other things with the effect that imposing liability will have on others beside the plaintiff and defendant. It is about the external effects of imposing, or not imposing, liability. And still others see tort law as a mix system that performs a combination of these and other factors.

A. Corrective justice

One important rights-based understanding of the function of tort liability is corrective justice. When one party wrongs another, correction of the wrong may help the moral balance between them. [. . .] The case of the intentional wrongdoer is most obviously an occasion for corrective justice. But in many cases of negligence, and even sometimes when there has been neither intention to cause harm nor negligence, corrective justice may have an appeal as a justification for imposing tort liability. [. . .]

B. Civil recourse

Whereas corrective justice focuses on what and why the defendant is obligated to pay the plaintiff, another group of rights-oriented scholars have focused on what the plaintiff is entitled to receive. These scholars argue that tort liability is better understood not as ensuring that injury is corrected, but by providing victims with recourse for civil wrongs. Under this view [...] the imposition of liability is a complex social practice that vindicates victims' needs for recognition that they have been wronged, in a manner that is proportional to the seriousness of the wrong and the seriousness of their injury. What both the corrective justice and civil recourse views of the function of tort law have in common [...] is that they both understand tort law as being mainly concerned with the moral or civil rights arising out of the relationship between the plaintiff and the defendant [...]. [...]

C. Optimal deterrence

The imposition of tort liability not only correct wrongs or provides civil recourse for wrongs that have already occurred; it also helps to prevent future tortious actions, by threatening potential wrongdoers with liability if they cause actionable harm. That is, tort law is not only backward looking, but may also be forward looking. [...] Not all risky activity is worth deterring, however, or we would be required to take endless safety precautions at unlimited cost. Rather, the function of tort liability in this respect is to promote *optimal* deterrence – that is, to deter excessively risky activity so that only those losses worth avoiding are avoided. [...]. Put harshly, some losses – and this includes some personal injuries – are not worth avoiding. Otherwise we would not require proof of negligence in a whole series of cases, but would instead always impose liability regardless of negligence. [...]

Some supporters of the principle of optimal deterrence promote it as an economic concept that compares the monetary costs of risking losses with the monetary costs of preventing losses. And some opponents of the principle object to it for precisely that reason, since it seems to them to ignore important human values. [...]

D. Loss distribution

Defendants who are held liable in tort actions often do not shoulder the burden of compensation themselves. Sometimes defendants are covered by liability insurance and the insurer literally pays the plaintiff on behalf of the policyholder/defendant. On other occasions even an uninsured defendant may be able to include its prospective liabilities in the price of the products it sells; or the defendant may have shareholders whose investments decline in value as a result of the payment of a liability by the company whose shares they own. In each of these situations the cost of the loss suffered by the plaintiff is not simply transferred to the defendant, but is distributed through the defendant to a larger number of individuals, Promoting the broad distribution of losses is therefore often considered one of the functions of tort liability. [...]

E. Compensation

It is sometimes said that a function of tort law is to promote the compensation of those who have suffered injury. For most analysts of tort law, this is only true in a very limited sense. There is no doubt that anytime tort liability is imposed, a plaintiff is awarded compensation. [...]

But if by the term "function" we mean a "goal" of tort law, the notion that providing compensation is a function of tort law is debatable. [...]

[. . .] Liability is not imposed in order to provide compensation to victims. Rather, victims are provided compensation in order to serve the other goals of tort law, such as corrective justice and deterrence. If it were otherwise then the basis of liability would be the suffering of misfortune, not the commission of a tort by another. Since in order to justify the imposition of liability, we require something in addition to the bare fact that the plaintiff suffered an injury caused by another party, describing "compensation" as one of the functions of tort liability cannot tell us why or when tort liability will or will not be imposed. At best, the desirability of providing compensation will be a factor that, when linked with others, makes it more likely that there will be tort liability for a particular category of conduct. And even on that view, proving compensation *under certain circumstances*, rather than in general is what is really going on when tort liability is imposed. For that reason, these "other circumstances" – whatever they turn out to be – are likely to reflect more clearly the actual functions, or goals of tort liability, than the goal of compensating victims. [. . .]

F. Redress of social grievances

[. . .] [A]nother view is that, even apart from these functions, the right to sue in tort promotes the redress of social grievances, especially against large, impersonal institutions. In this sense tort law is a populist mechanism that permits ordinary people to put authority on trial. Surely the lawsuits brought in the past involving [. . .] asbestos-related lung disease, and breast-implants exhibit some of this quality. Future suits may do so as well. Standing alone this justification for the imposition of tort liability may not be strong; but when allied with one or more of the other functions of tort liability, the possibility that imposing liability on an impersonal institution will help to redress social grievances will help to explain why some close cases are decided the way they are.

G. A mixed system?

A last possibility is that tort law does not perform only a single function or serve only a single goal, but a set of different functions whose importance is likely to vary with the situation. Tort law might thus perform a "mixed" set of functions. In some cases, concern for corrective justice or civil recourse might dominate, but in others deterrence or concern for loss distribution might be the key. Or in many instances the imposition of liability might be justified on both rights-based and instrumental grounds, because it simultaneously rights a wrong and deters future wrongdoing, for example. [. . .]

3. People's Republic of China

中华人民共和国侵权责任法 *(Tort Law Act)*

第一章 一般规定

第一条 为保护民事主体的合法权益，明确侵权责任，预防并制裁侵权行为，促进社会和谐稳定，制定本法。

Translation

Chapter I. General provisions

Art. 1. In order to protect the legitimate rights and interests of parties in civil law relationships, clarify the application of tort liability, prevent and punish[30] tortious conduct, and promote social harmony and stability, the present Law is formulated.

4. Principles of European Tort Law

Art. 10:101. Nature and purpose of damages. Damages are a money payment to compensate the victim, that is to say, to restore him, so far as money can, to the position he would have been in if the wrong complained of had not been committed. Damages also serve the aim of preventing harm.

VIII. Switzerland

I. Zivilgesetzbuch/Code civil (*Civil Code*)

Art. 28. (1) Wer in seiner Persönlichkeit widerrechtlich verletzt wird, kann zu seinem Schutz gegen jeden, der an der Verletzung mitwirkt, das Gericht anrufen.
(2) Eine Verletzung ist widerrechtlich, wenn sie nicht durch Einwilligung des Verletzten, durch ein überwiegendes privates oder öffentliches Interesse oder durch Gesetz gerechtfertigt ist.

Art. 28a. Der Kläger kann dem Gericht beantragen:
1. eine drohende Verletzung zu verbieten;
2. eine bestehende Verletzung zu beseitigen;
3. [. . .] Er kann insbesondere verlangen, dass eine Berichtigung oder das Urteil Dritten mitgeteilt oder veröffentlicht wird. Vorbehalten bleiben die Klagen auf Schadenersatz und Genugtuung sowie auf Herausgabe eines Gewinns entsprechend den Bestimmungen über die Geschäftsführung ohne Auftrag.

Translation

Art. 28. (1) Any person whose personality rights are unlawfully infringed may ask the court for protection against all those causing the infringement.

---

30 Regarding a potential punishment of the tortfeasor, see also below, pp. 489 ff.

(2) An infringement is unlawful unless it is justified by the consent of the person whose rights are infringed or by an overriding private or public interest or by law.

Art. 28a. The applicant may ask the court:
1. *To prohibit a threatened infringement;*
2. *To order that an existing infringement cease;*
3. *[. . .] In particular the applicant may request that the rectification or the judgment be notified to third parties or published. Claims for damages and satisfaction and for the handing over of profits in accordance with the provisions governing agency without authority are reserved.*

2. Obligationenrecht/Code des obligations (*Code of Obligations*)

Art. 49. (1) Wer in seiner Persönlichkeit widerrechtlich verletzt wird, hat Anspruch auf Leistung einer Geldsumme als Genugtuung, sofern die Schwere der Verletzung es rechtfertigt und diese nicht anders wiedergutgemacht worden ist.
(2) Anstatt oder neben dieser Leistung kann der Richter auch auf eine andere Art der Genugtuung erkennen.

Vierzehnter Titel: Die Geschäftsführung ohne Auftrag

Art. 419. Wer für einen anderen ein Geschäft besorgt, ohne von ihm beauftragt zu sein, ist verpflichtet, das unternommene Geschäft so zu führen, wie es dem Vorteile und der mutmasslichen Absicht des anderen entspricht.

Art. 423. (1) Wenn die Geschäftsführung nicht mit Rücksicht auf das Interesse des Geschäftsherrn unternommen wurde, so ist dieser gleichwohl berechtigt, die aus der Führung seiner Geschäfte entspringenden Vorteile sich anzueignen. [. . .]

Translation

Art. 49. (1) Any person whose personality rights are unlawfully infringed is entitled to a sum of money by way of satisfaction provided that this is justified by the seriousness of the infringement and that the infringement has not been remedied otherwise.
(2) The court may order that satisfaction be provided in another manner instead of or in addition to monetary compensation.

Title Fourteen: Benevolent intervention in another's affairs

Art. 419. Any person who benevolently intervenes in the affairs of another without authorisation is obliged to do so in accordance with his best interests and presumed intention of the other.

Art. 423. (1) Where the intervention was not carried out with the best interests of the other person (the principal) in mind, the principal is nonetheless entitled to claim any resulting benefits. [. . .]

3. Bundesgericht/Tribunal fédéral (*Federal Supreme Court of Justice*), 07.12.2006, *Schnyder* gegen *Ringier AG und Kraushaar*, BGE 133 III 153

A claim for the handing over of any resulting profits [. . .] and for compensatory damages can be awarded cumulatively (cons. 2.5). The claimant needs to prove an infringement of personality rights, a profit, and a causal link between the two; in the absence of compelling evidence, it is sufficient to demonstrate a strong probability (consid. 3.3). [. . .]

A.- Willy Schnyder (the plaintiff) is the father of the tennis player Patty Schnyder. The latter was involved in a love affair with Rainer Harnecker to the apparent disapproval of the plaintiff. To clear up his concerns, he hired a private detective by the name of Rainer Hofmann who then himself began a relationship with Patty Schnyder. The plaintiff later became aware of Hofmann's criminal past and once again raised objections over his daughter's choice of partner. The relationship between the plaintiff and Patty Schnyder deteriorated as a result.

In 2002, Beat Kraushaar [. . .] wrote a number of articles for *Sonntagsblick* (*Blick on Sunday*), owned by Ringier AG (the defendants [. . .]), including articles in which Patty Schnyder discussed her relationship with her father.

B.- On 28th May 2003, Willy Schnyder brought an action against the defendants claiming that they had unlawfully infringed his personality rights in the following editions of *Sonntagsblick*:

- 10th February 2002 edition: Front-page headline: "Pure Hate! – Patty Schnyder sues parents – 'They're like the Taliban'"; Article entitled: "Betrayal, Blackmail, Extortion – the accusations levelled by Patty Schnyder against her parents – Patty's hardest match yet";
- 17th February 2002 edition: Article entitled: "Patty Wants Money Back from Father and His Offshore Companies"; [. . .]
- 3rd November 2002 edition: Display: "Patty Schnyder gets millions from claim against father"; Front-page headline: "Patty Schnyder: Courtside Victory – against her own father"; Article [. . .]: "Patty Schnyder: 'Now I want my father in jail'".

The plaintiff is requesting a declaration that his personality rights were infringed and further requests that the decision be published, the article in question be deleted from the internet, and the defendants be ordered to pay CHF 7,395 in damages and CHF 5,000 as satisfaction, in addition to handing over any profits they have made.

[The lower instance courts held that the publications unlawfully infringed the plaintiff's personality rights. The courts dismissed the plaintiff's claim for the handing over of profits on the grounds that he had already requested damages and this therefore excluded him from claiming the handing over of profits.]

Extract from the Court's reasoning:

2. The plaintiff is requesting [. . .] that the defendants be ordered to hand over profits of CHF 75,000 made in relation to the publication of the articles in question. [. . .]

2.4 In such situations, ordering a person who has unlawfully infringed the personality rights of another to hand over profits has the purpose of stripping this person of any monetary advantage that he or she might have obtained through the unlawful infringement of the protected legal sphere of another. [. . .]

In cases of malevolent (rather than benevolent) intervention in another's affairs (*unechte Geschäftsführung ohne Auftrag*), the question arises as to whether the strict wording of the law in Art. 423 (1) of the Code of Obligations (*Obligationenrecht*) actually requires the intervener to have been "acting on behalf of" the principal [. . .] or whether it extends to activities which the injured party would either never have been able to perform, or never have been interested in doing. For example, the intervener is presumed to act on behalf of the principal when, through the unauthorised use of photographs of a model, the intervener makes a profit which the model could have made using these same photographs for commercial purposes; in the present case, however, it does not appear conceivable that the plaintiff might have launched a press campaign against himself for the purpose of making a profit.

The reference found in Art. 28a (3) of the Civil Code (*Zivilgesetzbuch*) [. . .] provides an answer to this point of contention; here, the legislator presumed that whenever a person unlawfully infringes the personality rights of another, the infringer is in principle bound to hand over any profit resulting from the infringement in accordance with the provisions on benevolent intervention in another's affairs. [. . .]

[. . .] The reference to the rules on benevolent intervention in another's affairs in Art. 28a (3) of the *Zivilgesetzbuch* should be construed as meaning that the legal consequences of these rules are to be the same regardless of whether the infringer was acting on behalf of the injured party or not; otherwise this provision would be largely devoid of purpose [. . .]. Where a person's personality rights are infringed by the press [. . .], it is indeed hardly conceivable that the victim might launch a media campaign against himself. [. . .]

In summary, it is clear that [. . .] the single decisive factor is the unlawful infringement of the personality rights of another, and that the rules on benevolent intervention in another's affairs extend to cases where the injured person would never have carried out the activities in question. [. . .][31]

2.5. [. . .] Should the infringing party – such as the one in the present case – unlawfully [. . .] interfere in the protected legal sphere of the victim [. . .], the latter may well incur [. . .] direct loss or damage (*damnum emergens*). For instance, the plaintiff might lose his job as a result of the incriminating report and therefore suffer loss or damage as a result of his unemployment. Lost profits are, however, distinct from the benefit obtained by the infringing party; consequently, it must be possible to claim both compensatory damages and the handing over of any resulting profits [. . .]. The same applies in the present case [. . .].

3. In view of what has been stated above, it results that the plaintiff may well be entitled to bring a claim for the handing over of profits, so we now need to examine the precise conditions of such a claim. [. . .]

---

31 The codifications in most other comprehensive jurisdictions also contain rules on benevolent intervention in another's affairs, see e.g. §§ 677 ff. of the *German* BGB. However, it appears that they have not yet been applied to shift the illegal gain made in situation such as the one in the above scenario. See for German law SEILER, in: *Münchener Kommentar zum BGB*, 6. Auflage, 2012, § 687 Rn. 20; GEHRLEIN, in: Bamberger/Roth/Hau/Poseck (Hrsg.) *BeckOK BGB*, 43th ed., Stand: 15.06.2017, § 687, Rn. 7; in favour of the application of these rules in such case scenarios: V. BEUTHIEN, Was ist vermögenswert, die Persönlichkeit oder ihr Image? – Begriffliche Unstimmigkeiten in den Marlene-Dietrich-Urteilen, *NJW* 2003, 1220 at 1222, and J. v. GERLACH, Gewinnherausgabe bei Persönlichkeitsverletzungen nach schweizerischem Vorbild?, *VersR* 2002, 917 at 926. See in comparative perspective *idem* with further references.

3.2 [. . .] The defendants allege that the plaintiff has failed to appropriately demonstrate that the magazine achieved record sales figures; they claim that only an effective increase in sales figures can give rise to an increase of profit and that mere speculation is an insufficient basis for calculation. [. . .]

3.3 To oblige the defendant to hand over any profits made in connection with the unlawful infringement of personality rights, the plaintiff must evidence that [. . .] his or her personality rights were infringed, that a profit was made, and that there is a causal link between the unlawful infringement and the profit made.

The fact that the two articles dated 10th and 17th February 2002 infringed the plaintiff's personality rights has been established [by the court of previous instance]. What remains to be examined is whether this led to a profit for the defendants [. . .]. With regard to the standard of evidence, it should be noted at the outset that, as a rule, full evidence needs to be provided both for the existence of profit and for causality. This requirement is fulfilled if the court finds the evidence convincing from an objective standpoint and is left with no reasonable doubt [. . .]. As far as causality is concerned, it is sufficient to demonstrate that it is more probable than not that a causal links exists, should direct evidence not be attainable in view of the nature of the matter at hand [. . .]. With regard to profits, the evidential requirements are lowered where the exact amount of such profit cannot be quantified; [. . .]; this less stringent requirement to provide evidence applies to both the existence and amount of profit [. . .].

[. . .] As will be explained below, the concept of profit cannot be understood as meaning that there necessarily has to be an increase in day-to-day sales figures and that there is some kind of gain in income. Further, it must be borne in mind that it is impossible to prove with certainty that there is a direct link between a certain article and the fact that a profit was made [. . .]. The court must refrain from imposing evidential requirements which would render illusory a claim for unlawful infringement of personality rights under Art. 28a (3) of the *Zivilgesetzbuch* in connection with the rules on benevolent intervention in another's affairs; especially since to do otherwise would almost entirely thwart the efforts made by the legislator to strengthen [. . .] the protection of personality rights. [. . .]

3.4 As a tabloid publication, *Sonntagsblick*'s sales figures are to be expected to fluctuate much more than those of other newspapers which rely almost entirely on subscriptions [. . .]; based on experience, many consumers decide which of the Sunday papers they would like to buy on the basis of newsagent displays, front pages and cover stories. [. . .] However, from a financial standpoint, it is even more important to consider the fact that the long-term sales figures of the Sunday paper depend significantly on the basic expectations of its readership and whether the paper regularly manages to satisfy its readers.

Sonntagsblick claims through its website that it sets itself apart from other Sunday papers by getting "up close and personal" [. . .]. To be up close and personal, the paper needs to raise, and at the same time satisfy, the public's natural curiosity for scandals, rumours, reports from disasters and other events, and particularly for (everyday) stories from the private, and sometimes intimate, lives of well-known personalities in the sports, politics, and entertainment worlds. [. . .]

If the economic prosperity or profitability of similar sectors of the media does not primarily depend upon coverage of individual issues but rather upon the long-term satisfaction of its readership, [. . .] then a causal link between the unlawful infringement of personality rights and the profit must be deemed as established if and to the extent that the reporting at hand is suitable, in content and form, to preserve readership numbers and thereby make profit.

3.5 Taking into account the above, evidence of the exact amount of profit generated in relation to the unlawful infringement of personality rights cannot be strictly required. Scholars are unanimous that [. . .] the amount is to be assessed at the discretion of the judge [. . .].

In forming this estimate, not only can factors such as sales, circulation, and readership play a role, but also the coverage, presentation, and positioning of the relevant article. The decision should subsequently be based on whether the injury occurred through a single article, a whole series, or indeed a full press campaign, in which case the article is particularly suited to further the aim of contributing long-term to the profit of the media. [. . .]

3.6 [. . .] The progression and presentation of the articles in question revealed not only the plaintiff's business activities, but also the tense relationship he had with his daughter; the story remained the "hot topic" of several issues and was brought back into the spotlight in November. *Sonntagsblick* [. . .] has uncovered all the necessary ingredients of a big story: love, hate, big business, and crime. Experience shows us that reports of this kind are effective at arousing the public's curiosity and are written to appeal to a specific readership, and that the articles in question have most likely had genuine repercussions for the [. . .] plaintiff's business operations. The conditions stated in para. 3.3 are thereby fulfilled and the defendant [. . .] is obliged by virtue of Art. 28a (3) of the Civil Code (*Zivilgesetzbuch*) in connection with Art. 423 (1) of the Code of Obligations (*Obligationenrecht*) to hand over its profits which resulted from the articles that infringed the claimant's personality rights.

3.7 With regard to fixing the amount of profit, [. . .] [this is] a question of fact [and the case is therefore referred back to the previous instance for decision]. [. . .]

IX. The Netherlands

Burgerlijk Wetboek (*Civil Code*)

> Art. 6:104. Indien iemand die op grond van onrechtmatige daad of een tekortkoming in de nakoming van een verbintenis jegens een ander aansprakelijk is, door die daad of tekortkoming winst heeft genoten, kan de rechter op vordering van die ander de schade begroten op het bedrag van die winst of op een gedeelte daarvan.

Translation

> *Art. 6:104. Estimation of damage and the handing over of profits. If someone, who is liable towards another person on the basis of tort or a default of complying with an obligation, has gained a profit because of this tort or non-performance, then the court may, upon the request of the injured person, estimate that damage in line with the amount of this profit or a part of it.*

X. Punitive or exemplary damages – alternative devices to set the right incentives?[32]

Note by the author: in order to set adequate incentives for potential tortfeasors to respect the law and to prevent them from infringing personality rights and the privacy of others, German courts have raised the maximum amount for violation of privacy up to € 400,000. Swiss law uses the rules on "benevolent intervention in the affairs of another" in order to transfer illegal benefits from the tortfeasor to the victim and to hereby prevent potential tortfeasors from benefitting from tortious conduct. Other jurisdictions have so far refused to follow any of these examples. This raises the question of whether exemplary or punitive damages, awarded in addition to compensatory damages, could be an alternative option to dissuade potential tortfeasors from breaching the law and from infringing the rights of others.

1. KENNETH S. ABRAHAM, *The Forms and Functions of Tort Law*, 4th ed., 2012, pp. 258–259

[. . .] In exceptional cases, the plaintiff is entitled not only to recover compensatory damages, but also to an award of damages designed to punish the defendant. These are known as "punitive" or "exemplary" damages. Punitive damages are awarded in only a small percentage of cases, but the threat that they may be awarded probably has more impact than the small percentage of awards reflects.

The states vary in their descriptions of the behaviour that warrants an award of punitive damages, but almost always behaviour more blameworthy than even gross negligence is [. . .] necessary. [. . .]

[. . .] [O]ver the past two decades, the US Supreme Court has reviewed punitive damages awards in a variety of cases in response to defendants' claims that excessive awards violate the Constitutional requirement of due process of law. In a series of decisions, the Court has articulated three factors to be used in evaluating the constitutionality of a punitive damages award; 1) the degree of reprehensibility of the defendant's conduct; 2) the disparity or disproportion between the harm or potential harm resulting from the defendant's conduct and the amount of compensatory damages awarded; and 3) the difference between this remedy and the civil or criminal penalties authorised to punish defendants in comparable cases. [. . .] [I]n *State Farm Insurance Company* v. *Campbell* [2003], the Court quantified the second factor holding that [. . .] awards that are more than nine times greater than compensatory damages are, in effect, presumably unconstitutional. [. . .]

---

32 In contemporary *English* law, the principle is that tort law clearly has a compensatory, rather than punitive, function. The leading case, *Rookes* v. *Barnard*, [1964] A.C. 11229 (per Lord DEVLIN), however, does not exclude punitive or exemplary damages entirely, and allows them in three situations, notably when the tortfeasor unduly profits from his or her deeds. So far, in cases of liability of the press, exemplary damages have exceptionally been awarded in case of *defamation* (i.e. the publication of *false*, defamatory statements), as opposed to the infringements of privacy via the publication of *true* statements. See the case: Court of Appeal, *Elton John* v. *MGN Ltd.*, 12.12.1995, [1997] Q.B. 586 at 618 (per BINGHAM M.R.): publication of the false allegation that Elton John suffered from bulimia; exemplary damages in the amount of £ 50,000 awarded.

2. Court of Appeals of California, Fourth District, *Grimshaw v. Ford Motor Co.*, 29.05.1981, 119 Cal. App. 3d 757, 174 Cal. Rptr. 348

GRIMSHAW v. FORD MOTOR CO.
Court of Appeals, Fourth District, 1981, 119 Cal. App.3d 757,
174 Cal. Rptr. 348

Docket No. 20095.

Court of Appeals of California, Fourth District, Division Two.
May 29, 1981.

OPINION

TAMURA, Acting Presiding Justice: A 1972 Ford Pinto hatchback automobile unexpectedly stalled on a freeway, erupting into flames when it was rear ended by a car proceeding in the same direction. Mrs. Lilly Gray, the driver of the Pinto, suffered fatal burns and 13-year-old Richard Grimshaw, a passenger in the Pinto, suffered severe and permanently disfiguring burns on his face and entire body. Grimshaw [et al.] sued Ford Motor Company and others. Following a six-month jury trial, verdicts were returned in favor of plaintiffs against Ford Motor Company. Grimshaw was awarded $ 2,516,000 compensatory damages and $ 125 million punitive damages; [. . .] On Ford's motion for a new trial, Grimshaw was required to remit all but $ 3 1/2 million of the punitive award [. . .].

Ford assails the judgment as a whole, [. . .] but the primary thrust of its appeal is directed against the punitive damage award. [. . .]

In 1968, Ford began designing a new subcompact automobile which ultimately became the Pinto. [. . .] Ford's objective was to build a car at or below 2,000 pounds to sell for no more than $2,000. [. . .]

Harley Copp, a former Ford engineer and executive in charge of the crash testing program, testified that the highest level of Ford's management made the decision to go forward with the production of the Pinto, knowing that the gas tank was vulnerable to puncture and rupture at low rear impact speeds creating a significant risk of death or injury from fire and knowing that "fixes" were feasible at nominal cost. He testified that management's decision was based on the cost savings which would inure from omitting or delaying the "fixes." [. . .]

PUNITIVE DAMAGES

[. . .] The concept of punitive damages is rooted in the English common law and is a settled principle of the common law of this country. [. . .] The doctrine was a part of the common law of this state long before the Civil Code [of California] was adopted. [. . .] When our laws were codified in 1872, the doctrine was incorporated in Civil Code section 3294, which at the time of trial read: "In an action for the breach of an obligation not arising from contract, where the defendant has been guilty of oppression, fraud, or malice, express or implied, the plaintiff, in addition to the actual damages, may recover damages for the sake of example and by way of punishing the defendant."

[. . .] As this court recently noted, numerous California cases [. . .] have interpreted the term "malice" as used in section 3294 to include, not only a malicious intention to injure the specific person harmed, but conduct evincing "a conscious disregard of the probability that the actor's conduct will result in injury to others." [. . .]

The interpretation of the word "malice" as used in section 3294 to encompass conduct evincing callous and conscious disregard of public safety by those who manufacture and market mass produced articles is consonant with and furthers the objectives of punitive damages. The primary purposes of punitive damages are punishment and deterrence of like conduct by the wrongdoer and others. [. . .] In the traditional noncommercial intentional tort, compensatory damages alone may serve as an effective deterrent against future wrongful conduct but in commerce-related torts, the manufacturer may find it more profitable to treat compensatory damages as a part of the cost of doing business rather than to remedy the defect. [. . .] Deterrence of such "objectionable corporate policies" serves one of the principal purposes of Civil Code section 3294. [. . .] Governmental safety standards and the criminal law have failed to provide adequate consumer protection against the manufacture and distribution of defective products. [. . .] Punitive damages thus remain as the most effective remedy for consumer protection against defectively designed mass produced articles. They provide a motive for private individuals to enforce rules of law and enable them to recoup the expenses of doing so which can be considerable and not otherwise recoverable.

[. . .] The [. . .] contention that the potential liability for punitive damages in other cases for the same design defect renders the imposition of such damages violative of Ford's due process rights also lacks merit. Followed to its logical conclusion, it would mean that punitive damages could never be assessed against a manufacturer of a mass produced article. [. . .] We recognize the fact that multiplicity of awards may present a problem, but the mere possibility of a future award in a different case is not a ground for setting aside the award in this case, particularly as reduced by the trial judge. If Ford should be confronted with the possibility of an award in another case for the same conduct, it may raise the issue in that case. We add, moreover, that there is no necessary unfairness should the plaintiff in this case be rewarded to a greater extent than later plaintiffs. [. . .]

Ford's final contention is that the amount of punitive damages awarded, even as reduced by the trial court, was [. . .] excessive [. . .].

[. . .] In deciding whether an award is excessive as a matter of law [. . .], the following factors should be weighed: The degree of reprehensibility of defendant's conduct, the wealth of the defendant, the amount of compensatory damages, and an amount which would serve as a deterrent effect on like conduct by defendant and others who may be so inclined. [. . .] Applying the foregoing criteria to the instant case, the punitive damage award as reduced by the trial court was well within reason.

[. . .] [T]he conduct of Ford's management was reprehensible in the extreme. It exhibited a conscious and callous disregard of public safety in order to maximize corporate profits. Ford's self-evaluation of its conduct is based on a review of the evidence most favourable to it instead of on the basis of the evidence most favourable to the judgment. [. . .] Ford's tortious conduct endangered the lives of thousands of Pinto purchasers. Weighed against the factor of reprehensibility, the punitive damage award as reduced by the trial judge was not excessive.

Nor was the reduced award excessive taking into account defendant's wealth and the size of the compensatory award. Ford's net worth was $ 7.7 billion and its income after taxes for 1976 was over $983 million. The punitive award was approximately .005 percent of Ford's net worth and approximately .03 percent of its 1976 net income. The ratio of the punitive damages to compensatory damages was approximately 1.4 to 1. [. . .]

Nor was the size of the award excessive in light of its deterrent purpose. An award which is so small that it can be simply written off as a part of the cost of doing business would have no deterrent effect. An award which affects the company's pricing of its product and thereby affects its competitive advantage would serve as a deterrent. [. . .] The award in question was far from excessive as a deterrent against future wrongful conduct by Ford and others.

[. . .] It is precisely because monetary penalties under government regulations prescribing business standards or the criminal law are so inadequate and ineffective as deterrents against a manufacturer and distributor of mass produced defective products that punitive damages must be of sufficient amount to discourage such practices. [. . .]

3. US Supreme Court, *Exxon Shipping Co. v. Baker*, 25.06.2008, 554 U.S. 471

[*Note by the author:* not all states in the USA allow the award of punitive damages. In the case *Exxon Shipping Co.* v. *Baker*, the US Supreme Court provided a short overview on the admissibility of punitive damages in the USA (and elsewhere):]

[. . .] State regulation of punitive damages varies. A few States award them rarely, or not at all. Nebraska bars punitive damages entirely, on state constitutional grounds. [. . .] Four others permit punitive damages only when authorized by statute: Louisiana, Massachusetts, and Washington as a matter of common law, and New Hampshire by statute codifying common law tradition. [. . .] Michigan courts recognize only exemplary damages supportable as compensatory, rather than truly punitive [. . .], while Connecticut courts have limited what they call punitive recovery to the "expenses of bringing the legal action, including attorney's fees, less taxable costs".

As for procedure, in most American jurisdictions the amount of the punitive award is generally determined by a jury in the first instance, and that "determination is then reviewed by trial and appellate courts to ensure that it is reasonable." [. . .] Many States have gone further by imposing statutory limits on punitive awards, in the form of absolute monetary caps [Virginia e.g. uses a $350,000 cap], a maximum ratio of punitive to compensatory damages [see, *e.g.*, Ohio: 2:1 ratio in most tort cases], or, frequently, some combination of the two [. . .]. The States that rely on a multiplier have adopted a variety of ratios, ranging from 5:1 to 1:1.

Despite these limitations, punitive damages overall are higher and more frequent in the United States than they are anywhere else. [. . .] In England and Wales, punitive, or exemplary, damages are available only for oppressive, arbitrary, or unconstitutional action by government servants; injuries designed by the defendant to yield a larger profit than the likely cost of compensatory damages; and conduct for which punitive damages are expressly authorized by statute. [. . .] Even in the circumstances where punitive damages are allowed, they are subject to strict, judicially imposed guidelines. The Court of Appeal in *Thompson* v. *Commissioner of Police of Metropolis*, [1998] Q. B. 498, 518, said that a ratio of more than three times the amount of compensatory damages will rarely be appropriate; awards of less than 5,000 are likely unnecessary; awards of 25,000 should be exceptional; and 50,000 should be considered the top.

For further contrast with American practice, Canada and Australia allow exemplary damages for outrageous conduct, but awards are considered extraordinary and rarely issued.

[. . .] Non-compensatory damages are not part of the civil-code tradition and thus unavailable in such countries as France, Germany, Austria, and Switzerland. [. . .] And some legal systems not only decline to recognize punitive damages themselves but refuse to enforce foreign punitive judgments as contrary to public policy [. . .] (noting refusals to enforce judgments by Japanese, Italian, and German courts [. . .]).

4. Bundesgerichtshof, BGH (*Federal Supreme Court of Justice*), 04.06.1992, BGHZ 118, 312

[*Note by the author*: when he was a minor of not yet 14 years old, the plaintiff, then living in California, was victim of sexual abuse by the defendant, a citizen of both Germany and the USA also living in California at the time. The defendant was convicted by a court in California to pay the plaintiff damages in the amount of $ 750,000 ($ 260 for past medical damages; a lump sum of $ 100,000 for future medical expenses; $ 50,000 for future costs of placement of the plaintiff; $ 200,000 for anxiety, pain, and suffering, and general damages of that nature; and $ 400,000 for exemplary and punitive damages). The court further ordered that 40% of these amounts were to be paid to the plaintiff's lawyers as a contingency fee.[33] The defendant is now living in Germany where he owns immovable property. The plaintiff requests the recognition and enforcement of the judgment in Germany:]

Grounds for the decision

66 [. . .] As many as four main objectives are pursued [. . .] when [a court orders payment of punitive damages]: the tortfeasor is to be punished for his socially unacceptable conduct, meaning that any vigilantism on the part of the victim shall be avoided; the tortfeasor and the general public are to be deterred from any similar future conduct which might prove detrimental for society, insofar as the mere risk of civil liability claims is not a sufficient incentive for behaving properly; the victim is to be rewarded for engaging in making sure that the law is fully enforced, hereby strengthening the legal system as a whole; and finally, the victim is to be entitled to receive an additional payment as compensation for damage which he may consider to have been improperly remedied in light of his limited access to social security etc. [. . .]; out-of-court expenses which are not otherwise recoverable may be taken into account here when fixing compensation. [. . .]

72 [. . .] [German] courts [. . .] regularly refuse to enforce United States court decisions ordering the payment of punitive damages on the grounds of *ordre public* [. . .].

73 [. . .] The modern German civil law system stipules that in response to an unlawful act, a court may only award compensation (§§ 249 ff. of the *BGB*), and not enrich the injured party [. . .]. [. . .] Punishment and [. . .] deterrence are both goals which are pursued under criminal law (§§ 46 and 47 of the Penal Code), where any fines which are imposed are thereafter awarded to the State; they are not goals of civil law.

76 In line with [. . .] *ordre public*, under German law satisfaction can only be provided to the victim [. . .] insofar as the "punitive damages" in question are intended to compensate the victim for his or her pain and suffering [. . .]. In the present case, however, the victim

---

33 See below, Chapter 17, p. 563.

has already received an award for his pain and suffering fully compensating him in this respect. [...]

88 aa) One of the fundamental principles of German law is the principle of proportionality, a foundation stone for the rule of law which extends to all civil law [...]. In civil law, it contributes *inter alia* to how we assess compensation in damages: the rules of civil procedure [...] aim to compensate victims for damage suffered through illegal acts, and the rules of procedure and evidence allow parties to exercise a decisive influence on the end result. [...]

89 On the other hand, the German view is that the power to impose sanctions which punish and deter – and therefore protect the legal system as a whole – fundamentally belongs to the State. The State protects the public interest by imposing sanctions exclusively in a special type of procedure [i.e. criminal procedure] which not only provides a higher degree of accuracy in investigating questions of fact, but also better protects the rights of the accused. From this point of view, it would seem intolerable that a civil court might levy a substantial cash payment which is not intended to compensate, but is instead determined in line with the interests of the general public and could conceivably lead to a situation of double jeopardy [...].

90 [In the present case] the punitive damages which have been imposed are higher than the total sum of compensation which was awarded for the damage suffered. [...] There is no evidence of any further damage. Under these circumstances, enforcement of punitive damages against this defendant would be excessive.

91 The courts in the USA have been known to impose (sometimes excessively high) awards in punitive damages which are not in any fixed relation to the actual harm suffered; as a result, liable parties are now required to shoulder a large financial burden making insurable risks difficult to measure and pushing liability insurance to its limits [...].

92 From a German perspective, recognising a decision founded on considerations which go above and beyond the protection of civil law [...] could ultimately lead to the current domestic liability system being dismantled. This recognition would have the effect of allowing foreign plaintiffs to claim much more money from tortfeasors than domestic plaintiffs even where the latter has sustained a substantially greater impairment. Placing plaintiffs from the few countries in the world where punitive damages are awarded into a better position [...] than all other plaintiffs is not justified by any interest worthy of protection under the German legal order. [...]

93 [...] For this reason, this judgment cannot be enforced in Germany as far as the part on punitive damages is concerned. [...]

94 The fact that the Superior Court's judgment is not capable of being declared enforceable in Germany in view of the imposition of punitive damages does not preclude recognition with respect to the award of compensatory damages in the same judgment. [...][34]

---

34 In other European jurisdictions as well, the recognition of foreign punitive damage awards has been rejected as contrary to public policy, e.g. in *Italy*, Corte di Cassazione Civile (*Court of Cassation, Civil Section*), 19.01.2007, no. 1183, Rep Foro it 2007, no. 13; translation by F. QUARTA, Recognition and Enforcement of U.S. Punitive Damages Awards in Continental Europe: The Italian Supreme Court's Veto, *HICLR* 2008, Appendix A, 780–782; see further: Corte di Cassazione (*Court of Cassation*), 08.02.2012, *Soc Ruffinatti v. Oyola-Rosado*, no. 1781/2012; *Poland*: Sąd Apelacyjny w Warszawie (*Court of Appeal in Warsaw*), 26.01.2012, I

5. Regulation (EC) No 864/2007 of the European Parliament and of the Council of 11 July 2007 on the law applicable to non-contractual obligations, [2007] OJ, L 199/40 (Rome II Regulation)[35]

Recital 32. [. . .] [T]he application of a provision of the law designated by this Regulation which would have the effect of causing non-compensatory exemplary or punitive damages of an excessive nature to be awarded may [. . .] be regarded as being contrary to the public policy (ordre public) of the forum.[36]

ACz 2059/11, cited according to K. OLIPHANT/B. C. STEININGER (eds.), *European Tort Law (ETL) 2012*, Berlin/Boston: De Gruyter, 2013, p. 21, nos. 36–42. In *Switzerland*, in line with the *obiter dictum* of the above BGH decision, the Court of First Instance of Basel, confirmed by the Basel Court of Appeal, recognised a Californian decision awarding punitive damages, arguing that "the main purpose of the punitive damages award was to compensate the claimant for unjust profit realized by the respondent, and that punishment played only a secondary role in the awarding of damages. [. . .]", Zivilgericht Basel-Stadt (*Basel Civil Court*), 01.02.1989, in: BJM 1991, 31 ff. According to scholars, "[i]t thus appears that Swiss courts will enforce a foreign award of punitive damages if they are primarily compensatory in nature", see J. Y. GOTANDA, *Supplemental Damages in Private International Law*, The Hague: Kluwer Law International, 1998, p. 203.

On the other hand, *French* and *Spanish* courts held that the recognition of foreign punitive damages awards does not violate public policy, as long as the amount is not disproportionate in relation to the damage suffered, French Cour de cassation (*Court of Cassation*), 01.12.2010, Schlenzka & Langhorne v. Fountaine Pajot SA, no. 09–13.303, D. 2011, 423: "le principe d'une condamnation à des dommages intérêts punitifs [. . .] n'est pas, en soi, contraire à l'ordre public, il est autrement lorsque le montant alloué est disproportionné au regard du préjudice subi et aux manquements aux obligations [. . .]" (translation: "The idea of imposing punitive damages [. . .] is not, in and of itself, contrary to public policy except where the amount imposed by the court is not proportionate to the harm suffered by the victim and the failure of the tortfeasor to comply with the obligations he was required to perform [. . .]"); Spanish Tribunal Supremo (*Supreme Court*), Miller Import Corp. v. Alabastres Alfredo, S.L., 13.11.2001, no. 2039/1999. The acceptable proportion seems to be set at 1:1 by *French* courts, and at 2:1 by the courts in *Spain*, comp. C. VANLEENHOVE, *Punitive Damages in Private International Law: Lessons for the European Union*, Cambridge: Intersentia, 2016, nos. 514 and 519. A similar position seems to prevail in *Greece*, see M. REQUEJO ISIDRO, Punitive Damages from a Private International Law Perspective, in: H. KOZIOL/V. Wilcox (eds.), *Punitive Damages: Common Law and Civil Law Perspectives*, Wien/New York: Springer, 2009, p. 247.

35 For the law applicable to cross-border torts, see below, Chapter 18, pp. 570 ff.
36 Note that the Rome II Regulation applies to most torts but does not, pursuant to its Art. 1 (2) (g), apply to "non-contractual obligations arising out of violations of privacy and rights relating to personality, including defamation". The reason is that the EU institutions could not find a compromise regarding which law should apply to this issue. The applicable tort law thus remains to be determined by the Private International Law rules of the forum.

Bibliography

On the right to privacy and benevolent intervention in another's affairs

XAVIER AGOSTINELLI, *Le droit à l'information face à la protection civile de la vie privée*, Aix-en-Provence: Libraire de l'Université d'Aix-en-Provence, 1994; ULRICH AMELUNG, *Der Schutz der Privatheit im Zivilrecht*, Tübingen: Mohr Siebeck, 2002; LISA M. AUSTIN, Privacy and Private Law: The Dilemma of Justification, *McGill L.J.* 2010, 165; KATHARINA VON BASSEWITZ, Hard Times for Paparazzi: Two Landmark Decisions Concerning Privacy Rights Stir Up the German and English Media, *IIC* 2004, 642–653; CATHERINE BERLAUD, Presse et vie privée: une publication ayant trait à l'intérêt général, *Gaz. Pal.* 2017, no. 11, p. 39; CHRISTINE BIGOT, Les exigences de l'information et la protection de la vie privée, *Légipresse* 1995, no. 126.II., pp. 83–93; THOMAS BINGHAM, Should There Be a Law to Protect Rights of Personal Privacy?, *E.H.R.L.R.* 1996, 455–462; OLIVIER D'ANTIN, Le domaine de la vie privée et sa délimitation jurisprudentielle, *Legicom* 1999, 154; EMMANUEL DERIEUX/FRANÇOIS GRAS, Vie privée et liberté d'informer. Le rôle du juge, *Légipresse* 1998, no. 148. II., pp. 1–10; SÉVERINE DUPUY-BUSSON, Respect de la vie privée et liberté d'informer: un délicat équilibre à trouver, *Gaz. Pal.* 2014, no. 100, p. 9; JEAN HAUSER, La protection de la vie privée et les nécessités de l'information, *RTD Civ.* 2017, 352; TILMAN HOPPE, *Persönlichkeitsschutz durch Haftungsrecht*, Berlin: Duncker Humblot, 2001; PIERRE KAYSER, *La protection de la vie privée*, 2ᵉ ed., Paris: Economica/Aix-en-Provence: P.U.A.M., 1990; HELMUT KOZIOL/ALEXANDER WARZILEK (eds.), *Persönlichkeitsschutz gegenüber Massenmedien/The Protection of Personality Rights against Invasion by Mass Media*, previously: Vienna/New York: Springer, now: Vienna: Verlag Österreich, 2005; ISABELLA LADSTÄTTER, *Benevolent Intervention in Another's Affairs im Draft Common Frame of Reference – Die Geschäftsführung ohne Auftrag im Rechtsvergleich*, Wien 2011, available at: https://core.ac.uk/download/pdf/11598246.pdf; AGATHE LEPAGE, Préjudice moral ou préjudice patrimonial, il faut choisir, *CCE* 2005, no. 1 comm. 17; AGATHE LEPAGE, Réparation du préjudice résultant d'une atteinte à la vie privée: refus de prendre en compte les profits réalisés par le journal, *D.* 2000, 269; TOM LEWIS/JONATHAN GRIFFITHS, The Human Rights Act 1998, Section 12 – Press Freedom over Privacy?, *Ent. L.R.* 1999, 36–41; NG-LOY WEE LOON, Emergence of a Right to Privacy from within the Law of Confidence?, *E.I.P.R.* 1996, 307–312; LAURE MARINO, *Responsabilité civile, activité d'information et médias*, Aix-en-Provence: P.U.A.M., 1997; CAROLINE MAS, L'intérêt général n'en finit pas d'irradier le droit de la presse, *Légipresse* 2017, 210–213; NICOLE MOREHAM, Privacy and Horizontality: Relegating the Common Law, *L.Q.R.* 2007, 373–378; ROGER NERSON, La protection de la vie privée en droit positif français, *R.I.D.C.* 1971, 737–764; TIMOTHY PINTO, Tiptoeing Along the Catwalk between Articles 8 and 10: Naomi Campbell v Mirror Group Newspapers Limited, *Ent. L.R.* 2004, 199–202; JACQUES RAVANAS, *La protection des personnes contre la réalisation et la publication de leur image*, Paris: L.G.D.J., 1978; BETH RICHARDS-BRAY, Human Rights: Privacy, Breach of Confidence and Freedom of Expression, *Cov. L.J.* 2002, 27–34; LYNN RICHMOND, Private Rights and Public Interest, *SLT* 2007, 233–235; WULF-HENNING ROTH, Persönlichkeitsschutz im Internet: Internationale Zuständigkeit und anwendbares Recht, *IPRax* 2013, 215–227; BLANCA R. RUIZ, *Privacy in Telecommunications: A European and an American Approach*, The Hague: Kluwer Law International, 1997; CHENG LIM SAW/GARY KOK YEW CHAN, The House of Lords at the Crossroads of Privacy and Confidence, *Hong Kong L.J.* 2005, 91; ARYE SCHREIBER, Confidence Crisis, Privacy Phobia: Why Invasion of Privacy Should Be Independently Recognised in English Law, *I.P.Q.* 2006, 160–192;

RABINDER SINGH, Privacy and the Media after the Human Rights Act, *E.H.R.L.R.* 1998, 712–729; HARTWIG SPRAU, Benevolent Intervention in Another's Affairs: Some Remarks on the Draft Report Presented by the Study Group on a European Civil Code, *Europäische Rechtsakademie: ERA-Forum* 2006, 220–233, also available at: https://link.springer.com/content/pdf/10.1007%2Fs12027-006-0005-0.pdf; JAMES STRACHAN/RABINDER SINGH, The Right to Privacy in English Law, *E.H.R.L.R.* 2002, 129–161; JAMES STRACHAN/RABINDER SINGH, Privacy Postponed?, *E.H.R.L.R.* 2003, Supp (Special issue: privacy 2003), 12–24; EMMA STOKER, Right to Privacy? David Murray v Big Pictures (UK) Ltd, *Ent. L.R.* 2008, 140–143; VERONIKA SZEGHALMI, The Definition of the Right to Privacy in the United States of America and Europe, *HYIEL* 2015, 397–410; RAYMOND WACKS, *Privacy and Media Freedom*, Oxford: OUP, 2013; SAMUEL D. WARREN/LOUIS D. BRANDEIS, The Right to Privacy, *Harv. L. Rev.* 1890, 194. STUDY GROUP ON A EUROPEAN CIVIL CODE, *Benevolent Intervention in Another's Affairs*, Munich: Sellier, 2006 (prepared by CHRISTIAN VON BAR); MAREK VRZAL, Die Entwicklung des Schmerzensgeldanspruchs anhand der neueren Rechtsprechung, *VersR* 2015, 284.

On the influence of the ECHR on the right to privacy

PATRICK AUVRET, L'équilibre entre la liberté et le respect de la vie privée selon la Cour européenne des droits de l'homme, *Gaz. Pal.* 2005, no. 102, 2; PATRICK AUVRET, Le Conseil de l'Europe et la protection de la vie privée en matière de presse, *Légicom*, 1999, no. 20, 97; ALEXANDRA BONN, *Die Europäisierung des Persönlichkeitsrechts – Harmonisierungswirkungen des "Caroline"-Urteils des EGMR in Deutschland und England unter Berücksichtigung prozessualer und kollisionsrechtlicher Aspekte*, Frankfurt am Main: Internationaler Verlag der Wissenschaften, 2013; FABRICE BURGAUD, Liberté d'expression et respect de la vie privée: quel équilibre au regard de la Convention européenne, *D.* 2015, 939; SOPHIE CANAS, L'influence de la fondamentalisation du droit au respect de la vie privée sur la mise en oeuvre de l'article 9 du Code civil, *Les nouveaux Cahiers du Conseil constitutionnel*, 01/06/2015, no. 48, 47; LAMIA EL BADAWI, Atteinte à la vie privée et droit à l'image, *J.D.I.* 2016, 1349–1353; ATTILA FENYVES/ERNST KARNER/HELMUT KOZIOL/ELISABETH STEINER (eds.), *Tort Law in the Jurisprudence of the European Court of Human Rights*, Berlin: De Gruyter, 2011; EIKE M. FRENZEL, Persönlichkeitsschutz und Pressefreiheit: Ein Blick auf Großbritannien, *AfP* 2011, 335–338; ANDREAS FRIEDRICH, *Grundrechtlicher Persönlichkeitsschutz und europäische Privatsphärengarantie*, Baden-Baden: Nomos, 2009; MATTHIAS LEHR, *Ansätze zur Harmonisierung des Persönlichkeitsrechts in Europa*, Baden-Baden: Nomos, 2009; SEVERIN MÜLLER-RIEMENSCHNEIDER, *Pressefreiheit und Persönlichkeitsschutz*, Hamburg: Kovac 2013; BRIAN O'BEIRNE, The European Court of Human Rights' Recent Expansion of the Right of Privacy: A Positive Development?, *Cov. L.J.* 2009, 14–22; CAROLINE PICHERAL, Evolutions de la jurisprudence de la Cour européenne des droits de l'homme, *RDLF* 2016, no. 29, available at: www.revuedlf.com/cedh/evolutions-de-la-jurisprudence-de-la-cour-europeenne-des-droits-de-lhomme-premier-semestre-2016/; KLAUS STERN/HANS PRÜTTING (eds.), *Das Caroline-Urteil des EGMR und die Rechtsprechung des Bundesverfassungsgerichts*, München: C. H. Beck, 2006; NATO TSOMAIA, *Der Konflikt zwischen BVerfG und EGMR im Spannungsfeld zwischen Medienfreiheit und Persönlichkeitsschutz*, Berlin: Lit Verlag, 2016; JAN VON HEIN, Die Europäisierung des Persönlichkeitsrechtsschutzes: Das Urteil des Europäischen Gerichtshofs für Menschenrechte in der Sache Caroline von Hannover gegen Deutschland, *GPR* 2004, 252–258.

On punitive or exemplary damages

Suzanne Carval, *De la fonction de peine privée de la responsabilité civile*, Paris: L.G.D.J., 1995; Sarah G. Cronan/J. Brittany Cross, Predictability in Punitive Damages: Considering the Use of Punitive Damage Multipliers, *Def. Couns. J.* 2012, 454; Phillip Dawkins, Damage Control: A Glimpse into Punitive Damage Reform, *Law & Soc'y J.* UCSB 2007–2008, 71; Hélène Gaudemet-Tallon, De la conformité des dommages-intérêts punitifs à l'ordre public, *Rev. Crit. DIP* 2011, 93; Robert E. Goodfriend, Preserving Error in Punitive Damage Cases, *Tex. B.J.* 1990, 1282; John Y. Gotanda, Charting Developments Concerning Punitive Damages: Is the Tide Changing?, *Colum. J. Transnat'l L.* 2007, 507; John Y. Gotanda, *Supplemental Damages in Private International Law*, The Hague: Kluwer Law International, 1998; Laurène Gratton, Le dommage déduit de la faute, *RTD Civ.* 2013, 275; Jean Hauser, Du cumul des sanctions en cas d'atteinte à la vie privée et du respect des décisions judiciaires, *RTD Civ.* 2008, 79; Jean Hauser, La protection de la vie privée: conditions et sanctions, *RTD Civ.* 1997, 632; Benjamin W. Janke/Francois-Xavier Licari, Enforcing Punitive Damage Awards in France after Fountain Pajot, *Am. J. Comp. L.* 2012, 775; Helmut Koziol/Vanessa Wilcox (eds.), *Punitive Damages: Common Law and Civil Law Perspectives*, Wien/New York: Springer, 2009; Jill W. Lens, Procedural Due Process and Predictable Punitive Damage Awards, 2012, *BYU L. Rev.* 2012, 1; Jill W. Lens, Pushing for the Injury: Tort Law's Influence in Defining the Constitutional Limitations on Punitive Damage Awards, *Hofstra L. Rev.* 2010–2011, 595; Agathe Lepage, Réparation du préjudice résultant d'une atteinte à la vie privée: refus de prendre en compte les profits réalisés par le journal, *D.* 2000, 269; François-Xavier Licari, La compatibilité de principe des punitive damages avec l'ordre public international: une décision en trompe-l'œil de la Cour de cassation ?, *D.* 2011, 423; Andrew C. W. Lund, The Road from Nowhere: Punitive Damage Ratios after BMW v. Gore and State Farm Mutual Automobile Insurance Co. v. Campbell, *Touro L. Rev.* 2004–2005, 943; Linda S. Mullenix, Nine Lives: The Punitive Damage Class, *U. Kan. L. Rev.* 2009–2010, 845; Stacey Obrecht, Tort Law – Punitive Damage Determinations: A Jury's Factual Inquiry or a Court's Mathematical Leash, *Wyo. L. Rev.* 2005, 637; William A. Reppy, Jr., Punitive Damage Awards in Pet-Death Cases: How Do the Ratio Rules of State Farm v. Campbell Apply, *J. Animal L. & Ethics* 2006, 19; Solange E. Ritchie, State Farm v. Campbell: The Trend towards Evidentiary and Constitutional Restrictions in Punitive Damage Awards, *W.St.U.L.Rev.* 2003–2004, 27; Jennifer K. Robbennolt, *Punitive Damages and Tort Reform: The Damage Award Decisions of Citizen and Judges*, Ann Arbor: UMI, 1998; Shaakirrah R. Sanders, Uncapping Compensation in the Gore Punitive Damage Analysis, *Wm. & Mary Bill Rts. J.* 2015–2016, 37; Victor E. Schwartz/Cary Silverman/Christopher E. Appel, The Supreme Court's Common Law Approach to Excessive Punitive Damage Awards: A Guide for the Development of State Law, *S. C. L. Rev.* 2008–2009, 881; Cedric Vanleenhove, *Punitive Damages in Private International Law: Lessons for the European Union*, Cambridge: Intersentia, 2016; Neil Vidmar/Mary R. Rose/Alan Calnan, Ending the Punitive Damage Debate, *DePaul L. Rev.* 1995, 101–122.

Chapter 16

Damage to public goods
The case of damage to the environment, pure ecological damage in particular

"Union policy on the environment shall [. . .] be based on the [. . .] principle [. . .] that the polluter should pay."[1]

"Compensation for environmental damage of a public nature, regarded as an infringement of the public and general interest in the environment, is solely a matter for the State".[2]

"Private law appears indispensable where public environmental law – or its enforcement – has not prevented environmental damage. Liability for damage remains the core task of private law".[3]

Scenario

A foundation dedicated to environmental protection is heading an international project aimed at reintroducing bearded vultures into their native environment. With a wingspan of 2.9 m, the bearded vulture is one of the largest birds in the world. Its numbers in Europe are extremely scarce, with only a few hundred viable breeding pairs.

The foundation cooperates with around 30 different zoological parks engaging in worldwide breeding programmes. Each year, it decides which of these captive birds are to be reintroduced into the wild. It then monitors the young birds' release into one of four designated sites in the Alps. Their movements are tracked on a regular basis by

---

1 Treaty on the Functioning of the European Union, Art. 191 (2).
2 Corte di cassazione penale italiana, sez. III (*Italian Supreme Court of Cassation, Sect. III*), 27.05.2011, sentenza no. 21311. In the Italian original: "Il risarcimento del danno ambientale di natura pubblica, in sé considerato come lesione dell'interesse pubblico e generale dell'ambiente, [. . .] spetta esclusivamente allo Stato"? The Court continues: "Tutti gli altri soggetti, singoli o associati [. . .] sono legittimati ad agire, ex art. 2043 c.c., per ottenere qualsiasi risarcimento del danno patrimoniale, ulteriore e concreto, che abbiano dato prova di avere subito dalla medesima condotta lesiva dell'ambiente in attinenza alla lesione di altri loro diritti patrimoniali, diversi dall'interesse pubblico e generale alla tutela dell'ambiente." Translation: "Any other parties, whether individuals or associations, [. . .] are entitled, pursuant to Art. 2043 of the Civil Code, to obtain compensation for pecuniary damage, whether direct or indirect, which they prove to have suffered as a result of conduct that is detrimental not only to the environment but also to their own protected rights and interests, the latter differing from the interest of the general public in the protection of the environment".
3 MICHAEL KLOEPFER, Umweltschutz als Aufgabe des Zivilrechts – aus öffentlich-rechtlicher Sicht, *Jb.UTR* 1990, 35 at 43. In the original German version: "Unverzichtbar erscheint das Zivilrecht gerade dort, wo das öffentliche Umweltrecht – oder sein Vollzug – Umweltschäden nicht verhindert hat. Die Schadenshaftung bleibt Kernaufgabe des Zivilrechts".

a volunteer observer network. In the past few years, more than 100 bearded vultures have been reintroduced into the wild, one among them being named *Republic V*.

During a hunt, B shoots down the bearded vulture *Republic V*. B is convicted of an offence and is made to pay a sum of € 20,000 to the State to "compensate" the loss of the bearded vulture.

The foundation then takes B to court, claiming damages of € 118,000 for the funds it had invested in breeding and reintroducing *Republic V* into the wild. This sum is required to breed and reintroduce a bearded vulture into nature.[4]

---

4 Scenario inspired by the *Swiss* case: Tribunal federal, 4C.317/2002, 20.02.2004 (see below, pp. 508–511). See also for *Spain*: the case STS, 01.04.1993, *RJ* 1993/9165 (killed bear), *Digest II*, 23/10 nos. 1–3 with comment by M. MARTIN CASALS/J. RIBOT; for *Germany*: VG Munich (*Munich Administrative Court of first instance*), 31.05.2007, M 11 K 06.4129 *NuR* 2007, 764 f. (killed brown bear "Bruno"), *Digest II*, 23/2 nos. 1–5 with comment by S. MARTENS/R. ZIMMERMANN; for *Norway*: Frostating lagmannsrett (Court of Appeal), 06.11.1978, *RG* 1979, 715 (shooting of ten Canadian geese), *Digest II*, 23/16 nos. 1–3 with comment by B. ASKELAND; for *Sweden*: Högsta domstolen (Supreme Court), 19.04.1995, *NJA* 1995, 249 (illegal shooting of two wolverines), *Digest II*, 23/17 nos. 5–7 with comment by H. ANDERSSON.

Introduction[5]

Who protects the public interest? Protecting the public interest, in particular the interest in preserving the natural environment, is in principle the role of public authorities.[6] However, it is often difficult for administrative authorities to efficiently ensure the respect of environmental laws and regulations, be it for lack of personnel and resources, or for the fact that public authorities are tasked with safeguarding multiple and potentially conflicting public interests (including the promotion of local businesses that engage in potentially polluting activities for the purpose of creating employment and taxable income for the community). It has been noted that this often leads to a certain *lack of enforcement of environmental protection rules* by administrative authorities.[7] Furthermore, ordinary citizens will generally not have any direct and personal interest in bringing a claim in compensation for injury to environmental interests, be it for lack of time, means, expertise, or because they may themselves have interests that conflict with the protection of the environment.

The participation of non-governmental non-profit associations. Unlike administrative authorities, private non-profit environmental associations focus exclusively on the protection of the environment and are not exposed to conflicts of interest. They often have a detailed knowledge of the local environment and the necessary expertise and dedication to effectively engage in the protection of natural resources. These qualities have led legislators in many countries, as well as the European Union, to create *participation rights* for environmental associations in *administrative procedures* which might have an adverse impact on the environment, and, under certain conditions, to allow them to *challenge* environmentally relevant *decisions made by administrative authorities* before the courts.

Remedies offered by public law. Administrative law relating to the environment focuses primarily on forward planning and on preventing harm to the environment. *Liability* and the *compensation of harm* are not its particular focus.[8] With regard to liability for damage to the environment, public law provides in many jurisdictions, at best, a patchwork of singular rules with many gaps. In addition, there is again the risk of a lack of enforcement. In this situation, *private law remedies* may play an important role in supplementing this system, filling gaps and making it more efficient.

Definition of environmental and of pure ecological damage. With regard to damage to the environment, two fundamentally different categories can be distinguished:

- There are situations in which both the environment and a private party's rights and interests (such as health or property) are injured concurrently. In these situations, the

---

[5] The present case addresses damage to the environment from a "micro" perspective, focusing on damage claims which may be covered by private law remedies. For cases addressing "macro" environmental damage, i.e. that of climate change and related litigation where the outer limits of private law remedies are tested and may arguably need to be (over)stretched to cover the issue, see M. Spitzer/B. Burtscher, Liability for Climate Change – Cases, Challenges & Concepts in Civil and Common Law, *JETL* 2017, pp. 137–176. See also M. Hinteregger, Civil Liability and the Challenges of Climate Change: A Functional Analysis, *JETL* 2017, pp. 238–260.
[6] See the quote above, fn. 2, taken from a judgment of the *Italian* Supreme Court of Cassation.
[7] Numerous references e.g. in T. Kadner Graziano, *Ersatz ökologischer Schäden – Ansprüche von Umweltverbänden*, Berlin: Duncker & Humblot, 1995, pp. 67–69 and 107–115.
[8] This applies in particular with respect to *pure ecological damage*, as defined in the next paragraph.

victim can claim damages according to the general rules, as set out in the previous chapters.[9]
- An environmental good may be harmed independently of any injury to a legally protected right or interest of a private party. This second category of damage is usually called *ecological* or *pure ecological damage*.[10]

In both situations, the particular expertise and determination of environmental associations may be used to efficiently claim compensation for damage done to natural resources.

Standing in private law. In private law, most jurisdictions traditionally require a person to be injured in his or her *own legally protected right or interest* to qualify for a claim. Many natural assets, however, do not belong to any particular individual. With respect to potential claims by environmental associations for damage done to natural resources (such as the killing of the rare protected bird in the above scenario), three particular key issues thus need to be addressed:

- Do environmental associations have standing to bring a claim in compensation for damage done to public goods and, if so, under which conditions?
- Which kind of damage can they claim compensation for in cases in which natural resources are impaired?
- How is this damage measured in monetary terms?

The present chapter focuses on private law remedies that environmental non-profit associations can enforce against persons who have caused damage to the environment.[11]

---

9 See e.g. the cases of the *Swiss* Federal Supreme Court of Justice: ATF 109 II 304 (an aluminium factory emits fluorine, polluting the air and causing damage to apricot trees owned by farmers); ATF 116 II 480 (an accident in a nuclear power plant leads to the radioactive contamination of the environment; consumers buy fewer vegetables, suspected to be contaminated, hereby causing farmers to lose income [Chernobyl case]).

10 *Ökologischer Schaden* or *rein ökologischer Schaden*; *dommage écologique* or *dommage pûrement écologique*, or in other terms: *dommage à l'environnement proprement dit* or *dommage environnemental au sens strict*.

11 In contrast with these remedies, US *citizen suits* have the aim of obliging public authorities to enforce environmental laws or to issue civil penalties or fines against polluters. See e.g. J. H. ADLER, Stand or Deliver: Citizen Suits, Standing, and Environmental Protection, *Duke Envtl. L. & Pol'y F.* 2001, 39; XIAO ZHU/CHARLES WHARTON, The Development of Legal Standing within Chinese Environmental Social Organizations and an American Comparative Perspective, *China Legal Sci.* 2013, 76 at 86 ff.

A similar approach was eventually chosen by the EU. See EU Directive 2004/35/CE of 21st April 2004 on environmental liability with regard to the prevention and remedying of environmental damage (Environmental Liability Directive), *OJ*, L 143, 30.04.2004, p. 56. According to the Directive, rights shall be given to require the remedial of environmental damage, or to remedy such damage and claim the costs of such measures, to "competent authorities" only. Interested natural or legal persons, and in particular "non-governmental organisations promoting environmental protection", are thus limited to request action by the "competent authorities". They are not in a position to bring a claim against the responsible person themselves under the Directive, see Art. 12 (Request for action) and Art. 3 (3) of the Directive: "Without prejudice to relevant national legislation, this Directive shall not give private parties a right of compensation as a consequence of environmental damage or of an imminent threat of such damage." See also Recital 25: "Persons adversely affected or likely to be adversely affected by environmental damage should be entitled to ask the competent authority to take action. [...]".

Questions

1) To be able to bring a claim before courts in private law, the *Swiss* Federal Act on Civil Procedure (*Code de procédure civile*) requires the claimant to have an "interest worthy of protection" (*un intérêt digne de protection*).[12]

   a) How did the non-profit environmental association in the *Republic V* case argue its right to *claim damages* for the shooting of the bird?

   b) Why did the foundation's claim fail? What does this reveal about the limits of traditional tort liability rules with respect to damage to public goods, and in particular to the environment?

2) If the foundation were granted standing before the civil courts (as defenders of the public interest in the environment), the second question would be whether it has suffered damage. In Swiss law, damage is defined as an "involuntary reduction of one's patrimony". In most jurisdictions, including Switzerland, it is thus difficult to recover expenses that have been "frustrated" (i.e. made useless) by a damaging event.[13] The reason is that these expenses would have been made anyway and were not induced by the tortious act.

   In view of the second Swiss case reproduced in the materials, do you think that the claim of the environmental association in the case of *Republic V* would have stood a better chance of success with regard to the issue of damage, had it been framed as a claim for the costs necessary to reintroduce another bearded vulture, rather than a claim in compensation for the money the association had already spent raising *Republic V*?

3) According to the *Dutch* Civil Code, an action in tort requires, in principle, a violation of the right of another person, which causes this other person to suffer damage. In addition to this, in 1994, the Dutch legislator introduced, in the Civil Code, the possibility of bringing a claim in the public interest. These include so-called group or class actions as well as pure public interest actions (*algemeenbelangacties* or *actio popularis*).

   a) What is the difference between these two forms of action?

   b) The provision of the Dutch Civil Code on public interest-related civil claims explicitly excludes damage claims. Why was the damage claim brought by an environmental association in the Dutch *Borcea* case nevertheless successful (and would be equally successful today)?

---

12 Article 59 (2) CPC. For actions of associations, see Art. 89 CPC ("*Action des organisations/Verbandsklage*") which grants a limited right for private associations and foundations to bring a claim when personality rights of their members are violated ("Les associations et les autres organisations d'importance nationale ou régionale qui sont habilitées aux termes de leurs statuts à défendre les intérêts d'un groupe de personnes déterminé peuvent, en leur propre nom, agir pour l'atteinte à la personnalité des membres de ce groupe."/ "Vereine und andere Organisationen von gesamtschweizerischer oder regionaler Bedeutung, die nach ihren Statuten zur Wahrung der Interessen bestimmter Personengruppen befugt sind, können in eigenem Namen auf Verletzung der Persönlichkeit der Angehörigen dieser Personengruppen klagen.") The associations can claim that an injunction against an ongoing violation be granted, that a violation be removed or that the court issues a statement confirming the illegality of the injury. Damage claims, on the contrary, can only be brought by members who suffered injury in their own rights.

13 See *Digest II*, nos. 16/2–30, in particular 16/30: Comparative Report (H. Koziol); T. Schobel (ed.), *Der Ersatz frustrierter Aufwendungen. Vermögens- und Nichtvermögensschäden im österreichischen und deutschen Recht*, Vienna: Springer, 2003.

c) In the bearded vulture scenario, could the association's claim succeed under Dutch law? How would you argue the case if you were acting as the association's lawyer?

4) In 2013, the *Belgian Cour de cassation* rendered a leading judgment on the standing of environmental associations to bring *damage claims* following the infringement of environmental interests. In a 2016 case that was ultimately brought before the Belgian Constitutional Court, the lower court had granted standing to an environmental association, hereby following the reasoning of the 2013 *Cour de cassation* decision.

   a) What were the arguments for granting standing to associations?

   b) What type of damage did the Belgian courts allow the association to claim compensation for? How was the compensation measured in monetary terms? Which clarification did the Constitutional Court bring to Belgian law in this regard?

5) *French* courts have always been particularly receptive to claims brought by environmental protection associations. In the 1982 case of *Centre ornithologique Rhône-Alpes c. association communale de chasse agréée de Saint-Martial (Ardèche)*, which category of damage was the environmental association awarded compensation for?

6) In the *Erika* case of 2008–12, the French courts were particularly concerned with different categories of environmental damage.

   a) Which categories of damage was the environmental association awarded compensation for, and which amounts were awarded for each category?

   b) Which of these categories of damage may fall under the new Arts. 1246 ff. of the French *Code civil* (as of October 2016), and which may remain governed by Arts. 1240 ff. (former Arts. 1382 ff.)?

7) What would be your suggested solution to the *Republic V* case under French law? Compare with Swiss, Dutch, and Belgian law.

8) Over the last two decades, *China* has enacted a large number of modern codifications, including the Civil Procedure Law Act (1991), the Tort Law Act (2009), and – in the particular field covered by the present chapter – the Environmental Protection Law Act (2014). In addition, the Supreme People's Court has issued precise and detailed guidelines on the interpretation of many laws, which have binding effect on the courts in China. The Civil Procedure Law Act together with the Environmental Protection Law Act allow "social organisations" to bring a claim before the courts following pollution of the environment, and the Tort Law Act explicitly addresses the issue of damage to the environment.

   a) What are the conditions environmental associations have to fulfil in order to have standing? Compare with the requirements existing in the European jurisdictions provided in the materials.

   b) Which are the remedies available for environmental associations, and what exactly can they require according to the above-mentioned laws and the relevant interpretations by the Supreme People's Court?

9) The European Group of Tort Law is considering updating and amending the PETL. Would you suggest adding a provision on liability for damage to the environment, natural resources, or ecological damage? Explain.

10) How would you argue the case in the scenario under the proposal reproduced in the annex?

Table of contents

I. Switzerland
1. Loi fédérale sur la protection de l'environnement/Bundesgesetz über den Umweltschutz (*Federal Act on the Protection of the Environment*), Art. 55 (1) – (3) .... p. 507
2. Loi fédérale sur la chasse et la protection des mammifères et oiseaux sauvages/ Bundesgesetz über die Jagd und den Schutz wildlebender Säugetiere und Vögel (*Federal Act on hunting and the protection of wild mammals and birds*), Art. 23 .... p. 508
3. Code des obligations/Obligationenrecht (*Code of Obligations*), Art. 41 .... p. 508
4. Tribunal fédéral/Bundesgericht (*Federal Supreme Court of Justice*), 20.02.2004 (*La Fondation X.* c. *La Masse en faillite de feu A.*), 4C.317/2002 .... p. 508
5. Tribunal fédéral/Bundesgericht (*Federal Supreme Court of Justice*), 15.12.1964 (*Etats de Fribourg et de Vaud* c. *Fibres de verre SA et Höganäsmetoder A.B.*), ATF 90 II 417 .... p. 511

II. The Netherlands
1. Burgerlijk Wetboek (*Civil Code*), Arts. 6:162, 3:305a (1) and (3) .... p. 512
2. BERTHY VAN DEN BROEK/LIESBETH ENNEKING, Public interest litigation in the Netherlands, *Utrecht L. Rev.* 2014, 77–90 .... p. 513
3. Rechtbank Rotterdam (*Rotterdam Court of First Instance*), 15.03.1991, NJ 1992, 91 (*Borcea case*) .... p. 515

III. Belgium
1. Code civil (*Civil Code*), Art. 1382 .... p. 516
2. Cour de cassation/Hof van Cassatie (*Court of Cassation*), 11.06.2013 (*P. P. et P. S. L. V.* c. *L'inspecteur régional de l'urbanisme et Milieusteunpunt Huldenberg, association sans but lucratif*), NDEG P. 12.1389.N, Pas. 2013, I, 361 .... p. 516
3. Cour constitutionnelle (*Constitutional Court*), 21.01.2016, F-20160121–1, 7/2016 .... p. 517

IV. France
1. Code civil (*Civil Code*), Art. 1240 (former Art. 1382) .... p. 519
2. Code de l'environnement (*Code on the environment*), Arts. L141–1 (1) and (4), L142–2 .... p. 519
3. Cour de cassation (*Court of Cassation*), 16.11.1982 (*Centre ornithologique Rhône-Alpes* c. *association communale de chasse agréée de Saint-Martial, Ardèche*), n° 81–15.550, Bull. 1982.1.282, n° 331, R.J.E. 1984, 225 .... p. 520

4. *Erika* case:
   a) Tribunal de Grande Instance de Paris (*High Court of Paris*), 16.01.2008, aff. n° 9934895010 .... p. 522
   b) Cour d'Appel de Paris (*Appellate Court of Paris*), 30.03.2010, aff. n° 08/02278 .... p. 523
   c) Cour de cassation, chambre criminelle (*Court of Cassation, Criminal Chamber*), 25.09.2012, n° 10–82.938, arrêt n° 3439 .... p. 524
5. Code civil (*Civil Code*, as of October 2016), Arts. 1246–1249, 1251 .... p. 524
6. MEMLOUK MALIK, La loi n° 2016–1087 du 8 août 2016 et la réparation du préjudice écologique (*Law n°2016–1087 of 8th August 2016 and the restoration of ecological damage*), BDEI 2016, 30–38 .... p. 526

V. People's Republic of China

1. 中华人民共和国侵权责任法 (*Tort Law Act*), Art. 65 .... p. 527
2. 中华人民共和国民事诉讼法 (*Civil Procedure Law Act*), Art. 55 .... p. 527
3. 中华人民共和国环境保护法 (*Environmental Protection Law Act*), Arts. 58, 64 .... p. 528
4. Supreme People's Court, 最高人民法院关于审理环境民事公益诉讼案件适用法律若干问题的解释 (*Interpretation of the Supreme People's Court on Several Issues concerning the Application of Law in the Conduct of Environmental Civil Public Interest Litigations*), Interpretation No. 1 [2015], Arts. 1, 2, 8, 11, 13, 14, 18, 20, 23, 24, 25, 29 .... p. 529

VI. Principles of European Tort Law and Draft Common Frame of Reference

BÉNÉDICT WINIGER/HELMUT KOZIOL/BERNHARD A. KOCH/REINHARD ZIMMERMANN (eds.), *Digest of European Tort Law, Vol. II: Essential Cases on Damage*, Berlin: De Gruyter, 2011, nos. 23/29/1 ff. (by THOMAS KADNER GRAZIANO) .... p. 531

VII. Annex: a 1995 proposal for reform

THOMAS KADNER GRAZIANO, *Der Ersatz ökologischer Schäden – Ansprüche von Umweltverbänden (Compensation for Ecological Damage – Remedies for Environmental Associations)*, Berlin: Duncker & Humblot, 1995, pp. 318–322 .... p. 533

Materials[14]

I. Switzerland

Several Swiss laws provide environmental associations with the right to bring a claim (i.e. to have *standing*) in administrative procedures that might have an impact on the environment. See for example:

1. Loi fédérale sur la protection de l'environnement (*Federal Act on the Protection of the Environment*)

Section 2. Recours des organisations contre les décisions concernant des installations

Art. 55. Organisations ayant qualité pour recourir. (1) Une organisation de protection de l'environnement a qualité pour recourir contre les décisions des autorités cantonales ou fédérales relatives à la planification, à la construction ou à la modification d'installations soumises aux dispositions sur l'étude d'impact [. . .] aux conditions suivantes:
   a. l'organisation est active au niveau national;
   b. l'organisation poursuit un but non lucratif; les éventuelles activités économiques servent le but non lucratif.
(2) L'organisation a le droit de recourir uniquement dans les domaines du droit visés depuis dix ans au moins par ses statuts.
(3) Le Conseil fédéral désigne les organisations qui ont qualité pour recourir. [. . .]

Translation

Section 2. Appeals brought by associations against planning decisions

Art. 55. Associations with the right of appeal [standing]. (*1*) *An environmental protection association is granted the right of appeal [i.e. has standing in administrative and court proceedings] in relation to any decision taken by the cantonal or federal authorities to plan, construct, or alter any installation for which the law requires an environmental impact assessment [. . .] subject the following requirements:*
   a. the association must operate nationally;
   b. the association must operate on a non-profit basis; economic activities in which it is engaged shall not be carried out in order to make a profit.
(2) The right of appeal shall be granted exclusively to associations which have acted for ten years or more in the domain as set out in their statutes of association.
(3) The Federal Government is to designate which associations have the right of appeal [standing]. [. . .]

---

14 For the original language versions of the materials reproduced in this chapter, see the companion website at www.routledge.com/9781138567733.

2. Loi fédérale sur la chasse et la protection des mammifères et oiseaux sauvages (*Federal Law on Hunting and the Protection of Wild Mammals and Birds*)

> **Art. 23. Dommages-intérêts.** Le locataire de la chasse, dans les régions où la chasse est affermée, le canton ou la commune, dans les autres régions, ont le droit d'exiger la réparation du dommage causé par un délit de chasse ou par une contravention. Pour le reste, les dispositions du code des obligations sur les actes illicites sont applicables.

Translation

> *Art. 23. Compensation. A tenant of land leased for hunting, or else the relevant canton or municipality, is entitled to request compensation for any damage incurred as a result of a violation of the present Act or relevant criminal provisions. In all other respects, the relevant provisions of the Code of Obligations on unlawful acts shall apply.*

3. Code des obligations (*Code of Obligations*)

> **Art. 41.** (1) Celui qui cause, d'une manière illicite, un dommage à autrui, soit intentionnellement, soit par négligence ou imprudence, est tenu de le réparer.
> (2) Celui qui cause intentionnellement un dommage à autrui par des faits contraires aux mœurs est également tenu de le réparer.

Translation

> *Art. 41. (1) Whoever unlawfully causes damage to another, whether wilfully or negligently, is obliged to provide compensation.*
> *(2) Whoever wilfully causes damage to another in an immoral manner is likewise obliged to provide compensation.*

4. Tribunal fédéral/Bundesgericht (*Federal Supreme Court of Justice*), 20.02.2004 (*La Fondation X. c. La Masse en faillite de feu A.*), 4C.317/2002

Facts

A. On 4th November 1997, B. shot down the bearded vulture *Republic V* during a hunt in an alpine pasture near Montana [in Valais, Switzerland].

B. was convicted of an offence under [. . .] the Protection and Hunting of Wild Birds and Mammals Act (hereinafter, the Protection and Hunting Act), and sentenced [. . .] to 10 days imprisonment, which was suspended for a 2-year period. His hunting licence was taken away from him for 1 year. The State of Valais launched a civil action within these criminal proceedings [. . .]. B. thereafter settled to pay a sum of CHF 20,000 to "compensate the loss of the bearded vulture", and the State of Valais withdrew their civil action.

B. The bearded vulture was hunted to near-extinction during the 19th century, officially disappearing from the Valais region in late February 1886. In the 1970s, the bird of prey was reintroduced into the Alps. [. . .] Between 1987 and 1995, 14 vultures were confirmed as having been sighted in the canton, among them Republic V, who was 5 years of age at the time of its death. [. . .]

Foundation X. (hereinafter, the Foundation) [. . .] heads an international project [. . .], supported by a mixture of public and private funding. Its goal is to repopulate the Alps with these birds. It coordinates exchanges with around 30 different zoological parks engaging in worldwide breeding programmes. Each year, it decides which of the birds in its project are to be reintroduced into the wild, and then, under its authority, the young are released into 1 of 4 designated sites in the Alps. [. . .] Their movements are then tracked on a regular basis by a volunteer observer network deployed across the Alps. By 2002, more than 100 bearded vultures had been reintroduced into the wild [among which Republic V].

C. On 12th May 2000, the Foundation brought a claim against B. in the amount of CHF 118,000 [. . .] to compensate the funds invested in Republic V. [. . .] [T]he second chamber of the Cantonal Court of Valais dismissed the claim. [. . .]

The Federal Supreme Court reasons:

[. . .] 2. This is an action for damages on the basis of an unlawful act [. . .].

3. The primary reason for which the Cantonal Court discarded the plaintiff's plea was that the latter did not have standing [*la qualité pour agir*]. [. . .]

As far as the conditions of extra-contractual liability are concerned, the question of standing is intertwined with the unlawfulness of the incriminating act [. . .]. Conduct is unlawful if it is contrary to a general duty, either because it infringes an absolute right of the injured party, or because it violates an injunction or legal provision which, whether contained within the written law or not, acts to safeguard the interest that was harmed [. . .]. Absolute rights include life and bodily integrity, personality rights, and both material and immaterial property rights [. . .]. Rules on the required conduct derive from the full body of Swiss law and may be written or unwritten, private or public, federal or cantonal [. . .].

4. – 4.1 The plaintiff, quite rightly, does not claim any kind of *right in rem* [i.e. property right] over the vulture. According to the learned trial judges [. . .], Republic V had been living in its natural habitat when it was shot down; the Foundation had, under its project to reintroduce the species, released the bird so that it could live in its natural habitat. Yet, the jurisprudence of the court is clear that wild animals are to be considered *res nullius* [i.e. belonging to no-one] [. . .]. [. . .]

4.2 The plaintiff's appeal first relies upon the applicable rules on possession. The Foundation asserts that while Republic V was indeed a *res nullius*, belonging to no-one, the

Foundation was nevertheless able to lawfully capture the bird at any given moment for scientific or health-related reasons without requiring any additional authorisation. In the plaintiff's view, such authority had the effect of affording it *de jure* control over bearded vultures, supported by the fact that such birds do not display a tendency to become frightened when around humans, evidence of its prior captivity.

This plea must be rejected. [. . .] The contested judgment outlines that the act whereby the Foundation released Republic V into the wild was a voluntary one, aimed at allowing the bird to live in its natural habitat [. . .]. This finding alone [. . .] ultimately dooms this plea to failure. Possession requires not only effective control of the object, but also implies a subjective will to possess such object [. . .]. [. . .]

5. – 5.1 Secondly, the Foundation is claiming a breach of Art. 23 of the Protection and Hunting Act, a provision whereby a tenant of land leased for hunting, or else the relevant canton or municipality, is entitled to request compensation for any damage incurred as a result of a violation of the present Act or relevant criminal provisions, specifying that Code of Obligations provisions on unlawful acts are otherwise applicable. The Foundation claims that wildlife sustainability and diversification are afforded a privileged status of protection under the Swiss legal system, one which is ingrained in the Federal Constitution (Art. 78 of the Constitution[15]) [. . .], and further affirms that the reintroduction of species into the wild is an act which serves the public interest, one which the State can perform itself or assign to a third party. [. . .]

According to the plaintiff, Art. 23 of the Protection and Hunting Act does not enable the State to claim a right in rem over all wild animals [. . .]; rather Art. 23 protects the State in its capacity as "administrator of the wildlife" ("*gestionnaire de la faune*"). The legislator hereby intended to impose a compensation requirement on those offenders responsible for the hunt independent of the property law regime applicable to the animal in question, taking into account the major expenditure associated with managing, and potentially breeding, wildlife. Given that the Foundation was required to obtain a permit to release vultures into the wild, the former could accordingly [. . .] be considered responsible for "wildlife management". For this reason, the economic interest of the Foundation in repopulating vultures is, according to its argument, protected by an analogous application of Art. 23 of the Protection and Hunting Act. [. . .] The Foundation thus argues that there is an omission in the text of Art. 23: had the federal legislator had in mind the role of associations participating in the reintroduction of wild species, he would have [. . .] provided them with a remedy to claim damages for illegal hunting.

5.2 In Keller's view [. . .], the legislator introduced Art. 23 of the Protection and Hunting Act so as to counter the issue that nobody has a right in rem over wild animals. [. . .] According to the official explanatory comments to this provision by the Federal Government, the compensation provision was primarily intended to serve as a means of obtaining a replacement for the illegally hunted species [. . .]. Associations for the protection of nature and of birds were involved in the drafting of the Act [. . .]. [. . .] Under these circumstances, the court cannot follow the plaintiff's interpretation of Art. 23 of the Protection and Hunting Act, whereby it argues that the absence of a reference to environmental protection associations

---

15 Art. 78 (Protection of natural and cultural heritage) provides (in English translation): "[. . .] (4) [The Confederation] shall protect endangered species from extinction. [. . .]".

is an unintended omission by the legislator and a gap that needs to be filled by granting standing to all persons or associations involved in wildlife management.

The Court is even less willing to accept that there is an unintended omission and a gap that the courts should fill, given that in the past few decades the legislator has consistently considered the issue of whether associations for the protection of animals, and more generally of nature, should have standing in this area. [. . .]

The trial judges cited Art. 40 of the French Act on the Protection of Nature of 10th July 1976 (*Loi française du 10 juillet 1976 relative à la protection de la nature*),[16] which allows any authorised association – e.g. the French Bird Protection Association (*Ligue française pour la protection des oiseaux*), the Savoy Ornithological Group (*Groupe ornithologique Savoyard*) etc. – to exercise the same rights as those granted to applicants in civil proceedings for an offence against a protected animal species where such act directly or indirectly harms the collective interest which they are set up to defend; the judges rightly noted that our law contains no analogous provision. [. . .] It is also worth noting in relation to France that the notion of "an association suffering personal harm" ("*préjudice subi personnellement par l'association*") has in the past been broadly interpreted by the courts [which in one case, for example, led the 1st Civil Chamber of the *Cour de cassation* to admit that an ornithological organisation committed to protecting migratory birds suffered non-material personal harm as a result of the fault committed by the organiser of a hunt in which a rare species of bird was shot down (Bull. cass. 1982.1.282 n° 331)[17]]. Such a broad interpretation acts to entrust certain legal persons with the task of defending the collective interest; such a wide and general task has in the past been considered as granting an implied right of action [and standing before the courts] otherwise not provided in law [Geneviève Viney, L'action d'intérêt collectif et le droit de l'environnement, pp. 12–13 [. . .]]. However, these solutions in [French] case law are not consistent with the present state of [Swiss] legislation. [. . .]

It follows from the above that in not affording the plaintiff standing for bringing a claim for compensation under Art. 23 of the Protection and Hunting Act, the cantonal court did not violate federal law.

6. Recognising that the plaintiff did not have standing to bring a claim, the Court shall not proceed to examine the further arguments relating to the tort law concept of "damage" [. . .].

For these reasons, the Federal Supreme Court of Justice holds: 1. The appeal is rejected. [. . .]

5. Tribunal fédéral/Bundesgericht (*Federal Supreme Court of Justice*), 15.12.1964 (*Etats de Fribourg et de Vaud c. Fibres de verre SA et Höganäsmetoder A.B.*), ATF 90 II 417

Summary of the facts

A. – [The defendant accidentally discharged contaminants into a river.] These [. . .] substances then killed all fish along a 23 kilometre stretch of the river [. . .]. The cantonal fishing authorities estimated that 74,200 kg of dead fish were later retrieved.

---

16 This provision has since been replaced in *French* law by the provisions below, pp. 519–520.
17 See below, pp. 520–521.

Following the spill, the cantons of Fribourg and Vaud took measures to replace the poisoned fish. [. . .]

[. . .] [T]he two cantons [are now seeking] [. . .] CHF 88,000 in restocking costs [. . .]. [. . .]

Extract from the court's reasoning:

[. . .] II. The scope of damages [. . .] 3. [. . .] The present legal proceedings have been brought as a civil action [. . .]. [. . .] [A]ccording to the relevant rules of private law, damage consists in a reduction in net wealth, in other words, the difference between the patrimony currently held by the injured party and his patrimony had the harmful event not taken place [. . .]. [. . .]

In the present case, irrespective of the expenses the plaintiff actually incurred [on these expenses, see below, 5.], the latter cannot be said to have suffered the type of damage defined above [. . .]. Firstly, the plaintiffs were not the owners of the poisoned fish, and secondly, they did not exercise any kind of right over them which could be equated with a property right [. . .]. Therefore, the plaintiffs cannot rely on the argument that they were injured in a property right [. . .]. Without injury to a property right [. . .], the plaintiffs cannot claim to have suffered a reduction of patrimony in proportion to the monetary value of the poisoned fish.

4. The plaintiff cantons cannot reclaim the monetary value of the poisoned fish [. . .] [because] they were not [. . .] the owners of the [. . .] fish which were killed. [. . .]

5. Subsidiarily, the plaintiffs are claiming [. . .] CHF 88,000 in restocking costs. Accordingly, the Court must consider whether the cantons are entitled to recover these expenses.

[. . .] Here, the plaintiffs' reduction in patrimony is substantial, a fact which is not disputed by the defendants. Nevertheless, the latter may only be held liable for this loss insofar as there exists an adequate causal link, in other words, the loss must have occurred with protection of a valid public interest in mind. This condition is fulfilled. [. . .] [I]n looking to replenish a natural resource [. . .] which is under the protection of the federal and cantonal authorities [. . .], the plaintiffs did indeed act [. . .] in the public interest. For this reason, their claim can generally be deemed valid insofar as the plaintiff is requesting the funds required to restore the resource to its previous state [. . .]. [This Court arrives to the conclusion that] the cost of the [fish] must be compensated in its entirety [. . .].

II. The Netherlands

1. Burgerlijk Wetboek (*Civil Code*)

Art. 6:162. (1) Hij die jegens een ander een onrechtmatige daad pleegt, welke hem kan worden toegerekend, is verplicht de schade die de ander dientengevolge lijdt, te vergoeden.
(2) Als onrechtmatige daad worden aangemerkt een inbreuk op een recht en een doen of nalaten in strijd met een wettelijke plicht of met hetgeen volgens ongeschreven recht in het maatschappelijk verkeer betaamt, een en ander behoudens de aanwezigheid van een rechtvaardigingsgrond.

(3) Een onrechtmatige daad kan aan de dader worden toegerekend, indien zij te wijten is aan zijn schuld of aan een oorzaak welke krachtens de wet of de in het verkeer geldende opvattingen voor zijn rekening komt.

Art. 3:305a. (1) Een stichting of vereniging met volledige rechtsbevoegdheid kan een rechtsvordering instellen die strekt tot bescherming van gelijksoortige belangen van andere personen, voorzover zij deze belangen ingevolge haar statuten behartigt. [. . .]
(3) Een rechtsvordering als bedoeld in lid 1 [. . .] kan niet strekken tot schadevergoeding te voldoen in geld. [. . .]

Translation

Art. 6:162. (1) A person who commits an unlawful act against another person that can be attributed to him or her, must repair the damage that this other person has suffered as a result thereof.
(2) As a tortious act is regarded a violation of someone else's right and an act or omission in violation of a duty imposed by law or of what according to unwritten law has to be regarded as proper social conduct, always as far as there was no justification for this behaviour.
(3) An unlawful act can be attributed to the person committing it if it results from his or her fault or from a cause for which he or she is accountable by virtue of law or by generally accepted common opinion.

Art. 3:305a. (1) A foundation or association with full legal capacity that, according to its articles of association, has the objective to protect specific interests, may bring to court a legal claim that intents to protect similar interests of other persons. [. . .]
(3) A legal claim as meant in paragraph 1 [. . .] cannot be filed in order to obtain compensatory damages. [. . .]

2. BERTHY VAN DEN BROEK/LIESBETH ENNEKING, Public Interest Litigation in the Netherlands, *Utrecht L. Rev.* 2014, 77–90

3. Public interest litigation before the Dutch civil courts: possibilities and limitations

3.1. Public interest-related civil claims

In the literature on Dutch civil procedural law, it has been recognized that one of the most important tendencies over the past century has been the increase in 'collective actions' pursued before the Dutch civil courts by a growing number of private law and public law interest groups in the Netherlands. These collective actions encompass two related but distinct types of actions: group actions and public interest actions (the latter are sometimes referred to as '*algemeenbelangacties*'). In group actions, the persons whose interests are sought to be promoted can be individualized. In public interest actions, by contrast, this is not possible since the interests at stake are of such a general nature that they concern many or potentially all members of society. It is these public interest actions that fall within the category of cases that are described in this article as public interest litigation, or, more specifically, public interest-related claims aimed at protecting environmental interests.

Over the past few decades, Dutch civil courts have on various occasions been confronted with public interest actions. A well-known example is a case in which a number of environmental organisations sued the city council of Amsterdam in pursuit of a judicial prohibition of the unlicensed dumping of (polluted) dredging from the Amsterdam canals into a nature reserve outside Amsterdam. [. . .]

3.2. Conditions for admissibility

In response to the increasing popularity of collective actions and a growing need for clarity surrounding the conditions under which such actions could be brought before the Dutch civil courts, in 1994 a separate provision was introduced into the Dutch Civil Code (DCC) (*Burgerlijk Wetboek*) dealing with collective actions (including both group and public interest actions): Article 3:305a DCC. [. . .] The provision's main objectives are to ensure a more effective or a more efficient legal protection of the collective interests involved [. . .].

According to Article 3:305a DCC, there are three basic conditions that need to be met in order for a collective action (or, more specifically: a public interest action) to be admissible. Firstly, the organisation initiating the action has to be a foundation or association with full legal capacity. Secondly, it must be clear from the articles of the foundation or the constitution of the association and from the activities it employs that (part of) its institutional objective is the promotion of the interests it seeks to further through the collective action. It should be noted that civil courts will generally be lenient when interpreting organisations' articles of association in this context, particularly if the pursuit of the action is likely to further the provision's main objectives of more effective and efficient legal protection and a reduction of claims. And, thirdly, the interests sought to be promoted must be analogous so as to be suitable for promotion through the collective action.

3.3. Possible claims

[. . .] An important restriction inherent in the Dutch collective action procedure of Article 3:305a DCC is the fact that because it involves legal actions by organisations representing the interests of others, it cannot be used to claim monetary compensation for the harm suffered. This does not necessarily exclude all types of financial claims, however; an example is a claim for the recovery of costs that the organisation itself has incurred in order to prevent or reduce (further) harm from occurring, as would be the case for instance when an environmental organisation takes action to save sea birds following an oil spill.[18] Also, the restriction leaves open the possibility of filing other types of claims seeking, for instance, declaratory judgments or injunctions ordering the defendant to take action or to cease certain activities, like illegal dumping of waste materials. It should be noted in this respect that a parliamentary motion seeking to lift the ban on monetary compensation in a collective action on the basis of Article 3:305a DCC was accepted in 2011 and is now being converted into a legal bill proposing an amendment to this article that will make it possible to claim monetary compensation in future collective actions.

Pending this amendment,[19] environmental NGOs seeking to bring public interest-related claims before civil courts [under Article 3:305a DCC] remain limited to claims seeking

---

18 *Note by the author*: see the *Borcea* case below, pp. 515–516.
19 On 16 November 2016, a legislative proposal to amend Art. 3:305a was sent to Parliament, see: Tweede Kamer der Staten-Generaal 2 Vergaderjaar 2016–2017, Nr. 2, 34 608, Wijziging van het Burgerlijk Wetboek en het Wetboek van Burgerlijke Rechtsvordering teneinde de afwikkeling van massaschade in een collectieve actie mogelijk te maken (*Amendment of the Civil Code and the Code of Civil Procedure in order to enable the settlement of mass damage in a collective action*). In early 2018, the amendment was still pending.

declaratory judgments holding that another actor is liable for environmental harm that has resulted from a particular activity (potentially followed by separate proceedings for the determination of damages) and/or claims seeking mandatory or prohibitory injunctions for imminent or ongoing polluting activities. [. . .]

3. Rechtbank Rotterdam (*Rotterdam Court of first instance*), 15.03.1991, NJ 1992, 91 (*Borcea case*)

Dutch Society for the Protection of Birds, a non-profit organisation based in Zeist (the plaintiff) [. . .],

against

Intreprindera de Exploatara a Floti Maritime Navrom, based in Constanţa (Romania) and incorporated under Romanian law (the defendant) [. . .].

Judgment

[. . .] On 4th January 1988, the hull of the bulk carrier *Borcea* was breached on the front-left side during a journey on the North Sea and around 75 m³ of oil leaked through a crack in the bottom of a bunker tank. As a result, the waters of the North Sea off the coast of Zeeland and South Holland and along the coastline became seriously contaminated by oil. The most serious damage was caused on 8th January 1988 when the slick reached Goeree-Overflakkee beach, between Brouwersdam and Ouddorp Lighthouse. Thousands of heavily oil-coated seabirds were later found on several beaches in the provinces of Zeeland and South Holland.

The defendant is the owner and operator of the *Borcea*. [. . .]

The plaintiff has as its statutory aim the protection of wild birds. In response to the *Borcea* oil spill, the plaintiff coordinated with bird sanctuaries and shelters to collect any oiled birds from the beaches, and subsequently incurred substantial costs collecting, cleaning, caring, sheltering, and eventually releasing the birds into the wild again. The *Dutch Association for Nature Conservation* has incurred similar costs. The aforementioned bird sanctuaries, bird shelters, and the *Dutch Association for Nature Conservation* have adjoined their claims to that of the plaintiff. [. . .]

The admissibility of the claim
Although seabirds have no link to any particular country and cannot be considered as belonging to any one person, it is in the general view of modern Dutch society that their conservation and protection is a valid public interest worthy of protection.

Given the mission of the plaintiff's association and the (undisputed) activities it has carried out in this respect for over 90 years, this public interest is also to be regarded as the plaintiff's own individual interest; consequently, if such interest is infringed, the plaintiff can not only require an injunction but also has the right to claim compensation for any damage suffered in limiting the effects of such infringement.

There is no reason why the plaintiff should be entitled to an injunction to protect the [environmental] interest it defends, but then be barred from claiming compensation from the responsible party for any subsequent loss it suffers or costs it incurs in limiting or preventing the effects resulting from the infringement. The plaintiff's claim is therefore admissible to the extent that it relates to the actual harm suffered. [. . .]

III. Belgium

1. Code civil (*Civil Code*)

> Art. 1382. Tout fait quelconque de l'homme, qui cause à autrui un dommage, oblige celui par la faute duquel il est arrivé, à le réparer.

Translation

> *Art. 1382. Any act of a person, which causes damage to another, obliges the person by whose fault it occurred, to compensate it.*

2. Cour de cassation (*Court of Cassation*), 11.06.2013 (*P. P. et P. S. L. V. c. L'inspecteur régional de l'urbanisme et Milieusteunpunt Huldenberg, association sans but lucratif*), NDEG P. 12.1389.N, Pas. 2013, I, 361

On the first ground of appeal:

4. The combined effect of [a number of provisions of the Aarhus Convention] is that Belgium has undertaken to ensure that associations promoting environmental protection have access to justice when looking to challenge acts which contravene domestic environmental law provisions and omissions by private persons and public authorities, provided that the associations meet the criteria laid down in domestic law. These criteria shall not be explained or interpreted in such a way as to deny associations access to justice. The judge may interpret the criteria set out by domestic law in line with the objectives [. . .] of the Aarhus Convention.[20]

5. According to [. . .] the preliminary part of the Code of Criminal Procedure (*Code de procédure pénale*), a claim in compensation [in accordance with Art. 1382 of the Belgian *Code civil*] may be brought by any party which suffers damage. This party must show that it has an interest which has been directly harmed.

---

20 *Note by the author*: the UNECE Convention on Access to Information, Public Participation in Decision-making and Access to Justice in Environmental Matters (Aarhus Convention), done at Aarhus, Denmark, on 25 June 1998 (UN Treaty Series, Vol. 2161, p. 447), is in force in 47 European States, including all EU Member States and Switzerland; the EU is also Party to the Convention. For a status table, see https://treaties.un.org/Pages/ViewDetails.aspx?src=IND&mtdsg_no=XXVII-13&chapter=27&clang=_en.

In this case, the *Belgian Cour de cassation* cites Arts. 3(4), 9(3) and 2(4) of the Aarhus Convention. Ultimately, the Court opts for a broad interpretation of the provisions and of the State's obligations under the Aarhus Convention. Not all courts of the Contracting States to the Convention share the interpretation that the Aarhus Convention affords environmental protection associations a right to pursue a civil claim for compensation.

If such an action is brought by a legal entity (*personne morale*) which, under its Statute, has as its objective the protection of the environment and works to contest acts and omissions carried out by private persons and public authorities in contravention of domestic environmental law provisions, then this legal entity shall be deemed to have an interest in opening legal proceedings and thereby passes the test of admissibility [and has standing]. [. . .]

6. The appellate judges declared the action against the second defendant admissible on the following grounds: [. . .] – the wrongful environmental interference which led to a violation of the plaintiff's [. . .] interest [in proper regional planning] allows a claim to be brought under Article 1382 of the *Code civil* since it represents a breach of a legitimate interest of the plaintiff; [. . .] – it cannot be denied that the violation of the plaintiff's interest in proper regional planning by the second defendant resulted in immaterial harm to the objectives set out in the plaintiff's Statute, in consideration for example of the importance of the illegal constructions with regard to proper regional planning. Therefore this interference can be said to harm the immaterial interests of this legal entity.

For these reasons, the decision of the appellate judges whereby it accorded a right of action against the second defendant was founded on a correct legal basis. [. . .]

For these reasons, the Court
Rejects the appeal; [. . .]

3. Cour constitutionnelle (*Constitutional Court*), 21.01.2016, F-20160121–1, 7/2016

The Constitutional Court (*Cour constitutionnelle*), [. . .] after due consideration, renders the following judgment:

B.2. The judgment referred to this Court indicates that the plaintiff, a legal entity (*personne morale*) established to promote the protection of the environment or aspects thereof has brought a civil law claim before the criminal courts to claim damages for the defendant's violation of the collective interest – an interest which the association in question is set up by statute to defend – for damage to a number of wild bird species, that is, to an environmental resource which is *res nullius* (belongs to no-one). [. . .]

B.5. In the case pending before the court *a quo*,[21] the environmental protection association's action was declared admissible, the court citing a 2013 case decided by the *Cour de cassation*.[22] Furthermore, the court *a quo* found that an association such as this can indeed suffer non-material damage for any violation of a collective interest which it is set up to defend. The claim, along with the question referred to this Court, relate only to how damages are to be quantified. [. . .]

B.6.2. The court *a quo* found that Art. 1382 of the *Code civil* precludes non-pecuniary damages from being awarded in excess of the nominal sum of € 1 in situations where there

---

21 The Court in question is the Criminal Court of East Flanders (*Tribunal correctionnel de Flandre orientale*), Ghent division, which had referred the case to the Constitutional Court for a preliminary ruling. Belgian law provides that the Criminal Court can also award civil damages.
22 See above, pp. 516–517.

is a violation of a collective interest which the environmental protection association is set up to defend and damage is caused to an environmental resource which does not specifically belong to anyone (*res nullius*).

B.6.3. The court *a quo* stated the following reasons for its decision:

This damage is non-material and cannot be assessed by assigning a specific value to each bird affected by the attested incident. The birds were rightly qualified as *res nullius*. In the absence of any specific legal framework, the plaintiff's non-material interest in preserving the bird population can only be assessed in line with the interest which each and every citizen has in this preservation. Since the standard is that of the interest each and every citizen has in the preservation of natural heritage, the outcome must be that infringement of this non-material interest can only result in a nominal sum being awarded. If the courts were to award a plaintiff a substantial amount in compensation, such reparation would have to be decided on an arbitrary basis, which would not be viable in practice. Recognising that a right has suffered infringement, the Court thus awards non-pecuniary damages of € 1. [. . .].

[. . .] B.7.2. For damage to be compensated on the basis of Art. 1382 of the *Code civil*, it must have been caused "to another [person]" and, thus, must have personally affected the plaintiff in some way.

B.8.1. It is true that much like a legal entity set up to protect the environment, each and every citizen has an interest in preserving nature – in the present case preserving a wild bird population. Nevertheless, there is a key distinction to be drawn between the citizen and an association such as this as regards initiating civil proceedings to claim compensation for damage suffered to an environmental resource which is *res nullius* (belongs to no-one).

The ordinary citizen will generally not have any direct and personal interest in bringing a claim in compensation for injury to such interest, precisely because such environmental resources are *res nullius*. On the other hand, a legal entity (*personne morale*) which was explicitly set up to protect the environment may [. . .] indeed have suffered non-material harm and hence bring an action. [. . .]

B.9.1. Pursuant to Art. 1382 of the *Code civil*, the judge is obliged to assess the damage occasioned by an unlawful act *in concreto* but has the option of quantifying the damage in equity where it is impossible to otherwise determine.

B.9.2. The rules of equity require that such compensation be quantified in line with the facts insofar as is possible, even where the damage in question is of a non-material nature. With this in mind, the situation of a legal entity (*personne morale*) is no different to that of an individual (*personne physique*) suffering non-material harm; neither can be calculated with mathematical certainty. [. . .]

B. 10.1. Although it is impossible to precisely assess the damage occasioned when a person damages an environmental resource which is *res nullius*, and although the non-material harm suffered by the legal entity (*personne morale*) does not correspond to the actual ecological damage occasioned to the environment, this does not prevent the judge from assessing the non-material harm suffered by the environmental protection association *in concreto*. The judge may take into account, *inter alia*: the purposes of the association as set out in its statute, the importance of its activities, and the association's efforts to achieve its stated aims. The judge may also consider the seriousness of the harm to the environment when assessing the non-pecuniary damages to be awarded to the association.

B.10.2. The judge may very well decide in any given case, after examining the damage *in concreto*, that non-pecuniary damages of € 1 are sufficient. However, to interpret Art. 1382 of the *Code civil* as meaning that damages of more than € 1 are to be refused whenever a legal entity (*personne morale*) suffers infringement to its collective non-material interest, is to go against the requirements of this provision (namely, that damages be quantified *in concreto* and reparation be awarded in full) without having objective and reasonable grounds for doing so.

B.10.3. Placing a restriction such as this also disproportionately affects the interests of environmental protection associations which play an important role in defending the Constitutionally-protected right to a healthy environment.

B.11.1. Thus, by interpreting Art. 1382 of the *Code civil* in such a way as to prevent a legal entity (*personne morale*) acting on behalf of a collective interest (such as the protection of the environment or aspects thereof) from being able to claim damages in excess of a nominal sum of € 1 following the violation of the collective interest it was set up to defend, the Court acted contrary to the Constitution. [. . .]

IV. France

1. Code civil (*Civil Code*)

> **Art. 1240 (ancien art. 1382).** Tout fait quelconque de l'homme, qui cause à autrui un dommage, oblige celui par la faute duquel il est arrivé, à le réparer.

Translation

> *Art. 1240 (former Art. 1382). Any act of a person, which causes damage to another, obliges the person by whose fault it occurred, to compensate it.*

2. Code de l'environnement (*Environmental Code*)

> **Art. L. 141–1.** (1) Lorsqu'elles exercent leurs activités depuis au moins trois ans, les associations régulièrement déclarées et exerçant leurs activités statutaires dans le domaine de la protection de la nature et de la gestion de la faune sauvage, de l'amélioration du cadre de vie, de la protection de l'eau, de l'air, des sols, des sites et paysages, de l'urbanisme, ou ayant pour objet la lutte contre les pollutions et les nuisances et, d'une manière générale, œuvrant principalement pour la protection de l'environnement, peuvent faire l'objet d'un agrément motivé de l'autorité administrative. [. . .]

(4) Ces associations sont dites "associations agréées de protection de l'environnement". [...]

Art. L. 142–2. Les associations agréées [de protection de l'environnement] peuvent exercer les droits reconnus à la partie civile en ce qui concerne les faits portant un préjudice direct ou indirect aux intérêts collectifs qu'elles ont pour objet de défendre et constituant une infraction aux dispositions législatives relatives à la protection de la nature et de l'environnement, à l'amélioration du cadre de vie, à la protection de l'eau, de l'air, des sols, des sites et paysages, à l'urbanisme, ou ayant pour objet la lutte contre les pollutions et les nuisances, la sûreté nucléaire et la radioprotection [...].

Translation

Art. L. 141–1. (1) Any duly-registered environmental protection association which has been active for at least three years and has worked under the scope of its statute: to protect nature; to manage wildlife; to improve the living environment; to protect water, air, soil, sites of interest, and landscapes; to promote urban and regional planning; or to combat pollution and obtrusions; may be approved by the competent administrative authority. [...]

(4) These associations are to be called "approved environmental protection associations". [...]

Art. L. 142–2. Any approved [environmental protection] association may exercise the same rights as any party to civil proceedings should the facts at hand present a direct or indirect infringement of the collective interest which it is set up to protect and such infringement violate legislative provisions governing: the protection of nature and the environment; improvement of the living environment; protection of water, air, soil, sites of interest, and landscapes; promotion of urban and regional planning; or otherwise designed to combat pollution and obtrusions, or to improve nuclear safety or protection against radiation [...].

3. Cour de cassation (*Court of Cassation*), 16.11.1982 (*Centre ornithologique Rhône-Alpes c. association communale de chasse agréée de Sant-Martial, Ardèche*), n° 81–15.550, Bull. 1982.1.282 n° 331, R.J.E. 1984, 225

[...] Whereas the Rhône-Alps Ornithological Centre (R.A.O.C.) brought a claim against the Registered Municipal Hunting Association (R.M.H.A.) of the commune of Saint-Martial to compensate the loss suffered through the death of an osprey, a legally protected bird of prey which was shot down during a hunt on land protected by the R.A.O.C. [...]

Whereas the osprey, a legally protected bird of prey with a wingspan of 180cm, was also migrating for the season and was shot and fatally injured by one or more of the hunters;

Whereas the following police investigation failed to identify a suspect;

Whereas the R.A.O.C., whose activities include the study and protection of birds of prey, brought a claim against Saint-Martial R.M.H.A. to compensate the loss suffered through the death of the osprey, the trial court holding that the R.M.H.A. was indeed liable and ordering the association to pay 2,000 francs in compensation;

Whereas Saint-Martial R.M.H.A. is appealing the ruling on the grounds that the court accused the association, or the president of the association, of being at fault [. . .];

Whereas however, the [. . .] trial court discovered that during a period of intense migration for various species of bird (some of which are protected by law or regulation), the president of the R.M.H.A. permitted a large number of non-members to join the hunt for the day outside of the conditions set out in its statutes of association without taking down details, requesting evidence of a hunting permit, ascertaining their hunting knowledge, or taking any measure whatsoever to publish hunting guidelines in an effort to protect legally protected migratory birds from being shot; [. . .]

Whereas [. . .] the trial court was able to deduce from these findings that, given the misconduct *(faute)* of Saint-Martial R.M.H.A. or its president, the association is liable in tort;

As a consequence, this ground of appeal must be rejected in its entirety;

On the two arguments of the third ground of appeal: whereas Saint-Martial R.M.H.A. further appeals the decision of the trial court on the grounds that there was no causal link between its supposed misconduct *(faute)* and the loss which the R.A.O.C. alleges to have suffered [. . .];

Whereas however, having held that due to the purpose of the association, which is to study and protect migratory birds, the R.A.O.C. was directly concerned by any acts jeopardising species which it was committed to protecting and that, through the death of a bird of prey, the latter suffered direct and personal non-material harm in connection with the goal and purpose of its activities [. . .];

Whereas the trial court could logically deduce without undermining its own reasoning that the misconduct of Saint-Martial R.M.H.A. or of its president [. . .] had encouraged and facilitated the facts leading to the death of the osprey and, therefore, there was a cause and effect with regard to the loss suffered by the R.A.O.C.;

As a consequence, this ground of appeal must be rejected in its entirety;

For these reasons: the Court dismisses the appeal against the judgment of the trial court of Tournon dated 28.4.1981;

4. *Erika* case

Note by the author: on 12th December 1999, the oil tanker *Erika* was on its way from Dunkirk (France) to Livorno (Italy). The vessel was Italian-owned, operating under a Maltese flag, and chartered by the French group TotalFinaElf. Sailing in strong winds off the coast of Brittany, with waves of between 10 and 14 meters in height, the ship broke in two while southwest of the port of Lorient. It sank and released into the sea around 17,000 of the 30,800 tons of heavy fuel oil it had onboard. The oil spill caused the deaths of between 150,000 and 300,000 seabirds.[23]

---

23 This was a criminal case; nevertheless, in France, the Criminal Court is authorised to award civil damages to the victim. In the criminal proceedings, which started in February 2007, it emerged that the Italian owner of the *Erika* had been aware of improperly executed repairs to the vessel. Surveyors from the Italian classification society RINA had acted against professional instinct in certifying that the ship was seaworthy. On 16 January 2008, the *Tribunal correctionnel de Paris* ordered TotalFinaElf, along with the owner and RINA, to pay fines and compensation amounting to a total of around € 200 million (not yet including environmental damage). Their subsequent appeal was dismissed in March 2010, and the matter reached the *Cour*

a) Tribunal de Grande Instance de Paris (*High Court of Paris*), 16.01.2008, aff. n° 9934895010

[...] 3 – Civil claim

3.1 – Civil claim resulting from an environmental pollution offence. For any civil claim resulting from an environmental pollution offence, the issue of standing (*constitution de partie civile*) must be distinguished from issues of compensation under tort law.

3.1.1 – Standing. Any person who has suffered individual and direct damage as a result of a legal transgression, as well as any association entitled by law to exercise the same rights as those afforded to civil parties, has standing in court. [...] Any objection made against the standing of victims or associations entitled by law to exercise the same rights as those afforded to civil parties to bring a claim in compensation before the criminal courts is thus ill-founded and must be rejected as such. [...]

3.1.2 – The claim for compensation. [...]

3.1.2.2.6 – Associations. According to Art. L. 142–2 (1) of the Environmental Code (*Code de l'environnement*), any "approved environmental protection association" as understood under [...] Art. L. 141–1 (1) of the Environmental Code may exercise the same rights as those afforded to civil parties whenever an act directly or indirectly harms the collective interest it is set up to defend and violates any of the legislative provisions [contained within Art. 141–1]. [...]

It results that whenever an act violates legislative provisions governing: natural and environmental protection, the improvement of the living environment, the protection of water, air, soil, sites of interest and landscapes, the promotion of effective regional planning, or provisions combating pollution and obtrusions; any association empowered by Arts. L. 142–2 (1) and 142–2 (2) of the Environmental Code (*Code de l'environnement*) to exercise the same rights as those afforded to civil parties may claim compensation *not only for (in)direct pecuniary and non-pecuniary loss suffered to the collective interests it is set up to defend, but also any loss arising from environmental damage* which directly or indirectly harms the aforementioned interests which it safeguards by virtue of its statutes of association.

The Bird Protection League (BPL)

Since January 1981, the BPL has held the status of an approved environmental protection association pursuant to Art. L.141–1 of the Environmental Code (formerly Art. 40 (1) of Law no. 76–629 of 10th July 1976) and has been recognised as an official public-interest organisation since 3rd July 1986. The purpose of this association is to protect birds and the ecosystems which they depend upon, especially animal and plant life. The association is well-renowned by public- and private-sector partners alike for its efficient and effective activities. When the first oiled bird arrived from Brittany to Aquitaine on 14th December 1999, it immediately implemented a national conservation campaign and set up four care centres with 8,000 volunteers working around the clock over a five-month period [...].

---

de cassation in September 2012. By way of amends, *Total Group* resolved to refrain from oil drilling in the Arctic, an area particularly susceptible to ecological damage, and urged other oil companies to follow its lead.

The pollution produced by the sinking of the ERIKA had a catastrophic effect on birdlife, with some 63,606 birds being sent to the BPL's temporary care centres for treatment. Only six percent of the birds arriving into these centres could be saved [. . .]. These birds belonged to various different species, one of which – the common eider – was never again found near the polluted shore. The advisory council of the association decided to bring a civil law claim on 1st March 2000. [. . .]

The appraisal of the pecuniary loss the association alleges to have suffered confirms the seriousness with which the association proceeds. The damage has been precisely measured against documentary evidence, notably including copies of invoices which depict the various expenses in detail. The requested sum of 242,040.94 euros is therefore awarded in that it relates to the operating costs of the BPL's care centres. Expenses relating to specific campaign drives, including the publication and diffusion of a special edition of "Bird Magazine" on the pollution produced by the sinking of the ERIKA, as well as the cost of two public exhibitions, are also within the scope of indirect loss which the law compensates. For the latter, the sum of € 61,126.19 is to be awarded to cover the expenses claimed by the association and proved by the items submitted into evidence. The BPL is therefore awarded a sum of € 303,167.13 for its pecuniary losses.

The BPL, which is requesting a further € 800,000 for non-pecuniary loss, is an association which is widely known for its long-standing commitment to the fight for the protection of birds and the ecosystems which they depend upon, including animal and plant life. Pollution of the extent seen following the ERIKA sinking has greatly thwarted advancements made in recent years. For this reason, the BPL has suffered non-pecuniary loss which must be remedied to the amount of € 100,000.

In the light of the purposes the association pursues according to its statutes, it may also recover the loss resulting from the environmental damage. In order to assess the relevant award in damages, the court must first take into account the extent of the pollution – the court has been left in no doubt that the event had disastrous consequences for birdlife since the birds had migrated to the Bay of Biscay in great numbers for the winter months – the court must then take into account the role that the BPL played in caring for the harmed birds over the relevant months, as well as the field work it invested to the benefit of local authorities and the public alike, and finally the national and international community it represents. In this regard, the association is to be compensated in the amount of € 300,000. [. . .]

b) Cour d'Appel de Paris (*Appellate Court of Paris*), 30.03.2010, affaire 08/02278

The Court, [. . .] on appeal against the judgment of 16th January 2008 by the 11th chamber of the *Tribunal de grande instance de Paris* (High Court of Paris), (P9934895010). Judgment under appeal affirmed in respect of: [. . .] – compensation ordered [. . .] to [. . .] the following associations:

- "Mouvement National de Lutte pour l'Environnement" (*National Environmental Action Movement*) in the amount of € 5,000 for its non-pecuniary losses,
- "Environnement 56" (*Environment 56*) in the amount of € 10,000 for its non-pecuniary loss, [. . .]

- "Ligue de Protection des Oiseaux" (*Bird Protection League*) in the amount of € 303,167.13 for its pecuniary losses, € 100,000 for its non-pecuniary losses, and € 300,000 for the environmental damage suffered, [. . .].

c) Cour de cassation, chambre criminelle (*Court of Cassation, Criminal Chamber*), 25.09.2012, n° 10–82.938, arrêt n° 3439

The Criminal Chamber of the *Cour de cassation* [. . .] has issued the following judgment: [. . .] given that [. . .] an act which adversely affects the preservation of the diverse natural environment, in all of its complexity, is distinct from an act which affects the material and immaterial interests of legal subjects; whereas the act in question adversely affected the wellbeing of seabirds in their natural environment, this being a collective interest which the BDL is committed to protecting; whereas since the association was adversely affected in the very objective it pursued, which forms and characterizes the very essence of its legal personality (*animus societatis*), the latter suffered individual harm and thus has standing; whereas the "pure" environmental harm suffered as a result of this act does not lend itself to reparation in kind [. . .], and that only monetary compensation can be awarded; whereas in order to assess the latter, the *Cour d'appel* was required to take into account any costs which the association might reasonably incur in the implementation of corrective measures in line with its associative purpose; whereas with respect to the number of birds of each species affected by the oil spill, but also of the capacity of nature to naturally repair the damage, and in particular that of the more common species to reproduce and offset losses following such an accident, whereas, on the other hand, other species of rarer birds or birds more susceptible to ecological change, will prove more difficult to restore and whereas, in order to maximise the effectiveness of corrective measures, it will be necessary to monitor the seabirds' progress and to pursue studies regarding the reintroduction of species which have disappeared from an area or are otherwise severely threatened, the *Cour d'appel* was authorised to discretionarily grant monetary compensation of € 300,000 for the "pure" environmental harm suffered by the BDL; [. . .][24]

5. Code civil (*Civil Code, as of October 2016*)[25]

Chapitre III: La réparation du préjudice écologique

Art. 1246. Toute personne responsable d'un préjudice écologique est tenue de le réparer.

Art. 1247. Est réparable, dans les conditions prévues au présent titre, le préjudice écologique consistant en une atteinte non négligeable aux éléments ou aux fonctions des écosystèmes ou aux bénéfices collectifs tirés par l'homme de l'environnement.

---

24 *Note by the author*: the *Cour de cassation* does not review the facts, and deals exclusively with the correct interpretation and application of the law.
25 Implemented by Art. 4 of Law No. 2016–1087 of 8 August 2016.

Art. 1248. L'action en réparation du préjudice écologique est ouverte à toute personne ayant qualité et intérêt à agir, telle que l'Etat, l'Agence française pour la biodiversité, les collectivités territoriales et leurs groupements dont le territoire est concerné, ainsi que les établissements publics et les associations agréées ou créées depuis au moins cinq ans à la date d'introduction de l'instance qui ont pour objet la protection de la nature et la défense de l'environnement.

Art. 1249. (1) La réparation du préjudice écologique s'effectue par priorité en nature.
(2) En cas d'impossibilité de droit ou de fait ou d'insuffisance des mesures de réparation, le juge condamne le responsable à verser des dommages et intérêts, affectés à la réparation de l'environnement, au demandeur ou, si celui-ci ne peut prendre les mesures utiles à cette fin, à l'Etat. [. . .]

Art. 1251. Les dépenses exposées pour prévenir la réalisation imminente d'un dommage, pour éviter son aggravation ou pour en réduire les conséquences constituent un préjudice réparable. [. . .]

Translation

Chapter III: Compensation for environmental damage

Art. 1246. Any person who causes ecological damage is under an obligation to remedy it.

Art. 1247. Subject to the conditions stipulated by the present chapter, ecological damage is recoverable for any act which causes a considerable adverse effect on the structure or function of an ecosystem, or environmental benefits enjoyed by society as a whole.

Art. 1248. A claim for ecological damage may be brought by any qualified person with an interest to act including the State, the French Biodiversity Agency (Agence française pour la biodiversité), local authorities and stakeholders, and any public entities and certified associations which promote the conservation of nature or the environment and were certified or established no less than five years before the institution of proceedings.

Art. 1249. (1) Ecological damage shall be restored to its previous state to the extent possible.
(2) In cases where restoration would be unfeasible, insufficient, or unlawful, the judge shall order the liable party to provide compensation to the plaintiff, the latter being bound to use the payment for the reparation of the damage, or to the government should the plaintiff be unable to carry out reparative measures. [. . .]

Art. 1251. All expenditure incurred in preventing an imminent threat of damage, avoiding further damage, or mitigating the consequences of damage, is to be compensated. [. . .]

6. MEMLOUK MALIK, La loi n°2016-1087 du 8 août 2016 et la réparation du préjudice écologique (*Law n°2016-1087 of 8th August 2016 and the restoration of ecological damage*), BDEI 2016, 30-38

[. . .] **A. – The definition of ecological damage**

If the *Cour de cassation*'s [. . .] decision on the Erika affair was indeed proof of the actionability of ecological damage, then our supreme court stayed well clear of providing a definition of what such damage is. [. . .] [The] Law of 8th August 2016 [. . .] has taken the positive step of imposing a statutory definition on the courts, which should in turn lead to a better harmonisation of the conditions required for its repair. Pursuant to Art. 1246 of the *Code civil*: "*Any person who causes ecological damage is under an obligation to remedy it.*" Art. 1247 of the *Code civil* notably provides reparation for "*any ecological damage [. . .] which, to a considerable degree, adversely affects the structure or function of an ecosystem, or environmental benefits enjoyed by society as a whole.*" [. . .]

One conclusion which we can draw from the new text is that individual harm and specific kinds of collective harm, such as direct or indirect harm to the collective interests defended by environmental associations, are not covered.[26] [. . .]

More importantly, the regime set out in the Law of 8th August 2016 is a model of strict liability. The new Law therefore looks to retain the polluter pays principle [. . .]. [. . .]

B. – Conditions required for the reparation of ecological damage

The most significant feature of the Law of 8th August 2016 [. . .] is the change to the way in which ecological damage is remedied. [. . .] To be more precise, the text looks to overcome a number of obstacles which the traditional rules of tort liability previously posed, thus allowing more satisfactory reparation of environmental damage. Art. 1249 of the *Code civil* does this, first and foremost, by prioritising reparation in kind. Proponents of "*pure*" ecological harm have always preferred this kind of reparation over awards of equivalent monetary value. [. . .] Reparation in kind is quite simply a better way of restoring the environment and wiping out any damage which has been caused: "*since it amounts to materially putting the situation back into the state in which it was, reparation in kind seems like the most adequate method of recovery since it generally wipes out the harm altogether.*" [. . .]

One particular sticking point [. . .] was the question of whether reparation in kind should be excluded where it would impose a disproportionate burden on the defendant. [. . .] Without giving particular reasons, the legislator has refused to qualify the cost burden posed by reparation in kind as grounds for its exclusion. This decision is up for debate. [. . .]

Since it is not always possible to order reparation in kind for ecological harm, Art. 1249 also provides the means to order ordinary compensation. [. . .]

One of the key achievements of the Law of 8th August 2016 is the exemption made from the principle that the beneficiary may freely dispose of the damage award. Under general civil liability law, the recipient of an award in damages is free to invest a compensation sum not

---

26 *Note by the author*: these types of damage will therefore remain governed by Arts. 1240 ff. (former Arts. 1382 ff.).

only for the remedying of the harm in question, but the recipient may also use it for any other appropriate purpose, or indeed "*squander it at his or her own pleasure.*" This principle, however, is particularly ill-suited when it comes to repairing collective harm such as ecological damage. As certain authors have underlined, when repairing collective harm, we should not look to fill the pockets of certain plaintiffs [. . .]. [. . .] It is for this reason [that there was a call for] an exception to be made to this principle for claims for ecological damage; this call was answered in the 2nd sentence of Art. 1249: "*the judge shall order the liable party to provide compensation to the plaintiff, the latter being bound to use the payment for repairing the damage, or to the government should the latter be unable to carry out such measures*".

It is worth pointing out from the outset that the primary aim of the legislation is to allocate compensation to the plaintiff. [. . .] [T]his approach [. . .] affords environmental protection associations the right to claim damages for ecological damage. These associations possess great technical knowledge and are able to target specific local issues. [. . .]

[. . .] [S]ubsidiarily, Art. 1249 anticipates [. . .] the problem of the plaintiff who is not in a position to use a compensation award for the reparation of the ecological damage in question. In these cases, the award shall go to the State. [. . .]

[. . .] Ultimately, bearing in mind the very complex nature of this field, it will no doubt be only a very small number of plaintiffs who can competently produce action plans for the restoration of affected environmental goods or other projects of investing the awards in order to make good the damage. [. . .]

V. People's Republic of China

1. 中华人民共和国侵权责任法 (Tort Law Act)

第八章环境污染责任第
六十五条 因污染环境造成损害的，污染者应当承担侵权责任。

Translation

Chapter VIII. Liability for environmental pollution

Art. 65. *Where harm is caused by environmental pollution, the polluter shall assume tort liability.*

2. 中华人民共和国民事诉讼法 (Civil Procedure Law Act)[27]

第五十五条 对污染环境、侵害众多消费者合法权益等损害社会公共利益的行为，法律规定的机关和有关组织可以向人民法院提起诉讼。

---

27 Amendment adopted on 31 August 2012, in force since 1 January 2013.

Translation

Art. 55. For conduct that pollutes the environment [. . .], an authority or relevant organisation as prescribed by law may bring a claim before the civil courts.[28]

3. 中华人民共和国环境保护法 (Environmental Protection Law)

第五十八条　对污染环境、破坏生态，损害社会公共利益的行为，符合下列条件的社会组织可以向人民法院提起诉讼：
（一）依法在设区的市级以上人民政府民政部门登记；
（二）专门从事环境保护公益活动连续五年以上且无违法记录。
符合前款规定的社会组织向人民法院提起诉讼，人民法院应当依法受理。
提起诉讼的社会组织不得通过诉讼牟取经济利益。
第六十四条　因污染环境和破坏生态造成损害的，应当依照《中华人民共和国侵权责任法》的有关规定承担侵权责任。

Translation

Art. 58. For an act polluting the environment or causing ecological damage in violation of the public interest, a social organisation which satisfies the following conditions may institute an action in a people's court:
(1) It has been legally registered with the civil affairs department of the people's government at or above the level of a districted city.
(2) It has specifically engaged in environmental protection for the public good for five consecutive years or more without any recorded violation of law.
Pursuant to this law, a civil court is required to accept any claim brought by a social organisation that satisfies the provision of the preceding paragraph.
A social organisation may not seek to benefit financially from any action it brings.

Art. 64. Those who cause damage due to environmental pollution and ecological destruction shall bear liability in tort in accordance with the provisions of the Tort Liability Law of the People's Republic of China.

---

28 For local legislation and court practice preceding Art. 55 and eventually leading to its adoption, and the legislative history of Art. 55, see Xiao Zhu/Charles Wharton, *China Legal Sci.*, 2013, 76 at 78 ff. and 96 ff.

4. Supreme People's Court, 最高人民法院关于审理环境民事公益诉讼案件适用法律若干问题的解释 (*Interpretation of the Supreme People's Court on Several Issues concerning the Application of Law in the Conduct of Environmental Civil Public Interest Litigations*), Interpretation No. 1 [2015][29]

Art. 1. Where an authority or relevant organisation as prescribed by law brings a claim against a party for environmental pollution and ecological harm which either damages the public interest or threatens to do so, in line with the joint provisions of Art. 55 of the Civil Procedure Law and Art. 58 of the Environmental Protection Law, [. . .], the People's Court shall accept such claim subject to [. . .] Art. 119 of the Civil Procedure Law [. . .].[30]

Art. 2. A social organisation, private non-enterprise entity, or foundation, among others, registered in the civil affairs administrative department of the People's Government [. . .] may be determined as a social organisation as prescribed under Art. 58 of the Environmental Protection Law [and may thus be entitled to bring a claim under Art. 55 of the Civil Procedure Law and the present rules].

Art. 8. The following materials shall be submitted for the filing of an environmental civil public interest action: [. . .]
(3) Where a social organisation files a lawsuit, it shall submit its registration certificate, articles of association, annual work reports or annual inspection reports of the five consecutive years before filing the lawsuit, and an official statement attesting that it has not committed any legal infringement [. . .].

Art. 11. The State prosecutor, the department responsible for the supervision of environmental protection, and any relevant administrative organ, authority, social organisation, business or public institution may [. . .] support a social organisation in an environmental civil public interest action by such means as providing legal consulting, submitting written opinions and assisting with investigations and the gathering of evidence.

Art. 13. Where the plaintiff requests that the defendant provide environmental information such as the names of its major pollutants, the discharge methods, the concentration and total volume of pollutants discharged, any discharge beyond the approved quota, and the construction and operation of pollution prevention and control installations, which shall be held by the defendant as provided for in any law, regulation or rule or is held as proved by evidence, but the defendant refuses to provide such information, if the plaintiff claims that the relevant facts are unfavourable to the defendant, the People's Court may presume that the claim is supported.

Art. 14. The People's Court shall, when it deems necessary, conduct investigations and collect the evidence required in relation to the environmental civil public interest action.

---

29 Adopted on 8 December 2014, in force since 7 January 2015.
30 Article 119 states (in English translation): "For a claim to be brought, the following conditions must be met: (1) The plaintiff is a citizen, legal person, or any other organisation with a direct interest in the case. (2) There is an identifiable defendant. (3) The nature, facts, and grounds for the claim can be demonstrated. (4) The case is within the scope of civil actions authorised by the people's courts and under the jurisdiction of the people's court in which the action is brought".

Art. 18. For any conduct that causes environmental pollution and ecological harm which either damages the public interest or threatens to do so, the plaintiff may request measures in relation to the defendant's civil liability including, but not limited to, the cessation of the tortious act, removal of the obstruction, elimination of the danger, restoration to the original state, compensation for losses, and an apology.

Art. 20. (1) Where the plaintiff requests that the damage be restored to its original state, the People's Court may render a judgment in accordance with the law that the defendant shall restore the environment to the state in which it was before the damage occurred. If complete restoration is impossible, the People's Court may permit the adoption of alternative restoration methods. The People's Court may, when rendering a judgment for the defendant to restore the environment to its previous state, determine the expenses that shall be borne by the defendant should the latter fail to perform such restoration obligation; or may directly render a judgment that the defendant shall assume the expenses for restoring the environment.
(2) The expenses relating to restoration of the environment include inter alia the expenses for preparing and implementing the restoration plan, monitoring, and supervision.

Art. 23. Where it is difficult to determine the expenses related to restoring the environment to its previous state or it is otherwise too costly to investigate such expenses, the People's Court may reasonably determine such expenses in light of the extent and degree of environmental pollution and ecological destruction, the scarcity of the ecological environment, the difficulty to restore the ecological environment, the operating cost of pollution prevention and control equipment, the benefits obtained by the defendant out of the tortious act, the extent of fault, and other factors, and may refer inter alia to the opinions of the department responsible for the supervision of environmental protection, relevant administrative bodies, and expert opinions.

Art. 24. The expenses required to restore the environment to its previous state [. . .] and other expenses that shall be assumed by the defendant according to the judgment rendered by the People's Court shall be used to restore the ecological harm in question.

Art. 25. (1) Where the parties to an environmental civil public interest litigation reach a mediation agreement or a settlement agreement by themselves, the people's court shall announce the content of the agreement for no less than 30 days.[31]
(2) After the expiration of the announcement period, if the people's court deems upon examination that the content of the mediation agreement or settlement agreement does not damage the public interest, it shall issue a mediation paper. The mediation paper shall state the claim, basic case facts and the content of the agreement, and shall be disclosed.

Art. 29. The filing of an environmental civil public interest litigation by any authority or social organisation prescribed by law shall not affect the filing of an action by any citizen, legal person or any other organisation that suffers from personal injury or property damage due to the same conduct that pollutes the environment and damages the ecology in accordance with the provisions of Article 119 of the Civil Procedure Law.

---

31 On the issue of settlements between environmental associations and persons having caused damage to natural resources, see T. KADNER GRAZIANO, *Ersatz ökologischer Schäden – Ansprüche von Umweltverbänden (Compensation for Ecological Damage – Remedies for Environmental Associations)*, Berlin: Duncker & Humblot, 1995, pp. 283 ff.

VI. Principles of European Tort Law and Draft Common Frame of Reference

BÉNÉDICT WINIGER/HELMUT KOZIOL/BERNHARD A. KOCH/REINHARD ZIMMERMANN (eds.), *Digest of European Tort Law, Vol. II: Essential Cases on Damage*, 2011, nos. 23/29/1 ff.
(by THOMAS KADNER GRAZIANO)

23. Environmental damage

[...] 29. Principles of European Tort Law and Draft Common Frame of Reference

Case 1

Facts

A tanker ship sinks in a storm and a massive oil spill ensues which causes considerable damage on the coast. A number of persons living in the area claim damages for the pollution and the degradation of the environment they are living in.[32]

Case 2

Facts

A company channels its waste into the coastal waters. The plaintiff files a petition for an injunction against this activity until a full system of biological purification, as required by law, is installed. The plaintiff alleges that the company's action illegally violates his personality rights due to the fact that he is impeded from using a good common to all such as the coastal sea, given that the sea is filled with waste consisting of indissoluble substances which modify the physical condition of sea water, its colour and essence and, as a consequence, cause serious ecological damage.[33]

Case 3

Facts

While hunting in the Alps, A shoots a bearded vulture. The bird was raised and released into the wild by a foundation working for the reintroduction and conservation of this rare species of birds in the Alps. The foundation claims CHF 118,000 from A as compensation for the money the foundation has invested for raising the animal and for reintroducing it into the local environment.[34]

---

32 See the *French* case: TGI Paris, 16.01.2008 (*Erika case*), D. 2008, 351 and 2681, J.C.P. 2008, II, 10053, *Digest II*, 16/6, nos. 1–5 with comment by J.-S. BORGHETTI.
33 See the *Greek* case: Nafplio Single Member Court of First Instance, 163/1991, NoV 39, 786, *Digest II*, 23/5 nos. 1–6 with comment by E. DACORONIA.
34 See the *Swiss* case: TF, 4C.317/2002, 20.02.2004, *Digest II*, 23/4 nos. 1–14 with comment by B. WINIGER/ P. FLEURY/P.-E. FEHR/P. AVRAMOV.

Solutions

a) Solution According to PETL. 'Damage requires material or immaterial harm to a legally protected interest', Art. 2:101 PETL. The protected interests are listed in Art. 2:102 and comprise human 'life, bodily or mental integrity, human dignity and liberty' (para 2), 'property rights, including those in intangible property' (para 3), and – more limited in scope – 'pure economic interests or contractual relationships' (para 4). The right to compensation for damage is linked to the infringement of one of these rights of the individual. The same is true for a claim for non-pecuniary damage (Art. 10:301 PETL) which requires, as a starting point, likewise that the victim has suffered, in principle, personal injury, injury to human dignity, liberty, or other personality rights.

If the damaged good belongs to no-one (*res nullius*) or to the community (*res communis omnium*) and if no individual property right or personality right is infringed, it will be difficult under the Principles to obtain compensation for damage to the environment. The Principles protect private property of individuals against damage that occurred 'on the path through the environment' ('*auf dem Umweltpfad*') whereas, pure ecological damage such as pollution of the environment *as such* or the loss of species or of ecosystems arguably does not trigger tortious liability. The Principles do, in particular, not give standing to environmental organisations that defend the infringed environmental interests.

In the first of the above scenarios, the [TGI Paris] classified the claimant's harm as non-pecuniary damage and ruled that, given the consequences the oil spill had on the environment the plaintiffs lived in (*cadre de vie*), each plaintiff deserved to be awarded compensation [for example] for his moral damage. This outcome, though arguably desirable in order to set the right incentives not to pollute common goods, seems however hard to achieve under the current version of the Principles.

In the second scenario the Greek courts held that the company's action illegally violated the plaintiff in his personality rights since it impeded him from using a common good, such as the coastal sea. Currently, under the Principles the scope of the protection of personality rights arguably does not reach that far.

In the third scenario of the rare bird that was shot, a claim by the foundation – framed as a claim for the recovery of the frustrated costs for raising the animal (i.e. the CHF 118,000 invested for raising the bird) – would hardly succeed given that frustrated expenses as such are not compensable damage under the Principles.

Based on the PETL, the claim in the third scenario would need to be framed differently: According to Art. 10:203(1), '[w]here a thing is lost, destroyed or damaged, the basic measure of damages is the value of the thing . . .' The foundation could argue that the value of the bird can be determined by taking into account the amount it would take to replace it by another bird yet to be raised. There would then still be the problem of the standing of the foundation since, once the bird was released, the foundation arguably did not own it anymore and could consequently not bring a claim as the bird's owner.[35]

---

35 This problem could be solved e.g. by modifying the rules on property on certain environmental goods (such as the property of an animal raised and released into nature), or by attributing standing to well-established and recognised environmental associations in case that the interests they are defending are harmed. See the *French* case: C. cass., 1st civ., 16.11.1982, Bull. Civ. I, n° 331 (Osprey), *Digest II*, 23/6 nos. 1–4 with comment by J.-S. Borghetti; the *Dutch* case: Court of Rotterdam, 15.03.1991, NJ 1992, 91 (Vogelbescherming/

b) Solution According to the DCFR. [...] The DCFR [...] explicitly addresses the issue of environmental damage in Art. VI – 2:209. The provision states: 'Burdens incurred by the State or designated competent authorities in restoring substantially impaired natural elements constituting the environment, such as air, water, soil, flora and fauna, are legally relevant damage to the State or the authorities concerned.' Art. VI – 2:209 DCFR thus attributes the State or any competent authority the right to claim compensation for measures taken in order to restore impaired environmental goods if the further conditions for liability are met. The DCFR gives standing to the State and the authorities concerned and hereby uses techniques of a private law in order to deal with damage to the environment.

In the above case scenarios, based on Art. VI – 2:209 DCFR the State or designated competent authorities could claim, for example, compensation for the costs incurred to clean up the oil spill (Case 1), for the costs incurred to clean up the coastal waters from waste (Case 2), or for the costs incurred to reintroduce another bearded vulture in the Alps (Case 3).

The provision does not grant any such rights to individual citizens, nor does it give standing to environmental organisations devoted to the protection of the harmed goods.[36] Only public authorities can claim compensation for pure ecological damage.

Conclusion

Whereas the PETL leave the issue of pure environmental or ecological damage open, the DCFR attributes to the State or any competent authority the right to claim compensation for measures taken in order to restore impaired environmental goods.

VII. Annex: a 1995 proposal for reform

THOMAS KADNER GRAZIANO, *Der Ersatz ökologischer Schäden – Ansprüche von Umweltverbänden (Compensation for Ecological Damage – Remedies for Environmental Associations)*, 1995, pp. 318–322

> Proposal of a private law remedy affording environmental associations the right to seek compensation for ecological damage

§ 1. **Duty to compensate loss.** Anyone who causes ecological damage is under an obligation to remedy it.

Exploatara a Floti Maritime Navrom), *Digest II*, 23/8 nos. 1–4 with comment by S. LINDENBERGH/H. T. Vos; the *Danish* case: Vestre Landsret (High Court of Western Denmark), 05.07.1988, U 1988.878/2V, *Digest II*, 23/15 nos. 1–3 with comment by V. ULFBECK/K. SIIG; see also the state of the law in *Portugal* where the right to bring a claim is assigned to an Ombudsman, and the *Portuguese* case Coruche Court, 23.02.1990, Process no 278/79; available at www.dgsi.pt (destruction of the natural habitat of 27 white storks), *Digest II*, 23/11 nos. 1–5 with comment by A. PEREIRA/M. M. VELOSO.

36 C. VON BAR/E. CLIVE (eds.), *Principles, Definitions and Model Rules of European Private Law: Draft Common Frame of Reference (DCFR)*, Oxford: OUP, 2010, Arts. VI-2:101 and VI – 2:209, Comment B, Environmental organization, p. 3364.

§ 2. Definition. (1) Ecological damage is any unlawful, considerable and ongoing impairment to natural resources, including the air, climate, water, earth, plant-life, and wildlife and the interactions between them.
(2) An impairment is considerable in particular where natural assets which are specifically protected under public law have been affected. An impairment is ongoing where nature is not likely to remedy it within a short period of time. The person who caused the harm has the burden of proving that nature can remedy the impairment within a short period of time [. . .]

§ 4. Persons entitled to a claim. Following an impairment to the environment, any certified association promoting the conservation of nature or the environment [. . .] is authorised to bring a claim in compensation for ecological damage under this Act provided such impairment adversely affects the interests it protects under its statutes of association.

§ 5. Nature and quantification of damages. (1) The person who caused the damage is liable to restore the situation that would exist had the circumstance that gave rise to the claim for compensation not occurred (restoration in kind). Instead of claiming restoration in kind, the person entitled to compensation may request the amount necessary to restore the situation to its original state. The award shall be used to restore the situation to its original state; this rule also applies to payments made under a settlement.
(2) If it is not possible to restore the situation to its original state at the place where the damage occurred, the person who caused the harm shall restore an ecologically similar state in the closest possible physical proximity to the damaged natural resource, or replace it with the most similar ecological resource possible at the place where the damage occurred or as close as possible to this place (replacement); section (1) 2nd and 3rd sentences apply accordingly.
(3) A claim in compensation shall also cover any expenditure necessary for assessing the nature and quantification of damages. [. . .]

§ 6. Limits to the obligation to restore the environment to its previous state or to provide a replacement. The expenses required to restore the situation to its previous state or to provide a replacement for the impairment (§ 5 (1) and (2) respectively) are not be awarded if they would impose a disproportionate burden on the liable party in relation to the ecological significance of the affected natural resource to the environment.
(2) In this instance, the person who caused the damage shall provide a reasonably equivalent to make good the damage or, at the request of the person entitled to the claim, pay the amount necessary for doing so.

§ 7. Compensation for permanent ecological harm. (1) Where it is not possible to restore the situation to its previous state or provide a replacement for the ecological harm, the person who caused the damage is to provide adequate monetary compensation. The amount in compensation is to be assessed by taking into consideration the cost that are necessary for the restoration in kind of goods of ecological value similar to that of the lost resource. Where such an assessment is impossible, the court may freely assess compensation with regard to all relevant circumstances and with particular regard to the ecological value of the lost natural resource.
(2) The person entitled to the claim is to employ the award for the purposes of natural conservation. The latter is to ensure the closest possible proximity in space and ecological value to the lost natural resource. [. . .]

§ 8. Damages for preventative costs. If an association that would be entitled under this Act takes measures to prevent the occurrence of ecological damage, the person who would be responsible for the damage under § 1 of this Act had it occurred, has to reimburse costs incurred that were necessary to prevent the occurrence of harm.

§ 9. Damages for work carried out. An association entitled under this Act can also claim an adequate amount of money for work carried out by its members that the latter could regard as necessary under the circumstances in order to remedy the ecological damage. [. . .]

§ 11. Adjoined claims. For any claim which is pending under the present Act, other persons entitled to a claim under § 4 may join the dispute at any stage regardless of the consent of the parties. Further independent actions regarding the same head of damage as the claim pending are inadmissible. If a decision about an individual head of damage has been rendered, then further claims regarding the same head are inadmissible. [. . .]

§ 12. Damage claims brought against land owners. The rights established under this Act also allow a claim to be brought against any person who has unlawfully caused ecological damage on his or her own site.

§ 13. Relationship between potential claimants. (1) If the ecological damage affects a land owner, then the parties entitled to a claim under § 4 may only claim an award in compensation from the person who caused the damage if they have already called upon the owner to assert a claim for the damage, and the owner has either agreed that the parties entitled under § 4 of the present Act may assert the claim for the damage, or he or she has failed to assert a claim within [an adequate relevant time limit].

§ 15. Injunctive relief. If ecological harm is likely to occur, the person who would be entitled to claim compensation under the present Act should the harm actually occur may request an injunction to prevent the impairment. If the claim for injunctive relief would be excluded under general principles of law, then injunctive relief under this Act shall also be excluded. [. . .]

§ 17. Limitation period. The limitation period applicable to actions in tort shall also apply to claims under the present Act [. . .].

Bibliography

BERTHY VAN DEN BROEK/LISBETH ENNEKING, Public Interest Litigation in the Netherlands: A Multidimensional Take on the Promotion of Environmental Interests by Private Parties through the Courts, *Utrecht L. Rev.* 2014, 77–90; BENOIT CHAPUIS, Le dommage environnemental: un état des lieux, in: David Sifonios (ed.), *Les entreprises et le droit de l'environnement: défis, enjeux, opportunités*, Lausanne: CEDIDAC, 2009, pp. 1–34; ANNE-SYLVIE DUPONT, *Le dommage écologique – Le rôle de la responsabilité civile en cas d'atteinte au milieu naturel*, Genève/Bâle: Schulthess, 2005; MICHAEL FAURE (ed.), *Deterrence, Insurability and Compensation in Environmental Liability: Future Developments in the European Union*, Vienna: Springer, 2003; MICHAEL FAURE/ALBERT VERHEIJ (eds.), *Shifts in Compensation for Environmental Damage*, Vienna: Springer, 2007; CHRISTINE GODT, *Haftung für ökologische Schäden: Verantwortung für Beeinträchtigungen des Allgemeingutes Umwelt durch individualisierbare Verletzungshandlungen*, Berlin: Duncker & Humblot, 1996; THOMAS KADNER GRAZIANO, *Der Ersatz ökologischer Schäden – Ansprüche von Umweltverbänden*, Berlin: Duncker & Humblot, 1995; THOMAS KADNER GRAZIANO, Das Rechtsschutzinteresse bei der Feststellungsklage und das Verbot der Popularklage im schweizerischen Recht, in: Götz Schulze (Hrsg.), *Europäisches Privatrecht in Vielfalt geeint – Der modernisierte Zivilprozess in Europa*, München: Sellier, 2013, pp. 57–75; ULRICH MAGNUS (ed.), *Unification of Tort Law: Damages*, The Hague: Kluwer Law International, 2001, Question 13; DENIS PIOTET, Commentaire de l'arrêt du 20.2.2004 de la Première Cour civile du Tribunal fédéral, La Fondation pour la conservation de gypaète barbu c/Masse en faillite de la succession répudié B., 4C.317/2002, *AJP/PJA* 2004, 1262; CLAIRE ROCA/BÉNÉDICTE RAJOT, *JurisClasseur Code civil, Art. 1382 à 1386, Fasc. 115: Droit à réparation – Conditions de la responsabilité délictuelle – Divers dommages réparables: Dommages à un groupement*, dernière mise à jour: 16 mai 2016; CHRISTOPH SEIBT, *Zivilrechtlicher Ausgleich ökologischer Schäden*, Tübingen: Mohr Siebeck, 1994; JAAP SPIER (ed.), *The Limits of Expanding Liability: Eight Fundamental Cases in a Comparative Perspective*, The Hague/London/Boston: Kluwer Law International, 1998, Case 4; AGATHE VAN LANG, La loi Biodiversité du 8 août 2016: une ambivalence assumée, Le droit nouveau: la course à l'armement (1ᵉ Partie), *AJDA* 2016, 2381; ANDREW WAITE, The Quest for Environmental Law Equilibrium, *Env. L. Rev.* 2005, 34–62; CUI ZHOU, Neue Verbandsklage in der VR China, *RIW* 2016, 202; XIAO ZHU/CHARLES WHARTON, The Development of Legal Standing within Chinese Environmental Social Organizations and an American Comparative Perspective, *China Legal Sci.* 2013, 76–105.

Chapter 17

Comparative tort litigation – an introduction, with a focus on the costs of lawsuits

"Of all the known methods of redressing grievances and settling disputes – pitched battle, rioting, duelling, mediating, flipping a coin, suing – only the latter has steadily won the day [. . .]."[1]

"Is a lawsuit an official quest for truth, or is it primarily a means of settling a dispute? [. . .] People don't litigate for fun. Lawsuits cost money. Worse, they are for most participants miserable experiences whether one wins or loses."[2]

Scenario

In the scenario of Chapter 11, Mr and Mrs Miller lost their three children in an accident at a set of crossroads. Having consulted a lawyer, Mr Miller seeks damages from the driver who caused the accident and the death of his three children. He claims damages for his loss of income and working capacity due to the loss of his employment following the events, for the costs of medical treatment relating to the psychiatric injury he suffered ("nervous shock" or post-traumatic stress disorder, PTSD), and for his pain and suffering following the impairment of his own health. Both parents are claiming compensation for the treatment and other accident-related costs (e.g. ambulance costs) incurred in relation to their children before their death, funeral costs, their emotional harm following the loss of their children, the damage caused to their car, and for legal fees.

The driver who caused the accident[3] agrees out of court to pay compensation for some of these heads of damages, while refusing to pay compensation for others. Mr and Mrs Miller thus consider bringing a lawsuit against the driver and/or his liability insurer. The value in litigation is, alternatively: € 5,000 / € 20,000 / € 200,000.

In deciding whether to litigate, Mr and Mrs Miller are considering the following questions:

a) What would be the costs of a lawsuit, in particular when it comes to lawyers' fees?
b) Which party would be required to bear these costs should they win or lose the case, totally or in part?
c) Would it be possible for the Millers to agree with their lawyers to pay lawyer's fees exclusively in the event of a successful outcome, based on a percentage of the compensation they receive (i.e. a contingency fee)?

---

1 JETHRO K. LIEBERMAN, *The Litigious Society*, New York: Basic Books, 1981, p. xi. See also: US Supreme Court, *Chambers v. Baltimore and Ohio Railroad Company*, 18.11.1907, 207 U.S. 142 at 148: "The right to sue and defend in the courts is the alternative of force. In an organized society, it is the right conservative of all other rights, and lies at the foundation of orderly government. It is one of the highest and most essential privileges of citizenship [. . .]".
2 STEPHEN C. YEAZELL/JOANNA C. SCHWARTZ, *Civil Procedure*, 9th ed., New York: Aspen Publishers, 2016, pp. 296, 299.
3 Or, in practice often, his road traffic accident liability insurer.

Questions

Having the right to receive damages does not necessarily mean that a person easily obtains compensation in practice. Should the person alleged to be liable, or the relevant liability insurer, refuse to pay compensation in full or in part, the victim may consider bringing a claim before the courts. With respect to the organisation of civil law trials, enormous differences exist between the national jurisdictions. These differences are particularly striking when comparing the procedures found in the USA with those on the European continent, particularly in Germany.

1) What do civil law trials in the *USA* and in *Germany* have in common according to the information provided in the materials? What are the main differences between them? Which reason(s) do ARTHUR TAYLOR VON MEHREN and JOHN LANGBEIN give for these fundamental differences?

2) What are the advantages and the disadvantages of the two systems when compared to each other?

3) In the event of a legal dispute before the courts, court[4] and lawyers' fees arise. Who bears the costs for lawyers in the USA? Who bears them in Germany? In what respect do the US and the German rules on costs differ, and what are the reasons for these differences? What are the strengths and weaknesses of the US rule on costs when compared with the European principle of causation?

4) In many European jurisdictions, like in the USA, parties can agree with their lawyers that fees shall be paid on an hourly basis. In the absence of such an agreement, lawyers' fees in Germany are fixed by law according to the provisions of the "Rechtsanwaltsvergütungsgesetz" (*Act on the Remuneration of Lawyers*). The Act provides a fee-table system, with fees largely depending on the amount in dispute and, albeit to a lesser degree, on the complexity and difficulty of the case.

   a) Imagine that the Millers' case is brought before the German courts and the amount claimed is € 5,000. Assume that the claimant either:
      - receives full compensation;
      - obtains 50% of the amount claimed;
      - obtains 20% of the amount claimed;
      - loses the claim.

   How much must the defendant and/or the claimant bear in lawyers' fees following each of these outcomes?

---

4 Court fees, which frequently amount only to a small fraction of the costs of the lawsuit, are often eventually borne by the losing party in both jurisdictions. See for the USA e.g. the Federal Rules of Civil Procedure, Rule 54(d)(1): "Costs Other Than Attorney's Fees. Unless a federal statute, these rules, or a court order provides otherwise, costs – other than attorney's fees – should be allowed to the prevailing party. [...]." In German law, first of all the plaintiff has to pay the general court fee required to start the procedure, see § 12 (1) ZPO. The question of who *finally* bears the court fees depends on the outcome of the lawsuit, see §§ 91, 92 ZPO. For details and examples of relevant calculations, see below pp. 557 ff. For more details, see the §§ 6 (1) 1, 12 (1) 1, 22 (1) 1 and 29 Nr. 1 of the German Gerichtskostengesetz, GKG (*Act on the Costs of Court Procedures*).

b) What are the costs each party has to bear following each of these outcomes before the German courts if the amount in litigation is € 20,000?
c) What if the amount in litigation is € 200,000?

5) What are the potential advantages and disadvantages of a fee-table system, such as the one used by the German courts, when compared to an hourly rate set by lawyers? Think, in particular, in terms of:
   - access to justice for clients who have a case with a moderate value in litigation;
   - the interests of, and incentives for, lawyers.

6) In the USA, contingency fee agreements are widespread. Which problem do such agreements address (and possibly solve)?

7) What is the position in Germany with respect to contingency fees? Which interests are involved and why is the German legislator, along with the legal community, reluctant to admit contingency fees?

Table of contents

A. **The organisation of civil lawsuits in the USA and Germany – a comparison**
   1. Constitution of the USA, 7th Amendment (1789/1792).................p. 542
   2. ARTHUR TAYLOR VON MEHREN/PETER MURRAY, *Law in the United States*, Cambridge: CUP, 2nd ed., 2007, pp. 162–178.................p. 542
   3. JOHN H. LANGBEIN, The German Advantage in Civil Procedure, *U. Chi. L. Rev.* 1985, 823–866.................p. 546

B. **The costs of lawsuits**

   I. The American rule of costs
   1. STEPHEN C. YEAZELL/JOANNA C. SCHWARTZ, *Civil Procedure*, 9th ed., New York: Aspen Publishers, 2016, pp. 340–342.................p. 555
   2. ARTHUR L. GOODHART, Costs, *Yale L. J.* 1929, 849 at 873.................p. 556
   3. GREGORY J. MYERS, When the Small Business Litigant Cannot Afford to Lose (or Win), *Wm. Mitchell L. Rev.* 2012–13, 140 at 141, 147.................p. 556
   4. U.S. Supreme Court, *Alyeska Pipeline Svc. Co.* v. *Wilderness Society*, 12.05.1975, 421 U.S. 240.................p. 557

   II. The European rule of costs – the example of Germany
   1. Zivilprozessordnung, ZPO (*Code of Civil Procedure*), §§ 91 (1), 92 (1)....p. 557
   2. Bundesgerichtshof, BGH (*Federal Supreme Court of Justice*), 30.05.2006, NJW 2006, 2490 at 2491.................p. 558
   3. SIMON M. BECK/TOBIAS SCHEEL, *Zivilprozessrecht im Assessorexamen (Civil Prodedure Law in the Second State Board Exam)*, 4th ed., Munich: C. H. Beck, 2016, nos. 635, 636.................p. 558
   4. Gesetz über die Vergütung der Rechtsanwältinnen und Rechtsanwälte, Rechtsanwaltsvergütungsgesetz, RVG (*Act on the Remuneration of Lawyers*), §§ 1 (1), 2 (1) and (2), 3a (1), 13 (1), 15 (1), and Annexe 2 to 13 (1) p. 3.................p. 558
   5. Bundesverfassungsgericht, BVerfG (*Federal Constitutional Court*), 17.10.1990, 1 BvR 283/85, BVerfGE 83, 1 at 14 (on the rationale behind the fee-table system).................p. 561
   6. Bundesverfassungsgericht, BVerfG (*Federal Constitutional Court*), 15.06.2009, 1 BvR 1342/07, NJW-RR 2010, 259 at 260 (on the rationale behind the amounts provided in the fee-table system).................p. 561
   7. CHRISTOPH HOMMERICH/MATTHIAS KILIAN/HEIKE JACKMUTH/THOMAS WOLF, Quersubventionierung im RVG: Fiktion oder Wirklichkeit? (*Cross-subsidisation: Fiction or Reality?*), *AnwBl.* 2006, 406 at 407.................p. 562
   8. STEFAN HARDEGE/BERND WAAS, *Rechtsanwaltsvergütung in Europa, Studie für die Bundesrechtsanwaltskammer (Remuneration of Lawyers in Europe, Study for the Federal Bar Association)*, Köln: Institut der Deutschen Wirtschaft, 2008, pp. 48 and 51.................p. 562

   III. Charging fees in case of success only? – contingency fees/ *Erfolgshonorare*
   1. ARTHUR TAYLOR VON MEHREN/PETER MURRAY, *Law in the United States*, Cambridge: CUP, 2nd ed., 2007, pp. 268–269.................p. 563

2. Bundesrechtsanwaltsordnung (*German Federal Act Regulating the Legal Profession*), § 49b (2) .... p. 563
3. Bundesverfassungsgericht, BVerfG (*German Federal Constitutional Court*), 12.12.2006, 1 BvR 2576/04, BVerfGE 117, 163, NJW 2007, 979 .... p. 564
4. Rechtsanwaltsvergütungsgesetz (*German Act on Lawyer's Fees*), § 4a (as of 01.07.2008) .... p. 566
5. JULIA VON SELTMANN, *Beck'scher Online-Kommentar RVG* (*Beck's Online Commentary on the German Act on Lawyer's Fees*), 35th ed., as of 01.06.2016, RVG § 4a .... p. 567
6. MATTHIAS KILIAN, Brennpunkte des anwaltlichen Berufsrechts (*Rules on the Profession of Lawyers in Focus*), *NJW* 2014, 1499 at 1500 .... p. 568
7. HANS-JOCHEM MAYER, Entwicklungen zum Rechtsanwaltsvergütungsgesetz (*Recent Developments on the Act on the Remuneration of Lawyers*) 2007 – 2011, *NJW* 2011, 1563 at 1565 .... p. 568
8. MATTHIAS KILIAN, Erfolgshonorare: Gründe für die verhaltene Nutzung durch die Anwaltschaft (*Success Fees: Reasons for Hardly Using Them in Practice*), *AnwBl.* 2014, 815 at 817 .... p. 568

Materials[5]

A. The organisation of civil lawsuits in the USA and Germany – a comparison

1. Constitution of the USA, 7th Amendment (1789/1792)

> In Suits at common law, where the value in controversy shall exceed twenty dollars, the right of trial by jury shall be preserved, and no fact tried by a jury, shall be otherwise re-examined in any Court of the United States, than according to the rules of the common law.

2. ARTHUR TAYLOR VON MEHREN/PETER MURRAY, *Law in the United States*, Cambridge: CUP, 2nd ed., 2007, pp. 162–178

6
American Civil Justice

This chapter does not seek to describe American first instance civil procedure in detail. Its purpose rather is to [. . .] consider why the style of American civil procedure differs so greatly from the style of continental European civil procedure. [. . .] As will be seen, the historical role of the jury is of central importance to most of these questions. [. . .]

C. AMERICAN CIVIL PROCEDURE AND THE CONTINUOUS TRIAL

That there are significant differences between American civil procedure and the procedural systems of most civil law jurisdictions is apparent to even the casual observer. The large role of American lawyers in the preparation and presentation of civil cases, the time-consuming and expensive discovery process, the dramatic, concentrated trial – often before the jury as audience – all appear strange and foreign to a jurist from the civil law tradition. [. . .] [I]t is now clear that many of the salient characteristics of American civil procedure can be linked to its use of a concentrated and continuous trial rather than a discontinuous or sequential process for determination of factual disputes and, indeed, the entire case. [. . .]

The use of a continuous trial may in turn be linked to the historical use of the jury and a strong commitment to preservation of the role of the jury even as times have changed. The use of *ad hoc* lay juries and the confiding of all determinations of disputed fact to their decision mean that trial processes must be adapted to permit the jury to function as efficiently as possible under the circumstances. So, for example, it would not be realistic to expect a given group of six, eight, or twelve laypersons to convene and reconvene several times over a period of several months to hear the evidence in a civil case. [. . .] The use of a fairly large group to hear the evidence and reach a decision means, as a practical matter, that the proceedings must be both concentrated and continuous for the institution to function at all.

The institution of the continuous trial is one that American civil procedure inherited from and continues to share with civil justice in Great Britain. [. . .] Only recently, with the

---

5 For the original language versions of the materials reproduced in this chapter, see the companion website at www.routledge.com/9781138567733.

adoption of the Woolf reforms, has English civil procedure taken a step in the direction of continental European forms, including greater toleration for sequential conferences and hearings.

1. Fundamental principles and basis institutional arrangements

Before considering differences, a basic similarity of great importance should be remarked: American and Western European procedural systems all accept, in essence, the adversarial rather than the inquisitorial principle. Inquisitorial procedure assigns to officials the basic responsibility for gathering and presenting to the adjudicator the materials for decision. In addition, officials prosecute the cause, moving the case forward through the investigatory and decisional stages. Enforcement of legal rights is looked upon as a duty that rests upon government and requires affirmative official action at every stage.

The adversarial principle, on the other hand, relies on party-prosecution. Each party controls and develops the preparation and presentation of its own cause; in essence, the enforcement of legal rights is left to the self-interest of those concerned. It is for them to prepare and prosecute the case and to move it forward through the investigatory and decisional stages. [. . .]

[However, t]he European and American procedural styles are very different. In the American system, the trial is concentrated in a single episode. Before trial, the lawyer for each side prepares with care the legal and factual issues that may arise. Discovery is had of the case materials available to the other side and prospective witnesses are insistently questioned. At the trial itself, the examination of witnesses is – subject to minor qualifications – conducted by the lawyers; the judge presides but is not responsible for the development of the case or for the questioning of witnesses.

On the other hand, in European systems such as that of the German Federal Republic, trials can be discontinuous. [. . .]. Pretrial discovery is not available as such. Even when prospective witnesses have been identified, lawyers are not expected to question them in the course of preparation for trial lest their testimony seem to have been influenced by such a contact. At the trial itself, the judge's role is central; the court has the basic responsibility for the questioning of witnesses as well as for developing the case to the point that it can be taken for decision.

2. The significance for first-instance procedure of concentrated trials

How are these real and important differences between first-instance procedural arrangements in the United States on the one hand and in Germany on the other to be explained? [. . .] [A]n important cause for the characteristic features of each procedural style is arguably institutional in nature: the presence in one system of the concentrated – and, in the other, of the discontinuous – trial. [. . .] What particular consequences can be said to flow then in adversarial systems from a system's use of one rather than the other of these alternative forms of trial, the concentrated and discontinuous?

If justice is to be administered on an informed and rational basis, both parties must be able to thoroughly prepare and present their positions before the adjudicator takes the matter for decision. Systems such as the American that combine the adversary principle with a concentrated trial have basically only two ways in which the foregoing can be ensured. One approach relies upon the parties' pleadings; the other utilizes pretrial exchanges and investigations to frame the issues and to give notice of the evidence upon which each party intends to rely.

If the avoidance of surprise is to be accomplished through the pleading process alone, the following are required: (1) Each party's pleadings must not only state his position fully but respond unequivocally to every position taken by the opposing party in his pleadings; (2) this exchange must continue until every point of agreement and disagreement between the parties has emerged; (3) only the issues thus defined can be considered at trial.

For the most part, the old common-law system of pleading exhibits these characteristics. [. . .]

In the United States, the pleading approach was supplanted by [. . .] arrangements which permit each party to familiarize himself before trial with the details of the positions that the other party may advance when the controversy is ultimately presented to the adjudicator. This solution requires elaborate pretrial interrogatory and discovery procedures. [. . .] Experience has shown that the pretrial procedures required can be cumbersome, extremely time-consuming, and very costly.[6]

Approaches along the foregoing lines to the problem of surprise are open to procedural systems like the German that combine the adversary principle with a discontinuous trial. However, such systems have another choice as well; surprise at the trial stage can be avoided by the simple device of providing for further appearances before the court at a later date. [. . .]

[. . .] [In the US, the] presence of a jury makes a discontinuous trial impractical. Great administrative difficulty and personal inconvenience would be involved in reconvening the jury from time to time over an extended period. Moreover, at least until relatively modern times, material presented at widely separated points in time could not be preserved in a form that would have enabled the jury to refresh its recollection when it ultimately came to deliberate and render the verdict.

[. . .] At least for simpler cases, the German system has long had as its ideal the concentration of oral-argument, proof-taking, and final argument in a single session. However, this ideal has proved to be elusive; in German practice the discontinuous trial is the norm in more complicated cases. In the United Kingdom, where the jury has fallen into disuse in civil litigation, recent reforms restricting discovery have been accompanied by an increase in the participation of judicial personnel to guide the proceedings through a series of discontinuous hearings. [. . .]

This situation is understandable. If the trial is to consist of a single episode pretrial procedures of one form or another must be developed to handle the surprise problem. [. . .]

Yet another reason can be advanced to support the proposition that a legal system – given a free choice – is not likely to resort to trial concentration in order to solve the surprise problem. [. . .] An adjudicator is not disposed to turn down plausible requests for postponements; indeed, to the extent that surprise is present, a refusal to grant a continuance may result in injustice. The stern discipline that concentration involves is, as a matter of human nature, unlikely to be imposed so long as, institutionally considered, the trial need not be a single episode.

---

6 *Note by the author*: for the impact of discovery procedures on the overall costs of litigation in the USA, see e.g. E. G. LEE/T. E. WILLGING, Defining the Problem of Cost in Federal Civil Litigation, *Duke L. J.* 2010–2011, 765 at 770: "In cases in which one or more types of discovery was reported, we found median litigation costs, including attorneys' fees, of $15,000 for plaintiffs and $20,000 for defendants."; at 779 f.: "The 2009 FCJ case-based study found that the median percentage of litigation costs accounted for by discovery was 20 percent for plaintiffs' attorneys and 27 percent for defendants' attorneys".

D. FURTHER PROCEDURAL CHARACTERISTICS ASSOCIATED WITH CONCENTRATED AND WITH DISCONTINUOUS TRIALS

The consequences that follow from the concentrated or discontinuous nature of the trial, respectively, are not limited to those discussed above. Other procedural characteristics have a strong affinity for each form of trial.

The combination found in the contemporary American system of the single-episode trial with extensive pretrial procedures makes it necessary, in matters of any complexity, for lawyers to play an active role in gathering and analyzing evidence and in shaping the case in the period before trial. Where the responsibility for such full preparation rests upon lawyers, it is unnatural and unreasonable to limit by legal rule or ethical canon their pretrial access to witnesses. Of course, such access involves appreciable risks that the witness's story will be affected by pretrial contact with the perspectives brought to the case by the lawyers who interview and question them.

Because of his or her active role in the pretrial phase, the lawyer typically has, when presentation of the controversy begins at the trial, a greater understanding of the case than does the judge (or *a fortiori*, the jury). The adjudicator is hardly in a position to play a dominant role in the presentation of the case. It is, therefore, natural for the lawyers to handle the questioning of witnesses and the general presentation of the matter. [. . .].

Another characteristic of concentrated-trial systems is that the problem of delay arises at the pretrial, rather than at the trial stage. [. . .]

Delay can also be caused, however, by one or both parties intentionally failing to proceed in a reasonably expeditious fashion. Where the trial is concentrated, such delay is found at the pretrial stage but is exceptional at the trial stage. [. . .]

Which further procedural characteristics are then typically exhibited by procedural systems that combine the adversarial principle with a discontinuous trial? As has already been remarked, in such systems relatively little emphasis is placed on pretrial procedures. It follows that there is relatively little need – and often only limited possibilities – for lawyers to be active at the pretrial stage. Accordingly, these systems can [. . .] strongly advance certain policies that must be largely ignored by systems using a concentrated trial. Thus, even though the system accepts the principle of party-presentation, that principle may be qualified by discouraging, as the German and French systems do, pretrial contact between lawyer and witness. The rationale advanced is that fresh and unrehearsed testimony is inherently more reliable than testimony given by witnesses who have already discussed the case with one of the lawyers. [. . .]

In these systems, lawyers thus often come to trial with [an understanding of the controversy similar to the one that] the adjudicator can have from the complaint and other documents filed with the court before trial. Accordingly, there is no built-in tendency for the lawyers to play a dominant role in the presentation of the controversy at the trial stage. As a result, the principle of party prosecution loses the support that it derives from the lawyer's pretrial preparation in systems such as the American.

Unlike systems that use the single-episode trial, in discontinuous systems the problem of delay centers, so far as procedure in first instance is concerned, upon the trial phase rather than upon the pretrial phase. [. . .]

Accordingly, adversarial systems using a discontinuous trial face a serious problem of delay at the trial stage, one that may be at least as serious as that encountered at the pretrial stage by adversarial systems using a concentrated trial. The only remedy ultimately available to discontinuous systems [. . .] is to assign greater directive power to the judge and to involve judges increasingly in the management of the litigation at the trial stage. The delay problem thus sets in motion forces that profoundly affect the principle of party-prosecution. The marked tendency in the twentieth century of continental European adversarial systems to emphasize the judges' directive role and increase their directive powers is, in this perspective, a natural and predictable phenomenon just as is the absence of a comparable trend in the American system.

3. John H. Langbein, The German Advantage in Civil Procedure, U. Chi. L. Rev. 1985, 823–866

Our lawyer-dominated system of civil procedure has often been criticized both for its incentives to distort evidence and for the expense and complexity of its modes of discovery and trial. The shortcomings inhere in a system that leaves to partisans the work of gathering and producing the factual material upon which adjudication depends.

We have comforted ourselves with the thought that a lawyerless system would be worse. The excesses of American adversary justice would seem to pale by comparison with a literally nonadversarial system – one in which litigants would be remitted to faceless bureaucratic adjudicators and denied the safeguards that flow from lawyerly intermediation.

The German advantage. The main theme of this article is drawn from Continental civil procedure, exemplified for me by the system that I know reasonably well, the [...] German. My theme is that, by assigning judges rather than lawyers to investigate the facts, the Germans avoid the most troublesome aspects of our practice. But I shall emphasize that the familiar contrast between our adversarial procedure and the supposedly nonadversarial procedure of the Continental tradition has been grossly overdrawn.

To be sure, since the greater responsibility of the bench for fact-gathering is what distinguishes the Continental tradition, a necessary (and welcome) correlative is that counsel's role in eliciting evidence is greatly restricted. Apart from fact-gathering, however, the lawyers for the parties play major and broadly comparable roles in both the German and American systems. Both are adversary systems of civil procedure. There as here, the lawyers advance partisan positions from first pleadings to final arguments. German litigators suggest legal theories and lines of factual inquiry, they superintend and supplement judicial examination of witnesses, they urge inferences from fact, they discuss and distinguish precedent, they interpret statutes, and they formulate views of the law that further the interests of their clients. I shall urge that German experience shows that we would do better if we were greatly to restrict the adversaries' role in fact-gathering. [...]

I. Overview of German Civil Procedure

There are two fundamental differences between German and Anglo-American civil procedure, and these differences lead in turn to many others. First, the court rather than the parties' lawyers takes the main responsibility for gathering and sifting evidence, although the lawyers exercise a watchful eye over the court's work. Second, there is no distinction between pretrial and trial, between discovering evidence and presenting it. Trial is not a single continuous event. Rather, the court gathers and evaluates evidence over a series of hearings, as many as the circumstances require.

Initiation. The plaintiff's lawyer commences a lawsuit in Germany with a complaint. Like its American counterpart, the German complaint narrates the key facts, sets forth a legal theory, and asks for a remedy in damages or specific relief. Unlike an American complaint, however, the German document[7] proposes means of proof for its main factual contentions. The major documents in the plaintiff's possession that support his claim are scheduled and often appended; other documents (for example, hospital files or government records such as police accident reports or agency files) are indicated; witnesses who are thought to know something helpful to the plaintiff's position are identified. The defendant's answer follows the same pattern. It should be emphasized, however, that neither plaintiff's nor defendant's lawyer will have conducted any significant search for witnesses or for other evidence unknown to his client. Digging for facts is primarily the work of the judge.

Judicial preparation. The judge to whom the case is entrusted examines these pleadings and appended documents. He routinely sends for relevant public records. These materials form the beginnings of the official dossier, the court file. All subsequent submissions of counsel, and all subsequent evidence-gathering, will be entered in the dossier, which is open to counsel's inspection continuously.

When the judge develops a first sense of the dispute from these materials, he will schedule a hearing and notify the lawyers. He will often invite and sometimes summon the parties as well as their lawyers to this or subsequent hearings. If the pleadings have identified witnesses whose testimony seems central, the judge may summon them to the initial hearing as well.

Hearing. The circumstances of the case dictate the course of the hearing. Sometimes the court will be able to resolve the case by discussing it with the lawyers and parties and suggesting avenues of compromise. If the case remains contentious and witness testimony needs to be taken, the court will have learned enough about the case to determine a sequence for examining witnesses.

Examining and recording. The judge serves as the examiner-in-chief. At the conclusion of his interrogation of each witness, counsel for either party may pose additional questions, but counsel are not prominent as examiners. Witness testimony is seldom recorded verbatim; rather, the judge pauses from time to time to dictate a summary of the testimony into the dossier. The lawyers sometimes suggest improvements in the wording of these summaries, in order to preserve or to emphasize nuances important to one side or the other.

Since the proceedings in a difficult case may require several hearings extending across many months, these summaries of concluded testimony – by encapsulating succinctly the results of previous hearings – allow the court to refresh itself rapidly for subsequent hearings. The summaries also serve as building blocks from which the court will ultimately fashion the findings of fact for its written judgment. If the case is appealed, these concise summaries constitute the record for the reviewing court. (We shall see that the first appellate instance in German procedure involves review de novo, in which the appellate court can form its own view of the facts, both from the record and, if appropriate, by recalling witnesses or summoning new ones.)

Anyone who has had to wade through the longwinded narrative of American pretrial depositions and trial transcripts (which preserve every inconsequential utterance, every false start, every stammer) will see at once the economy of the German approach to taking

---

7 *Note by the author*: see the *German* Zivilprozessordnung, ZPO (*Code of Civil Procedure*), § 253. Statement of claim (in English translation): "(1) The complaint shall be brought by serving a written pleading (statement of claim). (2) The statement of claim must include: 1. The designation of the parties and of the court; 2. Exact information on the subject matter and the grounds for filing the claim, as well as a precisely specified petition [stating e.g. the exact amount of damages that is claimed]. [. . .]".

and preserving evidence. Our incentives run the other way; we pay court reporters by the page and lawyers mostly by the hour.[8] [...]

Expertise. If an issue of technical difficulty arises on which the court or counsel wishes to obtain the views of an expert, the court – in consultation with counsel – will select the expert and define his role. (This aspect of the procedure I shall discuss particularly in Part IV below.)

Further contributions of counsel. After the court takes witness testimony or receives some other infusion of evidence, counsel have the opportunity to comment orally or in writing. Counsel use these submissions in order to suggest further proofs or to advance legal theories. Thus, nonadversarial proof-taking alternates with adversarial dialogue across as many hearings as are necessary. The process merges the investigatory function of our pretrial discovery and the evidence-presenting function of our trial. Another manifestation of the comparative efficiency of German procedure is that a witness is ordinarily examined only once. Contrast the American practice of partisan interview and preparation, pretrial deposition, preparation for trial, and examination and cross-examination at trial. These many steps take their toll in expense and irritation.

Judgment. After developing the facts and hearing the adversaries' views, the court decides the case in a written judgment that must contain full findings of fact and make reasoned application of the law.

II. Judicial Control of Sequence

From the standpoint of comparative civil procedure, the most important consequence of having judges direct fact-gathering in this episodic fashion is that German procedure functions without the sequence rules to which we are accustomed in the Anglo-American procedural world. The implications for procedural economy are large. The very concepts of "plaintiff's case" and "defendant's case" are unknown. In our system those concepts function as traffic rules for the partisan presentation of evidence to a passive and ignorant trier. By contrast, in German procedure the court ranges over the entire case, constantly looking for the jugular – for the issue of law or fact that might dispose of the case. Free of constraints that arise from party presentation of evidence, the court investigates the dispute in the fashion most likely to narrow the inquiry. A major job of counsel is to guide the search by directing the court's attention to particularly cogent lines of inquiry.

Suppose that the court has before it a contract case that involves complicated factual or legal issues about whether the contract was formed, and if so, what its precise terms were. But suppose further that the court quickly recognizes (or is led by submission of counsel to recognize) that some factual investigation might establish an affirmative defense – illegality, let us say – that would vitiate the contract. Because the court functions without sequence rules, it can postpone any consideration of issues that we would think of as the plaintiff's case – here the questions concerning the formation and the terms of the contract. Instead, the court can concentrate the entire initial inquiry on what we would regard as a defense. If, in my example, the court were to unearth enough evidence to allow it to conclude that the contract was illegal, no investigation would ever be done on the issues of formation and terms. A defensive issue that could only surface in Anglo-American procedure following full

---

8 For the *German* rule on costs, see below, pp. 557 ff.

pretrial and trial ventilation of the whole of the plaintiff's case can be brought to the fore in German procedure.

Part of what makes our discovery system so complex is that, on account of our division into pretrial and trial, we have to discover for the entire case. We investigate everything that could possibly come up at trial, because once we enter the trial phase we can seldom go back and search for further evidence. By contrast, the episodic character of German fact-gathering largely eliminates the danger of surprise; if the case takes an unexpected turn, the disadvantaged litigant can count on developing his response in another hearing at a later time. Because there is no pretrial discovery phase, fact-gathering occurs only once; and because the court establishes the sequence of fact-gathering according to criteria of relevance, unnecessary investigation is minimized. [. . .]

The episodic character of German civil procedure – Benjamin Kaplan called it the "conference method" of adjudication – has other virtues: It lessens tension and theatrics, and it encourages settlement. Countless novels, movies, plays, and broadcast serials attest to the dramatic potential of the Anglo-American trial. The contest between opposing counsel; the potential for surprise witnesses who cannot be rebutted in time; the tricks of adversary examination and cross-examination; the concentration of proof-taking and verdict into a single, continuous proceeding; the unpredictability of juries and the mysterious opacity of their conclusory verdicts – these attributes of the Anglo-American trial make for good theatre. German civil proceedings have the tone not of the theatre, but of a routine business meeting – serious rather than tense. When the court inquires and directs, it sets no stage for advocates to perform. The forensic skills of counsel can wrest no material advantage, and the appearance of a surprise witness would simply lead to the scheduling of a further hearing. [. . .]

In this business-like system of civil procedure the tradition is strong that the court promotes compromise.[9] The judge who gathers the facts soon knows the case as well as the litigants do, and he concentrates each subsequent increment of fact-gathering on the most important issues still unresolved. As the case progresses the judge discusses it with the litigants, sometimes indicating provisional views of the likely outcome. He is, therefore, strongly positioned to encourage a litigant to abandon a case that is turning out to be weak or hopeless, or to recommend settlement. The loser-pays system of allocating the costs of litigation[10] gives the parties further incentive to settle short of judgment.

III. Witnesses

Adversary control of fact-gathering in our procedure entails a high level of conflict between partisan advantage and orderly disclosure of the relevant information. Marvin Frankel put this point crisply when he said that "it is the rare case in which either side yearns to have the witnesses, or anyone, give the whole truth." If we had deliberately set out to find a means of impairing the reliability of witness testimony, we could not have done much better than the existing system of having partisans prepare witnesses in advance of

---

9 *Note by the author*: ZPO § 278 (1) imposes upon the court the duty to explore the possibility of a settlement at every stage of the proceeding. It provides (in English translation): "In all circumstances of the proceedings, the court is to act in the interests of arriving at an amicable resolution of the legal dispute or of the individual points at issue".

10 See below, pp. 557 ff.

trial and examine and cross-examine them at trial. Jerome Frank described the problem a generation ago:

> [The witness] often detects what the lawyer hopes to prove at the trial. If the witness desires to have the lawyer's client win the case, he will often, unconsciously, mold his story accordingly. Telling and re-telling it to the lawyer, he will honestly believe that his story, as he narrates it in court, is true, although it importantly deviates from what he originally believed.

Thus, said Frank, "the partisan nature of trials tends to make partisans of the witnesses." Cross-examination at trial – our only substantial safeguard against this systematic bias in the testimony that reaches our courts – is a frail and fitful palliative. Cross-examination is too often ineffective to undo the consequences of skillful coaching. Further, because cross-examination allows so much latitude for bullying and other truth-defeating stratagems, it is frequently the source of fresh distortion when brought to bear against truthful testimony. As a leading litigator boasted recently in an ABA [American Bar Association] publication: "By a carefully planned and executed cross-examination, I can raise at least a slight question about the accuracy of [an adverse] witness's story, or question his motives or impartiality."

When we cross the border into German civil procedure, we leave behind all traces of this system of partisan preparation, examination, and cross-examination of witnesses. German law distinguishes parties from witnesses. A German lawyer must necessarily discuss the facts with his client, and based on what his client tells him and on what the documentary record discloses, the lawyer will nominate witnesses whose testimony might turn out to be helpful to his client. As the proofs come in, they may reveal to the lawyer the need to nominate further witnesses for the court to examine. But the lawyer stops at nominating; virtually never will he have occasion for out-of-court contact with a witness. Not only would such contact be a serious ethical breach, it would be self-defeating. "German judges are given to marked and explicit doubts about the reliability of the testimony of witnesses who previously have discussed the case with counsel or who have consorted unduly with a party."

[. . .] German civil procedure preserves party interests in fact-gathering. The lawyers nominate witnesses, attend and supplement court questioning, and develop adversary positions on the significance of the evidence. Yet German procedure totally avoids the distortions incident to our partisan witness practice.

IV. EXPERTS

The European jurist who visits the United States and becomes acquainted with our civil procedure typically expresses amazement at our witness practice. His amazement turns to something bordering on disbelief when he discovers that we extend the sphere of partisan control to the selection and preparation of experts. In the Continental tradition experts are selected and commissioned by the court, although with great attention to safeguarding party interests. In the German system, experts are not even called witnesses. They are thought of as "judges' aides."

Perverse incentives. At the American trial bar, those of us who serve as expert witnesses are known as "saxophones." This is a revealing term, as slang often is. The idea is that the lawyer plays the tune, manipulating the expert as though the expert were a musical instrument on which the lawyer sounds the desired notes. I sometimes serve as an expert in trust and pension cases, and I have experienced the subtle pressures to join the team – to shade one's views, to conceal doubt, to overstate nuance, to downplay weak aspects of the case that one has been hired to bolster. Nobody likes to disappoint a patron; and beyond this psychological pressure is the financial inducement. Money changes hands upon the rendering of expertise, but the expert can run his meter only so long as his patron litigator likes the tune. Opposing counsel undertakes a similar exercise, hiring and schooling another expert to parrot the contrary position. The result is our familiar battle of opposing experts. [. . .]

[. . .] If the experts do not cancel each other out, the advantage is likely to be with the expert whose forensic skills are the more enticing. The system invites abusive cross-examination. Since each expert is party-selected and party-paid, he is vulnerable to attack on credibility regardless of the merits of his testimony. [. . .]

Thus, the systematic incentive in our procedure to distort expertise leads to a systematic distrust and devaluation of expertise. Short of forbidding the use of experts altogether, we probably could not have designed a procedure better suited to minimize the influence of expertise.

The Continental tradition. European legal systems are, by contrast, expert-prone. Expertise is frequently sought. The literature emphasizes the value attached to having expert assistance available to the courts in an age in which litigation involves facts of ever-greater technical difficulty. The essential insight of Continental civil procedure is that credible expertise must be neutral expertise. Thus, the responsibility for selecting and informing experts is placed upon the courts, although with important protections for party interests.

Selecting the expert. German courts obtain expert help in lawsuits the way Americans obtain expert help in business or personal affairs. If you need an architect, a dermatologist, or a plumber, you do not commission a pair of them to take preordained and opposing positions on your problem, although you do sometimes take a second opinion. Rather, you take care to find an expert who is qualified to advise you in an objective manner; you probe his advice as best you can; and if you find his advice persuasive, you follow it.

When in the course of winnowing the issues in a lawsuit a German court determines that expertise might help resolve the case, the court selects and instructs the expert. The court may decide to seek expertise on its own motion, or at the request of one of the parties. The code of civil procedure allows the court to request nominations from the parties – indeed, the code requires the court to use any expert upon whom the parties agree – but neither practice is typical. In general, the court takes the initiative in nominating and selecting the expert. [. . .] [T]he regional chambers of commerce and industry (Industrie- and Handelskammern) [. . .] identify experts in a wide variety or commercial and technical fields [. . .] who have exceptional knowledge of the particular specialty and to have these persons sworn to render professional and impartial expertise. The chamber circulates its lists of experts, organized by specialty and subspecialty, to the courts. [. . .]

Current practice. In 1984 I spent a little time interviewing judges in Frankfurt about their practice in selecting experts. [. . .] Among the judges with whom I spoke, I found unanimity on the proposition that the most important factor predisposing a judge to select an expert is favorable experience with that expert in an earlier case. Experts thus build reputations with the bench. Someone who renders a careful, succinct, and well-substantiated report and who responds effectively to the subsequent questions of the court and the parties will be remembered when another case arises in his specialty. Again we notice that German civil procedure tracks the patterns of decision-making in ordinary business and personal affairs: If you get a plumber to fix your toilet and he does it well, you incline to hire him again. When judges lack personal experience with appropriate experts, I am told, they turn to the authoritative lists described above. [. . .]

The American counterpart. It may seem curious that we make so little use of court-appointed experts in our civil practice, since "[t]he inherent power of a trial judge to appoint an expert of his own choosing is virtually unquestioned" [. . .]. The literature displays both widespread agreement that our courts virtually never exercise this authority, and a certain bafflement about why.

[. . .] The difficulty originates with the locktight segmentation of our procedure into pretrial and trial compartments, and with the tradition of partisan domination of the pretrial. Until lately, it was exceptional for the judge to have detailed acquaintance with the facts of the case until the parties presented their evidence at trial. By then the adversaries would have engaged their own experts, and time would no longer allow a court-appointed expert to be located and prepared. Effective use of court-appointed experts as exemplified in German practice presupposes early and extensive judicial involvement in shaping the whole of the proofs. [. . .]

V. Shortcomings of Adversary Theory

The case against adversary domination of fact-gathering is so compelling that we have cause to wonder why our system tolerates it. Because there is nothing to be said in support of coached witnesses, and very little to be said in favor of litigation-biased experts, defenders of the American status quo are left to argue that the advantages of our adversary procedure counterbalance these grievous, truth-defeating distortions. "You have to take the bad with the good; if you want adversary safeguards, you are stuck with adversary excesses."

The false conflict. This all-or-nothing argument overlooks the fundamental distinction between fact-gathering and the rest of civil litigation. Outside the realm of fact-gathering, German civil procedure is about as adversarial as our own. Both systems welcome the lawyerly contribution to identifying legal issues and sharpening legal analysis. German civil procedure is materially less adversarial than our own only in the fact-gathering function, where partisanship has such potential to pollute the sources of truth. Accordingly, the proper question is not whether to have lawyers, but how to use them; not whether to have an adversarial component to civil procedure, but how to prevent adversarial excesses. If we were to incorporate the essential lesson of the German system in our own procedure, we would still have a strongly adversarial civil procedure. We would not, however, have coached witnesses and litigation-biased experts.

The confusion with criminal procedure. Much of the rhetoric celebrating unrestrained adversary domination of judicial proceedings stems from the criminal process, where quite different policies are at work. [. . .]

Equality of representation. The German system gives us a good perspective on another great defect of adversary theory, the problem that the Germans call "Waffenungleichheit" – literally, inequality of weapons, or in this instance, inequality of counsel. [. . .] You cannot send me into a ring with Muhammed Ali if you expect a fair fight. [. . .] It is a rare litigator in the United States who has not witnessed the spectacle of a bumbling adversary whose poor discovery work or inability to present evidence at trial caused his client to lose a case that should have been won. Disparity in the quality of legal representation can make a difference in Germany, too, but the active role of the judge places major limits on the extent of the injury that bad lawyering can work on a litigant. In German procedure both parties get the same fact-gatherer – the judge. [. . .]

VI. JUDICIAL INCENTIVES

[. . .] Because German procedure places upon the judge the responsibility for fact-gathering, the danger arises that the job will not be done well. [. . .]

The answer to that concern in the German tradition is straightforward: The judicial career must be designed in a fashion that creates incentives for diligence and excellence. The idea is to attract very able people to the bench, and to make their path of career advancement congruent with the legitimate interests of the litigants.

The career judiciary. The distinguishing attribute of the bench in Germany (and virtually everywhere else in Europe) is that the profession of judging is separate from the profession of lawyering. Save in exceptional circumstances, the judge is not an ex-lawyer like his Anglo-American counterpart. Rather, he begins his professional career as a judge. [. . .]

Recruitment. [. . .] The judiciary is a prized career: influential, interesting, secure, and [. . .] prestigious and not badly compensated. "[O]nly the graduates with the best examination results have any chance of entering the judicial corps."

Specialization. [. . .] At the appellate level, including the first appellate instance (OLG) that proceeds by review de novo, there is extensive specialization. An OLG is quite large by our standards, sometimes staffed with more than a hundred judges, who sit in chambers containing four or five judges. Cases are allocated among these chambers on the basis of subject matter. All the medical malpractice cases go to one chamber, the maritime cases to another, and so forth. This system permits the judges to develop over the years just that sort of expertise in legal subspecialites that we expect of lawyers, particularly lawyers in large-firm practice, in the United States. The litigants get judges who know something about the field, in contradistinction to the calculated amateurism of our appellate tradition.

Political influence. Directly political concerns appear to be very subordinated in the selection and advancement of judges. [. . .] [P]olitical considerations de not materially affect appointment or promotion until the level of the Federal Supreme Court (BGH). Party balance is given weight in BGH appointments, but political connections do not substitute for merit. Positions on the BGH go to judges who have distinguished themselves on the OLG.

VII. APPELLATE REVIEW

[. . .] From the standpoint of comparison with American procedure, two attributes of German appellate practice appear especially noteworthy: (1) the requirement, meant to facilitate review, that the first-instance court disclose in writing its findings of fact and reasons of law; and (2) the de novo standard of review.

Disclosure of grounds. Unless the first-instance court is successful in encouraging the parties to settle, it must decide the case by means of a written judgment containing findings of facts and rulings of law. The thoroughness of the German judgment is legendary. Empirical study has shown how seriously the first-instance courts take their judgment-writing responsibility. [. . .] Good opinions reduce the reversal rate and win esteem in the peer evaluation process. Judges know that the reviewing court will have convenient access to the whole of the evidence and the submissions received at first-instance, since the dossier goes up with the appeal. Especially when coupled with searching review by an appellate court of great ability, the requirement of written findings and reasons is a bulwark against arbitrary or eccentric adjudication. In our system, by contrast, the conclusory general verdict of a jury is the antithesis of a reasoned judgment; nor do we insist on much better in the realm of bench trials. Fact-finding in American courts all too often resembles Caligula dealing with vanquished gladiators: thumbs up or thumbs down, yours but to wonder why.

Review de novo. Ultimately, it is the prospect of appellate review in German civil procedure that makes the other safeguards effective, both as deterrents and as correctives. The dissatisfied litigant has the right of appeal de novo (Berufung) in the first appellate instance (typically the OLG). No presumption of correctness attaches to the initial judgment. What makes this astonishingly liberal system of appellate review possible is the extreme economy of the technique [. . .] of recording in pithy summaries the evidence gathered at first instance. Retrial becomes for the most part only rereading. The OLG "may choose to rehear evidence and is likely to do so when demeanor of a witness seems important or when the record fails to give sufficient detail." The main task in review de novo is not, however, gathering new evidence, but considering afresh the record and the judgment from below. OLG review guarantees to the dissatisfied litigant a second look by a panel of long-experienced judges on all matters of law and fact. [. . .] OLG review is collegial; a panel of several judges decides the case. And because the OLG panels are specialized by subject matter, chances are that some of the judges who decide the case will be masters of the particular field of law. From the OLG there is a further level of review (by the BGH) according to a standard of review (Revision) that approximates the Anglo-American notion of review for error.

Adequacy of safeguards. There is no denying the power of the German judge, yet complaints about the misuse of judicial power are extremely rare. The career incentives and the system of appellate review have been designed to deter and correct abuse. Experience suggests that they work. [. . .]

VIII. [. . .]

[. . .] *Concentration.* When Kaplan sought "the grand discriminant, the watershed feature, so to speak, which shows the English and American systems to be consanguine and sets them apart from the German, the Italian, and others in the civil-law family," he found it in our "single-episode trial as contrasted with discontinuous or staggered proof-taking" on the Continent. Arthur von Mehren has advanced a similar view, showing in a recent article how extensively the concentrated trial has affected the rest of our civil procedure. [. . .]

The jury. "The common law system," writes von Mehren, "had to concentrate trials because of the jury ... The presence of a jury makes a discontinuous trial impractical." Historically, it is surely correct that concentration of the trial eliminated the problems of reassembling and controlling groups of laymen across long intervals, problems that would otherwise have bedeviled a system of routine but discontinuous jury trial. "Moreover, at least until relatively modern times, there was probably no way in which material presented at widely separate points in time could have been preserved in a form that would have enabled the jury to refresh its recollection when it ultimately came to deliberate and render the verdict." In an age of stenographically reported and now videotaped testimony, however, those concerns look less fundamental.

Although civil jury trial is a comparative rarity within the declining subset of our cases that go to any kind of trial, the jury entitlement is enshrined in the seventh amendment and in comparable state constitutional guarantees. There is a substantial body of opinion that the civil jury is a worthwhile safeguard, and that view can scarcely be gainsaid as long as our trial bench remains, at the margin, so unreliable.

The question arises, therefore, whether the jury guarantee will continue to dominate our increasingly juryless practice. In the context of comparative civil procedure, the question is whether the jury tradition that underlies the Anglo-American concentrated trial is a true "grand discriminant," capable of preventing convergence toward Continental procedure. [. . .]

B. The costs of lawsuits

I. The American rule of costs

1. Stephen C. Yeazell/Joanna C. Schwartz, *Civil Procedure*, 9th ed., 2016, pp. 340–342

1. The "American" and "English" Rules About Attorneys' Fees

Who pays for lawyers' work? Essentially, there are five candidates: the client, the opposing party, third-party financers, society generally (via subsidies or charity), and the lawyer herself (because she does the work for free). Each accounts for a portion of U.S. civil litigation.

The system in which each party pays its own legal fees has come to be known as the *American Rule*. Under the *English Rule* (which prevails not only in England but in most of the legal systems of the developed world), the losing party pays both its own fees and those of the other side. In practice, these distinctions are less than absolute: To an increasing extent someone other than the client pays U.S. legal fees, and in Great Britain less than the full amount of actual fees is generally taxed to the other side. Thus, these two "rules" do not accurately describe present practice in either country; they serve, however, as useful models and a starting point from which to explore the subject.

The English Rule in its pure form fully compensates a winning plaintiff: She gets both the damages (or other remedy) *and* the costs of litigation. By contrast, under the pure American Rule, a winning plaintiff has to subtract from any damages recovered the amount charged by his lawyer, and is to that extent made less than whole. Defenders of the American Rule point out that it permits litigants, typically plaintiffs, with tenable but less-than-certain cases to invoke the legal system without fear of having to bear the expense of both their own and the opposition's attorney. [. . .] Let us begin to explore the structure of fee arguments under the American Rule with a common situation – the client who agrees to pay the lawyer's fee[11] [. . .] One common form of agreement calls for the client to pay the lawyer at a specified hourly rate for legal services, plus various costs – photocopying, telephone calls, and the like.

The hourly fee is probably the most common financing mechanism for U.S. litigation. Most contract and commercial litigation, which, as you may recall, accounts for the majority of civil filings, is financed this way. One study done in 2000 found that the median hourly rate for legal fees was about $ 110 per hour; this average masks very wide variations, with senior lawyers in large urban practices charging over $ 1,000 per hour and rural solo practitioners charging as little as $ 75 per hour.[12]

Flat rates mean a lawyer charges a set amount for a particular matter: an uncontested divorce, a will, and so on. Some lawyers use flat rates alone or in combination with other kinds of compensation. Flat rates have the obvious advantage of a predictable, guaranteed fee. Their disadvantages are equally clear. Underestimates are possible: what begins as an uncomplicated conveyance can turn into a nightmare of legal research [. . .], forcing the lawyers to choose between malpractice and very expensive – and uncompensated – work. Yet if the lawyer tries to allow for such contingencies, she risks charging more than the matter warrants or the market will bear. As a consequence, flat rates are most often used for kinds

---

11 *Note by the author*: For the so-called "contingency fees" which are only paid out if the case is won, see below, p. 563
12 For the amounts of lawyers' hourly rates in numerous countries, see the excellent study by C. Hodges/ S. Vogenauer/M. Tulibacka (eds.), *The Costs and Funding of Civil Litigation – A Comparative Perspective*, Oxford: Hart, 2010, overview at pp. 180–183. Examples: *England*: £100–400; *France*: 220–500 €; *Switzerland*: 350–600 CHF; *Poland*: amounts equivalent to 50–200 USD.

of work that the lawyer thinks will have predictable investments of time: Wills are probably the most common example. Conversely, many lawyers have traditionally resisted handling contested litigation on a flat-rate basis. [. . .]

2. Arthur L. Goodhart, Costs, *Yale L. J.* 1929, 849 at 873

Why do the American rules differ so fundamentally from the English ones? Is the difference due merely to the accident of historical development, or is it based on some fundamental dissimilarity in social and economic conditions? Was the change from the English common-law practice [. . .] a conscious or an unconscious one when the common-law was established in the Colonies? [. . .]

Apart from purely historical reasons, the American rules as to costs may also be due in part to a vague feeling that they favor the poor man, and are therefore democratic, while the English system helps the wealthy litigant. The argument is that by imposing a liability for costs upon the losing party a poor man "might often become a prey of a dishonest adversary from sheer want of funds to protect his rights." [. . .]

Another objection to the introduction of substantial costs is based on the view that the law at best is a gamble, and that it is unfair to penalize the losing party. Perhaps this is a result of the sporting theory of justice [. . .]. It is unfair to hit a man when he is down, and to costs against the man who has lost seems to be perilously like it. This view has been strongly put in a recent article by Mr. Satterthwaite:

> The scheme urged [the loser to pay all costs] is based on the wholly unwarranted assumption that the losing party in litigation is always, or even ordinarily, in the wrong. Its sole justification must be that an adverse verdict by a jury or an unfavourable decision of the Court carries with it the necessary conclusion that the defeated party was morally culpable in bringing action, or in resisting suit, as the case may be. Nothing could be further from the actual facts of life. [. . .] An enlightened Judge must realize that, in spite of his most conscientious and painstaking efforts, he is, in a given case, as like as not to do injustice when he seeks to do justice.

Is not the answer to this that the costs must be paid by one party or the other, and that, in spite of Mr. Satterthwaite's pessimism, it is at least more probable that the losing party was in the wrong? [. . .]

3. Gregory J. Myers, When the Small Business Litigant Cannot Afford to Lose (or Win), *Wm. Mitchell L. Rev.* 2012–2013, 140 at 141, 147

[. . .] Hiring a lawyer to evaluate a dispute and prepare a complaint or answer can consume many thousands of dollars in fees. Preparing and responding to written discovery can be even more expensive, especially if it is coupled with motion practice and multiple depositions, which (including preparation time, testimony and transcript costs together) can cost between $2,000 to $10,000 per witness. Even a limited expert witness can add tens of thousands of dollars in additional costs and fees. Responding to or bringing a summary judgement motion can often exceed $40,000 in fees for a lawyer to brief and argue. These costly activities are only a partial list of costs and expenses that a litigant incurs – yet they could continue for six to twelve months or more before there is any prospect for settlement and before any trial. [. . .]

Each day of trial can involve two or more lawyers working twelve to eighteen hours a day, plus paralegal support, and possibly legal support in the office to work on trial motions and other matters. [. . .]

4. U.S. Supreme Court, *Alyeska Pipeline Svc. Co. v. Wilderness Society*, 12.05.1975, 421 U.S. 240 (1975)

[. . .] We do not purport to assess the merits or demerits of the "American Rule" with respect to the allowance of attorneys' fees. It has been criticized in recent years, and courts have been urged to find exceptions to it. [. . .] But the rule followed in our courts with respect to attorneys' fees has survived. It is deeply rooted in our history and in congressional policy, and it is not for us to invade the legislature's province by redistributing litigation costs [. . .]. [. . .]

II. The European rule of costs – the example of Germany[13]

1. Zivilprozessordnung, ZPO (*Code of Civil Procedure*)

Prozesskosten

§ 91. Grundsatz und Umfang der Kostenpflicht. (1) Die unterliegende Partei hat die Kosten des Rechtsstreits zu tragen, insbesondere die dem Gegner erwachsenen Kosten zu erstatten, soweit sie zur zweckentsprechenden Rechtsverfolgung oder Rechtsverteidigung notwendig waren. [. . .]

§ 92. Kosten bei teilweisem Obsiegen. (1) Wenn jede Partei teils obsiegt, teils unterliegt, so sind die Kosten gegeneinander aufzuheben oder verhältnismäßig zu teilen. Sind die Kosten gegeneinander aufgehoben, so fallen die Gerichtskosten jeder Partei zur Hälfte zur Last. [. . .]

Translation

Costs of the lawsuit

§ 91. (1) The party that loses the lawsuit shall bear the costs of the lawsuit, particularly the costs of the other party to the extent that they were required for a proper claim or defense. [. . .]

§ 92. (1) If both parties win and lose parts of the lawsuit, each party must bear the own costs or the costs are divided among the parties according to the percentage of the suit each party wins or loses. If both parties must bear their own costs, each of them shall bear half of the court fees. [. . .]

---

13 Many other continental jurisdictions, as well as *English* law, provide – like *German* law – a *loser-pays* principle for the costs of legal proceedings. However, many systems leave discretion to the judge when it comes to distributing the costs of the lawsuit. In e.g. *England and Wales*, courts grant the successful party an average reimbursement of 2/3 to 3/4 of their counsel's fees, see J. PEYSNER, England and Wales, in: Hodges/Vogenauer/Tulibacka (fn. 12), p. 289 at 296 and 299. The courts in *France* also "rarely order the losing party to pay the total amount of fees that have been paid to the lawyer by the winning party", see A.-L. VILLEDIEU, France – the Rules on Funding and Costs, in: *ibid.*, p. 335 at 346. Before German courts, on the other hand, the loser-pays principle is usually strictly applied.

2. Bundesgerichtshof, BGH (*Federal Supreme Court of Justice*), 30.05.2006, NJW 2006, 2490 at 2491

[. . .] In German procedural law, costs are assessed on the basis of equity, in particular on the basis of the "principle of causation" (*Veranlasserprinzip*). The losing party always bears any litigation costs in adversarial proceedings because he or she is deemed to have "caused" the dispute in question. [. . .]

3. SIMON M. BECK/TOBIAS SCHEEL, *Zivilprozessrecht im Assessorexamen (Civil Procedure Law in the Second State Board Exam)*, 4th ed., Munich: C. H. Beck, 2016, nos. 635, 636

[. . .] In accordance with the first sentence of § 91 (1), when a party loses a civil lawsuit, he or she is required to pay the costs of the other party. To provide adequate protection for the losing party, the proceedings must be carried out in a cost-effective manner; only those costs which were "necessary" to establish the claim or provide a defence are to be borne by the losing party. For this reason, any costs relating to the hiring of legal counsel are only reimbursed in an amount corresponding to the fees set out in the statutory tables, even if the winning party had agreed a different, higher fee with his or her lawyer. [. . .]

[. . .] If a party to a lawsuit is only partially successful and is (therefore) required to share the costs in part with the other party, then such costs shall be allocated in line with § 92. The degree to which each party won or lost the lawsuit is decisive, and the costs borne by each is to be **proportioned** accordingly. [. . .]

4. Gesetz über die Vergütung der Rechtsanwältinnen und Rechtsanwälte, Rechtsanwaltsvergütungsgesetz, RVG (*Act on the Remuneration of Lawyers*)

> § 1. **Geltungsbereich.** (1) Die Vergütung (Gebühren und Auslagen) für anwaltliche Tätigkeiten der Rechtsanwältinnen und Rechtsanwälte bemisst sich nach diesem Gesetz. [. . .]
>
> § 2. **Höhe der Vergütung.** (1) Die Gebühren werden, soweit dieses Gesetz nichts anderes bestimmt, nach dem Wert berechnet, den der Gegenstand der anwaltlichen Tätigkeit hat (Gegenstandswert).
> (2) Die Höhe der Vergütung bestimmt sich nach dem Vergütungsverzeichnis der Anlage 1 zu diesem Gesetz. [. . .]
>
> § 3a. **Vergütungsvereinbarung.** (1) Eine Vereinbarung über die Vergütung bedarf der Textform. [. . .] Sie hat einen Hinweis darauf zu enthalten, dass die gegnerische Partei [. . .] im Falle der Kostenerstattung regelmäßig nicht mehr als die gesetzliche Vergütung erstatten muss.
>
> § 13. **Wertgebühren.** (1) [. . .]. [. . .]. Eine Gebührentabelle für Gegenstandswerte bis 500 000 Euro ist diesem Gesetz als Anlage 2 beigefügt. [. . .]
>
> § 15. **Abgeltungsbereich der Gebühren.** (1) Die Gebühren entgelten, soweit dieses Gesetz nichts anderes bestimmt, die gesamte Tätigkeit des Rechtsanwalts vom Auftrag bis zur Erledigung der Angelegenheit.

Translation

§ 1. Scope of application. (1) This Act covers remuneration (fees and expenses) for legal services provided by lawyers. [. . .]

§ 2 Rate of remuneration. (1) Unless otherwise prescribed by this Act, fees are to be calculated in line with the amount in dispute in relation to which the legal services are provided (amount in dispute).
(2) The rate of remuneration is to be set according to the remuneration schedule found in Annex 1 of this Act. [. . .]

§ 3a. Agreements on remuneration. (1) Remuneration agreements must be made in writing. [. . .] The arrangement must indicate that the opposing party [. . .] is not obliged to pay more than the statutory fee in the event that he or she is required to pay the costs of the proceedings.

§ 13 Statutory fees. (1) [. . .]. [. . .]. Annex 2 contains a fee-table fixing fees for amounts in dispute up to 500,000 €. [. . .]

§ 15 Scope of fees. (1) Unless otherwise prescribed by this Act, fees cover all services provided by a lawyer from first commission up to the conclusion of the case.

Annex 2 (to § 13 (1) sent. 3)

Amount in dispute up to . . . €	Fee . . . €	Amount in dispute up to . . . €	Fee . . . €
500	45.00	50,000	1,163.00
1,000	80.00	65,000	1,248.00
1,500	115.00	80,000	1,333.00
2,000	150.00	95,000	1,418.00
3,000	201.00	110,000	1,503.00
4,000	252.00	125,000	1,588.00
5,000	303.00	140,000	1,673.00
6,000	354.00	155,000	1,758.00
7,000	405.00	170,000	1,843.00
8,000	456.00	185,000	1,928.00
9,000	507.00	200,000	2,013.00
10,000	558.00	230,000	2,133.00
13,000	604.00	260,000	2,253.00
16,000	650.00	290,000	2,373.00
19,000	696.00	320,000	2,493.00
22,000	742.00	350,000	2,613.00
25,000	788.00	380,000	2,733.00
30,000	863.00	410,000	2,853.00
35,000	938.00	440,000	2,973.00
40,000	1,013.00	470,000	3,093.00
45,000	1,088.00	500,000	3,213.00

Note by the author: Section 2 (2) RVG, together with Annex 1, determine the services for which a lawyer is entitled to claim fees. For example, once he or she is commissioned and starts acting for a client, he or she is entitled to charge a baseline fee plus a multiplier (*Geschäftsgebühr*) depending on the relevant tasks performed (with a multiplier of more than 1.3x the baseline fee only for matters which are particularly complex).

If the case goes to court, he or she is entitled to another 1.3x the baseline fee (divided by 2 if a *Geschäftsgebühr* has already been charged) (*Verfahrensgebühr*). Once the oral hearings have begun, an additional 1.2x the baseline fee is due (*Terminsgebühr*). In most cases that proceed to oral hearings, this makes it 2.5x the baseline fee.

Applied to the Millers' case and to the variations as exposed in question 4, this results in the following calculations:[14]

a) **The plaintiff claims damages in the amount of € 5,000 and the case goes before the court**

Type of fees	Legal basis	Calculation	Amount
Court fees	§ 48 (1) 1 GKG; §§ 3 ff. ZPO; 34 (1) GKG and annex 2; annex 1 GKG and no. 1210	3 × € 146.00	€ 438.00
Lawyers' fees	§ 23 (1) RVG; §§ 3 ff. ZPO; § 13 (1) RVG and annex 2 RVG; annex 1 RVG and nos. 3100, 3104, 7002, 7008.	[value in litigation € 5,000: 1 fee = € 303.00 (see table on p. 559)] *Verfahrensgebühr* (1,3 × € 303 =) € 393.90 + *Terminsgebühr* (1,2 × € 303 =) € 363.60 + flat rate for communication devices € 20.00 = € 777.50 + VAT 19% = € 147.73 = total amount of € 925.23	€ 925.23 for claimant's lawyer + € 925.23 for defendant's lawyer
Total costs		€ 438.00 + (2 × € 925.23)	**€ 2,288.46**

- **The plaintiff wins full compensation (€ 5,000 is awarded)**

  § 91 (1) 1 ZPO: The defendant bears the full costs of the lawsuit = **€ 2,288.46** (corresponding to approximately 50% of the amount claimed and in dispute)

- **The plaintiff is awarded 50% of the amount claimed (€ 2,500 is awarded)**

  § 91 (1) 2 ZPO: The plaintiff and the defendant each bear **€ 1,144.23** of the costs of the lawsuit (€ 219,00 = half of the court fees + € 925,23 for each party's own lawyer's fees)

- **The plaintiff is awarded 20% of the amount claimed (€ 1,000 is awarded)**

  § 91 (1) 1 ZPO (the parties share the costs in relation to the outcome of the claim)

---

14 For the costs of lawsuits and the calculation of lawyer's fees under the table, see https://anwaltverein.de/de/service/prozesskostenrechner.

The plaintiff bears 80% of the costs = € 2,288.46 × 0,8 = **€ 1,830.77**
The defendant pays 20% of the costs = € 2,288.46 € × 0,2 = **€ 457.69**

- **The plaintiff loses the lawsuit**

  § 91 (1) 1 ZPO: The plaintiff bears the full costs of the lawsuit = **€ 2,288.46**

b) **The plaintiff claims € 20,000 and the case goes before court**

   Court fees: € 1,035
   Lawyers' fees per party: € 2,231.25
   Total costs of the lawsuit: € 5,497.50 (approximately 30% of the amount claimed)

c) **The plaintiff claims € 200,000 and the case goes before court.**

   Court fees: € 5,238
   Lawyers' fees per party: € 6,012.48
   Total costs of the lawsuit: € 17,262.96 (approximately 10% of the amount claimed)

5. Bundesverfassungsgericht, BVerfG (*Federal Constitutional Court*), 17.10.1990, I BvR 283/85, BVerfGE 83, 1 at 14 (on the rationale behind the fee-table system)

[...] a) German law has implemented a comprehensive regulatory system for lawyers which fixes flat rates of remuneration for all types of legal service [...]. The purpose of fixing remuneration amounts in statute is to promote clarity and predictability with respect to any expenses arising out of a lawyer-client relationship [...]. It may therefore be the case that the fees charged by a lawyer for a particular case do not correspond exactly to the effort which the latter is required to put in. Nevertheless, this is not to be viewed as excessive legislative interference since the overriding aim of the measure is to ensure that, when all of these cases are added up, lawyers receive adequate remuneration for their services. While this does mean that lawyers are obliged to make long-term cost estimates (*Mischkalkulation*), at the same time they can benefit from the advantages offered by a comprehensive system of fixed tariffs and fees. [...]

6. Bundesverfassungsgericht, BVerfG (*Federal Constitutional Court*), 15.06.2009, I BvR 1342/07, NJW-RR 2010, 259 at 260 (on the rationale behind the amounts provided in the fee-table system)

[...] On the other hand, the fees provided for by statute do not seek to remunerate lawyers appropriately for every single case which they take up, and indeed in some cases the fees provided may not even cover the relevant costs. Instead, the underlying concept is that, when all of these cases are added up, the remuneration must cover the lawyer's operating costs and personal income [...]. The lawyer is thus required to make long-term cost estimates (*Mischkalkulation*) in a process known as "cross-subsidising" (*Quersubventionierung*), where the lawyer offsets less lucrative cases with more profitable ones. [...]

7. Christoph Hommerich/Matthias Kilian/Heike Jackmuth/Thomas Wolf, Quersubventionierung im RVG: Fiktion oder Wirklichkeit? (Cross-subsidisation: Fiction or Reality?), AnwBl. 2006, 406 at 407

[. . .] Based on [. . .] the data we have, it appears that in our diverse modern-day legal market the principle of cross-subsidisation (*Quersubventionierung*) can no longer entirely achieve the effects that the legislator of past intended it to have; small-scale, less-specialised law firms and/or firms with a smaller commercial clientele regularly report that they do not attract enough lucrative clients to outweigh those that are less profitable. This is all the more problematic since small-scale, less-specialised law firms rarely form remuneration agreements with their clients despite the fact that such agreements could, in theory, remedy the consequences of regulated tariffs. [. . .]

8. Stefan Hardege/Bernd Waas, *Rechtsanwaltsvergütung in Europa, Studie für die Bundesrechtsanwaltskammer* (Remuneration of Lawyers in Europe, Study for the Federal Bar Association), Köln: Institut der Deutschen Wirtschaft, 2008, pp. 48 and 51

[. . .] Any lawyer taking on a low-value dispute can, in theory, depart from the statutory payment threshold and earn higher fees through a remuneration agreement. The fact that this does not regularly occur in practice can be taken as an indication of intense competition between lawyers. [. . .]

[. . .] Statistics reveal that, in Germany, people with low-value claims are charged significantly less for legal services than those [. . .] in similar countries which do not use fee tables and fix pricing through statute. Charging lower prices for low-value claims has a positive effect on access to justice, in particular with regard to low-income groups. Almost 70 per cent of all civil lawsuits litigated before local courts fall into the category of low-value claims (awards of below 2,000 euros). In other countries, people find that it is not worth bringing a low-value claim and potential claimants are put off far more often by what they perceive to be excessive legal fees; in Germany, this problem exists to a much lesser degree.[15]

---

15 *Note by the author*: there is no problem finding qualified lawyers working at rates fixed in the tables, see e.g. M. Kilian, RVG-Mindestgebühren für Prozesse: Auslauf- oder Zukunftsmodell?, *AnwBl.* 2012, 409 (in English translation): "32 per cent of lawyers working in [international law firms] report [. . .] that they do not work for the minimum fees fixed by statute. [. . .] On the other hand, 97% of lawyers working in one man law firms and 95% of lawyers from medium-sized law firms are willing to act for the minimum statutory fees set out by the RVG." See also C. Hommerich/M. Kilian/H. Jackmuth/T. Wolf, Der Preis der Zeit – Stundensätze deutscher Rechtsanwälte, *AnwBl.* 2006, 473 (in English translation): "According to a study conducted in 1997 [. . .], between 40 and 60% of lawyers (this figure was found to vary for different specialisations) had no experience whatsoever with the hourly remuneration of their services."

For legal advice which is not linked to judicial proceedings, lawyers are recommended to agree on their fees, advice which is largely followed, see § 34 (1) RVG (in English translation): "For any oral or written advice, any drafting of a written opinion, or mediation [. . .] whereby information (counselling) is provided outside of the scope of any activity covered by statutory fees, lawyers are recommended to work on the basis of a fee agreement [. . .]".

III. Charging fees in case of success only? – contingency fees/ *Erfolgshonorare*

1. ARTHUR TAYLOR VON MEHREN/PETER MURRAY, *Law in the United States*, Cambridge: CUP, 2nd ed., 2007, pp. 268–269

4. Lawyers' fees and compensation

[. . .] Critics of the American Rule note that a defendant who defeats the plaintiff's claim is nonetheless burdened with the cost of doing so and that a successful plaintiff receives compromised compensation. On the other hand, the risk of having to pay the other party's fee if unsuccessful might deter plaintiffs of modest means from initiating meritorious litigation. Lawyers' heavy responsibility for successful outcomes in American litigation and the lack of a fee table or firm practice limiting potential fees also militate in favour of restricting liability for lawyers' fees to the party that retained the lawyer.

Fees are, for the most part, agreed upon between lawyer and client. The fee-table system, found in many European countries, is not used in the United States. An extreme result of this form of contractual freedom in the area of lawyer compensation is the "contingency fee", legal in every American state. Under a contingency fee arrangement, a plaintiff's lawyer can agree that he or she will only charge a fee if the plaintiff is awarded compensation in the litigation. If there is no recovery, there is no fee. On the other hand, if the case succeeds, the fee will typically be calculated as a percentage of the recovery. Percentages of 33 percent or even 40 percent of the amount recovered are typical, depending on the complexity of the case and the size of the potential recovery.

Contingency-fee arrangements are strictly regulated in most states, and the amount of compensation payable in individual cases is subject to court review for egregious unreasonableness. Contingent fees are especially frequent in personal-injury actions where these arrangements permit persons without means to litigate cases that their lawyers think are likely enough to produce recoveries and, hence, fees to justify the investment of their time and energy on a contingent basis.

2. Bundesrechtsanwaltsordnung, BRAO (*German Federal Act Regulating the Legal Profession*)

§ 49b. Vergütung. [. . .] (2) Vereinbarungen, durch die eine Vergütung oder ihre Höhe vom Ausgang der Sache oder vom Erfolg der anwaltlichen Tätigkeit abhängig gemacht wird oder nach denen der Rechtsanwalt einen Teil des erstrittenen Betrages als Honorar erhält (Erfolgshonorar), sind unzulässig, soweit das Rechtsanwaltsvergütungsgesetz nichts anderes bestimmt. [. . .]

Translation

§ 49b. Remuneration. [. . .] (2) Agreements under which remuneration or the amount of the award depend on the outcome of the case [success fee] or on the success of the lawyer's work, or any agreement under which the lawyer keeps a part of the award made by the court as a fee (contingency fee) are not permitted, unless the Act on the Remuneration of lawyers provides otherwise. [. . .]

3. Bundesverfassungsgericht, BVerfG (*German Constitutional Court*), 12.12.2006, 1 BvR 2576/04, BVerfGE 117, 163, NJW 2007, 979

Reasoning of the court

A.

1 The applicant is a lawyer. In this constitutional complaint she is challenging a disciplinary action which was brought against her after she made a contingency fee agreement (*pactum de quota litis*) with a client.

I.

2 1. According to the legal definition provided in § 49b (2) 1st sent. of the *Bundesrechtsanwaltsordnung* (Act Regulating the Legal Profession, hereinafter BRAO), a success fee ("*palmarium*"; success- or result-based remuneration) is agreed upon when the remuneration of the lawyer, or a part of it, depends on the outcome of the case or on the success of his or her professional legal activities. [...]

3 2. Since 1994, by virtue of § 49b II BRAO, lawyers have been prohibited from [...] entering into contingency fee agreements, by which they are entitled to a proportion of the amount that was awarded to their client, or any other kind of success fee arrangement.

4 a) [...] Since 1887, disciplinary tribunals have decided time and time again that success fee arrangements are inadmissible [...]. The inadmissibility of such forms of remuneration was justified by reference to the role of the lawyer. Playing a key role in the administration of justice ("*als Organ der Rechtspflege*"), a lawyer should not expose himself to any potential business interest in the client's lawsuit. The *Reichsgericht* consistently held that contingency fees constituted a serious breach of the rules of the profession and that such agreements were contrary to public policy [...] [and therefore void].

II.

17 1. By letter dated 24.09.1990, a woman living in the USA, Mrs Hanna N, approached the applicant's associate. She announced her intention to bring a claim in relation to a property in Dresden which had belonged to her grandfather and had been expropriated by the Nazi regime. She sought legal assistance to help enforce her financial interests. In her message she wrote: "Please let me know if you'd be interested in taking a one-third (33⅓ %) share in any gains as remuneration." The applicant's associate confirmed in a letter dated 10.10.1990 that they would be willing to take on the case and agreed with the proposal for remuneration. [...]

19 In October 1998, the courts awarded Mrs N an amount in compensation fixed at just under 262,000 DM in line with the rules established by the *Entschädigungsgesetz* (Compensation Act). In December 1998, she was awarded an additional 50,000 DM. On the basis of the agreement which they had reached, the applicant claimed a share of 104,000 DM for herself. The remainder [...] was paid to clients N and S.

20 2. a) A disciplinary tribunal found that by making a contingency fee agreement with her clients, N and S, the applicant acted in violation of her professional duties under § 43a (1) BRAO in conjunction with § 352 of the *Strafgesetzbuch* (Criminal Code, hereinafter StGB). The tribunal therefore issued a disciplinary warning and ordered the applicant to pay a fine amounting to 25,000 €. [...]

21 b) On appeal, the occupational court reduced the applicant's fine to 5,000 €.

III.

27 In her [. . .] constitutional complaint, the applicant asserts that her basic right to freely exercise her profession was infringed. [. . .]

B.

56 The constitutional complaint in question is partially well-founded. [. . .]

58 I. The blanket prohibition of success fee arrangements [. . .] violates the basic right of the applicant to freely exercise her profession (Art. 12 (1) of the *Grundgesetz*, hereinafter GG). [. . .]

60 2. Any measure which restricts the freedom to exercise a profession is only compatible with Art. 12 (1) GG where there is a lawful basis limiting such freedom on grounds of public policy [. . .]. The restriction in question must observe the principle of proportionality [. . .]. [. . .]

63 (1) By looking to protect the independence of lawyers, the legislator pursues the legitimate overriding aim of having a well-functioning judicial system. [. . .]

67 bb) Another legitimate aim of the blanket prohibition of success fee arrangements is to protect persons seeking legal advice from being subject to excessive rates of remuneration. [. . .]

69 cc) Finally, the statutory prohibition on success fee arrangements also pursues a public policy objective in that it promotes procedural equality of access to justice. [. . .] Although it is not impossible *per se* for a defendant to agree a success-based fee arrangement, he or she will have more difficulty than the claimant in proving that his or her claim has *de facto* succeeded and the extent to which it has succeeded, and thus in determining the remuneration which the lawyer is entitled to – for example if the case has been dismissed.

70 dd) Apart from this, all other public policy reasons provided to this Court to justify the prohibition of success fee arrangements do not meet the standards for constitutional review.

71 (1) The aim of avoiding a sharp increase in frivolous litigation is to be disregarded. The Court has seen no evidence which proves the assumption that by allowing success fee arrangements we will be threatened by a "flood of litigation." [. . .] The subsequent cost burden would generally act to deter clients who have no chance of success.

72 This point is proven by studies in the United States of America which show that people are encouraged to bring meritless claims not because of success-based remuneration but because of the ordinary law of costs by which the losing party is not required to bear the costs of the prevailing party (the "American rule"). For example, the number of unfounded medical malpractice claims brought in Florida fell significantly in the 1980s after the state installed a legal framework which took influence from the remuneration regime found under §§ 91 ff. of the *Zivilprozessordnung* (Code of Civil Procedure, hereinafter ZPO) even though proceedings remained governed by contingency fees (see Hughes/Snyder, Journal of Law and Economics 38 [1995], pp. 225 [229f., 234ff.]). [. . .]

[For the reasons outlined in nos. 63, 67 and 69, the prohibition of success fee arrangements is in line with constitutional requirements and thus permissible.]

97 bb) However, the prohibition is disproportionate insofar as § 49b (2) BRAO (previous version) does not allow any derogation. [. . .]. [. . .]

102 (3) [. . .] [T]he prohibition of success fee arrangements may result in blocking access to justice where a person seeking justice is afraid to bring a claim for fear of losing and being burdened with the costs of legal assistance which he or she cannot afford, or cannot afford in full, by virtue of his or her financial circumstances and where this prevents the latter from pursuing his or her rights.

111 2. The Court sets a deadline of 30.06.2008 for the legislator to revise the law in accordance with constitutional requirements.

4. Rechtsanwaltsvergütungsgesetz, RVG (*Act on the Remuneration of Lawyers*), as of 01.07.2008

§ 4a. Erfolgshonorar. (1) Ein Erfolgshonorar (§ 49b Abs. 2 Satz 1 der Bundesrechtsanwaltsordnung) darf nur für den Einzelfall und nur dann vereinbart werden, wenn der Auftraggeber aufgrund seiner wirtschaftlichen Verhältnisse bei verständiger Betrachtung ohne die Vereinbarung eines Erfolgshonorars von der Rechtsverfolgung abgehalten würde. In einem gerichtlichen Verfahren darf dabei für den Fall des Misserfolgs vereinbart werden, dass keine oder eine geringere als die gesetzliche Vergütung zu zahlen ist, wenn für den Erfolgsfall ein angemessener Zuschlag auf die gesetzliche Vergütung vereinbart wird. [. . .]

(2) Die Vereinbarung muss enthalten:

1. die voraussichtliche gesetzliche Vergütung und gegebenenfalls die erfolgsunabhängige vertragliche Vergütung, zu der der Rechtsanwalt bereit wäre, den Auftrag zu übernehmen, sowie
2. die Angabe, welche Vergütung bei Eintritt welcher Bedingungen verdient sein soll.

(3) In der Vereinbarung sind außerdem die wesentlichen Gründe anzugeben, die für die Bemessung des Erfolgshonorars bestimmend sind. Ferner ist ein Hinweis aufzunehmen, dass die Vereinbarung keinen Einfluss auf die gegebenenfalls vom Auftraggeber zu zahlenden Gerichtskosten, Verwaltungskosten und die von ihm zu erstattenden Kosten anderer Beteiligter hat.

Translation

§ 4a. Success fee (quota litis). (1) A success fee (quota litis, § 49b (2), first sentence of the Act Regulating the Legal Profession) may be agreed only for an individual case and only if the client, upon reasonable consideration, would be deterred from taking legal proceedings without the agreement on a success fee on account of his economic situation. In court proceedings, it may be agreed that in case of failure, no remuneration, or a lower amount than the statutory remuneration, is to be paid if it is agreed that an appropriate supplement is to be paid on the statutory remuneration in case of success. [. . .]

(2) The agreement must contain the following:

1. *the statutory fee that would potentially be due and, if relevant, the contractual remuneration other than a success fee for which the attorney would be willing to accept the mandate and*
2. *specification of which remuneration is to be earned upon fulfilment of which conditions.*

(3) The agreement shall also indicate the reasons that determined the assessment of the success fee (quota litis). In addition, it shall point out that the agreement has no influence on any court costs or administrative costs that the client may be required to meet, or on the costs of other participants that the client is required to reimburse.[16]

5. Julia von Seltmann, *Beck'scher Online-Kommentar RVG (Beck's Online Commentary on the German Act Regulating the Legal Profession)*, 35th ed., as of 01.06.2016, RVG § 4a

1 According to the first sentence of § 4a, a success fee may be agreed only for an individual case and only if the client, upon reasonable consideration, would be deterred from bringing legal proceedings without a success fee agreement on account of his economic situation. The legislator has decided against declaring success fees universally admissible and thus rejected a "very broad solution". The provision will, on the other hand, not only open up access to success fee agreements to "very poor clients", but to any clients who, upon reasonable consideration, would be deterred from bringing legal proceedings without a success fee agreement on account of their economic situation. [. . .] The provision provides a flexible standard which shall allow even for e.g. mid-sized businesses involved in large-scale construction project disputes to enter into success fee agreements.[17] [. . .]

3 It [. . .] does not apply in all circumstances. [. . .] Lawyers entering into a success fee agreement with a client are therefore advised to include a provision in the agreement which details the client's economic situation.

4 The requirement to assess on a case-by-case basis means that each individual case is to be considered separately. Lawyers are not permitted to advertise that they are generally willing to take on a case on the basis of a success fee agreement, nor may they conclude any agreement with a client according to which success fees are to apply to certain, or indeed all, further commissions with this same client.

---

16 For the admissibility of success fees and contingency fees in a large range of jurisdictions, see Hodges/Vogenauer/Tulibacka (fn. 12), pp. 132–133.

17 *Note by the author*: if at all, "success fees are usually only agreed between larger business consultancy firms and their commercial clients", see M. Kilian, Die Verwendung von Erfolgshonorarvereinbarungen durch die Anwaltschaft, *AnwBl.* 2012, 148 at 150 (translation from German).

6. Matthias Kilian, Brennpunkte des anwaltlichen Berufsrechts (*Rules on the Profession of Lawyers in Focus*), NJW 2014, 1499 at 1500

[. . .] Fewer than 1% of lawyers reported that they used success fee agreements on a regular basis at the time of the survey [2011].[18] [. . .]

7. Hans-Jochem Mayer, Entwicklungen zum Rechtsanwaltsvergütungsgesetz (*Recent Developments on the Act on the Remuneration of Lawyers*) 2007–2011, NJW 2011, 1563 at 1565

[. . .] The intense legal policy debate that preceded the Act on the Reform of the Prohibition of Success Fee Agreements (*Gesetz zur Neuregelung des Verbots der Vereinbarung von Erfolgshonoraren*), which introduced § 4a into the RVG, is in stark contrast to the relatively small practical impact that success fee agreements have had so far on the legal profession. This may be due not least to the fact that the legislator provided only a very narrow scope of application for success fee agreements. [. . .]

8. Matthias Kilian, Erfolgshonorare: Gründe für die verhaltene Nutzung durch die Anwaltschaft (*Success Fees: Reasons for Hardly Using Them in Practice*), AnwBl. 2014, 815 at 817

When the prohibition on success fees was partially lifted, many voiced concern that lawyers would jump at the opportunity to impose success fees on their clients on a regular basis and others would be forced to give in to the pressures of competition whether they liked it or not. This concern was clearly unfounded: the most significant reason why success fees have failed to gather momentum in the legal services market appears to be a lack of demand from parties. [. . .] We should not underestimate the fact that there is a sizeable portion of the legal profession that opposes these agreements as a matter of principle and, as a result, neither offers nor gets involved in them.

---

18 See further (translation from German): "As of spring 2011, only 29% of lawyers (i.e. a significant minority) had in some way agreed a success fee, 20% had agreed a fee entirely dependent on success, and 13% had agreed a contingency fee. Not only did those engaging in success fees constitute a minority, but some ¾ of the relatively small number of lawyers with experience in success fees reported that they used success-based remuneration only very rarely".

Bibliography

SIMON M. BECK/TOBIAS SCHEEL, *Zivilprozessrecht im Assessorexamen*, 4. Aufl., München: C. H. Beck, 2016, Rn. 623 ff.; KARL J. BINZ/JOSEF DÖRNDORFER/RAINER PETZOLD/WALTER ZIMMERMAN, *Gerichtskosten. Justizvergütungs- und -entschädigungsgesetz. Kommentar*, München: C. H. Beck, 2007; ALBERTO CASAGRANDE/MARCO SPALLONE, Investigating the Determinants of Pretrial Settlement Rates: Contingent versus Non-Contingent Lawyers' Fees, *Eur. J. L. & Econ.* 2007, 1–13; JOSEF DÖRNDORFER, *Der Streitwert für Anfänger*, 5. Aufl., München: C. H. Beck, 2009; HORST-REINER ENDERS, *RVG für Anfänger*, 15. Aufl., München: C. H. Beck, 2012; JONATHAN FISCHBACH/MICHAEL FISCHBACH, Rethinking Optimality in Tort Litigation: The Promise of Reverse Cost-Shifting, *BYU J. Pub. L.* 2005, 317–350; STEPHEN GOLDSTEIN, On Comparing and Unifying Civil Procedural Systems, in: S. Goldstein/M. J. Bonell (eds.), *Process and Substance: Lectures on Comparative Law*, London/Dublin/Edinburgh: Butterworths, 1995, pp. 1–43; REINHARD GREGER, Postkutsche auf der Autobahn – Ist der Zivilprozess noch zeitgemäß?, *NZV* 2016, 1–6; PETER HARTMANN, *Kostengesetze, Kurz-Kommentar*, 42. Aufl., München: C. H. Beck, 2012; MARTIN HENSSLER, Der europäische Rechtsanwalt zwischen Rechtspflege und Dienstleistung, *ZZP* 2002, 321–355; CHRISTOPHER HODGES/STEFAN VOGENAUER/MAGDALENA TULIBACKA (eds.), *The Costs and Funding of Civil Litigation: A Comparative Perspective*, Oxford: Hart, 2010; CHRISTOPH HOMMERICH/MATTHIAS KILIAN, Ein Jahr Erfolgshonorare – Empirische Ergebnisse zu einer erzwungenen Reform, *AnwBl.* 2009, 541–543; CHRISTOPH HOMMERICH/MATTHIAS KILIAN/HEIKE JACKMUTH/THOMAS WOLF, Die Vereinbarung der anwaltlichen Vergütung – Ergebnisse einer empirischen Untersuchung der Vergütungspraxis der deutschen Anwaltschaft, *BRAK-Mitt.* 6/2006, 253–258; CHRISTOPH HOMMERICH/MATTHIAS KILIAN, Die Praxis der Vergütungsvereinbarungen deutscher Rechtsanwältinnen und Rechtsanwälte – Zentrale Ergebnisse des Vergütungsbarometers 2009 des Soldan Instituts, *BRAK-Mitt.* 5/2009, 223–225; JAMES W. HUGHES/EDWARD A. SNYDER, Litigation and Settlement Under the English and American Rules: Theory and Evidence, *J. L. & Econ.* 1995, 225–250; KEITH N. HYLTON, Litigation Costs and the Economic Theory of Tort Law, *U. Miami L. Rev.* 1991, 111–148; Ronald Kandelhard, Das neue Berufsbild des Rechtsanwalts, *BRAK-Mitt.* 5/2002, 203–205; MATTHIAS KILIAN, Erfolgshonorare: Annäherung an die "contingent fee" – ein missverstandenes Phänomen des US-amerikanischen Rechts, *VersR* 2006, 751; MATTHIAS KILIAN, Die Vergütung des Anwalts – von der RAGebO über die BRAGO zum RVG, *AnwBl.* 2011, 877–889; MATTHIAS KILIAN, RVG-Mindestgebühren für Prozesse: Auslauf- oder Zukunftsmodell?, *AnwBl.* 2012, 409; MATTHIAS KILIAN, Die Verwendung von Erfolgshonorarvereinbarungen durch die Anwaltschaft, *AnwBl.* 2012, 148; MATTHIAS KILIAN, Brennpunkte des anwaltlichen Berufsrechts, *NJW* 2014, 1499; MATTHIAS KILIAN, Erfolgshonorare: Gründe für die verhaltene Nutzung durch die Anwaltschaft, *AnwBl.* 2014, 815; EMERY G. LEE/THOMAS E. WILLGING, Defining the Problem of Cost in Federal Civil Litigation, *Duke L. J.* 2010–2011, 765; JAMES R. MAXEINER, Cost and Fee Allocation in Civil Procedure, *Am. J. Comp. L.* 2010, 195–221; WILLIAM U. McCORMACK, Attorney's Fees in Civil Litigation, *FBI Law Enforc. Bull.* 1994, 28–32; DIETER MEYER, *Gerichtskosten der streitigen Gerichtsbarkeiten und des Familienverfahrens. Kommentar zum Gerichtskostengesetz (GKG) und zum Gesetz über Gerichtskosten in Familiensachen (FamGKG)*, 15. Aufl., Berlin: de Gruyter, 2015; DIETER MEYER, *Gerichtskostengesetz. Kommentar*, 10. Auflage, Berlin: de Gruyter, 2011; MATTHIAS REIMANN (ed.), *Cost and Fee Allocation in Civil Procedure: A Synthesis*, Wien/New York: Springer, 2013; EBERHARD SCHILKEN, *Zivilprozessrecht*, 6. Aufl., München: Verlag Franz Vahlen, 2010; CATHERINE T. STRUVE, The Paradox of Delegation: Interpreting the Federal Rules of Civil Procedure, *U. Pa. L. Rev.* 2002, 1099–1169; JOACHIM TEUBEL/HERBERT P. SCHONS, *Erfolgshonorar für Anwälte*, München: C. H. Beck, 2008; JOACHIM ZEKOLL, Comparative Civil Procedure, in: Mathias Reimann/Reinhard Zimmermann, *The Oxford Handbook of Comparative Law*, Oxford: OUP, 2006, Chapter 41.

Chapter 18

Cross-border torts

Coordinating legal diversity through Private International Law – an introduction

"According to data from the European Commission and previous calculations, the number of cross-border road traffic accidents in the EU might be assumed to 775,000 per year".[1]

Scenario

A family living in Germany goes on holiday to Spain. They drive in separate cars one after the other on a Spanish motorway. The son, who is driving the car out in front, approaches a long left-hand curve. In order to pass a lorry, he switches from the right-hand lane to the left when suddenly he notices a broken-down Seat Cordoba left immobile in the left-hand lane following an accident in which no other vehicle was involved. The young man makes an emergency stop, thereby avoiding a collision with the Seat Cordoba. His father, however, does not manage to stop in time and the two family cars collide. The son is severely injured and loses the capacity to work for the rest of his life. Both cars, driven by father and son, are registered and insured in Germany. The Seat (which was left untouched in the collision) is registered and insured in Spain.[2]

The young man seeks to obtain compensation for his personal injuries and for the lifetime loss of income. In which countries can he bring a claim and which law will be applied?

Variation: The son argues that the collision between the two family cars was caused by a faulty autonomous driving device installed in the father's car. The car was manufactured in Sweden by a company established there and marketed all around the European Union, notably in Germany, where the father of the victim had acquired it.[3]

---

1 European Parliamentary Research Service, *Study: Limitation Periods for Road Traffic Accidents*, PE 581.386, July 2016, p. 8 (by Christian Salm).
2 The scenario is inspired by the *Swiss* case: Bundesgericht (*Federal Supreme Court of Justice*), 05.11.2015 (*William Siegrist g. Helvetia Schweizerische Versicherungs AG*), 4A_41 3/2015. In that case, father and son had been living in Switzerland.
3 For the potential impact of new technologies on the rules on Private International Law (PIL), see: European Parliament, Directorate General for Internal Policies, Policy Department C: Citizens' Rights and Constitutional Affairs, *Study: Cross-Border Accidents in the EU – the Potential Impact of Driverless Cars*, June 2016 (by Thomas Kadner Graziano), available at: www.europarl.europa.eu/RegData/etudes/STUD/2016/571362/IPOL_STU(2016)571362_EN.pdf.

Introduction

Situation at the substantive law level. Regarding liability for road traffic accidents, domestic laws vary considerably between countries. Differences exist with regard to the applicable liability regimes (strict or fault-based liability), the conditions of liability, the damage covered, the amounts due, in particular with respect to loss of earnings or compensation of immaterial harm, and the rights of third parties.[4]

The present scenario has links with several countries:

- *Spain*, where the accident occurred, and where the Seat Cordoba was registered and insured;
- *Germany*, where the father and son were domiciled, and where their cars were registered and insured; and
- *Sweden*, where the father's autonomous car was manufactured (variation).

The differences between the domestic laws of these countries are of particular relevance for the injured young man. Whereas German and Swedish law, much like the laws of many other countries, apply the principle of full compensation to victims of traffic accidents,[5] Spanish law (or e.g. Portuguese law), on the other hand, uses binding tables, the so-called *Baremos*, under which compensation awards are calculated with regard to the economic climate in Spain.[6]

---

4 See above, Chapters 9–12 and 14. See also: European Commission DG Internal Market and Services, *Rome II Study: Compensation of Victims of Cross-Border Road Traffic Accidents in the EU: Comparison of National Practices, Analysis of Problems and Evaluation of Options for Improving the Position of Cross-Border Victims – Part II – Analysis*, November 2008 (by Demolin, Brulard, Barthelemy – Hoche, team leader: JEAN ALBERT), available at http://ec.europa.eu/civiljustice/news/docs/study_compensation_road_victims_en.pdf.

See also: European Commission, *Consultation Paper on the Compensation of Victims of Cross-Border Road Traffic Accidents in the European Union*, 2009, available at http://ec.europa.eu/internal_market/consultations/docs/2009/cross-border-accidents/rome2study_en.pdf; European Parliament, Directorate General for Internal Policies, Policy Department C: Citizens' Rights and Constitutional Affairs, *Note: Choice of Law for Cross-Border Road Traffic Accidents*, November 2012 (by JENNY PAPETTAS), available at: www.europarl.europa.eu/RegData/etudes/note/join/2012/462492/IPOL-JURI_NT(2012)462492_EN.pdf.

For a comparative overview with numerous references, see: T. KADNER GRAZIANO/C. OERTEL, Ein europäisches Haftungsrecht für Schäden im Straßenverkehr? – Eckpunkte de lege lata und Überlegungen de lege ferenda, ZVglRWiss 2008, 113–163.

For differences regarding third party rights, in particular with regard to damages for immaterial harm, see above, Chapters 11 and 12.

5 Compare, from a comparative perspective, Art. 10:101 (Nature and purpose of damages) of the PETL which consequently provides that "[d]amages are a money payment to compensate the victim, that is to say, to restore him, so far as money can, to the position he would have been in if the wrong complained of had not been committed. [. . .]".

6 Under the previous version of the *Baremo*, damage awards could end up being considerably lower than the damage actually suffered by a victim domiciled abroad, especially in regard to loss of income. Under the new version of the *Baremo*, applicable since 1 January 2016, the differences are much less striking.

For the revised *Baremo*, see: M. MARTÍN-CASALS, A New Spanish Compensation Scheme for Death and Personal Injury Resulting from Road Traffic Accidents, in: J. POTGIETER/J. KNOBEL/R. JANSEN (eds.), *Essays in Honour of Johann Neethling*, Durban: LexisNexis, 2015, pp. 301–322. See also: European Parliament, Directorate General Internal Policies of the Union, Policy Department C: Citizens' Rights and Constitutional Affairs, *Compensation of Victims of Cross-Border Road Traffic Accidents in the EU: Assessment of Selected Options*, 2007 (by ANDREA RENDA/LORNA SCHEFFLER), available at www.europarl.europa.eu/RegData/etudes/etudes/join/2007/378292/IPOL-JURI_ET%282007%29378292_EN.pdf.

Finally, limitation periods vary considerably, ranging from one year to ten years (or more) depending on which law applies, with the periods set by Spanish law being particularly short.[7] The question of the applicable law might thus be crucial for the outcome of the case.

In scenarios presenting cross-border elements, the injured party thus has an interest in knowing:

- where his or her claim can be brought (that is, which country or countries' courts have *jurisdiction* to hear the claim); and
- which will be the *applicable law* to govern the claim before these courts.

Situation at the Private International Law level. The answers to these two questions are provided by the rules on Private International Law (or Choice of Law or Conflict of Laws), which fulfil the task of *coordinating* the different national systems with respect to jurisdiction, the applicable law, and the recognition and enforcement of foreign decisions.[8]

In the European Union, the rules on Private International Law (PIL) are increasingly found in EU regulations providing uniform solutions that are, in principle, applicable throughout the EU. Regarding the question of *jurisdiction*, i.e. the determination of where a claim can be brought, the most important instrument in the EU is the "Brussels I Regulation".[9] As to the question of *applicable law*, i.e. the law a court will apply in a given case, the relevant instrument is the "Rome II Regulation" determining the law applicable to non-contractual obligations.[10]

Other PIL rules are found in international conventions, most importantly in the context of our scenario, in the 1971 Hague Convention on the Law Applicable to Traffic Accidents and the 1973 Hague Convention on the Law Applicable to Products Liability. These Hague Conventions are in force in some EU Member States but not in others.[11]

The criteria used in the Rome II Regulation and those found in the two Hague Conventions differ from each other. The law ultimately applicable to a particular case may thus be different depending on the courts having jurisdiction to hear the claim, and the PIL rules that these courts will apply.

---

7 For a European overview, see: European Parliamentary Research Service/European Added Value Unit, *Limitation Periods for Road Traffic Accidents*, PE 581.386, 2016, pp. 26, 28 (by CHRISTIAN SALM), available at www.europarl.europa.eu/RegData/etudes/STUD/2016/581386/EPRS_STU(2016)581386_EN.pdf.

8 See e.g. Art. 1 of the *Swiss* Private International Law Act (PILA), which provides (in English translation): "(1) In cases presenting a foreign element, this Act determines: a) jurisdiction [. . .]; b) the applicable law; c) the conditions for recognition and execution of foreign decisions; [. . .] (2) International treaties prevail."

9 Regulation (EU) No 1215/2012 of the European Parliament and of the Council of 12 December 2012 on jurisdiction and the recognition and enforcement of judgments in civil and commercial matters, [2012] OJ, L 351/1 (Brussels I Regulation, recast).

10 Regulation (EC) No 864/2007 of the European Parliament and of the Council of 11 July 2007 on the law applicable to non-contractual obligations, [2007] OJ, L 199/40 (Rome II Regulation).

11 The text of the Hague Conventions and up-to-date status tables are available at www.hcch.net.

Questions

1) In the above scenario, the injured young man claims damages for his personal injuries and for the loss of his life's income. Who belongs to the circle of persons who are potentially liable or who can be addressed to cover liability? Answer this question without consulting the materials.

2) Should the parties not achieve an out-of-court agreement, the victim (i.e. the young man in the above scenario) has the option to bring, alternatively:

- an action against the *driver of the Spanish car*,[12] before the courts of the country of his domicile, i.e. *Spanish courts*;[13]
- a direct claim against the *Spanish vehicle liability insurer*,[14] either before *Spanish courts*[15] or, at the choice of the victim, before the courts of the country of his own domicile, that is *German courts*;[16]
- an action against *his father* before *German courts*,[17] or, alternatively, before the *Spanish courts* for the place of the accident;[18] or
- a direct claim against *his father's German vehicle liability insurer* before *German courts*[19] or, alternatively, before the *Spanish courts* of the place of the accident.[20]

---

[12] In most European jurisdictions, strict liability for road traffic accidents focuses on the keeper of the car, whereas few jurisdictions (among which Spanish law) focus on the driver instead; see above, Chapter 9, and e.g. KADNER GRAZIANO/OERTEL (fn. 4), at pp. 123 ff. with references.

[13] Brussels I Regulation (recast), Art. 4(1): "persons domiciled in a Member State shall [. . .] be sued in the courts of that Member State".

[14] For the possibility of a direct claim, see: Directive 2009/103/EC of the European Parliament and of the Council of 16 September 2009 relating to insurance against civil liability in respect of the use of motor vehicles, and the enforcement of the obligation to insure against such liability (codified version), [2009] OJ, L263/11 (Motor Insurance Directive), Art. 3 (Compulsory insurance of vehicles): "Each Member State shall [. . .] take all appropriate measures to ensure that civil liability in respect of the use of vehicles normally based in its territory is covered by insurance. [. . .]." See also Art. 18: "Member States shall ensure that any party injured as a result of an accident caused by a vehicle covered by insurance as referred to in Article 3 enjoys a direct right of action against the insurance undertaking covering the person responsible against civil liability".

For direct claims in national legislations, see e.g. the *German* Versicherungsvertragsgesetz (*Insurance Contracts Act*) VVG, § 115 (1) n° 1.

[15] Brussels I Regulation (recast), Art. 11(1): "An insurer domiciled in a Member State may be sued: (a) in the courts of the Member State in which he is domiciled".

[16] Brussels I Regulation (recast), Art. 13(2): "Articles [. . .] 11 [. . .] shall apply to actions brought by the injured party directly against the insurer [. . .]"; Art. 11(1): "An insurer domiciled in a Member State may be sued: [. . .] (b) [. . .] in the case of actions brought by the policyholder, the insured or a beneficiary, in the courts for the place where the claimant is domiciled; [. . .]".

The Court of Justice of the European Union confirmed that a claim before the courts of the victim's own domicile is available not only to claimants specified in Art. 11(1)(b) (i.e. the policyholder, the insured or a beneficiary), but also, by application of Art. 13(2), to victims benefitting from a direct liability insurance claim against the insurer, such as the young man in our scenario (*FBTO Schadeverzekeringen NV* v. *Jack Odenbreit*, 13.12.2007, C-463/06).

[17] Brussels I Regulation (recast), Art. 4(1), see above, fn. 13.

[18] Brussels I Regulation (recast), Art. 7: "A person domiciled in a Member State may be sued in another Member State: [. . .] (2) in matters relating to tort, delict or quasi-delict, in the courts for the place where the harmful event occurred [. . .]".

[19] Brussels I Regulation (recast), Art. 11(1): "An insurer domiciled in a Member State may be sued: (a) in the courts of the Member State in which he is domiciled".

[20] Brussels I Regulation (recast), Art. 12 1st sent.: "In respect of liability insurance [. . .], the insurer may [. . .] be sued in the courts for the place where the harmful event occurred. [. . .]".

Spanish courts would thus have jurisdiction for a claim brought against any of the potential defendants. *German courts*, on the other hand, would have jurisdiction to hear a claim against the *liability insurer of the Spanish car*, the father of the injured young man or the father's *German vehicle liability insurer*.

Which law would *German courts*, on the one hand, and *Spanish courts* on the other, apply to determine the liability of:

a) the driver of the Spanish car?
b) the victim's father?

3) As a general rule, both the Rome II Regulation and the 1971 Hague Traffic Accident Convention designate the law of the place where the accident occurred. However, when it comes to making an exception to this rule, the two instruments apply different connecting factors. In the above scenario, the Rome II Regulation and the 1971 Hague Traffic Accident Convention therefore lead to the application of different laws (see the answer to question 2). Which of these connecting factors do you consider more appropriate taking into consideration the interests of the parties?

4) In the variation, the young man claims to have been injured by a faulty autonomous driving device. He wants to bring a products liability claim against the *Swedish manufacturer* of his father's car. He has the option of bringing this claim before the *Spanish* or *Swedish* courts. Which law would *Swedish courts* on the one hand, and *Spanish courts* on the other, apply to determine the car manufacturer's liability?

5) In our scenario, the Rome II Regulation and the 1973 Hague Products Liability Convention again designate different laws. Taking into consideration the interests of the parties involved, which of the connecting factors used in the two instruments do you consider more appropriate for the claim against the car manufacturer?

Table of contents

1. Regulation (EC) No 864/2007 of the European Parliament and of the Council of 11 July 2007 on the law applicable to non-contractual obligations, [2007] OJ, L 199/40 (Rome II Regulation), Arts. 1 (1), 3, 4 (1) and (2), 5 (1), 14 (1), 28 (1) ....p. 576
2. The Hague Convention of 4 May 1971 on the Law Applicable to Traffic Accidents, Arts. 1–4, 11 ....p. 577
3. Schweizerisches Bundesgericht (*Swiss Federal Supreme Court of Justice*), 11.11.2008, BGE 135 III 92 on the interpretation of Art. 4 of the 1971 Hague Traffic Accident Convention (with further references) ....p. 578
4. The Hague Convention of 2 October 1973 on the Law Applicable to Products Liability, Arts. 1 (1), 3–7, 11 ....p. 580

Materials[21]

Courts in EU Member States (except Denmark) determine the law applicable to a claim in extra-contractual, delictual, or tortious liability, in principle, according to the rules of the Rome II Regulation (below, 1.). Yet, with regard to road traffic accidents and products liability, pursuant to Art. 28(1) Rome II Regulation, the 1971 Hague Convention on the Law Applicable to Traffic Accidents (below 2.) and the 1973 Hague Convention on the Law Applicable to Products Liability (below, 4.) prevail over the Rome II Regulation for *claims brought in Contracting States* of the said Hague Conventions. Spain being a Contracting State to both of these Hague Conventions, Spanish courts determine the applicable law pursuant to the Hague Conventions. In Germany and Sweden, neither of the two conventions is in force, and therefore German and Swedish courts determine the applicable law according to the Rome II Regulation.

1. Regulation [EC] No 864/2007 of the European Parliament and of the Council of 11 July 2007 on the law applicable to non-contractual obligations, [2007] OJ, L 199/40 (Rome II Regulation)

Chapter I
SCOPE

Art. 1. Scope. (1) This Regulation shall apply, in situations involving a conflict of laws, to non-contractual obligations in civil and commercial matters. [. . .]

Art. 3. Universal application. Any law specified by this Regulation shall be applied whether or not it is the law of a Member State.

Chapter II
TORTS/DELICTS

Art. 4. General rule. (1) Unless otherwise provided for in this Regulation, the law applicable to a non-contractual obligation arising out of a tort/delict shall be the law of the country in which the damage occurs irrespective of the country in which the event giving rise to the damage occurred and irrespective of the country or countries in which the indirect consequences of that event occur.
(2) However, where the person claimed to be liable and the person sustaining damage both have their habitual residence in the same country at the time when the damage occurs, the law of that country shall apply. [. . .]

---

21 For the original language version of the Swiss court decision reproduced in this chapter, see the companion website at www.routledge.com/9781138567733.

Art. 5. Product liability. (1) Without prejudice to Article 4(2), the law applicable to a non-contractual obligation arising out of damage caused by a product shall be:

(a) the law of the country in which the person sustaining the damage had his or her habitual residence when the damage occurred, if the product was marketed in that country; or, failing that,
(b) the law of the country in which the product was acquired, if the product was marketed in that country; or, failing that,
(c) the law of the country in which the damage occurred, if the product was marketed in that country.

However, the law applicable shall be the law of the country in which the person claimed to be liable is habitually resident if he or she could not reasonably foresee the marketing of the product, or a product of the same type, in the country the law of which is applicable under (a), (b) or (c). [. . .]

Chapter IV
FREEDOM OF CHOICE

Art. 14. Freedom of choice. (1) The parties may agree to submit non-contractual obligations to the law of their choice:

(a) by an agreement entered into after the event giving rise to the damage occurred; or
(b) where all the parties are pursuing a commercial activity, also by an agreement freely negotiated before the event giving rise to the damage occurred. The choice shall be expressed or demonstrated with reasonable certainty by the circumstances of the case and shall not prejudice the rights of third parties. [. . .]

Chapter VI
OTHER PROVISIONS

Art. 28. Relationship with existing international conventions. (1) This Regulation shall not prejudice the application of international conventions to which one or more Member States are parties at the time when this Regulation is adopted and which lay down conflict-of-law rules relating to non-contractual obligations. [. . .]

2. The Hague Convention of 4 May 1971 on the Law Applicable to Traffic Accidents[22]

Art. 1. (1) The present Convention shall determine the law applicable to civil non-contractual liability arising from traffic accidents, in whatever kind of proceeding it is sought to enforce this liability.

---

22 The Convention is in force in *Austria, Belarus, Belgium, Bosnia & Herzegovina, Croatia, Czech Republic, France, FYR Macedonia, Latvia, Lithuania, Luxembourg, Montenegro, Morocco,* the *Netherlands, Poland, Serbia, Slovakia, Slovenia, Spain, Switzerland,* and *Ukraine*; status table available at www.hcch.net.

(2) For the purpose of this Convention, a traffic accident shall mean an accident which involves one or more vehicles, whether motorised or not, and is connected with traffic on the public highway, in grounds open to the public or in private grounds to which certain persons have a right of access.

Art. 2. The present Convention shall not apply – to the liability of manufacturers, sellers or repairers of vehicles; [. . .]

Art. 3. The applicable law is the internal law of the State where the accident occurred.

Art. 4. [. . .] [T]he following exceptions are made to the provisions of Article 3

(a) where only one vehicle is involved in the accident and it is registered in a State other than that where the accident occurred, the internal law of the State of registration is applicable to determine liability

- towards the driver, owner or any other person having control of or an interest in the vehicle irrespective of their habitual residence,
- towards a victim who is a passenger and whose habitual residence is in a State other than that where the accident occurred,
- towards a victim who is outside the vehicle at the place of the accident and whose habitual residence is in the State of registration.

(b) Where two or more vehicles are involved in the accident, the provisions of a) are applicable only if all the vehicles are registered in the same State.

(c) Where one or more persons outside the vehicle or vehicles at the place of the accident are involved in the accident and may be liable, the provisions of a) and b) are applicable only if all these persons have their habitual residence in the State of registration. The same is true even though these persons are also victims of the accident.

Art. 11. The application of Arts. 1 to 10 of this Convention shall be independent of any requirement of reciprocity. The Convention shall be applied even if the applicable law is not that of a Contracting State.

3. Schweizerisches Bundesgericht (*Swiss Federal Supreme Court of Justice*), 11.11.2008, BGE 135 III 92 on the interpretation of Art. 4 of the 1971 Hague Traffic Accident Convention

A. B. (the respondent) is keeper of a Mercedes Benz C 180 vehicle with registration plate ZG – His brother, A. (the appellant) was driving the aforementioned vehicle near D – in North-East Bosnia in the night of 16th August 2000. He lost control of the vehicle on a left-hand bend. He veered off the road and crashed into the wall of a farmhouse.

B. On 6th December 2005, the appellant filed suit against the respondent before the Cantonal Court of Zug (*Kantonsgericht Zug*), co-joining a claim against the latter's compulsory third-party liability insurer, C. [. . .]. The value of the claim amounts to CHF 200,000. In support of his claim, he maintains that he had been dazzled by an oncoming vehicle which had its lights on full beam. Panicking, he jerked his steering wheel, which is thought to have caused the car to skid and veer off the road. While his three passengers escaped with only minor injuries, he claims that he himself has suffered serious injury to his bodily integrity as a result of the accident, and that he has been bound to a wheelchair ever since. [. . .] The *Kantonsgericht* [. . .] dismissed the claim. [. . .] On 10th June 2008, the High Court (*Obergericht*) rejected his appeal and affirmed the judgment of the *Kantonsgericht*. It confirmed the view of the *Kantonsgericht* which had based its decision on [. . .] Art. 3 of the Hague Convention of 4 May 1971 on the Law Applicable to Traffic Accidents, leading to the application of the domestic law of Bosnia-Herzegovina. According to Bosnian law, the owner's liability is completely replaced by the liability of the person to whom the vehicle was entrusted. The appellant was therefore required to bear himself the damage he had sustained [. . .].[23] [. . .]

Extract from the court's reasoning:

3. [. . .] 3.1 The law applicable to the appellant's claim following his road traffic accident in Bosnia-Herzegovina [. . .] is determined by the Hague Convention of 4 May 1971 on the Law Applicable to Traffic Accidents ([. . .] hereafter: *the Convention*).

Art. 3 of the Convention sets out the basic principle that the applicable law is that of the State where the accident occurred. Arts. 4 and following of the Convention contain special connecting factors complementing this general rule. Notably, under Art. 4(a),[24] the liability of the keeper of the vehicle is to be determined by the State in which the vehicle was registered if only one vehicle was involved in the accident and this vehicle was registered in a Member State other than that where the accident occurred. If two or more vehicles were involved in the accident and all vehicles were registered in the same State, the State of registration is once again applicable (Art. 4(b) of the Convention[25]).

3.2 The appellant submits, contrary to the view of the court of previous instance, that the only vehicle involved in the accident was the one he was steering, and not that of the oncoming driver. Thus, according to Swiss law, the court of previous instance should have assessed his claim under Art. 4(a) of the Convention.

3.2.1 In order to interpret the term "*an dem Unfall beteiligt*" [in the German-language version of the Convention, German being the original language of the court's decision] in line with Art. 4 (a) and (b) of the Convention, the court must consult the wording of the original English- and French-language texts. The English-language text employs the term "involved" in Art. 4 (a) and (b) of the Convention, and the French-language text the term "impliqué". While the [English] term "involved" is indifferent as to whether fault played any part in the accident, such requirement could potentially be inferred from the [French] "impliqué" (ERIC W. ESSEN, Explanatory Report, Hague Conference on Private International Law, Acts and Documents of the Eleventh Session, 7–26 October 1968, Tome III, Traffic Accidents, 1970, Section 7.1 f. on Art. 4 of the Convention). However, the term "impliqué" as found in Art. 4

---

[23] Under *Swiss* law, on the contrary, the driver is among the beneficiaries of strict liability under Art. 58 (1) SVG (text above, Chapter 9, pp. 248–249); see e.g. Bundesgericht, 12.11.1991, BGE 117 II 609 at 620. Comparative overview in: KADNER GRAZIANO/OERTEL (fn. 4), at pp. 120 ff.
[24] See above, 2.
[25] *Ibid.*

(a) and (b) of the Convention, can only be understood in the neutral and objective sense of the word, without reading into it an element of fault [. . .]. The notion of involvement in the accident is to be broadly construed within the context of Art. 4 (a) and (b) of the Convention [. . .]. Any vehicle which has a role in the accident is deemed to be involved in the accident; in other words, any vehicle contributing to the accident, whether directly or indirectly, shall fall under the scope of Art. 4 (a) and (b) of the Convention [. . .]. [. . .]

3.2.2 It follows from the foregoing that the court of previous instance rightly rejected the assertion that the accident involved a single vehicle, and correctly stated that the oncoming vehicle was involved in the accident in line with Art. 4 (a) and (b) of the Convention. As the facts have shown, the accident was the result of not only driver error on the part of the appellant, but also of the actions of the oncoming driver who had dazzled the appellant with his headlights. Since this vehicle played a role in the accident, it is thus involved in the accident. The fact that there was no collision, nor indeed contact between the two vehicles, has no effect on the court's interpretation.

[. . .] [The Austrian Supreme Court has also] consistently held that the term *"beteiligt"* [involved] in the context of Art. 4 (a) and (b) of the Convention is to be understood in its broader, objective sense as encompassing any vehicle playing a direct or indirect role in the accident, insofar as its role is not wholly incidental (Judgment of the Austrian Supreme Court of 2nd September 1999; 2Ob48/93 of 16 September 1993; 2Ob59/89 of 14th November 1989).[26] The appellant failed to acknowledge on the basis of the facts that [. . .] the oncoming vehicle which dazzled him played more than a wholly incidental role in the accident. [. . .]

4. The Hague Convention of 2 October 1973 on the Law Applicable to Products Liability[27]

Art. 1. (1) This Convention shall determine the law applicable to the liability of the manufacturers and other persons specified in Article 3 for damage caused by a product [. . .].

Art. 3. This Convention shall apply to the liability of the following persons

1. manufacturers of a finished product or of a component part; [. . .]
2. suppliers of a product; [. . .]

---

26 *Note by the author*: see the further decisions, all following the same line of reasoning: **Austrian** Supreme Court of Justice (OGH), 21.05.1985, IPRE 2/90; OGH, 20.06.1989, IPRE 3/72 (an accident in Hungary involving vehicles registered in Hungary and Austria, respectively; claim for damages by the passenger against the driver of the *Austrian* vehicle and his liability insurance; application of the *lex loci delicti*); similarly, **Belgian** Court of Cassation, 15.03.1993, RW 1992/1993, 1446; **French** *Cour de cassation*, 04.04.1991 (*GAN Incendie-Accidents, Daniel Dubois* c. *Delle Pascale Marchot*), Clunet 1991, 981 (collision in *Yugoslavia* between a motorbike registered in *France* and a car registered in *Germany*; the passenger of the motorbike claimed damages from the driver of the motorbike and his insurer; application of *Yugoslav* law, that is the *lex loci delicti*); similarly, *French Cour de cassation*, 24.03.1987 (*Mutuelle Parisienne c Delfino*), Rev. crit. DIP 1987, 577; *French Cour de cassation*, 06.12.1988, Rev. crit. DIP 1990, 786; *French Cour de cassation*, 06.06.1990 (*L'Union et le Phénix espagnol et autres* c. *Mlle Beau*), Rev. crit. DIP 1991, 354.

27 The Convention is in force in *Croatia, Finland, France, FYR Macedonia, Luxembourg, Montenegro,* the *Netherlands, Norway, Serbia, Slovenia,* and *Spain*; status table available at www.hcch.net.

Art. 4. The applicable law shall be the internal law of the State of the place of injury, if that State is also

(a) the place of the habitual residence of the person directly suffering damage, or
(b) the principal place of business of the person claimed to be liable, or
(c) the place where the product was acquired by the person directly suffering damage.

Art. 5. Notwithstanding the provisions of Art. 4, the applicable law shall be the internal law of the State of the habitual residence of the person directly suffering damage, if that State is also

(a) the principal place of business of the person claimed to be liable, or
(b) the place where the product was acquired by the person directly suffering damage.

Art. 6. Where neither of the laws designated in Arts. 4 and 5 applies, the applicable law shall be the internal law of the State of the principal place of business of the person claimed to be liable, unless the claimant bases his claim upon the internal law of the State of the place of injury.

Art. 7. Neither the law of the State of the place of injury nor the law of the State of the habitual residence of the person directly suffering damage shall be applicable by virtue of Arts. 4, 5 and 6 if the person claimed to be liable establishes that he could not reasonably have foreseen that the product or his own products of the same type would be made available in that State through commercial channels.

Art. 11. The application of the preceding Articles shall be independent of any requirement of reciprocity. The Convention shall be applied even if the applicable law is not that of a Contracting State.

Solutions

Question 1: who may belong to the circle of persons who are potentially liable, or can be addressed to cover liability?

The circle of persons who are potentially liable, or who can be addressed to cover liability, include:

- the driver of the Spanish car, domiciled in Spain;
- the Spanish vehicle's liability insurer, established in Spain;
- the victim's father, domiciled in Germany; and
- the father's vehicle liability insurer, established in Germany.

Question 2: which law would Spanish or German courts apply to determine the liability of (a) the driver of the Spanish car, and (b) the victim's father?

In the European Union, questions of applicable law for liability for road traffic accidents are governed either by the Rome II Regulation (which applies in all EU Member States except Denmark) or the 1971 Hague Traffic Accidents Convention. Pursuant to **Art. 28 (1)** of the **Rome II Regulation**, the Hague Convention prevails over the Rome II Regulation for claims brought in Contracting States of the Hague Convention.

1. Applicable law before German courts

Germany is one of the 15 Member States of the EU that is *not* a Contracting State to the 1971 Hague Convention. Before German courts, the applicable law is thus determined by the Rome II Regulation, rather than by the 1971 Hague Convention. According to its Art. 1 (1), the Rome II Regulation determines the law applicable to non-contractual obligations in civil (and commercial) matters, such as the claim for damages brought by the young man in the scenario.

a) Liability of the driver of the Spanish car

According to the Rome II Regulation, liability following a road traffic accident is, in principle, governed by the law of the country in which the accident occurred, by virtue of Art. 4 (1). The liability of the driver of the Spanish car, domiciled in Spain, is thus governed by **Spanish law**.

b) Liability of the victim's father

The starting point for determining the liability of the victim's father is again Art. 4 (1) of the Rome II Regulation, leading in principle to the application of the law of the place where the accident occured. However, if the person claimed to be liable and the injured party both had their habitual residence in the same country at the time the damage occurred, Art. 4 (2) of the Rome II Regulation provides for the application of the law of that country instead of the law of the country in which the accident occurred. The reason is that both parties have to live with the consequences of the accident in the same country. The link with this country is thus closer than with the country of the accident, where the parties spent only a relatively short amount of time.

Before German courts, given that the father and his son (the parties to the claim in our example), had their habitual residence in Germany when the accident occurred, **German law** would apply (rather than Spanish law).

2. Applicable law before Spanish courts

Spain is a Member State of the EU and Contracting State to the 1971 Hague Convention on the Law Applicable to Traffic Accidents.[28] Before Spanish courts, the 1971 Hague Convention thus prevails over the Rome II Regulation. According to its Art. 1 (1) this Convention determines "the law applicable to civil non-contractual liability arising from traffic accidents, in whatever kind of proceeding it is sought to enforce this liability". Spanish courts would therefore

---

28 See above, Fn. 22.

determine the law applicable to a claim against the driver of the Spanish car, or against the young man's father, respectively, according to the rules of the 1971 Hague Convention.

a) Liability of the driver of the Spanish car

According to Art. 3 of the Hague Convention, liability following a road traffic accident is, in principle, governed by the law of the country where the accident occurred. Given that the accident happened in Spain, liability of the driver of the Spanish car is thus governed by **Spanish law**.

b) Liability of the victim's father

Here again, following Art. 3 of the Hague Convention, the liability of the victim's father is governed by the law of the country where the accident occurred, that is Spanish law. However, according to Art. 4 (b) of the Hague Convention, where several vehicles are involved, the law of the State of registration is applicable if all the vehicles are registered in the same state, which is also a State other than that where the accident occurred. The State of registration of the vehicles involved can thus allow/justify an exception to the principle of Art. 3.

The cars of both father and son were registered in Germany, whereas the Seat was registered in Spain. According to the case law of the Member States to the Hague Convention (such as the Swiss case provided in the materials[29]), if another car (like the Seat in our scenario) was a *potential cause* of the accident, it is considered to have been *involved* in the accident. Consequently, in the above scenario, not all cars involved in the accident were registered in the same State and, as a result, pursuant to Art. 3 of the Hague Convention, Spanish courts will apply **Spanish law**. The fact that both the injured person and the person claimed to be liable were domiciled in the same state, i.e. Germany, is thus irrelevant.

3. Conclusion

The liability of the driver of the Spanish car would, both before Spanish and German courts, be determined under Spanish law. Before Spanish courts, the liability of the victim's father would (in a claim against the father or the father's liability insurer) be determined under Spanish law, that is, the law of the place of the accident, whereas German courts would apply German law, given that both father and son were domiciled there when the accident occurred.

Question 3: when comparing the connecting factors used in the 1971 Hague Traffic Accident Convention, on the one hand, and those applied in the Rome II Regulation on the other, which connecting factors do you consider more appropriate taking into consideration the interests of the parties?

In principle, both PIL instruments provide for the application of the *lex loci delicti* rule, that is, the law of the country in which the accident happened and the damage occurred. The *lex loci delicti* rule presents many advantages. Firstly, in situations where the parties

---

29 See above, 3, with references also to *Austrian, French* and *Belgian* court decisions.

had no contact with each other before the damaging event occurred, which is the case, for example, in many road traffic accidents, the place of the accident is the only link between them. Secondly, the law of the place of the tort or accident is simple to apply, efficient and favours legal certainty. Parties know even before a tort is committed which law will apply to potential liability, and they might adapt their insurance cover accordingly. Thirdly, the application of the *lex loci delicti* is a neutral solution favouring neither party. Fourthly, it is in conformity with the interests of the State in which the damage occurred to have certain victims of accidents compensated, particularly those resident there. Lastly, this solution generally corresponds to the parties' expectations and interests, and is usually fair and recognised as such by the parties.

Article 4(2) of the Rome II Regulation makes an exception from the application of this rule "where the person claimed to be liable and the person sustaining damage both have their habitual residence in the same country at the time when the damage occurs". In that case, the law of that country shall apply. In the above scenario, this leads to the application of German law for an action of the victim against his father (or his father's liability insurer).

There are good reasons for making this exception to the *lex loci delicti* rule. Applying the law of the parties' common habitual residence has the advantage that the applicable tort rules are familiar to parties by virtue of their both living in this jurisdiction. Additionally, this is the jurisdiction in which the parties will bear the consequences of the accident. Under this rule, the case is thus treated as though it had occurred in the State in which the parties are habitually resident. The more superficial the link between the parties and the place of accident, the more justified this exception to the *lex loci delicti* rule appears.

When it comes to making an exception from the application of the *lex loci delicti*, the 1971 Hague Convention uses, on the contrary, the connecting factor of the country of registration of all vehicles involved in the accident, Art. 4(b). In the above scenario, not all vehicles involved in the accident were registered in the same country, and therefore the claim of the victim against his father is governed by Spanish law. Spanish law applies despite the fact that both father and son had their habitual residence in another, same country.

The explanatory report (*Rapport explicatif*) to the 1971 Hague Convention argues that the criteria of the place of registration (*lieu de l'immatriculation*) had the advantage of being easy to determine, coincided often with the country of habitual residence of the driver and the owner of the car and with the country where the car was insured.[30] Using the criteria of common habitual residence was considered too difficult to handle with respect to persons as diverse as the driver, owner, persons who rented a car, or passengers.[31]

The experiences with the Rome II Regulations and other PIL codifications that use the exception of common habitual residence, such as the Swiss PIL Act and many national PIL rules that preceeded the Rome II Regulation, illustrate, however, that the criteria of "habitual residence at the time when the accident occurred" is also easy to determine, that this exception is smooth to handle, and that it achieves very reasonable results. The place of registration may often lead to the same result, but not necessarily, as the above case illustrates. The aim of the exception rule is to identify the law which is the most closely connected to the case

---

30 Hague Conference on Private International Law, Convention on the Law Applicable to Traffic Accidents, Explanatory Report, at n° 5.1 (by Eric W. Essén), available at www.hcch.net/upload/expl19e.pdf.
31 *Ibid.*, at Art. 4, n° 2.

and to the parties of the claim. Regarding proceedings between parties who both live in the same country, this is the law of the country of their habitual residence, for the reasons set out above. It is thus submitted that the exception clause in Art. 4(2) of the Rome II Regulation leads to more appropriate results than that in Art. 4(b) of the 1971 Hague Traffic Accident Convention.

Question 4: which law would Swedish courts, on the one hand, and Spanish courts, on the other, apply to determine the car manufacturer's liability?

A liability claim against the manufacturer of the Swedish car could be brought before either (a) Swedish or (b) Spanish courts. In the European Union, questions of applicable law for liability for road traffic accidents are governed either by the Rome II Regulation (which applies in all EU Member States except Denmark) or by the 1973 Products Liability Convention (and not the 1971 Hague Traffic Accident Convention, since according to its Art. 2, this Convention does "not apply to the liability of manufacturers, sellers or repairers of vehicles"). Pursuant to Art. 28(1) of the Rome II Regulation, the Hague Convention prevails over the Rome II Regulation for claims brought in Contracting States of the Hague Convention.

1. Applicable law before Swedish courts

Sweden is *not* a Contracting State to the 1973 Hague Convention. Before Swedish courts, the applicable law is thus determined by the Rome II Regulation, rather than by the 1973 Hague Convention.

In the absence of a choice of the applicable law by the parties (Art. 14 Rome II), and if the parties to a non-contractual claim are not domiciled in the same country and are not in a contractual relationship with each other (Arts. 5(2) and 4(2) of the Rome II Regulation), "the law applicable to a non-contractual obligation arising out of damage caused by a product shall be: (a) the law of the country in which the person sustaining the damage had his or her habitual residence when the damage occurred, if the product was marketed in that country", Art. 5(1)(a) of the Rome II Regulation.

In the above scenario, the young man was domiciled in Germany where cars such as the one owned by his father were indeed marketed.[32] Contrary to Art. 5 of the Hague Products Liability Convention, Art. 5(1)(a) Rome II Regulation does not require that the claimant has purchased the product in this country. Rather, it is sufficient that products such as the one that caused the damage were marketed there. This follows in particular from the wording of Art. 5(1), 2nd sent., Rome II Regulation ("the marketing of the product, or a product of the same type"). The reason is that if the product was marketed there, it was *foreseeable* for the producer that victims may be injured in this country, should the product be defective.

---

32 According to CJUE case law, a product is marketed when it is offered to the public for use or consumption (C-127/04, *Declan O'Byrne* v. *Sanofi Pasteur and others*, [2006] ECR I-1313). The CJUE held in relation to the interpretation of the Products Liability Directive that "a product is put into circulation when it is taken out of the manufacturing process operated by the producer and enters a marketing process in the form in which it is offered to the public in order to be used or consumed".

Given that the young man who was injured in the car accident was domiciled in Germany and that the father's vehicle with the defective autonomous driving device was marketed there, **German law** applies to the claim of the young man against the Swedish car manufacturer.

2. Applicable law before Spanish courts

Spain is Member State of the EU and Contracting State to the 1973 Hague Convention on the Law Applicable to Products Liability.[33] Before Spanish courts, the 1973 Hague Conventions prevails over the Rome II Regulation (Art. 28 of the Rome II Regulation). Spanish courts would thus determine the applicable law according to the provisions of the 1973 Hague Products Liability Convention. According to its Art. 1 (1) this Convention determines the law applicable to the liability of the manufacturers and other persons specified in Article 3 for damage caused by a product.

The Hague Products Liability Convention combines four criteria, of which two generally need to be met in order to find the applicable law. The different combinations of criteria apply in a hierarchical order.

a) First, the law of the country of habitual residence of the party having suffered the damage applies, provided that the person alleged to be liable is also established there or the claimant has purchased the product in this country, Art. 5 Hague Products Liability Convention.

In the above scenario, the victim of the road traffic accident caused by the defective car had his habitual residence in Germany. However, the victim had not purchased the defective product there. In fact, the victim had not purchased the defective product (his father's car) at all, so that Art. 5 does not apply.

b) Second, the law of the country where the injury occurred, that is, where the legally protected interest was initially harmed, applies, provided that this is also "a) the place of the habitual residence of the person directly suffering damage, or b) the principal place of business of the person claimed to be liable, or c) the place where the product was acquired by the person directly suffering damage", per Art. 4 Hague Products Liability Convention.

The injury occurred on a Spanish motorway. However, the victim did not have his habitual residence in Spain, nor is Spain the principal place of business of the defendant car manufacturer or did the victim acquire the defective car in Spain. Consequently, Art. 4 does not apply either.

c) Finally, where the conditions of none of the above rules are met, the law of the country of the principal place of business of the person claimed to be liable applies, but the victim may opt instead for the law of the country where the injury occurred, per Art. 6 Hague Products Liability Convention.

The principal place of business of the car manufacturer alleged to be liable is in Sweden. Before Spanish courts, **Swedish law** thus applies to the products liability claim of the young man in our scenario. Given that the injury occurred in Spain, the young man may opt instead for the application of **Spanish law**.

---

33 See above, Fn. 22.

4. Conclusion

Regarding a products liability claim before Spanish courts, the 1973 Hague Convention on the Law Applicable to Products Liability would designate Swedish law, that is, the law of the country in which the car manufacturer is domiciled (with an option for the claimant to choose Spanish law instead, that is the law of the country where the injury occurred). Before Swedish courts, the Rome II Regulation would lead to the application of German law, that is, the law of the country where the young man was domiciled.

Question 5: when comparing the rules of the Rome II Regulation and of the 1973 Hague Products Liability Convention, which connecting factors do you consider more appropriate for the claim against the car manufacturer, taking into consideration the interests of the parties involved?

Faced with the difficulty of finding a satisfactory solution for the applicable law in products liability cases, both the 1973 Hague Convention and Art. 5 of the Rome II Regulation combine various criteria. In both instruments, the criteria are combined and arranged in a hierarchy, or cascading system, of connecting factors, so that if the criteria for applying the first rule are not met, then the second applies (and so on).

Under Art. 5 of the 1973 Hague Products Liability Convention, the law of the country of habitual residence of the party having suffered the damage applies, provided that the person claimed to be liable is also established there or the claimant has purchased the product in this country. For the latter alternative to apply, it is necessary that the party having suffered the damage has purchased the product that caused the damage in the country of his or her habitual residence. In the above scenario, the victim did not purchase the defective car himself. Consequently, Art. 5 does not apply. Instead, the law of the country of the principal place of business of the person claimed to be liable is eventually applicable (Swedish law). The victim may opt instead for the law of the country where the injury occurred (in the scenario: Spain), pursuant to Art. 6 of the 1973 Hague Convention.

Article 5(1)(a) Rome II Regulation also aims at protecting the person sustaining damage by the application of the law of the country in which the victim has his or her habitual residence. For Art. 5(1)(a) of the Rome II Regulation to be applicable, it is not necessary that the precise product that caused the damage was actually bought in the country of the injured person's habitual residence. It is sufficient that this line of products was marketed in that country (see Art. 5(1), 2nd sent. of the Rome II Regulation: "the marketing of the product, or a product of the same type"). This is particularly relevant for so-called bystanders injured by a product that they did not purchase. The rule achieves reasonable results, both in proceedings brought by the purchaser of a product, his or her family members or friends, and in proceedings brought by third parties that are not in relationship with the buyer but suffered damage from the product (so-called innocent bystanders).

For the victim, the application of the law of the country of his or her habitual residence is the simplest and, in principle, the least costly solution. It is also fair for the persons claimed to be liable, insofar as these persons are making a profit from the distribution of their products in this country and can reasonably expect the law of a country in which their products are distributed to apply when these products cause damage there.[34]

As the above scenario illustrates, when compared to the system of the 1973 Hague Convention, the Rome II Regulation leads more frequently to the application of the law of the country in which the victim has his or her habitual residence, while fully respecting the interests of the manufacturer. It is submitted that this is an advantage of Art. 5 of the Rome II Regulation when compared to the system of connecting factors in the 1973 Hague Convention.

---

34 See: European Commission, Proposal for a Regulation of the European Parliament and the Council on the Law Applicable to Non-Contractual Obligations ("Rome II"), COM(2003) 427 final, p. 16, and T. KADNER GRAZIANO, *Gemeineuropäisches Internationales Privatrecht – Harmonisierung des IPR durch Wissenschaft und Lehre (am Beispiel der ausservertraglichen Haftung für Schäden)*, Tübingen: Mohr Siebeck, 2002, pp. 278 ff.; T. KADNER GRAZIANO, Products Liability, in: J. Basedow/F. Ferrari/P. de Miguel Asensio/G. Rühl (eds.), *Encyclopedia of Private International Law*, Vol. 2, Cheltenham: Edgar Elgar Publishing, 2017.

Bibliography

Cross-border torts (in general)

WILLIAM BINCHY/JOHN AHERN (eds.), *The Rome II Regulation on the Law Applicable to Non-Contractual Obligations: A New Tort Litigation Regime*, Leiden: Martinus Nijhoff, 2009; ANDREW DICKINSON, *The Rome II Regulation on the Law Applicable to Non-Contractual Obligations*, Oxford: OUP, 2008; EUROPEAN PARLIAMENT, Directorate General Internal Policies of the Union, Policy Department C Citizens Rights and Constitutional Affairs, *Compensation of Victims of Cross-Border Road Traffic Accidents in the EU: Assessment of Selected Options* (authors: ANDREA RENDA and LORNA SCHEFFLER), 2007, available at: www.europarl.europa.eu/RegData/etudes/etudes/join/2007/378292/IPOL-JURI_ET%282007%29378292_EN.pdf; MARC FALLON, The Law Applicable to Specific Torts, in: Jürgen Basedow/Harald Baum/Yuko Nishitani (eds.), *Japanese and European Private International Law in Comparative Perspective*, Tübingen: Mohr Siebeck, 2008, p. 261; JAN VON HEIN, Protecting Victims of Cross-Border Torts under Article 7 No. 2 Brussels I *bis*: Towards a More Differentiated and Balanced Approach, *YbPIL* 2014–2015, 241; THOMAS KADNER GRAZIANO, Torts, in: Jürgen Basedow/Franco Ferrari/Pedro de Miguel Asensio/Gisela Rühl (eds.), *European Encyclopedia of Private International Law*, Cheltenham: Edgar Elgar Publishing, Vol. 2, 2017; THOMAS KADNER GRAZIANO, Freedom to choose the applicable law in tort – Articles 14 and 4(3) of the Rome II Regulation, in: William Binchy/John Ahern (eds.), *The Rome II Regulation on the Law Applicable to Non-Contractual Obligations*, Leiden: Martinus Nijhoff, 2009, p. 113; THOMAS KADNER GRAZIANO, General Principles of Private International Law of Tort in Europe, in: Jürgen Basedow/Harald Baum/Yuko Nishitani (eds.), *Japanese and European Private International Law in Comparative Perspective*, Tübingen: Mohr Siebeck 2008, p. 243; THOMAS KADNER GRAZIANO, *La responsabilité délictuelle en droit international privé européen*, Basel: Helbing Lichtenhahn, 2004; THOMAS KADNER GRAZIANO, *Europäisches Internationales Deliktsrecht*, Tübingen: Mohr Siebeck 2003; THOMAS KADNER GRAZIANO, *Gemeineuropäisches Internationales Privatrecht (am Beispiel der ausservertraglichen Haftung für Schäden)*, Tübingen: Mohr Siebeck, 2002; JOHN HUMPHREY CARLISLE MORRIS, The Proper Law of a Tort, *Harv. L. Rev.* 1951, 881; MATHIAS REIMANN, Comparative Law and Private International Law, in: Mathias Reimann/Reinhard Zimmermann, *The Oxford Handbook of Comparative Law*, Oxford: OUP, 2006, Chapter 42; SYMEON C. SYMEONIDES, Party Autonomy in Rome I and II from a Comparative Perspective, in: Katharina Boele-Woelki/Talia Einhorn/Daniel Girsberger/Symeon Symeonides (eds.), *Convergence and Divergence in Private International Law: Liber Amicorum Kurt Siehr*, Zürich: Schulthess, 2010, p. 513; also published in: *NIPR* 2010, 191; SYMEON C. SYMEONIDES, Rome II and Tort Conflicts: A Missed Opportunity, *Am. J. Comp. L.* 2008, 173.

International traffic accidents

ANDREA BONOMI, Accidents de la circulation à l'étranger: questions choisies, in: Franz Werro/Thomas Probst (eds.), *Journées du droit de la circulation routière*, Bern: Stämpfli, 2014, pp. 155–196; MIQUEL MARTÍN-CASALS, An Outline of the Spanish Legal Tariffication Scheme for Personal Injury Resulting from Traffic Accidents, in: Helmut Koziol/Jaap Spier (eds.), *Liber Amicorum Pierre Widmer*, Vienna: Springer, 2003, pp. 235–251; EUROPEAN COMMISSION, *Rome II Study on Compensation of Cross-Border Victims in the EU: Compensation of Victims of Cross-Border Road Traffic Accidents in the EU: Comparison of National Practices, Analysis of Problems and Evaluation of Options for Improving the Position of Cross-Border Victims: Final Report Prepared for the European Commission DG Internal Market and Services: Final Version of the Final Report – Part II – Analysis* (2008), available at: http://ec.europa.eu/civiljustice/news/docs/study_compensation_road_victims_en.pdf (author: Demolin, Brulard, Barthelemy – Hoche, team leader: JEAN ALBERT); EUROPEAN COMMISSION, *Consultation Paper on the Compensation of Victims of Cross-Border Road Traffic Accidents in the European Union* (2009), available at: http://ec.europa.eu/internal_market/consultations/docs/2009/

cross-border-accidents/rome2study_en.pdf; *Choice of Law for Cross Border Road Traffic Accidents, Note for the European Parliament, Directorate General for Internal Policies, Policy Department C: Citizens' Rights and Constitutional Affairs* (2012), available at: www.europarl.europa.eu/RegData/etudes/note/join/2012/462492/IPOL-JURI_NT(2012)462492_EN.pdf (author: JENNY PAPETTAS); *Cross-Border Accidents in the EU – the Potential Impact of Driverless Cars, Study for the European Parliament, Directorate for Internal Policies, Policy Department C: Citizens' Rights and Constitutional Affairs* (2016), available at: www.europarl.europa.eu/RegData/etudes/STUD/2016/571362/IPOL_STU(2016)571362_EN.pdf (author: THOMAS KADNER GRAZIANO); ROBERT FUCIK, Checkliste zum Haager Strassenverkehrsübereinkommen, *ZVR* 2011, 47; Hague Conference on Private International Law, Convention on the Law Applicable to Traffic Accidents, Explanatory Report (by ERIC W. ESSÉN), available at: www.hcch.net/upload/expl19e.pdf; THOMAS KADNER GRAZIANO, Traffic Accidents, in: Jürgen Basedow/Franco Ferrari/Pedro de Miguel Asensio/Gisela Rühl (eds.), *European Encyclopedia of Private International Law*, Cheltenham: Edgar Elgar Publishing, Vol. 2, 2017; THOMAS KADNER GRAZIANO, Internationale Straßenverkehrsunfälle im Lichte von Brüssel I, Rom II und des Haager Straßenverkehrsübereinkommens, *ZVR* 2011, 40; THOMAS KADNER GRAZIANO, Das auf außervertragliche Schuldverhältnisse anwendbare Recht nach Inkrafttreten der Rom II-Verordnung, *RabelsZ* 2009, 1; THOMAS KADNER GRAZIANO, Le nouveau droit international privé communautaire en matière de responsabilité extracontractuelle, *Rev. crit. DIP* 2008, 445; THOMAS KADNER GRAZIANO, The Rome II Regulation and the Hague Conventions on Tort Law – Interaction, Conflicts and Future Perspectives, *NIPR* 2008, 425; THOMAS KADNER GRAZIANO/CHRISTOPH OERTEL, Ein europäisches Haftungsrecht für Schäden im Strassenverkehr? Eckpunkte de lege lata und Überlegungen de lege ferenda, *ZVglRWiss* 2008, 113; BEATE LEMKE-GEIS/MARTIN MÜLLER, Internationale Unfallregulierung in der Europäischen Union, *SVR* 2009, 241; WERNER LORENZ, Das außervertragliche Haftungsrecht der Haager Konventionen, *RabelsZ* 1993, 175; CSONDOR ISTVAN NAGY, The Rome II Regulation and Traffic Accidents: Uniform Conflict Rules with Some Room for Forum Shopping – How So?, *J Priv Int L* 2010, 93; JENNY PAPETTAS, Direct Actions against Insurers of Intra-Community Cross-Border Traffic Accidents: Rome II and the Motor Insurance Directives, *J Priv Int L* 2012, 297; NORA REISINGER, *Internationale Verkehrsunfälle: Gerichtszuständigkeit und anwendbares Recht*, Wien: LexisNexis 2011; OSKAR RIEDMEYER, Internationale Zuständigkeit für Klagen bei Unfällen in der EU, in: René Schaffhauser (ed.), *Jahrbuch zum Strassenverkehrsrecht 2012*, Bern: Stämpfli, 2012, pp. 387–402; RODRIGO RODRIGUEZ, Gerichtsstände bei Unfällen im Ausland im Lichte der "Odenbreit"-Rechtsprechung und des revidierten Lugano-Übereinkommens, in: René Schaffhauser (ed.), *Jahrbuch zum Strassenverkehrsrecht 2012*, Bern: Stämpfli, 2012, pp. 365–386; IVO SCHWANDER, Das Internationale Privat- und Zivilprozessrecht der Ansprüche aus Strassenverkehrsunfällen, in: René Schaffhauser (ed.), *Jahrbuch zum Strassenverkehrsrecht 2009*, St. Gallen: Prisma Druck, 2009, pp. 211–258; THOMAS THIEDE, Strassenverkehrsunfall mit Auslandsberührung – Internationale Zuständigkeit und anwendbares Recht, *Zak* 2013, 407; THOMAS THIEDE/MARKUS KELLNER, Forum shopping zwischen dem Haager Übereinkommen über das auf Verkehrsunfälle anzuwendende Recht und der Rom II-Verordnung, *VersR* 2007, 1624; THOMAS THIEDE/KATARZYNA LUDWICHOWSKA, Kfz-Haftpflichtversicherung, *VersR* 2008, 631; JAN VON HEIN, Article 4 and Traffic Accidents, in: William Binchy/John Ahern (eds.), *The Rome II Regulation on the Law Applicable to Non-Contractual Obligations: A New Tort Litigation Regime*, Leiden: Martinus Nijhoff, 2009, p. 153.

Products liability

JAMES J. FAWCETT, Products Liability in Private International Law: A European Perspective, *Rec. des Cours* 1993, 9; TREVOR HARTLEY, Choice of Law for Non-Contractual Liability: Selected Problems under the Rome II Regulation, *ICLQ* 2008, 899; MARTIN ILLMER, The New European Private International Law of Product Liability: Steering through Troubled Waters, *RabelsZ* 2009, 269; THOMAS KADNER GRAZIANO/MATTHIAS ERHARDT, Cross-Border Damage Caused by Genetically Modified

Organisms: Jurisdiction and Applicable Law, in: Bernhard Koch (ed.), *Damage Caused by Genetically Modified Organisms*, Berlin: De Gruyter, 2010, p. 784; THOMAS KADNER GRAZIANO, Products Liability, in: Jürgen Basedow/Franco Ferrari/Pedro de Miguel Asensio/Gisela Rühl (eds.), *European Encyclopedia of Private International Law*, Cheltenham: Edgar Elgar Publishing, Vol. 2, 2017; THOMAS KADNER GRAZIANO, The Law Applicable to Product Liability: The Present State of the Law in Europe and Current Proposals for Reform, *ICLQ* 2005, 475; THOMAS KADNER GRAZIANO, Le nouveau droit international privé communautaire en matière de responsabilité extracontractuelle, *Rev. crit. DIP* 2008, 445; THOMAS KADNER GRAZIANO, *La responsabilité délictuelle en droit international privé européen*, Basel: Helbing Lichtenhahn/Bruxelles: Bruylant/Paris: L.G.D.J. 2004, p. 61; THOMAS KADNER GRAZIANO, *Europäisches Internationales Deliktsrecht*, Tübingen: Mohr Siebeck, 2003, p. 63; THOMAS KADNER GRAZIANO, *Gemeineuropäisches Internationales Privatrecht – Harmonisierung des IPR durch Wissenschaft und Lehre (am Beispiel der ausservertraglichen Haftung für Schäden)*, Tübingen: Mohr Siebeck 2002, p. 258; PHAEDON JOHN KOZYRIS, Values and Methods in Choice of Law for Products Liability: A Comparative Comment on Statutory Solutions, *Am. J. Comp. L.* 1990, 475; WILLIS L. M. REESE, The Hague Convention on the Law Applicable to Products Liability, *Int. Lawyer* 1974, 606; WILLIS L. M. REESE, Further Comments on the Hague Convention on the Law Applicable to Products Liability, *Ga. J. Int'l. & Comp. L.* 1978, 311; SYMEON C. SYMEONIDES, Choice of Law for Products Liability: The 1990s and Beyond, *Tul. L. Rev.* 2004, 1247; SYMEON C. SYMEONIDES, Party Choice in Product-Liability Conflicts, *Willamette J. Int'l L. & Disp. Resol.* 2004, 263; see also the reference on the website of the Hague Conference of Private International Law at www.hcch.net/index_de.php?act=conventions.publications&dtid=1&cid=84.

Chapter 19

Epilogue
Tort law in context – and potential alternatives to tort liability

> "*Je ne me dissimule point que je vais exposer [. . .] des opinions étrangères à celles qui règnent [dans notre pays]; mais soit qu'elles paraissent justes ou non, soit qu'on les adopte ou qu'on les combatte, elles donnent toujours à penser*".[1]

---

[1] Germaine de Stael, *De l'Allemagne*, Nouvelle éd., Paris: Librairie de Paris, 1844, Observations générales, p. 19. In English translation: "I shall not conceal that I will expose opinions differing from those prevailing [in our country]; but whether they seem right or wrong, whether we adopt or reject them, they will always motivate us to think."

Questions

Most tort liability systems strive to establish a careful balance between the interests of victims on the one hand, and of persons alleged to be liable on the other. A further consideration is the interest of society at large to keep the "floodgates of liability" under control and, despite empathy with potential victims, to somehow restrict the scope of liability.

1) In the previous chapters, the *French* liability system, when compared with most other tort liability systems, has proven to be particularly victim-friendly, and severe towards the person alleged to be liable.

   a) Which examples of this particular characteristic of French tort law could you give when looking back at the previous chapters?
   b) How does the French system avoid having its courts being flooded with claims and potential defendants being ruined or driven into insolvency?
   c) Which reasons does the French tort lawyer and comparatist Jean-Sébastien Borghetti give for the particular victim-friendliness of French tort law?

2) Looking back at the arguments for and against liability discussed in the previous chapters, which arguments speak in favour of the French approach, and which may speak against it? Also consider that in some countries (notably in France), general *liability (or third-party) insurance* is very widespread, whereas in others (such as *Italy*), it is not. Would a general requirement to contract liability insurance be an option and have an impact on your answer? What may be the limits of an approach that relies heavily on widespread (mandatory or voluntary) liability insurance coverage? Consider the issue regarding midwives in *Germany* related in the materials.

3) The Nordic countries focus, for certain types of relationships and damages, on *collective compensation schemes* rather than tort law remedies.[2] Which arguments may advocate a shift away from tort law to collective compensation mechanisms? What are the disadvantages of replacing tort law (fully or partially) with collective compensation schemes, and which (potentially positive) effects of tort law would be lost? Think, for example, of the cases of medical malpractice (Chapter 10) or cases of pure economic loss (Chapter 14).

4) Would you think that tort law sets incentives for socially desirable behaviour and contributes to *accident prevention*, complementing administrative and criminal law, as

---

[2] In other countries, some damage is covered by collective compensation schemes, whereas other damage is not. In e.g. *Germany* and *Switzerland*, costs for treatment are covered by mandatory health insurance, whereas there is no mandatory first-party insurance for immaterial harm or property damage. The case of loss of earning capacity is of particular importance: in Germany, in the event of an injury, the first six weeks of lost earnings are covered by the employer (if the victim is employed at the moment when the accident happens, which might not be the case for younger victims, self-employed persons, or persons working in their own household). If the loss of earning capacity lasts longer than 6 weeks, sickness benefits are granted by the social security system (§§ 47 and 48 of the SGB V) in the amount of 70% of lost earnings for a maximum duration of 78 weeks within three years for the same injury or illness. Beyond that period, there is no special coverage for loss of earnings.

On the relationship between social security and tort law, see e.g. G. Wagner, in: *Münchener Kommentar zum BGB*, Vol. 6, 7th ed., München: C. H. Beck, 2017, Vorbemerkungen zu §§ 823 ff., nos. 30–37; from a comparative perspective, see H. Koziol, Ausgleich von Personenschäden – Rechtsvergleichende Anregungen für ein Zusammenspiel von Schadensersatz- und Versicherungsrecht, *ALJ* 2015, 186, with further references.

suggested by STEPHEN SHAVELL and (many) others? What would this mean with respect to the proposal of replacing tort law (partially or totally) by collective compensation schemes and/or first-party insurance and/or third-party liability insurance?

5) In a speech delivered in 2015, the *English* judge Lord DYSON criticised what he calls "compensation culture". To what extent should tort law be driven by, and implement, moral values as opposed to focusing primarily on compensation of accident victims? In particular, to what extent does liability in tort depend on the individual's actual blameworthiness, and to what extent *should* blameworthiness, negligence, or fault be a necessary requirement of liability, alongside instances of strict liability?

6) As explained by MÅRTEN SCHULTZ, one particular feature of the Nordic systems is that victims shall receive full compensation even if they contributed to the occurrence of the damage. What is the advantage and what may be the drawbacks of diminishing, or even disregarding, the role of contributory negligence? Consider, for example, the case of sport accidents (Chapter 7), including the relevant case law, or road traffic accidents (Chapter 9), and evaluate this approach in terms of:

- compensation of damage inflicted and suffered;
- fairness;
- efficiency and costs of the compensation system;
- incentives to prevent accidents; and
- the interests of victims, potential defendants, and society in general.

7) What may this Epilogue tell us about aspects that should be taken into account when comparing tort liability systems, or about comparative methodology in general?

Table of contents

1. **France: floodgates of liability wide open**
   JEAN-SÉBASTIEN BORGHETTI, The Culture of Tort Law in France,
   JETL 2012, 158 ....p. 596

2. **Germany: a worst-case scenario**
   HANNES LEITLEIN, Geburtshilfe: Das Ende der Hebammen (*Obstetrics: The end of midwives*), *DIE ZEIT online*, 14.07.2015, www.zeit.de/ gesellschaft/2015-07/hebammen-elternprotest-versicherung ....p. 602

3. **The Nordic approach: using collective compensation schemes**
   MÅRTEN SCHULTZ, Disharmonization: A Swedish Critique of Principles of European Tort Law, *EBLR* 2007, 1305 at 1322–1326...................................p. 603

4. **Purposes of tort liability: compensating victims (only), accident prevention, both, or more?**
   STEVEN SHAVELL, *Economic Analysis of Accident Law*, Cambridge, Mass./London: Harv. Univ. Press, 2007, pp. 297–298..p. 606

5. **No alternatives needed? – The traditional response to trends towards "compensation culture": keeping the floodgates shut**
   LORD DYSON, Master of the Rolls, "Magna Carta and Compensation Culture", speech at the High Sheriff of Oxfordshire's Annual Law Lecture, Magna Carta Trust, 13th October 2015, *Judiciary of England and Wales, HMSO*, 2015..p. 606

Materials

1. France: floodgates of liability wide open

JEAN-SÉBASTIEN BORGHETTI, The Culture of Tort Law in France, JETL 2012, 158

[. . .] Tort law in France [. . .] is well known for being victim oriented. If a foreign lawyer were to look at the substantive rules of French tort law as they are outlined in the literature (both in France and abroad), or taught in France, he would be amazed, and probably also alarmed, at the breadth of tort law. In principle, all types of loss or damage can be compensated, including pure economic loss,[3] non-pecuniary damage,[4] values of affection, purely environmental damage[5] and loss of chance.[6] There is a general principle of liability for fault according to which any fault, that is, any act falling below the reasonable man standard whether it be a positive act or an omission, can be a source of liability. Besides this very broad principle, French tort law maintains several strict liability regimes including general liability for damage caused by things[7] and an extremely strict regime for traffic accidents.[8] It further supports various principles of liability for others including the liability of parents for any damage caused by their children.[9] [. . .]

[It is] difficult to come to any conclusion other than that the floodgates of litigation, which most legal systems strive to keep closed, are more than open in French law! They have been blown apart! French procedural rules seem to have no restraining effect; whilst there are often long delays in the judicial proceedings, legal aid is easily available and the financial obstacles to pursuing claims are thus limited. In such a context, courts could be expected to be flooded with tort claims and countless companies and individuals subject to potential ruin due to the ease with which liability claims can be brought. Yet this does not seem to be the case. The number of new liability claims filed before French civil courts in 2009 was around 45,000 and the number of registered *avocats* (attorneys), a profession that could be expected to thrive in a context of limitless liability, was only 51,758 in 2010[10] compared to the 146,910 *Rechtsanwälte* registered in Germany in 2009 and the 1,225,452 licensed lawyers in the United States in 2010. As for the potentially disastrous economic consequences of excessive civil liability, while they may exist, there is no documented evidence to this effect thus far and it has never arisen as a serious concern either in the media or amongst the general public. [. . .] [T]he above-mentioned figures [. . .] tend to indicate [. . .] that the effects of these rules are not as devastating as a non-French lawyer might think and as they probably would be in other countries or legal systems.

---

3 *Note by the author*: see above, Chapters 5 and 14.
4 Above, Chapters 11 and 12.
5 Above, Chapter 16.
6 Above, Chapter 10.
7 Above, Chapter 7.
8 Above, Chapter 9.
9 Above, Chapter 13.
10 *Note by the author*: for more recent figures, see http://cnb.avocat.fr/Les-Chiffres-cles-de-la-profession-actualises-pour-l-annee-2016-Observatoire-du-Conseil-national-des-barreaux-_a2222.html.

Why is this so? The obvious reason seems to be that the economic, social and cultural context underpinning French tort law and the way in which lawyers apply and understand the law are such that at least some of the potential negative effects of these rules are neutralised. In fact, it is possible that these rules would not have developed in the first place had the context been different. It is therefore essential to try to understand this context, however formidable a task this might be.

The first obstacle lies in determining the relevant non-legal (or, at least, not strictly legal) elements or factors, be they material or psychological, which are necessary to fully grasp the context of tort law rules. A simple way of describing these factors would be to say that they are those elements that make up the 'legal culture' in which tort law is embedded. [. . .] [T]he study will focus on various specific elements which the author believes are of particular significance to an understanding of how tort law is perceived and applied in his country. [. . .]

I. The context of French tort law

[. . .]

A. Tort law as an aspect of compensation law

[. . .] If one assumes that the primary aim of tort law is compensation, a thorough understanding of its context requires both that it be viewed within the wider frame of compensation mechanisms that exist in French law and that its close relationship to liability insurance be investigated.

1) Tort law and other compensation mechanisms

Three main compensation mechanisms, apart from tort law, must be mentioned here: social security, compensation funds and direct private insurance.

French social security, first of all, is rightly known for being relatively well developed. Despite efforts by the Government to curb the steady rise in the system's budget, the medical branch still offers generous coverage in respect of most health costs that may be incurred by individuals. This is especially true for serious medical treatment which may typically follow an accident. When the patient is prevented from working due to his illness or accident, the social security system will compensate for lost income up to a fixed amount. The result is that most victims of physical injury in France will receive at least partial compensation, through social security, for the financial loss resulting from their injury. As a consequence, compensation through tort law does not usually play the vital role that it does in other legal systems where this type of compensation may be the only means for victims of personal injury, who do not benefit from social security or health care coverage, to fund adequate medical treatment and stay financially afloat.

In addition to social security, in French law, a number of compensation funds exist. These funds come in all shapes and sizes but the common factor is that they usually provide compensation to victims of damage caused by specific sources of risk. One fund, for example, compensates victims of asbestos while another compensates victims of medical accidents not arising out of negligence. These funds normally offer compensation on top of social security payments and typically cover non-pecuniary damage.

Private direct insurance is another important compensation mechanism. It plays a major role in the medical sector. The majority of people subscribe to such insurance to top up social security payments. Sometimes, this additional insurance is financed by the employer. It is, however, rather cheap, at least in comparison to the price of private health insurance in countries where there is very little or no social security, as it only functions as a complement to social security. Private direct insurance is also widespread in the housing field. Most French families or individuals have 'household insurance' (*assurance habitation*) which covers damage accidentally caused to dwelling-places. Such insurance is normally required from the lessee in rented flats or houses and property-owners usually subscribe to such insurance on a voluntary basis. Another sector where private direct insurance is widespread is that of vehicles. Motor vehicle liability insurance for damage caused to third parties is compulsory in France. Most people, however, buy more extensive insurance which also covers damage caused to the subscriber's vehicle, his passengers or himself. Through private insurance in various forms, in many cases of damage the victim can thus rely on insurance payments in addition to social security payments. This further reduces the significance of tort law compensation for victims. Though damages paid by the tortfeasor may of course be very important for the claimant, both for financial and psychological reasons, such payments are not usually a matter of life or death. Rather than being the first or sole means of compensation, they are largely complementary.

The importance of social security, compensation funds and private direct insurance in France, as well as the resulting limited significance of tort law for victims, does not mean that tort law plays only a marginal role. Rather, the contrary is true. As a matter of fact, social security, compensation funds and private direct insurance seem to be the driving forces behind the development of tort law as social security, compensation funds and insurance companies often seek reimbursement for the payments they make to the victim from the tortfeasor when there is one.[11] The various compensation mechanisms are therefore not exclusive of one another. Rather, tort law appears as a natural extension of social security, compensation funds, and direct insurance.

2) Tort law and liability insurance

One question that arises is that if tortfeasors are forced to bear responsibility for a substantial portion of the financial burden of damage compensation, either through direct claims by victims or through regress claims by social security, compensation funds or insurance companies, does this not result in a large number of tortfeasors going into insolvency? The answer seems to be 'no', the reason being that most tortfeasors have civil liability insurance. Civil liability insurance is in fact extremely common in France. In some instances, it is compulsory: motor vehicle owners must, for example, have insurance covering any civil liability that may be incurred in respect of their vehicle and some professionals are required by statute to be insured.[12] Even when they are not bound to purchase such insurance many

---

11 Fn. 18: Unfortunately, the proportion of cases in which either social security or private insurers seek reimbursement from tortfeasors is not known, at least to the author. The proportion is said to be quite low as far as social security is concerned. Even if this is true, however, regress actions by the various social security entities still amount to a large number of claims, given the sheer size of social security and the number of accident victims it covers. A quick look at the name of the parties in the *Cour de cassation* rulings in matters of tort law further confirms that social security and insurance companies make up a significant proportion of litigants in that field.
12 Fn. 20: This is the case for medical practitioners and building contractors, for example.

professionals or companies still take out insurance to cover civil liability. Besides, all household insurance contracts, although they are intended foremost to provide direct insurance, also cover civil liability incurred by any person residing in the insured house or flat in the ordinary course of life.[13] In effect, most natural persons in France are therefore protected by liability insurance through their household insurance. In the event that someone does not have household insurance, they are able to purchase civil liability insurance at a very reasonable price.[14] As a consequence it is only seldom that a tortfeasor will bear the full financial weight of the damage that he caused or must answer for.[15]

This situation, in turn, creates an incentive for the further development of civil liability, especially for judges. French courts are all the more willing to extend the ambits of tort law knowing (or at least thinking) that potential defendants are likely to be insured. The liability of parents for damage caused by their children is probably the best example of how liability insurance can result in increased liability. The traditional rule in that field was that parents were responsible for any damage caused by their child provided that there was fault. In 2001, however, the *Cour de cassation* broadened this rule, holding parents liable for any damage caused by their child even in situations where there was no fault and the child had behaved in a 'normal' way.[16] While the *Cour de cassation* did not give any rationale for this new rule it seems clear that the rule would never have been adopted had the Court not relied on the common knowledge that most parents in France are insured against any liability they may incur through their children thanks to their household insurance. Tort law and liability insurance thus reinforce each other: the breadth of tort law in France creates a strong incentive to take out liability insurance and the generalisation of liability insurance makes further extensions of tort law more acceptable.

Tort law in France can therefore be better understood as an element of a wider set of compensation and insurance mechanisms which includes social security, direct insurance and liability insurance. This context accounts for the fact that tort law is both highly developed and not too burdensome for potential tortfeasors. Additionally, it helps to explain why tort law is so inconspicuous in French society at large.

B. Tort law as a social reality

An apparent French paradox, which the above-mentioned discussion helps to clarify, is that tort law is simultaneously very developed but also largely ignored by both the general public and the media and opinion-makers.

---

13 Fn. 21: Household insurance contracts do not cover liability that may arise from professional activity, from dangerous activities or from driving a motor vehicle; liability insurance for these activities must be bought separately.
14 Fn. 22: Civil liability insurance for damage that may be caused in the course of everyday life normally costs less than € 30 p.a.
15 Fn. 23: Civil liability insurance as included in household insurance contracts normally offers unlimited coverage for any damage caused by a source of liability covered by the contract. Professional insurance, on the contrary, very often sets a limit to the cover provided.
16 See above, Chapter 13.

1) Tort law and the general public

Anecdotal evidence suggests that many people in France do not have a clear understanding of what tort law is. Rather, they are simply aware that causing damage creates, at least in some circumstances, an obligation to compensate and conversely expect that if they suffer damage in similar circumstances someone will be liable to pay for it. [. . .]

Nothing indicates that people in France are particularly afraid of having to compensate damage that they, or those for whom they have to answer, may cause. [. . .] As a matter of fact, if they happen to be liable, they probably will not feel it, and might not even know about it. Why they will not feel it, or at least not fully, has been explained above: their insurance will pay for them. But their being insured might even result in their not being aware of the liability at all.

When a tortfeasor or an alleged tortfeasor is covered by insurance, compensation will normally be paid directly by the insurer to the victim. Article L 124–3 of the French insurance code (*code des assurances*) provides that the victim can request compensation directly from the insurer [. . .]. As a result, a victim of damage who seeks compensation on the basis of tort law will often turn to the (alleged) tortfeasor not to demand damages directly from him but rather to ask him for the name of his insurer. This typically happens in cases of traffic accidents; the standard procedure requires that the parties draft a statement of what happened which is then forwarded to their respective insurers. Should the victim request damages directly from the tortfeasor, the latter can call on his insurer to deal directly with the victim. Thus, in the majority of cases where the tortfeasor is insured, compensation and the whole compensation process is normally a 'private' matter between the victim and the insurer; the tortfeasor will usually not even be informed by the insurer of what compensation, if any, is paid to the victim. This suits the tortfeasor and is also usually easier for the victim as she will not have to concern herself with the tortfeasor's ability or willingness to pay and, if the latter is someone she knows (a neighbour, for example), not having to collect damages from him is just as good for the future of their relationship. As for the insurance company, it is in its interest to manage the compensation procedure, if only to control the amount of damages paid. As a rule, when the liability of the client is not disputed, insurance companies make a compensation offer to the victim based on their own compensation tables. Victims are often resentful that the amounts offered are low but prefer to accept them (perhaps after having negotiated a more favourable deal) rather than to sue. Should the victim nevertheless choose to sue, the tortfeasor is unlikely to be seriously put out – provided of course he is insured. For one thing, the victim may sue the insurance company directly on the basis of Art. L 124–3 of the insurance code. Alternatively, if she brings her claim directly against the tortfeasor, the latter can call in his insurer so that the order to pay damages will be directed against the latter. It also is possible that social security, a compensation fund or the direct insurer of the victim will bring a claim against the tortfeasor after having compensated the victim. However, these claims are often brought directly against the tortfeasor's insurer, when it is known, and damages may be paid without him even being aware of it. As for the victim, when she is fully compensated by her own direct insurer or a compensation fund she will normally not be informed of the recourse action brought against the tortfeasor or his insurer; she might thus not be aware that her damage was in fact a source of civil liability. Tortfeasors and victims are therefore only aware of a portion of all civil liability claims. A great number of claims are handled directly and exclusively by institutions, such as insurance companies, social security and compensation funds. Further, given that not all cases giving rise to civil liability convert into a claim and the payment of damages, this means that the social visibility of tort law in France is very low, especially when seen in light of the actual breadth of civil liability.

2) Tort law in the media and in public debate

Tort law's lack of social visibility translates into near inconspicuousness in public debate or discussion in France. [. . .] In fact, the system seems to be functioning so well that many people are not even aware of its existence and the role it plays. [. . .]

There seems to be only one field in which, occasionally, civil liability cases attract the attention of the media and of the general public, namely, medical liability and liability for pharmaceuticals. This is usually only the case, however, in the context of mass torts. In the 1980s, for example, a major tainted blood scandal broke out and in 2011 there was public uproar about Mediator, a weight-loss drug alleged to have caused hundreds of deaths among patients who had used it. In these cases, the media did report on the civil liability claims brought by the alleged victims against the producer. Here again, however, the attention focused on the potential criminal liability and the question of guilt: was someone guilty of having caused these casualties and if so, who? The public authority in charge of authorising pharmaceuticals was also accused of negligence. Interestingly, even before the role of Mediator in the suspicious deaths had been fully clarified, the Government, with the approval of Parliament, created a new compensation fund for the victims of this drug. [. . .]

II. The players of tort law

1) The dominant ideology

French *doctrine* in tort law is rightly known for being victim-oriented. [. . .] The strength of this concern for victims is such that values that tort law could embrace, such as the preservation of freedom of action or economic efficiency, are seldom explicitly taken into account. Indeed, many authors seem to regard the 'protection of victims' (*la protection des victimes*) as the only legitimate criterion with which to assess the need for and quality of tort law rules.

How can this be explained? One might be tempted to relate this orientation to general trends in French society, such as the idea that citizens deserve strong protection or a latent distrust of businesses and bosses (patrons), who are often the defendants in tort cases. In any case, this orientation is now quite old, and can be traced back at least to the end of the 19th century when various authors began to contend that the courts should not stick to liability for fault, as laid down in the *Code civil*, but should instead create categories of no-fault liability, even without the legislator's permission, in order to help compensate victims of industrial accidents. At that time, the political convictions of left-wing lawyers appeared to merge with the Christian concern for the poor and the afflicted. This established a strong pro-victim trend which has continued to thrive to this day. [. . .]

[. . .] Even if one assumes that tort law is first and foremost concerned with helping 'deserving' victims, for example, it does not follow that liability should necessarily apply whenever possible; in fact, there are many cases, in which an extension of tort law may profit a small number of victims but have negative side effects on numerous other people who are no less deserving.[17]

2. Germany: a worst-case scenario

Hannes Leitlein, Geburtshilfe: Das Ende der Hebammen (*Obstetrics: The end of midwives*), DIE ZEIT online, 14.07.2015

Midwives are vital. [...] Nevertheless, throughout Germany [...] the profession is on the brink of collapse. [...] An ever-increasing number of midwives are [...] dropping out of obstetrics altogether due to further rises in liability insurance premiums. With annual premiums rising to € 6,270 on 1st July, the Midwifery Association (*Habammen Verband*) claims that another 145 freelance midwives have joined those forced to leave obstetrics. For the 2,348 insured midwives who accompany mothers in labour on a freelance basis the insurance premiums may even exceed their salary.

There are still around 21,000 midwives [in Germany]. However, only a fraction of this number still perform the task of bringing babies into the world. The vast majority of midwives supply prenatal classes or postnatal support. [...] The shortage is already starting to have an impact on many women. Midwives who are still working are often overworked and require appointments several months in advance [...].

Also affected are the hospitals: in order to cut down on costs, centers are discharging midwives and instead hiring freelancers or shutting down labour wards entirely. As a result, those still working as midwives often have to attend to several mothers at once, a practice which often leads to complications at birth. [...]

Delivering a bad deal

For many years, obstetrics has been a loss-making venture for liability insurers. When something goes wrong during a birth, costs can spiral into the millions. According to the German Insurance Association (*Gesamtverband der Deutschen Versicherungswirtschaft*), midwives are not making more mistakes than before. The rise in premiums is simply a matter of costs: families are suing more often. A claim against the midwife's liability insurer

---

17 Fn. 65: Medical liability is of course a good example: extending it in order to help a victim in one case, out of legitimate compassion, may result in some medical services becoming more expensive due to an increase in insurance premiums, and many people no longer being able to afford them. This more or less happened in *France* after the *Cour de cassation* had accepted "wrongful life" claims in the *Perruche* case.
Note by the author: in this case (*Cour de cassation*, Plenary Assembly, 11.11.2000, no. 99–13701), the treating physician and the laboratory conducting testing on a pregnant woman failed to diagnose during her pregnancy that she was affected with rubella, a highly contagious disease, which led to the development of severe congenital disabilities of the child. The parents alleged that, had the diagnosis been conducted correctly, the pregnancy would have been terminated, and the birth of their child avoided. Both the parents and the disabled child brought damage claims (the latter for "wrongful life"). The Court of Cassation awarded damages to all claimants. The judgment led to a wide debate in France and was later overruled by Law no. 2002–303 of 04.03.2002, stating in Art. 1 that "Nul ne peut se prévaloir d'un prejudice du seul fait de sa naissance" (No one shall be entitled to prejudice on the sole basis of his or her birth).

covers not only a loss of earnings, but also offers compensation for pain and suffering. On top of this can be added any costs which have been paid off by health insurance schemes for the treatment and care of the mother or child. These costs also have to be covered, and eventually reimbursed, by the midwife's liability insurer. [. . .]

From a liability insurer's point of view, the reason why midwives are so expensive to insure is that unlike e.g. vehicle liability insurance, the costs of damage claims are not spread over millions of insurance-holders, but just a few thousand. [. . .]

A solution from Austria and the Netherlands

There is in fact [. . .] an [. . .] idea we can take inspiration from which could secure the work of midwives for years to come: a liability fund like that which already exists in Austria and the Netherlands [. . .]. Midwives in Austria pay a lump sum of € 100 per year towards their liability insurance. The rest is covered by the State. This way, obstetrics would be acknowledged to be a general good of society and freed from the pressures of business profit.[18]

3. The Nordic approach: using collective compensation schemes

MÅRTEN SCHULTZ, Disharmonization: A Swedish Critique of Principles of European Tort Law, *EBLR* 2007, 1305 at 1322–1326

[. . .] C. *Presentation of the Nordic Model*

The Nordic model towards tort law (with emphasis on personal injury law) can be characterized in different ways. The most fundamental and almost banal idea is that *personal injury should always be compensated* and that the cost of personal injury compensation is in general best carried by collective entities. To a lesser degree this also goes for property damages. The legal system has thus provided rules that promote that costs resulting from personal injuries are borne by collective entities.

A more detailed picture of the Nordic Model will reveal a complex interplay between social insurance and other kinds of collective compensation schemes as well as personal insurance, and – to a lesser extent – tort law. The Nordic Model is not the same as (the scurrilous picture of?) the New Zealand approach to personal injuries;[19] the idea was never that the taxpayer should cover all costs of personal injury. In fact one of the basic ideas was that

---

18 For first steps taken in Germany, see www.zeit.de/gesellschaft/2016-01/hebammen-haftpflichtversicherung-zuschuss-schiedsgericht-verband.
19 *Note by the author*: in 1974, *New Zealand* abolished compensation for personal injuries through tort law. In its place, the Accident Compensation Corporation (ACC) provides a universal no-fault compensation scheme. See e.g. L. N. KLAR, New Zealand's Accident Compensation Scheme: A Tort Lawyer's Perspective, *UTLJ* 1983, 80; R. MAHONEY, New Zealand's Accident Compensation Scheme: A Reassessment, *Am. J. Comp. L.* 1992, 159; P. H. SCHUCK, Tort Reform: Kiwi-Style, *Yale Law School Faculty Scholarship Series*, Paper 1679, 2008.

the costs instead should be covered by insurance paid for by the party responsible for activities that were thought to be particularly risky (and thus not by the taxpayer).

In a narrow sense the Nordic Model is sometimes used as a collecting term for four specific compensation schemes, covering traffic accidents, patient injuries, pharmaceutical injuries and work-related injuries. One important feature of these schemes is that they all intend to more or less replace the tort system in their respective fields and that insurance is mandatory. It is thus mandatory for someone (whether it is a private company or a public entity) that provides medical services to pay premiums to the patient insurance scheme. The patient insurance is supplied by a private insurance company and is supposed to cover all claims for personal injuries against the service provider. It is therefore very unusual to see for instance malpractice claims tried in the higher courts in Sweden since the compensation issue is normally dealt with under the special system set up under the Act on Patient Injuries that mainly deal with claims for compensation from the patient insurance.[20] Similar points can be made with regard to the kind of injuries that fall under the other three mentioned compensations schemes. The type of tort claims that have plagued for instance the American courts (associated with asbestos, DES, silicone implants, Agent Orange, etc.) are therefore by and large unheard of in the Nordic countries.

In a more extensive sense one can see the Nordic model as encompassing not only these comprehensive compensation schemes but a general outlook on the relationship between personal injury compensation and insurance. Many damages, including personal injuries, thus fall under other kinds of insurance, such as the private "home insurance" that covers most Swedish citizens. The view that the costs of damages to the highest extent possible should be covered by insurance has also had important influence on tort legislation. It has entailed not only that the victim will generally have a good chance of receiving compensation, especially in the case of personal injury, but also that the person that have caused the damage in many situations will be shielded from the risk of being subject of severe liability. I will give a couple of examples from the Swedish Tort Liability Act.

D. Swedish examples on the relationship between insurance and tort law

[...] 2. Contributory conduct of the victim in cases of personal injury

The Swedish system generally holds that social welfare concerns require that compensation for personal injuries is awarded also when a victim contributes to her own injury. Exceptions may be made in extraordinary cases but if the victim negligently contributed to her own injury full compensation is generally awarded (ch. 6, sect. 1).[21] Even in cases where the victim was injured in a traffic accident after having driven under the influence of alcohol or other substances full compensation (from the traffic insurance) will often be awarded.

---

20 Fn. 42: The victim still has a possibility to claim compensation in tort law for patient injuries according to a rule in the Act but this is seldom used since it is mostly more convenient to claim compensation from the insurance system. There is also a special procedural system that can be used when the (alleged) victim is unsatisfied with the decision by the insurance company that is often also more beneficial to the victim than the court system since it is generally free of charge (for the victim).
21 *Note by the author:* Chapter 9 (Common provisions) provides (in English translation): "§ 1. Compensation for personal injury can be adjusted if the victim contributed to the damage *intentionally* or through *gross negligence*. Compensation to the driver of a motor vehicle who is guilty of drunken driving can also be adjusted if the driver contributed to the damage through negligence. [. . .]"(emphasis added).

3. Reduction of damages in general

The Swedish Tort Liability Act includes a rule providing the court with an open possibility to reduce the amount of damages, when "needed" all the way to zero, if the obligation to pay damages would be unreasonably burdensome for the tortfeasor, ch. 6, sect. 2.[22] A factor to be regarded in the assessment of reduction of damages is whether the damage is covered by insurance.[23] If the tortfeasor has liability insurance there is generally no reason to reduce the damages but if the tortfeasor is not protected by liability insurance and the damage falls under insurance on the victim's side there may often be reasons to reduce the damages. The Swedish rule on reduction of damages may be used, and is in fact often used, even when the tortfeasor has caused the damage through an intentional criminal behaviour (for instance theft).

4. Reflections

These are only a couple of illustrations of how the idea that costs for damages should be allocated to insurance solutions has influenced the Swedish tort system. In addition one should also take into regard the protection provided by the social insurance system that means that most costs for medical treatment etc. will be covered by the taxpayer. There are several effects of this system. The most important effect is that the victim of personal injury in most situations will be able to receive compensation from an insurance, which means that she does not need to find and sue a solvent tortfeasor. This is even the case when the victim herself contributed in the production of the injury. Another important aspect of this is that private persons will often be protected from liability, also when they negligently cause damages.

This may seem like a very positive picture of the Swedish system but of course there are negative aspects as well. An exchange student recently said to me that Sweden seems like "the perfect country to be an idiot". (Adding: "Where do I sign up?") He had a point. Even if I negligently contribute to my own injury I will normally receive full compensation and even if I am grossly negligent in causing damage I will (in some circumstances) be protected from personal responsibility. In addition there is always the possibility to reduce the amount of damages if the obligation to pay damages will be regarded as too harsh. All in all these factors (among others) provide a picture of a Swedish tort system permeated with social concerns for both the victim and the tortfeasor.

These illustrations reveal a fundamental value underlying Swedish (and Nordic) tort law. Social policy has played an important part not only in forming social insurance law and legislation that can be said to belong to public law but also tort law as such. [. . .]

V. Conclusion

[. . .] The tradition in the field of tort law is something that I think many Swedish lawyers take pride in. The tort law model together with the insurance law solutions is (still!) generally thought progressive, pragmatic and efficient even if it is costly for the insurance collective and the taxpayers. [. . .]

---

22 *Note by the author*: it reads (in English translation): "Where liability to pay damages would be unduly burdensome for the person liable with regard to his financial situation, the amount of compensation may be adjusted according to what is reasonable, having regard also to the victim's need for compensation and other relevant factors".
23 See above, Chapter 6, question 8, p. 118 (in the context of liability in equity).

4. Purposes of tort liability: compensating victims (only), accident prevention, both, or more?

STEVEN SHAVELL, *Economic Analysis of Accident Law*, 2007, pp. 297–298

Purpose and future of accident liability

What is the purpose of accident liability? The answer to this question depends, in the first place, on the interpretation given to the word "purpose." Suppose that by the purpose of accident liability we mean what most participants in the legal system (or some wider class) *say* the purpose is. Then I would have to admit that the purpose of accident liability prominently includes the compensation of victims; it is my strong impression that the great majority of legal scholars, lawyers, and judges would state that the fair compensation of victims is an important (if not the important) purpose of accident liability.

Another interpretation of "purpose," however, refers to the difference that the presence of the liability system makes to actual outcomes. According to this *functional* definition, which I now adopt, compensation of victims cannot be said to be an important purpose of accident liability, since in its absence victims would probably be about as well compensated as they now are (certainly they could be). Compensation would be accomplished by private and social accident insurance. The main difference the presence of the liability system does make, therefore, is that it creates incentives toward safety. This, then, must be said to be the chief purpose of the liability system today. [. . .]

What should be the purpose of accident liability? The principal justification for use of accident liability today should not be compensation of victims because this can be accomplished with [a] well-developed and comparatively cheaply operating insurance system. Hence, if liability is to be employed in some area of accident, the major justification should be that liability creates incentives toward safety. [FN 12: More precisely, I mean that creation of incentives together with other goals different from compensation (such as providing a forum for victims and society to express disapproval of certain acts) must serve as the main justifications.] [. . .]

5. No alternatives needed? – The traditional response to trends towards "compensation culture": keeping the floodgates shut

LORD DYSON, Master of the Rolls, "Magna Carta and Compensation Culture", speech at the High Sheriff of Oxfordshire's Annual Law Lecture, Magna Carta Trust, 13th October 2015, *Judiciary of England and Wales*, HMSO, 2015

[. . .] 13. The so called compensation culture has been criticised as a form of abuse with [. . .] much passion [. . .]. An article by Professor Frank Furedi in 2012 complained about it 'poisoning our society'. A number of academic, government and Parliamentary studies have made recommendations as to how it should be tackled. [. . .]

17. There is [. . .] nothing new about the idea that the law requires the payment of fair compensation for harm which results from civil wrongs. It is long established. It is one of the

hallmarks of the Rule of Law and of the law of our land. But what is compensation culture [. . .]? Lord Falconer, who was Lord Chancellor at the time, gave an apt definition in 2005. He put it this way:

'Compensation culture' is a catch-all expression . . . It's the idea that for every accident someone is at fault. For every injury, someone to blame. And, perhaps most damaging, for every accident, there is someone to pay.

It is the idea that for every accident and every resultant injury or loss, someone other than the victim of the accident is to blame. The victim must, therefore, always be compensated. It is important not to confuse compensation culture with no fault compensation. No fault compensation is a legal principle according to which a person (C) is entitled to compensation for loss caused by another person (D) regardless of whether D was in any way at fault. This is an intellectually respectable principle which society may choose to embrace.[24] But in doing so, it must face up to its costs and economic consequences.

18. On the other hand, the compensation culture is not a legal principle at all. It has not displaced the principles of the law of negligence, whose essential elements remain as they were propounded in *Donoghue v Stevenson*[25]. Rather, to the extent that it exists, it is evidence of an [. . .] expectation that defendants will pay up rather than fight and risk losing. This has led to the idea that the compensation culture implies that there is no need to establish that a duty of care was owed to the injured party by whoever is viewed as being responsible; and there is no need to establish a breach of duty and causation of loss. All that the injured person has to do is to litigate (or even merely threaten to litigate) irrespective of the legal merits of the claim, and compensation will follow. [. . .]

19. One consequence of this is the view that as a society we have undergone a cultural shift. No longer is British society characterised by a somewhat philosophical and accepting approach to life. On the contrary, the view is taken that we are becoming more American in our approach; more ready to rush into litigation. To borrow from Tony Weir, we have become a 'wondrously unstoical and whingeing society with (an) endemic compensation neurosis', and which rather than sees us 'grin and bear it' sees us 'grit (our) teeth and sue'.

20. Perhaps even more dangerously, this shift in approach has been accompanied by a growing concern that an unjustified burden is now being placed on employers, businesses, schools, the NHS [National Health Service] and local and central government (as regards payment of compensation and, even worse, legal costs which often substantially exceed the amount of compensation[26]). To make matters worse, all of this is said to be giving rise to defensive practices on the part of such bodies. It is said that, as a consequence of the compensation culture, schools now ban conker fights on health and safety grounds; and school trips no longer take place. [. . .]

21. Media stories to this effect are commonplace. They tend to be about payments of large amounts of money for seemingly trivial injuries; [. . .]

---

24 See above, Chapters 8 and 9.
25 Related above, Chapter 5, pp. 76 ff.
26 For the costs of litigation, see above, Chapter 17, pp. 537 ff.

22. All of this acts as a spur to enterprising solicitors to encourage clients to launch speculative claims on a no-win no-fee basis. Clinical negligence claims are a good example. Some solicitors advertise their services on boards close to hospitals informing patients that, if they have not been satisfied with their treatment, they can sue the hospital authority at no cost to themselves. But many unsuccessful treatments are not the result of negligence. Patients may die despite the best possible surgery. The harsh commercial reality is that the legal costs to the NHS of defending a clinical negligence claim are often out of all proportion to the amount of damages that it will have to pay if the claim is successful. For this reason, the NHS is often willing to pay a claimant a sum to buy off a claim, even one which it considers is likely to fail. Claimant solicitors are only too aware of this. [. . .]

31. So what is the position in England and Wales? The perception is clear: compensation culture has taken firm root here and unwarranted and excessive compensation is routinely paid to claimants. This perception seems to persist despite studies and reports showing, as a Parliamentary enquiry put it, that the *'evidence does not support the view that increased litigation has created a "compensation culture"'*. It is worth asking whether the behaviour of our courts has contributed to this perception. Let me give you some examples which show that our judges are astute not to do anything to encourage the bringing of unjustified claims. [. . .]

33. [Take, for example, the case of] Tomlinson v Congleton Borough Council & Others which was decided by the House of Lords in 2003. One hot bank holiday in 1995, the claimant decided to go for a swim. He and friends were in the local park. They had been there many times before. In the park there was a flooded sand quarry, which had been made into a place for families to sunbathe and paddle in the water. As it was such a nice day and he was hot, the claimant decided to dive into the water to cool off. This was not the first time he had done this. Tragically however he hit his head on the bottom of the quarry. He broke his neck and, as a consequence was left a tetraplegic. He sued the local council. The House of Lords rejected the claim. In doing so Lord Hoffmann reiterated a principle that is entirely at odds with the idea that our courts are promoting a compensation culture. He said:

. . . the law does not provide such compensation simply on the basis that the injury was disproportionately severe in relation to one's own fault or even not one's own fault at all. Perhaps it should, but society might not be able to afford to compensate everyone on that principle, certainly at the level at which such compensation is now paid. The law provides compensation only when the injury was someone else's fault.

The law is fault-based. It requires a claimant to establish a duty of care, breach and causation of loss. These are not always straightforward matters and if a claimant fails to establish any one of them, his claim fails. The courts have not in recent years lowered the hurdles that a claimant must surmount. [. . .]

37. What do [the] cases illustrate? I think one answer is that our courts are well aware of the dangers of contributing to the idea that all injuries should result in compensatory awards. They are decisions that cannot be seen as encouraging the idea that anyone who suffers an injury has a remedy in damages. [. . .] A common theme is that accidents can and do happen and that the law does not compensate for accidents in the absence of legal responsibility. [. . .]

Bibliography

LORD BINGHAM OF CORNHILL, The Uses of Tort, *JETL* 2010, 3–15; PHILIPPE BRUN, *Responsabilité civile extracontractuelle*, 3rd ed., Paris: LexisNexis, 2014, pp. 429–450; GERT BRÜGGEMEIER, *Common Principles of Tort Law – a Pre-Statement of Law*, London: BIICL, 2004, pp. 267–274; GUIDO CALABRESI, Policy Goals of the "Swedish Alternative", *Am. J. Comp. L.* 1986, 657; HERMAN COUSY, Tort Liability and Liability Insurance: A Difficult Relationship, in: Helmut Koziol/Barbara C. Steininger (eds.), *European Tort Law* 2001, Vienna: Springer, 2002, pp. 18–55; JAMES DEMPSEY, Fault at the Crossroads, *A.B.A. Sec. Ins. Negl. & Comp. L. Proc.* 1971, 94; BILL W. DUFWA, Development of International Tort Law Till The Beginning of the 1990s from a Scandinavian Point of View, *Scand. Stud. L.* 2001, 87; ATTILA FENYVES/CHRISTA KISSLING/STEFAN PERNER/DANIEL RUBIN (eds.), *Compulsory Liability Insurance from a European Perspective*, Berlin/Boston: De Gruyter, 2016; JAN HELLNER, Compensation for Personal Injury: The Swedish Alternative, *Am. J. Comp. L.* 1986, 613; JAN HELLNER, Compensation for Personal Injuries in Sweden: A Reconsidered View, *Scand. Stud. L.* 2001, 249; HELMUT KOZIOL, *Basic Questions of Tort Law from a Germanic Perspective*, Vienna: Jan Sramek Verlag, 2012, pp. 1–92; RICHARD MAHONEY, New Zealand's Accident Compensation Scheme: A Reassessment, *Am. J. Comp. L.* 1992, 159–211; RICHARD LEWIS/ANNETTE MORRIS, Challenging Views of Tort: Part 1, *J.I.P.L.* 2013, 69–80; ROB MERKIN/JENNY STEELE, *Insurance and the Law of Obligations*, Oxford: OUP, 2013; CARL OLDERTZ, Security Insurance, Patient Insurance, and Pharmaceutical Insurance in Sweden, *Am. J. Comp. L.* 1986, 635; GERHARD WAGNER (ed.), *Tort Law and Liability Insurance*, Vienna: Springer, 2005; GERHARD WAGNER (ed.), in: *Münchener Kommentar Band 6: Schuldrecht Besonderer Teil*, 7th ed., München: C. H. Beck, 2017, Vor § 823; GERHARD WAGNER (ed.), Tort, Social Security, and No-Fault Schemes: Lessons from Real-World Experiments, *Duke J. Comp. & Int'l L.* 2012, 1–61.

Table of codal and statutory provisions

I. International conventions

European Convention on Human Rights
Art. 2 (1)	381
Art. 3	381
Art. 8	457
Art. 10	457
Art. 13	381

Hague Convention of 4 May 1971 on the Law Applicable to Traffic Accidents
Art. 1	577–578
Art. 2	578
Art. 3	578
Art. 4	578
Art. 11	578

Hague Convention of 2 October 1973 on the Law Applicable to Products Liability
Art. 1 (1)	580
Art. 3	580
Art. 4	581
Art. 5	581
Art. 6	581
Art. 7	581
Art. 11	581

II. European Union law

Regulation (EC) No 864/2007 of the European Parliament and the Council of 11 July 2007 on the law applicable to non-contractual obligations, [2007] OJ, L 199/40 (Rome II Regulation)
Recital 32	495
Art. 1 (1)	576
Art. 3	576
Art. 4 (1), (2)	576
Art. 5 (1)	577
Art. 14 (1)	577
Art. 28 (1)	577

III. National codes and statutes

Austria

Allgemeines Bürgerliches Gesetzbuch, ABGB *(General Civil Code)*
§ 21	139
§ 176	139
§ 1294	136
§ 1295 (1)	136, 336–337, 365
§ 1297	136–137
§ 1300	440
§ 1302	305
§ 1304	305
§ 1306	136–137
§ 1308	396
§ 1309	396
§ 1310	139
§ 1325	336–337, 365
§ 1327	367n29
§ 1328	368n34
§ 1329	368n35
§ 1331	368n33

Australia

Civil Liability Act
Sect. 33 (1), (2)	330

Belgium

Burgerlijk Wetboek/Code civil *(Civil Code)*
Art. 1382	176, 516
Art. 1383	176
Art. 1384 (1)	176
Art. 1386	176

Loi du 21 novembre 1989 relative à l'assurance obligatoire de la responsabilité civile en matière de véhicules automoteurs *(Act of 21st November*

1989 on Compulsory Motor Vehicle Liability Insurance)
Art. 29 *bis.* §§ 1er, 2, 5   257

Bulgaria

ЗАКОН ЗА ЗАДЪЛЖЕНИЯТА И ДОГОВОРИТЕ
(Law on Obligations and Contracts)
Art. 47 (1)   150
Art. 48 (1), (3)   407

Czech Republic

Občanský zákoník *(Civil Code)*
§ 444 (3)   372
§ 2899   170–171
§ 2920   150
§ 2950   439–440
§ 2959   72–73

Denmark

Erstatningsansvarsloven *(Liability for Damages Act)*
§ 24a   149
§ 24b   264–265

Lov om hæftelse for børns erstatningsansvar *(Act on Vicarious Liability for Children)*
§ 1   407

Bekendtgørelse af færdselsloven *(Road Traffic Act)*
§ 101   264

England and Wales

Water Industry Act
Sec. 209 (1), (2)   213

Fatal Accidents Act
Sect. 1A (1)–(4)   354

Power of Criminal Courts (Sentencing) Act 2000
Sect. 130   395
Sect. 131 (A1)   395
Sect. 131 (1)   395
Sect. 137 (1)   395

Estonia

Võlaõigusseadus *(Code of Obligations)*
§ 80   439n16
§ 81   439n16
§ 134 (2)   474
§ 134 (3)   371–372

§ 1043   90–91, 438–439, 474
§ 1045 (1)   90–91, 438–439, 474–475
§ 1046   474–475
§ 1048   438–439
§ 1050 (1)   184
§ 1052 (1), (3)   146–147
§ 1053   408
§ 1056 (1), (2)   221–222
§ 1057   265–266
§ 1058   221–222

Finland

Vahingonkorvauslaki *(Tort Liability Act)*
2 LUKU 1 §   93–94
2 LUKU 2 §   149
5 LUKU 1 §   93–94
5 LUKU 4a §   370

France

Code Civil *(Civil Code)*
Art. 9 (1)   462–463
Art. 1240   96–97, 171, 357, 519
Art. 1241   96–97, 171, 357
Art. 1242 (1)   171
Art. 1242 al. (4), (7)   402
Art. 1246   524–525
Art. 1247   524–525
Art. 1248   525
Art. 1249 (1), (2)   525
Art. 1251   525

Déclaration des droits de l'homme et du citoyen de 1789 *(Declaration of the Human Rights and the Rights of t he Citizen of 1789)*
Art. 11   463

Code de l'environnement *(Environmental Code)*
Art. L. 141–1 (1), (4)   519–520
Art. L. 142–2   520

Germany

Grundgesetz *(Basic Law)*
Art. 1 (1)   466
Art. 2 (1)   466
Art. 5 (1), (2)   466

Bürgerliches Gesetzbuch, BGB *(Civil Code)*

§ 249	82
§ 252	82
§ 253	331–332, 359, 467
§ 254 (1)	164, 245–246
§ 276	130
§ 630 h (5)	283
§ 675 (2)	434–435
§ 823 (1)	82, 164, 332, 359, 434, 467
§ 823 (2)	82, 434–435
§ 826	434–435
§ 828	131–132
§ 829	131–132
§ 832 (1)	396–397
§ 833	198
§ 836 (1)	198–199
§ 844	360n22
§ 845	360n22

Zivilprozessordnung, ZPO *(Code of Civil Procedure)*

§ 91 (1)	557
§ 92 (1)	557
§ 253 (1), (2)	547n7
§ 278 (1)	549n9

Haftpflichtgesetz *(Civil Liability Act)*

§ 1 (1), (2)	199–200
§ 2 (1), (3)	201

Produkthaftungsgesetz *(Product Liability Act)*

§ 1 (1)	199–200

Umwelthaftungsgesetz *(Environmental Liability Act)*

§ 1	199–200

Straßenverkehrsgesetz, StVG *(Road Traffic Act)*

§ 7 (1), (2)	244–245
§ 8	244–245
§ 9	244–245
§ 17 (1), (2)	244–245
§ 18 (1)	244–245

Gesetz über die Vergütung der Rechtsanwältinnen und Rechtsanwälte, Rechtsanwaltsvergütungsgesetz, RVG *(Act on the Remuneration of Lawyers)*

§ 1 (1)	558–559
§ 2 (1), (2)	558–559
§ 3a (1)	558–559
§ 4a	566–567
§ 13 (1)	558–559
§ 15 (1)	558–559
§ 34 (1)	562n15

Bundesrechtsanwaltsordnung, BRAO *(Federal Act Regulating the Legal Profession)*

§ 49b (2)	563

Gesetz betreffend das Urheberrecht an Werken der bildenden Künste und der Photographie, Kunsturhebergesetz *(Act Concerning the Copyright of Works of Visual Art and Photography, Art Copyright Act)*

§ 22	467
§ 23	467–468

Greece

Αστικός Κώδικας *(Civil Code)*

Art. 916	147
Art. 917	147
Art. 918	147
Art. 923 (1)	408
Art. 932	369

Ireland

Civil Liability Act

Sect. 47 (1)	354
Sect. 48 (1)	354
Sect. 49 (1)	355

Italy

Codice civile *(Civil Code)*

Art. 2043	179
Art. 2046	145
Art. 2047	145–146
Art. 2048 (1), (3)	408
Art. 2050	179, 219
Art. 2051	179
Art. 2054 (1), (2)	179–180
Art. 2054 (3)	262

Legge 24 dicembre 2003, n. 363: Norme in materia di sicurezza nella pratica degli sport invernali da discesa e da fondo *(Law no. 363/2003 of 24 December 2003)*

Art. 19 (1)	182

Japan

民法 *(Civil Code)*

Art. 711	375

Latvia

Civillikums *(Civil Code)*

Art. 1637	148
Art. 1780	148

Lithuania

Lietuvos Respublikos Civilinis kodeksas *(Civil Code)*

Art. 6.266	220–221
Art. 6.250	375–376
Art. 6.270 (1), (5)	220–221
Art. 6.284 (1)	376

The Netherlands

Burgerlijk Wetboek *(Civil Code)*

Art. 3:305a (1), (3)	513
Art. 6:104	488
Art. 6:162	512–513
Art. 6:164	146
Art. 6:165 (1)	146
Art. 6:169	408–409
Art. 6:173 (1)	217–218
Art. 6:174 (1)–(5)	217–218
Art. 6:175 (1), (3)	218–219

Wegenverkeerswet *(Road Traffic Act)*

Art. 185	260–261

Norway

Skadeserstatningsloven *(Compensatory Damages Act)*

§ 1-1	149
§ 1-2	409
§ 3-5 (2)	370–371

People's Republic of China

中华人民共和国侵权责任法 *(Tort Law Act)*

Art. 1	99–100, 482–483
Art. 2	100
Art. 6 (1)	100
Art. 32	411
Art. 33	266
Art. 48	266
Art. 65	527

电力法 *(Electric Power Law Act)*

Art. 60	101

中华人民共和国道路交通安全法 *(Road Traffic Safety Law Act)*

Art. 76	266–267

机动车交通事故责任强制保险条款 *(Compulsory Motor Vehicle Accident Liability Insurance Terms)*

Art. 8	267–268

中华人民共和国民事诉讼法 *(Civil Procedure Law Act)*

Art. 55	527–528

中华人民共和国环境保护法 *(Environmental Protection Law)*

Art. 58	528
Art. 64	528

Supreme People's Court, 最高人民法院关于审理环境民事公益诉讼案件适用法律若干问题的解释 *(Interpretation of the Supreme People's Court on Several Issues Concerning the Application of Law in the Conduct of Environmental Civil Public Interest Litigations), Interpretation No. 1 [2015]*

Art. 1	529
Art. 2	529
Art. 8 (3)	529
Art. 11	529
Art. 13	529
Art. 14	529
Art. 18	530
Art. 20	530
Art. 23	530
Art. 24	530
Art. 25	530
Art. 29	530

Poland

Kodeks cywilny *(Civil Code)*

Art. 426	147, 409
Art. 427	409
Art. 428	147
Art. 446 § 1	371
Art. 446 § 4	371

Portugal

Código civil *(Civil Code)*

Art. 488	148
Art. 491	409
Art. 494	370n38
Art. 496	369–370

Quebec, Canada

Code Civil/Civil Code

Art. 1457	379

Romania

Codul Civil *(Civil Code)*

Art. 1366	148

Art. 1372 410
Art. 1391 (1), (2) 374

Russian Federation

Гражданский кодекс Российской Федерации *(Civil Code)*

Art. 1064 (1), (2) 184
Art. 1073 (1) 147, 411
Art. 1074 (1) 147, 411
Art. 1074 (2), (3) 411
Art. 1075 411
Art. 1079 (1), (3) 219–220

Serbia

Zakon o obligacionim odnosima *(Law on Contracts and Torts)*

Art. 154 (1) 185
Art. 201 374–375

Slovenia

Obligacijski zakonik *(Code of Obligations)*

Art. 131 (1) 184–185
Art. 137 148
Art. 142 (1), (2), (4) 410
Art. 145 410
Art. 146 410–411
Art. 149 183
Art. 150 183
Art. 180 373–374

Slovakia

Občanský zákoník *(Civil Code)*

§ 422 (1), (2) 150

Spain

Códigó civil *(Civil Code)*

Art. 1902 404–405
Art. 1903 (1), (2), (6) 404–405

Ley orgánica 5/2000 de 12 de enero reguladora de la responsabilidad penal de los menores (Criminal Liability of Minors Act) (LORPM)

Art. 61 (3) 405

Sweden

Skadeståndslagen *(Tort Liability Act)*

1 kap. 2 § 91
2 kap. 1 §, 2 § 91–92
2 kap. 4 § 149
5 kap. 2 § 338–339
5 kap. 7 § 91–92

Switzerland

Code civil/Zivilgesetzbuch *(Civil Code)*

Art. 16 126–127
Art. 18 127
Art. 19 lit. 3 127
Art. 28 362, 483–484
Art. 28a 483–484
Art. 333 (1) 401

Code des obligations/Obligationenrecht *(Code of Obligations)*

Art. 41 (1) 87, 168, 333–334, 580
Art. 41 (2) 87, 508
Art. 42 301n16
Art. 44 (1) 129n16, 168
Art. 45 335n21
Art. 47 333–334, 361–362
Art. 49 361–362, 484
Art. 54 (1) 127
Art. 58 (1) 207
Art. 419 484
Art. 423 (1) 484

Code penal/Strafgesetzbuch *(Criminal Code)*

Art. 239 87–88

Loi fédérale sur les Chemins de fer, LCdF *(Federal Railway Act)*

Art. 40b (1) 203, 205

Loi fédérale sur l'aviation, LA *(Federal Aviation Act)*

Art. 64 (1) 203, 205

Loi fédérale sur les installations de transport par conduits de combustibles ou carburants liquids ou gazeux (Loi fédérale sur les installations par conduits, LIPC *(Federal Act on Pipelines for the Transport of Liquid or Gaseous Fuels)*

Art. 1 (1) 203–204, 205
Art. 33 (1) 204, 206

Loi fédérale sur les substances explosibles, Loi sur les explosifs, LExpl *(Federal Explosive Substances Act)*

Art. 27 (1), (2) 204, 206

Loi fédérale sur la responsabilité du fait des produits, LRFP *(Product Liability Act)*
Art. 1   204, 206

Loi sur la responsabilité civile en matière nucléaire, LRCN *(Federal Act on Nuclear Energy)*
Art. 3 (1)   204, 206

Loi fédérale sur la protection de l'environnement, LPE *(Federal Act on the Protection of the Environment)*
Art. 55 (1)-(3)   507
Art. 59a (1), (2)   204, 206
Art. 59a (3)   204–205, 205–206

Loi fédérale sur l'application du genie génétique au domaine non humain, Loi sur le genie génétique, LGG *(Federal Act on Non-Human Genetic Technology)*
Art. 30 (1), (4)   205, 207
Art. 31   205, 207

Strassenverkehrsgesetz/Loi fédérale sur la circulation routière *(Road Traffic Act)*
Art. 58 (1)   248–249
Art. 59 (1), (2)   248–249
Art. 60   248–249
Art. 62 (1)   248–249

Loi n° 85–677 du 5 juillet 1985 tendant à l'amélioration de la situation des victimes d'accidents de la circulation et à l'accélération des procédures d'indemnisation, Loi Badinter *(Law No. 85–677 of 5th July 1985, Aiming at the Improvement of the Conditions of Road Traffic Accident Victims and the Acceleration of the Compensation Procedure, Badinter Act)*
Art. 1   251
Art. 3   251–252
Art. 4   251–252
Art. 5   251–252

Loi fédérale sur la chasse et la protection des mammifères et oiseaux sauvages *(Federal Law in Hunting and the Protection of Mammals and Wild Birds)*
Art. 23   508

USA

Federal Law and Restatements

Constitution
7th Amendment   542

The American Law Institute, Restatement of the Law, Torts (3rd), Liability for Physical and Emotional Harm
§ 20   215
§ 48   329

The American Law Institute, Restatement of the Law, Torts (2nd)
§ 552 (1), (2)   428
§ 925   355

State Laws

Florida

Wrongful Death Act
Sect. 768.16   356
Sect. 768.17   356
Sect. 768.19   356
Sect. 768.21   357

New York

Estates Powers & Trusts Law
§ 5-4.1 (1)   356
§ 5-4.3   356

IV. Soft law principles

Draft Common Frame of Reference, DCFR

Art. VI. – 1:101 (1), (2)   108
Art. VI. – 2:101 (1)   108–109, 311
Art. VI. – 2:101 (2), (3)   108–109, 312
Art. VI. – 2:101 (4)   109
Art. VI. – 2:201-2:205 (Headlines)   109
Art. VI. – 2:206   109
Art. VI. – 2:207 (Headline)   109
Art. VI. – 2:207   446
Art. VI. – 2:208 (1)   109, 269
Art. VI. – 3:102   109, 269
Art. VI. – 3:103   154
Art. VI. – 3:104 (1), (3)   413
Art. VI. – 3:202   223
Art. VI. – 3:204-3:205 (Headlines)   224
Art. VI – 3:205   269
Art. VI. – 3:206   224

Principles of European Tort Law, PETL

Art. 1:101   103–104
Art. 2:101   104, 307
Art. 2:102 (1), (2)   104, 307, 443
Art. 2:102 (3), (4)   104, 444
Art. 2:102 (5), (6)   104

Art. 4:101	152, 268	Art. 5:101 (2)	223, 269
Art. 4:102	152	Art. 5:101 (3)	223
Art. 4:102 (1)	268, 444	Art. 6:101	412
Art. 4:102 (2)	268	Art. 10:101	483
Art. 4:201	187	Art. 10:301 (1)	384
Art. 5:101 (1)	222, 268		

Index

acting at one's own risk or peril 165, 170–171
alternative causation 305–306, 309–310
alternatives to tort liability 592 ff.; collective compensation schemes 603–605

benevolent intervention in another's affairs *see* shifting of illicit gain
bereavement, damages for *see* pure emotional harm
breach of confidence, tort 458 ff.
burden of proof, reversal 279, 283–287, 295, 308–309

cable cases 71 ff.
causation 277 ff.; alternative causation 305–306, 309–310; burden of proof, reversal of 279, 283–287, 295, 308–309; *conditio sine qua non* 56–57, 279, 300–302, 307–309; lawyer's liability 285–287, 299–300, 303–304, 310; loss of a chance 279, 287–303, 308; medical malpractice 279, 283–285, 289–303, 307
children *see* minors
collective compensation schemes 603–605
comparative law before the courts *see* judicial comparison
comparative methodology 5 ff.; benefits of multilateral comparison 17–18; range of jurisdictions for comparison 7–9
compensation culture 606–608
conditions of extra-contractual, fault-based liability 71 ff.
conditio sine qua non see causation
contributory negligence *see* fault-based liability
costs of lawsuits 537 ff.; American rule of costs 555–557; contingency fees/success fees/*Erfolgshonorar* 563–568; costs (USA) 556–557; European rule of costs 557 ff.; fee-table system 559–562; principle of causation 558
cross-border torts 570 ff.; *see also* Private International Law

dangerous activities *see* strict liability
Donoghue v. Stephenson 76–78, 212, 425, 427–428, 607

economic analysis 606; *see also* purposes and functions of tort law
economic loss 71 ff. (cable cases), 79 ff., 84, 88–89, 94–95, 101–103, 107, 419 ff. (wrongful advice)
emotional harm/mental harm 317–341, 343–387
environmental damage 199–200, 204–207, 499 ff.; *actio popularis* 503; class actions and public interest-related claims 503, 513–515; damage 503, 511–512, 521–527; Erika case 504, 521–524; non-governmental, non-profit environmental associations 501–511, 514–525, 528–530, 533–535; proposal for reform 533–535; pure ecological damage 499 ff., 501–502, 534; standing 502, 504, 507–511, 513–525, 528–530, 533–535
European Convention on Human Rights: protection of privacy and freedom of the press 451–452, 457, 461–462; secondary victims 381–384
European Court of Human Rights: protection of privacy and freedom of the press 452, 464–465, 470–471, 475–478; secondary victims 381–384

fault-based liability 115 ff., 158 ff.; challenges of establishing fault 158 ff.; contributory fault/negligence 164, 167–168, 170, 182–183; historical foundations 186–187; presumption of fault 185–186
frustrated expenses 503, 562

grief and sorrow *see* emotional harm; nervous shock

insurance: first-party insurance 118; insurance coverage as criterion for awarding claim 118,

134–135, 141–142, 145, 147–148; insurance dissociated from liability 231, 257–260; liability insurance/third-party insurance 118, 236–237, 267–268, 598–601, 602–603; social insurance 603–605

Jand'heur case 160, 171–173, 175, 231
judicial comparison 19 ff.; benefits 36–45; comparison in court practice 34–45, 318, 341; legitimacy 21–33

lawyer's liability 285–287, 299–300, 303–304, 310
legal families 7–8, 161
liability for others 389 ff.
liability without fault *see* strict liability
limits of extra-contractual liability 71 ff.
litigation, tort litigation 537 ff.; adversarial trial 543–546, 549, 552; concentrated and continuous trial 542–546; conference method of adjudication 549; experts 550–552; investigation of facts 546; jury 542–546, 549, 554; organisation of lawsuit 542 ff.; pre-trial discovery 542, 547, 549; role of the judge 547 ff.; witnesses 549–550; *see also* costs of lawsuits
loss of a chance 279, 287–303, 308
loss or severe injury of a loved one *see* secondary victims

medical malpractice 279, 283–285, 289–303, 307
minors, liability of 115; capacity of judgement 115 ff.; liability in equity 127, 130, 132, 134–135, 141–142

negligence, tort (basics) 76–78
nervous shock 317–341
non-pecuniary loss *see* emotional harm; nervous shock

objective liability *see* strict liability

parents' liability 389 ff.
personality rights *see* privacy, protection of
persuasive authority 31, 44, 125
perte d'une chance see loss of a chance
Principles of European Contract Law, PECL 47–50
Principles of European Tort Law, PETL 46–67; gaps to fill 59–65, 531–533; strengths 50–59
privacy, protection of, balanced against the freedom of the press 449 ff.
Private International Law 570 ff.; applicable law 572 ff.; Brussels I Regulation 572–573, 573nn15–20; Hague Convention on the Law Applicable to Products Liability 572, 580–581, 586–588; Hague Convention on the Law Applicable to Traffic Accidents 572, 576–580, 582–585; jurisdiction 572–573; Rome II Regulation 572 ff., 576, 582–88
psychiatric injury 317–341
PTSD *see* environmental damage; psychiatric injury; public goods, damage to
public goods, damage to 499 ff.
public interest, protection of through tort law *see* environmental damage
punitive or exemplary damages 489–495
pure economic loss *see* economic loss
pure emotional harm 343–387
purposes and functions of tort law 197–198, 209–212, 216–217, 449 ff., 452–454, 471–473, 478–483, 488–495, 596–608; 596–602 (France)

rationale behind strict liability *see* strict liability
res ipsa loquitur 213n21, 240
Restatement of Torts, USA, general information 150n36
risk-based liability *see* strict liability
road traffic accidents *see* traffic accidents

secondary victims 317–341, 343–387
shifting of illicit gain 453, 465, 484–488
sports accidents 158 ff.; sport federation rules 165–166, 188–189
standard of care, required 115 ff.; objective standard of care 116 ff.; subjective standard of care 117 ff., 137–138; *Übernahmeverschulden* 116–117; *see also* contributory negligence
strict liability 192 ff.; abnormally dangerous activities 213–215, 222–223; animals 182, 197–198, 202–203, 213; aviation 203, 205; dangerous activities 158 ff.; explosive substances 204, 206; function 197–198, 209–212, 216–217; *Gefährdungshaftung* 197–198, 202; general clauses 193; genetic technology 205, 207; *Kausalhaftung* 202–203; nuclear power or energy 197, 203, 206, 220–221; product liability 199–200, 204, 206, 224; railways 199–200, 203, 205; reciprocity of risk 194, 225; *Rylands v. Fletcher* 211–212, 214; source of danger/creation of risk 197, 202; things under one's control 171–176 (France), 176–179 (Belgium); unlawfulness of behaviour as a criterion 198

traffic accidents 193, 200–201, 224, 229 ff.; contributory negligence 244–248, 252, 254–256, 259–260, 262–263; damage to property 255; Dutch 50% rule 262; *fault-based liability* 236–244, 256; *force majeure*

246, 253–254; insurance 236–237, 267–268; insurance dissociated from liability 213, 257–260; liability of the (registered) keeper of a thing 244 ff.; *Loi Badinter* 251–256; physical incapacities 239, 243–244, 246–247, 250, 264–266, 269–271; strict liability 237, 240–241, 244 ff.

UNIDROIT Principles of International Commercial Contracts 47–50

wrongful information or advice 419 ff.; disclaimer 426–427, 433, 443; pecuniary interest/advice against remuneration 420, 428–430, 440–441